"During a time when there are so many astonishing and confusing things being claimed about the Bible, this volume brings exceptional clarity and careful scholarship to the task of introducing the New Testament. The authors not only provide the reader with a solid orientation to every NT book, but they also directly address a broad range of issues that scholars have raised. The end result is a richly informative text that is very readable and abundantly helpful. I enthusiastically recommend this volume to all who want to better understand their New Testament."

—***Clinton E. Arnold***, dean and professor of New Testament language and literature, Talbot School of Theology, Biola University

"*The Cradle, the Cross, and the Crown* is a comprehensive and informative introduction to the New Testament. Written from a convictional evangelical perspective, this marvelous volume carefully interacts with the most up-to-date issues in modern scholarship. This well-written textbook invites students to grasp the meaning of the various books of the New Testament in their historical, religious, political, cultural, and geographical setting while offering applicable theological insights into the New Testament's message for today. I have no doubt that this splendid work will become a standard resource for New Testament studies for years to come. I offer my heartiest congratulations to the authors for this fine publication."

—***David S. Dockery***, president, Trinity International University/Trinity Evangelical Divinity School

"Of making of New Testament introductions there seems to be no end, and the use of them is often a weariness of the flesh for the student. Yet from time to time, fresh breezes blow life into the genre, and such is the case with *The Cradle, the Cross, and the Crown.* Here we have a substantive, up-to-date introduction to the New Testament, for those preparing for ministry in the church. While broadly conversant with New Testament studies in general, the authors keep their target audience squarely in view, using information boxes, review questions, and even devotionals to good effect. Graded blocks of information for beginners, intermediate students, and those more advanced demonstrate an awareness of the range of competencies found in almost any classroom. This introduction should prove helpful to professors and edifying to students for many years to come."

—***George H. Guthrie***, Benjamin W. Perry Professor of Bible, School of Theology and Missions and senior fellow, R.C. Ryan Center for Biblical Studies, Union University

"This volume ranks among the finest such studies of recent decades in classic matters of New Testament introduction. What sets it apart includes: (1) attention to theology and the history of interpretation; (2) extended presentation of the history of New Testament times and the rise of the canon; (3) appropriate rigor; (4) frequently creative layout features; and (5) conceptual clarity. It is also written with Christian conviction. Beyond an impressive digest of scholarship, it is an appeal to faithful appropriation of the New Testament's message. It will and should see widespread graduate classroom use."

—***Robert W. Yarbrough***, professor of New Testament, Covenant Theological Seminary

SECOND EDITION

THE CRADLE, THE CROSS, AND THE CROWN

An Introduction to the New Testament

ANDREAS J. KÖSTENBERGER
L. SCOTT KELLUM
CHARLES L. QUARLES

Nashville, Tennessee

ISBN: 978-1-4336-8400-5

Published by B&H Academic

Nashville, Tennessee

Dewey Decimal Classification: 225.7

Subject Heading: BIBLE. N.T.—STUDY \ JESUS CHRIST—HUMANITY \ JESUS CHRIST—DIVINITY

Printed in the United States of America

4 5 6 7 8 9 10 • 22 21 20 19 18

BP

Contents

Abbreviations

AB	Anchor Bible
AnBib	*Analecta biblica*
ABD	*Anchor Bible Dictionary*
ABRL	Anchor Bible Reference Library
ACCS	Ancient Christian Commentary on Scripture
AGJU	Arbeiten zur Geschichte des antiken Judentums und des Urchristentums
ANRW	*Aufstieg und Niedergang der römischen Welt*
ASNU	Acta seminarii neotestamentici upsaliensis
AUSSDDS	Andrews University Seminary Studies Doctoral Dissertation Series
AUSS	*Andrews University Seminary Studies*
BA	*Biblical Archaeologist*
BAR	*Biblical Archaeology Review*
BBC	Blackwell Bible Commentaries
BBR	*Bulletin for Biblical Research*
BDAG	Bauer, W., F. W. Danker, W. F. Arndt, and F. W. Gingrich, *Greek-English Lexicon of the New Testament and Other Early Christian Literature* (Chicago, 1961)
BECNT	Baker Exegetical Commentary on the New Testament
BETL	Bibliotheca ephemeridum theologicarum lovaniensium
BGBE	Beiträge zur Geschichte der biblischen Exegese
Bib	*Biblica*
BibInt	*Biblical Interpretation*
BJRL	*Bulletin of the John Rylands University Library of Manchester*
BNTC	Black's New Testament Commentaries

BR	*Biblical Research*
BSac	*Bibliotheca sacra*
BST	The Bible Speaks Today
BT	*The Bible Translator*
BTB	*Biblical Theology Bulletin*
BTNT	Biblical Theology of the New Testament
BWA(N)T	Beiträge zur Wissenschaft vom Alten (und Neuen) Testament
BZ	*Biblische Zeitschrift*
BZNW	Beihefte zur Zeitschrift für die neutestamentliche Wissenschaft
CBQ	*Catholic Biblical Quarterly*
CGTC	Cambridge Greek Testament Commentary
CJ	*Classical Journal*
ConBNT	Coniectanea biblica: New Testament Series
CRINT	Compendia rerum iudaicarum ad Novum Testamentum
CTJ	*Calvin Theological Journal*
CTR	*Criswell Theological Review*
EB	Echter Bibel
EBC	The Expositor's Bible Commentary
EBS	Encountering Biblical Studies
ECC	Eerdmans Critical Commentary
EDRL	*Encyclopedic Dictionary of Roman Law*
EKKNT	Evangelisch-katholischer Kommentar zum Neuen Testament
EMS	Evangelical Missiological Society
EROER	Études préliminaires aux religions orientales dans l'Empire romain
EstBib	*Estudios biblicos*
ET	English translation
ETL	*Ephemerides Theologicae Lovanienses*
EvQ	*Evangelical Quarterly*
ExpTim	*Expository Times*
FFRS	Foundations and Facets Reference Series
GCS	Die griechischen christlichen Schriftsteller der ersten [drei] Jahrhunderte
HBT	*Horizons in Biblical Theology*
HNT	Handbuch zum Neuen Testament
HNTC	Harper's New Testament Commentaries
HTKNT	Herders theologischer Kommentar zum Neuen Testament
HTR	*Harvard Theological Review*
HTS	Harvard Theological Studies

IBS	*Irish Biblical Studies*
ICC	International Critical Commentary
Int	*Interpretation*
IRT	Issues in Religion and Theology
IVPNTC	InterVarsity Press New Testament Commentary
JAAR	*Journal of the American Academy of Religion*
JBL	*Journal of Biblical Literature*
JETS	*Journal of the Evangelical Theological Society*
JQR	*Jewish Quarterly Review*
JSNT	*Journal for the Study of the New Testament*
JSNTSup	Journal for the Study of the New Testament: Supplement Series
JSOT	*Journal for the Study of the Old Testament*
JSOTSup	Journal for the Study of the Old Testament: Supplement Series
JTS	*Journal of Theological Studies*
KD	*Kerygma und Dogma*
KEK	Kritisch-exegetischer Kommentar über das Neue Testament
LEC	Library of Early Christianity
LNTS	Library of New Testament Studies
MBPS	Mellen Biblical Press Series
MNTC	Moffat New Testament Commentary
MSJ	*The Master's Seminary Journal*
NABPR	The National Association of Baptist Professors of Religion
NAC	New American Commentary
NCB	New Century Bible
NCBC	New Cambridge Bible Commentaries
Neot	*Neotestamentica*
NHMS	Nag Hammadi and Manichaean Studies
NHS	Nag Hammadi Studies
NIB	*The New Interpreter's Bible*, Edited by Leander E. Keck. 12 vols. Nashville: Abingdon, 1994–2004
NIBC	New International Biblical Commentary
NIBCNT	New International Biblical Commentary on the New Testament
NICNT	New International Commentary on the New Testament
NIDNTT	*New International Dictionary of Old Testament Theology and Exegesis*. Edited by W. A. VanGemeren. 5 vols. Grand Rapids, 1997
NIGTC	New International Greek Testament Commentary

NIVAC	New International Version Application Commentary
NovT	*Novum Testamentum*
NovTSup	Supplements to Novum Testamentum
NS	New Series
NSBT	New Studies in Biblical Theology
NTD	Das Neue Testament Deutsch
NTL	New Testament Library
NTS	*New Testament Studies*
PG	Patrologia graeca [= Patrologiae cursus completus: Series graeca]. Edited by J.-P. Migne. 162 vols. Paris, 1857–1886
PL	Patrologia latina [= Patrologiae cursus completus: Series latina]. Edited by J.-P. Migne. 217 vols. Paris, 1844–1864
PNTC	Pillar New Testament Commentaries
PTMS	Pittsburgh Theological Monograph Series
QD	*Quaestiones Disputatae*
ResQ	*Restoration Quarterly*
RevBib	*Revue biblique*
RHR	*Revue de l'histoire des religions*
RNT	Regensburger Neues Testament
RTR	*Reformed Theological Review*
SacPag	Sacra Pagina
SANT	Studien zum Alten und Neuen Testament
SBAB	Stuttgarter biblische Aufsatzbände
SBEV	Service Biblique Evangile et Vie
SBL	Society of Biblical Literature
SBLDS	Society of Biblical Literature Dissertation Series
SBLMS	Society of Biblical Literature Monograph Series
SBLSBS	Society of Biblical Literature Sources for Biblical Studies
SBLSP	Society of Biblical Literature Seminar Papers
SBLSymS	Society of Biblical Literature Symposium Series
SBT	Studies in Biblical Theology
SC	Sources chrétiennes. Paris: Cerf, 1943–
Scr	*Scripture*
SE IV, TU	*Studia Evangelica IV,* Texte und Untersuchungen
SNT	Studien zum Neuen Testament
SNTSMS	Society for New Testament Studies Monograph Series
SR	*Studies in Religion*
SUNT	Studien zur Umwelt des Neuen Testaments
TANZ	Texte und Arbeiten zum neutestamentlichen Zeitalter
TBT	*The Bible Today*

TDNT	*Theological Dictionary of the New Testament.* Edited by G. Kittel and G. Friedrich. Translated by G. W. Bromiley. 10 vols. Grand Rapids, 1964–1976
Them	*Themelios*
Theol	*Theologica*
THNT	Theologischer Handkommentar zum Neuen Testament
TNTC	Tyndale New Testament Commentary
TrinJ	*Trinity Journal*
TRu	*Theologische Rundschau*
TSK	*Theologische Studien und Kritiken*
TU	Texte und Untersuchungen
TynBul	*Tyndale Bulletin*
VC	*Vigiliae Christianae*
WBC	Word Biblical Commentary
WTJ	*Westminster Theological Journal*
WUNT	Wissenschaftliche Untersuchungen zum Neuen Testament
WW	*Word and World*
ZAG	*Zeitschrift für alte Geschichte*
ZAW	*Zeitschrift für die alttestamentliche Wissenschaft*
ZCS	Zondervan Church Source
ZNW	*Zeitschrift für die neutestamentliche Wissenschaft und die Kunde der älteren Kirche*
ZRGG	*Zeitschrift für Religions- und Geistesgeschichte*
ZST	*Zeitschrift für systematische Theologie*

ABBREVIATIONS OF WORKS OF THE CHURCH FATHERS

1 Apol.	*1 Apologia,* Justin
Ant.	*Jewish Antiquities*, Josephus
Apol.	*Apologeticus,* Tertullian
Apion	*Against Apion*, Josephus
Barn.	*The Epistle of Pseudo-Barnabas*
Chron.	*Chronicle,* Eusebius
Comment. Matt.	*Commentarium in evangelium Matthaei*, Origen
Dial.	*Dialogus cum Tryphone,* Justin Martyr
Eccl. Hist.	*Ecclesiastical History,* Eusebius
Eph.	*To the Ephesians,* Ignatius
Hom. Luke	*Homilies on Luke,* Origen
Hom. Matt.	*Homiliae in Matthaeum,* John Chrysostom
J.W.	*Jewish Wars,* Josephus

Legat.	*Legatio ad Gaium,* Philo
Marc.	*Against Marcion,* Tertullian
Magn.	*To the Magnesians,* Ignatius
Nat.	*Ad nationes,* Tertullian
Or.	*De oratione,* Tertullian
Paed.	*Paedagogus,* Clement of Alexandria
Pol.	*To Polycarp,* Ignatius
Praef. in Ioann.	*Preface to John,* Theophylact
Praescr.	*De praescriptione hareticorum,* Tertullian
Quis div.	*Quis dives salvetur,* Clement of Alexandria
Scorp.	*Scorpiace,* Tertullian
Trall.	*To the Trallians, Ignatius*
Vir. ill.	*De viris illustribus,* Jerome

Abbreviations of other works (e.g., apocryphal, pseudepigraphical, Mishnaic, Talmudic, classical Greek and Roman writings, etc.) conform to *The SBL Handbook of Style.*

Preface to the Second Edition

For believers who look to Scripture as the authority for their faith and practice, the NT, with its twenty-seven books, presents both a wonderful, God-given treasure trove of spiritual insights and a formidable challenge for faithful, accurate interpretation. To be sure, "all Scripture is inspired by God and is profitable for teaching, for rebuking, for correcting, for training in righteousness, so that the man of God may be complete, equipped for every good work" (2 Tim 3:16–17). To be so equipped, however, the student of Scripture must follow Paul's exhortation to "[b]e diligent to present yourself approved to God, a worker who doesn't need to be ashamed, correctly teaching the word of truth" (2 Tim 2:15).

The diligence required for a correct understanding of God's "word of truth" involves a thorough acquaintance with the historical, literary, and theological aspects of the various NT writings. Ironically, the methodical study of these factors traces its modern origins back to the Enlightenment. We say "ironically" because the Enlightenment was also characterized by an antisupernatural bias and a critical—if not skeptical—spirit that emphasized studying the Bible just as one would approach any other book.[1] Clearly, for anyone who believes Scripture is *more* than just a piece of human literature, such an approach is unacceptable because it denies that Scripture is the product of divine inspiration.[2] But while Scripture ought not be reduced to a *mere* piece of human writing, we can gain much by paying careful attention to the historical, literary, and theological dimensions of the biblical writings and, in our case, particularly the NT.

[1] See especially W. Baird, *History of New Testament Research*, 3 vols. (Minneapolis, MN: Fortress, 1992, 2003, 2013).

[2] See the reference to the Scriptures as "inspired by God" in 2 Tim 3:16.

TITLE AND CONTENT OVERVIEW

Title

For this reason we present you, the serious student of the NT, with *The Cradle, the Cross, and the Crown.* The title attempts to capture the essence of NT theology: (1) *the cradle*, that is, Jesus's virgin birth and incarnation, which are narrated at the outset of the NT canon (Matt 1:18–25); (2) *the cross*, narrated in the Gospel Passion Narratives and explained in the NT epistolary literature; and (3) *the crown*, that is, the triumphant return of Christ and our eternal reign with him. Within this framework we advocate a holistic reading of the NT, and of the entire body of Scripture, along the lines of a salvation-historical framework that traces the story of God's progressive revelation and provision of redemption in the promised Messiah and Son of God, the Lord Jesus Christ.

The Nature of Scripture

The first part of this book attempts to set the stage for the ensuing study by presenting a discussion of the most critical foundational issues for NT interpretation: (1) the nature and scope of Scripture (chap. 1); and (2) the political and religious background of the NT (chap. 2). It is vital for all students of Scripture to have a proper understanding of the *doctrine* of Scripture, so chapter 1 discusses the formation of the NT canon, its inspiration and inerrancy, the preservation and transmission of the Bible over the centuries, and issues pertaining to the translation of Scripture.

Unfortunately, this kind of doctrinal instruction is increasingly neglected in many current publications on the topic.[3] But we judge it absolutely vital because only by understanding Scripture as divine revelation, in keeping with its own claims, will we be able to pursue our study all the way to its intended goal: the application of the "word of truth" to our personal lives and our relationships with others.[4] God has revealed himself in his inspired, inerrant Word; and because the Bible is the Word of God in written form, it is therefore without error, trustworthy, authoritative, and requires obedience and personal application.[5] James says it well:

> . . . humbly receive the implanted word, which is able to save your souls. But be doers of the word and not hearers only, deceiving yourselves. Because if anyone is a hearer of the word and not a doer, he is like someone looking at his own face in a mirror. For he looks at himself, goes away, and immediately

---

[3] The reason for this, at least in part, may be the continued hegemony of an approach to Scripture that holds doctrine—including the doctrine of Scripture—in abeyance and favors a primarily historical or literary mode of investigation. But this unduly neglects the third vital component of biblical interpretation, that is, theology. See A. J. Köstenberger, *Encountering John: The Gospel in Historical, Literary, and Theological Perspective*, EBS, 2nd ed. (Grand Rapids, MI: Baker, 2013), 14–15.

[4] See the classic article by W. A. Grudem, "Scripture's Self-Attestation and the Problem of Formulating a Doctrine of Scripture," in *Scripture and Truth*, ed. D. A. Carson and J. D. Woodbridge (Grand Rapids, MI: Zondervan, 1983), 19–59.

[5] See the doctrinal base of the Evangelical Theological Society (ETS), reproduced at www.etsjets.org/about (accessed April 11, 2016).

> forgets what kind of man he was. But the one who looks intently into the perfect law of freedom and perseveres in it, and is not a forgetful hearer but a doer who works—this person will be blessed in what he does (1:21–25).

Indeed, the purpose of Scripture is "training in righteousness, so that the man of God may be complete, equipped for every good work" (2 Tim 3:16–17).

In this regard, it is our desire that this present volume be more than a dry, academic compilation of various dates and facts. To be sure, the study of Scripture requires diligence—in other words, work!—but what ought to motivate our efforts is the payoff at the end of our research: a better understanding of the history, literature, and theology of the NT writings for the purpose of cultivating, in the power of the Holy Spirit, a deeper spiritual life within ourselves, our families, and our churches. This, in turn, will result in a more authentic and authoritative proclamation of the biblical message so that God's kingdom may be advanced in this world and so others may be subjected to his reign in their lives.

The Background of the New Testament

As we approach our study of the NT, we need to acquaint ourselves with the political and religious background of the NT (the contents of chap. 2). This ingredient is sometimes missing in standard NT introductions, an omission that when teaching NT survey courses in the past has sent us scrambling for other resources to prepare our students adequately for entering the world of the NT. In this chapter we cover the end of OT history (the exiles of Israel and Judah, the last prophets); the period between the Testaments (the Greeks, the Maccabees, and the Romans); and the political environment of Jesus's ministry (the Jewish sects, the Herodian dynasty, etc.). We also provide a survey of Second Temple literature and discuss relevant theological and philosophical issues.

History, Literature, and Theology

With this foundation laid, we analyze each NT book using the same pattern, which is called a "hermeneutical triad" in Köstenberger and Patterson's *Invitation to Biblical Interpretation*: (1) *history* (including a book's authorship, date, provenance, destination); (2) *literature* (genre, literary plan, outline, unit-by-unit discussion); and (3) *theology* (theological themes, contribution to the canon).[6] In keeping with the three major divisions of the NT canon, the material in the body of this book is then organized into the following three parts:

- *Part Two: Jesus and the Gospels*, which features a chapter on Jesus and the relationship among the four Gospels as well as introductions to each of the four Gospels.

[6] See A. J. Köstenberger and R. D. Patterson, *Invitation to Biblical Interpretation* (Grand Rapids, MI: Kregel, 2011); idem, *For the Love of God's Word: An Introduction to Biblical Interpretation* (Grand Rapids, MI: Kregel, 2015); cf. N. T. Wright, *The New Testament and the People of God*, Christian Origins and the Question of God, vol. 1 (Minneapolis, MN: Fortress, 1992).

- *Part Three: The Early Church and Paul,* which includes chapters on the book of Acts; the ministry and message of the apostle Paul; and the thirteen canonical Letters of Paul in likely chronological order of writing: Galatians; 1–2 Thessalonians; 1–2 Corinthians; Romans; the Prison Epistles; and the Letters to Timothy and Titus.
- *Part Four: The General Epistles and Revelation,* which are discussed in canonical order (except that Jude is kept with the Petrine Letters because of the missive's close relationship with 2 Peter): Hebrews; James; 1–2 Peter; Jude; 1–3 John; and Revelation.

The book closes with a chapter on unity and diversity in the NT and an epilogue tracing the biblical story line, concluding the volume as it began: with an emphasis on a holistic reading of Scripture.

RATIONALE AND DISTINCTIVES

Rationale

It is our belief, borne out of years of teaching on both undergraduate and graduate levels, that the pattern of organizing the material described above best reflects the organic growth of the NT material. It allows the classroom teacher (1) to cover the foundational material, that is, the doctrine of Scripture, the NT background, and Jesus and the Gospels; and (2) to use the template provided by the book of Acts as the basis for a study of the ministry and writings of the apostle Paul and the other NT witnesses.

While the NT is a collection of writings—a body of literature—to be appreciated in the sequence in which it is given, it also reflects a historical plan. It moves from God's promise of a Messiah, as described in the OT, to the coming of that Messiah, as depicted in the Gospels, to the growth of the early church as narrated in the book of Acts and the NT letters, and to the consummation of human history at the return of Christ as anticipated in Revelation.[7]

To give but one example, it will be helpful for the student to understand that Paul wrote the letter to the Galatians several years prior to his letter to the Romans so that the "Judaizing controversy" surrounding circumcision (discussed in Galatians) can be seen to provide the backdrop to the later, more general formulation of the gospel in the book of Romans. It will also be helpful to relate both Galatians and Romans to events in the book of Acts and to other events in early Christian history and in the ministry of Paul.

Distinctives

With this in mind, we aimed to produce a volume with the following distinctives.

1. *User-friendly.* We have written with the teacher and the student in mind. This book is scholarly, yet accessible; it is useful as a text for one- or two-semester

---

[7] See the chapter "Gospels, Acts, Epistles, and Apocalypse: The Fulfillment of the Old Testament in the New," in Köstenberger and Patterson, *Invitation to Biblical Interpretation.*

NT survey classes. One could cover all the material in one semester or go over the introduction and Jesus and the Gospels in semester 1 and the early church, covering Paul and the rest of the NT, in semester 2. User-friendly features include listings of Basic, Intermediate, and Advanced Knowledge at the beginning[8] and Study Questions and Resources for Further Study at the end of every chapter. An extensive glossary is found in the back of the volume.

2. *Comprehensive.* This book covers the entire NT canon, background, Jesus, the Gospels, the early church, and Paul's writings in order of composition, the General Epistles and Revelation, and the unity and diversity of the NT. Studying Paul's Letters in the order in which they were written helps integrate them with the historical framework of Acts. The second edition also includes discussions of how to interpret the various genres of Scripture (Gospels-Acts, parables, etc.) and an epilogue on the story line of Scripture, both OT and NT.
3. *Conservative.* All three writers of this book affirm that all twenty-seven books in the NT were written by the persons to whom they are ascribed (the four Gospels, the Letters). We have included a strong defense of the apostolic authorship of Matthew and John and a rebuttal of the alleged pseudonymity of the letters written by Paul and Peter, especially those to Timothy, Titus, and 2 Peter.
4. *Balanced.* We have attempted to follow sound hermeneutical procedure, modeling the study of each NT book in its historical, literary, and theological context. Hence, this volume is more (though not less) than just a NT introduction dealing with the introductory issues of authorship, date, provenance, destination, and so on. As mentioned under point 2 above, the second edition includes special discussions on how to interpret various NT genres.
5. *Up to date.* This volume includes comprehensive scholarly interaction with both older and more recent scholarship, with a primary focus on English-language sources. Where appropriate we draw on recent advances in the literary study of Scripture, following a narrative or discourse analysis approach in tracing the contents of various NT books. The second edition brings scholarly interaction up-to-date with regard to all matters of NT introduction.
6. *Spiritually nurturing and application oriented.* The style of writing consistently seeks to nurture the student's spirituality and encourages application of what is learned rather than giving an arid presentation of facts to be mastered merely on a cognitive level. This is reflected especially in the unit-by-unit discussions, in the

[8] We recommend that for one-semester courses and in Bible college settings, teachers aim for imparting (at least) what is identified as Basic Knowledge. If the NT survey sequence spans two semesters, especially in seminary settings, our recommendation is to make the Intermediate Knowledge listed at the beginning of each chapter the standard for learning and testing. The Advanced Knowledge is provided for particularly motivated students who, in some cases, may be called to pursue further study or even an academic career.

theological themes sections, and in the Something to Think About sidebars (a unique ingredient for NT introductions).

A BRIEF HISTORY OF NEW TESTAMENT INTRODUCTION

The Seventeenth and Eighteenth Centuries

Before commencing our study, we need to take a moment to set the larger context of the science of NT introduction. In fact, students of the NT may not always realize this field of research has a pedigree spanning centuries. Perhaps the first modern NT introduction was produced by the French Roman Catholic scholar Richard Simon, who in 1689 wrote *A Critical History of the Text of the New Testament*.[9]

Several decades later one of the most prolific Pietist scholars, Johann Bengel, wrote his massive *Gnomon of the New Testament*, though his work is written in commentary style rather than conforming to the conventional format of a NT introduction.[10] Shortly thereafter, J. D. Michaelis (1717–1791), professor at the University of Göttingen, produced his *New Testament Introduction*, in which he questioned the inspiration of non-apostolic NT literature.[11]

The Nineteenth and Twentieth Centuries

One of the most influential NT introductions in the nineteenth century was the massive two-volume *Introduction to the New Testament* by Heinrich Holtzmann. In it the author articulated the emerging critical consensus: the two-document hypothesis; the theological rather than historical character of John; the questionable reliability of Acts; the pseudonymity of Ephesians and the letters to Timothy and Titus; the problematic authorship of the General Epistles; and the importance of Hellenistic backgrounds for Paul and John.[12]

---

[9] R. Simon, *Histoire Critique du Texte du Nouveau Testament* (Rotterdam, Netherlands: Reinier Leers, 1689). See the discussion in Baird, *History of New Testament Research*, 1:17–25, who calls Simon "the founder of modern biblical criticism" (p. 17).

[10] J. A. Bengel, *Gmonon Novi Testamenti*, 3rd ed., M. E. Bengel and J. Steudel, eds., 2 vols. (Tübingen, Germany: L. F. Fues, 1850); English translation *Gnomon of the New Testament*, trans. J. Bandinel and A. R. Fausset, ed. A. R. Fausset, 5 vols. (Edinburgh, Scotland: T&T Clark, 1866); reissued as *New Testament Commentary*, 2 vols. (Grand Rapids, MI: Kregel, 1982). See the discussion in Baird, *History of New Testament Research*, 1:69–80.

[11] J. D. Michaelis, *Einleitung in die göttlichen Schriften des Neuen Bundes*, 4th rev. ed., 2 vols. (Göttingen, Germany: Vandenhoeck & Ruprecht, 1788); English translation *Introduction to the New Testament*, trans. H. Marsh, 2nd ed., 4 vols. (London, England: F. and C. Rivington, 1802). See the discussion in Baird, *History of New Testament Research*, 1:127–38, who called Michaelis "[a]nother wunderkind [*sic*; German for "child prodigy"] of the Aufklärung" (German for "Enlightenment").

[12] H. Holtzmann, *Lehrbuch der historisch-kritischen Einleitung in das Neue Testament*, 2nd ed. (Freiburg im Breisgau: Mohr Siebeck, 1886; this work has not been translated into English). See the discussion in Baird, *History of New Testament Research*, 2:111–22, who considered him to be an important figure moving NT research "toward critical consensus" (heading on p. 111).

The early twentieth century saw the publication of Theodor Zahn's 1,100-page *Introduction to the New Testament.*[13] Zahn affirmed the traditional authorship of all four Gospels. He reconstructed the order of writing of the NT letters as James, Galatians, 1–2 Thessalonians, 1–2 Corinthians, Romans, the Prison Epistles, and the Letters to Timothy and Titus. Zahn argued for the authenticity of both 1 and 2 Peter and believed the apostle John wrote not only the Gospel and the three Letters bearing his name but also the Apocalypse. Thus, Zahn provided a conservative counterpoint to Holtzmann and others representing the critical consensus, and his work became an important point of reference for subsequent conservative scholarship on matters of NT introduction.

Recent Contributions

More recently the British scholar Donald Guthrie (1990) and North Americans D. A. Carson and Douglas Moo (with Leon Morris, 1992; 2nd ed. Carson and Moo, 2005) have produced major evangelical NT introductions that set a high standard of scholarship while affirming conservative conclusions with regard to authorship, date, and other aspects of the NT literature.[14] Less conservative is the NT introduction by the Roman Catholic scholar Raymond Brown (1997).[15] Also noteworthy is the work of Donald Hagner, who does, however, frequently affirm critical positions regarding the authorship of NT books.[16] Several other NT introductions written from a more critical perspective in the last decade or two are available as well.[17]

CONCLUSION

As this brief survey of the history of NT introductions shows, the present volume stands in a long line of efforts by scholars with a variety of perspectives that range from conservative to critical. As mentioned at the outset, to a large degree this is a function of scholars' larger presuppositions with regard to the nature of Scripture. Nevertheless, we believe it is possible to meet on the common ground of the biblical text and of the available sources

---

[13] T. Zahn, *Einleitung in das Neue Testament*, 2 vols. (Leipzig, Germany: A. Deichert, 1897, 1899; repr. Wuppertal: R. Brockhaus, 1994); English translation *Introduction to the New Testament*, trans. Fellows and Scholars of Hartford Theological Seminary, ed. M. W. Jacobus, 2nd ed., three vols. in one (New York, NY: Scribner's Sons, 1917; repr. Edinburgh, Scotland: T&T Clark, 1971). See the discussion in Baird, *History of New Testament Research*, 2:367–73; see the discussion of Zahn's contemporary (and relative) A. Schlatter in ibid., 373–83. While Schlatter did not write a NT introduction as such, his two-volume *New Testament Theology* makes an important contribution to the understanding of the theological message of the New Testament. See A. Schlatter, *New Testament Theology*, 2 vols., trans. A. J. Köstenberger (Grand Rapids, MI: Baker, 1997, 1999); and A. J. Köstenberger, "T. Zahn, A. von Harnack, and A. Schlatter," in *Pillars in the History of New Testament Interpretation: Old and New*, ed. S. E. Porter and S. A. Adams (Eugene, OR: Wipf & Stock, forthcoming).

[14] D. Guthrie, *New Testament Introduction*, rev. ed. (Downers Grove, IL: InterVarsity, 1990); D. A. Carson, L. Morris, and D. J. Moo, *An Introduction to the New Testament* (Grand Rapids, MI: Zondervan, 1992); 2nd ed., D. A. Carson and D. J. Moo, *An Introduction to the New Testament* (Grand Rapids, MI: Zondervan, 2005).

[15] R. E. Brown, *An Introduction to the New Testament*, ABRL (New York, NY: Doubleday, 1997).

[16] D. A. Hagner, *The New Testament: A Historical and Theological Introduction* (Grand Rapids, MI: Baker, 2012).

[17] See, e.g., D. Burkett, *An Introduction to the New Testament and the Origins of Christianity* (Cambridge, MA: Cambridge University Press, 2002). For a recent survey of NT introduction from a German perspective, see F. W. Horn, "Einleitung in das Neue Testament 2001–2011," *TRu* 79 (2014): 294–327.

and evidence and to engage in scholarly work and dialogue. It will become apparent that the present work operates more closely in the conservative Zahn–Guthrie–Carson/Moo tradition than in the more critical vein of the Simon–Michaelis–Holtzmann–Brown trajectory.

As we release this second edition, we are well aware of the limitations associated with producing such a work. In this age of unprecedented proliferation of scholarly literature, who is adequate to such a task? Nevertheless, we believe it is a risk worth taking since the task of helping to equip another generation of Bible students with a portion of the knowledge of "the sacred Scriptures, which are able to give you wisdom for salvation through faith in Christ Jesus" (2 Tim 3:15) must not be left undone. On this side of heaven, our knowledge will of necessity be preliminary and incomplete: "For now we see only a reflection, as in a mirror," and long for the day when we will see Jesus "face to face" (1 Cor 13:12). In the meantime we invite you to join us to press on to full Christian maturity (Phil 3:12–14) as we grow in the knowledge and grace of our Lord Jesus Christ (2 Pet 3:18). May God be pleased to use this volume as a small tool toward that worthy and glorious end.

Acknowledgments

THIS BOOK REPRESENTS the product of collaboration among three authors. Each chapter was assigned to one of us, although all of us contributed our input throughout. Andreas served as general editor and wrote all the "Something to Think About" sections, and together we stand behind the final product. For this reason it would be counterproductive to identify the authors of individual chapters (though readers are, of course, welcome to venture educated guesses!).

We would like to express our appreciation to Jason Meyer for writing a first serious draft of the original chapter on the Prison Epistles and to Alan Bandy for doing so for the book of Revelation. Thanks are also due to Keith Campbell, Matt Lytle, Liz Mburu, and Nate Ridelhoover for their assistance in preparing the first edition, and gratitude extends to Chuck Bumgardner for his competent help in updating chapters 2, 5, 7, 15, 18, 20, and 21 for this second edition.

We also acknowledge our heartfelt thanks to our wives and families; our academic institution, Southeastern Baptist Theological Seminary; and our students past, present, and future. It is a great privilege and solemn responsibility to be involved in the serious study and teaching of Scripture, and we count ourselves blessed to serve our Lord Jesus Christ in this way and to partner in sharpening others as "iron sharpens iron" (Prov 27:17).

It is humbling to release our work to you, mindful that many have undertaken to write introductions to the NT before us. Inevitably, some of our scholarly colleagues who are less conservatively minded will beg to differ with regard to certain positions taken in the volume. Yet our reward is in serious students of Scripture finding in this book a measure of the spiritual wealth that Jesus alluded to when he said that "every student of Scripture instructed in the kingdom of heaven is like a landowner who brings out of his storeroom what is new and what is old" (Matt 13:52).

Soli Deo gloria—to God alone be the glory!

Andreas J. Köstenberger, L. Scott Kellum, and Charles L. Quarles
Wake Forest, North Carolina, May 1, 2016

Part One

INTRODUCTION

BEFORE INVESTIGATING THE Gospels and the rest of the NT in Parts Two through Four of this volume, it is appropriate to lay the groundwork for the study of the writings included in the canon of the NT by considering the nature and scope of Scripture (chap. 1) and by surveying the landscape of the political and religious background of the NT (chap. 2). This is appropriate because questions such as the extent of the NT canon, the inerrancy and inspiration of Scripture, the translation of Scripture, and its textual transmission (textual criticism) constitute preliminary issues that have an important bearing on the interpretation of the books included in the NT.

Unless these questions are adequately addressed, there is no proper foundation for NT introduction. When there is no proper foundation, the result is a doctrinal vacuum that leaves the student in a precarious and vulnerable position when confronted with challenges to the canonicity of certain NT books or to a high view of Scripture and its authority. Moreover, the Gospels, Acts, the NT letters, and the book of Revelation did not appear in a vacuum. For this reason it is vital to discuss the political and religious backgrounds that form the backdrop to the study of the various NT writings. Hence, NT introduction properly commences with treatments of the nature of NT Scripture and of the relevant NT background.

Chapter 1

The Nature and Scope of Scripture

CORE KNOWLEDGE

Basic Knowledge: Students should know the major issues involved in the formation of the canon, the doctrines of inerrancy and inspiration, the textual transmission of the NT, and translations of the Bible. They should have a basic grasp of the major figures and documents involved and issues addressed, including key dates.

Intermediate Knowledge: Students should be able to discuss more thoroughly the canonization process and the criteria of canonicity. They should be able to identify developments in the collection of the Gospels and the Pauline Letters. They should also be able to defend the reliability of the Bible on the basis of their knowledge of the relevant issues regarding the transmission and translation of Scripture.

Advanced Knowledge: Students should be able to provide definitions of *inerrancy* and *inspiration* on the basis of the major NT passages on the subject. They should be able to provide an overview of the history of the English Bible. They should also be prepared to discuss formal and functional equivalence in Bible translation.

INTRODUCTION

B. F. WESTCOTT noted long ago that a "general survey of the History of the Canon forms a necessary part of an Introduction to the writings of the New Testament."[1] For many students the discussion of the canon—the question of which books should be included in the Bible—seems moot: the canon is closed and limited to the books found in the Bible. But a study of the canon does more than merely determine the books of the OT and NT or furnish material for scholarly debate. It provides a basic orientation to how the Bible came into existence and therefore connects students more firmly to the foundations of their faith. In the context of the present volume, this opening chapter also serves the purpose of laying a basic framework for dealing with each NT book in more detail later on in this work.

This chapter begins a journey through the NT. The idea of a NT is traced along the lines of the historical development of this body of literature. As in the case of each individual NT book in the remainder of this volume, the discussion of the canon of the NT in the present chapter proceeds under the rubrics of history, literature, and theology.[2] First, the discussion of *history* scrutinizes the process of canonization in order to answer the question, Why these twenty-seven books? Second, the treatment of *literature* deals with the reliability of the Bible and seeks to adjudicate the question, Is the Bible today what was originally written? Finally, the canon is also significantly a function of the church's *theology*. Hence the chapter closes with an inquiry into the question, What is the nature of the canon?

THE NEW TESTAMENT CANON: WHY THESE TWENTY-SEVEN BOOKS?

The present investigation regarding the scope and extent of the NT—the NT canon—is concerned not so much with the production of these writings but with their recognition as Christian Scripture to the exclusion of all other possible candidates. What is a "canon"? Put succinctly, the word comes from the Greek word *kanōn*, which in turn derives from its Hebrew equivalent *kaneh* and means "rule" or "standard."[3] The term eventually came to refer to the collection of the Christian Scriptures. This modern concept of canon is clearly

---

[1] B. F. Westcott, *A General Survey of the History of the Canon of the New Testament* (London, England: Macmillan & Co., 1896), 1. Westcott defines *canon* as "the collection of books which constitute the original written Rule of the Christian Faith" (ibid., n. 1).

[2] Regarding the rubrics of history, literature, and theology, see A. J. Köstenberger and R. D. Patterson, *Invitation to Biblical Interpretation: Exploring the Hermeneutical Triad of History, Literature, and Theology* (Grand Rapids, MI: Kregel, 2011); idem, *For the Love of God's Word: An Introduction to Biblical Interpretation* (Grand Rapids, MI: Kregel, 2015).

[3] See L. M. McDonald, *The Biblical Canon: Its Origin, Transmission, and Authority*, 3rd ed. (Peabody, MA: Hendrickson, 2007), 38–39; and B. M. Metzger, *The Canon of the New Testament: Its Origin, Development, and Significance* (Oxford, UK: Clarendon, 1987), 289–93.

attested in the fourth century. How far the notion extends back beyond this to even earlier centuries is the subject of vigorous scholarly debate.[4]

The composition of the various NT writings took place starting in the late 40s and proceeded through the latter half of the first century. Subsequently, these books were copied and disseminated among the growing number of Christian congregations all over the Roman Empire, as is attested by the available manuscript evidence. The papyrus fragment $\mathfrak{P}^{52}$ contains John 18:31–33, 37–38 and most likely dates to the first half of the second century.[5] Its discovery in Egypt, many miles from the Gospel's origin in Asia Minor and only a few short decades after the Gospel was written, bears telling testimony to the speed with which the early Christian writings spread to various locales across a network of churches that one writer has called a "holy internet."[6]

Generally, the main subject of debate today is not whether the NT canon is closed (i.e., fixed and therefore unchangeable).[7] The discussion centers rather on the questions of how and when the closing of the canon occurred. The broad time frame during which this process of canonization took place spans from the period of the early church to the ecclesiastical councils of the fourth and fifth centuries that declared the canon closed.[8] Whether the canon was set earlier or later in this period is disputed. The limited evidence from second-century patristic literature and differing assumptions regarding the nature of Christianity and the Christian canon make the investigation into the process of canonization "a narrow path, roughly paved and poorly lit."[9]

---

[4] For helpful surveys see D. G. Dunbar, "The Biblical Canon," in *Hermeneutics, Authority, and Canon*, ed. D. A. Carson and J. D. Woodbridge (Grand Rapids, MI: Zondervan, 1986), 297–360, 424–46; and "The New Testament Canon," in D. A. Carson and D. J. Moo, *An Introduction to the New Testament*, 2nd ed. (Grand Rapids, MI: Zondervan, 2005), 726–43. See further the discussion below.

[5] K. and B. Aland, *The Text of the New Testament*, rev. and enl. ed., trans. E. F. Rhodes (Grand Rapids, MI: Eerdmans, 1988), 85; B. M. Metzger and B. D. Ehrman, *The Text of the New Testament: Its Transmission, Corruption, and Restoration*, 4th ed. (New York, NY: Oxford University Press, 2005), 55–56.

[6] M. B. Thompson, "The Holy Internet: Communication Between Churches in the First Christian Generation," in *The Gospels for All Christians: Rethinking the Gospel Audiences*, ed. R. Bauckham (Grand Rapids, MI: Eerdmans, 1998), 49–70.

[7] Some have sought to reopen this issue; see R. W. Funk, "The Once and Future New Testament," in *The Canon Debate*, 2nd ed., ed. L. M. McDonald and J. A. Sanders (Peabody, MA: Hendrickson, 2002), 541–57; and the discussion of reformist feminist proposals by E. S. Fiorenza, R. R. Ruether, and others in M. E. Köstenberger, *Jesus and the Feminists: Who Do They Say That He Is?* (Wheaton, IL: Crossway, 2008). McDonald (*Biblical Canon*, 427) has questioned the contours of the NT canon, particularly with regard to 2 Peter, the Pastorals, and other "nonapostolic" books. Certain Christian groups have historically had a different NT. The Nestorian churches in Eastern Syria still hold to a 22-book NT (B. M. Metzger, *The Bible in Translation* [Grand Rapids, MI: Baker, 2001], 25–29; Carson and Moo, *Introduction to the New Testament*, 735). Evangelicals and Roman Catholics continue to differ regarding the contents of the OT canon (see the discussion of the OT Apocrypha in chap. 2 below).

[8] J. Barton, *Holy Writings, Sacred Text: The Canon in Early Christianity* (Louisville, KY: Westminster John Knox, 1997), 1.

[9] W. R. Farmer, D. M. Farkasfalvy, and H. W. Attridge. *The Formation of the New Testament Canon: An Ecumenical Approach*, Theological Inquiries (New York, NY: Paulist, 1983), 125.

The Witness of the New Testament

The NT canon can be viewed from both a human and a divine perspective. The traditional evangelical view affirms God's activity in the formation of the canon. From this vantage point, it can be said that in one sense at least, the NT canon was closed the moment the last NT book was written. According to this view, God, through the agency of the Holy Spirit and the instrumentality of the NT writers, generated holy Scripture (a phenomenon called "inspiration"; see further below); and the church's task was not the *creation* of the canon but merely the *recognition* of the Scriptures God had previously chosen to inspire. This, in turn, has important ramifications with regard to authority: if the church's role is primarily passive in determining the Christian canon, then it is inspired Scripture, not the church, which is in the final position of authority.

Traditionally, the second century has been viewed as the pivotal period for the canonization process of the NT writings. By the end of that century, the books of the NT were largely recognized throughout the churches. In the two subsequent centuries, all that remained was a final resolution regarding the canonicity of smaller or disputed books such as James, 2 Peter, 2–3 John, Jude, and Revelation. What is more, the fact that traces of the church's canonical consciousness appear even in the NT itself suggests that the NT writers were aware that God was inspiring new documents in their day. In two important NT passages, the term "Scripture" *(graphē)*, used about fifty times in the NT to refer to the OT,[10] may refer to the emerging NT writings.

The first such passage is 1 Timothy 5:18: "For the Scripture says: 'Do not muzzle an ox while it is treading out the grain,' and, 'The worker is worthy of his wages.'" The text uses the word "Scripture" with reference to two quotations. The first, the prohibition against muzzling an ox, is taken from Deuteronomy 25:4. The second, "the worker is worthy of his wages," is in fact an exact verbal parallel of Luke 10:7.[11] While it is debated whether Luke's Gospel was the source for this quotation, it is clear that (1) the author used a written source (demanded by the word "Scripture," *graphē*); and (2) the source was considered to be authoritative on par with Deuteronomy. Whatever one's view is regarding the Pauline authorship of 1 Timothy, this furnishes a significant piece of evidence regarding the emerging canonical consciousness in NT times.

The same is true of 2 Peter 3:15–16. With reference to the apostle Paul, Peter writes that "[h]e speaks about these things in all his letters. There are some matters that are hard to understand. The untaught and unstable will twist them to their own destruction, as they also do with *the rest of the Scriptures*" (emphasis added). By implication, it follows that Peter

---

[10] E.g., Luke 4:21; 2 Tim 3:16; 2 Pet 1:20.

[11] I. H. Marshall, *The International Critical Commentary on the Pastoral Epistles*, ICC (Edinburgh, Scotland: T&T Clark, 1999), 615. He notes that some scholars try to lessen the implication of the statement by (1) making the reference to *graphē* apply only to the first quote; (2) a loose understanding of the word; or (3) the contention that the term is an inexact expression. However, as Marshall rightly says, "In any case, for the author the second citation had equal authority with the OT" (ibid.).

viewed Paul's Letters as "Scripture" on par with the writings of the OT. Strikingly, while NT writings were still being produced, 2 Peter indicates the acceptance of the Pauline Letters as Scripture and hence equally as authoritative as the Hebrew Scriptures.[12]

Given this kind of NT evidence, it is safe to conclude that, almost before the ink was dry, the earliest Christians, including leading figures in the church such as the apostles Paul and Peter, considered contemporaneous Christian documents such as Luke's Gospel and Paul's Letters as Scripture on the same level as the OT. From this it is not too difficult to trace the emerging canonical consciousness with regard to the formation of the NT through the writings of the early church fathers in the late first century and early second century. In fact, prior to the year 150, the only NT book not named as authentic or not unequivocally cited as authoritative in the extant patristic writings is 3 John.[13]

The Witness of the Early Church Fathers

A survey of the early patristic literature reveals that the early church fathers had no hesitancy whatsoever in quoting the various NT books as Scripture. Four examples must suffice. The author of *1 Clement*, the first extant non-biblical Christian document (ca. AD 96), tended to quote Scripture organically (i.e., without introductory formulas).[14] Clement cited the OT and the NT equally in this manner. He referred to the canonical Gospels, the book of Acts, 1 Corinthians, Philippians, Titus, Hebrews, 1 Peter, and perhaps James much as he did to the OT. Most likely, the earliest citation of a NT passage using the term "Scripture" in the subapostolic period (the period following the apostolic era) is *2 Clement* 2.4: "And another scripture says, 'I came not to call the righteous, but sinners.'"[15] This reference includes a clear citation of a passage in one of the canonical Gospels, most likely Mark 2:17, as early as the end of the first century.

---

[12] While the authors of this present book affirm the Pauline authorship of the letters to Timothy and Titus and the Petrine authorship of 1 and 2 Peter, respectively, the significance of the citations for the present debate is not diminished greatly if one assumes they are pseudepigraphical. Both books are normally considered first-century works.

[13] This silence can be explained by (1) the lack of complete records (3 John may have been cited in now-lost early patristic writings); (2) the brevity of the letter (only 14 verses); and (3) the fact that reference to 3 John may not have been as essential in the early church's proclamation, defense of the faith, or theological controversies, as those of other more weighty NT writings. But see C. E. Hill, *The Johannine Corpus in the Early Church* (New York, NY: Oxford University Press, 2004), 99, 369. Hill notes that the author of the *Epistula Apostolorum* used the phrase "to walk in truth," a possible echo of 3 John 3–4, and that Irenaeus (*Against Heresies* 4.26.3) may allude to 3 John 9 when referring to elders who "conduct themselves with contempt towards others, and are puffed up with pride of holding the chief seat." Hill also theorizes that the fifth- or sixth-century Codex Bezae may have originally included John, Revelation, and 1, 2 and 3 John in successive order, which would suggest a considerable prehistory as well as a "Johannine corpus" (ibid., 455). Given the size and content of 3 John, the question arises how such a manuscript could have survived unless it was attached to one or several larger works (at least 1 and 2 John).

[14] Generally, Clement uses *graphē* to refer to the OT, except for *2 Clem.* 23.3 where he cites an unknown writing (see also *2 Clem.* 11.2–4 for the same citation). There is some connection of this unknown writing to James.

[15] M. W. Holmes, *The Apostolic Fathers*, 3rd ed. (Grand Rapids, MI: Baker, 2007), 141: "This appears to be the earliest instance of a NT passage being quoted as *scripture*" (emphasis original). Holmes suggested the passage quoted is either Matt 9:13 or Mark 2:17.

Polycarp (ca. AD 69–155), whom Irenaeus called a disciple of the apostle John, also frequently referred to various NT writings in his letter to the Philippians. P. Hartog categorized Polycarp's use of NT documents according to three levels of certainty: (1) Polycarp *certainly* quoted Romans, 1 Corinthians, Galatians, Ephesians, Philippians, 1 Timothy, and 1 Peter; (2) he *probably* quoted Matthew, 2 Corinthians, 2 Timothy, and 1 John; and (3) he *possibly* quoted Luke, Acts, and 2 Thessalonians.[16] B. Metzger added an allusion to Hebrews to the list.[17] Thus Polycarp may have cited as many as fifteen NT books. By far Polycarp's most intriguing comment comes at *Phil.* 12.1: "For I am convinced that you are all well trained in the sacred scriptures. . . . Only as it is said in these scriptures, 'be angry but do not sin,' and 'do not let the sun set on your anger.'"[18] The clear implication is that there was a body of literature called "the Scriptures" of which the book of Ephesians was a part. Beyond this, it is more than likely that Polycarp viewed Paul's Letters in their entirety as Scripture.[19]

Papias (ca. AD 60–130), a contemporary of Polycarp and fellow disciple of John, wrote five books entitled *Expositions of the Lord's Sayings* that are no longer extant. From quotations in other books ("fragments") and reports from ancient writers, it is possible to ascertain that the books were a commentary on the words and deeds of Jesus from the canonical Gospels.[20] From these fragments it can be gleaned that Papias approved of Matthew, Mark, Luke, John, Acts, and Revelation. Reportedly, he also made use of 1 Peter and 1 John.[21] Since the word "sayings" or "oracles" *(logia)* is Paul's euphemism for the OT Scriptures (see Rom 3:2), it is likely that Papias considered his work an exposition of Scripture.

It follows from these observations that most NT documents were recognized as authoritative, even Scripture, as early as the end of the first or at least by the end of the second century of the Christian era. The four Gospels, the book of Acts, the letters of Paul, 1 Peter, and 1 John were universally recognized. With the exception of 3 John, the early church fathers cited all NT books as Scripture. Toward the end of the second century, the major contours of the NT had clearly emerged, setting the framework for the subsequent final resolution of the canonical status of several remaining smaller or disputed books.

---

[16] P. Hartog, *Polycarp and the New Testament*, WUNT 2/134 (Tübingen, Germany: Mohr Siebeck, 2002), 195.

[17] Metzger (*Canon*, 61) states, "Polycarp almost certainly knows the Epistle to the Hebrews; he calls Christ 'the eternal high priest' (xii.2; see Heb. vi.20; vii.3) and seems to echo Heb. xii.8 ('let us serve him with fear and all reverence,' vi.3)."

[18] The citation is from Eph 4:26, quoting Ps 4:5. Holmes, *Apostolic Fathers*, 295.

[19] Polycarp further seems rather enamored with *1 Clement*, which regularly uses the word translated "pore over" *(egkyptō)* to refer to studying the OT Scriptures. Yet Polycarp, for his part, uses Clement's favorite term, not with reference to the OT but to the Pauline Letters (*Phil.* 3.2). Clearly Polycarp understands the Pauline Letter collection to be Scripture. He certainly has access to Romans, 1 and 2 Corinthians, Galatians, Ephesians, Philippians, and 1 and 2 Timothy, and possibly 2 Thessalonians (Hartog, *Polycarp and the NT*, 195–97). Given this list, it is improbable that Polycarp's collection of Paul's Letters did not contain the rest of his letters (see below on the nature of ancient letter collections).

[20] C. E. Hill, "Papias of Hierapolis," *ExpTim* 117 (2006): 312.

[21] Ibid.

The Witness of the Muratorian Fragment

Most likely, in the late second century, an unknown writer composed a defense of the NT books that seems to corroborate the conclusion that most NT writings were recognized as Scripture by that time.[22] The writer referred to these writings as "held sacred," and he stated that pseudonymous works could not be "received" in the church because "gall should not be mixed with honey."[23] At the very least, the writer saw the books listed as a firm canon. The Muratorian Fragment, which was named for the eighteenth-century Italian historian and theologian who discovered it, lists at least twenty-two of the twenty-seven books in the NT canon.[24]

These works included the four Gospels, at least two of John's letters (and possibly the third), the Acts of the Apostles, Paul's thirteen letters, Jude, and Revelation. The books are not in a particular order, and the manuscript is fragmentary at the beginning and, most likely, at the end. Other books may well have been included in the church's canon at the time the Muratorian Fragment was written, such as Hebrews, the Petrine Letters, or the letter of James. From the third century to the fifth, questions regarding the rest of the General Epistles and the book of Revelation were resolved in the minds of most Christians.

We have considered the witness of the NT and of the early church fathers as well as the testimony of the Muratorian Fragment, which is likely the earliest extant canonical list that in all probability documents the existence of the concept of canon by the end of the second century.

Stimuli for Canonization and Criteria of Canonicity

Stimuli for Canonization There was likely a series of contributing factors for NT canonization. The treatment by N. Geisler and W. Nix is representative in suggesting the following five major stimuli for the church's determination of the NT canon.[25]

1. *The prophetic nature of the NT books.* The NT books themselves were prophetic, intrinsically valuable, and worthy of preservation.
2. *The church's need for authoritative Scriptures.* The demand for books that conformed to apostolic teaching to be read in the churches (see 1 Thess 5:27; 1 Tim 4:13) required a selection process.
3. *Heretical challenges.* Around 140, the heretic Marcion in Rome declared an edited Gospel of Luke and only ten letters of Paul as useful while rejecting all the other apostolic works, which necessitated a response by those in the apostolic mainstream of Christianity.

---

[22] See esp. E. J. Schnabel, "The Muratorian Fragment: The State of Research," *JETS* 57 (2014): 231–64.

[23] See Metzger, *Canon*, 305–7, citing Muratorian Fragment 60 and 66–67.

[24] See the discussion in ibid., 191–201.

[25] N. L. Geisler and W. E. Nix, *A General Introduction to the Bible*, rev. and exp. ed. (Chicago, IL: Moody, 1986), 277–78.

4. *Missionary outreach.* Since the Bible began to be translated into Syriac and Latin as early as the first half of the second century, determining the NT canon was important for deciding which books should be translated.
5. *Persecution.* When the edict of Diocletian in AD 303 ordered all the sacred books of the Christians burned (a fact that may, at least in part, account for the relative scarcity of pre-AD 300 NT manuscripts), this required believers to choose which books were part of Scripture and thus most worthy of preservation.

Criteria of Canonicity When the early church addressed the topic of the canon, it recognized which writings bore the stamp of divine inspiration. Four major criteria were used in this process.[26] The first was *apostolicity*, that is, direct or indirect association of a given work with an apostle. This criterion was met by Matthew, John, and Peter, all of whom were

SIDEBAR 1.1: PSEUDEPIGRAPHA IN THE EARLY CHURCH

There is no known example of a book falsely claiming to be written by an apostle (a "pseudepigraphical" work), orthodox or not, that was accepted by the early church as canonical. Serapion, bishop of Antioch (died AD 211), stated concerning the spurious *Gospel of Peter:* "For our part, brethren, we receive both Peter and the other apostles as Christ, but the writings which falsely bear their names we reject, as men of experience, knowing that such were not handed down to us."[1]

Tertullian (ca. AD 160–225) recorded the defrocking of an Asian elder, noting that, "in Asia, the presbyter who composed that writing [i.e. *Acts of Paul* and *3 Corinthians*], as if he were augmenting Paul's fame from his own store, after being convicted, and confessing that he had done it from love of Paul, was removed from his office."[2] Thus, when a book in the canon claims to have been written by a certain author, it may be assumed that the early church believed it was authentic.

[1] Eusebius, *Eccl. Hist.* 5.22.1.

[2] Tertullian, *On Baptism* 17, in *Ante-Nicene Fathers: The Writings of the Fathers Down to A.D. 325*, vol. III: *Tertullian*, ed. A. Roberts, J. Donaldson, A. C. Coxe, and A. Menzies (Peabody, MA: Hendrickson, 1994), 677. See also Eusebius's statement regarding apocryphal works: "in order that we might know them and the writings that are put forward by heretics under the name of the apostles containing gospels such as those of Peter, and Thomas, and Matthias, and some others besides, or Acts such as those of Andrew and John and the other apostles. To none of these has any who belonged to the succession of the orthodox ever thought it right to refer in his writings. Moreover, the type of phraseology differs from apostolic style, and the opinion and tendency of their contents are widely dissonant from true orthodoxy and clearly show that they are the forgeries of heretics" (*Eccl. Hist.* 3.25).

[26] For helpful treatments on the formation of the Christian canon, including criteria for canonicity, see Carson and Moo, *Introduction to the New Testament*, 726–43 (esp. pp. 736–37); M. J. Kruger, *Canon Revisited: Establishing the Origins and Authority of the New Testament Books* (Wheaton, IL: Crossway, 2012); idem, *The Question of Canon: Challenging the Status Quo in the New Testament Debate* (Downers Grove, IL: InterVarsity, 2013); and L. M. McDonald, "Canon," in *Dictionary of the Later New Testament and Its Development*, ed. R. Martin and P. H. Davids (Downers Grove, IL: InterVarsity, 1997), 134–44 (for ancient references regarding criteria for canonicity, see p. 135).

members of the Twelve (Matt 10:2–3 pars.), as well as Paul, an apostle commissioned by the risen Christ on the road to Damascus (Acts 9:1–9). It was also met by James and Jude, half brothers of Jesus (Matt 13:55; Mark 6:3; see Jas 1:1; Jude 1). Indirectly, the criterion was also satisfied by Mark, a close associate of Peter (1 Pet 5:13) and Paul (2 Tim 4:11), and Luke, a travel companion of Paul on some of his missionary journeys (see especially the "we" passages in the book of Acts).

The second criterion of canonicity was a book's *orthodoxy*, that is, whether a given writing conformed to the church's "rule of faith" (Lat. *regula fidei*). This allowed books such as Hebrews to be considered, though it appears that attribution to Paul or a member of the "Pauline circle" also played a major role in the acceptance of Hebrews into the canon. The question addressed under this rubric is whether the teaching of a given book conformed to apostolic teaching (see Acts 2:42).

SIDEBAR 1.2: ATHANASIUS'S EASTER LETTER OF AD 367

Athanasius, in his festal letter dated 367, lists the exact same canon as today. "There must be no hesitation to state again the [books] of the New Testament; for they are these: Four Gospels: according to **Matthew**, according to **Mark**, according to **Luke**, and according to **John**. Further, after these, also [The] **Acts** of [the] Apostles, and the seven so-called Catholic Epistles of the Apostles, as follows: One of **James**, but **two of Peter**, then, **three of John**, and after these, one of **Jude**. In addition to these there are fourteen Epistles of the Apostle Paul put down in the following order: The first to the **Romans**, then **two to the Corinthians**, and after these, [the Letter] to the **Galatians,** and then to the **Ephesians**; further, [the Letters] to the **Philippians** and to the **Colossians** and two to the **Thessalonians**, and the [Letter] to the **Hebrews**. And next two [Letters] to **Timothy**, but one to **Titus,** and the last [being] the one to **Philemon**. Moreover, also **the Apocalypse** of John."

The third criterion was a book's *antiquity*, that is, whether a given piece of writing was produced during the apostolic era. This served to corroborate the previous two criteria and excluded second-century and third-century apocryphal and pseudepigraphical literature (such as the Gospel of Thomas) that mimicked the authentic apostolic documents. It also ruled out documents such as the *Didache* or the *Shepherd of Hermas* that were produced subsequent to the apostolic era. Some of these latter writings reflected early church practice and were read with profit by the early Christians. In the end, however, they were not included in the canon because they failed to meet the criteria of apostolicity and antiquity.

The fourth and final major criterion of canonicity was that of *ecclesiastical usage*, that is, whether a given document was already widely used in the early church. As in the previous criterion, this benchmark was used in conjunction with the other standards stated above, and only documents that met all four criteria were included. The above list should not be taken to suggest that the early church used this exact list of criteria to arrive at the NT canon. Rather, these four criteria, used in conjunction with one another, adequately summarize the types of considerations that went into the early church's adjudication of individual books for possible inclusion in the canon. In fact, C. E. Hill notes that these types of criteria are digested from the churches' rejection of late contenders to be added to the Scripture.[27] It implies that these criteria were what is expressed in the existing canon and expected for any additions (if any).

Ecclesiastical Debates Regarding the Canonicity of Individual Books

Eusebius's* Ecclesiastical History *and Varying Opinions in the East and the West On the whole these were the major criteria used by the early church to determine the canonicity of a given piece of writing. But not everyone agreed in every specific instance. The historian and church father Eusebius (ca. AD 260–340), bishop of Caesarea, provided a valuable reflection of then current discussion in his *Ecclesiastical History*. Eusebius grouped the books of the NT into three categories. First were the commonly recognized books, that is, those writings widely acknowledged as canonical. These documents included the four Gospels, Acts, Paul's Letters, 1 John, 1 Peter, and Revelation. Second were the disputed books questioned by some, "but," as Eusebius noted, "nevertheless known [i.e., recognized as authentic and thus canonical] by most." These writings included James, Jude, 2 Peter, and 2–3 John. The third group encompassed the spurious books, which designated those works that at one time had been received by some but that had now been rejected. These writings included the *Acts of Paul*, the *Shepherd of Hermas*, the *Revelation of Peter*, and the *(Pseudo-) Epistle of Barnabas*.[28]

As the Roman Empire was divided into East and West, so also, to a certain extent, opinions were divided concerning certain NT books. In the West (Italy/Rome, North Africa, Gaul, etc.), doubts seemed to persist regarding Hebrews, James, 2 Peter, 3 John, and Jude. But these views were not universal since each of these books had its supporters.[29] In the East (Greece, Asia Minor, Syria, Palestine, and Egypt), the status of James, 2 Peter, 2–3 John, Jude, and Revelation continued to be debated.[30] But again this was not a universal opinion. For example, Athanasius, bishop of Alexandria (ca. AD 296–373), published

---

[27] Hill, "New Testament Canon," 119. Hill states, "They are internal qualities by which the authentic makes itself known and recognized. Also, they only seem to function negatively, when a given book is challenged, not positively, applied a priori before anything is to be considered as Scripture. Most of the books of the NT in fact never seem to have been significantly questioned within the church."

[28] Eusebius, *Eccl. Hist.* 3.25. Eusebius adds the book of Revelation to this because he cannot reconcile the thousand years of Rev 20:2–7 with his own antichiliast position, though this appears to be at least to some extent a function of his own personal bias rather than reflecting widespread rejection of Revelation by the church as a whole.

[29] Hilary of Poitiers (ca. 315–367/68) receives Hebrews and James; Philaster, bishop of Brescia (died ca. 397), receives the seven General Epistles and Hebrews; Rufinus (ca. 345–411) receives the entire 27-book NT, as did his friend and contemporary Jerome (ca. 345–420). Augustine (354–430) followed suit (see Metzger, *Canon*, 232–37).

[30] Revelation is the only book rejected by Cyril, bishop of Jerusalem (ca. 315–387), and Gregory Nazianzen (ca. 329/30–389/90); Amphilochius of Iconium (ca. 340–395) states that most reject Revelation.

his thirty-ninth festal letter in 367, in which he prescribed the same twenty-seven-book NT canon still affirmed by the vast majority of Christians.[31]

The Syrian church (Aramaic-speaking Christians in the East) hesitated to receive the General Epistles and Revelation. The Syrian translation of the NT (called "Peshitta") supports a twenty-two-book canon. It was not until the Philoxenian revision (ca. AD 500) that the remaining NT books were added to the church's canon.

Certain orthodox books for a time assumed canonical status in particular segments of the church or at least in the opinions of some of its representatives.[32] On the whole these writings were only rarely considered to be Scripture, but they were viewed as useful for the instruction of new Christians without being read during the church's worship. When some were included in the later complete codices (such as the fourth-century Codex Sinaiticus and the fifth-century Codex Alexandrinus), they were always placed subsequent to the book of Revelation. This suggests that the church considered these writings to be useful for believers' edification but not divinely inspired.[33] Thus, these codices, too large and bulky for personal use, among other things, served as "reference editions" of the Bible.[34]

Early Church Councils Only three known early church councils officially mention the canon of Scripture.[35] There may have been some earlier local councils, but we have only brief mentions of them.[36] The first, the Council of Laodicea, was a local meeting of bishops around AD 363. It only survives in an ancient summary of the individual canons. Canon LX contains a list of the Old and New Testaments. The list of specific books included in the extant documents was probably added at a later time and may not represent the council.[37] The description given of the canon shows the idea of "canon" is indeed present.

---

[31] As did Epiphanius of Salamis (ca. 315–403). See F. F. Bruce, *The Canon of Scripture* (Downers Grove, IL: InterVarsity, 1988), 210–14.

[32] These writings include the *Shepherd of Hermas* (received by Irenaeus, respected in Egypt, but not by Clement of Alexandria or Origen) as well as the Wisdom of Solomon and the *Apocalypse of Peter* (included in the Muratorian Fragment). *First Clement* is also received as Scripture by some (e.g., Clement of Alexandria). The *Epistle of Barnabas* is briefly believed to be canonical in Egypt. The *Didache* was at one time considered Scripture in Egypt according to Clement of Alexandria and Origen. See H. Y. Gamble, *The New Testament Canon: Its Making and Meaning*, Guides to Biblical Scholarship (Philadelphia, PA: Fortress, 1985), 48–49.

[33] Note that the Muratorian Fragment and Eusebius both discuss the books of the NT in these categories, as do many other patristic writers.

[34] Westcott (*Canon*, 439) notes regarding Codex Sinaiticus and the *Shepherd of Hermas* that "the arrangement of the quires shews *[sic]* that the *Shepherd*, like *4 Maccabees* in the Old Testament, was treated as a separate section of the volume, and therefore perhaps as an Appendix to the more generally received books."

[35] D. Brown (*The Da Vinci Code* [New York, NY: Doubleday, 2003], 234), in a widely popular novel, suggests that the canon was determined—what is more, significantly revamped—at the Council of Nicea (325). In fact the Council never even discussed the matter. Instead, this first ecumenical council presupposed the NT Scriptures, including the four canonical Gospels, as the arbiter of all disputes (see Westcott, *Canon*, 438).

[36] Tertullian appeals to "every council of Churches" who rejected the canonicity of the Shepherd of Hermas (*De pudicitia* 10). These would have predated the earliest of the known councils (*De pudicitia* was written around AD 210). Hill suggests that the Muratorian Fragment may possibly have been the report of one of these councils. (Hill, *Johannine Corpus*, 133–34).

[37] That list consists of the present NT, minus the book of Revelation. Westcott suggests the list is a copy from the list of Cyril of Jerusalem (ca. AD 315–387; Westcott, *Canon*, 505).

It states, "No psalms composed by private individuals nor any uncanonical books may be read in the church, but only the Canonical Books of the Old and New Testaments."[38] The second was the Council of Hippo Regius in North Africa (AD 393), which met and affirmed the present twenty-seven-book NT. The third was the Third Council of Carthage (AD 397), which read the previous affirmations and repeated them.[39] In no sense were these lists the result of great debate. The conciliar documents simply stated the books of the OT and NT and added the following note: "Let this be sent to our brother and fellow bishop, Boniface, and to the other bishops of those parts, that they may confirm this canon, for these are the things which we have received from our fathers to be read in church."[40] Rather than engaging in a sustained debate or a process of sorting and sifting, "the church," as P. Balla noted, "recognized as scripture in the fourth century those writings that had guided its life, at least in some regions, in the preceding centuries."[41]

In the next century the East came to receive Revelation and the rest of the General Epistles. Thus, by the close of the fifth century, virtually all questions regarding the extent of the NT canon were closed in the minds of most.

To sum up, the salient facts regarding the recognition of the NT canon thus far are as follows. First, most books of the present NT canon are found in every witness to a canon in antiquity. Almost immediately, twenty out of twenty-seven books were universally received; most accepted at least a twenty-two-book canon. Second, no book in the present canon had previously been universally rejected by the early churches. There is no post-second-century epiphany concerning a book in the NT that lacked ancient support. Third, no book was ever received into the NT canon that was believed to be pseudonymous.[42]

Finally, no council subjectively selected or rejected the books of the canon. Instead, after a period of sifting and sorting, the church recognized the divine inspiration of the books included in the NT canon and declined to accept the claims of canonicity of any competing works on the basis that they failed to meet the above-stated criteria of canonicity: apostolicity, orthodoxy, antiquity, and ecclesiastical usage.

Recent Developments in Scholarship on the NT Canon

The above survey of the major works and figures forms the basic framework for the study of the NT canon. The basic facts and data pertaining to the canonization process of the NT are not widely disputed. What has been the subject of considerable recent debate,

---

[38] P. Schaff, ed., *The Seven Ecumenical Councils: Nicene and Post-Nicene Fathers*, Series 2, vol. 14 (Edinburgh, Scotland: T&T Clark, n.d.), 14:158. Note also that earlier Canon XVI states, "The Gospel, apostle, and the other Scriptures are to be read on the Sabbath." The conjecture is that this is a reference to a Saturday worship and that the NT is to be read along with the OT (ibid., 133). For our purposes, note that "Gospel, apostle, and other Scriptures" sounds much like earlier descriptions of the books of the NT. See, e.g., Irenaeus who describes the four Gospels as "Gospel" and Paul as "the apostle."

[39] See Metzger, *Canon*, 314–15; Westcott, *Canon*, 448–49.

[40] Schaff, ed., *The Seven Ecumenical Councils*, 454.

[41] P. Balla, "Evidence for an Early Christian Canon (Second and Third Century)," in *Canon Debate*, 385.

[42] This is addressed in the discussion of pseudonymity later in this volume; see esp. the discussions in chap. 15 (Letters to Timothy and Titus) and chap. 18 (2 Peter).

however, is the interpretation of this data with regard to the question of the formation of the Christian canon. In fact, some, such as Sundberg, have called for a "revised history of the NT canon."[43] The discussion took its point of departure from the definition of the NT canon as "a closed list of authoritative books." Since this terminology is not found, at least explicitly, until the third or fourth centuries, these writers argued that characterizing the early church's deliberations in the second century as determining the "canonical" status of a given book committed the fallacy of anachronism. According to these writers, at this early stage of the canonical process, a particular work could have been viewed as "Scripture" (i.e., a piece of sacred writing) but not as "canonical" because this kind of canonical consciousness and sense of a "closed collection" of NT books only emerged in the third and fourth centuries.

What can be said in response to these claims? First, as mentioned above, on the assumption that the Muratorian Fragment is to be dated in the late second century, it would contradict these objections, for it clearly evidences this kind of canonical consciousness and presents a list of canonical books. This possible damaging counterevidence has been recognized by the proponents of this view. Consequently, scholars such as Sundberg and Hahneman have challenged the dating of the Muratorian Fragment to the second century, proposing instead a date in the fourth century.[44] But many continue to believe that a second-century date for the Muratorian Fragment is more likely.[45]

Another problematic aspect of Sundberg's thesis is that the early church in all probability did not only evidence a concept of canon but in fact possessed an already established canon: the OT. Again, Sundberg and others challenged the notion of a closed OT canon in the first two centuries, maintaining that the OT canon was not completed until at least the fourth century and that the early church received the OT canon before Judaism determined the canonical boundaries of the Hebrew Scriptures. According to these scholars, the collection of Scripture was a fluid process.[46]

In response, Sundberg and his followers focus unduly on *the church's* closing of the canon while failing to give adequate attention to *God's* activity of inspiring the NT writings in

---

[43] See A. C. Sundberg Jr., "Toward a Revised History of the New Testament Canon," *SE IV*, TU 102 (Berlin, Germany: Akademie, 1968), 452–61; idem, "Canon Muratori: A Fourth-Century List," *HTR* 66 (1973): 1–41.

[44] See Sundberg, "Canon Muratori"; G. M. Hahneman, *The Muratorian Fragment and the Development of the Canon*, Oxford Theological Monographs (Oxford, NY: Clarendon, 1992); and McDonald, *Biblical Canon*, 369–79. On the Muratorian Fragment, see already the brief summary earlier in this chapter as well as the discussion in Metzger (*Canon*, 191–201); and Schnabel, ""Muratorian Fragment.""

[45] E. Ferguson, "Canon Muratori: Provenance and Date," *Studia Patristica* 18 (1982): 677–83. Hahneman's arguments are solidly refuted by C. E. Hill, "The Debate over the Muratorian Fragment and the Development of the Canon," *WTJ* 57 (1995): 437–52 (see esp. p. 440); and Schnabel, "Muratorian Fragment." See also E. Ferguson, "Review of G. M. Hahneman, *The Muratorian Fragment and the Development of the Canon*," *JTS* 57 (1993): 696. For a helpful discussion of the date of the *Shepherd of Hermas*, see Holmes (*Apostolic Fathers*, 447), who suggests that the writing may be a composite document.

[46] See A. C. Sundberg, "The Bible Canon and the Christian Doctrine of Inspiration," *Int* 29 (1975): 352–71.

the first place.[47] Thus, these writers base their assessment primarily on definitive ecclesiastical pronouncements on the NT canon. Since this kind of final resolution does not occur until the fourth century, this is taken as evidence that "canon" was not an operative concept during earlier stages of the canonization process. Such reasoning is hardly convincing because it puts an undue emphasis on the church's role in the determination of canonicity. It also neglects to acknowledge that by the end of the second century, most NT books were recognized as part of the church's canon of sacred Scripture.

Viewing the determination of the church's canon of inspired, authoritative books primarily in terms of a "patristic accomplishment"[48] casts the debate along the lines of two possible options: wholesale acceptance or critical evaluation. Sundberg favors the first alternative. One of the entailments of such a full-scale acceptance of the fourth-century church's determination of the canon is the inclusion of the OT Apocrypha in the canon of Scripture on the basis that the same councils that enumerated the twenty-seven-book NT canon also included the OT Apocrypha.[49] C. D. Allert, likewise, seems to suggest that the church's proper response is to submit to this patristic decision. In doing so, he attempted to affirm inspiration and inerrancy but only through the lens of the church's interpretation, not as a function of the Bible's own testimony regarding itself.[50]

Conversely, while largely concurring with Sundberg, L. McDonald concluded his book with the following list of seven questions that suggests that he would prefer to evaluate, rather than merely accept, the "patristic accomplishment" in delineating the NT canon.[51] He asked,

1. Is the very notion of canon a Christian idea? In his view the earliest Christians had no concept of canon. So why should believers today entertain such a notion?
2. Should the contemporary church adhere to a canon that legitimizes abhorrent practices such as slavery or the subjugation of women?[52]

---

[47] See the discussion of inspiration later in this chapter.

[48] C. D. Allert, *A High View of Scripture? The Authority of the Bible and the Formation of the New Testament Canon*, Evangelical Resourcement: Ancient Sources for the Church's Future (Grand Rapids, MI: Baker, 2007), 175.

[49] A. C. Sundberg, "Protestant Old Testament Canon: Should It Be Re-examined?" *CBQ* 28 (1966): 194–203; and idem, "The 'Old Testament': A Christian Canon," *CBQ* 30 (1968): 143–55.

[50] Allert, *A High View of Scripture*, 175.

[51] McDonald, *Biblical Canon*, 426–27.

[52] This question addresses at least two major issues. First, there is the matter of proper exegesis: the NT endorses neither slavery nor the subjugation of women, though it does restrict certain ecclesiastical roles to men (see R. W. Yarbrough, "Progressive *and* Historic: The Hermeneutics of 1 Timothy 2:9–15," in *Women in the Church: An Analysis and Application of 1 Timothy 2:9–15*, 2nd ed., ed. A. J. Köstenberger and T. R. Schreiner [Grand Rapids, MI: Baker, 2005], 121–48). Second, there is the issue of the relationship between biblical revelation and contemporary culture. Especially since culture is always in a state of flux, if not entropy (a case in point being the advocacy of some, even in the church, of the permissibility of homosexuality today, which stands in conflict with the Bible's universal condemnation of this practice), culture must not be used to judge the appropriateness of biblical teaching. Instead, Scripture should constitute the standard by which the morality of the prevailing culture is assessed.

3. Does a move toward a closed canon limit the presence and power of the Holy Spirit in the church?
4. Should the church be limited to an OT canon to which Jesus and his first disciples were clearly not confined?
5. Should the church continue to recognize nonapostolic literature? Here McDonald affirms the criterion of apostolicity but rejects the authorship of the Pastoral Epistles, 2 Peter, and Jude.
6. Is it appropriate to tie the modern church to a canon that emerged out of the historical circumstances in the second to fifth centuries?
7. Does the same Spirit who inspired the written documents of Scripture not still speak today?

McDonald did not advocate replacing the Christian Bible, and he acknowledged that no other ancient document is, on the whole, more reliable than Scripture in its current configuration. But he did seek to listen to other voices to tell him about the Lord Jesus Christ. According to McDonald, the *agrapha* (supposedly true stories of Jesus that were not included in the canonical Gospels), the Apocrypha, the Pseudepigrapha, and other early Christian literature are valuable in informing the church's faith. While the questions raised by McDonald are certainly worthy of further reflection and discussion, his blurring of the edges of the canon is of doubtful merit.

Critique

How should one evaluate the various contributions by recent scholarship on the NT canon? To begin with, as noted above, the claim that the Muratorian Fragment was a fourth-century composition has been decisively refuted. Also, much of recent scholarship on the NT canon is beset by a series of methodological problems. One such difficulty is that the available relevant evidence is often judged as if "not extant" necessarily means "never existed." For example, Athanasius's list is sometimes declared to be the first time the present twenty-seven-book NT canon was listed as such.[53] But the truth is that we have precious little evidence from the previous centuries on any one subject. Is this the first complete list of NT canonical books ever compiled or the first such list extant today? The latter is more likely.

The same holds true with regard to terminological discussions. For example, concerning the term *canon*, Gamble stated, "It is important to notice that the word 'canon' did not begin to be applied to Christian writings until the mid-fourth century."[54] This is problematic for the following reasons. To argue that there was no concept of a canon in the previous centuries on the basis of the presence or absence of the word *canon* is an argument from silence that is notoriously difficult to substantiate. In fact, the argument constitutes

[53] E.g., Allert, *A High View of Scripture*, 141; Barton, *Holy Writing, Sacred Text*, 10; and Metzger, *Canon*, 212.
[54] Gamble, *New Testament Canon*, 17.

an instance of a semantic fallacy that fails to consider the possibility that another expression or set of terms may have been used to communicate the concept that was later called "canon."[55]

A third problem arises with regard to the significance placed on dissenting voices. How heavily does one weigh those who received a book versus those who rejected it or indeed the mere notation that some rejected or, more often, disputed the canonicity of a given book? Must one extrapolate from such discussions an unfinished collection of Scripture? If dissenting voices obviate the widespread mainstream consensus, there is still no canon today, nor was there ever a biblical canon, whether of the OT or the NT. Someone somewhere has always and will always object to a given book for often less than compelling reasons.[56] If unanimity, rather than consensus, is required, then there is no hope of ever having a canon of Scripture.

Thus, recent scholarship has been helpful in raising important questions regarding the NT canon but appears to be headed largely in the wrong direction by focusing on the final determination and closure of the NT canon by the church councils while unduly diminishing the significance of earlier developments in the canonization process. For this reason the conventional evangelical understanding continues to be preferred. In fact, closer scrutiny suggests that the traditional view may concede even more than is necessary by placing the closure of the canon at a date later than may be warranted by the available evidence. As seen below, there is good reason to believe that the core of the NT canon was established at least by the middle of the second century if not before.[57]

The Evidence for an Early Canon of Core New Testament Books

The Fourfold Gospel Even before the Gospels were written, there was an intense interest in the words and deeds of Jesus on the part of the church. J. D. G. Dunn argued that the oral pre-Gospel traditions were already functioning as canon in the first century.[58] He was undoubtedly correct when he stated, "It was the authority which it [the Gospel tradition] already possessed which ensured that it was written down."[59] His conclusion was that "the canonical process began with the impact made by Jesus himself."[60]

---

[55] E.g., M. G. Kline, *The Structure of Biblical Authority*, 2nd ed. (Eugene, OR: Wipf & Stock, 1997 [1987]), 75, who suggests that the covenantal nature of the canon may have led the early church writers to employ the term "covenantal" rather than "canon." Eusebius uses the term "the Covenantal Scriptures." The term is *endiathēkos*. Tertullian preferred the term "instruments" (Lat., *instrumentum*) that may mean "documents."

[56] E.g., E. Evanson attempts to reduce the Christian canon for theological reasons (*Dissonance of the Four Generally Received Evangelists and the Evidence of Their Respective Authenticity, Examined with That of Some Other Scriptures Deemed Canonical* [Gloucester, England: Walker, 1805], 340–41).

[57] See C. E. Hill, "The New Testament Canon: *Deconstructio ad absurdum?*" *JETS* 52 (2009): 114–20.

[58] J. D. G. Dunn, "How the New Testament Began," in *From Biblical Criticism to Biblical Faith: Essays in Honor of Lee Martin McDonald*, ed. W. Brackney and C. Evans (Macon, GA: Mercer University Press, 2007), 128. See also, *Jesus Remembered*, Christianity in the Making 1 (Grand Rapids, MI: Eerdmans, 2003).

[59] Dunn, "How the New Testament Began," 127.

[60] Ibid., 128.

Not too long after Jesus's earthly ministry the Synoptic Gospels were written (most likely, all before the fall of Jerusalem in AD 70). Originally, the four Gospels disseminated independently of one another. Their individual status as Scripture is usually not debated. Whether the collection of Gospels should be limited to these four is a different matter. There are about thirty known Gospels that appeared before the year 600,[61] but none were as popular as the canonical Gospels.[62] Only these four were recognized because, as Serapion—who died in 211—and others said, they were "handed down" to the church.[63] The other Gospels were rejected on the grounds that they did not agree with the commonly accepted four canonical Gospels. This implies not only antiquity of the collection but also the authority of the transmitters.[64]

The collection of the Gospels, and even the whole idea of a canon, is frequently attributed to a reaction to Marcion's rejection of all the NT Gospels but Luke.[65] Today most are less certain that Marcion is to be given as much credit, but many still see his canon as an important influence in the formation of the NT.[66] More importantly, Marcion's canon most likely presupposed a large portion of the present canon.[67] Ferguson noted that Marcion's contemporary, the gnostic teacher Basilides (ca. AD 117–138), "is our earliest full witness to the New Testament as scripture, but the offhand way he speaks shows that he was not the first to do this and was reflecting common usage."[68] An orthodox

---

[61] If limited to the first few centuries of the Christian era, the number is even smaller. B. D. Ehrman, *Lost Scriptures: Books That Did Not Make It into the New Testament* (New York, NY: Oxford University Press, 2003), includes only seventeen non-canonical Gospels, including the disputed Secret Gospel of Mark (see chap. 3 below). J. K. Elliott (*The Apocryphal New Testament* [Oxford, NY: Clarendon, 1993]) provided a fuller listing, but a perusal of the Gospels featured in his book shows that many of these Gospels (1) are fragmentary, late, and dependent on the canonical Gospels; (2) include dubious content; or (3) are otherwise transparently inferior to the canonical Gospels.

[62] The manuscript evidence alone suggests that the four canonical Gospels were far more popular than the rest. *Gospel of Thomas* has one whole manuscript (and three small fragments); the *Gospel of Peter* survives in only three small fragments; the *Egerton Gospel* in two small fragments; the *Gospel of the Hebrews* only in quotations (G. Stanton, *The Gospels and Jesus*, 2nd ed. [Oxford, NY: Oxford University Press, 2002], 122–35).

[63] See Eusebius, *Eccl. Hist.* 6.12.

[64] See especially R. Bauckham, *Jesus and the Eyewitnesses: The Gospels as Eyewitness Testimony* (Grand Rapids, MI: Eerdmans, 2006). He stresses the eyewitness character of the Gospels and argues that the Twelve served as an "authoritative collegium" in the Gospels' preservation of eyewitness testimony regarding Jesus in the Gospels.

[65] See A. von Harnack, *Marcion: Das Evangelium vom fremden Gott: Eine Monographie zur Geschichte der Grundlegung der katholischen Kirche*, Bibliothek klassischer Texte (Darmstadt, Germany: Wissenschaftliche Buchgesellschaft, 1996; repr. of 1924 ed.), 357; H. von Campenhausen, *The Formation of the Christian Bible* (Philadelphia, PA: Fortress, 1972), 148; and J. Knox, *Marcion and the New Testament* (Chicago, IL: University Press, 1942), 31, who wrote that "Marcion is primarily responsible for the idea of the New Testament."

[66] See the discussion of stimuli for canonization above. See Metzger, *Canon*, 99; and T. von Zahn, *Geschichte des neutestamentlichen Kanons I* (Erlangen/Leipzig, Germany: A. Deichert, 1888), 586.

[67] Tertullian's remark that Marcion "gnawed the Gospels to pieces" suggests that Marcion's separation of Luke from the rest of the Gospels was a disruption of an already existing collection (*Against Marcion*, in *The Ante-Nicene Fathers*, vol. III: *Latin Christianity: Its Founder, Tertullian*, ed. A. Roberts and J. Donaldson [Grand Rapids, MI: Eerdmans, 1986], 272). Tertullian further notes that Marcion's rejection of the other Gospels is purely an innovation, not a restoration movement, indicating that Marcion surely knew the other Gospels (*Against Marcion*, Book IV, chaps. III–IV, in ibid., 348–49).

[68] E. Ferguson, "Factors Leading to the Selection and Closure of the New Testament Canon," in *Canon Debate*, 313.

contemporary of Marcion, Justin Martyr (ca. 100–165), wrote of the Gospels ("the memoirs of the apostles") being read in the churches alongside the Prophets.[69] This reference has a bearing not only on worship in the early church, but it also indicates the status afforded the four Gospels.[70] They were Scripture on par with the OT.

In this context the question of format takes on special significance. When a given group of similar documents is gathered together, the writings that are included, by definition, constitute the limits of the collection. In terms of the Gospels, the creation of the fourfold Gospel codex says as much about the limits of the Gospel canon as it does about the Gospels chosen for inclusion. Rather than assigning the date of the Gospel collection to the *end* of the second century, it may well be that the canonical Gospels were circulating as a unit as early as the *beginning* of the second century.

It is not known whether Justin's Gospels were bound in one codex, but these four apostolic Gospels were being read in the churches.[71] What is known is that by the end of the second century the fourfold Gospel codex was common.[72] Irenaeus (ca. 130–200) is perhaps our strongest patristic witness to the fourfold Gospel. For him, the Gospels formed a fourfold unity. In fact, Irenaeus preferred the singular "Gospel" to the plural "Gospels."[73] While this is no doubt a theological conviction, it may well be reflected in the physical arrangement familiar to Irenaeus. In *Against Heresies* 3.11.8, he declared the Gospels to be precisely four in number, comparing them to the four winds, the four angelic creatures of Ezekiel, and the four covenants of God.

Irenaeus's argument is often understood to be limiting the number of the Gospels to only "these four and no more."[74] But this is only part of what Irenaeus sought to establish. His point was that there were four canonical Gospels—neither more *nor less*. He castigated the Ebionites for using only Matthew, the Docetists for only using Mark, the Marcionites for using only Luke, and the Valentinians for preferring John and audaciously creating a *Gospel of Truth*. In fact, Irenaeus wrote more about those who *reduced* the number of Gospels in the canon than about those who *added* to their number, which assumes a fixed Gospel collection in both directions.

T. C. Skeat has persuasively argued that Irenaeus's comparison to the four creatures of Ezekiel is both a citation of a previous work and an argument about the *order* of the

---

[69] See Justin, *1 Apol.* 67: "And on the day called Sunday, all who live in cities or in the country gather together to one place, and the memoirs of the apostles or the writings of the prophets are read, as long as time permits; then, when the reader has ceased, the president verbally instructs, and exhorts to the imitation of these good things" (*The Ante-Nicene Fathers*, vol. I: *The Apostolic Fathers—Justin Martyr—Irenaeus*, ed. A. Roberts and J. Donaldson [Grand Rapids, MI: Eerdmans, 1987], 186).

[70] Against von Campenhausen (*Formation of the Christian Bible*, 103), who maintained, "It is customary to talk of a 'canon of the Four Gospels,' a 'canon' of the Pauline Epistles, and an 'apocalyptic' canon even before the time of Marcion. Our sources certainly do nothing to justify such ideas."

[71] Justin's student Tatian created the *Diatessaron* ("through four"), a continuous Gospel harmony.

[72] G. N. Stanton, "The Fourfold Gospel," *NTS* 43 (1997): 316–46.

[73] M. Hengel, *The Four Gospels and One Gospel of Jesus Christ* (Harrisburg, PA: Trinity International, 2000), 10.

[74] E.g., McDonald (*Biblical Canon*, 290) argues that Irenaeus was an innovator here.

Gospels. If so, he rightly drew the following conclusion: "Any question of the order of the Gospels only makes sense when all four have been brought together in a single volume, which must be a codex, since no roll, however economically written, could contain all four Gospels."[75] As mentioned, Irenaeus referred to a four-gospel codex. Thus, it is more than just an abstract point that he declared that the gospel was in its very essence "fourfold."[76] Moreover, he concluded, "Now, these things being so, all these [men] are vain, unlearned, and moreover also audacious—these who destroy *the form of the gospel*,[77] and [by supposing] either more or less than what has been spoken, amend *the appearance of the gospels*."[78] In saying this, he was referring not only to the apostolic Gospels but very likely to a fourfold codex that was known and well established at the time he wrote.[79] Thus, this Gospel collection likely had a very early archetype, possibly one appearing a half-century earlier than Irenaeus.[80]

Evidence from the early Gospel manuscripts also points to an early canonical collection. There is ample manuscript evidence of a fourfold Gospel collection from the third century onward.[81] All of these have a different ancestor, which seems to suggest at least a mid-second century origin.[82] In fact, there may be physical evidence to this effect from the late second century from two manuscripts. First, $\mathfrak{P}^{75}$ contains a large portion of Luke and John, including the page where Luke ends and John begins. This sequence makes it likely that it originally included all four Gospels.[83] Second, T. C. Skeat argued that $\mathfrak{P}^{4}$, $\mathfrak{P}^{64}$, and $\mathfrak{P}^{67}$ (dated ca. 200) were all originally from the same codex and must have had an

---

[75] T. C. Skeat, "Irenaeus and the Four-Gospel Canon," *NovT* 34 (1992): 198–99. The order suggested is the so-called western order found in many Latin and Greek manuscripts (i.e., Matthew, John, Mark, and Luke). While this may cause one to doubt Skeat's thesis, J. Bingham and B. Todd Jr. have shown that text of the Gospels in Irenaeus show great affinity to the western text-type. They suggest it is possible that the Greek "Gospel text that Irenaeus used was closer to manuscripts from which the Latin manuscripts were derived." (D. J. Bingham and B. R. Todd Jr., "Irenaeus's Text of the Gospels in *Adversus haereses*," in *The Early Text of the New Testament*, ed. by C. E. Hill and M. J. Kruger [Oxford, NY: Oxford University Press, 2012], 392). Thus, it is no stretch of the imagination to suggest a western order of the Gospels in a Greek text that may have been related to the Old Latin's Greek parent.

[76] Irenaeus, *Against Heresies* 3.11.8 (Migne, *PG* 7.1, 889). Irenaeus's argument is that the *one* gospel is, literally, "*four-formed*" (*tetramorphē*).

[77] *Idean tou euangeliou* (emphasis added).

[78] Emphasis added; *prosōpon*, Lat. *personas*; lit. "face" or "mask." Irenaeus, *Against Heresies* 3.11.9 (Migne, *PG* 7.1, 890).

[79] Note also Irenaeus's final words: "Since God made all things orderly and neatly, it was also fitting for the outward appearance of the Gospel to be well arranged [Lat. *bene compositam*] and well connected [Lat. *bene compaginatam*]. Therefore, having examined the opinion of those men *who handed the Gospel down to us*, from their very beginnings, let us go also to the remaining apostles" (*Against Heresies* 3.11.9 [*PG* 71, 894]).

[80] Given an AD 170 or 180 date for *Against Heresies*, this would produce a date of ca. AD 120–130.

[81] The other early mss. that indisputably show more than one Gospel in a codex are $\mathfrak{P}^{45}$, containing all four Gospels and Acts (third cent.); possibly $\mathfrak{P}^{53}$ (including portions of Matthew and Acts, suggesting Mark–John lay between them; ca. 260); and Uncial 0171 (ca. 300). See Metzger and Ehrman, *Text of the New Testament*, 53–61.

[82] Ferguson, "Factors Leading to the Selection and Closure of the New Testament Canon," 303.

[83] Hill, *Who Chose the Gospels?*, 118. $\mathfrak{P}^{75}$ is officially dated ca. 200.

SIDEBAR 1.3: THE "CANONICAL EDITION" OF THE NEW TESTAMENT

D. Trobisch has advanced a fascinating theory concerning the canon of the NT. In essence Trobisch understands the NT to be a published book by no later than the middle of the second century. Trobisch originally assigned this "canonical edition" of the NT to unnamed "editors" in the early second century.[1] Later, he attributed it to Polycarp sometime between AD 156 and 168.[2] This, of course, is to place the "canonical edition" of the NT rather late.[3] While the internal evidence Trobisch marshals is often less than compelling due to the precarious nature of some of his presuppositions,[4] the most persuasive element of Trobisch's proposal is the empirical manuscript evidence.

Trobisch noted five phenomena in the manuscripts that point to an early archetype. Perhaps the most compelling are the first two. If correct, this would address two of the most nagging questions about the transmission of the Bible that have yet to receive a fully satisfactory answer. First, most biblical manuscripts display the *nomina sacra*, abbreviations of the divine names. These abbreviations usually consist of the first and last letter of the word for God *(theos)*, Jesus *(Iēsous)*, or the Spirit *(pneuma)* with a line above them to indicate that it is an abbreviation. These *nomina sacra* are found even in the earliest manuscripts.[5] No one has satisfactorily accounted for their pervasive presence. How did these abbreviations for the divine names become so widespread in the earliest manuscripts if there was no religious mechanism to control copying and no original archetype? Trobisch's answer is that the *nomina sacra* were the result of an editorial decision made in the original edition. This "canonical edition," then, was so popular that it quickly became the standard in the Christian world.

The second unanswered question addressed by Trobisch's proposal pertains to the surprising use of the codex format by the early Christians. It has already been noted that several theories have been proposed for the use of the codex in early Christian literature. None of these theories has gained universal acceptance. Trobisch's answer is that the codex was the choice of the editors of the canonical edition presumably on account of a variety of benefits accorded by the codex, most obviously that of providing the space needed to accommodate more easily such a large collection of writings.

The third piece of evidence for a canonical edition is the circulation units themselves. There is an amazing conformity of the manuscripts up until the seventh century in matters of content and order. The NT circulated in four smaller volumes: the fourfold Gospel Codex; Acts and General Epistles; the Letters of Paul (including Hebrews);

---

[1] D. Trobisch, *The First Edition of the New Testament* (New York, NY: Oxford University Press, 2000), 5–6.

[2] D. Trobisch, "Who Published the New Testament?" *Free Inquiry* 28 (Dec. 2007/Jan. 2008): 33.

[3] Manifestly, evidence for NT books that Trobisch considers to be forgeries at the time of publication (namely the Pastoral Epistles) predates this proposition. Attempts to describe these quotes as preliterary fragments have the ring of special pleading and are therefore unlikely.

[4] See L. S. Kellum, "Review of D. Trobisch, *The First Edition of the New Testament*," *Faith & Mission* 18/2 (2001): 84–87.

[5] L. W. Hurtado, "𝔓^{52} (P. Rylands Gk. 457) and the *Nomina Sacra*: Method and Probability," *TynBul* 54 (2003): 13. Hurtado suggested that the *nomina sacra* most likely appeared in our earliest extant NT manuscript, the above-mentioned 𝔓^{52}.

and Revelation. This order can be seen in the earliest manuscripts (i.e., before the fourth- and fifth-century church councils).

Fourth, the titles of the books in the collections are amazingly uniform. This virtual uniformity also suggests some sort of coordinated action early on in the canonical process. The uniformity of titles and arrangement of Paul's Letters was already noted above. The titles of the Gospels, likewise, are always some form of "According to Matthew," "According to Mark," and so on. "The Acts of the Apostles" appropriately captures the essence of this book. The titles of the General Epistles are different from those of Paul's Letters, yet they also display a marked degree of uniformity, following the format "From John A," "From John B," "From John C," "From Peter A," and so on. The fact that these letters were written by several different authors makes it likely that their collection and titling were the result of an editorial decision.

Finally, the title of the whole collection is "The New Covenant." This is the term for the collection used by Irenaeus (ca. AD 130–200); Clement of Alexandria (ca. AD 150–215); Tertullian (ca. AD 160–225); and Origen (ca. AD 185–254). Perhaps the most convincing statement is by Apolinarius's unknown associate (2nd c.): "I was somewhat reluctant, not from any lack of ability to refute the lie and testify to the truth, but from timidity and scruples lest I might seem to some to be adding to the writings or injunctions of the word of the new covenant of the gospel, to which no one who has chosen to live according to the gospel itself can add and from which he cannot take away."[6] From this quote it is apparent that this presbyter in the second century had a closed canon that he called "the writings of the new covenant of the gospel."

As mentioned, Trobisch's internal reconstructions as to the purpose and production of the NT are much less convincing. For him, the NT is by and large the result of the church's conflict with Marcion. Thus the editors included the LXX; added the General Epistles; and included Acts in order to rehabilitate Peter and Paul. That Marcion takes center stage is the Achilles heel of the theory. As argued above, Marcion's influence on

[6] Eusebius, *Eccl. Hist.* 5.16.3.

archetype earlier in the second century.[84] Clearly there was a fourfold Gospel codex circulating in the second century.

Skeat has proposed that this four-Gospel codex was the reason the early Christians preferred the codex over the roll. If so, their choice of the codex was a theologically driven decision. While it was possible to include these four Gospels in a codex, placing them in

[84] T. C. Skeat, "The Oldest Manuscript of the Four Gospels?" *NTS* 43 (1997): 1–34. See also P. W. Comfort, "Exploring the Common Identification of Three New Testament Manuscripts: $\mathfrak{P}^{4}$, $\mathfrak{P}^{64}$, and $\mathfrak{P}^{67}$," *TynBul* 46 (1995): 43–54. This identification has recently been questioned by P. M. Head, "Is $\mathfrak{P}^{4}$, $\mathfrak{P}^{64}$, and $\mathfrak{P}^{67}$ the Oldest Manuscript of the Four Gospels? A Response to T. C. Skeat," *NTS* 51 (2005): 450–57. Although C. P. Thiede has claimed a date near the year 100 for $\mathfrak{P}^{67}$, he has garnered few followers ("Papyrus Magdalen Greek 17 [Gregory-Aland $\mathfrak{P}^{64}$]: A Reappraisal," *TynBul* 46 [1995]: 29–42). Most recently S. Porter has patiently and fairly evaluated the objections to $\mathfrak{P}^{4}$, $\mathfrak{P}^{64}$, and $\mathfrak{P}^{67}$ coming from the same manuscript. He reports that the objections are not overwhelming and fall short of proof against a single codex. He states, "If these objections cannot be sustained (and they are not telling), we are still left with the possibility of $\mathfrak{P}^{4}$, $\mathfrak{P}^{64}$, and $\mathfrak{P}^{67}$ being the first testimony of a multiquire codex of the Gospels." S. Porter, *How We Got the New Testament: Text, Transmission, Translation* (Grand Rapids, MI: Baker, 2013), 99.

the NT canon most likely was less pronounced than is often supposed and almost certainly did not affect the specific contours of any collection of NT writings.

The identification of Polycarp as the editor of the canonical edition is also problematic. The citation of much of the NT—including the Pastoral Epistles—as Scripture in his letter to the Philippians thirty years prior to Marcion makes it unlikely that the canonical edition was his creation. The question also arises whether Polycarp could have had the ecclesiastical authority to publish a work that superseded all previous copies of the NT writings. This is rather unlikely. For example, Polycarp could not get the church in Rome to celebrate Easter at the Passover.

Ultimately, Trobisch has not definitively answered the question of the formation of the NT canon. Yet he has made an important contribution to the understanding of the early canonization process. The codex format, the ubiquitous appearance of the *nomina sacra*, and the near-uniform titles of the writings at least suggest a stream of convention that originated somewhere. It is not necessary to conclude that this convention was due to one canonical edition. It may well have started with one collection and may have been quickly imported into other such collections.

There is one more point made by Trobisch that is worth considering. It is often stated that the canon was in process until the fourth century when it was largely settled. Eusebius's list in his *Ecclesiastical History* acknowledges certain doubts regarding individual books in the NT canon. This list is often cited as evidence for a continuous state of turmoil from the very start. But is this necessarily the case? Could it be that the questions were not about which books were to be included in the canon but which books were in the canon in the first place? In other words, Eusebius's discussion regarding the different books included in the canon of the NT might constitute a fourth-century discussion rather than indicate a continuous stream of doubt from the first or second century onward. In fact, some of the sixteenth-century Reformers had similar questions about the canon.[7]

[7] W. Walden, "Luther: The One Who Shaped the Canon," *ResQ* 49 (2007): 1–10.

the same roll would have been impossibly cumbersome.[85] This is one of the more intriguing and plausible pieces of evidence accounting for Christians' preference for the codex in the early days of the church.

While by the latest count, about eight non-canonical "Gospels" may have been circulating in the second century, the manuscript evidence is telling regarding which of these Gospels the church considered canonical. First, whenever there is manuscript evidence of more than one Gospel that includes a canonical Gospel, the other Gospel was canonical as well. This means that no non-canonical Gospel appears bound with a canonical one, so there is no evidence for Matthew–Thomas or Luke–Peter, for example. This would indicate, by and large, that the issue of other Gospels having an equal scriptural status was a moot point among the orthodox.[86] Second, the manuscript evidence for non-canonical Gospels is amazingly

[85] C. H. Roberts and T. C. Skeat, *The Birth of the Codex* (London, UK: British Academy, 1983), 65.

[86] J. K. Elliott, "Manuscripts, the Codex, and the Canon," *JSNT* 63 (1996): 107.

thin when compared to the numbers of Greek manuscripts of the canonical Gospels. For example, there is only one known full copy of the Gospel of Thomas (and two fragmentary pages of other editions). In *Who Chose the Gospels?*, C. E. Hill notes that in the second and third centuries, "remnants of canonical Gospels outnumber remnants of non-canonical ones at least somewhere between two (plus) to one and three (plus) to one, and perhaps closer to four to one."[87] The evidence points to the fact that the apocryphal Gospels never had a wide hearing among the orthodox or quickly fell out of favor.

Exactly when the four-Gospel arrangement first occurred is unknown. But the outer limits can be deduced. The mid-second century seems the last possible date given the patristic and manuscript evidence. On the other end, the limit is set by the composition of the last Gospel, most likely the Gospel of John (conventionally dated in the AD eighties or nineties). Thus, sometime between the production of John's Gospel and the mid-second century, the status of these Gospels was so entrenched that they were bound and circulated together. This, by all accounts, should be taken as evidence for the church's recognition that the number of the Gospels was fixed and closed by the early or at least the middle of the second century.

The Pauline Letter Collection It is also known that Paul's Letters circulated together as a collective unit. The question is, How did this collection originate? Kümmel is representative of mainstream scholarship in assuming that Paul's Letters were a collection and (to some extent) a production of the late first century, as the letters were gradually formed into a collection.[88] S. E. Porter astutely noted, "One cannot help but think that the gradual collection theory . . . is one of expedience, designed to weave a narrative around the disparate evidence of the first four centuries, but without a firm foundation established as to how such a process actually occurred."[89]

Moreover, the time between Paul's death (mid- to late sixties) and the historical references to this collection is far too short to be explained by a gradual collection. By the production of 2 Peter (mid-sixties?), it is likely that there was at least a beginning collection of Paul's Letters. In about AD 96, Clement of Rome noted that Paul wrote "truly under the inspiration of the Spirit" (*1 Clem.* 47.3). Polycarp (ca. AD 69–155) quoted from a body of Scriptures that must have included the Pauline Letter collection. Finally, Marcion, in the first half of the second century, in formulating his truncated canon, edited an established Pauline Letter collection. Whatever the circumstances, the basic form of the collection can be shown to have rapidly circulated in the churches as Scripture. Moreover, the manuscript evidence seems to show that if there were "local collections," the full corpus was rapidly preferred.

---

[87] C. E. Hill, *Who Chose the Gospels?*, 18.

[88] W. G. Kümmel, P. Fein, and J. Behm, *Introduction to the New Testament* (Nashville, TN: Abingdon, 1966), 480–81. See also Aland and Aland, *Text of the New Testament*, 49.

[89] S. E. Porter, "When and How was the Pauline Canon Compiled? An Assessment of Theories," in *The Pauline Canon*, ed. S. E. Porter (Boston, MA: Brill, 2004), 103.

So how did such a collection come into existence? A host of "personal involvement theories" (Porter's term) explains the origins of this corpus. Whether Onesimus, Marcion, Luke, Timothy, or a "Pauline school" is credited with compiling a Pauline Letter collection, personal involvement is the common denominator. Most of these hypotheses, however, are based on speculative and often questionable judgments.[90] Nevertheless, it seems beyond question that a personality was involved by the very nature of what resulted: a collection.[91]

Many today suggest this person could have been none other than Paul himself. From what is known of ancient letter collections, the author would most likely have made a copy of the letter immediately, kept a copy for himself, and sent a copy to the recipient. Both Cicero's and Ignatius's letter collections began in this way.[92] Not only was this a known practice, it is unlikely that Paul would have sent a letter and not kept a copy for himself.[93]

D. Trobisch argued for three stages of development in the collection of ancient letters, with the author having been involved only in the first stage. The second and third phases were progressively removed from the author.[94] As Porter has shown, however, this is not a necessary conclusion.[95] While there might be evidence for some editing and arrangement of the edition (mainly in the titles and order of the letters), it seems likely that the collection originated with Paul's retained copies. The letter collection, or at least the beginnings of it, may be mentioned in 2 Timothy 4:13, where Paul wrote to Timothy, "When you come, bring the cloak I left in Troas with Carpus, as well as the scrolls, especially the parchments." The word translated "parchments" (*membrana*)

---

[90] Some suggest there was a long period of neglect of Paul because the antecedent judgment about the date of the earliest Gospels—post-70—meant that these Gospels had no knowledge of Paul. Thus, someone—perhaps reading the stirring account of Acts—was motivated to collect the letters some thirty years after Paul's death (see E. J. Goodspeed, *How Came the Bible?* [Nashville, TN: Cokesbury, 1940], 59–63); Goodspeed elsewhere suggests that the person responsible was Onesimus, the runaway slave mentioned in the book of Philemon. See *New Solutions to New Testament Problems* [Chicago, IL: University Press, 1927], 1–64; and his student J. Knox, *Philemon Among the Letters of Paul* [London, England: Collins, 1960]). However, Dunn ("How the New Testament Began," 133) rightly notes that "[t]hose [letters] which have been preserved were so because they were prized, read often, copied and circulated."

[91] Porter, "When and How Was the Pauline Canon Compiled," 109–13.

[92] For Cicero, see *Att.* 1.17; 3.9; for Ignatius's letters, see *Pol.* 13:1 (Polycarp's letter is in answer to the Philippians' request for Ignatius's letters). E. R. Richards (*Paul and First-Century Letter Writing: Secretaries, Composition and Collection* [Downers Grove, IL: InterVarsity, 2004], 156) cited Cicero and a papyrus find (PZen 10) and rightly concluded that this was "a common enough practice."

[93] H. Gamble, *Books and Readers in the Early Church: A History of Early Christian Texts* (New Haven, CT: Yale University Press, 1995), 100–1.

[94] D. Trobisch, *Paul's Letter Collection: Tracing the Origins* (Minneapolis, MN: Fortress, 2000 [1994]), 50. First, the author himself prepared some letters for publication (Trobisch argued for Romans, 1 and 2 Corinthians, and Galatians as this first level). Second, after the author's death these editions were expanded, and other editions were published from known letters of the author. Third, eventually all the editions were combined into a comprehensive edition. One of the reasons for this separation is that Galatians is shorter than Ephesians yet before it in the canonical arrangement. Trobisch saw this as evidence of the end of the original letter collection. But J. Murphy-O'Connor (*Paul the Letter Writer: His World, His Options, His Skills* [Collegeville, MN: Liturgical Press, 1995], 120–30) rightly notes that there were ways of measurement available to scribes other than the number of characters (such as the number of lines) that show very similar lengths for Galatians and Ephesians, and Colossians and Philippians, respectively.

[95] Porter, *Pauline Canon*, 115–21.

is actually a Latin word transliterated into Greek and most likely indicates a parchment codex.[96] Since the Pauline corpus could not fit on one scroll, it is likely that the letter collection was in a codex format.[97]

This decision to publish it involved arranging the letters and providing titles for them. Trobisch has well noted that the Pauline corpus regularly and invariably titles the letters "To the Romans," "To the Corinthians A," "To the Corinthians B," and so on.[98] This was most likely an editorial decision made when the letters were collected—maybe even by Paul himself. What is more, the arrangement is rather consistent in the manuscripts and in the basic order in which Paul's Letters are found in the NT today. Again this was likely an editorial decision. That the letters circulated widely in this arrangement would seem to suggest that the editing was done with publication in mind.

The exact content of the letter collection is a matter of debate. Specifically, the question of the placement of the epistle to the Hebrews and whether or not the Pastoral Epistles were included are debated. Regarding Hebrews, the patristic and manuscript evidence shows that it circulated among the Pauline Letters early.[99] The only question is, Where in the collection? It shows up in at least four places in the manuscripts.[100] Some claim this "indecision" suggests a later addition to the Pauline canon.[101] However, this is not the only or most likely explanation. It may point to a question about its exact nature, such as whether a letter was penned to a church or an individual. While it is not likely it was written by Paul, it certainly is connected to Paul.

Regarding the Letters to Timothy and Titus, some have suggested that the Pauline corpus was transmitted in two early editions. These are a fourteen-letter corpus and a ten-letter edition of Paul's Letters (minus 1–2 Timothy/Titus and Hebrews) that was a "seven-churches" edition (because it supposedly contains only letters to seven churches).[102] Marcion's canon, the so-called *Apostolikon*, is said to be a taking over of this canon with milder edits than usually suggested.[103] The theory (derived from noting similarity between

---

[96] Gamble, *Books and Readers*, 51–52.

[97] Gamble (ibid., 62–65) even promotes the idea that the Pauline Letter collection actually occasioned the Christian preference for the codex format. He is followed to some extent by Richards (*Paul and First-Century Letter Writing*, 223).

[98] Trobisch, *Paul's Letter Collection*, 22–24.

[99] See, e.g., 𝔓46, 𝔓13, and the citations in Clement of Rome (ca. AD 95).

[100] Porter, *How We Got the New Testament*, 119. The earliest Pauline manuscript (𝔓46) has it after Romans. Most early manuscripts, however, place it between 2 Thessalonians and 1 Timothy. The majority of Byzantine mss. place it at the end of the Pauline corpus.

[101] See, e.g., Trobisch, *Paul's Letter Collection*, 20.

[102] N. A. Dahl, "The Origin of the Earliest Prologues to the Pauline Letters," *Semeia* 12 (1978): 233–77.

[103] See, e.g., Ulrich Schmid, *Marcion und sein Apostolos: Rekonstruktion und historische Einordnung der marcionitischen Paulusbriefausgabe* (Berlin, Germany: de Gruyter, 1995); E. Gathergood, "Papyrus 32 (Titus) as a Multi-text Codex: A New Reconstruction," *NTS* (2013): 601; John J. Clabeaux, *A Lost Edition of the Letters of Paul: A Reassessment of the Text of the Pauline Corpus Attested by Marcion*, CBQ Monograph Series 21 (Washington, DC: The Catholic Biblical Association of America, 1989): 147–48; and Robert W. Wall, "The Function of the Pastoral Letters within the Pauline Canon of the New Testament: A Canonical Approach," in *The Pauline Canon*, 320–34. J. Quinn goes on to suggest a fourth collection, a "letters-to-individuals" corpus, featuring the letters to Timothy and Titus as well as to Philemon. In this view the

Marcion's Pauline collection and the Latin "Marcionite" prologues) suggests the prologues are not Marcionite and therefore predate the mid-second century.[104] Thus, the suggestion is that the "seven-churches" edition is the oldest, propping up the idea that the Letters to Timothy and Titus were pseudepigrapha added later (probably as a reaction to Marcion).

No doubt, that Paul wrote to seven churches was impressive to early Christians.[105] However, it may be more of a theological concept than proof of a letter-collection. Even if we were to grant that the edition existed, the nature of its composition is unknown. Specifically, can we say that it was the earliest collection or a reaction to a belief that the Letters to individuals have no universal application? In contrast, we should note that no manuscript evidence for a "seven-churches" edition exists. There is, however, clear and numerous manuscript evidence of the traditional Pauline corpus. In fact, Trobisch notes that there is no manuscript evidence that the corpus ever circulated apart from the Letters to Timothy and Titus.[106] Regarding literary evidence, these letters are cited 450 times by the second-century Fathers.[107] The earliest Fathers also show knowledge of the Letters.[108] Furthermore, the belief in the authenticity of the Letters to Timothy and Titus is never doubted until the modern era. Ultimately, the best evidence for the early shape of the Pauline Letter collection is the fourteen-letter collection.

So who was the compiling editor? It could have been Paul himself, a possibility neither demanded nor falsified by the limited available evidence. Another possibility is that the editor was one of Paul's close associates, who would likely have had access to copies retained by Paul. Most likely, the editor's contribution to the contents of the Letters was minimal, and the collection was published shortly after Paul's death and received rapid acceptance throughout the churches. Thus, there is every reason to believe that Paul's Letters attained canonical status no later than the last quarter of the first century.

While it is not possible here to pinpoint every stage of the production, the evidence thus far suggests an early recognition of the bulk of the NT canon. A scenario such as the following seems feasible. The Synoptic Gospels were written and received rapid acceptance in the churches as the authoritative source of the words of Christ. Roughly contemporaneous with them, Paul's Letters began circulating as a collection, probably soon after Paul's death. These Letters were immediately received and afforded *de facto* canonical status.[109] Shortly after the writing of John's Gospel, the Gospels were gathered and published as

---

"seven-churches" and "letters-to-individuals" collections are combined to form the 13/14-letter edition (J. D. Quinn and W. C. Wacker, *The First and Second Letters to Timothy: A New Translation with Notes and Commentary* [Grand Rapids, MI: Eerdmans, 2000], 3).

[104] See, e.g., Gamble, *New Testament Canon*, 42. Gamble suggests this edition is what Marcion inherited so that his rejection of the Letters to Timothy and Titus was due to this edition rather than perfidy on his part.

[105] See, e.g., the Muratorian Fragment, which states, "Paul . . . writes by name to only seven churches . . ."

[106] Trobisch, *Paul's Letter Collection*, 22.

[107] Quinn and Wacker, *First and Second Letters to Timothy*, 3.

[108] *1 Clement* (ca. AD 96), e.g., cites Titus and 1 Timothy (2.7; 60.4; and 61.2).

[109] Dunn, "How the New Testament Began," 137: "The *de facto* canon of Jesus and Paul, gospel and epistle, was already functioning with effect within the first thirty years of Christianity's existence."

a fourfold Gospel canon.[110] Regarding the manner in which the Acts and the General Epistles were gathered and published and by whom, less can be said with confidence. However, it is likely that the collection of these books was in some way related to the fourfold Gospel codex, for it was at that point that Luke and Acts were most likely separated.[111] It is possible (though far from certain) that the same person or persons were responsible for the collection of these various corpora. Finally, the book of Revelation, written in the mid- to late 90s by the aged apostle John, circulated independently from the rest, likely due to its late production. This reconstruction, purposefully painted in broad strokes, takes its point of departure from the undeniable fact of the early reception of the NT documents.

The Current Order of New Testament Books The collection of the canonical Gospels and the Pauline Letters, as well as the grouping together of Acts and the General Epistles and the separate circulation of the book of Revelation, were discussed above. The remaining question to be addressed is the current order of NT books. How did the existing order occur, and what is the theological and interpretive significance of the current order of the NT writings?

A case could be made for the order found in Athanasius's festal letter (also known as the Greek or Eastern order) as Trobisch and others do.[112] This order may well reflect the early collection units. But even among the collection units there was some degree of fluidity. The manuscripts of the fourfold Gospel codex are extant in different orders. Another case in point is the placement of the book of Hebrews, which seems to "travel" throughout the manuscripts, with most of them placing it between the letters to churches and the letters to individuals (i.e., between 2 Thessalonians and 1 Timothy). However, the oldest known manuscript containing Paul's letter collection ($\mathfrak{P}^{46}$) places Hebrews immediately after Romans. This is not unexpected in a hand-copied anthology such as the NT. Each scribe may have felt a certain amount of freedom to arrange his copy as he saw fit. This is even more likely in the case of personal copies.

The order of the books of the NT in our present English Bibles reflects the Western order found in the Vulgate (translated by Jerome) but has precursors back to the Old Italian translation.[113] In essence, it only differs from the Eastern order in the matter of placing the General Epistles after Paul's letter collection and setting Hebrews between the two

---

[110] John, it is stated, knew the other Gospels. See Eusebius (*Eccl. Hist.* 3.24.7)—identified by C. E. Hill ("What Papias Said About John (and Luke): A 'New' Papian Fragment," *JTS* 2 [1998]: 582–629) as a fragment of Papias—who writes, "John welcomed the three previous Gospels, which had been distributed to all, including himself, and testified to their truth, noting they omitted the first ministry." Another legend regarding John is found in a fragment of Origen that he claimed came from an "old writing." Commenting on the preface to Luke, he reports that "John collected the written Gospels in his own lifetime in the reign of Nero and approved of and recognized those of which the deceit of the devil had not taken possession; but refused and rejected those which he perceived were not truthful" (Origen, *Hom. Luke* 1 fr. 9).

[111] Ferguson, "Factors Leading to the Selection and Closure of the New Testament Canon," 304.

[112] Trobisch, *First Edition*, 103. Others include C. R. Gregory, *Canon and Text of the New Testament* (New York, NY: Charles Scribner's Sons, 1907), 467–68.

[113] This order is essentially found in the Muratorian Fragment and Eusebius. See R. Bauckham, *James: Wisdom of James, Disciple of Jesus the Sage*, New Testament Readings (New York, NY: Routledge, 1999), 115–16.

collections. Many Greek manuscripts of the late Byzantine period follow this order as well. Luther departed from this order, placing James and Hebrews toward the end of the Bible (and thus awarding them lesser status, implying a canon within the canon) together with Jude and Revelation. Tyndale followed suit—though possibly not for the same reasons—in his English version, as did Coverdale, Matthew's Bible, and others. However, when the Great Bible of 1539 was printed, the Western order was restored.[114] It has remained the basic order for the Bible in English ever since.[115]

The Gospels at the beginning of the NT transition from the OT quite nicely. This placement indicates their foundational nature. Virtually no arrangement of the NT starts elsewhere. The placement of Matthew first among the Gospels is most likely, at least in part, a function of the book's opening genealogy of Jesus; this provides a natural introduction to the presentation of Jesus in the four canonical Gospels as a whole. Luke's Gospel, while containing a genealogy in 3:23–37, places it immediately prior to the start of Jesus's public ministry instead of the beginning of the book.

Beyond this, there is no reason to suppose the order of the Synoptic Gospels (Matthew–Mark–Luke) is a necessary indication of the order of their composition, just as the order of the Pauline Letters (Romans–1 Corinthians–2 Corinthians–Galatians, etc.) is manifestly not a function of the chronological sequence of their composition, as is universally recognized. Conversely, it is likely that the placement of John's Gospel last among the four canonical Gospels indicates its later composition. More importantly, the ending of John's Gospel certainly provides a fitting conclusion, not only to John's Gospel, but to the four canonical Gospels in their entirety (see 21:24–25).[116]

Acts certainly bridges the gap between the Gospels and the Letters. As a sequel to Luke, it continues the narrative of the accomplishment of Christ (see Acts 1:1) and provides the foundation for a basic understanding of Paul and his correspondence. Anyone studying the Letters without knowledge of the book of Acts would lack a proper framework for interpretation. Who is this Paul who wrote these letters? When did James, half brother of Jesus, become a leader in the church at Jerusalem? When did the gospel spread to the

---

[114] Bruce, *Canon*, 243–46.

[115] The International Bible Society has issued a version of the TNIV called "the books of the Bible" that radically rearranges the NT. In a bold move, the committee removed the chapter and verse divisions of Robert Estienne (a.k.a. Stephanus) who introduced them in the fourth edition of his Greek NT in 1551 (see P. D. Wegner, *The Journey from Texts to Translations: The Origin and Development of the Bible* [Grand Rapids, MI: Baker, 1999], 269). Only the range is indicated at the bottom of the page. The NT begins with Luke-Acts, followed by a somewhat curious arrangement of Paul's Letters; Matthew is next, and then Hebrews and James; Mark is followed by 1–2 Peter and Jude; and John by 1–3 John and Revelation.

[116] See Trobisch, *First Edition*, 97–98.

SIDEBAR 1.4: WHAT IF ONE OF PAUL'S LOST LETTERS TO THE CORINTHIANS WERE FOUND TODAY?

A set of questions that is sometimes asked is, What if one of Paul's lost letters to the Corinthians were found today? Should the church add it to the NT canon, and on what basis should a decision be made? While a strong case can be made against including nonapostolic documents (such as the Gospel of Thomas) to the canon of Scripture, what if the writing in question were an authentic apostolic document? Should not such a book be included in the canon? In short, a strong case can be made that even in such a hypothetical scenario the correct response would be no.

To be sure, it would be appropriate to treasure such a document as historically important, and it would certainly be appropriate to use such a piece of writing to help interpret the existing NT documents. A host of historically important questions could be answered if we had the "previous letter" of 1 Cor 5:9 or the "painful letter" of 2 Cor 7:8. This would also help to adjudicate the various source-critical and rearrangement theories regarding 1 and 2 Corinthians.[1] But there are still good reasons these letters, if discovered, should not be added to the NT canon.

First, as Grudem points out, the fact that these letters, or any other now-lost apostolic documents, were missing from the canon collection from the beginning suggests that, for some reason, the apostles—and ultimately God the Holy Spirit—did not see fit to preserve these documents.[2] This is especially true if it were the case that the apostle Paul himself was behind the production of his letter collection. If such a document had been preserved, it would have survived—not by apostolic design—but because someone else preserved it when the apostles did not.

---

[1] See the discussion in chap. 12.

[2] W. Grudem, *Systematic Theology: An Introduction to Biblical Doctrine* (Grand Rapids, MI: Zondervan, 1994), 68 (the page number is the same in the 2000 edition).

Gentiles? These and other questions are answered when Acts is read first. Its place has always been between the Gospels and the Letters.

As far as the order of the Pauline Letters is concerned, it appears that it was for the most part the length of the document that proved decisive in the church's placement of these letters in canonical order.[117] This leads to an interesting dynamic in interpretation. Romans, read canonically, precedes Galatians and thus is, canonically speaking, foundational for it. Chronologically, however, Galatians preceded Romans and crystallized the issues at an earlier stage in the development of the early church that continued to be addressed at a later stage of Paul's ministry.

But one need not choose between the two dynamics of history and canon. Both are important with regard to our approach to the Bible. The reader who knows both dynamics

---

[117] "Length" may not necessarily be a function of word count but may pertain to the number of lines or some other form of measurement (Porter, "Pauline Canon," 115).

Second, the sovereignty of God in the production of the NT should be recognized. If he did not see fit to provide the letter for 2,000 years of Christian history, why would anyone suppose that a new letter should be added to the canon of Scripture now? What is more, in some sense, the addition of another document would potentially undermine believers' confidence in the sufficiency of Scripture. In such a case the canon would not truly be closed but only provisionally so. Inasmuch as the determination of the canon was a historical process that is bound up with the early centuries of the church, this era is forever past.

Finally, the above discussion assumed for argument's sake that such a document could be verified, but in truth this is highly unlikely. In all probability there would always be lingering questions surrounding the authenticity of such a document.[3] It is not hard to imagine that there would be a range of opinions, dissertations, and monographs defending authenticity or nonauthenticity, and sustained discussion in academic journals. If scholars cannot arrive at a consensus regarding the book of Ephesians, which is part of the existing NT canon, it is unlikely that they would come to a consensus regarding a "new" apostolic book.[4]

For reasons such as these it is not only highly unlikely that such a document will ever be found, but even if it were discovered, there are several weighty arguments against including it in the canon of Scripture. Such a document should be valued and could certainly be used with profit but not to the point of expanding the existing canon of Scripture. The Bible is complete as it stands, and the canon is closed and would not need to be reopened even if one of Paul's lost Corinthian letters or any other document written by one of the apostles were found today or tomorrow.

[3] Ibid

[4] Another related question is, Who would make the decision to include, say, 3 Corinthians in the NT canon? It is difficult to see how a mechanism could be found by which all of Christendom (or at least a sizable majority of Christians) were to arrive at such a momentous decision.

understands, for example, the importance of Galatians *chronologically* and Romans *canonically*. Galatians is the first of Paul's Letters to be written, which shows that Christian theology, far from evolving and changing, was basically the same from the first letter to the last.[118] That Romans stands at the beginning of the Pauline Letters begins the third section of the NT (the Letters) with the most prolonged and clear expositions of the gospel of God in the entire NT. Its position here certainly makes sense. Given that Paul may well have been the first to collect his own letters, it is even possible that this order reflects Paul's own chosen sequence.

Regarding the order of the General Epistles, it appears that Hebrews owes its place first in this collection and in immediate proximity to the Pauline Letters to the traditional attribution of authorship to Paul or a member of the "Pauline circle." Naturally, 1 and 2 Peter are grouped together, as are 1, 2, and 3 John. Beyond this, it is uncertain what led

[118] Regarding the question of development in Paul's theology, see chap. 21 below.

the compilers to place the writings in the order James, 1–2 Peter, 1–3 John, and Jude. But this arrangement is consistent in even the earliest manuscripts.

Without being dogmatic, certain observations can be made. The very Jewish James fits neatly next to the book of Hebrews, while 1–3 John sustain a certain amount of inter-textuality with the letters to the churches in the book of Revelation. Finally, Jude, with its apocalyptic references, certainly prepares the reader well for the Apocalypse.

Revelation is a fitting conclusion to the whole Bible, not just the NT.[119] The subjects of the return of Christ and the triumph of the Lamb over all evil are not only appropriate as the final messages of the NT, but are a nice *inclusio* ("bookend") with Genesis as well. The final state, as recorded in the Apocalypse, is in many ways a return to Eden (see Rev 22:1–5) that includes healing for the nations. There is no longer a curse on the earth and its inhabitants. The tree of life is once more in plain view of humans, although there is no tree of the knowledge of good and evil. In Revelation, "Eden has not only been restored but has been elevated and expanded for the people of God in eternity."[120]

Thus, there is a twofold dynamic to understanding the NT. It is important to read each individual book within its own context and frame of reference. In this regard, the critical issues of author, date, purpose, and so on (the standard fare for NT introductions) are important foundational issues in interpreting the NT. But each book must also be read within the larger canonical framework. In this way, attention can be given to all the major elements of a given piece of writing: (1) the unique set of historical circumstances that occasioned a given book; (2) its own narrative development or flow of argument; (3) significant theological themes; and (4) the way in which a particular NT document sustains a variety of historical, literary, and theological interrelationships with other books included in the biblical canon.[121]

The New Testament as a Collection of New Covenant Documents How is it that the early Christians so readily received new documents as Scripture—in fact, a whole new corpus of material? Some of the insights of M. Kline are helpful here.[122] With the new covenant having been instituted, these believers may have been expecting new covenant documents. The OT was clearly considered based on covenant documents, and portions of it were called "the book of the covenant" (see Exod 24:7; Deut 29:20; 31:9, 26; 2 Kgs 23:2, 21; 2 Chr 34:30). The same description can be found in Second Temple Jewish literature. When Antiochus IV sought to eliminate Judaism, he attempted to destroy the books of the OT. First Maccabees 1:56–57 chronicles this attempt: "The books of the law which

---

[119] See R. Bauckham, *The Theology of the Book of Revelation*, New Testament Theology (Cambridge, UK: Cambridge University Press, 1993), 144: "It is a work of Christian prophecy that understands itself to be the culmination of the whole biblical tradition."

[120] G. R. Osborne, *Revelation*, BECNT (Grand Rapids, MI: Baker, 2002), 768.

[121] The preceding observations provide the underlying rationale for why the material is treated in the remainder of this volume the way it is. (Note especially that the book follows a chronological, rather than canonical, order of Paul's Letters). The present remarks also provide the foundation for the final chapter on the subject of the unity and diversity of the NT.

[122] Kline, *Structure of Biblical Authority*.

they found they tore to pieces and burned with fire. Where the *book of the covenant* was found in the possession of any one, or if any one adhered to the law, the decree of the king condemned him to death" (emphasis added). Thus, both the OT itself and later Jews considered the OT or portions of it to be "book(s) of the covenant."

Since the establishment of the old covenant was accompanied by covenant documents, it would seem a reasonable expectation that there would be new covenant documents upon the institution of the new covenant. This expectation would not only explain the rapid reception of the NT writings in the churches but also the recognition that these documents were Scripture on par with the OT in virtually contemporaneous documents (1 Tim 5:18; 2 Pet 3:16). M. Kruger notes that the connection between canon and covenant can be seen among the Church Fathers. He mentions, (1) the use of *diathēkē* (Gk.: "covenant") to refer to the testaments, (2) by the time of Clement of Alexandria, the phrase "new covenant" is clearly the preferred title of the NT; and (3) Eusebius preferred the term *endiathēkous* (Gk.: "encovenanted") to refer to canonical books.[123]

If this assessment is accurate, the idea of a NT canon was not the notion of some fourth-century Christians or even the product of a second-century reaction to the truncated canon of Marcion. Rather, the concept of a NT flows organically from the establishment of a new covenant, predicted by the OT prophets and instituted in and through the Lord Jesus Christ himself, who thus became the very fount not only of all Christian salvation blessings but also of the NT canon. The early Christians clearly believed these books were "handed down to them." And as Hill notes of the Gospels, if asked who chose them, they would respond, "no one," similar to the way a son might reply if asked why he chose his parents. The early believers recognized that they were given a tremendous gift and they readily received it, little choice was involved at all.[124]

Conclusion

The canon of Scripture is therefore closed. In one sense the canon was closed around the year 95 when the book of Revelation was written as the last book to be included in the NT. Properly conceived, the church's duty was to recognize the canon of inspired writings and to proclaim the truths they contained. This is what the church did and is continuing to do. Moreover, as demonstrated above, this recognition of NT canonical books came quite early—earlier than many are prepared to concede—and differences in opinion regarding individual NT books were settled through a process of deliberation until one finds a virtual consensus regarding the contents of the canon of the NT by the fourth century.

---

[123] M. J. Kruger, *Canon Revisited: Establishing the Origins and Authority of the New Testament Books* (Wheaton, IL: Crossway, 2012), 168–69.

[124] Hill, *Who Chose the Gospels?*, 231.

SIDEBAR 1.5: DID THE WRITERS OF THE NEW TESTAMENT UNDERSTAND THAT THEY WERE WRITING SCRIPTURE?[1]

Some have suggested that the Gospels were composed to be read in the churches as part of a liturgical cycle.[2] If so, it is hard to dismiss the view that the Gospels were intended to be used as Scripture since the OT was already being read in the churches in such a way. Also, both Matthew and Luke saw themselves as continuing the biblical history of the OT.[3] By extension this applies also to the book of Acts because Luke-Acts was conceived as a two-volume work (see Acts 1:1). It is also likely that John understood the Apocalypse to be Scripture. The direct visions from God, the command for those with ears to hear, and the warning neither to take away nor to add to the prophecy of this book all sound like injunctions appropriate for Scripture.

The fact that all the Gospels were declaring the fulfillment of the OT promises in Christ also supports the notion that the NT writers understood themselves to be writing Scripture.[4] Like the Gospels, Paul's Letters were also to be read in the churches in keeping with Paul's explicit instruction (as in Col 4:16). It would seem that Paul, at least, understood his letters to be authoritative for the church. While they may not have foreseen the entire body of NT writings, the writers of the various NT documents most likely understood their work within the larger framework of Scripture. Thus the expectation of new covenant documents may have played a part in the production of the NT.

---

[1] For an affirmative answer with regard to the Gospels, see D. M. Smith, "When Did the Gospels Become Scripture?" *JBL* 119 (2000): 3–20 (the 1999 SBL presidential address).

[2] For Matthew, see G. D. Kilpatrick, *The Origins of the Gospel According to St. Matthew* (Oxford, UK: Clarendon, 1950); and M. D. Goulder, *Midrash and Lection in Matthew* (London, UK: SPCK, 1974); for Mark, see P. Carrington, *The Primitive Christian Calendar: A Study in the Making of the Marcan Gospel* (Cambridge, UK: Cambridge University Press, 1052). For a more recent defense, see Hengel, *Four Gospels*, 116.

[3] Smith, "When Did the Gospels Become Scripture?" 8–10.

[4] Ibid., 13.

THE TRANSMISSION AND TRANSLATION OF THE NEW TESTAMENT: IS THE BIBLE TODAY WHAT WAS ORIGINALLY WRITTEN?

The Bible was originally written in the languages in use at the time. The OT was written in Hebrew and Aramaic and the NT in Greek. The Bibles used today are translations from the original languages into English or other languages. Jesus most likely taught in Aramaic—though he probably also knew Hebrew and Greek—so that the Greek NT itself, for the most part, represents a translation of Jesus's teaching from the Aramaic into Greek.[125]

---

[125] See N. Turner, "The Language of Jesus and His Disciples," in *The Language of the New Testament: Classic Essays*, JSNTSup 60, ed. S. E. Porter (Sheffield, MA: JSOT, 1991), 174–90; J. Fitzmyer, "The Languages of Palestine in the First Century A.D.," *CBQ* 32 (1970): 501–31; S. E. Porter, *The Criteria for Authenticity in Historical-Jesus Research: Previous Discussion and New Proposals*, JSNTSup 191 (Sheffield, MA: Sheffield Academic Press, 2000), 126–80; and idem, "Greek of the New Testament," in *Dictionary of New Testament Background*, 426–35, esp. 433–34.

Answering the question "Is the Bible today what was originally written?" involves addressing two other important questions. First, are the available manuscripts of the Bible's books accurate representations of the original manuscripts (the autographs of Scripture)? This is an issue of textual *transmission*. Second, are the available translations faithful renderings of the Bible in the original languages? This is an issue of *translation*.

Textual Transmission: Are the Available Manuscripts Accurate and Reliable?

With regard to the first question, no original autographs exist of any biblical text; only copies are available. The word *manuscript* is used to denote anything written by hand, rather than produced by the printing press.[126] Textual evidence constitutes anything written on clay tablets, stone, bone, wood, various metals, potsherds (ostraca), but most notably papyrus and parchment (animal hides, also called vellum).[127]

Most ancient books were compiled and then rolled into scrolls.[128] Since a papyrus roll rarely exceeded thirty-five feet in length, ancient authors divided a long literary work into several "books" (e.g., the Gospel of Luke and the Acts of the Apostles comprised a two-volume set composed by Luke).[129] These were published by both individuals for private use and by professionals for sale. In both cases the books were copied laboriously by hand.

One of the mysteries of Christian literature is the preference for the codex rather than the roll. Even when only a page of an ancient book is found, it can easily be determined if it comes from a roll or a codex: the codex has writing on both sides of the page. The roll was considered the more literary form for books. It is likely that the NT always circulated as a codex. The origin of this preference has been suggested by Skeat to be the four-Gospel codex[130] and by Gamble to be the Pauline corpus.[131] In either case it was most likely a Christian innovation to publish sacred books in codex form.

Books eventually succumb to the ravages of time. They either wear out or deteriorate. This extended also to the original writings that comprise the NT. Although the autographs are no longer available, the original texts are preserved in thousands of copies. At times critics object that the loss of the scriptural autographs constitutes a major problem for those who defend the trustworthiness of the Bible. Yet this does not necessarily follow. At the outset, the lack of autographs helps to direct attention where it properly belongs: on the contents of Scripture rather than the physical objects on which it was first recorded.[132]

---

[126] N. R. Lightfoot, *How We Got the Bible*, 3rd ed. (New York, NY: MJF, 2003), 33.

[127] Metzger and Ehrman, *Text of the New Testament*, 4.

[128] Ibid., 5.

[129] Ibid.

[130] Elliott, "Manuscripts, the Codex, and the Canon," 107.

[131] Gamble, *Books and Readers*, 58.

[132] A case in point is the bronze snake that Moses crafted in the wilderness (Num 21:9), which was later worshipped under the name of "Nehushtan" and was eventually destroyed as part of Hezekiah's reforms. Similarly, the tomb of Irenaeus survived into the time of the Reformation, when it was destroyed by the French Calvinists because the Catholics were worshipping it. See G. W. Kitchin, *History of France*, vol. II: *A.D. 1453–1624*, 3rd rev. ed. (Oxford, England: Clarendon, 1896), 321.

More importantly, the extant manuscript evidence instills a high degree of confidence in the text of the Bible.[133] Both the OT and NT are attested by a large number of manuscripts in a variety of forms spanning many centuries.[134] The NT texts remain the best-attested documents in the ancient world. The witnesses to the NT fall into three broad categories: the Greek manuscripts; ancient translations (versions) into other languages; and quotations from the NT found in early ecclesiastical writers (the church fathers).[135] The Greek manuscripts include papyrus fragments, uncials (written in all capitals without spaces and punctuation), and minuscules (small cursive-like script).[136]

The papyri form the most significant group since their early date implies that they are chronologically the closest to the original autographs. For example, both 𝔓[52] (containing John 18:31–33, 37–38) and 𝔓[90] (containing John 18:36–19:7) are most likely dated to within thirty to fifty years of the original writing.[137]

The uncials follow the papyri in chronological importance. Codex Sinaiticus, an uncial written in approximately 350, is the earliest extant copy of the entire NT.[138] Other uncials, such as Codices Vaticanus, Alexandrinus, Ephraemi, and Bezae, constitute significant witnesses as well. The minuscules compose the largest group of Greek manuscripts, and they are dated considerably later. Even so, the representation in the first three centuries is substantial.[139]

---

[133] Against B. D. Ehrman, *Misquoting Jesus: The Story Behind Who Changed the Bible and Why* (San Francisco, CA: Harper, 2005). See D. B. Wallace, "The Gospel According to Bart: A Review Article of *Misquoting Jesus* by Bart Ehrman," *JETS* 49 (2006): 327–49.

[134] The primary witnesses to the OT come from the Masoretic text (the Masoretes were Jewish scribes), preserved in the Cairo Geniza (895), the Leningrad Codex (916), the Codex Babylonicus Petropalitanus (1008), the Aleppo Codex (ca. 900), the British Museum Codex (950), and the Reuchlin Codex (1105). See M. R. Norton, "Texts and Manuscripts of the Old Testament," in *The Origin of the Bible*, ed. P. W. Comfort (Wheaton, IL: Tyndale, 1992), 154–55. The Leningrad Codex remains the oldest complete manuscript and serves as the main source for the Hebrew text. See Wegner, *Journey from Texts to Translations*, 194. However, since the earliest of these manuscripts date from the ninth century, they are removed from the original autographs by a considerable period.

Other witnesses include the Talmud (Aramaic translations and commentaries), the Septuagint (or LXX, the Greek translation of the OT), the Samaritan Pentateuch, and the Dead Sea Scrolls (DSS). The latter, discovered during the 1940s and '50s, provide scholars with witnesses to the OT text that can be dated between 250 and 100 BC. Cave 4 (4Q), for example, has yielded about 40,000 fragments of 400 different mss, 100 of which are biblical, representing every OT book except Esther. Remarkably, a comparison of the Dead Sea Scrolls and the Masoretic text reveals that the number of discrepancies is not as great as might have been expected. Thus, the mss evidence for the OT suggests that the original OT texts were carefully preserved and are accurately represented in our modern Bible.

[135] Metzger and Ehrman, *Text of the New Testament*, 52.

[136] P. W. Comfort, "Textual Criticism," in *Dictionary of the Later New Testament and Its Developments*, 1171.

[137] P. W. Comfort, "Texts and Manuscripts of the New Testament," in *Origin of the Bible*, 179. See the depiction of 𝔓[52] in Aland and Aland, *Text of the New Testament*, 84.

[138] P. W. Comfort, "Texts and Manuscripts of the New Testament," 183.

[139] As Wallace notes, "Although the numbers are significantly lower for the early centuries, they are still rather impressive. Today we have as many as 12 MS from the second century, 64 from the third, and 48 from the fourth—a total of 124 mss within 300 years of the composition of the NT. Most of these are fragmentary, but the whole NT text is found in this collection multiple times." D. Wallace, "Lost in Transmission: How Badly Did the Scribes Corrupt the New Testament Text?" in *Revisiting the Corruption of the New Testament: Manuscript, Patristic, and Apocryphal Evidence*, ed. D. B. Wallace (Grand Rapids, MI: Kregel, 2010), 28.

Table 1.1: Extant Copies of Ancient Works

Printed editions of classical works often have very little source material in comparison to NT studies. At times these editions are forced to rely on quotations in other works and conjectural emendations to supplement their text. Below are representative samples from works in antiquity and two from Christian antiquity to highlight the confidence we can have in the transmission of the NT.
Homer: *The Iliad*: 2,200 copies;[1] *The Odyssey*, 141 copies.[2]
Julius Caesar's *Gallic Wars*: only nine or ten good copies, the earliest of which dates to 1,000 years after it was written.
Livy: 35 of 142 books of Roman history survive. In total about twenty principle manuscripts contain the volumes.[3]
Tacitus's *Histories* and *Annals*: Annals 1–6 survive in 1 copy; Annals 11–16 and the *Histories* survive in another copy (dated to the ninth and eleventh century respectively).[4]
Thucydides: The History of the Peloponnesian War is witnessed by some papyrus fragments and seven medieval manuscripts.[5]
Suetonius' De vita Caesarum: All extant copies are descendants of a single, now-lost, ninth-century manuscript.[6]
The writings of Plato: fragments date to the second and third century. However, the main sources for Plato are 51 medieval manuscripts beginning at about the ninth century.[7]
1 Clement, 5 manuscripts, only 2 in Greek, only 1 complete copy (so-called 2 Clement survives in 3 manuscripts, only 2 in Greek.[8]
Josephus' works survive in a total of 133 copies.[9] Not all of his works are equally supported, however. His *Life* is recorded in only 5 manuscripts. Furthermore, the manuscript for *Against Apion* descends from one incomplete Greek manuscript.[10]

[1] M. L. West, *Homeri Ilias*, vol. 1, *Rhapsodias I–XII Continens*, Bibliotheca Scriptorum Graecorum et Romanorum Teubneriana (Stuttgart, Germany: in Aedibus B. G. Teubneri, 1998), xxxviii-liv.

[2] Victor Berard, *L'Odyssee: Poesie Homerique*, vol. 1: *Chants 1–VII, Collection des Universités de France* (Paris, France: Societe D'Edition Les Belles Lettres, 1924), xxxvi–ccica. Van Thiel comprised his eclectic edition of the Odyssey from 10 major manuscripts. H. van Thiel, *Homeri Odyssea*, vol. 1, Bibliotheca Weidmanniana (n.p.: G. Olms, 1991), iii, xxi.

[3] All extant mss can be traced to these principal ancestors. L. D. Reynolds, "Livy," in *Texts and Transmission: a Survey of Latin Classics*, ed. L. D. Reynolds and P. K. Martin (Oxford, UK: Clarendon, 1983), 205–14. Note, however, that the individual "decades" are unevenly represented in the mss. E.g., Books 34–37 survive in seven principal mss. (J. Briscoe, *Books XXXIV-XXXVII* [Oxford, UK: Clarendon, 1981], 15); Books 41–45 are found in a single 5th-century mss (J. Briscoe, *A Commentary on Livy: Books 41–45* [Oxford, UK: Clarendon, 2012], 3).

[4] C. E. Murgia, "The Textual Transmission," in *A Companion to Tacitus*, ed. V. E. Pagàn (Blackwell's Companions to the Ancient World; n.p.: Wiley-Blackwell, 2012), 15–16. Copies of these mss exist but play little or no part in the reconstruction of the text.

[5] J. Mynott, ed., *The War of the Peloponnesians and the Athenians by Thucydides*, Cambridge Texts in the History of Political Thought (New York, NY: Cambridge University Press, 2013), xxvii.

[6] M. Winterbottom, "Suetonius," in *Texts and Transmission: A Survey of the Latin Classics*, ed. L. D. Reynolds and P. K. Marshall (Oxford, UK: Clarendon, 1983), 399.

[7] T. H. Irwin, "The Platonic Corpus," in *The Oxford Handbook of Plato* (New York, NY: Oxford University Press, 2011), 71.

[8] M. W. Holmes, ed., *The Apostolic Fathers: Greek Texts and English Translations*, 3rd ed. (Grand Rapids, MI: Baker, 2007), 38, 135–36.

[9] L. H. Feldman, "A Selective Critical Bibliography of Josephus," in *Josephus, the Bible, and History*, ed. L. H. Feldman and Gâohei Hata (n.p.: Brill, 1989), 332.

[10] J. M. G. Barclay, *Flavius Josephus: Translation and Commentary*, ed. S. Mason, vol. 10: *Against Apion: Translation and Commentary* (Boston, MA: Brill, 2007), LXIII.

Finally, the translations of Scripture into other languages prepared during the first several centuries of the church and citations of Scripture in the writings of the church fathers provide helpful information that can aid scholars in reconstructing the most plausible original readings. The total tally of 5,760 Greek manuscripts, more than 10,000 Latin Vulgate manuscripts, and more than 9,300 early versions results in over 25,000 early witnesses to the text of the NT.[140] When this is compared to other works in antiquity, no other book even comes close. Needless to say, classical scholars and historians would love to be working with books as well attested as the NT.

If there is bad news about this state of affairs, it is that with the sheer multiplicity of manuscripts come some variations in the text.[141] Because they were copied by hand, it is highly unlikely to have two manuscripts that are exactly alike from any handwritten book, sacred or otherwise.[142] Thousands of variant readings (most of them minor and inconsequential) exist among the manuscripts. While scribes exhibited great care in their effort to reproduce an exact copy,[143] they were not immune from human error. Scribal errors can take the form of unintentional and intentional errors.[144] Unintentional errors are the cause of the majority of textual variants.[145] These typically include errors of the eyes (e.g., skipping words or losing one's place); the hands (slips of the pen or writing notes in the margins); and the ears (confusing similar sounding words or misunderstanding a word).[146] Intentional errors resulted when scribes attempted to correct a perceived error in the text or altered the text in the interest of doctrine and harmonization.[147]

The presence of variants has often been used to undermine both the inspiration and reliability of the NT.[148] Ehrman declares there are 200,000 to 400,000 variants. Thus, "there are

---

[140] See Metzger and Ehrman (*Text of the New Testament*, 52), who state that there are "approximately 5,700 Greek manuscripts that contain all or part of the New Testament." D. B. Wallace, "Challenges in New Testament Textual Criticism for the Twenty-First Century," *JETS* 52 (2009): 96, puts the number of currently known Greek NT manuscripts at 5,760. Wallace's entire article provides a helpful survey of the current state of textual criticism and ably delineates the challenges and the remaining task ahead.

[141] G. D. Fee, "Textual Criticism," in *Dictionary of Jesus and the Gospels*, ed. J. B. Green, S. McKnight, and I. H. Marshall (Downers Grove, IL: InterVarsity, 1992), 828.

[142] It could only happen if only one ms survived and then confidence would be virtually zero. Muslim apologists have often made the claim that the Qur'ān has been preserved perfectly from its delivery to Mohammed (K. E. Small, *Textual Criticism and Qur'ān Manuscripts* [Lanham, MD: Rowman & Littlefield, 2011], 6). The implication is that it is superior to the NT because (1) there are variants in the NT mss tradition; and (2) no such variant exists in the Qur'ān. The assertion, however, is overstated. There are known variants in the post-canonization (i.e., after Uthman's recension) manuscripts (see Small, *Textual Criticism;* and Ibn Warraq, *Which Koran? Variants, Manuscripts, Linguistics* [Amherst, NY: Prometheus, 2008]). The point here is that all hand-written books have a textual history, including scribal errata.

[143] Metzger and Ehrman, *Text of the New Testament*, 16–33. See Comfort, "Textual Criticism," 1172.

[144] Lightfoot, *How We Got the Bible*, 61.

[145] For helpful charts describing the types of scribal errors, see Wegner, *Journey from Texts to Translations*, 225–36.

[146] Lightfoot, *How We Got the Bible*, 61.

[147] Comfort, "Textual Criticism," 1172.

[148] For an accessible treatment of this and related issues, see chap. 3: "Are the Biblical Manuscripts Corrupt?" in A. J. Köstenberger, D. L. Bock, and J. D. Chatraw, *Truth in a Culture of Doubt: Engaging Skeptical Challenges to the Bible* (Nashville, TN: B&H Academic, 2014), esp. 92–94.

more variations among our manuscripts than there are words in the New Testament."[149] This leaves the impression that textual certainty is a hopeless cause. Wallace, however, puts it in perspective. When we take the largest number and spread that over all NT manuscripts (versions included because the variant number does as well—ca. 25,000) an average of sixteen variants per manuscript appears. Using the lower number, the spread is eight.[150] Manuscripts and variants are not all equal, but it speaks highly of the stability of the text.

Therefore, the reliability of the NT is not materially affected by the existence of variants, which pertain to only a small portion of the NT. In fact, 94 percent of its content is exactly the same in virtually all the existing manuscripts.[151] Of the remaining 6 percent, 3 percent constitute nonsensical readings that are transparently not original but are the result of various scribal errors. Thus, only about 3 percent of the text is properly the subject of investigation. What is more, variants among the available manuscripts should cause no doubt that the correct reading can be found. There is virtually no possibility that among the thousands of manuscripts that exist today an original reading was lost. The correct reading is extant; the task that remains is to identify which of the variant readings most likely reflects the original. However, these efforts are regularly plagued by flawed underlying assumptions. First, the proper subject of investigation is not "Is the New Testament inspired?" but "What is the New Testament?"

In terms of classification of existing readings, all Greek manuscripts exhibit traits that enable scholars to group them into text families (Alexandrian, Western, or Byzantine) based on geographic origin, Greek style, and date. Through comparative analysis performed by the practitioners of a science called textual criticism, scholars sift through all the extant manuscripts in order to reproduce the most plausible reading of the original autographs in each individual case.[152]

Textual critics adjudicate between readings through exacting criteria such as dating, text type (geographic distribution), attested readings (how many manuscripts have a certain reading), and possible reasons for variants (such as smoothing out a theologically difficult reading). In addition to examining the Greek manuscripts, textual critics also consider all other relevant witnesses such as versions and the church fathers.

Although textual criticism is a complex and at times controversial science, it has provided students of Scripture with at least two assured results. First, none of the variant readings (including omissions) affect the central message or theological content of the Scriptures. Second, it can confidently be asserted that the text of the Bible today is an accurate and faithful representation of the autographs.

---

[149] B. D. Ehrman, *Misquoting Jesus: The Story Behind Who Changed the Bible and Why* (San Francisco, CA: Harper, 2005), 89.

[150] J. E. Komoszewski, M. J. Sawyer, D. B. Wallace, *Reinventing Jesus: What "The Da Vinci Code" and Other Novel Speculations Don't Tell You* (Grand Rapids, MI: Kregel, 2006), 82.

[151] P. D. Wegner, *A Student's Guide to Textual Criticism of the Bible: Its History, Methods, and Results* (Downers Grove, IL: InterVarsity, 2004), 298.

[152] See Aland and Aland, *Text of the New Testament*, esp. 275–77.

Translation: Are the Available Translations Faithful?

The second issue, namely that of *translation*, follows as a natural corollary once the question of *transmission* is settled. To assess the fidelity and accuracy of the Bible today compared to the original texts, one must investigate the issues of translation theory and the history of the English Bible. The task of translating the Bible from its source languages (Hebrew, Aramaic, and Greek) into a receptor language such as English involves a plethora of issues related to the nature of language and communication. Is word meaning found in some fixed form of inherent meaning, or is meaning determined by contextual usage? Is meaning located in the formal features of the original grammar or in the function of words within the grammar? These are just a few of the questions pertaining to translation theory.

Some translators maintain that accurate translation requires a word-for-word approach of formal equivalence (KJV, NKJV, NASB, ESV, CSB).[153] Others contend that construing a straightforward one-to-one correlation between two languages actually distorts meaning.[154] These translators employ a phrase-for-phrase approach[155] of dynamic or functional equivalence (NRSV, NIV, CEV, NLT).[156] The goal of all translators, no matter what translation theory they employ, is the production of a version that is an accurate rendering of the text and written in such a way that the Bible retains its literary beauty, theological grandeur, and, most importantly, its spiritual message.[157]

Table 1.2: Translation Continuum

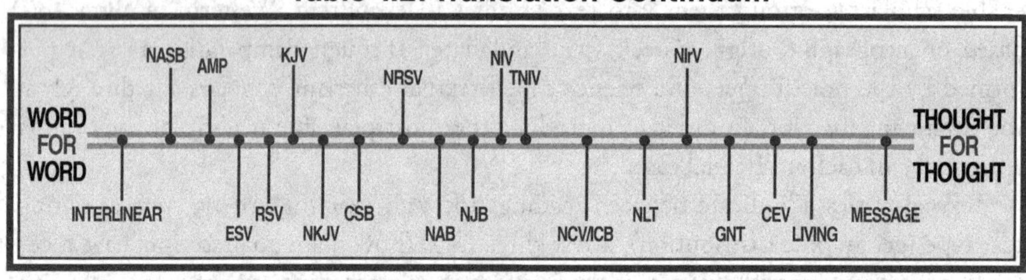

This continuum shows how different Bible translations fit into the word-for-word and thought-for-thought translation philosophies.

---

[153] V. S. Poythress and W. A. Grudem, *The Gender-Neutral Bible Controversy: Muting the Masculinity of God's Words* (Nashville, TN: B&H, 2000). See L. Ryken, *The Word of God in English: Criteria for Excellence in Bible Translation* (Wheaton, IL: Crossway, 2002).

[154] D. A. Carson, *The Inclusive Language Debate: A Plea for Realism* (Grand Rapids, MI: Baker, 1998), 47–76. See M. Silva, "Are Translators Traitors? Some Personal Reflections," in *The Challenge of Bible Translation*, ed. G. G. Scorgie, M. L. Strauss, and S. M. Voth (Grand Rapids, MI: Zondervan, 2002), 37–44.

[155] J. R. Kohlenberger III, "Inclusive Language in Bible Translation," in *Perspectives on the TNIV from Leading Scholars and Pastors* (Grand Rapids, MI: Zondervan, 2004), 11.

[156] D. A. Carson, "The Limits of Functional Equivalence in Bible Translation—and Other Limits, Too," in *Challenge of Bible Translation*, 65–113; K. L. Barker, "Bible Translation Philosophy with Special Reference to the New International Version," in *Challenge of Bible Translation*, 51–63. See M. L. Strauss, *Distorting Scripture?* (Downers Grove, IL: InterVarsity, 1998).

[157] G. G. Scorgie, "Introduction and Overview," in *Challenge of Bible Translation*, 25. The following chart is taken from "About Bible Translations," www.zondervan.com.

The good news is that there are faithful translations of the Bible in English available for a wide variety of readers. Whether a given person needs a rendition with a limited vocabulary and simple syntax or prefers an elevated style and grandeur of language, a faithful translation exists for him or her.

The history of the English Bible satisfactorily demonstrates that the Bible of today does indeed faithfully represent the Scriptures in their original languages.[158] For centuries the only Bible available to Western people was the Latin Vulgate prepared by Jerome (ca. AD 345–420), who was commissioned by Bishop Damasus toward the end of the fourth century.[159] The Vulgate served as the official version of the Bible throughout medieval Europe and its use was restricted to the clergy, monastic orders, and scholars.[160]

A British priest and Oxford scholar, John Wycliffe (1330–1384), was the first to make the entire Bible accessible to the common English-speaking people.[161] His translation was based on the Vulgate and not on the Hebrew and Greek.[162] William Tyndale published the first English NT based on the Greek text in 1526.[163] Two close associates of Tyndale, Miles Coverdale and John Rogers, finished his work by publishing their own respective translations of the entire Bible: the Coverdale Bible (1535) and Matthew's Bible (1537).[164] The Geneva Bible of 1560 provided a translation of the Bible entirely from the original languages.[165] This paved the way for King James I to issue a translation that would be a corrective to the partisan nature of the Geneva Bible.[166] Thus in 1611, the much-celebrated Authorized Version (AV or KJV), largely based on Tyndale's work, became the major English translation for approximately 270 years.[167]

The twentieth century has given rise to a number of new translations. Taking its point of departure from the revised Authorized Version in England in 1885, the American Standard Version (ASV) appeared in 1901. In 1952, the Revised Standard Version (RSV) was introduced. A Roman Catholic translation, the Jerusalem Bible, was released in 1966. The New English Bible (NEB), the New American Bible (NAB), and the New American Standard Bible (NASB) were all completed in 1970. The Good News Bible (GNB) or

---

[158] For a concise survey, see Chapter 1: "A Short History of Bible Translation," in A. J. Köstenberger and D. A. Croteau, *Which Bible Translation Should I Use? A Comparison of 4 Major Recent Versions* (Nashville, TN: B&H Academic, 2012), 4–23.

[159] D. France, "The Bible in English: An Overview," in *Challenge of Bible Translation*, 177.

[160] Ibid., 179.

[161] A. E. McGrath, *In the Beginning: The Story of the King James Bible and How It Changed a Nation, a Language, and a Culture* (New York, NY: Doubleday, 2001), 19–23.

[162] France, "Bible in English," 181. Compare *The Gospel of Saint John in West-Saxon*, ed. J. W. Bright (Boston, MA: D. C. Heath & Co., 1906), which presents the first English version of John's Gospel that precedes Wycliffe's translation by 400 years.

[163] *Tyndale's New Testament*, ed. D. Daniell (New Haven, CT: Yale University Press, 1995 [1989]).

[164] Ibid.

[165] McGrath, *In the Beginning*, 113–29.

[166] Ibid., 139–48.

[167] France, "Bible in English," 184.

Today's English Version (TEV) was produced in 1978, the year that also saw the publication of the New International Version (NIV).

The New King James Version (NKJV, 1982) was produced in the 1980s, the New Century Version (NCV, 1987), and the New Revised Standard Version (NRSV, 1989) came soon after. The pace did not slow in the 1990s, the Contemporary English Version (CEV, 1995), the updated New American Standard Bible (NASB, 1995), and the New Living Translation (NLT, 1996) were all released. At the turn of the 21st century additional significant translations were completed, including the English Standard Version (ESV, 2001), the Holman Christian Standard Bible (HCSB, 2004), Today's New International Version (TNIV, 2005), and its replacement, the updated New International Version (NIV, 2011).[168]

Such updating and production of new translations were necessitated by new manuscript discoveries, changes in the English language, and the advancement of modern linguistics. Today, when people open any English Bible, they may know that scholars have labored to deliver an accurate translation to the English speaking world. The great task ahead of us now is to translate the Bible into the languages that have no Bible available to them.

As the author of Hebrews states, "Long ago God spoke to the fathers by the prophets at different times and in different ways. In these last days, he has spoken to us by his Son. God has appointed him heir of all things and made the universe through him" (Heb 1:1–2). With this kind of revelation, there is no need to wait for another, greater revelation but to study, evangelize, preach, and teach the Word of God. The canon is the source of this information—inspired, illumined, and applied by the Holy Spirit. Truly, as one writer stated, the canon of Scripture is "the air we breathe."[169]

INSPIRATION AND INERRANCY: WHAT IS THE NATURE OF THE CANON?

The final topic for discussion in the present chapter relates to theology, that is, the doctrine of Scripture, and in particular the Bible's witness regarding itself. This consideration of the theological dimension of Scripture is needed in order to balance its historical development and the inclusion of particular books in the NT canon. This discussion deals with Scripture's witness regarding itself in the OT; the use of and approach to OT Scripture by Jesus and the early church; NT references to Scripture as "inspired" (2 Tim 3:16) and as deriving from men "carried along by the Holy Spirit" (2 Pet 1:21); and inerrancy (the doctrine that Scripture is free from error) and hermeneutics (biblical interpretation).

The Broader Notion of "Inspiration" in the Early Church Fathers

In the discussion of the criteria for canonicity above, we observed that when the ancient church compiled the canon, its essential task *historically* was to recognize which writings

[168] For a comparison of four major recent versions (ESV, NIV, CSB, NLT), see Köstenberger and Croteau, *Which Bible Translation?*

[169] S. J. Mikolaski, "Canon as the Air We Breathe," in *From Biblical Criticism to Biblical Faith*, 146–63.

bore the stamp of divine inspiration. Much of recent scholarship on the NT canon, however, rejects the *theological* notion of "inspiration" as a criterion of canonicity.[170] While it is difficult to deny that inspiration is a scriptural attribute, some argue that inspiration is not the sole prerogative of Scripture. Sundberg, for example, concluded not only that the church fathers did not include "inspired" in their criteria for canonicity but employed "inspired" versus "not inspired" language in polemical debates with heretical movements.[171] According to these scholars, "inspiration" terminology was used not only with reference to the Scriptures but also with regard to their own writings. Thus, Clement said that Paul wrote with "true inspiration" (*1 Clem.* 47.3) and that his own (Clement's) letter was "through the Holy Spirit" (*1 Clem.* 63.2) as well. Similar language is used in other patristic writings.

Sundberg further claimed that the doctrine of the *unique* inspiration of Scripture is not a Christian doctrine at all but rather a Jewish notion that arose after Christianity had received the Jewish Scriptures and broken with Judaism. Later on, according to Sundberg, this doctrine of inspiration was seized by Luther in the polemical debates of his day in order to exclude the Apocrypha.[172] Sundberg, for his part, claimed that everything that coheres with the Bible is inspired equally to the Bible. He stated,

> Thus, in forming the canon, the church acknowledged and established the Bible as the measure or standard of inspiration in the church, not the totality of it. . . . Christian inspiration parallels biblical inspiration, complementing it, and opening every Christian age to theological verisimilitude, like the books of the Bible and the periods in which they were written are verisimilar.[173]

This, of course, creates some difficulty for believers accustomed to understanding *inspired* to mean "from God" and therefore authoritative. If there were ancient or contemporary documents as equally inspired as the canonical writings, this would necessitate a broader definition of "Scripture." But this raises several important questions. For example, is it legitimate to consider a non-canonical document or utterance as inspired and authoritative if it goes beyond canonical Scripture and adds new revelatory content? Should such documents be added to the existing canon? Even Sundberg would say no, because the canon, settled in the fourth century, is the rule by which all other works are to be judged. Thus

---

[170] E.g., A. G. Patzia, *The Making of the New Testament: Origin, Collection, Text and Canon* (Downers Grove, IL: InterVarsity, 1995), 105.

[171] A modified form of this view is found in Metzger (*Canon*, 256) as well, though he clearly recognized the difference between a modern definition of biblical inspiration and the somewhat haphazard use of the word in antiquity.

[172] Sundberg, "Bible Canon," 371. See Walden ("Luther: The One Who Shaped the Canon," 1–10) for a somewhat different view.

[173] Sundberg, "Bible Canon," 371. There is irony in the fact that those who deny the connection between inspiration and canonicity are compelled to discuss it nonetheless.

the canon has a special place among the inspired writings. Yet Sundberg failed to adduce a proper biblical basis on which to exclude non-inspired, non-canonical books.

The all-important point in this regard is that the church fathers' use of inspiration terminology is not prescriptive for the church today. Although they made an indispensable contribution to our understanding of the early days of the church, it is Scripture's own witness and doctrine that are authoritative. Moreover, the church's role is best understood not as the acceptance of a certain group of writings on the basis of human criteria and deliberations but as the recognition of the books handed down to the church that bore the self-authenticating mark of divine inspiration.

For this reason it must be concluded that Sundberg's thesis is built on faulty presuppositions. The use of inspiration terminology in the church fathers is both unrefined and often generic, used to refer broadly to the participation of the Holy Spirit in their lives and writings. The church fathers should not be faulted for failing to utilize a modern theological construct drawn from centuries of discussion on the biblical texts. For this reason, rather than taking the writings of the early church fathers as one's point of departure, it is more appropriate to start with the scriptural witness regarding itself.

Of necessity, many of the relevant references pertain to the OT Scriptures. However, if the NT is the collection of new covenant documents in analogy with the OT being the collection of old covenant documents, it stands to reason that the NT writings will exhibit the same types of characteristics as the books of the OT. Thus, when Peter affirmed Paul's writings as being on a par with Scripture, and when Paul, as is likely, affirmed the Gospel of Luke as Scripture on the same level as Deuteronomy, then both NT writers were ascribing to the NT (or at least to Paul's Letters and the Gospels) the same characteristics as those found in the books of the OT.

The God portrayed in the OT is a communicating God. He speaks to his children, and he does so through his servants the prophets (hence the prophetic "Thus says the LORD"). Because it is God who speaks to and through his servants, he demands faith in and obedience to these utterances. Thus, King Jehoshaphat called on the Israelites to "believe in the LORD your God, and you will be established; believe in his prophets, and you will succeed" (2 Chr 20:20), and God himself is represented as addressing the wilderness generation with the following words:

> "Listen to what I say: If there is a prophet among you from the LORD, I make myself known to him in a vision; I speak with him in a dream. Not so with my servant Moses; he is faithful in all my household. I speak with him directly, openly, and not in riddles; he sees the form of the LORD. So why were you not afraid to speak against my servant Moses?" (Num 12:6–8).[174]

---

[174] One need not see a devaluation of the prophetic vision. The argument is from the lesser to the greater (common in Judaism). In essence, the logic presents itself this way: "If the prophetic word is to be obeyed, the word I speak directly to Moses should make you afraid to slander him."

God's word to his servants was expected to be believed and obeyed as God was to be believed and obeyed.

The Scripture's Witness Regarding Itself: The Old Testament

But what should be said about the written Word? Scripture itself contains information regarding the writing of Scripture. These, as W. Grudem noted, are "reports of men writing down words that God told them to write, words that are then understood as God's words."[175] Exodus 17:14 states, "The LORD then said to Moses, 'Write this down on a scroll as a reminder and recite it to Joshua.'" In subsequent generations, actions were to be performed in keeping with what was written in the law of Moses. This was explicitly commanded in passages such as Deuteronomy 28:58–59. Consequently, the command to Joshua was related to this book of the law: "This book of instruction must not depart from your mouth; you are to meditate on it day and night, so that you may carefully observe everything written in it. For then you will prosper and succeed in whatever you do" (Josh 1:8). Joshua also copied the law of Moses at its ratification (Josh 8:32). His last words to Israel were, "Be very strong, and continue obeying all that is written in the book of the law of Moses, so that you do not turn from it to the right or left" (Josh 23:6). Clearly, the written law of Moses, as the Word of God, was understood as authoritative and as the path of blessing for Israel. In later generations this continued to be the declaration of the OT (see 1 Kgs 2:3). Significantly, after a time of religious decline in Israel, Hilkiah the priest found "the book of the law" in the temple (2 Kgs 22:8; 2 Chr 34:14). When young King Josiah had the book read to him, it became to him a source of grief because "great is the LORD's wrath that is kindled against us because our ancestors have not obeyed the words of this book in order to do everything written about us" (2 Kgs 22:13). Josiah's subsequent reforms constituted a movement "back to the Bible." A similar thing happened after the return from the Babylonian captivity when Ezra read the book of the law "that the LORD had given Israel" to the assembled clans of Israel (Neh 8:1).[176]

The inclusion of the rest of the OT is directly related to the office of prophet that was central to the religious fidelity of Israel. The prophet's role was tied directly to the covenant relationship between Israel and God. The prophets were called not to be mere seers but to keep reminding Israel of her duties in the covenant. It is best to understand their role as covenant enforcers. What they speak is "the word of the LORD." The call of Jeremiah makes this explicit: "Then the LORD reached out his hand, touched my mouth, and told me: I have filled your mouth with my words" (Jer 1:9). Just as God commanded Moses to write down his words, so many of the writing prophets were enjoined to write down God's words (see Jer 36:28; Ezek 43:11; Hab 2:2). The recognition of an OT book as canonical

[175] W. A. Grudem, "Scripture's Self-Attestation and the Problem of Formulating a Doctrine of Scripture," in *Scripture and Truth*, ed. D. A. Carson and J. D. Woodbridge (Grand Rapids, MI: Zondervan, 1983), 25.

[176] It is obviously quite a large scroll, for it takes six hours to read only selected parts of the Pentateuch (Ezra "read in it," Hb. *wayyiqrā<-bô*, suggesting the whole was not read). See M. Breneman, *Ezra, Nehemiah, Esther*, NAC (Nashville, TN: B&H, 1993), 224.

also seems directly related to being written by one with the gift of prophecy.[177] R. L. Harris stated, "It seems that prophecy was the only institution in Israel for imparting new revelation of God's Word."[178] These works were considered authoritative almost immediately. Daniel, for example, read and received the book of Jeremiah as "the word of the LORD" (Dan 9:2; see Ezra 1:1; 2 Chr 36:22).

The character of these writings is directly related to their source, God. Two psalms are particularly explicit in their recognition of God's words in Scripture. Psalm 19 affirms the Scriptures to be "of the LORD." Thus, they are perfect and trustworthy (v. 7), right and pure (v. 8), and "reliable and altogether righteous" (v. 9). The longest chapter in the Bible, Psalm 119, is devoted in its entirety to the praise of the word of God. The psalmist describes the word as coming from God, and therefore as the "word of truth" (vv. 43, 142) in its entirety (vv. 86, 151, 160) and as altogether righteous (v. 172). Since it is God who is speaking in various forms and through various prophets, there are some clear assumptions about the veracity and authority of these words. Since God cannot lie (Num 23:19; 1 Sam 15:29; Prov 8:8; Ps 89:35), his word is truth (see Jesus's similar affirmation in John 17:17). And since God never fails (Zeph 3:5), neither can his word.

Moreover, God's word, as delivered to the prophets, was inviolate. It was not to be edited.[179] This was made explicit by Moses who stated, "You must not add anything to what I command you or take anything away from it, so that you may keep the commands of the LORD your God I am giving you" (Deut 4:2; see 12:32). What is more, the writer of Proverbs 30:5–6 extended the principle beyond the law to *every* word of God: "Every word of God is pure; he is a shield to those who take refuge in him. Don't add to his words, or he will rebuke you, and you will be proved a liar."

Thus, even though the OT books span a variety of genres, feature different rhetorical forms, and represent the work of different prophets, they all share as their major common element the divine source of their words. As Grudem stated, "The written words are seen as God's words in every way that direct speech by God and God's speech through the mouths of people are seen as God's words. The form of communication differs, but the character, authority, and truth status of the words do not."[180]

To be sure, these general observations are of necessity preliminary since it is impossible for the OT to proclaim regarding itself in its entirety something that, by definition, had to

---

[177] See R. L. Harris, *Inspiration and Canonicity of the Scriptures* (Grand Rapids, MI: Zondervan, 1969), 154–77; Bruce, *Canon of Scripture*, 255–69. This is contrary to E. J. Young, *Introduction to the Old Testament*, 2nd ed. (Grand Rapids, MI: Eerdmans, 1950), 41–42, although Young acknowledges the difference between the gift of prophecy and the prophetic office.

[178] Harris, *Inspiration and Canonicity*, 163; see R. H. Pfeiffer, *The Books of the Old Testament* (New York, NY: Harper, 1957), 13.

[179] This does not suggest that the collection into a canon was improper. See M. Grisanti, "Inspiration, Inerrancy, and the OT Canon: The Place of Textual Updating in an Inerrant View of Scripture," *JETS* 44 (2001): 577–98.

[180] Grudem, "Scripture's Self-Attestation," 27.

await the completion of its entire corpus of writings.[181] The NT looks back to the OT and registers some important affirmations regarding it and, by extension, regarding itself as well.

Jesus's Use of and Approach to Old Testament Scripture

First, it is instructive to consider Jesus's affirmations regarding OT Scripture. According to Jesus and his contemporaries, the OT Scriptures were the authority from which doctrine and practice were to derive. Thus Jesus challenged his opponents to understand the Scriptures: "Have you never read in the Scriptures?" (Matt 21:42/Mark 12:10). Likewise, Jesus asserted that ignorance with regard to the OT Scriptures was the reason his opponents were wrong: "You are mistaken, because you don't know the Scriptures or the power of God" (Matt 22:29/Mark 12:24). On another occasion Jesus judged a practical question—"Who is my neighbor?"—with an appeal to Scripture: "What is written in the law? . . . How do you read it?" (Luke 10:26). In John 5:39, Jesus observed that the Jews "pore over the Scriptures because you think you have eternal life in them, and yet they testify about me." A host of other Gospel citations describe the Word of God, the Scriptures, the Law, and the Prophets as the guide for life.[182] It is clear that Jesus and his hearers considered the OT to be the Word of God and authoritative. To this may be added the fulfillment quotations in the Gospels—OT quotes introduced with a formula such as "this happened in order that the words spoken by the prophet were fulfilled," occurring especially in Matthew and John—that presuppose that the readers had the highest regard for OT Scripture.[183]

Significantly, in the Gospel references there is no distinction between the human words of Scripture and the words of God. Men who spoke in the OT are described in the Gospels as God speaking. For example, Isaiah's words in Isaiah 7:14 are described by Matthew 1:22 as "spoken by the Lord through the prophet," which reveals that Scripture in its totality was considered to be the Word of God.[184] But this was not just a belief of the Gospel writers; it was also the view of Jesus himself. Luke's account of the encounter on the road to Emmaus records Jesus's affirmation that the disciples should have been quick to believe what was written about Jesus in "all the Prophets" (Luke 24:27). A few verses later, the reference is to "all the Scriptures" and "the Law of Moses, the Prophets, and the Psalms" (Luke 24:44).[185]

---

[181] Ibid., 28.

[182] E.g., Matt 4:4; 12:5; 15:6; 22:40; 23:23; Luke 2:23–24; 4:17; 8:21; 11:28; 16:29, 31; 24:25; John 7:19, 23, 49, 51; 8:17; 10:34; 18:31; 19:7.

[183] See Matt 1:22; 2:5, 15, 17, 23; 3:3; 4:14; 5:17; 8:17; 11:13; 12:17; 13:35; 21:4; 24:15; 26:54, 56; 27:9; Mark 1:2; Luke 1:70; 3:4; 4:21; 18:31; 24:27, 32, 44–45; John 1:23, 45; 2:22; 6:45; 7:38, 42, 52; 12:38; 13:18; 15:25; 17:12; 19:24, 28, 36–37; 20:9.

[184] Grudem, "Scripture's Self-Attestation," 38.

[185] The most common ascription of the OT is "the Law and the Prophets." This in no way affirms suspicion about the third division of the Hebrew Bible. This phrase and sometimes just "the Law" are a shorthand way of referring to the entire OT. See John 10:34 where Jesus cites "the Law" but actually quotes Ps 82:6 and Matt 13:35, where "prophet" introduces the quotation but the reference is to the Writings.

Not only were the OT Scriptures in their entirety the Word of God, but Jesus also affirmed their special nature. In John 10:35–36, Jesus countered the charge of blasphemy with an argument from the lesser to the greater: "If he called those whom the word of God came to 'gods'—*and the Scripture cannot be broken*—do you say, 'You are blaspheming,' to the one the Father set apart and sent into the world, because I said: I am the Son of God?"[186] The reminder that Scripture cannot be broken is a tacit acknowledgment of its status as the Word of God. Thus, the argument is that Scripture cannot be charged with error or it would be broken—that is, rejected as the Word of God.

Jesus succinctly said something similar in John 17:17: "your word is truth." But even here there may be a connection with new covenant documents. Thus when Jesus affirmed, "I have given them your word" (17:14), he may have implied more than merely "I taught them the Bible." In John's Gospel the statement is connected with the concept of truth. Jesus, who is "the truth" (14:6), gives the "Spirit of truth" (14:17; 15:26; 16:13), who leads believers "into all the truth" (16:13).[187] And this truth is "your [God's] word." This indicated what would serve as the foundation for new covenant documents: Jesus's words as the words of God. While this implies a connection to the NT as Scripture, other passages clearly point to the revelatory status of Jesus's words. For example, the affirmation that Jesus spoke God's word lies at the heart of the pronouncement in John 3:33–34: "The one who has accepted his testimony has affirmed that God is true. For the one whom God sent speaks God's words, since he gives the Spirit without measure."

One of the most striking passages related to Jesus's use of and approach to OT Scripture is found in Matthew 5:18, where Jesus affirmed that he would not destroy the law: "For truly I tell you: Until heaven and earth pass away, not the smallest letter or one stroke of a letter will pass away from the law until all things are accomplished."[188] The appeal here is to the smallest letter (*iota*, in Hebrew the *yodh*) or one stroke (*keraia*, lit. "a horn," most likely a tittle, an ornamental mark above a Hebrew letter, or a serif) being absolutely firm. Down to the minutest elements of an individual written word, Jesus affirmed the enduring authority of the OT.[189] The similar statement in Matthew 24:35 points to the equal status of Jesus's words: "Heaven and earth will pass away, but my words will never pass away." In both verses Jesus affirmed the dissolution of heaven and earth and offered a declaration regarding the enduring nature of God's words: in the first, the pronouncement pertains to the OT Scriptures; in the second, to the words of Jesus. While the immediate context is the Olivet Discourse, the parallelism is too strong to suggest only that the affirmation is

---

[186] Emphasis added. For a study of the use of the OT in John 10:34–36, see A. J. Köstenberger, "John," in *Commentary on the New Testament Use of the Old Testament*, ed. G. K. Beale and D. A. Carson (Grand Rapids, MI: Baker, 2007), 464–67.

[187] A. J. Köstenberger, *John*, BECNT (Grand Rapids, MI: Baker, 2004), 496.

[188] See Luke 16:17: "But it is easier for heaven and earth to pass away than for one stroke of a letter in the law to drop out."

[189] See L. Morris, *The Gospel According to Matthew*, PNTC (Grand Rapids, MI: Eerdmans, 1992), 109–10.

limited to this one speech. Jesus's words are the words of God on a par with the Law and the Prophets and thus are equally permanent and authoritative.[190]

Jesus's own use of Scripture also paves the way for the NT. Jesus's stance toward Scripture was striking on two fronts. First, Jesus submitted himself to the Scriptures as any human would. This can be seen in the account of Jesus's temptation by the Devil (Matt 4:1–11; Luke 4:1–13). When faced with these various temptations, Jesus did not assert divine privilege but simply affirmed and obeyed the word of God. As Bengel stated long ago, "Jesus does not appeal to the voice from heaven: He does not reply to the arguments of the tempter: against those arguments He employs the Scripture alone, and simply cites its assertions."[191] At other places, Jesus claimed to be the fulfillment of Scripture, such as in his address at the synagogue in Nazareth (Luke 4:18–21). He used Scripture in his arguments with religious opponents (Matt 21:13; Mark 7:6) and employed it in his teaching (Mark 9:13) and in his description of himself (Mark 14:21, 27). At the same time, he taught with unusual authority, not as one of the scribes (Matt 7:29; Mark 1:22). What was shocking to Jesus's hearers was that his interpretation was Christological in its focus. Jesus saw the contours of his ministry in the OT.[192] He thus became the fulfillment of God's purposes for and promises to Israel.[193]

The Early Church's Use of and Approach to Old Testament Scripture

Jesus passed on his approach to OT Scripture to his disciples.[194] In this way Jesus's method of interpretation and teaching "provides the groundwork for Jesus's authentication of the New Testament."[195] Jesus himself promised his disciples that the Holy Spirit "will teach you all things and remind you of everything I have told you" (John 14:26). From John's perspective, writing in the AD 80s or early 90s, this promise most likely served also as an affirmation of at least his memories of Jesus's words (if not of the memories of all the apostles) recorded in the Gospel(s).

The apostles and their followers continued to use the OT Scriptures as Jesus did, namely, as their authority for life and doctrine.[196] This can be seen in a variety of contexts, both in scriptural quotations and in explicit statements regarding the nature of

---

[190] R. Gundry, *Matthew: A Commentary on His Handbook for a Mixed Church Under Persecution*, 2nd ed. (Grand Rapids, MI: Eerdmans, 1994), 80.

[191] J. A. Bengel, *Gnomon of the New Testament*, vol. 1, trans. A. R. Fausset (Edinburgh, Scotland: T&T Clark, 1857–1858), 149.

[192] See especially R. T. France, *Jesus and the Old Testament: His Application of Old Testament Passages to Himself and His Mission* (London, UK: Tyndale, 1971).

[193] D. Dockery, *Christian Scripture: An Evangelical Perspective on Inspiration, Authority, and Interpretation* (Nashville, TN: B&H, 1995), 28.

[194] See especially R. N. Longenecker, *Biblical Exegesis in the Apostolic Period*, 2nd ed. (Grand Rapids, MI: Eerdmans, 1999).

[195] Dockery, *Christian Scripture*, 28.

[196] For a thorough treatment of the use of the OT in the NT, see Beale and Carson, *Commentary on the New Testament Use of the Old Testament.* See also D. A. Carson and H. G. M. Williamson, *It Is Written: Scripture Citing Scripture* (Cambridge, UK: Cambridge University Press, 1988), which also includes discussions of the use of earlier OT references in later

Scripture. Scripture provides the dual warrant for the replacement of Judas (Acts 1:20). At the Jerusalem Council, an OT citation helps adjudicate the issue of Gentile inclusion in the NT church (Acts 15:16–17). The Scriptures were the standard by which the Bereans judged Paul's claims concerning Christ (Acts 17:11). Key OT passages provide the basis for Paul's teaching in Romans regarding justification by faith (Rom 1:17; 4:3), the sinfulness of all humanity (Rom 3:10–18), and election (Rom 9:6–18). The same is true for other letters of Paul and the General Epistles.[197] Peter saw continuity between the OT and the word of the Lord that declared the gospel to his hearers (1 Pet 1:23–25).

The book of Revelation provides a fascinating and unique study in the use of the OT. It does not feature a single citation of an OT book by name. However, Revelation is replete with allusions and contextual references to the OT, which requires readers to be familiar with the OT. Clearly, the OT—particularly prophetic books such as Ezekiel and Daniel—is the key to unlocking the apocalyptic imagery found throughout the book.[198]

The apostles and NT writers, however, went beyond the mere affirmation and use of the OT. They continued to value the prophetic writings, but they also were deeply interested in the words of Christ. Acts 11:16 indicates that Peter confirmed direct Gentile Christian conversion because he remembered the "word of the Lord" (a reference to a saying of Jesus). Paul also cited an otherwise unwritten saying of Jesus (called an *agraphon*): "It is more blessed to give than to receive" (Acts 20:35). And he commanded the married—"not I, but the Lord" (1 Cor 7:10)—and later passed on what he "received from the Lord," namely, the institution of the Lord's Supper (1 Cor 11:23–24). The letter of James often echoes Jesus's teachings (see Jas 1:22 and Matt 7:24).

The NT writers also placed their remembrances of Jesus on par with the OT.[199] A case in point is the statement in 2 Peter 3:2 where Peter affirmed that he wrote "so that you recall the words previously spoken by the holy prophets, and the command of our Lord and Savior given through your apostles." That Paul had no direct word from the Lord in dealing with the unmarried (1 Cor 7:12) provides indirect evidence for the esteem of the words of Christ as authoritative. It is unclear whether Paul had in mind some sort of hierarchy, but he clearly expected his words on the matter to be obeyed as if they were the words of the Lord. Later in the book Paul made this explicit: "If anyone thinks he is a prophet or spiritual, he should recognize that what I write to you is the Lord's command. If anyone ignores this, he will be ignored" (1 Cor 14:37–38).

The writer of Hebrews declared the continuity between God's revelation in the OT and the NT: "Long ago God spoke to the fathers by the prophets at different times and in different ways. In these last days, he has spoken to us by his Son. God has appointed him

---

OT books and the helpful collection of essays in S. E. Porter, ed., *Hearing the Old Testament in the New Testament* (Grand Rapids, MI: Eerdmans, 2006).

[197] See Gal 3:22; 4:22, 27, 30; Jas 2:8; 4:52; 1 Pet 1:16.

[198] See G. K. Beale, "The Purpose of Symbolism in the Book of Revelation," *CTJ* 41 (2006): 53–66.

[199] Grudem, "Scripture's Self-Attestation," 46.

heir of all things and made the universe through him" (Heb 1:1–2). The communication of the word of God is continued in Hebrews 2:3: "This salvation had its beginning when it was spoken of by the Lord, and it was confirmed to us by those who heard him." The eyewitness nature of the apostles makes them the authoritative guarantors of the gospel message (see 1 John 1:1–5).[200] Their message is the very word of God (1 Thess 2:13). What they speak—the gospel message—is also called "the word of God."[201] Clearly, Paul and the other apostles understood their mission and message to be from God with all that followed from this conviction.

It was mentioned at the outset that two NT passages cite other NT books as "Scripture" on par with OT Scripture. First Timothy 5:18 most likely cites Luke's Gospel as Scripture alongside Deuteronomy, and Peter referred to Paul's Letters as "Scripture" on par with the OT (2 Pet 3:16). The book of Revelation also has a self-attesting character. The author presented the book as prophetic (Rev 1:3) and as a message from the Lord, conveying the words of Jesus (see the first vision and the letters to the churches in Rev 1:9–3:22). Moreover, the book contains the same injunction against adding to or taking away from it that the OT features regarding the law (Rev 22:18–19; see Deut 4:2; 12:32; Prov 30:6). This injunction, in turn, was common in ancient Near Eastern treaties, which suggests covenant implications.[202] By using this formula, the writer most likely understood the book to be afforded the same respect as the OT.[203] This is further supported by the possibility that Jesus himself issued the warning of Revelation 22:18.[204] One must be careful not to read too much into the formula, but surely the writer considered at least this book to possess scriptural status.[205]

This puts the self-attestation of the NT on the same level as the self-attestation of the OT.[206] The basic contours of God's Word are established by Jesus's teaching. This is further extended to the apostles' teaching and the various NT writers. Beyond this, some of the NT books are recognized as Scripture elsewhere in the NT. As the Word of God, the NT, as well as the OT, is from God. Thus, both are true, authoritative, irrevocable, and irreplaceable. What is more, there is an understanding and expectation that, accompanying the institution of the new covenant, new scriptural documents would be inspired.

---

[200] This is the central thesis argued by Bauckham, *Jesus and the Eyewitnesses*.

[201] See Acts 4:31; 6:7; 8:14; 11:1; 12:24; 13:5, 7, 46; 17:13; 18:11; 19:10; 1 Cor 14:37; 2 Cor 2:17; 4:2; Col 1:25; 1 Thess 1:8; 2 Tim 2:9; 1 Pet 1:23.

[202] Kline, *Structure of Biblical Authority*, 27–38.

[203] Against D. Aune (*Revelation 17–22*, WBC 52C [Nashville, TN: Thomas Nelson, 1998], 1231), who contends that this neither constitutes a "canonization formula" nor intends to place Revelation on par with the OT. He does affirm, however, that "he regarded his book as the record of a divine revelation that was both complete (and so unalterable) and sacred."

[204] G. R. Osborne, *Revelation*, BECNT (Grand Rapids, MI: Baker, 2002), 794.

[205] See R. Thomas ("The Spiritual Gift of Prophecy in Rev 22:18," *JETS* 32 [1989]: 201–16), who claimed that this marks the official closing of the canon as well as the cessation of prophecy. Neither contention is explicitly affirmed in the text itself.

[206] Grudem, "Scripture's Self-Attestation," 45.

Scripture as "Inspired": God the Source of Scripture (2 Tim 3:16–17)

The NT passage that addresses the issue of the inspiration of Scripture most directly is 2 Timothy 3:16–17: "All Scripture is inspired by God and is profitable for teaching, for rebuking, for correcting, for training in righteousness, so that the man of God may be complete, equipped for every good work." These verses raise several important interpretive questions; only the most salient points can be noted here.[207]

1. The term "all" (*pasa*) is singular and could be translated "every [individual passage of] Scripture." However, while the inspiration of individual passages of Scripture may be implied, it is better to think of "Scripture" in the present instance as a collective singular with Scripture being viewed in its totality.
2. The word "Scripture" (*graphē*) in the original context refers to the OT.
3. The phrase "all Scripture" in the immediate context refers to the entirety of the OT, and the logic of the verse applies by extension to the NT also (see 1 Tim 5:18, where Paul in all probability used the term *graphē* with reference to Luke's Gospel). This even includes potentially those NT books such as Revelation that were yet to be written at the time Paul penned 2 Timothy.
4. The term "inspired" (*theopneustos*; lit. "God-breathed" as in the NIV) designates the *source* of Scripture—God—rather than elaborating on the *process* of inspiration (though see below). Thus, the logic of the verse suggests that because Scripture has *God* as its source, it is true. What is more, because Scripture is true, it is therefore valuable for teaching, rebuking, correcting, and training in righteousness.
5. In part due to the absence of a form of the verb "to be" in 2 Timothy 3:16, the question arises whether *theopneustos* is an attributive adjective, in which case the proper rendering of the phrase would be "all inspired Scripture is also profitable"—which may suggest that there are two kinds of Scripture, one that is God-breathed and another that is not—or a predicate adjective (yielding the rendering "[a]ll Scripture is inspired by God and is profitable"). Of these alternatives, the latter is preferred if for no other reason than that it is inconceivable that Paul would have distinguished between inspired and uninspired Scripture.

These observations, among other reasons, suggest that the affirmation in 2 Timothy 3:16 is that "[a]ll Scripture is inspired by God and is [therefore] profitable."[208] What this means is that Scripture has God as its source, and it is therefore profitable for a variety of uses to equip "the man of God . . . for every good work" (2 Tim 3:17). This fits with Paul's earlier exhortation to Timothy to be diligent to present himself approved to God as a worker who correctly teaches "the word of truth" (2 Tim 2:15).

---

[207] See especially the helpful treatment by W. D. Mounce, *The Pastoral Epistles*, WBC (Nashville, TN: Thomas Nelson, 2000), 565–70; cf. A. J. Köstenberger, "1–2 Timothy, Titus," in *Expositor's Bible Commentary*, rev. ed., vol. 12, *Ephesians–Philemon* (Grand Rapids, MI: Zondervan, 2005), 591.

[208] Mounce, *Pastoral Epistles*, 565–70.

Men "Moved by the Holy Spirit": God as Superintending the Writing of Scripture (2 Pet 1:19–21)

While the term *theopneustos* in 2 Timothy 3:16 focuses on the *source* of Scripture rather than on the *mode* of inspiration, this does not mean the NT is silent regarding the latter. Second Peter 1:19–21 states, "We also have the prophetic word strongly confirmed. . . . Above all, you know this: No prophecy of Scripture comes from the prophet's own interpretation, because no prophecy ever came by the will of man; instead, men spoke from God as they were carried along by the Holy Spirit."

That the reference is to Scripture and not a spoken prophecy is clear from the designation "prophecy of Scripture." The phrase "one's own interpretation" (*idias epilysis*) may be better translated "from his own imagination" and be taken to refer to the reception and interpretation of a prophecy from God. The passage therefore asserts that Scripture is not merely human in origin but is the product of the Holy Spirit moving humans to speak the Word of God.[209]

SIDEBAR 1.6: SCRIPTURAL SELF-AFFIRMATIONS: KEY ATTRIBUTES OF INSPIRED SCRIPTURE

The Bible teaches the following truths regarding itself. First, Scripture is the *inerrant* Word of God.[1] In keeping with the divine attribute of truthfulness (Ps 19:7), written Scripture, as the Word of God, is completely truthful and thus, conversely, without error.

Second, "the Word of God" refers to each word down to the smallest parts—not even the tiniest letter will disappear (Matt 5:18). Biblical inspiration, then, is *verbal*, that is, it pertains to the very words, not merely the general concepts or ideas, that are used.[2]

Third, there is no indication that any portion of Scripture is "more inspired" than another: "*All* Scripture is inspired by God" (2 Tim 3:16). Inspiration of Scripture is therefore considered to be *plenary*, that is, "full" or "complete."

Fourth, the Scriptures are inviolate, that is, they may neither be supplemented nor edited by humans regarding their content, as the scriptural warning not to add to or take away from Scripture indicates (Rev 22:18–19; see Deut 4:2; 12:32).

Fifth, Scripture, being the Word of God, is the church's only authoritative source for doctrine and therefore the norm for life and practice for God's people ("profitable for teaching, for rebuking, for correcting, for training in righteousness"; 2 Tim 3:16).

[1] See N. L. Geisler, ed., *Inerrancy* (Grand Rapids, MI: Zondervan, 1980); see especially the classic definition of inerrancy by P. Feinberg (p. 294) which is quoted below with further discussion.

[2] Against N. T. Wright, *The Last Word: Beyond the Bible Wars to a New Understanding of the Authority of Scripture* (San Francisco, CA: HarperCollins, 2005), who says only the story line of Scripture, but not the very words of Scripture, is inspired.

[209] See the discussion in R. Bauckham, *Jude, 2 Peter*, WBC (Waco, TX: Word, 1983), 228–35.

The description of men "moved by the Holy Spirit" suggests that the Holy Spirit took the prime initiative in the writing of Scripture while humans cooperated with the Spirit in what B. B. Warfield termed "concursive operation."[210] In this process the human writers freely penned the words God desired them to use. Whether the writing of Scripture involved the use of sources, the reception of a prophetic message directly from God, or some other mechanism, the resulting product was inspired by the Holy Spirit.

Inerrancy and Hermeneutics

The above discussion has attempted to demonstrate that making Scripture's self-attestation primary leads inexorably to the conclusion that Scripture is inspired and inerrant. This both follows from specific scriptural references regarding the nature of Scripture as entirely trustworthy and also is required by the character of God as the ultimate source of Scripture.

Some might allege that this is essentially circular reasoning and constitutes an improper use of deduction. The argument is circular, those writers may claim, because Scripture is taken at face value as a witness regarding itself rather than biblical claims being subjected to critical evaluation by modern scholars. It is deductive because in essence the argument proceeds along the lines of the following syllogism: (1) the Bible is the Word of God; (2) God is true and does not err; (3) therefore, the Bible is truthful and inerrant.

Three responses may be made with regard to these concerns. First, while a certain amount of circularity in the above-made argument cannot be denied, it should be noted that this fact does not necessarily render the argument invalid or improper. Certainly there seems to be no good reason to deny Scripture a place, even a primary place, in attesting to its own nature. To the contrary, if Scripture were in fact found to be inerrant, it would inexorably follow that it speaks inerrantly regarding its own inerrant nature. In this case there would be nothing improper about accepting these claims of Scripture regarding itself.

Second, the character of God is properly a factor in assessing the nature of Scripture in light of its claims regarding itself. In fact, it may be countered that anything less than inerrant Scripture would be inconceivable as revelation of a God who is everywhere in the Bible represented as true. The burden of proof should instead be placed on critical scholars to explain how a less-than-inerrant Scripture can meaningfully function as an authoritative guide for the life of the church as well as individual believers. Are the mutually contradictory judgments of critical scholars truly superior to accepting Scripture's consistent self-affirmation regarding its nature?

Third, placing primary weight on Scripture's affirmations regarding itself, apart from being a necessary entailment of the Reformation principle of *sola Scriptura*, in no way obviates the need for hermeneutics and the interpretive process. To the contrary, this is clearly indicated by the classic definition of inerrancy by P. Feinberg, who wrote: "Inerrancy

---

[210] B. B. Warfield, "Revelation," in *The International Standard Bible Encyclopedia*, gen. ed. J. Orr (Chicago, IL: Howard-Severance, 1915), 4.2580a.

means that *when all facts are known*, the Scriptures in their original autographs and *properly interpreted will be shown to be wholly true in everything that they affirm*, whether that has to do with doctrine or morality or with the social, physical, or life sciences."[211]

This definition tacitly acknowledges the reality of apparent contradictions that must be subjected to appropriate harmonization as part of the need to deal satisfactorily with the actual phenomena of Scripture.[212] Hence, inductive approaches that address by exegetical means issues which are raised by individual texts and their relationship to other biblical texts ought to supplement the deductive, presuppositional affirmation that Scripture is the Word of God and therefore inerrant.[213]

As the above-stated definition makes clear, Scripture still requires interpretation, and only when it is "properly interpreted" will obstacles to understanding be resolved or apparent contradictions be removed. What is more, "all facts" may not always be known, so that at times it may be necessary to suspend judgment in the case of particularly vexing issues.[214] Yet even in those cases, judicious interpreters will not rush to judgment but will humbly acknowledge their own limitations and continue to seek a proper resolution of apparent incongruities, being slow to assume that an *apparent* contradiction necessarily represents a *real* contradiction.

In fact, the statement in the above definition, "will be shown to be wholly true," frankly acknowledges that finding Scripture free from actual contradictions will frequently involve an interpretive process that carefully weighs all the relevant issues before arriving at tentative conclusions regarding the interpretation of individual biblical passages.[215] At the same time, it expresses the confidence that when all the facts *are* known, the Scriptures will be found to be "wholly true" "in everything that they affirm."

The latter affirmation ("in everything that they affirm"), in turn, limits the scope of inerrancy to authorial intentionality. The interpreter must not misrepresent a given biblical

---

[211] Feinberg, "The Meaning of Inerrancy," in *Inerrancy*, 294 (emphasis added).

[212] See especially C. L. Blomberg, "The Legitimacy and Limits of Harmonization," in *Hermeneutics, Authority, and Canon*, ed. D. A. Carson and J. D. Woodbridge (Grand Rapids, MI: Zondervan, 1986), 135–74. See also idem, *The Historical Reliability of the Gospels*, 2nd ed. (Downers Grove, IL: InterVarsity, 2007); and idem, *The Historical Reliability of John's Gospel* (Downers Grove, IL: InterVarsity, 2001).

[213] This assumes, for the sake of argument, that such a procedure is indeed deductive. In fact, many would contend that their doctrine of an inerrant Scripture is the result of the sustained study of Scripture rather than a dogmatic presupposition brought to Scripture (though it may serve as a functional nonnegotiable for them). G. Osborne's concept of a "hermeneutical spiral" may be helpful here (*Hermeneutical Spiral*, passim). Indeed biblical interpretation requires humility and openness to the actual data on the part of the interpreter; a recognition that interpretation, as a human enterprise, of necessity deals with probability rather than absolute certainty; and a dialectical, transformative, and repeated process of applying oneself to the study of Scripture while being at the same time addressed and impacted by Scripture.

[214] For help in this area, see G. L. Archer Jr., *New International Encyclopedia of Bible Difficulties* (Grand Rapids, MI: Zondervan, 2001); W. C. Kaiser Jr., ed., *Hard Sayings of the Bible* (Downers Grove, IL: InterVarsity, 1996); and *The Holman Apologetics Bible Commentary*, vol. 1: *The Gospels and Acts*, by M. J. Wilkins, D. L. Bock, C. A. Evans, and A. J. Köstenberger (Nashville, TN: B&H, 2013). Note that this latter work is projected to eventually cover the entire OT and NT.

[215] In this day and age, interpreters have an unprecedented plethora of resources at their disposal, including a variety of reference tools such as Bible dictionaries, concordances, study Bibles, and scholarly commentaries and monographs. For recommended resources, see the appendix in Köstenberger and Patterson, *Invitation to Biblical Interpretation*.

author's intentions but rather be fair in his or her handling of the scriptural evidence.[216] This includes allowing for paraphrase in quotations, round numbering, accommodation, phenomenological language, and so on.[217] It also includes the recognition that inerrancy, properly understood, is claimed only for the scriptural autographs, which, although no longer extant, are well attested by the high number of available manuscript copies.[218]

All of this is to say that the inspiration and inerrancy of Scripture are not merely the products of circular reasoning or of improper deduction from the character of God. These can also be demonstrated inductively from the actual scriptural phenomena themselves, albeit requiring hermeneutics and occasional harmonization. Thus, doctrinal and exegetical efforts must work in tandem; both are essential if Scripture is to be properly appreciated and interpreted.[219]

When the well-known twentieth-century conservative scholar A. Schlatter was considered for a professorial appointment to the university in Berlin, he was asked by a churchman on the committee whether, in his academic work, he "stood on the Bible." Schlatter's reply: "No, I stand *under* the Bible!"[220] This well captures the proper stance of the biblical interpreter. A preparedness to obey and to order one's life on the basis of Scripture is an indispensable prerequisite and predisposition for the proper apprehension and appropriation of the biblical message. Rather than elevating oneself as a supposedly neutral critic of Scripture—and claiming to be totally objective—the student of the Bible ought to take his or her place "beneath Scripture" as one who is addressed by Scripture and who seeks to be changed by "the living and effective" Word of God (Heb 4:12).

---

[216] See P. Stuhlmacher, *Vom Verstehen des Neuen Testaments: Eine Hermeneutik*, Grundrisse zum Neuen Testament 6, 2nd ed. (Göttingen, Germany: Vandenhoeck & Ruprecht, 1986), especially 222–24, who advocates a "hermeneutic of consent." Such an approach stands in contrast to a "hermeneutic of suspicion," frequently employed by feminists such as E. S. Fiorenza (*In Memory of Her: A Feminist Theological Reconstruction of Christian Origins* [New York, NY: Crossroad, 1983]). N. T. Wright (*The New Testament and the People of God*, Christian Origins and the Question of God 1 [Minneapolis, MN: Fortress, 1992], 64) went even farther by calling for a "hermeneutic of love" as part of a critical realism that deals intelligently, but sympathetically, and in faith rather than doubt, with difficult passages in Scripture, in recognition of the fact that the understanding of "spiritual things" requires "spiritual people" (1 Cor 2:13). The importance of faith in biblical interpretation is also underscored by G. Maier, *Biblical Hermeneutics*, trans. R. W. Yarbrough (Wheaton, IL: Crossway, 1994; see chap. 14), who proposes the use of a "biblical-historical" in the place of a "historical-critical" method; and A. Schlatter, "Appendix D: Adolf Schlatter on Atheistic Methods in Theology," in W. Neuer, *Adolf Schlatter: A Biography of Germany's Premier Biblical Theologian*, trans. R. W. Yarbrough (Grand Rapids, MI: Baker, 1995), 211–25.

[217] With regard to paraphrase in quotations, compare Matt 5:3 ("Blessed are the poor in spirit") with Luke 6:20 ("Blessed are you who are poor"). With regard to round numbering, compare the reference to "70 persons" in Gen 46:27 with the mention of "75 people in all" in Acts 7:14. With regard to anthropomorphic language, see references to God "regretting," "changing His mind," or "relenting" (see Gen 6:6; Exod 32:14; Jonah 3:10). With regard to phenomenological language, see Matt 5:45 ("He causes His sun to rise").

[218] See the discussion below.

[219] For a helpful treatment, see D. A. Carson, "The Role of Exegesis in Systematic Theology," in *Doing Theology in Today's World: Essays in Honor of Kenneth S. Kantzer*, ed. J. D. Woodbridge and T. E. McComiskey (Grand Rapids, MI: Zondervan, 1991), 39–76.

[220] See W. W. Gasque, "The Promise of Adolf Schlatter," *Crux* 15/2 (June 1979): 8 (an article reprinted in *Evangelical Theological Review* 4 [1980]: 20–30).

STUDY QUESTIONS

1. What is the traditional evangelical position regarding the canon?
2. To what date does Sundberg point for the closing of the canon?
3. What is D. Trobisch's theory of the origins of the biblical canon?
4. According to Sundberg, what was the status of the OT canon in the first century?
5. What physical evidence points to an early reception of the four-Gospel canon?
6. Did an apocryphal Gospel ever circulate with a canonical Gospel?
7. When was the NT canon closed from a divine perspective?
8. Which NT books were slow to be universally received?
9. Which books in the present NT canon were universally rejected in the second century?
10. Which NT books are called "Scripture" in the NT?
11. What is "formal equivalence"?
12. What is "dynamic equivalence"?
13. What is an "autograph"?
14. What is one advantage resulting from the loss of the scriptural autographs?
15. Who was the first to translate the complete Bible into English?

FOR FURTHER STUDY

General Reference

Blomberg, C. L. *Can We Still Believe the Bible? An Evangelical Engagement with Contemporary Questions*. Grand Rapids, MI: Brazos, 2014.

Geisler, N. L., and W. E. Nix. *A General Introduction to the Bible*. Rev. and exp. ed. Chicago, IL: Moody, 1986.

Köstenberger, A. J., D. L. Bock, and J. D. Chatraw. *Truth in a Culture of Doubt: Engaging Skeptical Challenges to the Bible*. Nashville, TN: B&H Academic, 2014.

Patzia, A. G. *The Making of the New Testament: Origin, Collection, Text and Canon*. Downers Grove, IL: InterVarsity, 1995.

Roberts, M. D. *Can We Trust the Gospels? Investigating the Reliability of Matthew, Mark, Luke, and John*. Wheaton, IL: Crossway, 2007.

Canon

General

Bartholomew, C. G., S. Hahn, R. Parry, C. Seitz, and A. Wolters, eds. *Canon and Biblical Interpretation*. Scripture and Hermeneutics 7. Grand Rapids, MI: Zondervan, 2006.

Barton, J. *Holy Writing, Sacred Text: The Canon in Early Christianity*. Louisville, KY: Westminster John Knox, 1997.

Beckwith, R. *The Old Testament Canon of the New Testament Church*. Grand Rapids, MI: Eerdmans, 1985.

Bruce, F. F. *The Canon of Scripture*. Downers Grove, IL: InterVarsity, 1988.

Lightfoot, N. R. *How We Got the Bible*. 2nd ed. Grand Rapids, MI: Baker, 1988.

McDonald, L. *The Biblical Canon: Its Origin, Transmission, and Authority*. 3rd ed. Peabody, MA: Hendrickson, 2007.

McDonald, L. M., and J. A. Sanders, eds. *The Canon Debate*. 2nd ed. Peabody, MA: Hendrickson, 2002.

Metzger, B. M. *The Canon of Scripture: Its Origin, Development, and Significance*. Oxford, UK: Clarendon, 1987.

Miller, J. W. *How the Bible Came to Be: Exploring the Narrative and Message*. Mahwah, NJ: Paulist, 2004.

von Campenhausen, H. *The Formation of the Christian Bible*. Philadelphia, PA: Fortress, 1972.

NT Canon

Dunn, J. D. G. "How the New Testament Began." Pages 122–37 in *From Biblical Criticism to Biblical Faith: Essays in Honor of Lee Martin McDonald*. Edited by W. Brackney and C. Evans. Macon, GA: Mercer University Press, 2007.

Ellis, E. E. *The Making of the New Testament Documents*. Boston, MA: Brill, 2002.

Farmer, W. R., D. M. Farkasfalvy, and H. W. Attridge. *The Formation of the New Testament Canon: An Ecumenical Approach*. Theological Inquiries. New York, NY: Paulist, 1983.

Gamble, H. Y. *The New Testament Canon: Its Making and Meaning*. Guides to Biblical Scholarship. Philadelphia, PA: Fortress, 1985.

Hill, C. E. "The New Testament Canon: *Deconstrucio ad absurdum*?" *Journal of the Evangelical Theological Society* 52 (2009): 101–19.

Kruger, M. J. *Canon Revisited: Establishing the Origins and Authority of the New Testament Books*. Wheaton, IL: Crossway, 2012.

__________. *The Question of Canon: Challenging the Status Quo in the New Testament Debate*. Grand Rapids, MI: InterVarsity, 2013.

Porter, S. E. *How We Got the New Testament: Text, Transmission, Translation*. Grand Rapids, MI: Baker, 2013.

Trobisch, D. *The First Edition of the New Testament*. New York, NY: Oxford University Press, 2000.

Westcott, B. F. *A General Survey of the History of the Canon of the New Testament*. London: Macmillan, 1896.

The Fourfold Gospel Collection

Hengel, M. *The Four Gospels and One Gospel of Jesus Christ*. Harrisburg, PA: Trinity, 2000.

Hill, C. E. *Who Chose the Gospels? Probing the Great Gospel Conspiracy*. New York, NY: Oxford University Press, 2012.

Skeat, T. C. "Irenaeus and the Four-Gospel Canon." *Novum Testamentum* 34 (1992): 194–99.

Stanton, G. N. "The Fourfold Gospel." *New Testament Studies* 43 (1997): 316–46.

The Pauline Letter Collection

Murphy-O'Connor, J. *Paul the Letter Writer: His World, His Options, His Skills*. Collegeville, MN: Liturgical Press, 1995.

Porter, S. E. "When and How Was the Pauline Canon Compiled? An Assessment of Theories." In *The Pauline Canon*. Edited by S. E. Porter. Boston, MA: Brill, 2004, 95–127.

Richards, E. R. *Paul and First-Century Letter Writing: Secretaries, Composition and Collection*. Downers Grove, IL: InterVarsity, 2004.

Trobisch, D. *Paul's Letter Collection: Tracing the Origins*. Minneapolis, MN: Augsburg Fortress, 2000 [1994].

Inspiration and Inerrancy

Dockery, D. *Christian Scripture: An Evangelical Perspective on Inspiration, Authority, and Interpretation*. Nashville, TN: B&H, 1995.

Garrett, S. M., and J. Merrick, eds. *Five Views on Biblical Inerrancy*. Counterpoints. Grand Rapids, MI: Zondervan, 2013.

Geisler, N., ed. *Inerrancy*. Grand Rapids, MI: Zondervan, 1980.

Grudem, W. A. "Scripture's Self-Attestation and the Problem of Formulating a Doctrine of Scripture." In *Scripture and Truth*. Edited by D. A. Carson and J. D. Woodbridge. Grand Rapids, MI: Zondervan, 1983, 19–64.

Harris, R. L. *Inspiration and Canonicity of the Scriptures*. Grand Rapids, MI: Zondervan, 1969.

Henry, C. F. H. "The Authority and Inspiration of the Bible." In *The Expositor's Bible Commentary*. Vol. 1: *Introductory Articles*. Edited by F. E. Gaebelein. Grand Rapids, MI: Zondervan, 1979, 1–35.

Köstenberger, A. J., ed. *Quo Vadis? Perspectives on the Past, Direction for the Future: Nine Presidential Addresses from the First Fifty Years of the Journal of the Evangelical Theological Society*. Wheaton, IL: Crossway, 2007.

Pache, R. *The Inspiration and Authority of Scripture*. Chicago, IL: Moody, 1969.

Satterthwaite, P. E., and D. F. Wright, eds. *A Pathway into the Holy Scripture*. Grand Rapids, MI: Eerdmans, 1994.

Vanhoozer, K. J. *The Drama of Doctrine: A Canonical-Linguistic Approach to Christian Doctrine*. Louisville, KY: Westminster John Knox, 2005.

Warfield, B. B. *The Inspiration and Authority of the Bible*. Philadelphia, PA: Presbyterian & Reformed, 1948.

Hermeneutics and Harmonization

Archer, G. L., Jr. *The New International Encyclopedia of Bible Difficulties*. Grand Rapids, MI: Zondervan, 2001.

Blomberg, C. L. *The Historical Reliability of John's Gospel*. Downers Grove, IL: InterVarsity, 2001.

____________. *The Historical Reliability of the Gospels*. 2nd ed. Downers Grove, IL: InterVarsity, 2007.

____________. "The Legitimacy and Limits of Harmonization." In *Hermeneutics, Authority, and Canon*. Edited by D. A. Carson and J. D. Woodbridge. Grand Rapids, MI: Zondervan, 1986, 135–74.

Carson, D. A. "The Role of Exegesis in Systematic Theology." In *Doing Theology in Today's World: Essays in Honor of Kenneth S. Kantzer*. Edited by J. D. Woodbridge and T. E. McComiskey. Grand Rapids, MI: Zondervan, 1991, 39–76.

Fuhr, R. A., and A. J. Köstenberger. *Inductive Bible Study: Observation, Interpretation, and Application through the Lenses of History, Literature, and Theology*. Nashville, TN: B&H Academic, 2016.

Kaiser, W. C., Jr., ed. *Hard Sayings in the Bible*. Downers Grove, IL: InterVarsity, 1996.

Köstenberger, A. J., and R. D. Patterson. *Invitation to Biblical Interpretation: Exploring the Hermeneutical Triad of History, Literature, and Theology*. Grand Rapids, MI: Kregel, 2011.

____________. *For the Love of God's Word: An Introduction to Biblical Interpretation*. Grand Rapids, MI: Kregel, 2015.

Osborne, G. R. *The Hermeneutical Spiral: A Comprehensive Introduction to Biblical Interpretation*. 2nd ed. Downers Grove, IL: InterVarsity, 2006.

Textual Criticism

Aland, K., and B. Aland. *The Text of the New Testament: An Introduction to the Critical Editions and to the Theory and Practice of Modern Textual Criticism*. Translated by E. F. Rhodes. Grand Rapids, MI: Eerdmans, 1987.

Comfort, P. W. "Texts and Manuscripts of the New Testament." In *The Origin of the Bible*. Edited by P. W. Comfort. Wheaton, IL: Tyndale, 1992, 179–207.

Gamble, H. Y. *Books and Readers in the Early Church: A History of Early Christian Texts*. New Haven, CT: Yale University Press, 1995.

Hill, C. E., and M. J. Kruger. *The Early Text of the New Testament*. Oxford, UK: Oxford University Press, 2012.

Metzger, B. M., and B. D. Ehrman. *The Text of the New Testament: Its Transmission, Corruption, and Restoration*. 4th ed. New York, NY: Oxford University Press, 2005.

Wallace, D. B. "Challenges in New Testament Textual Criticism for the Twenty-First Century." *Journal of the Evangelical Theological Society* 52 (2009): 79–100.

____________. *Revisiting the Corruption of the New Testament: Manuscript, Patristic, and Apocryphal Evidence*. Text and Canon of the New Testament. Grand Rapids, MI: Kregel, 2010.

Wegner, P. D. *A Student's Guide to Textual Criticism of the Bible: Its History, Methods and Results*. Downers Grove, IL: InterVarsity, 2006.

____________. *The Journey from Texts to Translations: The Origins and Developments of the Bible*. Grand Rapids, MI: Baker, 1999.

Bible Translation

Beekman, J., and J. Callow. *Translating the Word of God*. Grand Rapids, MI: Zondervan, 1975.

Bruce, F. F. *The English Bible: A History of Translations*. New York, NY: Oxford University Press, 1961.

Carson, D. A. *The Inclusive Language Debate: A Plea for Realism*. Grand Rapids, MI: Baker, 1998.

Connolly, W. K. *The Indestructible Book: The Bible, Its Translators, and Their Sacrifices*. Grand Rapids, MI: Baker, 1996.

Daniell, D., ed. *Tyndale's New Testament*. New Haven, CT: Yale University Press, 1995.

De Hammel, C. *The Book: A History of the Bible*. New York, NY: Phaidon, 2001.

Köstenberger, A. J., and D. A. Croteau, eds. *Which Bible Translation Should I Use? A Comparison of 4 Major Recent Versions*. Nashville, TN: B&H Academic, 2012.

McGrath, A. E. *In the Beginning: The Story of the King James Bible and How It Changed a Nation, a Language, and a Culture*. New York, NY: Doubleday, 2001.

Metzger, B. M. *The Bible in Translation*. Grand Rapids, MI: Baker, 2001.

Noss, P., ed. *A History of Bible Translation*. New York, NY: United Bible Societies, 2007.

Poythress, V. S., and W. A. Grudem. *The Gender-Neutral Bible Controversy: Muting the Masculinity of God's Words*. Nashville, TN: B&H, 2000.

Ryken, L. *The Word of God in English: Criteria for Excellence in Bible Translation*. Wheaton, IL: Crossway, 2002.

Scorgie, G. G., M. L. Strauss, and S. M. Voth, eds. *The Challenge of Bible Translation*. Grand Rapids, MI: Zondervan, 2003.

Strauss, M. L. *Distorting Scripture? The Challenge of Bible Translation and Gender Accuracy*. Downers Grove, IL: InterVarsity, 1998.

Table 1.3: Dates of Church Fathers, Patristic Works, and Canonical Lists

Church Father, Patristic Work, Canonical List	Date(s) (Dates Are AD)*	Major Work(s)
Amphilochius of Iconium	ca. 340–395	Iambics for Seleucus
Anti-Marcionite Prologues	fourth century; Prologue to Luke: ca. 160–180	
Athanasius of Alexandria	ca. 296–373	Festal Letter of 367
Athenagoras of Athens	ca. 180	Supplication
Augustine of Hippo	354–430	Harmony of the Gospels; Confessions; City of God
Basil of Caesarea	ca. 330–379	On the Holy Spirit
Clement of Alexandria	ca. 150–215	The Instructor (Paedagogus); Miscellanies (Stromateis); Who Is the Rich Man That Will Be Saved? (*Quis dives salvetur?*)
Clement of Rome	ca. 96	1 Clement
Cyril of Jerusalem	ca. 315–387	Catecheses
Diatessaron	ca. 150–160?	Compiled by Tatian
Didache	Second half of first or early second century	
Epiphanius of Salamis	ca. 315–403	Refutation of All the Heresies = Panarion
Epistle of Pseudo-Barnabas	ca. 135?	
Epistle to Diognetus	second or third century	
Eusebius of Caesarea	ca. 260–340	Ecclesiastical History
Gregory of Nazianzus	329–390	Five Theological Orations, Philocalia
Hegesippus	ca. 110–180	Memoirs (cited by Eusebius)
Hippolytus of Rome	ca. 170–236	Refutation of All Heresies; Antichrist
Ignatius of Antioch	ca. 35–110	To the Ephesians; To the Magnesians; To the Philadelphians; To Polycarp; To the Trallians; To the Smyrnaeans
Irenaeus of Lyons	ca. 130–200	Against Heresies

Table 1.3: Dates of Church Fathers, Patristic Works, and Canonical Lists (continued)

Church Father, Patristic Work, Canonical List	Date(s) (Dates Are AD)*	Major Work(s)
Jerome	ca. 345–420	Vulgate; Commentaries; Book of Illustrious Men (*De Viris Illustribus*)
John Chrysostom	ca. 347–407	Homilies
Justin Martyr	ca. 100–165	Dialogue with Trypho; First Apology
Marcion of Sinope	Died ca. 160	Apostolicon
Melito of Sardis	Died ca. 190	Cited by Eusebius et al.
Monarchian Prologues	Late fourth or early fifth century?	
Muratorian Fragment	Later second century?	
Origen	ca. 185–254	Against Celsus; Commentaries
Orosius	ca. 385–420	Seven Books of History Against the Romans
Pantaenus	Died ca. 190	Mentioned by Eusebius
Papias of Hierapolis	ca. 60–130	Expositions of the Lord's Sayings
Philip Sidetes	Early fifth century	Christian History
Polycarp of Smyrna	ca. 69–155	To the Philippians
Serapion of Antioch	Died 211	Cited by Eusebius
Shepherd of Hermas	Early second century?	
Tertullian	ca. 160–225	Against Marcion; Apology; On Baptism
Theophilus of Antioch	Later second century	To Autolycus

* The dates generally follow *The Oxford Dictionary of the Christian Church*, ed. F. L. Cross and E. A. Livingstone, 3rd ed. (Oxford/New York: Oxford University Press, 1997). A question mark indicates the date is disputed. The date given reflects the authors' view.

Chapter 2

The Political and Religious Background of the New Testament

CORE KNOWLEDGE

Basic Knowledge: Students should know the eight periods of control over Palestine in the Second Temple era. They should have basic knowledge of the major figures and rulers and be acquainted with other major features of this period, including key dates, names of important works, and major groups and institutions that trace their origin back to this period.

Intermediate Knowledge: Students should have a more in-depth grasp of the dynamics operative in the transition from one empire to the other. They should also be able to discern and describe the major crises in Jewish history that confronted the nation.

Advanced Knowledge: Students should have a thorough command of the history of the Second Temple period, including major conflicts, specific dates, and names of rulers. They should be able to identify the various works commonly identified as Second Temple literature and be able to demonstrate how the various features described in this chapter constitute important background for the interpretation of the NT.

INTRODUCTION

WHEN THE OT era ended, the Persian Empire was in control of Jerusalem and Judea. When the NT era began, Rome was in charge. To gain an understanding of the political and religious background of the NT, we need at least a cursory grasp of the developments and events that led to the state of affairs in NT times.[1] Since there was no prophetic voice in Israel between Malachi and the ministry of John the Baptist, the time span from approximately 400 BC to the Christian era has been called "the silent years." This rightly underscores the absence of prophet-mediated divine revelation during this period, but the time was anything but quiet, as the remainder of this chapter demonstrates.

Table 2.1: From Babylon to Rome: The Second Temple Period

Period	*Time Frame*
Babylonian Period	606–539 BC
Persian Period	539–331 BC
Greek Period	331–167 BC
- the Great	331–320 BC
Ptolemaic Period	320–198 BC
Syrian Period	198–167 BC
Jewish Self-Rule	167–63 BC
Maccabean Period	167–135 BC
Hasmonean Period	135–63 BC
Roman Period	63 BC–AD 70

Formerly called the "intertestamental period," the term "Second Temple period" is now preferred by most scholars for the time from the building of the second temple in 515 BC by Zerubbabel until its destruction by the Romans in AD 70; this, of course, includes the time of Jesus and the early church. Thus, scholars are recognizing both the considerable body of literature (larger than the Christian Bible) and its importance to the interpretation of the NT. The following brief historical survey of this era and its literature and theology

---

[1] Major primary sources for this period include 1–2 Maccabees, Josephus, Philo, and the *Letter of Aristeas*. See also C. K. Barrett, ed., *The New Testament Background: Writings from Ancient Greece and the Roman Empire That Illuminate Christian Origins* (rev. and exp. ed.; San Francisco, CA: Harper, 1989), especially chaps. 1 (The Roman Empire), 7 (Jewish History), 9 (Qumran), 10 (Philo), and 11 (Josephus); Mark Harding, ed., *Early Christian Life and Thought in Social Context* (London, UK: T&T Clark, 2003). Additional information is found in E. Schürer, *The History of the Jewish People in the Age of Jesus Christ*, rev. and ed. G. Vermes, F. Millar, and M. Black, 3 vols. in 4 (Edinburgh, Scotland: T&T Clark, 1973, 1979, 1986, 1987); S. Safrai and M. Stern, ed., *The Jewish People in the First Century*, CRINT 1/1 (Philadelphia, PA: Fortress, 1974); Everett Ferguson, *Backgrounds to Early Christianity*, 3rd ed. (Grand Rapids, MI: Eerdmans, 2003); and Paul Barnett, *Jesus and the Rise of Early Christianity: A History of New Testament Times* (Downers Grove, IL: InterVarsity, 2002).

is intended to serve as a background for the study of Jesus and the Gospels and the other NT writings.[2]

Simply put, from the vantage point of Israel and biblical history, the Second Temple period is comprised of five eras demarcated by a series of occupational forces in Palestine and punctuated by five great crises for the Jewish people.[3] For much of this time Judea was essentially a "temple state" under the immediate control of the high priests who were themselves under the authority of foreign governors or rulers.[4] The following survey of the Second Temple period begins with the first great crisis, the rule of the Babylonian king Nebuchadnezzar and his destruction of the temple built by Solomon. This resulted in the Jews' loss of national sovereignty.

Table 2.2: The Second Temple Period: Important Events

I. End of Old Testament History: Babylonian and Persian Periods	
A. Babylonian Period (606–539 BC)	
606/5 BC	Nebuchadnezzar's conquest of Judea
587/86	Jerusalem temple destroyed; Judah goes into exile; origin of synagogue
539 BC	Babylon falls to Cyrus the Great of Persia; exiles are allowed to return to Israel
B. Persian Period (539–331 BC)	
515 BC	Second temple dedicated (Zerubbabel, Haggai, Zechariah)
ca. 400 BC	Last OT prophet Malachi: John the Baptist is predicted
II. Between the Testaments: Greek Rule, Jewish Self-Rule, Roman Rule	
A. Greek Period (331–167 BC)	
1. Alexander the Great and His Conquests (331–320 BC)	
334/333 BC	Alexander defeats Persians at battles of Granicus, Issus
331 BC	Alexander defeats Darius II at Arbela, which makes him the controlling player in the Middle East (including Israel); Hellenization begins (dissemination of the Greek way of life)
323 BC	Alexander dies; kingdom divided into four parts
By 320 BC	Israel falls to Ptolemy in Egypt

[2] See L. R. Helyer, "The Necessity, Problems and Promise of Second Temple Judaism for Discussions of New Testament Eschatology," *JETS* 47 (2004): 97–115.

[3] L. R. Helyer (*Exploring Jewish Literature of the Second Temple Period: A Guide for New Testament Students* [Downers Grove, IL: InterVarsity, 2002], 18–24) lists the crises as: (1) destruction of the First Commonwealth and the first temple; (2) collapse of the Persian Empire in the wake of Alexander the Great's invasion; (3) persecution by Antiochus IV Epiphanes; (4) domination by Rome; and (5) Roman destruction of the Jewish state and temple.

[4] R. A. Horsley, *Scribes, Visionaries, and the Politics of Second Temple Judea* (Louisville, KY: Westminster John Knox, 2007), 16–22; cf. M. Hengel, *Judaism and Hellenism: Studies in Their Encounter in Palestine During the Early Hellenistic Period*, vol. 1, trans. J. Bowden (Philadelphia, PA: Fortress, 1974), 25–27.

Table 2.2: The Second Temple Period: Important Events (continued)

2. Ptolemaic Period (320–198 BC)	
320–198 BC	Ptolemies rule Palestine from Alexandria, Egypt; Septuagint (the LXX, the Greek translation of OT) is produced
198 BC	Seleucid Antiochus III defeats Ptolemy V at Paneas (near Mount Hermon) and seizes control of Palestine
3. Seleucid or Syrian Period (198–167 BC)	
198–167 BC	Seleucids, centered in Antioch of Syria, rule Palestine Two parties arise among the Jews: "the house of Onias" (pro-Egyptian) and "the house of Tobias" (pro-Syrian)
168 BC	Antiochus IV (175–163 BC): type of antichrist; replaces Jewish high priest Onias III with Onias' brother Jason, a Hellenizer; invades Jerusalem, sacrifices pig on the altar ("abomination of desolation"; Dan 9:27; 11:31; 12:11; see Matt 24:15 and parallels); priest named Mattathias in village of Modein starts Maccabean revolt
B. Jewish Self-Rule: The Maccabees and Hasmoneans (167–63 BC)	
1. The Maccabees (167–135 BC)	
165/4 BC	Temple worship restored; Feast of Dedication (see John 10:22)
164–161 BC	Judas
161–143/2 BC	Jonathan
143/2–135/4	Simon
2. The Hasmoneans (135–63 BC)	
135/4–104 BC	John Hyrcanus I
104–103 BC	Aristobulus I
103–76 BC	Alexander Janneus
76–67 BC	Salome Alexandra
67–63 BC	Aristobulus II
C. Roman Period (63 BC–AD 70)	
63 BC	General Pompey enters Jerusalem and establishes Roman rule
44 BC	Julius Caesar assassinated in Senate by Brutus and others; "Caesar" becomes title for emperors
40 BC	Herod named king of Judea by Roman Senate
37 BC	Herod repulses the Parthians to take the kingdom
31 BC	Octavian ("Augustus") prevails in civil war against Mark Antony and Cleopatra (d. 30 BC); "Golden Age" of Rome, Roman law and order, *pax Romana* ("Roman peace"), emperor worship
ca. 5 BC	Jesus is born in Bethlehem (Matt 1:18–2:12; Luke 2:1–20)*
4 BC	Herod dies, leaves kingdom to Archelaus
AD 6	Archelaus replaced by Roman prefects
AD 26	Pontius Pilate becomes governor of Judea

Table 2.2: The Second Temple Period: Important Events (continued)

AD 33	Jesus is crucified*
AD 34	Conversion of Paul
III. Background to Jesus and the Early Church	
A. Roman Rulers	
31 BC–AD 14	Augustus: Jesus's birth; "Golden Age" of Rome (Luke 2:1)
14–37	Tiberius: Ministries of John the Baptist and Jesus take place during his reign (Luke 3:1–2, 21)
37–41	Caligula
41–54	Claudius: Expelled Jews from Rome (Acts 18:2)
54–68	Nero: Fire of Rome (64); martyrdoms of Peter and Paul (ca. 65/66)
68–69	Galba, Otho, and Vitellius
69–79	Vespasian
81–96	Domitian: Persecution of Christians (Revelation)**
B. Jewish Revolts	
66–73	First Jewish revolt
70	Titus destroys Jerusalem, temple (cf. Matt 24:1–2 and parallels)
132–135	Bar Kokhba revolt: Jews exiled until modern times
C. The Herodian Dynasty	
40/37–4 BC	Herod the Great: Edomite vassal-ruler over Palestine Slaughter of infants in Bethlehem (Luke 2:16); three sons:
4 BC–AD 33	Herod Philip: Tetrarch of northern provinces Iturea, Trachonitis, Gaulanitis, Auranitis, and Batanea
4 BC–AD 39	Herod Antipas: Tetrarch of Galilee and Perea: John the Baptist beheaded (Matt 14:3–12; Mark 6:17–29); Jesus called him "that fox" (Luke 13:32) and later stood trial before him (Luke 23:7–12)
4 BC–AD 6	Archelaus: Ethnarch of Judea and Samaria (banished by Augustus in AD 6); misrule caused Joseph to settle with Mary and Jesus in Nazareth after returning from Egypt (Matt 2:21–23); after AD 6, Galilee governed by Roman governors (prefects or procurators), except for the three-year rule of Herod Agrippa I
41–44	Herod Agrippa I: Grandson of Herod the Great; ruled as king over Judea and all Palestine; executed James the apostle and son of Zebedee and imprisoned Peter (Acts 12:1–3)
50–?	Herod Agrippa II: Great-grandson of Herod the Great; heard Paul's self-defense (Acts 25–26)

* See the discussion of the chronology of Jesus's life in chap. 3.
**See the discussion of the date of the book of Revelation in chap. 20.

HISTORY

The Babylonian Period (606–539 BC)

The account of the Babylonian occupation of Israel is included in the OT.[5] The Babylonian period began in 606/5 BC with Nebuchadnezzar's conquest of Judea; the northern kingdom of Israel had already fallen to the Assyrians in 722 BC (see 2 Kgs 24:12). The element of Nebuchadnezzar's foreign policy that most impacted the destiny of Judah was the deportation of the higher classes to Babylon. Nebuchadnezzar instituted this policy for Judah (including Daniel and Ezekiel) and placed Jehoiachin's uncle Mattaniah as king over Judah, renaming him Zedekiah (2 Kgs 24:17). Zedekiah's flirtation with Egypt forced Babylon to lay siege to Jerusalem until "the ninth day of the [fourth] month" of 586 BC.[6] Eventually tracked down and captured, Zedekiah saw the execution of his sons just before being blinded (2 Kgs 25:7). The pro-Babylonian Gedaliah was appointed in his place but was assassinated soon thereafter (2 Kgs 25:22–26).

This deportation created a theological crisis for the Jews in the Dispersion. The reason for the exile, from the theological point of view, was the breaking of the covenant. Babylon, however, by all accounts, had no idea what was going on in the mind of God. The theological dimensions of the exile are treated in more detail in chapter 22.

Historically, life outside the land of Israel presented some practical theological issues for Jews in exile. The dissolution of the monarchy, the loss of the central sanctuary, and the proximity to Gentiles all created moral and ceremonial problems for those living outside Judea.[7] The prophets had denounced Israel and Judah for emphasizing the ceremonial over the ethical aspects of their covenant with God. In the Dispersion it was evident that in the absence of the central sanctuary the Jews were led to focus on the moral dimension of God's law. With the ceremonial element remaining as only a lingering hope for the exiled Jews, law observance temporarily took the place of the temple ritual and animal sacrifice.[8]

Without a central place to meet and worship (the temple), the captives in all probability established the synagogue as a venue where they could gather to study and discuss the law. The synagogue is a well-established institution by NT times. It may be surprising to find that the emergence of the synagogue is not mentioned in the OT. Most likely, the synagogue had its origins in the exile.[9]

---

[5] See 2 Kgs 24–25; 2 Chr 36:5–21; and parts of Jeremiah, Daniel, and Ezekiel.

[6] 2 Kgs 25:3; see Jer 39:2: "In the fourth month of Zedekiah's eleventh year, on the ninth day of the month, the city was broken into" (i.e., July 18, 586 BC).

[7] J. J. Scott Jr., *Jewish Backgrounds of the New Testament* (Grand Rapids, MI: Baker, 2000), 108–12.

[8] M. Fishbane, *Biblical Interpretation in Ancient Israel* (Oxford, UK: Clarendon, 1985), 113.

[9] This represents conjecture on the part of scholarship. Strictly speaking, no one knows when and where the synagogue began. It appears that it did not exist prior to the exile, and the need for a meeting place for prayer and for the study of the Torah in the exile makes the exile a likely time for its origin. It is known that the synagogue did begin in the Dispersion and worked its way back into Palestine. See J. D. Newsome, *Greeks, Romans, Jews: Currents of Culture and Belief in the New Testament World* (Philadelphia, PA: Trinity Press International, 1992), 128; cf. the discussion below in this chapter.

Another development during the exile was the permanent renunciation of idolatry among the Jews. Idolatry, the worship of gods other than Yahweh, had been a major cause for the exile. During the Babylonian captivity, however, idolatry completely lost its appeal—as the apocryphal book of Judith exemplifies: "For never in our generation, nor in these present days, has there been any tribe or family or people or city of ours which worshiped gods made with hands, as was done in days gone by—and that was why our fathers were handed over to the sword, and to be plundered, and so they suffered a great catastrophe before our enemies" (8:18–19 RSV). The major lesson Israel learned from the exile was that God will not tolerate Israel's worship of other gods.

The Jews were also impacted on a basic level. Their very language changed. A closely related language, Aramaic, was the language of commerce in the Babylonian Empire. It soon took the place of ancient Hebrew. Thus, by the time of Jesus and the apostles, the basic language of Palestine was Aramaic. Hebrew eventually became only a literary language.[10]

The Persian Period (539–331 BC)

In due course Babylon came under attack from an upstart kingdom, the Persian Empire.[11] When Cyrus of Persia, a former vassal of Media (from around 550 BC), attacked the outlying city of Opis, his intentions to topple Babylon were clear. After Sippar fell to the Persian army, Babylon was Cyrus' next target. Nabonidus, king of Babylon, fled Sippar to make his stand at the capitol. It could have been a particularly foul conflict. Babylon had preparations to withstand a prolonged siege. However, Cyrus infiltrated the city through the diversion of the Euphrates River. A few days later, on October 29, 539 BC, Cyrus entered Babylon and proclaimed himself "King of Babylon." Thus began a new dynasty in the Middle East, without a major battle or prolonged siege.[12]

Several OT books describe events during the Persian period, including 2 Chronicles, Ezra, Nehemiah, Esther, selected psalms, Daniel, Haggai, Zechariah, Malachi, and perhaps most famously Isaiah 44–45. Cyrus's foreign policy (unlike that of Babylon) was to permit conquered peoples to maintain their local customs and religions in their homelands. Thus, when Ezra petitioned Cyrus to return to Judea, he agreed (Ezra 1:1–4). Subsequently, Persia became a real superpower, with succeeding kings expanding "from India to Cush" (i.e., Ethiopia; Esth 1:1). In light of the Persian Empire's conciliatory stance toward the Jews and in fulfillment of biblical prophecy (Isa 44:28–45:13), Cyrus allowed the Jews to return to their homeland (see Ezra 1:1–4). Thus, under Persian rule the captives returned and with them the temple furniture and provision for the rebuilding of Jerusalem, though

[10] A. J. Tomasino, *Judaism Before Jesus: The Events and Ideas That Shaped the New Testament World* (Downers Grove, IL: InterVarsity, 2003), 71–73.

[11] See L. L. Grabbe, "Jewish History: Persian Period," in *DNTB*, 574–76. This is often termed the "Medo-Persian period," but by the time Babylon was defeated, the Median Empire had been all but eradicated by Cyrus.

[12] P. Briant, *From Cyrus to Alexander: A History of the Persian Empire*, trans. P. T. Daniels (Winona Lake, IN: Eisenbrauns, 2002), 41–42.

this did not happen immediately. The return to the land and re-building of the temple begins the so-called "Second Temple period."

For our purposes, one of the most enduring developments of the Persian period was the completion of the OT. This is assuming traditional dates for the composition of these works. Malachi, the last of the books, was a fifth-century BC product. The canonization, by definition, comes later (see chap. 1). However, the impact of these thirty-nine books on Jews, Judaism, and the early church is undeniable.

The Persians ruled Palestine for more than 200 years. The empire eventually fell to the expansive campaigns of the Greeks. Organized as a vast alliance of semi-independent city-states, the Greeks over a period of time became aware of the inner weakness of Cyrus's successors. One of the more famous disclosures happened when Greek mercenaries were hired by Cyrus the Younger (no relation) to overthrow the present king, Artaxerxes II (404–358 BC). The story of these mercenaries is related in the Greek historian Xenophon's *Anabasis*. The internal divisions and weaknesses of the Persian Empire surely gave hope to the Greeks that the Eastern superpower was not the juggernaut it had previously been.

The Greeks had expanded off the Achaean mainland long before Alexander the Great's famous campaigns.[13] Persia had subdued the city-states in Asia Minor, but in 500–494 BC they revolted. Athens sent their navy to help and burned Sardis, while Persia (under King Darius) responded with a largely unsuccessful punitive expedition to the Greek peninsula.[14] Ultimately, Athens defeated the Persians at Marathon. Darius intended to return to Greece, but died in 486 BC before he could. The responsibility fell to his son, Xerxes (Esther's husband).[15] He responded with a full-scale invasion of enormous proportions. The Athenians pulled together an alliance of city-states (called the Hellenic League) to resist the invasion. The Persian land forces had initial success invading Athens. However, while the Persians were burning the Athenian Acropolis, the Greek navy won the decisive battle in the bay of Salamis in September of 480 BC. This demoralizing defeat was followed by a decisive land battle at Plataea in 479 BC, at which the Persians withdrew.[16]

The fifth century BC was characterized by the golden age of Athenian democracy. The Greeks and Persians remained in somewhat of a cold war with occasional battles, during which time the Persians gradually weakened. Judea was relatively unaffected by

---

[13] H. Koester, *History, Culture, and Religion of the Hellenistic Age*, 2nd ed. (Berlin, Germany: W. de Gruyter, 1995), 1.

[14] Briant notes that the expedition was to burn the acropolis in Athens as a reprisal for the Athenians burning the Persian temples at Sardis. According to Briant, the conquest of Greece was a side effect of the goal. Briant, *From Cyrus to Alexander*, 158.

[15] Ibid., 525.

[16] Ibid., 528–35. At the same time the Greek city of Mycale in Western Asia Minor was also liberated. The Greek sources do not mention that Xerxes had to defend a threat against Babylon at the same time. Thus, his withdrawal was a choice between defending the capitol Babylon or aggression on the frontier. His choice is understandable. (Ibid.).

the Greco-Persian wars, but Greek influence could be felt in Palestine. Yet, as had been prophesized in Daniel, Greece grew to become a significant empire.[17]

The Greek Period (331–167 BC)

The Greek period can be divided into three phases: (1) the conquests of Alexander the Great (331–320 BC); (2) the Ptolemaic period (320–198 BC); and (3) the Seleucid or Syrian period (198–167 BC). What is more, Greek influence was felt in Palestine well beyond the Grecian period through the pervasive impact of Greek culture called Hellenization. This "enculturation" is often said to begin with the conquests of Alexander the Great, however, other factors also play a significant role. Schiffman notes that the combination of the decline of the traditional powers in the Middle-East, a literary and intellectual vacuum, the Greek ideals of humanism, and a hunger for new spiritual thoughts had run far in advance of Alexander, so that "[t]he time was ripe for a new cultural movement. Thus, the peoples of the defeated Persian Empire could offer no more resistance to the Hellenic cultural onslaught than they had to the Macedonian army."[18]

Alexander the Great and His Conquests (331–320 BC) The impact of the rise of Alexander the Great can hardly be overestimated.[19] Macedonia, north of the Greek peninsula, had been ruled by Philip of Macedon, Alexander's father, who turned it into a fierce military machine. Philip subdued the Greek city-states, requiring tribute from them. As the leader of the newly formed "Corinthian league," he now had a vast military at his command. The military buildup was not merely for show. Philip was already engaged in hostilities with Persia, and his preparations were in view of a planned invasion.[20] However, he was assassinated by Pausanias in 336 BC before he could launch the war that had been officially declared the year before.[21] Thus, when Alexander took the throne as king of Macedonia, he inherited not only Philip's titles but also his ambitions.[22] The first step for Alexander was to subdue the Greek city-states that did not immediately bow to his

[17] See Dan 8:5–8. The vision is of a male goat that viciously destroys a ram with two asymmetrical horns. The ram is identified in Dan 8:20 as the Medo-Persian Empire, which advances northwest and south. The male goat with one conspicuous horn is Alexander the Great, king of Greece (see Dan 8:21). He pushes west with great intensity and speed. The end of Alexander's kingdom is presented as well. The kingdom is split into four horns, and a little horn (most likely Antiochus IV) persecutes Judea.

[18] L. H. Schiffman, *From Text to Tradition: A History of Second Temple & Rabbinic Judaism* (Hoboken, NJ: Ktav, 1991), 61.

[19] See L. L. Grabbe, "Jewish History: Greek Period," in *DNTB*, 570–74. For a broader description of the era, including a great deal of archaeological evidence, see A. M. Berlin, "Between Large Forces: Palestine in the Hellenistic Period," *BA* 60 (1997): 3–43. Greek influence continued unabated through the Ptolemaic and Seleucid dynasties and beyond into the NT era and thereafter.

[20] N. G. L. Hammond, *The Genius of Alexander the Great* (Chapel Hill, NC: The University of North Carolina Press, 1997), 20.

[21] Ibid.

[22] Pausanias was immediately killed as well, leaving speculation as to his motives. Suspects include the Persians, Olympias (Philip's ex-wife), and Alexander himself (possibly conspiring with his mother Olympias). See Newsome, *Greeks, Romans, Jews*, 4.

will—especially making an example of Thebes. Afterwards, he was free to turn his attention to Persia.[23]

Philip had invested heavily in Alexander's education both militarily and academically in preparation for this moment.[24] He had been tutored in philosophy, science, and culture by no less than Aristotle. His military training came from the Macedonian army.[25] The result was a man thoroughly groomed for a specifically Greek conquest. Persia was simply not ready to face a foe who was, as Briant puts it, "resolved to pursue total war to the end—that is, a war of conquest."[26]

Alexander's defeat of Persia was indeed swift. His invasion of Asia Minor began in 334 BC. One of the mysteries of history is the lack of a Persian naval response to Alexander's invasion.[27] One of the better explanations involves their problems elsewhere. When Egypt rebelled against Persia, Darius III had to reestablish his dominion. At least by January 14, 334 BC, he was hailed as king of Egypt but had to assign the bulk of his military forces there.[28] Whether shrewd or just lucky, with Darius's navy stationed in Egypt, Alexander crossed the Hellespont into Asia Minor and defeated the Persian forces at Granicus.[29] Alexander's swift victory at the battle of Issus (near Tarsus, 333 BC) caused Darius to retreat and rebuild his army in Babylon.[30]

Alexander then turned south, laying siege to and devastating Tyre of Phoenicia[31] and Gaza on his way to Egypt. The tactic cut off the powerful Persian navy from its seaports, thus protecting Alexander's weak rear flank.[32] This maneuver made it possible for Alexander to make the war one directional.

Thc Roman and Greek historians chronicling Alexander's campaigns do not specifically mention the Jews at all.[33] However, Arrian does note that between the fall of Tyre and the

---

[23] Ibid.

[24] E.g., intellectually, Philip hired Aristotle to be Alexander's tutor when the boy was 13 and militarily Alexander had been training and leading troops since the age of 16.

[25] B. W. R. Pearson, "Alexander the Great," in *DNTB*: 20.

[26] Briant, *From Cyrus to Alexander*, 867.

[27] Ibid., 820.

[28] See A. T. Olmstead, *History of the Persian Empire [Achaemenid Period]* (Chicago, IL: University of Chicago Press, 1948), 493, for a description of the revolt. Briant agrees that it is possible, but one cannot be certain of the dating of the documents involved. He concludes that we simply have no answer. Briant, *From Cyrus to Alexander*, 820.

[29] J. L. Berquist, *Judaism in Persia's Shadow: A Social and Historical Approach* (Philadelphia, PA: Fortress, 1995), 125. Alexander needed a swift victory. Ancient sources (see, e.g., *Quintus Curtius Rufus, History of Alexander*, X.2.24 and Ariann, VII.9.6) note that when he embarked he only had thirty days' worth of funds to support his army (60 talants). The swift victory at Granicus allowed him to continue his invasion.

[30] Briant, *From Cyrus to Alexander*, 830 (Diodorus Siculus, CVII.39.1–4; Quintus Curtius Rufus, *History of Alexander*, IV.6.1–2).

[31] The port supplying the Persian navy; see R. D. Milns, "Alexander the Great," *ABD* 1.147.

[32] Pearson, "Alexander the Great," 21.

[33] C. Seeman and A. K. Marshak, "Jewish History from Alexander to Hadrian," in *Early Judaism: A Comprehensive Overview*, ed. J. J. Collins (Grand Rapids, MI: Eerdmans, 2012), 32.

siege of Gaza "Palestinian Syria (as it is called) had already come over to him . . ."[34] It is highly likely that they provided no resistance whatsoever.[35] The Egyptians, who had never been fond of Persian rule and lacking the forces to resist, also surrendered peacefully,[36] so Alexander turned northward and pursued Darius across Syria and Persia. Darius's loss at the battle of Gaugamela (331 BC) sealed his fate. The import of the battle was lost on no one. At this point, Alexander began to call himself, "Lord of Asia."[37]

Darius was forced into captivity by his own noblemen. It is likely this outcome is due to resentment regarding his abandonment of Babylon (who surrendered quickly to Alexander) and his worsening political position.[38] Although Alexander sought to capture him alive, Darius was killed by his own men.[39] With no Persian heir to claim the throne, Alexander was declared the new world ruler.[40]

Alexander pushed east as far as the Indus River delta. Ultimately returning to Babylon, he set about ruling like a Persian king (to the consternation of his Macedonian troops). Before he could initiate further expansion, he caught a fever and died at the age of thirty-three, having conquered his empire in only thirteen years.[41]

The collapse of the Persian Empire with its lenient attitude toward self-identity and religious freedom constituted the second great crisis for the Jewish nation. The Jews would now have to deal with a series of Greek kings who had a strong belief in their cultural superiority and fully intended to implant that culture firmly in all the lands they occupied.[42]

In Daniel's vision the great horn of the male goat is suddenly struck, and four lesser horns grow up in four directions (Dan 8:8). Upon Alexander's death, his generals half-heartedly attempted to keep the empire together through Alexander's infant son (Alexander IV) by an Oriental princess, Roxanne, and then by Alexander's feeble-minded half-brother (Philip Arrhidaeus).[43] Over the next decades, wars for supremacy oscillated

---

[34] Arrian, *Anabasis of Alexander*, II.25.4. Hengel notes, "That means the majority of Palestinian peoples and cities had already surrendered to him by the time of the siege of Tyre, and supported his laborious efforts in implementing the siege." M. Hengel, *Jews, Greeks and Barbarians: Aspects of the Hellenization of Judaism in the pre-Christian Period* (Philadelphia, PA: Fortress, 1980), 6.

[35] According to Josephus, Jerusalem welcomed Alexander, showing him the book of Daniel. Josephus, *Ant.* 11.337. Most, however, believe that this is fantasy on the part of Josephus or his sources, for Alexander had his mind on the riches of Egypt and would have had no interest in Jerusalem. See Newsome, *Greeks, Romans, Jews*, 6; and Tomasino, *Judaism Before Jesus*, 108. Tomasino also denied the trip's veracity as a "trifling detour."

[36] Milns, "Alexander," 147.

[37] F. F. C. Fuller, "The Generalship of Alexander the Great," in *Alexander the Great: A Reader*, ed. Ian Worthington (New York, NY: Routledge, 2012), 89.

[38] Briant, *From Cyrus to Alexander*, 865 (see, also, Quintus Curtius Rufus, V.1.7–9).

[39] V. Tcherikover, *Hellenistic Civilization and the Jews* (Peabody, MA: Hendrickson, 1999), 4.

[40] Tomasino, *Judaism Before Jesus*, 109.

[41] See Arrian, *The Anabasis of Alexander*, VI–VII. At VII.27.28. Arrian describes his reign as 12 years and 8 months. He does not provide the starting point.

[42] Helyer, *Exploring Jewish Literature*, 19, 75–76.

[43] Milns, "Alexander," 149. Neither the infant Alexander nor the half-brother Philip survived the struggle for supremacy.

among Alexander's generals (the so-called *diadochi*[44] wars) until 301 BC. At the battle of Ippsus fought in Phrygia, the most ambitious of Alexander's lieutenants, Antigonus (the former satrap of Phrygia in Asia Minor), was defeated and killed.[45] At this point, all pretense of unification was over. The empire remained divided among Alexander's remaining generals. Of the original successors to Alexander's kingdom, only Ptolemy I Soter formed a successful kingdom. He was granted Egypt and kept it; Syria came under the control of the Seleucids; Lysimachus got Asia Minor, though he eventually lost much of it to Syria; and Cassander ruled Greece. Palestine first came under the jurisdiction of the Egyptian ruler Ptolemy in about 320 BC.[46]

The Ptolemaic Period (320–198 BC) Ptolemy set himself up as the progenitor of a ruling dynasty. Every ruler of Egypt until AD 30 bore the name "Ptolemy" regardless of actual descent.[47] The greatest contribution of the Ptolemies to later history was the city of Alexandria, the greatest metropolis of the Mediterranean world by 200 BC (only Rome would later surpass it). The famous library and museum (an academy dedicated to the muses) helped make Alexandria the intellectual and spiritual center of the Greek world.

Judea under Ptolemaic reign remains clouded in obscurity. According to the few trustworthy sources that survive, Judea evidently continued to govern itself as somewhat of a temple state under the high priest. Ptolemaic rule was mainly concerned with aggressive taxation through tax-farming and securing the trade routes in the trans-Jordan.[48]

The fate of Jews in Egypt varied. They were originally deported to Alexandria by Ptolemy I. Josephus described Ptolemy I's invasion of Jerusalem on the Sabbath, taking 120,000 Jews captive to Alexandria, where they stayed until Ptolemy's son Philadelphus (Ptolemy II) freed them. Their diffusion throughout the Mediterranean led many into prosperity.[49]

While the Ptolemies had gained control of Egypt, another Greek dynasty, the Seleucids, attained supremacy in Babylon. Seleucus I Nicator, the son of the Macedonian Antiochus,

---

[44] An Anglicized form of the Greek word for "successors" (*diadochoi*). See G. L. Thompson, "Diadochi," in *DNTB*, 278–81.

[45] Tcherikover, *Hellenistic Civilization and the Jews*, 9.

[46] The date 320 is set from Ptolemy's invasion and annexation of the region from the Lebanon Mountains to the Egyptian border (including Palestine) shortly after Alexander's death. Ptolemy eventually had to invade the land two more times to finally secure it. From 316–312 Antigonus's son Demetrius controlled the area but was repelled by Ptolemy. Several months later Ptolemy fled from an advancing Antigonus who held the area until 302. At that time, Ptolemy's part in finally getting rid of Antigonus was to retake Palestine. Tcherikover, *Hellenistic Civilization and the Jews*, 50–52.

[47] After Ptolemy XI, none were in the bloodline of Ptolemy I. Even Julius Caesar was hailed as Ptolemy XV due to his relationship with Cleopatra VII, the famous queen. This Cleopatra—thoroughly Greek in spite of Hollywood's portrayal of her—was the last of the Ptolemaic line. She ultimately chose to commit suicide by taking an adder's bite rather than submitting to Octavian.

[48] See Tomasino, *Judaism Before Jesus*, 116–17; and Horsley, *Scribes, Visionaries, and the Politics of Second Temple Judea*, 37–41.

[49] Josephus (*Ant.* 12.1–153) connects the freeing of the slaves to Philadelphus's desire to acquire the laws of the Jews and to translate them into Greek for the library at Alexandria. Aristeas, the high priest in Jerusalem, upon the request for the Law, granted the petition to free the Egyptian slaves, granting them citizenship.

was the first of the rulers *(diadochoi)* to govern Syria.[50] His heirs expanded the territory to the east and west.[51] Their influence covered part of Asia Minor (modern Turkey), Palestine, and parts of Mesopotamia. Originally, Seleucia had three nerve centers: Ionia (Sardis in Asia Minor), Syria (Antioch), and Babylonia. Eventually, the kingdom was reduced to Syria. In the deal struck after the defeat of Antigonus, Palestine was to be Seleucid territory. Yet, Ptolemy's possession was put off for another day in light of their friendship. The matter seemed to be somewhat of a raw nerve. It is not surprising, then, that the Seleucids and the Ptolemies engaged in constant battles over Palestine.[52] In the end, Ptolemy V lost Israel in 198 BC at Paneas to Antiochus III of Syria. After this battle, control of Palestine passed from Egyptian to Syrian hands, never to return.[53]

SIDEBAR 2.1: THE SEPTUAGINT (LXX)

According to tradition (*Epistle of Aristeas*; Philo, *Life of Moses*, 2.26–42), the OT was translated into Greek under Ptolemy II, Philadelphus (285–246 BC).[1] Legend has it that Philadelphus commissioned 70 or 72 scholars to translate the Hebrew Scriptures. Hence it was called the "Septuagint" (Greek for 70; abbreviated by the Roman numeral LXX). The translation was prepared in Egypt and designed for Jews who understood Greek better than Hebrew, a testimony to the success of Alexander's Hellenization program.

The LXX, though uneven in quality, proved widely influential. It served as the Bible of the early Christians. Many quotes of the OT in the NT are taken from the LXX. There are some places where the LXX differs from the Hebrew Masoretic Text (MT), but even in these cases the LXX rendering should not be dismissed too quickly. The LXX is one of the oldest witnesses to the Hebrew Bible, and some of the variants are attested in Hebrew manuscripts found at Qumran. The study of the LXX continues to be a vibrant field of scholarly research today.[2]

[1] See Barrett, *New Testament Background*, chap. 12, especially 292–98; cf. A. Wasserstein and D. J. Wasserstein, *The Legend of the Septuagint: From Classical Antiquity to Today* (Cambridge, UK: Cambridge University Press, 2006).

[2] See S. Jellicoe, *The Septuagint and Modern Study* (Winona Lake, IN: Eisenbrauns, 1989); K. H. Jobes and M. Silva, *Invitation to the Septuagint*, 2nd ed. (Grand Rapids, MI: Baker, 2015); and M. Hengel, *The Septuagint as Christian Scripture: Its Prehistory and the Problem of Its Canon*, trans. M. E. Biddle (Edinburgh/New York: T&T Clark, 2002).

The Seleucid or Syrian Period (198–167 BC) Syrian control over Palestine lasted only thirty-one years.[54] Although brief, the period proved one of the most difficult for

[50] Hence the alternation of the names "Seleucus" and "Antiochus" throughout the Seleucid dynasty.

[51] Scott, *Jewish Backgrounds*, 80.

[52] Tcherikover, *Hellenistic Civilization and the Jews*, 53.

[53] Ibid., 75. The kings marshaled were originally Ptolemy IV and Antiochus III. The first battles were decidedly in Ptolemy's favor. But, Antiochus bided his time. When the elder Ptolemy died and was replaced by his five-year old son, the instability was inevitable.

[54] For a helpful introduction, see D. W. J. Gill, "Seleucids and Antiochids," in *DNTB*, 1092–93.

the Jewish people. The Seleucid Empire struggled to keep the newly acquired territory and impress their culture on the area. The tenuous nature of this control is seen in their defeat at Magnesia when Antiochus III picked a fight with the Romans. Here the king had "made a poor decision and a bad enemy."[55] Not only was heavy tribute enacted, but his son, Antiochus IV, was sent to Rome as a hostage. The Romans imposed an exorbitant monthly tribute that in no small part impacted the political decisions of later kings. When Antiochus IV took over the region upon the death of his elder brother, Seleucus IV, in 176 BC, daily life in Jerusalem took a significant change.[56]

Antiochus IV called himself "Epiphanes"—"the Glorious One," implying he was the incarnation of Zeus on earth. But the Jews coined a play on words and dubbed him "Epimanes"—"the Madman." This was due to his program of aggressive Hellenization that outraged the Jews.[57] The desire for the spread of Greek culture and the need for great amounts of money to pay Rome led Antiochus IV to look to the Jerusalem temple treasuries with ever-increasing avarice.[58] This desire for cultural expansion and the need for additional financial resources presented an opportunity for Jason—the brother of the high priest Onias III, who was possibly pro-Egyptian and a theological conservative—to suggest Onias's removal as high priest. Jason promised Antioch some 440 talents of silver and offered to aid in the further Hellenization of Israel through the building of a gymnasium and granting citizenship to the men of Israel as citizens of Antioch.[59]

Even though Jason was Antiochus's main agent in turning Jerusalem into a Greek *polis*, his loyalty could not buy job security. Three years later, now as the high priest, Jason sent Menelaus with the yearly tribute to Antioch. Menelaus seized the opportunity and increased the bribe by 300 talents of silver, taking the high priesthood from Jason.[60] Selling the priesthood to Jason had been an unrighteous thing to do, but selling it to the non-Zadokite Menelaus showed a blatant disregard for the customs of the Jews. Consequently, sedition, brutality, and murder characterized Menelaus's reign.[61]

Antiochus was also a man with gigantic personal ambitions. This led him to attempt to annex Egypt with some early success. However, in 168 BC the Ptolemies enlisted the

---

[55] Tomasino, *Judaism Before Jesus*, 127.

[56] L. Grabbe, *Judaism from Cyrus to Hadrian, Volume One: The Persian and Greek Periods* (Minneapolis, MN: Fortress, 1992), 270.

[57] For a thorough treatment of Jewish history starting with the religious crisis and revolution in 175–164 BC and concluding with the Jewish revolt against Hadrian in AD 132–135, see Schürer, *Jewish History in the Age of Jesus Christ*, 1:125–557.

[58] Temples were often the financial centers of the ancient world as well as places of worship. The wealthy often stored sums of money in the temples in hopes that robbers would not dare invoke the wrath of the deity. See J. R. C. Cousland, "Temples, Greco-Roman," in *DNTB*, 1186–88.

[59] 2 Macc 4:7–13.

[60] 2 Macc 4:23–24. J. H. Hayes and S. R. Mandell, *The Jewish People in Classical Antiquity: From Alexander to Bar Kochba* (Louisville, KY: Westminster John Knox, 50–58).

[61] The author of 2 Maccabees summarizes: "But Menelaus, because of the cupidity of those in power, remained in office, growing in wickedness, having become the chief plotter against his fellow citizens" (2 Macc 4:50 RSV).

aid of the new world power on the horizon—Rome. Confronting Antiochus outside of Alexandria, the Roman Legate Popilius Laenas insisted that Antiochus retreat or face the wrath of Rome. Antiochus agreed to consider the request. But Laenas drew a circle around the Syrian monarch and, in essence, said, "Take all the time you need—but you must answer before you leave that circle." Antiochus withdrew, humiliated.[62]

While Antiochus was gone, Jason—who thought Antiochus dead—briefly ousted Menelaus. Antiochus savagely crushed the attempt, murdering men, women, and children. He confiscated the golden temple furniture (perhaps planning another attempt at securing Egypt), built a fortress on the western hill of Jerusalem, and filled it with his loyal troops. Not the least of his outrageous actions was Menelaus's admittance of a Gentile (Antiochus) into the temple.[63]

Antiochus, perhaps seeing the pious as the main source of the opposition, repressed the cultic practices of Israel.[64] His attempt to ban Judaism represented the third great crisis that affected the Jews and indelibly imprinted him in the social and religious consciousness of Judaism. In instituting the ban, he prohibited possession of the Torah, circumcision, festivals, and offerings to Yahweh. Perhaps the most devastating of all of Antiochus' measures was the dedication of the Jerusalem temple to Zeus, the head of the Greek pantheon. In so doing, Antiochus erected a statue of Zeus in the temple and sacrificed a pig on the altar.

Those families who resisted and clung to Judaism were horribly mistreated. Men and women were beaten with rods. Mothers who circumcised their children were crucified with their babies hung around their necks, and the sacred books were confiscated and those holding them executed.[65] These atrocities rightly outraged pious Jews.

The conflict came to a head when an emissary of Antiochus entered the village of Modein to gain the loyalty of its citizens. An old priest named Mattathias was offered the prestige of being a friend of the king plus gold and silver if he made an offering to the gods.[66] Mattathias refused. When a fellow Jew offered to take the money and make the sacrifice, Mattathias killed him and the envoy and then fled into the wilderness, sparking a Jewish resistance movement that would effectively end the Greek period.[67]

---

[62] Polybius, *Hist.* 6.36. Hayes and Mandell, *Jewish People in Classical Antiquity*, 58.

[63] 2 Macc 5:11–15.

[64] The practice of religious persecution was practically unheard of in the ancient world. Antiochus's program has thus provoked a good deal of speculation as to the cause and purpose of it. At the end of the day, the only certainty is that the attempt to stamp out Judaism, a religion different from all others, did in fact take place. See S. J. D. Cohen, *From the Maccabees to the Mishnah*, 3rd ed. (Louisville, KY: Westminster John Knox, 2014), 22.

[65] See Josephus, *Ant.* 12.250–56 and 1 Macc 1:61.

[66] According to Josephus (*Ant.* 12.265), Mattathias was the great-grandson of Hasmoneus. Tomasino, *Judaism Before Jesus*, 140, suggests that he was a gentleman farmer living off his priestly salary and migrating to Jerusalem for the two weeks of service and then returning home.

[67] 1 Macc 2:15–28.Tcherikover convincingly suggests that the movement actually began a year earlier with the Hasidim in Judea, however what they lacked was a leader "who could give to the guerrilla struggle the character of a regular planned war." (Tcherikover, *Hellenistic Civilization and the Jews*, 204). In Mattathias (and later his sons) they got one.

The Greek period saw a number of important developments. First, the conquests of Alexander the Great led to the Greek language becoming the language of commerce in the ancient world. Thus, only Jews in Palestine continued to speak Aramaic. Jews outside of Palestine (called the Diaspora) spoke Greek, creating a distinction among Jews in at least their heart language. Without a doubt, this led to the next development in some way.

Under the Ptolemies, sometime in the third century BC, a Greek translation of the Hebrew Bible was produced. Although it is not a document to completely trust at face value, the Letter of Aristeas gives us a glimpse into the origins of the translation.[68] The legend is that seventy-two Jewish scholars produced this translation, thus it is called the Greek word for "70," "Septuagint," often abbreviated "LXX."[69] The importance of the translation is multi-faceted. First, it served as the Scriptures of the early church. Many of the OT citations in the NT are LXX readings. Second, it is an independent early witness to the text of the Hebrew Bible. In many ways, it is the oldest surviving witness. Third, it provides insight into the lexical stock employed in the NT unlike any other source. Finally (for our purposes), the LXX provided the theological texture for the early church in many critical debates.[70]

Jewish Self-Rule (167–63 BC)

The Maccabees (167–135 BC) The Maccabean period is named for the third son of Mattathias, Judas.[71] Nicknamed "Maccabeus," "the hammer,"[72] he led a guerrilla war against the Seleucids. Although Judas was a brilliant tactician, leader, and diplomat, the Maccabees' success was due as much to Syria's problems with the Eastern Parthian Empire as to Judas's leadership. The Maccabees ultimately rose from a country priesthood to overthrow the metropolitan aristocracy and eventually replaced it with their own.[73]

Judas had been able to raise a rag-tag army and defeat, in order, Apollonius, Seron, and then the joint forces of Ptolemy, Nicanor, and Gorgias (all Syrian generals).[74] Lysias, Antiochus' governor over the region, then himself led a failed campaign.[75] Subsequently, in 164 BC Judas led in a cleansing of the temple, commemorated to this day as the Feast of Lights, an eight-day holiday known as Hannukah that falls in late December. Further skirmishes took place after the cleansing, but Judas held Jerusalem.

---

[68] The letter probably dates to the second century BC. It is, most likely, a response to those who questioned the validity of the translation. K. Jobes and M. Silva, *Invitation to the Septuagint* (Grand Rapids, MI: Baker, 2000), 34.

[69] We are using the broadest reference for the term "Septuagint" to refer to the entirety of the Greek translation. It is probably more precise to refer to the Pentateuch as the Septuagint and the rest of the OT as the "Old Greek," but this is cumbersome for our purposes. Ibid. 32.

[70] Ibid., 19–26.

[71] For a selection of readings in the primary sources, see Barrett, *New Testament Background*, chap. 7.

[72] Probably from the Hebrew word *maqqebeth*, meaning "hammer."

[73] Cohen, *From the Maccabees to the Mishnah*, 22–23.

[74] 1 Macc 3:10–24; 3:38–4:22.

[75] 1 Macc 4:26–35.

Nevertheless, the Maccabees wanted national autonomy. When Antiochus died in 163 BC, the struggle over his kingdom aided the Jewish quest for independence. Lysias, now the regent for young Antiochus V, was too distracted by rivals on the home front to eliminate Judas's army. Eventually, wary of the battle, Lysias formally rescinded Antiochus' ban on Judaism.[76] Demetrius I took control of Syria soon afterwards and attempted to suppress the rebellion.[77] Judas died in battle in 160 BC.

Judas's brother, Jonathan, took over in the instability caused by his death. Jonathan won further freedom from the Syrians in 157 BC. He masterfully worked the levers of political gamesmanship to secure a better position for Israel. However, in violation of the commands of Scripture, he accepted the office of high priest from one of the other claimants to the Syrian throne in 152 BC.[78] There is no record of local opposition to this irregularity, though many believe Jonathan's action prompted the exodus of the group that formed the Qumran community to the area near the Dead Sea.[79] In the continuing struggle Jonathan was captured by Trypho and executed in 142 BC, even though a ransom had been paid.[80]

The youngest and only surviving brother, Simon, continued the resistance and achieved the benchmark of national autonomy. Arguably, Simon was the greatest of the brothers.[81] The political theater that was Syria continued to play into the Hasmoneans' favor (named after Hasmon, great-grandfather of Mattathias).[82] In order to secure his support, Simon demanded release from tribute (taxation) from Demetrius II in return for military support against other claimants. Demetrius, desperate for help, agreed. In 141 BC, after securing the outer areas of the city, Simon captured the Syrian citadel in Jerusalem that was called the Akra. This marks the beginning of national autonomy for Israel.[83]

The Jewish nation gave Simon the high priesthood and vested in him military, religious, and executive privileges. Simon's installation in the executive and religious branches of government (a departure from the biblical teachings) marked the slide into despotism. From here, the descendants of the Maccabees declined into a selfish group of Hellenizing despots. After a reign characterized by economic prosperity and relative peace, Simon

---

[76] 1 Macc 6:55–64.

[77] 1 Macc 7:1–4. Lysias was put to death by Demetrius's army. Demetrius was the son of Seleucus IV (Antiochus's brother) who had taken Antiochus's place as a hostage in Rome. See B. Reicke, *The New Testament Era: The World of the Bible from 500 B.C. to A.D. 100*, trans. D. E. Green (Philadelphia, PA: Fortress, 1968), 59.

[78] 1 Macc 10:20.

[79] So Schürer (*Jewish History in the Age of Jesus Christ*, 2:587), who suggests that Jonathan was the person called the "Wicked Priest" in the Dead Sea Scrolls.

[80] 1 Macc 13:23.

[81] J. VanderKam, *An Introduction to Early Judaism* (Grand Rapids, MI: Eerdmans, 2001), 25.

[82] See J. Sievers, "Hasmoneans," in *DNTB*, 438–42.

[83] 1 Macc 13:31–42. The meaning of this was not lost on the Jews. First Maccabees 13:51 notes, "On the twenty-third day of the second month, in the one hundred and seventy-first year, the Jews entered it [the citadel] with praise and palm branches, and with harps and cymbals and stringed instruments, and with hymns and songs, because a great enemy had been crushed and removed from Israel" (RSV).

and two of his sons were murdered by his son-in-law Ptolemy. The surviving son, John Hyrcanus, escaped a similar attempt and defeated Ptolemy.[84]

The Hasmoneans (135–63 BC) Despite Simon's breakthrough, the years between 142 and 135 BC continued to be unsettled. John Hyrcanus (135/34–104 BC) was the first of the Hasmonean rulers from the start of his reign. The Syrians continued to be a persistent thorn in the flesh, but with their ever-present squabbles over succession they became less relevant.[85] Hyrcanus led an expansion of Judean territories into Moab and Idumea. While Hyrcanus is generally regarded as a theological conservative, he switched his association from the Pharisees to the Sadducees.[86] From this point on, only one Hasmonean ruler was associated with the Pharisees.

Upon the death of Hyrcanus I, his son Aristobulus I (104–103 BC) proclaimed himself king, becoming the first of the Hasmonean rulers to take that title. He conquered Galilee and founded Jewish settlements there. Aristobulus died of an unknown disease after only one year of rule.[87] Upon his sudden death in 103 BC, his widow, Salome Alexandra, appointed Alexander Janneus, Aristobulus's older brother, as high priest and king and then promptly married him.

Alexander Janneus (103–76 BC) ruled as a Hellenistic king.[88] He expanded the country to Solomonic proportions with the use of foreign mercenaries. However, he was an unpopular ruler. He alienated the populace and had to quell a rebellion with the use of his foreign mercenaries. The rebels, ironically, called on Demetrius III (a Syrian king!) to help them against the Hasmonean ruler. Alexander was on the verge of defeat, but at the last minute, for unknown reasons, 6,000 Jews reverted to Alexander and helped avert a certain rout.[89] Alexander took gruesome revenge on his opponents. While he was feasting with his concubines, 800 of his most die-hard opponents were crucified while their wives' and children's throats were slit at their feet.[90] Alexander continued his expansionist policies until he died from an alcohol-induced illness. Upon his death he gave the kingdom to his wife Salome Alexandra, who reigned from 76 until 67 BC.[91]

Salome Alexandra was the only queen of the Hasmonean line. She appointed her oldest son Hyrcanus II as high priest (who eschewed politics), and her youngest son Aristobulus II commanded the armies. She repaired the relationship with the Pharisees, who during her

---

[84] 1 Macc. 16:14; Josephus, *Ant.* 20:240; *Jewish War* 1:54.

[85] VanderKam, *Introduction*, 25.

[86] Josephus, *Ant.* 13:296.

[87] Josephus, *Ant.* 13:301–17.

[88] Josephus calls him *philellēn*, that is, "Greek-lover" (*Ant.* 13:318).

[89] Josephus, *Ant.* 13:372–97. Josephus attributed the switch of allegiance to pity (13:379).

[90] The response was so brutal that years later the author of one of the Dead Sea Scrolls interprets it as the prophecies of Nahum (4QpNah 3.4 i 2). See D. Flusser, "Pharisees, Sadducees, and Essenes in Pesher Nahum," in *Judaism of the Second Temple Period*, vol. 1: *Qumran and Apocalypticism*, trans. A. Yadin (Grand Rapids, MI: Eerdmans, 2007), 223.

[91] Josephus, *Ant.* 13:398–407.

reign dominated the Sanhedrin. Salome Alexandra reigned in relative peace for nine years.[92] Upon her death in 67 BC, her heirs contended for the kingdom.

At first the contest was between Hyrcanus II and Aristobulus II. Aristobulus had taken up a nearly open revolt during his mother's illness, securing a number of strategic strongholds. He also secured capitulation from his brother, who seemed content to return

SIDEBAR 2.2: THE ORIGINS OF THE PHARISEES AND SADDUCEES

Sometime during the Maccabean/Hasmonean reign the Pharisees came to prominence. They were "the most clearly recognizable and socially active group over the entire span of time."[1] Exactly when the Pharisees and Sadducees arose is unknown.[2] Josephus first mentioned them as established groups during the reign of Jonathan but did not explain their origins (*Ant.* 13.171–73). By the time of the reign of Hyrcanus, the two groups were clearly in opposition. Politically, the Pharisees were lay leaders who were the power brokers between the masses and the aristocracy. They were scrupulous about the law and viewed themselves as separate from those who were lax about keeping it.[3]

The Sadducees are even more shrouded in mystery. The derivation of the name Sadducee is uncertain. It is possible that it comes from the name Zadok, but this is far from certain; others trace the name back to the term *tsedek*, "righteousness." They were more connected to the aristocracy and observed only the Pentateuch. Josephus attributed to them a denial of divine sovereignty. The major discussion in the NT involving the Sadducees involves the resurrection, which they denied (Matt 22:23–33 and parallels; Acts 23:6–8). No known Sadducean document exists. The Sadducees were the major supporters of the Hasmonean dynasty.

The Hasidim, on the other hand, a pious Jewish group that had initially been supportive of the Hasmoneans, eventually turned against them. They split into two main groups: the Pharisees, who remained in Jerusalem; and the Essenes, who withdrew and most likely produced the Qumran sectarian literature known as the Dead Sea Scrolls.[4] Except for the reign of Salome Alexandra (see below), none of the Hasmoneans enjoyed the support of the Pharisees.

[1] R. Deines, "The Pharisees Between 'Judaisms' and 'Common Judaism,'" in *Justification and Variegated Nomism*, vol. 1: *The Complexities of Second Temple Judaism*, ed. D. A. Carson, P. T. O'Brien, and M. A. Seifrid (Grand Rapids, MI: Baker, 2001), 447.

[2] So much so that in Neusner's 2007 book on the Pharisees the question is not addressed in detail: see J. Neusner and B. D. Chilton, eds., *In Quest of the Historical Pharisees* (Waco, TX: Baylor University Press, 2007).

[3] See S. Mason, "Pharisees," in *Dictionary of New Testament Background*, 786.

[4] See further below.

[92] Josephus, *Ant.* 13:407–432.

to private life. However, Antipater, an Idumean governor, and the wealthy Jews he influenced, secured the help of the Nabatean kingdom and convinced Hyrcanus II that his life was in danger. His only choice was to rebel. He was briefly successful, pursuing Aristobulus II, who took refuge in the temple.[93]

In the meantime, Roman armies under the leadership of Pompey's agent Scaurus finally subdued the Seleucid kingdom. Scaurus then visited Jerusalem. Both brothers appealed to Scaurus for help, but Aristobulus was originally preferred. However, upon Pompey's arrival in Jerusalem, Aristobulus offended him and Rome's favor fell on Hyrcanus II. Aristobulus II and his group again barricaded themselves in the temple. Pompey defeated Aristobulus (eventually taking him captive to Rome), walked into the holy of holies, installed Hyrcanus II as high priest but not as king, and made Judea a client kingdom under the rule of an imperial governor in Syria. The independent Jewish state had come to an end, and Rome was now in charge of Palestine.[94]

At least four major developments regarding the NT occurred during the period of Jewish self-rule. First, the familiar political parties of the Sadducees and Pharisees seem to find official demarcation during the reign of Jonathan.[95] These will be the main conversation partners with Jesus in the NT.

Closely related to the rise of these parties is the falling out between the Pharisees and John Hyrcanus. Josephus notes that through the perfidy of a Sadducee named Jonathan, Hyrcanus became convinced of the ill will of the Pharisees.[96] They never completely recovered politically from this falling out.

Third, Jewish expansion by the Hasmoneans led to introducing neighboring areas to the Jewish religion not only by way of political assimilation but by religious assimilation as well. Both Idumea and Iturea submitted to circumcision—the former considering themselves Jews. This paved the way for Herod the Great in NT times, among other political entities.[97]

Finally, Roman control of the area dominates the attention of the Jews from this time forward. Whether one embraced, endured, or violently resisted Rome was at the heart of much self-identification throughout the period. Thus, the Jews had to deal with the fourth great crisis in their national identity: life under Roman rule.[98]

---

[93] Josephus, *Ant.* 14:4–28.

[94] Josephus, *Ant.* 14:29–79. Josephus laments, "Now the occasions of this misery which came upon Jerusalem were Hyrcanus and Aristobulus, by raising a sedition one against the other; for now we lost our liberty, and became subject to the Romans, and were deprived of that country which we had gained by our arms from the Syrians, and were compelled to restore it to the Syrians." (*Ant.* 14:77).

[95] Josephus, *Ant.* 13:171–73.

[96] Josephus *Ant.* 13:292–296.

[97] Josephus, *Ant.* 13:257–258.

[98] Helyer, *Exploring Jewish Literature*, 20.

Table 2.3: The Five Major Crises of the Jews in the Second Temple Period

1. Babylonian destruction of Jerusalem and the first temple
2. Collapse of the Persian Empire in the wake of Alexander the Great's invasion
3. Persecution by Antiochus IV Epiphanes
4. Domination by Rome
5. Roman destruction of the Jewish state and the second temple

The Roman Period (63 BC–AD 70)

Roman History and the Conquest of Palestine Outside of Palestine, Rome had been rising as a world power.[99] After Rome prevailed over the North African city of Carthage (146 BC), few rivals remained. They became a major player in Palestine in 63 BC (as stated above) when Pompey extended Roman rule to Palestine. At that time several men were jockeying for power—Antigonus (the heir of Aristobulus II), Hyrcanus II, Antipater (the Idumean), and Antipater's sons Phasael and Herod.

Hyrcanus II was not a particularly strong leader. His failures led the Roman governor to redraw the political lines and the duties of the high priest. He would no longer be the chief political leader of Jerusalem but had the "care of the temple." In essence, the temple state had come to an end.[100] Herod had been given Galilee, and Phasael received Judea. Antigonus, son of Aristobulus II (40–37 BC), would not give up easily. In an alliance with the Parthian Empire, he had Phasael imprisoned, where the man eventually committed suicide. Antigonus captured Hyrcanus II, and Josephus reported that Antigonus bit off Hyrcanus's ears himself so that he could no longer be the high priest.[101] Antigonus then was appointed king by the Parthians.[102] He held the crown for three years and was the last of the Hasmoneans.[103]

The Herodian Dynasty Meanwhile, Herod had fled to Rome, where he was named "king of Judea" by the Roman Senate in 40 BC.[104] Although assigned rule in 40 BC, Herod did not actually win his kingdom until 37 BC when he deposed Antigonus with the help of Marc Antony. Antony brutally dispatched Antigonus upon the urging of Herod by tying him to a cross, having him flogged, and then killed. According to Dio Cassius, this was a punishment no other king had suffered at the hands of the Romans.[105]

---

[99] For a survey of the Roman period, see L. L. Grabbe, "Jewish History: Roman Period," in *DNTB*, 576–80.

[100] Josephus, *Jewish War* 1:169; *Ant.* 14:91.

[101] Josephus, *Jewish War* 1:270.

[102] Josephus, *Ant.* 14:365; *Jewish War* 1:269.

[103] Josephus summarizes the time well: "These men lost the government by their dissensions one with another, and it came to Herod, the son of Antipater, who was of no more than a common family, and of no eminent extraction, but one that was subject to other kings. And this is what history tells us was the end of the Asamonean family" (Josephus, *Ant.* 14:491).

[104] For helpful primary source material, see Barrett, *New Testament Background*, 148–55; cf. H. W. Hoehner, "Herodian Dynasty," in *DNTB*, 485–94 (see esp. the chart on p. 321 and further bibliographic references on pp. 325–26).

[105] Dio Cassius, *Roman History* 49.2: "These people Antony entrusted to a certain Herod to govern; but Antigonus he bound to a cross and flogged—a punishment no other king had suffered at the hands of the Romans—and afterwards slew him."

Herod was technically a client king under the authority of Rome; thus, he was considered a friend and ally of the Roman people. Originally an ally of Antony, he quickly switched allegiance to Octavian after the famous battle at Actium. For the Romans, Herod proved to be "a stable and friendly ally on the eastern border and promoted economic development and Romanization in Judea."[106] He was an able administrator, but he was cruel and paranoid. His ability is seen in the agricultural and commercial enterprises he started that brought prosperity to the region. Moreover, Herod spent his wealth on many public works and building programs such as the expansion of the temple, which was considered one of the eight wonders of the ancient world.[107] But Herod was also brutal and deeply suspicious, which provoked him to take murderous actions, even on his own family. Neither his wife Mariamne (a Hasmonean princess) nor his sons she bore escaped his paranoia. Herod's reputation for cruelty and paranoia was well established. So much so that Caesar Augustus is reported to have said that it was better to be Herod's pig than his son.[108]

SIDEBAR 2.3: THE WIVES OF HEROD THE GREAT

Herod the Great had at least five wives, and they are listed here with their sons.

1. Doris became the mother of Antipater.
2. Mariamne, the Hasmonean princess, bore four children: two sons, Aristobulus (through whom came Herod Agrippa I and II) and Alexander, and two daughters, Salampsio and Cypros.
3. Another Mariamne, daughter of Simon the high priest, gave birth to Herod Philip (Mark 6:17).
4. Malthrace bore Archelaus (Matt 2:22), who was deposed as ethnarch of Judea in AD 6; and Herod Antipas (Mark 6:14; Luke 23:7), the tetrarch of Galilee.
5. Cleopatra was the mother of Philip, who became tetrarch of Iturea.[1]

[1] Scott, *Jewish Backgrounds*, 98.

In his later years, Herod suffered from dementia and died a grisly but natural death.[109] True to form, however, he sought to ensure mourning in Jerusalem for his passing. As his demise drew near, he had prominent citizens arrested and ordered them to be executed upon his death. Instead, contrary to his instructions, they were released.[110] Although the particular stories of Herod in the NT (see Matthew 2) are not corroborated by external

[106] C. Seaman and A. K. Marshak, "Jewish History from Alexander to Hadrian," in *Early Judaism: A Comprehensive Overview*, ed. J. J. Collins and D. C. Harlow (Grand Rapids, MI: Eerdmans, 2012), 51.

[107] See T. Mueller, "Herod: The Holy Land's Visionary Builder," *National Geographic* 214, no. 6 (December 2008): 34–59, which also chronicles the discovery of the Herodium, Herod's elaborate tomb. He built temples for his Gentile subjects as well.

[108] Macrobius, *Saturnalia* 2.4. A play on the Greek words for "pig" (*hus*) and "son" (*huios*).

[109] Josephus, *Ant.* 17:169.

[110] Josephus, *Ant.* 17:174–193.

sources, the cruel and paranoid picture painted there is in keeping with what we know of Herod's character elsewhere.[111]

Herod's sons were briefly given ruling positions. Archelaus was appointed ethnarch over Judea, Samaria, and Idumea, which included Jerusalem (4 BC). Rome dismissed and banished him to Gaul in AD 6 because of his incompetence. Archelaus was not a skillful administrator like his father, but he was like him in being cruel and paranoid. Ultimately, the most significant outcome of Archelaus's rule was that Jerusalem was placed under direct Roman control.[112]

Also in 4 BC, Philip, who married Salome, daughter of his half brother Herod Philip, was made tetrarch over Iturea and Trachonitis (areas northeast of the Sea of Galilee). On all accounts, Philip was an able and conscientious ruler.

Another of Herod's sons, and the one considered the most capable and astute, Herod Antipas, was made tetrarch over Galilee and Perea in 4 BC.[113] He divorced his wife (daughter of the Nabatean king Aretas IV) to marry the wife of his half brother, Herod Philip, and martyred John the Baptist for his condemnation of this act (Mark 6:14–29 and parallels). Subsequently, Aretas (see 2 Cor 11:32) inflicted a heavy defeat on Herod Antipas. Later, when Caligula took over the Roman Empire, Antipas fell into disfavor and was banished to Lyons in Gaul.[114]

Table 2.4: Roman Governors in Judea

(Note: Partial List; All Dates Are AD)

6–10	Coponius
10–13	M. Ambivius
13–15	Annius Rufus
15–26	Valerius Gratus
26–36	Pontius Pilate (Matthew 27 and parallels; John 18:28–19:42)
44–46	Fadus
46–48	Tiberius Julius Alexander
48–52	Camanus
52–59	Antonius Felix (Acts 23:24–24:27)
59–61	Porcius Festus (Acts 24:27–26:32)
62–64	Albinus
64–66	Gessius Florus (his provocation sparked the Jewish rebellion in 66)

---

[111] See P. L. Maier, "Herod and the Infants of Bethlehem," in *Chronos, Kairos, Christos II: Chronology, Nativity, and Religious Studies in Memory of Ray Summers*, ed. E. J. Vardaman (Macon, GA: Mercer University Press, 1998), 169–90.

[112] Josephus, *Jewish War*, 2:167; *Ant.* 17:342–44.

[113] On Herod Antipas, see H. W. Hoehner, *Herod Antipas*, SNTSMS 17 (Cambridge, UK: Cambridge University Press, 1972); and M. H. Jensen, *Herod Antipas in Galilee: The Literary and Archaeological Sources on the Reign of Herod Antipas and Its Socio-Economic Impact on Galilee*, WUNT 2/215 (Tübingen, Germany: Mohr Siebeck, 2006).

[114] Josephus, *Ant.* 18:252.

After AD 6, Judea was made a Roman province under the supervision of the legate of Syria and as such was under the rule of Roman imperial governors (prefects until Claudius, later procurators).[115] The governors lived in Caesarea and only went up to Jerusalem on feast days. However, they kept a strong military presence in Judea. They also built the fortress of Antonia directly across from the temple and high enough to look down on the open courts.

The Jews did enjoy some religious freedoms other provinces did not have. They were allowed to mint coins without offensive images, containing only names without ascriptions of deity. The yearly temple tax was sent to Jerusalem and not Rome. A sacrifice to Yahweh on behalf of the Roman government took the place of the required sacrifice to the gods. They also had limited autonomy through the rule of the Sanhedrin, over which the high priest presided. Roman control was demonstrated through the selection of the high priest. Furthermore, the garments of the high priest were kept in Roman custody until needed for festivals.[116]

The Roman Emperors and Governors of Palestine The NT takes place during what the Roman poet Virgil called the "Golden Age" of Rome under Caesar Augustus, who ruled from 31 BC until AD 14. This period was characterized by the rule of Roman law, providing it stability; the "Roman peace" (*pax Romana*), providing a climate conducive for the construction of roads and the unification of the empire; and general prosperity and affluence. Tiberius (14–37) succeeded Augustus and reigned during the lifetimes of John the Baptist and Jesus (Luke 3:1).[117]

The Roman governor of Palestine at the time of Christ's ministry was Pontius Pilate.[118] His tenure was characterized by bribery, insults, executions without trials, and grievous cruelty.[119] Pilate's early career was marked by arrogance and a willingness to offend the Jews, likely facilitated by the support provided by his powerful patron in Rome, Sejanus, prefect of the Praetorian Guard under Tiberius. This Sejanus administered the empire for Tiberius, while the latter stayed on the Isle of Capri. According to Philo, Sejanus had a

---

[115] See Barrett, *New Testament Background*, 155.

[116] J. S. Jeffers, *The Greco-Roman World of the New Testament Era: Exploring the Background of Early Christianity* (Downers Grove, IL: InterVarsity, 1999), 128.

[117] See J. E. Bowley, "Pax Romana," in *DNTB*, 771–75. This is the case whether Jesus's crucifixion is dated to the year 30 or 33, the two major options for dating the crucifixion. See the discussion on the chronology of Jesus's life in chap. 3 below.

[118] Matt 27:1–65; Mark 15:1–44; Luke 3:1; 13:1; 23:1–52; John 18:29–19:38; Acts 3:13; 4:27; 13:28; 1 Tim 6:13. The famous "Pilate Inscription," discovered in 1961 in Caesarea, reads as follows:

TIBERIEUM ("To Tiberius")
[PON]TIUS PILATUS ("From Pontius Pilate")
[PRAEF]ECTUS IUDA[EA]E ("Governor of Judea")

See Barrett, *New Testament Background*, 155–56; Schürer, *History of the Jewish People*, 1:358; and C. A. Evans, "Pilate Inscription," in *DNTB*, 803–4.

[119] According to Philo, *On the Embassy to Gaius*, 302.

particular dislike of the Jews and the Jewish nation, and Pilate may have been implementing Sejanus's policy toward Judea.[120]

But after Sejanus was executed in the year 31 for treason against Tiberius, Pilate no longer had the powerful patron on his side. Thus, Pilate's conciliatory attitude toward the Jews at the crucifixion of Jesus was most likely due to Sejanus's removal.[121] After a series of gaffes on Pilate's part, the Roman governor of Syria removed Pilate in the year 36 and sent him back to Rome to answer to Tiberius, who, fortunately for Pilate, died before he arrived. Pilate is not heard of again after his return to Rome, but Eusebius (ca. 260–340) recorded that he committed suicide.[122]

In Rome, Tiberius was succeeded by a series of emperors variously known for their cruelty and immorality: Caligula (AD 37–41); Claudius (AD 41–54), who expelled the Jews from Rome (Acts 18:2; see Suetonius, *Claudius* 25); Nero (AD 54–68), perpetrator of atrocious acts against Christians and responsible for the fire of Rome in the year 64 (Tacitus, *Annals* 15.44) and the martyrdoms of Peter and Paul (AD 65 or 66); Galba, Otho, and Vitellius (AD 68–69); Vespasian (AD 69–79); and Domitianus (AD 81–96; Suetonius, *Domitianus* 12–13), during whose reign the book of Revelation was likely written.[123]

After Pilate's death, Palestine was governed by Roman procurators, including Felix (AD 52–59) and Festus (AD 59–61). Finally, Florus's raiding of the temple treasury ignited a Jewish revolt in 66, which climaxed in the destruction of Jerusalem and the temple in 70. This precipitated the fifth major crisis for the Jewish people. With the destruction of the central sanctuary, temple worship and the sacrificial system ceased.[124]

From the time of the Babylonian captivity to the destruction of Jerusalem and the temple in the year 70, the Jewish nation was subjected to a series of occupational forces with only a brief interlude of self-rule during the Maccabean era. When Jesus was born and later began his public ministry, messianic expectations were widespread, and the Jewish hope of liberation—though construed primarily in political and nationalistic terms—was at a fever pitch.

---

[120] See Philo, *In Flaccum* 1.1; idem, *De Legatione ad Gaium* 24; and Eusebius, *Eccl. Hist.* 2.5, cited in P. L. Maier, "Sejanus, Pilate, and the Date of the Crucifixion," *Church History* 37 (1968): 3–13.

[121] See Maier ("Sejanus, Pilate, and the Date of the Crucifixion") for both a description and an explanation of Pilate's offenses against Jewish sensibilities. See also the discussion and further references in A. J. Köstenberger, *John*, BECNT (Grand Rapids, MI: Baker, 2004), 524–25.

[122] Eusebius, *Eccl. Hist.* 2.7. But Origen (*Against Celsus* 2.34)—and apparently his adversary Celsus—did not know of this report.

[123] For additional information on these and other Roman emperors, see E. Ferguson, *Backgrounds of Early Christianity*, 3rd ed. (Grand Rapids, MI: Eerdmans, 2003), 26–39; and Barrett, *New Testament Background*, chap. 1. See also chap. 20 on the book of Revelation below.

[124] Helyer, *Exploring Jewish Literature*, 20. Under Hadrian (117–138), the Jews rebelled again in what is known as the "Bar Kokhba revolt" (132–135). This uprising, too, was crushed by the Romans, resulting in a cessation of the Jewish state until 1948 (see Grabbe, *Judaism from Cyrus to Hadrian*, 2:601–605).

The "Fullness of Time"

Paul stated in his letter to the Galatians that the Lord Jesus appeared "when the fullness of time came" (Gal 4:4 NASB). The expression "fullness of time" (*to plērōma tou chronou*), among other things, conveys the notion that Jesus came "at just the right time." But what made the time of Christ's coming "just the right time"?[125]

In the context, Paul's reference to the "fullness of time" in Galatians 4:4 pertains to believers' adoption to sonship through the redemptive work of Christ (see vv. 5–7). This marked a new phase in salvation history subsequent to the period during which the law served as the primary point of reference (see Gal 3:16–26). The notion of fulfillment in Jesus is struck by both Jesus himself and the evangelists, especially Matthew and John.[126] R. Longenecker stated, "Set in the context of a fulfillment motif, the statement tells us that Jesus, God's Son par excellence, is the culmination and focus of all of God's redemptive activity on behalf of humanity."[127]

In addition to this salvation-historical point of reference of the phrase "fullness of time," which must remain primary, conditions were indeed ideally suited for the coming of Jesus due to factors such as (1) the Roman peace; (2) Roman roads; (3) the Greek language; and (4) Jewish messianic expectations.

First, the 200 years of unprecedented (though militarily imposed) peace known as the *pax Romana* provided "just the right time" for Jesus's appearing.[128] This peace enabled the spread of the Christian gospel during the days of the early church subsequent to Jesus's resurrection.

Second, there was a network of roads the Romans had built throughout the empire. The old saying is "All roads lead to Rome." These roads provided relatively easy travel. Thus, in God's providence the roads built by the Romans paved the way for the spread of the gospel of Jesus Christ from Jerusalem all the way to Rome (see the book of Acts, especially 1:8; 28:14–31).

Third, the conquests of Alexander the Great made Greek the language of commerce throughout the Roman Empire. The result was a common idiom that provided a universal vehicle for the spread of the gospel. In fact, the language became so influential that the OT was translated into Greek (the LXX) and the NT was written in Greek.[129]

---

[125] For helpful treatments, see H. N. Ridderbos, *When the Time Had Fully Come* (Grand Rapids, MI: Eerdmans, 1957); F. F. Bruce, *Commentary on Galatians*, NIGTC (Grand Rapids, MI: Eerdmans, 1982), 194; and R. N. Longenecker, *Galatians*, WBC (Dallas, TX: Word, 1990), 166–70. Longenecker (ibid., 167) noted that some view vv. 4–5 as representing a pre-Pauline confession drawn from the proclamation of the early church.

[126] Regarding Jesus, see Mark 1:15; 12:6; Luke 1:21. Regarding Peter and the preaching of the early church, see Acts 2:16–36; 3:18. Regarding the Matthean and Johannine fulfillment quotations, see the discussion in chap. 1 above. Regarding Paul, see also Acts 13:27; Rom 3:26; 5:6; Eph 1:10.

[127] Longenecker, *Galatians*, 170; cf. John 1:18; Heb 1:1–3.

[128] See D. Guthrie, *Galatians*, NCBC (Grand Rapids, MI: Eerdmans, 1974), 113.

[129] See the discussion above.

Fourth, the various strands of first-century Judaism, each in its own way, sustained a vibrant, albeit diverse, hope for a Messiah.[130] To be sure, many construed this messianic hope in nationalistic, political terms. Nevertheless, when Jesus came claiming to be the Messiah, he entered a world in which many were already expecting such a figure. Thus, from the perspective of salvation history and the providential elements of the day, Jesus came "at just the right time" indeed.

LITERATURE

While the production of canonical writings ceased in the intertestamental era, this does not mean there is no extant literature dating from this period. To the contrary, a large body of literature is available that sheds considerable light on the background of the NT. The purpose of the following brief survey of Second Temple literature is to acquaint the student with the vast array of relevant source material for the study of this era.[131] The OT itself is available in three versions: (1) in the original Hebrew; (2) in Greek translation (primarily the Septuagint or LXX; see above);[132] and (3) in Aramaic paraphrase (the Targums).[133] Alongside the OT, Jewish Second Temple literature may be examined under the following headings: (1) the Apocrypha; (2) the Pseudepigrapha; (3) the Qumran writings or Dead Sea Scrolls (DSS); (4) Philo; and (5) Josephus.

Table 2.5: Second Temple Jewish Literature

I. Apocrypha
1 and 2 Esdras (2 Esdras = 4 Ezra)
Tobit
Judith
Additions to Esther
Wisdom of Solomon
Sirach (Ecclesiasticus)
Baruch
Epistle of Jeremiah
Prayer of Azariah and the Song of the Three Young Men
Susanna
Bel and the Dragon

[130] See Scott, *Jewish Backgrounds*, 307–23; cf. the further discussion of messianism under the heading "Theology" below.

[131] See especially D. W. Chapman and A. J. Köstenberger, "Jewish Intertestamental and Early Rabbinic Literature: An Annotated Bibliographic Resource Updated," *JETS* 55 (2012): 235–72, 457–88 (posted at www.biblicalfoundations.org/articles).

[132] While the Septuagint was by far the most popular and enduring Greek translation of the OT, others were made as well, most notably by Aquila, Symmachus, and Theodotion. Origen included each of these translations alongside the Septuagint in his *Hexapla*, an edition of the OT that placed various Greek translations in columns paralleling the Hebrew text.

[133] On Targums, see B. D. Chilton, "Rabbinic Literature: Targumim," in *DNTB*, 902–9.

Table 2.5: Second Temple Jewish Literature (continued)

Prayer of Manasseh
1 and 2 Maccabees*
II. Pseudepigrapha (selected works)**
1 and 2 Enoch
2 and 3 Baruch (2 Baruch = Apocalypse of Baruch)
Sibylline Oracles
Testaments of the Twelve Patriarchs
Assumption of Moses
Martyrdom and Ascension of Isaiah
Jubilees
Psalms of Solomon
Letter of Aristeas
Joseph and Aseneth
3 and 4 Maccabees
III. Qumran Literature (Dead Sea Scrolls; selected works)***
CD (Damascus or Zadokite document)
1QS (Community Rule or Manual of Discipline)
1QM (War Scroll)
11QTemple (Temple Scroll)
1QpHab (Habakkuk *pesher* and other *pesharim* or commentaries)

* In addition, some canons including the Apocrypha also contain 3 and 4 Maccabees and Psalm 151 (see the Greek Orthodox Canon), but these books are usually classified as pseudepigraphical (see further below). See C. A. Evans, *Ancient Texts for New Testament Studies: A Guide to the Background Literature* (Peabody: Hendrickson, 2005), 341.

**See the fuller list in Evans, *Ancient Texts for New Testament Studies*, 26–27; and the contents of J. H. Charlesworth, ed., *The Old Testament Pseudepigrapha*, 2 vols. (Garden City: Doubleday, 1983, 1985).

***See the fuller list in Evans, *Ancient Texts for New Testament Studies,* 76–80.

The Apocrypha The Greek word *apocrypha* originally meant "things that are hidden."[134] The designation *Apocrypha* may also refer to the mysterious or esoteric nature of some of the contents of these books, to their spurious or heretical nature, or to both. Roman Catholics employ the label "deutero-canonical," by which they mean the books of the Apocrypha were added to the canon at a later time. Nevertheless, they consider the Apocrypha canonical rather than apocryphal.

The writings comprising the OT Apocrypha included in this category represent several different genres:

---

[134] D. A. deSilva, "Apocrypha and Pseudepigrapha," in *DNTB*, 58; see the entire entry on pp. 58–64, including additional bibliographic references.

1. Historical writings (1 Esdras, 1–2 Maccabees)
2. Moralistic novels (Tobit, Judith, Susanna, Bel and the Dragon)
3. Wisdom or devotional literature (Wisdom of Solomon; Sirach, also called Ecclesiasticus; Prayer of Manasseh; Prayer of Azariah; Song of the Three Young Men)
4. Pseudonymous letter (Letter of Jeremiah)
5. Apocalyptic literature (2 Esdras)

Except for 2 Esdras, these writings are found in the Septuagint. The Apocrypha are also included in the Vulgate, the Latin translation of the Bible prepared in the fourth century by Jerome, either as part of the OT or as an appendix but are not part of the canonical Scriptures.[135] Because of their inclusion in the Vulgate, the books of the Apocrypha were considered on par with the OT by the medieval church. In 1546, the Council of Trent declared them deuterocanonical, except for 1–2 Esdras and the Prayer of Manasseh.[136]

Protestants, not to mention other parts of Christendom, have traditionally distinguished between the Hebrew Scriptures and the Apocrypha, including only the former in their OT canon while setting off the latter in a category of its own. In Luther's 1534 German translation of the Bible, the Apocrypha are printed between the OT and the NT with the following superscription: "Apocrypha, that is, books which are not held equal to the sacred Scriptures, and nevertheless are useful and good to read." The King James Version of 1611 also included the Apocrypha.

The Thirty-Nine Articles of the Church of England (1571) declare that the Apocrypha, while useful for instruction, ought not to be used "to establish any doctrine"; and the Westminster Confession (1648) stipulates that the Apocrypha, "not being of divine inspiration, are no part of the Canon of Scripture; and therefore are of no authority in the Church of God, nor to be otherwise approved, or made use of, than other human writings." The available text of the Apocrypha is based primarily on the three major codices (ancient books): Vaticanus, Sinaiticus (both fourth century), and Alexandrinus (fifth century).

Apart from the OT Apocrypha of the Second Temple period, there are also NT Apocrypha that emerged in the second and subsequent centuries of the Christian era, consisting of spurious Gospels, Acts, and Apocalypses.[137] Many of these writings have in

---

[135] For a helpful English edition of the Apocrypha with a general introduction to the apocryphal/deuterocanonical books and introductions to the various writings and helpful explanatory notes, see Michael D. Coogan, ed., *The New Oxford Annotated Apocrypha: New Revised Standard Version*, 4th ed. (Oxford, NY: Oxford University Press, 2010). See also D. A. deSilva, *Introducing the Apocrypha: Message, Context, and Significance* (Grand Rapids, MI: Baker, 2002); Evans, *Ancient Texts for New Testament Study*, 1–8.

[136] For an older but still useful discussion of issues related to the canonicity of the OT Apocrypha and Pseudepigrapha, see N. L. Geisler and W. E. Nix, *A General Introduction to the Bible*, rev. and exp. ed. (Chicago, IL: Moody, 1986), chap. 15.

[137] See especially J. K. Elliott, *The Apocryphal New Testament* (New York, NY: Oxford University Press, 2005); and W. Schneemelcher, ed., *New Testament Apocrypha*, 2 vols., trans. R. M. Wilson (Louisville, KY: Westminster John Knox, 2003). Contrary to B. D. Ehrman (*Lost Scriptures* [New York, NY: Oxford University Press, 2005] and *Lost Christianities* [New York, NY: Oxford University Press, 2005]) who followed W. Bauer (*Rechtgläubigkeit und Ketzerei im ältesten Christen-*

common the underlying motivation to fill in perceived gaps in Scripture, frequently resulting in heterodox (false) teaching. The speculation of the apocryphal writers regarding what might have been said or what might have occurred in the literary gaps of Scripture gave rise to an imaginative "reading between the lines" that led to a body of literature lacking true divine inspiration but using familiar canonical biblical material as a point of departure for its exercise of imagination. This is the case both with the writings commonly grouped together as Apocrypha and with other Jewish Second Temple literature assembled under the amorphous rubric of Pseudepigrapha.[138]

Pseudepigrapha The Pseudepigrapha (from *pseudos*, "false," and *graphein*, "write") encompasses the following types of literature (selected works).

1. Apocalyptic and related literature (1–2 Enoch; 2–3 Baruch, 4 Ezra, Sibylline Oracles)
2. Testaments (Testaments of the Twelve Patriarchs)
3. Pseudonymous epistle (Letter of Aristeas)
4. Wisdom or devotional literature (Psalms of Solomon; Odes of Solomon; Psalm 151)
5. Expansions of OT material (Jubilees; Joseph and Aseneth; Jannes and Jambres; Assumption of Moses, Martyrdom and Ascension of Isaiah)
6. Religious novels and philosophical treatises (3–4 Maccabees)[139]

The evaluation of this Second Temple literature has been variously positive and negative. Positively, the historical information provided by books such as 1 Maccabees has been noted as an indispensable source for this particular period in Jewish history. Also, while not inspired or authoritative, many of these writings reflect the various religious beliefs of the Jewish people in the intertestamental period and thus provide helpful background information for the study of the NT.

---

tum [Tübingen, Germany: Mohr, 1934]; English translation *Orthodoxy and Heresy in Earliest Christianity*, ed. R. A. Kraft and G Krodel [Philadelphia, PA: Fortress, 1971]), the NT Apocrypha were not for a time put side by side with the canonical NT writings and were only later disqualified by the early Catholic church. See especially D. L. Bock, *The Missing Gospels: Unearthing the Truth Behind Alternative Christianities* (Nashville, TN: Thomas Nelson, 2006); C. A. Blaising, "Faithfulness: A Prescription for Theology," *JETS* 49 (2006): 6–9; P. Trebilco, "Christian Communities in Western Asia Minor into the Early Second Century: Ignatius and Others as Witnesses against Bauer," *JETS* 49 (2006): 17–44; and A. J. Köstenberger and M. J. Kruger, *The Heresy of Orthodoxy: How Contemporary Fascination with Diversity Has Reshaped Our Understanding of Early Christianity* (Wheaton, IL: Crossway, 2010).

[138] See Charlesworth, *Old Testament Pseudepigrapha*; B. N. Fisk, "Rewritten Bible in Pseudepigrapha and Qumran," in *DNTB*, 947–53.

[139] It is neither possible nor necessary to rehearse the contents of the apocryphal and pseudepigraphical literature here. On the Apocrypha, see the introductions in Coogan, *Annotated Apocrypha*; cf. Evans, *Ancient Texts for New Testament Studies*, chap. 1; deSilva, *Introducing the Apocrypha*. On the Pseudepigrapha, see the introductions in Charlesworth, *Old Testament Pseudepigrapha*; and Evans, *Ancient Texts for New Testament Studies*, chap. 2. On both, see M. E. Stone, ed., *Jewish Writings of the Second Temple Period*, CRINT 2 (Philadelphia, PA: Fortress, 1984); G. W. E. Nickelsburg, *Jewish Literature Between the Bible and the Mishnah*, 2nd ed. (Minneapolis, MN: Fortress, 2005); Schürer, *History of the Jewish People* 3.1; deSilva, "Apocrypha and Pseudepigrapha"; and the relevant sections in Helyer, *Exploring Jewish Literature*.

Negatively, scholars have stressed that some of the teachings in these writings are heterodox, that is, not in conformity with the doctrines affirmed in the canonical books. For example, 2 Maccabees teaches one to pray for the dead (2 Macc 12:38–46), and Tobit contains elements of magic and syncretism. This calls for discernment and a clear demarcation between the OT and the apocryphal and pseudepigraphical writings.[140] An added element requiring adjudication is the possible reference to two non-canonical writings in the book of Jude, which is discussed in chapter 18 below.

Dead Sea Scrolls The discovery of the Dead Sea Scrolls (DSS) began in 1947, constituted the major archeological find of the twentieth century, and greatly affected biblical and Jewish studies.[141] This discovery included both biblical manuscripts, which predate the previously earliest extant OT manuscripts by as many as a thousand years, and sectarian writings. The former include all OT books except for Esther, and the latter consist of writings such as the Damascus Document (CD); the Community Rule or Manual of Discipline (1QS); Thanksgiving Hymns (1QH); the War Scroll (1QM); the Habakkuk Pesher (1QpHab), and the Temple Scroll (11QTemple).[142] The biblical documents discovered at Qumran, including the famous Isaiah Scroll, have provided scholars with early readings of the Hebrew Scriptures. This has enabled them to make progress in ascertaining the original reading of specific OT passages.

In addition, the Dead Sea Scrolls provide a fascinating glimpse into the life of a Jewish sect that most likely arose in the Maccabean era around the middle of the second century BC and continued through the first Jewish revolt in AD 66–73.[143] The precise identity of the group(s) responsible for the Qumran literature remains uncertain. Most likely, the original impetus for the group's departure from Jerusalem and its withdrawal to the Dead Sea region was the corruption of the Jerusalem priesthood during the Maccabean period. Likely the Jewish high priest at the time of the community's formation is referred to in the Qumran literature as the "Wicked Priest" in contrast to the "Teacher of Righteousness" (see 1QpHab 1:13; 2:2; 8:7; 11:4–5), who presumably was the founder of the community.[144]

---

[140] See chap. 1.

[141] See especially J. C. Trever, *The Dead Sea Scrolls: A Personal Account* (Grand Rapids, MI: Eerdmans, 1977). Other helpful works include J. J. Collins, *Beyond the Qumran Community: The Sectarian Movement of the Dead Sea Scrolls* (Grand Rapids, MI: Eerdmans, 2009); J. C. VanderKam, *The Dead Sea Scrolls Today*, 2nd ed. (Grand Rapids, MI: Eerdmans, 2010); idem, *The Dead Sea Scrolls and the Bible* (Grand Rapids, MI: Eerdmans, 2012); the selected excerpts in Barrett, *New Testament Background*, chap. 9; and M. O. Wise, "Dead Sea Scrolls: General Introduction," in *DNTB*, 252–66.

[142] See F. García Martínez, *The Dead Sea Scrolls Study Edition*, 2 vols. (Grand Rapids, MI: Eerdmans, 2000); J. C. VanderKam, *An Introduction to Early Judaism* (Grand Rapids, MI: Eerdmans, 2000); L. H. Schiffman and J. C. VanderKam, eds., *Encyclopedia of the Dead Sea Scrolls*, 2 vols. (Oxford, NY: Oxford University Press, 2000); J. H. Charlesworth, ed., *The Bible and the Dead Sea Scrolls*, 3 vols. (Waco, TX: Baylor University Press, 2006); R. A. Kugler and E. M. Schuller, *The Dead Sea Scrolls at Fifty* (Atlanta, GA: Scholars Press, 1999); Schürer, *History of the Jewish People*, 380–469; Evans, *Ancient Texts for New Testament Studies*, chap. 3; and relevant entries in *DNTB*.

[143] See History above.

[144] As mentioned above, Schürer (*Jewish History in the Age of Jesus Christ*, 2:587), for example, suggests the Jewish high priest Jonathan was the person called the "Wicked Priest" in the Dead Sea Scrolls.

It is important to note that the Dead Sea Scrolls do not portray mainstream Judaism or Jewish attitudes during this era. This isolated community (or communities) was a sect that defined itself over against the Jerusalem establishment and engaged in its own distinctive religious and communal practices. These included a particular method of interpreting Scripture, the *pesher* method, which appropriated biblical material with reference to the community's contemporary situation (e.g., the "Habakkuk pesher").[145] Also, there is no reference to the NT or Jesus in the Dead Sea Scrolls. Thus, the Dead Sea Scrolls should be regarded as Jewish rather than Christian writings.[146]

The community's critical stance toward the corrupt Jerusalem priesthood thus provides an antecedent for Jesus's challenge of the corruption of the Jerusalem temple ritual during his ministry (Matt 21:12–17 and parallels; John 2:13–22). The community's use of Scripture also provides a fascinating precedent for John the Baptist's self-identification as "a voice crying in the wilderness" (taken from Isa 40:3). Interestingly, the Dead Sea community also appropriated the same passage of Scripture with reference to itself.[147] The community and the Dead Sea Scrolls provide a helpful background for understanding the NT in general and key NT figures such as John the Baptist and Jesus.[148]

Philo It has been said that "of all the Jews who have written in Greek, Philo of Alexandria is undoubtedly the greatest on the account of the breadth and richness of ideas, the number of his works and his brilliant literary qualities."[149] A contemporary of Jesus, Caius Julius Philo (ca. 20 BC–AD 50) was a prominent Jewish scholar and philosopher who lived in the important Egyptian city of Alexandria. He produced a variety of writings, including commentaries on the Torah, apologetic works, and philosophical treatises.[150] Arguably, his primary aim was to "show that Judaism, particularly as seen in the Scriptures of Judaism, constitutes a superior worldview,"[151] an aim he sought to accomplish by synthesizing Jewish tradition with Hellenistic philosophy through allegorical interpretation.[152] His surviving literary corpus—nearly fifty extant works of over seventy

---

[145] See R. N. Longenecker, *Biblical Exegesis in the Apostolic Period*, 2nd ed. (Grand Rapid, MI: Eerdmans, 1999), 24–30.

[146] Against erroneous claims in the tabloids and in popular literature such as D. Brown (*The Da Vinci Code* [New York, NY: Doubleday, 2003], 245), who claims that the Dead Sea Scrolls are among "the earliest Christian records."

[147] See A. J. Köstenberger, "John," in *Commentary on the New Testament Use of the Old Testament*, ed. G. K. Beale and D. A. Carson (Grand Rapids, MI: Baker, 2007), 421, 425–28.

[148] See J. Charlesworth, ed., *John and the Dead Sea Scrolls* (New York, NY: Crossroad, 1990); Kugler and Schuller, *Dead Sea Scrolls at Fifty*; Charlesworth, *Bible and the Dead Sea Scrolls*; VanderKam, *The Dead Sea Scrolls and the Bible*; and the helpful discussion in Evans, *Ancient Texts for New Testament Studies*, 3–6.

[149] C. Mondésert, "Philo of Alexandria," in *The Cambridge History of Judaism*, vol. 3: *The Early Roman Period*, ed. W. Horbury, W. D. Davies, and J. Sturdy (Cambridge, UK: Cambridge University Press, 1999), 877.

[150] The preferred translation of Philo for academic work is F. H. Colson, et al., *Philo*, 10 vols. plus 2 suppl., Loeb Classical Library (Cambridge, MA: Harvard University Press, 1929–1962). Note the ongoing commentary series: G. E. Sterling, gen. ed., *Philo of Alexandria Commentary Series* (Leiden, Netherlands: Brill, 2001–). Research on Philo may be followed via the scholarly journal *Studia Philonica Annual*.

[151] Evans, *Ancient Texts for New Testament Studies*, 168.

[152] Philo is generally painted as a (Middle) Platonist; Jerome noted sixteen centuries ago the common Greek proverb, "Either Plato philonizes or Philo platonizes" (*Vir. ill.* 11). Sterling's recent treatment nuances that estimation, noting that

attested—is valuable to students of the NT for the insights it provides into the history, ethics, moral philosophy, and interpretive practices of Hellenistic Judaism.[153] Debate continues on what, if any, direct influence Philo might have had on the writers of the NT,[154] but it is clear that "the NT authors do not . . . share the delight of Philo in allegorical interpretations."[155] In the NT corpus, John's Gospel, Hebrews, and the Pauline writings are most often studied in connection with Philo.[156]

Josephus It is difficult to overestimate the importance of the writings of Josephus (AD 37–ca. 100) for the student of the NT. Born into a priestly family in Jerusalem, Joseph ben Matthias led Galilean forces during the First Jewish Revolt against Rome. Surrendering to the Roman army in AD 67, he gained the favor of Roman General Vespasian by prophesying that he would become emperor—a prediction which shortly came to pass—and subsequently aided Rome in negotiations with the Jewish resistance. Traveling to Rome after the Jewish forces were quelled in AD 70, he lived comfortably under the patronage of Emperor Vespasian and his son Titus, taking on the Roman name Titus Flavius Josephus in honor of his patrons.

In Rome, Josephus published his four literary works.[157] (1) *Jewish War* narrates the First Jewish Revolt against Rome, from its roots in the second century BC to the destruction of the temple in AD 70 and subsequent mopping-up operations. (2) *Jewish Antiquities* reaches further back, giving a broad overview of Jewish history from the Genesis account of creation to the outbreak of war with Rome in AD 66. (3) Josephus's *Life* served as an

---

"his basic frame of thought was Platonic, but this was not an exclusive commitment for him. . . . Like most Hellenistic thinkers, he was eclectic," integrating Neopythagorean and Stoic concepts into his work as well. G. E. Sterling, "Philo," *The Eerdmans Dictionary of Early Judaism*, ed. J. J. Collins and D. C. Harlow (Grand Rapids, MI: Eerdmans, 2010), 1069.

[153] For a helpful topical index to Philo's writings, see K. Schenck, *A Brief Guide to Philo* (Louisville, KY: WJK, 2005), 119–38.

[154] For a competent treatment of this question, note F. Siegert, "Philo and the New Testament," in *The Cambridge Companion to Philo*, ed. A. Kamesar (Cambridge, UK: Cambridge University Press, 2009), 175–209; and the still-helpful D. T. Runia, "Philo and the New Testament," in *Philo in Early Christian Literature*, CRINT 3.3 (Minneapolis, MN: Fortress, 1993), 63–86. For a briefer summary, see T. Sealand, "Philo in the New Testament," in *The World of the New Testament: Cultural, Social, and Historical Contexts*, ed. J. B. Green and L. M. McDonald (Grand Rapids, MI: Baker, 2013), 408–12. Interestingly, Sealand notes the proposal that the Corinthian teaching of Apollos, who was from Alexandria (Acts 18:24), might have reflected Philonic influence (408).

[155] Sealand, "Philo in the New Testament," 409. Philo had a much stronger influence on early church fathers such as Clement of Alexandria and Origen.

[156] Ferguson, *Backgrounds of Early Christianity*, 482–83. Recent examples include V. Rabens, "Johannine Perspectives on Ethical Enabling in the Context of Stoic and Philonic Ethics," in *Rethinking the Ethics of John*, ed. J. G. van der Watt and R. Zimmermann, WUNT 291 (Tübingen, Germany: Mohr Siebeck, 2012), 114–39; S. N. Svendsen, *Allegory Transformed: The Appropriation of Philonic Hermeneutics in the Letter to the Hebrews*, WUNT 2/269 (Tübingen, Germany: Mohr Siebeck, 2009); and G. E. Sterling, "'The Image of God': Becoming Like God in Philo, Paul, and Early Christianity," in *Portraits of Jesus: Studies in Christology*, ed. S. E. Myers, WUNT 2/321 (Tübingen, Germany: Mohr Siebeck, 2012), 157–73.

[157] The standard translation of Josephus for academic work is H. St. J. Thackeray, et al., *Josephus*, 9 vols., LCL (Cambridge, MA: Harvard University Press, 1926–1965). The Greek text of Josephus's works and W. Whiston's eighteenth-century translation may be found in parallel at http://pace.mcmaster.ca/york/york/texts.htm. Note the ongoing commentary series: S. N. Mason, gen. ed., *Flavius Josephus: Translation and Commentary*, 10 vols. projected (Leiden, Netherlands: Brill, 1999–).

autobiographical appendix to *Jewish Antiquities*, concentrating on his military exploits. (4) *Against Apion* is an apologetic work defending Judaism against certain Roman detractors. In these four works Josephus provides a wealth of information about the background of first-century Judaism; in fact,

> it is Josephus that tells us almost everything we know about the non-Christian figures, groups, institutions, customs, geographical areas and events mentioned in the NT. He is the only surviving contemporary writer, for example, who describes John the Baptist, the Jewish high priests of the first century, the Pharisees and Sadducees, the various regions of Judea, Samaria and Galilee, Herod the Great, Agrippa II and Berenice, the Jerusalem temple renovated by Herod and its destruction in the revolt of 66-74, the census under Quirinius, Judas the Galilean, Theudas and the Egyptian prophet.[158]

Of particular interest is Josephus's testimony about John the Baptist, about James the brother of Jesus, and about Jesus himself.

> But to some of the Jews the destruction of Herod's army seemed to be divine vengeance, and certainly a just vengeance, for his treatment of John, surnamed the Baptist. For Herod had put him to death, though he was a good man and had exhorted the Jews to lead righteous lives, to practice justice towards their fellows and piety towards God, and so doing to join in baptism. In his view this was a necessary preliminary if baptism was to be acceptable to God. They must not employ it to gain pardon for whatever sins they had committed, but as a consecration of the body implying that the soul was already cleansed by right behavior. When others too joined the crowds about him, because they were aroused to the highest degree by his sermons, Herod became alarmed. Eloquence that had so great an effect on mankind might lead to some form of sedition, for it looked as if they would be guided by John in everything that they did. Herod decided therefore that it would be much better to strike first and be rid of him before his work led to an uprising, than to wait for an upheaval, get involved in a difficult situation and see his mistake. Though John, because of Herod's suspicions, was brought in chains to Machaerus, the stronghold that we have previously mentioned, and there put to death, yet the verdict of the Jews was that the destruction visited upon Herod's army was a vindication of John, since God saw fit to inflict such a blow on Herod.[159]
>
> [Ananus] convened the council of judges and brought before it the brother of Jesus—who was called "Christ"—whose name was James, and certain others. Accusing them of transgressing the law he delivered them up

---

[158] S. Mason, "Josephus," in *DNTB*, 596.

[159] *Ant.* 18.116–119 (Feldman, LCL).

for stoning. But those of the city considered to be fair-minded and strict concerning the laws were offended at this and sent to the king secretly urging him to order Ananus to take such actions no longer.[160]

SIDEBAR 2.4: MYSTERY RELIGIONS AND THE HISTORY-OF-RELIGIONS APPROACH

The history-of-religions approach is predicated upon an evolutionary model that views history primarily as the development of human religious consciousness rather than as the human response to actual divine revelation. If the possibility of divine revelation is ruled out at the very outset on a presuppositional level, it is no wonder that Christianity is construed in horizontal terms on a comparative religions scale. What is more, the question is not merely whether certain surface parallels exist between Christianity and non-Christian religions but in which direction the borrowing likely took place.

Caution with regard to apparent parallels is also needed since similarities are often more perceived than real. For example, while there are myths of dying and rising gods in pagan religions that may seem to resemble the NT teaching that Jesus died and rose from the dead, only Jesus brought redemption; only he was a recent historical figure; and only he died on a cross and rose bodily. Also, mystery religions were highly syncretistic and eclectic, incorporating a variety of elements from surrounding religions, while Christianity was exclusivistic, so that it is much more likely that mystery religions incorporated certain Christian features than that Christianity adapted pagan ones.

For reasons such as these it is much more likely that Christianity was grounded in the soil of Israel's religion as witnessed to in the OT, not in Hellenistic mystery religions.[1] This is strongly suggested by the extensive use of the OT by Jesus and many of the NT writers (including Paul), both in terms of explicit quotations and with regard to OT allusions and echoes.[2] What is more, the entire message of Jesus and the theology of the NT are built on the substructure of OT theology, binding the Testaments together along a salvation-historical continuum in which Jesus serves as the pivotal point of connection as the Messiah and fulfillment of OT predictions and typologies.

---

[1] See further the discussion of Judaism below.

[2] See especially Beale and Carson, *Commentary on the New Testament Use of the Old Testament*; see also Longenecker, *Biblical Exegesis in the Apostolic Period*; and D. A. Carson and H. G. M. Williamson, eds., *It Is Written: Scripture Citing Scripture* (Cambridge, UK: University Press, 1988). On echoes, see R. B. Hays, *Echoes of Scripture in the Letters of Paul* (New Haven, CT: Yale University Press, 1989).

About this time there lived Jesus, a wise man, if indeed one ought to call him a man. For he was one who performed surprising deeds and was a teacher of such people as accept the truth gladly. He won over many Jews and many of the Greeks. He was the Messiah. And when, upon the accusation of the principal men among us, Pilate had condemned him to a cross, those who

---

[160] *Ant.* 20.200 (Feldman, LCL).

> had first come to love him did not cease. He appeared to them spending a third day restored to life, for the prophets of God had foretold these things and a thousand other marvels about him. And the tribe of the Christians, so called after him, has still to this day not disappeared.[161]

The final excerpt, known as the *Testimonium Flavianum*, contains the earliest known reference to Jesus outside the NT, and its authenticity has been heavily disputed. Most likely Josephus did indeed speak of Jesus here, but his account was embellished at an early date to improve its apologetic value.[162]

THEOLOGY

The chapters on the various books of the NT investigate the specific background relevant for each book. At this stage it is helpful to provide a general backdrop of the first-century Jewish and Greco-Roman world in order to convey a general sense of the environment in which Jesus and the early church lived. The NT did not emerge in a vacuum but was rooted in a particular historical, cultural, and religious context. Understanding this context, at least in a general sense, puts the study of the NT into proper perspective. The following discussion presents the most significant background issues for the study of the NT: (1) Judaism; (2) paganism; (3) emperor worship; (4) mystery religions; (5) superstition and syncretism; (6) Gnosticism; and (7) philosophy.

Judaism

The first—and in many ways the most important—element of NT background is Judaism, which made several important contributions to early Christianity. In light of the importance of Judaism as a background for the study of the NT, the following treatment of Judaism is more extensive than the following sections. This section includes monotheism, the synagogue, the temple, the religious calendar, rabbinic schools, proselytes and God-fearers, messianism, and Jewish sects and institutions.[163]

Monotheism The most distinguishing mark of Judaism was that it held to *monotheism*, a firm commitment to the belief in one God as taught in the OT and proclaimed in the *Shema* (Hb. "Hear"): "Hear, O Israel: The Lord our God is one Lord" (Deut 6:4 KJV).[164]

---

[161] *Ant.* 18.3.3 (Feldman, LCL).

[162] See the discussion in chapter 3 below. Origen knows of Josephus, but notes that Josephus did not believe in Jesus as the Christ (*Cels.* 1.47; *Comm. Matt.* 10.17), an estimation at odds with the way the *Testimonium* presently reads. In addition, if Josephus understood Jesus to be the Messiah, it seems likely that he would have discussed him at other points in his works. See the important essay by J. P. Meier, "Jesus in Josephus: A Modest Proposal," *CBQ* 52 (1990): 72-103; and the detailed study by A. Whealey, *Josephus on Jesus: The Testimonium Flavianum Controversy from Late Antiquity to Modern Times* (Studies in Biblical Literature 36; New York, NY: Peter Lang, 2003).

[163] For general surveys and additional sources on Judaism, see J. C. VanderKam, "Judaism in the Land of Israel," 57–76; E. S. Gruen, "Judaism in the Diaspora," 77–96; M. Pucci Ben Zeev, "Jews among Greeks and Romans," 237–56; and D. C. Harlow, "Early Judaism and Early Christianity," *EDEJ*, 257–78.

[164] See A. J. Köstenberger and S. R. Swain, *Father, Son and Spirit: The Trinity and John's Gospel*, NSBT 24 (Downers Grove, IL: InterVarsity, 2008), chap. 1; and C. J. H. Wright, *The Mission of God: Unlocking the Bible's Grand Narrative* (Downers

The first two of the Ten Commandments (the Decalogue) forbade Israelites from worshipping other gods (Exod 20:2–6; Deut 5:6–10).

Monotheism set Israel apart from the polytheistic beliefs and practices of her pagan neighbors, including the Greco-Roman pantheon. This commitment became an important distinguishing characteristic of Jewish religion in a polytheistic environment and was recognized as a hallmark of the Jewish faith by Greco-Roman historians such as Tacitus, who writes, "The Jews conceive of one God only" (*Hist.* 5.5).

The Synagogue Although the origins of the synagogue are uncertain, its importance for Jewish life and for the early church is undisputed.[165] The synagogue provided the early church with a pattern in both liturgy (with its prayers, psalms, Scripture readings, sermons, and blessings or benedictions) and leadership (with its synagogue ruler, board of elders, and attendant).[166] For Jesus, Paul, and the early Christian mission, the synagogue provided a natural setting for proclaiming salvation through faith in Jesus as the Messiah (Luke 4:16–30; John 6:30–59; 18:20; Acts 13:13–52). The synagogue was also of critical importance for Jews in the Diaspora (Dispersion), especially after the destruction of the temple in AD 70.

The Temple Another important feature of Judaism was the Jerusalem temple,[167] which served as a vital symbol of national and religious unity. The original temple built by Solomon (1 Kings 5–8) was destroyed by the Babylonians in the sixth century BC. After the exile a new temple was built by Zerubbabel (Ezra 3; Haggai 1–2; Zechariah 4). The temple area and temple building included outer and inner courts and various rooms, including the holy place and the holy of holies. Later it was renovated and greatly expanded by Herod the Great, with the restoration of the building being completed in 18 BC and that of the outer courts in AD 64.

In the first century the temple was known for its magnificent appearance (Matt 24:1–2 and parallels; Josephus, *J.W.* 5.222–24; see *b. B. Bat.* 4a). Surrounded by porticoes, the temple consisted of an outer court (the Court of the Gentiles) and an inner court, made up of the Court of Women on the east and the Inner Court on the west. The first room was the holy place, which was separated from the outside by a heavy veil. The innermost room, the holy of holies, was separated from the holy place by another heavy veil. The high priest entered it but once a year on the Day of Atonement.

In Jesus's day, the temple, once the glorious symbol of God's dwelling with his people, had degenerated into a place of commerce and perfunctory ritual (John 2:14–16). With the destruction of the temple in the year 70, Judaism was forced to adjust its sacrificial and

Grove, IL: InterVarsity, 2006), "Part II: The God of Mission," especially 71–74 (both with further bibliographic references).

[165] See B. Chilton and E. Yamauchi, "Synagogues," in *DNTB*, 1145–53; L. I. Levine, "Synagogues," in *EDEJ*, 1260–71.

[166] See Schürer, *History of the Jewish People*, 2:415–63; Ferguson, *Backgrounds of Early Christianity*, 576–82.

[167] See Schürer, *History of the Jewish People*, 2:237–313; Ferguson, *Backgrounds of Early Christianity*, 562–65; B. Chilton, P. W. Comfort, and M. O. Wise, "Temple, Jewish," in *DNTB*, 1167–83; D. Instone-Brewer, "Temple and Priesthood," in *The World of the New Testament*, 197–206; and A. J. Köstenberger, "John," in *Zondervan Illustrated Bible Backgrounds Commentary*, ed. C. A. Arnold (Grand Rapids, MI: Zondervan, 2002), 2:30–31.

liturgical practices because the central element of its entire system of worship had been removed. In response to the loss of the temple, the Pharisees founded a rabbinic school at Javneh (Jamnia), while the Sadducees disappeared from the scene, as did the Essenes and the Zealots.

The Religious Calendar The OT Jewish religious calendar provides an important backdrop for the NT account of Jesus's life and for worship in the early church.[168] The institution of many important holy days in the life of Israel—including the Sabbath, Passover, the Day of Atonement—is recorded in Leviticus 23, and references to these festivals pervade the entire OT. These festivals dominated the religious life of observant Jews throughout the Second Temple period and beyond.

Table 2.6: Jewish Festivals

The Jewish religious calendar began in March/April and included the following festivals:
1. Passover (Exod 12:1–14; Lev 23:5; Num 9:1–14; 28:16; Deut 16:1–7)
2. Unleavened Bread (Exod 12:15–20; 13:3–10; 23:15; 34:18; Lev 23:6–8; Num 28:17–25; Deut 16:3–4,8), both celebrated at the beginning of wheat harvest (March/April) and commemorating God's deliverance of Israel at the time of the exodus
3. The Feast of Firstfruits (Lev 23:9–14)
4. The Feast of Weeks or Pentecost (Exod 23:16; 34:22; Lev 23:15–21; Num 28:26–31; Deut 16:9–12), celebrated at the end of the wheat harvest (May/June)
5. Trumpets or *Rosh Hashanah* (Lev 23:23–25; Num 29:1–6), commemorating the beginning of the civil year (September/October)
6. The Day of Atonement or *Yom Kippur* (Lev 16; 23:26–32; Num 29:7–11), a day of national repentance (September/October; technically not a feast)
7. Tabernacles or Booths or Ingathering (Exod 23:16; 34:22; Lev 23:33–36, 39–43; Num 29:12–34; Deut 16:13–15; Zech 14:16–19), commemorating the Israelites' living in tents in the wilderness after the exodus (September/October)
8. Lights or Dedication or *Hanukkah* (John 12:22), celebrating the rededication of the temple by Judas Maccabeus in 165 or 164 BC (December 25) after it had been desecrated by Antiochus Epiphanes
9. Purim (Esth 9:18–32), commemorating the deliverance of the Jews in the time of Esther (February/March).

Rabbinic Schools Another important element of Jewish background for the study of Jesus's ministry is that of the various rabbinic schools that existed in first-century Palestine. The rabbis in these schools sought to interpret the OT and as a result created a large body of oral tradition.[169] They maintained that the oral law could be traced back to Moses at

---

[168] See Schürer, *History of the Jewish People*, 2:521–27; B. D. Chilton, "Festivals and Holy Days: Jewish," 371–78; and S. Westerholm and C. A. Evans, "Sabbath," 1031–35, both in *DNTB*.

[169] See Barrett, *New Testament Background*, chap. 8; and B. D. Chilton, "Rabbis," in *DNTB*, 914–16. Compare H. L. Strack and G. Stemberger, *Introduction to the Talmud and Midrash*, trans. M. Bockmuehl, 2nd ed. (Minneapolis, MN: Fortress, 1996); and Schürer, *History of the Jewish People*, 2:314–80.

Mount Sinai and that it superseded the OT itself. Jesus, who charged them with revoking God's word because of their tradition (Matt 15:6), excoriated them for this:

> The scribes and the Pharisees are seated in the chair of Moses. Therefore do whatever they tell you and observe it. But don't do what they do, because they don't practice what they teach. They tie up heavy loads that are hard to carry and put them on people's shoulders, but they themselves aren't willing to lift a finger to move them. They do everything to be observed by others: They enlarge their phylacteries and lengthen their tassels. They love the place of honor at banquets, the front seats in the synagogues, greetings in the marketplaces, and to be called "Rabbi" by people (Matt 23:1–7; cf. Mark 7:1–13).

The Mishnah, a collection of Jewish teachings compiled around AD 200, attests to famous schools of rabbinic interpretation of the OT in the first and subsequent centuries.[170] Understanding this background proves helpful, for example, when one reads the following question posed by the Pharisees to Jesus: "Is it lawful for a man to divorce his wife on any grounds?" (Matt 19:3). The rabbinic dispute in this case revolved around the proper interpretation of the reference to "something indecent" in Deuteronomy 24:1, dealing with legitimate grounds for divorce. The stricter rabbinic school limited this offense to sexual impropriety, while the more liberal school extended it to a variety of lesser infractions as well. In response, Jesus affirmed the permanence of marriage on the basis of Genesis 2:24.[171]

Proselytes and God-Fearers Judaism attracted large numbers of proselytes (full converts to Judaism who observed the Sabbath, food laws, and male circumcision) and God-fearers (who only accepted the moral teachings and general religious practices of Judaism without submitting to circumcision).[172] These converts were attracted to Jewish monotheism and moral teaching, left behind pagan idolatry, and aligned themselves with the Jewish religion and way of life, though with varying degrees of conformity.

The NT, especially the Gospels and Acts, makes repeated references to proselytes and God-fearers.[173] God-fearers who approached Jesus in order to request healings include a Roman centurion (Matt 8:5–13 and parallels) and a royal official (John 4:46–54). A seminal account involving a God-fearer is that of Cornelius (Acts 10). The inclusion of

---

[170] See J. Neusner, "Rabbinic Literature: Mishnah and Tosefta," in *DNTB*, 893–97; S. J. D. Cohen, "Mishnah," in *EDEJ*, 960–61.

[171] See A Köstenberger (with D. W. Jones), *God, Marriage, and Family: Rebuilding the Biblical Foundation*, 2nd ed. (Wheaton, IL: Crossway, 2010), chap. 11, especially 224–25.

[172] See Ferguson, *Backgrounds of Early Christianity*, 546–51; S. McKnight, "Proselytism and Godfearers," in *DNTB*, 835–47.

[173] The word *theosebeis* ("God-fearer" or "worshipper of God") occurs in Acts 10:2, 22, 35; 13:6, 26; the related term *sebomenoi* ("worshipper[s] of God") is found in Acts 13:43, 50; 16:14; 17:4, 17; 18:7. See J. E. Burns, "God-fearers," in *EDEJ*, 681–82.

Gentiles on equal terms with Jews in the new messianic community was a revolutionary concept for many first-century Jews, including many early Christians (Acts 10:9–16; see 1 Cor 12:13; Gal 2:11–21; 3:28).

Jewish Theology There is no extant "systematic theology" of Judaism, only indications of Jewish beliefs on different topics in the Mishnah and the Talmuds.[174] Jewish theology took its starting point, not in mythology, mysticism, or philosophical speculation, but in the acts of God in history recorded in the Hebrew Scriptures (the OT). Many Jewish beliefs are significant as NT background, including those regarding the end-times, the nature of man, and the coming of the Messiah.

With regard to the end-times, Jews typically embraced the teaching of "two ages," whereby "the present (evil) age" preceded the "days of the Messiah" or "the Day of the LORD," inaugurating "the coming age." This is clearly seen in the Gospels.[175] Paradoxically, the Gospels indicate that with Jesus's coming, the "age to come" has already begun. Hence, Jesus taught that God's kingdom was already present (Luke 17:21), and those who believed in him already had eternal life (John 3:16; 10:10).

Another characteristic belief among the Jews, inferred from Genesis 2:7, was that God created man with a "good" and an "evil" impulse (*yetzer tov* and *yetzer ra*). The former was viewed as the moral conscience, the inner voice that reminded people of God's law when they desired to partake in the forbidden; the latter was essentially construed as self-centeredness.

Messianism One of the most important aspects of Jewish theology was messianism, that is, various beliefs regarding a coming figure called the "Messiah" or "Anointed One." Most Jews were looking for one, and in some cases several, Messiah(s).[176] Messianic expectations were anything but uniform, as the NT and Second Temple literature attest.[177] Some believed on the basis of Micah 5:2 that the Messiah was to be born in Bethlehem (Matt 2:5–6; see John 7:41–42); others held that the Messiah's origins would be shrouded in mystery (John 7:27; see Dan 7:13).

---

[174] See Ferguson (*Backgrounds of Early Christianity*, 537–61), who discusses Jewish beliefs in one God; Israel, the chosen people; Torah, tradition, and Scripture; Jewish mysticism; proselytes and God-fearers; messianism; the afterlife; festivals and holy days; and daily devotions. Compare J. Neusner, "Rabbinic Literature: Mishnah and Tosefta," 893–97; and H. Maccoby, "Rabbinic Literature: Talmud," 897–902, both in *DNTB*.

[175] See G. E. Ladd, *A Theology of the New Testament*, rev. ed., ed. D. A. Hagner (Grand Rapids, MI: Eerdmans, 1993), 54–67.

[176] See especially W. Horbury, *Jewish Messianism and the Cult of Christ* (London, UK: SCM, 1998); J. H. Charlesworth, ed., *The Messiah: Developments in Earliest Judaism and Christianity* (Minneapolis, MN: Fortress, 1987); J. Neusner, W. S. Green, and E. Frerichs, *Judaisms and Their Messiahs at the Turn of the Christian Era* (Cambridge, UK: Cambridge University Press, 1988); S. E. Porter, ed., *The Messiah in the Old and New Testaments* (Grand Rapids, MI: Eerdmans, 2007); J. J. Collins, *The Scepter and the Star: Messianism in Light of the Dead Sea Scrolls*, 2nd ed. (Grand Rapids, MI: Eerdmans, 2010); C. A. Evans, "Messianism," in *DNTB*, 698–707; and K. E. Pomykala, "Messianism," in *EDEJ*, 938–42.

[177] See J. A. Fitzmyer, *The One Who Is to Come* (Grand Rapids, MI: Eerdmans, 2007), 89–92; Schürer, *History of the Jewish People*, 2:488–545; Ferguson, *Backgrounds of Early Christianity*, 551–54.

The Dead Sea community apparently expected two separate Messiahs, a priestly one and a royal one (1QS 9:11).[178] Few (if any) expected that the Messiah would have to suffer (though this is suggested by Isa 52:13–53:12; see Matt 16:21–23 and parallels; John 12:34).[179] Most conceived of the Messiah in nationalistic terms, expecting him to establish an earthly rule with Israel at its center and delivering the Jews from their foreign oppressors (see John 1:49; 6:14; 12:12–13).

Jewish Sects and Other Groups of People The variety of sects in Palestine demonstrates that first-century Judaism was anything but monolithic. Several prominent Jewish sects that appear in the Gospels have their origin in the Maccabean period (mid-second century BC).[180] The main parties include (1) the Pharisees; (2) the Sadducees; (3) the Essenes; and (4) the Zealots.[181] The Pharisees, Jesus's primary antagonists, most likely originated from the God-fearing Hasidim, who practiced a form of righteousness that observed a complex system of oral traditions in an effort to flesh out the implications of scriptural commands for everyday life.[182] Unlike the Sadducees, the Pharisees believed in the resurrection and in angels (Acts 23:8).

The Sadducees traced their beginnings back to the Hasmonean period (late second century BC; Josephus, *J.W.* 2.404–15).[183] Their demise took place with the destruction of the Jerusalem temple in AD 70.[184] As the ruling aristocracy in Jerusalem, they had a vested interest in maintaining the status quo and allied themselves with the foreign overlords in Palestine. They held a majority on the Sanhedrin (the Jewish ruling council), accepted only the Pentateuch as Scripture, denied the future resurrection, and eschewed a belief in angels (Acts 23:8). The Sadducees allied themselves with the Pharisees to have Jesus crucified.

The Essenes, like the Pharisees, probably originated with the Hasidim, from whom they later separated (1 Macc 2:42; 7:13; Josephus, *J.W.* 2.555–97).[185] The Essenes were a group of pious and zealous Jews who participated with the Maccabees in a revolt against

---

[178] See C. Evans and P. W. Flint, *Eschatology, Messianism, and the Dead Sea Scrolls* (Grand Rapids, MI: Eerdmans, 1997); Schürer, *History of the Jewish People*, 2:550–54.

[179] See B. Janowski and P. Stuhlmacher, eds., *The Suffering Servant: Isaiah 53 in Jewish and Christian Sources*, trans. D. P. Bailey (Grand Rapids, MI: Eerdmans, 2004); Schürer, *History of the Jewish People*, 2:547–49.

[180] See "History" above; cf. S. Mason, "Theologies and Sects, Jewish," in *DNTB*, 1221–30.

[181] Josephus (*Jewish War* 2.119–20) referred to the first three of these: "Jewish philosophy, in fact, takes three forms. The followers of the first school are called Pharisees, of the second Sadducees, of the third Essenes." He also mentioned a fourth philosophy (*Jewish War* 2.108; *Ant.* 18.23), most likely the Zealots. See Schürer, *History of the Jewish People*, 2:599; Barrett, *New Testament Background*, 158–59; M. Lee-Barnewall, "Pharisees, Sadducees, and Essenes," in *The World of the New Testament*, 217–27; and Ferguson, *Backgrounds of Early Christianity*, 513–36, who also mentioned the Herodians and the Samaritans.

[182] See "History" above; cf. Schürer, *History of the Jewish People*, 2:388–403; and S. Mason, "Pharisees," in *DNTB*, 782–87.

[183] See G. G. Porton, "Sadducees," in *DNTB*, 1050–52.

[184] As a result, they are not mentioned in John's Gospel, which most likely was written after AD 70. See chap. 7 below in this volume.

[185] See Schürer, *History of the Jewish People*, 2:585–95; T. Beall, "Essenes," in *DNTB*, 342–48; J. Frey, "Essenes," in *EDEJ*, 599–602.

the Seleucids but later rejected the Maccabean corruption of the Jerusalem priesthood and temple system.[186] They may have formed the nucleus of the Dead Sea community that withdrew from Jerusalem to the desert in order to practice a form of communal living and pious religious observance. They engaged in the study of Scripture, ritual baths and washings, and worship liturgy; believed that they were the chosen end-time community; and some refrained from marriage. The Essenes are not mentioned in the NT.

The Zealots are first attested during the reign of Herod the Great (ca. 6 BC; Josephus, *J.W.* 2.598–606).[187] They ceased to exist as a movement after the fall of Masada, a Jewish fortress near the Dead Sea, at the end of the first Jewish revolt in the year 73. The Zealots resisted the foreign occupation of Palestine by the Romans and opposed payment of tribute or taxes to pagan emperors, which they held was owed only to God. They were fiercely loyal to Jewish traditions and stood opposed to any foreign influence in Palestine. Among them may have been the *sicarii*, a group of resistance fighters who concealed short daggers under their cloaks and murdered people in an effort to destabilize the political climate in the Holy Land.[188] One of Jesus's followers appears to have been a Zealot (Simon the Zealot; Matt 10:4).

The common people of Palestine, the "people of the land" (Hb. *am haarets*), were scorned by the religious leaders who considered them ignorant of the intricacies of their oral tradition and inadequately concerned with ritualistic piety and law observance. Typical is the Pharisees' attitude conveyed by the statement in John's Gospel: "But this crowd, which doesn't know the law, is accursed!" (7:49). It is also important to note the large number of Jews in the Diaspora outside of Palestine (see John 7:35). They worshipped in their synagogues and attracted a considerable number of proselytes and God-fearers.[189]

The Sanhedrin Variously called "Council," "the rulers," "chief priests, elders, and scribes," or a combination thereof in the NT, the Sanhedrin was the Jewish supreme council in all religious and political matters.[190] Ideally, it consisted of seventy members on the precedent of the elders appointed by Moses at the advice of Jethro, his father-in-law (Exodus 18), though this may not always have been their actual number. The Sanhedrin was convened by the high priest.[191] While Palestine was ruled by the Roman governor who reported to the emperor in Rome, the Jews enjoyed a considerable degree of religious and political autonomy in Jesus's day.

---

[186] See the historical survey of the Second Temple period above in this chapter.

[187] See M. Hengel, *The Zealots*, 2nd ed. (Edinburgh, Scotland: T&T Clark, 1977); cf. W. J. Heard and C. A. Evans, "Revolutionary Movements, Jewish," in *DNTB*, 936–47, especially 945–46.

[188] See Heard and Evans, "Revolutionary Movements," 944–45.

[189] See the discussion of proselytes and God-fearers above.

[190] See especially Schürer, *History of the Jewish People*, 2:199–226; Ferguson, *Backgrounds of Early Christianity*, 567–70; K. D. Litwak, "Synagogue and Sanhedrin," in *The World of the New Testament*, 268–71; and G. H. Twelftree, "Sanhedrin," in *DNTB*, 1061–65. The name "Sanhedrin" is from *synedrion*, "assembly."

[191] For a detailed discussion of Jewish high priests appointed by Herod the Great and his successors, see Schürer, *History of the Jewish People*, 2:229–36.

Paganism

People in the ancient world were profoundly religious whether they embraced the religion of Israel or Christianity.[192] Thus, when Paul healed a lame man in Lystra, the crowds exclaimed,

> "The gods have come down to us in human form!" Barnabas they called Zeus, and Paul, Hermes, because he was the chief speaker. The priest of Zeus, whose temple was just outside the town, brought bulls and wreaths to the gates because he intended, with the crowds, to offer sacrifice (Acts 14:11–13).

Greek mythology featured Zeus as the head of the hierarchy of gods. Apollos, son of Zeus, was cast as one who inspired poets and prophets. Roman religion appropriated much of the Greek pantheon, identifying Roman gods with Greek ones (Jupiter=Zeus, Venus=Aphrodite, etc.). The Roman emperor himself served as high priest *(pontifex maximus)*, merging the political and religious realms.

Emperor Worship

Following the common practice of ascribing divinity to rulers,[193] the Roman Senate instituted the emperor cult by deifying Augustus (31 BC–AD 14) and subsequent emperors after his death. Caligula (AD 37–41), Nero (AD 54–68), and Domitian (AD 81–96) claimed divinity while still living. Vespasian (AD 69–79) treated the emperor cult lightly and even joked when dying: "I think I am becoming a god."[194] Domitian, on the other hand, claimed the title *dominus et deus* ("lord and god"), to which the fourth evangelist may allude in his citation of Thomas's confession of Jesus as "my Lord and my God!" (John 20:28).[195] Emperor worship provides especially important background to the book of Revelation, which in all likelihood was written during the persecution of Christians under Nero or Domitian.[196]

Mystery Religions

The ancient world in the first few centuries of the Christian era was replete with "mystery religions," various cults that conceived of the heart of religion as mystical union with the divine.[197] There were Greek, Egyptian, and Oriental mystery religions, including the cults of Eleusis, Mithras, Isis, Dionysus, Cybele, and other local cults. Secret initiatory

---

[192] N. C. Croy, "Religion, Personal," in *DNTB*, 926–31, who discusses oracles, dreams, divination, prayer, magic, miracles, healing, superstition, and astrology, among other topics. Compare J. D. Charles, "Pagan Sources in the New Testament," in *DNTB*, 756–63.

[193] See N. Perrin, "The Imperial Cult," in *The World of the New Testament*, 124–34.

[194] Suetonius, *Vespasian* 23. See Ferguson, *Backgrounds of Early Christianity*, 37.

[195] Ibid., 38.

[196] See the discussion of the emperor cult in chap. 20.

[197] See Barrett, *New Testament Background*, chap. 6; Ferguson, *Backgrounds of Early Christianity*, 251–300; and M. Meyer, "Mysteries," in *DNTB*, 720–25; cf. A. J. Köstenberger, "The Mystery of Christ and the Church: Head and Body, 'One Flesh,'" *TrinJ* 12 NS (1991): 80–81.

rites involved ceremonial washings, sacred meals, intoxication, and emotional frenzies. The purpose of these rites was to enter into union with the deity. One such worshipper was Apuleius, a convert to the Mithras cult. The following excerpt illustrates the nature of these ancient mystery cults:

> In a dark night she appeared to me in a vision, declaring in words not dark that the day was come which I had wished for so long. . . . When I had heard these and the other divine commandments of the high goddess, I greatly rejoiced, and arose before day to speak with the great priest, whom I fortuned to espy coming out of his chamber. . . .
>
> Thereupon the old man took me by the hand, and led me courteously to the gate of the great temple, where, after that it was religiously opened, he made a solemn celebration, and after the morning sacrifice was ended, he brought out of the secret place of the temple certain books written with unknown characters. . . . Then he brought me, when he found that the time was at hand, to the next baths, accompanied with all the religious sort, and demanding pardon of the gods, washed me and purified my body according to the custom; after this, when two parts of the day was gone, he brought me back again to the temple and presented me before the feet of the goddess, giving me a charge of certain secret things unlawful to be uttered. . . .
>
> When morning came and that the solemnities were finished, I came forth sanctified with twelve stoles and in a religious habit. . . . In my right hand I carried a lighted torch, and a garland of flowers was upon my head, with white palm-leaves sprouting out on every side like rays; thus I was adorned like unto the sun, and made in fashion of an image, when the curtains were drawn aside and all the people compassed about to behold me. . . . [After this the initiate recites a lengthy prayer to the goddess.]
>
> When I ended my oration to the great goddess, I went to embrace the great priest Mithras, now my spiritual father, clinging upon his neck and kissing him often, and demanding his pardon, considering I was unable to recompense the good which he had done me: and after much talk and great greetings and thanks I departed from him straight to visit my parents and friends, after that I had been so long absent. . . . [The initiate voyages to Rome.] And the greatest desire which I had there was daily to make my prayers to the sovereign goddess Isis, who, by reason of the place where her temple was built, was called Campensis, and continually is adored of the people of Rome: her minister and worshipper was I, a stranger to her church, but not unknown to her religion.[198]

In the early part of the twentieth century, the history-of-religions school sought to establish parallels between these mystery cults and early Christianity, claiming that the latter

[198] The selection is from Barrett, *New Testament Background*, 127–29.

borrowed key elements of its religion from the larger Greco-Roman world.[199] For example, some argued that baptism was a Christian initiatory rite patterned after pagan initiation ceremonies, suggesting that the Lord's Supper was the equivalent of pagan sacred meals. Also, Christian beliefs at times appear to resemble elements found in pagan religions. However, there is little, if any, evidence that Christian practices are derived from other religions.[200]

Superstition and Syncretism

The ancient world was filled with superstition and syncretism, an eclectic mix of religious practices.[201] These practices included magic, horoscopes, oracles, and augury (the prediction of future events by observing birds' flight patterns). Many homes had household idols with images of gods. A letter addressed by a distressed father to an oracle illustrates the superstitious climate of this period:

> O Lord Sarapis Helios, beneficent one. [Say] whether it is fitting that Phanias my son and his wife should not agree now with his father, but oppose him and not make a contract. Tell me this truly. Goodbye.[202]

The book of Acts features numerous examples of superstition and syncretism in the first-century world. In Samaria, Simon the sorcerer, who had practiced magic, offered the apostles money so he too could confer the Holy Spirit on others (Acts 8:9–24). On the island of Cyprus, Elymas the magician opposed Barnabas and Paul (Acts 13:7). In Ephesus some who had practiced magical arts publicly burned their books (Acts 19:19). In Malta, when people saw a viper hanging on Paul's hand, they speculated that he was a murderer, but when he shook the snake into the fire and was unharmed, they changed their minds and concluded that he was a god (Acts 28:3–6).

Gnosticism

Gnosticism (from Gk. *gnōsis*, "knowledge") is rooted in the Platonic dualism that sharply distinguished between the invisible world of ideas and the visible world of matter.[203] Generally, this worldview equated matter with evil and viewed only the spirit realm as good. It is important to note that the NT era only documents an incipient form of

---

[199] See W. Bousset, *Kyrios Christos*, trans. J. E. Steely (Nashville, TN: Abingdon, 1970 [1913]); and R. Reitzenstein, *Hellenistic Mystery-Religions*, trans. J. E. Steely (Pittsburgh, PA: Pickwick, 1978 [1910]). Compare the discussion in S. Neill and T. Wright, *The Interpretation of the New Testament 1861–1986*, 2nd ed. (Oxford, NY: Oxford University Press, 1988), 165–85; and the sidebar below.

[200] See further the discussion of Gnosticism below.

[201] See B. W. R. Pearson, "Domestic Religion and Practices," in *DNTB*, 298–302.

[202] P. Oxy 1148, first century AD (A. S. Hunt and C. C. Edgar, *Select Papyri*, LCL [Cambridge, MA: Harvard University Press, 1932], 1:437).

[203] See Ferguson, *Backgrounds of Early Christianity*, 300–18; Neill and Wright, *Interpretation of the New Testament*, 185–95.

Gnosticism. Full-fledged Gnosticism did not emerge until the second century—well after the NT period.[204]

Gnostic thought, best attested in the Nag Hammadi Library (including the Gospel of Thomas) discovered in the 1940s in Egypt, led to the following opposing phenomena: (1) *asceticism*, the suppression of bodily passions because of their connection with evil matter; (2) *libertinism*, the indulgence of bodily passions because of the insignificance of matter. Some argued that if things done in the body do not matter, then the implication is that the body and its activities should be suppressed while the life of the spirit is nurtured. Others, on the opposite end of the spectrum, thought an immoral lifestyle could be pursued while a person claimed to be spiritual at the same time.

From its inception Gnosticism constituted the first serious heretical threat to Christianity. As a result of the gnostic dichotomization between matter and spirit, the notion of a *bodily resurrection* was abhorrent to the gnostics since matter was regarded as evil. Instead, the immortality of the soul was more desirable and was pursued through the knowledge and practice of secret religious activities. Also, as a result of this dichotomization, *human sinfulness* was denied; thus, the need for *redemption* became moot.

Although what is commonly called Gnosticism today did not exist in the first century, there may be foreshadows of it in the NT. For instance, in a possible reference to gnostic-type thought, Paul warned Timothy to avoid "irreverent, empty speech and contradictions from what is falsely called 'knowledge' [*gnōsis*]." (1 Tim 6:20). Paul also denounced false teachers who forbade marriage and demanded abstinence from certain foods, maintaining that, to the contrary, everything God created was good (1 Tim 4:1–5; see 1 Tim 2:15). He also condemned the Colossian heresy that advocated false asceticism and legalism (Col 2:4–23; see 1 Tim 4:7–8), though this may have been a unique form of syncretism.

Philosophy

Greek philosophy pervaded the first-century Mediterranean world as well.[205] The three most popular philosophies were (1) Epicureanism, (2) Stoicism, and (3) Cynicism. Epicureanism taught that pleasure (in the sense of happiness, not necessarily sensual pleasure) was the chief good in life.[206] This led to an advocacy of "hedonism," the pursuit of pleasure as a matter of ethical principle: "Let us eat and drink for tomorrow we die" (1 Cor 15:32; see Isa 22:13).

---

[204] The classic treatment is E. Yamauchi, *Pre-Christian Gnosticism: A Survey of the Proposed Evidences*, 2nd ed. (Grand Rapids, MI: Eerdmans, 1983 [1973]). See also idem, "Gnosticism," in *DNTB*, 414–18; C. B. Smith, *No Longer Jews: The Search for Christian Origins* (Peabody, MA: Hendrickson, 2004); and Barrett, *New Testament Background*, chap. 5. For a comprehensive resource, see W. J. Hanegraaff, ed., *Dictionary of Gnosis & Western Esotericism*, 2 vols. (Leiden, Netherlands: Brill, 2005).

[205] See J. M. Dillon, "Philosophy," in *DNTB*, 793–96.

[206] See Barrett, *New Testament Background*, 78–81; Ferguson, *Backgrounds of Early Christianity*, 370–79; and N. C. Croy, "Epicureanism," in *DNTB*, 324–27.

Stoicism taught the dutiful acceptance of one's fate—a form of fatalism—as determined by impersonal reason ruling the universe.[207] People were enjoined to face their destiny "stoically," that is, without emotion. In Athens, Paul encountered both Epicurean and Stoic philosophers who arrogantly considered him to be a pseudo-intellectual (Acts17:18). These philosophers mistakenly thought Paul believed "resurrection" to be a "foreign deity," indicating how foreign the Christian teaching of Jesus's bodily resurrection sounded to those steeped in Greek philosophy.

Advocates of Cynicism[208] were itinerant preachers who had forsaken worldly pursuits. They taught that simplicity was life's supreme virtue and that people ought to cultivate it instead of popular pursuits. In reality, superstition and syncretism largely prevailed among the masses.[209] Some, such as John Dominic Crossan and proponents of the "Jesus Seminar," have maintained on the basis of superficial similarities (such as Jesus's simple lifestyle and his itinerant ministry) that Jesus was a Cynic.[210] Yet this is unlikely if for no other reason than that Cynicism is not attested in first-century Palestine.

The preceding discussion illustrates that people in the first century adhered to various worldviews that the early Christians sought to engage. Similarly, many still adhere to these views today, though in modified forms. A basic knowledge of these philosophies—and insights into how the early Christians confronted them with the gospel—is therefore helpful not only for interpreting the NT documents but also for identifying ways in which the church might engage modern "Epicureans," "Stoics," and "Cynics."

CONCLUSION

It was the purpose of this chapter to lay the foundation for the study of the NT in the remainder of this volume. By acquiring a basic understanding of historical and political developments prior to the NT period as well as a familiarity with Second Temple literature and prevalent theological and philosophical currents, students will be equipped for dealing with each of the writings of the NT. That study occupies the remainder of this volume.

STUDY QUESTIONS

1. What is the significance of the following events or books for the NT?
   a. The Assyrian exile of Israel (the northern kingdom)
   b. The Babylonian exile of Judah (the southern kingdom)
   c. The book of Malachi
   d. The conquests of Alexander the Great
2. Which two Greek houses were in charge of Palestine from 320–167 BC?

---

[207] See Barrett, *New Testament Background*, 65–77; Ferguson, *Backgrounds of Early Christianity*, 354–69; and J. C. Thom, "Stoicism," in *DNTB*, 1139–42.

[208] See Barrett, *New Testament Background*, 81–91; Ferguson, *Backgrounds of Early Christianity*, 348–54; and B. Fiore, "Cynicism and Skepticism," in *DNTB*, 242–45.

[209] See the discussion of superstition above.

[210] See the discussion of the proposal of a "Cynic Jesus" in chap. 3.

3. What was the name of the Greek ruler who erected a statue of Zeus in the Jerusalem temple, and when did this event take place?
4. What was the name of the Jewish party supportive of the Maccabees?
5. What was the name of the dynasty following the Maccabees?
6. Which two parties divided from the Hasidim?
7. What are the years of rule for the following Roman emperors?
   a. Augustus
   b. Tiberius
   c. Nero
   d. Domitian
8. When did the Romans destroy the Jerusalem temple?
9. Who were Herod the Great's three sons who ruled over parts of Palestine, and which were the provinces or regions they ruled?
10. What are the names of at least five apocryphal books, five pseudepigraphical books, and three writings of the Qumran literature (Dead Sea Scrolls)?
11. What were the four major Jewish sects active in first-century Judaism?
12. What was the name of the Jewish ruling council?

FOR FURTHER STUDY

History

Berlin, A. M. "Between Large Forces: Palestine in the Hellenistic Period." *Biblical Archaeologist* 60 (1997): 3–43.

Berquist, J. L. *Judaism in Persia's Shadow: A Social and Historical Approach.* Philadelphia, PA: Fortress, 1995.

Bruce, F. F. *New Testament History.* Garden City, NY: Doubleday, 1980.

Briant, P. *From Cyrus to Alexander: A History of the Persian Empire.* Trans. P. T. Daniels. Winona Lake, IN: Eisenbrauns, 2002.

Burge, G. M., L. H. Cohick, and G. L. Green. *The New Testament in Antiquity: A Survey of the New Testament Within Its Cultural Contexts.* Grand Rapids, MI: Zondervan, 2009.

Chilton, B., and J. Neusner. *Trading Places: The Intersecting Histories of Judaism and Christianity.* Cleveland, OH: Pilgrim, 1996.

Cohen, S. J. D. *From the Maccabees to the Mishnah.* 2nd ed. Louisville, KY: WJK, 2006.

Davies, W. D., and L. Finkelstein. *The Cambridge History of Judaism.* 4 vols. New York, NY: Cambridge University Press, 1984–1999.

Evans, C. A., and S. E. Porter, eds. *Dictionary of New Testament Background: A Compendium of Contemporary Biblical Scholarship.* Downers Grove, IL: InterVarsity, 2000.

Flusser, D. "Pharisees, Sadducees, and Essenes in Pesher Nahum." Pages 214–57 in *Judaism of the Second Temple Period.* Vol. 1: *Qumran and Apocalypticism.* Translated by A. Yadin. Grand Rapids, MI: Eerdmans, 2007.

Grabbe, L. L. *An Introduction to First Century Judaism: Jewish Religion and History in the Second Temple Period.* London, UK: T&T Clark, 1996.

________. *Judaism from Cyrus to Hadrian. 2 Vols.* Minneapolis, MN: Fortress, 1991.

Green, J. B., and L. M. McDonald, eds. *The World of the New Testament: Cultural, Social, and Historical Contexts.* Grand Rapids, MI: Baker, 2013.

Hamerton-Kelly, R., and R. Scroggs. *Jews, Greeks, and Christians: Religious Cultures in Late Antiquity. Essays in Honor of William David Davies.* Leiden, Netherlands: Brill, 1976.

Helyer, L. R. *Exploring Jewish Literature of the Second Temple Period: A Guide for New Testament Students.* Downers Grove, IL: InterVarsity, 2002.

________. "The Necessity, Problems, and Promise of Second Temple Judaism for Discussions of New Testament Eschatology." *Journal of the Evangelical Theological Society* 47 (2004): 97–115.

Hengel, M. *Judaism and Hellenism: Studies in Their Encounter in Palestine During the Early Hellenistic Period.* Philadelphia, PA: Fortress, 1981.

Jeffers, J. S. *The Greco-Roman World of the New Testament Era: Exploring the Background of Early Christianity.* Downers Grove, IL: InterVarsity, 1999.

Luker, L. M., ed. *Passion, Vitality, and Foment: The Dynamics of Second Temple Judaism.* Harrisburg, PA: Trinity Press International, 2001.

Neusner, J., and B. D. Chilton, eds. *In Quest of the Historical Pharisees.* Waco, TX: Baylor University Press, 2007.

Newsome, J. D. *Greeks, Romans, Jews: Currents of Culture and Belief in the New Testament World.* Philadelphia, PA: Trinity Press International, 1992.

Niswonger, R. L. *New Testament History.* Grand Rapids, MI: Zondervan, 1988.

Nodet, E. *A Search for the Origins of Judaism: From Joshua to the Mishnah.* Journal for the Study of the Old Testament, Supplement Series 248. Sheffield, UK: Sheffield Academic Press, 1997.

Schiffman, L. H. *From Text to Tradition: A History of Second Temple & Rabbinic Judaism.* Hoboken, NJ: Ktav, 1991.

Scott, J. J., Jr. *Jewish Backgrounds of the New Testament.* Grand Rapids, MI: Baker, 2000.

Tomasino, A. J. *Judaism Before Jesus: The Events and Ideas That Shaped the New Testament World.* Downers Grove, IL: InterVarsity, 2003.

Witherington, B., III. *New Testament History: A Narrative Account.* Grand Rapids, MI: Baker, 2001.

Literature

Barrett, C. K., ed. *The New Testament Background: Writings from Ancient Greece and the Roman Empire that Illuminate Christian Origins.* Rev. ed. New York, NY: HarperCollins, 1989.

Bauckham, R., J. R. Davila, and A. Panayotov, eds. *Old Testament Pseudepigrapha: More Noncanonical Scriptures.* 2 vols. Grand Rapids, MI: Eerdmans, 2013.

Chapman, D. W., and A. J. Köstenberger. "Jewish Intertestamental and Early Rabbinic Literature: An Annotated Bibliographic Resource Updated." *Journal of the Evangelical Theological Society* 55 (2012): 235-72, 457-88.

Charlesworth, J. H., ed. *The Old Testament Pseudepigrapha.* 2 vols. Peabody, MA: Hendrickson, 2010.

________, ed. *The Bible and the Dead Sea Scrolls.* 3 vols. Waco, TX: Baylor University Press, 2006.

Collins, J. J. *Beyond the Qumran Community: The Sectarian Movement of the Dead Sea Scrolls*. Grand Rapids, MI: Eerdmans, 2009.

________. *The Dead Sea Scrolls: A Biography*. Lives of Great Religious Books. Princeton, NJ: Princeton University Press, 2012.

Collins, J. J., and D. C. Harlow. *The Eerdmans Dictionary of Early Judaism*. Grand Rapids, MI: Eerdmans, 2010.

Coogan, M. D. *The New Oxford Annotated Apocrypha: New Revised Standard Version*. 4th ed. Oxford, UK: Oxford University Press, 2010.

Crawford, S. W. *Rewriting Scripture in Second Temple Times*. Grand Rapids, MI: Eerdmans, 2008.

DeSilva, D. A. *Introducing the Apocrypha: Message, Context, and Significance*. Grand Rapids, MI: Baker, 2002.

Evans, C. A. *Ancient Texts for New Testament Studies*. Peabody, MA: Hendrickson, 2005.

Evans, C. A. and S. E. Porter, eds. *Dictionary of New Testament Background*. Downers Grove, IL: InterVarsity, 2000.

Ferguson, E. *Backgrounds of Early Christianity*. 3rd ed. Grand Rapids, MI: Eerdmans, 2003.

García Martínez, F., and E. J. C. Tigchelaar. *The Dead Sea Scrolls: Study Edition*. 2 vols. Leiden, Netherlands: Brill, 1997.

Harding, M. *Early Christian Life and Thought in Social Context: A Reader*. London, UK: T&T Clark, 2003.

Helyer, L. R. *Exploring Jewish Literature of the Second Temple Period: A Guide for New Testament Students*. Downers Grove, IL: InterVarsity, 2002.

Lim, T. H., and J. J. Collins, eds. *The Oxford Handbook of the Dead Sea Scrolls*. Oxford, UK: Oxford University Press, 2010.

Metzger, B. M., ed. *The Oxford Annotated Apocrypha*. Expanded ed., New York, NY: Oxford University Press, 1977.

Nickelsburg, G. W. E. *Jewish Literature Between the Bible and the Mishnah: A Historical and Literary Introduction*. 2nd ed. Minneapolis, MN: Fortress, 2005.

Schiffman, L. H. *Texts and Traditions. A Source Reader for the Study of Second Temple and Rabbinic Judaism*. Hoboken, NJ: KTAV, 1998.

Schiffman, L. H. and J. C. VanderKam, eds. *The Encyclopedia of the Dead Sea Scrolls*. 2 vols. Oxford, UK: Oxford University Press, 2000.

Scott, J. J., Jr. *Customs and Controversies: Intertestamental Jewish Backgrounds of the New Testament*. Grand Rapids, MI: Baker, 1995.

Stone, M. E. *Jewish Writings of the Second Temple Period: Apocrypha, Pseudepigrapha, Qumran Sectarian Writings, Philo, Josephus*. Compendia rerum iudaicarum ad Novum Testamentum. Section Two: *The Literature of the Jewish People in the Period of the Second Temple and the Talmud*. Assen: Van Gorcum, 1984.

Strack, H. L., and G. Stemberger. *Introduction to the Talmud and Midrash*. Translated by M. Bockmuehl. Minneapolis, MN: Fortress, 1992.

VanderKam, J. C. *The Dead Sea Scrolls Today*. 2nd ed. Grand Rapids, MI: Eerdmans, 2010.

________. *The Dead Sea Scrolls and the Bible*. Grand Rapids, MI: Eerdmans, 2012.

________. *An Introduction to Early Judaism*. Grand Rapids, MI: Eerdmans, 2000.

Vermes, G. *The Complete Dead Sea Scrolls in English*. 7th rev. ed. New York, NY: Penguin, 2011.

Theology

Evans, C. A., and S. E. Porter, eds. *Dictionary of New Testament Background.* Downers Grove, IL: InterVarsity, 2000.

Ferguson, E. *Backgrounds of Early Christianity.* 3rd ed. Grand Rapids, MI: Eerdmans, 2003.

Flusser, D. *Judaism of the Second Temple Period.* Vol. 1: *Qumran and Apocalypticism.* Translated by A. Yadin. Grand Rapids, MI: Eerdmans, 2008.

Grabbe, L. L. *Judaism from Cyrus to Hadrian.* London, UK: SCM, 1992.

Horbury, W., W. D. Davies, and J. Sturdy. *The Cambridge History of Judaism.* Vol. 3: *The Early Roman Period.* Cambridge, UK: Cambridge University Press, 1999.

Instone-Brewer, D. *Traditions of the Rabbis from the Era of the New Testament.* Vol. 2A: *Feasts and Sabbaths—Passover and Atonement.* Grand Rapids, MI: Eerdmans, 2008.

Safrai, S., and M. Stern, eds. *The Jewish People in the First Century.* Compendia rerum iudaicarum ad Novum Testamentum. Section One: *Historical Geography, Political History, Social, Cultural and Religious Life and Institutions.* 2 vols. Assen: Van Gorcum, 1974, 1987.

Sanders, E. P. *Judaism: Practice and Belief (63 BCE–66 CE).* London, UK: SCM, 1992.

Schiffman, L. H., and J. C. VanderKam, eds. *The Encyclopedia of the Dead Sea Scrolls.* 2 vols. Oxford, UK: University Press, 2000.

Schürer, E. *The History of the Jewish People in the Age of Jesus Christ (175 BC–AD 135).* Rev. and ed. G. Vermes, F. Millar, and M. Black. 3 vols. in 4. Edinburgh, Scotland: T&T Clark, 1973, 1979, 1986, 1987.

Vermes, G. *An Introduction to the Complete Dead Sea Scrolls.* London, UK: SCM, 1999.

Part Two

JESUS AND THE GOSPELS

PART 1 SOUGHT to lay a proper foundation for this comprehensive introduction to the NT by discussing the nature and scope of Scripture (chap. 1) and surveying the political and religious background of the NT (chap. 2). Part 2 provides discussions of Jesus and the Gospels (chap. 3) as well as treatments of the history, literature, and theology of each of the four Gospels: Matthew, Mark, Luke, and John, in canonical order (chaps. 4–7). Unlike part 3, which proceeds in chronological rather than canonical order to correlate Paul's Letters more closely with the book of Acts, the treatment of the Gospels follows a canonical order to avoid prejudging one's solution to the Synoptic Problem, that is, the presumed order of writing and interdependency of Matthew, Mark, and Luke.

The relationship of the Gospels to one another, especially Matthew, Mark, and Luke, as well as to Jesus, the main character in these four Gospels, are the subjects of the introductory chapter for part 2. The chapters on the individual Gospels consider each of these books in their own right, discussing the standard introductory matters for each as well as their literary plans, outlines, theological themes, and contributions to the canon. While they were most likely written subsequent to Paul's earlier letters, it is appropriate to treat the Gospels first due to their placement first in the NT canon and due to their foundational nature as presentations of Jesus as the Messiah, Savior, and Lord.

Chapter 3

Jesus and the Relationship Between the Gospels

CORE KNOWLEDGE

Basic Knowledge: Students should be able to identify key references to Jesus in Jewish and Roman extrabiblical materials and to describe and critique contemporary challenges to the NT portrayal of Jesus. They should also know major data in Jesus's life, including the date of his birth, the length of his ministry, and the date of the crucifixion.

Intermediate Knowledge: Students should be able to discuss the philosophical foundations of the modern study of the Gospels and to define and evaluate the major criteria of authenticity applied to Jesus material in the Gospels. They should also be familiar with the major views on the relationship between the Synoptic Gospels.

Advanced Knowledge: Students should be able to cite additional extrabiblical references to Jesus and to assess the value of the non-canonical "lost Gospels." They should be able to chronicle the four major "Quests for the Historical Jesus." They should also be able to provide a thorough description of the various synoptic theories, illustrating these options with examples from synoptic parallels.

INTRODUCTION

FOR THE CHRISTIAN, no study can be more important than that of Jesus and the Gospels. Jesus of Nazareth is the focus of the Christian faith. It is no accident that the earliest Christian councils were convened and creeds were written to address questions surrounding Jesus's nature and identity. The early church recognized that an understanding of Jesus's identity is essential to genuine Christianity and a prerequisite for experiencing salvation and enjoying a relationship with God.

While the OT predicted the coming of Jesus, and later portions of the NT frequently refer to him, the most thorough descriptions of Jesus's life and teachings are in the four canonical Gospels, properly titled "The Gospel According to Matthew," and so forth. These early titles capture the important fact that while there are four canonical Gospels, there is only one gospel of Jesus Christ, and, accordingly, the canonical Gospels, properly understood, are not four separate, independent presentations of Jesus Christ. They are four complementary perspectives or versions of the one gospel of Jesus Christ.

The study of the Gospels is enjoyable, even exciting, but it is no simple task. Those who study the Gospels need to be prepared to respond to the claim that Jesus never even existed or that other ancient descriptions of Jesus's life are more accurate than the NT documents. They must carefully evaluate contemporary portraits of Jesus. They must also grapple with questions related to such matters as the historical reliability of the Gospels, the sources used by the Gospel writers, and the relationship of the Gospels to one another. The purpose of this section is to prepare you for the lifelong study of the four Gospels by tackling these issues and addressing these challenges.

REFERENCES TO JESUS OUTSIDE THE GOSPELS

Non-believers sometimes challenge the Christian faith by claiming that Jesus never existed. They often incorrectly assert that no ancient texts outside of the NT even refer to him. Yet even if no texts outside of the NT mentioned Jesus, this would not be reasonable grounds for denying his existence. The NT should not be regarded as a single source since it is actually composed of twenty-seven books by at least eight different authors. The NT thus provides multiple independent attestations to Jesus's existence, life, teachings, miracles, death, and resurrection. Other early Christian writings by the apostolic and early church fathers offer further evidence regarding Jesus's existence.[1] In addition, several non-Christian extrabiblical texts, both Jewish and pagan, mention Jesus of Nazareth and offer brief descriptions of him. This section surveys those non-Christian extrabiblical references.[2]

---

[1] "Apostolic Fathers" is a technical label for the following writings: *1 and 2 Clement*; *The Letters of Ignatius*; *The Letter of Polycarp to the Philippians*; *The Martyrdom of Polycarp*; *The Didache*; *The Epistle of Barnabas*; *The Shepherd of Hermas*; *The Epistle to Diognetus*; the *Fragment of Quadratus*; and *Fragments of Papias*. See M. W. Holmes, *The Apostolic Fathers: Greek Texts and English Translations*, 3rd ed. (Grand Rapids, MI: Baker, 2007), especially pp. 5–6. Beyond this, other writings of early church fathers are gathered in various other collections.

[2] For a book-length treatment, see R. E. Van Voorst, *Jesus Outside the New Testament: An Introduction to the Ancient Evidence* (Grand Rapids, MI: Eerdmans, 2000); see also E. M. Yamauchi, "Jesus Outside the New Testament: What Is the

References to Jesus in Jewish Texts

Three extensive Jewish sources from the first century have been preserved: (1) the writings of Josephus (ca. AD 35–100); (2) the writings of Philo (ca. 20 BC–AD 50); and (3) the Dead Sea Scrolls. Neither Philo nor the Dead Sea Scrolls explicitly mention Jesus of Nazareth. The absence of a reference to Jesus in Philo is expected since he wrote from Alexandria, Egypt, and rarely mentioned contemporary events in Palestine.[3] The lack of a reference to Jesus in the Dead Sea Scrolls is likewise expected since references to historical figures in them are generally obscure references to important figures during the Second Temple period and since the Dead Sea Scrolls are Jewish pre-Christian documents that show no trace of influence from Christian sources.[4]

Matters are different with the Jewish historian Josephus. Two references to Jesus of Nazareth appear in one of Josephus's works called *Jewish Antiquities*. Josephus briefly referred to Jesus in a discussion of the identity of the Lord's half-brother James (*Ant.* 20.9.1 §§200–203):

> He [Ananus the high priest] seated the judges of the Sanhedrin Council and after he led to them the brother of Jesus who was called Messiah, the man whose name was James, and certain others, and accused them of having transgressed the Law, he handed them over to be stoned.[5]

The passage attests to the existence of Jesus of Nazareth as a historical person and to his relationship to James. It also confirms that some of Jesus's contemporaries recognized him as the Messiah.[6] The statement that some recognized Jesus as the Messiah is consistent with Josephus's grammar elsewhere. The reference does not imply that Josephus regarded Jesus as the Messiah and thus is not precluded by Josephus's Jewish faith. Elsewhere, for example, Josephus mentioned that Antiochus was called "god" by the Greeks (*Ant.* 12.3.2 §125), but this does not imply that Josephus accepted that claim.

J. Meier has pointed out that it is highly unlikely that this passage is a Christian interpolation. First, the NT and early Christian texts refer to James using the titles "brother of the Lord" and "brother of the Savior" rather than "brother of Jesus." Second, this account

---

Evidence?" in *Jesus Under Fire*, ed. M. J. Wilkins and J. P. Moreland (Grand Rapids, MI: Zondervan, 1995), 207–29.

[3] G. E. Sterling, "Philo," in *Dictionary of New Testament Background*, ed. C. A. Evans and S. E. Porter (Downers Grove, IL: InterVarsity, 2000), 789–93.

[4] See M. O. Wise, "Dead Sea Scrolls," in *Dictionary of Jesus and the Gospels*, ed. J. B. Green, S. McKnight, and I. H. Marshall (Downers Grove, IL: InterVarsity, 1992), 137–46, especially p. 141.

[5] Our translation.

[6] The participle *legomenou* ("who was called") could be pejorative and mean "so-called." Some interpreters take the usage here in this sense and appeal to this as evidence that the statement goes back to Josephus. See D. L. Bock, *Studying the Historical Jesus: A Guide to Sources and Methods* (Grand Rapids, IL: Baker, 2002), 54. However, an exhaustive examination of the use of this construction in Josephus's writings suggests it was not used in a disparaging manner (see *Ant.* 1.4.3 §§118–19; 8.5.3 §145; 12.10.5 §412; and *Apion* 1.18 §118). The construction is likely authentic because it reflects Josephus's characteristic grammar and style.

of James's death is significantly different from early Christian accounts that appear in the works of Hegesippus (ca. AD 110–180) and Eusebius (ca. AD 260–340). Third, one would have expected a Christian scribe to offer a more extensive description of James and Jesus. However, these are mentioned briefly and only in order to confirm the illegal behavior of Ananus. Consequently, few scholars seriously doubt the authenticity of this passage.[7]

Josephus has a more extensive reference to Jesus in a passage known as the *Testimonium Flavianum* (*Ant.* 18.3.3 §§63–64). Greek manuscripts of this text read,

> About this time, Jesus came. He was a wise man, if it is really proper to call him a man, because he was a person who did incredible works, a teacher of those people who gladly welcomed the truth. He won over many of the Jews and many of the Gentiles. He was the Messiah. And when Pilate condemned him to the cross based on evidence from the men of high standing from among us, the ones who loved him at the beginning did not abandon their love for him, because on the third day he appeared to them alive. And these and a thousand other wonderful things had been told about him by the divine prophets. And the tribe which is called "the Christians" has not died out even to this very day.[8]

The authenticity of portions of this passage is doubtful for several reasons. First, no Christian document in the first three centuries of the church cites this passage, even though it would have been helpful to them in some of their debates with non-Christians to appeal to Josephus's "Christian" faith. Second, Origen (ca. AD 185–254) claimed that Josephus did not regard Jesus as the Messiah.[9] Third, according to Josephus's own testimony in *Jewish War* (3.8.8–9 §§392–408), he regarded Vespasian as the Messiah of Judah.[10]

Nevertheless, although portions of the *Testimonium Flavianum* are likely Christian interpolations, strong evidence suggests that at least some elements of this statement are authentic.[11] First, the brevity of the reference to Jesus later in *Antiquities* (20.9.1 §§200–203) suggests that Josephus had already introduced Jesus of Nazareth earlier in his narrative. The *Testimonium Flavianum* is the only previous reference preserved in Greek manuscripts.[12]

---

[7] J. P. Meier, *A Marginal Jew: Rethinking the Historical Jesus*, 3 vols. (New York, NY: Doubleday, 1991), 1:57–58.

[8] Our translation.

[9] *Commentarium series in evangelium Matthaei* 10.50.17; *Against Celsus* 1.47.

[10] For a good introduction to the issues surrounding the *Testimonium Flavianum*, see C. A. Evans, "Jesus in Non-Christian Sources," in *Dictionary of Jesus and the Gospels*, 364–65.

[11] Meier noted that prominent scholars who affirm an authentic substratum plus some Christian interpolations include Jewish scholars L. Feldman and P. Winter; mainline Protestants such as J. H. Charlesworth; Catholic scholars such as C. M. Martini, W. Trilling, and A. M. Dubarle; and liberal scholars such as S. G. F. Brandon and M. Smith. L. H. Feldman, "Flavius Josephus Revisited: The Man, His Writings, and His Significance," in *Aufstieg und Niedergang der römischen Welt*, ed. W. Haase and H. Temporini (New York, NY: de Gruyter, 1984), II/21.2, 822, stated: "The great majority of modern scholars have regarded it as partly interpolated, and this is my conclusion as well."

[12] The Slavonic version of Josephus's *Jewish War* contains three additional passages which refer to Jesus (2.9.3 §§174-75; 5.5.4 §214; 5.5.2 §195). For a discussion of the Slavonic version, see Evans, "Jesus in Non-Christian Sources," 364–65.

Second, the Arabic version of the *Testimonium Flavianum* in Agapius's *History* lacks the distinctively Christian elements:

> At this time there was a wise man who was called Jesus. And his conduct was good, and he was known to be virtuous. And many people from among the Jews and the other nations became his disciples. Pilate condemned him to be crucified and to die. And those who have become his disciples did not abandon his discipleship. They reported that he had appeared to them three days after his crucifixion and that he was alive; accordingly he was perhaps the Messiah concerning whom the prophets have recounted wonders.[13]

Many scholars believe the Arabic version reflects the state of the text before Christian scribes added their interpolations. Third, the passage is saturated with vocabulary common in Josephus's writings and is generally consistent with his style.[14] Fourth, the passage contains statements that contradict the Gospels and thus are unlikely to have been composed by a Christian scribe. Such contradictory statements include the claim that Jesus had large numbers of Gentile followers during his public ministry. These statements were not likely to have been interpolated in the text by a Christian scribe familiar with the Gospels. They are much more likely claims by a first-century Jew who wanted to exonerate the Jews and blame the Romans for Jesus's death and who assumed that Jesus had large numbers of Gentile followers during his public ministry simply because large numbers of Christians were Gentiles in the writer's day.[15]

J. Meier summarized the significance of the *Testimonium Flavianum*:

> Independent of the Four Gospels, yet confirming their basic presentation, a Jew writing in the year 93–94 tells us that during the rule of Pontius Pilate (the larger context of "during this time")—therefore between A.D. 26 and 36—there appeared on the religious scene of Palestine a man named Jesus. He had the reputation for wisdom that displayed itself in miracle working and teaching. He won a large following, but (or therefore?) the Jewish leaders accused him before Pilate. Pilate had him crucified, but his ardent followers refused to abandon their devotion to him, despite his shameful death. Named Christians after this Jesus (who is called Christ), they continued in existence down to Josephus' day. The neutral, or ambiguous, or perhaps somewhat dismissive tone of the *Testimonium* is probably the reason why

---

[13] S. Pines, *An Arabic Version of the Testimonium Flavianum and Its Implications* (Jerusalem, Israel: Academy of Sciences and Humanities, 1971), 16.

[14] For example, the construction translated "about that time" appears five times in Josephus's writings. He used the adjective "wonderful/incredible" thirty-nine times. Other features of the text are unparalleled in Josephus, such as his description of the prophets as "divine." These and other vocabulary statistics are helpful in reconstructing Josephus's original statement and identifying the later Christian interpolations. See especially Meier, *Marginal Jew*, 1:80–83.

[15] Ibid., 1:64–66.

> early Christian writers (especially the apologists of the 2nd century) passed over it in silence, why Origen complained that Josephus did not believe that Jesus was the Christ, and why some interpolator(s) in the late 3rd century added Christian interpolations.[16]

The testimony of Josephus constitutes the most important early testimony about Jesus of Nazareth known outside of the Bible.

The Babylonian Talmud is a collection of rabbinic teachings that was finalized in the sixth century. The Talmud refers to Jesus of Nazareth several times. However, most of these references are of little historical value since they are relatively late, reflect secondhand knowledge of the Gospels, and are products of Jewish polemic with Christians. Other rabbinic literature—such as the Mishnah, Tosefta, Midrash, and the Jerusalem Talmud—may also be reactions to Christian claims and thus refer to Jesus.[17]

The Talmud challenges the Christian claim that Jesus was conceived by a virgin by arguing that Mary "who was the descendant of princes and governors, played the harlot with carpenters."[18] A chronologically confused account claims that Jesus fled to Egypt to escape King Janneus's slaughter of the rabbis in 87 BC. In Egypt Jesus was excommunicated and condemned for worshipping an idol.[19] The Talmud names five disciples of Jesus and claims that "Jesus the Nazarene practiced magic and led Israel astray."[20] Although two of the names are similar to Matthew and Thaddeus, the resemblance may only be coincidental since the names of the disciples in the Talmud serve as a basis for wordplays and do not appear to be serious attempts to record the actual names of Jesus's followers. The charge that Jesus practiced magic is significant since it parallels the accusation from Jesus's opponents in the Gospels that Jesus performed exorcisms through the power of Satan (see Mark 3:22). Rabbinic literature claims that Jesus taught heresy,[21] and it especially objected to Jesus's claims to be God, the Son of God, the Son of Man, the new Moses, and the Servant of the Lord.[22]

One of the most important references to Jesus in the Babylonian Talmud states,

> On the eve of Passover they hanged Jesus the Nazarene. And a herald went out before him for forty days, saying: "He is going to be stoned, because he practiced sorcery and enticed and led Israel astray. Anyone who knows

---

[16] Ibid., 1:68.

[17] An excellent summary of the rabbinic material with quotations of key texts appears in C. A. Evans, "Jesus in Non-Christian Sources," 366–67.

[18] *b. Sanh.* 106a. See also *b. Shab.* 104b; *b. Sanh.* 43a; *m. Yeb.* 4:13; *b. Yeb.* 49a.

[19] *b. Sanh.* 107b; *b. Sot.* 47a; *y. Hag.* 2:2; *y. Sanh.* 6:6.

[20] *b. Sanh.* 107b; see *t. Shab.* 11:15; *b. Sanh.* 43a; *b. Shab.* 104b; *b. Sot.* 47a.

[21] *b. Sanh.* 103a; *b. Ber.* 17a-b; *b. Abod. Zar.* 16b–17a; *t. Hul.* 2:24; *m. Avot* 4:19; *b. Shab.* 116a-b.

[22] *b. Shab.* 116a; *y. Taan.* 2:1; *Exod. Rab.* 29.5 on Exod 20:2; *Deut. Rab.* 2.33 on Deut 6:4; *Yal. Shim.* on Num 23:7; *Deut. Rab.* 8.6 on Deut 30:11–12; *b. Sanh.* 61b.

> anything in his favor, let him come and plead in his behalf." But, not having found anything in his favor, they hanged him on the eve of Passover.[23]

The passage is important for several reasons. First, it is identified as a *baraita*, a tradition that arose during the Tannaitic Period (AD 70–200). Thus, the reference probably preserves a tradition that is earlier than many of the other references to Jesus in the Talmud. Second, the passage probably emphasized a forty-day waiting period before Jesus's execution in response to Christian claims that the Jewish leaders did not follow proper procedures in the rushed hearings that led to Jesus's condemnation. Third, the execution of Jesus on the eve of the Passover fits with the chronology of Jesus's passion in the Gospel of John (John 18–19) in the view of many scholars.

The Babylonian Talmud also contains one clear and one probable reference to Jesus's resurrection. One manuscript of the Talmud states, "He then went and raised Jesus by incantation."[24] Another text says, "Woe to him who makes himself alive by the name of God."[25] Several texts also refer to disciples of Jesus miraculously healing others in Jesus's name. They forbade Jews to heal or to receive healing in Jesus's name.[26]

Several conclusions can be drawn from these rabbinic references. First, Jesus of Nazareth is not a myth or a legend. He was an actual historical person. As R. T. France noted,

> Uncomplimentary as it is, this is at least, in a distorted way, evidence for the impact Jesus's miracles and teaching made. The conclusion that it is entirely dependent on Christian claims, and that "Jews in the second century adopted uncritically the Christian assumption that he had really lived" is surely only dictated by a dogmatic skepticism. Such polemic, often using "facts" quite distinct from what Christians believed, is hardly likely to have arisen within less than a century around a non-existent figure.[27]

Second, Jesus performed works that could only be described as supernatural feats. It is significant that the rabbinic literature does not deny Jesus's resurrection, his miracles, or the healings performed in Jesus's name. Instead, it ascribes such events to magic or sorcery. These charges are identical to Jewish claims in the second and early third centuries preserved in the writings of early church fathers such as Justin Martyr (ca. AD 100–165) and Origen (ca. AD 185–254).[28] This strategy for dismissing the implications of Jesus's supernatural works suggests that both Christians and their Jewish opponents of the second

---

[23] *b. Sanh.* 43a.

[24] *b. Git.* 57a, MS. M.

[25] *b. Sanh.* 106a.

[26] See *t. Hul.* 2:22–23; *y. Shab.* 14:4; *y. Abod. Zar.* 2:2; *b. Abod. Zar.* 27b; *Qoh. Rab.* 10:5.

[27] R. T. France, *The Evidence for Jesus* (Downers Grove, IL: InterVarsity, 1986), 39.

[28] Justin Martyr, *Dialogue* 69.7; *First Apology* 30; Origen, *Against Celsus* 1.68.

century recognized that no one could reasonably dispute that Jesus actually performed miracles. The evidence for these acts was simply too compelling.

Instead, opponents of Christianity in the second century continued the strategy of Jesus's earlier opponents (Matt 12:24; Mark 3:22; Luke 11:15; John 10:19–21) and ascribed his miracles to Satan's power that he obtained through magic or sorcery. The admission in non-Christian sources that Jesus performed supernatural works constitutes convincing evidence not only for Jesus's historical existence but also for the historicity of his miracle-working ministry. Although the rabbinic testimony is questionable and clearly is often the imaginative creation of opponents of the Christian faith, the core of the descriptions of Jesus in the NT Gospels is confirmed by it.

References to Jesus by Roman Writers

Pagan writers generally showed little interest in Jesus of Nazareth. In a world teeming with a multitude of religions, Christianity was viewed as just another bizarre faith hardly worthy of mention. However, two Roman historians, a political official, a chronicler, a satirist, and a father referred to Jesus in their writings.

The Roman historian Tacitus (ca. AD 56–113) wrote his *Annals* in the early second century. His work originally covered the history of Rome (AD 14–68). Unfortunately, some of the books of the *Annals* have been lost, including the section discussing the years AD 29–32. Thus, if Jesus had been crucified AD 30 as many believe, the very section that may have described these events is no longer extant.[29]

But Tacitus did discuss the great fire of Rome that Nero blamed on the Christians to divert attention away from his own involvement in the arson. He wrote,

> Therefore, to squelch the rumor, Nero created scapegoats and subjected to the most refined tortures those whom the common people called "Christians," [a group] hated for their abominable crimes. Their name comes from Christ, who, during the reign of Tiberius, had been executed by the procurator Pontius Pilate. Suppressed for the moment, the deadly superstition broke out again, not only in Judea, the land which originated this evil, but also in the city of Rome, where all sorts of horrendous and shameful practices of every part of the world converge and are fervently cultivated (*Annals* 15.44).

The passage gives a far too negative depiction of Christianity to have come from the pen of a Christian scribe. Moreover, all the manuscripts of the *Annals* contain it. Thus, the passage is clearly authentic. Tacitus's statement comports with the claim of the Gospels that Jesus was executed during the reign of Tiberius (AD 14–37) and the governorship of Pontius Pilate (AD 26–36). Although it is possible that Tacitus derived his information regarding Jesus from Josephus, important differences between the accounts in Tacitus and

---

[29] But it is likely that Jesus was actually crucified AD 33. See the section on the chronology of Jesus's life below; cf. "The Date of Jesus's Crucifixion," in *The ESV Study Bible*, gen. ed. W. Grudem (Wheaton, IL: Crossway, 2008), 1809–10.

Josephus suggest that Tacitus was dependent on another source. Tacitus may have derived his information from common assumptions about Christians in the second-century Roman world or from the Roman archives.

Another Roman historian who referred to Jesus was Suetonius (ca. AD 120), who reported that "Claudius expelled the Jews from Rome who, instigated by Chrestus, never ceased to cause unrest."[30] This expulsion is probably that of AD 49 mentioned in Acts 18:2. Suetonius seems to have confused the name "Chrestus" (a name common among Roman slaves) with "Christus," a messianic title with which he was unfamiliar. Suetonius also assumed that Jesus was alive and in Rome at the time of the expulsion. He probably made this assumption because it was unusual for people to have the kind of devotion for a dead or distant figure that Christians in mid-first-century Rome expressed to Christ. The unrest to which Suetonius referred was likely tension between Jews and Jewish Christians over the claims of the Christian gospel.

In a letter to his son that compared Socrates, Pythagoras, and Jesus, Mara bar Serapion (ca. AD 73) asked, "For what advantage did . . . the Jews gain by the death of their wise king?" The letter added that it was just after the execution of their wise king that the kingdom of the Jews was abolished and they were ruined and driven from their land. The letter also claimed, "Nor did the wise king die for good; he lived on in the teaching he had given." The letter describes the execution of Jesus at the instigation of the Jews some time not long before the fall of Jerusalem.

In a letter to the Emperor Trajan, Pliny the Younger (ca. AD 110), proconsul of the province of Bithynia in Asia Minor, sought the emperor's approval of his handling of Christians. He mentioned that Christians gathered before dawn on a particular day to chant hymns "to Christ as to a god" and to partake of a meal together (*Ep.* 10.96).

Although his work is no longer extant, Thallus, who wrote a history of the eastern Mediterranean world around AD 52, was quoted by Julius Africanus (ca. AD 230) as claiming that the darkness that accompanied Jesus's crucifixion was related to an eclipse of the sun. Africanus dismissed Thallus's explanation since Passover occurs at the time of the full moon and a solar eclipse at this time is impossible.[31] Assuming that Africanus represented his source accurately, Thallus offered early independent verification of the phenomenon of darkness during Jesus's crucifixion.

Finally, Lucian of Samosata (ca. AD 115–200) wrote a satire titled *The Passing of Peregrinus*, an account about a Christian convert who eventually abandoned the Christian faith. The satire refers to Christians' worshipping "the man who was impaled in Palestine because he introduced this new cult into the world." Lucian later described Christians as "worshipping that crucified sophist himself and living under his laws."[32] The references

---

[30] Suetonius, *Life of Emperor Claudius* 25.4.

[31] Julius Africanus, *Frag.* 18.

[32] Meier, *Marginal Jew*, 1:92; cf. R. L. Wilken, *The Christians as the Romans Saw Them* (New Haven, CT: Yale University Press, 1984), 96–97.

acknowledge Jesus's death by crucifixion, his Palestinian origin, and his founding of a new faith.[33]

Some scholars see these descriptions of Jesus in Roman writings as offering little help for understanding Jesus of Nazareth or confirming NT accounts. In general, these writings seem to reflect secondhand knowledge about Christ that could have been derived from the Gospels, opponents of Christianity, or contemporary Christians. However, at the very least these references demonstrate that Jesus was widely regarded by Romans as a historical person who espoused controversial teachings and was executed by crucifixion.

Summary

The early non-Christian references to Jesus should be regarded as testimony about Jesus from hostile witnesses. Nevertheless, and significantly, this testimony at some points confirms the accounts of Jesus's life penned by his own followers. These corroborating testimonies offer strong evidence for the historicity of the general contours of Jesus's life as described in the NT. Although the non-Christian references add nothing new to the knowledge about Jesus gleaned from the Gospels, they do verify the NT at important points.

THE QUESTS OF THE HISTORICAL JESUS

Prior to the rise of the Enlightenment—during the "precritical" era—it was widely assumed that the Jesus presented in the Bible was the man who lived and died—and rose—in Palestine in the first century. Thus, to study Jesus was to study what *the Bible* had to say about Jesus. But the intellectual climate of the late 1700s set in motion a series of movements that called this approach to the study of Jesus into question, launching what is widely termed "the Quests of the Historical Jesus." This post-Enlightenment quest, which unfolded in a series of successive quests, was characterized by four basic configurations.[34]

The First Quest

The first quest (1778–1906) began with the posthumous publication of H. S. Reimarus's book released serially as *The Wolfenbüttel Fragments*.[35] Reimarus disputed the connection between the "Jesus of history" and the "Christ of faith." He proposed a radically different Jesus who was nothing but a Jewish revolutionary the apostles made the centerpiece of their new religion, "Christianity."[36] The firestorm ensuing from the publication of this

---

[33] Bock, *Studying the Historical Jesus*, 52; Meier, *Marginal Jew*, 1:102–20.

[34] For a more detailed description of Jesus studies since 1778, see N. T. Wright, *Jesus and the Victory of God*, Christian Origins and the Question of God 2 (Minneapolis, MN: Fortress, 1992), 3–121. Although we adopt the common categories used to describe the history of historical Jesus research, students must recognize that the periods cannot be sharply distinguished and often overlap. Wright (25) commented, "I should state at this point that I do not actually believe in rigid 'periods' in the history of scholarship, except as heuristic aids to help us grasp currents of thought."

[35] For a recent edition, see C. H. Talbert, ed., *Reimarus Fragments*, Scholars Press Reprints and Translations (Chico, CA: Scholars Press, 1985).

[36] Wright, *Jesus and the Victory of God*, 17.

book set off a whole series of books carrying the title "Life of Jesus," the most infamous being D. F. Strauss's *Das Leben Jesu* (German for "The Life of Jesus").[37]

Virtually all of the early exemplars of the first quest endeavored to show that Christianity stood in contradiction to historical reality and sought to introduce a new freedom for humanity.[38] Later works of the first quest typically propagated a Jesus who, in essence, constituted an expression of Protestant liberal theology.[39] Liberal theology, rooted in deism, advocated a religion that derived from reason alone. Such a theology, in turn, of necessity entailed an antisupernatural bias.

According to this kind of "enlightened" mind-set, miracles simply did not happen. Therefore, the Gospels, thoroughly infused with the miraculous, must be stripped of their miraculous content in order to make them palatable to a more "reasonable" approach to interpretation. This approach gave birth to various historical-critical methodologies. One such method was source criticism through which biblical scholars hoped to determine the earliest stratum of Gospel material. This was done in an effort to discover the "historical Jesus"—who he really was before the early church transformed him into a figment of its own imagination, the "Christ of faith."[40]

The inevitable result of the first quest was that Jesus looked more like the questers themselves than the first-century Jew Jesus was. According to many of these first questers, Jesus taught the brotherhood of man and the fatherhood of God, promulgated the ethics of the kingdom, and died a death that was exemplary in its self-giving, sacrificial nature rather than truly redemptive. Thus for first questers, the challenge was not to have faith *in* Jesus as much as it was to recover the faith *of* Jesus.[41]

The Abandoned Quest

The first quest came to an end in the first decade of the twentieth century. A series of works sent Jesus scholars looking in different directions. The chief among these was A. Schweitzer's *The Quest of the Historical Jesus*.[42] This period is commonly called "the Abandoned Quest" (1906–1953). According to these scholars, many of whom were existentialists, virtually nothing of the Jesus of history could be known. But this was not an

---

[37] For an English translation, see D. F. Strauss, *The Life of Jesus, Critically Examined*, Lives of Jesus (Philadelphia, PA: Fortress, 1973 [orig. German ed. 1835]).

[38] Wright, *Jesus and the Victory of God*, 17. It was the fear of this scandalous view that led Reimarus to avoid publication. Half a century later the proposal cost D. F. Strauss his post at Tübingen.

[39] One of the more famous "Lives" was that written by the Roman Catholic E. Renan, *Life of Jesus*, Modern Library (New York, NY: Random House, 1927).

[40] Source criticism thus was spawned—not from a mere exegetical vantage point, as was later the case with redaction criticism—but from a desire to identify the historic Jesus. Thus, H. J. Holtzmann, who "proved" the two-source hypothesis in the minds of many, was compelled to conclude his book with a chapter on the life of Jesus viewed from "Source A," truncated from Mark. See H. J. Holtzmann, *Die synoptischen Evangelien: Ihr Ursprung und geschichtlicher Charakter* (Leipzig, Germany: Engelmann, 1863), 468–96.

[41] W. B. Tatum, *In Quest of Jesus*, rev. and enl. ed. (Nashville, TN: Abingdon, 1999), 93–94.

[42] The most up-to-date English translation based on the 1913 German 2nd edition is A. Schweitzer, *The Quest of the Historical Jesus*, ed. J. Bowden (Minneapolis, MN: Fortress, 2001).

important loss since it was not the "Jesus of history" but the "Christ of faith" who had impacted the world.[43] As a result, virtually no important "life of Jesus" was written from the 1900s through the 1950s.[44]

Thus the Jesus of history became largely irrelevant to theological inquiry. Instead, scholars employed form criticism in order to investigate the early church that had preserved and adapted the stories of Jesus. For figures such as R. Bultmann, the important task was to demythologize the early church's stories about Jesus in order to isolate the kernel of truth they contained for Christian faith. As Tatum aptly summed up, for Bultmann a "faith which needed the external props of historical research into the life of Jesus was simply not faith. To Bultmann, therefore, both the nature of the Gospels and the nature of faith made the writing of a life of Jesus impossible and illegitimate."[45]

The Second Quest

The second quest began in 1954 and was, ironically, spawned by the students of R. Bultmann (see "Abandoned Quest" above). One of Bultmann's students, E. Käsemann, at a reunion of former students of Bultmann, delivered a paper in which he contended that something of the historical Jesus could be, and should be, recovered using Bultmann's methods. Käsemann proposed that a Christ divorced from history could be invoked to support almost any theological or political agenda. Many of these second questers had, all too starkly, seen the results of a Christ separated from his historical moorings as pre-World War II Nazi Germany created "a largely unJewish Christ."[46]

Thus, a new or second quest was quickly underway. These scholars held that Jesus must be connected in some way to early Christianity and that the church's preaching could provide information about that Jesus.[47] The second quest moved away from the canonical gospel proclamation and placed a higher value on other ancient sources such as the Gospel of Thomas, the Gospel of the Hebrews, and other non-canonical Gospel fragments. In the end a picture of Jesus was gleaned from glimpses of the earliest church's proclamation—an enterprise Bultmann would have disavowed.

Although a third quest has been launched (see below), the second quest has not passed off the scene. Modern advocates of its methods and conclusions are still working in the field, although the edges are blurred between second and third questers. The controversial Jesus Seminar is, in essence, a manifestation of the second quest. The major figures of the Jesus Seminar, B. Mack and J. D. Crossan, illustrate well the directions taken by the second

---

[43] This was the thesis of another important work in 1892 that helped end the first quest: English translation M. Kähler, *The So-Called Historical Jesus and the Historic, Biblical Christ*, trans. and ed. C. E. Braaten (Philadelphia, PA: Fortress, 1964).

[44] But see Bock (*Studying the Historical Jesus*, 145), who rightly noted that men such as A. Schlatter—and before him Westcott, Hort, and Lightfoot—approached Jesus from a more conservative point of view and held liberal theology at bay.

[45] Tatum, *In Quest of Jesus*, 99.

[46] Wright, *Jesus and the Victory of God*, 23.

[47] A term frequently used to describe the essence of this preaching was kerygmatic (from *kerygma*, "preaching") theology.

quest. Mack has promoted a Jesus who is a Cynic, nonapocalyptic, culturally and socially subversive, and who advocated a social experiment that was perceived as transformation.[48]

For Mack, earliest Christianity did not hold to the deity of Christ, nor did it view Christ as Savior but considered him to be a social reformer. The epithets of "deity" and of "Savior" were added subsequently by early Christians represented by the Gospel writers. Similarly, J. D. Crossan also held Jesus to be a Cynic, though he viewed Jesus at the same time as a Jewish peasant. Jesus's aim was to get all to rely on God, thus destroying the patron-client system in his day, announcing what Crossan calls "the brokerless kingdom of God."[49] The modern second questers have yet to win over the majority of scholars, but they remain a vocal minority in Jesus studies today.[50]

The Third Quest

The third quest[51] had precursors as early as 1965 with G. B. Caird's *Jesus and the Jewish Nation*.[52] This quest is characterized by a desire to place Jesus in the context of first-century, Second Temple Judaism. The scholars representing the third quest have in essence built on previous Jesus scholarship as they embark on a different type of quest. Their desire is to engage in serious historical research into first-century Judaism and to place Jesus within this cultural context. For many, the difference is that this investigation is separate from Christology; that is, it is conducted apart from traditional confessions regarding Jesus by the historic church. Instead, the goal of the historical research in the third quest is to locate Jesus as an actual historical figure.[53] N. T. Wright, an active advocate of the third quest, provided the following apt description of this quest:

> The Old [First] Quest was determined that Jesus should look as little like a first-century Jew as possible. Bultmann was determined that, though Jesus was historically a first-century Jew, his first-century Jewishness was precisely not the place where his "significance" lay. The renewed "New Quest," following this line, has often played down the specifically Jewish features of Jesus, stressing instead those which he may have shared with other Mediterranean cultures; it has also downplayed to a large extent the significance of Jesus's death, stressing that we know very little about it and suggesting that the earliest Christians were not particularly interested in it. . . . The present "Third Quest," by and large, will have none of this. Jesus

[48] B. Mack, *A Myth of Innocence: Mark and Christian Origins* (Philadelphia, PA: Fortress, 2006), 76–77; see below for further discussion of Mack's work.

[49] J. D. Crossan, *The Historical Jesus: The Life of a Mediterranean Jewish Peasant* (San Francisco, CA: Harper Collins, 1991), 422; see below for further discussion of Crossan's work.

[50] See B. Witherington III (*The Jesus Quest: The Third Search for the Jew of Nazareth* [Downers Grove, IL: InterVarsity, 1995], 11), whose comment that "the movement was dead in the water by the early 1970s" was obviously premature.

[51] For a monograph-length investigation, see Witherington, *Jesus Quest*.

[52] G. B. Caird, *Jesus and the Jewish Nation* (London, UK: Athlone, 1965).

[53] Tatum, *In Quest of Jesus*, 103.

> must be understood as a comprehensible and yet, so to speak, crucifiable first-century Jew whatever the theological or hermeneutical consequences.[54]

Two caveats should be registered here. First, if anyone were to claim that he or she is simply following where the evidence leads, this would be tantamount to asserting that it is possible to assume a truly neutral, objective stance as a researcher. But hermeneutical scholarship of the past century has shown that presuppositionless exegesis and even unbiased historical research are themselves myths.[55] No one is completely without preconceived notions as to who Jesus was, and to claim otherwise is either ignorant or naïve. This calls for caution in evaluating the claims of those engaging in Jesus research.

Second, the idea that Jesus should be understood in keeping with his first-century environment is not original to the third (or any) quest for the historical Jesus. Conservative scholars have generally sought to understand Jesus in this way as an outgrowth of their conviction that the Gospels' portrait of Jesus is historically accurate. In fact, this is why some evangelical scholars are drawn to the third quest in the first place. This is not to say that third questers are by and large conservative exegetes. They are not. Many of these authors have different theological and political agendas with widely divergent views on first-century Judaism and Jesus.

Wright identifies five crucial questions that third questers seek to answer: (1) How does Jesus fit into Judaism? (2) What were Jesus's aims? (3) Why did Jesus die? (4) How and why did the early church begin? (5) Why are the Gospels what they are?[56] How one answers these questions determines one's view of Jesus, and third questers differ in this regard. G. Vermes described Jesus in terms of a *hasid*, a Jewish holy man; E. P. Sanders and M. Casey, an apocalyptic prophet; B. Witherington, a sage, the embodiment of wisdom; J. P. Meier, a "marginal" Jew; Brandon, a Jewish revolutionary; and others, such as P. Stuhlmacher, hold that Jesus considered himself to be the Messiah of Israel.[57]

---

[54] Wright, *Jesus and the Victory of God*, 85–86.

[55] See the classic essay by R. Bultmann: "Is Exegesis Without Presuppositions Possible?" in *Existence and Faith*, trans. S. M. Ogden (New York, NY: World, 1960), 342–51; cf. chap. 5, "The Interpreter," in W. W. Klein, C. L. Blomberg, R. L. Hubbard Jr., *Introduction to Biblical Interpretation*, rev. and upd. ed. (Nashville, TN: Thomas Nelson, n.d.); and appendices 1 and 2 in G. R. Osborne, *The Hermeneutical Spiral: A Comprehensive Introduction to Biblical Interpretation*, rev. and exp. ed. (Downers Grove, IL: InterVarsity, 2006).

[56] Wright, *Jesus and the Victory of God*, 90–124.

[57] G. Vermes, "Jesus the Jew," in *Jesus's Jewishness: Exploring the Place of Jesus in Early Judaism* (New York, NY: Crossroad, 1991), 108–22; E. P. Sanders, *Jesus and Judaism* (Philadelphia, PA: Fortress, 1985); M. Casey, *From Jewish Prophet to Gentile God: The Origins and Development of New Testament Christology* (Louisville, KY: Westminster John Knox, 1991); Witherington, *Jesus Quest*, 185–96; Meier, *Marginal Jew*; S. G. F. Brandon, *Jesus and the Zealots: A Study of the Political Factor in Primitive Christianity* (Manchester, UK: Manchester University Press, 1967); P. Stuhlmacher, *Jesus of Nazareth—Christ of Faith*, trans. S. Schatzmann (Peabody, MA: Hendrickson, 1993).

Table 3.1: The Quests of the Historical Jesus*

	Prequest (prior to 1778)	First Quest (1778–1906)	Abandoned Quest (1906–1953)	Second Quest (1953–present)	Third Quest (1965–present)
Tools**	Exegesis of biblical texts	Source -criticism	Form criticism	Redaction and tradition criticism	Social-scientific and a retooled tradition criticism
Tenets regarding Jesus	Jesus of history identical with Christ of faith	Difference between Jesus of history and Christ of faith (emphasis on Jesus of history)	Difference between Jesus of history and Christ of faith (emphasis on Christ of faith)	Jesus of history less important than Christ of faith	Jesus of history, not Christ of faith, proper subject of investigation
Philosophical assumption	No problem and no quest	Methodologically possible and theologically necessary	Methodologically impossible and theologically unnecessary	Methodologically possible and theologically necessary	Methodologically possible and theologically neutral

* Adapted from Tatum, *In Quest of Jesus*, 109.

** See the discussion of some of these various methods later on in this chapter; cf. chaps. 1–2 in Carson and Moo, *Introduction to the New Testament*.

CONTEMPORARY CHALLENGES TO THE NEW TESTAMENT PORTRAYAL OF JESUS

Introduction

Sensational and unorthodox portrayals of the historical Jesus of Nazareth have become commonplace in the twenty-first century. One new account of the life of the "real Jesus" after another is hitting the shelves of bookstores and generating a heated controversy that quickly gains lucrative media attention.[58] Although they are often based on scanty evidence, these portrayals of Jesus become a part of urban legends about Jesus's identity that are propagated by the uninformed. Many Americans, whose knowledge of Jesus sometimes does not extend beyond the latest conspiracy theory that they read about in the newspaper

[58] For a helpful resource, see H. W. House, *The Jesus Who Never Lived: Exposing False Christs and Finding the Real Jesus* (Eugene, OR: Harvest House, 2008).

or a recent best-selling novel, assume that Jesus was married to Mary Magdalene, left a royal bloodline that still exists today, and lived temporarily in Western Europe.[59]

Unbiblical portrayals of Jesus are not only the work of novelists and conspiracy theorists. Many scholars engaged in serious historical Jesus research have proposed reconstructions of Jesus's life and teachings that are very different from the descriptions of Jesus in the NT. Views of Jesus affirmed by various scholars are nearly as diverse as the scholars who affirm them. This section briefly explores a few of the recent challenges to the NT portrayal of Jesus.[60] What several of these characterizations of Jesus have in common is that the canonical Gospels are set aside as primary historical sources in favor of other allegedly more pristine—and thus more authentic—writings, most commonly one or several of the gnostic Gospels. Thus, it should come as no surprise that such writers arrive at depictions of Jesus that are at variance with the NT Gospels.

The Traveling Cynic Philosopher

Scholars such as F. G. Downing, B. Mack, and J. D. Crossan have portrayed Jesus as a wandering Cynic philosopher.[61] Crossan in particular has argued in great detail that Jesus preached and practiced a radical egalitarianism that abolished all social hierarchies and distinctions.[62] In keeping with this radical egalitarianism, Jesus taught that the kingdom of God had no human broker and that a relationship with God required no human mediator. All people had equal and direct access to God. For Crossan, Jesus's death did not accomplish atonement for sin. Jesus was tragically crucified because he threatened to destroy the temple that he viewed as the seat of Jewish hierarchical authority, a symbol of the human inequality he had come to despise. Thus, Jesus's agenda was a social rather than a spiritual one, and his teachings consisted of a few wise sayings and parables that taught far more about human equality than about sin, judgment, forgiveness, or his own identity.

---

[59] See D. Brown, *The Da Vinci Code* (New York, NY: Doubleday, 2003) and further discussion below. For a critique of Brown's description of Jesus, see C. L. Quarles, "Revisionist Views About Jesus," in *Passionate Conviction: Contemporary Discourses on Christian Apologetics*, ed. Paul Copan and William Lane Craig (Nashville, TN: B&H Academic, 2007), 94–108. For a succinct critique, see A. J. Köstenberger, *The Da Vinci Code: Is Christianity True?* (Wake Forest, NC: SEBTS, n.d.; posted at www.sebts.edu/davinci). For other critiques, see T. P. Jones, *Misquoting Truth: A Guide to the Fallacies of Bart Ehrman's Misquoting Jesus* (Downers Grove, IL: InterVarsity, 2007); D. L. Bock, *Breaking the Da Vinci Code* (Nashville, TN: Thomas Nelson, 2004); and J. Garlow and P. Jones, *Cracking Da Vinci's Code* (Colorado Springs, CO: David C. Cook, 2004).

[60] More extensive summaries of many of the portraits of Jesus described below appear in Witherington, *Jesus Quest*; and M. A. Powell, *Jesus as a Figure in History: How Modern Historians View the Man from Galilee*, 2nd ed. (Louisville, KY: Westminster John Knox, 2013). See also W. S. Kissinger, *The Lives of Jesus: A History and Bibliography*, Garland Reference Library of the Humanities 452 (New York, NY: Garland, 1985); and W. P. Weaver, *The Historical Jesus in the Twentieth Century (1900–1950)* (Harrisburg, PA: Trinity Press International, 1999).

[61] See the brief description of cynicism in chap. 2 above. See also F. G. Downing, *Christ and the Cynic: Jesus and Other Radical Preachers in First Century Tradition* (Sheffield, UK: Sheffield Academic Press, 1988); idem, *Jesus and the Threat of Violence* (London, UK: SCM, 1987); Mack, *Myth of Innocence*; Crossan, *Historical Jesus*. On the latter two writers, see the survey of the "Quest of the Historical Jesus" above.

[62] Crossan's writings have also had considerable influence on feminist writers such as E. S. Fiorenza and R. R. Ruether. On the feminist Jesus, see further below.

As mentioned, Crossan could paint this portrait of Jesus only by dismissing large amounts of material about Jesus in the canonical Gospels and by preferring material in non-canonical sources. Yet his reconstruction of Jesus's life is only as good as the sources he used. As shown below, Crossan's preference for the non-canonical sources is unjustified since his favorite sources are either late revisions of material from the canonical Gospels, speculations about Jesus from second-century Christians, or even outright forgeries.

The Charismatic Faith Healer

M. Borg and G. Vermes have portrayed Jesus as a charismatic figure who had visionary or mystical experiences of God and somehow functioned as a channel of God's power for others.[63] Although these portraits are an improvement on views of Jesus that deny any supernatural activity by him due to modernist presuppositions, both reconstructions fail to comport with the fuller picture of Jesus presented in the NT.

Borg's Jesus had too much compassion for others to demand moral purity of them. Moreover, the "god" that this Jesus mediated was also more of an impersonal force than a personal deity. Borg claimed,

> God does not refer to a supernatural being "out there." . . . God refers to the sacred at the center of existence, the holy mystery that is all around us and within us. God is the non-material ground and source and presence in which . . . we live and move and have our being.[64]

Vermes's Jesus was a Galilean holy man (Hb. *hasid*) who performed miracles and operated outside the proper channels of normal religious authority. Vermes compared Jesus to two similar holy men described in the Talmuds, Hanina ben Dosa and Honi the Circle Drawer.[65] Just as these men performed miracles, Jesus healed the sick and conquered the forces of evil in individuals.

However, Vermes made the mistake of emphasizing similarities between Jesus and these figures and ignoring some important differences. For example, according to Vermes, the marks of a *hasid* included using prayer to produce cures for the sick and calling down rain. But the Gospels never describe Jesus as making rain. The Gospels portray Jesus as One who was more than just a mighty man of prayer and as One who had the personal power to heal directly.

The Apocalyptic Prophet

E. P. Sanders and M. Casey have written treatments of Jesus in which they argue that Jesus was an apocalyptic prophet who expected the climax of human history during his

---

[63] M. J. Borg, *Jesus: A New Vision* (San Francisco, CA: Harper, 1987); G. Vermes, *Jesus the Jew: A Historian's Reading of the Gospels*, 2nd ed. (New York, NY: Macmillan, 1983).

[64] M. J. Borg, *Meeting Jesus Again for the First Time: The Historical Jesus and the Heart of Contemporary Faith* (San Francisco, CA: Harper, 1995), 14.

[65] See C. A. Evans, "Holy Men, Jewish," in *Dictionary of New Testament Background*, 505–7.

lifetime or shortly after his death. Sanders argued that Jesus anticipated "the imminent direct intervention of God in history, the elimination of evil and evildoers, the building of the new and glorious temple, and the reassembly of Israel with himself and his disciples as leading figures in it."[66] Jesus prepared for God's judgment on the temple and the restoration of his people by offering unconditional forgiveness to even the most obdurate of the Jews. Jesus offered this forgiveness without requiring repentance. Sanders avoided the titles ascribed to Jesus in the Gospels but did identify Jesus as God's last envoy. Sanders tended to dismiss Jesus's miracles by arguing that they were cures of psychosomatic illnesses, intentional deceptions, and in a few cases mysterious manipulations of natural causes that are not presently understood by science. Sanders denied that Jesus experienced any serious conflict with the Pharisees.[67]

M. Casey argued that Jesus saw himself as the fulfillment of John the Baptist's prophecy about the Coming One. Jesus believed the climax of history would occur in his lifetime and urged the lost sheep of Israel to prepare for final judgment by repenting of their sins. Unlike Sanders's Jesus, Casey's Jesus experienced serious conflict with the Pharisees because of their attempts to impose strict purity regulations on Galilean Jews. This would have essentially excluded Galilean Jews, especially artisans and peasants, from the people of God. According to Casey, Jesus foresaw his own death and regarded it as an act that procured atonement that would redeem Israel. But this did not mean that Jesus was a messianic figure; rather, he simply viewed his death as having the same significance as the deaths of the Maccabean martyrs.

The research of Sanders and Casey rightly places Jesus in a first-century Jewish context, and to this extent their views are superior to treatments such as those of Crossan and Mack. But Sanders and Casey fail to capture the essence of the Jesus of the NT by suppressing or denying much of the Gospels' data. What is more, Sanders's Jesus was so similar to other Jewish contemporaries that it is difficult to explain why he was rejected and crucified. By contrast, the canonical Gospels make clear that ultimately the crucifixion was religiously motivated and that Jesus was accused of blasphemy on account of his claim to deity (Matt 26:63–65; John 19:7).

The Social Reformer

Scholars such as G. Theissen, R. A. Horsley, and R. D. Kaylor have argued that Jesus was more of a social reformer than an apocalyptic prophet.[68] Theissen, whose views were

---

[66] Sanders, *Jesus and Judaism*, 153.

[67] For more extensive summaries of Sanders's views, see Powell, *Jesus*, 113–29; Witherington, *Jesus Quest*, 116–36.

[68] G. Theissen, *Sociology of Early Palestinian Christianity* (Philadelphia, PA: Fortress, 1978); idem, *The Gospels in Context: Social and Political History in the Synoptic Tradition* (Edinburgh, Scotland: T&T Clark, 1992); R. A. Horsley and J. S. Hanson, *Bandits, Prophets and Messiahs: Popular Movements at the Time of Jesus* (Minneapolis, MN: Winston, 1985); R. A. Horsley, *Sociology and the Jesus Movement* (New York, NY: Crossroad, 1989); idem, *The Liberation of Christmas: The Infancy Narratives in Social Context* (New York, NY: Crossroad, 1989); R. D. Kaylor, *Jesus the Prophet: His Vision of the Kingdom on Earth* (Louisville. KY: Westminster John Knox, 1994). For helpful summaries of the presentation of Jesus as a social prophet, see Witherington, *Jesus Quest*, 137–60; and Powell, *Jesus as a Figure in History*, 52–54.

seminal for the later work of Crossan, Horsley, and others, viewed Jesus as a radical charismatic preacher. Jesus's committed followers accompanied him in his itinerant ministry and embraced a lifestyle that renounced possessions and family ties and was devoted to homelessness. Jesus founded a peace party that sought to extinguish the simmering spirit of revolt and violence popular in the various Jewish reform movements of his day. He and his followers encouraged commitment to an ethic of nonretaliation. Their refusal to defend themselves required them to be constantly on the move in order to escape harm. Jesus called individuals to this radical lifestyle because he was convinced that the end was near. When the kingdom of God was established, the poor would become wealthy; the weak, strong; and the least, the greatest.

Influenced by Theissen's theories, R. Horsley argued that Jesus was a social revolutionary who wished to restructure Galilean village life in order to establish equality between women and men, the poor and the wealthy, and the oppressed and the powerful. R. D. Kaylor also saw Jesus as a social reformer, but he further argued that Jesus's desire for reform was motivated by a desire to return to the egalitarianism that supposedly characterized Jewish agricultural communities before Israel's first monarchy.

Although Jesus was certainly concerned about human oppression and mistreatment, the theories of Theissen, Horsley, and to a lesser extent Kaylor generally overlook the spiritual dimension of Jesus's teaching. Abundant NT evidence shows that Jesus viewed himself as a messianic or kingly figure. This self-understanding precludes interpretations of Jesus as committed to a radical egalitarianism that abolishes all distinctions and challenges all authority structures. While Jesus clearly denounced the corrupt Jewish system (as at the temple cleansing, John 2:13–22), mere social or religious reform was not the primary thrust of his mission. As Jesus himself said, "My kingdom is not of this world" (John 18:36). Hence, any effort to understand Jesus predominantly or exclusively in human, political, or socioeconomic terms falls short of capturing the essence of Jesus's identity and calling.

The Feminist Jesus

E. S. Fiorenza, the leading proponent of feminist scholarship, viewed Jesus as a radical reformer who wished to liberate women and other marginalized people from male-dominated social structures and Roman imperialism.[69] She also argued that Jesus envisioned and worshipped God as Sophia, a feminine portrayal of deity. Fiorenza posited the theory that Proverbs 1–9 integrated language about Egyptian goddesses into its reflection of Yahweh. In keeping with this wisdom tradition, Jesus conceived of deity in feminine terms and worshipped God as Sophia rather than as Father or Abba.

Fiorenza's portrait of Jesus is driven more by the social agenda of championing female rights than by the actual data of the NT Gospels. Her claim that Jesus worshipped Sophia

---

[69] E. S. Fiorenza, *In Memory of Her: A Feminist Theological Reconstruction of Christian Origins* (New York, NY: Crossroad, 1984); idem, *Jesus: Miriam's Child, Sophia's Prophet: Critical Issues in Feminist Christology* (New York, NY: Continuum, 1994). For an excellent summary of Fiorenza's view of Jesus, see Witherington, *Jesus Quest*, 163–85.

is based largely on her questionable interpretation of Proverbs 1–9, her even more questionable handling of Matthew 11:19 (cf. Luke 7:35), and a casual dismissal of numerous texts in which Jesus described God as his Father. Her arguments never adequately explain why a radical egalitarian who wished to abolish all distinctions between men and women would appoint twelve men as his disciples and choose three of these men as his inner circle.[70]

Another major representative of feminist scholarship is R. R. Ruether. In 1998, Ruether set forth her thesis that Jesus was a "religious seeker" who was initially drawn to John the Baptist's apocalyptic message of repentance.[71] Later he broke with the Baptist, inspired by a vision of Satan falling from heaven like lightning (Luke 10:18). He concluded that he need no longer wait for God's future intervention but that Satan's power had already been broken. Around AD 30 he became convinced that his kingdom vision was about to be fulfilled. He gathered his followers, went to Jerusalem, and was arrested and crucified. Yet some of his disciples were persuaded that Jesus was not dead but alive and present with them "in the Spirit." Thus, the early church was born, with women playing an important role.

The Sage

B. Witherington has suggested that Jesus might best be understood as a teacher of wisdom or a sage who regarded himself as the embodiment or incarnation of God's Wisdom.[72] Witherington has shown that numerous sayings of Jesus have remarkable similarities to descriptions of divine Wisdom in the OT, Apocrypha, and Pseudepigrapha. This Wisdom was often personified in ancient texts such as Proverbs 8 to portray Wisdom as God's agent who was sent with a commission, possessed God's very mind and will, and revealed it to others.

As Witherington developed this thesis in his later work,[73] his view of Jesus as the embodiment of Wisdom explains the high Christology of John 1 and of the very early Christological hymns that appear in Colossians 1 and Philippians 2 portraying Jesus as the incarnation of deity. This early Christology was rooted in texts such as Proverbs 1, 8–9 and Sirach 24 that describe Wisdom as a personification of God that preexisted, assisted in creation, came to earth, called God's people to repentance, saved some but was rejected by others, and returned to the right hand of God.[74]

---

[70] For a fuller engagement and critique of the feminist Jesus, see M. E. Köstenberger, *Jesus and the Feminists: Who Do They Say That He Is?* (Wheaton, IL: Crossway, 2008).

[71] R. R. Ruether, *Women and Redemption: A Theological History* (Minneapolis, MN: Fortress, 1998), 16–20. The following summary is indebted to Köstenberger, *Jesus and the Feminists*, chap. 7. See also her assessment of Ruether's portrayal of Jesus (ibid).

[72] B. Witherington III, *The Christology of Jesus* (Philadelphia, PA: Fortress, 1990), 274–75 (though he noted that this contention is "more speculative" than others; p. 274).

[73] B. Witherington III, *Jesus the Sage: The Pilgrimage of Wisdom* (Minneapolis, MN: Fortress, 1994); see also idem, *John's Wisdom: A Commentary on the Fourth Gospel* (Louisville, KY: Westminster John Knox, 1995).

[74] But see A. H. I. Lee, *From Messiah to Preexistent Son: Jesus's Self-Consciousness and Early Christian Exegesis of Messianic Psalms*, WUNT 2/192 (Tübingen, Germany: Mohr Siebeck, 2005), who contends that it was not Jewish Wisdom traditions

Witherington's proposal has much to commend it. The criticism of the proposal is not primarily that it is incorrect but that by itself it is inadequate.[75] Witherington himself admitted this and conceded that no single title can fully describe Jesus.[76] He acknowledged that Jesus was not only the embodiment of Wisdom and a sage but that he was also a healer, a prophetic figure, and saw himself as Messiah.[77] As Witherington would acknowledge, although understanding Jesus as a sage and the embodiment of Wisdom explained aspects of his messianic consciousness, this understanding must be supplemented by other approaches and insights.

A Marginal Jew

J. P. Meier has suggested that the historical Jesus is best seen as a marginal Jew.[78] Jesus was marginal for several reasons. First, Jesus marginalized himself by abandoning his livelihood as a carpenter and undertaking a prophetic itinerant ministry that required him to depend on the generosity of others and thus invited the disgust of many ordinary working Jews. Second, Jesus's teachings and practices were marginal because they did not comport with the views and practices of the major Jewish sects of his time. Examples of Jesus's radical teachings and lifestyle include his prohibition of divorce, his rejection of fasting, and his voluntary celibacy. Jesus's rejection of standard Jewish convictions was viewed as particularly audacious since he had not received formal rabbinic training. Third, Jesus's shameful and brutal execution shows he had been pushed to the margins of society by both the political and religious establishment of Palestine.

The description of Jesus as a marginal Jew, however, is inadequate. First, the category does not adequately express Meier's view of the teachings and deeds of Jesus that can be historically verified. Meier's work affirms that Jesus performed what he and others regarded as miracles and exorcisms, that Jesus was a Jewish eschatological prophet who proclaimed the coming of God's kingdom, and that Jesus mediated the experience of the joys of salvation. These aspects of Jesus's ministry are not implied by the label "marginal Jew." Second, Meier's purpose in his research was merely to describe the Jesus who can be recovered and reconstructed by means of serious historical research and not to describe the Jesus who actually lived and is no longer recoverable. He wished to develop a portrait of Jesus that would satisfy any honest historian regardless of his philosophical or religious commitments. This required him to eliminate material that he regarded as probable from his reconstruction of Jesus's life. Despite these and other shortcomings of Meier's work, his portrait of Jesus is far more carefully and reasonably argued than most other contemporary portraits.

---

but Jesus's messianic consciousness that formed the basis for the early church's messianic exegesis of OT passages such as Pss 110:1 and 2:7; and the discussion of Lee's contribution in A. J. Köstenberger and S. R. Swain, *Father, Son and Spirit: The Trinity and John's Gospel*, NSBT 24 (Downers Grove, IL: InterVarsity, 2008), 39–41.

[75] See A. J. Köstenberger, *John*, BECNT (Grand Rapids, MI: Baker, 2004), 26–27.

[76] Witherington, *Christology of Jesus*, 267.

[77] Ibid., 263–77.

[78] Meier, *Marginal Jew*.

The Risen Messiah

One of the more biblically faithful portraits of Jesus in recent years has come from the pen of N. T. Wright. His first three volumes of a proposed six-volume work portray Jesus as a divine messianic figure who rose from the dead.[79] Wright's portrait of Jesus is not a mere repetition of the standard traditional view but one that breaks new ground in several ways. According to Wright, first-century Israel saw itself as still languishing in exile due to the Roman domination of Palestine. Israel desperately longed for God to return to deliver his people. Jesus was an eschatological prophet who came to announce that God was going to return to Zion to dwell with his people again. When he did, he would defeat Israel's enemies and liberate his people from their exile.

Jesus promised this coming deliverance in both word and deed. His miracles and exorcisms served as prophetic signs that demonstrated that God was already at work restoring Israel and defeating Satan, the nation's greatest enemy. His table fellowship with those rejected by Israel's religious authorities demonstrated Jesus's offer to forgive sinners and to include them in the restored Israel.

Jesus also replaced adherence to the temple cult and fidelity to the OT law with allegiance to himself. He believed that his own death would involve representative suffering for Israel in which he sacrificially bore the eschatological woes that were a necessary prelude to the end of Israel's exile. Jesus not only proclaimed the return of Yahweh to Israel; he enacted, symbolized, and personified that return. He recognized himself as the embodiment of Yahweh's return to Israel. Jesus "believed he had to do and be, for Israel and the world, that which according to scripture only YHWH himself could do and be."[80]

Finally, Wright argued convincingly and at great length that Jesus rose from the dead. He offered a devastating critique of the claim that Jesus experienced a mere spiritual resurrection, a claim lodged by scholars such as J. D. Crossan and B. Chilton. He insisted that both Jewish descriptions of resurrection and NT accounts of Jesus's resurrection demonstrated that Jesus experienced a bodily resurrection. This resurrection confirms the early church's belief that Jesus is both Lord and Christ.

Overall, Wright has offered a portrait of Jesus that accommodates more of the biblical data than the other contemporary views discussed above. At those points at which he departs from the traditional Christian view of Jesus and his teaching, the traditional view is generally superior. But Wright has succeeded in gaining a hearing again for a high view of Jesus that regards him as the risen Lord. What is more, Wright's outspoken defense of the

---

[79] N. T. Wright, *The New Testament and the People of God*, Christian Origins and the Question of God 1 (Minneapolis, MN: Fortress, 1992); *Jesus and the Victory of God*; Christians Origins and the Question of God 2 (Minneapolis, MN: Fortress, 1997) *The Resurrection of the Son of God*, Christian Origins and the Question of God 3 (Minneapolis, MN: Fortress, 2003). The fourth volume consists of two books titled *Paul and the Faithfulness of God*, Christian Origins and the Question of God 4 (Minneapolis, MN: Fortress, 2013).

[80] Wright, *Jesus and the Victory of God*, 653.

biblical teachings regarding Jesus's resurrection sets him apart from the leaders of the Jesus Seminar, such as J. D. Crossan, who do not accept the scriptural witness in this regard.

In a similar approach, Craig Keener has composed his own portrait of the historical Jesus. Keener sought to avoid both the minimalist approach (that affirms only what is "historically proved certainty") and the maximalist approach (that "grants as evidence whatever is possible").[81] He relied heavily on Mark and "Q" material in an appeal to "a consensus of scholarship regarding the most accepted sources for reconstructing Jesus's life."[82]

John the Baptist called Israelites to repentance and baptized the repentant in the wilderness. He warned of God's imminent judgment in the form of eternal torment. He proclaimed the coming One who was somehow both human and divine. John affirmed but later doubted Jesus's identity as the coming One since initially Jesus did not appear to fulfill John's vision of One who baptized with God's Spirit and poured out fiery judgment.[83]

Jesus grew up in Nazareth and later relocated to Capernaum. Some of his first disciples were fishermen. His milieu suggests that he was not a Cynic revolutionary or Pharisee (despite some similar convictions to those held by members of the sect). Jesus was a sage, possibily a charismatic one, who taught in parables. His parables emphasized the inauguration of God's kingdom and are probably connected to Jesus's understanding of himself as God's agent, one superior to the prophets.[84] Jesus urged people to get their lives in order in an effort to prepare for the impending kingdom. They needed to ready themselves to give up family ties, possessions, and even their lives for the sake of the kingdom. That kingdom would turn the present order upside down by exalting the lowly and demeaning the proud.[85]

Jesus's teachings emphasized love for God, inner purity, the importance of caring for aged parents, and the permanence of marriage.[86] Jesus had conflict with Pharisees and scribes over matters such as proper Sabbath observance, and he denounced these opponents in harsh terms.[87] Jesus functioned as an eschatological prophet, performed Elijah-like signs, and may have seen himself as a new Elijah and new Moses. As a prophet, Jesus foretold God's judgment on Israel, opposed commerce in the temple, and founded a restoration movement within Israel. Peter played a special role in the founding of this new community.[88]

Jesus saw himself as the Messiah and was ultimately executed for claiming to be Israel's true King. He did not view his Messiahship in mere political terms. He predicted his own death and saw his death as a necessary part of God's plan for his kingdom.[89] Jesus ate a final

---

[81] Craig Keener, *The Historical Jesus of the Gospels* (Grand Rapids, MI: Eerdmans, 2009), 163.

[82] Ibid., 164.

[83] Ibid., 163–77.

[84] Ibid., 178–95.

[85] Ibid., 196–213.

[86] Ibid., 214–22.

[87] Ibid., 223–37.

[88] Ibid., 238–55.

[89] Ibid., 256–82.

meal with his disciples in which he revealed the significance of his impending death: "Jesus was offering himself as a martyr to turn away God's anger from Israel, as Jewish traditions understood some other martyrs [to have done]."[90]

The general contours of the Passion Narrative are historical since they appear to be based on eyewitness testimony and fit so well with what is known of the personalities involved. After his crucifixion, Jesus's tomb was found to be empty and his disciples believed that Jesus rose from the dead because they believed they saw the risen Jesus. This belief was so firm that they gladly staked their very lives on this claim. For these disciples, "Jesus's resurrection cohered with his message: God was establishing a new order, and Jesus its proclaimer held first place in it."[91]

Keener's reconstruction is particularly intriguing since he began his personal quest to understand religion and biblical perspectives as not only an extreme skeptic, but an atheist. He commented, "As one who is now a Christian I approach the subject with a special interest I previously lacked, but an interest that I believe makes me more rather than less committed to investigating historical information about Jesus. When I was an atheist I never imagined that my life would take this turn, but I harbor no regrets that it has. Even when I was an atheist I valued pursuing truth, regardless of where it might lead."[92]

Table 3.2: Contemporary Portrayals of Jesus

Portrayal	Proponents	Description
Traveling Cynic Philosopher	J. D. Crossan, F. G. Downing	Jesus preached and practiced a radical egalitarianism that abolished social hierarchies and distinctions.
Charismatic Faith Healer	M. Borg, G. Vermes	Jesus as charismatic figure with visionary, mystical experiences of God who functioned as channel of God's power to others
Apocalyptic Prophet	E. P. Sanders, M. Casey	Jesus as prophet who expected the climax of human history in his lifetime or shortly after his death
Social Reformer	G. Theissen, R. A. Horsley	Jesus as itinerant preacher who renounced possessions, family ties, and violent revolts, calling for return to egalitarianism and renouncing social class system
Feminist Jesus	E. S. Fiorenza, R. R. Ruether	Jesus as liberator of women and the marginalized from male-dominated Roman social structures
Sage	B. Witherington	Teacher of wisdom who saw himself as the embodied Wisdom of God
Marginal Jew	J. P. Meier	Jesus renounced livelihood as carpenter and did not live by the rules of the Judaism of his day
Risen Messiah	N. T. Wright, Craig Keener	Jesus as risen Messiah who delivers Israel from exile

[90] Ibid., 283–302.
[91] Ibid., 348.
[92] Ibid., xxxv.

Summary

A. Schweitzer, in his famous survey of modern Jesus research, *The Quest of the Historical Jesus*, observed over a century ago that in many instances a scholar's portrait of Jesus is strangely reminiscent of the scholar responsible for the portrait.[93] As A. Loisy noted long ago, many reconstructions of Jesus appear to be pale reflections of the researcher himself.[94] More recently J. D. Crossan charged that it "is impossible to avoid the suspicion that historical Jesus research is a very safe place to do theology and call it history, to do autobiography and call it biography."[95] Feminists discover a feminist Jesus in the Gospels; liberal Protestants tend to find a liberal Jesus; and so forth. Crossan himself has been subjected to a creative and clever critique by N. T. Wright, who exposes the questionable criteria and sources underlying Crossan's work in the form of an entertaining parody.[96]

These tendencies demonstrate the powerful influence a scholar's presuppositions may exert on his research and conclusions. Thus, it is important to seek to understand and evaluate the presuppositions and philosophical commitments of scholars that may impact their reconstruction of Jesus's identity and teachings. In particular, the sources and methods utilized by scholars engaged in historical Jesus research can exert an influence on their conclusions that is as strong as their presuppositions. Not surprisingly, dependence on non-canonical sources for one's view of Jesus generally results in a portrait of Jesus that is quite different from the traditional Christian view. The next section therefore briefly examines some of these non-canonical sources and evaluates their usefulness in understanding Jesus.

DEPENDENCE ON NON-CANONICAL GOSPELS FOR AN UNDERSTANDING OF JESUS

Introduction

At the end of the twentieth century and the beginning of the twenty-first, North America witnessed an enormous increase of interest in the so-called lost Gospels, accounts of the life and teachings of Jesus excluded for various reasons from the NT canon.[97] Some have even claimed that literally thousands of written accounts of Jesus's life existed in the early church. According to these authors, although the canonical Gospels distort the true

---

[93] Schweitzer, *Quest of the Historical Jesus*.

[94] Although Schweitzer is normally credited with this criticism, it appears to have been made first by Loisy several years earlier in his criticisms of A. Harnack. See A. Loisy, *Evangile et l'Eglise* (Bellevue, France: Chez l'auteur, 1903); C. Brown, "Quest of the Historical Jesus," in *Dictionary of Jesus and the Gospels*, 331. For a helpful survey of the various quests of Jesus, see Tatum, *In Quest of Jesus*.

[95] Crossan, *Historical Jesus*, xxviii.

[96] N. T. Wright, "Taking the Text with Her Pleasure: A Post-Post-Modernist Response to J. Dominic Crossan, *The Historical Jesus: The Life of a Mediterranean Jewish Peasant* with Apologies to A. A. Milne, St Paul and James Joyce," *Theol* 96 (1993): 303–10.

[97] Although many North American scholars are insisting on the priority and independence of the lost Gospels, scholars in Europe have generally been unconvinced by their arguments.

story of the real Jesus because of theological and political agendas, the truth about Jesus of Nazareth is still preserved in these apocryphal works such as the Gospel of Philip and the Gospel of Mary Magdalene. One such author used these non-canonical Gospels to argue that Jesus's deity was an invention of a politically motivated Roman emperor and that Jesus was married to Mary Magdalene.[98]

Others writing for a scholarly audience have also preferred non-canonical works to Matthew, Mark, Luke, and John. For example, in his *Four Other Gospels*, J. D. Crossan argued that the Gospel of Thomas, an early stratum of the Gospel of Peter, and Secret Mark were earlier than the canonical Gospels and were utilized by the evangelists when they wrote their own Gospels.[99] In his *Historical Jesus*, Crossan placed these three sources along with Q in his first stratum of sources and utilized these sources to portray Jesus as a wandering Cynic philosopher.[100] Clearly, one's choice of sources in historical Jesus research has a significant impact on one's reconstruction of Jesus's life and teaching. Portraits of Jesus that take as their point of reference the canonical Gospels are *significantly* different from portraits of Jesus derived from alternative gospels.

In this section we discuss whether these alternative Gospels are helpful resources for understanding who Jesus really was. We briefly examine three of the lost Gospels on which some historical Jesus scholars rely, particularly the Gospel of Thomas, the Gospel of Peter, and Secret Mark. We suggest that these alternative Gospels are too late to reflect credible testimony about the Jesus of history. We also argue that the canonical Gospels remain our most helpful resources for understanding the life of Jesus of Nazareth—not merely because they are canonical, but because they are our earliest sources and reflect eyewitness testimony regarding Jesus's life and teachings.

The Gospel of Thomas

Some of the early church fathers of the third and fourth centuries referred to a Gospel associated with the name Thomas.[101] Fragments of this lost Gospel were discovered among the Oxyrhynchus Papyri in the 1890s,[102] but these fragments were not positively identified as belonging to the Gospel of Thomas until the discovery of the Nag Hammadi Codices, thirteen leather-bound books written in the Coptic language that were uncovered in Egypt in 1945. The second codex found at Nag Hammadi contained the full text of the Gospel of Thomas.[103]

---

[98] Brown, *Da Vinci Code*.

[99] J. D. Crossan, *Four Other Gospels: Shadows on the Contours of the Canon* (New York, NY: Harper & Row, 1985).

[100] Crossan, *Historical Jesus*.

[101] The earliest known reference is in *Hippolytus, Refutation of all Heresies* 5.7.20.

[102] P. Oxy. 1, 654 and 655 contain the Prologue, sayings 1–7, 24, 26–33, 36–39, 77.

[103] For a critical edition of the Coptic and Greek texts, see B. Layton, ed., *Nag Hammadi Codex II, 2–7 Together with XIII,2*, Brit. Lib. Or. 4296 (1), and P. Oxy. 1, 654, 655* (Leiden, Netherlands: Brill, 1989). For an introduction and English translation of the Coptic text, see J. M. Robinson, ed., *The Nag Hammadi Library in English* (San Francisco, CA: Harper, 1990).

The last twenty-five years have seen the Gospel of Thomas occupy an increasingly central role in attempts to reconstruct the life and teachings of Jesus of Nazareth. Of the scholars who rely heavily on the resource in providing a portrait of the historical Jesus, few have been more prolific or influential than Crossan. He listed Gospel of Thomas I (material in Thomas paralleled by the canonical Gospels) in his first stratum of sources for the Jesus tradition. According to Crossan, this earlier layer of tradition in Thomas "was composed by the fifties C.E., possibly in Jerusalem, under the aegis of James's authority (see *Gos. Thom.* 12)."[104] He asserts boldly that the Gospel of Thomas predated the canonical Gospels and preserved more reliable traditions of Jesus's sayings. But he overlooks considerable evidence supporting the older consensus view that the Gospel of Thomas was written in the mid-second century or later.

First, careful comparisons of the theological tendencies, vocabulary statistics, and preferred grammar of the canonical Gospels and Thomas strongly suggest that Thomas depended on the canonical Gospels and thus postdates them rather than vice versa. W. Schrage carefully examined every saying in the Gospel of Thomas that has a parallel in the Synoptic Gospels. He concluded that the evidence best supports Thomas's reliance on the Synoptic Gospels.[105] More recent publications have demonstrated that the very parallels to which some scholars have appealed as proof of the priority and independence of the Gospel of Thomas are better explained if Thomas depended on the Synoptic Gospels.[106] R. Bauckham recently noted that Gospel of Thomas 13 asserts an authority superior to that of the Gospels of Mark and Matthew and thus clearly postdates the composition and distribution of those Gospels.[107]

H.-M. Schenke's analysis of the compositional history of Thomas that he presented to the Jesus Seminar in 1991 concluded that the Gospel of Thomas was extracted from a commentary on the sayings of Jesus, probably Papias of Hierapolis's "Exposition of the Lord's Sayings." This suggests a date of composition somewhere around the year 140. Schenke pointed out that this date corresponds with evidence in saying 68, which he translated, "And they (i.e. your persecutors themselves) will no longer find a (dwelling-) place there where they persecuted you." Schenke argued that this statement clearly referred to the Bar Kokhba revolt in AD 132–135 that resulted in the expulsion of the Jews from Jerusalem by Roman authorities. Consequently, saying 68 provides an earliest possible date for the composition of Thomas. Schenke, who earlier identified himself as a "member of the Koester school of thought" that dates the Gospel of Thomas to the second half of

---

[104] Crossan, *Historical Jesus*, 427.

[105] W. Schrage, *Das Verhältnis des Thomas-Evangeliums zur synoptischen Tradition und zu den koptischen Evangelienübersetzungen*, BZNW 29 (Berlin, Germany: Töpelmann, 1964). A helpful summary of his conclusions appears on pp. 1–11.

[106] C. L. Quarles, "The Use of the Gospel of Thomas in the Research on the Historical Jesus of John Dominic Crossan," *CBQ* 69 (2007): 517–36.

[107] R. Bauckham, *Jesus and the Eyewitnesses: The Gospels as Eyewitness Testimony* (Grand Rapids, MI: Eerdmans, 2006), 236–37.

the first century, argued that the evidence of saying 68 calls for "a reabandonment of the early dating attempted within the Koester school of thought."[108]

S. J. Patterson joined S. Davies, H. Koester, J. D. Crossan, and the Jesus Seminar in dating the Gospel of Thomas to the middle of the first century.[109] But Patterson admitted that some portions of Thomas, such as saying 7, were composed and added to the collection as late as the third or fourth century. Saying 7 reads, "Jesus said: 'Fortunate is the lion that the human will eat so that the lion becomes human. And foul is the human that the lion will eat, and the lion will become human.'"[110] Patterson, appealing to the research of H. Jackson, argued that the text expressed imagery common among the ascetic monks of Upper Egypt beginning in the second century in which the lion symbolized the fleshly passions that the ascetics sought to suppress. Patterson suggested that the saying was added to the collection after it reached Egypt and was adopted by these ascetics.[111] Of course, if the saying is original to the Gospel, then Thomas would belong in the second century as was previously thought.

H. J. W. Drijvers, R. Schippers, and N. Perrin have dated the Gospel of Thomas close to 200. Perrin argued that the similarities between the Gospel of Thomas and Tatian's *Diatessaron*, which led Quispel to suggest that Tatian had used Thomas as a fifth Gospel in his harmony, were actually the result of Thomas's dependence on Tatian. Consequently, the Gospel of Thomas postdates the *Diatessaron*, which was most likely produced around AD 150–160. Perrin deduced the dependency of Thomas on Tatian using four steps: (1) the Gospel of Thomas was first composed in Syriac, a hypothesis Perrin defended persuasively by showing that numerous catchwords that link the sayings of Thomas depend on a Syriac original; (2) the Gospel of Thomas displays literary unity and reflects the work of one author; (3) due to the unity and compositional strategy behind the Gospel of Thomas, the author likely relied on written Syriac sources for his knowledge of Synoptic tradition; and (4) Tatian's *Diatessaron* is the only Syriac text of the Synoptic tradition that could have been available to Thomas.[112]

---

[108] H.-M. Schenke, *On the Compositional History of the Gospel of Thomas* (Claremont, CA: Institute for Antiquity and Christianity, 1998), 1–25, especially p. 25.

[109] S. Davies, *Thomas and Christian Wisdom* (New York, NY: Harper & Row, 1983), 3; H. Koester, *Ancient Christian Gospels: Their History and Development* (Philadelphia, PA: Trinity Press International, 1990), 85; S. Patterson, *The Gospel of Thomas and Jesus*, FFRS (Sonoma, CA: Polebridge, 1993), 113–18.

[110] M. Meyer, *The Gospel of Thomas: The Hidden Sayings of Jesus, New Translation, with Introductions and Notes* (San Francisco, CA: Harper, 1992), 25.

[111] S. Patterson, "Understanding the Gospel of Thomas Today," in *The Fifth Gospel: The Gospel of Thomas Comes of Age*, ed. S. J. Patterson, J. M. Robinson, and H.-G. Bethge (Harrisburg, PA: Trinity Press, 1998), 43–44; cf. H. Jackson, *The Lion Becomes Man: The Gnostic Leontomorphic Creator and the Platonic Tradition*, SBLDS 81 (Atlanta, GA: Scholars Press, 1985).

[112] N. Perrin, *Thomas and Tatian: The Relationship Between the Gospel of Thomas and the Diatessaron*, Academia Biblica 5 (Leiden, Netherlands: Brill, 2002), 193–94. Perrin acknowledged that the theory of Thomas's dependence on Tatian was earlier proposed by Drijvers and Schippers. See Drijvers, "Facts and Problems," 173; and R. Schippers, *Het Evangelie van Thomas: Aocriefe Woorden van Jezus: Vertaling, inleiding en kommentar* (Kampen, Netherlands: Kok, 1960). The theory that the Gospel of Thomas was first composed in Syriac or dependent on Syriac sources was proposed earlier by A. Guillamont, H. J. W. Drijvers, H. Quecke, K. Rudolph, F. Morard, and A. Strobel. See Perrin, *Thomas*, 6–7, for references; cf. the more

Since compelling evidence of the Gospel of Thomas's late date is prompting even scholars previously committed to an early date to abandon this theory, preference for Thomas over the canonical Gospels in reconstructing the life and teachings of Jesus is inappropriate. Although some scholars are attracted to the Gospel of Thomas because it has no miracles, no Passion Narrative, and no resurrection of Jesus, Thomas appears to have been composed too late to expect it to be more reliable than the canonical Gospels.

The Gospel of Peter

The church historian Eusebius of Caesarea (ca. AD 260–340) made mention several times of a heretical Gospel associated with the apostle Peter.[113] A narrative of the trial, crucifixion, and resurrection of Jesus that was discovered in excavations at Akhmim in Egypt in 1886–87 has been identified, perhaps incorrectly, as the lost Gospel of Peter.[114] As with the Gospel of Thomas, the scholar to make the most extensive use of the Gospel of Peter is Crossan.[115] After a detailed comparison of the Gospel of Peter with the canonical Gospels, he concluded that the earliest stratum in the Gospel of Peter was the hypothetical Cross Gospel.[116] He argued that this early narrative was utilized by the Synoptic writers and John and served as the only source of the canonical evangelists for the Passion Narrative.[117] Strong evidence suggests that the Gospel of Peter does not preserve reliable independent tradition about the death and resurrection of Jesus. Instead, the document was a revision of the canonical Gospels embellished with second-century legends.

In the narrative of the guard at the tomb, the content and vocabulary of the Gospel of Peter suggest a close relationship with Matthew.[118] Crossan noted one sustained verbal

---

recent work by Perrin, *Thomas: The Other Gospel* (Louisville, KY: Westminster John Knox, 2007); and the review by C. L. Quarles in *JETS* 51 (2008): 158–60.

[113] Eusebius, *Eccl. Hist.* 3.3.1–4; 3.25.6; 6.12.3–6.

[114] Present knowledge of the content of Gospel of Peter is limited since complete texts are no longer extant. The most extensive fragment of the Gospel of Peter begins at the end of Jesus's trial and breaks off at the beginning of a description of a postresurrection appearance of Christ to the Twelve. The original Gospel of Peter may have included an account of Jesus's birth, childhood, youth, and adult ministry. This supposition is supported by Origen's claim (*Comm. Matt.* 10.17) that the Gospel of Peter claimed that Joseph, Mary's husband, had children from a previous marriage. C. A. Evans, *Fabricating Jesus: How Modern Scholars Distort the Gospels* (Downers Grove, IL: InterVarsity, 2006), 78–85, has recently suggested that the Akhmim fragment may have been misidentified as the Gospel of Peter since Serapion described the Gospel as docetic (denying that Jesus had a physical body), but the Akhmim fragment has no docetic tendencies.

[115] For a more thorough discussion of the use of the Gospel of Peter in historical Jesus research, see C. L. Quarles, "The Gospel of Peter: Does It Contain a Precanonical Resurrection Narrative?" in *The Resurrection of Jesus: John Dominic Crossan and N. T. Wright in Dialogue*, ed. R. Stewart (Minneapolis, MN: Fortress, 2006), 106–20.

[116] Crossan, *Four Other Gospels*, 132–34; idem, *Cross That Spoke*, 16–30; idem, *Historical Jesus*, 429.

[117] Crossan acknowledged Koester's theory that Mark, John, and the Gospel of Peter may have independently relied on an earlier source. But he insisted, "Composed by the fifties C. E., and possibly at Sepphoris in Galilee, it [Cross Gospel] is the single source of the intracanonical passion narratives" (*Historical Jesus*, 429).

[118] The Greek text of the Gospel of Peter utilized is E. Klostermann's text that appears in full in various portions of K. Aland, *Synopsis Quattuor Evangeliorum* (Stuttgart, Germany: Deutsche Bibelgesellschaft, 1986). Klostermann's text differs from that of M. G. Mara, the most recent critical edition, in only a few conjectures. For a comparison of these two editions, see F. Neirynck, "Apocryphal Gospels and Mark," in *The New Testament in Early Christianity: La reception des écrits néotestamentaires dans le christianisme primitif*, ed. J.-M. Sevrin (Leuven, Belgium: Leuven University Press, 1989), 140–41.

parallel in Matthew and the Gospel of Peter that indicated one document was dependent on the other: "so that the disciples do not come and steal him" (*mēpote elthontes hoi mathētai autou klepsōsin auton*; Matt 27:64; *Gos. Pet.* 8:30). The sustained parallelism is best explained by a dependence of one Gospel on the other.[119] Although L. Vaganay had earlier argued that Gospel of Peter 8:30 was dependent on Matthew 27:64b, Crossan proposed that Matthew was in fact dependent on the Gospel of Peter.[120]

An examination of special features common to the Gospel of Peter or Matthew in the shared words provides the most objective means of determining the direction of the dependency. The vocabulary and grammar strongly suggest the Gospel of Peter's dependence on Matthew. R. Gundry described the words as a "series of Mattheanisms."[121] J. P. Meier concluded that "when it comes to who is dependent on whom, all the signs point to Matthew's priority. . . . The clause is a tissue of Matthean vocabulary and style, a vocabulary and style almost totally absent from the rest of the Gospel of Peter."[122] Since the shared series contains several prominent Mattheanisms, it seems more likely that the Gospel of Peter was dependent on Matthew than vice versa.[123]

Compositional strategies of the Gospel of Peter suggest that it is a second-century work dependent on the canonical Gospels. The author projected material from narratives describing Jesus's earlier life and teaching into his Passion Narrative using a compositional strategy also found in second-century works such as the Protevangelium of James.[124]

---

[119] Inferences drawn from the precise wording of the Gospel of Peter must be tentative since the text of the Gospel that is presently available is most likely significantly different from the original text. The two fragments of the Gospel of Peter from P. Oxy. 2949 are very brief. Based on the alignment of the two fragments suggested by Crossan (*Cross That Spoke*, 8–9), P. Oxy 2949 consists of portions of only thirteen lines of text. But even comparisons of the Akhmim text with P. Oxy. 2949 show that the two texts belong to significantly different recensions. Of the twenty-five words in P. Oxy. 2949, only fifteen are shared by the Akhmim mss. Although both mss. essentially agree, the later includes new phrases and words not found in the earlier text, employs different vocabulary, and frequently has different grammatical forms. One thus wonders whether the earliest text of the Gospel of Peter is sufficiently preserved in the Akhmim mss. to make conclusions drawn from redactional investigations truly reliable. For similar concerns from another scholar, see Koester, *Ancient Christian Gospels*, 219. For a more detailed comparison of the available fragments, see J. C. Treat, "The Two Manuscript Witnesses to the Gospel of Peter," SBLSP (Atlanta, GA: Scholars Press, 1990), 398–99.

[120] Crossan, *Cross That Spoke*, 271.

[121] R. Gundry, *Matthew: A Commentary on His Handbook for a Mixed Church Under Persecution*, 2nd ed. (Grand Rapids, MI: Eerdmans, 1994), 584.

[122] J. P. Meier, *The Roots of the Problem and the Person*, vol. 1 of *A Marginal Jew: Rethinking the Historical Jesus* (New York, NY: Doubleday, 1991), 117.

[123] This evidence for dependency was probably the result of the author of the Gospel of Peter's memory of Matthew's account. He apparently did not have copies of the four Gospels open before him as he wrote his Gospel, for in this case one would expect more numerous and sustained verbal parallels and more similarities in the sequence of the pericopes. Brown pointed out that unlike the Gospel of Peter, Tatian's *Diatessaron* is clearly recognizable in vocabulary and sequence as a harmonization. See R. E. Brown, *The Death of the Messiah: From Gethsemane to the Grave: A Commentary on the Passion Narratives in the Four Gospels*, ABRL (New York, NY: Doubleday, 1994), 2:1334–36.

[124] See C. L. Quarles, "The Protevangelium of James as an Alleged Parallel to Creative Historiography in the Synoptic Birth Narratives," *BBR* 8 (1998): 139–49, especially pp. 144–49. R. Brown (*Death of the Messiah*, 2:1135) also noted the similarity in the compositional strategies of the Gospel of Peter and the Protevangelium of James: "In terms of literary classification I would regard the *Protevangelium* as a cousin of *GPet* in the same species as the apocryphal gospels. The compo-

Moreover, the author tended to multiply miracles and to introduce new details into the narrative in an effort to defend Christian claims in a manner that closely parallels the tendencies of second-century literature.

Certain details of the Gospel of Peter also betray its comparatively late origin. The angel's question from heaven to the cross at the moment of Jesus's resurrection, "Did you preach to those who sleep?" in Gospel of Peter 9:38 (see below), betrays the author's knowledge of the later doctrine of Jesus's descent into Hades between his death and resurrection in order to preach to the believers held there. Scholars have questioned whether the doctrine is taught in the NT.[125] It is doubtful, in fact, that the doctrine arose earlier than the time of Justin Martyr (ca. AD 100–165). The first clear reference to it appears in the writings of Irenaeus in the late second century (*Against Heresies* 4.27.2). Thus, the reference to preaching to those who sleep in the Gospel of Peter suggests that the document was composed no earlier than the first quarter of the second century.

Matthew and the Gospel of Peter differ slightly in their descriptions of the sealing of Jesus's tomb. Matthew says simply that the tomb was sealed (Matt 27:66). The Gospel of Peter adds that it was sealed with seven seals (*Gos. Pet.* 8:33). The reference to seven seals suggests that the author of the Gospel of Peter embellished Matthew at this point out of apologetic concerns and probably in light of Revelation 5:1.[126] This suggests that the Gospel of Peter was written after Revelation, and it is likely a second-century work.

The use of the term "Lord's Day" may be particularly significant for dating the Gospel of Peter.[127] The earliest Christian documents to use the expression are Revelation 1:10,

---

sitional instincts are much the same, but the author of *Prot. Jas.* had access to written copies of Luke and Matt. On the one hand, it is more elaborately expanded over the canonical Gospels than is *GPet*; on the other hand, when it cites them, it does so with greater preservation of exact vocabulary. Dramatically both works describe eschatological events that the canonical Gospels were content to leave wrapped in silence: the actual birth of Jesus in *Prot. Jas.* 19 and the actual resurrection in *GPet* 10:39–41."

[125] J. Elliot, *1 Peter*, AB (New York, NY: Doubleday, 2000), 706–10; B. Reicke, *The Disobedient Spirits and Christian Baptism: A Study of 1 Peter III.19 and Its Context*, ASNU 13 (Copenhagen, Germany: Munksgaard, 1946), 115–18; E. G. Selwyn, "Unsolved New Testament Problems: The Problem of the Authorship of I Peter," *ExpTim* 59 (1947): 340.

[126] M. G. Mara (*Évangile de Pierre: Introduction, texte critique, traduction, commentaire et index*, SC 201 [Paris, France: Gabalda, 1973]) suggested that this reference to the apocalyptic imagery of Revelation is part of a string of such allusions. The glorious Christ's ability to break the seven seals closely matches Rev 5:1 (p. 170). The loud voice from heaven on the Lord's Day parallels John's experience in Rev 1:10. Revelation 11:11–12, like the Gospel of Peter, describes a loud voice, a resurrection, and an ascent to heaven (pp. 177–78). Revelation 10:1–3 describes a heavenly figure of enormous size (pp. 183–84). Brown (*Death of the Messiah*, 2:1296) commented, "The number seven is commonly symbolic in the Bible, but it is difficult to be certain whether here the seven is just part of the folkloric imagination or has special symbolism. One might appeal to Rev 5:1–5, which has a scroll sealed with seven seals that can be opened by no one in heaven or on earth save by the lion of the tribe of Judah, the root of David who has triumphed—that could reinforce the obvious meaning of *GPet* that everything was done to make opening the tomb difficult (but the power of God would break through all these human precautions)."

[127] Several others have independently recognized the significance of this reference for dating the document. See also A. Kirk, "Examining Priorities: Another Look at the Gospel of Peter's Relationship to the New Testament Gospels," *NTS* 40 (1994): 593. Wright (*Resurrection of the Son of God*, 594) listed this expression, along with seven other elements, as "conclusive evidence for the *Gospel of Peter* being later and more developed than the canonical parallels."

Didache 14:1, and Ignatius (*To the Magnesians* 9:1). The phrase the "first day of the week" (see the Synoptic Passion Narratives; John 20:1,19, 26; Acts 20:7; 1 Cor 16:2) is the more primitive form of reference to the day of Jesus's resurrection, which was common in the early church in the mid- and late first century. The absence of references to the "Lord's Day" in the early NT documents, coupled with the presence of the term in Revelation and the *Didache* (second half of first or early second century), suggests that the expression became popular in the final decades of the first century (alternatively, John coined the phrase in Rev 1:10). The use of "the Lord's Day," especially in its abbreviated form, suggests a second-century date for the Cross Gospel.[128]

Finally, the rather bizarre description of Jesus's resurrection in the Gospel of Peter is remarkably similar to second-century literature. Gospel of Peter 9:38 states that at the time of Jesus's resurrection a great sound or voice came from heaven. The heavens opened, and two men surrounded by a brilliant light descended through the gap in the heavens. The two heavenly figures entered the tomb to escort Jesus out. When the three figures emerged from the tomb, the heads of the angelic beings reached to the sky, but the head of Jesus extended even above the heavens (*Gos. Pet.* 10:39–40). As the angels and Jesus exited the tomb, a cross, apparently floating in thin air, followed behind them.[129] A heavenly voice asked, "Did you preach to those who are sleeping?" To this the cross replied, "Yes" (*Gos. Pet.* 10:39–42).

Second-century apocryphal literature was characterized by several of the features noted above. Other second-century texts also speak of independently moving crosses and ascribe a supernatural stature to the resurrected Christ.[130] Consequently, the descriptions of Jesus's stature and of the moving cross in the Gospel of Peter suggest a date of composition in the second century.

The date of the Gospel of Peter and its literary relationship to the canonical Gospels is an issue of great importance that has an enormous impact on one's reconstruction of the events surrounding Jesus's passion and resurrection. The Gospel of Peter is clearly a product of the author's creative literary imagination rather than a serious attempt to preserve eyewitness accounts of actual events. Thus, if the Gospel of Peter is the single source for the accounts of the passion and resurrection in the NT Gospels as Crossan claimed, the

---

[128] Crossan (*Historical Jesus*, 429) stated that the Cross Gospel was composed by the 50s, probably in Sepphoris of Galilee. Other scholars have pointed out additional historical problems in the Gospel of Peter. Brown (*Death of the Messiah*, 2:1232) noted that the author portrayed Herod as an observant Jew and as the supreme ruler of Palestine to whom even Pilate was subservient. The Gospel of Peter also has an enormous crowd of Jews from Jerusalem and the surrounding area travel to see the sealed tomb on the Sabbath, in apparent breach of Sabbath regulations (p. 1308). Brown also demonstrated that the author of the Gospel of Peter was confused about the chronology of Jewish feasts (p. 1340).

[129] Crossan (*Historical Jesus*, 389) described the cross as a "huge cruciform procession" of individuals who were resurrected along with Jesus; see Crossan, *Who Killed Jesus*, 197. Most scholars have been unconvinced by Crossan's interpretation of the speaking cross; see Wright, *Resurrection*, 595.

[130] We are indebted to B. J. Creel for pointing out these second-century parallels to the Gospel of Peter first compiled in L. Vaganay, *L'Évangile de Pierre*, 2nd ed. (Paris, France: Gabalda, 1930), 300. See *Epist. Apost.* 16; *Apoca. Pet.* 1; *Shep. Herm.* 83.1 (see 89.8; 90.1); 4 Ezra 2:43.

canonical Gospels are unreliable revisions of an imaginative tradition. But close examination of the Gospel of Peter indicates that the author was dependent on the canonical Gospels and wrote in the second century, long after the canonical Gospels were penned and the eyewitnesses of Jesus's ministry had passed from the scene.

Secret Mark

In 1958 Morton Smith, assistant professor of history at Columbia University, visited the monastery of Mar Saba near Jerusalem and photographed fragments of texts from the monastery library. In the end papers of an edition of the letters of Ignatius printed in 1646, Smith found a handwritten letter ascribed to Clement of Alexandria (ca. AD 150–215) in a Greek script resembling that common in the eighteenth century. In the letter, Clement claimed to have known three versions of Mark's Gospel: the canonical version used in public worship, a later version in which Mark added secret traditions to his earlier text for use in secret rituals of initiates, and an even later version containing additions by a gnostic group.

Clement quoted two additions from the second version that Smith identified as Secret Mark. The most extensive quotation described the resurrection of an unnamed figure that later came to Jesus wearing only a linen cloth. The man spent the night with Jesus, and Jesus taught him the mystery of the kingdom of God. The account appears to be modeled on John's account of the resurrection of Lazarus expressed in Markan terminology.[131]

Within two years of Smith's publication of his find, scholars began to challenge the authenticity of the text. Q. Quesnell suggested the text was a forgery.[132] Suspicion surrounded the text in part because after being photographed by Smith in 1958 and then a team of scholars in 1972, the text mysteriously disappeared, making it impossible to subject it to the testing necessary to authenticate it even as an eighteenth-century production.[133] The text still has its advocates. H. Koester maintained that the letter attributed to Clement was "probably genuine" and cautiously suggested that the canonical Gospel was dependent on this earlier version of Mark.[134] More recently, scholars such as B. Metzger and B. Ehrman have questioned the authenticity of Secret Mark and Smith's role in its discovery.[135] Despite such questions, J. D. Crossan has argued for both the authenticity of

---

[131] See M. Smith, *Clement of Alexandria and a Secret Gospel of Mark* (Cambridge, MA: Harvard University Press, 1973); and idem, *The Secret Gospel: The Discovery and Interpretation of the Secret Gospel According to Mark* (New York, NY: Harper & Row, 1973).

[132] Q. Quesnell, "The Mar Saba Clementine: A Question of Evidence," *CBQ* 37 (1975): 48–67.

[133] C. W. Hedrick, "Secret Mark: New Photographs, New Witnesses," *Fourth R* 13 (2000): 3–16.

[134] H. Koester, *History and Literature of Early Christianity*, vol. 2 of *Introduction to the New Testament* (Philadelphia, PA: Fortress, 1982), 168–69.

[135] B. M. Metzger, *Reminiscences of an Octogenarian* (Peabody, MA: Hendrickson, 1997), 128–32; B. D. Ehrman, *Lost Christianities: The Battles for Scripture and the Faiths We Never Knew* (Oxford, UK: Oxford University Press, 2003), 67–89.

Secret Mark and its priority to the canonical Gospel.[136] Crossan placed Secret Mark in his first stratum of sources for historical Jesus research.

S. C. Carlson has written an extensive examination of the authenticity of the letter of Clement and has produced compelling evidence supporting the suspicion that M. Smith created the text as part of a scholarly hoax.[137] First, Smith's account of the discovery of Secret Mark has several interesting parallels with an intriguing novel first published in 1940 titled *The Mystery of Mar Saba*. These parallels may be intentional clues showing that Secret Mark is a forgery like the Gospel of Nicodemus that is the focus of the novel. B. Ehrman has pointed out that the page opposite of Secret Mark in the 1646 edition of Ignatius expressed scorn for "impudent fellows" who have "interpolated" passages into ancient texts with "all kinds of nonsense." The placement of the copy of the Clementine letter in the book may be another clue expressing the true nature of the letter.

Second, certain characteristics of the script of the Clementine letter suggest it is a twentieth-century forgery. (1) The script bears signs of unnatural hesitations in the pen strokes that are consistent with a forger's tremor as well as pen lifts and signs of retouching that suggest that the characters were drawn rather than written. The characters also are inconsistently formed. (2) The script is dissimilar in several ways from that of other eighteenth-century manuscripts produced at Mar Saba. The script is more similar to scripts appearing in Western than Eastern Greek manuscripts of the period. The Western script is odd if the manuscript were produced at Mar Saba. Due to his previous research, Smith was far more familiar with the Western script. (3) The script is identical to that of another Mar Saba manuscript, manuscript 22, which Smith himself claimed was produced by a twentieth-century person whom he identified as M. Madiotes. Although the Greek suffix gives the name the appearance of being Greek, it is not a Greek proper name but a pseudonym meaning "baldy" and with a secondary figurative meaning, "swindler." The abbreviation "M." may well stand for "Morton." Moreover, Smith concluded from the manuscript that the scribe of the Clementine letter was an experienced writer and scholar with an interest in patristics and Western critical scholarship, conclusions completely unsupported by the evidence of the find unless the scribe was Smith himself and his description is autobiographical.

Third, the 1910 catalogue of books from the Mar Saba library contains no mention of this copy of Ignatius's works. This allows the possibility that the book was smuggled into the library after the forgery had already been penned. Smith's own survey of the library's

---

[136] H. Koester, "History and Development of Mark's Gospel (From Mark to *Secret Mark* and 'Canonical' Mark)," in *Colloquy on New Testament Studies: A Time for Reappraisal and Fresh Approaches*, ed. B. Corley (Macon, GA: Mercer University Press, 1983); Crossan, *Four Other Gospels*, 61–83.

[137] S. C. Carlson, *The Gospel Hoax: Morton Smith's Invention of Secret Mark* (Waco, TX: Baylor University Press, 2005). S. Brown attempts to challenge Carlson's claims by arguing that Smith did not have a reasonable motive for the hoax. See S. Brown, "The Question of Motive in the Case against Morton Smith," *JBL* 125 (2006): 351–83; idem, *Mark's Other Gospel: Rethinking Morton Smith's Controversial Discovery*, Studies in Christianity and Judaism (Waterloo, ON: Wilfrid Laurier University, 2005).

contents demonstrates that of the ten printed books in the collection: all were produced in Venice except for the Voss edition of Ignatius that was printed in Amsterdam. Moreover, the Voss edition is the only text in the library containing Latin as well as Greek.

Fourth, it seems rather suspicious that Smith's discovery corroborated claims made in Smith's earlier scholarly work. In his dissertation, *Tannaitic Parallels to the Gospels*, Smith associated Mark 4:11 with secrecy over forbidden sexual relationships.[138] Secret Mark hints at a forbidden sexual relationship between Jesus and the young man in the linen cloth. The find also confirmed his insistence that a source with Johannine traits lay behind miracle accounts in the Gospel of Mark.[139]

Fifth, as is often true of scholarly hoaxes, Smith seems to have left clues identifying himself as the true author of the Clementine letter. The preface to *Secret Gospel* stated, "No doubt if the past, like a motion picture, could be replayed, I should also be shocked to find how much of the story I have already invented."[140] The conclusion stated, "Truth is necessarily stranger than history."[141] Most intriguing is Smith's dedication of his book *Secret Gospel* "to the one who knows" that appears to match the dedication of the scholarly version of *Clement* to A. D. Nock, one of the scholars asked by Smith to examine the manuscript, who was skeptical about the text from the beginning. The dedications seem to suggest that Nock's suspicions about Secret Mark were correct.

Consequently, Secret Mark, which is important in the understanding of the historical Jesus and in reconstructing Gospel origins in the theories of prominent scholars such as Koester and Crossan, is probably a forgery. The evidence amassed by Carlson has been described by M. Goodacre of Duke University as "compelling, and utterly convincing,"[142] and by L. Hurtado as "persuasive, decisive, practically unanswerable."[143] Obviously, twentieth-century forgeries have nothing to contribute to serious discussions on the life and teachings of Jesus.

Gospel of Jesus's Wife

On September 18, 2012, Professor Karen King of Harvard Divinity School announced the discovery of a Coptic papyrus fragment to the International Association for Coptic Studies that met in Rome. The fragment contained a portion of a sentence which read, "And Jesus said, 'My wife . . .'" On the basis of this statement, King gave the fragment the controversial name "The Gospel of Jesus's Wife." She initially suggested the fragment was composed in the fourth century and was a translation of a Greek text likely composed in the second. Many scholars at the event responded to the announcement with skepticism. However, the announcement triggered a frenzy in the media, generating headlines such as

---

[138] M. Smith, *Tannaitic Parallels to the Gospels*, SBLMS 6 (Philadelphia, PA: SBL, 1951), 155–56.

[139] M. Smith, "Comments on Taylor's Commentary on Mark," *HTR* 48 (1955): 26.

[140] Smith, *Secret Gospel*, ix.

[141] Ibid., 148.

[142] Cover of Carlson, *Gospel Hoax*.

[143] Carlson, *Gospel Hoax*, xii.

"Harvard Scholar's Discovery Suggests Jesus Had a Wife," "Historian Says Piece of Papyrus Refers to Jesus's Wife," and even "Jesus Had a Wife, Newly Discovered Gospel Suggests."[144]

King later summarized her acquaintance with the fragment in this way:

> In July 2010, the owner contacted me, requested I look at a Coptic papyrus in his collection, and subsequently sent photographs. In December 2011, he delivered the GJW papyrus by hand to Harvard Divinity School for study and publication. In March 2012, the GJW fragment was examined at the Institute for the Study of the Ancient World in New York, by the Institute's director Roger Bagnall and by AnneMarie Luijendijk (Princeton University). Announcement of the discovery was made at the International Association for Coptic Studies meeting in Rome, September 18, 2012, and a draft edition with photographs was posted online. The open and lively discussion that followed gave helpful direction and focus to subsequent research, including further study of the papyrus and ink, detailed above.[145]

Within only a few days of the announcement, several scholars suggested the fragment was a forgery. Francis Watson demonstrated that the fragment could have been created by someone with little knowledge of Sahidic Coptic by cutting and pasting phrases from a modern edition of the Gospel of Thomas.[146] Andrew Bernhard demonstrated that a forger likely created the fragment using a specific modern edition available on the Internet, Michael Grondin's Interlinear version of the Gospel of Thomas.[147] Concerns raised by scholars prompted the Smithsonian Channel to postpone indefinitely the airing of a pre-filmed program on the Jesus's wife fragment.

The fragment was later subjected to intense analysis. Two different attempts to date the papyrus using radiocarbon analysis suggested two very different dates for the writing material, 404–209 BC or around AD 741, a difference of nearly one thousand years.[148] Amusingly, both analyses claimed a 95.4 percent probability, and the discrepancy was highlighted by critics who sensed that something was awry.[149] King affirmed the AD 741

---

[144] Associated Press, "Harvard Scholar's Discovery Suggests Jesus Had a Wife," *Fox News*, September 18, 2012, http://www.foxnews.com/science/2012/09/18/harvard-scholar-discovery-suggests-jesus-had-wife (accessed January 16, 2015); Laurie Goodstein, "A Faded Piece of Papyrus Refers to Jesus's Wife," *New York Times*, September 19, 2012, http://www.nytimes.com/2012/09/19/us/historian-says-piece-of-papyrus-refers-to-jesus-wife.html?pagewanted=all&_r=0 (accessed January 16, 2015); Live Science Staff, "Jesus Had a Wife, Newly Discovered Gospel Suggests," *Live Science*, September 18, 2012, http://www.livescience.com/23284-jesus-wife-gospel-suggests.html (accessed January 16, 2015).

[145] K. King, "'Jesus said to them, "My wife . . ."': A New Coptic Papyrus Fragment," *HTR* 107 (2014): 154.

[146] Francis Watson, "The Gospel of Jesus's Wife: How a Fake Gospel Fragment Was Composed," http://markgoodacre.org/Watson2.pdf (accessed January 16, 2015).

[147] A. Bernhard, "How *The Gospel of Jesus's Wife* Might Have Been Forged: A Tentative Proposal," http://www.gospels.net/gjw/mighthavebeenforged.pdf (accessed January 16, 2015).

[148] King, "New Coptic Papyrus Fragment,"135.

[149] See L. Depuydt, "The Alleged Gospel of Jesus's Wife: Assessment and Evaluation of Authenticity," *HTR* 107 (2014): 175.

date based on the second radiocarbon analysis, despite having originally claimed that the fragment dated to the fourth century. Micro-Raman spectroscopy determined that the ink used in the fragment was similar to that used in a Coptic manuscript of John that was part of the same collection and was assumed to be ancient. The analysis indicated that the inks used in the *Gospel of Jesus' Wife* and the John fragment were of a similar composition.

The paleographical analysis of the fragment by Malcolm Choat seemed to condemn the fragment with faint praise:

> Overall, if the general appearance of the papyrus prompts some suspicion, it is difficult to falsify by a strictly paleographical examination. This should not be taken as proof that the papyrus is genuine, simply that its handwriting and the manner in which it has been written do not provide definitive grounds for proving otherwise.[150]

The findings were published in an issue of the *Harvard Theological Review*, which was almost entirely dedicated to discussion of the Jesus's wife fragment.

Several factors have prompted most scholars to reject the fragment as a forgery. First, the text has a grammatical error that suggests it was copied from an online transcription of the Gospel of Thomas which contained the same error. Many scholars believe this betrays that the fragment is the work of a forger who did not know Coptic well and thus inserted segments of other Coptic works into the document in hopes of passing the scrutiny of Coptic scholars.[151]

Coptic scholar Christian Askeland observed that the inks used in the Jesus's wife and John fragments are very similar and the hands (appearance of the individual characters of the script) were identical. Thus the same scribe had produced both manuscripts belonging to this collection. However, Askeland discovered that the line breaks in all seventeen lines of the Coptic fragment of John were identical to Codex Qau, a Coptic manuscript of John discovered in 1923 and available on the Internet.[152] This indicated that a modern forger had created the John fragment based on the published codex. Since evidence indicated that the same "scribe" had produced both documents, by confirming the forgery of the John fragment Askeland demonstrated that the Jesus's wife fragment was also a modern forgery. Askeland also concluded that both the Jesus's wife fragment and the John fragment belonged to the Lycopolitan dialect, a dialect that died out well before the seventh or eighth century when the fragment was allegedly produced.

---

[150] M. Choat, "The Gospel of Jesus's Wife: A Preliminary Paleographical Assessment, *HTR* 107 (2014): 162.

[151] King, "Coptic Papyrus Fragment," 155–56. See also Michael Grondin, "Did A Forger Use My Interlinear?" October 14, 2012, http://gospel-thomas.net/x_gjw_ps2.htm (accessed January 16, 2015).

[152] C. Askeland, "Jesus Had a Sister-in-law," *Evangelical Textual Criticism*, April 24, 2014, http://evangelicaltextual-criticism.blogspot.co.uk/2014/04/jesus-had-ugly-sister-in-law.html. Askeland's critique is revised and expanded in "A Fake Coptic John and Its Implications for 'The Gospel of Jesus's Wife,'" *TynBul* 65 (2014): 1–10.

In addition, scholars and journalists began to dispute claims that the owner had made about the history of the possession of the fragment. The owner replied by offering a fresh account of the past ownership of the fragment which clearly conflicted with the account previously offered.[153]

Leo Depuydt of Brown University had expressed numerous concerns about the authenticity of the fragment. He was invited to publish his opinion in the *Harvard Theological Review* along with King's article. Depuydt's critique of the fragment and the sensational claims made regarding it were blunt:

> The following analysis submits that it is out of the question that the so-called Gospel of Jesus's Wife, also known as the Wife of Jesus fragment, is an authentic source. The author of this analysis has not the slightest doubt that the document is a forgery, and not a very good one at that.[154]

Although news agencies ranging from Fox News to the *Huffington Post* publicized King's claims and many assumed that the claim was as good as proven, by May 1, 2014, *The Wall Street Journal* published an opinion piece by J. Pattengale titled "How the Jesus's Wife Hoax Fell Apart."

This episode shows that readers should be cautious about accepting sensational claims by the media regarding recent discoveries. The public would be wise to wait until the scholarly community has had the opportunity to vet these claims before developing conclusions regarding the significance of new finds, which may well prove to be forgeries or to date significantly later than was originally claimed.

Conclusion

Our quick tour of some of the Gospels on which some scholars heavily depend in historical Jesus research raises disturbing questions about the reliability of these "lost Gospels." Evidence suggests that these Gospels generally date up to one hundred years, and sometimes significantly more, after the death of Jesus. Although these Gospels may be useful for understanding divergent religious movements of the second and third centuries, they are of little value for understanding who Jesus actually was or what he said and did. The four canonical Gospels remain the most helpful sources for historical Jesus research, not merely because they are canonical but because they are the most ancient sources and were written during the first century when eyewitness testimonies about Jesus were still available.[155]

---

[153] O. Jarus, "Gospel of Jesus's Wife": Doubts Raised about Ancient Text," http://www.livescience.com/45020-gospel-of-jesus-wife-questioned.html.

[154] Leo Depuydt, "The Alleged Gospel of Jesus's Wife: Assessment and Evaluation of Authenticity," *HTR* 107 (2014): 172.

[155] See R. Bauckham, *Jesus and the Eyewitnesses: The Gospels as Eyewitness Testimony* (Grand Rapids, MI: Eerdmans, 2006).

CHRONOLOGY OF JESUS'S MINISTRY

Introduction

Westerners in the twenty-first century tend to be concerned with times and dates. They frequently glance at their phones or watches and set appointments weeks, months, and sometimes even years in advance. Not surprisingly, they may be disappointed to find few references to precise dates in the NT. They may be shocked to discover that Jesus was not born on December 25, AD 1, and that modern scholars are not certain of the day, month, or even year of his birth. However, the lack of concern for precise chronology or frequent references to times and dates are to be expected from people from first-century agrarian societies. To expect a detailed chronology of Jesus's life to unfold in the Gospels is to impose modern Western concerns on the ancient text. In general, early Christians were far more concerned with the events of Jesus's life and their theological significance than issues of chronology. Modern believers could learn from the priorities of the early Christians.

Nevertheless, developing a chronology of Jesus's life is a worthy exercise and an important step in the historical study of the Gospels. Yet constructing a precise chronology is difficult for several reasons. First, the four evangelists provided few explicit references that enable scholars to relate the events of Jesus's life to the offices of important government officials, the normal way of establishing dates during this era. The only precise date explicitly mentioned in the Gospels is the date of the beginning of the ministry of John the Baptist, and even this reference appears in only one of the Gospels (Luke 3:1–3). Second, the Gospel writers mixed a basic chronological framework with some degree of topical arrangement, which makes it difficult to establish the precise order of key events in Jesus's ministry. Nevertheless, sufficient data exists for establishing an approximate chronology of Jesus's life and ministry. This section proposes approximate dates for Jesus's birth, baptism, ministry, and crucifixion.

The Birth of Jesus

Beginning students may assume Jesus was born in AD 1. Yet, as will shortly be evident, matters are not quite so straightforward. Matthew 2:1 and Luke 1:5 indicate that Jesus was born in the later years of the reign of Herod the Great. Josephus stated that an eclipse occurred shortly before Herod's death.[156] This eclipse may be dated from astronomical data to precisely March 12/13 in 4 BC.[157] Moreover, Herod died before Passover that same year. The Passover celebration in 4 BC began on April 11. Herod thus died between March 12 and April 11 in the year 4 BC. The date of Herod's death establishes the latest possible date *(terminus ad quem)* for Jesus's birth.

---

[156] Josephus, *Ant.* 17.6.5–6 and 17.8.1 §§ 167–81, 188–92.

[157] H. Hoehner, "Chronology," *Dictionary of Jesus and the Gospels*, 118–22.

Some scholars have argued that Herod the Great actually died in 1 BC.[158] However, theories of a later death of Herod either mistranslate key texts that refer to Herod's death, ignore the fact that all of Herod's successors point to the year 5–4 BC in dating the beginning of their reigns, or overlook Josephus's references to events contemporary with Herod's death. The majority of scholars continue to affirm 4 BC as the year Herod died.[159]

Luke stated that Jesus's birth occurred during the period of the Roman census ordered by Caesar Augustus. He further pinpointed the time of the census by associating it with Quirinius's governorship over Syria (Luke 2:1–2).[160] Unfortunately, to date no ancient historian refers to this particular census or to Quirinius's role in Syria in the Herodian period. H. Hoehner has suggested that other historical factors point to the years 6 to 4 BC as the most likely dates for the census in Palestine. Herod the Great had fallen into disfavor with Caesar. Herod was also extremely ill, and his sons were each competing for the throne. A census would have been a logical step toward assessing the situation in Palestine as Caesar prepared to appoint Herod's successor. Good historical reasons exist for affirming the accuracy of Luke's description of a census under Quirinius.[161] However, without extrabiblical references to the census or to Quirinius's term of office, the census does not really assist in determining the precise date of Jesus's birth.

Matthew 2:16 implies that Jesus may have been up to two years old at the time Herod ordered the slaughter of the innocents. This suggests Jesus was born by at least early 6 BC. However, it is possible that Herod extended the age of the children he slew in Bethlehem to two, even though the star appeared more recently than two years before to make sure that the Messiah did not escape his sword. Thus, Jesus may have been born any time between late 7 BC and early 4 BC.

Both the Western Church (December 25) and the Eastern Church (January 6) celebrate the birth of Jesus in the winter. None of the NT data is inconsistent with a

[158] W. E. Filmer, "The Chronology of the Reign of Herod the Great," *JTS* 17 (1966): 283–98; E. L. Martin, "The Nativity and Herod's Death," in *Chronos, Kairos, Christos: Nativity and Chronological Studies Presented to Jack Finegan*, ed. J. Vardaman and E. Yamauchi (Winona Lake, IN: Eisenbrauns, 1989), 85–92; A. E. Steinmann, *From Abraham to Paul: A Biblical Chronology* (St. Louis, MO: Concordia, 2011), 230–34; idem, "When Did Herod the Great Reign?," *NovT* 51 (2009): 1–29.

[159] See T. D. Barnes, "The Date of Herod's Death," *JTS* 19 (1968): 204–9; D. Johnson, "And They Went Eight Stades Toward the Herodeion," in *Chronos, Kairos, Christos*, 93–99; H. Hoehner, "The Date of the Death of Herod the Great," in *Chronos, Kairos, Christos*, 101–11; P. L. Maier, "The Date of the Nativity and the Chronology of Jesus's Life," in *Chronos, Kairos, Christos*, 113–30; R. E. Brown, *The Birth of the Messiah: A Commentary on the Infancy Narratives in Matthew and Luke* (New York, NY: Doubleday, 1979), 166–67.

[160] Some scholars, such as R. Brown (*Birth of the Messiah*, 547–55), are convinced that Luke was mistaken in his mention of both a census and the role of Quirinius in Syria during the reign of Herod the Great.

[161] Denials of the historical accuracy of Luke may be based on misinterpretations of Luke's statement. It does not require Quirinius to have been governor of Syria during Herod's reign. Quirinius may have simply been the administrator of the census (see D. J. Hayles, "The Roman Census and Jesus's Birth: Was Luke Correct? Part 2: Quirinius' Career and a Census in Herod's Day," *Buried History* 10 [1974]: 16–31, esp. 29) or the census may have begun under another governor and concluded during the tenure of Quirinius (see D. L. Bock, *Luke 1:1–9:50*, BECNT [Grand Rapids, MI: Baker, 1994], 909). Although English translations typically render Luke 2:2b "while Quirinius was governor of Syria," the Greek verb *hēgemoneuō* does not necessarily refer to filling the office of governor but could speak of virtually any administrative post (*BDAG*, s.v. "ἡγεμονεύω," gives the meaning as "to exercise an administrative position").

midwinter date.[162] If the traditional dates approximate the actual date of Jesus's birth, he was probably born in the winter of either 7–6 BC, 6–5 BC, or 5–4 BC, with a 6 or 5 BC date for Jesus's birth being perhaps the most likely.[163]

The Beginning of the Ministry of John the Baptist and Jesus

Luke 3:1–2 dates the beginning of the ministry of John the Baptist with greater precision than any other event in the Gospels: "In the fifteenth year of the reign of Tiberius Caesar, while Pontius Pilate was governor of Judea, Herod was tetrarch of Galilee, his brother Philip tetrarch of the region of Iturea and Trachonitis, and Lysanias tetrarch of Abilene, during the high priesthood of Annas and Caiaphas, God's word came to John the son of Zechariah in the wilderness."

The most precise method of dating the start of John's ministry is to determine what Luke considered to be the fifteenth year of Tiberius. Although Luke could have counted the fifteenth year of Tiberius's reign from the beginning of an alleged coregency with Augustus, this is unlikely. None of the ancient sources—including Josephus, Appian, Plutarch, Tacitus, Suetonius, or Dio Cassius—adopted such a system. More likely Luke counted from either the death of Augustus (August 19, AD 14), the vote of the Roman senate to approve Tiberius as Caesar (September AD 14), or the beginning of the first full calendar year of Tiberius's reign (AD 15).[164] This year may have begun on January 1 (Roman system), Nissan 1 (March or April; Jewish system), or even October 1 (Syro-Macedonian system).

Although it is impossible to be certain, the most probable views are (1) that Luke either began his calculation on the date of Augustus's death, in which case Tiberius's first year extended from August 19, AD 14, to August 18, AD 15; or (2) that Luke calculated using an ascension year system and reckoned time in accordance with the newly devised Julian calendar in which the year began on January 1. In this case Tiberius's first year of reign extended from January 1, AD 15, to December 31, AD 15.[165] Consequently, the

---

[162] See the helpful collection of data in J. Finegan, *Handbook of Biblical Chronology*, rev. ed. (Peabody, MA: Hendrickson, 1998), 320–28. Compare with O. Cullmann (*Der Ursprung des Weihnachtsfestes* [Zürich/Stuttgart, Germany: Zwingli, 1960]), who pointed to the uncertainty regarding the date of Jesus's birth in the first three centuries of the Christian era. He claimed that the traditional date was chosen by the church sometime in the fourth century (Cullmann specifies 325–54 as the most likely range, p. 24). According to Cullmann, Christmas served as the Christian equivalent to the Roman holiday of *sol invictus* ("the invincible sun god"), celebrated at the time of winter solstice, in the conviction that Jesus was Christians' true invincible "sun."

[163] This is affirmed by, among others, P. Maier, "Date of the Nativity," whose essay is the most authoritative on the subject. See also A. J. Köstenberger and A. E. Stewart, *The First Days of Jesus: The Story of the Incarnation* (Wheaton, IL: Crossway, 2015).

[164] For bibliographic references, see A. J. Köstenberger, *John*, BECNT (Grand Rapids, MI: Baker, 2004), 55–56n2. Ancient sources regarding the date of Augustus's death are listed in H. W. Hoehner, *Chronological Aspects of the Life of Christ* (Grand Rapids, MI: Zondervan, 1978), 32n13.

[165] For an excellent introduction to the various chronological options, see Finegan, *Handbook of Biblical Chronology*, 329–44; cf. Hoehner, *Chronological Aspects*, 29–38.

fifteenth year of Tiberius's reign likely fell within dates ranging from August 19, AD 28 to December 31, AD 29. John the Baptist's ministry began sometime during this period.

Jesus's ministry likely began only a few months after John's. Hoehner noted that if Jesus were born in the winter of 6/5 or 5/4 BC as suggested above and if he were baptized in the summer of the year 29, he would have been thirty-two or thirty-three years old at the time he began his public ministry.[166] This comports with the statement in Luke 3:23 that Jesus was "about" thirty years old when he began his public ministry.

This chronology fits nicely with another important clue that appears in John 2:20. During Jesus's first Passover in Jerusalem after the beginning of his ministry, Jesus's Jewish opponents provided an important reference that is helpful for establishing dates for Jesus's ministry by mentioning the construction of Herod's temple. Unfortunately, most of the major English translations of the Bible misconstrue the actual meaning of the Greek text. The translations of John 2:20 in the NIV, CSB, and NRSV imply that the conversation took place forty-six years after the construction of the temple *began* and that the temple was still under construction. However, the Greek grammar and extrabiblical references to the construction of the temple seem to imply that the conversation took place forty-six years after construction on the temple *had been completed.* Hence the translation, "This sanctuary was built forty-six years ago" may be superior to the translation, "This sanctuary took 46 years to build" (CSB).[167] According to one reference in Josephus, Herod began construction of the temple in the eighteenth year of his reign, the same year that Augustus arrived in Syria.[168] Augustus's arrival in Syria occurred in the spring or summer of 20 BC.[169] This means that Herod's eighteenth year would have extended from Nisan 1, 20 BC, to Nisan 1, 19 BC, if one assumes that Josephus used the ascension year method of calculating the duration of the reign. Although the construction of the entire temple complex *(hieron)* would continue until AD 64, Josephus noted that the inner sanctuary *(naos)* of the temple was completed by the priests in only eighteen months. Thus, when the Jews referred to the temple *(naos)* in John 2:20, they were speaking of the inner sanctuary that

---

[166] Hoehner, *Chronological Aspects*, 38.

[167] F. J. Badcock suggested the translation, "This temple (or sanctuary) was built (before you were born) forty and six years ago." See Badcock, "A Note on St. John ii.20," *ExpTim* 47 (1935): 40–41. John's use of the aorist verb "was built" is probably a "consummative aorist," which implies that the construction of the temple was completed, i.e. "this sanctuary was built." This tense would have been very odd if the temple were still under construction as most translations imply (in which case the imperfect tense would have been better suited). A more difficult question arises related to John's use of the dative "years." The only other use of the dative with "year" (etos) in the NT is Acts 13:20 where it clearly refers to an extent of time and thus supports the conventional translation. However, in the LXX, the dative form of "year" (etos) without a preposition almost always refers to a point in time. See the discussion in D. Wallace, *Greek Grammar Beyond the Basics: An Exegetical Syntax of the New Testament* (Grand Rapids, MI: Zondervan, 1996), 559–61, esp. nn. 15, 17, and 20. The most compelling argument for Badcock's translation is the meaning of "sanctuary" (*naos*, "temple building," rather than "temple area") in the Gospel of John. For a good answer to the objection that Badcock's translation does not fit this context, see Köstenberger, *John*, 109–10.

[168] Josephus, *Ant.* 15.11.1 §380; 15.10.3 §354.

[169] Dio Cassius 54.7.4–6.

had been completed in 18/17 BC.[170] The Passover forty-six years after the completion of the sanctuary would fall in the spring of AD 30. This date would confirm that Jesus began his ministry in the summer or fall of AD 29.[171]

The Duration of Jesus's Ministry

The Synoptic Gospels refer to Jesus's visiting Jerusalem only once during his entire ministry. But the Gospel of John refers to Jesus's visiting Jerusalem three times for the Passover, not counting visits related to other Jewish feasts.[172] Most scholars today affirm the accuracy of John's Gospel at this point. This does not mean that the Synoptic Gospels are in error. Although they mention only one Passover visit to Jerusalem, they do not deny that other Passover visits occurred during Jesus's ministry. In general, it appears that John was even more concerned with the chronology of Jesus's ministry than the Synoptic writers were. Moreover, John has a demonstrable interest in showing that Jesus fulfilled the symbolism underlying various Jewish festivals and thus narrates Jesus's visits to Jerusalem on the occasion of religious feasts including Passover.

Jesus's first Passover visit to Jerusalem during his ministry occurs in John 2:13, 23; a later Passover visit takes place in John 6:4; and a final Passover visit is recorded in John 11:55; 12:1; 13:1; 18:28, 39; and 19:14. However, John did not necessarily record every single Passover visit during Jesus's ministry. He may have omitted references to a particular Passover just as the Synoptic writers did. H. Hoehner has argued that a comparison of the Synoptics with John suggests that another Passover occurred between the Passover in John 2:13, 23 and the one in John 6:4.[173] An extra year of ministry between these two Passovers may be necessary to accommodate Jesus's ministry in Judea, Galilee, and Samaria during this period and to allow for the various seasons described in the Gospel accounts.[174]

---

[170] Hoehner (*Chronological Aspects*, 40–41) demonstrated that Josephus maintained the common distinction between *hieron* and *naos*. John's Gospel also maintains this distinction. John used *hieron* in his Gospel eleven times to refer to the entire temple complex (John 2:14, 15; 5:14; 7:14, 28; 8:2, 20, 59; 10:23; 11:56; 18:20). He used *naos* three times and only in this pericope. G. Theissen and A. Merz (*Historical Jesus*, 151–61, esp. 156) agreed that Herod's eighteenth year fell in 20/19 BC. However, they apparently calculated the date of the first Passover of Jesus's ministry from the beginning of the construction of the *naos* rather than its completion and dated the Passover to the spring of AD 27 or 28.

[171] This date should be viewed as only an approximation. Josephus may have calculated Herod's eighteenth year using either an inclusive or conclusive system. The inclusive system included any portion of reign leading up to the beginning of the calendar year as a full year. This is the system assumed by Hoehner. However, the conclusive system counted full years from the beginning of the reign. This would push the dates for Herod's eighteenth year a few months later. The chronology of Jesus's ministry is complicated by the fact that Josephus proposed another date for the beginning of temple construction in another of his works (*Jewish War* 1.21.1 §401), which dated the beginning of temple construction to Herod's fifteenth year rather than the eighteenth, that is, in 23/22 BC rather than 20/19 BC. This alternative date (which would yield an AD 26 date for Jesus's first Passover) may be the result of a scribal error or reflect Josephus's uncertainty as to the beginning date of construction.

[172] See the chart on the chronology of Jesus's ministry in John's Gospel in Köstenberger, *John*, 11–13.

[173] Hoehner, *Chronological Aspects*, 56–63.

[174] See the discussion of the possible chronological significance of Mark 2:23; 6:39 and John 6:4, 10 in Meier, *A Marginal Jew*, 1:413–14; cf. the chronological chart in Köstenberger, *John*, 11–12.

If one affirms that Jesus's ministry included only three Passovers, his ministry lasted approximately two and a half years.[175] If one allows for another Passover between the first and second Passovers explicitly mentioned by John, Jesus's ministry lasted approximately three and a half years, the latter being more likely.[176]

The Death of Jesus

Scholars typically date Jesus's death to either AD 30 or 33, and either date is possible. However, the preponderance of evidence examined above suggests that Jesus was crucified in AD 33.[177]

Jesus was crucified on a Friday and rose on a Sunday. The Gospels explicitly state that Jesus was executed on Friday, the day of preparation for the Sabbath (Matt 27:62; Mark 15:42; Luke 23:54; John 19:14, 31, 42). Because Jesus clearly rose from the dead on Sunday and because Matthew 12:40 stated that the Son of Man would be in the heart of the earth "three days and three nights," some interpreters have argued that Jesus was crucified on a Wednesday or Thursday. However, several OT texts suggest that "three days and three nights" (which occurs only in Matt 12:30) might function as an idiom for a portion of one day, then an entire day, plus a portion of another day (Gen 42:17–18; 1 Sam 30:12–13; 2 Chr 10:5, 12; Esth 4:16–5:1). This method of reckoning time was also affirmed in rabbinic literature.[178] Jesus apparently used the expression "three days and three nights" in a similar fashion. This is confirmed by the frequent references to his resurrection occurring "on the third day" (see Matt 16:21; 17:23; 20:19; 27:64).

The Gospels make clear that Jesus ate the Last Supper on the evening before his crucifixion (Matt 26:20; Mark 14:17; Luke 22:14; John 13:2), and this is confirmed by Paul (1 Cor 11:23). The Gospels also portray the Last Supper as shared in conjunction with the Passover meal.[179]

Some scholars have argued that John's Gospel does not portray the Last Supper as a Passover meal but instead presents Jesus's crucifixion as occurring at the time of the Passover in order to portray Jesus's death as the sacrifice of the Passover lamb. However, the most natural reading of the reference to the "preparation day for the Passover" refers to the day of preparation for the Sabbath during Passover week, the Friday of the Passover

---

[175] See D. A. Carson and D. J. Moo, *An Introduction to the New Testament*, 2nd ed. (Grand Rapids, MI: Zondervan, 2005), 125–26, especially n. 129 (with further bibliographic references).

[176] Some suggest John's account of Jesus's clearing of the temple at the beginning of his ministry is unhistorical, which would potentially reduce the span of Jesus's ministry according to John by one year. But see the discussion in Köstenberger, *John*, 111.

[177] See A. J. Köstenberger and J. Taylor with A. Stewart, *The Final Days of Jesus: The Most Important Week of the Most Important Person Who Ever Lived* (Wheaton, IL: Crossway, 2014).

[178] See *TDNT* 2:949–50.

[179] See A. J. Köstenberger, "Was the Last Supper a Passover Meal?," in *The Lord's Supper: Remembering and Proclaiming Christ until He Comes*, ed. T. R. Schreiner and M. R. Crawford, NAC Studies in Bible & Theology 10 (Nashville, TN: B&H Academic, 2010), 6–30.

celebration.[180] The word translated "day of preparation" *(paraskeuē)* was the normal word for Friday. This interpretation is confirmed by John 19:31: "Since it was the preparation day, the Jews did not want the bodies to remain on the cross on the Sabbath (for that Sabbath was a special day)." Both the Synoptics and John present the Last Supper as a Passover meal and show that Jesus was executed on the Friday of Passover week. Thus, no real conflict between the accounts exists.

The Passover meal was eaten by the Jews on Nissan 14. Thus, the year of Jesus's execution must be a year in which Nissan 14 fell on a Thursday. This possibly occurred in AD 30 and definitely occurred in the year 33.[181] Since AD 30 would not allow for sufficient time between Jesus's baptism and death for his extensive public ministry unless one posits that Josephus or Luke used unusual methods of reckoning time or that Jesus's ministry lasted only one or two years, the most likely year of Jesus's death is again AD 33.

Table 3.3: Chronology of Jesus's Life

Date	Event	Major Data for Dating Event
ca. 6/5 BC	Birth of Jesus	Death of Herod the Great (4 BC) (Matt 2:13–20)
AD 28–29	Beginning of John the Baptist's ministry	Fifteenth year of Tiberius's rule (Luke 3:1)
AD 29	Beginning of Jesus's ministry	Forty-six years since completion of renovation of temple (John 2:20)
AD 33	Death of Jesus	Occurrence of Nissan 14 on a Thursday

Conclusion

Jesus was probably born between 6 and 4 BC (6 or 5 BC being the most likely date) and began his public ministry around AD 29. His ministry apparently lasted about three and a half years and included three or four Passover celebrations. His crucifixion probably occurred in AD 33.

THE HISTORICAL RELIABILITY OF THE GOSPELS

As mentioned, contemporary portrayals of Jesus vary considerably. This is largely a function of which sources scholars privilege in their reconstruction of the identity of Jesus. Some scholars prefer sources such as the Gospel of Thomas or the Gospel of Peter to Matthew, Mark, Luke, and John because they are convinced that the four NT Gospels are unreliable accounts of Jesus's life and teachings. The Jesus Seminar, which categorized the Gospel of Thomas as a "fifth Gospel," shocked many Christians with their confident claim

---

[180] See the NIV rendering of John 19:14: "It was the day of Preparation of Passover Week."

[181] C. J. Humphreys and W. G. Waddington, "Dating the Crucifixion," *Nature* 306 (1983): 743–46.

that only 18 percent of the sayings attributed to Jesus in the Gospels were actually uttered by him.[182] Such sweeping dismissals of the Gospels by certain critics can easily make Christians wonder whether the historical value of the four Gospels is at all salvageable. The purpose of this section is to help readers understand the presuppositions and processes that lead some scholars to these conclusions. It also demonstrates that compelling evidence can be offered for the reliability of the Gospels.

The Philosophical Foundations of Modern Gospels Study

Many readers may assume that most scholars reject the reliability of the Gospels because careful analysis uncovered irreconcilable conflicts within the Gospels or with other historical accounts. In fact, many scholars reject the reliability of the Gospels for very different reasons. They do so because the Gospel accounts describe events that they consider impossible. Jesus could not have controlled the weather, cleansed lepers, given sight to the blind, or raised the dead because these scholars have a modernist worldview that denies the possibility of such occurrences. For such scholars the only events that are possible are those that can be explained as the effects of natural causes. In other words, many scholars approach history through their philosophical commitment to naturalism.

Denial of even the possibility of miraculous or supernatural occurrences is ultimately driven by atheism, deism, or monism. Atheism denies the existence of God. Deism acknowledges the existence of God but views him as One who governs the universe only through natural laws and apart from any direct intervention. Monism equates nature and its laws with deity. In these three worldviews, miracles in the sense of acts by a personal God simply do not occur—either because a personal God does not exist or because God does not act in a manner inconsistent with natural law.

Skepticism regarding the possibility of miracles has a long history. A century before the time of Christ, Cicero (106–43 BC) argued, "For nothing can happen without cause; nothing happens that cannot happen, and when what was capable of happening has happened, it may not be interpreted as a miracle. Consequently, there are no miracles."[183] About 300 years later, Lucian of Samosata expressed his skepticism about demon possession and exorcism.[184] Although ancient people are often assumed gullible, superstitious, and easily deceived by claims of miracles, some of the ancients were as skeptical as some modern thinkers. Rejection of supernatural occurrences is not a new phenomenon.

The widespread rejection of miracles in the modern era can be traced to the writings of the Jewish philosopher B. de Spinoza. His *Tractatus Theologico-Politicus*, published in 1670, provided a naturalistic critique of miracles in which Spinoza claimed that the idea of miracles was self-contradictory, since to say that God performed some action contrary

---

[182] R. W. Funk, R. W. Hoover, and the Jesus Seminar, *The Five Gospels: The Search for the Authentic Words of Jesus* (New York, NY: Polebridge, 1993).

[183] H. Van der Loos, *The Miracles of Jesus* (Leiden, Netherlands: Brill, 1965), 6–7.

[184] Lucian of Samosata, *The Love of Lies*, §16 cited in G. Twelftree, *Jesus the Miracle Worker: A Historical and Theological Study* (Downers Grove, IL: InterVarsity, 1999), 48.

to the laws of nature was to imply that God acts contrary to his own nature.[185] Spinoza identified the laws of nature with God's nature because he was a monist who viewed nature itself as God. Although Spinoza's work prompted some of the angriest and most vitriolic critiques of any published work in the seventeenth century, it would in many ways set the tone for the views of the supernatural in the Enlightenment period.

Spinoza's work paved the way for the critical deists who initiated what is now known as the "quest of the historical Jesus." The deists felt that the real Jesus had been obscured in the Gospels. In their philosophical system, the accounts of his miraculous activity in the Gospels were ruled to be impossible. In their view, pious notions of the inspiration of the Gospels could no longer be entertained by rational thinkers. The legends of Jesus's miracles and his claim to be divine had to be stripped from the Gospels in order to recover reliable traditions about Jesus.

In 1730, the English deist M. Tindal denied that the Bible was special revelation and called others to return to the original religion that was founded on the rational interpretation of natural revelation. Tindal's claims seriously undermined the authority of the Bible and weakened the assumption that one could trust the Gospels' accounts of Jesus's life and ministry simply because they were inspired Scripture.[186]

During the years 1727–30, T. Woolston published his *Six Discourses on the Miracles of Our Saviour and Defences of His Discourses* in which he claimed that Jesus's miracles were "Improbabilities, and Incredibilities, and grossest Absurdities." Woolston argued that a commonsense reading of the accounts of Jesus's miracles led to the conclusion that these acts were immoral or insane, actions that were never equaled by any "Quack-doctor." Woolston saved his most blistering critique of Jesus's miracles for the resurrection. He argued that the resurrection of Jesus was a fraud. Jesus's disciples had stolen his body, and then superstitious people who were given to seeing apparitions interpreted the empty tomb as a proof of resurrection. Woolston argued that the miracles of the Gospels were sensible and helpful only when interpreted allegorically. W. Baird commented, "This denial of the historicity of the miracles struck a responsive chord in an era when belief in the supernatural was evaporating, when the universe was believed to be ordered by Newton's law, and when physical phenomena were attributed to natural causes."[187] Although most of the deists were not biblical scholars and their work "could have been accomplished by any bright skeptic with the aid of the King James Bible," they did exert an influence on scholars of later generations.[188]

---

[185] B. de Spinoza, "Tractatus Theologico-Politicus (1670)," in R. H. M. Elwes, *The Chief Works of Benedict de Spinoza*, 2 vols. (London, England: George Bell & Son, 1883, 1884), 1:81–97.

[186] M. Tindal, *Christianity as Old as the Creation* n.p., 1730; (repr. Stuttgart-Bad Cannstatt, Germany: F. Frommann, 1967). For a brief summary of the work, see W. Baird, *From Deism to Tübingen*, vol. 1 of *History of New Testament Research* (Minneapolis, MN: Fortress, 1992), 41–43. For the deists' views of Jesus's resurrection, see W. L. Craig, *The Historical Argument for the Resurrection of Jesus during the Deist Controversy* (Lewiston, NY: Mellen, 1985), 71–352.

[187] Baird, *From Deism to Tübingen*, 56–57.

[188] Ibid.

D. Hume dismissed miracles in his *Enquiry Concerning Human Understanding*. He argued that no alleged miracle had been witnessed by a large enough group of observers to ensure that the witnesses either had not been deceived or were not misleading others themselves. He added that people generally wish for a display of the supernatural and believe miraculous accounts more readily than they should. He argued that miracles only occur among primitive and superstitious peoples. Finally, he claimed that since all major religions appeal to miracles to support their competing claims, appeals to miracles to support the truthfulness of Christianity are unconvincing.[189]

Spinoza's early critique of miracles greatly influenced F. Schleiermacher, the philosopher and theologian generally recognized as the father of liberal theology. Schleiermacher expressed Spinoza's critique with a new degree of sophistication, but the argument was essentially the same as that of Spinoza, whose influence is obvious in the following quotation:

> Now some have represented miracle in this [absolute] sense as essential to the perfect manifestation of the divine omnipotence. But it is difficult to conceive, on the one side, how omnipotence is shown to be greater in the suspension of the interdependence of nature than in its original immutable course which was no less divinely ordered. For, indeed, the capacity to make a change in what has been ordained is only a merit in the ordainer, if a change is necessary, which again can only be the result of some imperfection in him or in his work.[190]

Like Spinoza, Schleiermacher viewed history as a closed system of causes and necessary effects, a "divinely ordered" and "original immutable course" into which even God himself cannot intrude. W. Dembski offered a helpful summary of the view of Spinoza and Schleiermacher:

> Essentially Spinoza and Schleiermacher have God lock the door and throw away the key, and then they ask whether God can get back into the room. Since God presumably makes the best locks in the business, even God is not capable of getting back into the room without a key. By ordaining a system of nature, God builds a closed system of natural causes which has no way of accommodating miracles.[191]

---

[189] D. Hume, *Enquiries Concerning the Human Understanding and Concerning the Principles of Morals*, ed. L. A. Selby-Bigge, 2nd ed. (Oxford, UK: Clarendon, 1884), 308–14. For brief surveys and responses, see W. L. Craig, "The Problem of Miracles: A Historical and Philosophical Perspective," in *The Miracles of Jesus*, vol. 6 of *Gospel Perspectives*, ed. D. Wenham and C. L. Blomberg (Sheffield, PA: JSOT, 1986), 17–19, 22–27, 37–43; and Twelftree, *Jesus the Miracle Worker*, 40–43.

[190] F. Schleiermacher, *The Christian Faith*, trans. H. R. Mackintosh and J. S. Stewart (Philadelphia, PA: Fortress, 1976), 52.

[191] W. Dembski, *Intelligent Design: The Bridge Between Science and Theology* (Downers Grove, IL: InterVarsity, 1999), 66. The entire chapter titled "The Critique of Miracles" (pp. 49–69) is a helpful introduction and response to the arguments of Spinoza and Schleiermacher.

Similar ideas appear in the writings of the influential NT scholar R. Bultmann. Bultmann's famous dictum was "man's knowledge and mastery of the world have advanced to such an extent through science and technology that it is no longer possible for anyone seriously to hold the New Testament view of the world."[192] Bultmann led a sweeping movement in NT scholarship that rejected the notion of a three-storied universe as well as the virgin birth, resurrection, and miracles of Jesus. Like Spinoza and Schleiermacher, Bultmann presupposed that God could not intervene in natural processes.[193] Bultmann's worldview led him to dismiss the reliability of most of the material in the Gospels. He insisted, "It is impossible to use electric light and the wireless and to avail ourselves of modern medical discoveries, and at the same time to believe in the New Testament world of daemons *[sic]* and spirits."[194] He also maintained, "An historical event which involves a resurrection from the dead is utterly inconceivable."[195] Bultmann ultimately despaired of finding any reliable information about Jesus in the Gospels. He wrote, "I do indeed think that we can now know almost nothing concerning the life and personality of Jesus."[196] Bultmann's rejection of the testimony of the Gospels was grounded in his views of science and philosophy.

It is not the purpose of this introduction to prove the existence of a personal God or his intervention in the world today. Other excellent resources in Christian apologetics are available for guiding readers in exploring the evidence for these Christian claims.[197] However, readers should be alert to the philosophical presuppositions that underlie various approaches to Gospels study. The conclusions of the approach are no better than the presuppositions that guide them. Many Christians embrace particular approaches to Gospels study and affirm conclusions drawn from the application of these approaches without realizing that the philosophy that dictated the approach is antithetical to their most cherished convictions.

---

[192] R. Bultmann, "New Testament and Mythology," in *Kerygma and Myth*, ed. H. W. Bartsch (London, UK: SPCK, 1953), 4.

[193] R. Bultmann, *Faith and Understanding* (Philadelphia, PA: Fortress, 1987), 248.

[194] Bultmann, "New Testament and Mythology," 5.

[195] Ibid., 39.

[196] R. Bultmann, *Jesus and the Word* (New York, NY: Charles Scribner's Sons, 1958), 8. S. Porter has rightly questioned whether Bultmann's outlook on the possibility of recovering accurate information about Jesus from the Gospels was actually as grim as this quote implies. See S. E. Porter, *The Criteria for Authenticity in Historical-Jesus Research: Previous Discussion and New Proposals*, JSNTSup 191 (Sheffield, PA: Sheffield Academic Press, 2000), 45–47.

[197] See W. L. Craig, *The Existence of God and the Beginning of the Universe* (San Bernardino, CA: Here's Life, 1979); Dembski, *Intelligent Design*; J. P. Moreland and K. Nielsen, eds., *Does God Exist? The Great Debate* (Nashville, TN: Thomas Nelson, 1990); A. Plantinga, *God and Other Minds: A Study of the Rational Justification of Belief in God* (Ithaca, NY: Cornell University Press, 1990); R. Swinburne, *Is There a God?* (Oxford, UK: University Press, 1996). On the possibility of miracles, see N. L. Geisler, *Miracles and the Modern Mind: A Defense of Biblical Miracles* (Grand Rapids, MI: Baker, 1992); R. D. Geivett and G. R. Habermas, eds., *In Defense of Miracles: A Comprehensive Case for God's Action in History* (Downers Grove, IL: InterVarsity, 1997); C. Brown, *Miracles and the Critical Mind* (Grand Rapids, MI: Eerdmans, 1984); and especially the extensive defense of miracles in Craig Keener, *Miracles: The Credibility of the New Testament Accounts* (Grand Rapids, MI: Baker Academic, 2011).

It is becoming increasingly clear at the beginning of the twenty-first century that the philosophy that has guided the skeptical study of the Gospels has failed. Despite the reign of modernist philosophy in Western education for over a century, most Americans believe that the existence and intervention of God is self-evident. According to a survey conducted in 2006 by the Barna Research group, 71 percent of adult Americans believe in "the all powerful, all-knowing, perfect creator of the universe who rules the world today."[198] The 2003 Harris poll discovered that 84 percent of American adults believe in miracles and 72 percent of those who have postgraduate degrees believe in miracles.[199] This pervasive belief is likely a result of personal experiences that participants deemed to be miraculous or the result of personal testimonies about miracles experienced by people regarded as credible. Personal experiences have overridden the reigning philosophy and led to a widespread rejection of naturalistic claims. This rejection is legitimate since an acceptable philosophy should account for actual experiences.[200]

The point of this discussion is that the dismissal of the historical reliability of the Gospels by many contemporary scholars is not generally based on historical evidence that disputes the testimony of Gospel accounts. Rather, this dismissal is grounded in the scholars' philosophical presuppositions, presuppositions that most Americans rightly reject because they fail to explain personal experiences and perceptions of reality. When one overcomes philosophical prejudices against accounts that describe supernatural events such as incarnation, virgin birth, exorcism, miracle, and resurrection, one discovers that the evidence for the historical reliability of the Gospels is compelling.

The Criteria of Authenticity

Some scholars reject the historical reliability of the Gospels because they have attempted to use objective means to test whether particular sayings or events recorded in the Gospels can be traced back to Jesus. Many scholars believe that the only material that can be deemed reliable in the Gospels is material that satisfies particular criteria, which are called the "criteria of authenticity." These criteria were developed and refined by form and redaction critics of the early and mid-twentieth century. Although one scholar has compiled a list of twenty-five such criteria that have been applied in recent historical Jesus research,[201] this section treats only the four most widely recognized criteria: (1) multiple attestation or forms; (2) Palestinian environment or language; (3) dissimilarity; and (4) coherence.

---

[198] G. Barna, "Beliefs: General Religious," n.p. (cited May 1, 2007); posted at http://www.barna.org/FlexPage.aspx?Page=Topic&TopicID=2.

[199] H. Taylor, "The Religious and Other Beliefs of Americans, 2003," n.p. (cited May 8, 2007); posted at http://www.harrisinteractive.com/harris_poll/index.asp?PID=359.

[200] See R. Swinburne, "The Evidential Value of Religious Experience," in *The Sciences and Theology in the Twentieth Century*, ed. A. R. Peacocke (Stockfield, UK: Oriel, 1981), 182–96.

[201] D. Polkow, "Method and Criteria for Historical Jesus Research," in K. H. Richards, ed., *Society of Biblical Literature Seminar Papers*, SBLSP 26 (Atlanta, GA: Scholars Press, 1987), 336–56.

The Criterion of Multiple Attestation or Forms The criterion of multiple independent attestation suggests that material about Jesus is probably authentic if it appears in two or more ancient sources which did not rely on each other. F. C. Burkitt first suggested that locating material that appeared in both Mark and Q was "the nearest approach that we can hope to get to the common tradition of the earliest Christian society about our Lord's words."[202] Later scholars expanded the criterion to include not only material in Mark and Q but also material in M (material unique to Matthew), L (material unique to Luke), John, other NT writings, and extrabiblical sources such as the Gospel of Thomas. Jesus's teaching on divorce, for example, is attested by three independent sources: Mark 10:2–12 (Matt 19:3–12); Q (Matt 5:32//Luke 16:18); and Paul (1 Cor 7:10–11) and thus should be regarded as authentic according to this criterion.

C. H. Dodd argued that material that appeared in multiple forms was also probably early and possibly authentic.[203] The various forms had been defined by form critics who sought to trace the history of the oral traditions behind the Gospels. The designated forms included aphorisms, parables, dialogues, and miracle stories. For example, since Jesus proclaimed that the kingdom of God had arrived in multiple forms including an aphorism (Matt 5:17), parables (Matt 9:37–38; Mark 4:26–29), poetic sayings (Matt 13:16–17), and dialogues (Matt 12:24–28), the insistence that the kingdom of God had arrived was likely an authentic theme of Jesus's teaching.

S. Porter has pointed out several problems related to applying this criterion.[204] Most importantly, the criterion is able to establish general themes of the teaching of Jesus but does not usually enable scholars to reconstruct Jesus's actual words. Moreover, the appeal to multiple independent sources is now complicated by recent rejection of the once widely held solution to the Synoptic problem.[205] Most importantly, while the criterion of multiple attestation may enable the researcher to confirm the authenticity of Gospels material on the positive side, conversely, it is inadequate to rule out from consideration material that is attested in only one source since there is no good reason for someone to reject material as authentic merely because, for example, a given feat of Jesus is recorded only once. This points to an egregious limitation in the use of this criterion.

The Criterion of Palestinian Environment or Language From the seventeenth century until modern times, the criterion of Palestinian environment or language has served as an index for evaluating material associated with Jesus. This criterion suggests that a section of material in the Gospels is probably authentic if it appears to be a fairly literal translation of a Semitic (Hebrew or Aramaic) original into Greek. The rationale behind this criterion

---

[202] F. C. Burkitt, *The Gospel History and Its Transmission*, 3rd ed. (Edinburgh, Scotland: T&T Clark, 1911), 147. Burkitt examined Mark and Q for double attestation. After the publication of B. H. Streeter's work (on which see further below), the criterion was expanded to include material in M and L as well.

[203] C. H. Dodd, *The Parables of the Kingdom*, rev. ed. (New York, NY: Charles Scribner's Sons, 1961), 26–29; idem, *History and the Gospel* (London, UK: Nisbet, 1938), 91–102.

[204] Porter, *Criteria of Authenticity*, 86–89.

[205] See the discussion of the various theories regarding the relationship of the Synoptic Gospels below.

is the observation that Greek quickly became the predominant language of the church. Material created by the church would have been originally composed in Greek and would not possess Semitic characteristics. Therefore, material that preserves Semitic vocabulary, grammar, or style is very early and likely to be authentic.

An example of Palestinian language appears in Matthew 5:13. Although most modern translations refer to salt "losing its taste," the verb translated in this fashion *(mōranthē)* does not mean "to lose taste" anywhere else in all of ancient literature. The verb normally means "to become foolish, lose one's mind, or be mentally incapacitated," a meaning that does not quite make sense in this context. The puzzling use of the Greek verb here is likely a by-product of the Greek translation of an original Aramaic saying. In Hebrew and Aramaic, the root *tpl* can mean either "be foolish" (Job 1:22; 24:12; Jer 23:13) or "be saltless, dull, insipid" (Job 6:6). The evidence of an Aramaic original here suggests both the antiquity and authenticity of the saying.[206]

The criterion of Palestinian environment suggests that material is probably early and possibly authentic if it refers to customs, geographical features, or beliefs characteristic of first-century Palestine. The probability of the antiquity and authenticity of the material increases if the knowledge of the Palestinian environment exhibited in the account would have been possessed only by someone with a personal acquaintance with that environment. For example, the very specific description of the five colonnades of the pool of Bethesda near the Sheep Gate in John 5:2 has been confirmed through archaeological excavations.[207] The description strongly suggests that the author of John's Gospel was personally familiar with the city of Jerusalem before the fall of the city in AD 70 and who thus had access to authentic traditions about Jesus or was indeed an eyewitness of Jesus's ministry.

As in the case of the criterion of multiple attestation, the present criterion of Palestinian environment or language may serve positively as an indication of the authenticity of material included in the Gospels. At the same time, caution should be exercised not to disqualify material whose authenticity cannot be established by the use of this criterion since other criteria may affirm its authenticity. Moreover, the intrinsic limitations of any criterion of authenticity of Gospels material should be kept in mind.

The Criterion of Dissimilarity The criterion of dissimilarity suggests that material in the Gospels is authentic if the sayings or deeds of Jesus recorded in the account are dissimilar to those expected from the Judaism of his day or from the practices and theology of the early church. This criterion was first formulated by W. Heitmüller and P. W. Schmiedel. It was popularized by R. Bultmann who wrote, "We can only count on possessing a genuine similitude of Jesus where, on the one hand, expression is given to the contrast between

---

[206] See C. L. Quarles, *The Sermon on the Mount: Restoring Christ's Message to the Modern Church,* NAC Studies in Bible and Theology 11 (Nashville, TN: B&H Academic, 2009), 81.

[207] See U. C. von Wahlde, "Archaeology and John's Gospel," in *Jesus and Archaeology*, ed. J. H. Charlesworth (Grand Rapids, MI: Eerdmans, 2006), 560–66 (with additional references); R. Brown, *The Gospel According to John I–XII*, AB 29 (Garden City, NY: Doubleday, 1966), 206–7; and Köstenberger, *John*, 178.

Jewish morality and piety and the distinctive eschatological temper which characterized the preaching of Jesus; and where on the other hand we find no specifically Christian features."[208] The intent of the criterion is to rule out material that may have originated in Jewish circles or may have been invented by early Christians. Application of the criterion establishes the authenticity of material such as Matthew 8:22 according to which Jesus said, "Let the dead bury their own dead." Such a saying was unlikely to have originated from Jewish traditions or the teaching of the Christian community.[209]

Unfortunately, this criterion has often been misapplied. Not only is material that satisfies the criterion accepted as authentic, material that does not satisfy the criterion is sometimes rejected as inauthentic. This misapplication of the criterion results in the absurd portrait of a first-century Jew who in no way reflects his Jewish background and a teacher whose teachings were completely abandoned by the church he founded. For this reason, many current scholars rarely apply this criterion, and some have called for the abandonment of the criterion altogether.[210]

G. Theissen and D. Winter recently urged that the criterion be replaced by a criterion of historical plausibility. This criterion has four elements:

1. Contextual appropriateness: "What Jesus intended and said must be compatible with the Judaism of the first half of the first century in Galilee."
2. Contextual distinctiveness: "What Jesus intended and did must be recognizable as that of an individual figure within the framework of the Judaism of that time."
3. Source coherence: "The coherence of enduring features that persisted despite the variety of tendencies at work within pluralistic early Christianity."
4. Resistance to tendencies of the tradition: "Those elements within the Jesus tradition that contrast with the interests of the early Christian sources, but are handed on in their tradition, can claim varying degrees of historical plausibility."[211]

N. T. Wright has suggested a similar modification of the criterion of dissimilarity. He called his modification "the criterion of double similarity and double dissimilarity." Wright argued that no historical person differs too radically from his immediate context. One would also expect significant continuity between the founder of a movement and his earliest followers. However, a truly distinctive leader will differ from others in his context in important ways, and his followers may prove incapable of fully imitating him. Thus, the historical Jesus should both be similar and dissimilar to other first-century Jews and his

---

[208] See Porter, *Criteria of Authenticity*, 71; Bultmann, *History of the Synoptic Tradition*, 205.

[209] M. Hengel, *The Charismatic Leader and His Followers*, trans. J. C. G. Greig (Edinburgh, Scotland: T&T Clark, 1981), 5.

[210] For the call to abandon the criterion of double dissimilarity, see G. Theissen and D. Winter, *The Quest for the Plausible Jesus: The Question of Criteria*, trans. E. M. Boring (Louisville, KY: Westminster John Knox, 2002), 27–171.

[211] Ibid., 211.

earliest disciples.[212] Modifications such as these are necessary in order for this criterion to make a positive contribution to Jesus studies.

The Criterion of Coherence This criterion, also called "criterion of consistency or conformity," simply stipulates that material is likely early and authentic if consistent with material judged to be authentic based on other criteria. As J. P. Meier noted, "The criterion of coherence holds that other sayings and deeds of Jesus that fit in well with the preliminary 'data base' established by using our first three criteria have a good chance of being historical (e.g., sayings concerning the coming of the kingdom of God or disputes with adversaries over legal observance)."[213]

Used appropriately, the application of this criterion has the potential to enlarge significantly the amount of material deemed by critics to be authentic in the Gospels. At the same time, Meier rightly cautioned that "[o]ne must, however, be wary of using it [the criterion of coherence] negatively, i.e., declaring a saying or action inauthentic because it does not seem to be consistent with words or deeds of Jesus already declared authentic on other grounds."[214] One should not discard the possibility that Jesus uttered statements that set him apart from other religious leaders of his day.

Table 3.4: Historical Jesus Research: Criteria of Authenticity

Criterion	Definition
Criterion of Multiple Attestation	Material about Jesus is probably authentic if it appears in two or more independent ancient sources.
Criterion of Palestinian Environment	A section of material in the Gospels is probably authentic if it appears to be a fairly literal translation of Semitic (Hebrew or Aramaic) idiom into Greek.
Criterion of Dissimilarity	Material in the Gospels is authentic if the sayings or deeds of Jesus recorded in the account are dissimilar to those expected from the Judaism of his day or from the practices and theology of the early church.
Criterion of Coherence	Material is likely early and authentic if it is consistent with material judged to be authentic based on other criteria.

Evaluation of the Criteria

These criteria can be helpful for demonstrating the historical reliability of the Gospels if they are properly applied. However, at least three problems are associated with these criteria.

First, some scholars do not apply the criteria consistently. Instead, they manipulate them to create a portrait of Jesus that accords with their expectations. The Jesus Seminar, for example, claimed to value the standard criteria of authenticity but casually dismissed

[212] Wright, *Jesus and the Victory of God*, 90.

[213] J. P. Meier, "Criteria: How Do We Decide What Comes from Jesus?" in *The Historical Jesus in Recent Research*, ed. J. D. G. Dunn and S. McKnight (Winona Lake, IN: Eisenbrauns, 2005), 134.

[214] Ibid., 135.

much material that is authenticated by the criteria.[215] Second, some scholars abuse the criteria by automatically assuming that material not established as authentic by applying the criteria is necessarily inauthentic, an imaginative creation of the early church. Third, and most importantly, the criteria of authenticity place an unreasonable burden of proof on the Gospel material. Historians generally accept the historical reliability of ancient sources unless there are good reasons for not doing so. In legal parlance, the sources are deemed innocent until proven guilty. However, the criteria of authenticity are often applied as if the NT Gospels are guilty until proven innocent. C. Blomberg noted,

> Once one accepts that the Gospels reflect attempts to write reliable history or biography, however theological or stylized its presentation may be, then one must immediately recognize an important presupposition which guides most historians in their work. Unless there is good reason for believing otherwise one will assume that a given detail in the work of a particular historian is factual. This method places the burden of proof squarely on the person who would doubt the reliability of a given portion of the text. The alternative is to presume the text unreliable unless convincing evidence can be brought forward in support of it. While many critical scholars of the Gospels adopt this method, it is wholly unjustified by the normal canons of historiography. Scholars who would consistently implement such a method when studying other ancient historical writing would find the corroborative data so insufficient that the vast majority of accepted history would have to be jettisoned.[216]

Although the criteria of authenticity represent a bias against the reliability of the Gospels that does not generally characterize historians' treatment of other ancient records, these criteria can serve to establish the historical reliability of a large percentage of the material in the Gospels if they are fairly and consistently applied. Unless one imposes a dual function on the criteria in which they authenticate some material and invalidate all other material, the large percentage of material authenticated by the criteria strongly implies the general historical reliability of the Gospels. More simply put, if the authors of the four Gospels preserved accurate history in the large percentage of material established by the criteria of authenticity, scholars are justified in assuming that the evangelists preserved accurate history in the other material in their Gospels. What is more, these criteria of authenticity establish the historical reliability of the Gospels' accounts of Jesus's supernatural activity including exorcisms, miracles, and his own resurrection.[217] Thus, these criteria

---

[215] See C. L. Quarles, "The Authenticity of the Parable of the Warring King: A Response to the Jesus Seminar," in *Authenticating the Words of Jesus*, ed. B. Chilton and C. A. Evans (Leiden, Netherlands: Brill, 1999), 409–30.

[216] C. L. Blomberg, *The Historical Reliability of the Gospels*, 2nd ed. (Downers Grove, IL: InterVarsity, 2007), 303–4.

[217] See J. P. Meier, *Mentor, Message, and Miracles*, vol. 2 of *The Marginal Jew* (Garden City, NY: Doubleday, 1994), 617–970; Twelftree, *Jesus the Miracle Worker*; N. T. Wright, *The Resurrection of the Son of God*, Christian Origins and the Question of God 3 (Minneapolis, MN: Fortress, 2003).

demand a fresh appraisal of the philosophical commitments that provided the original incentive for skeptical treatments of the Gospels.

The Transmission of Gospel Traditions

The study of the Gospels during much of the twentieth century was dominated by an approach called form criticism. Form criticism involved three basic steps: (1) classifying the form of the Gospel materials as parable, miracle story, proverb, and such; (2) assigning the form to the context in the life of the early church in which it was probably used; and (3) tracing the history of the oral transmission of each form until it was written down.[218] As a part of the third step, form critics developed detailed laws that described how early oral traditions about Jesus were adapted as they were passed down. Form critics generally assumed that by the time the oral traditions were written down, they had become a mixture of both history and legend. Claims about Jesus became increasingly exaggerated each time stories about him were passed on until Jesus evolved from a fairly ordinary man into a miracle-working deity.

Although form criticism has been largely abandoned in recent NT scholarship, some assumptions associated with the method are still widely (and uncritically) accepted. Most important of these is the assumption that accounts of Jesus's words and deeds were significantly altered and embellished during a lengthy period of oral transmission before the accounts were preserved in writing.[219] Bauckham summarized the three major types of oral transmission that have been proposed for Gospel traditions: (1) informal uncontrolled (Bultmann); (2) informal controlled (Bailey, followed by Dunn); and (3) formal controlled (the Scandinavian school; Gerhardsson, following Riesenfeld).[220]

By way of overall critique, the informal uncontrolled model insufficiently recognizes the presence of eyewitnesses throughout the transmission period, which safeguarded the control of accuracy. The informal controlled model uses a questionable model of transmission, that is, the way oral material is transmitted in rural settings, while early Christianity was significantly transmitted in large urban centers. The formal controlled model asserts that Jesus's followers memorized large portions of his teaching or took written notes during his ministry, so it is often judged as too rigid and inadequately supported by the evidence. The following specific points of critique may be noted.

First, recent research has demonstrated that accounts transmitted orally in first-century Palestine were much more stable than many form critics believed. K. Bailey and J. Dunn have recently argued that the stories about Jesus would have been transmitted in a process

---

[218] For a good introduction to form criticism, see E. P. Sanders and M. Davies, *Studying the Synoptic Gospels* (Philadelphia, PA: Trinity Press International, 1989), 123–200.

[219] But see Darrell L. Bock, *The Missing Gospels: Unearthing the Truth behind Alternative Christianities* [Nashville, TN: Thomas Nelson, 2006], 83–96, 115–30, 147–64, 183–214, who explains how theology was being taught and understood in its core while the NT was being written. All the things the whole church did—whether reading Hebrew Scripture, singing hymns, reciting doctrinal summaries, and practicing church rites—allowed early believers to be taught core theology while these works were being produced. See also Darrell L. Bock and Daniel B. Wallace, *Dethroning Jesus: Exposing Popular Culture's Quest to Unseat the Biblical Christ* (Nashville, TN: Thomas Nelson, 2007).

[220] See Bauckham, *Jesus and the Eyewitnesses*, chap. 10, and the literature cited there, to whose treatment the following discussion is indebted; see especially his critique of Bailey and Dunn on pp. 257–63.

best described as informal controlled oral tradition.[221] Those who transmitted the traditions sought to preserve faithfully the key features of the tradition that expressed the meaning and significance of that tradition, especially when stories or teachings were important for a community's identity. To this R. Bauckham added the important insight that the major tradition-controlling element in the case of Gospel tradition was the presence of the original eyewitnesses throughout the transmission process.[222]

Second, compelling evidence suggests that the Synoptic Gospels were written between twenty to thirty years after Jesus's death. At this early date numerous eyewitnesses of Jesus's ministry would have been available to serve as sources of traditions about Jesus and to correct the tradition as necessary. The time between the witnessed events and the penning of the Gospels is simply not long enough to accommodate the drastic evolution of the oral tradition that is often suggested. The more widely accepted dates of composition for the Synoptic Gospels (late fifties to mid-eighties) allow only slightly more time for the adaptation of the accounts but not enough to explain the rather drastic differences between original forms of the tradition and the forms preserved in the Gospels that many scholars suppose. Abundant NT evidence demonstrates that the early church respected the authority of eyewitnesses over the tradition and sought to preserve accurate testimony about Jesus that was based on eyewitness accounts. Luke's preface (Luke 1:1–4), Paul's appeals (1 Cor 15:1–8), and the qualifications of the apostles (Acts 1:21–22) are but a few of the numerous indications of the importance of eyewitness testimony for the early church.

Third, the supposition that the Gospels contain highly evolved accounts of Jesus's ministry ignores significant evidence suggesting that the early church was correct in its claim that the four Gospels were based on eyewitness testimony. Luke's preface explicitly claims that his Gospel was based on the recollections of eyewitnesses (Luke 1:2; *autoptai*). Papias claimed that Mark's Gospel preserved the reminiscences of Jesus's ministry by Simon Peter.[223] Papias, who may have written as early as AD 110, based his testimony on tradition received from a certain Aristion and a "John the Elder," both of whom were personal disciples of Jesus.[224] Moreover, internal features of the book confirm Mark's reliance on Peter as his primary source. Papias's claim that the apostle Matthew wrote the Gospel that bears his name is consistent with the details of the Gospel itself. Finally, the Gospel of John explicitly claims to have been written by an eyewitness (John 21:24). Although no discussion of the authorship of the Fourth Gospel by Papias has survived, Bauckham has convincingly argued that the discussion of the Gospel of John in the Muratorian Canon (late second century) borrowed heavily from Papias.[225] Thus the claim that the Gospel of

---

[221] K. E. Bailey, "Informal Controlled Oral Tradition and the Synoptic Gospels," *Asia Journal of Theology* 5 (1991): 34–54; idem, "Middle Eastern Oral Tradition and the Synoptic Gospels," *ExpTim* 106 (1995): 363–67; J. D. G. Dunn, *Jesus Remembered*, Christianity in the Making 1 (Grand Rapids, MI: Eerdmans, 2003), 173–254.

[222] Bauckham, *Jesus and the Eyewitnesses*, chaps. 10 and 11.

[223] Eusebius, *Eccl. Hist.* 3.39.14–16.

[224] Some scholars suggest that Papias wrote his "Expositions of the Lord's Sayings" around the year 130. But Bauckham (*Jesus and the Eyewitnesses*, 12–14) demonstrated that this date is based on unreliable evidence.

[225] Bauckham, *Jesus and the Eyewitnesses*, 425–33.

John was written by a disciple, which is preserved in the Muratorian Canon that probably dates to the late second century, can actually be traced back to Papias around the year 110. Ascription of this Gospel to an eyewitness was also confirmed by Polycrates (ca. AD 130–196) and Irenaeus (ca. AD 130–200) in the late second century.

Bauckham has recently demonstrated that the claim that the Gospels preserve eyewitness testimony is confirmed by features within the Gospels. These features include an "*inclusio* of eyewitness testimony" similar to those employed by Lucian and Porphyry in their Greek biographies. This literary device involves the reference to the primary eyewitness source of a given document source by name at the beginning and at the end of that particular piece of writing. The *inclusio* in the Gospel of Mark identifies Peter as Mark's primary witness (Mark 1:16; 16:7). Similar uses of the device acknowledge the importance of Peter's testimony in the Gospels of Luke and John.[226]

Scholars who assume a lengthy period of oral transmission of Gospel stories occurred before the Gospels were written typically argue that many of the details of the narratives were secondary additions made by later storytellers. These new details, they suggest, included the naming of important characters in the narrative.[227] But Bauckham used recent statistics on the use of Jewish names in Palestine between 330 BC and AD 200 to demonstrate that the names of the Palestinian Jews in the Gospels and Acts coincide very closely with the names of Palestinian Jews known from ancient Jewish texts and ossuary inscriptions.

At the same time, the names of Palestinian Jews in the Gospels and Acts were quite dissimilar from the names of Jews in the Diaspora during that same period. Bauckham concluded, "In this light it becomes very unlikely that the names in the Gospels are late accretions to the traditions. Outside Palestine the appropriate names simply could not have been chosen. Even within Palestine, it would be very surprising if random accretions of names to this or that tradition would fit the actual pattern of names in the general population."[228] The testimony of the early church regarding the authorship of the Gospels and the internal features of the Gospels led Bauckham to this conclusion:

> The Gospel texts are much closer to the form in which the eyewitnesses told their stories or passed on their traditions than is commonly envisaged in current scholarship. This is what gives the Gospels their character as testimony. They embody the testimony of the eyewitnesses, not of course without editing and interpretation, but in a way that is substantially faithful to how the eyewitnesses themselves told it, since the Evangelists were in more or less direct contact with eyewitnesses, not removed from them by a long process of anonymous transmission of the traditions.[229]

---

[226] See ibid., 114–47.

[227] Bultmann, *History of the Synoptic Tradition*, 68, 215, 241, 283, 310, 345, 393; M. Dibelius, *From Tradition to Gospel*, trans. B. L. Woolf (London, UK: Nicholson & Watson, 1934), 50–53.

[228] Bauckham, *Jesus and the Eyewitnesses*, 73–74.

[229] Ibid., 6. For Bauckham's views on the authorship of John's Gospel and a critique of his views, see chap. 7 below.

Both the antiquity of the Gospels and their connections to eyewitnesses strongly affirm the historical reliability of the Gospels.

The Legitimacy of Harmonization

Scholars in the early church—including Tatian (ca. 175), Irenaeus (ca. 130–200), Origen (ca. 185–254), Chrysostom (ca. 347–407), and Augustine (354–430)—generally believed that the four Gospels were complementary rather than contradictory accounts. When they discovered apparent discrepancies between one Gospel and another, they sought explanations that would reconcile or harmonize the accounts. They acknowledged differences between the Gospels but generally denied that there were actual disagreements between them.[230]

Augustine, for example, noted that differences in order between the Gospels did not constitute disagreements since the Gospels should be assumed to be arranged chronologically only in those cases in which the author explicitly mentioned chronological sequencing. He also argued that the Gospels preserve the same sense of Jesus's sayings even when they vary in wording. Finally, Augustine suggested that apparent parallels in the Gospels that had significantly different details might actually record similar events that occurred on separate occasions in Jesus's ministry.[231]

During the Enlightenment period, scholars increasingly frowned on attempts at harmonization. The Gospels were viewed more and more as mere human literature in which contradictions should be expected. Efforts to reconcile apparent discrepancies between the Gospels were assumed to involve manipulating the evidence in order to force conformity with misguided notions of divine inspiration.

Sometimes well-intentioned scholars have resorted to unreasonable extremes in harmonization,[232] but this should not discredit all attempts to harmonize the Gospels. Historians often find apparent discrepancies in various accounts of the same event in ancient sources. They generally explore ways in which the accounts might be reconciled before assuming that one or more of the sources are inaccurate. The apparent discrepancies may simply result from the fragmentary nature of the reports that nonetheless unite to give a more complete picture of the event. At other times the apparent discrepancy results from the historian's own misinterpretation of the data.

Several considerations assist scholars in addressing apparent discrepancies between Gospel accounts.[233] The most important of these relates to the nature of the references to Jesus's sayings in the Gospels. The Gospel writers were committed to preserving the

---

[230] Blomberg, *Historical Reliability*, 25–30.

[231] Ibid., 30.

[232] See H. Lindsell, *Battle for the Bible* (Grand Rapids, MI: Zondervan, 1976), 174–76. In order to explain variations in wording between the Gospels, Lindsell claimed that Peter denied Jesus six times. But this claim conflicts with Jesus's own prophecy that Peter would deny him three times before the rooster crowed.

[233] For a more extensive discussion of legitimate approaches to harmonization, see Blomberg, *Historical Reliability*, 152–240; idem, "The Legitimacy and Limits of Harmonization," in *Hermeneutics, Authority, and Canon*, ed. D. A. Carson and J. D. Woodbridge (Grand Rapids, MI: Zondervan, 1986), 139–74.

original sense or gist of Jesus's sayings but were not confined to reporting these sayings word for word. Variations in the wording of Gospel sayings do not constitute historical errors since the Gospel writers preserved the *ipsissima vox* (exact voice or true sense) even when they did not record the *ipsissima verba* (exact words) of Jesus. The evangelists were free to summarize, abbreviate, paraphrase, or clarify Jesus's words as necessary. Although modern readers expect greater precision in quotations and may be troubled by the freedom exercised in quotations by ancient writers, their disappointment should be alleviated if they consider that many of the quotations of sayings in the Gospels are more along the lines of indirect quotes or paraphrases than verbatim direct quotations. Sometimes modern readers assume the sayings of Jesus in the Gospels are verbatim quotations because they are placed in quotation marks. But ancient writers did not use literary conventions like quotation marks to distinguish direct and indirect quotations. The quotation marks in English translations are the creation of translators and editors of modern texts.

This text cannot discuss all of the alleged contradictions between the Gospels and the possible means of harmonizing them.[234] However, scholars have posed plausible and often persuasive solutions to all of the apparent discrepancies. Comparative analysis of the Gospels strongly supports their historical reliability.

THE RELATIONSHIPS BETWEEN THE GOSPELS

Scholars often refer to Matthew, Mark, and Luke as the Synoptic Gospels. The term *synoptic* means "to see together, to have the same view or outlook," so the first three Gospels are "synoptic" because they offer similar presentations of the life and teachings of Jesus. Despite remarkable similarities, differences between these Gospels exist as well. Today scholars generally refer to questions regarding this puzzling combination of differences and similarities between these three Gospels—especially questions about the possible sources the Gospel writers used—as the Synoptic Problem. This terminology is less than ideal, however, in that it seems already to presuppose that there is a "problem" needing to be solved rather than an opportunity to view Jesus from a variety of complementary perspectives that enrich rather than contradict one another.

This section explores the similarities between the Gospels and surveys various explanations scholars have offered to account for those similarities. It also highlights the strengths and weaknesses of the various ways in which the relationship between the Synoptic Gospels has been construed. It should be pointed out at the outset, however, that one's view on this issue should not be taken as a test of orthodoxy, especially since the available evidence does not allow for a definitive resolution of all the issues involved. This does not mean it is illegitimate to attempt to construct a plausible hypothesis on the basis of all the available data. But it does mean that dogmatism should be avoided and that neither Matthean nor

---

[234] Helpful resources include G. L. Archer Jr., *The New International Encyclopedia of Bible Difficulties* (Grand Rapids, MI: Zondervan, 2001 [1982]); N. L. Geisler and T. Howe, *When Critics Ask: A Popular Handbook on Bible Difficulties* (Grand Rapids, MI: Baker, 1992); and W. C. Kaiser Jr., ed., *Hard Sayings of the Bible* (Downers Grove, IL: InterVarsity, 1996).

Markan priority, nor any other model, should be disparaged as being incompatible with a high view of Scripture.

Similarities among the Gospels

Scholars seek to identify the similarities and differences among the Gospels by using a tool called a Gospels Synopsis.[235] This tool places similar accounts in the various Gospels side by side in parallel columns so scholars can compare them more easily. Scholars typically use a color-coding system to highlight the material shared by all four Gospels, by the Synoptic Gospels, or other combinations of the Gospels. They then analyze the common material to attempt to make decisions about the possible literary relationships between the Gospels. This comparison is best conducted using a Greek Synopsis since some similarities and differences in English versions may be due to the translator rather than the original authors of the Gospels. This quest to determine the literary relationships among the Gospels is called "source criticism." Comparisons of the Synoptic Gospels highlight four major similarities: (1) in wording; (2) in order; (3) in parenthetical and explanatory material; and (4) in OT quotations.

Similarities in Wording Some of the wording of the Synoptic Gospels, especially the wording of Jesus's sayings, is identical or almost identical, as seen in the following comparison of Jesus's first prediction of his sufferings (Matt 16:21–23; Mark 8:31–33; Luke 9:22).

Table 3.5: Synoptic Comparison of Jesus's First Passion Prediction

Matt 16:21–23	Mark 8:31–33	Luke 9:21–22
From then on Jesus ***began*** to point out to his disciples THAT he MUST go to Jerusalem and SUFFER MANY THINGS from THE ELDERS, CHIEF PRIESTS, AND SCRIBES, BE KILLED, AND be raised the third day. ***And Peter took him aside and began to rebuke him,*** "Oh no, Lord! This will never happen to you!" ***But the one turning*** told Peter, "***Get behind me, Satan***! You are a hindrance to me ***because you're not thinking about God's concerns but human concerns.***"	Then he ***began*** to teach them THAT *the Son of Man* must SUFFER MANY THINGS *and be rejected* by THE ELDERS, the CHIEF PRIESTS, and the SCRIBES, BE KILLED, AND rise after three days. He spoke openly about this. ***And Peter took him aside and began to rebuke him. But the one turning*** around and looking at his disciples, rebuked Peter and said, ***"Get behind me, Satan, because you are not thinking about God's concerns but human concerns."***	But he strictly warned and instructed them to tell this to no one, saying THAT *the Son of Man* MUST SUFFER MANY THINGS *and be rejected* by THE ELDERS, CHIEF PRIESTS, AND SCRIBES, BE KILLED, AND be raised the third day.

In the example above, the CSB translation has been slightly adapted to show agreements that exist in the Greek texts of the Gospels. Small caps indicate agreements in all

[235] See K. Aland, ed., *Synopsis of the Four Gospels* (New York, NY: United Bible Societies, 1982; repr., Peabody, MA: Hendrickson, 2006); idem, *Synopsis Quattuor Evangeliorum*, 15th ed. (Stuttgart, Germany: Deutsche Bibelgesellschaft, 2001).

three Synoptics; italics indicate exact agreements between Mark and Luke; bold italics indicate exact agreements between Matthew and Mark; underlines indicate exact agreements between Matthew and Luke. An examination of the parallels shows that the three Synoptics agree on the essence of Jesus's saying.

The similarity in wording is sufficiently close to suggest the possibility of a literary relationship, as if one or more of the Gospel writers was familiar with one or more of the other Gospels. Mark seems to have a special connection to the other two Gospels. Mark shares material with Matthew that Luke lacks, particularly the rebuke of Peter in which Mark and Matthew have extensive verbatim agreements.

On the other hand, Mark also shares important features with Luke that are absent in Matthew, such as the use of the title "Son of Man" and the reference to Jesus's rejection. The only material that Luke and Matthew share that differs from Mark is the phrase "be raised the third day" in contrast to Mark's "rise [a different Greek verb from the one used by Matthew and Luke] after three days." This minor agreement may suggest Matthew knew Luke or vice versa. However, the parallel is not extensive enough to require a literary dependence between Matthew and Luke. They may have both coincidentally adapted Mark in an identical fashion.

The only clear conclusion to be derived from these parallels is the special connection of Mark to Matthew and Luke. But this special connection may be explained in two different ways: (1) Mark wrote his Gospel first, and Matthew and Luke used Mark in writing their own Gospels; (2) Matthew and Luke wrote first, and Mark used both of these earlier Gospels in writing his Gospel. These two possible interpretations of the parallels constitute the two major solutions to the Synoptic Problem. The view that Mark wrote first and was used by the other two synoptic writers is called "Markan priority." The view that Matthew and Luke wrote first, and Mark used both of these earlier Gospels is called the "Griesbach (or Two Gospel) hypothesis."

Similarities in Order The Gospels contain numerous pericopes, self-contained units of narrative such as the account of Jesus's healing of the leper in Mark 1:40–45. Although these pericopes could be arranged in a number of different ways in the individual Gospels—topically, chronologically, or geographically (based on the locations in which they occurred)—the Gospels share a remarkable similarity in the order of the pericopes. The following chart shows how the Synoptic Gospels order pericopes describing the early ministry of Jesus.

Table 3.6: Synoptic Comparison of Early Ministry of Jesus

Pericopes (arranged in Markan order)	Matthew	Mark	Luke
1. Jesus's teaching in Capernaum synagogue		1:21–22	4:31–32
2. Healing of demoniac in Capernaum		1:23–28	4:33–37
3. Jesus's healing of Peter's mother-in-law	8:14–15	1:29–31	4:38–39

Table 3.6: Synoptic Comparison of Early Ministry of Jesus (continued)

Pericopes (arranged in Markan order)	Matthew	Mark	Luke
4. Jesus's healing in the evening	8:16–17	1:32–34	4:40–41
5. Jesus leaves Capernaum		1:35–38	4:42–43
6. Jesus's preaching in Galilee	*4:23*	1:39	4:44
7. Miraculous catch of fish			5:1–11
8. Jesus's healing of the leper	8:1–4	1:40–45	5:12–16
9. Jesus's healing of the paralytic	9:1–8	2:1–12	5:17–26
10. Calling of Levi	9:9–13	2:13–17	5:27–32
11. Controversy over fasting	9:14–17	2:18–22	5:33–39
12. Controversy over plucking grain	12:1–8	2:23–28	6:1–5
13. Controversy over Sabbath healing	12:9–14	3:1–6	6:6–11
14. Healing by the sea	*4:24–25* 12:15–16	3:7–12	6:17–19
15. Choosing of the Twelve	*10:1–4*	3:13–19	*6:12–16*

In this table, italics indicate pericopes Matthew or Luke place in an order different from Mark's.[236] A close analysis of this data leads to several observations. First, a remarkable similarity in order exists between Mark and Luke. Luke differed from Mark in order in his placement of only one pericope, the choosing of the Twelve. Although Luke included a pericope that both Matthew and Mark lack, the miraculous catch of fish, this difference did not disrupt the order shared with Mark.

Second, Matthew follows the same order as Mark with only a few exceptions. Matthew gathered summary statements about Jesus's preaching and healing ministry in Galilee and placed them in an introduction positioned at the beginning of the Galilean ministry. However, he repeated the summary of Jesus's Galilean healing ministry in Matthew 12:15–16 in keeping with the order in Mark and Luke. Matthew, like Luke, placed the choosing of the Twelve earlier than Mark did but positioned it even earlier than Luke.

The shared order of the pericopes suggests a literary relationship among the Synoptic Gospels. But the similarities and differences in order can be explained according to either of the major theories of Gospel composition: Markan priority or the Griesbach (Two-Gospel) hypothesis. Analysis of the order of pericopes by itself cannot prove one theory over the other but must be used in conjunction with the study of other types of similarities and differences.

[236] This table was adapted from R. Stein, *The Synoptic Problem: An Introduction* (Grand Rapids, MI: Baker, 1987), 35. Using Mark as the standard of comparison for the order of pericopes can prejudice a discussion in favor of Markan priority. That is not the intention here. The order of one of the Gospels must serve as a basis for comparison, and the great similarity in order between Mark and Luke justifies using either Mark or Luke in this way.

Similarities in Parenthetical and Explanatory Material Similarities in the wording of Jesus's sayings in the Synoptic Gospels might be explained in terms of accuracy in reporting Jesus's words rather than literary dependence. Such explanations are not completely satisfactory, however, since Jesus's original Aramaic words could be translated into Greek in a number of different ways and thus not yield the frequent verbatim agreements that exist among the Gospels. But where the Gospels share identical editorial comments or parenthetical material, this strongly implies literary dependence between the Gospels.

One famous example of a shared parenthetical statement is "let the reader understand" (Matt 24:15–18; Mark 13:14–16; lacking in Luke 21:20–22). If this parenthetical statement is a note from the Gospel writer to the readers of the Gospel, the fact that both Matthew and Mark contain it would imply that one writer used the other's Gospel. But many scholars interpret the comment as Jesus's words to the readers of Daniel, in which case the statement shared by Matthew and Mark would demonstrate accuracy in reporting Jesus's words rather than literary dependence.

Those who argue that the statement is a note by the Gospel writer contend that Jesus typically referred to his audience "hearing" the OT rather than reading the OT. Since only wealthy first-century Jews had their own copies of the OT, most became familiar with it by hearing it read in synagogues rather than by reading it themselves (Luke 16:29, 31).[237] But some scholars who affirm a literary dependence between the Gospels argue that Jesus himself uttered the words "let the reader understand" and that he addressed them to readers of Daniel. This seems confirmed by Jesus's rather frequent references to reading the OT (Matt 12:3, 5; 19:4; 21:16, 42; 22:31; Mark 12:10, 26; Luke 10:26).[238]

Other shared editorial comments are not so easily dismissed. One such comment is Mark 15:10: "For he knew it was because of envy that the chief priests had handed him over." The statement is closely paralleled by Matthew 27:18, "For he knew it was because of envy that they handed him over."[239] Since these verses are editorial comments that describe Jesus's thoughts rather than transcriptions of his spoken words, the similarity in content and wording strongly suggests literary dependence. Similar examples are frequent in the Synoptics.

Similarities in Old Testament Quotations Quotations of the OT in the NT assume a variety of forms. Sometimes the quotation seems to be a strict translation of the Hebrew OT into Greek. Sometimes the quotation is a verbatim reproduction of

---

[237] Stein, *Synoptic Problem*, 38; cf. E. Best, "The Gospel of Mark: Who Was the Reader?" *IBS* 11 (1989): 124–32.

[238] For commentators who affirm that the parenthetical statement was Jesus's call to careful interpretation of Daniel, see D. A. Carson, "Matthew," in *Matthew, Mark, Luke*, EBC 8 (Grand Rapids, MI: Zondervan, 1984), 500; C. Keener, *A Commentary on the Gospel of Matthew* (Grand Rapids, MI: Eerdmans, 1999), 576; W. D. Davies and D. Allison, *Matthew 19–28*, ICC (London, UK: T&T Clark, 1997), 346. J. Nolland (*The Gospel of Matthew*, NICGT [Grand Rapids, MI: Eerdmans, 2005], 972) argued that the words refer to readers of Daniel rather than the Gospels but that they were inserted by the evangelists.

[239] Our translation. In addition to the slight differences that are obvious in the translation ("chief priests" and different tenses of the verb "handed over"), the evangelists used two different verbs for "know."

the rendering in the Septuagint (LXX). Sometimes the quotation appears to be a verbatim translation of the rendering that appears in one of the Targums. Occasionally, the quotation appears to be the Gospel writer's own paraphrase. Sometimes NT quotations conflate or blend together references to several different texts. By examining the form of OT quotations used in the Gospels, scholars can better understand their literary relationships.[240]

Matthew 11:10, Mark 1:2, and Luke 7:27 contain quotations of the OT that blend together Exodus 23:20 and Malachi 3:1 in precisely the same way.

Table 3.7: Synoptic Comparison of Use of Old Testament

OT	Matt 11:10	Mark 1:2	Luke 7:27
Exod 23:20 (LXX)			
Look, I [myself] am sending my messenger before You	See, I am sending my messenger ahead of you;	Look, I am sending my messenger ahead of you,	See, I am sending my messenger ahead of you;
Mal 3:1 (LXX)			
And he will examine the way before Me	he will prepare your way before you	who will prepare your way	he will prepare your way before you
Mal 3:1 (MT)			
and he will clear the way before Me			

Several observations support the literary dependence of the Gospels. The Synoptics agree verbatim in the quotations with only two exceptions. Mark lacks the final words "before you" that appear in Matthew and Luke. Matthew, in agreement with the Septuagint, states the pronoun after "Look," making "I" mildly emphatic ("I [myself]"). This verbatim agreement is remarkable since it required all three evangelists to link the same two texts together at precisely the same point and to translate Malachi 3:1 identically, even though their translations differ from both the Hebrew text and the Septuagint. The best explanation for the similarity in the OT quotations seems to be literary dependence between the Gospels.

A similar example is the quotation of Isaiah 29:13 in Mark 7:6–7 and Matthew 15:8–9. The renderings in Mark and Matthew are identical except for a minor variation in word order in the first clause. Their quotations seem to follow the Septuagint, although they differ from it at several important points. Matthew and Mark use a singular verb in the first clause, although the Septuagint uses a plural form. Moreover, in the Septuagint, the last line of the quotation reads "teaching commandments and doctrines of men" rather than "teaching as doctrines the commandments of men," which appears in Matthew and Mark. The fact that

---

[240] See especially G. K. Beale and D. A. Carson, eds., *Commentary on the New Testament Use of the Old Testament* (Grand Rapids, MI: Baker, 2007).

Matthew and Mark deviate from the Septuagint at precisely the same points and in precisely the same way seems more than a coincidence. It appears that either Matthew was aware of Mark's translation of Isaiah 29:13 or that Mark was aware of Matthew's translation.

Explanations of the Similarities Among the Gospels

The similarities in wording, order, editorial comments, and OT references described above have been explained in several different ways in the history of NT scholarship.

Literary Independence Some scholars argue that these similarities are products of the divine inspiration of the Synoptic Gospels rather than indicating the use of one Gospel by another. They argue that since these three Gospels share the same divine author, the Holy Spirit, readers should not be surprised by the remarkable similarities found in Matthew, Mark, and Luke. But if divine inspiration alone accounts for the similarities between the Synoptics, it is difficult to account for the differences between the Synoptics and especially the differences between the Synoptics and John.

Similarly, other scholars argue that the similarities among the Gospels simply reflect history. Similarities are a byproduct of the Gospel writers' faithful reporting of what actually happened. Although this explanation could account for the similar reporting of events and sayings in the Gospels, it is not an adequate explanation of other remarkable similarities. This explanation does not account for the parallels in parenthetical references, editorial comments, or the similarities in OT quotations described earlier.[241]

Literary Dependence The most commonly accepted explanation of the similarities among the Synoptic Gospels is that the later Synoptic writers used the earlier Synoptic Gospel(s). Theories of such literary dependence can be traced back to as early as the fifth century.[242] For example, Augustine suggested that the canonical order of the Gospels (Matthew, Mark, Luke, John) was the order in which the Gospels were written. The later writers used the material of the earlier writers: "Each of them is found not to have desired to write in ignorance of his predecessor" (Augustine, *De Consensu Evangelistarum* 1.4).[243] According to this theory Matthew, an eyewitness, wrote the first Gospel; Mark used Matthew in the compilation of his Gospel; and Luke used Matthew (and Mark) in the compilation of his.

---

[241] Proponents of the independence of the Gospels include H. Alford, *The Four Gospels* (London, England: Rivington's, 1863), 2–6; B. F. Westcott, *An Introduction to the Study of the Gospels* (London, England: Macmillan, 1895); B. Reicke, *The Roots of the Synoptic Gospels* (Philadelphia, PA: Fortress, 1986); and E. Linnemann, *Is There a Synoptic Problem? Rethinking the Literary Dependence of the First Three Gospels* (Grand Rapids, MI: Baker, 1992).

[242] See the brief history of the early church discussion in D. Bock, *Studying the Historical Jesus: A Guide to Sources and Methods* (Grand Rapids, MI: Baker, 2002), 164–67. For a more extensive history, see part 1 of D. L. Dungan, *A History of the Synoptic Problem: The Canon, the Text, the Composition, and the Interpretation of the Gospels*, ABRL (New York, NY: Doubleday, 1999), 11–144.

[243] Some claim that the "Augustinian hypothesis" is a misnomer. H. J. de Jonge ("Augustine on the Interrelations of the Gospels," in *The Four Gospels 1992: Fs. Frans Neirynck*, ed. F. van Segbroeck et al., BETL 100 [Leuven, Belgium: Leuven University Press, 1992], 3:2417) stated: "The so-called 'Augustinian hypothesis' does not reflect Augustine's views on the origin and interrelations of the Gospels. It is a recent invention, possibly not older than the sixteenth century." On p. 2410, de Jonge notes the singular "predecessor" in the above-cited reference by Augustine.

Illustration 3.1: Augustinian View

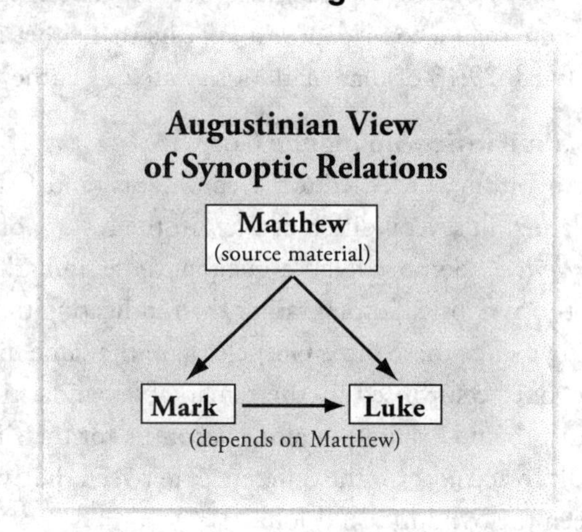

Although Augustine's solution to the Synoptic Problem has a few modern supporters, most scholars support one of the following two theories.[244]

The Two-Gospel Hypothesis In 1783 J. J. Griesbach proposed that Matthew wrote his Gospel first. In contrast to Augustine, Griesbach argued that Luke was the second Gospel and Mark the third. Griesbach's view regarding Luke's possible usage of Matthew is unclear. But modern supporters of Griesbach's view, known today as the two-Gospel hypothesis, generally argue that Luke used Matthew in writing his own Gospel. More importantly, Griesbach argued that Mark was the last of the Synoptics and that he used both Matthew and Luke in his writing.

Several factors support the two-Gospel hypothesis. First, early church tradition was all but unanimous that Matthew's Gospel was the first to be written. Matthew's placement in the canon is probably due to the early church's opinion that his Gospel was the first. As Griesbach noted, it is easier to explain (at least to the minds of some) why a non-apostle, Mark, would use the Gospel of an apostle than to explain why an apostle like Matthew would use a Gospel written by someone who was not an apostle.[245]

Second, the two-Gospel hypothesis offers a reasonable explanation for those texts in which Matthew and Luke are identical or similar but differ from Mark. The most influential proponent of the two-Gospel hypothesis in recent years, W. Farmer, argued that these Matthean-Lukan agreements are consistently of minor importance and "do not seriously

---

[244] The Augustinian solution to the Synoptic Problem has been defended recently by B. C. Butler, *The Originality of St. Matthew* (Cambridge, UK: Cambridge University Press, 1951); and J. Wenham, *Redating Matthew, Mark, and Luke: A Fresh Assault on the Synoptic Problem* (London, UK: Hodder & Stoughton, 1991). Compare D. A. Black, *Why Four Gospels? The Historical Origins of the Gospels* (Grand Rapids, MI: Kregel, 2001).

[245] This argument is weakened by the insistence of the early church that Mark's Gospel preserves Peter's reminiscences of Jesus's ministry. See the testimony of Papias, Clement of Alexandria, and Origen in Eusebius, *Eccl. Hist.* 3.39.15; 6.14.5–7; and 6.25.5 respectively; Irenaeus, *Against Heresies* 3.1.2; Tertullian, *Against Marcion* 4.5; and the Muratorian Canon. See particularly the discussion in Bauckham, *Jesus and the Eyewitnesses*, 202–39.

affect the literary purpose or theological intention of the passages concerned."[246] Mark's policy was to copy the text of his predecessor when it was identical with the exception of these minor elements that did not affect the sense of the passage.

Third, the hypothesis offers a reasonable explanation for the so-called Markan redundancies. Mark contains 213 "redundancies" in which a statement is made and then followed by a nearly equivalent but unnecessary statement. Mark 1:32 says, "When evening came, after the sun had set." If Mark used both Matthew and Luke, the redundancy can be easily explained, since Matthew 8:16 says, "When evening came," and Luke 4:40 says, "When the sun was setting."

Finally, unlike the two-document hypothesis, the two-Gospel hypothesis does not require hypothetical sources such as "Q" (probably from the German word *Quelle* meaning "source").[247]

Proponents of alternative hypotheses point to several problems with the two-Gospel hypothesis. First, despite its claim to honor church tradition, the hypothesis conflicts with an important element of church tradition regarding the composition of the Gospels. The two-Gospel hypothesis states that Mark wrote his Gospel last and used Matthew and Luke. But early church testimony insists that Mark wrote his Gospel independently of the other Gospels based on the memoirs of Peter (as stated by Papias) and that Luke's Gospel was the last Gospel to be written, not the second (as stated by Origen, the Anti-Marcionite Prologue, and Augustine).[248]

Second, most agreements of two-Gospels readings are best explained by Markan priority. Redaction critics who seek to explain why a later evangelist adapted the wording of his source have been able to offer reasonable explanations for Matthew or Luke changing Mark's wording. But it is often more difficult to explain why Mark would have adapted readings from Matthew or Luke in accordance with the two-Gospel hypothesis. Many of the differences between Mark and the other two Synoptics can be easily explained as Matthew and Luke making grammatical or stylistic improvements or theological clarifications to Mark. Often the differences between Mark and the other two Synoptics so particularly suit the emphases of Matthew and Luke that they appear to be a product of Matthew's or Luke's revision of Mark.[249]

---

[246] W. R. Farmer, *The Synoptic Problem* (Dillsboro, NC: Western North Carolina Press, 1976), 215–17.

[247] See further discussion below.

[248] R. Stein, "Synoptic Problem," in *Dictionary of Jesus and the Gospels*, 787. The church fathers uniformly described Matthew as first and John as last, but there is less clarity regarding the respective positions of Luke and Mark. For example, Irenaeus (ca. 130–200) described the order as Matthew, Mark, Luke, and John (*Against Heresies* 3.1.1–4), as do a great many other church fathers. This order may be reflective of the shape of the fourfold Gospel codex, although Irenaeus himself may have known it in the Western order Matthew, John, Mark, Luke. But Clement of Alexandria (ca. 150–215), in a passage preserved in Eusebius (*Eccl. Hist.* 6.14.5–7), described the order as Matthew, Luke, Mark, and John.

[249] Stein, "Synoptic Problem," 787. For a more detailed discussion with examples, see Stein, *Introduction to the Synoptic Problem*, 52–58, 62–67, 76–88.

Third, although the explanation of the Markan redundancies by the two-Gospel hypothesis may initially appear compelling, closer examination raises serious questions. There are only seventeen clear redundancies in Mark where Matthew has one and Luke the other. In many more instances of Markan redundancy, Matthew or Luke share the same element of the redundancy and Mark adds another or Matthew and Luke have neither. This suggests the redundancies were more a product of Markan style than a result of his sources.[250]

Fourth, alternative views do not require hypothetical sources. One variation of the Markan priority view eliminates the need for hypothetical documents by asserting that Luke used Matthew's Gospel in writing his own Gospel.

Illustration 3.2: Two-Gospel Hypothesis

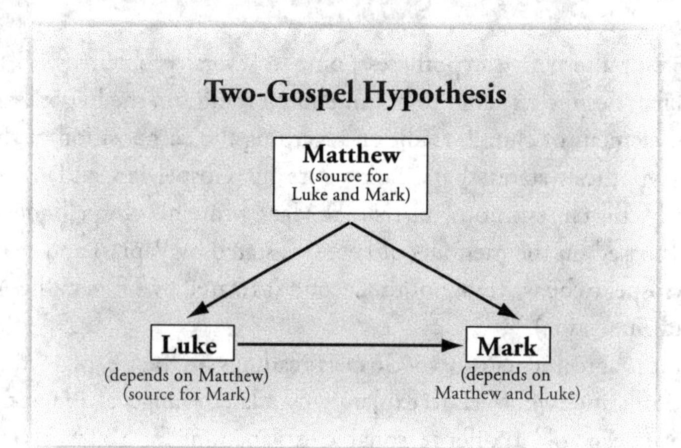

Markan Priority Careful analysis of the similarities among the Synoptic Gospels indicates that Mark has a special relationship to both Matthew and Luke. Mark shares more material and verbatim agreement with Matthew and Luke than they share with each other. The special relationship of Mark to Matthew and Luke has commonly been explained in two opposite ways. Some assert that the similarity results from Mark's using both Matthew and Luke in his Gospel. The Markan priority hypothesis suggests that Mark served as a primary source for the other two.

Several lines of evidence support Markan priority. First, Mark's Gospel is the shortest of the three Synoptic Gospels. Contrary to the two-Gospel hypothesis, Mark's brevity does not appear due to his effort to abbreviate or summarize the other two Gospels. A comparison of the length of the individual pericopes in the Synoptics shows that Mark's version of pericopes shared by Matthew and Luke tend to be longer and more detailed than those in the other two Gospels. Mark's Gospel is shorter than the other two Synoptics not because individual pericopes were abbreviated but because Mark lacks large blocks of material in

[250] Ibid., 787.

the other Gospels, such as the narratives of Jesus's birth and the Sermon on the Mount. It is difficult to explain why Mark would lengthen individual pericopes from the other two Gospels and then eliminate such important material. It is easier to explain Matthew and Luke expanding Mark than Mark abbreviating Matthew and Luke at the expense of such significant testimonies to Jesus.

Additional evidence for Markan priority comes from Mark's Aramaic expressions. Mark frequently transliterates Aramaic words into Greek characters. Generally, Matthew and Luke either omit these words altogether or give a Greek translation in place of Mark's transliteration. Many scholars believe it is more probable that Matthew and Luke translated the lesser-known Aramaic into Greek than that Mark reverted from the better-known Greek to the lesser-known Aramaic. Similarly, Mark's Greek is less refined than that of the other two Synoptic Gospels. Many scholars reason that it is more likely that Matthew and Luke improved Mark's Greek than that Mark diminished the quality of the grammar and style of the other Synoptics.[251]

Third, Mark has more difficult readings. For instance: "'Why do you call me good?'" Jesus asked him. "'No one is good except God alone.'" (Mark 10:18). This could be taken as a denial of Jesus's deity. Matthew's reading carefully avoids confusion by rendering the statement, "'Why do you ask me about what is good?'" he said to him. "'There is only one who is good'" (19:17). Scholars reason that it makes more sense for Matthew to have attempted to clarify an important theological statement than for Mark to have muddled it.[252]

Fourth, Matthew and Luke seldom agree against Mark in wording or in order. In 1835 K. Lachmann observed that the order of pericopes in Matthew and Luke is very similar when Mark also contains the pericope and that the order of pericopes in Matthew and Luke is often different if Mark does not contain the pericope. Lachmann also noted that Matthew and Luke never agree in order against Mark. Moreover, when Matthew and Mark agree in order against Luke, or Luke and Mark agree in order against Matthew, the deviation from Markan order can be explained plausibly. But if one presumes that Mark changed the order of pericopes that he found in his sources, Matthew or Luke, such changes by Mark are much more difficult to explain.[253]

Moreover, as discussed earlier, redaction critics who seek to explain why a later evangelist adapted the wording of his source have been able to offer reasonable explanations for Matthew or Luke changing Mark's wording. But it is often more difficult to explain why Mark would have adapted readings from Matthew or Luke in accordance with the two-Gospel hypothesis. Many of the differences between Mark and the other two Synoptics can be easily explained in one of three ways: (1) Matthew's and Luke's improvements of grammar or style; (2) Matthew's and Luke's theological clarifications to Mark; and (3) Matthew's and Luke's adaptation of Mark's text in a way that heightens the

---

[251] Stein, *Introduction to the Synoptic Problem*, 52–58.

[252] Ibid., 62–67.

[253] Ibid., 67–76.

themes and emphases that permeate the materials in their Gospels that are not paralleled by Mark's.[254]

Generally, differences among the Synoptics can be more reasonably explained when one assumes Markan priority. For example, Matthew and Luke place greater emphasis on high Christology than Mark does. They both apply the title "Lord" to Jesus far more frequently than Mark. It seems more likely for Matthew and Luke to adapt Mark in order to highlight Jesus's deity than for Mark to edit such material out.[255]

Finally, certain stylistic features in Mark appear in Matthew almost exclusively in the material he has in common with Mark. Mark was particularly fond of using the temporal adverb "immediately," which appears forty-one times in his Gospel. The adverb appears eighteen times in Matthew's Gospel. Fourteen of these occurrences appear in material that Matthew shares with Mark. R. Stein has calculated that the adverb appears once for every 778 words in material shared with Mark but only once for every 1,848 words in the material not shared. This suggests that the frequency of occurrences of the adverb "immediately" in Matthew was influenced by his dependency on Mark.[256]

Illustration 3.3: Markan Priority

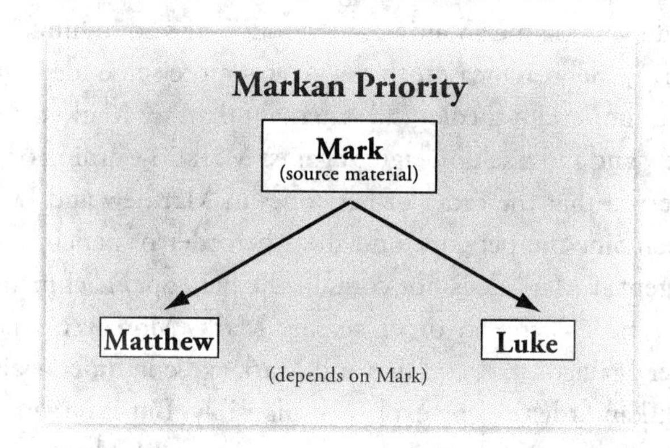

The Two-Document Hypothesis The two-document hypothesis argues that Mark was written first (Markan priority). When Matthew and Luke wrote their Gospels, they wrote independently of each other but relied heavily on Mark (or perhaps an early version of Mark that is slightly different from the canonical version) and an additional now-lost

---

[254] Stein, "Synoptic Problem," 787. For a more detailed discussion with examples, see Stein, *Introduction to the Synoptic Problem*, 52–58, 62–67, and 76–88.

[255] See especially P. M. Head, *Christology and the Synoptic Problem: An Argument for Markan Priority*, SNTSMS 94 (Cambridge, UK: Cambridge University Press, 1997); cf. M. C. Williams, *Two Gospels from One: A Comprehensive Text-Critical Analysis of the Synoptic Gospels* (Grand Rapids, MI: Kregel, 2006).

[256] Stein, "Synoptic Problem," 787.

document known as "Q."[257] Although many scholars attribute the origins of the two-document hypothesis to H. J. Holtzmann who wrote in 1863, the origins of the hypothesis actually date nearly a century earlier.[258] As early as 1794, J. Eichhorn argued that Matthew and Luke independently used a presynoptic source. In 1798, H. Marsh argued for the existence of a proto-Gospel and a sayings source. In 1836, K. A. Credner suggested that Matthew and Luke independently used a sayings collection in addition to an early version of Mark's Gospel as their primary sources. C. H. Weisse proposed a similar hypothesis a few years after Credner. However, Weisse argued that the version of Mark used by Matthew and Luke was the canonical form of Mark rather than an earlier version.[259] The two-document hypothesis was popularized in the English-speaking world by B. H. Streeter in 1924.[260]

Illustration 3.4: Two-Document Hypothesis

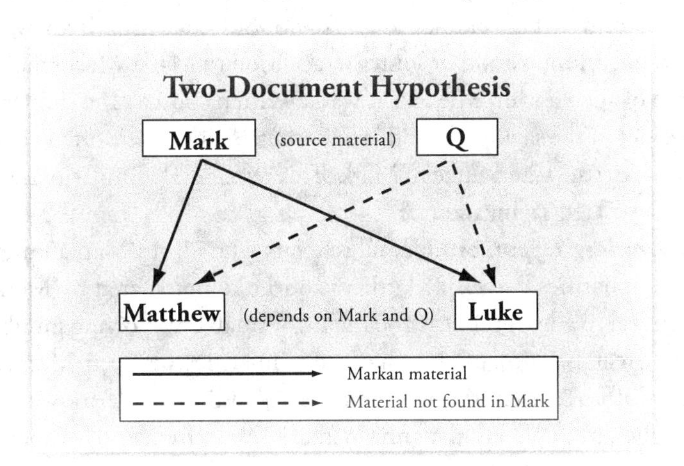

Evidence for Q Some scholars argue that the material shared by Matthew and Luke but not by Mark—mostly discourse material containing Jesus's teachings and sayings—must be explained by an appeal to another shared document because Matthew could not have used Luke and Luke could not have used Matthew. These scholars point to three major

[257] Earlier supporters of the two-document hypothesis used designations other than Q to refer to the hypothetical sayings source that lay behind Matthew and Luke. Marsh used the Hebrew *bet.* Holtzmann used the Greek *lambda*, an abbreviation for *logia* meaning "sayings source."

[258] H. J. Holtzmann, *Die synoptischen Evangelien: Ihr Ursprung und geschichtlicher Charakter* (Leipzig, Germany: Engelmann, 1863).

[259] C. H. Weisse, *Die evangelische Geschichte kritisch und philosophisch bearbeitet*, 2 vols. (Leipzig, Germany: Breitkopf & Härtel, 1838).

[260] B. H. Streeter, *The Four Gospels: A Study of Origins, Treating of the Manuscript Tradition, Sources, Authorship and Dates* (London, UK: Macmillan, 1924).

lines of evidence that suggest the literary independence of Matthew and Luke and necessitate their reliance on a hypothetical document.

First, when a parallel account appears in all three Synoptics but either Matthew or Luke contains additional material, they rarely share the same additions. Similarly, it is difficult to explain why Luke or Matthew would have omitted material unique to the other Gospel if one Gospel had used the other. It seems unlikely, for example, that Matthew would eliminate Luke's parable of the Prodigal Son or that Luke would have omitted Matthew's visit of the magi. This makes it improbable that either writer knew the other's work.[261]

Second, Luke places the material that he shares with Matthew but not with Mark in different contexts than Matthew.[262] Matthew divided the material into five blocks of teaching and Luke into two. Third, Matthew and Luke never share the same order of pericopes when they are absent from Mark and never agree in order against Mark.[263]

Many scholars reason that since Matthew and Luke share similar material that is absent from Mark and since Matthew did not use Luke nor did Luke use Matthew, Matthew and Luke must share in common another source in addition to Mark. Most scholars who argue for the existence of such a source believe it was a written source. The similarities in wording and in the order of the sayings from this hypothetical source are often even greater than the similarities of Matthew and Luke to Mark. This remarkable similarity is taken to imply the existence of a written sayings source.

The Farrer-Goulder Hypothesis Not all scholars who affirm Markan priority are convinced that the similarities between Matthew and Luke not shared by Mark are best explained by an appeal to a hypothetical document. A small but growing number of scholars (particularly in Great Britain) believe that the similarities between Matthew and Luke are best explained if Luke used Matthew's Gospel in addition to Mark when he wrote his own. Interestingly, although Holtzmann's name is most frequently associated with the two-document hypothesis, Holtzmann abandoned that hypothesis only a few years after he proposed it and suggested that Luke knew and used Matthew.[264] In 1955 A. M. Farrer argued that Luke did indeed use Matthew's Gospel in addition to Mark and that this made Q completely unnecessary.[265] In 1989 M. Goulder wrote an entire commentary on Luke that examined the hypothesis of Luke's use of Matthew.[266]

---

[261] See Stein, *Introduction to the Synoptic Problem*, 91–95.

[262] For an extensive discussion of the minor agreements of Matthew and Luke against Mark, see F. Neirynck, *Evangelica II*, BETL 99 (Leuven, Belgium: University Press, 1991), 1–138.

[263] Stein, *Introduction to the Synoptic Problem*, 70. But J. K. Verbin (*Excavating Q: The History and Setting of the Sayings Gospel* [Minneapolis, MN: Fortress, 2000]) found agreement in order in the double tradition in 27 or 67 pericopes (40%).

[264] H. J. Holtzmann, "Zur synoptischen Frage," *Jahrbücher für protestantische Theologie* 4 (1878): 145–88, 328–82, 533–68, esp. 553–54.

[265] A. M. Farrer, "On Dispensing with Q," in *Studies in the Gospels: Essays in Memory of R. H. Lightfoot*, ed. D. E. Nineham (Oxford, UK: Blackwell, 1955), 55–88.

[266] M. Goulder, *Luke: A New Paradigm*, JSNTSup 20 (Sheffield, UK: Sheffield Academic Press, 1989).

The most important evidence supporting Luke's use of Matthew is the so-called minor agreements of Matthew and Luke against Mark. Based on different methods of identifying such minor agreements, various scholars have suggested that anywhere from 770 to 3,785 such minor agreements exist. Some of these may be explained as coincidental agreements in improving Mark. However, other agreements are more significant and may indicate Luke's dependence on Matthew. Such agreements include Mark 1:7–8; 2:12; 3:24, 26–29; 5:27; 6:33; 8:35; 9:2–4, 18–19; 10:29; 14:65, 72 and the parallel texts in Matthew and Luke.

Recent research by R. Vinson concluded that these verbatim agreements by Matthew and Luke in their revision of Mark could not have been accidental. They are best explained if Luke used Matthew. Vinson established an experiment in which he collected ten paragraphs from three student term papers then submitted these paragraphs to ten doctoral students for revision. He then examined the revisions to determine the number of verbal agreements. He considered every possible pairing of the revisions and calculated the average rate of verbal agreement. He next counted the number of minor verbal agreements between Matthew and Luke. Finally, he compared the rates of verbal agreement in his experiment against agreements in Matthew and Luke utilizing the Ustatistic, a method that ensures that the agreements were compared on an appropriate scale. The calculations demonstrated that the agreement between Matthew and Luke was significantly higher than the pairs of modern editors and too high to be dismissed as merely coincidental.[267]

Scholars who affirm the two-document hypothesis have sought to explain these minor agreements in the following ways.[268] First, Mark and Q may have overlapped in their contents at a number of points. When Mark and Q shared the same material but had slightly different readings, Matthew and Luke may have both opted for the Q reading at the same place. Second, the minor agreements may sometimes be products of textual corruption. Matthew's Gospel was the favorite Gospel of many people in the early church. Scribes may have produced some of the minor agreements by conforming Luke's readings to Matthew. Third, both Matthew and Luke may have been familiar with oral traditions that overlapped with Mark and prompted them to revise Mark in the same way at the same point.

---

[267] R. Vinson, "The Significance of the Minor Agreements as an Argument Against the Two-Document Hypothesis" (Ph.D. diss., Durham, NC: Duke University, 1984). For a summary of the research, see Vinson, "How Minor? Assessing the Significance of the Minor Agreements Against the Two-Source Hypothesis," in *Questioning Q: A Multidimensional Critique*, ed. M. Goodacre and N. Perrin (Downers Grove, IL: InterVarsity, 2004), 151–64. For criticisms of Vinson's research, see T. A. Friedrichsen, "The Minor Agreements of Matthew and Luke Against Mark: Critical Observations on R. B. Vinson's Statistical Analysis," *ETL* 65 (1989): 395–408.

[268] See Stein, *Introduction to the Synoptic Problem*, 113–28; idem, "Synoptic Problem," 791.

Table 3.8: Theories of Literary Dependence of the Synoptic Gospels

Theory	Definition
Augustinian View	Canonical Gospels are listed in the order they were written.
Two-Gospel Hypothesis	Gospels were written in the order of Matthew, Luke, then Mark.
Markan Priority	Mark wrote first; Matthew and Luke wrote independently of each other, both using Mark as a source.
Two-Document Hypothesis	Matthew and Luke used Mark as a source; Matthew and Luke also used "Q," a document containing the similar material found in Matthew and Luke, but not found in Mark.
Farrer-Goulder Hypothesis	Luke used Mark and Matthew as sources.

Value of the Study Source criticism is a complex and difficult exercise. Although the two-document hypothesis was the consensus view of Gospel relationships in the mid- and late twentieth century, at present no single theory of Gospel relationships can be described as the scholarly consensus—though Markan priority is held by a majority of scholars. This thorny issue may not be fully resolved until (and unless) new evidence comes to light. In the meantime, questions surrounding Gospel relationships remain important for several reasons.

First, source criticism is an important preliminary step in the historical investigation of Jesus's life. The discussion of the criteria of authenticity earlier in this chapter demonstrates that one of the most widely accepted criteria is the criterion of multiple independent attestation. However, various theories of source criticism have different views of what is necessary to satisfy this criterion. If one accepts the two-document hypothesis, a saying or theme of Jesus's teaching that appears in at least two of the Gospel sources—Mark, Q, M, L, or John—is likely authentic. But if one accepts the Farrer-Goulder hypothesis, material shared by Matthew and Luke is a result of Luke's dependence on Matthew. Thus, a claim attested by Q (material that Matthew and Luke shared) and M (material unique to Matthew) satisfies the criterion of multiple independent attestation in the two document hypothesis but would belong to a single source in the Farrer-Goulder hypothesis.

Second, source criticism is a prerequisite for redaction criticism in which scholars examine how Gospel writers adapted their sources in order to understand the theological purpose that prompted this adaptation. Thus, the potential benefits of source criticism are well worth the effort invested in this difficult enterprise.

Redaction Criticism

As mentioned, form criticism emerged in the 1920s as a quest to discern the prehistory of individual pericopes included in the Gospels in the form of units of oral tradition as they were passed on by the community on the basis of certain laws of oral transmission. Source criticism, in turn, sought to discern the use of written and/or oral sources by the evangelists. For example, the possible use of Mark and Q and other sources by Matthew and Luke was examined in order to see what light such use might shed on the final text of these Gospels. Also, scholars speculated as to John's possible use of sources such as a "signs" or "discourse source" in his Gospel.[269] One other important interpretive methodology should be mentioned in conjunction with form and source criticism: redaction criticism.[270]

Redaction criticism was first practiced in the 1950s by students of R. Bultmann, including G. Bornkamm, W. Marxsen, and H. Conzelmann. The primary concern of redaction criticism is to view a given document as a composition and literary whole. Consequently, the focus is not on the work of the community at large (form criticism) or on the use of sources by the evangelists (source criticism) but on the theological contributions made by the evangelists in their own right as they processed and shaped their source material. (In this regard redaction criticism is predicated on source criticism in that it presupposes a certain source-critical view, such as Mark's use by Matthew.) When it appears that one of the evangelists has adapted one of his sources, the theological implications of his revision are explored.

For example, redaction criticism might observe that Matthew's treatment of the disciples' understanding of Jesus's words is markedly more positive than that of Mark, who repeatedly and consistently focused on the disciples' failure to comprehend the true meaning of Jesus's teaching and of his messianic identity. On the basis of this observation, it is concluded that Mark sought to demonstrate that it is only after the resurrection, and as aided by the Holy Spirit, that anyone was able to understand Jesus's true nature as the Son of God. Hence a comparison of Mark with Matthew reveals a difference in perspective (or at least emphasis) that has the potential of helping the reader to better understand the distinctive contributions and theological emphases of the respective evangelists.

INTERPRETING THE GOSPELS

The NT letters are sometimes misinterpreted by modern readers who simply read them as books of the Bible addressed directly to them. However, readers who recognize that these books were originally letters written by specific people to specific individuals or groups often seem to know intuitively how the NT letters should be interpreted. They recognize that one should seek to understand the meaning intended by the original author to the original recipients.

---

[269] See especially R. T. Fortna, *The Gospel of Signs: A Reconstruction of the Narrative Source Underlying the Fourth Gospel* (Cambridge, UK: Cambridge University Press, 1970); idem, *The Fourth Gospel and Its Predecessors: From Narrative Source to Present Gospel* (Philadelphia, PA: Fortress, 1988). Compare G. van Belle, *The Signs Source in the Fourth Gospel: Historical Survey and Critical Evaluation of the Semeia Hypothesis*, BETL (Leuven, Belgium: University Press, 1994).

[270] Helpful resources include F. G. Downing, "Redaction Criticism," in *Dictionary of Biblical Criticism and Interpretation*, ed. S. E. Porter (London, UK: Routledge, 2007), 310–12; N. Perrin, *What Is Redaction Criticism?* (London, UK: SPCK, 1970); and G. R. Osborne, "Redaction Criticism," in *Interpreting the New Testament: Essays on Methods and Issues*, ed. D. A. Black and D. S. Dockery (Nashville, TN: B&H, 2001), 128–49.

They recognize this based on modern parallels. They know well that if a postal worker accidentally delivers to their home a piece of mail addressed to a neighbor, they cannot simply open the mail and interpret it as if it were written directly to them. Despite the words on the paper that they hold in their hands, they will not likely pay the neighbor's electrical bill, answer the neighbor's call to jury duty, or cash the neighbor's employment check. They will not interpret the neighbor's Valentine's Day card as an expression of a stranger's love for them personally. Anyone who has accidentally sent an e-mail or text to the wrong recipient only to have the person grossly misinterpret the correspondence because he or she did not understand the original context of the message has likely learned the importance of this hermeneutical principle: an interpreter must seek to understand the meaning intended by the original author to the original reader. Because of the modern reader's familiarity with the genre of "letter," he generally knows how to handle the interpretation of ancient letters.

Unfortunately, modern readers struggle greatly to interpret the Gospels or other biblical narratives because they lack clear modern parallels. The Gospels do not read like modern history books, novels, news articles, letters, or memorandums. They seem to belong to a category of their own.

Although few Christians will be comfortable with this blunt assessment, a good argument can be made that most readers intuitively approach the stories of the Gospels as if they are fables. Like most fables, the stories of the Gospels are very old. As is in the case of fables, many Americans were taught these stories as children. They assume that the Gospel stories, like fables, were written in order to teach a particular moral. They learned long ago that the question of whether or not the events in the fable actually occurred is ultimately irrelevant. Discovering the moral of the story and living in light of its wisdom is what matters. This principle common to fables, they assume, must apply to the Gospels too.

Consequently, many readers approach the Gospel stories on a quest to discover their morals, to learn their life lessons. Just as the fable of the "Boy Who Cried 'Wolf!'" taught that sounding a false alarm is dangerous, Jesus's cleansing of the temple teaches that it is wrong to make merchandise of holy things. Just as the fable of "The Tortoise and the Hare" teaches that overconfidence leads to failure and perseverance leads to success, Jesus's stilling of the storm teaches that "Jesus calms the storms of life." Unfortunately, the search for the moral of the story often results in the reader missing the real point of the narrative.

If the Gospels are not fables designed to teach morals, what is the nature of the Gospels? How should one interpret them? This section will attempt to address those questions. The following list of steps for Gospel interpretation is not exhaustive. This section is not intended to replace hermeneutics textbooks by giving comprehensive instructions for interpretation. Rather, it is merely intended to describe some of the most important practical steps for interpreting Gospel narratives. Texts on hermeneutics will offer more guidance and good commentaries will provide helpful models to follow in applying sound hermeneutical principles to the study of the Gospels.

Scholars often refer to two important approaches to Gospel study: vertical reading and horizontal reading.[271] Vertical reading (sometimes called holistic analysis) refers to reading a particular Gospel without reference to the other Gospels, at least initially. Horizontal reading (sometimes called comparative analysis) refers to comparing and contrasting the Gospels that share the same account. Both approaches are useful and enlightening.

Vertical Reading

One should begin the study of a Gospel with the vertical reading. The interpreter should read the Gospel from start to finish without taking an extended break. This step is probably the most important one, since the Gospel writers likely assumed that this was the manner in which most readers would approach their accounts. Unfortunately, many modern Gospel readers seldom approach the Gospels in this way. They typically read a pericope here and a pericope there, detaching each from the rest of the Gospel and without much sensitivity to the flow of the narrative. In the process, they miss the connections between the pericope and the Gospel as a whole and often overlook how the pericope fits with the material that immediately precedes and follows the account.

As the interpreter reads through the Gospel, he should pay careful attention to details. As he reads, he should ask himself the questions that a news journalist or criminal investigator often asks when interviewing witnesses: Who? What? When? Where? Why? and How?[272] If the reader completes a pericope and cannot answer these basic questions, he has not read with sufficient care. Answering these questions will help the reader gain a basic understanding of the narrative. Additional insight may be gleaned by taking the following steps.

1. *Seek to understand how individual pericopes relate to the purposes of the Gospel as a whole.* A survey of the introductions to the Gospels in this text will show that the Gospels were written primarily to reveal who Jesus is and who his disciples ought to be. As A. Köstenberger and R. Patterson noted, "All four Gospels have as their primary subject the life, death, and resurrection of Jesus Christ and the training of his followers, the new messianic community."[273] So first, the Gospels were written to serve as testimonies about Jesus and to bring people to faith in him. John's Gospel clearly indicates that John selected the accounts that he included in his Gospel to prompt readers to "believe that Jesus is the Messiah, the Son of God, and that by believing you may have life in his name" (John 20:31). Thus, as one reads each pericope or discourse in the Gospel, he should seek to understand how the account points to Jesus's messianic nature, his identity

---

[271] See, e.g., W. Klein, C. Blomberg, R. Hubbard, *Introduction to Biblical Interpretation* (Nashville, TN: Word, 1993), 327–30; A. J. Köstenberger and R. D. Patterson, *Invitation to Biblical Interpretation: Exploring the Hermeneutical Triad of History, Literature, and Theology* (Grand Rapids, MI: Kregel, 2011), 376, 385–86; M. Strauss, *Four Portraits, One Jesus: A Survey of Jesus and the Gospels* (Grand Rapids, MI: Zondervan, 2002), 32–35; G. Fee and D. Stuart, *How to Read the Bible for All Its Worth*, 4th ed. (Grand Rapids, MI: Zondervan, 2014), 140–46.

[272] J. S. Duvall and J. D. Hays, *Grasping God's Word: A Hands-On Approach to Reading, Interpreting, and Applying the Bible* 2nd ed. (Grand Rapids, MI: Zondervan, 2005), 250.

[273] Köstenberger and Patterson, *Invitation to Biblical Interpretation*, 376, repeated on p. 383.

as the Son of God, his power to impart spiritual life, and the significance of "his name." Mark's introduction indicates that he wished to highlight Jesus's identity as the Christ, the Son of God; thus, readers should also seek to understand how each episode of Mark's account points to that identity (Mark 1:1). Matthew's introduction shows that he wishes to affirm Jesus's identity as Son of David, Son of Abraham, and Immanuel the Son of God (Matt 1:1–25). Luke's introduction to Jesus identifies him as the virginally conceived Son of the Most High who will reign from the throne of David over an eternal kingdom (Luke 1:31–33). The conclusion of Luke's Gospel presents Jesus as the One concerning whom all the Scriptures bear testimony, the crucified and resurrected Messiah who offers forgiveness of sins to those who obey his call to repentance, the One who sends the Holy Spirit in fulfillment of the new covenant, the One enthroned in heaven and worthy of worship (Luke 24:44–49).

Even the most cursory reading of the Gospels shows that all four of the Gospel writers intended for their Gospels to be interpreted *primarily* as Christological documents. The Gospel writers "used a Christ-centered approach that presented a theologically motivated account of the life and work of Jesus."[274] The Gospels teach about other topics too, topics such as discipleship, the kingdom, and Christian ethics; thus, the Gospels are not *exclusively* Christological. However, all of these topics are secondary in comparison with the identity and mission of Jesus. Consequently, as the reader studies each pericope, the question he must constantly ask is, "What does this text tell me about Jesus?" Because the Gospels are Christocentric documents, any approach to them that is not likewise Christocentric distorts their message.[275]

Second, the Gospels were written to serve as a guide for the beliefs and behavior of Jesus's followers. Jesus's discourses to his disciples offer helpful instructions to his disciples today. Furthermore, the actions of Jesus in the Gospels often serve as an example that believers are to emulate in some way. Thus, readers should seek to determine what obligation Jesus's words and actions impose on his disciples of all times. This secondary purpose of the Gospels is intrinsic to the nature of true discipleship. Jesus's invitation to discipleship normally took the form of the command, "Follow me" (e.g. Matt 4:19; 8:22; 9:9; 10:38; 16:24; 19:21). This command did not mean merely to accompany Jesus on his travels from one village to another but to follow Jesus's leadership and to emulate his example. In the original context, the command would have been interpreted against the background of the relationship of the rabbis and their disciples. First-century discipleship was comparable to a modern apprenticeship. The disciple would listen to the master's words and repeat them. He would watch his master's movements and imitate them in hopes that he would become like his master. Christian discipleship involves more than mere imitation of an example. It requires willingness to forsake all else out of allegiance to Jesus and even a

[274] Ibid., 372.

[275] For an excellent statement of this principle, see Stein, *Basic Guide to Interpreting the Bible*, 159.

readiness to die for his sake. Nevertheless, imitation of the Master is intrinsic to discipleship and assumed by the command to "follow" Jesus.[276]

The call to the disciple to imitate Jesus is prominent in the NT letters. Paul commended the believers at Thessalonica because they "became imitators of us and of the Lord" (1 Thess 1:6). Similarly, Peter wrote that "Christ also suffered for you, leaving you an example, so that you should follow in his steps" (1 Pet 2:21). Based on these texts, important church figures such as Augustine of Hippo, Francis of Assisi, Thomas à Kempis, and John Calvin called for Christians to practice the *imitatio Christi*, the imitation of Christ.

Thus, modern believers should seek to "follow" Jesus by examining the Gospel accounts of his life and seeking to live by the ethic of Jesus and in conformity with the character of Jesus. Applying this hermeneutical principle requires wisdom and discernment. The command "follow me" does not imply that modern believers must reside in Nazareth or Capernaum, wear sandals and seamless robes, or observe the Passover. The interpreter must consider the geographical, cultural, and historical differences between modern Western readers of the Gospels and the original disciples. Even more importantly, in seeking to follow the example of Jesus, the interpreter must not depreciate the uniqueness of Jesus. Christ, as deity incarnate, acted in ways that modern believers cannot replicate. Modern believers will not be conceived by virgins, control the weather, or feed thousands with a few loaves and fish. On the other hand, they can and should oppose injustice, express compassion to the helpless, humbly serve the lowly, embrace suffering for the cause of righteousness, protect the sanctity of marriage, and show love to their enemies. Jesus did not just demand such practices by his teaching; he modeled them by his example. Consequently, the Gospel narratives were written both to inspire certain beliefs and encourage certain behavior. So after asking, "What does this passage teach about Jesus?," readers should ask, "Did Jesus offer an example that I am to follow and, if so, how?"

2. *Examine themes in the headings, introductions, and programmatic statements.* These elements of the Gospels in particular inform the reader of the most important themes in each Gospel. The reader should focus on these elements, read them several times, and consult several different translations in his reading. He will also profit greatly from reading the treatment of these specific passages in respected commentaries, like those recommended at the end of each chapter of this text. Below are a few examples of insights that may be gleaned from a careful study of some of these important sections of the Gospels.

a. *Headings*. Mark began his Gospel with the words, "The beginning of the gospel of Jesus Christ, the Son of God."[277] These words appear to serve as a heading or title for the Gospel.[278] The heading suggests that Jesus's identity as (a) the Christ or Messiah and

---

[276] See D. A. Hagner, *Matthew 1–13*, WBC 33A (Dallas, TX: Word, 1993), 76–77.

[277] For a brief discussion of the textual issue in Mark 1:1, see Sidebar 5.1 "Textual Issues in Mark's Gospel."

[278] For an explanation of this position, see R. T. France, *The Gospel of Mark*, NIGTC (Grand Rapids, MI: Eerdmans, 2002), 49–53. France notes that other scholars have seen Mark 1:1 merely as the title for the first section of the Gospel, which is variously seen as extending to 1:3, 8, 13, or 15.

(b) the Son of God will be prominent themes in the Gospel. Interestingly, the first half of the Gospel climaxes with Peter's confession that Jesus is the Messiah (Mark 8:29), and the second half climaxes with the centurion's confession that Jesus is the Son of God (Mark 15:39). These themes are developed through the Gospel in numerous ways. For example, Jesus is described as the "Son" or "Son of God" in Mark 1:1, 11; 3:11; 5:7; 9:7; 12:6; 13:26; 14:61; and 15:37. Mark signaled his intention to present the good news that Jesus is the Christ, the Son of God from the very first line.

The opening line of Matthew's Gospel likewise introduces the reader to three of the Gospel's most prominent themes. The title "Son of David" highlights Jesus's identity as the Messiah, the King of God's people. The body of the Gospel then emphasizes Jesus's Davidic lineage repeatedly, more often than any other Gospel. The theme comes to its climax in the final statement of the Gospel when the resurrected Messiah claims, "All authority has been given to me in heaven and on earth" (Matt 28:18).[279]

The title "son of Abraham" emphasizes Jesus's identity as the founder of a new spiritual Israel. This theme also surfaces repeatedly in the Gospel.[280] Perhaps most importantly, the words which begin Matthew's Gospel and are deemed by many scholars as the original title of the Gospel ("the historical record of Jesus Christ") are best translated as "book of genesis of Jesus Christ."[281] The title implies that Matthew regarded his work as Scripture, and thus on a par with the first book of the OT. Furthermore, the title implies that Matthew regarded his Gospel as a creation account, a record of a new beginning wrought by the Messiah.[282] After alluding to this theme in subtle ways, Matthew 19:28 clearly states that the reign of the Messiah initiates a new beginning. The term translated "Messianic Age" in the CSB literally refers to the era of "beginning again" or "new beginning."[283] The final words of the Gospel refer to "the end of the age" and thus imply a new coming age (Matt 28:20).

b. *Introductions.* In addition to these headings, readers should pay close attention to the lengthier introductions or prologues to the Gospels. Mark's prologue extends from Mark 1:1 to Mark 1:13 (or possibly 15). The prologue is saturated with important themes that frequently resurface in the Gospel.[284] The citation of Isaiah 40:3 in Mark 1:2–3 shows that Jesus is the fulfillment of prophecy—not merely prophecy about the coming of Messiah, but prophecy about the coming of Yahweh himself! The reference to the baptism with

---

[279] See R. T. France, *Matthew: Evangelist and Teacher* (Grand Rapids, MI: Zondervan, 1989), 284–86; C. L. Quarles, *A Theology of Matthew: Jesus Revealed as Deliverer, King, and Incarnate Creator* (Philipsburg, NJ: P&R, 2013), 71–96; Mark Strauss, *Four Portraits, One Jesus*, 223, 239–40.

[280] See France, *Matthew: Evangelist and Teacher*, 206–41; Quarles, *Theology of Matthew*, 97–130; Strauss, *Four Portraits*, 223.

[281] W. D. Davies, *Setting*, 67–73; Craig A. Evans, *Matthew*, NCBC (New York, NY: Cambridge University Press, 2012), 32; France, *Matthew*, 28–29.

[282] See W. D. Davies and Dale Allison, *Matthew*, ICC, 1:149–56; Quarles, *Theology of Matthew*, 177–85; D. Turner, *Matthew*, BECNT (Grand Rapids, MI: Baker, 2008), 56–57.

[283] The NRSV and NIV attempt to express this in the translation "the renewal of all things." The Geneva Bible, KJV, and NASB translate the word as "the regeneration." The NLT uses the paraphrase "when the world is made new." Similarly, the NET renders the term "the age when all things are renewed."

[284] See especially the discussion in France, *The Gospel of Mark*, NIGTC (Grand Rapids, MI: Eerdmans, 2002), 54–55.

the Spirit performed by Jesus shows that Jesus will fulfill the new covenant promised in Ezekiel 36:25–27. The descent of the Spirit on Jesus at his baptism confirms his identity as the One who will baptize with the Spirit. The pronouncement of the Father at Jesus's baptism, "You are my beloved Son," is a profound confirmation of the theme announced in Mark 1:1, Jesus's divine Sonship. Finally, Jesus's temptation experience demonstrates his victory over Satan and shows that he is one of such greatness that even angels serve him. Thus, Jesus's deity, divine Sonship, supremacy, authority, fulfillment of prophecy, and role in fulfilling the new covenant are all premiered in the brief intro to the Gospel. Mark emphasizes each of these themes in various ways later in his Gospel.

Few will contest that the prologue to John's Gospel (1:1–18) likewise introduces the reader to the primary themes which guide the reader in interpreting the remainder of the Gospel. The prologue stresses Jesus's deity, his role in the creation of the universe, his rejection by sinners, his role in granting new birth, and his embodiment of divine glory. Carson aptly wrote, "The Prologue is a foyer to the rest of the Fourth Gospel (as John's Gospel is often called), simultaneously drawing the reader in and introducing the major themes."[285] After summarizing the major themes of the prologue and pointing to later echoes of these same themes, he added, "The rest of the book is nothing other than an expansion of this theme."[286] Köstenberger, following J. A. T. Robinson, shows that the prologue introduces the great themes of the Gospel like "the overture to an opera."[287] The full implications of the prologue are in fact too rich to explore adequately in this brief discussion. Nevertheless, the prologue provides a helpful template to the reader for understanding the remainder of the Gospel.

c. *Programmatic statements.* In addition to the introduction and conclusion, ancient books sometimes contained a "programmatic statement" that states the agenda of the narrative that follows. Such programmatic statements often appear early in the work. They may be embedded in the introduction or separate from it. This material was intended to serve as a guide to the reader's interpretation of the narrative that followed.[288] Scholars generally recognize that Matthew 1:21 serves as the programmatic statement of the Gospel of Matthew.[289] Since the "angel of the Lord" announced the identity and mission of Jesus in this text, readers should know intuitively that the announcement is of great importance

---

[285] D. A. Carson, *John*, PNTC (Grand Rapids, MI: Eerdmans, 1991), 111.

[286] Ibid.

[287] A. J. Köstenberger, *John*, BECNT (Grand Rapids, MI: Baker Academic, 2004), 19, esp. note 1.

[288] W. Carter, borrowing the term from M. Perry, referred to the strong impact that material at the beginning of the Gospel had on the audience's understanding of the book as a whole as the "primacy effect." See Carter, *Matthew: Storyteller, Interpreter, Evangelist*, rev. ed. (Peabody, MA: Hendrickson, 2004), 93.

[289] M. A. Powell, "The Plot and Subplots of Matthew's Gospel," *NTS* 38 (1992): 195; W. Carter, "To Save His People from Their Sins (Matt 1:21): Rome's Empire and Matthew's Salvation as Sovereignty," SBLSP 39 (2000): 381, 397; M. Nakano, "Jesus the Savior of God's People from Sin: A Study of Matthew's Soteriology" (Ph.D. diss., Claremont Graduate University, 2001), 4, 117; Carter, *Matthew: Storyteller, Interpreter, Evangelist*, 93; D. D. Kupp, *Matthew's Emmanuel: Divine Presence and God's People in the First Gospel*, SNTSMS 90 (Cambridge, UK: Cambridge University Press, 1996), 57; K. McDaniel, *Experiencing Irony in the First Gospel: Suspense, Surprise, and Curiosity* (London, UK: T&T Clark, 2013),

and is completely accurate, for it reflects the heavenly perspective on Jesus rather than the clouded judgments of mere humans that are sometimes reported later in the Gospel. The statement announces Jesus's purpose of saving his people from their sins. The statement prompts two questions: Who are "his people," and how will Jesus save them? In many ways, the material that appears later in the Gospel shows that Jesus's disciples are his people and that he saves them by his sacrificial sufferings.

Although most scholars identify Matthew 1:21 as the programmatic statement, the statement probably includes verses 22 and 23 as well. These introduce two additional major themes of Matthew's Gospel: Jesus's fulfillment of Scripture and Jesus's identity as Immanuel. Many scholars have noted that the name "God is with us" in 1:23 parallels the promise "I am with you" at the conclusion of the Gospel (28:20). The theme is further reinforced by the promise "I am there among them" in the middle of the Gospel (18:20). Kingsbury concluded that "the entire first Gospel may be regarded as an attempt on the part of Matthew to draw out the implications of what it means to say in 1:23 that in him God dwells with his people."[290]

Modern readers often miss the message of the Gospels because they do not pay close attention to the clues to the author's purpose given in the headings, introduction, conclusion, and programmatic statements. Some of the clues discussed above are far clearer in some translations than in others. Thus, interpreters unable to do their vertical reading in Greek should consult multiple translations if possible. Unfortunately, no modern translations properly express the allusion to the book of Genesis in Matthew 1:1. Interpreters without knowledge of the Greek text must refer to commentaries based on the Greek text for such insights. Consulting several respected commentaries for a detailed discussion of the introduction and conclusion to each Gospel is an exercise that will normally lead to very helpful insights into the purpose and primary themes of each Gospel writer.

3. *Examine repeated themes, titles, phrases, and theological emphases.* The Gospel writers often used repetition to stress the themes that they especially wanted their readers to notice. Köstenberger and Patterson observe,

> It was noted earlier that repetition is perhaps the most widespread and widely recognized stylistic feature of biblical narratives. All four Gospels and Acts employ repetition in their narratives. Repetition extends to words, sequence of words, themes, imagery, signs, and scenes. Repetition is also achieved through inclusio and other structural devices such as chiasms. While repetition may seem tedious by modern literary standards, this stylistic device serves a very important purpose. It was always used to emphasize or clarify a point.[291]

117; L. Novakovic, *Messiah, the Healer of the Sick: A Study of Jesus as the Son of David in the Gospel of Matthew*, WUNT 170 (Tübingen, Germany: Mohr Siebeck, 2003), 74.

[290] J. D. Kingsbury, *Matthew: Structure, Christology, Kingdom* (Philadelphia, PA: Fortress, 1975), 69.

[291] Köstenberger and Patterson, *Invitation to Biblical Interpretation*, 394–95.

Thus, highlighting or underlining examples of repetition as one performs the vertical reading is a helpful step.[292] For example, as the reader works through the first few chapters of Mark's Gospel, he will likely notice the repetition of the word "authority" (Mark 1:22, 27; 2:10; 3:15; 6:7; 11:28–29, 33; 13:34). The emphasis on Jesus's authority in Mark is confirmed by statistical analysis. For every thousand words, Matthew uses the word "authority" 0.45 times, John 0.43 times, Luke 0.68 times, but Mark uses the word 0.73 times. Mark uses the word "authority" nearly twice as often as Matthew or John.[293] After the reader observes Mark's emphasis on authority, particularly Jesus's authority, he may then reread the narratives questioning whether Jesus's authority is emphasized even in passages in which Mark did not explicitly use the term. He quickly discovers that the theme of Jesus's authority is more pervasive than the initial reading may have revealed. Mark 1:12–13 implies Jesus's authority over Satan and angels. Mark 1:16–20 implies Jesus's complete authority over his disciples. Mark 1:21–28 affirms Jesus's authority in interpreting the Scripture and his authority over demons, including his power to destroy demonic spirits. Mark 1:29–32, 40–45 display Jesus's authority over sickness and disease. Mark 2:1–12 affirms Jesus's authority to forgive sins, a divine prerogative. In pericope after pericope, Mark emphasizes Jesus's great authority. Mark likely intends for his readers to ask the question posed to Jesus by the chief priests, scribes, and elders: "By what authority are you doing these thing? Who gave you this authority to do these things?" (Mark 11:28). Although Jesus's initial response to the question is enigmatic, his counter question shows that only two options existed. Jesus either acted on human authority or on divine authority. The parable that immediately follows the discussion (Mark 12:1–12) shows that Jesus's authority was that of God's own Son.

Similarly, a careful reader will notice that the Gospel of John places emphasis on knowledge. The verbs related to knowing appear about three or four times more frequently in John than in the other Gospels.[294] The verbs are used to emphasize and contrast the ignorance of sinful humanity, a theme introduced in John 1:10, and the amazing knowledge of Jesus.[295] In John 1:43–51, Jesus displayed supernatural knowledge of Nathanael's character and past experiences. John 2:24–25 states that Jesus did not entrust himself to the many individuals who followed him because of his miracles since he "knew them all" and "knew what was in man."[296] John 4:1–26 shows that Jesus knew deeply personal information about the Samaritan woman's past, even though they had not previously met. In John 4:39

---

[292] For other examples of the importance of this step in both OT and NT narratives, see R. Stein, *A Basic Guide to Interpreting the Bible: Playing by the Rules* (Grand Rapids, MI: Baker, 1994), 163. See also Köstenberger and Patterson, *Invitation to Biblical Interpretation*.

[293] Statistics were generated by Accordance software.

[294] The rates of usage of γινώσκω per 1,000 words are Matthew (.91), Mark (.88), Luke (1.20), and John (3.04). For οἶδα, the rates are Matthew (1.09), Mark (1.54), Luke (1.07), and John (4.48).

[295] Köstenberger, *John*, 37.

[296] Köstenberger notes, "Jesus knew what was in people's hearts. . . . Perhaps the closest OT parallel is Solomon's statement at the occasion of the dedication of the temple that God alone knows the hearts of all people (1 Kings 8:39; see Morris 1995: 183). The present statement implies that Jesus is God or at least possesses a divine attribute." *John*, 117.

the woman testified: "He told me everything I ever did." This theme continues throughout the Gospel and ultimately climaxes with the ascription of omniscience to Jesus in the disciple's confession in 16:30: "You know everything" and in Peter's confession, "Lord, you know everything!" (21:17). This theme is specifically related to Jesus's identity at several points. For example, Nathaniel concludes from Jesus's display of supernatural knowledge that he is the Son of God (John 1:49). The Samaritan woman recognizes that Jesus's supernatural knowledge confirms his identity as the Messiah (John 4:25, 29). Thus, the display of Jesus's supernatural knowledge, knowledge so extensive that it may be properly called "omniscience," prompts John's readers to believe that Jesus is the Messiah, the Son of God; this fulfills the primary purpose for which John writes (John 20:31).[297]

4. *Examine editorial comments that interpret the significance of the event.* The Gospel writers often embedded clues to the proper interpretation of the narratives in brief comments that they inserted into the account.[298] In many of these statements, the author ceased to serve as a narrator and took up the role of a commentator. This is somewhat like the work of a sportscaster on a radio program. When the clock is running and a play is in motion, the sportscaster offers a mere description of the action. But between plays, while the clock is stopped, he ceases to be a mere narrator and becomes a commentator, explaining the significance of what just took place. The Gospel writers fulfilled the roles of both narrator and commentator. Sometimes their "comments" (explanations of the significance of the event) are woven into the narrative itself. Sometimes the commentary comes at the beginning of the narrative and sometimes at the end of it. These brief commentaries are often the most important key for interpretation of the narrative.[299]

John 2:11 is an example of commentary at the conclusion of a pericope. After telling the story of Jesus's miracle of transforming water into wine in Cana, John adds this: "Jesus did this, the first of his signs, in Cana of Galilee. He revealed his glory, and his disciples believed in him." The commentary echoes themes from the prologue and programmatic statement by referring to the display of Jesus's glory (John 1:14) and referring to belief in Jesus (John 1:12; 20:31). The commentary shows that the purpose of the pericope has little to do with whether Christians today should consume alcoholic beverages, a discussion often generated by this text. The nature of the wine Jesus produced is not the focus of the narrative. Rather, the commentary shows that the reader should seek to understand how the episode displayed Jesus's glory and why it resulted in the faith of Jesus's disciples.[300] This should influence the reader's approach to other miracles recorded in the Gospel of

---

[297] Köstenberger, *John*, 479; Strauss, *Four Gospels*, 328, 330–31.

[298] See Köstenberger and Patterson, *Invitation to Biblical Interpretation*, 387–91.

[299] For several examples from the OT and NT, see Stein, *A Basic Guide to Interpreting the Bible*, 161–62.

[300] Strauss' *Four Gospels*, 303.

John. These signs not only reveal Jesus's identity as the Messiah, but they manifest Jesus's glory as "the incarnate Word, God's one-of-a-kind Son (1:14)."[301]

John 13:1–3 is an example of a relatively extensive editorial comment that appears at the beginning of a pericope. The comment guides the reader in understanding the significance of the narrative that follows. The comment shows that Jesus's act of washing the feet of his disciples was a profound expression of his love for his own. This expression was all the more profound because Jesus performed it while fully aware of his own divine origin and authority on the one hand and the impending betrayal of Judas Iscariot on the other. The editorial comment emphasizes that Jesus's act was not merely one of mild condescension from noble teacher to humble servant but of radical condescension from King of heaven to servant of humans. Furthermore, Jesus lavished humble service not only on dear friends but even on an enemy in Satan's grip.[302]

5. *Note the response of the original witnesses to an event.* Sometimes original witnesses model the response the Gospel writer wishes to elicit in his readers. This, of course, is not always the case. Sometimes the response of the original witnesses is completely wrong, such as when the Pharisees argued that Jesus cast out demons by the ruler of demons (Mark 3:22). Sometimes the response of the original witnesses mixes good insight with dangerous error, such as when the scribes responded to Jesus's healing of the paralytic by saying, "He's blaspheming! Who can forgive sins but God alone?" (Mark 2:7). Jesus did not dispute their theological premise that only God can forgive sins; this suggests he affirmed it. However, he disputed the charge of blasphemy by demonstrating his power to forgive through his act of healing. Thus, when determining whether the reader should respond to the event like the original witnesses did, one must carefully examine 1) the context and 2) the characterization of those particular persons elsewhere in the Gospel. The generally negative portrayal of the Jewish leaders elsewhere in Mark (e.g., 3:3) and Jesus's many rebukes of the Pharisees and scribes suggests that their reaction is one Jesus's disciples should avoid.

Sometimes the crowds react to Jesus's actions and words in ways modern readers should emulate. This includes moments when the crowds are amazed by Jesus (Mark 1:27; 5:20), glorify God because of Jesus (Mark 2:12), and believe in Jesus (John 4:39–42, 53). The characterization of the crowds in the Gospel of Mark is mixed, most often presented positively (11:8–11, 18; 12:12, 37; 14:1–2) but sometimes also portrayed negatively (Mark 6:4–6; 15:13; cf. John 7:20). The negative portrayals are generally due to manipulation of the crowd by characters consistently portrayed as wicked (Mark 15:11). Thus, the natural response of the crowds to Jesus is often an indication of how the reader should respond to Gospel accounts.[303]

---

[301] Köstenberger, *Theology of John's Gospel and Letters*, 192. Carson mentioned that the use of the word "beginning" in John 2:11 "may also hint of the 'new creation' theme" in light of the use of the word in 1:1 and the reference to the number of days in 2:1. See his *John*, 175.

[302] Köstenberger, *John*, 400–403; Carson, *John*, 458–61.

[303] In the Gospel of John, the characterization of the crowd is more mixed than in Mark. For example, in John 7:20 the crowd accuses Jesus of having a demon and naively assumes that their leaders had no intention to harm Jesus. In 7:25–26

Very often Jesus's disciples modeled proper response to his words and deeds. Once again, there are clear exceptions. The disciples sometimes misunderstood his actions, his teachings, and earned his rebuke for their lack of faith in the process. One can normally discern whether the response of the disciples should be emulated by whether or not Jesus issued a rebuke or whether an editorial comment refers to their lack of understanding. For example, Jesus clearly rebuked the disciples for their expression of doubt that he truly cared for them (Mark 4:38–40). However, other reactions of the disciples are described at the climax of the pericope in a manner that implies they are worthy of imitation. Mark clearly desires that his readers respond to the account of Jesus's stilling of the storm like Jesus's disciples reacted to the event. They are to ask, "Who then is this? Even the wind and the sea obey him" (Mark 4:41).

Jesus's miracle of stilling the storm (Mark 4:35–41) is often used to seek to comfort people who are facing difficult problems. Such people are assured that their problems will soon be resolved because "Jesus calms the storms of life." However, this interpretation may miss the most important truth taught by this text. Jesus controlled the weather! He did not still some mere metaphorical "storm of life," but a real and fierce storm that caused fishermen who had navigated the Sea of Galilee since childhood to fear for their lives. The reaction of the disciples reminds us that the real point of the narrative rests in the repercussions that his authority over nature have for the understanding of his identity. The exclamation that the wind and sea obey him recalls descriptions of Yahweh in the OT (Job 38:8–11; Pss 65:5–8; 89:8–9; and esp. 107:23–32). The account is especially reminiscent of Psalm 107:28–29: "Then they cried out to the Lord in their trouble, and he brought them out of their distress. He stilled the storm to a whisper, and the waves of the sea were hushed." The disciples recognized that Jesus's authority over the wind and sea had staggering implications for the answer to the question, "Who is this?" Mark wanted his readers to recognize that too. The implicit answer to the question is that Jesus is the Lord, just as the application of a prophecy about Yahweh to Jesus in the prologue implied. The response of the original witnesses to an event can be an important clue guiding the proper interpretation.

6. *Look for possible connections between narrative and discourse material in the immediate context.* Sometimes the sayings of Jesus that are closely connected to the deeds of Jesus help explain the significance of those deeds. One of the clearest examples of this appears in John 9. Verses 1–12 record Jesus's miracle of healing a man born blind, a miracle without historical precedent (9:32). Amazingly, the Pharisees refused to believe that a miracle had occurred despite extensive interviews of eyewitnesses (9:13–34). The pericope ends with a dialogue between Jesus and these Pharisees. Jesus said, "I came into this world for judgment, in order that those who do not see will see and those who do see will become blind." The Pharisees recognized that the statement was an indictment against them, and Jesus confirmed this. His statement refers to spiritual blindness and spiritual sight. The

---

the crowd is confused because it sees evidence of Jesus's messiahship but doubts that he is the Messiah because they wrongly think that they know Jesus's origin. In response to the doubts of the crowd, Jesus affirmed his divine and heavenly origin. Again the response was mixed. Some wished to seize him but others cautiously affirmed his identity as Messiah (7:30–31).

statement implies that he intended for his miracle to serve as an object lesson about man's spiritual condition and his own power to cure it.[304] Sinners are spiritually blind, and they will remain so until Jesus grants them spiritual sight. This statement regarding spiritual blindness is closely related to a statement from John's prologue: "He was in the world, and the world was created through him, and yet the world did not recognize him" (1:10).[305]

7. ***Carefully examine all OT quotations and allusions.*** Even brief OT allusions often refer to the broader context of the OT passage and provide keys for the proper interpretation of the Gospel narrative.[306] For example, in Matthew 2:20 the angel of the Lord told Joseph it was safe to return to Israel "because those who intended to kill the child are dead." These words are a clear allusion to Yahweh's words to Moses in Exodus 4:19. Despite the differences between the statements in English translations, the phrases in Matthew 2:20 and Exodus 4:19 in the LXX are almost identical. Most scholars recognize that the allusion to Exodus serves to portray Jesus as the new Moses who will lead his people on a new exodus that rescues them from their slavery to sin.[307] Other allusions to the OT in Matthew confirm this view. For example, the words spoken by the Father at Jesus's transfiguration are identical to those he spoke at Jesus's baptism, but with one important addition: "Listen to him!" (Matt 17:5). This command is an allusion to Deuteronomy 18:15, in which Moses promised that God would raise up a prophet like him (Moses) and urged: "You must listen to him." The allusion confirms Jesus's identity as the prophet like Moses and the long-awaited fulfillment of the promise in Deuteronomy 18:15.[308]

Some good study Bibles mention these allusions and their significance.[309] Some study or reference Bibles list the OT passages as cross references.[310] Unfortunately, many English Bibles do not. Perhaps the best resource for quickly identifying these allusions is the "Index of Allusions and Verbal Parallels" contained in the back of the United Bible Society's edition of the Greek NT. The index is simple to use and does not require familiarity with the Greek language. These allusions were probably more obvious to the original readers of the Gospels who were likely far more familiar with the OT than many modern readers are. Looking up these allusions and carefully examining them in their original context is well worth the effort and may shed enormous light on the Gospel narratives.[311]

8. ***Consider the significance of events against the background of OT teaching and first-century Jewish theology.*** Even when the Gospels do not directly quote or allude to

---

[304] Köstenberger, *John*, 277–96.

[305] For a helpful discussion of the theological implications of this passage, see Köstenberger, *A Theology of John's Gospel and Letters* (Grand Rapids, MI: Zondervan, 2009), 223–25. For cautions regarding this step, see Wiarda, *Interpreting Gospel Narratives*, 107–10.

[306] Köstenberger and Patterson, *Invitation to Biblical Interpretation*, 384.

[307] See D. C. Allison, *The New Moses: A Matthean Typology* (Minneapolis, MN: Fortress, 1993), 142–44; France, *Matthew*, 90; Quarles, *Theology of Matthew*, 36–37.

[308] See C. Blomberg, *Matthew*, NAC (Nashville, TN: Broadman, 1992), 264; Quarles, *Theology of Matthew*, 44.

[309] See the discussion in CSB Study Bible notes on Matt 2:20 and 17:1–6.

[310] The NIV Study Bible and the ESV list Exod 4:19 as a cross-reference for Matt 2:20 but do not list Deut 18:15 as a cross-reference for Matt 17:5.

[311] For cautions regarding this step, see Wiarda, *Interpreting Gospel Narratives*, 117–26.

a specific OT text, the general teaching of the OT remains important for a proper understanding of Gospel narratives. Gospel writers sometimes assumed that the worldview of their readers had been heavily influenced by OT teaching. The OT functioned like an encyclopedia of general knowledge that informed the interpretation of the Gospel narratives. For example, Mark 6:45–52 records Jesus's miraculous crossing of the Sea of Galilee. When early Christian readers of Mark's Gospel encountered that narrative, they would likely have recalled similar events recorded in the OT such as Israel's miraculous crossing of the Red Sea during the exodus. Thus, they would have associated Jesus's miracle with the miraculous deeds of Yahweh through his servant Moses in Israel's history. They may have also recalled descriptions of Yahweh in other OT texts, such as Psalm 77:19 and Isaiah 44:16. The closest OT parallel to Jesus's action is Job 9:8: "[God] alone stretches out the heavens and treads on the waves of the sea."[312] Other features of Mark's description of the event are also paralleled in Job 9. Mark mentioned that Jesus "wanted to pass by them" (Mark 6:48). Similarly, Job 9:11 says, "If he passed by me, I wouldn't see him." Mark 6:49 says the disciples did not recognize Jesus, but thought him a ghost. The next line of Job 9:11 says, "If he [God] went by, I wouldn't recognize him." Such parallels suggest that Mark may have had Job 9 in mind when he remembered Peter's recounting of this episode in Jesus's ministry. Familiarity with OT descriptions of Yahweh as One who walks on the sea guides the reader in understanding this account as a powerful testimony to Jesus's identity as Yahweh.

In Mark 1:40–45 Jesus healed a man of leprosy, a serious skin disease. Readers familiar with the OT would likely have recalled that only three persons in the OT were healed of leprosy: Moses (Exod 4:6–7), Miriam (Num 12:10–16), and Naaman (2 Kings 5:1–19). In particular, they may have remembered the words of the king of Israel in response to the plea for Naaman's healing in the letter from the king of Aram: "Am I God, killing and giving life that this man expects me to cure a man of his skin disease?" Mark's readers knew well that only God could cleanse someone of leprosy. Thus, Jesus's miraculous healing of the leper was a strong indication of Jesus's deity.

Horizontal Reading

Horizontal reading involves careful comparison of a pericope in a particular Gospel to parallel accounts in other Gospels. This practice is sometimes called "comparative analysis" and is an important component of source and redaction criticism. Source criticism compares the Synoptic Gospels, analyzes the differences among them, and seeks to determine which Gospel writer most likely used and adapted the work of another Gospel writer. Redaction criticism goes beyond source criticism by seeking to explain the theological motivations behind a Gospel writer's adaptation of his sources. The accuracy of the findings of redaction criticism often depends on whether the solution to the Synoptic problem assumed or argued by the research is accurate. Scholars today tend to be less confident about

---

[312] The cross references in the margin of the NA28 lists Job 9:8 as a parallel to Mark 6:48. See the note on Matt 14:33 in the CSB Study Bible; R. T. France, *The Gospel of Mark*, NIGTC (Grand Rapids, MI: Eerdmans, 2002), 270; W. Lane, *The Gospel of Mark*, NICNT (Grand Rapids, MI: Eerdmans, 1974), 235–37; and especially J. Edwards, *The Gospel According to Mark*, PNTC (Grand Rapids, MI: Eerdmans, 2002), 198–99.

prevailing solutions to the Synoptic problem than scholars of the previous generation. However, an interpreter can engage in comparative analysis of the Gospels without necessarily seeking to explain literary dependency among the Gospels. Elements in a particular Gospel that are unique to that Gospel likely reflect the special emphases of the author, whether or not his particular Gospel depended on another.[313]

Before practicing comparative analysis, the interpreter should consider several cautions. First, when analyzing the differences among the Gospels, one must not lose sight of the remarkable similarities between them. The Gospels have an amazing agreement in detail, which lends support to their historical accuracy. Second, one must not confuse differences between Gospel parallels with disagreements. Despite the differences among the Gospels, the accounts can be harmonized. Properly interpreted, the Gospels contain no contradictions. After thorough consideration of the similarities and differences between the Gospels, Blomberg wrote,

> Harmonizing the Gospels and analyzing their redactional distinctives are not contradictory but complementary methods. With a full appreciation of all the variations in wording between parallel accounts, not one example has come to light which demands an abandonment of belief in the Gospel's accuracy, provided that accuracy is measured by standards of precision appropriate to the cultures and expectations of the original authors and their audiences.[314]

Comparative analysis should proceed according to these steps:

1. Locate parallel accounts in the Gospels, preferably by using a Gospel harmony or Gospel synopsis that arranges the text of the Gospels in parallel columns.
2. Examine the similarities and differences between the parallel texts. Mark differences by highlighting or underlining.
3. Consider whether the unique elements of a particular Gospel highlight theological emphases of that Gospel.
4. Test the hypothesis regarding theological emphases by determining whether that same emphasis is reflected in other passages in that particular Gospel.

The usefulness of this approach may be seen through the following example. Let's suppose a pastor intends to preach a sermon on Jesus's exorcism as recorded in Matthew 15:21–28. He consults a harmony or synopsis and discovers that the account is also recorded in Mark, but not in Luke. He then highlights the distinctive elements of Matthew's account. These are placed in bold type in the following text box.

---

[313] See the brief discussion in Köstenberger and Patterson, *Invitation to Biblical Interpretation*, 376.

[314] C. Blomberg, *Interpreting the Parables* (Downers Grove, IL: InterVarsity, 1990), 130. See also idem, "The Legitimacy and Limits of Harmonization," in *Hermeneutics, Authority, and Canon*, ed. D. A. Carson and J. D. Woodbridge (Grand Rapids, MI: Zondervan, 1986), 139–74; idem, *The Historical Reliability of the Gospels*, 2nd ed. (Downers Grove, IL: InterVarsity, 2007), 152–95.

Matthew 15:21–28	Mark 7:24–30
When Jesus left there, he withdrew to the area of Tyre and Sidon.	He got up and departed from there to the region of Tyre. He entered a house and did not want anyone to know it, but he could not escape notice.
Just then a **Canaanite** woman from that region came and kept crying out, "**Have mercy on me, Lord, Son of David!** My daughter is severely tormented by a demon."	Instead, immediately after hearing about him, a woman whose little daughter had an unclean spirit came and fell at his feet.
Jesus did not say a word to her. His disciples approached him and urged him, "Send her away because she's crying out after us."	The woman was Gentile, a Syrophoenician by birth, and she kept asking him to cast the demon out of her daughter.
He replied, "**I was sent only to the lost sheep of the house of Israel.**"	
But she came, knelt before him, and said, "**Lord, help me!**"	
He answered, "It isn't right to take the children's bread and throw it to the dogs."	He said to her, "Let the children be fed first, because it isn't right to take the children's bread and throw it to the dogs."
"Yes, Lord," she said, "yet even the dogs eat the crumbs that fall from their masters' table."	But she replied to him, "Lord, even the dogs under the table eat the children's crumbs."
Then Jesus replied to her, "**Woman, your faith is great.** Let it be done for you as you want." And **from that moment** her daughter was healed.	Then he told her, "Because of this reply, you may go. The demon has left your daughter."
	When she went back to her home, she found her child lying on the bed, and the demon was gone.

The pastor then begins to consider whether the unique elements of Matthew's account point to his special theological emphases. The pastor is familiar with Matthew's Gospel because he conducted the "vertical reading" at the beginning of his study of the Gospel and because he has been preaching through the Gospel pericope-by-pericope up to this point.

He first notices that Mark referred to the mother of the demon-possessed girl as a Gentile and a Syrophoenician. Matthew described her as a Canaanite. On the surface, this may appear a contradiction. But careful examination leads to the conclusion it is not. The noun used in the Greek text of Mark means "Greek woman" and may describe the woman as one who spoke the Greek language or was immersed in Greek culture. Often in the NT, the masculine counterpart to the term ("Greek man") is roughly equivalent to "Gentile" (hence the translation in the CSB). It was the district in which Tyre and Sidon were located. It belonged to the region designated "Canaan" in the OT. Even in the NT era, it was inhabited by descendants of the Canaanites whose language and religion were similar to those of the OT Canaanites. Mark used the term most commonly used by his contemporaries to designate people from this region. Matthew used an archaic term drawn from the OT. No contradiction exists.

The pastor must ask, however, why Matthew used an archaic term. Why did he use the geographical terminology of the OT era rather than that commonly used by his contemporaries like Mark chose to do? He recalls that the Canaanites were the arch-enemies of the Israelites in the OT. He would likely note that the background and identity of the woman made Jesus's display of compassion to her and her daughter all the more remarkable. He should note that Jesus's compassion to a Canaanite fits well with the theme of Jesus's inclusion of the Gentiles in his redemptive plan. A plan which climaxes with the command to make disciples of "all nations" (Matt 28:19–20).[315] He might also recall from his study of Matthew's genealogy of Jesus that of the four mothers named in the genealogy, all four were Gentiles and two (Tamar and Rahab) were Canaanites specifically.[316] Thus, Matthew's unique description of the woman seems intended to highlight Jesus's compassion to Gentiles—even the most notorious and hated of the Gentiles.

The pastor will also notice that the woman's appeal to Jesus, "Have mercy on me, Lord" is unique to Matthew. This appeal is reiterated with another unique statement: "Lord, help me." Again, these unique elements are fully compatible with Mark's account. Mark says that the woman "kept asking him" to cast out the demon. Matthew chose to give the actual content of the repeated requests, which Mark only summarized. At the very least, Matthew's version emphasizes the helplessness, humility, and total dependence on Jesus that the request expressed. The pastor notes that although the woman refers to Jesus as "Lord" once in Mark, she used this title for Jesus three times in Matthew's pericope. He concludes that Matthew intended to emphasize Jesus's identity as Lord and explores the meaning of this title in Matthew's Gospel. If he takes the time to explore how these appeals were used in the OT, he will discover that these petitions were the very phrases used consistently in the OT in a petitioner's appeals to God. This suggests the title "Lord" connotes Jesus's deity and not merely his authority.[317]

The pastor notes that only Matthew refers to Jesus as the Son of David. A quick scan of Matthew's Gospel will reveal that it uses this title more frequently than any other Gospel. He should recall from his study of the title of the Gospel and the genealogy that introduces the Gospel that Jesus's identity as the Son of David is one of Matthew's primary theological themes. The title identifies Jesus as the fulfillment of God's covenant with David, the One who will rule eternally over people of every nation, tribe, and tongue.

Jesus's statement "I was sent only to the lost sheep of the house of Israel" is also unique to Matthew's Gospel. Hopefully, the pastor will recall that Jesus also used the expression "lost sheep of the house of Israel" in Matthew 10:6. Even if not, his search of cross references recommended in the vertical reading will lead to this discovery. The repetition highlights the importance of the phrase. If he takes the time to search for a paragraph in the OT in which the terms "lost," "sheep," and "Israel" all appear, the search will direct him to Ezekiel 34. The text is an indictment against Israel's "shepherds," her corrupt spiritual leaders. The text promises that God will judge Israel's wicked leaders, shepherd his people himself, and send the Messiah to serve as their shepherd:

---

[315] For a thorough discussion of this theme in Matthew, see Quarles, *Theology of Matthew*, 119–24.

[316] See France, *Matthew*, 592 and esp. 590n12; Keener, *Matthew*, 415.

[317] On the forms of the petitions and their significance, see Quarles, *Theology of Matthew*, 142–46.

> I will establish over them one shepherd, My servant David, and he will shepherd them. He will tend them himself and will be their shepherd. I, the Lord, will be their God, and my servant David will be a prince among them. I, the Lord, have spoken.[318]

Thus, Jesus's statement that he was sent (by God) to the "lost sheep of the house of Israel" implies that he is the fulfillment of the Ezekiel 34 prophecy. The statement confirms that Jesus is, as the Canaanite woman earlier confessed, the "Son of David," the promised Messiah.[319]

Finally, Jesus's commendation of the Canaanite woman's faith is unique to Matthew. The pastor will likely remember that Jesus gave a similar commendation in 8:10: "I have not found anyone in Israel with so great a faith!" This commendation given to a Roman centurion was followed by Jesus's promise that he would include many people "from east and west" in his kingdom. This second commendation confirms the genuineness and greatness of the faith of Gentiles and Jesus's gracious acceptance of Gentiles who believed. This suggests that the statements that Jesus made to the Gentile woman earlier are not the harsh rejections that they initially appear to be. These statements are tests of faith, not blunt insults.[320]

The exercise in comparative analysis will open the interpreter's eyes to important themes he may otherwise have overlooked. His understanding of the text and his proclamation of it will be enriched as he recognizes that Jesus is not merely One who bears authority over demons; he is the merciful Lord, the Savior who accepts believing Gentiles (even the worst of them), and the King promised by the OT prophets.

Readers should not assume that following the steps suggested above will enable them to discover everything they need to know about a Gospel passage. Biblical interpretation cannot be reduced to a mechanical process. Nevertheless, these steps serve as a useful starting point for the interpretation of most Gospel narratives. If the reader undertakes them consistently, he is not likely to miss the most important truths of the stories of the Gospels.

INTERPRETING THE PARABLES

Although the discourses of Jesus in the Gospels are fairly straightforward and their interpretation will not be discussed in this brief guide, an exception must be made for one element of Jesus's discourses, his parables. This discussion is necessary due to the frequent mishandling of the parables. Gordon Fee correctly observed, "For all their charm and simplicity, the parables have suffered a fate of misinterpretation in the church second only to the Revelation."[321]

---

[318] Ezek 34:23–24.

[319] On the Son of David theme in Matthew, see Quarles, *Theology of Matthew*, 71–96.

[320] See the helpful comments in France, *Matthew*, 590–91.

[321] G. D. Fee and D. Stuart, *How to Read the Bible for All Its Worth*, 4th ed. (Grand Rapids, MI: Zondervan, 2014), 154.

Modern interpreters face two dangers as they approach the parables. One danger is the tendency to over-interpret the parables by seeing every detail as symbolic. Augustine's interpretation of the parable of the Good Samaritan (Luke 10:30–37) is commonly cited as an example of this approach. The following chart summarizes Augustine's interpretation.

Symbol	Referent
Wounded man	Adam
Jerusalem	heavenly city from which Adam fell
Jericho	Mortality
Thieves	Satan and his demons
Stripping	loss of immortality
Beating	Enticement to sin
Half-dead	Oppression by sin
Priest and Levite	the OT law that was unable to save
Samaritan	Jesus
Bandaging wounds	restraint of sin
Oil	comfort that comes from hope
Wine	encouragement to work fervently
Animal	Jesus's human flesh
Putting on animal	belief in the incarnation
Two denarii	two great commandments: love God and love neighbor
Inn	Church
Innkeeper	Paul
Promise of additional payment	Paul's celibacy or his willingness to forego financial support by the church

This approach to the interpretation of parables was challenged by church leaders like Chrysostom, Aquinas, and Calvin. Nevertheless, even at the close of the nineteenth century, one prominent scholar argued that interpreters should assume that every detail of a parable is symbolic unless it is contested by strong evidence.[322]

Another danger is the tendency to under-interpret the parables by attempting to reduce the meaning of each parable to a single simple truth. This approach is a relic of the influence of the German scholar A. Jülicher on parable interpretation. Jülicher argued that the parables, as originally told by Jesus, were pure similes that highlighted one point of comparison between the kingdom and some object or action. Many modern interpreters fail to understand that Jülicher's description applied only to the hypothetical "original form" of the parable as reconstructed by him. Even Jülicher recognized that the parables recorded

---

[322] R. C. Trench, *Notes on the Parables of Our Lord* (New York, NY: Appleton, 1873), 37.

in the Gospels often contain allegorical elements. However, based on his presuppositions about the forms of communication Jesus must have used, he rejected these allegorical elements and regarded them as later additions made by the church. In the course of time, some elements of Jülicher's hypothesis came to be misapplied as interpreters attempted to understand the Gospel parables in their current canonical form as simple stories teaching single truths. Nevertheless, parallels between Jesus's parables and the parables in the OT and rabbinic literature suggest that Jesus's parables are allegories in which multiple elements are symbolic. For those who affirm that the Gospels faithfully preserve Jesus's teaching, Jesus's interpretation of his parables in texts like Mark 4:1–20 confirms that his parables contained multiple allegorical elements.

The best approach to parable interpretation steers a middle course between these two extremes.[323] The interpreter should recognize that not every detail of the parable is symbolic. Some details simply serve to move the plot forward or to make the parable realistic. On the other hand, the parables are not pure similes that make only one point of comparison between a scene and a spiritual truth. They often contain several symbols, each communicating an important spiritual truth.[324]

The parables of Jesus are neither simple stories teaching single morals nor pure allegories. In most parables, some details are symbolic and some are not. The key to proper interpretation is to distinguish the symbolic and non-symbolic elements and then determine the referents of each symbol. Osborne aptly wrote that "only the context may decide which details provide local color without spiritual significance (part of the story world) or have individual theological meaning themselves (meant to be contextualized)."[325] This section will offer a preliminary guide to that process.

1. *Identify the main characters of the parable.* Main characters within a parable are often symbolic. They are often composed of an authority figure and his subordinates. The authority figure represents God while the subordinates represent people. Jesus's parables, like rabbinic parables, often use stock imagery like a king and his subjects, a master and his slaves, a shepherd and his sheep, a land-owner and his hired hands, and a groom and the wedding party to portray God and people respectively. Subordinates who are positively portrayed often represent those who belong to and serve God, such as Jesus's disciples or

---

[323] For the sake of brevity, this brief guide cannot discuss the history of parable interpretation or interact with current debates regarding it. See the outstanding discussion in Blomberg, *Interpreting the Parables*, esp. "Part 1: Methods and Controversies in Interpreting the Parables," 26–169. The discussion here has been heavily influenced by Blomberg. For a briefer introduction also consistent with the principles affirmed by Blomberg, see Köstenberger and Patterson, *Invitation to Biblical Interpretation*, 422–46. The most comprehensive, recent guide to the interpretation of Jesus's parables that is written in English is K. R. Snodrass, *Stories with Intent: A Comprehensive Guide to the Parables of Jesus* (Grand Rapids, MI: Eerdmans, 2008).

[324] See the helpful discussion of the range from short simile to long allegory in Köstenberger and Patterson, *Invitation to Biblical Interpretation*, 426–27.

[325] Osborne *Hermeneutical Spiral*, 293.

the OT prophets. Those negatively portrayed represent the wicked, normally those who reject Jesus or who are false disciples.

Exceptions to these guidelines do exist, however. For example, the sons of a father portray people such as Jesus's disciples or those who reject him in parables in which multiple sons are mentioned. Examples of this include the parable of the Lost Son (Luke 15:11–32) and the parable of the Two Sons (Matt 21:28–32). On the other hand, some parables refer to a single son of a king or landowner and this son represents Jesus. Examples include the parable of the Wicked Tenants (Matt 21:33–46) and the parable of the Wedding Banquet (Matt 22:1–14).

2. *Identify objects given special importance.* Not only do the persons described in the parables function as symbols, objects sometimes do so as well. In some of Jesus's parables, certain objects are emphasized in a way that suggests they have some special significance. This is somewhat like watching a play in which the spotlight moves from the actors and shines on a particular prop. The illumination of the prop definitely means something: the spectators intuitively know that prop is important. Similarly, when the parable of the Sower moves the spotlight from the farmer to the seed and to the soils, readers almost intuitively know that the seed and soils are symbolic. Likewise, when the parable of the Talents shifts the focus from the landowner and his slaves to a detailed discussion of talents, readers intuitively know that the talents symbolize something. In a sense, these objects are more than mere props. Although they are inanimate, they function as major characters in the parable.

3. *Examine the structure of the parable.* Jesus's parables often have two or three major sections. These sections are like different scenes in the act of a play or episodes in a drama. Each emphasizes a particular truth. For example, the parable of the Prodigal Son (Luke 15:11–32) appears to have three major sections: verses 11–20a focus on the son's rebellion and return; verses 20b–24 focus on the father's compassion and restoration of the son; verses 25–32 focus on the elder son's understandable, but unjustified, resentment. Each scene focuses on a different character. This confirms that each scene, like each character, communicates a particular truth.

4. *Identify details of the parable that seem shocking, extraordinary, unnatural, or unrealistic.* Some details of a parable simply move the story line forward or serve to aid hearers and readers in creating a more vivid mental picture of the scene. Such details may or may not have symbolic significance. However, elements that catch the hearer and reader by surprise, that are unexpected twists in the plot, are almost certainly allegorical. Examples include a landowner who pays those who worked only for minutes the same amount as those who worked all day, a mustard seed growing to such enormity that birds roost on its branches, seed that produces many times more than a bumper crop, or subjects ignoring a king's summons to the wedding banquet for his son. Readers must familiarize themselves with the customs and practices of the first-century Jewish world to be able to identify these surprising elements. They must also learn to read the parables with fresh eyes. Sometimes familiarity may prevent the reader from spotting extraordinary details.

5. *Examine connections to introductions or conclusions to the parable.* Occasionally, Jesus explained the meaning of his parables at length. Sometimes the Gospel writers explain the basic significance of a parable in introductions or conclusions to it. Luke's Gospel is particularly helpful in this regard. For example, as he introduces the parable of the Persistent Widow (Luke 18:1–8), he writes that this parable is about the "need for them to pray always and not become discouraged." Then Jesus further explained the parable in a conclusion in verses 6–8. Similarly, as Luke introduces the parable of the Pharisee and the Tax Collector (Luke 18:9–14), he writes, "He also told this parable to some who trusted in themselves that they were righteous and looked down on everyone else" (Luke 18:9).

Sometimes the discussions that formed the prelude to a parable (or group of parables) are an important guide to interpretation. For example, Jesus told the parables of the Lost Sheep (Luke 15:3–7), Lost Coin (Luke 15:8–10), and Lost Son (Luke 15:11–32) in response to an indictment against him from the Pharisees and scribes: "This man welcomes sinners and eats with them!" (Luke 15:2). This context prompts readers to expect the parables that follow to address Jesus's relationship to sinners.

6. *Examine connections to other parables in the same grouping.* Sometimes the Gospel writers grouped parables dealing with the same topic. Thus, truths gleaned from the study of one parable in the group may serve as a helpful guide to the interpretation of other parables in the group. For example, the three parables in Luke 15 are presented one after another with no breaks between them. They were told on the same occasion. They also share similar themes. One may refer to Luke 15 as the "lost and found section" of the Gospel because each parable focuses on the loss of something that was precious to someone. The loss of this precious item, animal, or person prompted a desperate search. The discovery of this lost person or thing inspired lavish celebration. The proximity of these parables and their shared themes suggest that they communicate basically the same message.

Readers should not assume, however, that the parables use particular symbols in exactly the same way simply because they are grouped together. For example, Matthew 13 groups several parables related to the kingdom of God. Seed serves as a symbol in three of these parables: the parable of the Sower (Matt 13:3–9), the parable of the Wheat and Tares (Matt 13:24–30), and the parable of the Mustard Seed (Matt 13:31–32). However, the symbol of the seed has a different referent in each parable. In the parable of the Sower, the seed represents the message about the kingdom (Matt 13:19). In the parable of the Wheat and Tares, the seed represents the "sons of the kingdom" (Matt 13:38). In the parable of the Mustard Seed, the seed represents the kingdom itself.

On the other hand, Matthew 13:31–33 contains two closely related parables: the parable of the Mustard Seed and the parable of the Yeast. In this case, two different symbols (seed and yeast) have the same referent (kingdom). Both parables portray the expansion of the kingdom and its advancement throughout the world. Another close connection exists between the parable of the Hidden Treasure and the parable of the Priceless Pearl in Matthew 13:44–45. Again, two different symbols (treasure and precious pearl) have essentially the same referent (the kingdom, which is worth any sacrifice necessary to attain it).

7. ***Apply steps for Gospel interpretation previously discussed.*** The steps outlined above are intended to supplement, not replace, those suggested earlier for Gospel interpretation. Steps such as considering the major themes of the Gospel, comparing Gospel parallels, and examining OT allusions may be invaluable for better understanding Jesus's parables. An example of the helpfulness of a couple of these steps should suffice.

Differences between the wording of the parables in Gospel parallels are sometimes due to a Gospel writer's effort to emphasize correct interpretation of the parable. For example, Mark's version of the parable of the Mustard Seed ends with the statement that the mustard plant grows enormous branches "so that the birds of the sky can nest in its shade" (Mark 4:32). An enormous tree in which birds nest and enjoy shade was a common prophetic portrayal for the expansion of a world-wide empire (Dan 4:10–12, 20-22; Ezek 17:23; 31:6). However, Mark's readers might overlook this connection. Although he merely describes the mustard as "taller than all the garden plants," Matthew and Luke specifically describe the adult mustard as a "tree." Some modern readers have heavily criticized this description because they assume it indicates Matthew's and Luke's ignorance in the field of biology since a mustard plant is an herb or vegetable rather than a tree. This criticism, of course, completely misses the point. Matthew and Luke specifically use the word "tree" to encourage the reader to recall imagery used by the OT prophets. They are using this clue to nudge the reader toward the proper interpretation of the parable's conclusion. If the reader affirms that all three Gospel writers are faithful to Jesus's intention, the clue in Matthew and Luke assists in the interpretation of the parable in Mark. The allusions to the prophet's imagery portray the kingdom of God as a world-wide empire stretching to the ends of the earth and encompassing all nations.

On the other hand, Mark's version assists in the interpretation of the parable in the other Synoptic Gospels too. All three versions of the parable make clear and definite allusions to Daniel 4:11–12 (both LXX and Theodotian) and thus portray the kingdom of God as a world-wide empire that will encompass all kingdoms of the earth. Mark's version adds to those allusions an unmistakable reference to Ezekiel 17:23. Both Mark's version and Ezekiel's prophecy refer to birds under the shade of a tree's branches, and Mark and the LXX use precisely the same phrase for this. The parable in Ezekiel 17:22–24 appears to be a description of the messianic kingdom that extends throughout the entire world and encompasses Gentiles as well as Jews. The allusion to Ezekiel in Mark reminds readers that the kingdom of God, which will extend throughout the world, is distinctly messianic. This clue in Mark can give clarity to interpretations of the parallels in Matthew and Luke.

Now let's apply these steps to the interpretation of a single parable. The parable of the Wicked Tenants appears in Mark 12:1–12, Matthew 21:33–46, and Luke 20:9–19. We will focus on Mark's version, but will later use insights from Matthew and Luke to guide our interpretation.

1. *Identify the main characters of the parable.* The main characters are 1) the vineyard owner, 2) the tenant farmers, 3) the servants of the vineyard owner, and 4) the son of the vineyard owner. Thus, the main characters consist of an authority figure and two groups of subordinates. One group, the tenant farmers, are negatively portrayed. The other group, the servants and the son, are positively portrayed. The authority figure represents God, the servants and son represent those who faithfully serve God, and the tenant farmers represent those who rebel against God.

2. *Identify objects given special importance.* A considerable amount of attention is given to the vineyard in the parable. The word "vineyard" appears four times. The description of the vineyard in 12:1 is rather extensive, certainly more extensive than the story line required. This suggests that the vineyard is not merely the incidental scene for the parable or a meaningless prop; the vineyard likely has symbolic significance.

3. *Examine the structure of the parable.* The parable seems to have three major sections. Verse 1 describes the preparation and leasing of the vineyard. Verses 2–8 describe the lessees' refusal to fulfill the terms of the lease. Verses 9–10 focus on the owner's reaction to the lessees' horrible actions. Thus, one might at first assume the parable teaches three major truths, one corresponding to each of the three sections. These truths might be summarized this way:

1. God entrusted something very valuable to a group of people.
2. These people failed to fulfill their responsibility to God and rejected multiple appeals from God, even badly abusing those who were faithful to God.
3. God will punish those unfaithful people and entrust their responsibility to others.

However, the middle section has two subsections: the abuse of the servants (vv. 2–5) and the murder of the son (vv. 6–8). These subsections are each as long (or longer) than the first and last major sections. This suggests the treatment of the servants and that of the son should be regarded as distinct episodes. They likely teach distinct truths. This alerts the reader to expect the parable to relate four major truths corresponding to four sections.

4. *Identify details of the parable that seem shocking, extraordinary, unnatural, or unrealistic.* Although most of the parable would make perfect sense to first-century readers who understood the hazards of being a distant landlord, one element was certain to prompt a gasp. The unrelenting patience of the vineyard owner in sending servant after servant after servant only to have them be abused and even killed sets the reader up to expect the landowner to employ a drastically different strategy for handling the tenants. A realistic strategy might be to send someone accompanied by armed mercenaries to force the tenants into submission. Shockingly, the vineyard owner sent his son instead. Even before the parable continues, the reader intuitively knows what the result will likely be—the abuse and murder of the son. When the owner at last destroys the tenants, no sensible reader will fault him. His patience and forbearance climaxing in the sending of the son have already strained credulity.

The shock factor associated with the sending of the son suggests that this element of the parable is symbolic. The son likely represents a special individual similar to but distinct from the servants of the owner.

5. *Examine connections to introductions or conclusions to the parable.* The immediately preceding context to the parable may offer some guidance in interpretation. Jesus's cleansing of the temple and cursing of the fig tree were symbolic acts that threatened God's judgment on Israel. The Jewish leaders responded by "looking for a way to kill him" (Mark 11:18) and by verbally challenging Jesus's authority. This suggests that Jesus himself may be represented by either the servants or the son killed in the parable. The conclusion to the parable offers an even clearer clue for interpretation. Mark noted that the Jewish leaders sought to arrest Jesus "because they knew he had spoken this parable against them" (Mark 12:12). The original audience recognized that the villains of the parable, the tenants, represented the Jewish leaders.

6. *Examine connections to other parables in the same grouping.* In Mark and Luke, this parable stands alone. However, Matthew groups this parable with two others: the parable of the Two Sons (Matt 21:28–32) and the parable of the Wedding Banquet (Matt 22:1–14). All three parables share one important feature in common: the noun "son." The parable of the Wicked Tenants seems to have an especially close connection to the latter of these parables. Both describe the destruction of those who do not show proper respect to the son of an authority figure. This confirms the suspicion that the "son" of this parable is a main character with symbolic significance.

7. *Apply steps for Gospel interpretation previously discussed.* To prevent this section from becoming unwieldy in length, we will undertake just a few of these steps here: comparative analysis, examination of OT allusions, and consideration of the parable's relationship to the Gospel's major themes.

Matthew's account has several differences with Mark's that appear significant. First, in Matthew 21:34, Matthew places more emphasis on the "fruits" of the vineyard. Although Mark and Luke refer to the occasion in which the owner attempts to collect from the tenants as "harvest time," Matthew calls this occasion "time . . . to harvest fruits" (Matt 21:34).[326] Furthermore, though Mark and Luke state at the end of the parable that the owner will destroy the tenants and hand the vineyard over to others, only Matthew adds, "who will give him his fruit at the harvest." Notice that the literal translation in the margin of the CSB refers to "the fruits in their seasons." Furthermore, although the feature is obscured in several English translations, Mark and Luke used the singular form of the noun "fruit" and Matthew used the plural form. Although Mark and Luke refer to the harvest as a whole, Matthew's grammar focuses on the individual pieces of fruit that make up the harvest.

---

[326] See the literal translation in the margin of the CSB.

One might dismiss these differences as insignificant if not for the emphasis on fruits and fruit-bearing elsewhere in Matthew's Gospel (Matt 3:8, 10; 7:16, 17[2x], 18[2x], 19–20; 12:33[3x]; 13:8, 26; 21:19, 34, 41, 43). Although Mark's Gospel used the word "fruit" five times and Luke used it twelve, Matthew used the word nineteen times. That means he refers to "fruit" more than Mark and Luke combined! Even when one accounts for the different lengths of the three Synoptic Gospels, the difference is significant. Mark used the noun .37 times per thousand words. Luke used the term .51 times per thousand words. Matthew's usage climbs to .86 times per thousand words. In all of these usages, the word "fruits" refers either directly or symbolically to the actions and words of an individual that reflect his true character. For example, Matthew 7:16–20 states,

> You'll recognize them [false prophets] by their fruit. Are grapes gathered from thornbushes or figs from thistles? In the same way, every good tree produces good fruit, but a bad tree produces bad fruit. A good tree can't produce bad fruit; neither can a bad tree produce good fruit. Every tree that doesn't produce good fruit is cut down and thrown into the fire. So you'll recognize them by their fruit.[327]

Most likely, Matthew emphasized "fruits" due to the vineyard owner because he recognized that these symbolized "fruits consistent with repentance" (Matt 3:8), actions that displayed proper submission and devotion to God.

In Matthew 21:35 another significant difference appears. Both Mark and Luke refer to the humiliation, beating, and murder of the servants by the tenants. Only Matthew refers to the stoning of the servants. The reference would likely have struck the original readers as a bit odd and out of place. The tenants would not have been forced to resort to stoning to kill the servants since their pruning knives could have more easily accomplished the task. Furthermore, in Jewish law, stoning was reserved for sexual felons, idolaters, blasphemers, and sorcerers, although the character of the tenants suggests they would not have been concerned about such scruples.[328] More importantly, Matthew 23:37 used this term to describe Jerusalem's treatment of the prophets: "Jerusalem, Jerusalem who kills the prophets and stones those who are sent to her." Matthew's description of the servants as those "sent" and "stoned" makes unmistakable reference to this later passage. Thus, the use of the verb "stoned" guides the reader in identifying the servants of the parable. They are the prophets sent by God to Israel to call his people to repentance.

Matthew 21:43 states that "the kingdom of God will be taken away from you and given to a people producing its fruit." This confirms that the vineyard represents the kingdom of God, the tenants represent the chief priests and Pharisees, and the new tenants represent a new people who express genuine repentance and enjoy the benefits of the kingdom.

---

[327] For the meaning of this text and its OT background, see Quarles, *Sermon on the Mount*, 323–28.

[328] m. *Sanh.* 7.

The OT quotation and possible allusions in the parable are also helpful for understanding its meaning. At the conclusion of the parable, in all three Gospel parallels, Jesus quoted Psalm 118:22–23. His original audience and the Gospels' original readers should have recognized the quotation as referring to the Messiah. The crowds had chanted this psalm during the triumphal entry only a few verses before as they praised Jesus as the "Son of David," the Messiah (Matt 21:9). The NT interprets this Psalm as Messianic and applies it to Jesus (Acts 4:11; 1 Peter 2:7). This implies that Jesus, the Messiah, is a referent for one of the symbols of the parable. The obvious choice is the son of the vineyard owner. Mark and Luke suggest this interpretation by specifically describing the son as the father's "beloved son," a description that prompts readers to recall the utterance of the Father at Jesus's baptism and transfiguration: "You are my beloved Son" (Mark 1:11; 9:7).

Finally, Mark 12:1 contains an allusion to the Song of the Vineyard in Isaiah 5:1–7. In the OT context, the passage is an indictment of Israel for its disobedience to God. The attention lavished by the vineyard owner on the vineyard illustrated God's gracious and lavish care for Israel. The failure of the vineyard to produce good fruit attested to Israel's failure to produce good deeds. The destruction of the vineyard symbolized God's judgment of Israel. The allusion to Isaiah reminds the hearers and readers of the parable of Israel's sin and God's just response. This suggests the transfer of the vineyard (kingdom) to a new people pictures the transfer of the kingdom of God from national Israel to Jesus's disciples, composed of both believing Jews and Gentiles.

The truths of the parable discovered so far may be summarized this way:

1. God loved Israel and appointed spiritual leaders over her to ensure that her people produced works that expressed a proper relationship with God.
2. Israel's leaders neglected their duty and violently persecuted the OT prophets that called them to repentance. Nevertheless, God patiently sent one prophet after another.
3. God finally sent his Son to Israel. Shockingly, Israel's leaders rejected Jesus and executed him.
4. God would transfer the kingdom from Israel to a new people, Jesus's followers, who would properly express repentance before God.

Admittedly, the parable contains some truths this examination missed. For example, the use of the "stone" prophecy to describe the son is probably related to a wordplay since in Jesus's original Aramaic the words for "stone" and "son" rhymed and differed by only one letter.[329] This highlights the importance of the "son" in the parable and confirms that the son refers to the Messiah, Jesus. Still, although other steps could be taken to gain a fuller understanding of the parable, these are sufficient to glean the most important

[329] John the Baptist employs the same word play in Matt 3:9.

truths. Carefully following these steps is certain to shed new light on some of Jesus's most important teachings.

STUDY QUESTIONS

1. Name the work from which this quote is taken: "On the eve of Passover they hanged Jesus the Nazarene."
2. From where is this quote taken? "Therefore, to squelch the rumor, Nero created scapegoats and subjected to the most refined tortures those whom the common people called 'Christians.'"
3. From where is this quote taken, and what is the special name assigned to it? "At this time there was a wise man who was called Jesus. And his conduct was good, and he was known to be virtuous."
4. What are three contemporary portrayals of Jesus that prefer extrabiblical sources over the canonical Gospels?
5. According to the authors, what are the dates for Jesus's birth and death, and what, according to the authors, is a critical datum for dating Jesus's death?
6. What is a critical datum for dating Jesus's birth?
7. What is a simple definition of the "Criterion of Multiple Attestation"?
8. What is a simple definition of the "Criterion of Dissimilarity"?
9. Where do critical scholars assign the burden of proof regarding the authenticity of Jesus material in the Gospels?
10. What are the two major possibilities regarding the relationship among the Gospels?
11. In what order were the Gospels written, according to the Augustinian hypothesis?
12. In what order were the Gospels written, according to the two-Gospel hypothesis?
13. In what order were the Gospels written, according to the Markan priority view?
14. What is the two-document hypothesis?
15. What is Q?
16. List the steps for interpretation of a Gospel pericope.
17. List the steps for the interpretation of a parable.

FOR FURTHER STUDY

Jesus

Beilby, J. K., and P. R. Rhodes, *The Historical Jesus: Five Views*. Downers Grove, IL: IVP Academic, 2009.

Bock, D. L. *Jesus According to Scripture: Restoring the Portrait from the Gospels*. Downers Grove, IL: InterVarsity, 2002.

__________. *Studying the Historical Jesus: A Guide to Sources and Methods*. Grand Rapids, IL: Baker, 2002.

Bock, D. L., and G. J. Herrick, eds. *Jesus in Context: Background Readings for Gospel Study*. Grand Rapids, MI: Baker, 2005.

Bock, D. L., and B. I. Simpson. *Jesus the God-Man: The Unity and Diversity of the Gospel Portrayals*. Grand Rapids, MI: Baker, 2016.

Bowman, R., J. E. Komoszewski, and R. M. Bowman Jr. *Putting Jesus in His Place: The Case for the Deity of Christ.* Grand Rapids, MI: Kregel, 2007.

Brown, C. "Historical Jesus, Quest of." Pages 326–41 in *Dictionary of Jesus and the Gospels.* Edited by J. B. Green, S. McKnight, and I. H. Marshall. Downers Grove, IL: InterVarsity, 1992.

Dunn, J. D. G. *Jesus Remembered.* Christianity in the Making 1. Grand Rapids, MI: Eerdmans, 2003.

Dunn, J. D. G., and S. McKnight, eds. *The Historical Jesus in Recent Research.* Sources for Biblical and Theological Study. Winona Lake, IN: Eisenbrauns, 2005.

Eddy, P. R., and G. A. Boyd. *The Jesus Legend: A Case for the Historical Reliability of the Synoptic Tradition.* Grand Rapids, MI: Baker, 2007.

Evans, C. A. *Fabricating Jesus: How Modern Scholars Distort the Gospels.* Downers Grove, IL: InterVarsity, 2006.

________. "Jesus in Non-Christian Sources." Pages 364–68 in *Dictionary of Jesus and the Gospels.* Edited by J. B. Green, S. McKnight, and I. H. Marshall. Downers Grove, IL: InterVarsity, 1992.

Harris, M. H. *Jesus as God: The New Testament Use of* Theos *in Reference to Jesus.* Grand Rapids, MI: Baker, 1992.

Hoehner, H. W. *Chronological Aspects of the Life of Christ.* Grand Rapids, MI: Zondervan, 1977.

________. "Chronology." Pages 118–22 in *Dictionary of Jesus and the Gospels.* Edited by J. B. Green, S. McKnight, and I. H. Marshall. Downers Grove, IL: InterVarsity, 1992.

Keener, Craig. *The Historical Jesus of the Gospels.* Grand Rapids, MI: Eerdmans, 2009.

Köstenberger, M. E. *Jesus and the Feminists: Who Do They Say That He Is?* Wheaton, IL: Crossway, 2008.

Levine, A.-J., D. C. Allison Jr., and J. D. Crossan, eds. *The Historical Jesus in Context.* Princeton Readings in Religions. Princeton, NJ: Princeton University Press, 2006.

Meier, J. P. *A Marginal Jew.* 3 vols. New York, NY: Doubleday, 1991, 1994, 2001.

Powell, M. A. *Jesus as a Figure in History: How Modern Historians View the Man from Galilee.* 2nd ed. Louisville, KY: Westminster John Knox, 2013.

Schlatter, A. *Do We Know Jesus?* Translated by A. J. Köstenberger and R. W. Yarbrough. Grand Rapids, MI: Kregel, 2005 [1938].

Schweitzer, A. *The Quest of the Historical Jesus.* Translated by J. Bowden. Minneapolis, MN: Fortress, 2001 [1910].

Stein, R. H. *The Method and Message of Jesus' Teachings.* Louisville, KY: Westminster John Knox, 1978.

Van Voorst, R. E. *Jesus Outside the New Testament: An Introduction to the Ancient Evidence.* Grand Rapids, MI: Eerdmans, 2000.

Wilkins, M. J., and J. P. Moreland, eds. *Jesus Under Fire.* Grand Rapids, MI: Zondervan, 1995.

Witherington, B., III. *The Jesus Quest: The Third Search for the Jew of Nazareth.* Downers Grove, IL: InterVarsity, 1995.

Wright, N. T. *Jesus and the Victory of God.* Christian Origins and the Question of God 2. Minneapolis, MN: Fortress, 1996.

__________. *The Resurrection of the Son of God.* Christian Origins and the Question of God 3. Minneapolis, MN: Fortress, 2003.

The Gospels

Bauckham, R. *Jesus and the Eyewitnesses: The Gospels as Eyewitness Testimony*. Grand Rapids, MI: Eerdmans, 2006.

Bauckham, R., ed. *The Gospels for All Christians: Rethinking the Gospel Audiences*. Grand Rapids, MI: Eerdmans, 1997.

Black, D. A. *Why Four Gospels? The Historical Origins of the Gospels*. Grand Rapids, MI: Kregel, 2001.

Black, D. A., and D. R. Beck, eds. *Rethinking the Synoptic Problem*. Grand Rapids, MI: Baker, 2001.

Blomberg, C. L. *Interpreting the Parables*. 2nd ed. Downers Grove, IL: IVP Academic, 2012.

__________. *The Historical Reliability of the Gospels*. 2nd ed. Downers Grove, IL: InterVarsity, 2007.

Bock, D. L., and R. L. Webb, eds. *Key Events in the Life of the Historical Jesus: A Collaborative Exploration of Context and Coherence*. Wissenschaftliche Untersuchungen zum Neuen Testament 247. Tübingen, Germany: Mohr Siebeck, 2009.

Burridge, R. A. *What Are the Gospels? A Comparison with Graeco-Roman Biography*. 2nd ed. Grand Rapids, MI: Eerdmans, 2004.

Carlson, S. C. *The Gospel Hoax: Morton Smith's Invention of Secret Mark*. Waco, TX: Baylor University Press, 2005.

Dungan, D. L. *A History of the Synoptic Problem: The Canon, the Text, the Composition, and the Interpretation of the Gospels*. Anchor Bible. New York, NY: Doubleday, 1999.

France, R. T. "The Authenticity of the Sayings of Jesus." Pages 101–41 in *History, Criticism, and Faith*. Edited by Colin Brown. Downers Grove, IL: InterVarsity, 1976.

France, R. T., D. Wenham, and C. Blomberg, eds. *Gospel Perspectives*. 6 vols. Sheffield, PA: JSOT, 1980–1986.

Goodacre, M. *The Case Against Q: Studies in Markan Priority and the Synoptic Problem*. Harrisburg, PA: Trinity Press International, 2002.

Green, J. B. *How to Read the Gospels and Acts*. Downers Grove, IL: InterVarsity, 1987.

Green, J. B., S. McKnight, and I. H. Marshall, eds. *Dictionary of Jesus and the Gospels*. Downers Grove, IL: InterVarsity, 1992.

Hays, R. B. *Reading Backwards: Figural Christology and the Fourfold Gospel Witness*. Waco, TX: Baylor University Press, 2014.

Head, P. M. *Christology and the Synoptic Problem: An Argument for Markan Priority*. Society for New Testament Studies Monograph 94. Cambridge, UK: Cambridge University Press, 1997.

Hengel, M. *The Four Gospels and the One Gospel of Jesus Christ*. Harrisburg, PA: Trinity Press, 2000.

__________. *Studies in the Gospel of Mark*. Philadelphia, PA: Fortress, 1985.

Linnemann, E. *Is There a Synoptic Problem? Rethinking the Literary Dependence of the First Three Gospels*. Translated by R. W. Yarbrough. Grand Rapids, MI: Baker, 1992.

Marsh, S. *Jesus and the Gospels*. 3rd ed. T&T Clark Approaches to Biblical Studies. New York, NY: Bloomsbury T&T Clark, 2015.

McKnight, S. *Interpreting the Synoptic Gospels*. Guides to New Testament Exegesis 2. Grand Rapids, MI: Baker, 1988.

Pennington, J. T. *Reading the Gospels Wisely: A Narrative and Theological Introduction*. Grand Rapids, MI: Baker, 2012.

Porter, S. E., ed. *Reading the Gospels Today*. McMaster New Testament Studies. Grand Rapids, MI: Eerdmans, 2004.

Porter, S. E., and B. R. Dyer, eds. *The Synoptic Problem: Four Views*. Grand Rapids, MI: Baker, 2016.

Roberts, M. D. *Can We Trust the Gospels? Investigating the Reliability of Matthew, Mark, Luke, and John*. Wheaton, IL: Crossway, 2007.

Snodgrass, K. R. *Stories with Intent: A Comprehensive Guide to the Parables of Jesus*. Grand Rapids, MI: Eerdmans, 2008.

Stein, R. H. "Synoptic Problem." Pages 784–92 in *Dictionary of Jesus and the Gospels*. Edited by J. B. Green, S. McKnight, and I. H. Marshall. Downers Grove, IL: InterVarsity, 1992.

___________. *The Synoptic Problem: An Introduction*. Grand Rapids, MI: Baker, 1987.

___________. *Studying the Synoptic Gospels: Origin and Interpretation*. Grand Rapids, MI: Baker, 2001.

Strauss, M. *Four Portraits, One Jesus: A Survey of Jesus and the Gospels*. Grand Rapids, MI: Zondervan, 2007.

Streeter, B. H. *The Four Gospels: A Study of Origins, Treating of the Manuscript Tradition, Sources, Authorship and Dates*. London, UK: Macmillan, 1924.

Stuhlmacher, P., ed. *The Gospel and the Gospels*. Grand Rapids, MI: Eerdmans, 1991.

Wenham, J. *Redating Matthew, Mark, and Luke: A Fresh Assault on the Synoptic Problem*. Downers Grove, IL: InterVarsity, 1992.

Wiarda, T. J. *Interpreting Gospel Narratives: Scenes, People, and Theology*. Nashville, TN: B&H Academic, 2010.

Williams, M. C. *Two Gospels from One: A Comprehensive Text-Critical Analysis of the Synoptic Gospels*. Grand Rapids, MI: Kregel, 2006.

Chapter 4

The Gospel According to Matthew

CORE KNOWLEDGE

Basic Knowledge: Students should know the key facts of Matthew's Gospel. With regard to history, students should be able to identify the Gospel's author, date, provenance, destination, and purpose. With regard to literature, they should be able to provide a basic outline of the book and identify core elements of the book's content found in the Unit-by-Unit discussion below. With regard to theology, students should be able to identify Matthew's major theological themes.

Intermediate Knowledge: Students should be able to present the arguments for historical, literary, and theological conclusions. With regard to history, students should be able to discuss the evidence for Matthean authorship, date, provenance, destination, and purpose. With regard to literature, they should be able to provide a detailed outline of the book. With regard to theology, students should be able to discuss Matthew's major theological themes and the ways in which they uniquely contribute to the NT canon.

Advanced Knowledge: Students should be able to discuss whether Matthew's Gospel was originally written in Hebrew or Aramaic, to compare Matthew and Mark's structure, and to interact critically with alternative proposals regarding Matthew's structure and the role of the five discourses. In addition, students should be able to discuss the function of the fulfillment quotations and the Great Commission in Matthew's Gospel.

KEY FACTS

Author:	Matthew
Date:	AD 50s or 60s
Provenance:	Unknown
Destination:	Jewish audience in unknown location
Purpose:	To demonstrate that Jesus is the Messiah predicted in the OT
Theme:	Jesus is Immanuel, the Messiah, and the Savior of God's people
Key Verses:	16:13–20

INTRODUCTION

IT IS LITTLE wonder that Matthew's Gospel quickly became the favorite Gospel of the early church. Matthew's Gospel is one of only two Gospels written directly by one of the twelve disciples, and it is also richly theological with a great emphasis on such truths as Jesus's identity as the virgin-born Immanuel. With its frequent citations of the OT, Matthew's Gospel emphasizes Jesus's fulfillment of God's messianic promises.

It is no accident that lists of Gospel books and collections of Gospel texts in the early church consistently place Matthew first, despite differences in the ordering of the other Gospels.[1] It provided a connecting link between the OT and the NT. Matthew's Gospel is also a remarkable piece of literature. Matthew communicated his message not only through explicit statements but also through his structure, literary devices, and *gematria*.

Although modern scholars tend to prefer Mark to the other NT Gospels based on the opinion that it was the earliest to be written, Matthew was the favorite Gospel of the early church. R. T. France wrote, "It is a fact that mainstream Christianity was, from the early second century on, to a great extent Matthean Christianity."[2] Matthew's Gospel contains rich material on Jesus's infancy, the Sermon on the Mount (only partially paralleled in Luke), and a valuable collection of Jesus's parables.

Moreover, Matthew's Gospel demonstrates with special clarity that Jesus's death was sacrificial and that he rescued his disciples from the penalty for their sins. Thus, it is no

---

[1] R. V. G. Tasker (*The Gospel According to St. Matthew*, TNTC [London, UK: Tyndale, 1961], 15–16) pointed out that this is probably due to more than a conviction that Matthew's Gospel was the first to be written. The priority of Matthew in the canon was inspired by the conviction that Matthew formed an appropriate bridge between the Testaments. For rare deviations in order, see Tertullian, Adv. Marc. 4.2, 5 and the Synopsis of the OT and NT attributed to John Chrysostom. R. T. France, *Matthew: Evangelist and Teacher* (Grand Rapids MI: Zondervan, 1989), 13n3.

[2] France, *Matthew: Evangelist and Teacher*, 16.

surprise that E. Renan identified Matthew's Gospel as the most important book ever written.[3] Careful study of Matthew uncovers a message of such theological depth and literary artistry as to convince the reader that Renan's assessment was hardly an exaggeration.

HISTORY

Author

Like the other canonical Gospels, Matthew is formally anonymous, since the author did not explicitly identify himself in the body of the book. However, the title that ascribes the Gospel to Matthew is clearly early if not original.[4] The title would have been necessary to distinguish one Gospel from the others when the four Gospels began to circulate as a single collection. Especially if the author were aware of an earlier Gospel and used it in the composition of his own work as most scholars suspect, he may have felt that a title was necessary to distinguish his book from the earlier writing (Mark, on the assumption of Markan priority). Although D. Allison suggested the ascription to Matthew may date as early as AD 125, he argued that the title *KATA MATHTHAION* ("According to Matthew") is not indisputable evidence of Matthew's authorship of the Gospel since other titles appear in the manuscript tradition.[5] But since all variations of the title of the Gospel in the early manuscripts ascribe it to Matthew, the early titles remain important evidence regarding the identity of the author.

The earliest external evidence—that is, evidence derived not from the document itself (internal evidence) but from sources outside the Gospel like attributions of authorship by the early church fathers—is from a statement of Papias, bishop of Hierapolis, in his *Expositions of the Lord's Sayings*.[6] Papias's testimony is especially significant because he claims to have received his information directly from those who personally heard Jesus's closest disciples,

---

[3] L. Morris, *The Gospel According to Matthew*, PNTC (Grand Rapids, MI: Eerdmans, 1992), 1.

[4] M. Hengel argued that the Gospels have always had their headings and that "according to" *(kata)* implies authorship. See Hengel, *The Four Gospels and the One Gospel of Jesus Christ: An Investigation of the Collection and Origin of the Canonical Gospels*, trans. J. Bowden (Harrisburg, PA: Trinity Press International, 2000), 48–53, 77. Compare with France, *Matthew: Evangelist and Teacher*, 50–80; and the discussion of objections to Hengel's proposal in D. A. Carson and D. J. Moo, *An Introduction to the New Testament*, 2nd ed. (Grand Rapids, MI: Zondervan, 2005), 141–42.

[5] W. D. Davies and D. C. Allison Jr., *Matthew*, ICC (London, UK: T&T Clark, 1988–1997), 1:8.

[6] Papias's works have not survived but are quoted by Eusebius of Caesarea in his *Ecclesiastical History* from the early fourth century. Although many scholars date Papias's original work to 130–140 (based on a statement of Philip Sidetes who wrote in the early fifth century), Eusebius, who wrote 100 years earlier and was generally more reliable than Philip, stated that Papias was well-known during the time of Ignatius (ca. 35–110) and Polycarp (ca. 69–155). Moreover, Eusebius recounted the testimony of Papias that precedes his description of Christian persecution under Trajan between 98 and 117. This suggests that Papias's testimony dates most likely to the early second century. See especially the discussion in R. Gundry, *Matthew: A Commentary on His Handbook for a Mixed Church Under Persecution*, 2nd ed. (Grand Rapids, MI: Eerdmans, 1994), 610–11, who argued that Philip depended on Eusebius for his information about Papias but garbled the testimony of his source. For an excellent examination of evidence for both the late and early dating of Papias with a defense of the early dating and a discussion of its implications for Gospel research, see R. W. Yarbrough, "The Date of Papias: A Reassessment," *JETS* 26 (1983): 181–91.

including Matthew.[7] Irenaeus (ca. 130–200) claimed that Papias was a disciple of the apostle John who had direct access to John's testimony regarding the early years of the Christian church.[8] Papias wrote, "Therefore, on the one hand Matthew arranged in order the sayings in the Hebrew dialect; on the other hand, each translated these as he was able."[9]

Most scholars dispute Papias's claim that the Gospel was first written in Hebrew. Consequently, many doubt the reliability of other elements of his description such as the claim that Matthew wrote the Gospel. Most scholars believe that Matthew's Gospel utilized accounts from Mark's Gospel, and they doubt that an apostle and eyewitness like Matthew would have chosen to rely on the work of a non-apostle like Mark. However, even if Papias and other early church fathers were wrong about the original language of Matthew's Gospel, this does not necessarily mean they were mistaken regarding the identity of the author.[10] Also, Matthew's role as an apostle would not make his use of Mark's Gospel implausible, especially since the early church recognized Mark's Gospel as a transcription of Peter's reminiscences of Jesus's life and Peter was the recognized leader of the Twelve.

After carefully reviewing two recent extensive treatments of Papias's account, D. Allison correctly observes, "In light of the general considerations adduced and of the work of Kennedy and Kürzinger, the simplistic understanding of Papias which dismisses him out of hand must be questioned if not abandoned."[11] The early church unanimously affirmed that the Gospel was authored by the apostle Matthew. This view was not seriously challenged until the late nineteenth century.

Clues from the Gospel itself (internal evidence) tend to confirm the early church's ascription to Matthew. Based on the internal evidence of the Gospel, most scholars recognize that the author was a Jewish Christian. Although the internal evidence is not specific enough to trace the identity of the author, it is compatible with and suggestive of Matthean authorship as affirmed by Papias. First, Matthew affirmed that the tax collector named "Levi" whom Jesus appointed to be one of the Twelve (see Mark 2:14; Luke 5:27) was also called "Matthew" (Matt 9:9). Matthew, a Hebrew name meaning "gift of Yahweh" or "gift of the Lord," appears to be the apostolic name Jesus gave to the tax collector after he chose to follow

---

[7] See the discussion in Gundry, *Matthew*, 611–17. For the argument that Papias had actually heard the teachings of two eyewitnesses to Jesus's ministry, see R. Bauckham, *Jesus and the Eyewitnesses: The Gospels as Eyewitness Testimony* (Grand Rapids, MI: Eerdmans, 2006), 12–38.

[8] Irenaeus, *Against Heresies* 5.33.4.

[9] Eusebius, *Eccl. Hist.* 3.39. Our translation.

[10] This does not mean to suggest that Papias *was* likely wrong, however. For a defense of Papias, see C. L. Blomberg (*Matthew*, NAC 22 [Nashville, TN: B&H, 1992], 40), with reference to R. Glover, "Patristic Quotations and Gospel Sources," *NTS* 31 (1985): 234–51; A. C. Perumalil, "Are Not Papias and Irenaeus Competent to Report on the Gospels?" *ExpTim* 91 (1980): 332–37; and G. Howard, *The Gospel of Matthew According to a Primitive Hebrew Text* (Macon, GA: Mercer University Press, 1987). Compare with D. A. Hagner (*Matthew 1–13*, WBC 33A [Dallas, TX: Word, 1993], xliii–xlvi), who suggested that Matthew may have collected Jesus's sayings in Aramaic or perhaps even the body of Jesus's teachings in the form of five major discourses, which is one of Matthew's most distinctive contributions.

[11] Davies and Allison, *Matthew*, 1:16.

Christ. This is much like the way Jesus renamed Simon "Peter" (John 1:42; reaffirmed in Matt 16:18). The use of the name here may be Matthew's personal touch.

Some scholars have explained this feature as a mark of pseudonymity.[12] But an examination of other pseudepigrapha suggests that an author seeking to gain credibility for his work by attributing it to an apostle would likely have focused more attention on that apostle in his Gospel than the Gospel of Matthew does. Matthew is mentioned in this Gospel only twice (9:9; 10:3). The Gospel does not describe Matthew as the recipient of special revelations in either reference. They simply refer to his call to discipleship and name him as one of the twelve apostles. These brief references are not likely a mark of pseudonymity.

Second, in the discussion of the payment of the imperial taxes (Matt 22:15–22), Mark and Luke both used the Greek term *denarion*, but Matthew also included the more precise term *nomisma* ("state coin"). The use of more precise terminology in referring to currency may suggest the expertise of a former tax collector.[13] Similarly, among the Gospels only Matthew includes the pericope about Jesus and Peter paying the temple tax (17:24–27). Although this evidence is inconclusive, it does lend support to the strong tradition of authorship preserved by the early church. Based on the impressive external and internal evidence for Matthean authorship, modern readers may confidently affirm Matthew's authorship of this Gospel and recognize it as a testimony to the life of Jesus written by both an eyewitness and an apostle.[14]

Date

Internal Evidence Most contemporary NT scholars date the Gospel of Matthew to the mid- to late 80s.[15] R. Schnackenburg gives the rationale for this late date:

> Matthew wrote after the Jewish War and the destruction of Jerusalem (22:7). The break with Judaism, which had become strong under the leadership of

[12] E.g., G. D. Kilpatrick, *The Origins of the Gospel of Matthew* (London, UK: Oxford University Press, 1946), 138.

[13] D. Guthrie, *New Testament Introduction*, rev. ed. (Downers Grove, IL: InterVarsity, 1990), 52–53.

[14] In our affirmation of Matthean authorship, we go against the prevailing winds of scholarship that prompt commentators to reject the apostle Matthew as author of this Gospel or at least to limit his role in the process. E.g., R. Bauckham's rejection of Matthean authorship led him to neglect Matthew's Gospel almost completely in his otherwise excellent work *Jesus and the Eyewitnesses*; and U. Luz (*Matthew 1–7*, Continental Commentary [Minneapolis, MN: Fortress, 1989], 94–95) also rejected Matthean authorship—though he also noted that Matthew as the author is too flippantly dismissed and evidence for Matthean authorship ignored with "gratuitous silence." More cautious were Davies and Allison (*Matthew*, 1:7–58), who did not explicitly reject Matthew as the author but who nonetheless could muster only the minimalistic conclusion that the author was Jewish and whose preference for a date between 80 and 95 seemed to all but preclude Matthean authorship. C. S. Keener (*A Commentary on the Gospel of Matthew* [Grand Rapids, MI: Eerdmans, 1999], 40), who at one time rejected Matthean authorship but who rethought his view while writing his commentary and "presently [is] inclined to accept the possibility of Matthean authorship on some level, although with admitted uncertainty," viewed as the most probable scenario "the presence of at least a significant deposit of Matthean tradition in this Gospel, edited by the sort of Matthean school scholars have often suggested." Hagner (*Matthew 1–13*, xliii–xlvi) suggested that Matthew may have been responsible for the collection of the major discourses of the Gospel not contained in Mark or that Matthew collected the sayings now known as "Q."

[15] See the discussion in Keener, *Commentary on the Gospel of Matthew*, 42–44.

> the Pharisaic scribes, had occurred (see 27:25; 10:17; 23:34). The tension with these circles who now lived according to the strict interpretation of the law is discernible (see chap. 23), and the self-awareness of the church as the true "people of God" has been reinforced (21:43). Accordingly, the composition of this work is to be dated around A.D. 85–90.[16]

Schnackenburg assumes that Jesus's reference to the fall of Jerusalem in Matthew 22:7 was not possible unless the fall of Jerusalem had already occurred. This assumption is based on the modernist presupposition that Jesus was incapable of predicting the future. Since Jesus "predicted" the fall of Jerusalem in Matthew 24:2 and elsewhere, some scholars argue that Matthew must have written this "prediction" after this event *(vaticinium ex eventu)* and deceptively presented it to his readers as "prophecy." J. Nolland recently challenged this assumption:

> NT critical scholarship has a curious capacity to identify as "genuine" prophecy that which failed to be fulfilled and, all too often, to insist that fulfilled prophecy is only after-the-event description dressed up as prophecy. . . . The possibility of "touched up" prophecy is quite real, but to base the dating of Matthew on an assumption that the text could not have spoken so confidently of the coming judgment on Jerusalem and the temple if these had not already taken place represents an uncalled-for imposition.[17]

If one believes Jesus was capable of predictive prophecy (and abundant evidence supports this conviction), a date prior to AD 70 is plausible.

Schnackenburg also claims that references to strong tensions between Jews and Christians in Matthew implied a complete break of the church from the synagogue. He listed AD 85 as the earliest possible date for the Gospel since this was the approximate time that the curse against heretics was added to the Eighteen Benedictions *(Shemoneh Esreh)* of the Jewish *Tefillah*, a prayer to be recited by faithful Jews three times a day. The Twelfth Benediction is called the *Birkath ha-minim* or "Curses against the Heretics" and says,

> And for apostates let there be no hope; and may the insolent kingdom be quickly uprooted, in our days. And may the *notsrim* and the *minim* perish quickly; and may they be erased from the Book of Life and may they not be inscribed with the righteous. Blessed are you, Lord, who humbles the insolent.[18]

---

[16] R. Schnackenburg, *The Gospel of Matthew*, trans. R. R. Barr (Grand Rapids, MI: Eerdmans, 2002), 6. See the summary and critique in Carson and Moo, *Introduction to the New Testament*, 152–56.

[17] Nolland, *Matthew*, 14. Nolland did not affirm a pre-70 date for Matthew out of a desire to defend Matthean authorship, which he rejected. Nolland argued that Jesus's prophecy contained exaggerations that were not completely and literally satisfied through the events surrounding the fall of Jerusalem and that Matthew would have softened them if he wrote after 70.

[18] Palestinian recension. See P. L. Mayo, "The Role of the *Birkath Haminim* in Early Jewish-Christian Relations: A Reexamination of the Evidence," *BBR* 16 (2006): 325–44.

SIDEBAR 4.1: DID MATTHEW WRITE HIS GOSPEL IN HEBREW?

A close examination of Papias's statement that Matthew "therefore" arranged Jesus's sayings "in the Hebrew dialect" leads to several observations. First, the expression "therefore" closely linked the statement regarding Matthew's authorship of his Gospel to the preceding discussion in Papias. In Eusebius's quotation the statement immediately follows a description of the authorship of Mark's Gospel which mentioned that Mark wrote his Gospel based on Peter's reminiscences of the Lord's ministry but that he did not attempt to provide an ordered arrangement of the teachings of Jesus. If Eusebius quoted Papias in order without skipping any material, the "therefore" links the statement about Matthew's composition to the preceding description about Mark's composition and implies that Matthew wrote his Gospel to provide an account characterized by the order that Mark's Gospel lacked. If so, Papias's statement implies that Mark's Gospel was written first and that Matthew wrote later, possibly utilizing pericopes from Mark but giving them a new order.[1] Moreover, such a connection would indicate that the account of the composition of Matthew, like the account regarding the composition of Mark, was attributed by Papias to a still earlier source called "the elder," most likely John the elder.[2] According to other statements by Papias quoted in Eusebius, this elder was at least an eyewitness of Jesus's ministry, a bearer of important traditions in the early church, and likely the apostle John, son of Zebedee.[3]

Second, Papias claimed that Matthew wrote his Gospel "in the Hebrew dialect."[4] Recently some scholars have argued that Papias's language merely implies that Matthew wrote "in the Semitic style of composition."[5] Others have contended that the context strongly implies that Matthew actually wrote his Gospel in either the Hebrew or Aramaic language.[6] Many modern scholars have disputed Papias's testimony regarding the authorship of Matthew. They have argued that Papias was clearly wrong about the

[1] Gundry, *Matthew*, 614. Bauckham (*Jesus and the Eyewitnesses*, 222) suggested that Eusebius may have omitted material with which he disagreed. But the several verbal parallels between the statements regarding Mark and Matthew suggest a close relationship between the two statements. Unfortunately, only a new discovery of this portion of Papias's work would indicate the precise relationship between the two statements.

[2] Eusebius, *Eccl. Hist.* 3.39.14–16. See J. Kürzinger, *Papias von Hierapolis und die Evangelien des Neuen Testaments* (Regensburg, Germany: Pustet, 1983), 45.

[3] A. J. Köstenberger and S. O. Stout, "The Disciple Jesus Loved: Witness, Author, Apostle: A Response to Richard Bauckham's *Jesus and the Eyewitnesses*," *BBR* 18 (2008): 209–31.

[4] Other church fathers also described Matthew as originally writing in Hebrew, including Irenaeus (ca. AD 130–200; *Against Heresies* 3.1.1), Pantaenus (died ca. 190), Origen (ca. 185–254; *Commentary on the Gospel of John* 1.6; 6.32), Eusebius (ca. 260–340; *Eccl. Hist.* 3.24.6), Cyril of Jerusalem (ca. 315–387; *Catecheses* 14), Epiphanius (ca. 315–403; *Against Heresies* 2.1.51), Jerome (ca. 345–420; Prologue in *Commentary on Matthew Book IV*), and Augustine (354–430; *Harmony of the Gospels* 1.2.4). For a more complete list of references, see Davies and Allison, *Matthew*, 1:8–9.

[5] Kürzinger, *Papias von Hierapolis*, 9–24. Gundry (*Matthew*, 619–20) posited a similar view (relying in part on preliminary research published by Kürzinger in 1960) and equated Hebrew style with midrashic style.

[6] This is implied especially by the combination of the noun *dialektos* ("language") and the verb *hermeneuō* ("translate"). For a succinct discussion of some of the relevant linguistic data, see C. A. Evans, "Hebrew Matthew," in *Dictionary of New Testament Background*, 463–64.

original language of the Gospel since the Greek of Matthew does not appear to be translation Greek. Some scholars who affirm Markan priority question whether an author would have utilized Mark's Greek Gospel at all in producing a Hebrew or Aramaic Gospel. They further argue that if Papias were wrong about the original language of the Gospel, he was likely incorrect about the author as well. Many scholars dismiss Papias's claim regarding Matthean authorship because they view an apostle's reliance on a Gospel written by a nonapostle as inconceivable.[7]

However, the excellent Greek of Matthew could have been produced by a skilled translator of an original Hebrew text. Allison noted that many of the early church fathers who affirmed Matthew's authorship of a Hebrew Gospel were native Greek speakers who knew Greek better than most, if not all, modern scholars and were in a better position to determine whether the Greek Gospel could have been a translation of a Hebrew original.[8] Moreover, hints of Hebraic influence appear in this Gospel, suggesting that Papias could have been correct about a Hebrew original. Many commentators, for example, believe that the emphasis on the number 14 in Matt 1:17 is due to *gematria* (numerical symbolism) in which 14 is the numerical equivalent of the Hebrew name *David*.[9] Yet the *gematria* works only in Hebrew since the Greek transliteration of the name "David" has a different numeric value. The onomastic play on the name *Jesus* ("Yahweh saves") in Matt 1:21, with the explanation "because he will save his people from their sins," likewise, works only in Hebrew, not in Greek (see also Matt 1:23).

Such texts make a Hebrew/Aramaic original of the Gospel plausible despite the high quality of the Greek in the extant version. Since Aramaic quickly ceased to be the language of the early church as the church expanded into Gentile territories and this required the Gospel to circulate in Greek translation, the absence of ancient Hebrew/Aramaic texts of Matthew is not surprising.

Nevertheless, other evidence speaks against the theory that Matthew's Gospel was originally penned in Hebrew or Aramaic. As Carson and Moo note, the numerous OT quotations in Matthew do not reflect a single text form.[10] The lack of uniformity of text forms in Matthew's OT citations may suggest an author who wrote in Greek but knew Hebrew and thus was able to vary the form of his quotes. Also, if Matthew wrote after Mark (as many believe), it is unlikely that Matthew's Gospel, while using Mark's Gospel, was first written in Hebrew or Aramaic. Third, to some at least, the Greek text of Matthew's Gospel does not read as if it were the product of translation from Hebrew or Aramaic (though others disagree). Fortunately, while vigorously debated among scholars, the question of a Hebrew or Aramaic original of Matthew's Gospel is of little (if any) doctrinal consequence and has yet to be settled conclusively.[11]

---

[7] E.g., the arguments adduced against Matthean authorship in J. Nolland, *The Gospel of Matthew*, NIGTC (Grand Rapids, MI: Eerdmans, 2005), 3.

[8] Davies and Allison, *Matthew*, 1:12.

[9] The name *David* in the consonantal Hebrew text is made up of the three letters *daleth*, *waw*, and *daleth*. Since *daleth* is the fourth letter in the Hebrew alphabet (as "d" is in the English), and *waw* is the sixth letter, 4 + 6 + 4 = 14.

[10] Carson and Moo, *Introduction to the New Testament*, 143–44.

[11] See ibid., 102: "All in all, the hypothesis of an earlier, Semitic-language edition of Matthew cannot certainly be either proven or disproven."

However, even if this Twelfth Benediction was focused on Christians (which is possible but far from certain), this does not support the claim that frequent references to Jewish persecution of Christians in Matthew require a post-85 date for the Gospel. Such a conclusion fails to take into account the references to Jewish persecution of believers in the book of Acts very early in the history of the church, which demonstrate that intense anti-Christian persecution occurred and prompted some Christians to separate from the synagogue half a century before AD 85.

Schnackenburg also suggests that the belief that the disciples of Jesus constituted the true people of God requires a late date for the Gospel. He specifically cited Matthew 21:43 as evidence. This passage teaches that the kingdom of God will be taken from the Jewish leaders and be entrusted to others who produce the fruits of the kingdom. But this affirmation coheres with NT teaching elsewhere (see Acts 13:46; 18:5–6; 1 Pet 2:9).

Jesus's selection of twelve disciples is one of the deeds of Christ that has been verified by historical Jesus research.[19] The selection of twelve disciples expresses Jesus's intention to build a new Israel from a faithful remnant. The assumption that Christians began to regard themselves as the true people of God only in the final decades of the first century is simply false and is poor evidence for a late Matthean date.

External Evidence External evidence requires a first-century date of composition. Although it is possible the authors of John's Gospel and 1 Peter may have known Matthew's Gospel, the earliest definite allusions to Matthew appear in the writings of Ignatius (ca. AD 35–110) and the *Didache* (second half of first or early second century).[20] Polycarp (ca. AD 69–155) knew and quoted Matthew in the first half of the second century.[21] The Epistle of Pseudo-Barnabas (ca. AD 135?) quoted Matthew and described the Gospel as inspired Scripture with authority comparable to the OT.[22] The author of the Gospel of Peter also

---

[19] E. P. Sanders, *Jesus and Judaism* (Philadelphia, PA: Fortress, 1991), 98–106; S. McKnight, "Jesus and the Twelve," in *Key Events in the Life of the Historical Jesus: A Collaborative Exploration of Context and Coherence*, ed. D. L. Bock and R. L. Webb, WUNT 247 (Tübingen, Germany: Mohr Siebeck, 2009), 181–214.

[20] E.g., compare Matthew 2 with Ignatius, *To the Ephesians* 19:1–3; Matt 3:15 with Ignatius, *To the Smyrnaeans* 1.1; and Matt 10:16 with Polycarp, *To the Philippians* 2.2. When Ignatius referred to "the Gospel" in *To the Philippians* 5:1–2; 8:2, he was likely referring to Matthew's Gospel. Compare also Matt 6:9–11 with *Didache* 8:2.

[21] Compare Matt 5:3, 10; and Polycarp, *To the Philippians* 2.3. See also C. L. Quarles, "The Use of the Gospel of Thomas in the Research on the Historical Jesus of John Dominic Crossan," *CBQ* 69 (2007): 517–36; and H. Koester, *Synoptische Überlieferung bei den apostolischen Vätern*, TU 65 (Berlin, Germany: Akademie, 1957), 13, 116–18. Some research suggests that the *Didache* may be even earlier. J. P. Audet (*La Didache, Instructions des Apôtres* [Paris, France: Gabalda, 1958]) and M. W. Holmes (*The Apostolic Fathers: Greek Texts and English Translations*, 3rd ed. [Grand Rapids, MI: Baker, 2007], 337–38) suggested that the *Didache* reflects a time closer to Paul and James (both died in the 60s) than Ignatius (died ca. 110). If this date of composition of the *Didache* is correct, this would require a pre-70 date for Matthew's Gospel on the assumption of the *Didache's* dependence upon Matthew, though this is less than conclusive (see the discussion in Holmes, *Apostolic Fathers*, 338).

[22] Compare *Barn.* 4.14 with Matt 24:14.

knew and used Matthew's Gospel, probably in the mid-second century.[23] External evidence alone, however, cannot guide interpreters to a more specific date of composition.

Determining the date of the first Gospel depends largely on the relationship of the Gospels to one another. Most scholars believe that Matthew used Mark's Gospel in writing his.[24] If this is correct, Matthew's Gospel must postdate Mark. But the date of Mark's Gospel is also ambiguous. Irenaeus (ca. AD 130–200) apparently claimed that Mark wrote his Gospel after Peter's death in the mid-60s. Yet Clement of Alexandria (ca. AD 150–215), who wrote only twenty years after Irenaeus, claimed Mark wrote his Gospel while Peter was still alive. Given the ambiguity of the historical evidence concerning a Markan date, a decision must be based on other factors.

The date of composition for Mark is best inferred from the date of Luke-Acts. The abrupt ending of Acts, which leaves Paul under house arrest in Rome, implies that Acts was written before Paul's release. Since one of the major themes of Acts is the legality of Christianity in the Roman Empire, one would have expected Luke to mention Paul's release by the emperor if it had already occurred. This evidence dates Acts to the early AD 60s. Luke and Acts were two volumes of a single work as the prologues to these books demonstrate. Luke was clearly written before Acts (Acts 1:1). Given the amount of research that Luke invested in writing Acts and the travel that eyewitness interviews probably required, a Gospel completion date in the late AD 50s is reasonable. If Luke used Mark in writing his own Gospel, Mark was written sometime before the late AD 50s, perhaps in the early to mid-50s. Thus, if Matthew used Mark's Gospel, Matthew may have written his Gospel anytime beginning in the mid-50s or, perhaps more likely, in the early AD 60s. The earliest historical evidence is consistent with this opinion since Irenaeus (ca. AD 130–200) claimed Matthew wrote his Gospel while Peter and Paul were preaching in Rome (early AD 60s).[25]

Other evidence in Matthew suggests that the Gospel was written before AD 70 when Roman armies destroyed the Jerusalem temple and devastated the Holy City. Matthew 17:24–27 contains Jesus's instruction regarding the payment of the two-drachma temple tax. Jesus taught that his disciples should pay the tax in order to avoid offending fellow Jews. However, after the destruction of the temple, the temple tax was collected by the Romans in order to support the pagan temple of Jupiter Capitolinus in Rome.[26] It is doubtful that Matthew would have included the account in his Gospel at a date at which it would have been interpreted as support for pagan idolatry (see Matt 4:10).[27] Moreover, Jesus taught Peter that although Christian disciples should pay the tax for social reasons, they were not obligated

[23] See C. L. Quarles, "The Gospel of Peter: Does It Contain a Pre-canonical Passion Narrative?," in *The Resurrection of Jesus: John Dominic Crossan and N. T. Wright in Dialogue*, ed. R. Stewart (Minneapolis, MN: Augsburg Fortress, 2006), 106–20, especially 110–18.

[24] See the discussion of Markan priority in the previous chapter.

[25] Irenaeus, *Against Heresies* 3.1.1.

[26] Josephus, *Jewish War* 7.218; Dio Cassius, 65.7.2; Suetonius, *Domitian* 12. Consequently, *m. Sheq.* 8.8 taught that the shekel laws applied only as long as the temple stood.

[27] Gundry, *Matthew*, 606.

to do so since kings demanded taxes from their subjects but not their sons. This implies that Jesus's disciples were sons of the great divine King to whom the taxes were paid. But the same argument after AD 70 might be taken as identifying the disciples as sons of Jupiter, who were exempt from the tax but should pay it to pacify the Romans!

Matthew's special references to sacrifice also make the most sense if written before the fall of Jerusalem. Although Matthew permitted Jewish Christians to offer sacrifices in the temple, he consistently portrayed such sacrifices as gifts that expressed gratitude to God rather than rituals that effected atonement. He further taught that Jesus was the fulfillment of Isaiah 53, the Suffering Servant whose sacrificial death accomplished atonement for sin.[28] Matthew's carefully articulated sacrificial theology and particularly his concern for clarifying the significance of temple offerings fit best with a date of composition before AD 70 when the temple was destroyed and the sacrificial system ended.

Only Matthew contains Jesus's teaching regarding swearing by the temple or its gold (Matt 23:16–22). Such vows meant, "May the temple or related objects be destroyed if I do not fulfill my promise." Obviously, such vows would be meaningless if the temple had already been destroyed. These clues and many others suggest a date for Matthew sometime prior to the destruction of Jerusalem in AD 70.[29]

This early date of Matthew is significant for two reasons. First, an early date is more consistent with Matthean authorship than a late first-century date. Second, an early date tends to confirm the historical reliability of the Gospel accounts. If the accounts of Jesus's life and ministry were transmitted orally for several generations before being written down, some details might have changed during this period of oral transmission. But if Matthew wrote his Gospel within a few decades of Jesus's lifetime while eyewitnesses of Jesus's ministry survived, his Gospel arguably preserves accounts of Jesus's life and teachings that are accurate in detail.

Provenance and Destination

Scholars have proposed a variety of theories regarding possible places of origin for Matthew's Gospel. Suggestions include Jerusalem or Palestine, Caesarea Maritima, Phoenicia, Alexandria, Pella, Edessa, Syria, and Antioch. Allison correctly noted, "Given the nature of the available evidence, it is quite impossible to be fully persuaded on the issue at hand. We shall never know beyond a reasonable doubt where the autograph of Matthew was completed."[30]

The theories of origin that have gained the most scholarly support view the Gospel as written in either Palestine or Syria. The early church fathers who insisted on a Hebrew or Aramaic original for Matthew probably assumed that Matthew wrote his Gospel in

---

[28] See section on theological themes in Matthew.

[29] See the extensive and compelling defense of the early date of Matthew in Gundry (*Matthew*, 599–609), who concluded that Matthew was probably written during the 50s or early 60s.

[30] Davies and Allison, *Matthew*, 1:139.

Palestine. Jerome (ca. AD 345–420) specifically identified Judea as the place of authorship.[31] But the majority of scholars today opt for Syria, more specifically Antioch of Syria, as the place of origin. Several clues support this location. First, Matthew combined both Jewish and Gentile interest, and Antioch had a large Jewish population while also being the hub of Gentile missionary activity. Second, Matthew was first quoted by Ignatius, bishop of Antioch (ca. AD 35–110).

B. H. Streeter appealed to a third line of evidence, which was deemed especially persuasive support for a Syrian provenance by many scholars in the twentieth century. Streeter pointed out that Matthew 17:24–27 describes the official *stater* (an ancient coin of Greek or Lydian origin) as exactly equal to the *didrachmae* or two *drachma* (another ancient Greek coin). He claimed that the only two cities known to have placed this exact value on the *stater* are Antioch and Damascus.[32] Unfortunately, Streeter did not cite any sources to support his claims, and it now appears the claim was incorrect. A *stater* equaled the *didrachmae* in value in several currencies of the ancient world, including the Attic and Ptolemaic currencies.[33]

The questions of the provenance and destination of this Gospel are closely linked. Scholars who accept a Palestinian provenance generally see the church in Palestine as the intended audience. Likewise, scholars who accept a Syrian provenance generally see the church in Syria as the intended audience.

Regardless of one's view, Matthew's Gospel clearly circulated widely soon after its composition. This is demonstrated by the geographical distribution of early quotations of the book that appear in the writings of Ignatius (ca. AD 35–110; Antioch), Polycarp (ca. AD 69–155; Smyrna), Pseudo-Barnabas (ca. AD 135?; possibly Alexandria), Justin Martyr (ca. AD 100–165; Ephesus), and *2 Clement* (probably Alexandria) in the late first or early second century.[34]

Purpose

In part because Matthew's Gospel itself does not include an explicit purpose statement, scholars have suggested a number of possibilities. Some have proposed that Matthew should be read as a theological rather than a historical document. M. Goulder and R. Gundry argue that Matthew belongs to a genre of literature known as "midrash," a non-historical genre that wove together narrative motifs from the OT into an imaginative

---

[31] For a defense of a Palestinian provenance, see J. A. Gibbs, *Matthew 1:1–11:1*, Concordia Commentary (St. Louis, MO: Concordia, 2006), 67.

[32] B. H. Streeter, *The Four Gospels* (London, UK: Macmillan, 1951), 500–523.

[33] U. Luz (*Matthew 1–7* [Minneapolis, MN: Augsburg, 1983], 1:91n184) challenged Streeter's claim.

[34] Koester noted that the early church suggested that the Epistle of Barnabas was composed in Alexandria. But the church based its opinion on the Alexandrian mode of interpretation used in the book. Koester later stated that modern scholars know almost nothing about the provenance of the book (*Introduction to the New Testament: History and Literature of Early Christianity* [Philadelphia, PA: Fortress, 1982], 2:220, 277). Koester dated the Epistle of Barnabas to the end of the first century since in his opinion it did not refer to any NT books.

tale that highlighted Jesus's theological significance.[35] They also claimed that parallels between Matthew's narrative and OT texts indicate that Matthew created stories about Jesus based on scattered OT texts, stories that had no relationship to actual events in Jesus's life. For example, Gundry claims that Matthew had an angel announce Jesus's birth to Joseph through a dream not because such a dream actually occurred but in order to conform Joseph's experience to the famous dreams of his OT namesake, Joseph the patriarch.[36]

Such an analysis of Matthew faces several serious problems. First, the genre of literature to which Goulder and Gundry assign Matthew is not actually "midrash," which simply referred to biblical interpretation, but what Paul described as "Jewish myth" (Titus 1:14). Paul's adamant rejection of such myths (1 Tim 1:4) makes it unlikely that Matthew would have been so freely and widely accepted by early Christians if it truly were a mere "theological tale."[37] Second, midrash critics are frequently guilty of what S. Sandmel called "parallelomania," the tendency to find parallels where there are none or where these are of doubtful merit.[38] These critics analyze similarities between Matthew's narrative and OT texts but fail to account adequately for differences between them. These differences often make Matthew's dependence on a particular text highly unlikely. Finally, classifications of Matthew as midrash fail to appreciate important features of the Gospel which suggest that Matthew intended to write a historical narrative. In particular, Matthew's insistence that certain events in Jesus's life happened in order to fulfill the OT indicates that Matthew wrote a careful record of actual events.[39]

Goulder attempts to combine his assessment of Matthew as midrash with the theory of Matthew as lectionary.[40] He contends that the first-century synagogue used an annual lectionary cycle consisting of prescribed OT readings for each Sabbath. Goulder maintains that Matthew is organized so as to correlate with this lectionary cycle. Goulder argued, for example, that the narrative of Jesus's birth in Matthew was based on the fifth Sabbath lectionary reading (Gen 23–25:18); the visit of the magi on the sixth Sabbath reading (Gen 25:19–28:8); and the slaughter of the innocents on the seventh Sabbath reading (Gen 28:9–31:55).[41] Goulder's thesis has failed to convince most scholars for several reasons. Scholars have not yet determined whether any lectionary cycle was used in the first-century synagogue, much less the one that Goulder proposed. Moreover, Goulder's

---

[35] M. D. Goulder, *Midrash and Lection in Matthew: The Speaker's Lectures in Biblical Studies 1969–71* (London, UK: SPCK, 1974); Gundry, *Matthew*. Gundry's commentary was originally subtitled, "A Commentary on His Literary and Theological Art." For summaries of these two volumes, see C. L. Quarles, *Midrash Criticism: Introduction and Appraisal* (Lanham, MD: University Press of America, 1998), 7–15.

[36] Gundry, *Matthew*, 22.

[37] See C. L. Quarles, "Midrash as Creative Historiography: The Portrait of a Misnomer," *JETS* 39 (1996): 457–64.

[38] S. Sandmel, "Parallelomania," *JBL* 81 (1962): 2–13.

[39] For an analysis of the questionable premises, methodological weaknesses, and tenuous conclusions of midrash criticism, see Quarles, *Midrash Criticism*, 68–103. Compare with the interchange between D. J. Moo and R. H. Gundry in *JETS* 26 (1983): 31–86.

[40] Goulder, *Midrash and Lection*.

[41] For a more thorough summary of Goulder's view, see Quarles, *Midrash Criticism*, 7–9.

own analysis of OT themes in Matthew did more to demonstrate dependence by Matthew on narrative motifs outside of the lectionary readings than in the proposed readings.

Other recent scholars have demonstrated that Matthew's Gospel shares much in common with ancient biographies of revered figures. Matthew is most similar to ancient biographies about the founding figure of a philosophical school. Such biographies demonstrate that the founder was responsible for the insights that defined the movement. They also portrayed the founder as a person whose example was worthy of imitation.[42]

Nolland has suggested that Matthew intended to write an account of Jesus's life that paralleled OT accounts of the lives of key figures in the history of Israel. These OT biographies focused not merely on the human figure but also on God and his dealings with Israel. Nolland stated, "The story of Jesus is told as a continuation—indeed, as some kind of culmination—of the long story of God and his people."[43] He also offered an important qualification to his comparison. Although such OT accounts were designed to link people to a figure from the past, Matthew's concern was to link them to a figure who was still their contemporary, to lead his readers to an encounter with the risen Christ.

Although Matthew did intend to demonstrate that Jesus was the source of the foundational teachings of the church and to commend Jesus's example to his readers, Matthew's primary focus was Jesus's identity. Matthew's Gospel stressed four aspects of Jesus's identity.[44] First, Jesus is the Messiah, the long-awaited King of God's people. Second, Jesus is the new Abraham, the founder of a new spiritual Israel consisting of all people who choose to follow him, including both Jews and Gentiles. Third, Jesus is the new Moses, the deliverer and instructor of God's people. Fourth, Jesus is the Immanuel, the virgin-born Son of God who fulfills the promises of the OT.[45] Thus, although Matthew's Gospel is similar in some ways to ancient biographies, it remains distinct. Matthew was concerned not only to preserve Jesus's teachings, to record his deeds, or to commend his example, but especially to explain who Jesus is. Matthew's Gospel might best be described as a "theological biography," a historical account of Jesus's life and teachings that explains his spiritual significance.

Although the book of Matthew functions primarily as a theological biography, several scholars have pointed out that it has a secondary purpose. The Gospel was written to serve as a manual for discipleship. The subtitle to R. Gundry's massive commentary on Matthew describes the Gospel as a "handbook for a mixed church under persecution." Matthew's topical arrangement of lengthy discourses, his emphasis on the ethical demands of the kingdom of God, and especially the climactic statement regarding teaching new disciples to observe all Jesus commands—all of these combine to offer guidance for Christian living.

---

[42] Nolland, *Matthew*, 19. Compare with the section "Matthew as Biography" in Keener, *Commentary on the Gospel of Matthew*, 16–24.

[43] Nolland, *Matthew*, 19.

[44] See the similar discussion in Carson and Moo, *Introduction to the New Testament*, 158.

[45] For more information on these themes, see Charles L. Quarles, *A Theology of Matthew* (Phillipsburg, NJ: P&R, 2013).

LITERATURE

Literary Plan

Papias's comments regarding the authorship of Matthew's Gospel have already been discussed above. Papias also commented on the literary structure of Matthew's Gospel. According to him, "Matthew arranged in order the sayings [of Jesus]" (Eusebius, *Eccl. Hist.* 3.39). Most likely, Papias meant that Matthew's Gospel had a more orderly arrangement than Mark's. Since Matthew generally shares the same order of pericopes as Mark when the two overlap, Papias probably referred to the fact that Matthew began with a genealogy and an account of Jesus's birth, gave a more thorough treatment of Jesus's postresurrection appearances, and arranged Jesus's teaching into five major sections.[46]

Although portions of Matthew's Gospel are clearly arranged topically, the Gospel follows a general chronological order: genealogy, birth, baptism, Galilean ministry, journey to Jerusalem, trial, crucifixion, and resurrection.[47] In addition to the general chronological arrangement, scholars have observed other markers that appear to divide the book into major sections.

B. W. Bacon found clues suggesting that Matthew intended to divide his Gospel into five major sections plus a prologue (chaps. 1–2) and an epilogue (26:3–28:20).[48] Each major section concluded with the statement, "And when Jesus finished." This was followed by some reference to Jesus's sayings, instruction, or parables (7:28–29; 11:1; 13:53; 19:1; 26:1). These major sections were similarly designed because they contained narrative segments followed by major discourses. Bacon suggested the organization of Matthew into five major sections was a part of Matthew's attempt to present his Gospel as a new Pentateuch. The five sections mirrored the five books of Moses (Genesis to Deuteronomy) in the OT.[49] The major flaw in Bacon's analysis of the structure was the reduction of the accounts of Jesus's birth and infancy to a mere prologue and the passion and resurrection narratives to a mere epilogue.

J. D. Kingsbury argued that Matthew divided his Gospel into three major sections.[50] Matthew introduced new major sections with the words "from that time on Jesus

---

[46] Bauckham (*Jesus and the Eyewitnesses*, 226–30) argues that Papias's concern was over the lack of chronological order in Mark and the disruption of Matthew's superior order in the Hebrew original when the Gospel was adapted by Greek translators. He concludes that Mark and the Greek of Matthew lacked chronological order by comparing these Gospels to John.

[47] See Hagner, *Matthew 1–13*, liii, also citing D. C. Allison, "Matthew: Structure, Biographical Impulse and the *Imitatio Christi*," in *The Four Gospels 1992:* Festschrift F. Neirynck, ed. F. van Segbroeck et al. (Leuven, Belgium: University Press, 1992), 1208.

[48] B. W. Bacon, *Studies in Matthew* (New York, NY: Holt, 1930).

[49] See the collection of the Hebrew Psalter into five books. Another instance of the number five in Matthew is the inclusion of five women in the opening genealogy in 1:1–17: Tamar (v. 3), Rahab and Ruth (v. 5), Uriah's wife (v. 6), and Mary the mother of Jesus (v. 16).

[50] J. D. Kingsbury, *Matthew: Structure, Christology, Kingdom*, 2nd ed. (Minneapolis, MN: Fortress, 1989). See J. C. Hawkins, *Horae Synopticae* (Oxford, UK: Clarendon, 1899); cf. the critique by F. Neirynck, "*Apo tote erchato* and the Structure of Matthew," *ETL* 64 (1988): 21–59, cited in Hagner, *Matthew 1–13*, li.

began to" (4:17; 16:21). According to Kingsbury, these transitional statements divide the Gospel into the introduction (1:1–4:16), body (4:17–16:20), and conclusion (16:21–28:20). Kingsbury labeled these sections: The Person of Jesus Messiah (1:1–4:16); The Proclamation of Jesus Messiah (4:17–16:20); and The Suffering, Death, and Resurrection of Jesus Messiah (16:21–28:20). However, these captions do not adequately describe the contents of these sections. For example, although three of the five major discourses of the Gospel appear in the "Proclamation" section, two appear in the section labeled "Suffering, Death, and Resurrection." This suggests the transitional statement in 16:21 had a purpose other than marking a shift from Jesus's discourses to the Passion Narrative. Nevertheless, Kingsbury's observation that the constructions in 4:17 and 16:21 were important structural markers is sound. Most likely, 4:17 marks a chronological transition by pinpointing the beginning of Jesus's adult ministry. The construction in 16:21 marks a geographical transition and a chronological one. At this point, Jesus heads toward Jerusalem and predicts his coming suffering, death, and resurrection.

Bacon's analysis of Matthew's structure seems affirmed by the majority of scholars.[51] The repetition of the concluding formula after segments of narrative followed by discourse is too consistent to be merely coincidental. Moreover, the division into five sections fits tightly with one of Matthew's major theological emphases, Jesus's identity as the new Moses.[52]

In support of the fivefold proposal, Gundry has observed that other ancient books had a five-part arrangement that reflected the influence of the Pentateuch. Such books include the book of Psalms, the Megilloth, the history of the Maccabees by Jason of Cyrene, 1 Enoch, the original Perekim (sayings) that lay behind the Pirke Aboth ("Sayings of the Fathers"), and Papias's *Expositions of the Lord's Sayings*.[53] At the same time, Gundry objected that Matthew's five "books" do not parallel the five books of Moses and that Matthew has five major discourses but six major narrative sections.[54] But Gundry's concerns notwithstanding, it is best to view the structure of Matthew as centered on five major discourses of Jesus within a framework that oscillates between narrative and discourse.[55]

This does not mean, however, that Kingsbury's insights should be ignored. Matthew's structure is complex and combines several different strategies. The major discourses are clearly important. However, the transitional markers in 4:17 and 16:21 suggest Matthew's

---

[51] See Hagner (*Matthew 1–13*, lii–liii), who further lists chiastic and other proposals, none of which prove compelling.

[52] See the section on major Matthean theological themes below.

[53] Gundry, *Matthew*, 10–11.

[54] Ibid. See Hagner (*Matthew 1–13*, li), who objects that "certain parts of the Gospel do not fit into this structure at all." He cited Matthew 11 and 23 as well as the infancy and Passion Narratives and contends that the fivefold structure is "a subsidiary structure rather than the primary one."

[55] See the discussion in Carson and Moo (*Introduction to the New Testament*, 134–36), who write, "That Matthew reports extensive teaching of Jesus outside the five discourses is no criticism of the outline: the fivefold sequence of narrative and discourse does not assume that Jesus is not portrayed as speaking in the narrative sections. . . . The point, rather, is that the five discourses are so clearly marked, from a literary point of view, that it is well-nigh impossible to believe that Matthew did not plan them."

Gospel is driven by chronological and geographical movement as well. Craig Evans has noted that if Matthew's Gospel utilized Mark as most scholars believe, the importance of chronological and geographical movement is heightened since Mark's Gospel followed a simple outline that followed a basic chronological order and was based on Jesus's geographical movement (ministry in Galilee, journey south to Judea and Jerusalem, and passion and resurrection in Jerusalem).[56]

This suggested outline attempts to incorporate the insights of Bacon, Kingsbury, and Evans:

Table 4.1: The Five Discourses in the Gospel of Matthew

Discourse	Reference	Theme
1. Sermon on the Mount	5–7	Jesus's vision for establishing the kingdom of God
2. Instruction of the Twelve	10	Disciples are to spread gospel; warning of coming persecution
3. Parables of the Kingdom	13	Explains rejection of gospel by some and presence of evil; growth and ministry of the kingdom of God in the face of opposition
4. Parables of the Kingdom	18	Explains how disciples are to relate to Jesus and to each other
5. Olivet Discourse, More Kingdom Parables	24–25	Prophecy of destruction of the temple and events preceding the Second Coming

OUTLINE

I. INTRODUCTION (1:1–4:16)
   A. The Ancestry, Birth, and Early Boyhood of Jesus (1:1–2:23)
      1. Genealogy of Jesus Christ (1:1–17)
      2. The Birth of Jesus (1:18–25)
      3. King Herod and the Visit of the Wise Men (2:1–12)
      4. Flight to Egypt, Bethlehem Massacre, Return to Nazareth (2:13–23)
   B. Prolegomena to Jesus's Ministry (3:1–4:16)
      1. The Ministry of John the Baptist (3:1–12)
      2. Jesus's Baptism (3:13–17)
      3. Jesus's Temptation (4:1–11)
      4. Jesus's Move to Capernaum (4:12–16)

II. JESUS'S GALILEAN MINISTRY (4:17–16:20)
   A. First Part of Galilean Ministry (4:17–25)
      1. Jesus Begins to Preach (4:17)
      2. Call of Disciples (4:18–22)
      3. Summary (4:23–25)

---

[56] Craig A. Evans, *Matthew*, New Cambridge Bible Commentary (New York, NY: Cambridge University Press, 2012), 9.

Discourse 1: Sermon on the Mount (5:1–7:29)

B. Second Part of Galilean Ministry (8:1–9:38)
   1. Healing Ministry (8:1–17)
   2. Discipleship (8:18–27)
   3. Healing Ministry (8:28–9:8)
   4. Discipleship (9:9–17)
   5. Healing Ministry (9:18–34)
   6. Summary (9:35–38)

Discourse 2: Instruction to the Twelve (10:1–11:1)

C. Third Part of Galilean Ministry (11:2–12:50)
   1. Jesus and John the Baptist (11:1–19)
   2. Judgment and Discipleship (11:20–12:8)
   3. Healing Ministry (12:9–45)
   4. Discipleship (12:46–50)

Discourse 3: Parables of the Kingdom (13:1–53)

D. Withdrawal from Galilee to the North (13:54–16:20)
   1. Rejected in Hometown (13:54–58)
   2. John the Baptist Beheaded (14:1–12)
   3. Feeding of the Five Thousand (14:13–21)
   4. Walking on Water (14:22–36)
   5. Discipleship (15:1–20)
   6. Healing (15:21–28)
   7. Feeding of the Four Thousand (15:29–39)
   8. Warning Against Pharisees and Sadducees (16:1–12)
   9. Peter's Confession of Christ (16:13–20)

III. JESUS'S JOURNEY TO JERUSALEM AND MINISTRY THERE (16:21–25:46)

A. Return to Galilee (16:21–17:27)
   1. Prediction of Death, Resurrection, and Exaltation (16:21–28)
   2. Transfiguration (17:1–13)
   3. Healing (17:14–23)
   4. Temple Tax (17:24–27)

Discourse 4: Parables of the Kingdom (18:1–35)

B. Journey through Judea (19:1–20:34)
   1. Teaching on Divorce (19:1–12)
   2. Little Children (19:13–15)
   3. Discipleship and Parable of Workers (19:16–20:16)
   4. Second Passion Prediction (20:17–19)
   5. Greatness in the Kingdom (20:20–28)
   6. Healing (20:29–34)

C. Final Ministry in Jerusalem (21:1–23:39)
   1. Triumphal Entry (21:1–11)

2. Cleansing of the Temple (21:12–17)
3. Withering of a Fig Tree (21:18–27)
4. Parables of Two Sons, Wicked Tenants, Wedding Banquet (21:28–22:14)
5. Controversial Questions (22:15–46)
6. Jesus's Denunciation of the Pharisees (23:1–39)

Discourse 5: Olivet Discourse, Kingdom Parables (24:1–25:46)

IV. JESUS'S PASSION AND RESURRECTION (26:1–28:20)
A. Jesus's Passion (26:1–27:66)
1. The Plot to Kill Jesus (26:1–5)
2. The Anointing (26:6–16)
3. The Passover (26:17–30)
4. Prediction of Peter's Denials (26:31–35)
5. Gethsemane, the Betrayal and Arrest (26:36–56)
6. The Trial before the Sanhedrin and Peter's Denials (26:57–75)
7. Judas's Suicide (27:1–10)
8. The Trial before Pilate (27:11–26)
9. Jesus Mocked and Crucified (27:27–56)
10. Jesus's Burial (27:57–61)
11. The Posting of the Guards (27:62–66)
B. The Resurrection and the Great Commission (28:1–20)
1. The Resurrection (28:1–10)
2. The Guards' Report (28:11–15)
3. The Great Commission (28:16–20)

UNIT-BY-UNIT DISCUSSION

I. Introduction (1:1–4:16)

A. The Ancestry, Birth, and Early Boyhood of Jesus (1:1–2:23) Matthew begins his Gospel with a brief introduction. Matthew 1:1 may have served as the original title of the Gospel. A literal translation of the introductory phrase is "the book of genesis of Jesus Christ." The phrase suggests that the coming of Jesus will introduce a period of new beginnings, a new creation.[57] The titles of Jesus, "Son of David" and "Son of Abraham," introduce major themes of the Gospel and prepare for the genealogy of Jesus that confirms his descent from Abraham and David (1:1–17).[58] This genealogy does far more than merely satisfy curiosity about Jesus's family tree. It shows that Jesus is the fulfillment of

[57] See Davies and Allison, *Matthew*, 1:149–55; David Hill, *The Gospel of Matthew*, New Century Bible (London, UK: Oliphants, 1972), 74–75; Morris, *Matthew*, 18–19; Quarles, *Theology of Matthew*, 177–85; Michael J. Wilkins, *Matthew, NIV Application Commentary* (Grand Rapids, MI: Zondervan, 2004), 55.

[58] For a thorough discussion of Matthew's genealogy, see D. L. Turner, *Matthew*, BECNT (Grand Rapids, MI: Baker, 2008), 25–32 (including the chart comparing Matthew's and Luke's genealogy of Jesus on p. 29). Compare D. S. Huffman, "Genealogy," in *Dictionary of Jesus and the Gospels*, ed. J. B. Green, S. McKnight, and I. H. Marshall (Downers Grove, IL: InterVarsity, 1992), 253–59; D. R. Bauer, "Genealogy," in *Dictionary of Jesus and the Gospels*, 2nd ed., ed. J. B. Green, J. K. Brown, and N. Perrin (Downers Grove, IL: InterVarsity, 2013), 299–302.

God's covenants with Abraham and David. God promised Abraham that through him all the nations of the earth would be blessed (Gen 12:1–3). God promised David that one of his royal descendants would reign over God's people forever (2 Sam 7:12–16). As Son of David Jesus is the promised messianic king. As Son of Abraham Jesus is the One who will bless all nations by saving repentant and believing Gentiles in addition to the Jews who follow Jesus. The inclusion of the Gentiles in God's redemptive plan is probably the purpose for the mention of the four mothers (Tamar, Rahab, Ruth, and Bathsheba) in the genealogy since all four were considered Gentiles, yet were part of the line of the Messiah.[59] The genealogy also underscores Jesus's supremacy over the OT patriarchs.

The account of Jesus's conception and birth (1:18–25) portrays these events as absolutely unique. It demonstrates that Jesus was the fulfillment of God's promises given through the OT prophets. Even more importantly, the account emphasizes Jesus's identity as the virgin-born Immanuel, God living among humans, and the Savior who would rescue his people from their sins. The reference to Isaiah 7:14 in Matthew 1:22–23 is the first in a series of fulfillment quotations that document the fact, all-important for Matthew's Jewish audience, that virtually every major event in Jesus's life—including his birth, his identity as "God with us," his miracles, his healing ministry, and the circumstances surrounding his death, burial, and resurrection—took place in order to fulfill, and in keeping with, OT Scripture.[60]

The visit of the wise men to worship the infant Jesus (2:1–12) further demonstrates that though Jesus's mission was first directed to the Jews, its scope transcended Israel and reached to Gentiles as well. Their time-consuming and difficult journey from the east to Bethlehem, their valuable gifts, and especially their worship of Jesus highlight his supremacy and imply his deity. The failure of the chief priests and scribes to travel to Bethlehem in search of Jesus betrays indifference toward the Messiah that later developed into animosity. The account foreshadows the rejection of Jesus by his own people, particularly the Jewish leaders.

The flight from Herod and the slaughter of the innocents (2:13–18) are reminiscent of the murder of Hebrew children at the order of Pharaoh and the flight of Moses (Exodus 1–2). The account begins a portrayal of Jesus as the new Moses, the instructor and deliverer of God's people. Despite its tragic nature, the event is in keeping with OT prophecy (Jer 31:15 cited in Matt 2:18). Matthew's account is fully consistent with descriptions of Herod's character by ancient historians.[61] The temporal relationship of Jesus's

---

[59] R. Bauckham, "Tamar's Ancestry and Rahab's Marriage: Two Problems in the Matthean Genealogy," *NovT* 37 (1995): 313–29; Davies and Allison, *Matthew*, 1:170–72; C. S. Keener, *A Commentary on the Gospel of Matthew* (Grand Rapids, MI: Eerdmans, 1999), 78–80; U. Luz, *Matthew*, Hermeneia (Minneapolis, MN: Augsburg Fortress, 2001–7), 1:66–67; Quarles, *Theology of Matthew*, 119–22.

[60] See Table 4.4 under Major Theological Themes. On Jesus as "Immanuel," see D. D. Kupp, *Matthew's Emmanuel: Divine Presence and God's People in the First Gospel*, SNTSMS 90 (Cambridge, UK: Cambridge University Press, 1996).

[61] Josephus, *Ant.* 17.167–69; *J.W.* 1.437, 443–44, 550–51, 659–60, 664–65. See Keener, *Commentary on the Gospel of Matthew*, 110–11; R. T. France, "Herod and the Children of Bethlehem," *NovT* 21 (1979): 98–120.

birth to Herod's death is the most significant factor in establishing a chronology of Jesus's early life.[62]

The account of Jesus's infancy ends with a description of the holy family settling in Nazareth (Matt 2:19–23). Matthew saw a connection between the name of the town and the similar-sounding Hebrew word for "branch" (Hb. *netser*). The connection portrayed Jesus as the fulfillment of the "Branch prophecies" of the OT (Isa 4:2; 11:1; Jer 23:5; 33:15).[63] These prophecies told of a righteous descendant of David whose wise and just rule would be empowered by the Spirit and who would bring salvation to Judah. Matthew thus saw Jesus's hometown as a clue to his identity as the Messiah, continuing the pattern of the fulfillment of OT passages in the life of Jesus.

B. Prolegomena to Jesus's Ministry (3:1–4:16) This section begins with a description of the ministry of John the Baptist, again in keeping with OT expectation (3:1–6). Matthew's application of Isaiah 40:3 to John the Baptist says as much about Jesus's identity as it does about John's role. John is a "voice of one crying out in the wilderness," calling the Jewish people to repentance and thus preparing the way for God himself to come in the person of Jesus the Messiah. While Matthew uses the prophecy to describe John's preparation for the coming of Jesus, in its original context the prophecy spoke of one who prepared for the coming of Yahweh God. By using a text about the coming of Yahweh to describe the coming of Jesus, Matthew implies that Jesus is divine, the Immanuel, God with us.

John announced the coming kingdom and called his Jewish hearers to repentance (3:7–12). In particular, he urged them to abandon the assumption that physical descent from Abraham guaranteed salvation. He called on them to express their repentance by accepting his baptism and producing the fruit of good works. He also promised that another person would come after him who was more powerful and vastly superior. This messianic figure would offer sinners a choice between two baptisms: either a baptism effected by the Spirit that would transform them or a baptism of fire that would burn them as fire burned wheat chaff.

Matthew's description of Jesus's baptism (3:13–17) is packed with theological significance. When Jesus approached John requesting baptism, John identified Jesus as the One he had promised by arguing that it was more appropriate for Jesus to baptize John than for John to baptize him. The descent of the Holy Spirit on Jesus like a dove may indicate that Jesus possessed the power of new creation (Gen 1:1–2; cf. 8:8–12). The voice of the heavenly Father described Jesus using two OT texts that identified Jesus as the Messiah and the Suffering Servant who would provide forgiveness to sinners by becoming their sacrifice (Ps 2:7; Isa 42:1).

---

[62] See the discussion on the chronology of Jesus's life in chap. 3 above.

[63] Isaiah 11:1 uses *netser*. The other texts use the synonymous term *tsemach*.

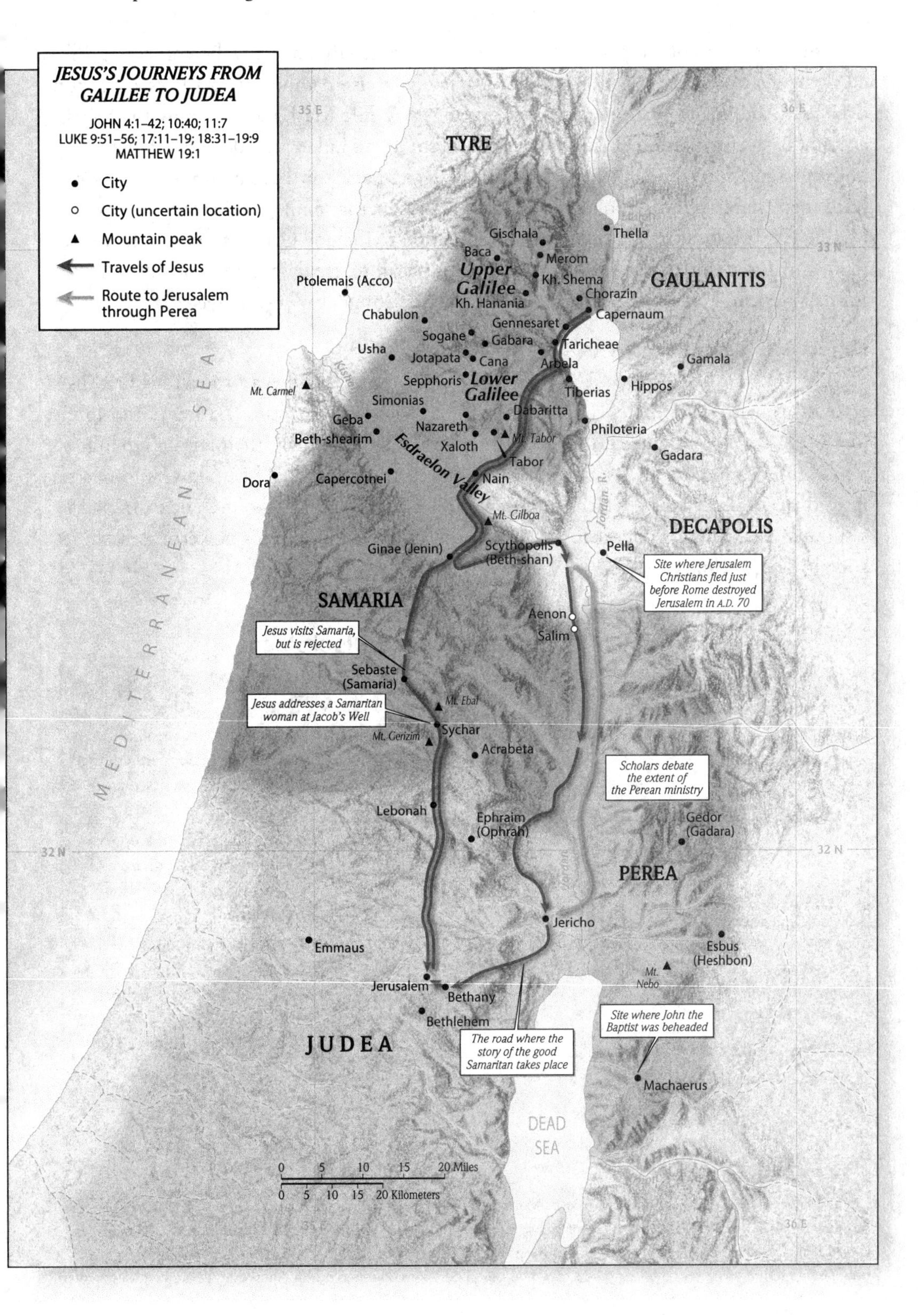
JESUS'S JOURNEYS FROM GALILEE TO JUDEA
JOHN 4:1–42; 10:40; 11:7
LUKE 9:51–56; 17:11–19; 18:31–19:9
MATTHEW 19:1
City
City (uncertain location)
Mountain peak
Travels of Jesus
Route to Jerusalem through Perea
TYRE
GAULANITIS
DECAPOLIS
SAMARIA
PEREA
JUDEA
MEDITERRANEAN SEA
DEAD SEA
Upper Galilee
Lower Galilee
Esdraelon Valley
Gischala
Thella
Baca
Merom
Kh. Shema
Kh. Hanania
Chorazin
Capernaum
Ptolemais (Acco)
Chabulon
Gennesaret
Sogane
Gabara
Taricheae
Usha
Jotapata
Cana
Arbela
Gamala
Mt. Carmel
Sepphoris
Tiberias
Hippos
Simonias
Dabaritta
Geba
Nazareth
Philoteria
Beth-shearim
Mt. Tabor
Xaloth
Tabor
Gadara
Dora
Capercotnei
Nain
Jordan R.
Mt. Gilboa
Ginae (Jenin)
Scythopolis (Beth-shan)
Pella
Site where Jerusalem Christians fled just before Rome destroyed Jerusalem in A.D. 70
Aenon
Salim
Jesus visits Samaria, but is rejected
Sebaste (Samaria)
Mt. Ebal
Jesus addresses a Samaritan woman at Jacob's Well
Sychar
Mt. Gerizim
Acrabeta
Scholars debate the extent of the Perean ministry
Lebonah
Ephraim (Ophrah)
Gedor (Gadara)
Jericho
Emmaus
Esbus (Heshbon)
Mt. Nebo
Jerusalem
Bethany
Bethlehem
The road where the story of the good Samaritan takes place
Site where John the Baptist was beheaded
Machaerus
35 E
36 E
33 N
32 N
0 5 10 15 20 Miles
0 5 10 15 20 Kilometers

Jesus's forty days of temptation (4:1–11) demonstrated that he truly did come to "fulfill all righteousness" (3:15).[64] The temptation experience also demonstrated Jesus's authority over Satan and his own supremacy over the angels. While Mark includes only the tersest account of the temptation (1:12–13), Matthew, similar to Luke, provides a much more detailed presentation (though Luke's order of the second and third temptations is reversed). Jesus then established his ministry headquarters in Capernaum in "Galilee of the Gentiles" (4:12–16). This location confirmed God's intention to include Gentiles in his redemptive plan, a major theme of Matthew's Gospel. Jesus began to proclaim a message identical to John's: "Repent, because the kingdom of heaven has come near" (4:17; see 3:2).

II. Jesus's Galilean Ministry (4:17–18:35)

A. First Part of Galilean Ministry (4:17–25) Jesus then began to call his first disciples, two pairs of brothers who were fishermen: Peter and Andrew, and James and John (4:18–22). Their willingness to abandon their occupation and leave their families to follow Jesus demonstrates that Jesus was worthy of any sacrifice he called his followers to make. Jesus then commenced to preach the gospel of the kingdom throughout Galilee (4:23–25, a summary statement). Great crowds followed him in response to his powerful preaching and amazing healing miracles.

Table 4.2: Jesus's Twelve Disciples

Name	Key Scriptures	Description
Simon Peter	Matt 4:18; 16:13–17, 21–23; Luke 22:54–62; John 21:15–19	Fisherman before called to discipleship; one of inner circle of disciples; often brash and hotheaded
Andrew	Matt 4:18; John 1:40; 6:8; 12:22	Peter's brother; fisherman prior to following Jesus; disciple of John the Baptist before following Jesus
James	Matt 4:21; Mark 3:17; 9:2; 14:33; Acts 12:1–5	Former fisherman; John's brother; one of the two "Sons of Thunder," possibly due to temper; one of inner circle of disciples; martyred at the hand of Herod

[64] "Righteousness" is an important theme in Matthew's Gospel, especially in the early portions of Matthew: see the reference to those who "hunger and thirst for righteousness" (5:6); Jesus's requirement that his followers' "righteousness" exceed that of the Pharisees (5:20); and his injunction that his disciples seek first "the kingdom of God and His righteousness" (6:33).

Table 4.2: Jesus's Twelve Disciples (continued)

Name	Key Scriptures	Description
John	Matt 4:21; Mark 3:17; 9:2; 14:33; John 1:35–39?; 13:23; etc.; 21:2	Former fisherman; one of the two "Sons of Thunder," possibly due to temper, but also called "disciple whom Jesus loved"; one of inner circle of disciples
Philip	John 1:43–48; 6:5–7; 12:21–22;	Called as disciple and brought Nathanael to Jesus
Bartholomew (Nathanael)	Matt 10:3 pars.; John 1:43–49	Also known as Nathanael; seen by Jesus "under the fig tree," confessing Jesus as "Son of God" and "King of Israel"
Thomas	John 11:16; 14:5; 20:24–29	Well known as a "doubter," but later called Jesus "my Lord and my God"
Matthew (Levi)	Matt 9:9–13; 10:3; Mark 2:18; Luke 6:15	Former tax collector who left all to follow Jesus; possibly brother of James the son of Alphaeus (Mark 2:14)
James son of Alphaeus	Matt 10:3; Mark 3:18; Luke 6:15; Acts 1:13	Possibly brother of Matthew (Mark 2:14)
Thaddaeus (Judas son of James)	Matt 10:3; Mark 3:18; Luke 6:16; John 14:22; Acts 1:13	Also known as Judas son of James; the "other Judas" (not Iscariot; see below)
Simon the Zealot	Matt 10:4; Mark 3:18; Luke 6:15; Acts 1:13	Former zealot (Jewish freedom fighter/terrorist)
Judas Iscariot	Matt 10:4; 26:14–16; 27:3–10; John 6:70–71; 12:4–6; 13:21–30; 17:12; Acts 1:16–20	The traitor; keeper of the disciples' moneybag who eventually betrayed Jesus for thirty pieces of silver and subsequently hanged himself

Discourse 1: The Sermon on the Mount (5:1–7:29)

The introduction to Jesus's first discourse, the Sermon on the Mount (5–7), clearly portrays him as the new Moses.[65] Jesus's ascent of the mountain is reminiscent of Moses's as-

[65] E.g., D. C. Allison Jr., *The New Moses: A Matthean Typology* (Minneapolis, MN: Fortress, 1993). On the Sermon on the Mount, see R. A. Guelich, *The Sermon on the Mount: A Foundation for Understanding* (Dallas, TX: Word, 1982); D. A. Carson, *The Sermon on the Mount: An Evangelical Exposition of Matthew 5–7* (Grand Rapids, MI: Baker, 1978); J. Jeremias, *The Sermon on the Mount*, Facet Books 2, trans. N. Perrin (Philadelphia, PA: Fortress, 1963); W. D. Davies, *The Setting of the Sermon on the Mount* (Cambridge, UK: Cambridge University Press, 1964); D. M. Lloyd-Jones, *Studies in the Sermon on the Mount*, 2nd ed. (Grand Rapids, MI: Eerdmans, 1976); J. R. W. Stott, *Christian Counter-culture* (Leicester, UK: InterVarsity, 1978); and D. Bonhoeffer, *The Cost of Discipleship*, rev. ed., trans. R. H. Fuller (New York, NY: Macmillan, 1963). Compare C. Quarles, *The Sermon on the Mount: Restoring Christ's Message to the Modern Church*, NAC Studies in Bible & Theology (Nashville, TN: B&H, 2011).

cent of Mount Sinai (Exod 19:3; 24:13, 18). As in the OT (e.g., Mount Sinai; Exod 19:3), mountains in Matthew are places of divine revelation (e.g., the Mount of Transfiguration in 17:1–3, with Moses and Elijah joining Jesus).[66] Moreover, the blessings pronounced by Jesus recall Moses's blessing on the tribe of Israel (Deut 33:29). The Beatitudes (5:3–12) identify Jesus's disciples as the new true spiritual Israel on whom God's blessings rest.

Jesus urged his disciples to live lives characterized by purity that served to glorify God. In this way they will be "salt" and "light" in the world (5:13–16). He affirmed the inspiration of the OT and ordered his disciples to be characterized by complete obedience to even the least of the OT commands as interpreted by him in his teaching. Unless their righteousness exceeds that of the Pharisees, Jesus's followers will be unable to enter God's kingdom (5:17–20). Rightly interpreted, the OT demands that disciples control their tempers, pursue sexual purity, honor the covenant of marriage, speak with integrity, refrain from acts of vengeance, and love their enemies (5:21–48). Jesus insisted that only his disciples were capable of such righteousness since he graciously imparted this righteousness to his followers by his blessing (5:6).

Jesus also gave instructions regarding the so-called three pillars of Judaism: prayer, fasting, and almsgiving (6:1–18). He especially cautioned his disciples against performing acts of religious devotion in order to please a human audience. He stressed that true acts of devotion must be focused exclusively on pleasing God. He promised God would reward such expressions of genuine piety. Jesus urged his disciples to value eternal and spiritual matters above temporal and material things. In particular, he warned them about the allurement of materialism. He commanded his disciples to be free from anxiety by trusting in God's ability to provide for their needs and by letting God's priorities define theirs (6:19–34).

Jesus prohibited hypocritical judgment of others (7:1–6). He taught that disciples may assist others in conquering sinful habits only as they gain victory over their own. Jesus promised his disciples that those who asked for good gifts would receive them. Those who sought the kingdom would find it. Those who knocked on the narrow gate that led to the kingdom would be granted entrance. However, Jesus warned that the life of the true disciple would entail difficulty and persecution. Few would be willing to suffer this hardship for the sake of receiving eternal life (7:7–14).

Jesus warned his disciples about false prophets and false disciples (7:15–23). Disciples could recognize counterfeits by their "fruits," the actions and words that attested to their true inner character. Jesus taught that false disciples would be exposed on judgment day for what they truly were. He would personally unmask them and banish them from the kingdom of heaven. Jesus concluded the Sermon on the Mount with a parable that taught that hearing and obeying his teaching were the only effective means of preparing for

---

[66] See T. L. Donaldson, *Jesus on the Mountain: A Study in Matthean Theology*, JSNTSup 8 (Sheffield, UK: Almond, 1985).

eschatological judgment. Matthew noted that the people recognized the unusual authority of Jesus's teaching in comparison with their scribes and teachers of the law (7:24–29).

B. Second Part of Galilean Ministry (8:1–9:38) The narrative section that follows the Sermon on the Mount is saturated with accounts of Jesus's miracles. He cleansed a leper, healed the paralyzed servant of a Roman centurion, cooled the fevered brow of Simon's mother-in-law, controlled the weather by his mere command, delivered the man from Gadara from a legion of demons, raised a synagogue ruler's daughter from the dead, stopped a woman from hemorrhaging when she simply touched the hem of his garments, gave sight to the blind, and enabled a mute man to speak.

These miracles served several purposes. First, they confirmed Jesus's identity as God the Savior since Isaiah 35:5–6 promised that when God came to save his people, he would open the eyes of the blind, unstop the ears of the deaf, enable the lame to leap like deer, and cause the mute to shout for joy. Second, some of the miracles, particularly the healing of the centurion's servant and the exorcism of the Gadarene demoniac, demonstrated Christ's compassion for Gentiles and clearly stated God's intention to grant them salvation. Third, because Matthew explained Jesus's healing power by quoting Isaiah 53:4 (Matt 8:17), the miracles showed that Jesus was the Servant of the Lord who would offer his life as a sacrifice to atone for the sins of God's people. Fourth, one healing miracle and the accompanying dialogue clearly expressed Jesus's authority to forgive sins (9:1–8). Finally, several of Jesus's healing miracles displayed his compassion toward people regarded as unclean who were rejected by the religious community and treated as untouchable. These miracles demonstrated that Jesus's grace and mercy extended even to the most despised and unworthy people.

This section concludes with Jesus's observation that the crowds were like sheep without a shepherd (9:35–38; see Num 27:17 with reference to the leadership transition from Moses to Joshua), an indictment against the Jewish leaders (see Ezek 34:5).

Discourse 2: Instruction to the Twelve (10:1–11:1) Jesus followed his indictment of the Jewish leaders with the appointment of the Twelve to serve as shepherds of the lost sheep of the house of Israel. These twelve disciples would serve as the nucleus of a newly reconstituted spiritual Israel. Jesus commanded them to proclaim the message of the coming kingdom, to perform miracles similar to his to demonstrate that the messianic age had dawned, and to live in dependence on God's gracious provision.

Jesus also warned his disciples about persecutions they would endure because of their association with him. These would give them the opportunity to testify about Jesus before rulers and kings. They need not be anxious regarding their testimonies in such cases because the Holy Spirit would give them the words to say. Jesus's disciples were to fear God more than others since God could destroy both their bodies and souls while people could only destroy bodies.

C. Third Part of Jesus's Galilean Ministry (11:2–12:50) This section describes the wide variety of responses to Jesus's ministry, ranging from the doubt of figures such as John the Baptist to his hearers' refusal to repent. Jesus alleviated John's doubts by pointing to his own miraculous works that fulfilled OT prophecy and confirmed his messianic identity (11:1–19). Jesus pointed out that he and John the Baptist had been different in several ways. John had lived an austere lifestyle, but Jesus had associated with sinners. By rejecting both Jesus and John, the people demonstrated that their problem was with the shared message about the coming kingdom and the necessity to repent rather than personalities or lifestyle differences. Jesus identified John as the Messiah's forerunner, thereby implicitly identifying himself as the Messiah.

Jesus warned unrepentant cities of the terrifying judgment awaiting them if they did not repent of their rejection of Jesus (11:20–24). He explained that no one knows God the Father except Jesus his Son and "anyone to whom the Son desires to reveal him" (11:25–30). The following pericopes display the intensifying rejection of Jesus by the Jewish leaders. The Pharisees first challenged Jesus's disciples for breaking one of their Sabbath laws. Jesus replied by identifying himself as the Lord of the Sabbath, a title the Pharisees would have recognized as belonging to Yahweh alone. When Jesus later healed a paralyzed man on the Sabbath, the Pharisees began to plot to take Jesus's life (12:1–14).

Again, Jesus is identified as the Servant of Yahweh (see 8:17), fulfilling OT messianic prediction not only with regard to his miraculous healing ministry of universal scope but even with regard to the meek and humble manner of his ministry (12:15–21). The Pharisees' rejection of Jesus climaxed when they identified the ruler of the demons as the source of Jesus's ability to cast out demons (12:22–37). Jesus warned them that ascribing to Satan the activities of the Spirit through his ministry constituted the sin of blasphemy against the Spirit, a sin for which no forgiveness was offered. He further warned that the words of the Pharisees would result in their condemnation on judgment day.

The Pharisees asked Jesus to perform a sign for them to confirm his claims (12:38–45). Jesus replied that the only sign they would be given was his own resurrection (the "sign of Jonah"; this is the only "sign" of Jesus in the Synoptics, while John features a series of signs to show that Jesus is the promised Messiah). However, Jesus warned that the Pharisees and many others of that generation would reject that sign and that their spiritual condition would only grow worse, like a man liberated from one demon only to be inhabited by more evil spirits. Finally, Jesus taught another lesson on faith and discipleship by identifying all those who performed his Father's will as his spiritual brothers and sisters (12:46–50).

Discourse 3: Parables of the Kingdom (13:1–53) In his third major discourse, Jesus told a number of parables related to the kingdom of God.[67] The parable of the Sower

---

[67] Note that Matthew's preferred term is "kingdom of heaven" (used thirty-two times, though "kingdom of God" does occur five times; Mark, Luke, and John do not use the term "kingdom of heaven"). For an explanation of Matthew's unique phrase, see J. T. Pennington, *Heaven and Earth in the Gospel of Matthew* (Grand Rapids, MI: Baker, 2007), esp. 310–11. Cf. J. B. Green, "Kingdom of God/Heaven," in *Dictionary of Jesus and the Gospels*, 2nd ed., ed. J. B. Green, J. K. Brown, and N. Perrin (Downers Grove, IL: InterVarsity, 2013), 468–81, who believes "Matthew prefers 'kingdom of heaven' not because of his aversion to referring to Yahweh as God, but rather to emphasize the heavenly origins and nature of the kingdom" (p. 474).

(13:1–23) explained the reasons for which many rejected Jesus's message. Jesus invoked the message of Isaiah (Isa 6:9–10), who also faced serious rejection, and noted that Israel's rejection of Jesus as Messiah fulfilled OT prophecy. Jesus's parable also emphasized the amazing production of righteous deeds and words by those who heard and accepted Jesus's message.

Table 4.3: Parables of Jesus in the Synoptics

Parable	Mark	Matthew	Luke
Guests of the Bridegroom	2:19–20	9:15	5:33–39
Unshrunk Cloth	2:21	9:16	5:36
New Wine in Old Wineskins	2:22	9:17	5:37–39
Strong Man	3:22–27	12:29–30	11:21–23
The Sower	4:1–9, 13–20	13:1–9, 18–23	8:4–8, 11–15
A Lamp Under a Bowl	4:21–25	5:14–15	8:16–18
Secretly Growing Seed	4:26–29		
Mustard Seed	4:30–32	13:31–32	13:18–19
Wicked Tenants	12:1–12	21:33–46	20:9–19
Budding Fig Tree	13:28–32	24:32–36	21:29–33
Watchful Servants	13:34–37		12:35–38
Father and Son		7:9–11	11:11–13
Two Gates		7:13–14	13:23–27
Good and Bad Trees		7:16–20	
Wise and Foolish Builders		7:24–27	6:47–49
Weeds Among Wheat		13:24–30, 36–43	
Yeast		13:33	13:20–21
Hidden Treasure		13:44	
Pearls		13:45–46	
The Net		13:47–50	
Owner of a House		13:52	
The Lost Sheep		18:12–14	15:1–7
Unmerciful Servant		18:23–35	
Workers in the Vineyard		20:1–16	
Two Sons		21:28–32	
Wedding Feast		22:1–14	14:15–24
Thief in the Night		24:42–44	12:39–40
Faithful and Wise Servant		24:45–51	12:42–46
Wise and Foolish Maidens		25:1–13	

Table 4.3: Parables of Jesus in the Synoptics (continued)

Parable	Mark	Matthew	Luke
The Talents		25:14–30	19:11–27
Sheep and Goats		25:31–46	
Two Debtors			7:41–50
The Good Samaritan			10:25–37
The Persistent Friend			11:5–8
Rich Fool			12:13–21
Unfruitful Fig Tree			13:6–9
Lowest Seat			14:7–14
Great Banquet			14:16–24
Tower Builder			14:28–30
Warring King			14:31–33
Lost Sheep			15:1–7
Lost Coin			15:8–10
Lost Son			15:11–32
Shrewd Manager			16:1–8
Rich Man and Lazarus			16:19–31
Humble Servant			17:7–10
Persistent Widow			18:1–8
Pharisee and Tax Collector			18:9–14

Jesus's parable of the Weeds (13:24–30, 36–43) was his response to those who wondered why he did not immediately destroy the wicked if he were the promised Son of Man. The parable demonstrated that Jesus was not the source of evil in the world (compare 13:27–28 with 13:36–39), that the entire earth belongs to the Son of Man, that the Devil had no right to bring evil into the world, and that the Son of Man would assert his kingship over the world by punishing the wicked and blessing the righteous at the appropriate time.

The parables of the Mustard Seed and the Leaven (13:31–35) portray the remarkable growth of the kingdom and its extensive influence on the world. The parables of the Hidden Treasure and the Valuable Pearl (13:44–46) show that the kingdom of God is worthy of any sacrifice Jesus's disciples may be called to make.

The parable of the Dragnet (13:47–51) portrayed the separation of Jesus's righteous disciples from the wicked people of the world in final judgment and the punishment that the wicked will face. The parable of the Scribe (13:52) depicted Jesus's disciples as better qualified than the scribes and Pharisees to serve as teachers of the law. In their storeroom of instruction, they had both old (the OT) and new treasures (the teachings of Jesus).

D. Withdrawal from Galilee to the North (13:54–16:20) This section of the Gospel begins with another reference to Jesus's rejection by his own people, this time, the people of Nazareth, in his own hometown (13:54–58). The beginning of the close of the Galilean ministry is further signaled by the execution of John the Baptist by Herod the Tetrarch in 14:1–12. John was last heard from in 11:1–19. In God's plan John's mission as a voice preparing the way for the Lord has been fulfilled, and he passes from the scene, with Jesus's mission in full swing.

Jesus sought to retreat to a place of solitude after John's death, but the crowds followed him wherever he went. He miraculously provided for the crowds through the miracle of the loaves and the fish (14:13–21). He also amazed his disciples by the miracle of walking on water (14:22–36). The two miracles were reminiscent of the provision of the manna in the wilderness and the crossing of the Red Sea; they thus contribute to Matthew's emphasis on Jesus's identity as the new Moses. Jesus's miracles resulted in his even greater popularity among the common people who thronged around him in hopes that they might just touch the hem of his garments and be healed.

This popularity stirred the resentment of the Pharisees and scribes. They traveled from Jerusalem to Galilee to challenge Jesus for breaking their traditions (15:1–20). Jesus denounced them as hypocrites who elevated their own traditions above the commandments of God. He also charged the scribes and Pharisees with caring too much about matters related to Jewish rituals and with neglecting the more important matter, the condition of their hearts.

The faith of the Canaanite woman (15:21–28) provides a striking contrast with the disbelief of the Jewish leaders. Jesus's willingness to heal her demon-possessed daughter and his words of commendation, "Your faith is great," imply that Jesus would call disciples from among the Gentiles as well as from among the Jews—though for now Jesus affirms the salvation-historical privilege of the Jews and indicates that they are the primary focus of his earthly mission (15:24, 26; see 10:5–6).

Jesus continued his miraculous ministry by ascending a mountain and healing people who suffered from various conditions. He also performed another miraculous feeding reminiscent of the miraculous feedings that God provided through Moses during the wilderness wanderings (15:29–39). However, unlike the previous miraculous feeding, this time the participants were Gentiles rather than Jews. By repeating his miracles performed for the benefit of the Jewish people now for the Gentiles, Jesus confirmed his love for the Gentiles and his intention of including both believing Jews and Gentiles in his kingdom.

Despite these frequent, public miracles, the Pharisees and Sadducees approached Jesus and requested another miraculous sign (16:1–12). Jesus insisted again that they would receive only one sign, the sign of Jonah mentioned earlier. This is a reference to Jesus's resurrection.

Jesus warned his disciples to avoid the teaching of the Pharisees and Sadducees, perhaps particularly their constant demand for another miracle to prove his identity.

Jesus's disciples, particularly Peter (16:13–20), recognized Jesus's identity as God's Son as Peter stated in the watershed confession at Caesarea Philippi. According to Jesus, this was the result of divine revelation, and he would build his messianic community on Peter on the basis of his confession.[68]

III. Jesus's Journey to Jerusalem and Ministry There (16:21–25:46)

A. Return to Galilee (16:21–17:27) Matthew 16:21 is a major turning point in the Gospel. At Caesarea Philippi, about twenty-five miles north of the Sea of Galilee, Jesus predicted his suffering, death, and resurrection. He then began to move south through Galilee, then Judea, and on to Jerusalem to fulfill this destiny. When Jesus began to predict his suffering, death, and resurrection, Peter protested. This indicates that despite his confession of Jesus as the Messiah, Peter still did not understand that the Messiah must suffer. Jesus explained that all Christian disciples had to be prepared to bear their own cross just as Jesus was prepared to bear his. He promised his disciples they would see the dawn of the kingdom before they died.

This promised kingdom arrived six days later during the transfiguration of Jesus (17:1–13). Several features of the event are paralleled in Exodus 34:29–35. This suggests the event served to confirm Jesus's identity as the new Moses, the Savior and Redeemer of God's people. However, the event transcends Moses's experience and demonstrates that Jesus is vastly superior to Moses. The description of Jesus echoes descriptions of God in the OT and strongly implies Jesus's deity. Jesus proceeded to cast out a demon which his disciples were unable to expel. He explained that their inability was due to their lack of faith. If the disciples had faith the size of a mustard seed, nothing would be impossible for them.

The section continues with the account of Jesus's paying the temple tax (17:24–27). Jesus described himself as the Son of the heavenly King and thus under no obligation to pay the tax. But he performed a miracle that displayed his authority over the animal kingdom so that he and Peter could pay the tax and avoid unnecessarily offending the Jews.

Discourse 4: Parables of the Kingdom (18:1–35) Jesus began the fourth major discourse in Matthew by describing the childlike humility of his disciples, which enabled them to submit to his authority like a child submitted to his parents' authority (18:1–9). Jesus warned that those who attempted to bring about the downfall of his disciples would be severely punished. He stressed the importance of his disciples to God by promising that their angelic representatives had access to the heavenly throne room and always remained in God's presence. Moreover, God's sovereign will determined that all of Jesus's disciples

---

[68] Note this is one of only two instances of *ekklēsia* in all the Gospels (the other reference is in 18:17). For this reason, a nontechnical translation such as "messianic community" seems preferable to the standard rendering "church" in Matt 16:18 and 18:17. The term was used in the OT to describe the gathering of God's people. Thus, the term is part of Jesus's portrayal of his disciples as the new Israel. See Quarles, *Theology of Matthew*, 109–110.

should remain true to him. Though they may wander from him, they will not be permanently lost (18:10–14).

Jesus outlined a disciplinary process that would encourage true disciples to repent and isolate false disciples from the Christian fellowship (18:15–20). He promised to be present with his disciples when they gathered to seek his leadership regarding what behavior was acceptable or unacceptable for disciples. He also promised to answer their fervent prayer for the sinning brother's forgiveness and restoration.

Finally, Jesus used a powerful parable to urge his disciples to offer gracious forgiveness to others (18:21–35). This forgiveness expressed the great grace that God had expressed to the disciples. Failure to offer forgiveness to others showed utter disregard for the magnitude of mercy that God exhibited in forgiving the disciple's sin. True disciples will forgive. Those who refuse to forgive others who repent demonstrate by their refusal that they are not true disciples. They will suffer God's wrath for their hypocrisy.

B. Journey through Judea (19:1–20:34) Jesus ended his ministry in Galilee and crossed the Jordan River to enter Judean territory (which extended beyond the Jordan River on the east) and begin his journey to Jerusalem. The Pharisees sought to trap Jesus with a question regarding divorce (19:1–12). Jesus affirmed the sanctity and permanence of marriage. He taught that divorce had been permitted in OT law because of the hardheartedness of God's people. The implication was that since Jesus's disciples were characterized by pure hearts (see 5:8), they were also capable of marital love that fulfilled God's original ideal.

After blessing the children brought to him (19:13–15), Jesus explained to a questioner the requirements for inheriting eternal life (19:16–30). Jesus urged him to keep the commandments and named all of the commandments from the second table except for the tenth, which was related to possessions. Jesus's command, "[S]ell your belongings. . . . Then come, follow me," was designed to show the young man that he defied the spirit of the Tenth Commandment by his covetousness and the commandment to love his neighbor by his neglect of the poor. Jesus's teaching was intended to shake the man's dependence on his own good works and to shatter his arrogant refusal to acknowledge his sinfulness and need for divine grace. Such a spirit of prideful self-dependence made entrance into the kingdom difficult for the rich. Kingdom entrance required giving up this self-dependence and humbly relying on the gracious forgiveness of God.

Jesus taught that the sacrifices his disciples made to follow him would be rewarded. The disciples would reign over the twelve tribes of Israel. Jesus's disciples would receive back one hundred times more than what they had sacrificed for him. This teaching was followed by a parable that demonstrated that just as a rich landowner was free to dispense his wealth as he saw fit, God is free to dispense his grace as he determines (20:1–16).

Jesus then gathered his disciples privately and foretold explicitly his betrayal, trial, mockery, scourging, crucifixion, and resurrection (20:17–19) in greater detail than before. The mother of James and John approached Jesus, asking that her sons be granted special positions in the kingdom (20:20–28). Jesus urged his disciples to offer humble service to others rather than seek to dominate them. He concluded with a powerful statement that portrayed his death as an atoning sacrifice, a ransom for many. As Jesus passed through Jericho, he healed two blind men by touching their eyes (20:29–34).

C. Final Ministry in Jerusalem (21:1–23:39) As Jesus and his disciples approached Jerusalem, Jesus fulfilled OT prophecy by riding a donkey into the city in triumphal procession (21:1–11; see Zech 9:9). The crowds in Jerusalem praised Jesus as both a prophet and as the Son of David, the long-awaited Messiah.

Jesus entered the temple and threw out those who sold currency for temple offerings and animals for temple sacrifice (21:12–17), and he quoted Isaiah 56:7 as justification for his actions. He also healed the blind and the lame in the temple. Jesus's display of miraculous power and the praises of the children who proclaimed him as the Son of David incited the anger of the Jewish leaders. He then defended the testimony of the children with an appeal to Psalm 8:3.

On his way from Jerusalem back to Bethany, Jesus cursed a fig tree whose green leaves gave it the appearance of life though it produced no figs (21:18–22). The tree immediately withered. The cursing of the fig tree foreshadowed the destruction of Jerusalem, which had failed to produce the fruits of righteousness that God expected of it.

When Jesus returned to the temple, the Jewish leaders attempted to trap him in his words (21:23–27). He evaded the trap by laying a clever trap for them. He then contrasted the Jewish leaders with his own disciples by telling a parable about two sons: one who rebelled but later humbly submitted to his father's authority and another who promised obedience but then did not obey (21:28–32). Jesus compared the first son to sinners who repented in response to John's preaching; the second son he linked to the Jewish leaders who refused to believe and obey John's message.

Jesus then told the parable of the Wicked Tenants, which describes the Jewish leaders' abuse of the OT prophets and their murder of God's Son. These leaders were motivated by their refusal to offer to God the fruits of righteousness he demanded (21:33–46). Jesus warned that God would punish the Jewish leaders by stripping his kingdom from their hands and entrusting it to Jesus's disciples, who would produce the righteousness God expected. The parable enraged the Jewish leaders, and they resolved again to kill Jesus.

The parable of the Wedding Feast reiterated Jesus's warning by portraying the Jewish leaders as those who insulted the heavenly King by refusing an invitation to honor his Son and by mistreating and killing his servants, the OT prophets (22:1–14). The king in the story destroyed both them and their city, thus foreshadowing the impending destruction of Jerusalem. The king then invited other guests, who represent Jesus's disciples, to participate in the great messianic feast.

Another trap was laid when the Pharisees asked Jesus whether they should pay taxes to the Roman Emperor (22:15–22). If so, he would have acknowledged the Romans' right to tax God's people. If not, they would have had grounds to accuse Jesus of political subversion against Rome. Jesus cleverly, and memorably, responded that people must give to Caesar what is Caesar's and to God what is God's. Jesus's reply evaded the trap and taught the important principles that (1) subjects and citizens should pay taxes and (2) since humans were created in the image and likeness of God, all they have and are belong to him. The Sadducees also attempted to trap Jesus by offering what they thought was irrefutable evidence against the doctrine of the resurrection. Jesus demonstrated from the law of Moses that individuals continued to exist even after death (22:23–33), thus refuting the annihilationism affirmed by the Sadducees.

The Pharisees attempted to trap Jesus again with a question regarding the most important commandment (22:34–40). He replied that the most important commandments required wholehearted devotion to God and love for others and insisted that all other aspects of the law were related to and dependent on these two central commands. Finally, Jesus questioned the Pharisees about the lineage of the Messiah, and they could not answer him. He demonstrated that the Messiah was superior to David and was recognized by David himself as Lord (22:41–45). Jesus's response so thwarted the Jewish leaders' ploys that no one dared to challenge Jesus's teaching in a public forum again (22:46).

In a series of blistering woes (chap. 23), Jesus warned the crowds that although the teaching of the scribes and Pharisees was generally reliable, their example should not be followed since their lives were inconsistent with their teachings (23:1–39). He challenged the egotistical way that these religious leaders sought honor from other people. He urged his followers to be characterized by humility. Jesus pronounced judgment on the scribes and Pharisees for the way they prevented others from entering the kingdom, sentenced to destruction those who embraced their teaching, used legal loopholes to evade the clear demands of the commandments, and focused on the minutiae of the law to the neglect of the more important matters such as justice, mercy, and faith. He rebuked them for focusing on matters related to external purity and for giving no attention to their inner corruption. Although the Jewish leaders piously claimed to be morally superior to their ancestors, Jesus insisted their abuse of his disciples would make them accountable for the blood of all righteous martyrs that had been shed in history. Jesus concluded his cry against the Jewish leaders with a warning that God would abandon the temple and that Jesus would not return to Jerusalem until his Second Coming.

Discourse 5: Olivet Discourse, Kingdom Parables (24:1–25:46) Jesus's final discourse in Matthew commences with a section on the impending destruction of the Jerusalem temple and the Second Coming. He prophesied that the temple would be completely destroyed and then outlined the events that would precede this destruction. He explained the horrible suffering his people would endure during that period of tribulation and assured them he would shorten the period of suffering for their sakes. He also assured his chosen ones that they would not be deceived by the false messiahs and false prophets who would appear. Jesus's own coming would be unmistakable and easily distinguished from the appearance of the false messiahs.

Jesus taught that the events surrounding the destruction of Jerusalem would occur within one generation. However, he implied that the Second Coming would occur in the distant future and taught that no one but the Father knew the day or hour of that great event. He used a powerful parable to urge his disciples to remain in a state of constant preparation (24:42–50), and he challenged them to live every day as if it were the day he would return.

Jesus continued by telling several other parables related to the importance of preparing for his return. The parable of the Ten Virgins (25:1–13) warned the disciples to prepare immediately for the Second Coming but to anticipate a lengthy delay. The parable of the Talents (25:14–30) emphasized the importance of living faithfully and responsibly during the lengthy delay before the Lord's return. The parable of the Sheep and Goats (25:31–46) demonstrated that one of the most important steps in preparing for Jesus's return was treating Jesus's followers kindly and compassionately.

IV. JESUS'S PASSION AND RESURRECTION (26:1–28:20)

A. Jesus's Passion (26:1–27:66) After the conclusion of Jesus's final discourse, several Matthean features indicate that Jesus's death is drawing close. Jesus offered another prediction of his crucifixion (26:1–2). The Jewish leaders met to conspire to kill him (26:3–5). A woman anointed Jesus with myrrh in preparation for his burial (26:6–16). One of Jesus's own disciples approached the Jewish leaders, offering to betray Jesus for a price (26:17–25).

While Jesus shared the Passover meal with his disciples, he announced that one of them would betray him (26:26–30). Then he specifically identified Judas as the betrayer. Jesus instituted the Lord's Supper by using the bread and cup from the Passover to portray his body and blood that would be sacrificed to seal the new covenant and provide forgiveness of sins.

After this Jesus quoted an OT prophecy to demonstrate that his disciples would abandon him after his arrest (26:31–35). Peter and the other disciples strongly denied that this was possible, yet Jesus predicted Peter would deny him three times before the rooster crowed at sunrise. At this Jesus led his disciples into the garden of Gethsemane (26:36–46), gathering his inner circle (Peter, James, and John) to join him in prayer. Jesus asked that the Father might allow him to escape the cross, but he submitted himself to the Father's will whatever it might be. Then Jesus approached the disciples, and when he found them sleeping, he urged them to remain alert and to pray.

This scene was repeated three times until Judas entered Gethsemane accompanied by an armed mob dispatched by the Jewish officials (26:47–56). Judas identified Jesus by greeting him with the kiss of friendship, and Jesus was seized by the mob. One of the disciples intervened, drew his sword, and struck off the ear of a servant of the high priest. Jesus rebuked the disciple and reminded him that his Father was more than capable of

Something to Think About: All Authority Is Jesus's

"All authority has been given to me in heaven and on earth" (28:18). Who is the man who can claim to have been given all authority in heaven and on earth? Has a more amazing statement ever been made, a more startling claim ever been registered? In the climactic moment in Matthew's entire Gospel, here is Jesus, with the Eleven, in Galilee, ascended onto the mountain, uttering what has become known as "the Great Commission": "Go, therefore, and make disciples of all nations, baptizing them in the name of the Father and of the Son and of the Holy Spirit, teaching them to observe everything I have commanded you. And remember, I am with you always, to the end of the age" (28:19–20).

How can Jesus have all authority in heaven and on earth? In the context of Matthew's Gospel, the reader is reminded of the gambit proposed to Jesus by "the tempter," the Devil, Satan, who took Jesus "to a very high mountain" and showed him all the kingdoms of this world and their splendor and said to him, "I will give you all these things if you will fall down and worship me" (4:8–9). Jesus refused, rebuking the Devil, "Go away, Satan!" Later in the Gospel, Jesus told his closest followers that he must suffer, and be killed, and be raised the third day; and when Peter took him aside and rebuked him, denying the necessity of the cross, Jesus, in similar terms, told Peter, "Get behind me, Satan!" (16:21–23).

Only after the crucifixion does Jesus claim to have all authority in heaven and on earth. The risen Christ, in the manner of a conquering, victorious general, ascends the mountain and commissions his followers to go and conquer the world, similar to Alexander the Great and other military leaders who set out to subdue the universe and subject it to their will. But Jesus's conquest would be gentle, in keeping with his invitation, "Come to me, all of you who are weary and burdened, and I will give you rest. Take up my yoke and learn from me, because I am lowly and humble in heart, and you will find rest for yourselves. For my yoke is easy and my burden is light" (11:28–30).

And as his followers go into all the world in order to disciple the nations, Jesus himself, Isaiah's Immanuel, which is translated "God is with us" (1:23), would be with them: "And remember, I am with you always, to the end of the age." How, then, can the church's mission possibly fail, if Jesus, the risen Christ, the conquering general, will himself be present with his people in the power of the Holy Spirit? Indeed, "This good news of the kingdom will be proclaimed in all the world as a testimony to all nations, and then the end will come" (24:14). In the original scene, as Matthew tells us, "When they saw him, they worshiped, but some doubted" (28:17). Will you and I worship, or will we doubt?

rescuing him if he chose to do so but that his arrest and death were necessary to fulfill the promises of Scripture.

After this Jesus was led to Caiaphas, the high priest, and an assembly of the scribes and elders (26:57–68). Peter followed closely but discretely and waited in the courtyard to hear the outcome of the proceedings. The Jewish leaders sought false witnesses whose testimony might justify executing Jesus. Two witnesses appeared, charging that Jesus had claimed that he was able to destroy the temple and rebuild it in three days. Jesus remained silent in the face of the charges until the high priest placed him under oath and demanded to know if he were the Messiah, the Son of God. Jesus replied by quoting Psalm 110:1 and Daniel 7:13. The high priest accused Jesus of blasphemy. Then the assembly sentenced Jesus to death. Members of the assembly began to abuse Jesus by spitting in his face, punching him with their fists, and slapping him.

In the meantime, others present in the courtyard recognized Peter as a disciple of Jesus (26:69–75). He denied knowing Jesus three different times. Each denial was more adamant and angrier than the previous one. Immediately after the third denial, the rooster crowed, signaling the fulfillment of Jesus's prophecy and sending Peter out to weep.

While Jesus was led away to Pilate, Judas regretted his decision to betray Jesus (27:1–10). He returned the betrayal price to the Jewish leaders, proclaimed Jesus's innocence, and then hanged himself. The Jewish leaders used the money to purchase a plot of land for the burial of foreigners who visited Jerusalem.

When Jesus was questioned by Pilate and accused by the Jewish leaders, he remained silent (27:11–26). Although Pilate attempted to release Jesus by appealing to a Passover custom in which he released one prisoner, the people, prompted by their leaders, pled for Pilate to release Barabbas instead and to crucify Jesus. Pilate washed his hands in a symbolic attempt to alleviate his guilt in Jesus's execution while the Jews accepted full responsibility for Jesus's death; he had Jesus scourged and handed him over to be crucified.[69]

Soldiers from the Roman cohort responsible for Jesus's execution stripped him and ridiculed his messianic claims by adorning him with a mock robe, crown, and scepter, and bowing before him in fake homage (27:27–50). They then spit on Jesus and brutally beat him. Due to weakness from his severe scourging, and since Jesus was unable to carry his cross to the place of execution, the soldiers forced Simon of Cyrene to carry the cross for him. Jesus was offered a mixture that could have diminished his sufferings, but he refused to drink it. While he was suffering, onlookers mocked Jesus, particularly the chief priests, scribes, and elders, as well as those crucified along with him.

Several remarkable signs accompanied Jesus's sufferings and death (27:51–56). While he hung on the cross, the sky was black although it was midday. When Jesus died, the heavy curtain that separated the holy of holies from the rest of the temple complex was torn from the top to the bottom while an earthquake split the rocks and opened the tombs

---

[69] For recent treatments of crucifixion, see D. W. Chapman, *Ancient Jewish and Christian Perceptions of Crucifixion*, WUNT 2/244 (Tübingen, Germany: Mohr Siebeck: 2008); J. G. Cook, *Crucifixion in the Mediterranean World*, WUNT 327 (Tübingen,Germany: Mohr Siebeck, 2014).

of the city. The Roman centurion and soldiers who supervised the crucifixion were terrified by these supernatural events and confessed that Jesus truly was the Son of God.

Joseph of Arimathea buried Jesus in his own new tomb and sealed it with a stone (27:57–66). Mary Magdalene and Mary, mother of two of Jesus's disciples, observed the burial and thus were aware of the location of the tomb. This familiarity with its location ensured that the tomb that they later found empty was, in fact, the tomb where Jesus had been buried. At the request of the Pharisees, Pilate secured and sealed Jesus's tomb and ordered a Roman *custodia* to guard it in order to prevent Jesus's disciples from stealing the body and staging a resurrection.

B. The Resurrection and the Great Commission (28:1–20) At dawn on Sunday morning, the two women who observed Jesus's burial returned to the tomb (28:1–10). Another earthquake occurred as an angel appeared and rolled back the stone that sealed Jesus's tomb. The Roman guard was immobilized with terror. The angel announced that Jesus had risen from the dead and commanded the women to report this to the disciples and to urge them to travel to Galilee where Jesus would meet them. As they raced to obey, Jesus himself intercepted them. The women fell to the ground, threw their arms around Jesus's feet, and worshipped him.

Meanwhile, some of the soldiers from the Roman *custodia* reported to the chief priests what had happened (28:11–15). The Sanhedrin gathered and decided to bribe the soldiers to give the false report that the disciples had stolen Jesus's body while they were asleep. Later Jesus appeared to his disciples in Galilee and commanded them to acknowledge his authority over both heaven and earth by making disciples of people from all ethnic groups (28:16–20). These new disciples should be baptized and taught to obey all of Jesus's commands. Jesus promised his presence would empower his disciples to fulfill this commission.

THEOLOGY

Theological Themes

Jesus as the Fulfillment of Old Testament Messianic Predictions One of the most significant theological themes in Matthew's Gospel is that Jesus is the Messiah predicted in the Hebrew Scriptures. This fulfillment is highlighted, especially in Matthew 1–4, in the form of several fulfillment quotations. Virtually every significant event in Jesus's life is shown to fulfill Scripture:

The OT substructure of Matthew's theology is also evident in his portrayal of Jesus in relation to major OT characters. At the beginning Matthew presented Jesus as *the Son of David and the Son of Abraham* (1:1–18). Jesus is also *the new Moses*, who in his "inaugural address" in the Gospel, the Sermon on the Mount, ascends a mountain and instructs his followers in his law (chaps. 5–7).

Table 4.4: Jesus's Fulfillment of OT Prophecy in Matthew's Gospel

Gospel Event in Jesus's Life	Matthew	OT Passage
The virgin birth and name of Jesus	1:22–23	Isa 7:14; 8:8, 10
Jesus's birthplace, Bethlehem	2:5–6	Mic 5:2
The flight to Egypt	2:15	Hos 11:1
The slaying of infants by Herod	2:18	Jer 31:15
Jesus called a Nazarene ("branch")	2:23	Isa 11:1; 53:2
John the Baptist's ministry	3:3; 11:10	Isa 40:3; Mal 3:1
The temptation of Jesus	4:1–11	Deut 6:13, 16; 8:3
The beginning of Jesus's ministry	4:15–16	Isa 9:1–2
Jesus's healing ministry	8:17; 11:5; 12:17–21	Isa 53:4; 35:5–6; 42:18; 61:1
Division brought by Jesus	10:35–36	Mic 7:6
Jesus's gentle style of ministry	12:17–21	Isa 42:1–4
Jesus's death, burial, resurrection	12:40	Jonah 1:17
Hardened response to Jesus	13:14–15; 15:7–9; 21:33, 42	Isa 5:1–2; 6:9–10; 29:13; Ps 118:22–23
Jesus's teaching in parables	13:35	Ps 78:2
Jesus's triumphal entry	21:5, 9	Isa 62:11; Ps 118:26
Jesus's cleansing of the temple	21:13	Isa 56:7; Jer 7:11
Jesus as Son and Lord of David	1:1; 22:44	Ps 110:1
Lament over Jerusalem	23:38–39	Jer 12:7; 22:5; Ps 118:26
Judas's betrayal of Jesus	26:15	Zech 11:12
Peter's denial	26:31	Zech 13:7
Jesus's arrest	26:54, 56	"The Scriptures, the Prophets"
Judas's death	27:9–10	Zech 11:12–13; Jer 32:6–9
Jesus the righteous sufferer	27:34–35, 39, 43, 46, 48	Pss 22:1, 7–8,18; 69:21

Jesus as the New Moses As mentioned, a number of features in Matthew's Gospel suggest the evangelist intended to highlight important parallels between Jesus and Moses. These parallels first appear in Matthew's account of the circumstances surrounding Jesus's birth described in Matthew 2. Herod the Great sought to prevent any threat to his throne by killing the infant that the wise men recognized as the Messiah. He demanded that all male children in Bethlehem age two and under be slain. To Jewish Christian readers, Herod's action would have been reminiscent of Pharaoh's order to kill all male Israelite infants in Exodus 1.

Matthew 2 reverberates with similarities to popular Jewish traditions about Moses's birth that are preserved in texts such as Josephus's *Antiquities of the Jews*. In that account, a "sacred scribe" in Pharaoh's court foretold that an Israelite boy would be born who would bring down the Egyptian dominion, raise the Israelites, be more righteous than any other man, and obtain a glory that would be remembered through all ages. The frightened ruler responded by ordering that all male Israelite infants be cast into the Nile (Josephus, *Ant.* 2.210–16). In both Matthew's account and Josephus's, a pagan king ordered the slaughter of male Israelite infants because he feared a single child of promise.

The parallels between Jesus and Moses are emphasized even more in Matthew 2:20b. The words "those who sought the child's life are dead" are a clear and direct quotation of the Greek version (LXX) of Exodus 4:19 with only minor changes, which were necessary to adapt the statement to a new context. The angel of the Lord seems to quote these exact words in order to signal that Jesus would somehow be like Moses.

Similarly, Jesus's ascent of a mountain to deliver his authoritative interpretation and application of God's law to his people is reminiscent of Moses's ascent of Sinai to receive and deliver the law of God (Exod 19:3). Three details suggest Matthew wanted his readers to notice this parallel. First, the words "he went up on the mountain" (*anebē eis to oros*) in 5:1 are exactly parallel to the description of Moses ascending Mount Sinai in Exodus 19:3. This particular construction appears only three times in the Greek OT, and all three occurrences describe Moses's ascent of Mount Sinai (Exod 19:3; 24:18; 34:4). Second, the definite article "the" may highlight the importance of the mountain and imply a comparison with Mount Sinai. Third, many Jewish interpreters took the Hebrew text of Deuteronomy 9:9 to mean that Moses sat on the mountain when he received the law. Although the Hebrew verb *yasab* may mean to "remain" or "dwell," the most common meaning in the Hebrew OT was "sit," and references in the Talmud show that many rabbis took the verb in this sense.[70] The description of Jesus's posture on the mountain in 5:1–2 would thus constitute another parallel with Moses on Mount Sinai.

Matthew used this construction "he went up on the mountain" again in 14:23 and "he went up on a mountain" in 15:29.[71] Matthew 14:23 introduces Jesus's miracle of walking on the water, which may have been reminiscent of the miraculous crossing of the sea in Exodus 14:15–31. Similarly, Matthew 15:29 immediately precedes the miraculous feeding of the 4,000, which is reminiscent of the miracle of the manna in the wilderness. Matthew did not create or invent events in Jesus's life to make him similar to Moses. However, it seems he consciously highlighted the parallels between actual events in Jesus's life and Moses's experiences.[72]

---

[70] See *b. Megillah* 21a and *b. Sotah* 49a; cf. the reference to Jesus's ascending the mountain and sitting in Matt 15:29.

[71] The "mountain motif" constitutes an important Matthean motif in its own right, spanning all the way from the above-mentioned mountain on which Jesus delivered his first major body of teaching (chaps. 5–7) to the mountain at the end of the Gospel where he uttered his Great Commission (28:16–20). See Donaldson, *Jesus on the Mountain.*

[72] Davies and Allison (*Matthew* 1:423–24), Stott (*Christian Counter-culture*, 20–21), and Hagner (*Matthew 1–13*, 85–86) agree that the Moses typology is present here. Guelich (*Sermon on the Mount*, 52) and D. A. Carson ("Matthew," in EBC 9, rev. ed. [Grand Rapids, MI: Zondervan, 2010], 159) disagree due to the force of arguments in Davies (*Setting of*

Finally, as B. W. Bacon observed, Matthew divided his Gospel into five major sections that may be a conscious imitation of the structure of the five books of Moses.[73] Although Bacon's theory has not met with universal acceptance, it has much to commend it. Other Jewish literature consciously imitated the Pentateuch's five-book structure, and this structure closely matches the parallels Matthew established between Jesus and Moses in his narrative details and OT quotations.

The parallels between Jesus and Moses identify Jesus as the new Moses and the fulfillment of Moses's prophecy in Deuteronomy 18:15–19. The prophecy offers three descriptions of the One who would fulfill it. First, he would be an Israelite. Twice Moses described him as coming "from among your own brothers" (Deut 18:15, 18). Second, he would speak with divine authority, and the people were obligated to obey whatever he said. Third, God told Moses that the prophet would be "like you" (Deut 18:15, 18). Deuteronomy 34:10–12 listed two important features of Moses's unique prophetic ministry: Moses's intimate relationship with God and Moses's miracles. Thus, being "like Moses" would at least involve an intimate relationship with God and numerous amazing miracles. First-century Jews recognized that the prophecy foretold the coming of a Messiah-like figure (John 6:14; 7:40). The apostle Peter recognized the text as a messianic prophecy (Acts 3:11–26) and applied it specifically to Jesus.

Matthew's presentation of Jesus as the prophet like Moses fulfilled an important theological purpose: it identified Jesus as the Savior of his people in a powerful way. Although modern Christians think of Moses primarily as a lawgiver, to the ancient Jews he was far more. Moses was recognized as a redeemer, deliverer, and savior. Stephen, the first martyr of the Christian church, presented Jesus as the fulfillment of the prophet-like-Moses prophecy. His sermon emphasized that Jesus, like Moses, was a rejected redeemer and deliverer. Stephen emphasized Moses's role as deliverer in Acts 7:25: "He assumed his people would understand that God would give them deliverance through him, but they did not understand." He emphasized Moses's role as redeemer in Acts 7:35: "This Moses, whom they rejected when they said, 'Who appointed you a ruler and a judge?'—this one God sent as a ruler and a deliverer through the angel who appeared to him in the bush. This man led them out and performed wonders and signs in the land of Egypt, at the Red Sea, and in the desert for forty years."

By showing that Jesus is the prophet like Moses, Matthew demonstrated that Jesus was not only a prophet or a miracle worker, but he was also One who would redeem and deliver his people. Whereas Moses delivered Israel from their slavery in Egypt, Jesus would rescue God's people from their sins and from their deserved punishment. Matthew 1:21 clearly stresses that Jesus "will save his people from their sins." Later, 20:28 insists that Jesus came "to give his life as a ransom for many." Jesus led his people out of their spiritual bondage much like Moses led his people out of political bondage. Jesus delivered his

---

the Sermon on the Mount, 93, 99). In fact, Davies later changed his position as the ICC commentary reflects. See the list of interpreters in Keener (*Commentary on the Gospel of Matthew*, 164n.10).

[73] Bacon, *Studies in Matthew*. See discussion above.

people from their slavery to sin much like Moses delivered his people from their slavery in Egypt. Jesus will lead his people into a spiritual promised land (5:5) much like Moses led his people to inherit the land of Canaan. Jesus's name in Hebrew *(Yeshua)* is the same as that of Moses's immediate successor, Joshua, implying that Jesus was Moses's true successor who would continue Moses's ministry in a far greater sense. As the angel announced to Joseph, "You are to name him Jesus, because he will save his people from their sins" (1:21).

The theme of Jesus as the new Moses is intensified even more by two of the OT texts Matthew quoted. In 2:15, he quoted Hosea 11:1: "Out of Egypt I called my Son." In the context of Hosea, the "son" was the nation of Israel, and the call from Egypt refers to the exodus when Pharaoh released the enslaved Hebrew people. At first it seems strange that Matthew would use this text to describe the holy family's journey from Egypt to Galilee. However, Matthew applied this text about the exodus to Jesus in order to identify Jesus as the new Moses who would lead a new exodus, who would liberate God's people from their bondage to sin much like Moses liberated his from their bondage to Pharaoh. It is no accident that the second text that Matthew applied to Jesus in 2:17 was a passage from Jeremiah 31:15 about Israel's bondage (this time in Babylon), which was immediately followed by a promise of deliverance and restoration. Matthew appealed to OT texts about bondage and redemption, slavery and deliverance, to show that Jesus was a deliverer who rescues God's people from the worst plight of all: sin and its consequences.

Jesus's identity as Savior and deliverer of those enslaved to sin is not only a theme of great texts in the NT letters but of the Gospel of Matthew as well. Moses was a savior and deliverer whose name brought to mind images of redemption and rescue. Although centuries had passed since Moses led his people to freedom from bondage to Pharaoh, his name still evoked images of rescue, deliverance, and salvation to Matthew's original readers. Through his motif identifying Jesus as the new Moses, Matthew beautifully and powerfully emphasized that Jesus came to rescue his people, to break the power of sin, and to set its captives free.

Jesus as the Davidic King Just as the Gospel of Matthew closely associates Jesus with Moses, it also closely associates King Jesus with King David. From the first verse of the Gospel, Matthew identified Jesus as "the Son of David, the Son of Abraham." The order of the two titles is significant. The genealogy itself was arranged in chronological order. Thus, it began with the most ancient ancestor, Abraham, and concluded with the final legal descendant, Jesus. By listing the titles "Son of David" and "Son of Abraham" in 1:1 in reverse chronological order, Matthew placed emphasis on Jesus's descent from David's line.

Matthew also stressed Jesus's Davidic descent by his arrangement of the genealogy. Matthew 1:17 divided Jesus's genealogy into three sets of fourteen generations. This arrangement is clearly artistic since it does not match the number of generations in each period listed in the preceding verses. The three periods actually contain thirteen, fourteen, and thirteen generations (or fourteen, fifteen, and fourteen, if each person is identified as a generation); thus, David is included twice for emphasis, ending the second and beginning the third consecutive generations respectively. Matthew's artistic arrangement in 1:17 was not a result of a simple count of generations in the genealogy but was intended to communicate a message about Jesus's identity. Matthew was utilizing a literary device common among the rabbis of his day. This device was called *gematria,* which used the numeric value of the letters of the Hebrew alphabet to communicate an encoded message. The code was simple, and Matthew's readers would have been familiar with it. The first letter of the Hebrew alphabet represented the number 1, the second letter represented the number 2, and so forth. Using this device, the numeric value of the consonants of David's name was *daleth* (four), *waw* (six), and *daleth* (four), which made a total of fourteen. In Hebrew *gematria*, the number fourteen thus represented King David. Hence, the artistic arrangement of the genealogy, like the title, emphasized Jesus's Davidic descent.[74]

The important role of David in Jesus's lineage was stressed again in the heart of the genealogy. Although the genealogy of Jesus contained the names of many kings, ranging from David to Jechoniah, only David was specifically identified as a king. This implies that Matthew stressed Jesus's Davidic lineage in order to demonstrate that Jesus was qualified to reign as King. Old Testament prophecies foretold that the Messiah, the eternal King of God's people, would be a descendent of David. In 2 Samuel 7:11–16, Nathan prophesied that God would raise up a descendant of David and establish the throne of his kingdom forever. In light of this prophecy, many first-century Jews recognized that the Messiah would be a descendant of David. The Davidic Messiah was described in clear terms in Isaiah 9:1–7, a text Matthew explicitly quoted in 4:15–16 that has close connections with the prophecy in Isaiah 7:14 that Matthew quoted in 1:23. The climax of the messianic prophecy in Isaiah 9 says,

> For a child will be born for us, a son will be given to us, and the government will be on his shoulders. He will be named Wonderful Counselor, Mighty God, Eternal Father, Prince of Peace. The dominion will be vast, and its prosperity will never end. He will reign on the throne of David and over his kingdom, to establish and sustain it with justice and righteousness from now on and forever. The zeal of the Lord of Armies will accomplish this. (Isa 9:6–7)

Matthew presented Jesus as this long-awaited King, the rightful heir to David's throne, the ruler of God's people.[75]

Matthew emphasized Jesus's identity as the Davidic Messiah again in 2:23. He explained that after Joseph, Mary, and Jesus returned from Egypt, they chose to settle in the city of Nazareth. Matthew added that this fulfilled "what was spoken by the prophets."

---

[74] See the list of commentators in Keener, *Commentary on the Gospel of Matthew*, 74n6. Keener himself downplayed the numerical symbolism, conjecturing that "perhaps fourteen was simply Matthew's average estimate of the generations" or that "Matthew preferred a round number for each set of generations, perhaps for ease of memorization."

[75] For a biblical-theological study, see A. J. Köstenberger and A. E. Stewart, *The First Days of Jesus: The Story of the Incarnation* (Wheaton, IL: Crossway, 2015), "Part 1: Virgin-Born Messiah," 29–91.

He summarized the prophetic message, "He will be called a Nazarene." No single OT prophecy suggests that the Messiah would live in Nazareth. However, the plural noun "prophets" suggests that Jesus's identity as a Nazarene was foretold in multiple places in the OT and belonged to a broad prophetic theme. The best explanation of this is that Matthew saw a connection between the name Nazarene and the "branch" prophecies of the OT.[76] The prophets used the image of the branch to describe the descendant of David who would reign over God's people. Isaiah 11:1 referred to the Messiah as a branch *(neser)* from Jesse, father of David: "Then a shoot will grow from the stump of Jesse, and a branch from his roots will bear fruit." This prophecy promised that the Spirit of Yahweh would rest on this branch. He would be characterized by righteousness, knowledge, and justice. He would also serve as eschatological judge: "He will strike the land with a scepter from his mouth, and he will kill the wicked with a command from his lips" (Isa 11:4).

The promised branch is also mentioned in other texts (see Isa 4:2; Jer 23:5; 33:15).[77] An examination of these shows that the branch would be a descendent of David (or of David's father, Jesse) who would reign with wisdom and justice forever, who would judge the earth for sins, and who would save God's people. Matthew observed that the consonants of Jesus's hometown matched the consonants of one of the Hebrew words for branch and used this to point to Jesus as the long-awaited branch, Israel's Messiah.

Matthew confirmed Jesus's identity as the Messiah in many other ways and in many other texts. Material that Matthew shares with Mark and Luke also clearly expresses Jesus's messianic identity. However, the texts discussed above are especially important for an understanding of Matthew's theological emphases since they are unique to Matthew's Gospel. These and numerous other texts in Matthew demonstrate that one of his major theological purposes was to explain that Jesus is the Messiah. Matthew wanted his readers to recognize that Jesus was the One whom the Father appointed to reign over his eternal kingdom. He wanted those same readers to bow in homage before Jesus and surrender to his authority as King.

Jesus as the "Son of Man" The exact meaning of the title "Son of Man" is debated in biblical scholarship. Jesus was especially fond of this designation and frequently used it as a self-reference. Each of the four Gospels contains references to Jesus as the "Son of Man." (It occurs more often in the Synoptics than in John; even Mark's short Gospel contains more references than John does.) Matthew alone used this title of Jesus some thirty-one times. The abundance of Jesus's self-references as the "Son of Man" indicates that this was not only how Jesus viewed himself but also how he wanted others to view him. The question remains, What meaning is the term "Son of Man" supposed to convey?

---

[76] See Hagner, *Matthew 1–13*, 41; Gundry, *Matthew*, 40; and Davies and Allison, *Matthew*, 1:277–79 (though they see this as a "secondary" allusion). Others who affirmed this view include M. Black, K. Stendahl, U. Luz, A. Schlatter, and B. Weiss.

[77] Hebrew terms other than *netser* are used to identify the branch in these texts. See also Zech 3:8 and 6:12.

The OT contains a notable reference to "One like a son of man" in Daniel 7:13. In this passage Daniel has a vision of four beasts, the last of which is blasphemous and boastful. In the midst of the fourth beast's boasting, thrones appear, and the Ancient of Days takes his seat (Dan 7:9). The four beasts are judged, and the "One like a son of man" enters the scene. As he stands before the Ancient of Days, this "son of man" is given authority to rule over everything with an everlasting dominion. In a number of his references to himself as Son of Man, Jesus clearly alludes to this OT text (24:30; 25:31; 26:64). Thus, as Son of Man, Jesus is the One whom God has appointed to rule over people of every nation, tribe, and tongue forever.

However, this "son of man" figure is far more than a mere human king. Daniel 7:14 says that "all peoples, nations, and languages should serve him." The verb translated "serve" (*plkh*) elsewhere refers exclusively to the worship of God or gods (Dan 3:12, 17–18, 28). Furthermore, the connection between the Ancient of Days vision and the Son of Man vision in Daniel implies that the Son of Man was enthroned beside the Ancient of Days and reigned as his coregent. The oldest manuscript of the Septuagint actually identified the Son of Man as the Ancient of Days. Intertestamental Jewish literature even assigned the divine name Yahweh to the Son of Man. This shows that the title Son of Man strongly implies Jesus's deity. The notion that the title merely asserts Jesus's humanity is terribly mistaken.[78]

Jesus's Atoning Death Matthew affirmed the presentation of temple sacrifices by Jewish Christian disciples in accordance with Jesus's own teaching (5:23–24). However, he insisted on referring to sacrifices as "gifts" (*dōron*; 5:23–24; 8:4; 15:5; 23:18–19) except in cases in which he is directly quoting the OT (9:13; 12:7) or criticizing Jewish ritualism that devalued devotion to God and love for other people (12:33). Although a wide range of vocabulary was used in the Septuagint to refer to specific types of offerings, common terms for sacrifice in general were "sacrifice" *(thysia)* and "offering" (*dōron*). However, the term "sacrifice" was far more common than "offering" or "gift." In the Pentateuch the term *thusia* was used to describe sacrifices 179 times, but the term *dōron* was used in that sense only 85 times. Against this background Matthew's consistent use of *dōron* for sacrifices seems significant.

Matthew's preference for the term is especially striking in 8:4. In the parallel in Mark 1:44, Jesus commanded the leper whom he had healed to offer "what Moses prescribed for your cleansing, as a testimony to them," which could be taken to imply that the offering actually accomplished ritual cleansing. However, Matthew preferred to describe the sacrifice for lepers required by Leviticus 14:10–20 as "the *gift* Moses prescribed" and removed the reference to cleansing. The OT clearly presented this offering as an atoning sacrifice. Although Leviticus 14:10–20 is rich with sacrificial terminology, the term "gift" was not used to speak of this particular sacrifice. But apparently Matthew departed from

---

[78] For more background to the title "Son of Man," see C. L. Quarles, "Lord or Legend? Jesus as the Messianic Son of Man," in *Can We Trust the New Testament on the Historical Jesus? Bart Ehrman and Craig Evans in Dialogue* (Minneapolis, MN: Fortress, forthcoming); idem, *Theology of Matthew*, 87–95, 134–38.

the precedent in Leviticus and Mark in order to describe the offering as a gift, more an expression of gratitude than a ritual that secures atonement.[79]

This tendency in Matthew's Gospel suggests he was determined to make his readers rethink the significance of sacrifice. Although they were encouraged to continue participation in the temple rituals, they were to view sacrifices as gifts that expressed thanksgiving for forgiveness and cleansing already received rather than as offerings that accomplished forgiveness. This Matthean tendency is likely related to Matthew's view of Jesus's sacrificial death as the means of atonement for sin. Matthew's quotation of Isaiah 53:4 in 8:17 shows that he recognized Jesus as the fulfillment of Isaiah 53, the One whose sacrifice would remove the guilt of God's people. Echoes of Isaiah 53 also abound in Matthew: he seems to have alluded to Isaiah 53:2 (Matt 2:23), 53:5 (Matt 26:67), 53:7 (Matt 26:63; 27:12, 14), 53:9 (Matt 26:24), and 53:12 (Matt 27:38).[80] There are more quotations and allusions to Isaiah 53 in Matthew than in any other NT book.[81]

Matthew's sacrificial theology recognized Jesus as the one true and effective sacrifice. Consequently, all other sacrifices that sought atonement were now *passé*. Sacrifices were appropriate only when they expressed gratitude for forgiveness and cleansing by Jesus's atoning work, not when they sought atonement through rituals performed. This sacrificial theology also surfaced in 20:28 where Jesus said that "the Son of Man did not come to be served, but to serve, and to give his life as a ransom for many." It climaxed with Jesus's statement during the Last Supper: "For this is my blood of the covenant; it is shed for many for the forgiveness of sins" (26:28).

Thus, the Gospel of Matthew emphasizes that Jesus was the Savior of sinners who secured their atonement through his sacrificial death. Like the writer of Hebrews, Matthew stressed that the animal sacrifices offered in the temple could not effect atonement. Matthew also shared the conviction that "it is impossible for the blood of bulls and goats to take away sins. . . . We have been sanctified through the offering of the body of Jesus Christ once for all time" (Heb 10:4, 10).

The Great Commission and the Inclusion of the Gentiles Matthew was a Jewish Christian who originally wrote for a predominantly Jewish Christian audience. One of his purposes in writing the Gospel was to demonstrate that Israel's Messiah did not come for the benefit of Israel alone. Rather, he came to offer salvation to all the peoples of the earth.[82] This theological theme surfaces at a number of points in Matthew's Gospel, beginning in his genealogy of Jesus. Although scholars have suggested a variety of motives for Matthew's inclusion of the names of four women in the genealogy, one possible reason is that all four

---

[79] In the Pentateuch (LXX), "gifts" are described as effecting atonement only twice (Lev 9:7; Num 15:25).

[80] See the "Index of Quotations" and "Index of Allusions and Verbal Parallels," in *The Greek New Testament*, 4th ed., ed. B. and K. Aland et al. (Stuttgart, Germany: United Bible Societies, 1993), 887–901.

[81] One quotation and seven allusions to Isaiah 53 appear in Matthew, and 1 Peter is only slightly behind Matthew with one quotation and six allusions—a remarkable concentration for such a brief letter.

[82] See A. J. Köstenberger and P. T. O'Brien, *Salvation to the Ends of the Earth: A Biblical Theology of Mission*, NSBT 11 (Downers Grove, IL: InterVarsity, 2001), 87–109 (with further bibliographic references).

of the women were Gentiles. Ancient Jewish texts describe Tamar as a "foreigner" (Philo, *Virt.* 220–22) and particularly as an Aramean (*Jub.* 41:1–2; *Test. Jud.* 10:1–2). Rahab was a Canaanite from Jericho (Josh 2:8–24). Ruth was a Moabite (Ruth 1:4). Bathsheba was probably viewed as possessing the status of a Hittite, like her husband Uriah (2 Sam 11:3). The mention of these four thus may have signaled God's intention to include Gentiles in his redemptive plan.

This theme surfaced again in Matthew's account of the summons of the wise men to worship Jesus in Bethlehem (Matt 2:1–12). First-century Eastern wise men mixed together the false religion of Zoroastrianism with astrology, the interpretation of dreams and visions, and black magic. Eastern wise men are described in some detail in the book of Daniel (2:2, 4–5, 10), where the magi are associated with "diviner-priests," "mediums," and "sorcerers" in the court of the king of Babylon. The wise men thus represented the leaders of the false religions of the Gentile world (see Acts 13:6–10). Their humble and reverent worship of Jesus stands in stark contrast to the apparent apathy of the Jewish leaders and their refusal to investigate the possibility that the Messiah had been born. This foreshadows Jesus's rejection by the Jewish leaders and his acceptance by Gentiles later in the Gospel.

In Matthew 3:6, John's warning that God could raise up children for Abraham from the stones hints that God may form a new Israel that is not necessarily composed of Abraham's physical descendants. Matthew 4:12–16 describes Jesus's decision to establish his ministry headquarters in Capernaum as a fulfillment of God's promise in Isaiah 9:1–2 to bring light to "Galilee of the nations." In Matthew 4:24, people from Syria, probably including Gentiles, began to bring sick and diseased friends and family members to Jesus for healing. The crowds from the Decapolis that followed Jesus (4:25) were probably largely composed of Gentiles.

In Matthew 8:5–13, Jesus offered to enter the house of a Roman centurion. This would have defied the Jewish taboo against entering the house of a Gentile (Acts 10:28). Jesus exclaimed that the faith of this Gentile exceeded any faith he had encountered in Israel. He clearly implied the inclusion of the Gentiles in the kingdom of God by claiming that many from the east and the west would enter the kingdom and feast with Abraham, Isaac, and Jacob. He also warned that many "sons of the kingdom," Jews who rejected Jesus, would be excluded from the kingdom.

Matthew 12:15–21 identifies Jesus as the fulfillment of Isaiah 42:1–4, a prophecy climaxing with the promise "the nations will put their hope in his name." In Matthew 12:41–42, Jesus reminded the scribes and Pharisees of the Ninevites and the queen of the South who had repented and sought true wisdom from the ends of the earth. He warned that these Gentiles would stand up on the day of judgment and condemn Jewish leaders who rejected Jesus. Matthew 15:21–28 describes Jesus's kindness to a Gentile woman, and she is specifically called a "Canaanite" (cf. Mark 7:26), probably in order to associate this woman with the most notorious pagan enemy of Israel. Jesus's kindness to her shows that the Gentiles, whom first-century Jews regarded as most despicable, may follow Christ and be blessed by him. In Matthew 15:29–31, Jesus healed the sick on the northern shores of the Sea of Galilee in what was apparently Gentile territory. The people's praise "to the God of Israel" implies Gentiles were glorifying the God associated with the Israelites.

The theme of God's inclusion of the Gentiles climaxed at Jesus's crucifixion with the confession of the Roman centurion and his guards who exclaimed, "This man really was the Son of God!" (27:54). Their bold confession is in stark contrast to the refusal of the Jewish leaders to believe even after the soldiers reported Jesus's resurrection. Finally, the theme was clearly stated in the Great Commission in which Jesus urged his followers to make disciples of "all nations" (28:19–20).

Although it is Luke's Gospel that is commonly recognized as the Gospel that emphasizes that God has incorporated Gentile believers into the new Israel, this great theological theme is just as prominent in the Gospel penned by one of Jesus's own Jewish followers. If this theme had been fully appreciated by other Jewish Christians in the early church, the tensions between Jewish and Gentile Christians that Paul had to address so frequently in his letters might never have arisen. Although Paul is recognized as the great apostle to the Gentiles, Matthew's Gospel demonstrates that at least one of the Twelve was equally committed to Gentile outreach. The convictions Paul expressed in Ephesians 2:11–22 were cherished by Matthew also. Though Gentiles had once been "without Christ, excluded from the citizenship of Israel, and foreigners to the covenants of promise, without hope and without God in the world," now those who were far away had been "brought near by the blood of Christ." Gentile disciples of Jesus were "no longer foreigners and strangers, but fellow citizens with the saints, and members of God's household."

CONTRIBUTION TO THE CANON

- Genealogy of Jesus Christ, the Son of Abraham, the Son of David (1:1–17)
- Account of the virgin birth of Christ (1:18–25)
- Fulfillment quotations showing that Jesus is the Messiah (1–4)
- Five major discourses or teaching sections of Jesus, including the Sermon on the Mount (5–7), the commissioning of the Twelve (10), Jesus's parables of the kingdom (13; 18), and his final teachings, including the Olivet Discourse on the end times (23–25)
- The Great Commission (28:16–20)

STUDY QUESTIONS

1. Who does the earliest extant external evidence suggest wrote Matthew's Gospel?
2. Did Matthew write his Gospel in the Hebrew language? Explain your answer.
3. When did Matthew most likely write his Gospel? Why is an early date significant?
4. What are the two most likely locations where Matthew's Gospel may have been written?

5. To what geographical area did Matthew write? What demonstrates this?
6. What are the primary and secondary purposes of Matthew's Gospel?
7. What is the most prominent feature of Matthew's structure?
8. Which phrase used by the evangelist enables the interpreter to identify the overall structure of Matthew's Gospel?
9. What are two instances in which Matthew used numerical symbolism to make his theological point?
10. What are the chapters in Matthew that correspond to the Sermon on the Mount and the final eschatological discourse?
11. Which feature is particularly prominent in Matthew 1–4?

FOR FURTHER STUDY

Allison, D. C., Jr. *The New Moses: A Matthean Typology*. Minneapolis, MN: Fortress, 1993.

________. *Studies in Matthew: Interpretation Past and Present.* Grand Rapids, MI: Baker, 2005.

Aune, D. E., ed. *The Gospel of Matthew in Current Study*. Grand Rapids, MI: Eerdmans, 2001.

Blomberg, C. L. *Matthew*. New American Commentary 22. Nashville, TN: Broadman, 1992.

________. "Matthew." Pages 1–109 in *Commentary on the New Testament Use of the Old Testament*. Edited by G. K. Beale and D. A. Carson. Grand Rapids, MI: Baker, 2007.

Brown, J. K. "Matthew, Gospel of." Pages 570–84 in *Dictionary of Jesus and the Gospels*. 2nd ed. Edited by J. B. Green, J. K. Brown, and N. Perrin. Downers Grove, IL: InterVarsity, 2013.

Carson, D. A. "Matthew." Pages 23–670 in *Matthew, Mark, Luke*. Vol. 9 of *The Expositor's Bible Commentary*. Rev. ed. Grand Rapids, MI: Zondervan, 2010.

Davies, W. D., and D. C. Allison. *Matthew*. 3 vols. International Critical Commentary. Edinburgh, Scotland: T&T Clark, 1988–1997.

Evans, C. A. *Matthew*. New Cambridge Bible Commentary. New York, NY: Cambridge University Press, 2012.

France, R. T. *The Gospel of Matthew*. New International Commentary on the New Testament. Grand Rapids, MI: Eerdmans, 2007.

________. *Matthew: Evangelist and Teacher*. Grand Rapids, MI: Zondervan, 1989.

Gundry, R. *Matthew: A Commentary on His Handbook for a Mixed Church Under Persecution*. 2nd ed. Grand Rapids, MI: Eerdmans, 1994.

Gurtner, D. M., and J. Nollands, eds. *Built upon the Rock: Studies in the Gospel of Matthew.* Grand Rapids, MI: Eerdmans, 2008.

Hagner, D. A. *Matthew*. 2 vols. Word Biblical Commentary 33. Dallas, TX: Word, 1993.

Keener, C. S. *A Commentary on the Gospel of Matthew.* Grand Rapids, MI: Eerdmans, 1999.

Kingsbury, J. D. *Matthew: Structure, Christology, Kingdom*. Philadelphia, PA: Fortress, 1975.

Luz, U. *Matthew in History: Interpretation, Influence, and Effects*. Minneapolis, MN: Fortress, 1994.

________. *Matthew*. 3 vols. Hermeneia. Minneapolis, MN: Fortress, 2001–2007.

McKnight, S. "Matthew, Gospel of." Pages 526–41 in *Dictionary of Jesus and the Gospels*. Downers Grove, IL: InterVarsity, 1992.

Nolland, J. *The Gospel of Matthew*. New International Greek Testament Commentary. Grand Rapids, MI: Eerdmans, 2005.

Osborne, G. *Matthew*. Exegetical Commentary on the New Testament. Grand Rapids, MI: Zondervan, 2010.

Pennington, J. T. *Heaven and Earth in the Gospel of Matthew*. Grand Rapids, MI: Baker, 2007.

Powell, M. A., ed. *Methods for Matthew*. Methods in Biblical Interpretation. New York, NY: Cambridge University Press, 2009.

Quarles, C. L. *A Theology of Matthew: Jesus Revealed as Deliverer, King, and Incarnate Creator.* Philipsburg, NJ: P&R, 2013.

________. *Sermon on the Mount: Restoring Christ's Message to the Modern Church.* NAC Studies in Bible and Theology 11. Nashville, TN: B&H Academic, 2011.

Stanton, G. N. *A Gospel for a New People: Studies in Matthew*. Edinburgh, Scotland: T&T Clark, 1992.

__________. "Matthew." Pages 205–19 in *It Is Written: Scripture Citing Scripture.* Cambridge, UK: Cambridge University Press, 1988.

Turner, D. L. *Matthew.* Baker Exegetical Commentary on the New Testament. Grand Rapids, MI: Baker, 2008.

Wilkins, M. J. *Matthew*. NIV Application Commentary. Grand Rapids, MI: Zondervan, 2004.

Chapter 5

The Gospel According to Mark

CORE KNOWLEDGE

Basic Knowledge: Students should know the key facts of Mark's Gospel. With regard to history, students should be able to identify the Gospel's author, date, provenance, destination, and purpose. With regard to literature, they should be able to provide a basic outline of the book and identify core elements of the book's content found in the Unit-by-Unit Discussion. With regard to theology, students should be able to identify Mark's major theological themes.

Intermediate Knowledge: Sudents should be able to present the arguments for historical, literary, and theological conclusions. With regard to history, students should be able to discuss the evidence for Markan authorship, date, provenance, destination, and purpose. With regard to literature, they should be able to provide a detailed outline of the book. With regard to theology, students should be able to discuss Mark's major theological themes and the ways in which they uniquely contribute to the NT canon.

Advanced Knowledge: Students should be able to interact with theories about Mark's identity. In addition, they should be able to evaluate critically Peter's role in the writing of Mark's Gospel, assess the originality of the various proposed endings to the Gospel, and be able to discuss the theological significance of the Markan "messianic secret" motif.

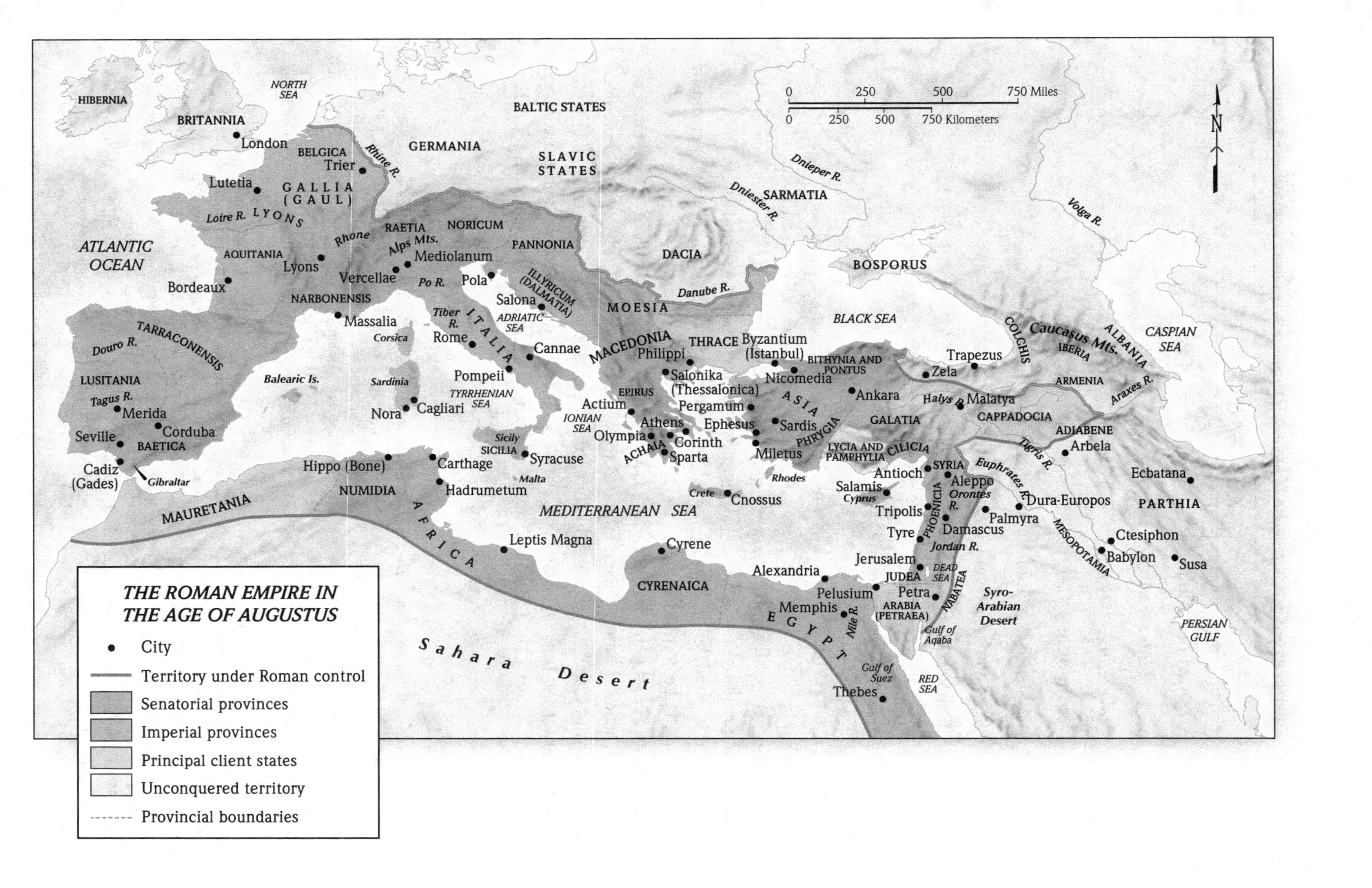
THE ROMAN EMPIRE IN THE AGE OF AUGUSTUS
City
Territory under Roman control
Senatorial provinces
Imperial provinces
Principal client states
Unconquered territory
Provincial boundaries
0 250 500 750 Miles
0 250 500 750 Kilometers
N
HIBERNIA
BRITANNIA
London
NORTH SEA
BALTIC STATES
GERMANIA
SLAVIC STATES
BELGICA
Trier
Rhine R.
Lutetia
GALLIA (GAUL)
LYONS
Loire R.
ATLANTIC OCEAN
AQUITANIA
Lyons
Rhone
Bordeaux
NARBONENSIS
Massalia
RAETIA
NORICUM
Alps Mts.
Mediolanum
Vercellae
Po R.
PANNONIA
Pola
ILLYRICUM (DALMATIA)
Salona
ADRIATIC SEA
Tiber R.
ITALIA
Rome
Cannae
Pompeii
Corsica
Sardinia
TYRRHENIAN SEA
Nora
Cagliari
Sicily
SICILIA
Syracuse
Malta
IONIAN SEA
TARRACONENSIS
Douro R.
LUSITANIA
Tagus R.
Merida
Corduba
Seville
BAETICA
Cadiz (Gades)
Gibraltar
Balearic Is.
MAURETANIA
NUMIDIA
Hippo (Bone)
Carthage
Hadrumetum
AFRICA
Leptis Magna
MEDITERRANEAN SEA
Sahara Desert
DACIA
Danube R.
MOESIA
MACEDONIA
THRACE
Philippi
Salonika (Thessalonica)
EPIRUS
Actium
Olympia
ACHAIA
Athens
Corinth
Sparta
Crete
Cnossus
Byzantium (Istanbul)
BITHYNIA AND PONTUS
Nicomedia
Pergamum
ASIA
Ephesus
Sardis
Miletus
PHRYGIA
Rhodes
BLACK SEA
BOSPORUS
SARMATIA
Dnieper R.
Dniester R.
Volga R.
Ankara
GALATIA
LYCIA AND PAMPHYLIA
CILICIA
Cyprus
Salamis
Trapezus
Zela
COLCHIS
Caucasus Mts.
IBERIA
ALBANIA
CASPIAN SEA
ARMENIA
Araxes R.
Halys R.
Malatya
CAPPADOCIA
ADIABENE
Arbela
Tigris R.
Euphrates R.
SYRIA
Antioch
Aleppo
Orontes R.
PHOENICIA
Tripolis
Tyre
Damascus
Palmyra
Dura-Europos
MESOPOTAMIA
Jordan R.
Jerusalem
JUDEA
DEAD SEA
NABATEA
Petra
ARABIA (PETRAEA)
Syro-Arabian Desert
Gulf of Aqaba
Cyrene
CYRENAICA
Alexandria
Pelusium
Memphis
Nile R.
EGYPT
Gulf of Suez
RED SEA
Thebes
Ecbatana
PARTHIA
Ctesiphon
Babylon
Susa
PERSIAN GULF

KEY FACTS

Author: John Mark, "interpreter" of Peter

Date: Mid- to late 50s

Provenance: Rome

Destination: Gentiles in Rome

Purpose: Apologetic for the cross, discipleship

Theme: Jesus is the authoritative, miracle-working Son of God

Key Verses: 10:45; 15:39

INTRODUCTION

THE GOSPEL OF Mark is the shortest of the four Gospels and has the least unique material. While it does not use the word *euangelion* as a title, it is the only Gospel to refer to its message about Jesus as the "gospel" (1:1).[1] It is regarded by many as foundational to the other two Synoptic Gospels, Matthew and Luke. About 92 percent of it is paralleled in Matthew, about 48 percent in Luke, and about 95 percent in Matthew and Luke combined.

A minority of scholars have alleged that Mark created the story of Jesus for the church.[2] A majority believe Mark pioneered the literary genre of "Gospel."[3] His opening reference to his account as "the gospel" most likely set the stage for the use of that term as a literary designation for the four distinctive literary works we now call "Gospels" and contributed to the use of "Gospel" in a literary sense in the early church (e.g., Irenaeus, *Haer 3.1.2).*[4]

[1] While it is possible that this phrase serves as the title for the Gospel as a whole, it most likely refers, as in Paul, to the saving message about Jesus and the salvation he provides (see M. Hengel, *Studies in the Gospel of Mark*, trans. J. Bowden [Philadelphia, PA: Fortress, 1985], 53). The beginning of Mark's account sets forth the prolegomena to Jesus's ministry, including the ministry of John the Baptist (1:2–8) and Jesus's baptism and temptation (1:9–13). For a helpful discussion, see D. A. Carson and D. J. Moo, *An Introduction to the New Testament*, 2nd ed. (Grand Rapids, MI: Zondervan, 2005), 169.

[2] See B. L. Mack, *A Myth of Innocence: Mark and Christian Origins* (Philadelphia, PA: Fortress, 1988); W. Schmithals, *Das Evangelium nach Markus* (Gütersloh, Germany: G. Mohn, 1979).

[3] R. A. Guelich, "Mark, Gospel of," *Dictionary of Jesus and the Gospels*, 1st ed., ed. J. B. Green, S. McKnight, and I. H. Marshall (Downers Grove, IL: InterVarsity, 1992), 512. See also the summary in Perrin, "Mark, Gospel of," *Dictionary of Jesus and the Gospels*, 2nd ed., ed. J. B. Green, J. K. Brown, and N. Perrin (Downers Grove, IL: InterVarsity, 1992), 554; and J. Diehl, "What Is a 'Gospel'? Recent Studies in the Gospel Genre," *Currents in Biblical Research* 9.2 (2011): 171–99.

[4] R. A. Guelich, *Mark 1–8:26*, WBC 34A (Dallas, TX: Word, 1989), xviiii. Marcus makes the interesting suggestion that "Mark is more the biography of a movement, or at least that movement's beginnings (*archē*), than it is the biography of an individual, and the narrative points toward the continuation of that movement after Jesus's death, both through explicit prophecies (e.g. chapter 13) and through the way in which Jesus and his followers and opponents constantly become symbols for groups in the Markan present" (J. Marcus, *Mark 1–8*, AYB 27 [New Haven, CT: Yale University Press, 2000], 66).

In terms of its relationship to the other canonical Gospels, the most widely accepted view today is that Mark was written first (Markan priority).[5] Relevant factors include, but are not limited to, the following: (1) the agreements in order and wording; (2) the less sophisticated Greek used by Mark; (3) his less developed theology; (4) the brevity of the Gospel; and (5) the awkwardness of its style. Most likely Matthew and Luke used Mark as a primary source, as well as other written and oral sources (two- or four-document hypothesis), to compose their Gospels. While the exact nature of the literary interdependence between the Synoptic Gospels remains uncertain, this is nonetheless the working hypothesis adopted by most scholars.[6]

The Gospel of Mark is a fast-paced portrayal of the life of Jesus Christ, most likely patterned after the blueprint of Petrine preaching.[7] Peter's sermon in Acts 10:34–43 provides us with a brief summary of the basic structure of the four canonical Gospels.[8] It tells us a story, the "Gospel," about Jesus (1:1; see 1:14–15; 8:35; 10:29; 13:10; 14:19).[9] The emphasis lies on the person of Christ rather than his discourses or parables. In particular, Mark focused on Jesus's performance of a variety of miraculous feats, showing himself to be the Son of God. At the same time, Mark's Gospel most keenly of any of the Synoptic Gospels accentuates the lack of understanding of Jesus's true identity by his first followers.

For this and other reasons, Mark's Gospel has been called both "paradoxical" and "enigmatic."[10] As N. Perrin notes, "The Gospel of Mark is a case study in paradox. . . . If the kerygma—the proclamation of the early church—was essentially a narrative about divine triumph despite and indeed through human suffering, then arguably there is no other text in which this paradox comes into crisper expression than the Gospel of Mark."[11]

Throughout most of Christian history, Mark's lack of unique content has led scholars to view it as an abridgment of Matthew and Luke, and this in turn contributed to its lack of popularity.[12] However, in the nineteenth century the proposal of Markan priority as a

---

[5] See the discussion in chap. 3 above.

[6] For an alternative view advocating Matthean priority, see D. A. Black, *Why Four Gospels? The Historical Origins of the Gospels* (Grand Rapids, MI: Kregel, 2001).

[7] See Bauckham, *Jesus and the Eyewitnesses*, chap. 7: "The Petrine Perspective in the Gospel of Mark." Compare with W. L. Lane, *The Gospel of Mark: The English Text with Introduction, Exposition, and Notes*, NICNT (Grand Rapids, MI: Eerdmans, 1974), 10–11.

[8] Guelich, "Mark," 513.

[9] Controversy surrounds the understanding of the term "gospel" as used here. Is it the message preached *by* Jesus the Messiah, the Son of God (see Mark 1:14); the message *about* Jesus the Messiah, the Son of God, as understood and proclaimed by the church; or the story that follows? See D. E. Garland, "Mark," in *Zondervan Illustrated Bible Backgrounds Commentary*, ed. C. E. Arnold (Grand Rapids, MI: Zondervan, 2002), 1:207. Most likely, "gospel" refers to the story about Jesus narrated in the text, but it also includes the oral tradition that supplements the text. It comprises Jesus's words, deeds, death, and resurrection as God's direct intervention into history, and it challenged imperial cult propaganda that promoted a message of good tidings and a new age of peace through the Roman emperor (Guelich, "Mark," 513).

[10] C. Focant, *The Gospel according to Mark: A Commentary*, trans. L. R. Keylock (Eugene, OR: Pickwick, 2012), 14.

[11] Perrin, "Mark," 553.

[12] J. A. Brooks, *Mark*, NAC 23 (Nashville, TN: Broadman, 1991), 17–19. Augustine (*Cons.* 1.2) considers Mark to be Matthew's "follower and abbreviator" (*Marcus eum subsecutus tamquam pedisequus et breviator eius videtur*).

solution to the Synoptic Problem, and the claim that Mark was the most historical of the Gospels, in conjunction with the quests for the historical Jesus, led to a revival of interest in this Gospel.[13] The high number of related works written over the past forty years is evidence of the rise in prominence of Mark's Gospel.[14] In recent years literary studies of Mark's narrative have rehabilitated Mark as a skillful writer and evangelist.[15]

HISTORY

Author

Like the other Gospels, Mark is formally anonymous, since the author did not explicitly identify himself. However, as in the case of Matthew and the other Gospels, the title that ascribes the Gospel to Mark is clearly early if not original.[16] If Mark was the first to write his Gospel (Markan priority) and affixed the title to the Gospel himself, the other evangelists would likely have followed suit. In any case, the titles would have become necessary as soon as the Gospels were gathered and began to circulate in a single collection.

As R. Bauckham has shown, Mark's Gospel, by way of a literary device called the "*inclusio* of eyewitness testimony" (the practice of naming first and last in the document the major eyewitness underlying an account), purports to be based on the witness of the apostle Peter (see the references to Peter in 1:16 and 16:7).[17] Another feature, the "plural-to-singular device," which singles out one individual from a group in order to tell an

---

[13] At the turn of the century, A. Schweitzer, in his monumental work *Quest of the Historical Jesus* (New York, NY: Macmillan, 1910), showed that scholars had not based their "lives" on the Gospels but on their own preconceived notions of Jesus as merely a liberal, ethical teacher. W. Wrede claimed that Mark struggled to reconcile two contrasting traditions in the early church, one that Jesus became Messiah at his resurrection and another that Jesus's earthly ministry was already messianic. Wrede believed that Jesus did not claim to be the Messiah during his earthly ministry and that Mark represented this fact by what Wrede termed the "messianic secret." About two decades later the form critics K. L. Schmidt, M. Dibelius, and R. Bultmann argued that Mark collected a number of short, independent accounts of the sayings and deeds of Jesus and invented a framework for them in order to produce a continuous account. (Form criticism is the analysis of a text according to typical and identifiable forms by which people express themselves linguistically.) From their perspective, therefore, the Markan outline, which Matthew and Luke followed, is of doubtful historical merit (Brooks, *Mark*, 19).

[14] "The traditional 'Second Gospel' became the first gospel." F. J. Moloney, *The Gospel of Mark: A Commentary* (Grand Rapids, MI: Baker, 2002), 2.

[15] See D. M. Rhoads and D. M. Michie, *Mark as Story: An Introduction to the Narrative of a Gospel*, 3rd ed. (Minneapolis, MN: Fortress, 2012); and E. Best, *Mark: The Gospel as Story* (Edinburgh, Scotland: T&T Clark, 1983). D. J. Harrington, *What Are They Saying about Mark?* (Mahwah, NJ: Paulist, 2004), 7, notes the shift in emphasis from the world behind the text to the text itself. Harrington also notes the emergence of literary, rhetorical, social-scientific, feminist, and political readings of the Gospel. See also J. C. Anderson and S. D. Moore, eds., *Mark and Method: New Approaches in Biblical Studies* 2nd ed. (Minneapolis, MN: Fortress, 2008).

[16] See M. Hengel, *The Four Gospels and the One Gospel of Jesus Christ: An Investigation of the Collection and Origin of the Canonical Gospels*, trans. J. Bowden (Harrisburg, PA: Trinity Press International, 2000), 48–53, 77. Guelich ("Mark, Gospel of," 514) suggested the title "according to Mark" was most likely added several decades subsequent to the composition of Mark's Gospel.

[17] R. Bauckham, *Jesus and the Eyewitnesses* (Grand Rapids, MI: Eerdmans, 2006), chaps. 6–7. See further below.

account from his perspective, makes Peter's the dominant perspective in the narrative, reproducing his eyewitness recollection in first-person terms.[18]

External Evidence Ancient tradition has consistently attributed this Gospel to Mark, who was believed to have been closely associated with the apostle Peter. The earliest and most important attestation of Markan authorship is that of Papias, bishop of Hierapolis in Phrygia in Asia Minor (ca. AD 60–130), whose five-volume work *Expositions of the Lord's Sayings* is cited by Eusebius in the early fourth century (*Hist.* eccl. 3.39). Papias claims to have learned of Mark's authorship from an individual he referred to as "the Elder" or "the Presbyter," thus preserving a tradition that dates at least as far back as the early second century.[19] Papias also claims that Mark was not an eyewitness but derived his material from Peter, affirming the Gospel's apostolic connection. He does not view the Gospel as having been written in a chronological fashion but rather as following the occasional nature of Peter's preaching. He states,

> And John the Presbyter also said this, Mark being the interpreter of Peter whatsoever he recorded he wrote with great accuracy but not however, in the order in which it was spoken or done by our Lord, for he neither heard nor followed our Lord, but as before said, he was in company with Peter, who gave him such instruction as was necessary, but not to give a history of our Lord's discourses: wherefore Mark has not erred in any thing, by writing some things as he has recorded them; for he was carefully attentive to one thing, not to pass by any thing that he heard, or to state any thing falsely in these accounts.[20]

Later testimony from the middle and late second century appears to rely on this tradition. Although Marcion (first half of the second century) rejected Mark's Gospel (as he did Matthew's and John's), this rejection was not related to Markan authorship, and the Anti-Marcionite Prologue affirms Markan authorship. Justin Martyr (ca. AD 100–165) makes reference to "Memoirs" that contained the following words found only in Mark's Gospel: "named Boanerges, which means 'sons of Thunder'" (*Dial. 106).*[21] Tatian used Mark's Gospel in compiling his *Diatessaron,* a synopsis of all four Gospels (ca. AD 150–160). Irenaeus of Lyons (ca. 130–200) states that Mark, Peter's disciple and interpreter, wrote this Gospel subsequent to Peter's death (*Haer.* 3.1.1). Clement of Alexandria (ca. AD 150–215; cited by Eusebius, *Hist. eccl. 6.14*), Tertullian (ca. AD 160–225), and Origen (ca. AD 185–254) all believed Mark wrote this Gospel and that Peter was his source.[22] Tradition

---

[18] Ibid., 156–64.

[19] Lane, *Gospel of Mark,* 8.

[20] Eusebius, *Ecclesiastical History,* new updated ed., trans. C. F. Cruse (Peabody, MA: Hendrickson, 1998), 104–5.

[21] As Perrin ("Mark," 559) notes, Justin Martyr speaks of "his memoirs," which could refer either to Jesus ("the memoirs about Jesus") *or* Peter ("the memoirs connected with/approved by/written 'by' Peter").

[22] Brooks, *Mark,* 18.

may vary with respect to certain details, such as Peter's exact role in connection with the composition of the Gospel and the date of authorship, but all agree that Mark wrote this Gospel and that Peter's preaching in Rome played a central role.[23]

Portrait of Mark The association of Mark with Peter by both Papias and church tradition suggests that this Mark is most likely the John Mark referenced by Luke (Acts 12:12, 25; 13:13; 15:37–39), Peter (1 Pet 5:13), and Paul (Col 4:10; Phlm 24; 2 Tim 4:11).[24] He may be the young man referred to at the end of the Gospel who fled from the scene of Jesus's arrest, leaving his linen garment behind (Mark 14:51–52), but this is less than certain.[25] His mother was a prominent member of the early Jerusalem church (Acts 12:12). It was this same Mark who accompanied his cousin Barnabas and Paul on the first missionary journey (Acts 12:25).[26] The book of Acts records that his failure to complete this journey resulted in a breach between Barnabas and Paul over Mark, which was later mended (Acts 13:13; 15:37–40; see Phlm 24; Col 4:10). In 2 Timothy 4:11, Paul wrote of his desire to have Mark join him in Rome, showing that God can restore to effective Christian ministry those who have previously failed.

Although some scholars have attempted to distinguish between the evangelist Mark, a companion of Peter (1 Pet 5:13), and John Mark, the associate of Paul in Acts and the Pauline corpus, these efforts have been largely unsuccessful.[27] Later tradition asserts that Mark was at one time bishop of Alexandria in Egypt, and Hippolytus of Rome (ca. 170–236) described him as "stump-fingered" (*Haer. 7.30;* see also the Anti-Marcionite Prologue to Mark). The Paschal Chronicle (seventh century) claims he died a martyr's death. However, the validity of these three traditions is impossible to determine.[28]

Modern Doubts Modern scholarship has frequently sought to discredit the traditional notion of Markan authorship. Several arguments stand behind this denial: (1) the occurrence of Latinisms, which are taken to reflect non-Jewish authorship; (2) the general lack of Jewish coloring; (3) the explanation of Hebrew terms and customs; and (4) the allegedly confused topography of Mark 7:31, which records Jesus traveling to Galilee and

---

[23] W. Hendriksen, *Exposition of the Gospel According to Mark,* NTC (Grand Rapids, MI: Baker, 1975), 12–13.

[24] Guelich, "Mark," 514.

[25] See Bauckham (*Jesus and the Eyewitnesses*, chap. 8, especially 197–201), who, on the basis of G. Theissen's theory of "protective anonymity," suggests that the young man mentioned in Mark 14:51–52 is Lazarus.

[26] Barnabas was probably Mark's cousin rather than his uncle. Although the AV refers to Mark as "sister's son to Barnabas" in Col 4:10, scholarly opinion understands *o` avneyio.j Barnaba/* to mean "his cousin Barnabas." So J. Dunn, *Colossians and Philemon*, NIGTC (Grand Rapids, MI: Eerdmans, 1996), 277; M. Harris, *Colossians and Philemon*, EGGNT (Grand Rapids, MI: Eerdmans, 1991), 206; BDAG 78d; EDNT 1:98. D. W. Pao notes, "The term ἀνεψιός has been misunderstood to mean nephew . . ., but ancient sources consistently use it in the sense of "cousin"; Num 36:11; Tob 7:2; Philo, *Embassy* 67; Josephus, *War* 1.662; *Ant.* 1.290" (*Colossians & Philemon*, ZECNT [Grand Rapids, MI: Zondervan, 2012], 313).

[27] Apart from the absence of any solid basis for this distinction in the tradition, the mention of both Silvanus and Mark in 1 Pet 5:12–13 makes clear that "Mark" was the "John Mark" of Acts and the Pauline corpus who with Silvanus (Silas) had also been a companion of Paul. Therefore, Mark was the companion of both Peter and Paul, and a member of the primitive community in Jerusalem that met in the upper room of his mother's home (Acts 12:12) where Jesus might have celebrated the Last Supper (see Mark 14:14–15; Acts 1:13–14). Guelich, "Mark," 514.

[28] Brooks, *Mark*, 27.

the Decapolis, southeast of Tyre, by means of Sidon to the north. Additional reasons are (5) the alleged lack of contact with Pauline theology, which indicates that Mark could not have been Paul's travel companion; (6) the negative way in which the author portrayed the disciples, especially Peter; and (7) the complex history of tradition demonstrated by form, source, and redaction criticism, which rules out any single primary witness to the life and ministry of Christ.

In response to these objections it should be noted that Mark intended his Gospel for a Gentile audience and hence accommodated his presentation to this audience while also using Semitisms that reflected his Jewish origin. Further, the circuitous itinerary of 7:31 would have been natural for an itinerant preacher. Pauline theology is reflected in Mark's emphasis on the cross, and the negative view of the disciples may have been Peter's way of counteracting the early church's tendency to exalt these first followers of Jesus.[29] As to the final objection, the use of Peter as a primary source does not necessarily rule out other sources, whether written or oral. In addition to the fact that nothing suggests that Mark had no other sources, the identification of the origins and growth of traditions is not as assured as many critics assert.[30]

Moreover, as Carson and Moo point out, the modern approach to the Gospels as a product of a long and complex process of tradition history need not conflict with the emphasis on the direct relationship between Mark and Peter that has endured from Papias through the centuries, a connection that is further confirmed in the Gospel itself. Of the four evangelists Mark most scrupulously recorded Peter's sins and weaknesses while omitting positive commendations the apostle received elsewhere (such as Matt 16:17). In some instances where Matthew did not mention Peter by name, Mark did (5:37; 11:21; 16:7).[31] Moreover, since Mark was a relatively obscure figure with a mixed record of ministry, it is unlikely he would have been chosen as a candidate for authorship by anyone desiring to attribute the Gospel to an authoritative witness.[32]

Other factors that may support Markan authorship include (1) the vividness and the rapidity of movement and detail with which this Gospel is written, which may suggest an eyewitness account (in association with Peter); (2) the harsh and negative picture of the disciples that is most plausibly explained on the assumption of an apostolic connection;[33] (3) Peter's prominence in the Gospel; (4) references to Peter that may derive from Peter himself (such as the references to Peter's "remembering" in 11:21; 14:72); (5) the overall pattern followed by the Gospel that appears to reflect Peter's preaching elsewhere

---

[29] C. Blomberg, *Jesus and the Gospels: An Introduction and Survey,* 2nd ed. (Nashville, TN: B&H, 2009), 140.

[30] Carson and Moo, *Introduction to the New Testament,* 176.

[31] Hendriksen, *Mark,* 12–13.

[32] Blomberg, *Jesus and the Gospels,* 140. And so, "as the renowned Oxford scholar B. H. Streeter once aptly opined, in the case of Matthew and John the burden of evidence remains on anyone seeking to establish traditional authorship, but in the case of Mark (and Luke) the onus falls on anyone wishing to deny traditional authorship" (Perrin, "Mark," 558).

[33] Based on the "criterion of embarrassment," one might expect the Gospel authors or their sources to omit details that would prove embarrassing to them, thus the inclusion of such potentially embarrassing material suggests authenticity.

(Acts 10:36–41); and (6) evidence of a close relationship between Peter and Mark as indicated by Peter's reference to Mark as "my son" in 1 Peter 5:13.[34]

Date

The date of Mark's Gospel continues to be the subject of considerable debate. The earliest tradition, the Anti-Marcionite Prologue, and Irenaeus (*Haer.* 3.1.1; ca. 130–200) date this Gospel after Peter's death (assumed to be ca. AD 65–66) and hence during Nero's rule.[35] Clement of Alexandria (ca. AD 150–215), on the other hand, suggests a date during Peter's time in Rome, which he claimed was sometime between the years 45 and 65.[36]

On the basis of historical and other considerations, some have proposed a date as early as the late 30s or early 40s.[37] Thus it has been alleged, for example, that the "abomination that causes desolation" in 13:14 refers to the Emperor Caligula's effort in AD 40 to put up his image in the Jerusalem temple. A date in the 50s and no later than 60 has also found proponents based on Peter's being in Rome in the 50s and on an acceptance of Markan priority and a date for Luke no later than 62. Carson and Moo propose a date in the late 50s or the 60s.[38]

If, as tradition suggests, Peter had significant input in Mark's Gospel, then a very early date is unlikely because Peter probably did not arrive in Rome much before AD 62. This may be supported by the fact that Peter is not mentioned in Paul's Prison Epistles.[39] For this reason some believe that Mark's Gospel was written sometime in the mid- to late 60s after Peter's death.

According to tradition, Peter died a martyr's death in Rome during the persecution of Christians by Nero (AD 64–66), so his martyrdom is usually dated to AD 65 or 66.[40] With reference to Mark 13, taken to reflect the time of the Jewish revolt between AD 66 and 70, Guelich and others suggest AD 66–67 as the most likely date.[41] A late date in the 70s has also been proposed by some who see Mark 13 as reflecting the actual sacking of Jerusalem by the Roman armies.

However, Mark 13 is best taken as prophetic rather than contemporary to the time of writing, and a late date on the basis of Mark 13 should therefore be judged as unnecessary

---

[34] Carson and Moo, *Introduction to the New Testament*, 176–77; Hendriksen, *Mark*, 12–13.

[35] Guelich, "Mark," 514; Anti-Marcionite Prologue; Irenaeus, *Haer.* 3.1.1 (ca. 160–80).

[36] Though see discussion below. See Guelich, "Mark," 514; Eusebius, *Hist. eccl.* 6.14.5–7.

[37] E.g., James G. Crossley, *The Date of Mark's Gospel: Insight from the Law in Earliest Christianity* (London, UK: T&T Clark, 2004), who holds that "abomination of desolation" refers to Caligula's actions. See also the discussion in Carson and Moo, *Introduction to the New Testament*, 179–82.

[38] Carson and Moo, *Introduction to the New Testament*, 182. See their entire discussion on pp. 179–82.

[39] Brooks, *Mark*, 28.

[40] Ibid.

[41] The only relevant data in Mark may come in 13:14, when read against the historical background of the Jewish War of the years 66–73. Mark set the discourse in 13:3–37 in the context of the predicted fall of Jerusalem. Not only does the "abomination" lack a personal referent in the events of the destruction of the temple, but the summons to "flee to the hills" makes little sense after Rome completely surrounded Jerusalem with a tight military blockade in the years 67–69 that prevented all entrances and exits. See Guelich, "Mark," 514.

and unlikely.[42] If Mark was the first to write his Gospel and if Luke used Mark in writing his, and since the book of Acts was likely written in the early 60s and Luke before that, then all these factors would place the most probable date for the writing of Mark's Gospel in the second half of the 50s.

Provenance

It is difficult to determine where Mark was when he wrote his Gospel. Various possibilities have been suggested: Galilee, the Decapolis, Tyre, Sidon, Syria, the East, and Rome. Traditionally, the provenance of Mark's Gospel was identified as the "regions of Italy" by the Anti-Marcionite Prologue, and Clement of Alexandria, (ca. AD 150–215) in his *Hypotyposes*, located it in Rome during Peter's ministry (Eusebius, *Hist. eccl.* 2.15; 6.14.6). John Chrysostom (*Hom. Matt.* 1.7; ca. AD 347–407) even set Mark's Gospel in Egypt, a notion that probably originated with the insufficiently attested tradition that Mark once served as bishop of Alexandria.[43] For the most part, tradition associates Mark's Gospel with Peter and consequently with Rome.[44]

Although internal evidence is scanty, what little there is points to an origin in Rome. Mark used a considerable number of Latinisms. For instance, the two copper coins *(lepta)* the poor widow cast into the offering box are explained as amounting to one Roman *quadrans* (also called "penny," padram; 12:42), and the palace (*aulē*) into which the soldiers led Jesus is called the *praetorium* (the governor's official residence; 15:16).[45] Guelich noted that readers in the East would not have needed any clarification of the underlying Greek expressions but that such would have been necessary for a Western audience in Rome. But he also pointed out that this argument from language "is hardly conclusive, since many of the Latinisms do reflect semi-technical expressions common to military and trade and would be found in any area, such as the East, occupied by Roman forces."[46] Nevertheless, this does not disqualify Rome as the most likely place of origin, even though Latin was spoken in areas outside of Rome as well.

Another possible piece of evidence pointing to a Roman provenance is the mention of Rufus in 15:21. As Hendriksen notes, "Mark is also the only Gospel that informs us (15:21) that Simon of Cyrene was 'the father of Alexander and Rufus,' who were evidently

---

[42] Carson and Moo, *Introduction to the New Testament*, 182: "Mark 13 shows very little evidence of being influenced by the course of events in A.D. 70. Jesus's predictions reflect stock Old Testament and Jewish imagery having to do with the besieging of cities rather than the specific circumstances of the siege of Jerusalem."

[43] Brooks, *Mark*, 27.

[44] Garland (*Mark*, 206) notes that a Palestinian origin of the Gospel should not be discounted since a good case can be made for it.

[45] Robert H. Stein, *Mark*, BECNT (Grand Rapids, MI: Baker, 2008), 11–12.

[46] As with date and author, the lack of explicit references supporting any one locale means that the issue of place has little to do with how one reads or understands the Gospel. Consequently, time and space locators in Mark belong strictly to the narrative rather than to the historical setting of when and where the Gospel was written. See Guelich, "Mark," 515.

well-known in Rome (see Rom 16:13)."[47] Mark also reckoned time in accordance with the Roman method, referring to the four watches of the night rather than the traditional three in Jewish reckoning (6:48; 13:35).[48] Moreover, references to suffering and persecution in Mark's Gospel may reflect the persecution of believers in Rome. Other NT evidence includes 1 Peter 5:13, which places Mark together with Peter in "Babylon" (i.e., Rome) in the early 60s—roughly at the same time Mark likely wrote his Gospel.[49] For these and other reasons, an origin in Rome is most likely.

Destination

The universal character of this Gospel has been noted by many, and this makes it difficult to pinpoint a specific audience for Mark's Gospel. But a non-Jewish destination is supported by the fact that several Aramaic terms and expressions are translated into Greek: *boanerges* ("Sons of Thunder"; 3:17), *talitha cumi* ("Little girl, I say to you, get up!"; 5:41), *corban* ("an offering"; 7:11), *ephphatha* ("Be opened!"; 7:34), *Bartimaeus* ("son of Timaeus"; 10:46), *abba* ("Father"; 14:36), *Golgotha* ("Place of the Skull"; 15:22), and *Elōi, Elōi, lemá sabachtháni*? ("My God, my God, why have you abandoned me?"; 15:34).

In addition, Jewish laws and customs are often explained, such as the washing of hands (7:3–5), the custom to sacrifice the Passover lamb on the first day of the Feast of Unleavened Bread (14:12), and the "day of preparation" being the day before the Sabbath (15:42).[50] Moreover, Mark displayed an interest in the cessation of ritual elements in the Mosaic law, especially food laws (see 7:19).[51] While this most probably provides evidence of their non-Jewish ethnic background, it may only reflect the original readers' unfamiliarity with certain forms of Judaism.[52]

As mentioned above, in support of a Roman provenance are the frequent Latinisms, the reference to Rufus, and the use of the Roman method of reckoning time, all of which may point not only to the Gospel's origin in Rome but to a Roman destination as well. The mention of Roman coins (*lepta*; 12:42) and other Latin loan words, such as "Legion" (*legiōn*; 5:9), "executioner" (*spekoulator*; 6:27), "flogged" (*phragelloō*; 15:15), "praetorium" (*praitōrion*; 15:16), and "centurion" (*kentyriōn*; 15:39), combine to lend Mark's Gospel a distinct Roman flavor that renders a Roman provenance and/or destination plausible.

---

[47] Hendriksen, *Mark,* 13. However, "[the use of Rufus in both Mark 15:21 and Rom 16:13] could be a mere coincidence, if one takes into account that Rufus was one of the most widespread names in Rome. In Lampe's list (*Stadtrömischen Christen*, 189) it comes in third place in frequency, with 374 known cases, after more than 1,400 occurrences of Julia and 841 of Hermes. The argument is thus fragile." Focant, *Gospel according to Mark*, 7–8.

[48] Lane, *Gospel of Mark*, 24.

[49] Or, perhaps more likely, a few years after Mark wrote his Gospel (see the discussion under Date above). Cf. Carson and Moo, *Introduction to the New Testament*, 177, and their entire discussion on pp. 177–79.

[50] Hendriksen, *Mark*, 13.

[51] Carson and Moo, *Introduction to the New Testament*, 183.

[52] Hence, Guelich ("Mark," 515) suggests that claiming more goes beyond the evidence. See L. W. Hurtado, *Mark,* NIBC (Peabody, MA: Hendrickson, 1989), 6: "The only positive conclusion to draw is that Mark wrote for Gentile Christians located somewhere outside of Palestine."

Another possible piece of evidence in this regard is that this Gospel reaches its climax in the confession of Jesus's deity by a *Roman centurion* (15:39). Hence, many believe it is no coincidence that a Roman utters the climactic confession of Jesus as the Son of God in this Gospel. Most likely Mark carefully crafted his narrative so as to culminate his presentation of Jesus as the Son of God in the Roman centurion's confession. Consequently, "Roman Christianity found in the Gospel an account peculiarly appropriate to its life and problems."[53]

To sum up, this internal evidence suggests Mark's first readers were most likely Greek-speaking individuals who did not know Aramaic or Hebrew and were for the most part unfamiliar with certain Jewish customs. At the same time, they seem to have possessed at least a basic knowledge of the OT and a familiarity with early Christian traditions about Jesus.[54] Together with the fact that early external evidence also points to a Roman audience, it may be concluded that Mark's intended audience was most likely comprised of Gentile Christians, probably situated in Rome.[55] Beyond this, the Gospel is addressed to "all Christians" who care to read it.[56]

Purpose

Numerous attempts have been made to identify the purpose of Mark's Gospel. The context of theological struggles and the negative social and political circumstances of the early church have often been marshaled as evidence for a particular purpose.[57] For instance, Garland indicates that if Mark wrote in AD 65–70, the context of this Gospel is one of persecution and crisis (see esp. Mark 13). If Jerusalem was either on the verge of being sacked by a Roman legion or this event had recently happened, Mark may have written his Gospel (1) in order to fortify the faith of those in danger of being overwhelmed by fear; (2) to account for the present circumstances of believers; (3) to admonish, encourage, and prevent believers from being deluded by end-time speculation; (4) to equip Christ's followers to engage in worldwide missionary outreach; and/or (5) to strengthen their faith in Jesus their Lord.[58]

Others note that the overall context of Mark's writing was probably one of severe persecution of Christians during Nero's reign (AD 54–68). In fact, Mark's language challenges the imperial myth by claiming that the good news for the world is tied up with Jesus Christ, the

---

[53] Lane, *Gospel of Mark*, 24.

[54] See the discussion by R. H. Stein, "Is Our Reading the Bible the Same as the Original Audience's Hearing It? A Case Study in the Gospel of Mark," *JETS* 46 (2003): 66–67. Mark's readers may have experienced persecution (see especially 10:30: "with persecutions," not found in the Synoptic parallels Matt 19:29 and Luke 18:29).

[55] This is the reasoned conclusion of Stein (ibid., 63–78, esp. 63–67), who provided a detailed assessment of all the available evidence.

[56] R. Bauckham, ed., *The Gospels for All Christians: Rethinking the Gospel Audiences* (Grand Rapids, MI: Eerdmans, 1997).

[57] Guelich, "Mark," 513.

[58] Garland, *Mark,* 206.

true Son of God.[59] Blomberg, who states that a Roman origin is likely and comports well with the internal evidence of the Gospel, writes:

> The negative portrait of the disciples prior to the formation of the church, along with Mark's emphasis on the way of the cross as the precursor to glory, suggests a concern *to reassure a struggling community that it too could eventually cope and that victory comes only through suffering.* Given the Jewish Christians' expulsion from Rome in AD 49, growing tensions within the community and with the government after their return in the mid-50s, and the Neronic persecution from AD 64–68, *Roman Christians would have formed an audience much in need of such comfort and encouragement.* In other words Mark's concerns may have been first of all pastoral in nature.[60]

Other scholars have identified Mark's purpose as (1) eschatological: to prepare Christians for Jesus's imminent return;[61] (2) Christological: a polemic against a divine man (*theios anēr*) myth;[62] or (3) apologetic: an attempt to mask the political implications of Jesus's life and death.[63] However, the rather general nature of the Gospel does not permit specific historical or theological reconstructions of this nature.

As with the other Gospel writers, the primary problem confronting Mark is to account for Jesus's crucifixion. Why should anyone believe in a miracle-working messianic pretender who ended up being crucified as a common criminal? In response to this objection, Mark wrote "an apology [or apologetic] for the cross," contending that it is precisely as the crucified that Jesus proved himself to be the messianic King and the Son of God.[64] Not only was the Messiah's death predicted in OT Scripture, it was also repeatedly predicted by Jesus (8:31; 9:31; 10:33–34), and it was required as "a ransom for many" (10:45), that is, as a substitutionary, atoning sacrifice for sin.

An additional avenue for ascertaining Mark's likely purpose is the opening statement of his Gospel, which indicates that the major thrust of Mark's narrative is the demonstration

---

[59] "This emperor, [Nero,] increasingly hated and despised by his own people, promoted his deification (which at his death was denied by the Senate). More than any emperor before him, he encouraged the use of the honorific titles 'god,' 'son of god,' 'lord,' 'savior,' and 'benefactor.'" C. A. Evans, "Mark," *NDBT*, 269.

[60] Blomberg, *Jesus and the Gospels*, 136 (emphasis original).

[61] W. Marxsen, *Mark the Evangelist* (Nashville, TN: Abingdon, 1969), 133–35.

[62] T. J. Weeden, *Mark: Traditions in Conflict* (Philadelphia, PA: Fortress, 1971). Weeden's argument to this effect is helpfully summarized on pp. 159–68. Though note that Harrington (*What Are They Saying*, 9) considers the "'divine man' Christology" issue to "have faded away" (i.e., it is now passé).

[63] S. G. F. Brandon, *Jesus and the Zealots* (Manchester, UK: University Press, 1967), 221–82.

[64] This is the subtitle of R. Gundry's commentary on Mark's Gospel: *Mark: A Commentary on His Apology for the Cross* (Grand Rapids, MI: Eerdmans, 1993). Cf. A. J. Köstenberger and P. T. O'Brien, *Salvation to the Ends of the Earth: A Biblical Theology of Mission*, NSBT 11 (Downers Grove, IL: InterVarsity, 2001), 74. Mark shared this concern with John (see esp. John 12:30–36). For references to the kingdom of God, see 1:15; 4:11, 26, 30; 9:1, 47; 10:14–15, 23–25; 12:34; 14:25; 15:43; for references to Jesus as King, see 15:2, 9, 12, 18, 26, 32.

Sidebar 5.1: Textual Issues in Mark's Gospel

Mark's Gospel has two important textual problems related to its beginning and its end. In 1:1, "Son of God" (*huios theou*) is omitted in a few important earlier manuscripts, which may be due to an oversight in copying. However, the phrase is found in the majority of both early and significant manuscripts. While scribes had a tendency to expand titles and quasi-titles of books, the textual evidence in favor of this reading is nonetheless extremely strong.[1]

With regard to the ending of Mark, four different endings are found in the extant manuscripts. The shorter ending, which does not have the final 12 verses after Mark 16:8, is supported by the two oldest Greek manuscripts, Codex Sinaiticus and Codex Vaticanus, an Old Latin codex, and other Syriac, Armenian, and Georgian manuscripts. Neither Clement of Alexandria (ca. AD 150–215) nor Origen (ca. AD 185–254) appears to have known of the existence of a longer ending.[2]

The traditional ending of Mark (16:9–20), with which many readers are familiar and which includes some of Jesus's resurrection appearances, his commissioning of the disciples, and his ascension, comes to us through the AV and other translations of the Textus Receptus. It is present in the great majority of witnesses, including Codex Alexandrinus.[3] The other two longer endings include a version that inserts a verse between v. 8 and v. 9, and an expanded form of the traditional ending.[4]

The conflicting nature of the external evidence supporting the longer ending seems to suggest that none of the longer endings is likely original with Mark. Internal evidence strongly supports this conclusion. The longer endings contain non-Markan vocabulary and expressions, in some cases display a different style, and do not flow smoothly from v. 8. There are also dubious references to drinking poison and snake handling (16:18), which places the longer endings in the more likely category of second- or third-century apocryphal legendary material than the time of Jesus and the apostles.

For these and other reasons, the external evidence and internal considerations point to the likelihood that the longer ending of 16:9–20 was not written by Mark. Mark's Gospel ends rather suddenly at 16:8. Metzger suggests three possibilities for this abrupt ending: (1) Mark intended to close his Gospel at this point; (2) the Gospel was never finished; or (3) it accidentally lost its last leaf before it was multiplied by transcription (or the original ending was lost for some other reason). Of these, some judge the last to be the most likely option, though there seems to be no compelling reason not to accept Mark 16:8 as the original ending intended by Mark.[5]

---

[1] B. M. Metzger, ed., *A Textual Commentary on the Greek New Testament,* 2nd ed. (New York, NY: United Bible Societies, 2002), 62.

[2] Both Eusebius and Jerome attested that this passage was absent "from all Greek copies of Mark known to them" (Metzger, *Textual Commentary,* 103).

[3] Ibid.

[4] Ibid. It has a short section after verse 14 (found in only one Greek manuscript, Codex Washingtonianus); contains several non-Markan words and expressions; has extremely limited external evidence; and bears an apocryphal flavor. Most probably it is the insertion "of a second or third century scribe who wished to soften the severe condemnation of the Eleven in 16:14" (ibid., 104).

[5] See Metzger, *Textual Commentary*, 104–6, for a fuller discussion; Carson and Moo (*Introduction to the New Testament*, 189–90) noted that the most popular option is that Mark stopped at v. 8; but cf. R. H. Stein ("The Ending of Mark," *BBR* 18 [2008]: 79–98), who contended that the present text is incomplete and who pointed to other major commentaries supporting this conclusion. For a recent survey of positions, see D. A. Black, ed., *Perspectives on the Ending of Mark: 4 Views* (Nashville, TN: B&H, 2008).

that Jesus is the Son of God (1:1).[65] In the ensuing Gospel, persons as diverse as God (who refers to Jesus as his "beloved Son" at Jesus's baptism and the transfiguration; 1:11; 9:7); demons (1:25; 3:11–12; 5:7); Jesus himself (12:6; 14:61); and a Roman centurion (15:39) concur that Jesus is the Son of God.[66] In support of this claim, Mark's Roman audience was treated to a dazzling display of Jesus's miracle-working power that attests to his authority over the realms of nature, sickness, and death, and even the supernatural (4:35–5:43).[67]

Overall, therefore, it is possible to discern four interrelated purposes in Mark's Gospel, all of which revolve around Jesus's identity as Son of God: (1) a *pastoral* purpose: to teach Christians about the nature of discipleship; (2) a *missionary-training* purpose: to explain how Jesus prepared his followers to take on his mission and to show others how to do so as well; (3) an *apologetic* purpose: to demonstrate to non-Christians that Jesus is the Son of God because of his great power and in spite of his crucifixion; and (4) an *anti-imperial* purpose: to show that Jesus, not Caesar, is the true Son of God, the Savior, and Lord.

LITERATURE

Literary Plan

Mark is an action-rich Gospel with a style characterized by compactness, concreteness, vividness, and orderliness. Mark's frequent use of the word "immediately" (*euthus*), particularly in the first half of the Gospel, advances the narrative at a fast pace, while his more detailed descriptions add color (see shorter parallel accounts in 2:1–12; 5:1–20). Hendriksen observes Mark's vivid style expressed in his graphic descriptions of Jesus's acts, gestures, and emotions, his attention to detail with regard to place and time, and his frequent change of tense.[68]

But Mark also has the least polished Greek of the four Gospels, and his sentences are often simple and straightforward, a style that has earned his Gospel the reputation of being "barbarous" or "unrefined."[69] However, Lane suggests "it is better to understand [Mark's style] as supporting a conscious literary or even theological intention. Simple sentence construction, parataxis, direct speech and the historical present serve to make Jesus the contemporary of those who hear or read the account."[70] Voelz has recently argued at length

---

[65] Guelich, "Mark," 513. See Peter's sermon in Acts 10:34–43.

[66] Köstenberger and O'Brien, *Salvation to the Ends of the Earth*, 74.

[67] See Gundry, *Mark*, 237; Guelich, *Mark*, 261–63.

[68] Hendriksen, *Mark*, 18. Perrin also summarizes several other features of Mark's Gospel: Mark's apparent penchant for threefold repetitions, his use of irony, his predilection for questions, and suspense. Perrin, "Mark," 557–58.

[69] Lane, *Gospel of Mark*, 26. See D. A. Black, "Some Dissenting Notes on R. Stein's *The Synoptic Problem* and Markan 'Errors,'" *Filologia neotestamentaria* 1 (1988): 95–101. See also Perrin, "Mark, Gospel of," 556: "Lacking in the subordinate clauses and similar signs of stylistic smoothness that are so characteristic of Matthew and Luke, Mark is a rough-and-ready Gospel." But see Perrin's further comment: "Despite all initial appearances, Mark's Gospel is extremely sophisticated and yields up a level of complexity that is sometimes mind-boggling" (557).

[70] Lane, *Gospel of Mark*, 26.

that Mark's Greek is characterized by "complexity and sophistication" and suggests that his Gospel is "a carefully crafted work." [71]

Mark often juxtaposed contrasting accounts either by placing them one after the other or by inserting one account into the other (see 3:7–19 and vv. 20–35), as well as including parallel accounts for the sake of emphasis (see 6:35–44 and 8:1–10).[72] Throughout his Gospel, Mark sought to demonstrate by way of both direct quotations and OT allusions that the coming of Jesus constituted the fulfillment of OT prophecy and that his powerful acts proved that he is the Son of God.

Mark's Gospel consists of two main sections that portray Jesus as the powerful Messiah (1:1–8:26) and the Suffering Servant (8:27–16:8).[73] The plot is centered on the "Gospel of Jesus Christ, the Son of God" (1:1). The development of this plot involves conflict. However, as Rhoads and Michie explain with regard to the Markan narrative, "Although Jesus is the immediate cause of the conflicts, the story shows that God is the ultimate origin of many of the actions and events of the story."[74] The question of Jesus's identity also surfaces as a corollary to this conflict motif, further complicated by Jesus's own injunctions to have his identity kept secret (the "messianic secret" motif) and the failure of the disciples to comprehend who Jesus really was (the "discipleship failure" and "misunderstanding" motifs).

Focant characterizes the gospel this way:

> The world to which the gospel of Mark introduces its reader is a world of conflicts and suspense, enigmas and secrets, questions and overturning of evidence, irony and surprise. Its principal actor, Jesus, is perplexing in the extreme. He is evidently so for the religious authorities who oppose him. But he is so also for his disciples who shift from astonishment to opposition and flight through incomprehension. He is so finally for an ambivalent crowd that will end up clamoring for his death. Questions of meaning, life and death, good and evil are constantly broached. . . . The narrative is a subtle invitation to leave its first plainness to enter into a new world, that of the

---

[71] J. W. Voelz, *Mark 1:1—8:26* (St. Louis, MO: Concordia, 2013), 22. He writes, "An assessment arguing for linguistic sensitivity and sophistication runs counter to the last several centuries of scholarship on the Second Gospel, but the Greek of the Marcan text supports such an assessment at virtually every point" (24). See also R. Decker, "Markan Idiolect in the Study of the Greek of the New Testament," in *The Language of the New Testament: Context, History, and Development*, ed. S. E. Porter and A. W. Pitts, Early Christianity in Its Hellenistic Context 3, Linguistic Biblical Studies 6 (Leiden, Netherlands: Brill, 2013), 43–66.

[72] Note Mark's strong use of Isaiah in the overall program of his book. See esp. R. E. Watts, *Isaiah's New Exodus In Mark*, WUNT 2/88 (Tübingen, Germany: Mohr Siebeck, 1997). See also R. Schneck, *Isaiah in the Gospel of Mark, I-VIII* BIBAL Dissertation Series 1 (Vallejo, CA: BIBAL Press, 1994).

[73] J. W. Voelz, *Mark 1:1—8:26* (St. Louis, MO: Concordia, 2013), 22. He writes, "An assessment arguing for linguistic sensitivity and sophistication runs counter to the last several centuries of scholarship on the Second Gospel, but the Greek of the Marcan text supports such an assessment at virtually every point" (24). See also R. Decker, "Markan Idiolect in the Study of the Greek of the New Testament," in *The Language of the New Testament: Context, History, and Development*, ed. S. E. Porter and A. W. Pitts, Early Christianity in Its Hellenistic Context 3, Linguistic Biblical Studies 6 (Leiden, Netherlands: Brill, 2013), 43–66.

[74] Rhoads and Michie, *Mark*, 74. See their entire discussion on pp. 73–100.

> coming reign of God, in which the first are last and the one who wants to save his life loses it.[75]

The story itself is set in an unspecified time frame between Jesus's baptism and death, and within shifting geographical locales encompassing Galilee and the surrounding regions, the Transjordan, finally coming to a dramatic close in Jerusalem.[76] This compactness may suggest that the events occurred within a one-year period, especially in view of the fact that only one Passover is mentioned. But Guelich correctly stated, "Though seeking to provide the reader with a connected narrative, the evangelist makes no claim about either the extent of the chronology or the completeness of his story."[77] The first section is action-packed and centers on Jesus's miracles and stories that focus on healings, controversies, and parables. Mark presented Jesus's ministry first in Galilee and then in Jerusalem. Blomberg noted, "Mark has just described significant opposition to Jesus, appears to bring a section to a close, and then starts afresh with Jesus withdrawing from hostility and calling or commissioning his disciples for further service in a new location (3:7; 6:6b)."[78]

The major turning point in the Gospel is Peter's confession of Jesus on the road to Caesarea Philippi (8:27–30), which also provides an apt introduction to the second section. In the second half of his narrative, Mark focused on Jesus's teaching concerning his impending suffering and death. Two key markers in this second half include Jesus's triumphal entry into Jerusalem and the reference to the coming Passover (11:1; 14:1).[79] The events of the cross occupy center stage, both thematically and in the proportion of time spent on them, showing the significance of this event for Mark.[80] Throughout his Gospel, Mark featured selected references to Jesus as Son of God, beginning with the opening sentence in 1:1 and peaking with the centurion's confession at 15:39 (see also 1:11; 3:11; 5:7; 9:7; 12:6; 13:32; 14:61).

---

[75] Focant, *Gospel according to Mark*, 1.

[76] Focant's observations are perceptive: "Jesus's journey is inserted between two baptisms, the one in water in the Jordan and the one of the passion, according to a metaphor used by Jesus himself to characterize the way of rejection and suffering through opposition to the glorious way two disciples dream of: 'Can you drink the cup that I drink or be baptized with the baptism I am baptized with?' (10:38). With these two baptisms are associated two tearings, figures of God's revelation. There is first of all the tearing of the heavens through which the heavenly voice and the Spirit pass and through which the divine Sonship of Jesus is recognized (1:9–11). This revelation authenticates Jesus's mission that he is going to begin in what follows in the narrative. At the other end of it there is the tearing of the veil of the temple (15:38), by which is meant God's absence from the Holy of Holies; it is in the Crucified One that he allows himself from now on to be encountered, which confirms the confession of the Roman centurion, 'Truly, this man was Son of God' (15:39). It is thus confirmed that the divine Sonship is only truly understood if it includes the passion, suffering and death of Jesus." Focant, *Gospel according to Mark*, 17.

[77] Guelich, *Mark*, xxv.

[78] Blomberg, *Jesus and the Gospels*, 129.

[79] Ibid.

[80] For recent treatments of crucifixion, see D. W. Chapman, *Ancient Jewish and Christian Perceptions of Crucifixion*, WUNT 2/244 (Tübingen, Germany: Mohr Siebeck: 2008); J. G. Cook, *Crucifixion in the Mediterranean World*, WUNT 327 (Tübingen, Germany: Mohr Siebeck, 2014).

Outline

The structure of Mark's Gospel presents itself this way:[81]

I. JESUS THE SON OF GOD AS THE POWERFUL MESSIAH (1:1–8:26)
  A. Preparation for Jesus's Ministry in the Wilderness (1:1–13)
    1. Opening (1:1)
    2. The Preaching of John the Baptist in the Wilderness (1:2–4)
    3. The Baptizing Work of John in the Jordan (1:5–8)
    4. The Baptism of Jesus in the Jordan (1:9–11)
    5. The Temptation of Jesus in the Wilderness (1:12–13)
  B. Jesus's Initial Ministry in Galilee (1:14–3:35)
    1. Summary and Initial Response (1:14–45)
    2. Controversy with Religious Leaders (2:1–3:6)
      a. Jesus Heals a Paralytic (2:1–12)
      b. The Call of Matthew and Jesus's Ministry to Sinners (2:13–17)
      c. On Fasting and the Sabbath (2:18–28)
      d. Jesus Heals a Paralytic (3:1–6)
    3. Summary and Initial Decision (3:7–35)
      a. Jesus's Messianic Ministry (3:7–12)
      b. The Calling of the Twelve (3:13–19)
      c. Jesus's True Mother and Brothers (3:20–35)
  C. Jesus's Ministry on and Around the Sea of Galilee (4:1–8:26)
    1. Cycle 1: Responses to Jesus and Proofs of His Authority (4:1–5:20)
      a. The Parable of the Sower and the Purpose of Parables (4:1–20)
      b. Other Parables and Illustrations (4:21–41)
      c. Casting Out a Legion of Demons (5:1–20)
    2. Interval: Faith and Unbelief (5:21–6:29)
      a. Healing of Jairus's Daughter and an Ailing Woman (5:21–43)
      b. Jesus Rejected at Nazareth (6:1–6a)
      c. Commissioning of the Twelve (6:6b–13)
      d. The Beheading of John the Baptist (6:14–29)
    3. Cycle 2: More Demonstrations of Jesus's Messianic Authority (6:30–56)
      a. Feeding the 5,000 (6:30–44)
      b. Walking on Water (6:45–52)
      c. Miraculous Healings (6:53–56)
    4. Interval: Matters of the Heart (7:1–37)
      a. The Tradition of the Elders and True Uncleanness (7:1–23)
      b. The Faith of the Syrophoenician Woman (7:24–30)
      c. Jesus Heals a Deaf Man (7:31–37)
    5. Cycle 3: Mounting Opposition and Jesus's Continued Messianic Ministry (8:1–26)
      a. Feeding the 4,000 (8:1–10)

---

[81] The broad contours of the outline are adapted from J. F. Williams, "Does Mark's Gospel Have an Outline?," *JETS* 49 (2006): 505–25. See also K. W. Larsen, "The Structure of Mark's Gospel: Current Proposals," *Currents in Biblical Research* 3, no. 1 (2004): 140–60.

b. The Leaven of the Pharisees and Herod (8:11–21)[82]
c. Jesus Heals a Blind Man (8:22–26)

II. JESUS THE SON OF GOD AS THE SUFFERING SERVANT (8:27–16:8)
A. Jesus's Ministry on the Way to Jerusalem (8:27–10:52)
1. First Passion Prediction and Response (8:27–38)
2. Interval: Jesus as Powerful Son of God (9:1–29)
a. The Transfiguration (9:1–13)
b. Healing a Demon-Possessed Child (9:14–29)
3. Second Passion Prediction and Response (9:30–50)
4. Interval: Jesus as Authoritative Teacher (10:1–31)
a. Jesus's Teaching on Divorce (10:1–12)
b. Jesus Welcomes Children (10:13–16)
c. The Rich Young Ruler and Following Jesus (10:17–31)
5. Third Passion Prediction and Response (10:32–45)
6. Healing of Blind Bartimaeus (10:46–52)
B. Jesus's Ministry at the Temple (11:1–13:37)
1. First Trip to the Temple: The Triumphal Entry (11:1–11)
2. Second Trip to the Temple: Cleansing the Temple (11:12–19)
3. Third Trip to the Temple: Challenges and Teachings (11:20–13:37)
a. The Lesson of the Fig Tree (11:20–26)
b. Rebuffing a Challenge to Jesus's Authority (11:27–33)
c. The Parable of the Wicked Tenants (12:1–12)
d. Paying Taxes to Caesar (12:13–17)
e. Challenging Jesus on the Resurrection (12:18–27)
f. The Two Most Important Commandments (12:28–34)
g. Other Teachings of Jesus (12:35–40)
h. The Widow's Great Gift (12:41–44)
i. Jesus's Teaching on the End Times (13:1–37)
C. Jesus's Death on the Cross and the Empty Tomb (14:1–16:8)
1. Anointing at Bethany and Betrayal Plot (14:1–11)
2. The Last Supper (14:12–25)
3. Prayer and Arrest at Gethsemane (14:26–52)
4. Trial Before Sanhedrin and Denials by Peter (14:53–72)
5. Trial Before Pilate and Mocking by Soldiers (15:1–20)
6. Crucifixion and Burial (15:21–47)
7. The Empty Tomb (16:1–8)

---

[82] "Leaven" is preferable to "yeast." According to Stein (*Mark*, 381): "The reference to 'leaven' (ζύμης, *zymēs*) refers not to yeast but to unbaked dough containing the yeast culture that when added to new dough would cause it to rise." BDAG notes that "the rendering 'yeast' . . . popularly suggests a product foreign to ancient baking practices" (429d). In C. L. Mitton's important article on this ("New Wine in Old Wineskins: iv, Leaven," *ExpTim* 84 (1973): 339–43), he notes, "'Leaven' is not quite the same as yeast. In ancient times, instead of yeast, a piece of dough was held over from one week's baking to the next. By then it was fermenting, and so could cause fermentation in the new lot of dough, causing it to rise in the heat." See further Thiselton, *The First Epistle to the Corinthians*, NIGTC (Grand Rapids, MI: Eerdmans, 2000), 401.

UNIT-BY-UNIT DISCUSSION

I. Jesus the Son of God as the Powerful Messiah (1:1–8:26)

A. Preparation for Jesus's Ministry in the Wilderness (1:1–13) In his prologue Mark informs his readers that he is about to narrate the story of "Jesus Christ, the Son of God" (1:1).[83] He begins by grounding his story in the OT, in the words of Isaiah the prophet (actually a conflation of Mal 3:1 and Isa 40:3), hence effectively announcing that "John's ministry fulfills divine prophecy and then identifies Jesus as the beloved Son and the conveyer of the Spirit."[84] John the Baptist performed his God-ordained role as he baptized in the desert, a place that is eminently appropriate because of its symbolism as a place of new beginnings and renewal (see Exod 2:15; 1 Sam 23:14; 1 Kgs 19:3–4),[85] and it was a baptism he performed as preparatory for God's coming Messiah and kingdom. Before Jesus began his work, he submitted to John's baptism, at which significant juncture his Sonship was declared by God himself as the Holy Spirit descended on him (Mark 1:11). He was subsequently driven into the desert by the Holy Spirit to undergo a period of temptation by Satan. His victory over the Devil set the pattern for the narrative that continues to unfold.

B. Jesus's Initial Ministry in Galilee (1:14–3:35) Rooting Jesus's mission in the ministry of John the Baptist (1:2–3), the evangelist showed how Jesus began to call and train a select group of followers for their missionary task. In Mark's account of Jesus's activities in Galilee, Jesus's preaching and healing ministry is held up as the pattern for his disciples to emulate (see 1:14–15, 21–28, 34; and 6:12–13).[86]

As the narrative progresses, Jesus drew his followers more fully into his own messianic mission: he called them away from their natural vocations to follow him (1:16–20; 2:13–17); he chose the Twelve "and they came to him" (3:13–19); and at the climax of the first part of this Gospel he sent them on a mission (6:6b–13). Early in his ministry, Jesus dissociated himself from blood ties and affirmed new forms of kinship. He redefined who his true mother and brothers are (3:31–35) and was rejected in his hometown of Nazareth (see 6:1–6a).

---

[83] Some of the following material is adapted from Köstenberger and O'Brien, *Salvation to the Ends of the Earth*, 73–86. As Focant perceptively notes, "The gospel of Mark follows the life and death course of an adult. Unlike Matthew and Luke, no reading key is provided through a birth and childhood narrative. Unlike John, no evocation of preexistence brings a clarification from the beginning." Focant, *Gospel according to Mark*, 16.

[84] Garland, *Mark*, 207. By singling out Isaiah as the source, Mark informed his readers that the story "is to be understood against the backdrop of Isaian themes" (J. Marcus, *The Way of the Lord: Christological Exegesis of the Old Testament in the Gospel of Mark* [Louisville, KY: Westminster John Knox, 1992], 20).

[85] As Garland (*Mark*, 209) notes, "It was also the place one went to elude persecution and to flee iniquity, since it was beyond the control of the cities. The desert was also viewed as the mobilizing area for God's future victory over evil and the place where Elijah (Mal. 4:5) and the Messiah were thought to appear (Matt. 24:26)."

[86] Note the *inclusio* of 1:14 and 6:29, which records John's imprisonment and death at Herod's hands.

The important principle of access on the basis of spiritual rather than ethnic distinctives paves the way for the future extension of the gospel to non-Jews.[87] It also demonstrates the nature of true discipleship: following Jesus involves conflict, rejection by one's own, even the bearing of one's cross. By distancing himself from his own biological family, Jesus modeled in his own life a stance toward kingdom membership that the disciples are to emulate in their relationships with one another and in their mission.[88]

C. Jesus's Ministry on and Around the Sea of Galilee (4:1–8:26) Already in 3:6, the reader is told of the Pharisees' plot with the Herodians to kill Jesus (cf. 8:15; 12:13). While this rejection of Jesus by the official representatives of Judaism did not cause him to forsake his mission to the Jews, it did give him increased exposure to Gentiles.[89] This includes Jesus's healing of the Gerasene demoniac in 5:1–20; his encounter with the Syrophoenician woman in 7:24–30; and his feeding of the multitude in 8:1–10, which is reminiscent of Elisha's miraculous feeding of Gentiles in 2 Kings 4:42–44.[90] Nevertheless, when Jesus, for instance, restored the Gerasene demoniac to sanity, he did not invite the healed Gentile to join his messianic mission but sent him home to tell his own people what had happened to him.

In his account of the sending of the Twelve, Mark, unlike Matthew (Matt 10:5–6), did not explicitly limit their mission to Israel (6:6b–13). Nevertheless, Jesus's ministry in the first part of the Gospel is primarily devoted to the Jews (see esp. 7:26a). After Herod's mistaken identification of Jesus as the resurrected John the Baptist (6:14–29), Jesus's feeding of the 5,000, and his walking on the water (6:30–52), mounting opposition to Jesus caused him to withdraw from Galilee. He first moved to the region of Tyre and Sidon north of Galilee (7:24–30), then to the Decapolis east of Galilee (7:31–8:12), and finally to the far north in Caesarea Philippi (8:27–9:32).

Throughout his entire narrative Mark not only emphasizes the disciples' misunderstanding and hardness of heart, but he also portrays their increased involvement in Jesus's mission (see 6:41). The primarily Jewish context of Jesus is gradually broken up. This is accomplished by Jesus's indictment of the Jews' unbelief (7:6–7; cf. Isa 29:13); his frequent withdrawals from Galilee (7:24–9:32); and his declaration that all food is clean (7:19). But most pronounced is the incident with the Gentile Syrophoenician woman, who wants Jesus to exorcize a demon from her daughter but who is initially rebuffed by Jesus (7:24–30). Only after the woman accepts the fact that Jesus's mission is first and foremost directed to the Jews does Jesus grant her request.[91]

---

[87] D. Senior and C. Stuhlmueller, *Biblical Foundations for Mission* (Maryknoll, NY: Orbis, 1983), 222.

[88] See J. F. Williams, "Mission in Mark," in *Mission in the New Testament: An Evangelical Approach*, ed. W. J. Larkin Jr. and J. F. Williams (Maryknoll, NY: Orbis, 1998), 146: "Following a Messiah who came to die on a cross involves sacrifice, suffering, and service."

[89] W. Telford, "Introduction: The Gospel of Mark," in *The Interpretation of Mark*, IRT 7, ed. W. Telford (Philadelphia, PA: Fortress, 1985), 23; F. Hahn, *Mission in the New Testament*, SBT 47 (London, UK: SCM, 1965), 113.

[90] See Z. Kato, *Die Völkermission im Markusevangelium*, Europäische Hochschulschriften 23/252 (Bern, Switzerland: Peter Lang, 1986), 191.

[91] Ibid., 190.

Something to Think About: Walking on the Water of Life

Few of Jesus's miracles are as astounding as his walking on the water (6:45–52). Like his turning a large amount of water into wine, this nature miracle defies human explanation—not that unbelievers have not tried to account for the event by supplying some naturalistic explanation. Just recently, for example, someone suggested that Jesus was simply skipping from rock to rock, the stones hidden just barely beneath the surface of the water. This theory may get first prize for creatitivty, but it is such a transparent attempt to explain the unexplainable that it is instantaneously self-defeating and reveals more about the unbelief of the person proposing the "solution" than about what most likely happened.

Ever since the period of the Enlightenment, deists and other antisupernaturalists have sought to devise mere cause-and-effect scenarios that drained the miraculous from Scripture. One of them was an important founding father of the United States, Thomas Jefferson. He set forth the "principles of a pure deism" supposedly taught by Jesus, "omitting the question of his deity." The Jefferson Bible, *not published until 1895 by Jefferson's grandson, begins with an account of Jesus's birth that omits all mention of angels, prophecy, miracles, the Trinity, or the deity of Jesus. It concludes with the words, "Now in the place where he was crucified there was a garden; and in the garden a new sepulchre, wherein never man yet laid. There laid they Jesus: and rolled a great stone to the door of the sepulchre, and departed." End of story! No resurrection.*

How different this is from the unpredictable eyewitness accounts concerning Jesus in Scripture. It is highly unlikely that anyone would have fabricated the kind of story where Jesus walked on the water, plus told Peter to come out of the boat to walk on the water toward him, unless he actually remembered such an unusual event. Walking on the water, in turn, would clearly have evoked the memory of Scripture, according to which God "alone . . . treads on the waves of the sea" (Job 9:8). Upon seeing Jesus, his followers were so startled they thought he was a ghost and screamed. Afterward, Mark says that "they were completely astounded" and "their hearts were hardened" (6:51–52). Yet when Jesus breathed his last, the Roman centurion at the cross cried out, "Truly this man was the Son of God!" (15:39).

"What kind of man is this? Even the winds and the sea obey him!" (Matt 8:27).

II. Jesus the Son of God as the Suffering Servant (8:27–16:8)

A. Jesus's Ministry on the Way to Jerusalem (8:27–10:52) Subsequent to Peter's confession of Jesus as the Christ (8:29–30)—which occasions a thrice-repeated pattern of passion prediction, discipleship failure, and instruction regarding true discipleship (8:27–9:1; 9:30–41; 10:32–45)—the "messianic secret" is gradually lifted, at least for the disciples (1:34, 44–45; 3:12; 5:43; 7:36–37; 8:26, 29–30; 9:9). Nevertheless, as long as the disciples fail to understand the inner dynamics of the cross, they do not yet recognize their mission, since this mission is contingent upon the disciples' following Jesus in the way of the cross (see 8:34).[92]

Jesus ministered in Galilee up to 8:26, not leaving it permanently until 10:1. The entire section of 8:27–10:52 is cast as a journey from Caesarea Philippi to Jerusalem (see 9:30, 33; 10:1, 17, 32, 46, 52).[93] Intriguingly, Mark limited instances of gospel proclamation entirely to Galilee (see 1:14, 38–39, 45; 3:14; 5:20; 6:12; 7:36). The only two references to preaching the gospel in the Jerusalem section of Mark refer to the *future* proclamation of the good news to the Gentiles. Moreover, a future meeting between Jesus and the disciples is intimated in 14:28 and 16:7, which further directs the reader's attention to Galilee.

B. Jesus's Ministry at the Temple (11:1–13:37) Following Jesus's entry into Jerusalem (11:1–11), scenes from the Jewish temple draw attention to the shift that will ensue as a result of Jesus's ministry and his rejection by the Jews.[94] Thus, Mark refers to the temple as a house of prayer *for all the nations* (see the quotation of Isa 56:7 in 11:17), indicating that the particularism of Jewish worship had come to an end and that the temple would soon be replaced by an eschatological "house of prayer."[95] The cursing of the fig tree, with accompanying lessons regarding its significance (11:12–14, 20–26; 13:28–31), likewise draws attention to the rejection of the Jews as a result of their rejection of Jesus as Messiah. Lane called Jesus's cursing of the fig tree "a prophetic sign warning of God's judicial action against the nation . . . equivalent in function to Ch. 12:9."[96]

The climax is reached in the parable of the Tenants of the Vineyard (12:1–2), where Jesus declared that God's vineyard would be taken away from the Jews and given *to others* (see 12:9). These "others" come into view particularly during Jesus's eschatological discourse in chapter 13, which is once again occasioned by a scene at the temple. Jesus, after predicting the temple's destruction, informed his disciples that the glorious coming of the Son of Man would be preceded by the preaching of the gospel *to all the nations*. Thus, "Mark in effect identifies the community's activity between Jesus's own ministry and the cataclysmic end of the world as a time of universal proclamation and witness."[97]

C. Jesus's Death on the Cross and the Empty Tomb (14:1–16:8) The last major section of Mark's Gospel begins with Jesus's anointing and the institution of the Lord's

---

[92] Senior and Stuhlmueller, *Biblical Foundations for Mission*, 226.

[93] See W. Kelber, *The Kingdom in Mark* (Philadelphia, PA: Fortress, 1974), 67–85; R. Pesch, *Das Markusevangelium*, HTKNT (Freiburg, Germany: Herder, 1980) for the "way" or "journey" motif in Mark.

[94] J. R. Donahue, *Are You the Christ?*, SBLDS 10 (Missoula, MT: SBL, 1973), 137; D. Juel, *Messiah and Temple*, SBLDS 31 (Missoula, MT: SBL, 1977), 212.

[95] See Telford, *Mark*, 224–25; K. Stock, "Theologie der Mission bei Markus," in *Mission in Neuen Testament*, ed. K. Kertelge, QD 93 (Freiburg, Germany: Herder, 1982), 142; Donahue, *Are You the Christ?* 114; Senior and Stuhlmueller, *Biblical Foundations for Mission*, 223.

[96] Lane, *Gospel of Mark*, 402.

[97] Senior and Stuhlmueller, *Biblical Foundations for Mission*, 224.

Supper. This intimate scene is contrasted with the harsh reality of Jesus's trial before the Sanhedrin (14:53–65).[98] At the high point of the Jewish trial, Jesus responded to the high priest's question of whether he is the Messiah (v. 61), the Son of the Blessed One (see John 20:30–31), in the affirmative. In contrast, Jesus refrained from answering Pilate's question of whether he is the king of the Jews, presumably owing to the title's political overtones (15:2). Thus, the reader is led to understand that Jesus is the Messiah in terms of Jewish OT expectations but not a king in Roman political terms (see John 18:36).

Finally, at the climax of Mark's Gospel, the Roman centurion exclaimed at the foot of the cross, "Truly this man was the Son of God!" (15:39), indicating that now the messianic secret has been lifted even for the (Roman) Gentiles, so that the missionary power of Jesus's suffering and death has been extended also to non-Jews. If there is a genuinely Markan equivalent to the Matthean "Great Commission," the centurion's confession would certainly qualify. Indeed, the fact that it is not a Jew but a Gentile who confessed Jesus at the end of Mark is highly significant for the Gospel's narrative thrust.[99] At the same time, it is certainly no coincidence that a Christological confession by a Gentile (see Peter's "Jewish" confession in 8:29) is not issued until *after* Jesus's death.

The final verses (16:1–8) end on the hopeful note of the empty tomb and the news of Jesus's resurrection. At the same time, if 16:8 is indeed the original ending of Mark's Gospel, the account does not include any of Jesus's resurrection appearances but concludes on a note of fearfulness on the part of Jesus's followers, a state of affairs that may resemble the state of Christianity in Rome at the time of writing.[100] The abrupt ending leaves open for the reader how Jesus's announcement that he would meet the disciples in Galilee would be fulfilled (see 14:28; 16:7). As M. Hooker aptly notes, "Mark's ending disturbs us, because it seems so inconclusive. We long to complete the book—and that, of course, is precisely what Mark wants us to do!"[101]

---

[98] As Focant observes, "the series of mockeries against Jesus (14:65; 15:16–20,29–32,35–36) . . . all have a christological meaning: in them Jesus is ironically proclaimed prophet, king, Messiah, savior. And these sarcastic remarks point to a hidden truth: in suffering, in being rejected and executed on a cross, Jesus turns out to be truly prophet, king, Messiah and savior, who never puts his power to his own service." Focant, *Gospel according to Mark*, 19.

[99] Kato, *Völkermission*, 193.

[100] "Mark is the only Gospel in which the risen Christ never appears" (Perrin, "Mark," 558).

[101] M. D. Hooker, *Endings: Invitations to Discipleship* (Peabody, MA: Hendrickson, 2003), 23. See also Marcus: "For Mark and his readers, Jesus's *bios* is not complete, indeed can never be completed, which is perhaps part of the reason that the Gospel ends as abruptly as it does (if the original ending is 16:8): Mark's writing describes only the *beginning* of the good news of Jesus (1:1), because in Mark's day Jesus's good news *continues through his presence with the church and in the world.*" J. Marcus, *Mark 1–8*, 67.

THEOLOGY

Theological Themes[102]

Jesus as the Son of God The preeminent theological theme in Mark's Gospel is that Jesus is the miracle-working, authoritative Son of God. Beginning with Mark's opening statement in 1:1, strategic references to Jesus as the Son of God are distributed throughout the Gospel.

Table 5.1: Jesus as the Son of God in Mark's Gospel

Introduction		Galilean Ministry		Way to the Cross		Trial and Crucifixion	
1:1	1:11	3:11	5:7	9:7	13:32	14:61	15:39
Mark	God	Demons	Demons	God	Jesus	Caiaphas	Roman Centurion

The chart indicates that this theme forms the all-inclusive bookends of the Markan narrative. The evangelist frames his telling in terms of Jesus being the Son of God in the opening verse and in the Roman centurion's climactic confession in 15:39. This is no coincidence since Mark's audience was the church in Rome, and it is only appropriate that the final reference to Jesus as Son of God in the Gospel should be uttered by a Roman. Evans notes, "The centurion's confession that Jesus was 'truly' the son of God (15:39) is the equivalent of Roman deification of their deceased emperors, but the discovery of the empty tomb and the (angelic?) announcement that he has risen (16:4–7) provide divine confirmation of the truth of Jesus's predictions."[103]

Earlier in the narrative, Jesus is declared by the heavenly voice to be the Son of God at his baptism (1:1) and at the transfiguration (9:7). Apart from Jesus's two self-references (12:6; 13:32) and Caiaphas's question at Jesus's trial (14:61), the only other characters in Mark's Gospel who acknowledge that Jesus is the Son of God are demons (though Peter's confession of Jesus as the Messiah is, however, immediately revealed as lacking full understanding, 8:31–33). Remarkably, demons are the only ones to acknowledge Jesus as the Son of God throughout his entire Galilean ministry (1:16–8:26; see 3:11; 5:1–6).

In Mark's Gospel, other than God, Jesus, and demons, no one understands that Jesus is the Son of God prior to the crucifixion. This lack of understanding works hand in hand

---

[102] In addition, a number of writers highlight the "journey" or "way" motif, particularly beginning with the discussion that led to Peter's confession in 8:27ff (cf. 1:2–3; 8:27; 9:33–34; 10:17, 32, 52; 11:8). See, e.g., Edwards, *The Gospel according to Mark*, 19–20. See also W. R. Telford, *The Theology of the Gospel of Mark*, NTT (Cambridge, UK: Cambridge University Press, 1999), 28, who lists as important emphases (1) the secrecy motif and the interest in the true but hidden identity of Jesus; (2) the passion of Jesus and its significance for Christology; (3) the nature and coming of the Kingdom of God and Jesus's return as the Son of Man; (4) an interest in Galilee; (5) the term "gospel" (*euangelion*); (6) an interest in Gentiles and the Gentile mission; (7) an interest in persecution, suffering, and martyrdom and the true nature of discipleship; (8) Mark's harsh treatment of the Jewish leaders, Jesus's family, and the original disciples.

[103] Evans, "Mark," 273.

with two other major Markan themes, the "messianic secret" and the "discipleship failure" motifs. Evans said, "Despite rejection at the hands of his own people(and the most important people, according to contemporary measures of importance) and a shameful death at the hands of the most powerful people, Jesus was indeed the son of God, humanity's true Savior and Lord."[104]

In a context where Roman emperors frequently ascribed deity to themselves, Mark's presentation of Jesus as the Son of God is profoundly countercultural. At the same time, the OT background in which the Davidic King was considered to be God's Son was clearly a factor as well (see esp. Ps 2:7; cf. Ps 110:1).[105] And indeed, Mark's Gospel has an appeal to Jew and Gentile alike. Blomberg contended that in his account of Jesus, Mark's concern was to achieve a balance between two essential truths that pertain to Jesus as well as his disciples: the centrality of the cross and Jesus's glory through suffering (see esp. 8:31–9:1).[106] Indeed, Jesus frequently alluded to his coming death and resurrection (8:31; 9:31; 10:33–34) and in a direct way spoke to Caiaphas, the Jewish high priest, of his glorious return (14:62).

This is also the contention of R. Martin, who says of Mark's Gospel that it skillfully balances an emphasis on Jesus's divinity with his humanity.[107] The Christological titles that Mark uses, particularly the title "Son of God," which occurs at significant junctures in this Gospel, exemplify this balance. Mark's juxtaposition of Christ's "successes" and "failures," his mighty deeds and his suffering and death, highlights this distinctively Markan theological perspective on the life and work of Jesus.[108]

The Kingdom of God Another important Markan motif is the kingdom of God proclaimed by Jesus (1:15), featured in several parables (4:11, 26, 30), and addressed in the form of entrance requirements (9:47; 10:14–15, 23–25; 11:10; 12:34; cf. 9:1; 14:25; 15:43). The entrance of the kingdom means the beginning of the end of Satan's dominion over humanity and the liberation of those who repent (1:15). Indeed, John's water baptism is only preparatory as people plunge into the Jordan, signifying their repentance to ready themselves for God's coming kingdom (1:7). Evans writes, "The 'beginning of the good news' (1:1), as inhabitants of the Roman Empire would have understood it, would have to entail restoration and renewal. Jesus's remarkable ministry, in which he overpowers Satan and his allies and brings about healing and restoration, dramatically validates his message."[109]

---

[104] Ibid.

[105] See also Mark 10:46–48 (Bartimaeus: "Jesus, Son of David, have mercy on me"); and 12:35–37.

[106] Blomberg, *Jesus and the Gospels*, 131.

[107] R. Martin, *Mark: Evangelist and Theologian* (Grand Rapids, MI: Zondervan, 1973), cited in Blomberg, *Jesus and the Gospels*, 131 (emphasis Blomberg's).

[108] Blomberg, *Jesus and the Gospels*, 131–32.

[109] Evans, "Mark," 270.

Mark's use of "kingdom of God" is synonymous with Matthew's "kingdom of heaven," and both of these evangelists view the kingdom as intimately tied to and demonstrated through Jesus's miracles. In the development of this theme, Mark progresses from Jesus's proclamation of the kingdom, which serves to announce the kingdom of God, and then develops an outline of the coming kingdom by focusing on the ministry of Jesus.[110] The miracles that Mark's Gospel record demonstrate Jesus's authority over four different things: (1) nature (4:35–41); (2) demons (5:1–20); (3) death (5:21–24, 35–43); and (4) sickness (5:35–43). While Mark consistently affirms that the kingdom of God is in opposition to Satan and his demons, he made clear that Jesus is the victor (1:24, 34; 3:11, 27; 5:6–10; 9:20, 25). Indeed, the message conveyed by the miracles Jesus performed is significant in revealing the "manifestations of the kingdom of God, that is, the powerful presence of God."[111] That the kingdom is hidden to outsiders is also a vital part of Mark's presentation. Jesus used parables to demonstrate this "hiddenness" of the kingdom, a kingdom that has both present and future aspects (4:11, 26–32, 33–34).

The "Messianic Secret" Mark's Gospel refers to Jesus's title of Messiah at least seven times, beginning with Peter's confession of Jesus as the Christ (8:29–30), which occasions a thrice-repeated pattern of passion prediction, discipleship failure, and instruction regarding true discipleship (8:27–9:1; 9:30–41; 10:32–45). However, this portrayal of Jesus shows a man who was not yet willing to have his messiahship unveiled. Of the four Gospels, Mark most frequently records that Jesus told people not to reveal who he was. In the Matthean parallel (16:17–19), Jesus bestowed praise and promises on Peter for his confession of his messiahship, while no such praise accompanies Peter's confession in Mark 8:30. Other instances include his refusal for insight into parables to be given to "outsiders" (4:10–12), his rebuke of demonic confessions of his true identity (1:25, 34; 3:12), and his orders that spectacular miracles are to be reported to no one (1:44; 5:18–19, 43).[112]

In an effort to explain this "messianic secret," nineteenth-century theologian W. Wrede held that Mark himself created this motif because, although he believed Jesus was the divine Christ and Son of God, Jesus made no such claims. As Blomberg has noted, "In other words, by creating both the claims and the 'cover-up,' Mark could account for why earlier stages of Christianity had not believed in Jesus as Messiah, and yet Mark himself could still promote the notion."[113] A more probable explanation is that although Jesus was aware of

---

[110] G. Goldsworthy, "Kingdom of God," *NTBT*, 616.

[111] Evans, "Mark," 270.

[112] Blomberg, *Jesus and the Gospels*, 132.

[113] Ibid., 119, with reference to W. Wrede, *The Messianic Secret* (trans. J. C. G. Greig; Library of Theological Translations; London: J. Clark, 1971). Note, however, that Wrede apparently later revised his view, at least in part. In a 1905 letter to A. Harnack, Wrede wrote, "I am now more inclined than previously to believe that Jesus chose to regard himself as the Messiah" (H. Rollmann and W. Zanger, "Unveröffentlichte Briefe William Wredes zur Problematisierung des messianischen Selbstverständnisses Jesu," *ZNThG* [2001], 317, cited in U. Schnelle, *Theology of the New Testament* (trans. M. E. Boring; Grand Rapids, MI: Baker, 2007), 44n8. For a survey of approaches to the messianic secret, see D. F. Watson, *Honor Among Christians: The Cultural Key to the Messianic Secret* (Minneapolis, MN: Fortress, 2010), 3–12. Most plausible is the presen-

his messianic status, he was wary of accepting the title from the Jewish people because of the prevailing Christological expectations, which tended to focus more on a political messiah and left little room for a suffering one (see 10:45).[114] In addition, Hurtado has suggested that the prominence of the "messianic secret" is to be understood as part of a larger Markan theme. Since Jesus's crucifixion was his key work, "In Mark's view, no one could understand the true meaning of Jesus and his work until Jesus had actually completed it by his death as a ransom for others (10:45)."[115] Guelich states that this messianic secret is further enhanced by Jesus's rejection by the religious authorities (see 3:22–30; 14:63–65), his parents (see 3:21), his hometown (see 6:1–6), and even the misunderstanding of his disciples (see 4:35–41; 6:45–52; 8:31–33). He also notes, "Furthermore, Jesus's silencing of the demons and his disciples whenever his true identity is involved, as well as his exclusive use of the ambiguous 'Son of man' to refer to himself, enhances this 'messianic secret.'"[116] This secret is lifted at the climax of Mark's Gospel, when the Roman centurion exclaims at the foot of the cross, "Truly this man was the Son of God!" (15:39), indicating that now the messianic secret has been removed even for the (Roman) Gentiles, so that the missionary power of Jesus's suffering and death has been extended also to non-Jews.

The Nature of Discipleship In Mark's account of the calling of the disciples, he reveals the authority Jesus wields over people. When he called the first four disciples, first Simon and Andrew, and then James and John the sons of Zebedee, his call was abrupt and the response was prompt (Mark 1:16–20). In this introduction to Jesus, "the abruptness of the call and the promptness of compliance casts [*sic*] Jesus in an impressive, commanding light; he summons people and they obey."[117] As Mark progresses in his narrative, he reveals the nature of true discipleship: following Jesus involves conflict, rejection by one's own, even the bearing of one's cross. By distancing himself from his own family, and through the cross, Jesus modeled in his own life a stance toward kingdom membership that the disciples are to emulate in their relationships with one another and in their mission.[118]

The initial picture of the disciples is soon overshadowed by Mark's portrayal of their frequent failures and misunderstandings, an emphasis that is absent in the other Gospels.[119]

---

tation of J. D. G. Dunn, "The Messianic Secret in Mark," in *The Christ and the Spirit: Collected Essays of James D. G. Dunn*, vol. 1, *Christology* (Grand Rapids, MI: Eerdmans, 1998), 57–77.

[114] As Blomberg (*Jesus and the Gospels*, 133) aptly sums up, "For Mark, however, 10:45 may be the most important verse in the Gospel in summarizing his emphasis on Jesus's road to the cross. . . . Although Mark never uses the exact expression, the concept of *suffering servant* (as in Isa. 52:13–53:12) perhaps best encapsulates this very human side of Jesus's nature and mission. In short, the Gospel of Mark is about why Jesus died."

[115] Hurtado, *Mark*, 10.

[116] Guelich, "Mark," 516.

[117] Evans, "Mark," 271.

[118] For a treatment of the Markan discipleship theme, see E. Best, *Following Jesus: Discipleship in the Gospel of Mark*, *JSNT* (Sheffield, PA: Sheffield Academic, 1981).

[119] It is intriguing to contemplate that there may be a connection between Mark's "discipleship failure" motif and Mark's own "discipleship failure" referenced in Acts 15:36–41. See, e.g., Marcus: "Might not the searing Markan portrait of the (temporary) abandonment of Jesus by the disciples, particularly by Peter (14:27–31, 50, 66–71), partly reflect the traumatic experience of John Mark himself, who had similarly abandoned Paul at one point in his career (Acts 13:13; 15:38)? Both

Of the four evangelists, Mark duly notes the disciples' obduracy and magnifies their failure, which is displayed through a lack of understanding despite the repetition of Jesus's feeding miracle, while at the same time portraying their increased involvement in Jesus's mission.[120] W. Lane finds in "the juxtaposition of rejection and mission, a pattern confirmed in the rejection of Jesus by the nation, climaxed by crucifixion and resurrection, which created the apostolic mission."[121] The disciples fail to grasp Jesus's parables (4:11–13, 33–34); where one expects to see a response of faith, one reads instead of their hardened hearts, their little faith, and their perplexity after crucial miracles (4:40; 6:51–52; 8:4, 14–21), and where one expects them to exercise their Christ-given authority over demons, they fail miserably (9:14–21). After his confession, Peter himself is cast in an extremely negative light for failing to leave room in it for a suffering Messiah (8:33).[122]

Hence, Mark frequently depicted the disciples in a manner that reveals they do not understand Jesus's mission. Their blindness is brought even more sharply into focus as Mark narrated two stories in which spiritual and literal blindness are set in stark contrast (8:22–26; 10:46–52). As long as the disciples failed to understand the true meaning of the cross, they would not recognize their mission since it is contingent upon their following Jesus in the way of the cross (see 8:34).[123] The record of Peter's denial, Judas's betrayal, and the desertion by the rest of the disciples demonstrates how patently true this observation is (chaps. 14–15).

The disciples' response to Jesus is often frustrating to readers. Guelich writes,

> Called and privileged to be with Jesus (1:16–20; 3:7–12), privately taught by him (e.g., 4:10–20, 33–34), commissioned to participate in his ministry (e.g., 6:7–13, 30), they continually fail to understand him or accurately recognize who he really is and the implications of who he is for their discipleship (e.g., 8:27–10:45). They waffle between having their mind on "divine things" and having their mind on "human things" (8:33).[124]

Evans accurately summarizes Mark's purpose in this negative portrayal:

> The evangelist's purpose in portraying the disciples in this way is not to denigrate them, or to correct an unhealthy triumphalist Christianity that

---

of the words used to describe Mark's defection in these Acts passages, *apochōrein* and *aphistanai*, can have the nuance of apostasy (see e.g. 3 Macc 2:33; Luke 8:13; 1 Tim 2:19; Heb 3:12), and as we shall see in the exegesis of the story of Peter's denial, that narrative also has been shaped by early Christian experiences of defection from the faith. Mark, therefore, may have highlighted the disciples' desertion of Jesus partly because it was so similar to his own desertion of Paul." Marcus, *Mark 1–8*, 24.

[120] E.g., 3:5; 4:41; 6:45–52; 7:18; 8:14–21, 32–33; 9:10, 18, 28, 32; 10:35–45; 16:8; note esp. 6:52 and 8:17–21. See Köstenberger and O'Brien, *Salvation to the Ends of the Earth*, 77.

[121] Lane, *Gospel of Mark*, 205.

[122] Blomberg, *Jesus and the Gospels*, 133.

[123] Senior and Stuhlmueller, *Biblical Foundations for Mission*, 226.

[124] Guelich, "Mark," 515.

identifies with them. The purpose is to highlight the contrast between the masterful, commanding Jesus on the one hand, and the much weaker and less comprehending disciples on the other. The evangelist wishes to present Jesus to the Roman world as a compelling figure, as the true savior.[125]

Jesus as the Son of Man Apart from the designation "Son of God," Jesus is identified in Mark's Gospel also as the "Son of Man." Notably, people in general are called "sons of men" in Mark (see 3:28). Thus, in one sense the title "Son of Man" marks Jesus as fully human (though clearly Jesus is portrayed also as fully divine in Mark's Gospel).

In another sense, however, the epithet "Son of Man" designates Jesus as a messianic figure in keeping with Daniel's reference to the mysterious figure of one "like a son of man" (Dan 7:13; see especially Mark 8:38; 13:26; 14:62). Jesus as the Son of Man claimed to have authority to forgive sins (2:10), and he claimed to be Lord over the Sabbath (2:28). Jesus also referred to himself as the Son of Man when predicting his suffering and resurrection (8:31; 9:9, 12, 31; 10:33, 45; 14:21, 41). The title, therefore, is bound up with Jesus's vicarious death on the cross for humanity.

Hence, Jesus's use of the title "Son of Man" in Mark's Gospel (a use similar to that of the other Gospels) identifies him both as fully human—and thus able to render substitutionary atonement for sin—and as the Messiah and Son of God who came in fulfillment of OT predictions to establish the kingdom of God.

CONTRIBUTION TO THE CANON

- Presentation of a Gospel of Jesus narrating his ministry from Galilee to Jerusalem
- Jesus as the miracle-working Son of God (1:1, 11; 5:7; 9:7; 15:39)
- Jesus displaying his power over nature, demons, sickness, and death (4:35–5:43)
- Discipleship failure (4:40; 6:51–52; 8:16–21, 33; 9:18–19; 14:66–72; 16:8)
- Jesus's sacrificial, vicarious death as a ransom for many (10:45)

STUDY QUESTIONS

1. Who does ancient tradition suggest wrote Mark's Gospel? Who was believed to be his close associate?
2. Why do some posit a late date for Mark?
3. What linguistic evidence points to a Roman destination?
4. What is the major Christological title in Mark?
5. How does the structure of Mark fit with his purpose?
6. What reasons support the theory that Mark's Gospel was penned in the second half of the 50s?
7. According to this chapter, what are four interrelated purposes of Mark's Gospel?
8. What is the textual issue in Mark 1:1?

---

[125] Evans, "Mark," 272.

9. According to the authors, what are at least two reasons the longer endings of Mark should not be considered original?
10. Why is Mark's Gospel called "action rich"?
11. How many major parts are in the structure of Mark's Gospel, and which verse is the turning point?
12. To what does the "messianic secret" refer?

FOR FURTHER STUDY

Anderson, J. C., and S. D. Moore, eds. *Mark and Method: New Approaches in Biblical Studies.* 2nd ed. Minneapolis, MN: Fortress, 2008.

Bauckham, R., ed. *The Gospel for All Christians: Rethinking the Gospel Audiences.* Grand Rapids, MI: Eerdmans, 1998.

———. *Jesus and the Eyewitnesses: The Gospels as Eyewitness Testimony.* Grand Rapids, MI: Eerdmans, 2006.

Best, E. *Mark: The Gospel as Story.* Edinburgh, Scotland: T&T Clark, 1983.

Blomberg, C. L. *Jesus and the Gospels: An Introduction and Survey.* 2nd edition. Nashville, TN: B&H, 2009.

Bolt, P. *Jesus' Defeat of Death: Persuading Mark's Early Readers.* Study for the New Testament Monograph Series 125. Cambridge, UK: Cambridge University Press, 2003.

Breytenbach, C. "Current Research on the Gospel according to Mark: A Report on Monographs Published from 2000–2009." Pages 13–32 in *Mark and Matthew I: Comparative Readings: Understanding the Earliest Gospels in their First-Century Settings.* Edited by E.-M. Becker and A. Runesson. Wissenschaftliche Untersuchungen zum Neuen Testament 271. Tübingen, Germany: Mohr Siebeck, 2011.

Brooks, J. A. *Mark.* New American Commentary 23. Nashville, TN: Broadman, 1991.

Burridge, R. A. *What Are the Gospels? A Comparison with Graeco-Roman Biography.* Society for New Testament Studies Monograph Series 70. Cambridge, UK: Cambridge University Press, 1992.

Bryan, C. *A Preface to Mark: Notes on the Gospel in Its Literary and Cultural Settings.* New York, NY: Oxford University Press, 1993.

Chilton, B., D. Bock, D. M. Gurtner, J. Neusner, L. H. Schiffman, and D. Oden, eds. *A Comparative Handbook to the Gospel of Mark: Comparisons with Pseudepigrapha, the Qumran Scrolls, and Rabbinic Literature.* The New Testament Gospels in their Judaic Contexts 1. Leiden, Netherlands: Brill, 2010.

Decker, R. "Markan Idiolect in the Study of the Greek of the New Testament." Pages 43–66 in *The Language of the New Testament: Context, History, and Development.* Edited by S. E. Porter and A. W. Pitts. Early Christianity in Its Hellenistic Context 3. Linguistic Biblical Studies 6. Leiden, Netherlands: Brill, 2013.

Edwards, J. R. *Mark.* Pillar Commentary on the New Testament. Grand Rapids, MI: Eerdmans, 2002.

Evans, C. A. "Mark." Pages 199–318 in *The Holman Apologetics Commentary on the Bible: The Gospels and Acts.* Nashville, TN: B&H, 2013.

———. *Mark 8:27–16:20.* Word Biblical Commentary. Nashville, TN: Thomas Nelson, 2001.

France, R. T. *The Gospel of Mark: A Commentary on the Greek Text.* New International Greek Testament Commentary. Grand Rapids, MI: Eerdmans, 2002.

Garland, D. E. "Mark." In *Zondervan Illustrated Bible Backgrounds Commentary*. Vol. 1. Edited by C. E. Arnold. Grand Rapids, MI: Zondervan, 2007.

__________. *Mark*. NIV Application Commentary. Grand Rapids, MI: Zondervan, 1996.

__________. *A Theology of Mark's Gospel: Good News about Jesus the Messiah, the Son of God*. Biblical Theology of the New Testament. Grand Rapids, MI: Zondervan, 2015.

Gray, T. C. *The Temple In the Gospel of Mark: A Study in Its Narrative Role*. Wissenschaftliche Untersuchungen zum Neuen Testament 2/168. Tübingen, Germany: Mohr Siebeck, 2008.

Guelich, R. A. *Mark 1–8:26*. Word Biblical Commentary 34A. Dallas, TX: Word, 1989.

__________. "Mark, Gospel of." Pages 511–25 in *Dictionary of Jesus and the Gospels*. 1st ed. Edited by J. B. Green, S. McKnight, and I. H. Marshall. Downers Grove, IL: InterVarsity, 1992.

Gundry, R. H. *Mark: A Commentary on His Apology for the Cross*. Grand Rapids, MI: Eerdmans, 1993.

Hahn, F. *Mission in the New Testament*. Studies in Biblical Theology 47. London, UK: SCM, 1965.

Harrington, D. J. *What Are They Saying about Mark?* Mahwah, NJ: Paulist, 2004.

Hengel, M. *Studies in the Gospel of Mark*. Philadelphia, PA: Fortress, 1985.

Hurtado, L. W. *Mark*. New International Biblical Commentary. Peabody, MA: Hendrickson, 1989.

Iverson, K. R. *Gentiles in the Gospel of Mark: Even the Dogs Under the Table Eat the Children's Crumbs*. Library of New Testament Studies 339. London, UK: T&T Clark, 2007.

Juel, D. *Messiah and Temple*. SBL Dissertation Series 31. Missoula, MT: SBL, 1977.

Kato, Z. *Die Völkermission in Markusevangelium*. Europäische Hochschulschriften 23/252. Bern, Switzerland: Peter Lang, 1986.

Kelber, W. *The Kingdom in Mark*. Philadelphia, PA: Fortress, 1974.

Lane, W. L. *The Gospel According to Mark: The English Text with Introduction, Exposition, and Notes*. Grand Rapids, MI: Eerdmans, 1974.

Lincoln, A. T. "The Promise and the Failure: Mark 16:7, 8." *Journal of Biblical Literature* 108/2 (1989): 283–300.

Malbon, E. S. *In the Company of Jesus: Characters in Mark's Gospel*. Louisville, KY: WJK, 2000.

Marcus, J. *Mark 1–8*. Anchor Yale Bible. New Haven, CT: Yale University Press, 2000.

__________. *Mark 9–16*. Anchor Yale Bible. New Haven, CT: Yale University Press, 2009.

Martin, R. *Mark: Evangelist and Theologian*. Grand Rapids, MI: Zondervan, 1972.

Perrin, N. "Mark, Gospel of." Pages 553–66 in *Dictionary of Jesus and the Gospels*. 2nd ed. Edited by J. B. Green, J. K. Brown, and N. Perrin. Downers Grove, IL: InterVarsity, 2013.

Pesch, R. *Das Markusevangelium*. Herders theologischer Kommentar zum Neuen Testament. Freiburg, Germany: Herder, 1980.

Rhoads, D., J. Dewey, and D. Michie. *Mark as Story: An Introduction to the Narrative of a Gospel*. 3rd ed. Minneapolis, MN: Fortress, 2012.

Stein, R. H. *Mark*. Baker Exegetical Commentary on the New Testament. Grand Rapids, MI: Baker, 2008.

Stock, K. "Theologie der Mission bei Markus." Pages 130–44 in *Mission in Neuen Testament*. Quaestiones disputatae 93. Edited by K. Kertelge. Freiburg, Germany: Herder, 1982.

Telford, W. R. "Introduction: The Gospel of Mark." Pages 1–41 in *The Interpretation of Mark*. Issues in Religion and Theology 7. Edited by W. R. Telford. Philadelphia, PA: Fortress, 1985.

_________. *The Theology of the Gospel of Mark*. Cambridge, UK: Cambridge University Press, 1999.

_________. *Writing on the Gospel of Mark*. Guides to Advanced Biblical Research. Blandford Forum, UK: Deo, 2009.

Watts, R. E. *Isaiah's New Exodus in Mark*. Wissenschaftliche Untersuchungen zum Neuen Testament 2/88. Tübingen, Germany: Mohr (Siebeck), 1997.

_________. "Mark." Pages 111–249 in *Commentary on the New Testament Use of the Old Testament*. Edited by G. K. Beale and D. A. Carson. Grand Rapids, MI: Baker, 2007.

Williams, J. F. *Mark*. Exegetical Guide to the Greek New Testament. Nashville, TN: B&H, 2014.

_________."Mission in Mark." Pages 137–51 in *Mission in the New Testament: An Evangelical Approach*. Edited by W. J. Larkin Jr. and J. F. Williams. Maryknoll, NY: Orbis, 1998.

_________. "Literary Approaches to the End of Mark's Gospel." *Journal of the Evangelical Theological Society* 42 (1999): 21–35.

_________. *Mark*. Exegetical Guide to the Greek New Testament. Nashville, TN: B&H Academic, forthcoming.

Winn, A. *The Purpose of Mark's Gospel: An Early Christian Response to Roman Imperial Propaganda*. Wissensgchaftliche Untersuchungen zum Neuen Testament 2/245. Tübingen, Germany: Mohr Siebeck, 2008.

Witherington, B., III. *The Gospel of Mark: A Socio-Rhetorical Commentary*. Grand Rapids, MI: Eerdmans, 2001.

Wrede, W. *The Messianic Secret*. Translated by J. C. G. Greig. Library of Theological Translations. London, UK: James Clark & Co., 1987. Translation of *Das Messiasgeheimnis in den Evangelien*. Göttingen, Germany: Vandenhoeck & Ruprecht, 1901.

Chapter 6

The Gospel According to Luke

CORE KNOWLEDGE

Basic Knowledge: Students should know the key facts of Luke's Gospel. With regard to history, students should be able to identify the Gospel's author, date, provenance, destination, and purpose. With regard to literature, they should be able to provide a basic outline of the book and identify core elements of the book's content found in the Unit-by-Unit discussion. With regard to theology, students should be able to identify Luke's major theological themes.

Intermediate Knowledge: Students should be able to present the arguments for historical, literary, and theological conclusions. With regard to history, students should be able to discuss the evidence for Lukan authorship, date, provenance, destination, and purpose. With regard to literature, they should be able to provide a detailed outline of the book. With regard to theology, students should be able to discuss Luke's major theological themes and the ways in which they uniquely contribute to the NT canon.

Advanced Knowledge: Students should be able to evaluate the role played by the "we" passages in the book of Acts in determining the date and authorship of Luke-Acts. In addition, they should be able to assess the literary and theological significance of the "Lukan travel narrative" for Luke's Gospel.

Map 6.1: Provenance and Destination of Luke

KEY FACTS

Author:	Luke, the beloved physician
Date:	ca. 58–60
Provenance:	Rome, perhaps Achaia
Destination:	Theophilus
Purpose:	A defense of the Christian faith, useful for both evangelism and discipleship
Theme:	Jesus brings universal salvation in fulfillment of OT promises to Israel.
Key Verse:	19:10

INTRODUCTION

IN 1977, THE filmmaker, John Heyman produced and directed a movie titled, *The Jesus Film*. While most passion plays are based on the shortest Gospel, Mark, Heyman preferred the Gospel of Luke as his narrative backbone. It was an ambitious choice. The Gospel of Luke is the longest book in the NT. It comprises a little over 14 percent of the NT and is almost 10 percent longer than the second longest NT book, the book of

Acts. (By contributing these two volumes, Luke composed 27 percent of the NT).[1] Heyman, consulting biblical scholars, chose Luke for two basic reasons. First, it is a complete narrative covering Christ's birth to his ascension. Second, it is "an international Gospel for Gentiles and shows Jesus as the Son of Man as well as the Son of God."[2] While we would not necessarily remove Jews from Luke's audience, one could hardly argue with the basic accuracy of these statements. Nor could one argue with the film's results. The movie, translated into 1,305 languages, has been seen by billions; remarkably, more than 200 million decisions for Christ are associated with it.[3] The choice and the results highlight the literary and theological masterpiece that is the third Gospel.

In the literary realm, Luke has produced a highly readable, highly engaging narrative of the life of Christ. He wrote in an elegant Greek, mastered the vocabulary and prose of an educated man, and was able to employ a variety of genres and styles.[4] He could write like an OT narrator, record prophet-like oracles, and stitch it all together in rather fluid presentation. Furthermore, he insisted that he kept an eye on historical accuracy. It is no wonder, then, that E. Renan called the Gospel of Luke "the most beautiful book" ever written.[5]

Luke's artistry is in service to his theological message. Luke especially emphasized the universal nature of the Gospel. It is for all people. This theme reveals one of his major (and somewhat surprising) contributions to the Gospel portrait of Jesus: Jesus's concern for the poor, women, children, the sick, and others of low status in society. Jesus is shown mingling freely with outcasts; he is a "friend of . . . sinners" who came "to seek and to save the lost" (19:10). According to Luke, Jesus was the physician who came to heal not the healthy but the sick and to provide righteousness to those who knew themselves to be poor spiritually while resisting the spiritually proud and self-sufficient.

In the midst of this theological artistry, Luke paid careful attention to accuracy. While not an eyewitness of Jesus's ministry, Luke claims he carefully investigated these matters from those who were (1:1–4), especially Peter (5:3) and the women who followed Jesus from Galilee (8:2–3).[6] He was careful to relate major events in the Christian story to world history (called "synchronisms"), such as Jesus's birth in relation to Caesar Augustus and the

---

[1] If, as postulated by some, Luke was Paul's amanuensis for the Letters to Timothy and Titus, it is even more remarkable how much Luke contributes to the content of the NT. See S. G. Wilson, *Luke and the Pastoral Epistles* (London, UK: SPCK, 1979), 139–40.

[2] From the director's notes. See http://www.historicjesus.com/1/index.html.

[3] http://jesusfilm.org/film-and-media/statistics/statistics

[4] A. Plummer (*A Critical and Exegetical Commentary on the Gospel According to S. Luke*, 5th ed. [Edinburgh, Scotland: T&T Clark, 1922], xlix) notes that Luke is the most versatile of all the Gospel writers: "He can be as Hebraistic as the LXX, and as free from Hebraisms as Plutarch. And, in the main, whether intentionally or not, he is Hebraistic in describing Hebrew society, and Greek in describing Greek society."

[5] E. Renan, *Les Évangiles et la seconde génération chrétienne* (Paris, France: Calmann Lévy, 1877), 283: "C'est le plus beau livre qu'il y ait" (English translation *The Gospels* [London: Mathieson, n.d.]).

[6] See Richard Bauckham, *Jesus and the Eyewitnesses: The Gospels as Eyewitness Testimony* (Grand Rapids, MI: Eerdmans, 2006), 114–24, 129–32. We will address the charges leveled against Luke's accuracy below.

governor Quirinius (2:1),[7] and the beginning of John the Baptist's and Jesus's ministries to Tiberius Caesar, the governor Pontius Pilate, Herod Antipas, and others (3:1).

In spite of its aesthetics, elegant theology, and historical attention, Luke's Gospel—as well as the book of Acts—has been the subject of considerable controversy in the academy. S. E. Porter wrote, "With few exceptions, Luke-Acts has been the center of more debate than almost any of the other books in the NT."[8] Until the 1950s, Luke's Gospel was largely viewed as a historical book since scholars in the nineteenth century and the early twentieth generally saw him as a Hellenistic doctor, a follower of Paul, and not overly interested in theology.

With the writings of H. Conzelmann, however, Luke began to be seen as a revisionist who reinvented the story of Jesus in order to impose a new theology on the history of the church, and he was disparaged for doing so.[9] This prompted W. C. van Unnik's now-famous article that declared Luke a theological "storm center," which continues to hold true into the present.[10] In recent years many have studied Luke primarily in literary terms.[11] However, as will be seen below, Luke is both a historian *and* a theologian. Thus, his literary art is in service to both these related subjects.

HISTORY

Author

The traditional view is that Luke, Paul's beloved physician, wrote both this Gospel and the book of Acts. If so, Paul referred to this Luke three times in the NT (Col 4:14; 2 Tim 4:11; Phlm 24), and Luke obliquely referred to himself repeatedly in the book of Acts in the "we" passages. Although the author remains unnamed in both the Gospel and Acts, this does not necessarily mean that these writings were originally anonymous[12] since one can assume that the person to whom the book was dedicated (Theophilus) and its first readers knew who the writer was.

---

[7] On Quirinius, see the discussion below and chap. 3 above.

[8] S. E. Porter and L. M. MacDonald, *Early Christianity and Its Sacred Literature* (Peabody, MA: Hendrickson, 2000), 291.

[9] See H. Conzelmann, *The Theology of St. Luke*, trans. G. Buswell (London, UK: Faber & Faber, 1960).

[10] W. C. van Unnik, "Luke-Acts, a Storm Center in Contemporary Scholarship," in *Studies in Luke-Acts*, ed. L. E. Keck and J. L. Martyn (Nashville, TN: Abingdon, 1966), 15–32.

[11] A. Thiselton, "The Hermeneutical Dynamics of 'Reading Luke' as Interpretation, Reflection and Formation," in *Reading Luke: Interpretation, Reflection, Formation*, ed. C. G. Bartholomew, J. B. Green, A. Thiselton, Scripture and Hermeneutics 6 (Grand Rapids, MI: Zondervan, 2005), 3. For a literary approach, see W. S. Kurz, *Reading Luke-Acts: Dynamics of Biblical Narrative* (Louisville, KY: Westminster John Knox, 1993).

[12] See D. A. Carson and D. J. Moo, *An Introduction to the New Testament*, rev. ed. (Grand Rapids, MI: Zondervan, 2005), 205–6 (citing M. Dibelius, *Studies in the Acts of the Apostles* [London, UK: SCM, 1956], 89 and 148), who note "that it is unlikely that the books ever circulated without a name attached to them in some way."

Whoever this Luke was, the preface to the Gospel, to go no further, evinces a refined use of the Greek language that points to an author who was well educated.[13] It is apparent that the author was male,[14] that he had access to a variety of sources about the life of Jesus,[15] that he was not an eyewitness of Jesus's ministry,[16] and that he had the opportunity to investigate the story about Jesus fully (v. 3). On these points most are agreed.[17] Beyond this, however, many have disputed the traditional attribution. For this reason it is necessary to examine the internal and external evidence in turn.

Internal Evidence The common authorship of Luke and Acts is virtually assumed in modern scholarship.[18] First, the preface to the book of Acts appears to introduce a sequel (Acts 1:1 refers to "the first narrative"). Second, both books are dedicated to the same person, Theophilus (Luke 1:3; Acts 1:1). Third, the contents of Acts readily follow the story of Jesus presented in Luke (see the reference to "all that Jesus *began* to do and teach" in Acts 1:1). Fourth, Luke ends and Acts begins with Jesus's ascension. This was an ancient method of connecting one book to another. Finally, both books display similar styles and interests.[19]

The strongest evidence for Lukan authorship are the so-called "we" passages in Acts (16:10–17; 20:5–15; 21:1–18; 27:1–28:16). A natural reading of these texts suggests that

---

[13] See Luke 1:1–4. In 1882 W. K. Hobart wrote his famous book, *The Medical Language of St. Luke* (repr. Grand Rapids, MI: Baker, 1954), in which he argues that where Matthew and Mark used common expressions, Luke often employed medical terms to describe Jesus's healings. But this was challenged by H. J. Cadbury, *The Style and Literary Method of Luke* (Cambridge, MA: Harvard University Press, 1920), who points out that Luke's terminology is not necessarily specialized though it is the language used by educated people. The enduring result of this interchange is that the writer of Luke-Acts was assuredly an educated person.

[14] The Greek participle *parēkolouthēkoti* ("having carefully investigated") in 1:3 is masculine.

[15] See the reference to "many" others in 1:1.

[16] See the reference to "the original eyewitnesses" in 1:2.

[17] But see the opinion of W. G. Kümmel, *Introduction to the New Testament*, rev. ed., trans. H. C. Kee (Nashville, TN: Abingdon, 1975), 149: "The only thing that can be said with certainty about the author, on the basis of Lk, is that he was a Gentile Christian."

[18] E.g., J. Verheyden, "The Unity of Luke-Acts: What Are We Up To?" in *The Unity of Luke-Acts*, ed. J. Verheyden (Leuven, Belgium: University Press, 1999), 3. For overviews of the debate, see M. F. Bird, "The Unity of Luke-Acts in Recent Discussion," *JSNT* 29 (2007): 425–48; P. E. Spencer, "The Unity of Luke-Acts: A Four-Bolted Hermeneutical Hinge," *CurBR* 5 (2007): 341–66. The most recent volume on the topic is A. F. Gregory, and C. K. Rowe, eds., *Rethinking the Unity and Reception of Luke and Acts* (Columbia, SC: University of South Carolina Press, 2010), which contains essays pro and con. Against unified authorship is A. C. Clark, *The Acts of the Apostles* (Oxford, UK: Clarendon, 1933); P. Walters, *The Assumed Authorial Unity of Luke and Acts: A Reassessment of the Evidence*, SNTSMS 145 (Cambridge, UK: Cambridge University Press, 2010). For unified authorship: R. C. Tannehill, *The Narrative Unity of Luke-Acts: A Literary Interpretation*, 2 vols. (Minneapolis, MN: Fortress, 1990); J. B. Green, "Luke-Acts, or Luke and Acts? A Reaffirmation of Narrative Unity," in *Reading Acts Today: Essays in Honour of Loveday C. A. Alexander*, ed. S. Walton, et al., LNTS 427 (London, UK: T&T Clark, 2011), 101–19.

[19] L. Morris, *The Gospel According to St. Luke: An Introduction and Commentary*, TNTC 3 (Grand Rapids, MI: Eerdmans, 1974), 14. The unity of Luke and Acts extends beyond the mere question of common authorship. The more complicated hermeneutical implications of Luke and Acts being two volumes of a single work are taken up in the chapter on the book of Acts.

the author was a traveling companion of Paul, a view attested as early as Irenaeus (ca. AD 130–200; see *Against Heresies* 3.1.2).[20]

But C. J. Hemer lists three alternative views.[21] First, many see the "we" passages as reflecting a source composed by the author himself, a travel diary of sorts.[22] Although this is possible, the theory cannot be proven and may be based on the (now largely discarded) assumption that all sources must be written. Second, some argue that the "we" passages are from a travel diary written by someone other than the author.[23] Yet if these sections are from someone else's diary, Luke has stamped his unique style on all but the first-person plural pronouns. Also, such literary inconsistency would be out of character for an author who elsewhere displays great elegance and care in his writing. Third, many suggest that these sections are merely literary devices.[24] If this is true, the writer would be so subtle as to confuse (if not mislead) part of his audience.[25]

Assuming, then, that the author would not normally employ first- and third-person plurals at the same time, the people named in these sections alongside the author may be removed from consideration for authorship. Thus, the author could not have been Paul, Silas (Acts 16:19), Sopater, Aristarchus, Secundus, Gaius, Timothy, Tychicus, or Trophimus (Acts 20:4). Moreover, since the writer of the book of Acts was with Paul during his first Roman imprisonment (Col 4:14), it is possible that Paul mentioned him in one or several of the letters written during this period, namely, in the Prison Epistles: Philippians, Ephesians, Colossians, and Philemon.[26] Paul names six such companions: Mark, Demas, Jesus Justus, Epaphroditus, Epaphras, and Luke.

Regarding these six, Mark wrote the Gospel that bears his name. Demas deserted Paul because he "loved this present world" (2 Tim 4:10), which renders him an unlikely candidate for authoring Acts. Jesus Justus was a Jew (Col 4:11); the writer of Luke-Acts was probably not.[27] Epaphroditus was most likely from Philippi (Phil 4:25), which makes it

---

[20] E.g., Carson and Moo, *Introduction to the New Testament*, 204; F. F. Bruce, *The Acts of the Apostles* (Grand Rapids, MI: Eerdmans, 1951), 2–3; and most conservative scholars; but see S. E. Porter, "The 'We' Passages," in *The Book of Acts in Its First-Century Setting*, vol. 2: *The Book of Acts in Its Greco-Roman Setting*, ed. D. W. J. Gill and C. Gempf (Grand Rapids, MI: Eerdmans, 1994), 545–74.

[21] C. J. Hemer, *The Book of Acts in the Setting of Hellenistic History* (Winona Lake, IN: Eisenbrauns, 1990), 312–13.

[22] C. K. Barrett, *Luke the Historian in Recent Study* (Philadelphia, PA: Fortress, 1979), 22; Porter, "'We' Passages," 574.

[23] Kümmel, *Introduction*, 184.

[24] So E. Haenchen, *The Acts of the Apostles* (Philadelphia, PA: Westminster, 1971), 85–90; P. Vielhauer, "On the 'Paulinism' of Acts," in *Studies in Luke-Acts*, 33–34; and F. Bovon, *Luke 1*, Hermeneia, trans. C. M. Thomas (Minneapolis, MN: Fortress, 2002), 8–9. Cf. V. K. Robbins ("The We-Passages in Acts and Ancient Sea-Voyages," *BR* 20 [1975]: 5–18), who understands the "we" references as characteristic of a genre recounting ancient sea voyages; but C. J. Hemer ("First Person Narrative in Acts 27–28," *TynBul* 36 [1985]: 79–109) refuted this view.

[25] Most of those proposing such an understanding do so not on the basis of the phenomenon itself but due to their prior belief that the writer of Luke-Acts was so distant from the historical Paul that he could not have been his traveling companion. See D. Wenham, "The Purpose of Luke-Acts," in *Reading Luke: Interpretation, Reflection, Formation*, 81.

[26] B. D. Ehrman (*The New Testament: A Historical Introduction to the Early Christian Writings*, 4th ed. [New York, NY: Oxford University Press, 2008], 159) unduly reduces these multiple references to a single one (Phlm 24). Cf. the treatments of Paul's authorship of Colossians and of the Letters to Timothy and Titus later on in this volume.

[27] See Col 4:10–14 (esp. vv. 10–11a) and the discussion in Carson and Moo, *Introduction to the New Testament*, 206.

difficult to explain why he would have first joined Paul in Asia Minor before Philippi was evangelized (Acts 16:10). Epaphras is noted in the NT primarily for his role in founding the Colossian church (Col 1:7–8; 4:12–13; see Phlm 23). This leaves Luke as the best viable candidate.

External Evidence The early church clearly understood the author of Luke-Acts to be Paul's "beloved physician." This is attested in the title "according to Luke," appearing in the earliest manuscript (e.g., $\mathfrak{P}^{75}$); in the stated opinion of the early church fathers such as Irenaeus (ca. AD 130–200], Theophilus of Antioch (later second century), and Justin Martyr (ca. AD 100–165); and in early canonical lists. One of the earliest extrabiblical indications of authorship comes from Justin Martyr (ca. AD 100–165), who mentioned a quote from Luke as from one who followed the apostles.[28]

The earliest and clearest extant reference to the author of Luke-Acts by name is found in the Muratorian Canon (later second century), followed by Irenaeus (ca. AD 130–200) and the Anti-Marcionite Prologue to Luke (ca. AD 160–180). That Luke was mentioned rather late has led many to speculate that Luke was little known in the first half of the second century.[29] However, this conclusion is premature since Polycarp (ca. AD 69–155) quotes both Luke and Acts (*Phil.* 1.2; 2.1, 3). Also, Papias (ca. AD 60–130) named Luke as the author of the Gospel (cited in Eusebius, *Eccl. Hist.* 3.24.5–13).[30]

Another fragment of Papias is found in an Armenian writer who quoted Luke 10:18.[31] Moreover, Papias apparently had a lengthy discussion on the putrification of Judas in the book of Acts.[32] Hence, both Papias and Clement in all likelihood knew and used both Luke's Gospel and Acts early on.

It should also be noted that some early heretics also made use of Luke's Gospel. Marcion (ca. AD 150) severely edited the Gospel of Luke, removing all Jewish elements, to include it in his canon. The gnostic Heracleon wrote a commentary on Luke's Gospel.[33] The references to the Gospel of Luke in the works of both men also strongly suggest that Luke's Gospel was already in use in the early church prior to the middle of the second century.

Finally, no candidate for authorship other than Luke has ever been set forth in the history of the church. Taken together, this data provides strong evidence for Luke as the author of both the Gospel and Acts, especially since it seems unlikely that the early church would have attributed these weighty books to an otherwise unheralded fellow worker of

---

[28] The exact quote is, "For in the memoirs which I say were drawn up by his apostles and those who followed them, [it is recorded] that his sweat fell down like drops of blood while he was praying, and saying, 'If it be possible, let this cup pass'" (*Dial.* 103). While this falls short of a citation of Luke as the author, the reference comports with the early church's view of the authorship of the Gospels.

[29] J. T. Townsend, "The Date of Luke-Acts," in *Luke-Acts: New Perspectives from the Society of Biblical Literature*, ed. C. Talbert (New York, NY: Crossroad, 1984), 47.

[30] C. E. Hill, "What Papias Said About John (and Luke): A 'New' Papian Fragment," *JTS* 49 (1998): 588–89.

[31] F. Siegert, "Unbeachtete Papiaszitate bei Armenischen Schriftstellern," *NTS* 27 (1981): 606.

[32] Holmes, *Apostolic Fathers*, 755–57.

[33] So F. Godet, *A Commentary on the Gospel of St. Luke*, trans. W. W. Shalders and M. D. Cusin (New York, NY: Funk & Wagnalls, 1890), 1–3.

Paul unless he were the real author. The relative insignificance of Luke elsewhere in the NT remains a grave difficulty for those who would deny the attribution of the Gospel to Luke as traditionally conceived.[34]

Not until the mid-nineteenth century did anyone doubt the tradition that Luke wrote this Gospel and Acts. Then the identification of the author of Luke-Acts as the beloved physician of Colossians 4:10 was considered to be nothing but faulty guesswork.[35] Most modern scholars who reject Lukan authorship do so contending that Luke's theology and historical detail differ substantially from Paul's. Many are willing to see "a Luke" as the author of the Gospel, but one who was not a disciple of Paul and who wrote after the year 70.[36]

To conclude, there is ample reason to hold to the Lukan authorship of Luke-Acts. In particular, the external evidence provides strong support for Lukan authorship, with virtually no dissenting voice. Indeed, it is unclear why anyone would have attributed the Gospel to him unless he was in fact the author. What is more, Luke-Acts was evidently written by a well-educated author, which fits what is known of Luke, Paul's travel companion and "beloved physician" (Col 4:14).

Date

Since Luke and Acts are related volumes, it is necessary to discuss both in order to determine accurately the date of Luke. While some have argued that Acts precedes Luke, this is highly unlikely.[37] The "first narrative" mentioned in Acts 1:1 doubtless refers to the Gospel of Luke. Thus, Luke's Gospel predates the book of Acts; hence, the date of writing for Acts is to some extent predicated upon the date of composition for Luke.

Many date Luke's Gospel in keeping with their solution to the Synoptic Problem. More conservative scholars frequently date Mark in the 50s on the assumption that Luke used Mark. On the other end of the spectrum, critical scholars often assign to Luke-Acts a date subsequent to the year 70 based on their dating of Mark at about AD 65.[38]

Perhaps more importantly, the historical evidence in Luke's Gospel and especially in the book of Acts provides an independent point of reference for the dating of these two

---

[34] Bovon (*Luke*, 10) writes, "Why anyone would happen upon the name Luke remains a riddle. Perhaps a student of Paul was desired for this work. The names Titus and Timothy were already taken, if only as the addressees, and not the writers, of the Pastoral Epistles. Among the remaining frequently appearing names in the Pauline corpus, Luke all but jumped out." Bovon's remarks well illustrate the difficulty: would the name "Luke" leap at us from the biblical pages independent of the church's tradition?

[35] H. J. Cadbury (*The Making of Luke-Acts* [London: SPCK, 1927, repr., 1958], 354–60) seems to capture the spirit of critical opinion when he explains the early church's identification of the author as Luke as little more than guesswork based on the faulty understanding of the "we passages" and an equally faulty belief that Paul wrote all the letters that bear his name.

[36] These matters are taken up further in the chapter on Acts below.

[37] J. A. Fitzmyer, *The Gospel According to Luke I–IX* (Garden City, NY: Doubleday, 1981), 53.

[38] E.g., R. E. Brown (*An Introduction to the New Testament* [New York, NY: Doubleday, 1997], 273–74) dates Luke at around 85 because he assigns Mark an approximate date of 68–73.

books.[39] This requires some distance between the events of Christ's life and the writing of Luke's Gospel, but it does not demand a half century or more, as some surmise.[40]

Dates proposed for the book of Acts fall into three broad eras: (1) prior to AD 70; (2) around AD 80; and (3) near the end of the first century or in the early second century.[41] Predominantly, those who adhere to the first or second position suggest that the historical Luke of church tradition accurately represented history in his writing of Acts. These proponents divide generally over the issue of the fall of Jerusalem in the year 70. Those who understand Jesus's description in Luke 21:20 as a "prophecy after the fact" conclude that Luke wrote around AD 80 or later.

But the evidence for an early date for Luke-Acts (prior to AD 70) is compelling for six reasons. First, Luke does not mention any significant event subsequent to the early 60s in the book of Acts,[42] such as the persecution of the church by Nero, the destruction of Jerusalem, and the deaths of Peter, Paul, and James the Just.[43]

Second, the stance toward the Roman Empire in the book of Acts is decidedly neutral if not friendly. This would seem to favor a time prior to Nero's persecution of Christians that culminated in Paul's and Peter's martyrdoms (AD 64–66).

Third, the failure to mention Jerusalem's destruction in Luke's Gospel also favors a pre-70 date. Since Luke consistently noted the fulfillment of prophecy, both written and oral,[44] why would he not mention that Jesus's prediction of the destruction of the Jerusalem temple had been fulfilled?[45] Moreover, the temple plays a prominent role in both Luke and Acts; in fact, Luke's Gospel begins and ends in the temple (1:9; 24:53). This prominence seems unlikely if the Gospel were written after the temple's destruction. Also, the relevance and impact of the Stephen episode in Acts 7 are predicated upon the temple still being in existence. At the very least the author missed a great opportunity to underscore Stephen's point (the corruption of the temple system) by failing to mention the destruction of the temple.

[39] See Carson and Moo, *Introduction to the New Testament*, 180.

[40] Kümmel (*Introduction*, 150) maintains that "by the year 60 'many' gospel writings could not have been in existence, including Mk." But this is unwarranted since there were three decades between Jesus's resurrection and the writing of Luke.

[41] Hemer, *Book of Acts in the Setting of Hellenistic History*, 365.

[42] Morris, *Gospel According to St. Luke*, 22.

[43] Some have claimed that Acts does not mention the fate of its participants. But both Stephen and James the son of Zebedee meet their fate in Acts 7 and 12 (see Hemer, *Book of Acts in the Setting of Hellenistic History*, 378).

[44] E.g., Luke 7:20 see Isa 28:18; 35:5; 61:1; Luke 7:27 see Mal 3:1; Luke 24:6 see Luke 9:21–44; 18:31–33; Acts 11:28; and Acts 21:10–14.

[45] Fitzmyer (*Luke*, 56) tries to explain the omission of the temple's destruction by proposing that the Christian church had long since been removed from its Palestinian origins and was simply more interested in the spread of Christianity into the Mediterranean world among European Gentiles.

A fourth indication of an early date is that Paul's Letters are not mentioned in Acts. As L. T. Johnson stated, "It is far more likely for Paul's Letters to be ignored before the time of their collection and canonization than after."[46]

A fifth piece of evidence important for dating the book of Acts is its conclusion (Acts 28:30–31). For many the ending is uncomfortably brusque. Paul finally reaches Rome under the protection of the emperor, but the reader is left without knowing the outcome of the trial. The book ends with Paul preaching the gospel in Rome without hindrance. The logical question is, Why didn't Luke write a paragraph or two describing the outcome of the trial? The response that Luke had accomplished his purpose by showing the progress of the gospel from Jerusalem all the way to Rome, implying that any mention of the outcome of Paul's trial would have been superfluous, is unsatisfactory.[47] The natural conclusion is that Luke caught up with Paul in time and that when Luke concluded Acts, Paul was still under house arrest in Rome and awaiting trial before Emperor Nero.

Sixth, in Acts 20:25 Paul told the Ephesian elders he would never see them again. However, the Letters to Timothy and Titus suggest that Paul continued to sustain close ties with the Ephesian church after his release from the first Roman imprisonment (1 Tim 1:3). The inclusion of this statement in Acts 20 is difficult to explain if it was written after the Letters to Timothy and Titus.[48]

A late date for Acts is therefore far more problematic than an early one. Therefore, the most likely date for Luke is sometime before the composition of the book of Acts, which was probably written in the early 60s.

By how many years does Luke's Gospel precede the book of Acts? It is impossible to be certain. If Luke conceived of Luke-Acts as a two-volume work, which seems likely (see Acts 1:1–3), it would seem reasonable to conclude that Luke wrote his Gospel and the book of Acts within a few years of each other—though this falls, of course, short of proof. If one assumes that Luke used Mark, as well as other written and oral sources, in writing his Gospel (see Luke 1:1–4), this would require Mark and other accounts of Jesus's life to have been written prior to Luke's writing of his Gospel. If Mark is dated in the mid-50s and time is allowed for Luke to access Mark's Gospel, this would narrow the most likely window for the composition of Luke's Gospel to the mid to late 50s. If Luke was traveling with Paul during this time, he would have had ample opportunity to do the necessary research and to compose his Gospel during Paul's two-year stay at Caesarea Maritima

---

[46] L. T. Johnson, "Book of Luke-Acts," *ABD* 4:404. For efforts to explain the lack of reference to Paul's Letters in Acts on the assumption of a late date of Acts, see W. O. Walker, "Acts and the Pauline Corpus Reconsidered," *JSNT* 24 (1985): 3–23; idem, "Acts and the Pauline Corpus Revisited: Peter's Speech at the Jerusalem Conference," in *Literary Studies in Luke-Acts: Essays in Honor of Joseph B. Tyson*, ed. R. P. Thompson and T. E. Phillips (Macon, GA: University Press, 1998), 77–86.

[47] The claim by deSilva (*Introduction*, 309) that after Paul reached Rome "any explicit mention of the events of the mid- to late-60s [is] out of place and superfluous" still does not answer the question of why the outcome of Paul's first Roman trial or subsequent events are not mentioned.

[48] Though it is true that some date the Letters to Timothy and Titus very late as well.

(AD 55–57). Thus, a date in the mid- to late 50s seems most plausible, with a likely date of the early 60s for the book of Acts, though certainty remains elusive.[49]

Provenance

Internally, the Gospel gives no indication of its place of origin. Externally, both the Anti-Marcionite Prologue to Luke (allegedly written against Marcion; ca. AD 160–180) and the Monarchian Prologue (short introductions prefixed in many Vulgate manuscripts to the four Gospels, probably written in the fourth or fifth century) claim that the Gospel was written from Achaia (Greece).[50] But both of these documents connect Matthew to Judea (uncertain) and Mark to Italy (more likely), so the linkage of Luke to Achaia may or may not be accurate. Achaia as a place of composition is not ruled out by a date in the early 60s since Luke may have temporarily left Paul when the latter was in Rome. Ancient tradition also places Lukan provenance in Boeotia and Rome. Ultimately, we have little evidence in the apostolic fathers beyond the regions of Greece, and this data may be quite late. Fitzmyer was on target when he stated that the provenance of Luke's Gospel is "anyone's guess."[51] But if it is correct that Luke compiled his sources while Paul was in prison in Caesarea and was with Paul during the first Roman imprisonment (as is indicated by Col 4:14), the Gospel of Luke could have been written anywhere between Caesarea and Rome.

Destination

The recipient of Luke's Gospel is clearly Theophilus (Luke 1:3). Luke's preface tells us at least three things about him. First, he was a man of high rank, for Luke addressed him as "most honorable" (*kratistos*; Luke 1:3), a term used elsewhere in the NT only by the same author in Acts with reference to the Roman government officials Felix and Festus (see Acts 23:26; 24:3; 26:25).[52] Second, Theophilus had received previous instruction regarding the Christian faith ("you have been instructed"; Luke 1:4). Third, Luke offered his Gospel to give Theophilus further assurance regarding this instruction ("so that you may know the certainty"; Luke 1:4).

Several views regarding Theophilus's identity surface in the scholarly literature.[53] Perhaps most common is the view that Theophilus was the monetary backer and literary patron who sponsored the publication of Luke's work.[54] Some have suggested he was an

---

[49] E.g., Bock, *Luke*, 1:16–18; Carson and Moo, *Introduction to the New Testament*, 208; I. H. Marshall, *The Gospel of Luke: A Commentary on the Greek Text*, NIGTC (Grand Rapids, MI: Eerdmans, 1978), 33–35; and Morris, *Luke*, 22–26.

[50] H. Koester (*Ancient Christian Gospels: Their History and Development* [Harrisburg, PA: Trinity, 1990], 243) attributes the mention of the provenance in the Anti-Marcionite Prologue to a fourth-century emendation.

[51] Fitzmyer, *Luke*, 57.

[52] Though note the opposing view by Theophrastus (*Characters* 5), who maintains that the address is "simple flattering speech" (cited and promptly discarded by Bock, *Luke*, 63; Bock also cites the dissenting opinion of F. Bovon, *Das Evangelium nach Lukas*, vol. 1: *Lk 1,1–9,50*, EKKNT 3/1 [Zürich, Germany: Benzinger/Neukirchen-Vluyn: Neukirchener, 1989], 39n34).

[53] See the discussion and bibliographic references in Bock, *Luke*, 1:63.

[54] E.g., E. E. Ellis, *The Gospel of Luke*, 2nd ed., New Century Bible (Grand Rapids, MI: Eerdmans, 1974), 66.

influential unbeliever with an interest in Christianity.[55] Others proposed that Theophilus was a new Christian in need of further instruction[56] or even the Roman official overseeing Paul's trial.[57] Finally, some see the name "Theophilus" as a euphemism for all who love God (*theos* = "God"; *philos* = "friend"; *Theophilus* = "friend or lover of God")[58] or as a designation used to protect the real identity of the patron or recipient of the letter. However, the reference to him as "most excellent" almost certainly points to a real person, especially in light of the above-mentioned parallels in Acts (23:26; 24:3; 26:25).[59]

Most likely, then, Theophilus was Luke's literary patron who supported the production of the books and made them available for viewing and copying. It was customary in ancient historiography for the patron's name to appear in the preface of a work.[60] The stated purpose ("so that you may know the certainty of the things about which you have been instructed," Luke 1:4) implies that Theophilus was more than merely interested but had received some previous Christian instruction,[61] although it is impossible to determine his precise spiritual status.

Although Luke specifically addressed his Gospel to Theophilus, it is unlikely that he limited his audience to just one person. If Theophilus was indeed Luke's literary patron, his identity would be less important since his name would appear more because of custom than because of direct address.[62]

Luke's Gospel reveals several characteristics about this broader audience. Virtually all scholars suggest that Luke wrote for a Gentile audience since he tended to substitute Greek names and titles for overtly Jewish ones[63] and since he traced Jesus's genealogy back to

---

[55] E.g., W. J. Larkin, *Acts*, IVPNTC (Downers Grove, IL: InterVarsity, 1995), 20; and J. Nolland, *Luke 1–9:20*, WBC 35A (Dallas, TX: Word, 1989), xxxiii (on whose view see further under Purpose below).

[56] E.g., Carson and Moo, *Introduction to the New Testament*, 210: "He was probably a recent convert to the faith."

[57] That Theophilus was a Roman official overseeing Paul's trial was frequently discussed in the early part of the twentieth century. Bruce (*Acts*, 29) cited both J. I. Still (*St. Paul on Trial: A New Reading of the History in the Book of Acts and the Pauline Epistles* [London, UK: Student Christian Movement, 1923], 84) and G. S. Duncan (*St. Paul's Ephesian Ministry: A Reconstruction with Special Reference to the Ephesian Origin of the Imprisonment Epistles* [London, UK: Hodder & Stoughton, 1929], 97).

[58] See Plummer (*Luke*, 5), who first said that the epithet *kratistos* ("most excellent") "is strongly in favour of the view that Theophilus was a real person" but went on to say, "it was a name likely to be used to represent any pious reader."

[59] Bock, *Luke*, 1:63; Marshall, *Luke*, 43; and Fitzmyer, *Luke*, 299.

[60] See Josephus's reference in two subsequent books to a "most excellent" *(kratiste)* and "most esteemed" *(timiōtate)* Epaphroditus (*Against Apion* 1.1; 2.1).

[61] The Greek word for "instruct" is *katēcheō*, which can mean "to report, inform" (Acts 21:21, 24) or "to instruct" (Acts 18:25; Rom 2:18; 1 Cor 14:19; Gal 6:6). Hence, Theophilus may have simply been informed about the story of Jesus or had received formal instruction. Based on the meaning of *katēcheō*, some have argued that Theophilus was an interested non-Christian (Larkin, *Acts*, 20). If so, Luke's purpose may have been at least in part evangelistic, while others contend he was a believer (see Bock, *Luke*, 64).

[62] L. Alexander ("Ancient Book Production and the Gospels," in *The Gospels for All Christians: Rethinking the Gospel Audiences*, ed. R. Bauckham [Grand Rapids, MI: Eerdmans, 1998], 98–99) notes that the patron would house and feed the writer while the book was being written and thus give access to the book to be copied. This would not have been the sole source of publication but an important one. Patrons also had varying interests in the books themselves.

[63] Plummer (*Luke*, xxxiv) notes the following: *zelotēs* ("zealot") for *kananiaos* ("canaanite"); *kranion* ("Skull") for Aramaic *golgotha*; *nomikos* ("lawyer") for *grammateus* ("scribe"); the terms "rabbi" or *rabbouni* do not occur in Luke, but they do

Adam (Luke 3:38), the first human, not just to Abraham, the Jewish patriarch, as Matthew did (see Matt 1:1–2, 17). Also, Luke situated the Gospel historically by referring to the dates of the Roman emperors Augustus and Tiberius (see Luke 2:1; 3:1), and this would be of particular interest to Gentiles in the Greco-Roman world. Moreover, compared to Matthew and Mark, Luke featured few original quotations of the OT, with the notable exception of Luke 4:18–19.[64] Finally, Luke's use of the term "Judea" in a generic sense for all of Palestine seems to indicate an audience removed from the Holy Land.[65] Thus, the internal evidence from Luke's Gospel points to a Gentile writing for Gentiles.

This is not to suggest that Luke's Gospel bore little or no interest for his Jewish readers.[66] Luke's vivid emphasis on the temple at both the beginning and the end of the Gospel (Luke 2:27, 37, 46; 24:53) and the Jewish expression of Christianity described in Acts (see Acts 21:20) would certainly resonate with a Jewish audience. Moreover, Luke took pains to show that the religion of God does not change (Luke 16:16–17). Luke may have had a specific target audience in mind but most likely wrote his Gospel for all who would read it. As Blomberg concluded, "Luke . . . is often considered the most universal of all the Gospels. Perhaps that is the reason his purposes and circumstances are so hard to pin down; he may have been deliberately trying to reach a wide audience."[67]

Purpose

The purpose of Luke's Gospel has been the subject of considerable disagreement. A multitude of suggestions have been offered from evangelism to a defense of the memory of Paul.[68] It seems most natural to allow Luke's stated purpose in his preface in correlation with the Gospel's structure to dictate the book's purpose. Indeed, Luke's Gospel does contain a purpose clause. Luke stated that he wrote his treatise to Theophilus "so that you may know the certainty of the things about which you have been instructed" (Luke 1:4). The word "instructed" indicates that Theophilus, and perhaps Luke's target audience, had been instructed but not necessarily converted.[69] The word *asphaleia* ("certainty")

---

appear in the Matthean and Markan parallels; Luke has only seven (six in UBS5) instances of the Hebrew particle *amēn* ("let it be so" or "amen") compared with Matthew's thirty (Luke prefers forms of "truly" [*alēthōs or alētheias*]).

[64] Plummer, *Luke*, xxiv–xxv.

[65] Fitzmyer (*Luke*, 58) listed Luke 1:5; 4:44; 6:17; 7:17; 23:5; Acts 2:9; 10:37 as specific instances.

[66] J. Jervell, *Luke and the People of God: A New Look at Luke-Acts* (Minneapolis, MN: Augsburg, 1979); R. L. Brawley, *Luke-Acts and the Jews: Conflict, Apology, and Conciliation* (Atlanta, GA: Scholars Press, 1987).

[67] Blomberg, *Jesus and the Gospels*, 152.

[68] E.g., R. Maddox (*The Purpose of Luke-Acts*, Studies of the New Testament and Its World [Edinburgh, Scotland: T&T Clark, 1982], 19–23) lists the following views on Luke's purpose: evangelism; an apology for Paul's trial; defending Christians before the Roman government; a defense of the memory of Paul; an explanation of the delay of the Second Coming; a defense against Gnosticism; and the confirmation of the gospel. For other discussions of the purpose(s) of Luke-Acts, see Bock (*Luke*, 14–15), who provides a list of eleven possible Lukan interpretations. See also Carson and Moo (*Introduction to the New Testament*, 301–6), who discuss conciliation; evangelism/apologetics; theological polemics; and edification.

[69] See note above.

indicates absolute certainty but also carries the nuance of stability.[70] Thus, Luke wanted Theophilus to know that the message about Jesus was reliable. This would imply that both Theophilus and Luke's larger audience were about to read a treatise defending the truthfulness of Christianity.

This apologetic character of the Gospel is clearly expressed in Luke's concern for accuracy. Luke first claimed to have had access to eyewitness traditions: "just as the original eyewitnesses and servants of the word handed them down to us" (Luke 1:2).[71] This is corroborated by Jesus's statement in Luke 24:48: "You are witnesses of these things" (cf. Luke 12:12). Luke also claimed to have engaged in a thorough investigation of the story of Jesus: "since I have carefully investigated everything from the very first" (Luke 1:3). Moreover, Luke described his first narrative in Acts as a description of "all [the things] that Jesus began to do and teach" (Acts 1:1). Together these references suggest that Luke wants to impart basic, reliable information about the life and teachings of Jesus. This included not only an accurate historical account of Jesus's ministry but also the interpretation of its theological significance and relevance.

D. Bock contended that the emphases of the Gospel pointed to Gentile Christians who struggled with the success of the Gentile mission and the apparent failure of the church's outreach to the Jews. Luke and Acts answered the doubts of a Gentile who found himself worshipping a Jewish Messiah that the Jews largely reject.[72] The following Lukan themes validate these emphases: texts pertaining to faithfulness, Jewish-Gentile relations (especially in Acts), the hope of Jesus's return, and the plan of God.[73] The primary purpose of Luke's Gospel, then, is the edification of Gentile Christians in need of instruction.

Luke's Accuracy

Luke's self-professed commitment to accuracy has already been referenced above. This claim, however, has not been taken at face value in the academy. One major issue is chronology. R. Brown, for example, stated, "[A]lthough Luke likes to set his Christian drama in the context of well-known events from antiquity, sometimes he does so inaccurately."[74] Brown's comments come in the midst of his discussion of Luke 2:1–2, which has become the premier example of Luke supposedly getting it wrong.

The reference is to the census mentioned in Luke 2:1–2: "In those days a decree went out from Caesar Augustus that the whole empire should be registered. This first registration

---

[70] C. Spicq, "ἀσφάλεια, ἀσφαλή, ἀσφαλῶ," in *Theological Lexicon of the New Testament,* vol. 1: ἀγα-ἐλπ (Peabody, MA: Hendrickson, 1994), 216.

[71] See R. Bauckham, *Jesus and the Eyewitnesses: The Gospels as Eyewitness Testimony* (Grand Rapids, MI: Eerdmans, 2007), especially 58–60 and 129–32.

[72] Bock, *Luke,* 1:15.

[73] Ibid. See Theological Themes below.

[74] R. Brown, *Introduction,* 233. Brown goes on to list the census at Luke 2, the eclipse of the sun at Passover AD 30 or 33, and Gamaliel's speech at Acts 5:36–37. He asserts, "Those convinced of Bible literalism are hard pressed to explain away all these inexactitudes" (ibid.) No such pressure is felt in the present work. We'll discuss the first claim here. The assumption of a purely natural eclipse is the (unwarranted) basis for the second claim. Gamaliel's speech is discussed in chap. 8.

took place while Quirinius was governing Syria." From this simple statement a series of objections have been raised that can be summarized into two points. (1) The kind of census Luke describes is neither recorded nor possible; and (2) Quirinius was not governor of Syria at the time of Christ's birth.[75] Josephus (*Ant.* 18:1–2, 26–29; 20:102) describes Quirinius as settling the estate of Archelaus and performing a tax registration about AD 6. This is, of course, about a decade too late. Thus, Conzelmann suggests (and many agree) that all attempts to rescue Luke from the charge of error are "hopelessly contrived."[76]

We can certainly dismiss the charge that Luke's census was impossible. D. Bock registers the following observations. Although we have no official records of all census activities, we do know that Augustus ordered three censuses, and periodic cycles of censuses did occur (in Egypt it was a fourteen-year cycle). Cycles in Syria, Gaul, and Spain occurred at or near the birth of Christ. The reference to Caesar's edict may simply reflect the ongoing census activity of the empire in which every jurisdiction participated (including, at times, vassal kingdoms). Furthermore, the fact that the Romans sometimes did allow a census to be taken based on local customs may explain the trip to Bethlehem.[77] So, then, the charge that the type of census taken was not possible is unfounded.

It is the governorship of Quirinius and the date of the census that is the weightier problem for interpreters. The current question is obscured by the sketchy and loosely connected nature of the historical evidence. The Roman records of the era are sparse and fractured. As a result, each interpreter, to varying degrees, expresses differing opinions regarding the timeline of events. Putting all the pieces of the evidence together presents a rather large puzzle with missing or isolated pieces. However, even operating on minimal evidence, we can affirm Luke's accuracy. So what do we know?

Quirinius shows up in two basic literary sources outside of Luke and in a few inscriptions.[78] Altogether, these show a man who rose up through the ranks from humble origins to have made more than moderate achievements as a soldier and politician.[79] There is some anecdotal evidence of Quirinius holding a high office in the province of Syria.[80] Inscriptional evidence shows him active in Asia Minor (Pisidian Antioch) and even conducting a census in Syria.[81] Finally, he served as the governor (propraetorial imperial leg-

---

[75] J. M. Compton, "Once More: Quirinius's Census," *Dallas Baptist Seminary Journal* 14 (2009): 46.

[76] H. Conzelmann, *History of Primitive Christianity* (Nashville, TN: Abingdon, 1973), 30. Cited in Compton, "Once More," 45.

[77] D. Bock, *Luke*, 1:904–905.

[78] Tacitus, *Annals*, 3; the aforementioned passages in Josephus; and three inscriptions (the full texts are recorded at *Inscriptiones* Latinae *Selectae* #2683, #9502, and #9503, the last two are duplicates of the same inscription).

[79] Tacitus reports that his public service included the consulship, that he was awarded a triumph for a war against the Homonadensians in Cilicia, that he died childless in Rome, and that he was awarded a public funeral. Tacitus, *Annals, 3.48.*

[80] W. M. Ramsay, *The Bearing of Recent Discovery on the Trustworthiness of the New Testament*, 2nd ed. (New York, NY: Hodder & Stoughton, 1915), 280. Ramsay notes that the Homonadensian wars would have been employing the Roman legions in Syria.

[81] Known as the *Lapis Venetus,* the inscription (#2683 above) is the funeral stone for Aemilius Secundus who served under Quirinius (identified as a legate of Caesar but not a propraetor) regarding Apamena, Syria.

ate) of Syria from AD 6–12. In summary, all the evidence points to Quirinius serving in the East (mainly Syria) from at least 12 BC. We can be fairly sure he was not the governor of Syria at the time of Christ's birth, although who exactly was governor from 4 to 1 BC is unknown.[82]

So then, did Luke get his facts wrong? Not necessarily. Of the many solutions to the problem, three seem the most likely.[83] First, the fact that he was not the governor of Syria in 6 or 5 BC (the most likely dates for the birth of Jesus) would not prevent his name from being attached to a census.[84] We can conclude that the names of lower-level officials are connected to matters such as a census—in this case Quirinius himself. In this light, it is important to note that neither Luke nor Josephus ever used terms that necessarily describe Quirinius as governor.[85] If there was a census going on about 6 or 5 BC, there is no reason why Quirinius's name could not be attached to it.[86] Given what we know about the Roman provincial censuses (or, more precisely, what we *don't* know), a now-unknown census is likely.

Second, the adjective "first" (*prōtē*) should be carefully weighed. The most natural reading of Luke 2:2 is, "This was the first census." This terminology would allow for at least a second or even a series of registrations. In this understanding, an AD 6 census would probably be the second census. It would make sense that the later census was more famous and serves as a reference point, for it caused a riot according to both Josephus and Luke.[87] In a similar vein, some have suggested that "first" should be translated "before."[88] Thus, the translation would be "this was the census before Quirinius was governor of Syria."

---

[82] For a full list of Imperial governors, see http://www.worldheritage.org/articles/List_of_Roman_governors_of_Syria. Even if Quirinius was governor during this time period, it is after the birth of Christ in 6 or 5 BC.

[83] Porter lists six views: (1) ignore the major issues; (2) leave the issues as unresolved or unsolvable; (3) Quirinius had two legateships; (4) "first" means "before"; (5) Luke actually means AD 6; and (6) Luke conflates conflicting accounts. S. E. Porter "The Reasons for the Lukan Census," in *Paul, Luke and the Graeco-Roman World: Essays in Honour of Alexander J. M. Wedderburn*, JSNTSupp 217 (London, UK: T&T Clark, 2003), 170–71. There are more; see below.

[84] Inscriptional evidence does show Quirinius's name attached to a Syrian census (the *Lapis Venetum* cited above). The census described is variously dated. Often it is dated to the census of AD 6, based essentially on Josephus (see, e.g., D. Kennedy, "Demography, the Population of Syria and the Census of Q. Aemilius Secundus," *Levant* 38 [2006]: 109–24). However, see the questions below regarding Josephus and the census. The terminology used in the inscription for Quirinius is simply "legate"; that is not necessarily propraetorial legate (governor). Even if the inscription is an AD 6 census, it does not disqualify an earlier census.

[85] J. H. Rhoads, "Josephus Misdated the Census of Quirinius," *JETS* 54 (2011): 82. Josephus never refers to Quirinius as the governor of Syria. Luke uses a genitive absolute construction that is literally translated "while Quirinius was leading Syria." The term "leading" (Gr. *hēgemoneuontos*) does not demand the imperial office but one having power. It could be translated "the one having Syrian hegemony." Luke uses the same term at Luke 22:26 to refer to the greatest of the disciples; in Acts 7:10 to refer to Joseph; in 14:12 to refer to Paul the "chief speaker;" and in 15:22 to reference the representatives of the Jerusalem Council. Only Joseph could be considered something like a governor in Luke's usage.

[86] This is the view put forth by D. J. Hayles, "The Roman Census and Jesus's Birth: Was Luke Correct? Part 2: Quirinius's Career and a Census in Herod's Day," *Buried History* 10 (1974):16–31. Thus, Ramsay's argument that Quirinius was twice the governor of Syria (based on questionable inscriptional evidence) is unnecessary *(Bearing of Recent Discovery*, 277).

[87] See Acts 5:37.

[88] See, e.g., J. Nolland, *Luke 1:1-9:20*, WBC 35a (Dallas, TX: Word, 1989), 102; for a solid defense of this position, see A. J. Köstenberger and A. E. Stewart, *The First Days of Jesus: The Story of the Incarnation* (Wheaton, IL: Crossway, 2015), 234–39.

While this is within the semantic range of *prōtē* (first), it would be a highly unusual use of the adjective."[89] An infrequent use of a word, however, does not make such a reading impossible. At any rate, under either interpretation, the AD 6 census is referred to as a later census. Thus, given that Quirinius is not named with the title of propraetorial legate (governor), there is no chronological issue at Luke 2:2.

Recently, a third viable option has been suggested. In an article published in the *Journal of the Evangelical Theological Society*, J. H. Rhoads asserts that there *was* an error in the literature; only Josephus is the one who made it. Employing source criticism to Josephus, Rhoads posits that the historian has misread his source(s) and confused similar events. He suggests that the accounts that contain the census and the revolt of a Galilean named Judas are actually duplicates of earlier accounts. Thus, Josephus misplaced them at the end of Archelaus's reign. Rhoads's study is a detailed and lengthy *tour de force* through a mountain of evidence, so reproduction here is not feasible. Suffice it to say that his arguments, if not compelling, are certainly possible.[90] Josephus manifestly makes obvious errors elsewhere; it is not impossible that here the error is more subtle.[91]

Thus, it is not necessary to assert that Luke made an error here. In fact, only an unwarranted preference for Josephus over Luke would demand that conclusion. Instead, we suggest that given Luke's track record elsewhere regarding accuracy, the general nature of Luke's statement at 2:2 (nothing really pointing to AD 6), and the possibility of duplication on Josephus's part should lead interpreters to avoid hasty conclusions regarding Luke's accuracy. He has withstood scrutiny on a level not usually applied to other documents. He should certainly be given the benefit of the doubt in this case.

LITERATURE

Literary Plan

Overall, Luke follows a geographical pattern in his presentation of Jesus's ministry similar to that of Mark and Matthew. Similar to Matthew (but not Mark), Luke begins

---

[89] Typically the word appears as a neuter when it means "before" (see, e.g., John 15:18). The adjective is a nominative here, agreeing with "registration." The nominative, however, is used in John 1:15 and 30 with the meaning "before," but there are complicating factors there. If Luke uses *prōtos* here as meaning "before," this would be the only time he does so in Luke-Acts.

[90] Rhoads, "Misdated," 65–87. Rhoads is not the first to make this assertion. He acknowledges T. Zahn, "Die Syrische Statthalterschaft und die Schätzung des Quirinius," *NKZ* 4 (1893): 633–54; W. Lodder, Die Schätzung des Quirinius bei Flavius Josephus. Eine Untersuchung: Hat sich Flavius Josephus in der Datierung der bekannten Schätzung (Luk 2,2) geirrt? (Leipzig, Germany: Döffling & Franke, 1930); F. Spitta, "Die Chronologische Notizen und die Hymnen in Lc 1 U. 2," ZNW 7 (1906): 281–317; W. Weber, "Der Census des Quirinius nach Josephus," ZNW 10 (1909): 307–19.

[91] Keener notes that Josephus is known to contradict himself regarding the rise of the Sicarii, in names, in numbers, and in the order of events. He does so also with biblical events. He confuses people with similar names (Agrippa I with Agrippa II) and gets the placement of public buildings wrong (as exposed by archaeology). Furthermore, he can even get the most notable of relationships wrong (Germanicus was not the nephew of Tiberius as stated in *Ant.* 18.206). C. Keener, *Acts: An Exegetical Commentary*, vol. 2: *3:1–14:28* (Grand Rapids, MI: Baker, 2013), 1233. The suggestions made by Rhoads are no more spectacular than these examples.

his Gospel with a birth narrative—though Luke's Gospel reflects Mary's and Elizabeth's perspectives rather than Joseph's, who is primary in Matthew's Gospel—and provides a genealogy of Jesus. Unlike Matthew, however, Luke places Jesus's genealogy not at the beginning of his Gospel but just prior to the beginning of Jesus's ministry (3:23–38). Luke opens his Gospel with a polished literary preface in which he acknowledges his indebtedness to other accounts about Jesus and stresses the accuracy of the information he provides.

After this, Luke—again similar to Matthew—provides an account of Jesus's temptation by the Devil, though the order of the second and third temptations is reversed in Matthew (Luke 4:1–13). Luke's functional substitute for Matthew's Sermon on the Mount (5–7) is Jesus's inaugural sermon at his hometown synagogue of Nazareth. Matthew reveals Jesus as the new Moses who gives to his followers a new law, but Luke presents Jesus as Isaiah's Servant of the Lord who is endowed with the Spirit and anointed to preach good news to the poor (4:18–19, citing Isa 61:1–2). This sounds a major Lukan emphasis throughout his Gospel, namely, Jesus's coming first and foremost to the disenfranchised in society. This group includes women, children, Gentiles, tax collectors and "sinners," the sick and disabled, and the poor.

Subsequently, Luke mainly follows the familiar pattern (especially from Mark) of tracing the various stages of Jesus's initial ministry in Galilee, including major teachings (though some of Matthew's larger body of Jesus's teaching material is most likely broken up, such as the contents of the Sermon on the Mount) and healings. Some of these healings, such as that of a widow's son in the town of Nain, are unique to Luke (7:11–17). Luke also documents Jesus's calling of his disciples and, in another Lukan emphasis, his support by a number of devoted women (8:1–3) who follow Jesus all the way to the cross (23:49). As in Matthew and Mark, Peter's confession of Jesus as the Messiah is a watershed moment (9:18–20) and is followed by predictions of Jesus's passion with important implications for discipleship (9:21–27).

As noted in greater detail below, Luke breaks new ground in his lengthy "Travel Narrative" (9:51–19:27). This section is introduced by a curious reference to Jesus's ascension only a third of the way into the Gospel (9:51) and records Jesus's approach to Jerusalem, the place where he will be tried and rejected by the Jewish people, in considerable detail. Luke builds suspense by including a significant amount of teaching material, particularly parables of Jesus. Many of these parables are unique to Luke, including the parables of the Good Samaritan (10:25–37) and the Prodigal Son (15:11–32). A beloved character also unique to Luke's Gospel is Zacchaeus, the tax collector who converts to faith in Jesus and restores the money he took, prompting Jesus's programmatic declaration that "the Son of Man has come to seek and to save the lost" (19:10).

Luke's Passion Narrative follows largely familiar lines in keeping with the presentations by Mark and Matthew. But Luke again breaks new ground in his account of several resurrection appearances not found in any of the other Gospels, most notably Jesus's appearance to two disciples on the road to Emmaus. (One of these men was Cleopas, the possible source of this narrative, 24:13–35). Luke's Gospel, similar to Matthew's, concludes with a commissioning narrative (24:46–49). References to the giving of the Spirit and the disciples' witness to all the nations, beginning in Jerusalem, and to Jesus's ascension prepare the reader for Luke's second volume, the book of Acts.

OUTLINE

Preface: Luke's Purpose (1:1–4)

I. INTRODUCTION TO JESUS AND HIS MISSION (1:5–4:13)
   A. John the Baptist and Jesus (1:5–2:52)
      1. Prediction of the Births of John and Jesus (1:5–38)
      2. Mary's Visit to Elizabeth and Mary's Song (1:39–56)
      3. Birth of John the Baptist and Zechariah's Song (1:57–80)
      4. Jesus's Birth and Boyhood (2:1–52)
   B. Preliminaries to Jesus's Ministry (3:1–4:13)
      1. John the Baptist and Jesus's Baptism (3:1–22)
      2. Jesus's Genealogy (3:23–38)
      3. Satan's Temptation of Jesus (4:1–13)
II. JESUS'S GALILEAN MINISTRY (4:14–9:50)
   A. First Part of Galilean Ministry (4:14–7:50)
      1. Initial Ministry: Nazareth Sermon, Exorcism, Healings (4:14–5:39)
      2. Sabbath Controversy (6:1–11)
      3. Choosing of the Twelve (6:12–16)
      4. Sermon on the Plain (6:17–49)
      5. Major Healings: Centurion's Servant, Widow's Son (7:1–17)
      6. John the Baptist: Doubts and His Role (7:18–35)
      7. Anointing of Jesus by Sinful Woman (7:36–50)
   B. Second Part of Galilean Ministry (8:1–39)
      1. Female Supporters of Jesus (8:1–3)
      2. Parables of the Kingdom and Related Teaching (8:4–21)
      3. Trip Across Galilee: Stilling of Storm, Gerasene Demoniac (8:22–39)
   C. Third Part of Galilean Ministry and Withdrawal (8:40–9:50)
      1. Miracles and Ministry, Raising of Jairus's Daughter (8:40–9:9)
      2. Feeding of 5,000 (9:10–17)
      3. Caesarea Philippi: Peter's Confession, Transfiguration (9:18–50)
III. JESUS'S JOURNEY TO JERUSALEM AND HIS PASSION (9:51–24:53)
   A. The Journey to Jerusalem (9:51–19:27)
      1. Following Jesus (9:51–62)
      2. Mission of the Seventy (10:1–24)
      3. Parable of the Good Samaritan (10:25–37)
      4. Mary and Martha (10:38–42)
      5. Teachings on Prayer, Beelzebub, Sign of Jonah (11:1–13:21)
      6. The Narrow Door, Warning (13:22–35)

7. At a Pharisee's House (14:1–23)
8. Teachings and Parables of Jesus: Prodigal Son, Rich Man and Lazarus (14:24–16:31)
9. Additional Teachings, Healing of Ten Lepers (17:1–18:17)
10. Rich Young Ruler (18:18–30)
11. Jesus Foretells His Death (18:31–34)
12. Healing of a Blind Man (18:35–43)
13. Zacchaeus (19:1–10)
14. Parable of Ten Minas (19:11–27)

B. Final Ministry in Jerusalem (19:28–22:38)
1. Triumphal Entry (19:28–44)
2. Cleansing of the Temple (19:45–48)
3. Final Controversies with Jewish Leaders (20:1–47)
4. Olivet Discourse (21:1–38)
5. Last Supper (22:1–38)

C. Jesus's Crucifixion, Resurrection, and Ascension (22:39–24:51)
1. Gethsemane (22:39–46)
2. Arrest (22:47–65)
3. Trial (22:66–23:25)
4. Crucifixion (23:26–56)
5. Resurrection (24:1–12)
6. Postresurrection Ministry (24:13–49)
7. Ascension (24:50–51)

Epilogue: The Disciples Return to Jerusalem (24:52–53)

UNIT-BY-UNIT DISCUSSION

Preface: Luke's Purpose (1:1–4)

In his elegantly worded preface, Luke sets the ministry of Jesus in the scope of God's plan of salvation and states his reason and purpose for taking up his narrative. He announces the continuity of what happened in and through Jesus with God's past dealings with his people, the thoroughness of his research, and his plan to write an orderly account in order to give assurance to Theophilus regarding the truthfulness of Christianity.

I. Introduction to Jesus and His Mission (1:5–4:13)

A. John the Baptist and Jesus (1:5–2:52)

This portion of the Gospel provides the foundation for Jesus and his messianic mission. Luke describes Jesus's supernatural birth and sets forth its significance through repeated pronouncements by God's messengers. Gabriel tells Zechariah that his son John will come in the power of Elijah and that "he will turn many of the sons of Israel to the Lord their God" (1:16). The same angel announces to Mary that her virgin-born child is the Son of the Most High God (1:32). Zechariah prophesies that the Lord will bring salvation to his people and that John will proclaim forgiveness of sins (1:77).

At Jesus's birth the angelic hosts proclaim to the shepherds that a Savior has been born in Bethlehem (2:11). When Jesus is circumcised at the temple on the eighth day, Simeon identifies him as the Messiah who will bring salvation and revelation to both Jews and Gentiles (2:30–32). Anna the prophetess declares the redemption of Israel (2:36–38). Finally, Jesus at age twelve is already fully aware of his true identity and calling: he must be in his Father's house, the temple, and be about his Father's business (2:49).

B. Preliminaries to Jesus's Ministry (3:1–4:13)

The first steps of the narrative—the baptism, genealogy, and temptation accounts—identify Jesus as the Coming One who will save his people from their sins.

This section presents Jesus as an adult about to enter his ministry and includes references to the ministry of John the Baptist, the genealogy of Jesus, and an account of Jesus's temptation by Satan. Luke begins this new section by fast-forwarding from Jesus at age twelve to the presentation of John in the wilderness. Although Luke includes information on John's teaching, his primary emphasis is on John's declaration about Jesus. After this transition in the Gospel, Luke's emphasis shifts from John to Jesus.

Luke chooses to place Jesus's genealogy (3:23–38) at the onset of Jesus's ministry rather than at the beginning of his book as Matthew does (see Matt 1:1–17). Also, Luke follows a different line of ancestry than Matthew, which reflects a different purpose on Luke's part. Moreover, by tracing Jesus's genealogy back to Adam, the "son of God" (3:38), Luke endeavors to be inclusive by beginning with the progenitor of the entire human race.[92]

The final preliminary to Jesus's ministry is his temptation by the Devil (4:1–13). Luke presents a different sequence for the three temptations than Matthew does (4:1–11): (1) turning stones into bread; (2) worshipping Satan in exchange for all the world's kingdoms; and (3) jumping off the pinnacle of the temple to be protected by angels. Most assume that Matthew follows the chronological order[93] and that Luke inverts the last two temptations.[94] Starting at 4:14, Jesus's ministry begins in earnest.

---

[92] For a comparison between Matthew's and Luke's genealogies, see D. R. Bauer, "Genealogy," in *Dictionary of Jesus and the Gospels*, 2nd ed., 299–302.

[93] Matthew employed several chronological markers in his version of the temptation narrative: "then" *(tote)* in vv. 5, 10 and "again" *(palin)* in v. 8.

[94] The temptations seem to parallel Gen 3:6: (1) stone to bread/ "good for food"; (2) kingdoms of the world/ "delightful to look at"; (3) pinnacle of the temple/ "desirable for obtaining wisdom." If so, Luke's presentation is similar to Paul's teaching on Jesus as the last Adam (see Rom 5:14–21; 1 Cor 15:22). So Godet, *Luke*, 207–8; Plummer, *Luke*, 109; Bock, *Luke*, 371; Hendriksen, *Luke*, 233–34; contra Fitzmyer, *Luke*, 512.

II. Jesus's Galilean Ministry (4:14–9:50)

A. First Part of Galilean Ministry (4:14–7:50)

Jesus's Galilean ministry begins with his inaugural sermon in the synagogue at Nazareth (4:14–30) where Jesus presents himself as Isaiah's Servant of the Lord (see Isa 61:1–2) and publicly announces the commencement of his mission to a hostile and unbelieving congregation in his hometown. Then Jesus casts out demons and heals Peter's mother-in-law and many others (4:31–41). After this Luke provides a summary of the results of Jesus's preaching and a statement of his purpose, echoing the Isaiah quote in 4:18 (4:43).

Another series of events during the first stage of Jesus's Galilean ministry is the calling of Jesus's first disciples: Simon Peter and his partners, the sons of Zebedee (5:1–11), and Levi, the tax collector (5:27–32). After the narration of a controversy ensuing from Jesus's healing of an invalid on the Sabbath (6:1–11), the selection of Jesus's twelve apostles (6:12–16) ensues. Luke also documents a series of instructions that Jesus gives his disciples, culminating in the Sermon on the Plain (6:17–49), the shortened Lukan equivalent to Matthew's Sermon on the Mount (chaps. 5–7). In this Jesus advocates rejection of worldly pleasures and goods, love for others, and radical following after him.

Another set of major healings ensues: the centurion's servant is restored to health (7:1–10) and a widow's son is raised from the dead (7:11–17). At this point John the Baptist expresses doubts, so Jesus points to the fulfillment of OT messianic prophecy in his ministry to reassure the Baptist (7:18–35), who apparently is unsettled by the popular understanding of Jesus as a mere prophet. The unit concludes with Jesus's anointing by a sinful woman in the house of Simon the Pharisee (7:36–50).

B. Second Part of Galilean Ministry (8:1–39)

The second part of Jesus's Galilean ministry begins with a reference to a group of faithful women who sacrifice to minister to Jesus out of their own means (8:1–3).[95] This is followed by the parable of the Soils, which highlights the proper reception of Jesus by those who, "having heard the word with an honest and good heart, hold on to it" (8:15). The parable of the Soils is followed by another brief parable on "the light on a lampstand" (8:16–18). Continuing on the theme of proper response to Jesus, he identifies "those who hear and do the word of God" as his true family (8:21).

After this Luke shows Jesus journeying across Galilee (8:22–39), highlighting his authority. The first vignette is known as the "Stilling of the Storm," where Jesus calms a strong wind on the Lake of Tiberias (8:22–25). The climactic pronouncement sets the stage for the pericopes to follow: "Who can this be? He commands even the winds and the waves, and they obey him!" (8:25). Jesus also has authority over demons, as the encounter with the demoniac Gadarene makes clear (8:26–39).

---

[95] So Bock, *Luke*, 1:629.

C. Third Part of Galilean Ministry and Withdrawal (8:40–9:50)

The account of the third part of Jesus's Galilean ministry continues to emphasize Jesus's authority over disease and death. The pericope of the woman with the issue of blood (8:43–48) interrupts the raising of the daughter of Jairus where Jesus showed his authority over death (8:40–42, 49–56). Jesus grants authority over demons and disease (but not nature or death) to the Twelve (9:1–6), and their mission is so successful it even perturbs Herod Antipas (9:7–9).

Sidebar 6.1: The Lukan "Travel Narrative"

One of the most striking features of Luke's Gospel is the extraordinarily long "Journey to Jerusalem" section. It takes up nearly 38 percent of the Gospel.[1] Much of the material in this section is unique to Luke. The section is dominated by Jesus's discourses and fewer miracles. This is predicated on the fact that Luke had established who Jesus is in his narration of the Galilean ministry, and then he moved on to what it means to follow Jesus as he journeyed inexorably to Jerusalem where crucifixion awaited him.

The journey to Jerusalem covers 9:51 to 19:27 and is followed by Luke's Passion Narrative, which includes Jesus's final ministry in Jerusalem (19:28–22:38) and an account of his crucifixion, resurrection, and ascension (22:39–24:53). The strategic significance of 9:51 is impossible to exaggerate. After a little more than a third of his Gospel, Luke wrote, "When the days were coming to a close for him to be taken up, he determined to journey to Jerusalem."

It is striking for Luke to speak of Jesus's ascension that early in the narrative, leapfrogging, as it were, over the ensuing events including Jesus's arrest, trial, crucifixion, burial, and resurrection. With its reference to Jesus's ascension, 9:51 introduces the entire remainder of the Gospel and provides a literary inclusion with the ending of Luke's narrative in 24:50–53, which in turn corresponds to the narration of Jesus's ascension in Acts 1:9–11.

[1] Of course, the number varies whether one counts words, verses, or lines. The present calculation is based on the number of words.

Jesus then withdraws with his disciples (9:10). The final miracle in this section is the feeding of the 5,000 (9:10–17), which is followed by several narrative units dealing with the nature of discipleship. Peter's confession of Jesus as the Messiah (9:18–27) marks a significant transition in Jesus's preaching and ministry. Until this point Jesus has sought to reveal himself to his disciples; here his attention turns to preparing his disciples in light of his impending death in Jerusalem.

In the wake of Peter's confession, Jesus explains to his disciples that they must deny themselves and "take up [their] cross daily" as they follow him. In fact, some will see the kingdom of God, which likely anticipates the transfiguration of Jesus narrated in the following pericope (9:28–36). Moses and Elijah appear and speak with Jesus about his upcoming "departure" (9:31 NIV; Gk. *exodos*). This indicates that Jesus's death would provide deliverance for God's people similar to the exodus for Israel.

As Jesus descends the Mount of Transfiguration, he encounters two instances of inadequate discipleship. First, he exorcises a demon from a boy whom his disciples could not help. Jesus castigates them for being part of an "unbelieving and rebellious generation" (9:41). Second, Jesus confronts a spirit of self-aggrandizement in the disciples as they argue about who is the greatest among them (9:46–48). Jesus rebukes them for their ungodly attitude. He also tells them not to prevent others from casting out demons in his name (9:49–50).

III. Jesus's Journey to Jerusalem and His Passion (9:51–24:53)

A. The Journey to Jerusalem (9:51–19:27)

The first portion of the Lukan travel narrative discusses the nature of discipleship. The key thematic thread running through 10:42 is that following Jesus often requires separation from the familiar and comfortable and commitment to proclaim the kingdom of God. The journey begins when Jesus and his disciples pass through a Samaritan village that does not receive Jesus. He rebukes his followers who want him to destroy the village supernaturally (9:52–56).

Would-be disciples must be willing to leave behind their familiar surroundings, occupation, and loved ones to follow Jesus (9:57–62). This is followed by the mission of the seventy whom Jesus sends out after giving them specific instructions (10:1–20). Jesus's private instruction to his disciples is succeeded by a question from a scribe, which Jesus answers in the parable of the Good Samaritan (10:25–37). After this Jesus visits Mary and Martha and commends Mary for making the right choice by sitting at his feet (10:38–42).

Jesus then teaches in Judea while still on his journey to Jerusalem (11:1–13:21). As he makes clear, following him entails a call to prayer. The unit begins with the Lukan version of the Model Prayer (11:1–4) and continues with an encouragement to be faithful in prayer (11:5–13). In 11:14, the narrative takes a dramatic turn toward the controversies that followed in Jesus's wake. The distinctive thread through 11:54 is the call for a proper response to Jesus. He answers the question regarding the source of his power in the Beelzebul controversy: it is from God (11:14–26).

After commending those who "hear the word of God and keep it" (11:27–28), Jesus berates his generation for seeking signs, pointing them to "the sign of Jonah" (11:29–36). Rather than demanding additional signs, people should recognize that in the Son of Man, "something greater than Jonah is here" (11:32). Jesus also pronounces woes against the Pharisees and experts in the law (11:37–54), castigating the Jewish leaders for rank hypocrisy and for leading people to destruction. The result is that the Pharisees start trying to trap Jesus with his own words (11:54).

The events Luke selects in the next portion of the journey highlight the necessity of responding to Jesus in faith. In particular, Jesus identifies three obstacles to the reception of his message: hypocrisy, greed, and sluggishness. First, he warns against the "leaven" of the Pharisees, that is, hypocrisy (12:1–12). Second, he takes the opportunity provided by a request from the crowd to settle a family dispute to speak out against greed (12:13–34), urging his followers to be about the business of the kingdom: "For where your treasure is, there your heart will be also" (12:34). Finally, he enjoins watchfulness because he will return at an unexpected time (12:49–59). This is particularly relevant because he will come to "bring fire on the earth"—judgment is coming (12:49). Consequently, 13:1–9 focuses on the urgent necessity of repentance in light of God's patience.

The next phase of the journey sustains a long thread of teaching concerning the question of who is allowed to enter God's kingdom.[96] Another Sabbath controversy ensues in a stern warning against the hypocrisy of the religious leaders (13:10–17). The section focuses on the marked reversal of expectations brought by Jesus's ministry. Contrary to popular expectations, only a few will be saved. What is more, the few who are saved are not the religious leaders but those who "enter through the narrow door" (13:24–30). Ironically, Jerusalem herself is the owner of a desolate house (13:35).

While attending a banquet, Jesus shares his wisdom with the guests. The Pharisees are a foil for Jesus's teaching on the proper attitude of those who inherit the kingdom. He begins by noting the pride of jockeying for exalted positions at the banquet and counsels that "everyone who exalts himself will be humbled, and the one who humbles himself will be exalted" (14:11). He proceeds to instruct his listeners to invite those who cannot repay so that their reward will come at the resurrection.

Jesus's teaching regarding ministering to the outcast results in controversy: "This man welcomes sinners and eats with them!" (15:2). The answer is given by way of the famous trio of parables on "lost things"—a sheep, a coin, and a son—highlighting people's joy over finding that which was lost. This series constitutes a defense of Jesus's practices of fraternizing with "sinners" and a response to the sustained criticism of the Pharisees embodied in the older son in the final parable.

Chapter 16 returns to the matter of wealth (the subject of the second warning at 12:13–34). The surprising hero of Jesus's parable is the shrewd manager who conveys the lesson that one's wealth should be used in ways that count for eternity (16:9). The Pharisees are again the foil as they scoff at Jesus because they were "lovers of money" (16:14). The parable of Lazarus and the Rich Man points to the folly and idolatry of serving money.

The disciples are then warned not to cause others to sin or to harbor an attitude of bitterness or self-aggrandizement (17:1–10). The final portion of the journey to Jerusalem focuses on several aspects of the kingdom. At 17:11–19, ten lepers are healed, but only one Samaritan among them is grateful. Jesus notes that his faith saved him. When the

---

[96] See Green, *Luke*, 516.

Pharisees ask Jesus about the coming of God's kingdom, he declares that the kingdom is both a present and a future reality to which many are oblivious, just as were the contemporaries of Noah and Lot.

Next, Jesus enjoins his hearers to faithful prayer through the parable of the Unjust Judge and the Persistent Widow (18:1–8). The parable is still related to the coming of the Son of Man, for Jesus asks, "Nevertheless, when the Son of Man comes, will he find faith on earth?" (18:8). The parable of the Pharisee and the Tax Collector (18:9–14) prohibits self-righteous prayer, "because everyone who exalts himself will be humbled, but the one who humbles himself will be exalted" (18:14). Little children are the preeminent example of those who come to the kingdom (18:15–17).

Luke proceeds to cite the negative example of the rich young ruler, who turned away sad because he would not part with his wealth (18:18–23). Jesus then makes the point that there is "no one who has left a house, wife or brothers or sisters, parents or children because of the kingdom of God, who will not receive many times more at this time, and eternal life in the age to come" (18:29–30).

The concluding portion of the journey shows Jesus bringing salvation to Jerusalem. Luke 18:31–34 contains yet another announcement of why Jesus is going to Jerusalem: to be beaten, killed, and raised the third day, in fulfillment of the message of the prophets and thus in keeping with the plan of God. This announcement sets the stage for the final segment of the journey. Jesus first heals a blind beggar (18:35–34, Mark's Bartimaeus) as the first aspect of salvation emphasized by Luke, a humble cry for mercy.

The second aspect is highlighted by Zacchaeus (19:1–10): repentance evidenced by works, in his case restoration of dishonest gain and giving the rest to the poor.[97] The parable of the Pounds addresses the expectation by some that the kingdom will come immediately (19:11–27). The parable demonstrates not only that there will be a delay but also stresses the need for faithfulness in the interim.

B. Final Ministry in Jerusalem (19:28–22:38)

The triumphal entry (19:28–44) marks the end of the journey section and the beginning of the end for Jesus in accomplishing salvation. Jesus first mounts a donkey and rides into Jerusalem in fulfillment of prophecy (Zech 9:9), entering the city not to assume kingship but to announce it (19:38, citing Ps 118:26). The Pharisees object to this display of royalty, and Jesus promptly rebukes them (19:39–40). Finally, Jesus laments the impending fate of Jerusalem (19:41–48).[98] Fully cognizant of what will soon happen to him, Jesus grieves over the great devastation to come upon Jerusalem because of its part in the crucifixion and rejection of him, the Messiah.

The following sections show the opposition of the Jewish leadership and the ultimate consequences of the nation's rejection of the Messiah (19:45–48; chap. 20). When Jesus

---

[97] Bock, *Luke*, 2:1501.

[98] See Green, *Luke*, 683–89.

arrives in Jerusalem, he clears the temple and makes it the center of his teaching. His enemies cannot take him into custody because the crowd is "captivated by what they heard" (19:48). This sets the stage for the temple controversy (20:1–8), where Jesus reminds the Jewish leaders that John witnessed to them about him.

This controversy, in turn, leads to the parable of the Wicked Tenants (20:9–19). In this parable, the tenants of a vineyard mistreat the farmer's servants and kill his heir, which rightly makes them the object of the farmer's wrath. The leaders immediately recognize that the parable is addressed to them. Jesus then appeals to Psalm 118:22–23: "The stone that the builders rejected has become the cornerstone," and ominously notes that this stone will crush those who oppose it. The following section chronicles several attempts to trap Jesus, all in vain (20:20–40). The unit ends with another denunciation of the pride and hypocrisy of the scribes (20:41–47).

With his demise imminent Jesus delivers the Olivet Discourse, outlining the scenario for the end-times (21:1–36). First, he announces the impending destruction of the temple. The disciples ask a twofold question: When will these things be, and what are the warning signs? Jesus's answer pertains to the temple's destruction and his return. There will be false messiahs, wars, and natural disasters, but first the disciples will be persecuted. Jesus encourages them to endure (21:19).

When Jerusalem is surrounded by armies, the end will be near. Jerusalem will be trampled until the time of the Gentiles is completed—a reference to the intervening time between the destruction of Jerusalem and Jesus's return (21:20–24). Jesus's return will be preceded by terrifying supernatural environmental disasters that make the world faint from fear, and then the Son of Man will appear with power and great glory. Jesus's concluding call for watchfulness (21:34–36) is prefaced by the parable of the Fig Tree (21:29–33).

In chapter 22, Luke begins to relate the events leading up to the crucifixion. His narration essentially has three parts: preparation, confrontation, and crucifixion. First is the preparation for the event. This includes both the betrayal and the last Passover. Satan enters Judas to betray Jesus (22:1–6). Jesus also prepares the disciples for his crucifixion and subsequent absence by transforming the Passover meal (22:7–38). He announces Judas's betrayal and squelches a debate about who will be the greatest. He also tells the disciples to be prepared for his departure, referring to the ensuing persecution and Peter's denial.

C. Jesus's Crucifixion, Resurrection, and Ascension (22:39–24:51)

The arrest and trials of Jesus mark the beginning of his demise. Jesus endures agony at Gethsemane (22:39–46) and then is betrayed and arrested. Jesus does not allow his disciples to resist the arrest and considers it appropriate that the chief priests seize him in the dark because darkness is their domain (22:53). Peter's denials are recorded as the trial phase begins (22:55–62).

The trial emphasizes Jesus's innocence and the guilt of those who condemn him. At the trial before the Sanhedrin (22:63–71), the charge against Jesus is blasphemy for his claiming to be the Son of God. Yet since the Sanhedrin lacks the power of capital punishment, they send him to Pilate (23:1–7). Pilate finds no guilt in Jesus, declaring him innocent three times. Neither does Herod (23:15), but Pilate succumbs to the demands of the bloodthirsty mob. Hence a triangle of enemies—Pilate, Herod, and the Jewish leaders—have come together to execute this plot.

Table 6.1: Phases of Jesus's Trial

Trial	Scripture	Description
Trial Before Annas	John 18:19–23	Annas questions Jesus about his teaching; Jesus is struck in the face and challenges his accusers for striking him illegally; no witnesses produced
Trial Before Caiaphas	Matt 26:57–68; Mark 14:53–65; John 18:24–28	When asked if he is the Messiah, Jesus claims to be the divine Son of Man; convicted of blasphemy and sent to Herod
Trial Before Pilate	Luke 23:1–6	Jesus falsely accused; affirms his messianic status; sent to Herod
Trial Before Herod	Luke 23:7–11	False charges against Jesus; Herod finds no guilt; Jesus sent to Pilate
Trial Before Pilate (continued)	Matt 27:1–25; Mark 15:1–15; Luke 23:12–25; John 18:29–19:6	No formal charges brought against Jesus; no witnesses produced; Jesus sentenced to crucifixion without conviction from Pilate, who states three times that he finds no fault in Jesus.

The rest of chapter 23 records the events surrounding the crucifixion. Jesus is crucified and mocked repeatedly (23:24–33). He is mocked by the soldiers who crucify him, the thieves on either side of him, and the scribes and Pharisees.[99] But it is apparent that something more than a criminal execution is taking place as the sun darkens and the veil of the temple is torn (23:44–46). Thus, the mood changes: a soldier declares Jesus's righteousness, and the crowds leave beating their chests (23:47–48).

The resurrection appearances serve to reinforce and explain the meaning of the cross. An angel confronts the women at the startlingly empty tomb and reminds them of Jesus's claim that he will rise again (24:1–8). The apostles' response to the report is not laudatory, but Peter does examine the empty tomb. The most prominent event is Jesus's appearance to two disciples on the road to Emmaus (24:13–33). The fact that this is God's plan is pointedly reinforced (esp. at 24:26). Jesus then appears to the Eleven in Jerusalem and establishes that he is really resurrected and not a ghost (24:34–49). For the second time

[99] For recent treatments of crucifixion, see D. W. Chapman, *Ancient Jewish and Christian Perceptions of Crucifixion*, WUNT 2/244 (Tübingen, Germany: Mohr Siebeck: 2008); J. G. Cook, *Crucifixion in the Mediterranean World*, WUNT 327 (Tübingen, Germany: Mohr Siebeck, 2014).

Jesus interprets the Scriptures to his disciples. Finally, the fulfillment of 9:51 occurs at 24:50–51: Jesus ascends into heaven from Bethany near Jerusalem.

Table 6.2: Jesus's Resurrection Appearances

Recipients/ Location	Date/ Time	Matt	Mark	Luke	John	Acts	1 Cor
Number of appearances		**2**	**0**	**4**	**4**	**2**	**4 [5]**
First Sunday							
1. The women/ Tomb	Early morning	28:8–10					
2. Mary Magda-lene/ Tomb	Early morning				20:11–18		
3. Peter/Jerusalem	Late morning?			24:34			15:5
4. Two Disciples/ Emmaus Road	Midday/ Afternoon			24:13–32			
5. Ten Disciples/ Upper Room	Evening	24:36–43		20:19–25			
Second Sunday (One Week Later)							
6. Eleven/Upper Room	Evening				20:26–29		15:5
Subsequently							
7. Seven Disciples/ Sea of Galilee	Daybreak				21:1–23		
8. Eleven/Moun-tain in Galilee	Sometime later	28:16–20					
9. More than 500	Sometime later						15:6
10. James	Sometime later						15:7
11. Disciples/ Mount of Olives	Forty days later			24:44–49		1:3–8	
12. Paul/Road to Damascus	Sometime later					9:3–6	[15:8]

Epilogue: The Disciples Return to Jerusalem (24:52–53) The final two verses form an epilogue to the book. The disciples returned to Jerusalem rejoicing. When they arrived, they went to the temple, continually blessing God. This ending prepares the reader for the second treatise, the book of Acts, which continues the Gospel's emphasis on God's plan of salvation in history and its fulfillment in Jesus.

THEOLOGY

Theological Themes

Salvation and Salvation History Many of the major themes in Luke are related to the fulfillment of God's purposes in Jesus as the culmination of salvation history.[100] God is the architect of human history, which is driven by his purposes and will. H. Conzelmann contended that Luke viewed salvation history in three stages: (1) Israel; (2) Jesus's ministry; and (3) the *ecclesia pressa* ("the church under pressure").[101] Indeed, Luke's apologetic purpose centers on the demonstration that in Jesus, God fulfilled his salvation promises to his people.[102] Perhaps more accurately, however, Luke's conception of salvation history may be described along the lines of "promise and fulfillment," with John the Baptist marking the end of the period of promise (16:16: "The Law and the Prophets were until John") and the following stages denoting the fulfillment of that promise (Jesus and the church).[103]

The beginning of the Gospel implies that through Jesus, God was fulfilling his previously planned purpose of salvation ("fulfilled among us"; 1:1). It is not long until the reader is told that what God has fulfilled by sending Jesus is the provision of a Savior (1:31–33; see 1:68–71). Indeed, salvation is one of the most prominent themes in this Gospel. The word "salvation" *(sōtēria)* is used four times in Luke; it is not used in Matthew or Mark and only once in John. The first three of these references occur in Zechariah's song, where the ministry of the coming Messiah is described (1:69, 71, 77; the fourth reference is 19:9). The word "salvation" also occurs six times in Acts (4:12; 7:25; 13:26, 47; 16:17; 27:34).

Other words in the same semantic range are prominent in Luke as well. Both God and Jesus are called "Savior" (*sōtēr*; 1:47; 2:11; again, the word is not used in Matthew and Mark and only once in John). The verb "to save" *(sōzō)* is often used as a synonym for conversion (see 7:50; 8:12; 13:23; also frequent in Matthew and Mark). A particularly prominent and memorable instance of the word "to save" in Luke's Gospel is found in 19:10, where Jesus defined his mission: "For the Son of Man has come to seek and to save the lost." Importantly, as shown below, the salvation provided by Jesus encompasses all people—in particular those of low status in society, bringing about a "great reversal" in and through Jesus's ministry.

Jesus's Fulfillment of Prophecy Closely related to the theme of salvation in Luke's Gospel is the motif of the fulfillment of scriptural prophecy in and through Jesus. In 1:1, the events of the ensuing narrative are said to have been "fulfilled among us." And in

---

[100] Note the fuller treatment of Bock (*A Theology of Luke and Acts*, 239–77) regarding "the Many Dimensions of Salvation." Note particularly his discussions on the act of proclaiming good news; the scope of salvation; the authentication of the message; the objective aspect of salvation; the subjective side of salvation; and the benefits of salvation.

[101] Conzelmann, *Theology of St. Luke*, 16–17.

[102] See F. Thielman, *Theology of the New Testament: A Canonical and Synthetic Approach* (Grand Rapids, MI: Zondervan, 2005), 111–16.

[103] Ibid., 117. Thielman notes that a two-stage understanding is possible, but since the repetition of the ascension at Acts 1:9–11 points to the period of Jesus as a separate period (see v. 22), it is safe to assume three stages.

24:44–49, the disciples are told that "everything written about me in the Law of Moses, the Prophets, and the Psalms must be fulfilled." Thus, both the beginning and the end of Luke's Gospel frame the narrative by focusing on the theme of fulfillment.

The fulfillment of prophecy also figures prominently throughout the book as part of Luke's emphasis on the fulfillment of God's plan.[104] While Luke's OT quotations are not extensive, the reference to Isaiah 61:1–2 regarding Jesus's inaugural sermon at the synagogue of Nazareth is highly significant in that it presents Jesus as Isaiah's Servant of the Lord (4:18–19). Also, when John the Baptist questioned Jesus, Jesus pointed to his activities as fulfilling OT messianic expectations (7:20; see Isa 29:18; 35:5; 61:1).

There is also an interest in what Johnson called "literary prophecy," that is, the fulfillment of prophecies made by characters in the narrative itself.[105] Both Simeon and Anna prophesied regarding Jesus without otherwise having been told of the nature of his birth. A large number of Jesus's own prophecies are fulfilled as well. This includes the fulfillment of Jesus's predictions regarding his suffering, death, and resurrection (9:22); his rejection by Israel (9:22, 44); his death at the hands of Gentiles (18:31–33); the destruction of Jerusalem (21:24); and the Spirit's coming (24:49). These fulfillments constitute a "proof from prophecy" that served Luke's apologetic purpose of showing Christianity to be true.

In both Luke's Gospel and the book of Acts, God is shown to be in absolute control of the events in the story as his plan continued to unfold. In the infancy narratives, all proceeded at God's direction. Jesus's death occurred by the will of God. In 7:30, the Pharisees are shown to reject the plan of God for themselves. Equally striking is the use of the "divine must" in Luke's Gospel. Jesus described his earthly ministry in terms of divine compulsion: he must be in his Father's house (2:49); he must preach the gospel of the kingdom in many cities (4:43); he must die on the cross (9:22; 17:25; 22:37; 24:7); he must heal the woman with an issue of blood (13:16); he must be killed in Jerusalem (13:33); and he must eat at Zacchaeus's house (19:5). Jesus's entire earthly ministry was driven by divine necessity (24:44).

Jesus's description of his death occurs using the word "must" *(dei)* as well, indicating that the crucifixion proceeded in keeping with God's plan. The first occurrence is found in 9:22: "It is necessary that the Son of Man must suffer many things and be rejected by the elders, chief priests, and scribes, be killed, and be raised the third day" (see 9:44).[106] In 18:31–33, the reader is told that everything written through the prophets regarding Jesus's death and resurrection will be accomplished. The crucifixion is not the regrettable death of

---

[104] L. T. Johnson (*The Gospel of Luke*, SacPag 3 [Collegeville, MN: Liturgical Press, 1991], 16) describes Luke's use of proof from prophecy as his "most important literary device."

[105] Ibid.

[106] This is repeated nearly verbatim in 24:7: "It is necessary that the Son of Man be betrayed into the hands of sinful men, be crucified, and rise on the third day." See 13:33: He must die in Jerusalem; and also 17:25: "But first it is necessary that he suffer many things and be rejected by this generation."

a good man, or a mere instance of the plight of all prophets, but is a fulfillment of God's long-standing plan of salvation.

Related to this is the portrayal of Israel and the Jewish people in Luke's Gospel. Some have claimed that the Jews are presented in a negative light by Luke, but this conclusion is unnecessary.[107] Although Israel is depicted as a nation that has, by and large, strayed from their God and is comprised of sinners,[108] Jesus remains the One who "fulfills the hopes and aspirations of Israel."[109] The ultimate goal of God's plan for Israel is the restoration, not destruction, of Israel (Acts 1:6).

Both Mary and Zechariah understood Jesus to be the fulfillment of God's promises to Israel (1:54, 68). Simeon was also looking for "Israel's consolation" (2:25). When he saw the infant Jesus, he blessed God for letting him see God's salvation (2:30). Jesus was going to be a revelation to the Gentiles but also a glory to Israel. Yet not all Israel was in view, for Jesus was "destined to cause the fall and rise of many in Israel and to be a sign that will be opposed" (2:34). Thus, Jesus's coming is seen at the outset as a sign of both hope and warning for Israel.

But Jesus's coming also brings about a further development in God's plan of salvation. This point is driven home by the parable of the New Wineskins (5:33–39), and later a similar note of advance is struck (16:16). The Law and the Prophets were in effect until John; then the good news of the kingdom of God was preached in and through Jesus. Consequently, the dividing line between the world and the people of God is faith in Christ, not ethnic identity or adherence to the law. For Jerusalem, the embodiment of the Jewish nation, rejecting Jesus brings destruction rather than peace, "because you did not recognize the time when God visited you" (19:44). Salvation in Luke is a matter of faith, repentance, and following after Jesus.

Jesus's Concern for the Lowly Among the evangelists, Luke puts special emphasis on Jesus's concern for those of lowly status in society—Gentiles, the poor, tax collectors and "sinners," the sick and disabled, women and children. This is part of Luke's understanding of the salvation brought by Jesus, a salvation that is inclusive of all people. In this Luke echoed Paul's statement in Galatians 3:28 that in Christ "there is no Jew or Greek, slave or free, male and female." Rather, God's offer of salvation in Christ extends to all humanity.

In order to indicate the universal scope of Jesus's salvation, Jesus's genealogy is traced back not just to Abraham, as in Matthew, but all the way to Adam (4:1–13). In the infancy narrative, the angel announced, "I proclaim to you good news of great joy that will be for *all the people*" (2:10, emphasis added). "All the people" means that the salvation brought

---

[107] E.g., J. T. Sanders (*The Jews in Luke-Acts* [Philadelphia, PA: Fortress, 1987], 317) states, "In Luke's opinion, the world will be much better off when 'the Jews' get what they deserve and the world is rid of them." For a fuller review of scholarship, see J. B. Tyson *Luke, Judaism, and the Scholars: Critical Approaches to Luke-Acts* (Columbia, SC: University of South Carolina Press, 2010).

[108] I. H. Marshall, *New Testament Theology* (Downers Grove, IL: InterVarsity, 2004), 142.

[109] Wenham, "Purpose," 88.

Something to Think About: Jesus's Concern for the Lowly

In his wisdom God gave us not one but four inspired accounts of Jesus's life and ministry. Without contradicting one another, each of the evangelists captured unique aspects of Jesus's heart and mission. Matthew showed how Jesus fulfilled the scriptural predictions regarding the long-awaited Jewish Messiah. Mark presented Jesus as the powerful, miracle-working Son of God, recognized even by the Gentile world. John extolled Jesus as the preexistent Word who was made flesh and revealed God's glory through an escalating series of messianic signs.

But what about Luke, Paul's "beloved physician"? In striking humility, Luke frankly acknowledged at the outset of his Gospel that he was not an eyewitness and that he was not the first to write an account of Jesus's life and ministry (1:1–4). Yet in compiling his presentation, he consulted many of the original eyewitnesses and "carefully investigated everything from the very first" (1:3) in order to document "the events that have been fulfilled among us" (1:1).

What kind of God has been revealed through Jesus? Luke allowed Mary, the mother of Jesus, to do the talking: "He has done a mighty deed with His arm; He has scattered the proud because of the thoughts of their hearts; He has toppled the mighty from their thrones and exalted the lowly. He has satisfied the hungry with good things and sent the rich away empty" (1:51–53). As Jesus proclaimed: "The Spirit of the Lord is on me, because he has anointed me to preach good news to the poor" (4:18; see Isa 61:1). For this reason:

Blessed are you who are poor, because the kingdom of God is yours.
Blessed are you who are hungry now, because you will be filled.
Blessed are you who weep now, because you will laugh (Luke 6:20–21).

What Luke captured in Jesus's heart is his concern for the lowly—the poor, women, children, non-Jews (Samaritans and Gentiles), the hated tax gatherers who collaborated with the Romans and were consequently viewed as traitors by the Jews, the sick and disabled, orphans and widows, aliens and strangers. Read Luke's Gospel and meditate on the way in which it portrays Jesus as the "friend of sinners" and as the physician who came to heal. His healing is not for those who consider themselves righteous but for those who know they need mercy from God.

And in this "great reversal," depicted in many of Jesus's parables in Luke's Gospel, those of low status in this world are exalted while those who are part of the establishment find themselves on the outside of God's saving purposes.

by Jesus is not only for God's people, the Jews, but also for *the Gentiles*. Thus even Simeon, upon seeing the infant Jesus, prophesied that Jesus would be "a light for revelation to the Gentiles" as well (2:32).

During the course of his ministry, Jesus commended the widow of Zarephath and Naaman the Syrian, both Gentiles (4:25–27); he praised a Gentile centurion's faith (7:9); he made a Samaritan the hero of his parable of the Good Samaritan (10:30–37) and commended another Samaritan for being the only one of ten cleansed lepers to return to give thanks (17:16); and he repeatedly hinted at the inclusion of Gentiles in the orbit of salvation (e.g., 14:23). At the end of Luke's Gospel, Jesus sent the disciples to all nations (24:46–48), and the book of Acts narrates the irresistible march of the gospel to Rome (Acts 1:8), with Paul affirming that God's gift of salvation has now come to the Gentiles (Acts 28:28).

Luke's emphasis on the universality of salvation brought by Jesus extends significantly to those of low status in society, most notably *the poor*.[110] Related to this is Luke's emphasis on the "great reversal" brought about by Jesus's ministry. Thus, Mary declared at the outset of the Gospel that the humble would be exalted and the lofty would be humbled (1:48–49). In his inaugural sermon at the synagogue of Nazareth, Jesus stated that he was sent to "preach good news to the poor," in fulfillment of Isaiah's prophecy about the Servant of the Lord (4:18; see 7:22). The Beatitudes in the Sermon on the Plain (6:20–23) are balanced with woes against the rich and well fed (6:24–26).

A major issue in Luke is the use and abuse of wealth with regard to discipleship. Luke consistently emphasized that Jesus strongly opposed the notion that wealth and position were indicative of a person's status before God. Instead, Jesus accepted anyone who repented and turned to him, while one's possessions, status, and power constituted major obstacles to the reception of Jesus's message. The parables of the Rich Fool (12:13–21) and of the Rich Man and Lazarus (16:19–31) expose the idolatry and ultimate futility of wealth. Jesus counseled believers to "sell your possessions and give to the poor. Make money-bags for yourselves that won't grow old, an inexhaustible treasure in heaven, where no thief comes near and no moth destroys" (12:33). Jesus painted a terrifying picture of those who were exalted on earth but who will find themselves shut out when wanting to enter God's kingdom (13:28–30). Those who hold a feast ought to invite the poor and lowly (14:13, 21–24).

Ultimately a person's attitude toward his possessions is indicative of his relationship to Jesus: "In the same way, therefore, every one of you who does not renounce all his possessions cannot be my disciple" (14:33). In the parable of the Unjust Steward, Jesus instructed his listeners to invest their money with eternity in mind (16:9). Jesus also explained that only a work of God can bring a rich man into the kingdom (18:24–25). Zacchaeus, upon salvation, voluntarily gave half of his money to the poor and used the other half to repay those he had wronged—one suspects Zacchaeus made some quick calculations that reserved little or none for himself (19:8). Faithful servants invest in their master's work

---

[110] See especially C. L. Blomberg, *Neither Poverty nor Riches: A Biblical Theology of Material Possessions*, NSBT (Grand Rapids, MI: Eerdmans, 1999), 111–46, 160–74.

(19:11–27), and the widow who parted with her mite receives Jesus's highest commendation (21:1–4).

Throughout his Gospel, Luke also emphasized Jesus's teaching among the lowly and outcasts in society: the hated *tax collectors*, despised as traitors due to their service to the Roman authorities, and *"sinners."* Levi, a tax collector, was included among the Twelve, and Jesus fellowshipped with tax collectors and other "sinners" at Levi's house, stating that he had come to call such people to repentance (5:30, 32). Among the people Jesus was known as "the friend of . . . sinners" (7:34; see 7:36–50). When reproached by his opponents for "welcoming sinners" (15:1–2), Jesus responded by telling a trilogy of parables highlighting the joy of finding that which had been lost. In fact, this is why Jesus came: "to seek and to save the lost" (19:7).

Another disenfranchised group that was the recipient of Jesus's special ministry according to Luke was the large number of *sick, demon-possessed, and disabled.* Among the many healed were Peter's mother-in-law (4:38–41); a centurion's servant (7:1–10); a widow's son (7:11–17, raised from the dead); the Gadarene demoniac (8:26–39); a woman with abnormal blood flow, and the daughter of Jairus, a synagogue ruler (8:40–56; the latter was raised from the dead); and a blind beggar on the road to Jericho (18:35–43). In his healing ministry Jesus epitomized the OT portrait of the Messiah who would make the blind see and the lame walk, who would cleanse lepers, make the deaf hear, raise the dead, and preach the gospel to the poor (7:22; see 4:18).

Yet another part of this "great reversal" brought about by Jesus's coming involves *women.* Women played a prominent role in Luke's Gospel, which mentions thirteen women not featured in the other Gospels.[111] Many of these women are characterized by unusual devotion to Jesus. Among these were a sinful woman who anointed Jesus (7:36–50); Mary Magdalene; Joanna the wife of Chuza, Herod's steward; and Susanna, among others who supported Jesus out of their own means (8:2–3); and Mary and Martha, who learned from him, served him, and were his close friends (10:38–42). Women also had an important part in the events surrounding Jesus's crucifixion and resurrection (23:55–24:10). The considerable number of women among Jesus's followers stood in contrast with the male-oriented ministry of other Jewish rabbis in Jesus's day. Women are also featured prominently in many of Jesus's parables in Luke's Gospel, often parallel with male characters.[112]

Another group receiving special attention by Jesus according to Luke is *children.* In his early years Jesus himself is frequently called "child" by Luke (2:17, 27, 40). Repeatedly, Jesus held up children as examples of the kind of humility required for people to enter God's kingdom (9:46–48; 18:15–17). At one point in his ministry, Jesus pronounced woes on those who cause little ones to stumble, saying it would be better for them to have a

---

[111] M. Strauss, *Four Portraits, One Jesus: An Introduction to Jesus and the Gospels* (Grand Rapids, MI: Zondervan, 2007), 339.

[112] See T. K. Seim, *The Double Message: Patterns of Gender in Luke-Acts* (Edinburgh, Scotland: T&T Clark/Nashville, TN: Abingdon, 1994).

millstone hung around their neck and to be thrown into the sea (17:2). When his disciples wanted to prevent people from bringing children to him, he sternly rebuked them and told them to let the children come to him (18:15–17).

Table 6.3: Jesus and the Lowly in Luke's Gospel

Group of People	Passages in Luke's Gospel
Gentiles	2:10, 32; 4:25–27; 7:9; 10:30–37; 14:23; 17:16
The poor	1:46–55; 4:18; 6:20–23; 7:22; 10:21–22; 14:13, 21–24; 16:19–31; 21:1–4
Tax collectors and "sinners"	5:27–32; 7:28, 30, 34, 36–50; 15:1–2; 19:7
The sick and disabled	4:31–41; 5:12–26; 6:6–11, 17–19; 7:1–17; 8:26–9:2; 9:37–43; 17:11–19; 18: 35–43
Women	7:36–50; 8:1–3, 48; 10:38–42; 13:10–17; 24:1–12
Children	2:17, 27, 40; 9:46–48; 17:2; 18:15–17

The Holy Spirit Luke emphasizes the Holy Spirit as part of the new epoch being inaugurated with Jesus (see Acts 2:16–21, citing Joel 2:28–32). The Holy Spirit is given more prominence in Luke's Gospel than in any other—with the possible exception of John 14–16. Luke's emphasis, rather than being confined to isolated teaching, permeates the Gospel, occurring some sixteen times. In comparison, Mark has six references and Matthew twelve.[113] The Spirit was active in the infancy narratives and at the outset of Jesus's ministry. John the Baptist and his parents were filled with the Spirit (1:15, 41, 67). Jesus was conceived when the Holy Spirit came upon Mary (1:35). Simeon was a man upon whom the Spirit rested (2:25). Jesus was described as filled with the Spirit (Luke 3:22; 4:1, 14). John predicted that Jesus would baptize with the Spirit (Luke 3:16).[114] And in his inaugural sermon, Jesus stated that it was the Spirit who anointed him "to preach good news to the poor" (4:18).

In Luke's Gospel, Jesus explained that the ministry of the Spirit would continue beyond his earthly ministry. Jesus made reference to the Father giving the Spirit to all those who ask for him (11:13); he warned of the blasphemy of the Spirit (12:10); he showed that the Spirit would speak through the disciples when they suffered persecution on account of their association with Jesus (12:12); and he promised the coming of the Spirit subsequent to his resurrection (24:49). Importantly, by salvation-historical necessity, the coming of the Spirit must await the period subsequent to the ascension of Jesus. Hence, the Spirit's arrival marked Jesus's exaltation with the Father as proof of his resurrection (Acts 2:14–36).

---

[113] D. L. Bock, *A Theology of Luke and Acts: God's Promised Program, Realized for All Nations*, BTNT (Grand Rapids, MI: Zondervan, 2011), 211.

[114] Bock describes this passage as "the most important text on the Spirit and its central role in God's program" (ibid., 213). The reference is to two groups of people. Those who receive the gospel receive the Holy Spirit; those who do not receive fire (i.e., condemnation).

Prayer A final Lukan motif related to his emphasis on the Holy Spirit is that of prayer. Jesus himself often prayed, expressing his total dependence on God during his earthly ministry and modeling a prayerful approach to ministry and all of life for his followers (5:16; 6:12; 11:1; 22:41–42).

Notably, prolonged and persistent prayer was Jesus's habitual practice. Luke told his readers that Jesus "often withdrew to deserted places and prayed" (5:16). Prior to his selection of the Twelve, Jesus "went out to the mountain to pray and spent all night in prayer to God" (6:12). Once, when the disciples heard Jesus praying, and when he finished, they asked him to teach them how to pray (11:2–4).

Luke also recorded Jesus's extensive teaching on prayer, some in parables (11:5–6; 18:1–14). In these pieces of instruction, Jesus enjoined his listeners "to pray always and not give up" (18:1). Jesus also urged his disciples to pray so they would not fall into temptation (22:46; see 11:4).

CONTRIBUTION TO THE CANON

- Jesus as the son of Adam, the Son of God (3:37)
- Jesus as the Spirit-anointed Suffering Servant (4:18–19)
- Jesus as the compassionate healer and physician (5:31–32)
- Jesus as the Messiah sent to the poor, Gentiles, women, children, sick, and others of low status in society
- Jesus as the "friend of tax collectors and sinners" (7:34) and seeker of the lost (19:10)

STUDY QUESTIONS

1. Concerning the authorship of Luke, on what points are most scholars agreed?
2. Why do the internal and external evidence support Lukan authorship?
3. What does the "medical" terminology of Luke suggest?
4. To whom is Luke-Acts dedicated? What is the recipient's likely identity? Explain.
5. Why is it necessary to discuss the date of Acts in order to assess the date of Luke's composition?
6. Where was the most likely place for Luke to gather information for his Gospel?
7. What is the significance of Jesus's genealogy in Luke?
8. How does Luke's use of parables differ from that of the other Synoptics?
9. According to the authors, which two individuals or groups are the major eyewitness sources for Luke's account?
10. What is the most natural way, according to the authors, to understand Luke's purpose in writing?
11. What is Luke's "Travel Narrative," and why do the authors suggest that it "breaks new ground"?
12. What are the phases of Jesus's trial?

FOR FURTHER STUDY

Alexander, L. C. A. *The Preface to Luke's Gospel: Literary Convention and Social Context in Luke 1:1–4 and Acts 1:1.* Society for New Testament Studies Monograph Series 78. Cambridge, UK: Cambridge University Press, 1993.

Barrett, C. K. *Luke the Historian in Recent Study.* Philadelphia, PA: Fortress, 1979.

Bartholomew, C. G., J. B. Green, and A. C. Thiselton, eds. *Reading Luke: Interpretation, Reflection, Formation.* Scripture and Hermeneutics 6. Grand Rapids, MI: Zondervan, 2005.

Blomberg, C. L. "Midrash, Chiasmus, and the Outline of Luke's Central Section." Pages 217–61 in *Gospel Perspectives.* Vol. 3. Edited by R. T. France and D. Wenham. Sheffield, PA: JSOT, 1983.

Bock, D. L. *A Theology of Luke and Acts: God's Promised Program, Realized for all Nations,* BTNT. Grand Rapids, MI: Zondervan, 2011.

__________. *Luke.* 2 vols. Baker Exegetical Commentary on the New Testament. Grand Rapids, MI: Baker, 1994.

__________. "Luke, Gospel of." Pages 495–510 in *Dictionary of Jesus and the Gospels.* Edited by J. B. Green, S. McKnight, and I. H. Marshall. Downers Grove, IL: InterVarsity, 1992.

Bovon, F. *Luke 1.* Hermeneia. Translated by C. M. Thomas. Minneapolis, MN: Fortress, 2002.

Brawley, R. L. *Luke-Acts and the Jews: Conflict, Apology, and Conciliation.* Atlanta, GA: Scholars Press, 1987.

Cadbury, H. J. *The Style and Literary Method of Luke.* Cambridge, MA: Harvard University Press, 1920.

Fitzmyer, J. A. *The Gospel According to Luke.* 2 vols. Anchor Bible. New York, NY: Doubleday, 1981–85.

Green, J. B. *The Gospel of Luke.* New International Commentary on the New Testament. Rev. ed. Grand Rapids, MI: Eerdmans, 1997.

Hill, C. E. "What Papias Said about John (and Luke): A 'New' Papian Fragment." *JTS* 49 (1998): 582–629.

Hobart, W. K. *The Medical Language of St. Luke.* Grand Rapids, MI: Baker, 1954.

Jervell, J. *Luke and the People of God: A New Look at Luke-Acts.* Minneapolis, MN: Augsburg, 1979.

Kealy, S. P. *The Interpretation of the Gospel of Luke.* Vol. I: *From Apostolic Times Through the Nineteenth Century.* Studies in the Bible and Early Christianity 63. Lewiston, NY: Mellen, 2005.

Keck, L. E., and J. L. Martyn, eds. *Studies in Luke-Acts.* Nashville, TN: Abingdon, 1966.

Kurz, W. S. *Reading Luke-Acts: Dynamics of Biblical Narrative.* Louisville, KY: Westminster John Knox, 1993.

Liefeld, W. L., and D. W. Pao. "Luke." In *The Expositor's Bible Commentary.* Rev. ed. Vol. 10. Grand Rapids, MI: Zondervan, 2007.

Maddox, R. *The Purpose of Luke-Acts.* Studies of the New Testament and Its World. Edinburgh, Scotland: T&T Clark, 1982.

Marshall, I. H. *Commentary on Luke.* New International Greek Testament Commentary. Grand Rapids, MI: Eerdmans, 1978.

__________. *Luke: Historian and Theologian.* 2nd ed. Grand Rapids, MI: Zondervan, 1988.

Morris, L. *The Gospel According to St. Luke: An Introduction and Commentary.* Tyndale New Testament Commentary. 2nd ed. Grand Rapids, MI: Eerdmans, 1988.

Nolland, J. *Luke. Word Biblical Commentary.* 3 vols. Dallas, TX: Word, 1990–93.

Pao, D. W., and E. J. Schnabel. "Luke." Pages 251–414 in *Commentary on the New Testament Use of the Old Testament.* Edited by G. K. Beale and D. A. Carson. Grand Rapids, MI: Baker, 2007.

Rhoads, J. H. "Josephus Misdated the Census of Quirinius." *JETS* 54 (2011): 65–87.

Sanders, J. T. *The Jews in Luke-Acts.* Philadelphia, PA: Fortress, 1987.

Strauss, M. *Four Portraits, One Jesus: An Introduction to Jesus and the Gospels.* Grand Rapids, MI: Zondervan, 2007.

Thiselton, A. "The Hermeneutical Dynamics of 'Reading Luke' as Interpretation, Reflection and Formation." In *Reading Luke: Interpretation, Reflection, Formation.* Edited by C. G. Bartholomew, J. B. Green, and A. Thiselton. Scripture and Hermeneutics 6. Grand Rapids, MI: Zondervan, 2005.

Townsend, J. T. "The Date of Luke-Acts." In *Luke-Acts: New Perspectives from the Society of Biblical Literature.* Edited by C. Talbert. New York, NY: Crossroad, 1984.

Verheyden, J. "The Unity of Luke-Acts: What Are We Up To?" In *The Unity of Luke-Acts.* Edited by J. Verheyden. Leuven, Belgium: Leuven University Press, 1999, 3–56.

Wenham D. "The Purpose of Luke-Acts." In *Reading Luke: Interpretation, Reflection, Formation.* Edited by C. G. Bartholomew, J. B. Green, and A. C. Thiselton. Scripture and Hermeneutics 6. Grand Rapids, MI: Zondervan, 2005.

Wilson, S. G. *Luke and the Pastoral Epistles.* London, UK: SPCK, 1979.

Chapter 7

The Gospel According to John

CORE KNOWLEDGE

Basic Knowledge: Students should know the key facts of John's Gospel. With regard to history, students should be able to identify the Gospel's author, date, provenance, destination, and purpose. With regard to literature, they should be able to provide a basic outline of the book and identify core elements of the book's content found in the Unit-by-Unit discussion. With regard to theology, students should be able to identify John's major theological themes.

Intermediate Knowledge: Students should be able to present the arguments for historical, literary, and theological conclusions. With regard to history, students should be able to discuss the evidence for Johannine authorship, date, provenance, destination, and purpose. With regard to literature, they should be able to provide a detailed outline of the book. With regard to theology, students should be able to discuss John's major theological themes and the ways in which they uniquely contribute to the NT canon.

Advanced Knowledge: Students should be able to survey the history of Johannine scholarship and to explain and critique the "Johannine community hypothesis." They should be able to evaluate critically the internal and external evidence that John, the son of Zebedee, wrote John's Gospel, and they should be able to interact critically with Richard Bauckham's work *Jesus and the Eyewitnesses* in this regard. They should also be able to assess the authenticity of the pericope of the adulterous woman in John 7:53–8:11.

Map 7.1 Provenance and Destination of John

KEY FACTS

Author:	John
Date:	Mid- or late 80s or early 90s
Provenance:	Ephesus
Destination:	Ephesus
Purpose:	To demonstrate that Jesus is the Messiah so that people would believe in him and have eternal life (20:30–31)
Theme:	Selected signs show that Jesus is the Messiah
Key Verse:	3:16

INTRODUCTION

JOHN'S GOSPEL AND the book of Romans may well be considered the two highest peaks in NT theology. Known from antiquity as the "spiritual Gospel," John's Gospel soars like an eagle over the canonical landscape.[1] It likely was written by John the apos-

[1] A. J. Köstenberger, "John," in *NDBT*, 280–85. Taking their point of reference from the four beasts in Ezek 1:10 and Rev 4:6–15, the Fathers describe John as an eagle. See Augustine, *Cons. 6*, cited in A. Volfing, *John the Evangelist in Medieval German Writing: Imitating the Inimitable* (Oxford, UK: University Press, 2001), 45n67: "John flies like an eagle above the clouds of human weakness and gazes most keenly and steadily with the eye of his heart at the light of unchangeable truth." The reference to John as a "spiritual Gospel" is to Clement's *Hypotyposeis*, found in Eusebius, *Hist. eccl.* 6.14.

tle (the "beloved disciple," as he preferred to call himself) at the culmination of his long life and ministry. Most likely due to the fact that its author was closer to Jesus than anyone else during his earthy ministry, John's Gospel penetrates more deeply into the mystery of God's revelation in his Son than the other canonical Gospels and perhaps more deeply than any other biblical book. From the majestic prologue to the probing epilogue, the evangelist's words are as carefully chosen as they must be thoughtfully pondered by every reader of his magnificent work.

Over the course of history, John's Gospel has exercised a remarkable influence commensurate with the profundity of its message. John's Christology, particularly affirmations of Jesus's deity and of his human and divine natures, has decisively shaped the formulations adopted by the early church councils and creeds.[2] Many of the great minds of the Christian church, from the early church fathers to modern times, have written commentaries or monographs on John's Gospel.[3] Despite the massive assault on John's trustworthiness in the wake of the Enlightenment, especially by liberal German scholars, John's Gospel now stands widely rehabilitated as a reliable witness to the life, words, and deeds of our Lord Jesus Christ,[4] although there continue to be many critical scholars who affirm John's Gospel is unhistorical.[5]

---

[2] See J. N. Sanders, *The Fourth Gospel in the Early Church* (Cambridge, UK: Cambridge University Press, 1943); T. E. Pollard, *Johannine Christology and the Early Church*, SNTSMS 13 (Cambridge, UK: Cambridge University Press, 1970); F. -M. Braun, *Jean le théologien*, vol. 1: *Jean le théologien et son évangile dans l'église ancienne* (Paris, France: Gabalda, 1959); A. Grillmeier, *Christ in Christian Tradition*, vol. 1: *From the Apostolic Age to Chalcedon (451)*, trans. J. Bowden, 2nd rev. ed. (Atlanta, GA: John Knox, 1975), esp. 26–32.

[3] On the Latin background, see Volfing, *John the Evangelist*, 11–59; cf. the works referenced in J. N. Sanders, *Fourth Gospel*; Pollard, *Johannine Christology*; Braun, *Jean le théologien*; and Grillmeier, *Christ in Christian Tradition*.

[4] The Fourth Gospel's integrity is not compromised by the inimitable Johannine style enveloping narrative as well as discourse portions. For positive assessments of the historical reliability of John's Gospel, see C. L. Blomberg, "To What Extent Is John Historically Reliable?" in *Perspectives on John: Method and Interpretation in the Fourth Gospel*, ed. R. B. Sloan and M. C. Parsons, NABPR Special Studies Series (Lewiston, NY: Mellen, 1993), 27–56; idem, "The Historical Reliability of John: Rushing in Where Angels Fear to Tread?" in *Jesus and Johannine Tradition*, ed. R. T. Fortna and T. Thatcher (Louisville, KY: Westminster John Knox, 2001), 71–82; and idem, *The Historical Reliability of John's Gospel* (Leicester, UK: InterVarsity, 2002); contra M. Casey, *Is John's Gospel True?* (London, UK: Routledge, 1996). See also other recent reevaluations of John's historicity in P. N. Anderson, *The Fourth Gospel and the Quest for Jesus: Modern Foundations Reconsidered* (London, England: T&T Clark, 2006); R. Bauckham, *The Testimony of the Beloved Disciple: Narrative, History, and Theology in the Gospel of John* (Grand Rapids, MI: Baker, 2007), 93–112, 173–89; D. M. Smith, *The Fourth Gospel in Four Dimensions: Judaism and Jesus, the Gospels and Scripture* (Columbia, SC: University of South Carolina Press, 2008). Note also C. E. Hill's groundbreaking work, *The Johannine Corpus in the Early Church* (Oxford, UK: University Press, 2004).

Nevertheless, there continues to be skepticism on the part of many; see the survey by R. Kysar, *Voyages with John* (Waco, TX: Baylor University Press, 2005), chap. 15: "The Expulsion from the Synagogue: The Tale of a Theory"; the largely positive assessment by M. M. Thompson, "The 'Spiritual Gospel': How John the Theologian Writes History," in *John, Jesus, and History*, vol. 1: *Critical Appraisals of Critical Views*, ed. P. N. Anderson, F. Just, and T. Thatcher (Atlanta, GA: SBL, 2007), 103–7; and the negative evaluation by H. W. Attridge, "Responses to 'The Dehistoricizing of the Gospel of John' by Robert Kysar" (presented at the annual SBL meeting, Toronto, November 23–26, 2002).

[5] For example, Anderson notes, "Whereas the question in traditionalist circles used to be whether or not one believed in the historicity of John, the litmus test for the modernist biblical scholar has come to be: Do you believe in the *ahistoricity* of John?" Paul N. Anderson, "Why This Study Is Needed, and Why It Is Needed Now," in *John, Jesus, and History*, vol. 1: *Critical Appraisals of Critical Views*, ed. P. N. Anderson, F. Just, and T. Thatcher (Atlanta, GA: SBL, 2007), 14. But Anderson

SIDEBAR 7.1: WAS JOHN'S GOSPEL WRITTEN BY ANOTHER "JOHN"?

A major challenge to the apostolic authorship of John's Gospel came from R. Bauckham. In his work *Jesus and the Eyewitnesses*, Bauckham argued persuasively that the Gospels reflect eyewitness testimony. According to Bauckham, the ideal source in ancient Greco-Roman literature was not the dispassionate observer but the eyewitness.[1] The written Gospels, according to Bauckham, contain oral history related to the personal transmission of eyewitness testimony, not merely oral tradition resulting from the collective and anonymous transmission of material.[2] "In this context," Bauckham contended, "the twelve served as 'an authoritative collegium.'"[3]

Especially important in this regard is the phrase "from the beginning," which is found at several strategic points in the Gospels and the rest of the NT record (see Luke 1:2; John 1:1; 1 John 1:1). Several other literary devices are used to stress the Gospels' character of eyewitness testimony, such as "the *inclusio* of eyewitness testimony" (see Mark 1:16–18; 16:7 for Peter; and John 1:40; 21:24 for John). According to Bauckham, the transmission process of the Jesus tradition resulting in our written canonical Gospels is best understood as a formal controlled tradition in which the eyewitnesses played an important and continuing part.[4]

With regard to John's Gospel, Bauckham agreed that the "disciple Jesus loved" should be regarded as the author, but he identified John the elder—not John the apostle, the son of Zebedee—as the author. His view is primarily (it seems) the result of his reading of patristic evidence (Papias, Polycrates, Irenaeus) and his understanding of the reference to the "sons of Zebedee" in John 21:2.[5] Regarding the latter point, Bauckham found the beloved disciple's anonymity throughout the Gospel an insurmountable obstacle to the apostolic authorship of John's Gospel since the "sons of Zebedee" are named. He believed the beloved disciple is one of the two unnamed disciples in that list.

This may be so, but there seems to be no good reason that John the apostle (if he was the author) could not have put himself inconspicuously at the scene without lifting his anonymity as the author. Put a different way, since the "disciple Jesus loved" must be one of the seven disciples mentioned in John 21:2, but since he cannot be Peter, Thomas, or Nathanael, there is at least a one-in-four possibility that he is John the son of Zebedee, and if his brother James is ruled out (as he should be; see above), the probability rises to one in three. The argument for John the apostle as the author becomes all the more compelling when one considers the following list of concerns with Bauckham's argument:[6]

1. Mark 14:17–18 and Luke 22:14 clearly place the Twelve in the Upper Room with Jesus at the Last Supper; this militates against Bauckham's thesis that the author

---

[1] Bauckham, *Jesus and the Eyewitnesses*, 8–11.

[2] See especially ibid., 36.

[3] Ibid., 94.

[4] Ibid., 264, and throughout.

[5] But see the critique by A. J. Köstenberger and S. O. Stout, "The Disciple Jesus Loved: Witness, Author, Apostle: A Response to Richard Bauckham's *Jesus and the Eyewitnesses*," *BBR* 18 (2008): 209–32.

[6] This list is adapted from A. J. Köstenberger and S. R. Swain, *Father, Son and Spirit: The Trinity and John's Gospel*, NSBT 24 (Downers Grove, IL: InterVarsity, 2008), 31–33.

was not one of the Twelve and seems to pit one apostolic eyewitness (Peter as the source for Mark) against another (that of the "disciple Jesus loved").[7]

2. Apart from the question of whether other persons may have been *present* at the Last Supper, what is the historical plausibility of someone other than one of the Twelve being *at Jesus's side* at the Last Supper, even more so as we know that Judas (one of the Twelve) was on Jesus's other side? The answer would have to be, "Slim to none."

3. Bauckham made nothing of the strong historical link between Peter and John the apostle in all of the available NT evidence (all four Gospels, Acts, and Galatians; see above). This is especially significant in light of the fact that Peter and the "disciple Jesus loved" are indisputably and consistently linked in John's Gospel.

4. The presence of the phrase "I suppose" *(oimai)* in John 21:25 as a device of authorial modesty (in keeping with the label "the disciple Jesus loved") supports the integrity of the entire Gospel as from the same author, identified in the Gospel as an eyewitness at strategic points (e.g., 13:23; 19:35).[8]

5. Methodologically, the question arises how legitimate it is to put a large amount of weight on one's reading of the patristic evidence over against the internal evidence of the Gospels themselves. It would seem that, in the end, the most plausible reading of the internal evidence ought to be given the most weight.

6. How likely is it, in light of Bauckham's own theory, that the primary eyewitness behind John's Gospel is not an apostle? In this regard the question arises whether the early church would ever have received such a Gospel, especially if written a generation after the Synoptic Gospels and in light of the crucial importance placed on apostolicity in the canonization process.

7. Why did the author leave out the name John, other than for the Baptist? Surely it is surprising that someone as important as John the apostle would not be mentioned in

[7] R. Bauckham, *The Testimony of the Beloved Disciple: Narrative, History, and Theology in the Gospel of John* (Grand Rapids, MI: Baker, 2007), 15, citing D. E. H. Whiteley, "Was John Written by a Sadducee?" in Wolfgang Haase, ed., *Aufstieg und Niedergang der Römischen Welt* 2.25.3 (Berlin, Germany: de Gruyter, 1985), 2481–505, ventured the conjecture that the "disciple Jesus loved" at Jesus's side at the Last Supper was the host and owner of the Upper Room. This is certainly a novel hypothesis, but highly unlikely.

[8] See A. J. Köstenberger, "'I Suppose' (οἶμαι): The Conclusion of John's Gospel in Its Literary and Historical Context," in *The New Testament in Its First Century Setting: Essays on Context and Background in Honour of B. W. Winter on His 65th Birthday*, ed. P. J. Williams, A. D. Clarke, P. M. Head, and D. Instone-Brewer (Grand Rapids, MI: Eerdmans, 2004), 72–88.

Almost from its inception the interpretation of John's Gospel was hotly contested. In the days of the early church, the Gnostics laid claim to this Gospel, alleging that it supported their message of salvation through knowledge (revelation) apart from redemption and forgiveness of sins.[6] John's first epistle may be the first to bear witness to the way in

goes on to point out that "many, perhaps even most, of the leading Johannine scholars over the last two centuries would not have agreed to John's patent ahistoricity" (15).

[6] See J. N. Sanders, *Fourth Gospel*, 47–87; Pollard, *Johannine Christology*, 25.

the Gospel at all (apart from John 21:2). Would it not be considerably more likely that he is in fact the "disciple Jesus loved" and the author of the Fourth Gospel?

8. Which other John was ever credited with the authorship of the Gospel of John in the early church? Apart from the above-cited ambiguous Papias quote in Eusebius, and an extremely doubtful reference to a John mentioned in Acts 4:6 by Polycrates,[9] the answer is, once again, "None."

9. The clear implication of John 21:2 is that the men listed are seven of the Eleven apostles, which excludes the elusive "John the elder" altogether.

The cumulative force of the list suggests that Bauckham's argument, while generally sound in affirming the importance of eyewitness testimony for the Gospels, is unduly biased when examining the evidence for the authorship of John's Gospel. In fact, it is hard to avoid the impression that the nonapostolic authorship of the Fourth Gospel is all but assumed at the outset of Bauckham's argument. This is all the more surprising as apostolic authorship seems to be the most natural corollary of Bauckham's overall thesis. After all, Bauckham's point is not merely that eyewitness testimony—any eyewitness testimony—is important for the Gospels but that we are dealing here with *apostolic* eyewitness testimony, that is, eyewitness testimony that is credible because it comes from those who were closest to Jesus during his earthly ministry. In this regard it is difficult to see how the testimony of one largely unknown "John the Elder"—not mentioned in any of the Synoptics or other non-Johannine NT writings—would satisfy Bauckham's own criterion. On the other hand, the apostolic authorship of John's Gospel would fit perfectly with Bauckham's overall theory.

For these and other reasons we welcome and concur with Bauckham's overall thesis regarding the Gospels' eyewitness character, yet we do not find his case against the apostolic authorship of John's Gospel convincing. Much more likely, in our opinion, is the view that John's Gospel, like the other three canonical Gospels, is founded on apostolic eyewitness testimony, and that John's, in fact, is the Gospel written by the apostle who was closest to Jesus during his earthly ministry. This claim, in turn, fits historically only with the apostle John, who, according to the unified witness of Matthew, Mark, and Luke, was one of three members of Jesus's inner circle together with Peter and John's brother James.

[9] Adduced by Bauckham, *Jesus and the Eyewitnesses*, 439.

which the Gospel was misunderstood if not intentionally misrepresented (see 1 John 1:1–3; 4:2–3).[7]

Subsequent to the Reformation, English deists as well as liberal German scholars initially preferred John's Gospel to the Synoptics due to its lack of emphasis on demon exorcisms. But in the wake of the Enlightenment, from E. Evanson in England to K. Bretschneider and D. F. Strauss in Germany, attacks were mounted alleging contradictions between John's "spiritual Gospel" and the Synoptics, pitting "history" against "theology," as if a Gospel that stresses the importance of eyewitness testimony and the careful

[7] See the discussion of the relationship between John's Gospel and 1–3 John in chap. 19 of this volume.

evaluation of evidence must necessarily bend historical fact for the sake of theological expediency.[8] In the twentieth century the towering figure R. Bultmann enlisted John in his program of demythologization.[9]

Also, efforts have been made in recent years to transfer John's Gospel from the mainstream of apostolic Christianity to the margins of sectarianism at the end of the first century. Some allege that the "Johannine community," "school," or "circle" (rather than John the apostle) was responsible for compiling the Gospel in the wake of its struggles against a parent synagogue that expelled a portion of its members for their faith in Jesus as Messiah.[10] This reconstruction, it should be noted, is significantly based on the charge that the references to synagogue expulsion in John (esp. 9:22) are anachronistic.

Still more recently, however, the historical value of such reconstructions has itself come under serious scrutiny and has been increasingly questioned.[11] In a stunning "confession," Robert Kysar chronicles the rise and fall of the Martyn/Brown-style "Johannine community hypothesis" and expresses personal regret for ever having endorsed it. While opting for a postmodern paradigm that acknowledges the validity of a variety of "readings" of the Fourth Gospel, Kysar's critique opened the way for a thorough reassessment of a paradigm that until recently was almost beyond question.[12]

---

[8] On the history of Johannine scholarship in the late eighteenth and early nineteenth centuries, see A. J. Köstenberger, "Early Doubts of the Apostolic Authorship of the Fourth Gospel in the History of Modern Biblical Criticism," in *Studies in John and Gender* (New York, NY: Peter Lang, 2001), 17–47. L. Morris's essays on history and theology in the Fourth Gospel and on the question of its authorship (*Studies in the Fourth Gospel* [Grand Rapids, MI: Eerdmans, 1969], 65–292) still repay careful study. For an interesting application of Clement's statement, see F. Thielman, "The Style of the Fourth Gospel and Ancient Literary Critical Concepts of Religious Discourse," in *Persuasive Artistry: Studies in New Testament Rhetoric in Honor of George A. Kennedy*, ed. D. F. Watson, JSNTSup 50 (Sheffield, PA: JSOT, 1991), 183, in the context of his entire article.

With regard to the designation of John's Gospel as the "spiritual Gospel," cf. Thompson ("Spiritual Gospel," 103), who rightly notes that "whatever Clement meant in calling John 'a spiritual Gospel,' it is doubtful that he meant to contrast 'facts,' in the modern sense, and 'interpretation.' . . . [A] 'spiritual' Gospel gives the inner meaning of an event or reality, and, hence its truth must be spiritually discerned." Thompson rightly alleges that "the modern view" that calls into question the historicity of any item in John that "stands in the service of his theological or interpretive agenda" constitutes "a very strange way to imagine how theology works, and perhaps it could only have been thought of by people actually *not* doing theology" (p. 104; emphasis original). Thompson proceeds to call for greater sophistication in biblical scholars' philosophy of history. D. A. Carson (*The Gospel according to John*, PNTC [Grand Rapids, MI: Eerdmans, 1991], 29) similarly disavows attributing to Clement a dichotomy between "spiritual" and "historical"; he suggests "spiritual" may mean "allegorical" or "symbol-laden."

[9] See Carson, *Gospel according to John*, 31–33.

[10] See J. L. Martyn, "Glimpses into the History of the Johannine Community," in *L'Évangile de Jean: sources, rédaction, théologie*, BETL 44, ed. M. de Jonge (Gembloux, Belgium: Duculot, 1977), 149–75; idem, *History and Theology in the Fourth Gospel*, 3rd ed., NTL (Louisville, KY: Westminster John Knox, 2003); R. E. Brown, *The Community of the Beloved Disciple* (New York, NY: Paulist, 1979); cf. O. Cullmann, *The Johannine Circle* (London, England: SCM, 1976).

[11] M. Hengel, *Die johanneische Frage*, WUNT 67 (Tübingen, Germany: Mohr Siebeck, 1993); R. Bauckham, *The Gospels for All Christians: Rethinking the Gospel Audiences* (Grand Rapids, MI: Eerdmans, 1998). See A. Schlatter (*Der Evangelist Johannes*, 2nd ed. [Stuttgart, Germany: Calwer, 1948], x), who comments that the term "Johannine school" appears to him to be "completely divorced from reality" (*völlig phantastisch*).

[12] R. Kysar, "The Dehistoricizing of the Gospel of John," in *John, Jesus, and History*, 75–101. As late as 1990, D. M. Smith could write, "Martyn's thesis has become a paradigm. . . . It is a part of what students imbibe from standard works, such as commentaries and textbooks, as knowledge generally received and held to be valid." D. M. Smith, "The Contribu-

Currently the "John, Jesus, and History" section of the Society of Biblical Literature (SBL) is in the process of investigating John's historicity. Some have even called for a "Fourth Quest" of the historical Jesus in which criteria are used that do not inherently favor the Synoptics.[13] Especially if John, as is now widely supposed, drew on traditions independent from the Synoptics, it should not be surmised at the outset that John, rather than Mark (on the widely-held supposition of Markan priority) is unhistorical. Rather, the possibility should be seriously considered that John, rather than Mark, is historical in a given instance or that both (not to mention the other canonical Gospels) may be historical.[14] Yet others believe that the theory of Johannine independence is itself subject to revision and that it is more plausible to suppose that John knew one or more of the Synoptics even though he apparently made little use of them.[15]

HISTORY

Author

John's Gospel, like the Synoptics, is formally anonymous.[16] In fact, it is "often viewed as somehow *more* anonymous than the other three [Gospels], by those who prefer to speak of Matthew, Mark, Luke, and 'the Fourth Gospel.'"[17] But the author left tantalizing clues in his Gospel (see Internal Evidence), which, when examined in conjunction with the testimony of the early church fathers (see External Evidence), points convincingly to authorship by John, the son of Zebedee and apostle of Jesus Christ.

Internal Evidence The author identifies himself as "the disciple Jesus loved" (21:20, 24; frequently referred to as "the disciple whom Jesus loved"), a prominent figure in the

---

tion of J. Louis Martyn to the Understanding of the Gospel of John," in *The Conversation Continues: Studies in Paul and John in Honor of J. Louis Martyn*, ed. R. T. Fortna and B. R. Gaventa (Nashville, TN: Abingdon, 1990), 293n30. J. van der Watt, *An Introduction to the Johannine Gospel and Letters*, Approaches to Biblical Studies (London, England: T&T Clark, 2007), 145, notes that the history of Johannine scholarship has been characterized by continual pendulum swings moving "between Gnostic, Hellenistic and Jewish frameworks; from documents containing several sources to documents that must be read as single units; from general messages to all Christians to documents that are aimed at specific groups."

[13] Possible proposed criteria include primitivity, corroborative impression, critical realism, and open coherence (per P. N. Anderson). See A. J. Köstenberger, "Who Were the First Disciples of Jesus? An Assessment of the Historicity of the Johannine Call Narrative (John 1:35–51)," in *John, Jesus, and History*, vol. 3: *Glimpses of Jesus through the Johannine Lens*, Early Christianity and Its Literature 18, ed. Paul N. Anderson, Felix Just, and Tom Thatcher (Atlanta: Society of Biblical Literature/Leiden: E. J. Brill, 2016), 189–99.

[14] See, e.g., D. M. Smith, *The Fourth Gospel in Four Dimensions: Judaism and Jesus, the Gospels and Scripture* (Columbia, SC: University of South Carolina Press, 2008).

[15] See A. J. Köstenberger, "John's Transposition Theology: Retelling the Story of Jesus in a Different Key," in *Earliest Christian History: History, Literature, and Theology: Essays from the Tyndale Fellowship in Honor of Martin Hengel*, ed. M. F. Bird and J. Maston, WUNT 2/320 (Tübingen, Germany: Mohr Siebeck, 2012), 191–226. See further the brief discussion of the relationship between John and the Synoptics at the end of this chapter.

[16] See the discussion of this issue in the chapters on the Synoptic Gospels above. See also Blomberg, *Historical Reliability of John's Gospel*, 32, for a brief treatment of the "anonymity" of John's Gospel.

[17] J. R. Michaels, *The Gospel of John*, NICNT (Grand Rapids, MI: Eerdmans, 2010), 5.

Johannine narrative (13:23; 19:26; 20:2; 21:7, 20).[18] Although this disciple's identity is elusive, he leaves sufficient clues in the narrative to ascertain it beyond reasonable doubt. The first such clues appear in 1:14 and 2:11. The author uses the first person in 1:14, "we have observed his glory," revealing that he is an eyewitness to the accounts contained in his Gospel. The "we" of 1:14 refers to the same people as does 2:11, Jesus's disciples.[19] Thus the writer is an apostle, an eyewitness, and a disciple of Jesus.

An examination of the phrase "the disciple Jesus loved" later on in the Gospel offers further clues to his identity.[20] The expression first appears in 13:23 at the Last Supper where only the Twelve are gathered (Matt 26:20; Mark 14:17; Luke 22:14), indicating that "the disciple Jesus loved" must have been one of the Twelve.[21] Since the author never refers to himself by name, he cannot be any of the named disciples at the Last Supper: Judas Iscariot (13:2, 26–27), Peter (13:6–9), Thomas (14:5), Philip (14:8–9), or Judas the son of James (14:22).

The writer offers more clues to his identity in the final chapter of the Gospel, where he mentions "the disciple, the one Jesus loved" as one of seven other apostles: "Simon Peter, Thomas (called 'Twin'), Nathanael from Cana of Galilee, Zebedee's sons, and two others of his disciples" (21:2; see 21:7). In addition to Peter and Thomas who have already been eliminated (see above), Nathanael is also ruled out as a possible author since, as previously noted, the author remains unnamed in John's Gospel.

---

[18] The first occurrence of the label "the disciple Jesus loved" in the second major portion of John's Gospel (i.e., at 13:23) is in keeping with the marked shift in perspective in chaps. 13–17, where the disciples' mission is viewed from the perspective of Jesus's exaltation (A. J. Köstenberger, *The Missions of Jesus and the Disciples according to the Fourth Gospel* [Grand Rapids, MI: Eerdmans, 1998], 153). Hence, the casting of John in more elevated terms in chaps. 13–21 is not unique in John's Gospel and may be seen as indicating that the apostle, as "the disciple Jesus loved," has an important part to play in the postexaltation mission of Jesus carried out through his commissioned followers. For an argument against "the disciple Jesus loved" as the author of the Gospel, see G. R. Beasley-Murray, *John*, WBC 36, 2nd ed. (Nashville, TN: Thomas Nelson, 1999), lxx–lxxv.

[19] The connection between "we" and "his disciples" is clear because of the parallel between the related references to "his [Jesus's] glory" in 1:14 and 2:11. For a discussion on John's use of "we" (21:24) and "I" (21:25), see G. L. Borchert, *John 1–11*, NAC 25A (Nashville, TN: B&H, 1996), 89–90. See also the works referenced in the following note.

[20] See the excellent and concise treatment in Carson, *Gospel According to John*, 472–73. The epithet "the disciple Jesus loved" is plausibly understood as an instance of authorial modesty. See K. J. Vanhoozer ("The Hermeneutics of I-Witness Testimony: John 21:20–24 and the 'Death' of the Author," in *Understanding Poets and Prophets: Essays in Honour of George Wishart Anderson*, ed. A. G. Auld, JSOTSup 152 [Sheffield, PA: JSOT, 1993], 374), who cites Augustine and Westcott, against C. K. Barrett, *The Gospel according to St. John*, 2nd ed. (Philadelphia, PA: Westminster, 1978), 117; and A. J. Köstenberger, "'I Suppose' (*Oimai*): The Conclusion of John's Gospel in Its Literary and Historical Context," in *The New Testament in Its First Century Setting: Essays on Context and Background In Honour of B. W. Winter on His 65th Birthday*, ed. P. J. Williams, A. D. Clarke, P. M. Head, and D. Instone-Brewer (Grand Rapids, MI: Eerdmans, 2004), 72–88.

[21] Contra Bauckham, *The Testimony of the Beloved Disciple: Narrative, History and Theology* (Grand Rapids, MI: Baker, 2007), 15–16; see the critiques by A. J. Köstenberger, *A Theology of John's Gospel and Letters: The Word, the Christ, the Son of God*, BTNT (Grand Rapids, MI: Zondervan, 2009), 75–79; and A. J. Köstenberger and S. O. Stout, "The Disciple Jesus Loved: Witness, Author, Apostle: A Response to Richard Bauckham's Jesus and the Eyewitnesses," BBR 18 (2008): 209–32. Michaels, John (NICNT), 13–14, speculates that the beloved disciple who authored the Gospel was one of Jesus's brothers, with Joses/Joseph a "marginally better candidate" (23). Some commentators (e.g., Beasley-Murray, *John*, lxx) suggest that the author is unclear as to how many disciples are present at the Lord's Supper.

Thus, the author must be either one of "Zebedee's [two] sons" or one of the "two other of [Jesus's] disciples." Of the two sons of Zebedee, James and John, James can safely be ruled out since he was martyred in the year 42 (see Acts 12:2). The remaining three possibilities are John the son of Zebedee and the "two other disciples." These latter two could be Matthew (Levi), Simon the Zealot, James the son of Alphaeus, Bartholomew, or Thaddaeus.[22] Matthew is an unlikely candidate since a Gospel is already attributed to him.[23] Simon the Zealot, James the son of Alphaeus, Bartholomew, and Thaddaeus are unlikely candidates as well due to their historical obscurity and lack of historical support (see "External Evidence" below). This leaves John the son of Zebedee as the most plausible option.

External Evidence During the second half of the second century, Irenaeus (ca. AD 130–200) attributed John's Gospel to John the apostle: "John the disciple of the Lord, who leaned back on his breast, published the Gospel while he was a resident at Ephesus in Asia" (*Haer.* 3.1.2). Clement of Alexandria (ca. AD 150–215) followed suit: "John, last of all . . . composed a spiritual Gospel" (quoted by Eusebius, *Eccl. Hist.* 6.14.7). From this point forward, the church unanimously attributed authorship to the apostle John for almost eighteen centuries with virtually no dissent.

Those who doubt apostolic authorship take their point of departure from a quote of Papias (ca. AD 60–130) by Eusebius (ca. AD 260–340), in which the former appears to refer to a John other than the apostle:

> If anyone chanced to come who had actually been a follower of the elders, I would enquire as to the discourses of the elders, what Andrew or what Peter said, or what Philip, or what Thomas or James, or what *John* or Matthew or any other of the Lord's disciples; and the things which Aristion and *John the Elder*, disciples of the Lord, say (Eusebius, *Eccl. Hist.* 3.39.4–5, emphasis added).

If these two Johns were different people, the Gospel bearing that name could have been penned by either one. But it is more likely that Papias referred to John the son of Zebedee by two different names, distinguishing between deceased eyewitnesses of Jesus's ministry and those who were still alive in his day.[24] The Papias quote wanes in importance when set in the context of other early evidence.

---

[22] The named apostles in the Gospels and Acts include Peter, his brother Andrew, James and John the sons of Zebedee, Philip, Thomas, Judas Iscariot (replaced by Matthias per Acts 1:15–26), Judas the son of James, Matthew/Levi, Simon the Zealot, who might be the same man sometimes called Thaddaeus, James the son of Alphaeus, and Bartholomew, perhaps also known as Nathanael; see Matt 10:2–4; Mark 3:16; Luke 6:14; Acts 1:13. Cf. R. Bauckham, *Jesus and the Eyewitnesses: The Gospels as Eyewitness Testimony* (Grand Rapids, MI: Eerdmans, 2006), 113.

[23] In addition, since Matthew's and John's style and vocabulary differ significantly, it is unlikely that the same author wrote both Gospels. On Johannine style, see Köstenberger, *Theology of John's Gospel and Letters*, 133–35.

[24] See D. A. Carson and D. J. Moo, *An Introduction to the New Testament*, 2nd ed. (Grand Rapids, MI: Zondervan, 2005), 229–54. Cf. Carson and Moo's discussion of Papias's quote (pp. 233–34). For a dissenting monograph that attributes

Reaching back further than Irenaeus, C. Hill persuasively argues in an important scholarly work that first-century believers used John's Gospel widely and authoritatively. By a scrupulous examination of the primary data, Hill refutes the previous notion (which he calls "orthodox Johannophobia") that early orthodox Christians avoided John's Gospel while the early Gnostics embraced it and that John's Gospel was not regarded as orthodox until the time of Irenaeus.[25] To the contrary, Hill demonstrates that John's Gospel was in all probability known by Polycarp (ca. AD 69–155), Ignatius (ca. AD 35–110), and the *Shepherd of Hermas* (early second century?), and that the first use of John's Gospel is likely found as early as in 1 John (as well as possibly in 2 and 3 John). One important implication of Hill's work is that the alleged non-use of John in the first half of the second century can no longer be used legitimately as an argument against its apostolic authorship.[26]

The Synoptic Gospels and Paul's Letters also provide corroborating data for John's authorship. The author of John's Gospel consistently shows "the disciple Jesus loved" to be a close companion of Peter (13:23–24; 18:15–16; 20:2–9; 21:7, 20–23), while other NT writers also note the close companionship of the apostles John and Peter (Luke 22:8; Acts 1:13; 3:1–4:23; 8:14–25; Gal 2:9). Taken by itself, this connection may be considered inconclusive. In conjunction with the internal and external evidence adduced above, however, it further confirms the likelihood that John the apostle is the author of the Gospel that bears his name, since, as the "disciple Jesus loved," John was the most likely close companion of Peter and thus the author of the Fourth Gospel.

A close examination of the available internal and external evidence, therefore, provides plausible grounds for the following three conclusions about the authorship of John's Gospel:[27] (1) the author is an apostle and eyewitness (1:14; see 2:11; 19:35); (2) he is one of the Twelve (13:23; see Mark 14:17; Luke 22:14); (3) he is John, the son of Zebedee (by far the strongest candidate on the basis of the above-adduced evidence). While the hypothesis of the apostolic authorship of the Fourth Gospel is regularly the object of skepticism if not derision in contemporary Johannine scholarship, the hypothesis has never been decisively refuted and continues to be eminently viable and certainly at least as plausible as alternative explanations.[28]

Johannine authorship to Papias's "John the elder," see M. Hengel, *The Johannine Question* (Philadelphia, PA: Trinity Press International, 1989). However, even Hengel himself acknowledges that his "hypothesis may sound fantastic" (p. 130).

[25] For an explication of this view, see W. Bauer, *Orthodoxy and Heresy in Earliest Christianity* (Philadelphia, PA: Fortress, 1971 [orig. German ed. 1934]).

[26] Hill, *Johannine Corpus in the Early Church.*

[27] Köstenberger, "John," 280. For a discussion of John as fisherman, son of thunder, beloved disciple, elder and seer, apostle in second-century interpretation, saint depicted as an eagle, and as hero and icon, see R. A. Culpepper, *John, the Son of Zebedee: The Life of a Legend* (Columbia, SC: University of South Carolina Press, 1994; repr. Minneapolis, MN: Fortress, 2000).

[28] See Carson, *Gospel according to John*, 68–81; Carson and Moo, *Introduction to the New Testament*, 229–54; Köstenberger, *Theology of John's Gospel and Letters*, 75–79; and C. S. Keener, *The Gospel of John: A Commentary*, 2 vols. (Peabody, MA: Hendrickson, 2003), 114–15, who states, "It is somewhat surprising, then, to discover the degree to which internal

Date

The date of John's Gospel depends on a complex matrix of questions regarding the author, his original audience, purpose, occasion for writing, and other factors. In the quest for the most likely date of composition, AD 65 and 135 serve, respectively, as the *terminus a quo* and *terminus ad quem* (the earliest and latest plausible dates).[29] The first of these dates is established by John's reference to Peter's martyrdom (21:19), which occurred in AD 65 or 66, and by John's depiction of Jesus as the replacement of the temple, whose destruction took place in the year 70.[30] The second date is determined by the twentieth-century discovery of the earliest NT manuscript of John's Gospel to date (𝔓[52], ca. 135), which contains John 18:31–32 and 37–38.

Within this time frame John most likely wrote his Gospel in the mid-80s or early 90s based on the following evidence.[31] First, although the Synoptics and Paul's Letters refer to Jesus's divinity, John's language seems closer to the "less restrained language of Ignatius [ca. AD 35–110]—in particular the ease and frequency with which Ignatius refers to Jesus as God."[32] In other words, it seems that sufficient time needed to elapse after Jesus's resurrection in order for John to articulate his theology in such terms.[33]

Second, if the reconstruction of John's occasion for writing—the destruction of the temple—is correct, the Gospel was most likely written ten to twenty years after the year 70, since a certain amount of time had to pass between the temple destruction and its composition: "[It is] hard to believe that . . . the date was *immediately* after AD 70 [the destruction of the temple]. . . . The reverberations around the Empire, for both Jews and Christians, were doubtless still too powerful. A little time needed to elapse . . . before a

---

and external evidence appear to favor John son of Zebedee as the Fourth Gospel's author. . . . one may therefore attribute the Gospel as a whole to an eyewitness."

[29] These scholars suggest a pre-70 date for John: R. M. Grant, *A Historical Introduction to the New Testament* (London, England: Collins, 1963), 152–53, 60; L. Morris, *The Gospel according to John*, NICNT (Grand Rapids, MI: Eerdmans, 1971), 30–35; and J. A. T. Robinson, *Redating the New Testament* (London, England: SCM, 1976), 254–84. For a summary of their arguments, see Beasley-Murray, *John*, lxxvi; for a refutation, see A. R. Kerr, *The Temple of Jesus' Body: The Temple Theme in the Gospel of John*, JSNTSup 220 (Sheffield, PA: Sheffield Academic Press, 2002), 19–25; cf. Carson, *Gospel according to John*, 82–86; L. Morris, *The Gospel according to John*, rev. ed., NICNT (Grand Rapids, MI: Eerdmans, 1995), 25–30; and D. B. Wallace, "John 5, 2 and the Date of the Fourth Gospel," *Bib* 71 (1990): 177–205.

[30] See "Occasion" for a brief explanation and additional bibliographic references.

[31] See D. A. Croteau, "An Analysis of the Arguments for the Dating of the Fourth Gospel," *Faith and Mission* 20/3 (2003): 47–80.

[32] Carson and Moo, *Introduction to the New Testament*, 267.

[33] Though note that this argument should not be pressed too far. Worship of Jesus as God is attested very early in Christian history. See, e.g., 1 Cor 8:6 (ca. AD 55): "yet for us there is one God, the Father, from whom are all things and for whom we exist, and one Lord, Jesus Christ, through whom are all things and through whom we exist." See L. W. Hurtado, *Lord Jesus Christ: Devotion to Jesus in Earliest Christianity* (Grand Rapids, MI: Eerdmans, 2003); R. Bauckham, *Jesus and the God of Israel: God Crucified and Other Studies on the New Testament's Christology of Divine Identity* (Grand Rapids, MI: Eerdmans, 2008); M. F. Bird *et al.*, *How God Became Jesus: The Real Origins of Belief in Jesus' Divine Nature* (Grand Rapids, MI: Zondervan, 2014).

document like the Fourth Gospel could be free *not* to make an *explicit* allusion to the destruction of the temple."[34]

Third, John's Gospel lacks reference to the Sadducees.[35] Since they play such an important role in the Synoptics (written prior to John) and since they were less influential after the destruction of the temple, their omission in John makes sense if he wrote subsequent to the temple's demise.

Fourth, John's use of the designation "Sea of Tiberias" in clarifying the "Sea of Galilee" (6:1; 21:1) suggests a mid-80s/early 90 date of composition. Herod Antipas founded the city of Tiberias on the Galilean seashore around AD 17–18 (Josephus, *Ant.* 18.2.3 §36). Gradually, the Sea of Galilee took on the name "Sea of Tiberias." On a popular level this shift probably took place in the 80s or 90s.[36]

Fifth, if Thomas's confession of Jesus as "my Lord and my God" is intended to evoke associations of emperor worship under Domitian (AD 81–96), this would seem to require a date subsequent to AD 81.[37]

Thus, a date of composition in the mid-80s or early 90s best fits all the evidence. This date also allows plenty of time for the Gospel to gain the popularity needed for a copy (𝔓[52]) to make it to Egypt by about AD 135.

Provenance

Early patristic testimony lends support to the notion that John wrote his Gospel in Ephesus.[38] Eusebius states that after the Jewish War (AD 66–73) dispersed the early apostles, John went to serve in Asia (*Eccl. Hist.* 3.1.1), which placed him in or near Ephesus during the 80s and 90s. Irenaeus writes that "John, the disciple of the Lord . . . published the gospel while living in Ephesus in Asia" (*Against Heresies* 3.1.2 [ca. AD 130–200]). However, some who believe that John's Gospel and the book of Revelation were written by different authors allege that Eusebius mistook the writer of the Gospel for the author of the Apocalypse.[39]

Opponents of the Ephesian provenance of John's Gospel set forth three major alternatives. First, some propose an Alexandrian provenance because John seems to bear affinities

---

[34] Carson, *Gospel according to John*, 85.

[35] Schlatter, *Evangelist Johannes*, 44, but note Carson's caution (*Gospel according to John*, 84).

[36] A. J. Köstenberger, *John*, BECNT (Grand Rapids, MI: Baker, 2004), 199.

[37] Ibid., 8. Some have suggested that since John was not quoted in works prior to the late second century, he probably wrote much later than 100 (H. Nun, *The Authorship of the Fourth Gospel* [Oxford, UK: Alden & Blackwell, 1952], 20–32; R. Brown, *The Gospel according to John I-XII*, AB 29 [Garden City, NY: Doubleday, 1966], lxxxi). But see C. E. Hill (*Johannine Corpus in the Early Church*), who demonstrated that many early second-century writers did in fact use John's Gospel (see discussion under "Author" above).

[38] For a magisterial study of the life of the early Christians in Ephesus, see P. Trebilco, *The Early Christians in Ephesus from Paul to Ignatius* (Grand Rapids, MI: Eerdmans, 2008).

[39] See Beasley-Murray, *John*, lxxix; Carson and Moo, *Introduction to the New Testament*, 254.

to Philo.[40] Second, others suggest an Antiochian origin because they see affinities between John's Gospel and Ignatius, bishop of Antioch (ca. AD 35–110), as well as with the *Odes of Solomon*, presumably written in Syria (of which Antioch was the capital).[41] Third, still others maintain that John's Gospel originated in Palestine because of apparent cultural influences and John's familiarity with certain topographical details.[42]

But these proposals are not without problems. For example, Philo was read outside of Alexandria as well; the literary influence of Ignatius and the *Odes of Solomon* in all likelihood reached beyond Antioch; and John was probably aware of, and influenced by, Palestinian culture dating back to his role in the ministry of Jesus and thereafter, but may have written the Gospel at a later time.[43] Overall, then, Eusebius and Irenaeus provide the most reliable data available, though it is less than conclusive. Thus, John most likely wrote in Ephesus in the province of Asia Minor.

Destination

Since John does not explicitly identify his audience, the arguments above regarding authorship and providence also relate to the question of the destination of the letter. If Irenaeus and others are correct that John was the author of the Gospel and that he wrote in Ephesus (see above), it is reasonable to assume that people living in and around Ephesus, primarily Diaspora Jews and Gentiles, were at least part of his intended readership.[44]

Beyond this, John's Gospel, like the other canonical Gospels, was likely written for "all Christians" rather than for readers in only one geographical location.[45] If so, John most likely wrote with Diaspora Jews, proselytes, and other Gentiles in mind without intending to limit his audience exclusively to any one group. This is also indicated by the genre of John's book: "After all, John's gospel is a *gospel*, heralding the universal good news of salvation in Christ."[46]

Occasion

The destruction of the Jerusalem temple in the year 70 was a traumatic event that left Judaism in a national and religious void and caused Jews to look for ways to continue their

---

[40] K. Lake, *An Introduction to the New Testament* (London, England: Christophers, 1948), 53; J. N. Sanders, *Fourth Gospel*, 85–86.

[41] W. G. Kümmel, *Introduction to the New Testament*, rev. ed., trans. H. C. Kee (Nashville, TN: Abingdon, 1975), 246–47.

[42] Martyn, "Glimpses into the History of the Johannine Community," 151–75.

[43] These critiques are offered by Carson and Moo, *Introduction to the New Testament*, 254.

[44] See Carson, *Gospel according to John*, 91.

[45] Bauckham, *Gospels for All Christians*, 9–48.

[46] Köstenberger, *Encountering John*, 8. For a detailed assessment, see idem, "The Genre of the Fourth Gospel and Greco-Roman Literary Conventions," in *Christian Origins and Greco-Roman Culture: Social and Literary Contexts for the New Testament*, vol. 1: *Early Christianity in Its Hellenistic Context*, ed. S. E. Porter and A. W. Pitts, Texts and Editions for New Testament Study (Leiden, Netherlands: Brill, 2012), 435–62.

SIDEBAR 7.2: TEXTUAL ISSUES IN JOHN'S GOSPEL

John's Gospel raises several important textual issues.[1] One of them pertains to the variant readings in 1:18. Some versions have *monogenēs huios* ("One and Only Son"), while others have *monogenēs theou* ("One and Only, [himself] God"). The discovery of 𝔓[66] and 𝔓[75], both of which read *monogenēs theos,* now seems to favor this "harder" reading. Most likely, John intended to open and close his prologue with references to Jesus as God (an *inclusio*), and the reading "one-of-a-kind Son" was introduced by scribes who were familiar with the reading at 3:16, 18 (a scribal assimilation).

Another interesting textual issue is raised in 1:34, where some early manuscripts read "the Son of God" (the reading adopted in the NIV, NASB, NRSV, NKJV, ESV, NLT, and CSB), while others (such as the Codex Sinaiticus and the recently published papyrus 𝔓[106]) have "the Chosen One of God" (adopted by the NIV). The former reading used to be the consensus view; but now the latter reading is favored by major commentators such as L. Morris, D. A. Carson, C. K. Barrett, R. Brown, R. Schnackenburg, and others.[2]

John 5:3b–4, which describes the periodic stirring of the water by a descended angel and the resulting healing of the first to enter the pool, also raises an interesting set of text-critical issues. The passage is clearly inauthentic, that is, was written not by the author of John's Gospel but added by a later hand, perhaps to elaborate on the passing reference to the stirring of the water in verse 7. The early attestation of this verse is poor, and there are as many as seven non-Johannine words in this one sentence.[3]

---

[1] For a more thorough treatment of these and other textual issues in John's Gospel, see Köstenberger, *John*, 50, 88, 245–49 (with further bibliographic references).

[2] For these and other references, see ibid., 50.

[3] See the discussion and further bibliographic references in Köstenberger, *John*, 195.

ritual and worship.[47] The temple's destruction likely served as one of the major catalysts for John to write his Gospel. The destruction threw late first-century Jews into turmoil since their faith was inextricably connected with the temple through the sacrificial system and the priesthood. In the same way that the Babylonian exile (606/586 BC) precipitated a

---

[47] S. Motyer, *'Your Father the Devil'? A New Approach to John and 'the Jews'* (Carlisle, UK: Paternoster, 1997); Kerr, *Temple of Jesus' Body*; P. W. Walker, *Jesus and the Holy City: New Testament Perspectives on Jerusalem* (Grand Rapids, MI: Eerdmans, 1996), 195; J. A. Draper, "Temple, Tabernacle and Mystical Experience in John," *Neot* 31 (1997): 264, 285. See especially P. S. Alexander, "'The Parting of the Ways' from the Perspective of Rabbinic Judaism," in *Jews and Christians: The Parting of the Ways, A.D. 70 to 135*, ed. J. D. G. Dunn (Tübingen, Germany: Mohr Siebeck, 1992), 1–25; and M. Goodman, "Diaspora Reactions to the Destruction of the Temple," in ibid., 27–38. For a fuller development and further bibliography, see A. J. Köstenberger, "The Destruction of the Second Temple and the Composition of the Fourth Gospel," *TrinJ* 26 NS (2005): 205–42; slightly revised in *Challenging Perspectives on the Gospel of John*, ed. J. Lierman, WUNT 2/219 (Tübingen, Germany: Mohr Siebeck, 2006), 69–108. For a critique of the Brown-Martyn-style "Johannine community hypothesis," see Carson, *Gospel according to John*, 35–36, 87–88, 369–72. The major evidence cited in support of a pre-70 date of writing is the lack of reference to the destruction of the temple and the present tense verb in John 5:2. But these are not determinative and are capable of alternative explanations (see Schlatter, *Evangelist Johannes*, 23–24; and Köstenberger, *John*, 177–78).

The most significant textual issue in John's Gospel is doubtless the *pericope adultera*, the story of the adulterous woman (7:53–8:11). There are serious doubts regarding the original inclusion of this passage in John's Gospel. As a result, virtually all modern translations place the pericope in square brackets. In terms of internal evidence, virtually every verse of this account features Greek words not found elsewhere in the Gospel. Conversely, much standard Johannine vocabulary is absent from the pericope. To this should be added different style characteristics and syntactical constructions.

On a literary level this pericope interrupts the narrative flow from 7:52 to 8:12 and breaks up the literary unit 7:1–8:59. On a historical level the setting of 7:53–8:1 suggests most plausibly Jesus's pattern during the week before his passion (Mark 11:11, 19; 13:3; and esp. Luke 21:37). Thus the preponderance of the internal evidence, including vocabulary, style, syntax, and literary flow, speaks decisively against the notion that the author of John's Gospel penned the pericope and included it at 7:52 in his Gospel.

In terms of external evidence, there are strong doubts regarding the originality of the passage in John's Gospel. (1) The pericope is absent from all pre-fifth-century manuscripts (though there is a certain amount of debate regarding this). (2) It appears in no fewer than six different places in the manuscript tradition: after John 7:36; after 7:44; after 7:52; at the end of John's Gospel; after Luke 21:38; and at the end of Luke's Gospel. (3) There is a lack of citation of this pericope in early patristic writings up to the fourth century (though this is debated).

The obvious conclusion, therefore, from studying both the internal and the external evidence regarding this pericope is that the account was almost certainly not a part of the original Gospel and should therefore not be regarded as divinely inspired, authoritative, or canonical. This does not mean the account is necessarily unhistorical. It is certainly possible (though impossible to verify) that the encounter between Jesus and this woman took place in the way recounted in this story. Nevertheless, like the longer ending of Mark, the story should be treated with caution.

deep crisis in Jewish worship removed from the first temple,[48] the destruction of the second required a major reorientation of Jewish ritual. In the wake of the temple's fall, John likely saw a window of opportunity for Jewish evangelism, seeking to encourage fellow believers to reach out to their Jewish and Gentile neighbors in the Diaspora.[49] He did so by arguing that the crucified and risen Messiah providentially replaced the temple (2:18–22; see 1:14; 4:21–24) and fulfilled the symbolism inherent in Jewish festivals (esp. 5–12).[50]

---

[48] See the discussion under "History: The Babylonian Period" in chap. 2 above.

[49] See Bauckham, *Gospels for All Christians*. Some might contend that in light of the strained relations between Jews and Christians subsequent to AD 70, it is unlikely that John would have sought to evangelize Jews. To the contrary, it is improbable that John would have ceased to desire the conversion of his fellow Jews to the Messiah, the only pathway to their covenant God (14:6), especially if, as suggested above, the destruction of the temple provided a new impetus to commend Jesus to unbelieving Jews and others attracted to the Jewish faith.

[50] Köstenberger, "Destruction of the Second Temple"; P. M. Hoskins, *Jesus as the Fulfillment of the Temple in the Gospel of John*, Paternoster Biblical Monographs (Carlisle, UK: Paternoster, 2007); Draper, "Temple, Tabernacle and Mystical Experience," 264–65.

In addition to the temple's destruction, the early Christian Gentile mission (Acts 9:16; Rom 1:13) and the emergence of early gnostic thought likely served as part of the matrix that occasioned the writing of John's Gospel. Since John wrote in the Diaspora for both Jews and Gentiles attracted to Judaism and since he wrote fifty years after the formation of the church when the Gentile mission was well underway, it stands to reason that this mission directly affected John's writing. Gnosticism, which began to emerge in the latter half of the first century but did not come to full fruition until the second century, provides part of the backdrop as well. Though John did not embrace or promote gnostic teachings,[51] like many evangelistic writings ever since he used the conceptual categories of his audience to contextualize his message (see John 1:1, 14). These three important factors—the temple's destruction, the Gentile mission, and gnostic thought—combine as possible occasions for John's Gospel.[52]

Purpose

John states his purpose toward the end of his Gospel: "But these [signs] are written so that you may believe that Jesus is the Messiah, the Son of God, and that by believing you may have life in his name" (20:31).[53] On a surface reading, "so that you may believe" suggests an evangelistic purpose, that is, leading John's readers to first-time faith in Jesus as Messiah.[54] At the same time, John's Gospel seems to presuppose an audience already familiar with Scripture since it contains detailed instructions for believers, especially in the second half of the Gospel. What is more, there are few examples of directly evangelistic first-century documents. For reasons such as these, it seems that John's purpose encompasses both aspects, evangelism of unbelievers and edification of believers, and that John pursues an indirect evangelistic purpose, aiming to reach an unbelieving audience through the Christian readers of his Gospel.[55]

---

[51] U. C. von Wahlde, "The Johannine Literature and Gnosticism: New Light on Their Relationship?" in *From Judaism to Christianity: Tradition and Transition: A Festschrift for Thomas H. Tobin, S. J., on the Occasion of His Sixty-fifth Birthday*, ed. P. Walters, NovTSup 136 (Leiden, Netherlands: Brill, 2010), 221–54, argues that "the features commonly thought to reflect a Gnostic world view can be accounted for more consistently and systematically by seeing them as prerogatives of the eschatological outpouring of God's Spirit as this is articulated within non-apocalyptic, OT Judaism" (228). He proceeds to discuss eleven elements of John's Gospel that are often understood to indicate Gnostic influence and finds each "better explained as consistent with the ('traditional') Jewish outlook rather than by some relationship to Gnosticism" (252). While the resemblance was "accidental" (252), the Gnostics later found this work helpful for their use. See also the overview of scholarship on the relationship between John's Gospel and Gnosticism (221–25).

[52] In addition to these, there were also other influences that may have affected his writing, such as the OT, rabbinic Judaism, Qumran, the Samaritans, Jewish persecution, Philo, and the Corpus Hermeticum. For an excellent examination of these factors, see Borchert, *John 1:1–11*, 60–80.

[53] Compare the purpose statement in 1 John 5:13: "I have written these things to you who believe in the name of the Son of God, so that you may know that you have eternal life."

[54] The phrase "so that you may believe" in 20:31 is represented in textual variants as either in the present (*pisteuēte*) or the aorist subjunctive (*pisteusēte*). Some have suggested that the former would point to an edificatory purpose while the latter would suggest an evangelistic purpose, but matters are considerably more complex, and the tense of *pisteuō* in 20:31 hardly resolves the ambiguity, which may be deliberate. See the discussion in Carson and Moo, *Introduction to the New Testament*, 270.

[55] Bauckham, *Gospels for All Christians*, 10.

Thus, according to 20:31, John's purpose is to show evidence that Jesus is the Messiah, the Son of God, so that people might believe in him and as a result have life in his name.[56] The purpose statement corresponds to the opening chapter of the Gospel where John set forth Jesus's messianic identity (see 1:1–3, 14, 29, 34, 41). The body of John's Gospel presents a series of Jesus's messianic "signs" and narrates his death, resurrection, and appearances in order to elicit faith in Jesus as the Messiah.[57] "Believing" in John's Gospel goes beyond mere intellectual assent; it involves putting one's trust in Jesus.[58] "Life" refers to eternal communion with Jesus entered into already in the here and now (see 5:24; 8:12; 10:10; 17:3).

Finally, it is important not to confuse John's likely *purpose* with possible *effects* of his Gospel. Carson and Moo aptly note, "Just because John's gospel can be used to offer comfort to the bereaved in the twenty-first century does not mean that is why the evangelist wrote it."[59] John explicitly states his purpose (20:30–31), which, as mentioned, against the backdrop of his provenance and occasion, is best understood as indirect evangelism. All other purposes must be seen as subordinate to this larger purpose or as effects that result from it.

LITERATURE

Literary Plan

There is wide agreement that John's Gospel breaks down into an introduction (1:1–18), a first major unit frequently called "The Book of Signs" (1:19–12:50; focusing on Jesus's messianic "signs" for the Jews), a second major unit best termed "The Book of Exaltation" (13:1–20:31; anticipating Jesus's exaltation with the Father subsequent to his crucifixion, burial, and resurrection), and an epilogue (chap. 21).[60] There is also considerable support for the notion that chapters 11–12 represent a transition from "The Book of Signs" to "The Book of Exaltation," featuring Jesus's climactic "sign," the raising of Lazarus, which, in turn, foreshadows Jesus's own resurrection.[61]

---

[56] The terms "Messiah" and "Son of God" are most likely used interchangeably (e.g., Acts 9:20, 22). See the interchange between D. A. Carson, "The Purpose of the Fourth Gospel: John 20:30–31 Reconsidered," *JBL* 108 (1987): 639–51; G. D. Fee, "On the Text and Meaning of John 20,30–31," in *The Four Gospels 1992: Festschrift Frans Neirynck,* ed. F. van Segbroeck, C. M. Tuckett, G. van Belle, and J. Verheyden, vol. 3, BETL 100 (Leuven, Belgium: Leuven University Press, 1992), 2193–205; and D. A. Carson, "Syntactical and Text-Critical Observations on John 20:30–31: One More Round on the Purpose of the Fourth Gospel," *JBL* 124 (2005): 693–714. The debate revolves around the issue of whether John's purpose is to identify Jesus as the Messiah or the Messiah as Jesus.

[57] See the discussion of the structure of John's Gospel and of major Johannine themes below.

[58] E.g., 1:12; 3:15–16, 36; 4:50; 5:24; 6:29, 40, 47, 69; 9:38; 11:25–27; 12:44, 46; 14:1; 16:27, 30; 17:8, 20; 19:35. See D. A. Croteau, "An Analysis of the Concept of Believing in the Narrative Contexts of John's Gospel," Th.M. thesis (Southeastern Baptist Theological Seminary, 2002).

[59] Carson and Moo, *Introduction to the New Testament*, 270.

[60] Many commentators, such as F. J. Moloney, *The Gospel of John*, SacPag (Collegeville, MN: Liturgical Press, 1998), v–viii, call the second major unit "Book of Glory," though references to glory are prevalent also in the first major unit.

[61] Carson, *Gospel according to John*, 106–7; Ridderbos (*Gospel of John*, viii) calls John 11–12 "Prelude to the Passion Narrative"; as does Keener (*Gospel of John*, xvii), who labels the unit "Introducing the Passion."

With regard to the structure of "The Book of Signs," many believe, on the basis of literary *inclusios*, that this unit is made up of two major cycles narrating Jesus's ministry, a "Cana cycle" (2:1–4:54; see 2:11; 4:54) and a "festival cycle" (5:1–10:42; see 1:19–34; 10:40–41).[62] Some also see a division between chapters 5–6 and chapters 7–10 in light of the watershed defection of many of Jesus's followers at the end of chapter 6.[63]

"The Book of Exaltation" breaks down into the Farewell Discourse (13–17), which can be subdivided into a preamble (13:1–30), the Farewell Discourse proper (13:31–16:33), Jesus's final prayer (17), and the Passion Narrative (18–20), culminating in a declaration of John's purpose (20:30–31). Thus, John's Gospel reveals a deliberate literary plan that reflects the evangelist's theological message.

By way of brief summary, John achieved his purpose of demonstrating that Jesus is the Messiah, the Son of God (20:30–31; see "Purpose" above) by weaving together several narrative sections that function within an overall structure. The introduction to John's Gospel places the entire narrative in the framework of the eternal, preexistent Word made flesh in Jesus (1:1–18).

The first major section, "The Book of Signs," sets forth evidence for Jesus's messiahship in the form of seven selected signs. The narration of these serves as the framework for the first half of John's Gospel (1:19–12:50; see esp. 12:37–40; cf. 20:30–31).[64]

John also includes Jesus's seven "I am" sayings (see chart on facing page) and calls numerous (seven?) witnesses in support of Jesus's claims, including Moses and the Scriptures, John the Baptist, the Father, Jesus and his works, the Spirit, the disciples, and the evangelist himself. Representative questions concerning Jesus's messiahship serve to lead the Gospel's readers to the author's intended conclusion, namely that Jesus is the Messiah (e.g., 1:41; 4:25; 7:27, 31, 52; 10:24; 11:27; 12:34).

The second major section of John's narrative, "The Book of Exaltation," shows how Jesus ensured the continuation of his mission by preparing his new messianic community for its mission. This portion opens with Jesus's Farewell Discourse (chaps. 13–17), in which the new messianic community is cleansed, prepared, and prayed for. The cleansing is effected by the footwashing and Judas's departure (chap. 13); the disciples' preparation involves instructions regarding the coming of the Holy Spirit (chaps. 14–16); and Jesus's followers are prayed for in his final prayer (chap. 17).

John's Passion Narrative (chaps. 18–19) presents Jesus's death both as atonement for sin (see 1:29, 36; 6:48–58; 10:15, 17–18), though largely without the Synoptic emphasis on shame and humiliation, and as prolegomenon of Jesus's return to the Father (see 13:1; 16:28). The resurrection appearances and the disciples' commissioning constitute the focal point of John's penultimate chapter (chap. 20), where Jesus is cast as the paradigmatic

---

[62] Moloney, *Gospel of John*, v–vi.

[63] E.g., Keener, *Gospel of John*, xvi; Ridderbos, *Gospel of John*, vii; Köstenberger, *John*, 52, whose structural proposal includes both the "festival cycle" in chaps. 5–10 and a break at a "moment of major crisis" at 6:60–71.

[64] A. J. Köstenberger, "The Seventh Johannine Sign: A Study in John's Christology," *BBR* 5 (1995): 87–103.

Table 7.1: The "I Am" Sayings of Jesus in John's Gospel

Statement	Reference in John's Gospel	Significance
"I am the bread of life."	6:35, 48, 51	Spoken after feeding of multitude; in analogy with God's provision of manna for wilderness-dwelling Israel; Jesus is the true bread of heaven able to satisfy people's spiritual hunger.
"I am the light of the world."	8:12; 9:5	Jesus as fulfillment of Feast of Tabernacles; Jesus is the salvation foreshadowed by the lamps of the Feast; "light" and "life" are related in John's Gospel, so Jesus is the "light of life" (8:12).
"I am the door."	10:7, 9	Jesus is the exclusive way to salvation—all must be saved through him; spoken in context of Good Shepherd Discourse.
"I am the good shepherd."	10:11, 14	In contrast to the Pharisees as worthless shepherds (see Zech 11:17), Jesus is the shepherd-king in the tradition of David; the good shepherd lays down his life for the sheep (substitutionary atonement).
"I am the resurrection and the life."	11:25	Jesus is the resurrection that Mary and Martha (and most of Israel) are waiting for in the last day; spoken prior to the raising of Lazarus.
"I am the way, the truth, and the life."	14:6	Jesus asserts that he himself is the exclusive way to the Father; Jesus's use of articles (*the* way, *the* truth, *the* life) further reiterates Jesus's status as the exclusive way to salvation.
"I am the true vine."	15:1	The OT used vine imagery to describe Israel (Isa 5:1–7; 27:2–6; Jer 2:21; Ezek 15; 19:10–14; Hos 10:1; Ps 80:9–16); Jesus is therefore the new Israel (as well as the replacement of the temple and Jewish festivals).

"Sent One" (see 9:7), who now sends the representatives of his new messianic community as he himself was sent by the Father (20:21–23). The purpose statement of 20:30–31 reiterates the major motifs of the Gospel: signs, believing, (eternal) life, and the identity of Jesus as Messiah and Son of God.

The Epilogue (chap. 21), John's final major section, brings closure to the joint characterization of Peter and the "disciple Jesus loved"—especially in the second half of John's Gospel. It portrays their relationship in terms of differing yet equally legitimate roles of service within the believing community, predicting Peter's martyrdom (21:19) and offering a further glimpse into the identity of the Gospel's author (21:24–25).

OUTLINE

I. INTRODUCTION: THE WORD MADE FLESH (1:1–18)

II. THE BOOK OF SIGNS: THE SIGNS OF THE MESSIAH (1:19–12:50)

- A. The Forerunner and the Coming of the Messiah (1:19–51)
  - 1. The Testimony of John the Baptist (1:19–34)
  - 2. The Beginning of Jesus's Ministry (1:35–51)
- B. The Cana Cycle: Jesus's Inaugural Signs and Representative Conversations (2–4)
  - 1. Sign 1: Changing Water into Wine at the Wedding in Cana (2:1–12)
  - 2. Sign 2: One of Jesus's Jerusalem Signs: The Clearing of the Temple (2:13–22)
  - 3. Representative Conversations: Nicodemus the Jewish Ruler, the Samaritan Woman (2:23–4:42)
  - 4. Sign 3: The Second Sign in Cana: The Healing of the Royal Official's Son (4:43–54)
- C. The Festival Cycle: Additional Signs amid Mounting Unbelief (5–10)
  - 1. Sign 4 at an Unnamed Feast in Jerusalem: The Healing of the Lame Man (5:1–47)
  - 2. Sign 5: Galilean Passover: Feeding the Multitude and Bread of Life Discourse (6:1–71)
  - 3. Jesus at the Feast of Tabernacles (7–8)
    - a. First Teaching Cycle (7:1–52)[65]
    - b. Second Teaching Cycle (8:12–59)
  - 4. Sign 6: The Healing of the Blind Man and the Good Shepherd Discourse (9–10)
    - a. Jesus Heals a Blind Man (9)
    - b. Jesus the Good Shepherd (10)
- D. Final Passover: Climactic Sign, the Raising of Lazarus, and Other Events (11–12)
  - 1. Sign 7: The Raising of Lazarus (11)
  - 2. Final Events of Jesus's Public Ministry (12)
    - a. The Anointing at Bethany (12:1–11)
    - b. The Triumphal Entry into Jerusalem (12:12–19)
    - c. The Dawning Age of the Gentiles (12:20–36)
    - d. Final Indictment: Jesus's Rejection by the Jews (12:37–50)

III. THE BOOK OF EXALTATION: PREPARING THE NEW MESSIANIC COMMUNITY AND THE PASSION OF JESUS (13–20)

- A. The Cleansing and Instruction of the New Covenant Community, including Jesus's Final Prayer (13–17)
  - 1. Cleansing the Community (13:1–30)
    - a. The Footwashing (13:1–17)
    - b. The Betrayal (13:18–30)
  - 2. The Farewell Discourse (13:31–16:33)
    - a. Jesus's Departure and Sending of the Spirit (13:31–14:31)
    - b. Jesus the True Vine (15:1–17)
    - c. The Spirit and the Disciples' Witness to the World (15:18–16:33)
  - 3. Jesus's Parting Prayer (17)
- B. The Passion Narrative (18–19)
  - 1. The Betrayal and Arrest of Jesus (18:1–11)
  - 2. Jesus Questioned by the High Priest and Denied by Peter (18:12–27)

---

[65] John 7:53–8:11 is not included in the outline because the passage was most likely not part of the original Gospel.

        3. Jesus Before Pilate (18:28–19:16a)
        4. Jesus's Crucifixion and Burial (19:16b–42)
    C. Jesus's Resurrection and Appearances, Commissioning of Disciples (20:1–29)
        1. The Empty Tomb (20:1–10)
        2. Jesus's Encounter with Mary Magdalene (20:11–18)
        3. Jesus's First Appearance, to His Disciples (20:19–23)
        4. Jesus's Second Appearance, to Thomas (20:24–29)
    D. Concluding Purpose Statement (20:30–31)
IV. EPILOGUE: THE COMPLEMENTARY ROLES OF PETER AND THE BELOVED DISCIPLE (21)
    A. Jesus's Third Appearance, to Seven Disciples in Galilee (21:1–14)
    B. Jesus and Peter (21:15–19)
    C. Jesus and the Disciple Jesus Loved (21:20–25)

UNIT-BY-UNIT DISCUSSION

I. Introduction: The Word Made Flesh (1:1–18)

John's striking prologue sets the course for his entire Gospel by drawing a road map for the reader that projects in eloquent language the path on which the Gospel will travel.[66] From 1:1 onward, John makes a startling assertion: Jesus is God. This God "became flesh" and "took up residence" (literally, "pitched his tent") among God's people (1:14) as the "One and Only Son from the Father," who was himself God (1:14, 18). Going beyond Matthew and Luke, who link Jesus with Abraham and/or Adam, John traces Jesus's origins back to creation (see Gen 1:1), thus anchoring him not simply in temporal historical events but in eternity past.

Anticipating later unbelief and the rejection of Jesus as Messiah by both the Jews and the world (chaps. 5–10, 18–19), John distinguishes between two groups of people: those who recognize the incarnate Word (1:12–13; believers) and those who do not (1:10–11; unbelievers). All must respond to Jesus based on the testimony of John the Baptist (1:6–9, 15) and on the Fourth Evangelist's presentation of Jesus throughout the rest of his Gospel, especially his setting forth of Jesus's seven messianic "signs" (chaps. 2–12; see 20:30–31).

II. The Book of Signs: The Signs of the Messiah (1:19–12:50)

After introducing Jesus as the Word made flesh in the introduction, John starts the first of his two "books"—"The Book of Signs" (1:19–12:50) and "The Book of Exaltation" (chaps. 13–20). The first book, "The Book of Signs," establishes by way of seven selected signs that Jesus is the Messiah sent from God (2:1–11, 13–22; 4:46–54; 5:1–15; 6:1–15; 9:1–41; 11:1–44). The second book, "The Book of Exaltation," records how the God-sent

---

[66] Brown notes, "The choice of the eagle as the symbol of John the Evangelist was largely determined by the celestial flights of the opening lines of the Gospel." Raymond Brown, *Gospel according to John*, AB 29A 1:18.

Something to Think About: By Their Fruit You Will Know Them

In the Sermon on the Mount, Jesus warned people against false prophets. With simple logic, Jesus pointed out that "every good tree produces good fruit, but a bad tree produces bad fruit.... So you'll recognize them by their fruit" (Matt 7:17, 20). For not everyone who says to Jesus, "Lord, Lord!" will enter the kingdom of heaven but only the one who does the will of his Father in heaven (Matt 7:21).

Later on toward the close of his ministry, Jesus challenged his followers with similar words. Earlier there were those who appeared to place their trust in Jesus, but Jesus was not fooled by outward expressions of faith that were unaccompanied by obedience (John 2:23–25). The many who had believed in him, he urged, "If you continue in my word, you really are my disciples" (8:31). Sadly, most did not heed Jesus's words.

So on his way to Gethsemane, Jesus reiterated his challenge once again: "If you remain in me and my words remain in you, ask whatever you want and it will be done for you. My Father is glorified by this: that you produce much fruit and prove to be my disciples" *(15:7–8). Are we easily satisfied with our new status in Christ and slack in our obedience? Let us not forget that it is* by our fruit *that we prove to be Jesus's followers and glorify our Father in heaven.*

Messiah became the sender of his disciples and thus the One who establishes God's new messianic community.

A. The Forerunner and the Coming of the Messiah (1:19–51) John begins the narrative proper by expounding on the testimony of John the Baptist (1:19–36; see 1:6–8, 15). To a delegation from Jerusalem, the Baptist bears witness regarding his own identity (1:19–28): he is not the Messiah but the "voice of one crying out in the wilderness" envisioned by the OT prophet Isaiah (1:23; see Isa 40:3; cf. Matt 3:3; Mark 1:3; Luke 3:4). He also directs his followers to Jesus, "the Lamb of God, who takes away the sin of the world" (1:29; see 1:36) and makes clear that the purpose of his ministry of baptism is so that Christ "might be revealed to Israel" (1:31). The remainder of the chapter shows Jesus calling his first disciples and identifying himself to them as the new Bethel (1:50–51; cf. Gen 28:12).

B. The Cana Cycle: Jesus's Inaugural Signs and Representative Conversations (2–4) After these introductory matters, chapter 2 opens with Jesus's ministry beginning in earnest. His first sign in Cana—turning water into wine—"displayed his glory," so that his disciples "believed in him" (2:11). Another possible sign, the clearing of the temple (2:13–22), anticipates Jesus's resurrection (2:19) and signals the temple's replacement with Jesus (2:20). After intermittent conversations with Nicodemus, the Jewish rabbi (3:1–21), and a Samaritan woman (4:1–42), Jesus performs another sign at Cana, healing an official's son (4:43–54). This closes the Cana cycle that spans chapters 2–4, which features Jesus's messianic ministry through both inaugural signs and extended conversations with representative individuals.

C. The Festival Cycle: Additional Signs amid Mounting Unbelief (5–10) In chapters 5–10, Jesus's public ministry is shown to continue amid escalating controversy due to the unbelief foreshadowed in 1:10–11 and 2:24–25. This intensifying unbelief is further exposed by additional messianic signs of Jesus. His fourth sign, the healing of a lame man (5:1–15), takes place at an unnamed festival (possibly Tabernacles) and is performed on the Sabbath, resulting in the Jews' persecution of Jesus (5:16). In the ensuing controversy, Jesus defends himself against the charge of blasphemy, calling on God the Father, his own works, John the Baptist, Moses, and others as his witnesses (5:17–47).

After this Jesus crosses the Sea of Galilee to celebrate Passover, where he performs his fifth sign, feeding the multitude (6:1–15). After the intervening account of Jesus's walking on the water (6:16–21), typically paired with the account of the feeding of the multitude in the Gospels (see Matt 14:13–33 and parallels), Jesus, in the "bread of life" discourse, reveals himself as the life-giving "bread," which is to be given sacrificially for the life of the world (6:22–59). After this, even many of Jesus's disciples stop following him, and he is left with the Twelve—and even one of them proves a traitor (6:60–71).

Continuing on the theme of growing escalation between belief and unbelief (7:1, 10, 12), the evangelist proceeds to narrate Jesus's journey to Jerusalem for the Feast of Tabernacles (7:1–8:59), presented in the form of two teaching cycles of Jesus (7:1–52; 8:12–59).[67] Sometime after the festival, Jesus performs the sixth of his seven signs, the healing of a blind man (9:1–12), which prompts further tension between Jesus and the Jewish authorities (9:13–41). Their failure to recognize Jesus as Messiah leads to severe division and mounting unbelief, with the plot to have Jesus killed inexorably moving toward a climax, even in the midst of a series of compelling messianic signs (chap. 10).

Table 7.2: Jesus's Fulfillment of Old Testament Festivals

Festival	Scripture	Description/Fulfillment
Feast of Passover	Exod 12:1–4; Lev 23:4–5; John 1:29–36; 2:13; 6:4; 11:55; 12:1	Also known as *Pesach*; a lamb was killed in commemoration of God's deliverance of Israel from Egypt **Fulfillment:** Jesus is the Lamb of God whose death causes God to pass over judging those covered by the blood of Jesus
Feast of Unleavened Bread	Exod 12:15–20; Lev 23:6–8	Also known as *Hag Hamatzot*; Israel must eat unleavened bread for seven days; in Scripture leaven often represents sin **Fulfillment:** Jesus is the Bread of Life who is free from sin (leaven)

[67] Regarding the noninclusion of the Pericope of the Adulterous Woman (7:53–8:11), see Sidebar 7.2: Textual Issues in John's Gospel above.

Table 7.2: Jesus's Fulfillment of Old Testament Festivals (continued)

Festival	Scripture	Description/Fulfillment
Feast of Firstfruits	Lev 23:9–14	Also known as *Yom HaBikkurim*; Israel offered first ripe sheaf of barley to the Lord; the sheaf was set aside on Passover and offered on the third day of the Passover feast **Fulfillment:** Jesus rose on the third day of the Passover feast as the "firstfruits of those who have fallen asleep" (1 Cor 15:20)
Feast of Pentecost	Lev 23:15–22; Acts 2:1–40	Also known as "Feast of Weeks" or *Shavnot*; occurs fifty days after Sabbath of Unleavened Bread; Israel offered new grain of summer harvest **Fulfillment:** Holy Spirit poured out on disciples forty-nine days after Jesus's resurrection (fifty days after the Sabbath preceding it)
Feast of Trumpets	Lev 23:23–35; Num 29:1–11; Matt 24:31; 1 Cor 15:51–52; 1 Thess 4:16–17	Also called *Rosh HaShana*; trumpet blown to call people into a time of introspection and repentance **Fulfillment:** Traditionally associated with judgment and the Book of Life, represents the Second Coming of Jesus as judge; Jesus's coming will be announced by a trumpet blast
Day of Atonement	Lev 23:26–32, 44–46; Rom 3:21–25; Heb 9:11–28	Also called *Yom Kippur*; high priest makes atonement for sin in the holy of holies where the ark of the covenant rested; final day of ten days of repentance of Feast of Trumpets; two goats (atonement sacrifice and scapegoat) represented atonement of Israel's sin for another year **Fulfillment:** Jesus as high priest entered heaven (the holy of holies) and made eternal atonement for sin with his blood
Festival of Tabernacles	Lev 23:34–43; John 1:14; 7:38–39; 8:12; 9:5	Also called *Sukkot*; the Jews dwelled in tents for one week; reminder of God's protection during Israel's wilderness wanderings; priest would pour out water to symbolize the world knowing God at coming of Messiah **Fulfillment:** Jesus made his dwelling among us; Jesus as source of living water that will flow from believers (Jesus's address at Festival of Tabernacles)

D. Final Passover: Climactic Sign, the Raising of Lazarus, and Other Events (11–12) In this bridge section the evangelist narrates Jesus's climactic sign, the raising of Lazarus (11:1–44), as well as mounting opposition to Jesus by the Jewish authorities (11:45–57). The startling demonstration of Jesus's messiahship at the raising of Lazarus adds the final exclamation point to Jesus's claim of being the messianic Son of God (see 12:36–41; 20:30–31). In light of the mounting pressure following Jesus's final sign in this Gospel, Jesus decides to avoid the open public and withdraws with his disciples (11:54).

With the seven signs behind Jesus and with the plot against him escalating, John moves the reader from the "Book of Signs" (1:19–12:50) to the "Book of Exaltation" (chaps. 13–20), featuring the following events: Mary's anointing of Jesus at Bethany (12:1–8), which anticipates his death and burial; Jesus's triumphal entry into Jerusalem, which underscores his messianic identity (12:12–19);[68] and the coming of some Greeks, which signify the dawning age of the Gentiles (12:20–36). These three public events precede the final indictment of Jewish rejection (12:37–50). With this Jesus shifts his focus from his revelation to Israel to the preparation of his new messianic community.

Table 7.3: Jesus's Signs in John's Gospel

Sign	Reference	Christological Significance
1. Changing water to wine	2:1–11	Display of glory; results in disciples' belief
2. Clearing of the temple	2:13–22	Signals replacement of temple; anticipates Jesus's resurrection
3. Healing of official's son	4:46–54	Performance of "hard miracles"; rejection theme
4. Healing of lame man	5:1–15	Performed on Sabbath; leads to persecution
5. Feeding of multitude	6:1–15	Shows Jesus as "Bread of Life"
6. Healing of blind man	9:1–41	Jesus, the light of the world, can cure spiritual blindness
7. Raising of Lazarus	11:1–44	Foreshadows Jesus as the risen, messianic Son of God

III. The Book of Exaltation: Preparing the New Messianic Community and the Passion of Jesus (13–20)

After narrating Jesus's seven "messianic signs" in "The Book of Signs," and climaxing in his rejection by the Jews (chaps. 1–12), John proceeds to anticipate Jesus's resurrection and ascension in "The Book of Exaltation" (chaps. 13–20). The focus is squarely on Jesus's preparation of the new messianic community, which is followed by an account of Jesus's passion, including his arrest, crucifixion, and burial, and the first two of his resurrection appearances. A purpose statement concludes the narrative proper (20:30–31).

---

[68] H. N. Ridderbos, *The Gospel according to John*, trans. J. Vriend (Grand Rapids, MI: Eerdmans, 1997), 423.

A. The Cleansing and Instruction of the New Community, Including Jesus's Final Prayer (13–17) With the line of demarcation between believers and unbelievers now clearly drawn, Jesus turns his attention to the Twelve (or Eleven) in order to prepare them for the time subsequent to his imminent departure. This preparation, presented in a section unique to John's Gospel that is commonly called the "Upper Room Discourse" or "Farewell Discourse" (chaps. 13–17), proceeds in three stages: (1) Jesus cleanses the community (13:1–30); (2) Jesus offers an encouraging and challenging farewell (13:31–16:33); and (3) Jesus utters a parting prayer (chap. 17).

First, the new messianic community is cleansed, both literally through Jesus washing the disciples' feet (13:1–17) and spiritually through the removal of Judas the traitor from the disciples' midst (13:18–30). With the community cleansed and Jesus's departure imminent, he turns to a period of extended instruction of the Eleven in order to prepare his followers for the time when he will no longer be physically present with them (the "Farewell Discourse" proper, 13:31–16:33). In this John presents Jesus's parting instructions to his followers against the backdrop of Moses's farewell in Deuteronomy.[69]

After announcing that his departure is imminent, Jesus comforts his disciples by telling them that he is going to prepare a place for them in his "Father's house" (14:2). In order to follow him there, they must remember that Jesus is the only way to the Father (14:6). Jesus further comforts his followers by promising to send "another Counselor" (14:16), "the Spirit of truth" (14:17). Once Jesus is exalted, the disciples must remain connected to the "true vine" (15:1), for apart from him they can do nothing (15:5). They must witness to a world that will hate and persecute them (15:18–16:33), knowing that Jesus's victory has already been secured (16:33).

While the community's cleansing serves as a preamble to Jesus's Farewell Discourse, his parting prayer (17:1–26) provides a postlude. Jesus first prays for himself (17:1–5); then for his disciples (17:6–19); and finally for all those who are going to believe on account of his disciples' proclamation (17:20–26). This provides a fitting conclusion to the Farewell Discourse and a suitable introduction to the events of the Passion Narrative that ensue in rapid order.

B. The Passion Narrative (18–19) After praying, Jesus, knowing what is about to happen to him (18:4), is arrested by a group of soldiers aided by Judas the betrayer under the cover of night. Johannine irony thickens as the passion events unfold. From the world's perspective, the high priest's questioning of Jesus (18:19–24), Peter's denials (18:15–18, 25–27), and Pilate's sentencing (18:28–19:16) reveal the misfortunes of a Jewish pretender who sought to mislead his followers by claiming to be the long-awaited Messiah. From John's perspective, however, Jesus is the otherworldly King who has come to this world as

---

[69] See John 6:14–15 and Jesus's "signs." Possible antecedents for Jesus's Farewell Discourse in John's Gospel include Moses's farewell discourse (Deuteronomy 31–33), other similar OT and Second Temple farewells (see *Jub.* 22:1–30; 1 Macc 2:49–70), and the patriarchal deathbed blessings and final words. For specific additional references, see Köstenberger, *John*, 396–97.

a witness to the truth; he is the One who will one day serve as its Judge but who now is to give his life for the sins of the world. He is the crucified, buried, and risen Messiah, whose resurrection constitutes the final act of the "elusive Christ" who has continued to evade the world's grasp.[70]

As John makes clear, all of these final events in Jesus's earthly ministry unfold according to the predetermined, sovereign plan of God (12:37–41; 13:1–3; 18:4), a perspective that is particularly evident throughout the Passion Narrative (see esp. the fulfillment quotations in 19:24, 28, 36–37).[71] At the trial and crucifixion, the Jewish nation, represented by its religious leaders, is shown to join the world in its unbelief and rejection of the Messiah. The carefully planned structure of an oscillating pattern of outdoor and indoor scenes of Jesus before Pilate (18:28–19:16a)[72] is intended "to exhibit the paradoxical outcome of the whole process—how they [Pilate and the Jewish leaders] found each other in a single unprincipled alliance against Jesus."[73] Their alliance leads to Jesus's crucifixion and the apparent success of Jesus's enemies (19:16b–42).

Table 7.4: The Seven Words of Jesus at the Cross

Sayings of Jesus	NT Reference
"Father, forgive them, because they do not know what they are doing."	Luke 23:34
"I assure you: Today you will be with me in paradise."	Luke 23:43
"Woman, here is your son. . . . Here is your mother."	John 19:26–27
"*Eloi, Eloi, lemá sabachtháni*?" ("My God, My God, why have You forsaken Me?")	Matt 27:46// Mark 15:34
"I'm thirsty!"	John 19:28
"It is finished!"	John 19:30
"Father, into Your hands I entrust my spirit."	Luke 23:46

C. Jesus's Resurrection and Appearances, Commissioning of Disciples (20) Jesus's resurrection and related appearances provide the conclusion to the Passion Narrative and the penultimate conclusion to the entire Gospel. The empty tomb offers the first hopeful glimmer of the return that Jesus promised in the Farewell Discourse (20:1–10). This hope reaches its initial fruition in Jesus's first postburial encounter with Mary Magdalene (20:11–18). Appearances to the disciples continue first without Thomas (20:19–23) and then with him (20:24–29).

---

[70] M. W. G. Stibbe, *John as Storyteller: Narrative Criticism and the Fourth Gospel*, SNTSMS 73 (Cambridge, UK: Cambridge University Press, 1992), 111–12.

[71] See Köstenberger, "John," in *Commentary on the New Testament Use of the Old Testament*, 500–506.

[72] Outside (18:29–32); inside (18:33–38a); outside (18:38b–40); inside (19:1–3); outside (19:4–7); inside (19:8–11); and outside (19:12–15).

[73] Ridderbos, *Gospel according to John*, 587.

Climaxing the "sending" motif in this Gospel, Jesus commissions his disciples ("As the Father has sent me, I also send you"; 20:21). He breathes on them and, in a symbolic gesture, confers on them the Holy Spirit (20:22) and a message of forgiveness (20:23).[74] Jesus's appearance to Thomas concludes with the latter's climactic confession, "My Lord and my God!" (20:28), which recalls the opening identification of Jesus as God in the prologue (1:1, 18).

D. Concluding Purpose Statement (20:30–31) The end purpose statement in 20:30–31 features virtually every major theme from the preceding narrative: (1) certain selected signs; (2) the necessity of believing that Jesus is the Messiah and the Son of God; and (3) the promise of life, both present and eternal.

IV. Epilogue: The Complementary Roles of Peter and the Beloved Disciple (21)

At a first glance it seems that John's Gospel should have come to an end with the concluding purpose statement in 20:30–31 and that the epilogue was most likely added by a later writer subsequent to John's death. On the contrary, however, most likely the epilogue serves as the closing bookend that corresponds to the opening bookend of the prologue. The epilogue resolves the relationship between Peter and the "disciple Jesus loved" in terms of noncompetition and resolves the identity of Johannine authorship. Thus, the epilogue most likely came from John's hand: its language and style are similar to chapters 1–20; no textual evidence exists that John's Gospel ever circulated without it. Therefore, John's epilogue appears to be part of John's overall literary plan.[75]

A. Jesus's Third Appearance, to Seven Disciples in Galilee (21:1–14) After appearing to the disciples without Thomas and then with him (see above), Jesus shows himself to them a third time, further validating his resurrection.[76] The disciples return to the Sea of Tiberias (the Sea of Galilee; see 6:1, 23) to fish, a return to Peter's former profession (see Matt 4:18).[77] When Jesus calls to them from the shore, they fail to recognize him (21:4). Yet after he instructs them on where to cast their net, the "disciple Jesus loved" does recognize the "Lord," prompting Peter to plunge into the water and swim ashore. The disciples' fishing trip introduces the next two important sections of the epilogue by providing the context for these subsequent events.

B. Jesus and Peter (21:15–19) Earlier Peter openly denied knowing Jesus three times (18:15–18, 25–27). Now, correspondingly, Jesus openly affirms and commissions Peter before his fellow disciples. Despite his failure, Peter will become the leader of the church

---

[74] For a book-length study, see Köstenberger, *Missions of Jesus and the Disciples.*

[75] See ibid., 583–86.

[76] See 21:14: "This was now the third time Jesus appeared to the disciples after he was raised from the dead" (cf. 20:19–23, 24–29). Note that this numbering does not include Jesus's appearance to Mary Magdalene (20:11–18), indicating that the Fourth Evangelist did not include her among Jesus's disciples known as the Twelve (or Eleven).

[77] The disciples' return to fishing may indicate unbelief. This is also suggested by the fact that they catch no fish. See the discussion with further bibliographic references in Köstenberger, *John*, 588–89.

(see Matt 16:16–19; Acts 1–12) and glorify God by dying a death similar to that of his Lord (21:18–19; the phrase "stretch out your hands" was a common ancient euphemism for crucifixion).

C. Jesus and the Disciple Jesus Loved (21:20–25) The Fourth Evangelist concludes his Gospel with an interchange between Jesus, Peter, and the "disciple Jesus loved." The rumor is dispelled that this disciple will not die prior to Jesus's return (21:23), and the "disciple Jesus loved" is identified as the author of the Gospel (21:24; see 21:20; 13:23; cf. "Author" above). As noted, this brings proper closure to the Gospel by resolving the relationship between Peter and "the disciple Jesus loved" in terms of noncompetition and by revealing the identity of the Gospel's author.

Finally, the concluding hyperbole recalls similar concluding statements in Greco-Roman and Jewish writings (21:24–25; cf. Eccl 12:9–12; *Soperim* 6.8). As one commentator observes, "John's hyperbole . . . extols neither the books people write nor the wisdom people acquire, but rather the deeds Jesus performed. Taken together with the prologue's stress on Jesus's person, the epilogue's reference to his works renders John's christological portrait not exhaustively comprehensive but sufficiently complete."[78]

THEOLOGY

Theological Themes[79]

Jesus as the Word, the Lamb of God, and the Messianic Son of God John's Gospel concludes the Gospels portion of the NT canon by stating that the whole world could not contain the books that would need to be written if everything Jesus did and said were recorded (21:25). This statement serves as a fitting conclusion to both John's Gospel and to all four Gospels in their entirety. With its presentation of Jesus as the preexistent Word who was with God in the beginning and who was himself God (1:1), yet who was made flesh (1:14) and as the "Lamb of God" provided substitutionary atonement for sin (1:29, 36), John's Gospel makes an indispensable contribution to the NT canon.

Indeed, Jesus is at the heart of John's narrative. He presents Jesus as both divine (1:1; 8:58; 12:41; 17:5; 20:28) and human (4:6–7; 11:33, 35; 19:28).[80] It is not possible to explore the full depth of John's depiction of Jesus here. The following survey briefly discusses

---

[78] Ibid., 606.

[79] For a comprehensive treatment of major themes in Johannine theology, see Köstenberger, *Theology of John's Gospel and Letters*. See also more briefly on John's Gospel, C. R. Koester, *The Word of Life: A Theology of John's Gospel* (Grand Rapids, MI: Eerdmans, 2008); on all the Johannine writings from a more systematic theological perspective, P. A. Rainbow, *Johannine Theology: The Gospel, the Epistles and the Apocalypse* (Downers Grove, IL: InterVarsity, 2014); and on selected Johannine themes (divine and human community, God's glory, the cross and the resurrection, the sacraments), R. Bauckham, *Gospel of Glory: Major Themes in Johannine Theology* (Grand Rapids, MI: Baker, 2015).

[80] See A. J. Köstenberger and S. R. Swain, *Father, Son and Spirit: The Trinity and John's Gospel*, NSBT 24 (Downers Grove, IL: InterVarsity, 2008), chap. 1, who contend that John's Christology neither minimizes nor sacrifices his Jewish monotheistic views.

interrelated aspects of John's Christology: Jesus as the Word *(Logos)*; Jesus as the Son of God; Jesus as the Lamb of God; and Jesus's signs and their relation to faith.[81]

At the outset John's account is grounded in the OT teaching that God sends forth his divine Word (see 1:1: *logos*) to achieve his aims (see Isa 55:10–11). This squarely places John's Christology within the framework of OT salvation history. The opening phrase "in the beginning" recalls the first words of Genesis, which recount the creation of the world (1:1; see 1:3). According to John, the coming of the Word into the world and his being made flesh in Jesus constitute an event of comparable magnitude (1:1, 14). Jesus is presented as the Word sent from heaven to accomplish a mission and, once the mission had been accomplished, to return to the place from which he came (1:1, 14; 13:1–3; 16:28; see Isa 55:11).

People must believe that God sent Jesus not only as the king of Israel (1:49) but also as the "Lamb of God" (1:29, 36). In his Gospel, John echoes OT theology and typology by alluding to the sacrificial Passover lamb. John is the only evangelist to call Jesus "the Lamb of God," and he states that Jesus "takes away the sin of the world" (1:29). This provides the remedy for people's sin (see 8:24, 34), which is ultimately the sin of unbelief in Jesus (16:9). The sacrificial and substitutionary nature of Jesus's death is also highlighted in references to Jesus as "the bread of life" given for the life of the world (6:31–59) and as the "good shepherd" who gives his life for his sheep (10:11–17). A vital part of Jesus's mission, therefore, is the sacrificial removal of sin.

Perhaps most pervasively, John's Gospel presents Jesus as the Son sent by the Father (3:17, 35–36; 5:19–26; 6:40; 8:35–36; 14:13; 17:1). This metaphor is taken from the Jewish concept of the *šālîah*, according to which the sent one is like the sender himself, faithfully pursuing the sender's interests (see 13:16, 20). Jesus's messianic mission thus derives from God and is thoroughly grounded in Jewish forms of thought. Yet Jesus is not just any messenger; he is the messianic Son of God (20:30–31), the One and only Son from the Father, himself God, who has come to give a full account of him (1:14, 18; 3:16, 18).

The Signs The significance of the signs in John's Gospel can hardly be overstated. Jesus's performance of selected messianic signs dominates the first half of John's Gospel (chaps. 1–12) as it builds inexorably to its first climax, the Jewish rejection of Jesus as Messiah (12:36b–41). Notably, Jesus's performance of messianic signs culminates in the raising of Lazarus, anticipating his own resurrection. Overall it appears that John's selection of particular acts of Jesus as signs proceeds on the criterion of particularly startling or stunning displays of Jesus's *messianic* power. In each case this is made clear by specific references provided by the evangelist, often involving large numbers.

In the case of Jesus's turning water into wine, John notes the large quantity of water that is turned into wine (2:6). In the clearing of the temple, the long time span that elapsed

[81] John features many other Christological themes. Beasley-Murray (*John*, lxxxi) notes the following: only Son (1:18; 3:16, 18); the Son (3:17, 36; 5:19–27); a teacher from God (3:2); a prophet (4:19; 9:19); the Messiah (1:41; 4:29; 11:11, 20, 31); King of Israel (1:49; see 6:15; 12:13); King of the Jews (19:19); and Lord (20:18, 28; 21:7).

since the completion of the temple is contrasted with the short time span in which Jesus's body, the "new temple," will be raised (2:19–20). Jesus's healing of the centurion's son is a difficult long-distance miracle (note that attention is drawn to the perfect coincidence between when Jesus spoke the word and when the healing takes place [i.e., 1:00 p.m.; 4:52–53]). The lame man healed by Jesus has been in that condition for thirty-eight years (5:38). In the feeding of the multitude the evangelist notes the large amount of leftovers, twelve basketsful (6:13). The blind man healed by Jesus has been blind since birth (9:1). Finally, Lazarus is not only dead when Jesus arrives on the scene; he has been dead for four days and is already decomposing (11:39).

All of these features underscore the amazing nature of Jesus's displays of his messianic identity, which renders Jewish unbelief all the more inexcusable (a function of John's theodicy, showing God to be just in condemning unbelief).[82] The significance of the signs in John's Gospel is further highlighted by the strategic references to Jesus's signs at the end of the first half of John's Gospel (12:36–40) and in the purpose statement at the end of the Gospel proper (20:30–31). This shows that for John, the signs are both a key Christological motif and a structural component of his Gospel.

Similar to the sending motif in John's Gospel, the signs concept is deeply grounded in Jewish thought.[83] The trajectory of OT theology reaches back all the way to the signs and wonders performed by Moses at the exodus. Building on this trajectory, Jesus's signs point to a new exodus and deliverance for God's people from their sins (see Luke 9:31). Hence, in this Gospel, more so than in the Synoptic accounts, the supernatural nature of Jesus's works—his "miracles" (Gk. *dynamis*), a term used consistently in the Synoptics but not in John, who uses the equivalent *sēmeion*—is placed within the larger framework of their prophetic and messianic symbolism. Jesus's miracles are not only powerful works; they show him to be the Messiah.

Similar to the signs performed by Moses and later prophets (cf. Isa 20:3), Jesus's signs thus serve primarily to authenticate the One performing them as God's true representative. People are severely criticized for demanding spectacular evidence of Jesus's authority (4:48); at the same time, signs are graciously offered as an aid to faith (10:38). And while blessing is pronounced on "those who have not seen and yet believe" (20:29), Jesus's signs are clearly designed to elicit faith from his audience, and when they fail to do so, people are held responsible. The desired outcome of Jesus's mission is that people will believe in him as the Messiah. His signs, then, serve as evidence for his identity and as an aid to lead unbelievers to faith.

The New Covenant Community and John's Portrayal of "the Jews" A primary goal of Jesus's messianic mission in John is the formation of a new messianic community. Like

---

[82] Together with Romans and Revelation, John's Gospel provides the most extensive and explicit theodicy in the NT, vindicating the righteousness of God by showing that his condemnation of sinners is just since they rejected his love expressed in the sending of his Son (3:16; 12:36b–41). See further the discussions of theodicy in chaps. 13 and 20 below.

[83] Köstenberger, "Seventh Johannine Sign," 87–103.

his portrait of Jesus, John's presentation of this community follows a salvation-historical pattern.[84] In keeping with OT typology, believers are described as a "flock" (10:1–20) and as "branches" of the vine (15:1–8). Yet John does not teach that the church replaces Israel. Instead, he identifies *Jesus* as Israel's replacement: *he* is God's "vine" who takes the place of Israel, God's OT "vineyard" (Isaiah 5).[85] John acknowledges that "salvation comes from the Jews" (4:22), yet he portrays Israel as part of the unbelieving world that rejects Jesus. Jesus's "own"—the Jews—do not receive him (1:11), and in their place the Twelve (except for Judas), who are now "his own," are the recipients of his love (13:1; see chap. 17). The Jewish leaders, on the other hand, never did belong to Jesus's flock (10:26).

Jesus's replacement of Israel raises the question of the new messianic community's relationship with the Jewish people. It has at times been alleged that John is anti-Semitic, since he seems to use the term "the Jews" (*Ioudaioi*) predominantly in a negative sense. But of the sixty-eight times he uses the expression, many of them mean either "Judeans" (as opposed to Galileans; 1:19) or "Jewish leaders" (see 19:7, 12). Frequently, the phrase refers to the majority of the Jewish people or the Jewish nation as a whole that rejected Jesus (10:33).[86] Thus, John does not mean to suggest that the Jews are now shut out from God's salvation-historical program—especially since "salvation is from the Jews" (4:22)—but that they, like everyone else, must come to Jesus *in faith* rather than presuming upon their Jewishness.

Once someone is incorporated into the new messianic community by Jesus through faith, that person's standing is secure. God gives believers to Jesus, and he will not lose any of them (6:39). Moreover, no one can snatch them out of Jesus's hand because the Father, who gave them to him, is greater than all (10:29). Even Jesus's twelve disciples did not choose him, but he chose them (15:16). Only the betrayer, Judas Iscariot, was doomed to destruction "so that the Scripture would be fulfilled" (17:12).

---

[84] J. W. Pryor, *John, Evangelist of the Covenant People: The Narrative and Themes of the Fourth Gospel* (Downers Grove, IL: InterVarsity, 1992).

[85] Hutchinson notes, "The seven ["I am"] images in John's Gospel were carefully chosen because of their rich association with stories and symbols from the Old Testament. Thus Jesus's messianic ministry is contrasted with the Old Covenant much like the fulfillment of a type" (79; cf. 72–73). J. C. Hutchison, "The Vine in John 15 and Old Testament Imagery in the 'I Am' Statements," *BSac* 168 (2011): 63–80.

[86] C. Blomberg (*Jesus and the Gospels: An Introduction and Survey,* 2nd ed. [Nashville, TN: B&H, 2009], 193) rightly notes that "John recognizes as readily as the Synoptics that Jesus's first followers were all Jewish, so there is no universal indictment of an entire ethnic group here." See also the judicious assessment by D. A. Hagner, "Anti-Semitism," *Dictionary of Jesus and the Gospels,* 2nd ed., ed. J. B. Green, J. K. Brown, and N. Perrin (Downers Grove, IL: InterVarsity, 2013),18–23, esp. 21–23 , who observes that (1) the Gospels are anti-Judaic, not anti-Semitic; (2) the negative view of the Jews in the Gospels is not universal and there is no condemnation of Jews merely because they are Jews; (3) the Romans crucified Jesus at the instigation of the Jewish authorities; (4) historically, anti-Judaism has fueled anti-Semitism, but the solution to this is not to reject or recast the Gospels but to interpret them correctly; (5) Jesus was a Jew, and so were the apostles, which indicates the special importance of the Jewish people in God's eyes; (6) the ultimate cause of Jesus's death is the universal sin of humanity, Jew and Gentile alike. See also L. Kierspel, *The Jews and the World in the Fourth Gospel: Parallelism, Function, and Context,* WUNT 2/220 (Tübingen, Germany: Mohr Siebeck, 2006).

Something to Think About: No Partiality with God

Jewish rabbis in Jesus's day typically avoided women and stayed away from Samaritans. Thus, the Samaritan woman who came to the well in Sychar had at least two strikes against her. Add to this her immoral lifestyle, and Jesus had every reason to evade contact with this individual. Even the woman herself was surprised that Jesus was talking to her: "How is it that you, a Jew, ask for a drink from me, a Samaritan woman?" (4:9). John added, "For Jews do not associate with Samaritans." Jesus's disciples, upon their return from grocery shopping in town, also "were amazed that he was talking with a woman" (4:27).

By contrast, everyone in Jesus's day would have been honored to engage in conversation with Nicodemus, a member of the Sanhedrin, the Jewish ruling council. Jesus called him "Israel's teacher" (3:10 NIV). This teacher visited Jesus by night to inquire covertly as to the nature of his teaching. Similarly, the Jewish authorities had looked into John the Baptist's activities (1:19). Later, at the Jewish trial preceding Jesus's crucifixion, the high priest asked Jesus about his disciples and his teaching (18:19). Yet when Nicodemus showed up on Jesus's doorstep, Jesus was not intimidated. To the contrary, he challenged him to be born again.

Ever since NT times, the church has had trouble treating the rich and the poor alike. Paul and James both exhorted believers not to give preferential treatment to the wealthy (1 Tim 6:17–19; Jas 2:1–7). By not showing partiality, Jesus exhibited a divine trait, for God is no respecter of persons. You and I should not think that because of our status—say, as a seminary professor or as an upright citizen of our community—we will be treated by God any differently than anyone else. As God told Samuel, "Humans do not see what the LORD sees, for humans see what is visible, but the LORD sees the heart" (1 Sam 16:7 NIV).

The chosen ones in the community, however, must "remain" in Jesus and "bear fruit" for him (15:4–8). Anyone who does not remain in Jesus will be thrown aside like a withered branch fit only to be burned (an emblem of divine judgment). Such branches are gathered, thrown into the fire, and burned (15:6). Election and perseverance, however, are but two sides of the same coin, as John indicates elsewhere: "They went out from us, but they did not belong to us; for if they had belonged to us, they would have remained with us. However, they went out so that it might be made clear that none of them belongs to us" (1 John 2:19).[87]

The community is formally constituted in the commissioning narrative where Jesus breathes on his gathered disciples and brings into being a new creation (20:22), recalling

[87] For further study, see D. A. Carson, *Divine Sovereignty and Human Responsibility: Biblical Perspectives in Tension* (Atlanta, GA: John Knox, 1981), 99–122; Blomberg, *Jesus and the Gospels*, 190–91.

the creation of the first human, Adam (Gen 2:7).[88] Jesus's parting preparation of his followers comes in terms reminiscent of Moses's Deuteronomic farewell discourse, another instance of John's drawing on OT antecedents.[89] At this salvation-historical juncture, however, it is not *Israel* but *believers in Jesus* who represent the core group through which God will pursue his redemptive purposes. In this, Jesus's dependent and obedient relationship to his sender, the Father, is made the paradigm for the disciples' relationship with their sender, Jesus.[90] Thus the Father sent his Son, the Messiah, to establish his new messianic community, and he commissions his new messianic community, whose mission it is to believe in, remain in, and proclaim the message of Jesus the Messiah.

God the Father As mentioned, in John, God is preeminently God the Father. In his 120 references to God the Father, however, John does not focus primarily on God in and of himself but more specifically on God as the Father (5:17–23) and sender (5:37; see 10:30–39) of Jesus Christ. The reason for this is that John's audience, including Jewish people and Gentile God-fearers and proselytes, already believed in God (see 14:1). John's purpose was to lead them from the common belief in God to faith in Jesus as the God-sent Messiah and Son of God (20:30–31). Nevertheless, God's existence in John's Gospel is pervasively present and unequivocally assumed.[91]

The unequivocal identification of Jesus as God *(theos)* in John's Gospel (1:1, 18; 20:28; see 5:18; 10:30) leads to the Jewish charge of blasphemy, ultimately resulting in Jesus's crucifixion (5:18; 19:5). Jesus's contemporaries allege that his claim of deity clashes with the Jewish belief in one God (monotheism), which is rooted in the Deuteronomic confession of God as "one" (Deut 6:4) and enshrined in the first two of the Ten Commandments (Exod 20:2–6; Deut 5:6–10)—a fact distinguishing Israel from the other surrounding nations (see 8:41). This apparent ditheism (belief in "two gods") is an objection Jesus himself addresses with reference to Psalm 82:6 in John 10:34–38.

By claiming unity with God the Father in both his works and his essence (see esp. 5:19–20; 10:30; 14:9–11), Jesus expands the horizons of Jewish monotheism by showing that there is indeed one God, yet this God includes two, and in fact, three Persons (including the Holy Spirit), who sustains an exceedingly intimate relationship of love and cooperates in God's plan in salvation-history (see 14:15–26, where the Father, the Son, and the Spirit are all said to come to reside in believers). In this demonstration of Jesus's deity as compatible with Jewish monotheistic beliefs, John provides an indispensable apologetic for the viability of Christianity for his Jewish readers and those attracted to the Jewish faith.[92]

---

[88] On the Johannine "new creation" motif, see esp. Köstenberger, *Theology of John's Gospel and Letters*, chap. 8 (for further research, see the Bibliography in ibid., 336–37).

[89] Compare the terminology of "love," "obey," and "keep commandments" (chaps. 13–17; cf. 1:17).

[90] Köstenberger, *Missions of Jesus and the Disciples*, 190–98.

[91] See Köstenberger and Swain, *Father, Son and Spirit*, chap. 3.

[92] See further ibid., chap. 1, with additional bibliographic references.

Salvation and Substitutionary Atonement According to John, God's purpose in sending Jesus is the salvation of the world, resulting in eternal life (see 3:16–17). In fact, the giving of life may be the most consistently stated purpose of Jesus's mission in John's Gospel (see 6:57; 10:10; 17:2; cf. 5:24).[93] Salvation comes only through Jesus (14:6) and is offered to everyone who believes (3:16).[94] As the "Savior of the world" (4:42), Jesus provides substitutionary atonement, a concept some allege is missing in John. Instead, they argue that for John, salvation came through mere revelation.[95] This argument assumes that John understood salvation like his gnostic counterparts, who believed salvation came through knowledge of divine revelation and mystical experience.

But John makes clear that Jesus indeed provided substitutionary atonement. First, John the Baptist refers to Jesus as "the Lamb of God" (1:29, 36), which is reminiscent of the substitutionary role of the sacrificial lamb in the OT. Second, Caiaphas unwittingly prophesies that Jesus will die "for the people," indicating the vicarious nature of Jesus's death (11:49–52). Third, John refers to Jesus's sacrificial, vicarious death in the "bread of life" and "good shepherd" passages (6:51; 10:15–18). While John does stress the revelatory aspect of Jesus's mission, he does not echo the gnostic notion that knowledge of revelation by itself equals salvation. Rather, he teaches that God's love is savingly revealed in the "lifting up" of Jesus on the cross, and it is only by believing in Jesus's substitutionary, vicarious death that people receive eternal life (3:16).[96]

The Holy Spirit John's teaching regarding the Holy Spirit is significant, especially in the second half of his Gospel.[97] In the first half, reference is made to the Spirit in only a few passages. The Baptist testifies that the Spirit rested on Jesus during his earthly ministry (1:32–33) and did so to an unlimited degree (3:34). Jesus notes that his words are life-giving and Spirit-infused (6:63), and the evangelist tells his readers that the Spirit is to be given only subsequent to Jesus's earthly ministry (7:39). Other possible references to the Spirit turn out at closer scrutiny more likely to be generic references to spirit in contrast to flesh (that is, the material contrasted with the spiritual realm; 3:5–8) and identifying God as spirit (that is, he is a spiritual being; 4:23–24).

The primary impetus for the teaching about the Spirit in the second half of the Gospel is Jesus's imminent departure, the occasion for the Farewell Discourse. The purpose for the teaching is to ensure a connection between the teaching of Jesus and the explanation

---

[93] See J. McPolin, "Mission in the Fourth Gospel," *ITQ* 36 (1969): 118.

[94] For a detailed study of John 3:16 in its first-century Jewish context, see A. J. Köstenberger, "Lifting Up the Son of Man and God's Love for the World: John 3:16 in Its Historical, Literary, and Theological Contexts," in *Understanding the Times: New Testament Studies in the 21st Century: Essays in Honor of D. A. Carson on the Occasion of His 65th Birthday*, ed. A. J. Köstenberger and R. W. Yarbrough (Wheaton, IL: Crossway, 2011), 141–59.

[95] J. T. Forestell, *The Word of the Cross: Salvation as Revelation in the Fourth Gospel*, AnBib 57 (Rome, Italy: Biblical Institute Press, 1974).

[96] See D. A. Carson, "Adumbrations of Atonement Theology in the Fourth Gospel," *JETS* 57 (2014): 513–22.

[97] John used three terms to identify the Holy Spirit: "Paraclete" ("helping presence"; 14:16, 26; 15:26; 16:7); "Holy Spirit" (14:26; focusing on his holiness); and "Spirit of truth" (14:17; 15:26; 16:13; focusing on his truthfulness). See Köstenberger and Swain, *Father, Son and Spirit*, chap. 5.

of that teaching that the Spirit was tasked to give. Once Jesus has been exalted with the Father subsequent to his resurrection, the Holy Spirit will come and take his place with his followers as the "other Counselor" (14:16). However, this does not mean that Jesus will disappear from the scene. To the contrary, from his exalted position with the Father, he will continue to direct the disciples' mission, answering prayer directed to God in his name (14:12–13; see Acts 1:1).

In the Farewell Discourse, the Spirit is presented as the connecting link between the believer, Jesus, and God. The Spirit serves as an abiding presence in believers (14:17); teaches and reminds them of Jesus's teaching (14:26); bears witness to him (15:26); convicts the world (16:7); guides believers into all truth (16:13); and declares things to come (16:13). This latter function includes the formation of the NT canon as apostolic testimony about Jesus. In all of this, the Spirit does not act independently of God or Jesus. Rather, he depends on them and their mission while being one with them.[98] The Holy Spirit is also prominently featured in the Johannine commissioning scene, where Jesus is shown to impart the Spirit to his disciples, constituting them as his new covenant community (20:22).[99] Thus, only in the power of the Spirit will they be able to fulfill their mission, which is patterned after Jesus's own sending from the Father.

Jesus's Fulfillment of Typology Inherent in Jewish Festivals, Sacred Space[100] The first half of John's Gospel, especially chapters 5–10, revolve around Jesus's fulfillment of the symbolism inherent in Jewish religious festivals and other institutions. This includes Passover (6:4; Jesus is "the bread of life," 6:48) and Tabernacles (7:2; Jesus is the "light of the world," 8:12; 9:5). In these cases, Jesus is shown by the evangelist to embody and fulfill the symbolism and typology inherent in these antecedent Jewish religious festivals, which adds to the author's portrait of Jesus as Messiah, along with his performance of signs and his self-identification as the divine "I am."

Along similar lines, John also shows Jesus as embodying sacred space. In an allusion to the OT tabernacle, John said that Jesus "took up residence" (literally "pitched his tent," *skenoō*) among God's people (1:14). John's Gospel also features Jesus's prediction to the Jewish authorities that the temple will be destroyed and rebuilt in three days, a veiled reference to his crucifixion and resurrection, which John interprets with reference to "the sanctuary of His body" (2:21; see vv. 19–20). This shows that the old covenant sanctuary, the Jerusalem temple, is soon going to be obsolete; in fact, it was destroyed by the Romans in the year 70.[101] In its place, proper worship should be directed to Jesus, the crucified and risen Savior of the world and Messiah of the Jews.

---

[98] See Köstenberger and Swain, *Father, Son and Spirit*, chap. 5.

[99] Most likely, this represents a symbolic promise of the soon-to-be-given gift of the Spirit, not the actual giving of him about fifty days later at Pentecost. See Köstenberger, *John*, 574–76, with further bibliographic references.

[100] For a thorough treatment, see chap. 10: "Salvation History: Jesus' Fulfillment of Festal Symbolism," in Köstenberger, *Theology of John's Gospel* (see also the Bibliography on p. 403 in ibid.).

[101] On the destruction of the temple as one possible occasion for the composition of John's Gospel, see the discussion under Purpose above. See also Köstenberger, "Destruction of the Second Temple" (with further bibliographic references).

Similarly, when asked by the Samaritan woman about the proper place of worship, whether Mount Gerizim (the Samaritan sanctuary) or Jerusalem, Jesus responds that proper worship must be offered to the Father "in spirit and truth," for "God is spirit, and those who worship him must worship in Spirit and truth" (4:23–24). Taken together with the previous reference to Jesus's body replacing the temple as the proper "sacred space" for worship, this worship "in spirit and truth" involves worship of Jesus as the divinely sent, crucified, and risen Son of God, who is himself God. In fact, this is Thomas's conclusion in the climactic Christological confession at the end of John's Gospel. There he worships Jesus and exclaims, "My Lord and my God!" (20:28; see also the response of the healed man in 9:38 who was born blind).

Taken as a whole, John's programmatic, methodical presentation of Jesus as the fulfillment of typology associated with Jewish religious festivals and sacred space makes the powerful point that Jesus has become the one and only proper object of worship—subsequent to his resurrection and exaltation with God the Father. All previous sanctuaries, including the tabernacle and temple, have been replaced and rendered obsolete by Jesus; all previous religious festivals have been shown to point typologically to Jesus and have found their fulfillment in him. To speak in the language of the writer of Hebrews, those who insist on continuing to worship through following the OT ritual are dealing in "shadows" and "copies" of the reality that has come in Jesus.[102]

Realized Eschatology John's teaching on the end time, while not in conflict with that of other NT documents (including the Synoptic Gospels), is distinctive in that it accentuates more keenly than some of the other NT writings the extent to which the end of time has already begun in and through Jesus. This does not mean that the future is entirely swallowed up in the present or that John denies the second coming of Jesus in the future, as some have claimed. Yet John does point out the way in which the future has invaded the present through Christ.

For John, eternal life is not merely a matter of life after death; it begins and is experienced already in the here and now (a teaching called "realized eschatology," indicating that aspects of the *eschaton* or "end time" are becoming a reality already in the present). Thus, when someone believes in Jesus as the Messiah, that person at that moment possesses eternal life (3:16) while simultaneously possessing future life (6:40). Already, he "has eternal life and . . . has passed from death to life" (5:24).

Nevertheless, this "Johannine dualism" (as it is often called) is not the same as the gnostic dualism of matter and spirit; rather, it is more akin to the Jewish distinction between "this age" and "the age to come," which flows from the Jewish understanding of redemptive history.[103] John's theology of the end time roots the future in the present or has the

---

[102] See Heb 8:5; 9:24; 10:1.

[103] On John's worldview, see especially Köstenberger, *Theology of John's Gospel and Letters*, 275–99.

present anticipate the future, but John also stresses the necessity for believers to persevere in their commitment to Christ (see 8:31; 15:4–8).

Relationship with the Synoptic Gospels and the Other Johannine Writings

The relationship between John's Gospel and the Synoptics is a vast and complex topic that cannot be treated exhaustively here.[104] The relationship has been described in terms of mutual independence or varying degrees of literary dependence.[105] Despite efforts to demonstrate literary dependence, it seems difficult to establish on purely literary grounds that John knew or used one or several of the Synoptic Gospels. Historically, however, it seems difficult to believe that the Fourth Evangelist had not heard of the existence of the Synoptics and read at least portions of them. But whether or not the author of the Fourth Gospel knew these other Gospels, he clearly did not make extensive use of them in composing his own narrative. Apart from the feeding of the 5,000, the anointing, and the Passion Narrative, John does not share any larger blocks of material with the Synoptic Gospels.[106]

Unlike the Synoptics, John's Gospel has no birth narrative, no Sermon on the Mount or Lord's Prayer, no transfiguration, no Lord's Supper, no narrative parables, no demon exorcisms, and no eschatological discourse. Clearly John has written his own book. But this does not make his a sectarian work apart from the mainstream of apostolic Christianity.[107] Rather, it appears John frequently transposed elements of the Gospel tradition into a different key.[108] The Synoptics' teaching on the kingdom of God corresponds to the Johannine theme of "eternal life"; narrative parables are replaced by extended discourses on the symbolism of Jesus's signs. Moreover, all four Gospels present Jesus as the Son of Man and as the Messiah fulfilling OT predictions and typology. Thus, the differences between the Synoptics and John ought not to be exaggerated.

---

[104] For a brief survey, see the treatment in chap. 21.

[105] See the monograph-length treatment by D. M. Smith, *John among the Gospels*, 2nd ed. (Columbia, SC: University of South Carolina Press, 2001).

[106] But note the "interlocking traditions" enumerated in Carson and Moo, *Introduction to the New Testament*, 260–62; and the internal evidence for John's awareness of Synoptic tradition, if not one or more of the written Gospels, listed in Köstenberger, *Encountering John*, 23, who cites 1:40 (Andrew "Simon Peter's brother"); 3:24 ("since John [the Baptist] had not yet been thrown in prison"); 4:44 ("a prophet has no honor in his own country"; see Mark 6:4 and parallels); 11:1–2 (Bethany, the "village of Mary and her sister Martha"; see Luke 10:38–41); and 6:67, 71 (the Twelve, Judas "one of the Twelve").

[107] D. Wenham, "The Enigma of the Fourth Gospel: Another Look," *TynB* 48 (1997): 149–78.

[108] For a detailed exploration, see Köstenberger, "John's Transposition Theology," 191–226. Stuhlmacher ("My Experience with Biblical Theology," in *Biblical Theology: Retrospect and Prospect*, 185–87) contends that John and the Synoptics do not merely represent different perspectives (what M. Hengel calls "aspective") but that the Fourth Gospel "cultivates a[n] . . . idealized type of memory concerning Jesus." He urges that "the Johannine witness therefore needs to be consistently realigned with the Synoptics, the Pauline corpus and the OT, so that faith in Jesus Christ does not lose its historical roots" (p. 187). But his seems to be merely a nice way of saying that John's Gospel is historically unreliable and that there are real contradictions between John and the Synoptics (see Stuhlmacher's more direct statement in "Der Kanon und seine Auslegung," in *Jesus Christus als die Mitte der Schrift: Studien zur Hermeneutik des Evangeliums*, ed. C. Landmesser *et al.*, BZNW 86 [Berlin, Germany: de Gruyter, 1997], 287). Current evidence denies both.

With regard to the relationship between John's Gospel, the Letters of John, and the book of Revelation, in all probability John the apostle was not only the author of the Gospel but of the other books as well.[109] This is indicated, among other things, by the numerous verbal and conceptual parallels among these writings.[110] The differences, such as the lack of OT references in the Letters and the symbolic nature of Revelation, are likely attributed to the different purposes and genres of these writings. Most likely, John's Gospel was written first, and the Letters dealt with issues and challenges that arose subsequently. The designation "elder" in the Johannine Letters (2 John 1; 3 John 1) may refer both to John's advanced age and his stature among the congregations he addressed.

CONTRIBUTION TO THE CANON

- Jesus as the preexistent Word made flesh (1:1, 14)
- Jesus as the One and only Son of the Father (1:14, 18; 3:16, 18) who sends his followers on a mission as the Father sent him (17:18; 20:21)
- Jesus as the Lamb of God who took away the sins of the world (1:29, 36)
- Jesus as the glorified, exalted Lord who directs the mission of his followers through the "Other Helping Presence," the Holy Spirit (14:16–18, 26; 15:26–27; 16:7–15)
- Jesus as the Messiah who performed a series of startling signs (20:30–31)

STUDY QUESTIONS

1. Who is "the disciple Jesus loved"?
2. What three conclusive reasons do the authors provide for believing that John wrote the Gospel bearing his name?
3. What are the two major divisions that comprise the structure of John's Gospel?
4. How do these two divisions fulfill the purpose statement of 20:30–31?
5. What is one major theological theme in John's Gospel that points to a late date of composition?
6. Who was probably John's general audience?
7. How does John 1:1–18 serve as a road map for the entire Gospel?
8. What is the major purpose of the signs included in the first half of John's Gospel?
9. What were the two major catalysts for the production of John's Gospel?
10. What is the major purpose of the "I am" statements?
11. Why do some reject the originality of John 21? How do the authors defend it?
12. What are the implications of Jesus being the sent Son of God?

---

[109] See the discussions of authorship in chaps. 19 and 20 below.

[110] For a list and brief discussion of important parallels between John's Gospel, his Letters, and Revelation, see Köstenberger, *Encountering John*, 194–97; cf. chaps. 19 and 20 below.

FOR FURTHER STUDY

Anderson, P. N. *The Fourth Gospel and the Quest for Jesus: Modern Foundations Reconsidered.* Library of New Testament Studies 321. New York, NY: T&T Clark, 2006.

Anderson, P. N., F. Just, and T. Thatcher. *John, Jesus, and History.* 2 vols. Society of Biblical Literature Symposium Series 44. Atlanta, GA: Society of Biblical Literature, 2007, 2009.

Anderson, P. N., F. Just, and T. Thatcher. *John, Jesus, and History.* Vol. 3: *Glimpses of Jesus through the Johannine Lens.* Atlanta, GA: Society of Biblical Literature. Leiden, Netherlands: Brill, forthcoming.

Ashton, J., ed. *The Interpretation of John.* 2nd ed. Studies in New Testament Interpretation. Edinburgh, Scotland: T&T Clark, 1997.

Barrett, C. K. *The Gospel according to St. John.* 2nd ed. Philadelphia, PA: Westminster, 1978.

Bauckham, R. *Gospel of Glory: Major Themes in Johannine Theology.* Grand Rapids, MI: Baker, 2015.

__________. *Jesus and the Eyewitnesses: The Gospels as Eyewitness Testimony.* Grand Rapids, MI: Eerdmans, 2006.

__________. *The Testimony of the Beloved Disciple: Narrative, History, and Theology in the Gospel of John.* Grand Rapids, MI: Baker, 2007.

__________, ed. *The Gospels for All Christians: Rethinking the Gospel Audiences.* Grand Rapids, MI: Eerdmans, 1998.

Beasley-Murray, G. R. *John.* Word Biblical Commentary 36. 2nd ed. Waco, TX: Word, 1999.

Bennema, C. *Encountering Jesus: Character Studies in the Gospel of John.* 2nd ed. Minneapolis, MN: Fortress, 2014.

Blomberg, C. L. *The Historical Reliability of John's Gospel: Issues and Commentary.* Downers Grove, IL: InterVarsity, 2002.

Borgen, P. *The Gospel of John: More Light from Philo, Paul and Archaeology. The Scriptures, Tradition, Exposition, Settings, Meaning.* Novum Testamentum Supplement 154. Leiden, Netherlands: Brill, 2014.

Brown, R. E. *The Gospel according to John.* Anchor Bible 29-29A. 2 vols. Garden City, NY: Doubleday, 1966, 1970.

__________. *An Introduction to the Gospel of John.* Edited by F. J. Moloney. Anchor Bible Reference Library. New York, NY: Doubleday, 2003.

Carson, D. A. *The Gospel according to John.* Pillar New Testament Commentary. Grand Rapids, MI: Eerdmans, 1991.

Coloe, M. *God Dwells with Us: Temple Symbolism in the Fourth Gospel.* Collegeville, MN: Liturgical Press, 2001.

Culpepper, R. A. *Anatomy of the Fourth Gospel: A Study in Literary Design.* Philadelphia, PA: Fortress, 1983.

Culpepper, R. A., and C. C. Black, eds. *Exploring the Gospel of John. Fs. D. Moody Smith.* Louisville, KY: Westminster John Knox, 1996.

Dodd, C. H. *The Interpretation of the Fourth Gospel.* Cambridge, UK: Cambridge University Press, 1953.

Duke, P. D. *Irony in the Fourth Gospel.* Atlanta, GA: John Knox, 1985.

Edwards, R. *Discovering John: Content, Interpretation, Reception.* 2nd. ed. London, UK: SPCK, 2014.

Farelly, N. *The Disciples in the Fourth Gospel: A Narrative Analysis of Their Faith and Understanding.* Wissenschaftliche Untersuchungen zum Neuen Testament 2/290. Tübingen, Germany: Mohr Siebeck, 2010.

Frey, J., J. G. van der Watt, and R. Zimmermann, eds. *Imagery in the Gospel of John: Terms, Forms, Themes, and Theology of Johannine Figurative Language.* Wissenschaftliche Untersuchungen zum Neuen Testament 200. Tübingen, Germany: Mohr Siebeck, 2006.

Harris, M. J. *Jesus as God: The New Testament Use of* Theos *in Reference to Jesus.* Grand Rapids, MI: Baker, 1992.

__________. *John.* Exegetical Guide to the Greek New Testament. Nashville, TN: B&H Academic, 2015.

Hengel, M. *The Johannine Question.* Translated by J. Bauden. London, UK: SCM, 1989. Translation of *Die johanneische Frage.* Wissenschaftliche Untersuchungen zum Neuen Testament 67. Tübingen, Germany: Mohr Siebeck, 1993.

Hill, C. E. *The Johannine Corpus in the Early Church.* Oxford, UK: Oxford University Press, 2004.

Hunt, S. A., D. F. Tolmie, and R. Zimmermann, eds. *Character Studies in the Fourth Gospel: Narrative Approaches to Seventy Figures in John.* Wissenschaftliche Untersuchungen zum Neuen Testament 314. Tübingen, Germany: Mohr Siebeck, 2013.

Kealy, S. P. *John's Gospel and the History of Biblical Interpretation.* 2 vols. Lewiston, NY: Mellen, 2002.

Keener, C. S. *The Gospel of John: A Commentary.* 2 vols. Peabody, MA: Hendrickson, 2003.

__________. "John, Gospel of." Pages 419–36 in *Dictionary of Jesus and the Gospels.* 2nd ed. Edited by J. B. Green, J. K. Brown, and N. Perrin. Downers Grove, IL: InterVarsity, 2013.

Kellum, S. L. *Preaching the Farewell Discourse: An Expository Walk-Through of John 13:31–17:26.* Nashville, TN: B&H Academic, 2014.

Kierspel, L. *The Jews and the World in the Fourth Gospel: Parallelism, Function, and Context.* Wissenschaftliche Untersuchungen zum Neuen Testament 2/220. Tübingen, Germany: Mohr Siebeck, 2006.

Kobel, E. *Dining with John: Communal Meals and Identity Formation in the Fourth Gospel and Its Historical and Cultural Context.* Biblical Interpretation Series 109. Leiden, Netherlands: Brill, 2011.

Koester, C. R. *The Word of Life: A Theology of John's Gospel.* Grand Rapids, MI: Eerdmans, 2008.

Köstenberger, A. J. *Encountering John: The Gospel in Its Historical, Literary, and Theological Perspective.* Encountering Biblical Studies. 2nd ed. Grand Rapids, MI: Baker, 2013.

__________. *John.* Baker Exegetical Commentary on the New Testament. Grand Rapids, MI: Baker, 2004.

__________. "John." Pages 415–512 in *Commentary on the New Testament Use of the Old Testament.* Edited by G. K. Beale and D. A. Carson. Grand Rapids, MI: Baker, 2007.

__________. "John." Pages 499–634 in *The Holman Apologetics Commentary on the Bible: The Gospels and Acts.* Nashville, TN: B&H, 2013.

__________. "John." Pages 1–216 in *Zondervan Illustrated Bible Backgrounds Commentary*, vol. 2. Edited by C. E. Arnold. Grand Rapids, MI: Zondervan, 2001.

__________. *The Missions of Jesus and the Disciples According to the Fourth Gospel.* Grand Rapids, MI: Eerdmans, 1998.

__________. *Studies in John and Gender: A Decade of Scholarship.* Studies in Biblical Literature 38. New York, NY: Peter Lang, 2001.

__________. *A Theology of John's Gospel and Letters: The Word, the Christ, the Son of God.* Biblical Theology of the New Testament. Grand Rapids, MI: Zondervan, 2009.

__________, and S. R. Swain. *Father, Son and Spirit: The Trinity and John's Gospel.* New Studies in Biblical Theology 24. Downers Grove, IL: InterVarsity, 2008.

Kysar, R. *John, the Maverick Gospel.* 3rd ed. Louisville, KY: Westminster John Knox, 2007.

Le Donne, A., and T. Thatcher, eds. *The Fourth Gospel in First-Century Media Culture.* Library of New Testament Studies 426. New York, NY: T&T Clark, 2011.

Lee, D. A. *Symbolic Narratives of the Fourth Gospel: The Interplay of Form and Meaning.* Journal for the Study of the New Testament Supplement 95. Sheffield: JSOT, 1994.

Lierman, J., ed. *Challenging Perspectives on the Gospel of John.* Wissenschaftliche Untersuchungen zum Neuen Testament 2/219. Tübingen, Germany: Mohr Siebeck, 2006.

Lincoln, A. T. *The Gospel according to Saint John.* Black's New Testament Commentaries. London, UK: Continuum, 2005.

__________. *Truth on Trial: The Lawsuit Motif in the Fourth Gospel.* Peabody, MA: Hendrickson, 2000.

Martyn, J. L. *History and Theology in the Fourth Gospel.* 3rd ed. Louisville, KY: Westminster John Knox, 2003.

McHugh, J. F. *John 1–4.* Edited by Graham Stanton. International Critical Commentary. New York, NY: T&T Clark, 2009.

Michaels, J. R. *The Gospel of John.* New International Commentary on the New Testament. Grand Rapids, MI: Eerdmans, 2010.

Moloney, F. J. *The Gospel of John.* Sacra Pagina 4. Collegeville, MN: Liturgical Press, 1998.

Morris, L. *The Gospel according to John.* New International Commentary on the New Testament. rev. ed. Grand Rapids, MI: Eerdmans, 1995.

__________. *Jesus Is the Christ: Studies in the Theology of John.* Grand Rapids, MI: Eerdmans, 1989.

__________. *Studies in the Fourth Gospel.* Grand Rapids, MI: Eerdmans, 1969.

Motyer, S. *"Your Father the Devil"? A New Approach to John and "the Jews."* Carlisle, UK: Paternoster, 1997.

Painter, R. J. *The Gospel of John: A Thematic Approach.* Eugene, OR: Wipf & Stock, 2011.

__________. "Johannine Literature: The Gospel and Letters of John." Pages 344–72 in *The Blackwell Companion to the New Testament.* Edited by David E. Aune. Chichester, UK: Wiley-Blackwell, 2010.

Pate, C. M. *The Writings of John: A Survey of the Gospel, Epistles, and Apocalypse.* Grand Rapids, MI: Zondervan, 2011.

Pollard, T. E. *Johannine Christology and the Early Church.* Society for New Testament Studies Monograph Series 13. Cambridge, UK: Cambridge University Press, 1970.

Porter, S. E., and A. K. Gabriel. *Johannine Writings and Apocalyptic: An Annotated Bibliography.* Johannine Studies 1. Leiden, Netherlands: Brill, 2013.

Pryor, J. W. *John: Evangelist of the Covenant People: The Narrative and Themes of the Fourth Gospel.* Downers Grove, IL: InterVarsity, 1992.

Quast, K. *Peter and the Beloved Disciple: Figures for a Community in Crisis.* Journal for the Study of the New Testament Supplement 32. Sheffield: JSOT, 1989.

Rainbow, P. A. *Johannine Theology: The Gospel, the Epistles and the Apocalypse.* Downers Grove, IL: InterVarsity, 2014.

Ridderbos, H. N. *The Gospel of John: A Theological Commentary.* Translated by J. Vriend. Grand Rapids, MI: Eerdmans, 1997.

Schlatter, A. *Der Evangelist Johannes: Wie er spricht, denkt und glaubt.* 2nd ed. Stuttgart, Germany: Calwer, 1948.

Schnackenburg, R. *The Gospel according to St. John.* 3 vols. New York, NY: Crossroad, 1990.

Scholtissek, K. "The Johannine Gospel in Recent Research." Pages 444–72 in *The Face of New Testament Studies: A Survey of Recent Research.* Edited by S. McKnight and G. R. Osborne. Grand Rapids, MI: Baker, 2004.

Skinner, C. W. *Characters and Characterization in the Gospel of John.* Library of New Testament Studies 461. London, UK: Bloomsbury T&T Clark, 2013.

Sloyan, G. S. *What Are They Saying About John?,* rev. ed. New York, NY: Paulist, 2006.

Smalley, S. S. *John: Evangelist and Interpreter.* 2nd ed. Downers Grove, IL: InterVarsity, 1998.

Smith, D. M. *John among the Gospels.* 2nd ed. Columbia, SC: University of South Carolina Press, 2001.

__________. *The Theology of the Gospel of John.* New Testament Theology. Cambridge, UK: Cambridge University Press, 1995.

Stibbe, M. W. G. "The Elusive Christ: A New Reading of the Fourth Gospel." *Journal for the Study of the New Testament* 44 (1991): 19–38.

__________. *John as Storyteller: Narrative Criticism and the Fourth Gospel.* Society for New Testament Studies Monograph Series 73. Cambridge, UK: Cambridge University Press, 1992.

Thatcher, T., ed. *What We Have Heard from the Beginning: The Past, Present, and Future of Johannine Studies.* Waco, TX: Baylor University Press, 2007.

Thatcher, T., and Stephen D. Moore, eds. *Anatomies of Narrative Criticism: The Past, Present, and Futures of the Fourth Gospel as Literature.* Atlanta, GA: Society of Biblical Literature, 2008.

Thompson, M. M. "John, Gospel of." Pages 368–83 in *Dictionary of Jesus and the Gospels.* Edited by J. B. Green, S. McKnight, and I. H. Marshall. Downers Grove, IL: InterVarsity, 1992.

Tovey, D. *Narrative Art and Act in the Fourth Gospel.* Journal for the Study of the New Testament Supplement 151. Sheffield: Sheffield Academic Press, 1997.

Van Belle, G., ed. *The Death of Jesus in the Fourth Gospel.* Bibliotheca Ephemeridum Theologicarum Lovaniensium 200. Leuven, Belgium: Leuven University Press, 2007.

Van Belle, G., J. G. van der Watt, and F. Maritz, eds. *Theology and Christology in the Fourth Gospel: Essays by Members of the SNTS Johannine Writings Seminar.* Bibliotheca Ephemeridum Theologicarum Lovaniensium 184. Leuven, Belgium: Leuven University Press, 2005.

Van der Watt, J. G. *Family of the King: Dynamics of Metaphor in the Gospel according to John.* Biblical Interpretation Series 47. Leiden, Netherlands: Brill, 2000.

__________. *An Introduction to the Johannine Gospel and Letters.* London, UK: T&T Clark, 2007.

Verheyden, J., G. Van Oyen, M. Labahn, and R. Bieringer, eds. *Studies in the Gospel of John and Its Christology: FS Gilbert Van Belle.* Bibliotheca Ephemeridum Theologicarum Lovaniensium 265. Leuven, Belgium: Leuven University Press, 2014.

Von Wahlde, U. C. *The Gospel and Letters of John.* Eerdmans Critical Commentary. 3 vols. Grand Rapids, MI: Eerdmans, 2010.

Walker, P. W. L. *Jesus and the Holy City: New Testament Perspectives in Jerusalem.* Grand Rapids, MI: Eerdmans, 1996.

Part Three

THE EARLY CHURCH AND PAUL

IN THIS PORTION of this work, the book of Acts (chap. 8) forms the basic framework for the discussion of Paul's life and ministry (chap. 9) and subsequent chapters treating Paul's letters in chronological sequence in their presumed order of writing (chaps. 10–15): Galatians; 1 and 2 Thessalonians; 1 and 2 Corinthians; Romans; the Prison Epistles (Philippians, Ephesians, Colossians, and Philemon); and the Letters to Timothy and Titus.

Organizing the material this way enables the student to get a sense of the development of the early church and first-century Christianity throughout Paul's missionary career. Since Paul wrote thirteen of the twenty-seven books of the NT, and since his letters probe the major implications of Jesus's mission and saving cross-work for NT believers, part 3 forms the heart of this introduction to the NT. It is complemented and completed by the discussion of the General Epistles and the book of Revelation in part 4 (chaps. 16–20) and a concluding chapter on unity and diversity in the NT (chap. 21).

Chapter 8

The Book of Acts

CORE KNOWLEDGE

Basic Knowledge: Students should know the key facts about the book of Acts. With regard to history, students should be able to identify the book's author, date, provenance, destination, and purpose. With regard to literature, they should be able to provide a basic outline of the book and identify core elements of the book's content found in the Unit-by-Unit discussion. With regard to theology, students should be able to identify the major theological themes in the book of Acts.

Intermediate Knowledge: Students should be able to present the arguments for historical, literary, and theological conclusions. With regard to history, students should be able to discuss the evidence for Lukan authorship, date, provenance, destination, and purpose. With regard to literature, they should be able to provide a detailed outline of the book. With regard to theology, students should be able to discuss the major theological themes in the book of Acts and the ways in which they uniquely contribute to the NT canon.

Advanced Knowledge: Students should be able to evaluate critically and to assess the historical accuracy of the speeches, the Jerusalem Council, and the miracles recorded in Acts. They should also be able to evaluate accurately the sources that lie behind the composition of Acts.

KEY FACTS

Author: Luke

Date: Early 60s

Provenance: Rome

Destination: Theophilus

Purpose: A defense of the Christian faith showing the expansion of the early church from a Jewish sect to a worldwide movement

Theme: Salvation history: the birth and mission of the early church

Key Verse: 1:8

INTRODUCTION

WHEN OSCAR WILDE was studying the classics at Oxford, he had to take an oral exam to test his knowledge of Greek. The examiners looked at him, sensed he was "an effete and 'difficult' young man," and assigned him the most difficult text to translate in the Greek NT: the account of Paul's shipwreck in Acts 27 with its extensive use of nautical language. "That will be all, Mr. Wilde," the examiners said, when Oscar, a brilliant Greek student, provided an effortless translation. "Oh, please," exclaimed Wilde, "do let me go on—I am longing to know how the story finishes."[1]

This anecdote illustrates two facets of the book of Acts. To begin with, it is the account of a grand adventure, taking us from Palestine to the center of the Gentile world: Rome. Along the way, it includes the exciting story of encounters with hostile people and governments, sailing adventures, shipwrecks, and even courtroom dramas. No doubt about it: the book of Acts is an exciting adventure. But the anecdote not only underlines the exciting tale that is the book of Acts, it also leaves us (like Wilde) longing to know how the story finished because the book ends rather suddenly, with Paul remaining under arrest in Rome and awaiting trial.

[1] A. N. Wilson, *Paul: The Mind of the Apostle* (New York, NY: W. W. Norton, 1997), 21–22. Ironically, of course, Wilde would *not* have found out how the story finishes even *if* he had read through the end of the book of Acts, since the story is open-ended.

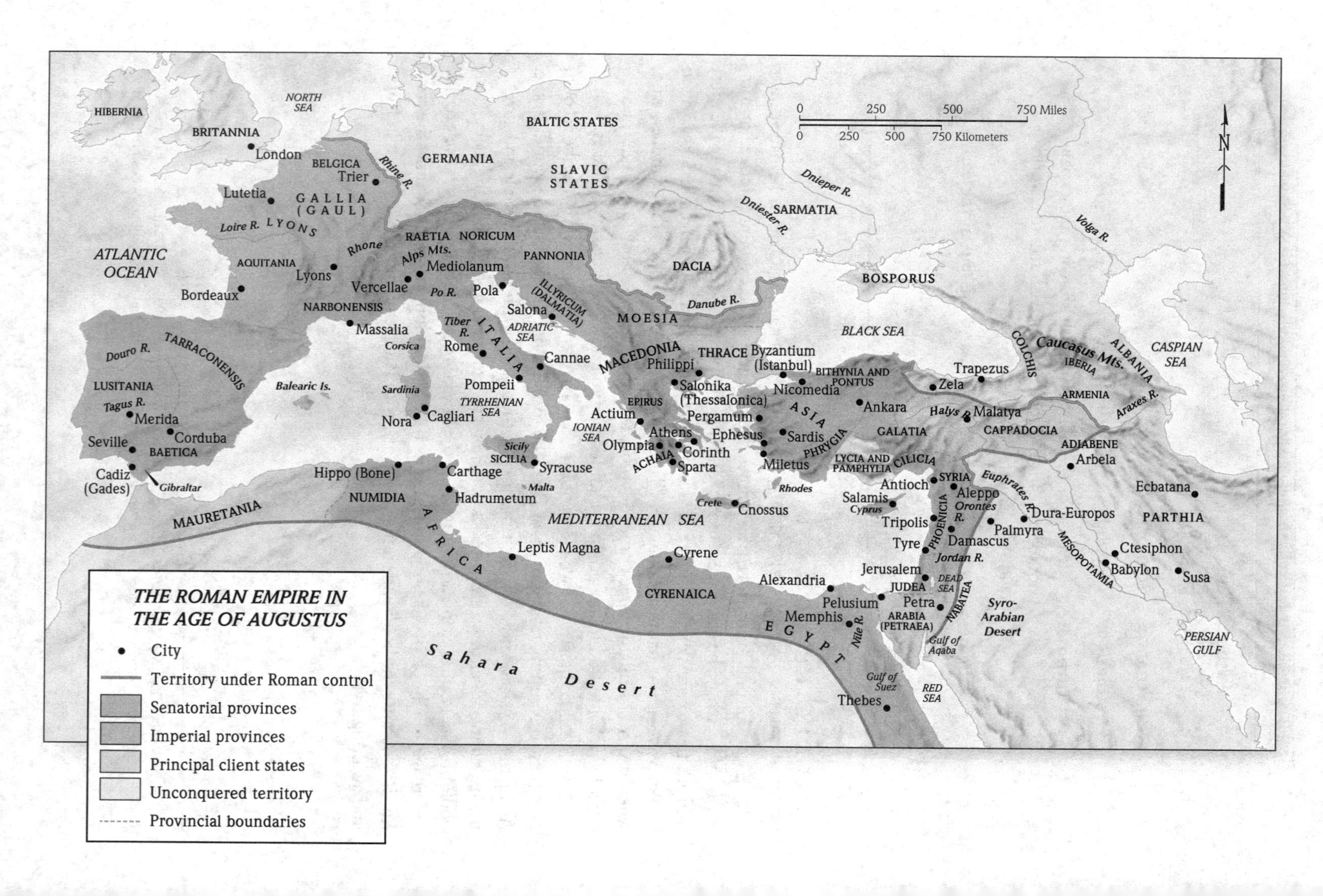
THE ROMAN EMPIRE IN THE AGE OF AUGUSTUS
City
Territory under Roman control
Senatorial provinces
Imperial provinces
Principal client states
Unconquered territory
Provincial boundaries
0 250 500 750 Miles
0 250 500 750 Kilometers
N
HIBERNIA
BRITANNIA
London
NORTH SEA
ATLANTIC OCEAN
BELGICA
Trier
GALLIA (GAUL)
LYONS
Lutetia
Loire R.
AQUITANIA
Bordeaux
Lyons
Rhine R.
Rhone
NARBONENSIS
Massalia
Vercellae
Balearic Is.
TARRACONENSIS
Douro R.
Tagus R.
LUSITANIA
Merida
Corduba
BAETICA
Seville
Cadiz (Gades)
Gibraltar
MAURETANIA
Hippo (Bone)
NUMIDIA
AFRICA
Carthage
Hadrumetum
Leptis Magna
Sahara Desert
GERMANIA
RAETIA
NORICUM
Alps Mts.
Mediolanum
Po R.
Corsica
Sardinia
Nora
Cagliari
BALTIC STATES
SLAVIC STATES
PANNONIA
Pola
ITALIA
Tiber R.
Rome
TYRRHENIAN SEA
Pompeii
Sicily
SICILIA
Salona
ADRIATIC SEA
ILLYRICUM (DALMATIA)
Cannae
Syracuse
Malta
IONIAN SEA
MEDITERRANEAN SEA
MOESIA
DACIA
Danube R.
MACEDONIA
Philippi
Salonika (Thessalonica)
THRACE
Byzantium (Istanbul)
EPIRUS
Actium
Olympia
ACHAIA
Athens
Corinth
Sparta
Pergamum
Ephesus
Sardis
Miletus
ASIA
PHRYGIA
Crete
Cnossus
Rhodes
Cyrene
CYRENAICA
SARMATIA
Dniester R.
Dnieper R.
Volga R.
BOSPORUS
BLACK SEA
Nicomedia
BITHYNIA AND PONTUS
Ankara
GALATIA
LYCIA AND PAMPHYLIA
CILICIA
Salamis
Cyprus
Alexandria
EGYPT
Pelusium
Memphis
Nile R.
Thebes
Gulf of Suez
RED SEA
Zela
Trapezus
COLCHIS
Caucasus Mts.
IBERIA
ALBANIA
CASPIAN SEA
ARMENIA
Araxes R.
Halys R.
Malatya
CAPPADOCIA
ADIABENE
Arbela
SYRIA
Antioch
Aleppo
Orontes R.
Euphrates R.
PHOENICIA
Tripolis
Tyre
Damascus
Palmyra
Jordan R.
DEAD SEA
JUDEA
Jerusalem
Petra
ARABIA (PETRAEA)
NABATEA
Gulf of Aqaba
Syro-Arabian Desert
Dura-Europos
MESOPOTAMIA
Ctesiphon
Babylon
Ecbatana
PARTHIA
Susa
PERSIAN GULF

HISTORY

Author

In a previous chapter, we identified Luke the beloved physician as the author of both the Gospel bearing his name and the book of Acts.[2] To recapitulate, Luke was a well-educated man, steeped in the OT (especially the LXX). He knew the geography of Palestine and the Mediterranean world. He was not an original disciple (see Luke 1:2) but was a traveling companion of Paul (thus the use of the first-person plural pronoun in the "we" passages starting at Acts 16:8–17; see Table 8.1 below) and revealed great respect for Paul in his writings.[3] Thus, while Luke was not an eyewitness of the events recorded in his Gospel, he was an eyewitness of a significant portion of events narrated in the second half of the book of Acts. Luke's close association with the apostle Paul ensured that the canonical criterion of apostolicity was met. Furthermore, if Paul endorsed the Gospel of Luke at 1 Timothy 5:18, it is no stretch to apply it to the second volume as well.

Table 8.1: The "We" Passages in Acts

Passages in Acts	Journeys and Locations	Event
16:8–17	Troas to Philippi	Ministry in Philippi
20:5–15	Philippi to Troas to Miletus	On way to Jerusalem
21:1–18	Miletus to Jerusalem via Caesarea	On way to Jerusalem
27:1–28:16	Caesarea to Rome	All the way to Rome

Date

Like its authorship, the date of the book of Acts was established in the chapter on the Gospel of Luke. The following brief discussion summarizes the major views on the subject.

[2] P. Walters (*The Assumed Authorial Unity of Luke and Acts: A Reassessment of the Evidence*, SNTSMS 145 [Cambridge, UK: Cambridge University Press, 2009]) recently has challenged the near-universal affirmation of common authorship. She investigates the literary seams and summaries of both Luke and Acts, applying a statistical (chi-square) analysis of her findings. J. B. Green (http://www.bookreviews.org/pdf/7084_7695.pdf) suggests Walters's work is hindered by a small set of data, a lack of a control set, questionable criteria to evaluate, and questionable assumptions. At the end of the day, he applauds the attempt but doubts the results. Likewise, the more sympathetic M. C. Parsons and H. M. Gorman ("The assumed Authorial Unity of Luke and Acts: a Review Essay," *Neot* 46 [2012]: 139–52) add that Walters's segmentation (essentially clause/sentence length) is questionable (we would suggest a *modern* imposition); they could not consistently reproduce the same results. They also question Walters's assumption that there is no outlying factor (especially lapse of time between writings) to affect stylistic differences. Quoting K. Lake, they deem her work a "failure, though a splendid one" suggesting that to this point the thesis's flaws cause doubt, but it might show future promise with refined methods (ibid., 149). On the whole, issue of author attribution through statistical analysis is often flawed on just such bases. For more information, see L. S. Kellum, *The Unity of the Farewell Discourse: The Literary Integrity of John 13:31–16:33*, JSNTSupp 256 (London, England: T&T Clark, 2005).

[3] C. Keener (*Acts: An Exegetical Commentary, Vol. 1, Introduction and 1:1–2:47* [Grand Rapids, MI: Baker, 2012], 407) notes that the "we passages" indicate eye-witness testimony and are "our most secure available observation regarding authorship."

There are basically three positions set forth in the relevant literature: (1) a date prior to AD 70;[4] (2) a date of AD 70–100;[5] and (3) a date in the second century.[6]

Few scholars today date Acts in the second century.[7] The more popular date (especially among less conservative commentators) is one sometime after AD 75.[8] This is usually based on these scholars' solution to the Synoptic Problem (typically in terms of Markan priority) and a dating of Mark in the mid- to late 60s.[9] The abrupt ending of Acts is then explained in terms of Luke completing his purpose.[10]

An early date, however, remains the best option for the book of Acts. The aforementioned abrupt ending; the neutral, if not friendly, presentation of the Roman Empire;[11] the lack of mention of the Pauline Letters; and the lack of mention of the Jewish war and its events all point to an early date for Acts.[12] The ending of Acts is best explained as Luke having recorded everything that has happened up to this point in Paul's mission. Although not universally accepted, an early date is thus most plausible in light of the available evidence.[13]

---

[4] See, e.g., D. L. Bock, *Acts*, BECNT (Grand Rapids, MI: Baker, 2007), 27. He prefers a date just before AD 70.

[5] See, e.g., Keener, *Acts*, 1:400. For Keener, a late date of Mark, Synoptic solutions, and a date during the lifetime of an eye-witness necessitate this date. D. G. Peterson (*The Acts of the Apostles*, PTNC [Grand Rapids, MI: Eerdmans, 2009], 5) is non-committal: "A date in the 70s seems entirely reasonable and consistent with the evidence from the documents themselves." However, he affirms that a good case can be made for an AD 62–64 date (ibid.)

[6] See, e.g., R. I. Pervo, "Dating Acts," *Forum* 5, no. 1 (2002): 53–72 and M. C. Parsons, *Acts*, Paideia Commentary on the New Testament (Grand Rapids, MI: Baker, 2008), 3, 17.

[7] A second-century date for Acts was proposed more frequently in the past. For example, the Tübingen School posited a reconciling tendency in the book of Acts and assigned the book to the second century. A few have suggested a later date on other grounds: see F. C. Burkitt, *The Gospel History and Its Transmission*, 3rd ed. (Edinburgh, Scotland: T&T Clark, 1911), 105–10; M. S. Enslin, "Once Again, Luke and Paul," *ZNW* 61 (1970): 253, 271; and J. C. O'Neill, *The Theology of Acts in Its Historical Setting* (London, England: SPCK, 1961), 21, 26.

[8] How one dates the book of Acts is not in itself a litmus test for a high view of Scripture. See, e.g., Polhill, *Acts*, 31.

[9] For this argument, see J. A. Fitzmyer, *The Acts of the Apostles: A New Translation with Introduction and Commentary*, AB 31 (Garden City, NY: Doubleday, 1998), 54–55.

[10] E.g., D. J. Williams, *Acts*, NIBC 5 (Grand Rapids, MI: Zondervan, 1990), 13; and W. G. Kümmel, *Introduction to the New Testament*, rev. ed., trans. H. C. Kee (Nashville, TN: Abingdon, 1975), 186. It must also be noted that this is not just a "liberal" versus "conservative" option, for the generally conservative D. Wenham dates Acts rather late: D. Wenham and S. Walton, *Exploring the New Testament: A Guide to the Gospels and Acts*, vol. 1 (Downers Grove, IL: InterVarsity, 2001), 297.

[11] P. Parker ("The 'Former Treatise' and the Date of Acts," *JBL* 84 [1965]: 53) noted, "For any Christian to write, thereafter, with the easy optimism of Acts 28 would require almost subhuman obtuseness."

[12] For a slightly different track to reach the same conclusion, see A. J. Matill Jr., "The Date and Purpose of Luke-Acts: Rackham Reconsidered," *CBQ* 40 (1978): 335–50.

[13] The usual objections are well summarized in a recent monograph by T. M. Troftgruben (*A Conclusion Unhindered: A Study of the Ending of Acts within its Literary Environment,* WUNT 2, vol. 280 [Tübingen, Germany: Mohr Siebeck, 2010], 8–11). He discounts the theory for three basic reasons. 1) The majority of scholars do not accept an early date for Acts. This "counting scholars" technique is, frankly, far too pervasive and philosophically flawed. The majority opinion on any matter is fluid from generation to generation and often reverts to previous paradigms. For example, John's philosophical background has, in the academy, moved from Jewish to Hellenistic, now back to Jewish. The "majority opinion" is by nature fluid. Thus, it is not a particularly strong appeal. In this case, it is further complicated by appeals to a synoptic theory that places Mark both late and the first Gospel written. So then, the argument is actually based on two appeals to "the majority opinion." 2) Troftgruben asserts that Paul's speech at Miletus (Acts 20:17–38) hints at Paul's death (vv 23–25, 28). Thus, Luke did know events after AD 62. We would suggest, first, that if it were really a prophecy of Paul's death why would Luke, who is very interested in fulfilled prophecy (see below) not note the fulfillment of it? The literary artistry is not foiled in any way by the

If Paul (1) was released from his first Roman imprisonment in which he found himself at the end of the book of Acts; (2) engaged in several years of further missionary travels and ministry as the Pastorals suggest; (3) his martyrdom was preceded by a second, significantly harsher, Roman imprisonment as 2 Timothy seems to indicate; and (4) as tradition indicates, was martyred in ca. AD 65/66 during the persecution under Nero (reigning from AD 54 to 68) subsequent to the great fire in Rome (AD 64), 60 is the most reasonable date for the conclusion of the book of Acts and a date of composition shortly thereafter.

Provenance

If the evidence for the date has been rightly evaluated, the only option for the provenance of the book is the city of Rome. If Luke had caught up in time with Paul so that the apostle was awaiting trial in Rome at the time of writing and if the "we" sections are an indication of personal involvement, then Luke was with Paul when he wrote the book. This was the view of Irenaeus (ca. AD 130–200), Eusebius (ca. AD 260–340), and Jerome (ca. AD 345–420).[14] The Anti-Marcionite Prologue mentions Achaia as the place of publication for Luke's Gospel, though it does not identify a provenance for the book of Acts, unless an identical provenance is assumed, and no Anti-Marcionite Prologue for Acts is extant. Jerome's belief that Luke wrote from Rome was self-admittedly adduced from the ending of Acts.[15] The other church fathers may well have come to the same conclusion. Ultimately, we are left with a few contradictory snippets in the tradition. This makes the provenance difficult to pinpoint. Like Irenaeus, Jerome, and Eusebius, one may deduce from the ending that Luke was with Paul in Rome at the time of writing without staking any undue weight on this deduction. (Also, at a later point, Luke is said to be the only one left with Paul in Rome; 2 Tim 4:11.)

Destination

Theophilus, like Josephus's Epaphroditus, goes unnamed in the rest of the narrative. As discussed in chapter 6 on Luke's Gospel, little is known about him other than that he may have been a Roman official (see the designation "most honorable" in Luke 1:3; it also occurs in Acts 23:26; 24:3; 26:25 with reference to Felix and Festus) and that he had received

---

notation. Second, the text is not so plain as portrayed. Troftgruben is again operating under antecedent judgments regarding the speeches in Acts. Maybe, instead of a purely Lukan composition (see below), the text accurately portrays Paul's readiness to face death. 3) Troftgruben asserts that if the ending of Acts is due to Luke catching up to Paul in time, the ending is haphazard. Instead Troftgruben will suggest the ending has a literary appropriateness for Luke's purposes. We would suggest that catching up to Paul in time and literary appropriateness are not necessarily mutually exclusive. Troftgruben's ultimate thesis that the ending (due to its openness) points to "an expansive story that stretches to the end of the age" (ibid., 188) is certainly worthy of consideration. It is not, however, dependent on disproving an early date nor the sole explanation for the abrupt ending. As noted above, the ending is only one of a series of evidences that point to an early date. All things considered, it is more probable that Luke's conclusion is the way that it is due to both chronological and literary concerns. In other words, he expresses the ending the way he does because there's no more to say at the time and he expresses it in a way that fits his theological concerns.

[14] Irenaeus, *Against Heresies* 3.1.1; 3.14.1; Eusebius, *Eccl. Hist.* 2.22.6; and Jerome, *De Viris Illustribus* 7.

[15] Jerome, *De Viris Illustribus* 7.

previous information regarding the Christian faith (Luke 1:4). Most likely, he was Luke's literary patron, in which case he would not only have paid the price of publication but may have housed Luke during the book's production and made the manuscript available for copying subsequent to its completion.

In addition, Luke likely had a target audience beyond Theophilus. In determining the makeup of Luke's intended readers, it is instructive to look at the kind of information that Luke expected or did not expect his audience to know. On the one hand, he did not expect his readers to know the basic details of Judean topography, as in the statement that Mount Olivet was near Jerusalem (Acts 1:12). Nor did he expect them to know the local language: Aramaic terms are explained (see 1:12, 19; 4:36; 9:36; 13:8). At the same time, no explanation is given with regard to Jewish institutions such as Pentecost (2:1; 20:16), "a Sabbath day's journey" (1:12), uncleanness (10:14), and "Passover" (12:4), which suggests that Luke expected his audience to be familiar with this kind of information.[16] Likewise, it may be assumed that since the OT quotes are from the LXX, this was the Bible of choice among Luke's readers.

Finally, the apologetic thrust of the book, setting forth the expansion of Christianity from a Jewish sect to a worldwide movement, may also indicate a particular target audience: anyone interested in the astonishing rise of the Christian movement from humble beginnings in Jerusalem to the empire's capital, Rome. On the whole, then, Acts is a book that would resonate well with non-Aramaic speakers familiar with the Greek OT. This would have included Gentile Christians, and it would not have ruled out Diaspora Jews or Jewish Christians living outside of Palestine. Beyond this, anyone interested in the nature and phenomenal rise of Christianity in the first few decades of the church would have found the book of Acts valuable and informative.

Purpose

Numerous proposals have been made regarding the purpose of Acts. These include evangelism,[17] an apology or defense of the Christian faith,[18] Paul's legal defense,[19] various

---

[16] C. J. Hemer, *The Book of Acts in the Setting of Hellenistic History* (Winona Lake, IN: Eisenbrauns, 1990), 107.

[17] E.g., W. J. Larkin, *Acts*, IVPNTC (Downers Grove, IL: InterVarsity, 1995), 19–20; W. Neil, *Acts*, New Century Bible Commentary (Grand Rapids, MI: Eerdmans, 1981), 28.

[18] R. H. Gundry, *A Survey of the New Testament,* 4th ed. (Grand Rapids, MI: Zondervan, 2003), 304; F. F. Bruce, *The Book of Acts,* NICNT (Grand Rapids, MI: Eerdmans, 1987), 20; D. A. deSilva, *An Introduction to the New Testament: Contexts, Methods, and Ministry Formation* (Downers Grove, IL: InterVarsity, 2004), 354; L. T. Johnson, *The Acts of the Apostles,* SacPag 5 (Collegeville, MN: Liturgical Press, 1992).

[19] B. H. Streeter, *The Four Gospels: A Study of Origins* (London, England: St. Martins, 1953), 539. Kümmel (*Introduction,* 162) also lists Munck, Sahlin, and Koh.

Something to Think About: Christianity Takes the World by Storm

If the first generation of the Christian church proves anything, it is this: the power of God is infinitely greater than any human obstacles in its way. A humble Galilean craftsman, who suffered an untimely death and accumulated no earthly possessions, wrote no books, and left behind nothing but a small band of disheartened followers, spawned a movement so powerful that it took the Roman Empire by storm.

How was this possible? There is only one satisfying answer: the same Jesus who was crucified on a hill outside of Jerusalem rose again from the dead three days later and was exalted to the right hand of God. As Peter proclaimed at Pentecost, "God has raised this Jesus; we are all witnesses of this. Therefore, since he has been exalted to the right hand of God and has received from the Father the promised Holy Spirit, he has poured out what you both see and hear" (2:32–33).

The rest of the book of Acts records the amazing, astounding, breathtaking, irresistible progress of the Christian gospel in a world where the Jews fiercely oppose the early church's mission and where, ironically, the Romans protect Paul and the early Christians from certain death. Internal obstacles, whether dishonesty or potential disunity, are overcome, as are persecution and various external threats. Not clever strategy but humble trust in God and faithful witness to him empower the early Christians, who prove victorious again and again.

Luke's account of the spiritual exploits of the early church can serve as a mighty inspiration to the church of all ages, which is faced with the same challenge of bearing witness to the living, resurrected Christ in a world hostile to the gospel message. As we continue this godly legacy, we must make sure our trust, as that of the first Christians, is in the same God who raised Jesus from the dead and for whom no obstacle is too great if we only put our trust in him and his awesome power rather than in our own ability to overcome.

theological concerns,[20] the historical basis of the establishment and growth of the kingdom of God,[21] and evangelism and edification.[22]

In considering the purpose of Acts, it must be remembered that the work is a sequel to Luke's Gospel. This does not necessarily mean that the purpose of Acts is identical to

---

[20] These include the geographical movement of the gospel (T. Zahn, *Die Apostelgeschichte des Lukas* [Leipzig, Germany: A. Deichert, 1919–21], 14–15); the adjudication of church controversies (E. Trocmé, *Le 'Livre des Actes' et l'Histoire* [Paris, France: University of France Press, 1957]); or the explanation of the delay of the *parousia* or Second Coming (H. Conzelmann, *The Theology of St. Luke* [New York, NY: Harper & Row, 1961]).

[21] I. H. Marshall, *The Acts of the Apostles*, TNTC (Grand Rapids, MI: Eerdmans, 1980), 17–22.

[22] So D. A. Carson and D. J. Moo, *An Introduction to the New Testament,* 2nd ed. (Grand Rapids, MI: Zondervan, 2005), 305; R. E. Brown, *An Introduction to the New Testament* (New York, NY: Doubleday, 1997), 272–73; and Kümmel, *Introduction,* 163.

the purpose of Luke's Gospel; it means that the former should be related appropriately to the latter (see esp. Acts 1:1). If the preface to Luke applies to Acts as well—and given the brevity of Acts' preface, this is most likely the case—then Luke set out to write an orderly account and to provide assurance and an apology or defense of the Christian faith. But what kind of defense did Luke provide?

The first and best indication of purpose is the literary structure of Acts, which revolves around showing the early expansion of the church from a local sect to a worldwide movement as empowered by God. Each expansion is brought about by the leading of the Holy Spirit rather than by the disciples' own initiative. In this theological emphasis, the book manifests the same focus on God's plan (including promise and fulfillment) that is prominent in Luke's Gospel. This also answers the question of why a sequel to Luke's Gospel was needed in the first place. The Gospel is "about all that Jesus began to do and teach" (Acts 1:1), and Acts narrates the continuation of that which was begun there. The story of Jesus is not complete until the gospel has moved from the Jewish capital to "the end of the earth" (Acts 1:8).

It is sometimes claimed that Luke's Gospel is continually journeying toward Jerusalem (especially the "Lukan Travel Narrative") and that the book of Acts is moving away from Jerusalem to the "ends of the earth." But this is an oversimplification. More precisely, the book of Acts *spirals* out from Jerusalem and Palestine. In the second half of the book, Paul was continually returning to Jerusalem, only to set out deeper and deeper into the Gentile world. Three factors point to a sustained apologetic for Gentile inclusion on the basis of the Jewish rejection of the Messiah. First is the sustained apologetic for Gentile inclusion in the first part of the book that culminated in the Jerusalem Council (Acts 15:1–29). Second is Paul's consistent pattern of preaching in the local synagogue in each city before moving on to the Gentiles, which is followed by his repeated returns to Jerusalem.

This prominently surfaces in Acts 28:25–27, where Paul, upon reaching Rome, first speaks to the Jewish leaders there. Some of them believe, but to those who do not Paul cites Isaiah 6:9–10:

> And [the Lord] replied: Go! Say to these people: Keep listening, but do not understand; keep looking, but do not perceive. Make the minds of these people dull; deafen their ears and blind their eyes; otherwise they might see with their eyes and hear with their ears, understand with their minds, turn back, and be healed.

Having thus explained the rejection of the gospel by the Jews, Paul drew the following implication: "Therefore, let it be known to you that this salvation of God has been sent to the Gentiles; they will listen" (28:28). With this, the book of Acts closes.

The literary structure of the book thus points to a historical apologetic that explains God's plan of extending the gospel to the Gentiles while including believing Jews as well. While it can be surmised that Luke's target audience included non-Aramaic speakers familiar with the OT, the apologetic presented is wide-ranging, including the evangelism of Diaspora Jews as well as the edification of Gentile Christians who worship the Jewish Messiah whom the Jews had rejected. Luke's purpose was to write an accurate historical narrative designed to edify his Christian readers and to help them evangelize unbelievers.

LITERATURE

Genre

The question regarding the genre of Acts is more than merely a matter of curiosity. The answer helps one to identify the expectations one should have when approaching the book. Certain genres of literature have no or little expectation of trustworthiness or historical veracity (e.g., a fairy tale or a novel). It matters, therefore, if the book of Acts was written as a collection of legends or as a serious historical narrative. For this reason, identifying the genre of Acts is a significant aid in understanding Luke's purpose.

As with the Gospels, the literary genre of Acts is difficult to determine with certainty. There are few (if any) works of a similar nature prior to the publication of Acts. Also, again similar to the Gospels, a host of apocryphal "Acts" were written in imitation of the canonical book.[23] This is not to say that the term "Acts" is original. In literary circles, "Acts" (*praxeis*) referred to the heroic deeds of mythical or historical figures, but this kind of writing was most likely not an established literary genre (even less was the term featured in titles) when Luke penned this volume.[24]

The Gospels have been identified by some as a specialized form of biography, with the words and deeds of Jesus at the center. If so, at first sight, Luke's second volume does not seem to fit this description, as it features the deeds of more than one person: Peter, Stephen, Philip, Paul, and so on. There are several significant human agents, but there is one, and only one, major divine agent underlying the entire plot of the book of Acts: the Holy Spirit. For this reason, rather than identifying the book as presenting the "Acts of the Apostles," it may be more accurate to say that at its heart are the "Acts of the Holy Spirit." But even this needs to be adjusted, for his acts are the acts of the risen Christ.[25]

---

[23] E.g., The Acts of Paul and Thecla; The Acts of John; The Acts of Peter; et al.

[24] Fitzmyer, *Acts of the Apostles*, 47; and Carson and Moo, *Introduction to the New Testament*, 301.

[25] Thompson rightly asserts, "As important as the Holy Spirit is in Acts, it should be noted that even this designation does not quite capture the emphasis of Luke in Acts. Acts 1:1 indicates that the book is going to be about what Jesus is continuing to do and teach; therefore, the 'Acts of the Risen Lord Jesus's would be a better title. It must be said, though, that this could also be understood as a shorthand expression for something like 'the Acts of the Lord Jesus, through his people, by the Holy Spirit, for the accomplishment of God's purposes'!" A. J. Thompson, *The Acts of the Risen Lord Jesus: Luke's Account of God's Unfolding Plan*, NSBT 27 (Downer's Grove, IL: InterVarsity, 2011), 48–49.

In fact, this unity of what Jesus began to do during his earthly ministry and what he began to do in the power of the Holy Spirit subsequent to his ascension seems to be precisely what Luke himself implies in the opening verse of Acts: "I wrote the first narrative, Theophilus, about all that Jesus began to do and teach until the day he was taken up, after he had given instructions through the Holy Spirit to the apostles he had chosen" (Acts 1:1–2). This may constitute the common ground between Luke's Gospel and Acts and mark both books as a literary unity.[26]

In recent times the genre of Acts has been identified by some as related to the romance literature of its time, as if it were a kind of novel.[27] This is ultimately unproven and unhelpful.[28] More likely, the genre of Acts is bound up with historiography. The early church fathers, familiar with the different literary genres, referred to the book as a "history."[29] Although Luke did not use the term himself, there is good evidence that he set out to write a historical account. He wrote in a septuagintal style resembling OT narratives.[30] It thus appears that Luke saw himself as writing sacred history.[31]

Another good indication of this comes from the prefaces of Luke and Acts. D. Aune suggested that Luke's Gospel exhibits the following four of seven features of ancient historiography: (1) requests and dedications; (2) mention of predecessors; (3) use of appropriate methodology; and (4) reasons for writing.[32] If the preface to the Gospel covers both

---

[26] Against M. C. Parsons and R. I. Pervo (*Rethinking the Unity of Luke and Acts* [Minneapolis, MN: Fortress, 1993], 20–44), who identified Acts as a "romance" and registered concerns about what they see as a shift in genre between Luke and Acts. Also, Luke mentioned other Gospels in Luke 1:1, but he did not mention any such predecessors in the case of the book of Acts (see B. Witherington III, *The Acts of the Apostles: A Socio-Rhetorical Commentary* [Grand Rapids, MI: Eerdmans, 1998], 9).

[27] See R. I. Pervo, *Profit with Delight* (Philadelphia, PA: Fortress, 1987). However, just because the work is entertaining does not mean that it must be in the novel genre. Pervo's genre identification is followed by the Westar Institute's "Acts Seminar." This seminar, of which Pervo is a fellow, is a sequel to the notorious "Jesus Seminar." D. E. Smith ("Was There a Jerusalem Church? Christian Origins According to Acts and Paul," *Forum* 3 [Spring 2000]: 57) said, "Today some scholars still propose that Acts can be defined under the genre of ancient history in some sense, but the burden of proof has now shifted to those who would claim historicity for Acts." In that same volume, D. R. MacDonald ("Luke's Emulation of Homer: Acts 12:1–17 and Illiad *[sic]* 24," *Forum* 3 [Fall 1999]: 197) stated that "the Acts of the Apostles is a self-conscious fiction. . . . The historical stratum, if any, is extremely thin and from my perspective quite uninteresting." Lucian, in the second-century work *How to Write History*, noted that the historian's task was not free from providing entertainment value. He wrote, "The task of the historian is . . . to give a fine arrangement to events and illuminate them as vividly as possible" (51).

[28] Marshall, *Fresh Look*, 19–21.

[29] See Clement, *Stromateis* 5.12; Jerome, *Epistles* 53.8. Jerome called it "unadorned history"; Lat. *nuda historia*, which is lit. "naked history."

[30] Since Luke demonstrated an ability to write in other styles, this is most likely deliberate (so I. H. Marshall, *Acts*, TNTC [Grand Rapids, MI: Eerdmans, 1980], 18). J. Polhill (*Acts*, NAC 26 [Nashville, TN: B&H, 1992], 43) noted, "Throughout Acts there is a verisimilitude in the narrative. Jews speak with a Jewish accent, Athenian philosophers speak in Atticism, and Roman officials speak and write in the customary legal style. Luke showed not only a familiarity with such linguistic idiosyncrasies but also the ability to depict them through his style of writing."

[31] Whether Luke understood himself to be writing an inspired work is another question.

[32] The full list includes requests and dedications, an apology for defective style, comments on the value and utility of history, mention of predecessors, assurance of impartiality, use of appropriate methodology, and reasons for writing (D. Aune, *New Testament in Its Literary Environment*, 89–90). L. Alexander (*The Preface to Luke's Gospel: Literary Convention and Social Context in Luke 1:1–4 and Acts 1:1*, SNTSMS 78 [Cambridge, UK: Cambridge University Press, 1993]) disagreed and

volumes, then Luke claimed to have written an account that is trustworthy, emphasizing the veracity of his research. Moreover, Luke produced a linear historical writing. He was careful to set events clearly at a point in history (called "synchronisms") and, in line with Greek historiography, arranged his work geographically.[33]

However, Acts does not seem to fit any one genre of historiography. Like Plutarch's *Lives*, Acts features the lives and words of well-known people like Peter, Stephen, and Paul. At the same time, the book shifts from person to person. Stephen is only important in Acts 6 and 7, Philip in Acts 8. After Acts 15, Peter drops off the scene altogether; and then the main character is Paul, as the gospel moves through the known world. It seems that the personalities involved serve a purpose; thus, the book of Acts is not meant as a mere chronicle of their lives.

The genre of Acts is also similar to OT historiography. Similar to the Gospels, the history is properly seen as ancient historiography, with a theological focus. Blomberg called it a "theological history,"[34] which seems a satisfying way of capturing the nature of the book. Keener summarizes it well: "Acts is history, probably apologetic history in the form of a historical monograph with a narrow focus on the expansion of the gospel message from Jerusalem to Rome."[35] If so, the reader should expect the book to set forth a historical narrative that strives not only for accuracy in its portrayal of events but also seeks to be God-centered in its approach to history. In Acts, God is engendering salvation history. Thus, the next question: How accurate is this history?

The Historical Reliability of Acts

Introduction Assessments of Luke's accuracy in Acts range from complete affirmation to total denial.[36] Some, such as Pervo, complimented Luke's literary ability while denigrating his accuracy in recording historical details. Pervo claimed that Luke was "bumbling and incompetent as an historian."[37] Those advocating a radical denial of historicity include M. Dibelius, H. Conzelmann, O. Vielhauer, and E. Haenchen. On the other side of the spectrum, F. F. Bruce, C. Hemer, W. Gasque, and I. H. Marshall, among others, strongly defend Luke's accuracy. In recent days many have sought to find middle

---

posited that the prefaces in Luke-Acts are more akin to scientific and technical treatises that were written for a less educated audience. She drew the conclusion that Luke was written for an audience with the same level of education. Of course, not every element had to appear for a work to be considered historiography. When the prefaces to Luke and Acts are compared to Josephus's *Against Apion*, there is an amazing similarity. See Josephus's preface in the second book against Apion: "In the former book, most honored Epaphroditus, I have demonstrated our antiquity, and confirmed the truth of what I have said, from the writings of the Phoenicians, and Chaldeans, and Egyptians" (Josephus, *Apion* 2.1).

[33] See especially the works of Ephorus (Witherington, *Acts of the Apostles*, 34–35).

[34] C. L. Blomberg, *From Pentecost to Patmos: An Introduction to Acts through Revelation* (Nashville, TN: B&H, 2006), 17.

[35] Keener, *Acts*, 1:115.

[36] For the former, see W. W. Gasque, *A History of the Criticism of the Acts of the Apostles*, BGBE 17 (Tübingen, Germany: J. C. B. Mohr, 1975); for the latter, see E. Haenchen, *The Acts of the Apostles: A Commentary*, trans. B. Noble, G. Shinn, H. Anderson, and R. M. Wilson (Philadelphia, PA: Westminster, 1971), 14–50.

[37] Pervo, *Profit with Delight*, 3.

ground. One of these scholars is J. Fitzmyer, who noted, "It is clear today that a middle ground has to be sought between the skeptical approach and a conservative reaction to it. One has to admit that at times Luke's information is faulty and that he has confused some things in his narrative, but by and large he does present us with a reliable account of much of what he recounts."[38] Bumbling and incompetent, historically accurate, or somewhere in between—which is it?

Geography, Sociology, and Specific Events Luke's general reliability in verifiable matters has been well attested. In matters of geography, he knew the topography of Jerusalem (e.g., Acts 1:12, 19; 3:2, 11). He was also familiar with the geography of Asia Minor. In 13:4–5, the natural crossing is correctly called "ports." In 16:1, Paul passes through the "Cilician gates," and Luke correctly chronicled Derbe as the first city on the route. Luke was also well acquainted with the Greek peninsula. In 16:12, Philippi is correctly described as a Roman colony. In 17:6, the board of magistrates in Thessalonica is properly identified as "politarchs." More examples could be given. Suffice it to say that C. Hemer's fifty-one-page treatment "Specific Local Knowledge of Luke" has conclusively settled the matter of Luke's geographical and provincial accuracy in the affirmative.[39]

Luke's descriptions are also accurate in terms of specific people. The title of the emperor was "Augustus" (transliterated *Augoustos* in Luke 2:1), but on the lips of a Roman official it was formally and correctly rendered *Sebastos* (Acts 25:21, 25). Cyprus was governed by a proconsul at Paphos (13:7). Luke correctly stated that Ananias was the high priest (23:2). The Roman governor of Malta was known to be the "first man" (*prōtos*) of the island (28:7). Gallio was proconsul of Achaia (Greece) in Corinth starting in the year 44 (18:12).[40]

Luke also correctly portrayed elements of ancient culture. He accurately noted that the people at Lystra spoke their own dialect (14:11). They were also particular worshippers of Hermes and Zeus (see the ascription of the titles "Hermes" and "Zeus" to Paul and Barnabas in 14:12). Also, Luke accurately detailed ancient navigation (chap. 26). Classicist A. N. Sherwin-White ably demonstrated that Luke presented an accurate description of Roman jurisprudence.[41] Because Luke narrated many encounters with the Roman courts in Acts (especially in the last quarter of the book), this covers a large portion of the narrative.

Further, Luke correctly narrated events recorded elsewhere in ancient historiography. These included a famine during the reign of Claudius (11:28), the death of Herod Agrippa I (12:19–23), the edict of Claudius (18:2), and the replacement of the proconsul Felix by Porcius Festus (24:27).

---

[38] Fitzmyer, *Acts*, 124.

[39] Hemer, *Book of Acts in the Setting of Hellenistic History*, 108–58.

[40] These and other examples can be found under the headings "Common Knowledge" and "Specialized Knowledge" in Hemer, *Book of Acts in the Setting of Hellenistic History*, 107–8.

[41] A. N. Sherwin-White, *Roman Law and Roman Society in the New Testament* (Grand Rapids, MI: Baker, 1963).

On only a few points is Luke severely criticized in verifiable matters outside of Scripture. The first is found in the short speech of Gamaliel when he mentioned a certain Theudas and Judas (5:34–37). Theudas, according to Gamaliel, claimed to be someone important, gathered 400 men, but was killed and his followers scattered. A Theudas whom we know from Josephus appeared ten to fifteen years after Gamaliel's speech.[42] This is seen by many as an anachronism on Luke's part.[43] Others suggest that it was Josephus who mixed up his chronology.[44] A possible key to unlocking this puzzle may be the mention of a certain Judas who is said to have come after Theudas. The Judas of Galilee we know comes from the time near Jesus's birth (at the death of Herod the Great). It is possible that Gamaliel's Theudas was not the same man as Josephus's.[45] Since Theudas was a common name, and after the death of Herod numerous uprisings occurred, this otherwise unknown Theudas may be one of them.[46]

The second specific charge against Luke's accuracy is related to his use of numbers in the case of the number of the Egyptian's band of 4,000 (21:38). Josephus also knows of an Egyptian terrorist but said he had 30,000 men.[47] But in this instance Luke should be preferred over Josephus since Josephus had a well-demonstrated tendency to inflate numbers.[48]

---

[42] Josephus wrote, "During the period when Fadus was procurator of Judaea [ca. AD 44], a certain impostor named Theudas persuaded the majority of the masses to take up their possessions and to follow him to the Jordan River" (*Ant.* 20.97). But Fadus would have none of it, and Theudas was captured and his head cut off.

[43] See, e.g., Barrett, *Acts*, 1:296 and Keener, *Acts*, 2:1236; both suggest it is minor and need not impinge on Luke's overall accuracy.

[44] See Witherington, *Acts*, 238–39. Witherington suggests either a mistake by Josephus or another Theudas as the answer to this problem. In Josephus's account (*Ant.* 20.97–99) Theudas's revolt is followed by a revolt of Judas of Galilee's sons. We noted in chap. 6 that J. H. Rhoads ("Josephus Misdated the Census of Quirinius," *JETS* 54 [2011]) has made a compelling case that Josephus misdated the census of Quirinius. If so, he may have done something similar here. For a number of problems in Josephus, see S. Cohen, *Josephus in Galilee and Rome: His Vita and Development as a Historian* (Leiden, Netherlands: Brill, 1979).

[45] While Gamaliel's summation is brief, there are some differences. For example, Gamaliel said that Theudas gathered an army of 400 men, while Josephus referred to "the majority of the masses." Furthermore, Barrett (*Acts*, 295) notes that the western MS D and Eusebius (*Eccl. Hist.* 2.11.1) both describe Theudas's death by suicide. This is in stark contrast to Josephus's account.

[46] K. F. Nögren (*Commentar* über *die Apostelgeschichte des Lukas* [Leipzig: Dörfling und Franke, 1882], 147) noted that Josephus related four Simons in a 40-year time span, and three men named Judas in a 10-year span, who each led a rebellion. Cf. Josephus, *Ant.* 17.269: "Now, at this time there were ten thousand other disorders in Judea, which were like tumults." According to *Ant.* 17.285, this state lasted a long time.

[47] The account is found in Josephus, *Jewish War* 2.261–63; *Ant.* 20.169–72. See P. W. Barnett, "The Jewish Sign Prophets, A.D. 40–70—Their Intentions and Origin," *NTS* 27 (1981): 679–97. Another complaint against Luke's accuracy occurs in this passage in Lysias's use of the latinized term for "terrorist" (Gr.: *sicarii*). It is said that from Josephus, the term's usage here is an anachronism. However, M. A. Brighton ("The Sicarii in Acts: A New Perspective" *JETS* 54 (2011):547–58) has ably demonstrated that a closer reading of Josephus vindicates the usage in Acts.

[48] Keener, *Acts* 3:3176. Polhill, *Acts*, 455, notes that it has been suggested that a scribal error accounts for Josephus's inflation. The uncial letter D (4 in Greek) was accidentally replaced by a L (30 in Greek). In Greek, it is an easy mistake of the eye, for the capital letters are very similar; cf. Δ (D) with Λ (L). A hazy or defective baseline moves the number by 26!

Those striking the middle ground often concede the point of Luke's accuracy in historical matters but do not necessarily extend it to the story he told.[49] These scholars take issue with Luke at three major points. Fitzmyer's threefold charge is representative: (1) the speeches in Acts are Lukan compositions; (2) there are tendentious story lines (Fitzmyer cites Acts 15 as a conflation of two councils); and (3) the recounting of miracles and heavenly interventions are judged problematic in terms of historicity.[50] It is therefore necessary to address these three issues next. As will be seen, in each case closer scrutiny vindicates Luke's accuracy.

The Speeches of Acts The speeches take up about 25 to 30 percent of the book, depending on how one identifies a speech. Some have suggested that the speeches in Acts are wholly Luke's invention, so much so that some theologians do not even use Paul's speeches in Acts to develop a Pauline theology.

Although some claim that the precritical understanding of the speeches in Acts considered them *verbatim* reports, this is not the case. Many pre-Enlightenment exegetes considered them to be summaries rather than dictated notes.[51] Indeed, *verbatim* reports are a virtual impossibility given the textual evidence. First, in some cases the receptor language is different from the original speech. Luke said that Paul's defense against the mob in the temple was in Aramaic (21:40), as was the heavenly voice at Paul's conversion (26:14). On other occasions the language used would most likely have been Greek, such as Paul's speech in the synagogue at Pisidian Antioch (13:15) or the conversation between Paul and the commander of the guard (21:37). But in none of these cases is the conclusion warranted that these were *verbatim* reports.

Second, the text itself indicates at places that the speeches have been summarized. For example, Peter's sermon at the temple square lasted from three p.m. to evening (see 3:1; 4:3), but what we have of it only covers seventeen verses. No one suggests that these seventeen verses represent the totality of the original speech.

Finally, in matters of literary and linguistic style, Luke's diction is evident even in the speeches. But the rhetorical style (i.e., the shape of the speeches) is suitable to the context. For instance, Peter's Pentecost sermon reads like that of an OT prophet (2:14–36), but Stephen spoke like a Hellenistic Jew (chap. 7).[52] Paul's speech at the synagogue in Pisidian Antioch resembles that of a rabbi (13:16–41), while he used the structure of a philosopher

---

[49] C. K. Barrett ("The Historicity of Acts," *JTS* 50 [1999]: 525) stated, "The accurate accounts of the working of Greek cities cannot prove that Luke's main plot is not wholly or in part fictitious."

[50] Fitzmyer, *Acts*, 127.

[51] W. W. Gasque, *History of the Criticism of the Acts of the Apostles* (Grand Rapids, MI: Eerdmans, 1975), 20.

[52] J. J. Scott Jr. ("Stephen's Defense and the World Mission of the People of God," *JETS* 21 [1978]: 172) noted regarding Stephen, "His speech employs literary forms, ideas and emphases that suggest the influence of a culture other than that of OT Judaism." Cf. B. Gärtner, *The Areopagus Speech and Natural Revelation* (Uppsala, Sweden: C. W. K. Gleerup, 1955), 27.

in Athens (17:22–31).[53] This suggests that while the speeches are not *verbatim* reports, neither are they "free compositions" by Luke.[54]

Nevertheless, many object to this conclusion and challenge Luke's accuracy. Hemer summarized the arguments: (1) ancient historians often invented speeches to suit their purposes; (2) the unity of style also suggests that the material was fabricated (or at least embellished) by Luke rather than accurately recording the actual original content of the speeches; and (3) the speeches display a continuity of content that spans from speech to speech and from speaker to speaker.[55] Fitzmyer, modifying Schweizer, identified a series of elements that commonly appear in the major speeches of Acts. He proposed that these elements allowed him to characterize them as "Lukan compositions."[56] But these objections can be met by the following rejoinders.

Regarding the first objection, B. Witherington III noted that in the matters of ancient historians and source materials, "there was no *convention* that ancient historians were free to create speeches."[57] Ancient historians were highly influenced by rhetorical conventions but not to the detriment of accuracy, so they had two concerns: "fidelity to the truth and perfection of style."[58] Ancient historians fell into a continuum between those who elevated oratorical style and those who were less so inclined.[59] Those on the latter end of the continuum were less likely to manipulate speeches for oratorical flavor. Studies in Luke's style show that he is no Atticizer, writing in rhetorical flourishers, but is more in line with writers of serious Hellenistic history (especially Polybius).[60] He therefore falls on the latter end of the continuum as one less inclined to create oratorical compositions with his speeches.

Witherington also noted that the speeches in Acts show some disjunction with Hellenistic historical works such as those by Thucydides. To begin with, the speeches in Acts are considerably shorter, which diminishes the possibility that Luke used a speech to impress his readers with his own oratorical skill. Also, the speeches in Acts are grounded more strongly in their historical setting than the speeches in Thucydides's works. Finally, the speeches in Acts do not comment on the events; they are the events—proclamations of the word of God.[61]

---

[53] See Witherington, *Acts*, 518.

[54] J. W. Bowker, "Speeches in Acts: A Study in Proem and Yelammedenu Form," *NTS* 14 (1967–68): 96–111.

[55] Hemer, *Book of Acts in the Setting of Hellenistic History*, 420.

[56] Fitzmyer, *Acts*, 107. The list is limited to "Missionary and Evangelizing Speeches" (excluding apologies) and includes items such as "Direct Address" and "Appeal for Attention" that ostensibly any impromptu speech would have, as well as items such as "Christological-theological Kerygma."

[57] Witherington, *Acts*, 40.

[58] Ibid., 41, citing H. F. North, "Rhetoric and Historiography," *Quarterly Journal of Speech* 42 (1956): 242.

[59] Witherington, *Acts*, 41.

[60] Ibid., 43. Polybius stated that the "whole genus of orations . . . may be regarded as summaries of events and as the unifying element in historical writing" (*Hist.* 12.25a-b; see 36.1).

[61] Witherington, *Acts,* 46. Thucydides is often cited at this point by both sides of the argument. He stated, "As to the speeches that were made by different men . . . , it has been difficult to recall with strict accuracy the words actually spoken, both for me as regard that which I myself hear, and for those who from various other sources have brought me reports. Therefore the speeches are given in the language which, as it seemed to me, the several speakers would express on the subjects

Regarding the second objection, the unity of style is conceded by all. But this can also be seen in Luke's Gospel when Luke cited his source. The fact that Luke stamped his sources with his own style in no way undermines the view that the speeches are summaries of what was actually said.

The third objection is based on a continuity of content across the speeches, something Hemer shows "is clearly not the case."[62] To be sure, Psalm 16 is cited twice by different people as a messianic proof text, but Peter was less refined than Paul in his usage. The speeches also show a remarkable suitability to their own context. For example, Paul cited a Stoic philosopher (Epimenides) when dealing with the Stoics (Acts 17:28).

One should also include certain verbal affinities that point away from Lukan free compositions. Peter's speeches have certain vocabulary words that occur in 1 Peter. One example is the use of "tree" (Gk. *xylon*) for the cross (see Acts 5:30; 10:39; 1 Pet 2:24). It should also be noted that Peter's outline of the ministry of Jesus is remarkably similar to that found in the Gospel of Mark (Acts 10:36–41; ostensibly based on Peter's preaching).[63] Finally, Paul's "Miletus speech is widely conceded to contain Pauline characteristics" (Acts 20:18–35).[64]

Therefore, no real reason to doubt the accuracy of Luke's speeches exists if these are understood as reliable summaries of real speeches. Whatever redaction Luke performed does not seem to have robbed the speeches of their situation in history or of the substance of what was said. If, then, the speeches most likely are not free compositions of Luke, it is also less probable that the story line is invented.

The Jerusalem Council Another important matter pertaining to Luke's accuracy is the reporting of the Jerusalem Council in Acts 15. Not only is the event central to the theological message of the book, but how one interprets it also bears heavily on how Luke has composed his book. As Witherington observed, "It raises all the key questions of what Luke's relationship to Paul was, what the relationship is between Acts 15 and Galatians 2, and therefore what sort of history Luke is writing."[65]

A number of scholars see problems in Acts 15. They allege that the problem of Gentile inclusion apparently went unsolved after the council (as seen in Galatians). They also contend that Paul never mentioned the decree later on in the book, and they object that he would not have liked it. Their solution is to propose a conflation of meetings from an Antiochene source. At first, Paul was present and in agreement with the conclusion to continue the

---

under consideration, the sentiments most befitting the occasion, though at the same time I have adhered as closely as possible to the general sense of what was actually said" (*War* 1.22). The troublesome issue comes when Thucydides is interpreted as saying that he gave what his subjects *ought* to have said. Witherington observed that he should be interpreted as noting what it seems likely that they said (ibid., 47).

[62] Hemer, *Book of Acts in the Setting of Hellenistic History*, 424.

[63] W. Lane, *The Gospel of Mark*, NICNT (Grand Rapids, MI: Eerdmans, 1974), 10–11.

[64] Hemer, *Book of Acts in the Setting of Hellenistic History*, 425. See also the word *chairein* ("greetings") in Acts 15:23 and Jas 1:1.

[65] Witherington, *Acts*, 439.

SIDEBAR 8.1: TEXTUAL ISSUES IN THE BOOK OF ACTS

Textual critics distinguish four basic text types of the NT that were handed down to us: Alexandrian, Caesarean, Byzantine, and Western. The so-called Western text is generally regarded as secondary and unremarkable until one arrives at the book of Acts, where it is about 8.5 percent longer than the established text. A comparison of a typical Alexandrian edition with a Western edition results in a difference of 1,582 words. A similar comparison between the Robinson-Pierpont Byzantine and Eclectic text indicates that only 222 words are different, an approximate 2 percent difference in length (i.e., about twice as many words as in the present paragraph).[1]

The Western text of Acts tends to smooth out grammatical "difficulties," clarifies ambiguous points, expands references to Christ, and adds notes of historical details at unprecedented levels.[2] Some examples will suffice to show the flavor of these readings. At Acts 11:28, Luke is identified as a native of Antioch (employing a first-person plural, constituting this as a "we" passage). At Acts 19:9, Paul rented the school of Tyrannus of Ephesus "from the fifth hour to the tenth" (i.e., 11 a.m. to 4 p.m.). At Acts 15:20, 29, the Western text omits "things that are strangled" and adds "and not to do to others what they would not like to be done to themselves" at the end of the apostolic decree. Many other similar changes occur throughout Acts.

That the Western text adds historical details is the most interesting, and ultimately the most valuable, phenomenon. While not Scripture, these notes may preserve ancient understandings. Where did these additions come from? Some say from Luke himself;[3] others name an early reviser (before 150);[4] yet others propose a later revision.[5] Ultimately, very little of these readings can be considered original. In the ultimate analysis, these additions may give more insight into a single scribe's practice than they add any significant historical information.[6]

---

[1] The figures for a comparison between the Alexandrian and Western are from F. G. Kenyon, *The Western Text in the Gospels and Acts*, Proceedings of the British Academy 24 (London, UK: H. Milford, 1938), 26, cited in B. M. Metzger, *A Textual Commentary on the Greek New Testament*, 2nd ed. (New York, NY: United Bible Societies, 1994), 223.

[2] Metzger's textual commentary on Acts comprises nearly a third of the book, due mainly to discussions of the Western text type. For a nice but rather brief discussion, see Haenchen, *Acts*, 50–60.

[3] This is the opinion of F. Blass, *Acta Apostolorum sive Lucae ad Theophilum liber alter edition philologica* (Göttingen, Germany: Vandenhoeck & Ruprecht, 1895). He viewed the Western text as an earlier draft of the book, as did T. Zahn, *Die Urausgabe der Apostelgeschichte des Lucas* (Leipzig, Germany: A. Deichert, 1916). Although criticized early, the theory has had some new life breathed into it by M.-E. Boismard and A. Lamouille, *Texte Occidental des Actes des Apôtres: Reconstitution et Réhabilitation*, 2 vols., Synthèse 17 (Paris: Editions Recherche sur les Civilisations, 1984). Their view that the Western recension of Acts shows Lukan style traits has been adequately critiqued by T. C. Geer Jr., "The Presence and Significance of Lucanisms in the 'Western' text of Acts," *JSNT* 39 (1990): 59–76.

[4] See J. H. Ropes, *The Beginnings of Christianity: Part I the Acts of the Apostles*, ed. F. J. Foakes Jackson and K. Lake, *Vol. III: The Text of Acts* (London, UK: Macmillan, 1926), ccxliv–ccxlvi.

[5] B. Aland, "Entstehung, Charakter und Herkunft des sog. Westlichen Textes untersucht an der Apostelgeschichte," *ETL* 62 (1986): 5–65.

[6] For recent discussions of the Western text of Acts, see T. Nicklas and M. Tilly, eds., *The Book of Acts as Church History*, BZNW 120 (New York, NY: W. de Gruyter, 2003); and P. M. Head, "Acts and the Problem of Its Texts," in *The Book of Acts in Its First Century Setting*, vol. 1: *Ancient Literary Setting*, ed. B. W. Winter and A. D. Clarke (Grand Rapids, MI: Eerdmans, 1993), 415–44.

Gentile mission. At a later meeting, a new law was imposed on the Gentiles, something to which Paul never would have agreed.[66] Thus, conceiving of the speeches as free compositions is an integral part of "solving" an apparent incongruity.

But each of these objections is based on debatable antecedent judgments. The theory that the speeches were free compositions has already been critiqued. The assumption that Galatians 2 chronicles (at least in part) Acts 15 is debated and unlikely as well. It is more probable that Galatians 2 refers to the famine relief visit of Acts 11:30.[67] Thus, Paul did not mention the results of the decree in Galatians because the Jerusalem Council had not yet taken place. As for the theory that the decree imposed a new law on Gentile believers, Blomberg noted, "When the council writes its letter to believers in Antioch and nearby regions explaining their decision (vv. 22–29), it concludes simply by stating, 'you will do well to avoid these things' (v. 29), hardly a way to refer to mandatory legislation."[68] Therefore, a hypothetical conflation theory is not necessary to explain the phenomenon of the Jerusalem Council.

Miracles in Acts No doubt the most problematic area for some regarding the veracity of Acts is the miraculous elements in the book. Indeed, the book features some astonishing miracles, such as healings of men lame from birth (3:1–10; 14:8–10); Peter's repeated angelic deliverances from prison (5:19–20; 12:6–11; cf. the violent earthquake in 16:26); Philip being carried away by the Spirit of the Lord from the Ethiopian's presence (8:39–40); Paul's vision of the resurrected Jesus on the road to Damascus (9:3–9); Peter healing a paralyzed man named Aeneas (9:33–34); Peter raising Dorcas from the dead (9:36–41); visions by Cornelius and Peter (10:3–16); Paul striking Elymas the sorcerer with blindness (13:9–11); God speaking directly to Paul in his Macedonian vision, in Corinth, and in Jerusalem (16:9–10; 18:9–10; 23:11); and Paul raising young Eutychus from the dead (20:8–12). Perhaps among the more astonishing feats recorded is at Paul's ministry in Ephesus: "God was performing extraordinary miracles by Paul's hands, so that even facecloths or aprons that had touched his skin were brought to the sick, and the diseases left them, and the evil spirits came out of them" (19:11–12; see also 5:12–16).

Are these accounts of astonishing miracles performed by the apostles and other supernatural manifestations credible, or should these be regarded as reflections of an outmoded, superstitious frame of mind? To some, the existence of these references as part of a historical narrative is unacceptable. But the heart of the issue is not historical; it is a matter of philosophical and theological presuppositions.[69] Those who reject divine intervention reject the veracity of the miracles; those who accept divine intervention have no problems with these events based on the appearance of the miraculous. The more moderate commentators leave

[66] Barrett, "Historicity," 530.

[67] See the discussion of the date of Galatians in chap. 10 below.

[68] Blomberg, *From Pentecost to Patmos*, 53.

[69] See the discussion of Philosophical Foundations of Modern Gospels Study in chap. 3 above (including bibliographic references). See "Chapter 3: Miracles" in C. L. Blomberg, *The Historical Reliability of the Gospels*, 2nd ed. (Downers Grove, IL: InterVarsity, 2007).

them in the category of "unprovable." It should be affirmed, however, that in light of Luke's proven credibility elsewhere, there seems no good reason to doubt his reliability with regard to the supernatural events mentioned previously—especially since post-Enlightenment skepticism regarding the possibility of miracles and God's supernatural intervention in human affairs has itself been shown to be of doubtful merit.[70]

Conclusion Ultimately, there is no substantial reason to doubt Luke's accuracy on empirical grounds. Where sources are available, Luke's information is shown to be reliable. Unlike in his Gospel where Luke relied on the accounts of eyewitnesses (Luke 1:3), Luke himself was an eyewitness to a substantial part of Paul's missionary travels recorded in the book of Acts. This assumes that the "we" passages indicate Luke's participation in these portions of the narrative. In light of Luke's proven reliability where this is borne out by the available sources, it seems reasonable to hold him innocent until proven guilty where his information cannot be currently corroborated by extant extrabiblical material. As W. Ramsay stated, "You may press the words of Luke in a degree beyond any other historian's, and they stand the keenest scrutiny and the hardest treatment, provided always that the critic knows the subject and does not go beyond the limits of science and justice."[71]

The Sources of Acts

Arising from the scholarly quests for the historical Jesus, where everything must have a written source of some kind, Luke's sources for writing Acts have been a field of inquiry as well.[72] This kind of procedure is the next logical step once one rejects the notion that the writer was a follower of Paul. Hypothetical sources include a "Jerusalem A and B source,"[73] "an Antiochene Source,"[74] and a "travel diary/itinerary."[75] Haenchen left open the possibility that Luke traveled to the great Pauline centers, gathering information from local sources.[76] Fitzmyer is representative of much of mainstream scholarship on the issue. He posited a Palestinian source (generally chronicling Peter's activities); an Antiochene source

---

[70] For more, see C. S. Keener, *Miracles: The Credibility of the New Testament Accounts*, 2 vols. (Grand Rapids, MI: Baker, 2011); G. H. Twelftree, *Jesus the Miracle Worker: A Historical and Theological Study* (Downers Grove, IL: InterVarsity, 1999); and idem, *Paul and the Miraculous: A Historical Reconstruction* (Grand Rapids, MI: Baker, 2013).

[71] W. Ramsay, *The Bearing of Recent Discovery on the Trustworthiness of the New Testament* (London, England: Hodder & Stoughton, 1915), 89.

[72] E.g., F. Schleiermacher, *Einleitung ins Neue Testament, in Friedrich Schleiermacher's Sämtliche Werke*, ed. G. Wolde, div. 1, vol. 8 (Berlin, Germany: Reimer, 1834–1864), 360. According to Meyer, Schleiermacher held that Luke simply strung together other written documents. See H. A. W. Meyer, *Critical and Exegetical Handbook to the Acts of the Apostles*, 2nd ed., trans. P. J. Gloag (New York, NY: Funk & Wagnalls, 1889), 9.

[73] von Harnack, *Acts of the Apostles*, 162. He based this on apparent doublets in the narrative in Acts 1–15, that is, two Petrine sermons, two arrests, two defenses before the Sanhedrin, two estimates of converts, and two accounts of the community sharing all things. But Bruce showed that this is unnecessary (*Acts*, 23).

[74] R. E. Brown (*An Introduction to the New Testament* [New York, NY: Doubleday, 1997], 317) contended that today this source is probably the most widely held.

[75] Dibelius, *Studies in the Acts of the Apostles*, 126. Dibelius's work largely ended the quest for solely written sources for Acts, preferring to describe Luke as a creative author (Neil, *Acts*, 24).

[76] Haenchen, *Acts*, 86.

(Stephen, Gentile inclusion issues, the Dispersion, and the Jerusalem Council); a "we" sections source; and a Pauline source (encompassing Paul's conversion and activities).[77] Much of this is conjecture based on the research of someone—not a follower of Paul—who wrote a generation after Paul's death, a theory critiqued above.

So what kind of sources can be suggested for Acts? Acts 16–28 is dominated by the "we" passages, and this is best explained as discussed above under the authorship of the Gospel of Luke. This section reflects either (1) the reminiscences of the author; or (2) a diary, of sorts, of the author. The greater details in the latter part of the book point to recent events and more than likely to the first option.[78] For the events outside of the "we" passages in the second half of Acts, one needs to look no further than Luke's personal acquaintance with Paul himself.[79]

The question remains concerning Luke's sources for Acts 1–15, when he was not present at the events. Hemer, in a rather extensive look at how Luke treated his sources, concluded that "Luke obtained parts of his material by interviewing participants, and that he sometimes edited older traditions by re-interviewing such surviving participants as may have been accessible to him, and that this process accounts for some of the significant 'L-nuances' in the Third Gospel."[80]

Hemer further suggested that a close connection to Peter (such as a personal interview) can be sustained, so that Luke was not necessarily dependent on second-hand sources.[81] This, then, would coincide with Luke's declaration of his sources in the preface to Luke (Luke 1:1–4); some written sources (see Acts 15:23–29; 23:25–37); eyewitness testimony; and personal investigation. Luke's extensive travels would have allowed for sufficient opportunities to make contact with individuals who could supply him with information regarding events in which he was not personally involved.

Literary Plan

As stated above, and as widely agreed upon, the basic blueprint of Acts is given at Acts 1:8: "But you will receive power when the Holy Spirit has come on you, and you will be my witnesses in Jerusalem, in all Judea and Samaria, and to the end of the earth." The rest of the book shows the fulfillment of Jesus's command and the unfolding of God's plan from the church in Jerusalem and Judea (1:1–6:7) to Samaria (6:8–9:31) and to the ends

---

[77] Fitzmyer, *Acts*, 85–88.

[78] See the discussion of the authorship of Luke's Gospel in chap. 6 above.

[79] Since he was strongly connected to the Sanhedrin, Paul could even have been the source for speeches and events at which it was impossible for Luke or the early Christians to be present, such as the speech of Gamaliel given to the Sanhedrin (Acts 5:35–39) or Stephen's speech and stoning (Acts 7).

[80] Hemer, *Book of Acts in the Setting of Hellenistic History*, 351. Cf. S. J. Kistemaker's treatment that shows that Peter and Paul spoke in terms familiar to the Peter and Paul known outside of Acts but not available to Luke at the time of writing (*An Exposition of the Acts of the Apostles* [Grand Rapids, MI: Baker, 2002], 9–12).

[81] Hemer, *Book of Acts in the Setting of Hellenistic History*, 356–62.

of the earth (9:3–28:31).[82] Luke took pains to show that the expansion of Christianity was at God's direction, including the Gentiles, while at the same time continuing salvation "to the Jews first."

At the heart of the book is the Jerusalem Council (chap. 15) where the church regulated the inclusion of the Gentiles in the rapidly growing Christian movement. Paul's ministry is presented through three missionary journeys (one before and two after the Jerusalem Council). Similar to Luke's Gospel, where the extended "Lukan Travel Narrative" shows Jesus on his way to Jerusalem, the action slows down during the last quarter of the book of Acts as Paul made his way to trial in Rome. Unlike Luke's Gospel—where Jesus is arrested, tried, and crucified, and on the third day rises from the dead—Acts ends on an inconclusive note, with Paul still awaiting trial in Rome.[83]

Table 8.2: Alternate Structural Proposals for Acts

F. F. Bruce	D. L. Bock
I. Birth of the Church (1:1–5:42)	I. Ascension and Commission (1:1–11)
II. Persecution & Expansion (6:1–9:31)	II. Early Church in Jerusalem (1:12–6:7)
III. Beginnings of Gentile Christianity (9:32–12:24)	III. Judea and Samaria (6:8–9:31)
IV. Extension from Antioch (12:25–15:35)	IV. Gospel to the Gentiles (9:32–12:25)
V. Movement to the Aegean World (15:36–19:20)	V. Mission from Antioch and Incorporation of Gentiles (13:1–15:35)
VI. Paul Travels to Rome (19:21–28:31)	VI. Expansion to Greece (15:36–18:23)
	VII. Arrest and Trip to Rome (21:17–28:31)

OUTLINE

I. THE EQUIPPING OF THE CHURCH FOR ITS MISSION (1:1–2:47)
  A. Preliminary Steps (1:1–14)
    1. Review of Jesus's Ministry and Instructions (1:1–5)
    2. The Ascension of Jesus (1:6–14)
  B. The Replacement of Judas (1:15–26)

---

[82] Commentators outline the book in slightly different ways. Table 8.2 reproduces in simplified form the outlines by Bruce, *Acts*, vii–xiv; and D. L. Bock, *Acts*, BECNT (Grand Rapids, MI: Baker, 2007), vii–viii. For other outlines, see Marshall, *Acts*, 51–54; J. R. W. Stott, *The Spirit, the Church, and the World: The Message of Acts* (Downers Grove, IL: InterVarsity, 1990), 3–4; and Larkin, *Acts*, 34–36.

[83] A few of the headings in the outline below are borrowed from the useful book by H. A. Kent Jr., *Jerusalem to Rome: Studies in Acts* (Grand Rapids, MI: Baker, 1972), 7.

- C. Pentecost: The Church Is Born (2:1–47)
  1. The Event: The Exalted Jesus Sends the Spirit (2:1–4)
  2. The Evidence of the Spirit's Coming: Foreign Languages (2:5–13)
  3. The Explanation: Peter's Message (2:14–40)
  4. The Expansion: The Growth of the Early Church (2:41–47)

II. THE EARLY CHURCH IN JERUSALEM (3:1–6:7)
- A. A Miracle and Its Aftermath (3:1–4:31)
  1. The Miracle (3:1–10)
  2. Peter's Defense (3:11–26)
  3. The Aftermath: Peter and John's Arrest and Bold Witness (4:1–31)
- B. Trouble Within and Without (4:32–6:7)
  1. The Sharing of Property in the Early Church: Good Example (4:32–37)
  2. The Sharing of Property in the Early Church: Bad Example (5:1–11)
  3. Further Growth in Numbers and Geographical Extension (5:12–17)
  4. Another Arrest (5:18–42)
  5. Serving the Hellenists' Widows: Potential Conflict Avoided (6:1–7)

III. INITIAL EXPANSION: STEPHEN, SAMARIA, AND SAUL (6:8–9:31)
- A. Suffering: One of the Servants Arrested and Martyred (6:8–7:60)
  1. The Charges Against Stephen (6:8–15)
  2. Stephen's Defense (7:1–53)
  3. Stephen's Martyrdom (7:54–60)
- B. Palestine and Syria: Philip, Saul, and Peter (8:1–9:30)
  1. Saul the Persecutor (8:1–3)
  2. The Gospel Spreads to Samaria Through Philip (8:4–25)
  3. Philip and the Ethiopian Eunuch (8:26–40)
  4. Saul's Conversion (9:1–19a)
  5. Saul's Postconversion Days (9:19b–30)
- C. Summary: Judea, Galilee, and Samaria (9:31)

IV. CONTINUED EXPANSION: THE FIRST GENTILE CONVERT (9:32–12:24)
- A. The Proof of Gentile Conversion (9:32–11:18)
- B. Gentile Conversion in Antioch and the Return of Paul (11:19–26)
- C. Events in Jerusalem (11:27–12:24)

V. THE GENTILE MISSION (PART 1, ASIA MINOR): FIRST JOURNEY, JERUSALEM COUNCIL (12:25–16:5)
- A. First Missionary Journey (12:25–14:28)
  1. Syrian Antioch: Sent Out (13:1–3)
  2. Cyprus: Proconsul Sergius Paulus Believes (13:4–12)
  3. Pisidian Antioch: Gentiles Believe Despite Jews (13:13–52)
  4. South Galatia: Iconium, Derbe, Lystra (14:1–23)
  5. Return to Syrian Antioch (14:24–28)
- B. Jerusalem Council (15:1–35)
  1. Setting (15:1–4)

2. Apostles and Elders Convene (15:5–6)
3. Reports by Peter, Paul, and Barnabas (15:7–12)
4. James' Response on Behalf of Jerusalem Church (15:13–21)
5. The Council's Decree (15:22–29)
6. Return to Syrian Antioch (15:30–35)

C. Second Missionary Journey Begins (15:36–16:5)
1. Paul and Barnabas Separate (15:36–41)
2. Paul and Silas Deliver Decisions of Jerusalem Council, Take Timothy (16:1–5)

VI. THE GENTILE MISSION (PART 2, GREECE): SECOND AND THIRD JOURNEYS (16:6–19:20)

A. Second Missionary Journey Continues (16:6–18:22)
1. Paul's Vision of the Man of Macedonia: Ministry in Philippi (16:6–40)
2. Ministry in Thessalonica (17:1–9)
3. Ministry in Berea (17:10–15)
4. Ministry in Athens (17:16–34)
5. Ministry in Corinth (18:1–17)
6. Return Trip (18:18–22)

B. Third Missionary Journey (18:23–19:20)
1. Apollos Instructed by Priscilla and Aquila (18:23–28)
2. Apollos Goes to Corinth, Paul Ministers in Ephesus (19:1–20)

VII. THE GENTILE MISSION (PART 3, ITALY): JOURNEY TO ROME (19:21–28:31)

A. From Ephesus to Jerusalem (19:21–21:16)
1. Ephesus: Opposition by Demetrius (19:21–41)
2. Paul's Journey to Macedonia and Greece, Seven Days in Troas (20:1–13)
3. From Troas to Miletus (20:14–16)
4. Farewell to Ephesian Elders (20:17–38)
5. Paul's Journey to Jerusalem (21:1–16)

B. Paul's Final Visit to Jerusalem and His Removal to Caesarea (21:17–23:35)
1. Paul's Visit with James and the Elders (21:17–26)
2. Paul Arrested at the Temple (21:27–40)
3. Paul's Defense (22:1–29)
4. Paul Before the Sanhedrin (22:30–23:11)
5. Paul's Removal to Caesarea (23:12–35)

C. Paul's Defenses Before Felix, Festus, and Agrippa (24:1–26:32)
1. The Jews' Charges Against Paul (24:1–9)
2. Paul's Defense Before Felix (24:10–27)
3. Paul's Defense Before Festus and His Appeal to Caesar (25:1–12)
4. Paul Before Agrippa: Charges Specified (25:13–26:32)

D. Paul's Trip to Rome (27:1–28:31)
1. Sea Voyage and Shipwreck on Malta (27:1–28:14)
2. Paul Preaches the Gospel Openly in Rome (28:15–31)

INTERPRETING ACTS

The procedures for interpreting biblical narratives apply to the book of Acts as well. In the section on interpreting the Gospels, we advocated both a vertical and a horizontal reading. In Acts, no horizontal reading is necessary or even possible since it is a volume with no known literary sources.[84] That said, most of the vertical reading procedures for interpreting narratives are still valid with certain adjustments regarding terminology and categories.[85] These principles are apropos:

1. Seek to understand how individual scenes relate to the purposes of the book as a whole. Acts 1:4–11 is the first and ultimate example of a scene in Acts relating to the rest of the book. Jesus's discussion with the disciples first of all sets the events of the book in a salvation history framework. The Holy Spirit as the Father's promise sets the present time in an eschatological light as does the angel's promise of his return (1:11).[86] It is the last times. Thus, the question from the disciples about restoring the kingdom is normal and natural. Jesus's answer, however, continues the theme of God's plan begun in the Gospel of Luke (1:7). Most of all, 1:8 defines the mission of the disciples, the power behind the mission, and the scope of the mission. Literarily, it lays out the contents of the book of Acts for Jesus's prophecy is precisely fulfilled.[87] All these themes take prominent roles in the book.

2. Examine themes in the heading, introduction, conclusion, and programmatic statement. We have already highlighted themes in the introduction, and we will return to this topic in the conclusion. That leaves one to consider any programmatic statement in Acts. In Acts, like Luke, the programmatic statement is a sermon based on primarily three OT texts (Joel 2:28–32; Pss 16:8–11; 110:1).[88] The sermon is an explanation of the manifestation seen publicly at Pentecost. Peter's sermon has four movements that together explain the plan of God.[89] First, Peter asserts that the phenomena people observed marked the fulfillment of the prophesied gift of the Spirit (2:14–22). Peter continues the citation of Joel 2 until he gets to "then everyone who calls on the name of the Lord will be saved." The second movement (2:22–31) cites Psalm 16 to identify Jesus as the Lord on whom they must call. The final movement (33–36) employs Psalm 110:1 to describe Jesus as both Lord and Messiah. Those who repent and identify with Jesus Christ are forgiven, for the

---

[84] See W. Klein, C. Blomberg, and R. Hubbard Jr., *Introduction to Biblical Interpretation* rev. and upd. ed. (Nashville, TN: Thomas Nelson, 2004), 420.

[85] First, "scenes" replaces "pericopes" as the latter tends to be reserved for Gospel literature. Second, the earlier suggestion to note the response of the original witnesses to an event is not as prominent in Acts. And, finally, the suggestion to look for possible connections between narrative and discourse material in the immediate context is also less of an interpretive tool since in Acts, the discourse materials are the speeches that are an organic part of the narrative and (often) less subtle than in the Gospel genre.

[86] See Marshall's statement, "Thus, the promise of the parousia forms the background of hope against which the disciples are to act as the witnesses to Jesus. In effect the present passage corresponds to Jesus's statement in Mark 13:10 that the gospel must first be preached to all nations before the end can come." Marshall, *Acts*, 62.

[87] Johnson, *Acts*, 30.

[88] Peterson, *Acts*, 130. In Luke 4:14–30, it is the sermon at Nazareth that explicates Jesus's fulfillment of Isaiah 61.

[89] Bock, *Acts*, 108.

promise is for all. It is evident that these movements in Peter's Pentecost Sermon set the theological stage for the book of Acts.

3. Examine repeated themes, titles, phrases, and theological emphases. Quite a number of themes are prominent. Peterson lists "witness, prayer, word, Spirit, salvation, resurrection, faith, repentance, baptism, signs and wonders."[90] These topics understandably occur rather frequently in Acts. However, it is not only the repetition of synonyms that are theologically significant. Luke also repeats similar narrative events that display important theological emphases. For example, Peter, Paul, Stephen, and Philip share similar experiences (e.g., commissioning, proclamation, suffering), teaching, and miracles. This pattern of activity among Luke's main protagonists displays a prophetic continuity among earliest Christianity and highlights the expansion of Christianity as a product of God's work and not merely a human phenomenon.[91]

4. Examine editorial comments that interpret the significance of the event. The most significant of Luke's editorial comments come when he summarizes the previous narrative events (see, e.g., 1:12–14; 2:42–47; 4:32–37; 6:7; 9:31; 12:24; 16:5; 19:20). More than simple summaries, these passages often highlight the church's growth and maturity.[92] However, sometimes these summaries, as transitional statements, add important information for the following context. For example, 6:7 notes that "a large group of priests became obedient to the faith." This casts the charge of blasphemy against the temple brought against Stephen in the following section (6:13) in a curious light. Some suggest it puts Stephen and Christians like him in a theological bind.[93] However, there is no textual indication of internal difficulties among believers on the subject. Much of this interpretation seems based on the assumption that the charges against Stephen—blasphemy against the Law and temple—are true! Luke, however, plainly calls the witnesses against Stephen, false witnesses (6:13). Furthermore, nothing in Stephen's speech is particularly inflammatory against either.[94] The picture Luke paints is of an enraged mob engaging in a first-century lynching.[95] Instead, it is more likely that the reference in the summary is to show that many priests had no problems with the message of Christianity, serving to highlight that Stephen is murdered as an innocent man.

5. Carefully examine all OT quotations and allusions. Like most of the NT, Acts is saturated in OT allusions and quotations.[96] As stated above, the programmatic statement

---

[90] Peterson, *Acts*, 43.

[91] A. C. Clark, *Parallel Lives: The Relation of Paul to the Apostles in the Lucan Perspective*, Paternoster Biblical and Theological Monographs (Waynesboro, GA: Paternoster, 2001), 335–38.

[92] Peterson, *Acts*, 42.

[93] See, e.g., ibid., 232 and Bruce, *Acts*, 131–32.

[94] See the comments below on "jumping to conclusions."

[95] See Witherington's assessment: Witherington, *Acts*, 258–64. We would also add that even if Stephen were critical of the temple, this was not generally worthy of the death penalty. The covenanters at Qumran were very critical of the priesthood and the temple.

[96] Keener notes that Acts contains at least twenty direct quotations of the LXX and a host of allusions. Keener, *Acts*, 1:478. Scholars commonly quote C. K. Barrett: "The influence, whether literary or theological, of the Old Testament upon

is found in Peter's Pentecost sermon (2:5–39). It is largely a citation and interpretation of three OT texts. What is often missed is that when the book concludes with an appropriation of the OT, that is equally programmatic.[97]

When preaching to the Jews in Rome, Paul ultimately cites the well-known Isaiah 6:9–10 ("You will listen and listen, yet never understand"; Acts 28:26–27), and they depart debating. Paul's parting shot to them is, "Therefore, let it be known to you that this salvation of God has been sent to the Gentiles; they will listen" (Acts 28:28). Most likely, this is an appropriation of Psalm 67 (66 LXX): "so that your way may be known on earth, your salvation among all nations" (Ps 67:2).[98]

The combination of the allusion and the citation is climactic, explanatory, and, in some sense, recursive.[99] It is climactic in that Paul has faithfully proclaimed the gospel to Jews and Gentiles alike throughout the Mediterranean world. By appropriating the citation, Paul puts himself in the prophetic position of proclaiming a warning to Israel ("go and say") who has seen and heard the message (seeing and hearing).[100] Its use here as the final parting word of Paul to the Jews suggests a completion, at least for Paul.

It is explanatory in that Luke's point is that the failure of the Jewish people to receive their Messiah, promised in their Scriptures, proclaimed by their fellow Jews is because of their own individual callousness, blindness, and deafness. (It in no way rules out a future restoration of Israel.)[101] Yet there remains a note of hope, for even now not all are callous, blind, and deaf because "Some were persuaded" (Acts 28:24).

The citation is also recursive in that it completes the first programmatic statement. The first citation was an offer to the house of Israel (and to all nations) to receive the gospel. That offer, patiently made throughout the Jewish world, has now largely been rejected. The citation highlights the fact that this was prophesied long ago. The inclusion of the allusion to Psalm 67(66) shows the plan of God is in full force. It is not invalidated by the Jews' rejection. As Dunn says, "It is simply a phase in the larger purposes of God to include all, Jew and Gentile, within his saving concern."[102] So, then, through Paul's solemn announce-

---

the Lucan writings . . . is profound and pervasive" (C. K. Barrett, "Luke/Acts," in *It is Written: Scripture Citing Scripture: Essays in Honour of Barnabas Lindars, SSF*, ed. D. A. Carson and H. G. M. Williamson [Cambridge, UK: Cambridge University Press, 1988], 231).

[97] Keener, *Acts*, 1:479.

[98] Barrett, *Acts*, 2:1246 and J. D. G. Dunn, *The Acts of the Apostles*, Narrative Commentaries (Valley Forge, PA: Trinity Press International, 1996), 354.

[99] Peterson states, "So Luke's work ends where it began, with a declaration of the fulfillment of Scripture in the events he records." D. Peterson, "The Motif of Fulfillment and Purpose of Luke-Acts," in *The Book of Acts in its First Century Setting*, vol. 1: *Ancient Literary Setting*, ed. B. W. Winter and A. D. Clarke (Grand Rapids, MI: Eerdmans, 1993), 100.

[100] Bock, *Acts*, 755.

[101] I. H. Marshall, "Acts," in *Commentary on the New Testament Use of the Old Testament*, ed. G. K. Beale and D. A. Carson (Grand Rapids, MI: Baker, 2007), 601; Witherington, *Acts*, 804.

[102] Dunn, *Acts*, 356.

ment that the gospel has "been sent to the Gentiles," the program, announced in Peter's speech, is ongoing. "Nothing can or will prevent the spread of the gospel."[103]

"Luke-Acts" or "Luke and Acts"?

Those who describe Luke and Acts as separate volumes often express it as "Luke and Acts." Likewise, those who see it as a multi-volume work call it "Luke-Acts."[104] While we have addressed the issue above and in chapter 6, it was mostly in terms of historical questions such as authorship and date. The question of unity also affects how one interprets both Luke and Acts. Canonical criticism does not deny unity but chooses to interpret Luke in light of its position after John in the canon. Some suggest the reception history of a document should guide our interpretation as well. This group of scholars often thinks Luke and Acts are interpreted separately in the early church and so should we should follow suit.[105] So, then, do we interpret the books along the lines of canonical criticism and reception history as un- (or dis-) connected entities? We suggest neither should trump the intent of the authors (both human and divine) as the books were written. In other words, the unity of Luke and Acts is a legitimate interpretive key as we investigate either book. But how do we understand "unity"?

It is unlikely that we should consider the Gospel of Luke as incomplete without the book of Acts. It does end with a future promise of the Spirit's empowerment for mission (Luke 24:49). However, as Green points out, it has a beginning (birth), middle (ministry), and end (ascension) of the life of Jesus. It is a complete story.[106] Whatever the narrative unity (to use cinematic examples), it is not like the trilogy of *The Lord of the Rings* that continually cycles forward until the ring of power is destroyed in Mordor. It is more like *Rocky I* and *II,* where the sequel continues the story but *Rocky I* did not end on a cliffhanger; it is a complete story.

The second book, however, is manifestly connected to the Gospel. Luke recapitulates the Gospel in the prologue of Acts, picking up where the first story stops. The author clearly saw Acts as a continuation of the previous book. Noting this, Green says, "Interpretation of Luke and Acts as narratives, and particularly as narrative representations of history, however, can scarcely escape the text's own intention to be read not as two discrete accounts . . . but as a single narrative of the coming of salvation in all its fullness to all people."[107] Thus,

---

[103] Barrett, *Acts*, 2:1246.

[104] This is, of course, not universal. H. J. Cadbury ["Lexical Notes on Luke-Acts, I," *JBL* 44 (1925): 214–27] argued strongly for unity and was the first to insert the dash. For more in-depth discussion of the modern questions of unity, see M. F. Bird, "The Unity of Luke-Acts in Recent Discussion" *JSNT* 29 (2007): 425–48 and J. B. Green "Luke-Acts or Luke and Acts? A Reaffirmation of Narrative Unity," in *Reading Acts Today: Essays in Honour of Loveday C. A. Alexander*, ed. S. Walton, *et al.* (London, England: T&T Clark, 2011), 101–36.

[105] A. Gregory, *The Reception of Luke and Acts in the Period before Irenaeus: Looking for Luke in the Second Century*, WUNT 2, 169 (Tübingen, Germany: Mohr Siebeck, 2003); and C. K. Rowe, "History, Hermeneutics and the Unity of Luke-Acts," *JSNT* 28 (2005): 131–57.

[106] Green, "Luke-Acts, or Luke and Acts?," 115.

[107] Ibid, 119.

the term "sequel" is preferred here for Acts; it keeps narrative unity and the completion of Luke. This leads to three simple principles as we interpret the books.

First, it is legitimate to see a theological unity throughout Luke-Acts. Theological unity can be embraced if the latter interprets or informs the former. As L. T. Johnson states, in Acts "Luke provides the first, authoritative *interpretation* of his Gospel."[108] Thus, it has often been stated that the Gospel has no concept of a substitutionary atonement. However, the sequel certainly does. Paul states in Acts 20:28, ". . . shepherd the church of God, which he purchased with his own blood." This text and others in Acts clarifies what Luke does not emphasize in his Gospel. Theological unity also can be seen going from Luke to Acts as well. This is especially true in the areas of theological framework. As Marshall states, "The Gospel thus to some extent constitutes the matrix for Acts in that it establishes the first part of the story and sets the programme [*sic*] for what is to follow, namely the way in which good news spread and embraced the Gentiles."[109]

Second, it is legitimate to see forward-pointing references in Luke that might be missed until one has read the book of Acts. For example, John the Baptist proclaims, "I baptize you with water, but one is coming who is more powerful than I. I am not worthy to untie the strap of his sandals. He will baptize you with the Holy Spirit and fire" (Luke 3:16). Acts 1:4–5 (and Luke 24:49); 2; 10–11; 13; 15:8; and 19:4 can all legitimately find conceptual links to John's statement.[110] Bock is certainly correct when he states, "Luke 3:16 extends its shadow over the two volumes."[111]

In contrast, we would warn against maximizing intertextuality markers between the two works. Both volumes could refer to OT passages rather independently. Luke 20:42–43 and Acts 2:34–35 both cite Psalm 110:1. It is unlikely contextually that there is a link between Luke and Acts beyond the messianic import of the Psalm. Likewise, both volumes could use similar terminology without necessarily forming a direct conceptual link. This is especially true for common themes. For example, both Luke and Acts make several references to Christ and David in the same context. It is unlikely that they all form a specific intertextuality beyond the Davidic messianic expectation. Instead, one should look for both contextual and linguistic markers to suggest a strong connection.

Normative or Descriptive?

Interpreting the meaning of the book of Acts is an exercise in closely reading a narrative. Most who read it as it stands, generally come to similar interpretations regarding the major contours of the book. It is, however, not what it meant that is the most vexing problem in Acts. It is in what it means. In other words, how do we apply the book to our context? Most of the interpretive issues with the book arise right here. The question is

[108] L. T. Johnson, *The Writings of the New Testament,* 3rd ed. (Philadelphia, PA: Fortress, 2010), 96.

[109] I. H. Marshall, "Acts and the 'Former Treatise,'" in *The Book of Acts in Its First-Century Setting,* vol. 1, *Ancient Literary Setting,* ed. B. W. Winter and A. D. Clarke (Grand Rapids, MI: Eerdmans, 1993), 181.

[110] See Bock, "Theology of Luke-Acts," 216–17.

[111] Ibid., 216.

usually framed by asking what is *normative* (i.e., what we should do?) versus what is *descriptive* (i.e., what did people do, or what happened?). Duvall and Hays assert, "Without a doubt this is the most significant issue we face as we learn to interpret Acts."[112]

The question is twofold. First, it regards discerning the theology of the passage. For example, does the experience of the Samaritans (Acts 8:5–17) who received the Spirit significantly after they believe describe the normative experience of the believer? Most Pentecostals would say, "Yes." Many others would say, "No." Second, it regards the practice of the early disciples. For example, does Paul's encounter with a demon-possessed young woman in Acts 16:16–18 provide a template for dealing with the demonic? Does it teach not to accept the affirmation of the enemy? Does it teach waiting to cast out the spirit until one's spirit is vexed? A variety of opinion exists regarding this event.

This problem is not unique to Acts, but it is especially acute here, for it is the only narrative in the NT apart from the Gospels. We don't readily identify our spiritual condition with Jesus's. Because he walked on water doesn't mean we can do the same. In ethics it is appropriate to ask, "What would Jesus do?" However, few would attempt to practice Jesus's actions at a funeral! We obviously are more comfortable identifying in these ways with the apostles. But what controls allow us to wisely apply the book of Acts? We offer the following suggestions to interpret and apply the book.

1. Note the transitional nature of particularly the early part of Acts. The book takes place within a shift from the old to the new covenant. The early church's awareness of the particulars of this shift does not seem particularly evident at the beginning. For example, the casting of lots to determine God's will is fairly common in the OT (appearing there about fourteen times) and in antiquity in general.[113] However, in the NT it is only recorded at Jesus's crucifixion (for Jesus's robe) and at the selection of Matthias to replace Judas (Acts 1:26). When similar choices are to be made (the Seven, Acts 6; ministry sites, Acts 16), no such device is suggested. We are safe in insisting that casting lots is not a NT practice to determine God's will.[114] The indwelling Holy Spirit surely makes the practice obsolete (although not necessarily wrong for the pre-Pentecost disciples).[115] Peter's kosher diet (10:15); the early church's worship in the temple (e.g., 3:1; 21:26; and 22:17); and the hesitancy to accept the Gentiles directly (cf. 10:45; 11:1–3, 18; and 15:5) can all be understood from this perspective.

2. Don't jump to conclusions. No one advocates jumping to conclusions, yet we are all guilty of this from time to time. There are many texts that upon a cursory reading seem to advocate something unusual. Normally, these texts do not explicitly give a command but a model seems to be offered. Patient exegesis often answers the questions when no

---

[112] J. S. Duvall and J. D. Hays, *Grasping God's Word: A Hands-on Approach to Reading Interpreting and Applying the Bible*, 3rd ed. (Grand Rapids, MI: Zondervan, 2012), 299.

[113] Barrett, *Acts*, 1:104.

[114] Peterson, *Acts*, 129.

[115] Klein, Blomberg, and Hubbard, *Biblical Interpretation*, 423; Witherington, *Acts*, 126.

direct command is given. Matters that may seem normative are shown by textual indicators and wider patterns to be merely descriptive.

For example, it is a common misunderstanding that the early church's "sharing of all things" is a model for modern believers to follow. The narrative at Acts 4:32–5:11 is usually cited as the basis for this.[116] In this view, Ananias and Sapphira received the ultimate discipline for keeping part of the proceeds of a sold parcel of land for themselves. However, upon a closer look we note that Peter criticizes Ananias and Sapphira for lying, not for keeping the money for themselves. In fact, Peter affirms their legitimate control of personal property. He states, "Wasn't it yours while you possessed it? And after it was sold, wasn't it at your disposal? Why is it that you planned this thing in your heart? You have not lied to men but to God!" (Acts 5:4). The problem, then, was not keeping the money. The issue was self-serving dishonesty.

The apostle's reaction suggests permission rather than prescription. Although believers are not commanded to live in a "commune" of sorts, we are certainly free to do so. As Bock states, "Nothing Luke does or says about this pattern indicates that selling everything was a command (see Zacchaeus) or that it was wrong."[117]

3. Ask if the narrative presents the event as extraordinary. We can expect an all-powerful God to occasionally do things to glorify himself by breaking expected patterns. Similar to the call to a close inspection of the text, this suggests we look at the passage and the book as a whole to see whether an event is out of the ordinary. Here we look for overt statements and actions that are unusual.

Two examples immediately come to mind. First, nothing could be stranger than the church's preoccupation with so-called "prayer cloths" supposedly based on Acts 19:12. Quite a number of media evangelists have promoted their version of this item. Acts 19:12 states, "so that even facecloths or aprons that had touched his skin were brought to the sick, and the diseases left them, and the evil spirits came out of them" (Acts 19:12). Does this reference support the modern practice? This is highly doubtful. In Acts 19, Luke describes the event in the passive voice; thus, it is unclear whether Paul was personally involved in distributing the items. At any rate, the idea of healing power associated with touching something closely associated with an important person was a common belief in antiquity. Similar things are reported about Jesus (Luke 8:44–48) and Peter (Acts 5:14–16). These are described as "extraordinary miracles," that is, ones that are uncommon. It is most likely that God accommodated the ancient belief for his own purposes rather than

---

[116] The Christian communes of the 1960s–80s used this passage and certain Gospel passages to defend their practice. D. Tidball, "The New Gospel of Community: Derek Tidball Questions the Current Emphasis on Christian Community Living," *Third Way* (April 1980): 15.

[117] D. Bock, *A Theology of Luke and Acts: God's Promised Program, Realized for All Nations*, BTNT (Grand Rapids, MI: Zondervan, 2011), 445.

indicating repeatable "magic" activity.[118] Surely something described as extraordinary cannot rightly be viewed as commonplace.

The second example is the reception of the Spirit by Samaritans in Acts 8. This, too, represents an event that breaks the normal pattern. In Acts 8:5–13, Philip preaches Christ to the Samaritans and they believe and are baptized. After the apostles lay hands on them, they observably receive the Spirit of God. This sequence has been suggested as affirmation that receiving the Spirit at a later point subsequent to faith is the norm for Christian experience.[119] However, indications in the text and the pattern outside the passage point to a better understanding. Regarding the text, the apostles Peter and John were sent to Samaria upon hearing that the Samaritans had only been baptized in the name of Jesus. In other words, they were expecting to receive the Holy Spirit as well, but the problem was that this did not happen. Thus, Luke notes that something was wrong in the Samaritans' experience. It was something that created the need for an urgent reply from Jerusalem.[120] So, then, the clues in the text suggest that the Samaritans believed but did not receive the Spirit, thus constituting an unusual event.

If this were the norm for Christian experience, we should see the pattern elsewhere in the book. As we investigate the issue, however, we find the Samaritan sequence is clearly exceptional. Everywhere in the book, receiving Christ and the Spirit occur without such a large interval.[121] In fact, in 10:44, only the reception of the Spirit is noted (assuming belief), making the two virtually synonymous. The presence of such a gap here again suggests an event that is out of the ordinary. So, then, the text indicates that this is not a normal pattern. So what do we make of the event? What was God up to? Elsewhere when the gospel moves into strategic people groups, the sign gifts appear as irrefutable indicators that people had received the new covenant Spirit promise: Jews (2:1–4), Gentiles (10:44–45), and disciples of John the Baptist (19:1–7). Through the exceptional event, the apostles are

---

[118] Peterson, *Acts,* 537.

[119] This is typically referred to as "separability and subsequence." Turner describes the Pentecostal views as either two-stage or one-stage reception of the Spirit. In the first, the Spirit is involved in salvation upon belief. Later the believer receives an empowerment of the Spirit of prophecy for miraculous gifts and service (see, e.g., J. R. Williams, *Renewal Theology: Systematic Theology from a Charismatic Perspective, Three Volumes in One* [Grand Rapids, MI: Zondervan, 2011]). In the second, the Spirit is only received in the latter event (see, e.g., R. P. Menzies, *Empowered for Witness: The Spirit in Luke-Acts* [Sheffield, PA: Sheffield Academic Press, 1994], 204–25). M. Turner, "Interpreting the Samaritans of Acts 8: The Waterloo of Pentecostal Soteriology and Pneumatology?" *PNEUMA: The Journal of the Society for Pentecostal Studies* 23 [2001]: 266–68). For an insider discussion of the Pentecostal position on Acts 8, see, G. Fee, "Baptism in the Holy Spirit: The Issue of Separability and Subsequence," *PNEUMA: The Journal of the Society for Pentecostal Studies* 7 (1985): 87–99.

[120] Keener suggests Luke is referring to prophetic empowerment (*Acts,* 2:1522–26). However, as important as it is, it is unlikely that it would inspire the urgency the apostolic visit seems to indicate. Furthermore, as Keener admits, the Samaritans do no prophetic activities afterwards. Like Dunn's view that the Samaritans were not fully converted (J. D. G. Dunn, *Baptism in the Holy Spirit: A Re-examination of the New Testament Teaching on the Gift of the Spirit in Relation to Pentecostalism Today,* 2nd ed. [London, England: SCM, 2010], 55–72), this view does not seem to fit the evidence either.

[121] It is highly unlikely that the disciples of John the Baptist who received the Spirit in Acts 19 were actually believers before Paul preached Christ to them. Note that there they are baptized again (Acts 19:5), signifying their previous baptism was not Christian baptism.

given convincing evidence that the Samaritans had received the gospel without becoming Jews first.[122] These "half-Jews" (already circumcised) are paving the way to open the minds of the early church to Gentile conversion as well. It is beyond question now that God has acted in Samaria.[123]

Conclusion

The book of Acts is certainly more than mere history. As theological history, the book teaches many truths regarding the nature of God, salvation, and mission. It is, after all, Scripture and "is profitable for teaching, for rebuking, for correcting, for training in righteousness" (2 Tim 3:16). As a narrative, it requires interpretation in keeping with the normal rules of the genre. However, as we've seen, it includes some challenging portions as we seek to apply the text to our lives and to the church today. Keeping in mind the above-mentioned principles and cautions, we will be better equipped to avoid some of the interpretive pitfalls and to faithfully live out the theology of the book of Acts.

UNIT-BY-UNIT DISCUSSION

I. The Equipping of the Church for Its Mission (1:1–2:47)

A. Preliminary Steps (1:1–14) The book of Acts opens by referring to the "first narrative," Luke's Gospel, which told of what Jesus began to do and teach. By implication, Acts, the sequel, sets forth the continuation of God's plan by recording what Jesus *continued* to do and teach through the Holy Spirit and the apostolic church. The resurrected Jesus reminded the disciples of the promised Holy Spirit and commanded them to wait for his imminent coming in Jerusalem.

The disciples asked when Jesus would establish his kingdom, but Jesus just told them that they would be his Spirit-empowered witnesses. A period of waiting and praying followed as the early believers prepared for the coming of the Spirit (1:6–14).

B. The Replacement of Judas (1:15–26)

Acts 1:15–26 shows the replacement of Judas by the Eleven. After they set the ground rules, Matthias was selected by lot. It is a matter of debate whether Matthias's selection was approved by God.[124] However, Luke makes no specific comment on the matter.

C. Pentecost: The Church Is Born (2:1–47) When the day of Pentecost arrived, the gathered disciples experienced the coming of the Holy Spirit (2:1–13), which took place in fulfillment of Jesus's promise (see 1:8). Because devout Jews from every nation were

---

[122] See Polhill, *Acts*, 217–18.

[123] Bock, *Acts*, 331.

[124] The silence may suggest no problem with the selection. However, the following concerns can be raised: (1) Jesus's command was for the apostles to wait until the giving of the Spirit; Peter's initiative to replace Judas appears to violate that command; (2) casting lots is an OT mode of decision-making, hardly normative for NT times; (3) Matthias is not heard of again in the narrative of Acts subsequent to his selection; (4) instead, Luke narrated Christ's selection of Paul in Acts 9, apparently as the twelfth apostle and replacement of Judas (though this point is not explicitly made); (5) Peter and the other apostles did not possess the Holy Spirit at this point prior to the giving of the Spirit at Pentecost.

present, all Israel was represented. These worshippers heard the word of God in their own languages and witnessed the power of the Spirit, a sign of the end time. In this way the coming of the Spirit at Pentecost highlights the worldwide implications of the gospel, reversing the confusion of languages that ensued at the tower of Babel incident (Gen 11:1–9).

Peter explained the significance of the events that had transpired (2:14–40). In essence, the logic of Peter's address is that (1) the Spirit had now been poured out; (2) Jesus predicted that this would occur once he had been exalted with God subsequent to his ascension (Luke 24:49; see Acts 1:8–9); (3) hence the coming of the Spirit proved that Jesus had now been exalted: "Therefore, since he has been exalted to the right hand of God and has received from the Father the promised Holy Spirit, he has poured out what you both see and hear" (2:33).

Peter quoted the prophecy of Joel 2:28–32 to explain that this was the promised coming of the Holy Spirit (2:14–21). The last line of Joel's prophecy, "Then everyone who calls on the name of the Lord will be saved," transitions into Peter's evangelistic appeal (2:22–36). He concluded with a call to repentance (2:37–40), with the result that 3,000 were converted! The citation of Joel 2:28–32 can be compared to the citation of Isaiah 61:1–2 in Luke 4:18–19 in that it sets the stage for the rest of the book by narrating the coming of the Spirit to all those who called on the name of the Lord.

Luke concluded his account of these preliminary events with the first of several summaries that mark the transitions (2:41–47). The church devoted itself to the apostles' teaching (the standard of doctrinal orthodoxy prior to the formation of the NT), to fellowship, to the breaking of bread (i.e., celebrating the Lord's Supper), and to prayers (note the plural in the original Greek, which may suggest set prayers). Many miraculous signs and wonders were performed by the apostles. The believers shared everything in common, worshipped God in gladness, and continually grew in number.

II. The Early Church in Jerusalem (3:1–6:7)

Subsequent to the foundational narrative of the ascension of Jesus and the coming of the Spirit in the first two chapters, this unit presents the establishment of the church in Jerusalem: stage one of the three-part expansion of the gospel predicted by the risen Jesus at the beginning of the book of Acts (1:8). At this early juncture the church is wholly Jewish and expanding rapidly, which is further underscored by the reference to a number of priests coming to the faith, which concludes this section (6:7). Jesus's promise that his followers would be witnesses in Jerusalem was powerfully fulfilled.

A. A Miracle and Its Aftermath (3:1–4:31) God performed a remarkable miracle through Peter who, together with John, was on his way to the hour of prayer in the temple (3:1–10). When approached for money by a man born lame, Peter healed the man, whose great rejoicing drew a large crowd. Peter's ensuing speech at the temple (3:13–26) charged the people with putting Jesus to death but acknowledged that they had done so out of ignorance. Peter told the crowd that they would experience "times of refreshing" if they repented and followed Jesus.

At this, Peter and John were seized by the Jewish leaders (4:1–4). This gave Peter the opportunity to extend a similar message to the Sanhedrin, albeit without an appeal to repent. Subsequently, Peter and John were released with orders to stop talking about Jesus (4:5–22). Upon their return to the community of believers, the place was shaken, and the Christ-followers were all filled with the Holy Spirit to "speak the word of God boldly" (4:31).

B. Trouble Within and Without (4:32–6:7) This section of Acts shows the nature of the new community and the lengths to which God was prepared to go to protect her purity. Barnabas, first mentioned here, sold a piece of property and donated the proceeds to the church (4:32–37). This spurred a couple in the church, Ananias and Sapphira, to do the same though keeping back a portion for themselves. By itself, this was unobjectionable, but lying about it in order to increase one's stature was an affront to God. The couple was severely judged: first Ananias and then his wife were struck dead on the spot (5:1–11). As a result, great fear came upon the church.

Undaunted, the apostles preached continually in the temple, boldly healing in Jesus's name (5:12–16). Once more the apostles were arrested but freed by an angel who told them to go on so they could "tell the people all about this life" (5:20). When arrested again and forbidden to preach about Jesus, the apostles retorted, "We must obey God rather than people" (5:29). Gamaliel's advice to his fellow Sanhedrin members was to wait and see. If this movement was not from God, it would fail, as other movements had done in the past. After receiving a flogging, the apostles returned joyfully to preaching the gospel, in direct disobedience to the Sanhedrin (5:40) but in obedience to God.

The section is rounded out by a return to the community life of the young church. A potential crisis was averted by the church's selection of seven qualified, Spirit-filled men to meet the needs of a group of Hellenistic widows (6:1–7). Stephen, the main character of chapter 7, is introduced as a man full of faith and the Holy Spirit. Luke summarized the state of the church by highlighting the effective witness borne in Jerusalem. In particular, Luke noted that even a large number of priests came to the faith (6:7).

III. Initial Expansion: Stephen, Samaria, and Saul (6:8–9:31)

A. Suffering: One of the Servants Arrested and Martyred (Acts 6:8–7:60) Stephen, introduced in the previous section, was falsely accused of speaking against "Moses and God" before the Sanhedrin by those of "the Freedmen's Synagogue" (6:8–15). Stephen's defense (chap. 7) shows how throughout Israel's history, the nation opposed God's plan: Joseph was sold into slavery, Moses's leadership was rejected, and the people worshipped idols. In a sense this unit serves as the completion of the last section in its emphasis on Jewish responsibility. Stephen's martyrdom and vision led to the events narrated in the following chapters.

B. Palestine and Syria: Philip, Saul, and Peter (8:1–9:31) Stephen's death sparked a period of great persecution for the church. Saul, who had played a major role in Stephen's stoning, was ravaging the church (8:1–3). The believers, except for the apostles, were scattered throughout the surrounding regions, which resulted in the extension of the gospel beyond Judea to Samaria, in fulfillment of Jesus's mandate (see 1:8).

Philip, one of the seven (6:5), performed signs in Samaria and preached Christ to the Samaritans (8:4–8). However, the Samaritans did not receive the Spirit upon salvation until Peter and John, representing the apostles, came and laid hands on them. This served to authenticate God's work among them. In the process, Simon the sorcerer, who sought to purchase the power of the Holy Spirit from Peter for money, was rebuked (8:9–25).

Subsequently, Philip, again at the direction of the Holy Spirit, encountered a court official for Candace, the queen of Ethiopia, and led him to Christ (8:26–38). Although Gentile by birth, he was probably a proselyte, perhaps a God-fearer. The Holy Spirit miraculously transported Philip to Azotus, where he evangelized the coastal regions all the way to Caesarea (8:39–40). The gospel then moved throughout the regions of Judea and Samaria.

The final chapter in this section records the conversion of Saul in preparation for the Gentile mission (9:1–31). While on the road to Damascus to persecute Christians, Saul encountered the risen Christ and was converted. This marks a momentous occasion in the mission of the early church. The major opponent of Christianity became the greatest protagonist of the church's mission, and—amazingly—he would take the gospel to the "ends of the earth."

To Ananias, a disciple charged with ministering to Saul, Jesus described Saul as his "chosen instrument to take my name to Gentiles, kings, and the Israelites" (9:15). Although first met with skepticism, Saul preached the gospel powerfully in Damascus. Later, the Jerusalem church received him at the intercession of Barnabas. Saul preached boldly in the name of Jesus until an assassination attempt forced the brothers to take him to Tarsus via Caesarea.

Luke concluded this section with a summary that includes a reference to the church enjoying a period of peace and increase in numbers. Thus, Luke chronicled the plan of God as expressed in 1:8, taking the gospel through Jerusalem and Judea and Samaria. His next step was to provide a clear demonstration that Gentiles can be saved without converting to Judaism first, and this is the subject of the next two major sections.

IV. Continued Expansion: The First Gentile Convert (9:32–12:24)

A. The Proof of Gentile Conversion (9:32–11:18) Peter apparently had an itinerant ministry in Palestine. The healing of Aeneas the paralytic in Lydda led to raising Dorcas in Joppa (9:32–43). It also set up the account of the encounter with the Roman centurion Cornelius (chap. 10). While in Joppa, Peter received a vision which impressed on him that he should not consider anyone "unclean" (10:9–29). Meanwhile, Cornelius received a vision to call for Peter in Joppa. When Cornelius believed, Peter was convinced that God had accepted a Gentile into the church (10:24–48). Peter, in turn, convinced skeptics among the Jewish Christians that Cornelius's conversion was genuine (11:1–18).

B. Gentile Conversion in Antioch and the Return of Paul (11:19–26) Those scattered because of the persecution of Stephen reached Syrian Antioch, preaching only to Jews. But men from Cyprus and Cyrene preached to the Gentiles (the term "Hellenists" means "speakers of Greek," which refers to Gentiles). The Lord was with them, and a large number converted. Barnabas was sent to investigate, observed the genuineness of the conversions, and sought out Saul in Tarsus, teaching daily for the period of a year. Also, believers were first called "Christians" in Antioch.

C. Events in Jerusalem (11:27–12:24) The events in Jerusalem are sandwiched between references to Saul's and Barnabas's relief mission in response to a famine (11:27–30; 12:25). This indicates not only the solidarity the new Gentile believers had with the Jerusalem church but also that God was still moving among the Jews.

Peter's miraculous release apparently so infuriated Herod Agrippa I that when he could not find Peter, he executed the guards and left town.[125] Having given an oration and received the adoration of men as if he were indeed a god, Herod was "eaten by worms and died" (12:1–23).

Another Lukan summary statement concludes the section, noting that the word of God continued to spread. Barnabas and Saul returned to Antioch from their mission to Jerusalem, accompanied by John Mark, who would later go with them on the first part of their first missionary journey and, later still, write the Gospel that bears his name.

V. The Gentile Mission (Part 1, Asia Minor): First Journey, Jerusalem Council (12:25–16:5)

Luke has described the progress of the gospel geographically through Palestine and parts of Syria, and ethnically or religiously from Jews to proselytes, God-fearers, and Gentiles. His agenda here was to describe the Lord's work of sending the gospel to the uttermost parts of the earth. At each stage, progress was achieved through the work of God and not human efforts.

A. First Missionary Journey (12:25–14:28) The gospel's penetration into the Gentile world began with a specific call by the Holy Spirit through the prophets at Antioch to separate Barnabas and Saul for the missionary enterprise. Ironically, what Saul, prior to his conversion, sought to prevent by persecuting Christians in Damascus (also in Syria), he now actively brought about: the spread of the gospel to Syria and beyond. Once commissioned, they began their journey at Barnabas's home on the island of Cyprus (13:4; see 4:26). There Paul blinded Elymas the sorcerer because he "opposed them and tried to turn the proconsul away from the faith" (13:8). But the proconsul Sergius Paulus was converted.

---

[125] This is implied by the force of the word "and" (*kai*) in v. 19.

Paul and Barnabas then traveled through Pisidian Antioch, and 13:16–41 details Paul's sermon in the local synagogue. The Jews and proselytes begged Paul to preach again the next Sabbath, and the ensuing crowds sparked jealousy and derision from the members of the synagogue. Paul then turned to the Gentiles, and the gospel spread throughout the area. But the Jews instigated a persecution against Paul and Barnabas, expelling them from the region. This, then, forms the pattern throughout the first journey: synagogue, reception, rejection, persecution.

The results in Iconium were similar to those in Pisidian Antioch (14:1–7). Paul preached in the synagogue and then suffered persecution. At Lystra, Barnabas and Paul were met with a warm reception that almost turned to idolatry after the healing of a man who had been lame from birth. But the Jews from Iconium and Antioch swayed the crowds to stone Paul, and they left him for dead. Paul then evangelized Derbe (14:8–20) and made a return trip through Derbe, Iconium, and Lystra, establishing elders in every church, on his way to Antioch in Syria (14:21–28).

B. Jerusalem Council (15:1–35) The Jerusalem Council is a pivotal event for the Gentile mission. The question of Gentile converts is settled by this special meeting of the apostles and elders in Jerusalem. The issue was whether Gentiles had to become Jewish proselytes before they could become Christians (see 15:1, 5). The matter was settled by the testimonies of Peter, Paul, and Barnabas, and ultimately James adjudicated the matter by citing Amos 9:11. At the conclusion of the meeting, a letter was sent (see 15:23–29) that encouraged the Gentiles to abstain from things particularly repulsive to Jews (15:20, 29).

C. Second Missionary Journey Begins (15:36–16:5) Traditionally, 15:36 has been seen as marking the beginning of Paul's second missionary journey. This journey is presented in terms of encouraging the church in Syrian Antioch and the young churches planted during the first journey. The letter mentioned in the previous section was taken to the churches of South Galatia. Silas replaced Barnabas after Barnabas and Paul disagreed on whether to take John Mark with them. Paul said no because of Mark's desertion early in the first missionary journey. But Barnabas wanted to give his nephew another chance, so they parted company. While Paul was in Lystra, Timothy was highly recommended by the churches and joined Paul and Silas. The section concludes with a summary that notes the growth and encouragement of the churches.

VI. The Gentile Mission (Part 2, Greece): Second and Third Journeys (16:6–19:20)

A. Second Missionary Journey (16:6–18:22) As in every genuine new movement of the gospel into new lands or people groups, God is the One who instigated the irresistible spread of the gospel in the mission of the early church. Paul's plan was to continue through Asia Minor, but the Spirit prevented him from doing so. When he had a dream about a Macedonian calling him for help, Paul proceeded to go there, "concluding that God had called us to preach the gospel to them" (16:10).

Paul's first stop after crossing the Hellespont was Philippi, where the first "we" section occurs (starting in 16:10). Paul's pattern, consistent with God's salvation-historical plan, was to begin with the Jewish residents of a given city or region and then turn to the Gentiles. The first convert to the Christian gospel in Europe was Lydia, a female merchant selling an expensive purple cloth.

The confrontation with a demon-possessed young woman led to a painful but fruitful encounter with the magistrates of the city. Paul and his companions were jailed but found this incident to be a platform for the gospel. The jailer was converted, and the magistrates offered to release Paul. But Paul, appealing to his Roman citizenship, would not let them beat him and his associates in public and then release them secretly. Paul demanded, and received, a public apology, but he and his coworkers were urged to leave town.

In Thessalonica, Paul stayed consistent in following the pattern "to the Jew first, and also to the Gentile" (see 17:2, "as usual"). Preaching in the synagogue for at least three Sabbaths, Paul used the Scriptures to show people "that it was necessary for the Messiah to suffer and rise from the dead" and that that Messiah was Jesus (17:3). When Gentiles came to Christ in large numbers, the Jews became jealous and hired scoundrels to persecute the believers. When this was brought to the attention of the magistrates, they fined Paul's host while Paul and the missionary team departed for Berea. After their early success there, the Jews from Thessalonica followed them to Berea and stirred up more violence until Paul was forced to go to Athens.

Athens, a major intellectual center, provided Paul with a great challenge in his missionary preaching. He found the city full of idols and reasoned with Epicurean and Stoic philosophers, who considered the apostle a "pseudo-intellectual" (lit. a "seed picker," that is, one who picks up scraps; 17:18). Some thought Paul spoke of "foreign deities" because he proclaimed Jesus and the resurrection (17:18). Paul began his address by referring to an altar he had observed that bore the inscription "To an unknown God" (17:23). From this Paul declared the good news of Jesus and his resurrection from the dead. Some ridiculed Paul, but a few believed, among them Dionysius the Areopagite and a woman named Damaris (17:34). On the whole, Paul met with less positive response there than on other occasions in his missionary preaching.

The next stop was Corinth, where Paul met with Aquila and Priscilla, Jewish Christians recently expelled from Rome. Again Paul reasoned in the synagogues. When the people there steadfastly resisted, Paul turned to the Gentiles. Crispus, the leader of the synagogue, was converted along with many other Corinthians. Paul stayed in Corinth for eighteen months. Ultimately, the conflict with the Jews ended up with Paul standing before the Roman proconsul Gallio, who decided he had no jurisdiction in Jewish religious matters. Paul then left for Syria via Ephesus.

B. Third Missionary Journey (18:23–19:20) Although from here on Paul traveled to Jerusalem and on to Antioch, the focus is on Ephesus. When Paul left Corinth, he briefly went to Ephesus. After preaching in the synagogue there, Paul was asked to stay longer but declined by saying, "I'll come back to you again, if God wills" (18:21). His return occurred two verses later. In the meantime, he traveled to Caesarea, Jerusalem, Antioch, and back, visiting some of the churches of the first journey, and then arrived back in Ephesus. There Paul encountered a residual John the Baptist movement (18:24–19:7), engaged in some initial missionary work (19:8–10), and performed extraordinary acts of ministry (19:11–20).

VII. The Gentile Mission (Part 3, Italy): Journey to Rome (19:21–28:31)

A. From Ephesus to Jerusalem (19:21–21:16) Paul planned to go to Rome after visiting Macedonia, Achaia, and Jerusalem, and this itinerary dominates the concluding section of the book. Paul's later vision (see 23:11) reinforces this plan, and Rome is the target on the horizon throughout this last section of the book of Acts. Before Paul departed from Ephesus, however, there was a strong pagan uprising. Once again, the Christians brought before the crowd were shown to be innocent of the charges brought against them. Paul traveled through Macedonia and Greece and set sail for Miletus. There he met with the Ephesian elders and gave them farewell instructions. The final unit of this section (21:1–16) marks the beginning of Paul's last journey before his arrest, and at every stop he was warned about difficulties awaiting him in Jerusalem.

B. Paul's Final Visit to Jerusalem and His Removal to Caesarea (21:17–23:35) Upon arriving in Jerusalem, Paul was invited to pay for a Jewish vow to alleviate suspicion among the Jewish believers. But a charge from Jews of Asia Minor that Paul brought a Gentile into the temple created a riot. Paul was seized by the Roman soldiers garrisoned at the fortress of Antonia. (Ironically, the false charge that Paul brought a Gentile into the temple caused Gentiles to enter the temple to rescue Paul.)

C. Paul's Defenses Before Felix, Festus, and Agrippa (24:1–26:32) After being allowed to give his defense before the crowd, Paul, over a period of at least two years, was brought before Felix (24:1–27), Porcius Festus (25:1–12), and Agrippa (25:13–27). Paul's appeal to Caesar necessitated the trip to Rome even though Paul was declared innocent of the charges at each interrogation (26:1–32).

D. Paul's Trip to Rome (27:1–28:31) The actual seafaring journey comprises almost two-thirds of the final two chapters of the book. Just as God had been the major impetus behind the church's missionary expansion, he was also the driving force on the journey to Rome. While Paul was not in control of his movements, neither were the Romans. God's providence is clearly accentuated through this final section of the book. It ultimately brought Paul to Rome and proved God's power throughout the journey.

When Paul arrived in Rome, he followed the pattern set throughout his ministry and met with the Jews first, with moderate success. Regarding those who rejected the message, Paul cited Isaiah 6:9–10 in order to show that the rejection of the Jews was not unexpected. After this, the Gentiles were invited to trust in Christ. Thus, Luke concluded the book with Paul under house arrest in Rome yet preaching unhindered to all who would listen, Jews and Gentiles alike.

THEOLOGY

In the past century, up until perhaps Conzelmann's work, Luke was not considered to be much of a theologian. Upon closer inspection, we should be able to appreciate Luke's theological underpinning. Witherington states, "Luke should have never been accused of not being much of a theologian. . . . In fact, he proves to be one of the theologians and ethicists in the New Testament who does the best job of integrating history, theology, ethics, rhetoric, and religious praxis in an intentional way."[126]

Theological Themes

Salvation History Luke's organizing principle is best described as "salvation history." His intent throughout Luke-Acts was to narrate the unfolding of God's salvation plan.[127] This, of course, was impacted by the identification of the genre of Acts as historiography and the nature of Acts as being a sequel to Luke. In describing this approach, one must avoid importing all the negative conclusions reached by proponents of *Heilsgeschichte* (German for "salvation history") to the interpretation of Luke-Acts. For Luke, focusing on salvation history was not a necessary correction to an embarrassing delay in the apocalyptic expectation within the lifetime of the early disciples.[128] Rather, Luke presented God's plan throughout history as one that brings about individual redemption through Jesus Christ. This redemption, in the fullness of time, was announced and offered through the proclamation of this historical event, that is, the gospel.[129] As Köstenberger and O'Brien observed, "Luke's Gospel tells the story of Jesus and his salvation, while the book of Acts traces the movement of that salvation to the Gentiles."[130]

One of the more prominent themes throughout Acts is the sovereignty of God in moving the gospel out of Palestine "and to the end of the earth" (1:8). This can be seen in a variety of ways. To begin with, Luke was clearly interested in the fulfillment of Scripture. The vast majority of the OT quotations occur in the evangelistic speeches in Jewish contexts (see esp. Peter's appeals in 2:14–36 and 3:12–26; Stephen's speech in 7:2–53; and Paul's address in the synagogue at Pisidian Antioch in 13:16–41).[131] In Gentile contexts (e.g., 17:22–31), this was a less effective appeal, but among those who hold to the inspiration of

---

[126] B. Witherington, III, *Invitation to the New Testament: First Things* (Oxford, UK: Oxford University Press, 2013), 120.

[127] See the essays in "Part I: The Salvation of God," in *Witness to the Gospel: The Theology of Acts*, ed. I. H. Marshall and D. Peterson (Grand Rapids, MI: Eerdmans, 1998). D. Peterson (ibid., 523) speaks of the "centrality of salvation theology" in Luke-Acts.

[128] As proposed by H. Conzelmann, *The Theology of St. Luke* (Philadelphia, PA: Fortress, 1961), 137–69.

[129] See F. Thielman, *Theology of the New Testament: A Canonical and Synthetic Approach* (Grand Rapids, MI: Zondervan, 2005), 113–14.

[130] A. J. Köstenberger and P. T. O'Brien, *Salvation to the Ends of the Earth*, NSBT 11 (Downers Grove, IL: InterVarsity, 2001), 157.

[131] All but two of the citations are in chaps. 1–15. The last two instances are in 23:5 and 28:26–27.

the Torah it was quite successful. The fulfillment of the OT was essential to the conversion of the Ethiopian eunuch (8:30–35). Beyond these specific instances, there are also unspecified appeals in Acts to the fulfillment of the OT that point to God's activity in sending Christ (e.g., Peter speaks of what "all the prophets testify," 3:18, 24; 10:43; cf. the summaries of Paul's preaching in 17:3; 24:14; 26:22; and of Apollos's preaching in 18:28). Thus, the message to Israel is, "Your Messiah has come, *according to the Scriptures*."

This fulfillment of God's desire is seen in the continued emphasis on God's plan. The "divine must" (*dei*) is a continued phenomenon from Luke's Gospel (see 1:16, 21). At many places in the narrative it is used to show the plans of God (see 3:21; 4:12; 9:6; 14:22; 17:3; 19:21; 23:11; 27:24; 27:26).

From a structural and literary standpoint, Luke shows that the expansion of the gospel to the ends of the earth was a movement of God. Above all else, it was in obedience to and in fulfillment of the explicit command of Jesus (1:8). The rest of the book unfolds as Jesus foretold (i.e., "Jerusalem, in all Judea and Samaria, and to the end of the earth"). But more than that, each step happened with God's interested involvement. The evangelization of Jerusalem came after the outpouring of the Spirit at Pentecost. In 8:4, the door was opened to Judea and Samaria. The persecution at the stoning of Stephen and the subsequent Dispersion proved providential. Philip evangelized some Samaritans and then a Gentile God-fearer (the Ethiopian) at the command of an angel.

The door was further opened to Gentiles with the salvation of Cornelius, who received a vision to talk to a man named Peter (10:1–5). Meanwhile, Peter, in Joppa, received a vision not to exclude anyone (10:9–16). At about that time the invitation from Cornelius arrived.

The outline of Acts is centered geographically: Jerusalem, Judea and Samaria, Asia Minor, Macedonia and Greece, and Rome. At the entrance of the gospel to each of these regions, Luke was careful to note that the gospel penetrated these areas at the direction of God. In 13:2, Paul and Barnabas were selected by the Holy Spirit to take the gospel to Asia Minor. On the return trip, a Macedonian vision was interpreted as a message from God to go there (16:9). Paul was determined to go to Rome, but this happened in such a way that could only be considered providential (19:21). The purposes of God were clearly announced to Paul on his final trip to Jerusalem. In the end he was arrested, appealed to Caesar, and was sent to Rome at state expense, all of which was articulated to Paul as the decree of God (e.g., 21:10–14; 23:11; 27:23–24).

The Universal Scope of the Gospel The second, unmistakable theme related to salvation history is that the gospel is for all nations. Luke stresses in Acts 1:8 that Jesus commanded the apostles to go to the ends of the earth. Yet he also documents that the steps to the inclusion of the Gentiles were slow and hesitating. Moreover, these steps were certainly not the result of human planning. For example, Peter had to be convinced by miraculous, divine means that Gentiles could receive the gospel apart from Judaism (10:1–48).

Although the inclusion of the Gentiles is widely accepted, it is often forgotten (and sometimes denied)[132] that salvation includes the restoration of Israel through Jesus (see esp. the question at 1:6 and Peter's invitation at 2:36). Jesus's reply to the question at 1:6 ("Lord, are you restoring the kingdom to Israel at this time?") was not that the kingdom would not be restored but that this would take place in the Father's timing. F. Thielman was certainly correct when he stated, "This implies that such a restoration is coming, although Christians should not calculate the timing of its arrival."[133] Throughout the book of Acts, the pattern—as Paul announced it in Romans 1:16—is "to the Jew, and also to the Gentile." Thus Luke demonstrated that the gospel was initially proclaimed "to the Jews first."

The Holy Spirit Related to the accentuation on the sovereignty of God in moving the gospel forward is an emphasis on the Holy Spirit as the agent of the church's life and growth. Luke describes his Gospel as recording "all that Jesus began to do and teach" (Acts 1:1), implying that the book of Acts is about the continuing activity of Christ. This activity was accomplished through the Holy Spirit.[134] Hence, the disciples were commanded to wait for the promise of the Spirit (1:4, 8). His coming at Pentecost signaled the beginning of the church's advance (2:1–4, 33).

Since God promised to give the Spirit at salvation (2:38; 9:17), his reception is proof of salvation. Speaking in tongues is the evidence that three key people groups have been saved: Jews (2:4), Gentiles (10:46), and some disciples of John the Baptist (19:6). Since it is evident that the Samaritans had received salvation as well (8:16), it is possible that they spoke in tongues at salvation too—though this is not stated explicitly in the text. It is a mistake, however, to assume that salvation is always accompanied by speaking in tongues. The account of Paul's conversion, for example, makes no mention of tongues. Tongues in Acts are an indisputable sign that salvation has taken place with regard to specific people groups. The phenomenon strongly underscores the inclusiveness of the gospel.

The Holy Spirit sovereignly directed the Christian mission. Jesus gave orders through the Holy Spirit (1:2). Philip was ordered by the Holy Spirit (8:29, 39). Peter was instructed by the Holy Spirit to receive Gentiles (10:19–20). The Holy Spirit set apart Barnabas and Saul and directed them to depart (13:2, 4). The Holy Spirit initiated Paul's departure to the Greek peninsula (16:6–10; cf. 20:22–23, 28; 21:4).

The Holy Spirit not only directed the mission; he empowered it. This was in keeping with the promise of Jesus (1:8), affirmed repeatedly in the narrative (4:8, 31; 6:10; 7:55; 9:31; 11:28–29; 13:9–10; 21:11). Peter's citation of Joel 2:28 (2:16–21), where the Lord promised an eschatological outpouring of the Spirit that would inaugurate salvation on

---

[132] See J. T. Sanders, *The Jews in Luke-Acts* (Philadelphia, PA: Fortress, 1987).

[133] Thielman, *Theology of the New Testament*, 133.

[134] A few times in Acts the Lord Jesus himself appears and communicates (1:4–8; 7:56; 9:1–18; and 23:11), although these occasions can hardly be separated from the ministry of the Holy Spirit.

a universal scope, is programmatic for the entire book. Thus it is difficult to overstate the Spirit's post-Easter role in salvation history.[135]

The Resurrection and Ascension of Jesus The key point in salvation history is the death, resurrection, and exaltation of Jesus. In the proclamation of the gospel, this cluster of significant events is the pivot point of history and the culmination of God's plan from long ago. This plan was commanded by God (4:23), predicted by the prophets (26:22), accomplished in Christ (13:28–39), and proclaimed by faithful witnesses (4:33).[136]

Luke's teaching on the resurrection of Christ entails not merely a restoration from the dead but an unprecedented exaltation. Even though others, such as Enoch or Elijah, had ascended to heaven, Jesus was elevated to the right hand of God. The importance of the ascension in Luke's theology is seen by strategic references to it in Luke-Acts at the end of the Gospel and at the beginning of Acts. Paul likewise, in the synagogue in Pisidian Antioch, connected the resurrection of Jesus to his Sonship (13:33–34). Thus, Jesus reigns as God's Messiah from the heavenly throne—not only as the Son of David but also as the Son of God.

The resurrection of Jesus is the proof of Jesus's claims (see 3:15; 5:20; 25:19). It is also the guarantee of a personal resurrection for chosen humanity (see 24:15; 26:23). Finally, as noted above, it is also the starting point for the restoration of Israel. This is the first question asked of the resurrected Jesus in the book of Acts (1:6), and he is the "hope of Israel" (28:20). This restoration begins with the reception of the Messiah and his purging of sin, a message powerfully proclaimed by Peter at Pentecost and marked especially by the pouring out of the Spirit as an inaugural sign of the last days (2:38).

The restoration includes a powerful "reconstituting" of the people of God to include the poor and oppressed in Israel and ultimately the inclusion of "all who are far off, as many as the Lord our God will call" (2:39).[137] Peter's words thus provide a fitting summary: "Let it be known to all of you and to all the people of Israel, that by the name of Jesus Christ the Nazarene—whom you crucified and whom God raised from the dead. . . . This Jesus is the stone despised by you builders, who has become the cornerstone. There is salvation in no one else, for there is no other name under heaven given to people by which we must be saved" (4:10–12).

CONTRIBUTION TO THE CANON

- Volume 2 of Luke-Acts: what Jesus continued to do through the Holy Spirit (1:1)

---

[135] Although Luke clearly understood that the Spirit was involved in the writing of the OT (e.g., some OT passages are identified as having come through the Holy Spirit: 1:16; 4:25–26; 28:25), the reception of the Spirit is clearly something eschatological.

[136] This is a far cry from Conzelmann's understanding that Jesus was the "middle of time." Luke's presentation of the resurrection and exaltation of Jesus is not an eschatological correction of inaccurate prophecy, but an integral part of God's plan.

[137] See the fine treatment in Thielman, *Theology of the New Testament*, 123–24.

- Account of the spread of Christianity from Jerusalem to Rome (1:8) and of the life and practices of the early church (see 2:42)
- Giving of the Spirit at Pentecost and birth of the NT church (chap. 2)
- Ministry of Peter, John, James (Jesus's half brother), and others (chaps. 1–12)
- Inclusion of the Gentiles by decree of the Jerusalem Council (chap. 15)
- Ministry of Paul "to the Jew first and also to the Gentiles" in locations to which Paul addressed letters included in the canon (chaps. 13–28; see especially 28:23–28)

STUDY QUESTIONS

1. Who wrote Acts? Was the author an apostle? If not, what ensures that the criterion of apostolicity was met?
2. When was Acts most likely written, and what is the major reason usually given for this date?
3. Who was Theophilus; how do we know; and what was his likely role with regard to Luke-Acts?
4. Where was the book of Acts most likely completed?
5. What are the major proposals regarding the purpose of Acts? According to the authors, what is the most likely purpose?
6. Why is the question regarding genre important for studying Acts?
7. Why is the book of Acts considered historically reliable?
8. What are the sources that lay behind the composition of Acts?
9. What is the basic "blueprint" for Acts, and why?
10. What is the logic underlying Peter's Pentecost sermon?
11. What major issue was discussed at the Jerusalem Council?
12. What role does the Holy Spirit play in the book of Acts?

FOR FURTHER STUDY

Alexander, L. C. A. *Acts in Its Ancient Literary Context: A Classicist Looks at the Acts of the Apostles.* Library of New Testament Studies 298. London, UK: T&T Clark International, 2005.

Barnett, P. *The Birth of Christianity: The First Twenty Years.* Vol. 1: *After Jesus.* Grand Rapids, MI: Eerdmans, 2005.

Barrett, C. K. *A Critical and Exegetical Commentary on the Acts of the Apostles.* International Critical Commentary. 2 vols. Edinburgh, Scotland: T&T Clark, 1994, 1998.

Bauckham, R., ed. *The Book of Acts in Its First Century Setting.* Vol. 4: *Palestinian Setting.* Grand Rapids, MI: Eerdmans, 1995.

Bird, M. F. "The Unity of Luke-Acts in Recent Discussion." *JSNT* 29 (2007): 425–48.

Blomberg, C. L. *From Pentecost to Patmos: An Introduction to Acts through Revelation.* Nashville, TN: B&H, 2006.

Bock, D. L. *Acts.* Baker Exegetical Commentary on the New Testament. Grand Rapids, MI: Baker, 2007.

________. *A Theology of Luke and Acts: God's Promised Program, Realized for All Nations*. Biblical Theology of the New Testament. Grand Rapids, MI: Zondervan, 2011.

Bruce, F. F. *The Book of Acts*. Rev. ed. New International Commentary on the New Testament. Grand Rapids, MI: Eerdmans, 1988.

Conzelmann, H. *Acts of the Apostles*. Hermeneia. Translated by J. Limburg, A. T. Kraabel, and D. H. Juel. Philadelphia, PA: Fortress, 1987.

Fitzmyer, J. A. *The Acts of the Apostles*. Anchor Bible. New York, NY: Doubleday, 1999.

Gasque, W. W. *A History of the Criticism of the Acts of the Apostles*. Beiträge zur Geschichte der biblischen Exegese 17. Tübingen, Germany: Mohr Siebeck, 1975.

Gill, D. W. J., and C. Gempf, eds. *The Book of Acts in Its First Century Setting*. Vol. 2: *Greco-Roman Setting*. Grand Rapids, MI: Eerdmans, 1994.

Haenchen, E. *The Acts of the Apostles: A Commentary*. Translated by B. Noble, G. Shinn, H. Anderson, and R. M. Wilson. Philadelphia, PA: Westminster, 1971.

Hemer, C. J. *The Book of Acts in the Setting of Hellenistic History*. Winona Lake, IN: Eisenbrauns, 1990.

__________. "First Person Narrative in Acts 27–28." *Tyndale Bulletin* 36 (1985): 79–109.

Hengel, M. *Acts and the History of Earliest Christianity*. Philadelphia, PA: Fortress, 1979.

Johnson, L. T. *The Acts of the Apostles*. Sacra Pagina 5. Collegeville, IN: Liturgical Press, 1992.

Keck, L. E., and J. L. Martyn, eds. *Studies in Luke-Acts*. Nashville, TN: Abingdon, 1966.

Keener, C. S. *Acts: An Exegetical Commentary*, 4 vols. Grand Rapids, MI: Baker, 2012–2015.

Kent, H. A., Jr. *Jerusalem to Rome: Studies in Acts*. Grand Rapids, MI: Baker, 1972.

Köstenberger, A. J., and P. T. O'Brien. *Salvation to the Ends of the Earth*. New Studies in Biblical Theology 11. Downers Grove, IL: InterVarsity, 2001.

Larkin, W. J. *Acts*. IVP New Testament Commentary. Downers Grove, IL: InterVarsity, 1995.

Levinskaya, I. *The Book of Acts in Its First Century Setting*. Vol. 5: *Diaspora Setting*. Grand Rapids, MI: Eerdmans, 1996.

Longenecker, R. N. "Acts." In *The Expositor's Bible Commentary*. Rev. ed. Vol. 10. Grand Rapids, MI: Zondervan, 2007.

Marshall, I. H. *The Acts of the Apostles*. Tyndale New Testament Commentary. Grand Rapids, MI: Eerdmans, 1980.

__________. "Acts." Pages 513–606 in *Commentary on the New Testament Use of the Old Testament*. Edited by G. K. Beale and D. A. Carson. Grand Rapids, MI: Baker, 2007.

Marshall, I. H., and D. Peterson, eds. *Witness to the Gospel: The Theology of Acts*. Grand Rapids, MI: Eerdmans, 1998.

Nicklas, T., and M. Tilly, eds. *The Book of Acts as Church History*. Beihefte zur neutestamentlichen Wissenschaft 120. New York, NY: de Gruyter, 2003.

Pao, D. W. *Acts and the Isaianic Exodus*. Wissenschaftliche Untersuchungen zum Neuen Testament 2/130. Tübingen, Germany: Mohr Siebeck, 2000. Repr. Biblical Studies Library. Grand Rapids, MI: Baker, 2000.

Polhill, J. *Acts*. New American Commentary 26. Nashville, TN: B&H, 1992.

Porter, S. E. *The Paul of Acts*. Wissenschaftliche Untersuchungen zum Neuen Testament 115. Tübingen, Germany: Mohr Siebeck, 1999.

__________. "The 'We' Passages." In *The Book of Acts in Its First-Century Setting*. Vol. 2: *The Book of Acts in Its Greco-Roman Setting*. Edited by D. W. J. Gill and C. Gempf. Grand Rapids, MI: Eerdmans, 1994, 545–74.

Rapske, B. *The Book of Acts in Its First Century Setting*. Vol. 3: *The Book of Acts and Paul in Roman Custody*. Grand Rapids, MI: Eerdmans, 2004.

Robbins, V. K. "The We-Passages in Acts and Ancient Sea-Voyages." *Biblical Research* 20 (1975): 5–18.

Ropes, J. H. *The Beginnings of Christianity*. Part I: *The Acts of the Apostles*. Edited by F. J. Foakes Jackson and K. Lake. Vol. III: *The Text of Acts*. London, England: Macmillan, 1926.

Schlatter, A. *The Theology of the Apostles: The Development of New Testament Theology*. Translated by A. J. Köstenberger. Grand Rapids, MI: Baker, 1999.

Schnabel, E. J. *Early Christian Mission*. 2 vols. Downers Grove, IL: InterVarsity, 2004.

Stott, J. R. W. *The Spirit, the Church, and the World: The Message of Acts*. Downers Grove, IL: InterVarsity, 1990.

Tannehill, R. C. *The Narrative Unity of Luke-Acts: A Literary Interpretation*. 2 vols. Minneapolis, MN: Fortress, 1990.

Thompson, A. J. *The Acts of the Risen Lord Jesus: Luke's Account of God's Unfolding Plan*. NSBT 27. Downer's Grove, IL: InterVarsity, 2011.

Vielhauer, P. "On the 'Paulinism' of Acts." Pages 33–50 in *Studies in Luke-Acts*. Edited by L. E. Keck and J. L. Martyn. Nashville, TN: Abingdon, 1966.

Walton, S., ed. *Reading Acts Today: Essays in Honour of Loveday C. A. Alexander*. London, UK: T&T Clark, 2011.

Chapter 9

Paul: The Man and His Message

CORE KNOWLEDGE

Basic Knowledge: Students should be able to list several of Paul's quotations of and allusions to Jesus's teachings. They should be prepared to describe the three major historic views with regard to Paul and the law including Scholasticism, Lutheranism, and the New Perspective. They should know the major dates associated with Paul's life, including his conversion, missionary journeys, imprisonments, and death.

Intermediate Knowledge: Students should be able to provide evidence to refute the claim that Paul was disinterested in the historical Jesus. They should be able to explain the three major challenges to Sanders's description of the Jewish view of salvation in the first century. They should know the approximate dates and occasions of each of Paul's Letters.

Advanced Knowledge: Students should be able to give a brief overview of the history of the debate over the relationship of Paul's theology to Jesus's teaching. They should be able to describe the adaptations of the "New Perspective on Paul" by J. D. G. Dunn and N. T. Wright. Finally, they should be prepared to identify and explain important references outside of the Bible that aid in establishing a Pauline chronology.

THE ROMAN EMPIRE IN THE AGE OF AUGUSTUS
City
Territory under Roman control
Senatorial provinces
Imperial provinces
Principal client states
Unconquered territory
Provincial boundaries
0 250 500 750 Miles
0 250 500 750 Kilometers
N
HIBERNIA
NORTH SEA
BRITANNIA
London
BALTIC STATES
GERMANIA
SLAVIC STATES
BELGICA
Trier
Rhine R.
Lutetia
GALLIA (GAUL)
Loire R.
LYONS
ATLANTIC OCEAN
AQUITANIA
Lyons
Rhone
Bordeaux
NARBONENSIS
Massalia
RAETIA
NORICUM
Alps Mts.
Mediolanum
Vercellae
Po R.
PANNONIA
Pola
ILLYRICUM (DALMATIA)
Salona
ADRIATIC SEA
DACIA
Danube R.
MOESIA
SARMATIA
Dnieper R.
Dniester R.
Volga R.
BOSPORUS
BLACK SEA
Douro R.
TARRACONENSIS
LUSITANIA
Tagus R.
Merida
Corduba
Seville
BAETICA
Cadiz (Gades)
Gibraltar
Balearic Is.
Corsica
Sardinia
Nora
Cagliari
Tiber R.
ITALIA
Rome
Pompeii
Cannae
TYRRHENIAN SEA
Sicily
SICILIA
Syracuse
Malta
MAURETANIA
NUMIDIA
Hippo (Bone)
Carthage
Hadrumetum
AFRICA
Leptis Magna
Sahara Desert
MEDITERRANEAN SEA
IONIAN SEA
MACEDONIA
EPIRUS
Actium
Olympia
ACHAIA
Athens
Corinth
Sparta
Philippi
Salonika (Thessalonica)
THRACE
Byzantium (Istanbul)
BITHYNIA AND PONTUS
Nicomedia
Pergamum
Ephesus
Sardis
ASIA
PHRYGIA
Miletus
Rhodes
Crete
Cnossus
Ankara
GALATIA
LYCIA AND PAMPHYLIA
CILICIA
Salamis
Cyprus
Zela
Trapezus
COLCHIS
Caucasus Mts.
IBERIA
ALBANIA
CASPIAN SEA
ARMENIA
Araxes R.
Halys R.
Malatya
CAPPADOCIA
ADIABENE
Arbela
Ecbatana
PARTHIA
SYRIA
Antioch
Aleppo
Euphrates R.
Orontes R.
PHOENICIA
Tripolis
Palmyra
Dura-Europos
Damascus
Tyre
Jordan R.
MESOPOTAMIA
Ctesiphon
Babylon
Susa
Jerusalem
DEAD SEA
JUDEA
NABATEA
Petra
ARABIA (PETRAEA)
Syro-Arabian Desert
Gulf of Aqaba
PERSIAN GULF
RED SEA
Gulf of Suez
Cyrene
CYRENAICA
Alexandria
Pelusium
Memphis
Nile R.
EGYPT
Thebes

INTRODUCTION

ONE CANNOT MASTER the content of the NT and ignore the apostle Paul. After encountering the risen Jesus on the road to Damascus, Saul of Tarsus became the outstanding missionary, theologian, and writer of the early church.[1] He was a central figure both in the NT and in the history of Christianity. He wrote thirteen Letters that comprise almost one-fourth of the NT. Approximately sixteen chapters of the book of Acts (13–28) focus on his missionary labors, describing him as the most effective missionary in all of history. Consequently, Paul was the author or subject of nearly one-third of the NT and the most influential interpreter of the teachings of Christ and of the significance of his life, death, and resurrection. This chapter introduces his message and important current debates about the theology and significance of this great apostle.

FOLLOWER OF JESUS OR FOUNDER OF CHRISTIANITY?

Most readers of the NT automatically assume that Jesus was the founder of Christianity and that Paul was a faithful follower of Christ who propagated Jesus's teachings throughout the world. However, recent NT scholarship has frequently challenged this traditional view. Some interpreters argue that Paul was the real founder of the Christian movement by introducing so many new ideas and emphases into the Christian faith that he essentially abandoned the original religion of Jesus of Nazareth.[2]

A Brief History of the Debate

One of the first significant modern scholars to argue for a strong dichotomy between the teachings of Jesus and Paul was F. C. Baur, whose work first appeared in 1845.[3] Baur insisted that Paul's teachings display irreconcilable differences with the teachings of the Jerusalem apostles and Palestinian churches that had been influenced by and sought to be faithful to the original teachings of Jesus. Paul consciously departed from the Jesus tradition, especially in his Christology and his view of the validity of the law. Baur's thesis sparked lively debate. Several scholars in Germany and France argued that significant differences existed between the teachings of Jesus and Paul. Radical scholars began to call for an abandonment of Pauline Christianity and a return to the simple teachings of Jesus.[4]

At the beginning of the twentieth century, W. Wrede, an influential German NT scholar, argued that Paul's thought was influenced by Jewish apocalyptic messianic expectations rather than by Jesus. Paul was an independent, free-thinking theologian whom Wrede

---

[1] See esp. Eckhard J. Schnabel, *Paul the Missionary: Realities, Strategies, and Methods* (Downers Grove, IL: InterVarsity, 2008).

[2] This organically develops from the quest for the historical Jesus (see chap. 3 above). If there is a discontinuity between the "Jesus of history" and the "Christ of faith," the question naturally arises, "From where did Paul get his religion?"

[3] F. C. Baur, *Paul, the Apostle of Jesus Christ*, trans. A. Menzies, 2 vols. (London, England: Williams & Norgate, 1875).

[4] For an excellent survey of the early history of the debate, see J. M. G. Barclay, "Jesus and Paul," in *Dictionary of Paul and His Letters*, ed. G. F. Hawthorne, R. P. Martin, and D. G. Reid (Downers Grove, IL: InterVarsity, 1993), 492–503.

called "the second founder of Christianity."[5] Wrede argued that Paul saw the life and teachings of Jesus as insignificant. All that mattered for Paul was Jesus's death and resurrection. The risen Christ who appeared to Paul on the Damascus road, rather than the earthly Jesus who walked the dusty roads of Galilee, was the focus of Paul's teachings. Wrede argued that Paul's teaching had exerted on Christianity "the stronger—not the better—influence," by which he echoed the earlier slogan of radical critics who called for a return "back from Paul to Jesus."[6] Several years later W. Bousset argued that Paul had been influenced by popular Hellenistic religion to transform Jesus from a Galilean prophet into a cultic god, a notion unprecedented in the teachings of Jesus or the earliest Palestinian community of believers.[7]

Wrede's theories received a forceful response from both liberal Protestant theologians in Germany and more conservative British and American scholars.[8] These scholars argued that Paul did not make many explicit references to Jesus's teachings because he had emphasized Jesus's message in his initial missionary preaching and assumed his readers' familiarity with them. Moreover, the theological differences in the teachings of Jesus and Paul had been grossly exaggerated by the critics. Although Paul's teachings developed those of Jesus, Paul did not contradict Jesus. The developments of Jesus's original teachings by Paul were grounded in a legitimate interpretation of Jesus's message and in no way perverted it.

R. Bultmann severely critiqued the responses to Wrede by scholars such as J. G. Machen. Bultmann saw so little historical continuity between Jesus and Paul that he could state, "Jesus's teaching is—to all intents and purposes—irrelevant for Paul."[9] Bultmann noted that Paul rarely alluded to or quoted from the teachings of Jesus and that these quotations and allusions were typically related to ethical rather than theological matters. This lack of reference to Jesus's life and teachings demonstrates that Paul was concerned only with the theological truths established by Jesus's crucifixion and resurrection and the implications of these events for an understanding of Jesus's identity as preexistent Son of God and Lord. However, Bultmann did see a significant theological consistency between the teachings of Jesus and Paul. Both of them attacked Jewish legalism and the sin of self-dependence for salvation. He even noted a material congruity between the Christologies of Jesus and

---

[5] W. Wrede, *Paul* (London, England: Green, 1907), 179. The original German edition is W. Wrede, *Paulus*, Religionsgeschichtliche Volksbücher 1 (Tübingen, Germany/Halle: Mohr, 1904). An important evangelical critique of Wrede's work was J. G. Machen, *The Origin of Paul's Religion* (New York, NY: Macmillan, 1921).

[6] Wrede, *Paul*, 180.

[7] W. Bousset, *Kyrios Christos: A History of Belief in Christ from the Beginnings of Christianity to Irenaeus*, trans. J. Steely (Nashville, TN: Abingdon, 1970; original German ed., 1913).

[8] The German responses came from A. von Harnack, A. Jülicher, and A. Resch. English responses included those of J. Moffatt, C. A. A. Scott, and J. G. Machen.

[9] R. Bultmann, "The Significance of the Historical Jesus for the Theology of Paul," in *Faith and Understanding: Collected Essays* (London, England: SCM, 1952), 223.

Paul.[10] Bultmann argued that the radical cry of scholars influenced by Wrede, "back from Paul to Jesus," was nonsense, since one could only discover Jesus through Paul.[11]

In the last half of the twentieth century, the relationship of Paul to Jesus did not receive the attention it deserves. J. M. G. Barclay has identified several factors leading to this neglect: (1) a parting of the ways between theology and NT study; (2) a widespread uncertainty about the meaning of the messages of Jesus and Paul; and (3) the general opposition in NT scholarship to attempts to develop a synthesis of the theologies of NT writers and early Christian figures and particularly Jesus and Paul.[12] Nevertheless, several scholars have made important contributions to an understanding of the relationship of Pauline thought to Jesus's message. In 1971, D. L. Dungan carefully analyzed Paul's appeal to the sayings of Jesus in 1 Corinthians and suggested that the Corinthians were already familiar with this material.[13] This confirmed the view of earlier scholars who responded to Wrede by arguing that references to the teachings of Jesus were prominent in Paul's missionary preaching. Dungan's research encouraged other scholars such as D. Wenham and D. Allison to explore the possible dependency of Paul's eschatological teaching on the eschatological discourses of Jesus.[14] M. Thompson carefully defined the sometimes nebulous terms "quotation," "allusion," and "echo" to aid in discussions of Pauline dependency on Christ's teachings and developed reasonable criteria for identifying each category in Paul's Letters.[15] In the last two decades of the twentieth century, scholars such as A. J. M. Wedderburn, B. Witherington, V. Furnish, and D. Wenham published important studies of the relationship of Paul to Jesus.[16] These works argue for a more extensive dependence of Pauline thought on the teachings of Jesus than has generally been accepted by scholars since Wrede.

Despite the new emphasis in the late twentieth century on the consistency of Paul's teachings with Jesus's, some scholars continue to portray Paul as the true founder of Christianity who perverted or ignored the teachings of Christ. The most important scholarly defense of this view in recent years was H. Maccoby's book, *The Mythmaker: Paul and the Invention of Christianity*, which was published in 1986. Maccoby revived the old arguments of the history-of-religions school which had its heyday in the early 1900s and argued that Paul invented the myths of Jesus's divinity and sacrificial death under the influence of the Greek mystery religions. He viewed Paul as single-handedly responsible

[10] For an excellent discussion of Bultmann's contribution to the debate, see Barclay, "Jesus and Paul," 494–96.

[11] See especially R. Bultmann, "Jesus and Paul," in *Existence and Faith* (London, England: Hodder & Stoughton, 1936), 201.

[12] Barclay, "Jesus and Paul," 497–98.

[13] D. L. Dungan, *The Sayings of Jesus in the Churches of Paul* (Oxford, UK: Blackwell, 1971).

[14] D. Wenham, *Gospel Perspectives 4: The Rediscovery of Jesus's Eschatological Discourse* (Sheffield: JSOT, 1984); D. Allison, *The End of the Ages Has Come* (Philadelphia, PA: Fortress, 1985).

[15] M. Thompson, *Clothed with Christ: The Example and Teaching of Jesus in Romans 12.1–15.13* (Sheffield: JSOT, 1991).

[16] V. Furnish, *Jesus According to Paul* (Cambridge, UK: Cambridge University Press, 1993); A. J. M. Wedderburn, ed., *Paul and Jesus: Collected Essays* (Sheffield: JSOT, 1989); D. Wenham, *Paul: Follower of Jesus or Founder of Christianity?* (Grand Rapids, MI: Eerdmans, 1995); B. Witherington III, *Jesus, Paul and the End of the World* (Downers Grove, IL: InterVarsity, 1992).

for injecting into Christianity the most offensive elements of the faith such as negative attitudes toward women and sexuality, anti-Semitism, authoritarian tendencies, and pro-slavery sentiments.[17] Many modern and especially postmodern readers were offended by perceived elements of Paul's teachings and were reviving the slogan "back from Paul to Jesus." As Wenham noted,

> It is not only scholars who have argued this. Many ordinary Christians, as well as non-Christians, have found Paul extremely difficult, and feel that Christianity would be very much better off without some of the dogmas that he propounds (e.g., the divinity of Jesus and Jesus's death as a blood sacrifice), not to mention his teachings of sex, women, and slaves. They would be quite happy if we could keep Jesus, but quietly lose Paul.[18]

Evidence for Paul's Lack of Concern for the Teachings and Life of Jesus

The paucity of references to Jesus's earthly life in Paul's Letters has convinced many that Paul was unconcerned with the Jesus of history. Thus, R. Bultmann appealed to 2 Corinthians 5:16, which states, "From now on, then, we do not know anyone in a purely human way. Even if we have known Christ in a purely human way, yet now we no longer know him like that." Bultmann interpreted the verse as indicating that Paul once had an interest in the historical Jesus but was only concerned with the death and resurrection of Jesus—rather than with his life—after his own conversion.[19]

However, as competent subsequent critiques by scholars such as M. J. Harris or N. T. Wright revealed, Bultmann's interpretation of the verse was flawed at two crucial points. First, Bultmann regarded the phrase "according to the flesh" as an adjectival phrase modifying "Christ," although the preceding sentence clearly identifies the phrase as adverbial, modifying "known." Second, Bultmann overlooked the clear importance of the historical Jesus in 2 Corinthians 4–5 and particularly in 2 Corinthians 4:7–15. Hence, in context, the statement means that Paul was

> repudiating (in v. 16b,c) as totally erroneous his sincere yet superficial preconversion estimate of Jesus as a misguided messianic pretender, a crucified heretic, whose followers must be extirpated (Acts 9:1–2; 26:9–11), for he had come to recognize the Nazarene as the divinely appointed Messiah whose death under the divine curse (Gal. 3:13; see Deut. 21:23) in fact brought life (vv. 14–15).[20]

---

[17] H. Maccoby, *The Mythmaker: Paul and the Invention of Christianity* (London, England: Weidenfeld & Nicholson, 1986).

[18] Wenham, *Paul*, 3.

[19] R. Bultmann, *Theology of the New Testament*, trans. K. Grobel (New York, NY: Scribner's, 1951–55), 1:237–39; idem, *The Second Letter to the Corinthians* (Minneapolis, MN: Augsburg, 1985), 155–56.

[20] M. J. Harris, *The Second Epistle to the Corinthians*, NIGTC (Grand Rapids, MI: Eerdmans, 2005), 429. Cf. N. T. Wright, *The New Testament and the People of God*, Christian Origins and the Question of God 1 (Minneapolis, MN: Fortress, 1992), 408.

Although, as has been seen, Bultmann's interpretation of this text has been ably refuted, Bultmann's influence is still seen and felt in those who argue for a sharp dichotomy between the Christ of Paul and the Jesus of history.

Scholars also point to the scarcity of direct quotations of Jesus in Paul's writings. Many scholars see a direct appeal to the teachings of Jesus in Paul's Letters only in 1 Corinthians 7:10 (which refers to the tradition preserved in Matt 5:27–28; 19:3–9; Mark 10:2–12; Luke 16:18) and 1 Corinthians 9:14 (which refers to the tradition preserved in Matt 10:10; Luke 10:7), that is, only two references in a single letter. That Paul here alluded to the Jesus tradition is difficult to dispute since he introduced the statements as the Lord's command and since his teaching so closely parallels that of Jesus both linguistically and thematically.

Some scholars even see these two clear allusions to Jesus's teachings as evidence for Paul's low estimation of the Jesus tradition since Paul cited these teachings rather loosely and seemed to have no concern to preserve Christ's exact words. Moreover, in 1 Corinthians 9:14 Paul cited Jesus's teaching that those who proclaim the gospel should receive financial support for their labors in the context of an explanation as to why he personally refused such support. Thus, the critics charge, Paul practiced the opposite of what Jesus actually commanded!

On the other hand, Paul's references to Jesus's teachings bespeak Paul's recognition of the authoritative nature of Jesus's utterances. Paul's admission in 1 Corinthians 7:12 and particularly 7:25 ("Now about virgins: I have no command from the Lord, but I do give an opinion as one who by the Lord's mercy is faithful") demonstrates the special authority assigned to Jesus's teachings in the view of Paul and the early church. Similarly, Paul's practice of supporting himself financially did not involve a dismissal of Jesus's teaching as some have suggested. Jesus's words, "The worker is worthy of his wages" (quoted in 1 Tim 5:18), while showing that the minister deserves support and that beneficiaries of the ministry are obligated to offer it, fall short of issuing a command that would render Paul's practice disobedient. Paul probably saw the command he referenced in 1 Corinthians 9:14 as a command to the *beneficiaries* of gospel ministry rather than to the gospel minister himself. Jesus's teachings established Paul's "right" to such support but did not demand that he actually receive it, especially if this had rendered him vulnerable to the charge that his ministry was financially motivated.[21]

Scholars who see little connection between Paul and Jesus also point to the divergent doctrines of the two teachers. Jesus, for example, affirmed the OT law; Paul disparaged it. Jesus saw himself as a prophet, but Paul transformed him into a cultic deity to be worshipped. The kingdom of God constituted the central focus of Jesus's preaching; however, kingdom language is almost completely absent from Paul's Letters. In response, other scholars have pointed out that much of the tension between the teachings of Jesus and those of Paul results from a misinterpretation of Jesus, Paul, or both. Jesus's teachings and

[21] Notice the emphasis on "rights" and the "authority" of the gospel messenger in 1 Cor 9:2, 12, 15, 18.

Paul's Damascus road experience defined the contours of Paul's theology. He faithfully interpreted Jesus's teachings in order to address the theological and ethical challenges of the churches to which he wrote.

Evidence of Paul's Concern for the Teachings and Life of Jesus

Significant evidence supports Paul's dependence on the teachings of Jesus. First, allusions to Christ's teachings in Paul's Letters are far more extensive and frequent than many scholars have recognized. Identifying actual intentional allusions to Jesus's teachings in Paul's Letters can be difficult. However, allusions are likely when (1) Paul used an explicit tradition indicator such as "the Lord commanded" or "word from the Lord"; (2) the suspected allusion contains linguistic or thematic echoes from the Gospels; or (3) a series of several possible allusions appears in a particular context.

An investigation by D. Wenham concluded that "there is massive evidence of Pauline knowledge of Jesus-traditions."[22] Wenham categorized allusions in Paul to the sayings of Jesus as highly probable, probable, or plausible. The chart below summarizes some of the most important of Wenham's findings.

Table 9.1: Highly Probable Allusions to Jesus in Paul's Letters

Sayings and Acts of Jesus	Allusions by Paul
Last Supper (Matt 26:26–30; Mark 14:22–26; esp. Luke 22:14–23)	1 Cor 11:23–26
Resurrection narratives (Luke 24:36–49; John 20:19–29; 21:1–14)	1 Cor 15:3–5, 35–57; Phil 3:21
Divorce (Mark 10:1–12; Matt 19:1–12)	1 Cor 7:10–11
Support of preachers (Matt 10:10; Luke 10:7)	1 Cor 9:14; 1 Tim 5:18
Eschatological teaching (Matthew 24; Mark 13; esp. Luke 21)	2 Thess 2:1–12
Eschatological parables: Thief in the night (Matt 24:43–44) Watchman (Luke 12:36–38) Stewards (Matt 24:45–51; Luke 12:42–48) Wise and foolish virgins (Matt 25:1–13)	1 Thess 4:1–5:11
Mountain-moving faith (Matt 17:20)	1 Cor 13:2
Nonretaliation (Matt 5:38–42; Luke 6:29–30)	Rom 12:14
Love and the law (Matt 22:37–40)	Rom 13:8–10; Gal 5:14
Nothing unclean (Matt 15:10–20; Mark 7:17–23)	Rom 14:14
Abba (Mark 14:36)	Rom 8:15; Gal 4:6

Wenham also argued for the probability of Paul's knowledge of many other sayings and events, including Jesus's baptism by John the Baptist (Matt 3:13–17 and parallels);

[22] Wenham, *Paul*, 381.

Jesus's sayings about taking up the cross (Matt 16:24–26 and parallels); the sayings about drinking his cup and sharing his baptism (Mark 10:38); the commissioning of Peter (John 21:15–19); Jesus's transfiguration (Matt 17:1–13 and parallels); the story of James's and John's competition (Matt 20:20–24); the ransom saying (Matt 20:28//Mark 10:45); the parable of the Sower (Matt 13:1–9, 18–23 and parallels); the discussion of paying taxes (Matt 22:15–22); teaching about peacemaking (e.g., Matt 5:9); and the instruction about cutting off offending limbs of the body (Matt 5:29–30). Wenham argued too for the plausibility of Paul's knowledge of other details recorded in the Gospels, such as the traditions of Jesus's birth (Matt 1:18–25; Luke 2:1–20); temptation (Matt 4:1–11 and parallels); the Sermon on the Mount (Matthew 5–7); his use of the title "Son of Man" (e.g., John 1:51); and the parable of the Prodigal Son (Luke 15:11–32). Although space does not permit a discussion of the contextual and linguistic evidence supporting the probability and plausibility of these allusions, the evidence for many of the allusions that Wenham deemed highly probable or probable is compelling.

Data collected by Wenham suggests Paul's extensive knowledge of the life of Jesus. Wenham remarked, "The sheer quantity of evidence assembled is impressive. Indeed, if Paul knew all the gospel traditions which we have noted, then he knew most of the story of Jesus as the Gospels present it (at least in content, if not in order)—from the infancy of Jesus to his baptism, his ministry, and on to his death, resurrection, and ascension."[23] Notably, the evidence presented by Wenham has been deemed persuasive by a number of scholars well versed in both Paul's teachings and Jesus's Gospels sayings. R. Bauckham commented, "Allusions to Jesus traditions in Paul's writings are in fact much more numerous than an older stereotype of Paul allowed."[24] Similarly, after comparing a number of examples of allusions in Paul's writings to Jesus's teaching, J. D. G. Dunn concluded,

> In short, once granted the likelihood that Paul and the churches to which he wrote shared a good deal of common Jesus tradition, familiar enough on both sides to be a matter of allusion and implicit reference, the probability becomes strong that Paul would have naturally and without contrivance referred to that tradition in just that way. Against that plausible background several passages in Paul gain additional illumination and resonance. And the conclusion becomes increasingly persuasive that knowledge of and interest in the life and ministry of Jesus was an integral part of his theology, albeit referred to only *sotto voce* [i.e. under his breath] in his written theology.[25]

However, not all of the Pauline allusions to the Jesus tradition argued by Wenham are equally convincing. The process of identifying allusions is often subjective, despite

---

[23] Ibid., 385.

[24] R. Bauckham, *Jesus and the Eyewitnesses: The Gospels as Eyewitness Testimony* (Grand Rapids, MI: Eerdmans, 2006), 267.

[25] J. D. G. Dunn, *The Theology of Paul the Apostle* (Grand Rapids, MI: Eerdmans, 1998), 195.

Wenham's attempt to objectify the process as much as possible by pointing to specific textual features. Nevertheless, Wenham has demonstrated ably that Paul's knowledge of Jesus's teachings extended far beyond 1 Corinthians 7:10 and 9:14 and that the continuity between Jesus and Paul is significantly greater than much recent NT scholarship has affirmed.[26]

Not only are verbal allusions to Jesus's teachings more frequent in Paul than many scholars assumed, but the theological similarities between the two figures are also much greater than many have acknowledged. Although some have argued that Jesus viewed himself as a mere mortal prophet or sage whom Paul deified under the influence of pagan mystery religions, recent research has demonstrated that Jesus's self-understanding was quite similar to Paul's view of him. For example, many scholars today believe that a source (identified as "Q") that was utilized by Matthew and Luke was likely the earliest source for the Gospels.[27] Several have suggested that "Q" reflects a low Christology in which Jesus is merely an inspiring sage. However, L. Hurtado recently argued,

> Instead, Q reflects a very high view of Jesus's role, powers, and person. He is directly associated with God in crucial eschatological functions, and he has unquestioned authority in the lives of his followers. He is uniquely endowed with God's Spirit, and in his powerful activities that include healing, exorcism, and other remarkable miracles, as well as in his proclamation, God's kingdom comes to eschatological expression. Through him, his followers are privileged to participate in declaring and demonstrating God's kingdom, and he is paradigmatic for all their activities. They suffer opposition precisely for his sake, and on his account; he promises them a spectacular vindication that will involve sharing his kingdom.[28]

The earliest canonical Gospel, the Gospel of Mark, also reflects a high Christology. Mark portrays Jesus's coming as the fulfillment of OT prophecies about the coming of Yahweh (Mark 1:2–3), thereby identifying Jesus as God. Numerous scenes in Mark from Jesus's life may be described as "epiphanic" in that they echo descriptions of the acts of Yahweh in the OT. For example, in Mark 6:45–52 Jesus walked on the water, an act of which God alone is capable according to Job 9:8. He identified himself with the words "I am" *(egō eimi)* in a manner reminiscent of the self-identification of Yahweh in Exodus 3. Marcus correctly stated that "the overwhelming impact made by our narrative is an impression of

---

[26] Wenham, *Paul.* See also S. Kim ("Jesus, Sayings of," in *Dictionary of Paul and His Letters*, 474–92), who identified twenty-five instances in which Paul certainly or probably referred to or alluded to a saying of Jesus and over forty possible echoes of a saying of Jesus. Kim's findings are similar to those of Wenham. Kim's discovery of extensive parallels between the teachings of Jesus and Paul led him to pose this thesis: "When in the Pauline Letters an echo of a dominical logion is disputed, the burden of proof lies more heavily on those who would deny it, than on those who would accept it."

[27] See chap. 3 above.

[28] L. Hurtado, *Lord Jesus Christ: Devotion to Jesus in Earliest Christianity* (Grand Rapids, MI: Eerdmans, 2003), 254.

Jesus' divinity."[29] Moreover, Jesus's preferred title "Son of Man" constitutes a clear allusion to Daniel 7:13–14 and describes Jesus as a divine King of heavenly origin who will reign over a universal and eternal kingdom.[30] Consequently, Paul's affirmations of Jesus's eternal existence and deity are consistent with the portrayals of Christ in the earliest Gospel material and are closely associated with Jesus's own self-understanding.

Continuity and Development

The strict "founder" versus "follower" dichotomy, in which the debate over Paul's relationship to Jesus has often been cast, unnecessarily prompts the interpreter to gravitate to one of two extremes. The most reasonable interpretation of the data suggests that Paul both respected and relied on the teachings of Jesus but felt free to develop and augment those teachings based on his own reflection on the significance of his Damascus road experience and his study of the OT. As in a comparative study of the four Gospels, so here, in comparisons of the teachings of Jesus and Paul, one must not assume that all differences amount to disagreements.

Several important factors in the mission of Paul required him both to develop and to modify the message of Jesus: (1) Jesus's passion, resurrection, and glorification demanded an emphasis on the exalted Christ; (2) the death and exaltation of the Messiah and the outpouring of the Spirit introduced a new eschatological era and enacted a new covenant between God and his people; and (3) the differences between Jesus's Jewish audience and Paul's Gentile audience required Paul to use different idioms and thought forms in order to relate to his own cultural context.[31] After an extensive comparison of the theologies of Paul and Jesus, which highlighted more differences than Wenham's research, Barclay concluded,

> The central question is whether in essence Paul's theology is harmonious with, and a legitimate development of, the message of Jesus. As we have seen, this question cannot be answered simply by discovering or denying the presence of echoes of the words of Jesus in Paul. That issue, which lies on the level of historical continuity between Jesus and Paul, cannot by itself determine whether Paul's theology is congruous with that of Jesus. But there is sufficient evidence to show that, whether consciously or otherwise, Paul did develop the central insights of the teaching of Jesus and the central meaning of his life and death in a way that truly represented their dynamic and fullest significance.[32]

---

[29] J. Marcus, *Mark 1–8: A New Translation and Commentary*, AB (New York, NY: Doubleday, 2000), 432.

[30] G. E. Ladd, *A Theology of the New Testament*, rev. ed. (Grand Rapids, MI: Eerdmans, 1993), 143–57. The interpretation of the meaning of the title suggested by Ladd has been challenged in recent scholarship. See J. D. G. Dunn, *Jesus Remembered*, vol. 1 of Christianity in the Making (Grand Rapids, MI: Eerdmans, 2003), 724–64.

[31] See Barclay, "Jesus and Paul," 502; A. J. Köstenberger, "Review of David Wenham, *Paul: Follower of Jesus or Founder of Christianity?*" *TrinJ* NS 16 (1995): 259–62.

[32] Barclay, "Jesus and Paul," 502.

Conclusion

Although Paul's contributions to the Christian faith should not be underestimated, Paul should be recognized as a faithful follower of Jesus Christ rather than as the founder of a form of Christianity that deviated drastically from Jesus's teachings. Paul's teachings originated from his reflection on the life and teachings of Jesus, his study of the OT, and his contemplation on the significance of his Damascus road experience.[33] Although the major motifs of his theology are rooted in the message of Jesus himself, Paul was necessarily an innovator who pored over the Hebrew Scriptures as he addressed the unique challenges raised by the churches he influenced.

The fact that Paul's mission primarily addressed Gentile congregations whereas Jesus's ministry was primarily focused on Palestinian Jews meant that Paul often had to look beyond Jesus back to the OT to understand the implications of Jesus's death, burial, and resurrection and put them in terms his audience could grasp. However, the differences between Jesus's teaching and Paul's Letters are like the difference between the seed and the mature plant, the foundation and the superstructure built upon it. In Paul's Letters to the churches, one hears not only the voice of the Spirit that inspired the OT Scriptures but also the voice of Jesus, Paul's Savior and Lord.

THE "NEW PERSPECTIVE" ON PAUL

In the last quarter of the twentieth century, a paradigm shift in the interpretation of Paul's Letters and theology occurred. Ever since the Reformation, Protestant scholars and some leading Catholic scholars viewed Paul's Letters as a polemic against Jewish legalism, which insisted that individuals could save themselves by their efforts to keep the OT law. Paul countered this arrogant theology by maintaining that salvation was by grace through faith alone. Since the 1977 publication of E. P. Sanders's *Paul and Palestinian Judaism*, many scholars concluded that such legalism did not exist in first-century Judaism. This "new perspective" on first-century Judaism has required a reexamination of Paul's gospel, that is, his teachings about the law, good works, and justification. For this reason it is helpful to provide a brief review of the history of scholarship on this issue.[34]

The Scholastic Perspective

Scholasticism was a philosophical movement dominant in Western Christian civilization from the ninth century to the fourteenth. It sought to reconcile the teachings of the classical philosophers with Christian theology.[35] One of the most important scholastics

---

[33] For the significance of the Damascus road experience for Paul's theology, see S. Kim, *The Origin of Paul's Gospel* (Grand Rapids, MI: Eerdmans: 1982). For the significance of the OT for Paul and his methods of OT exegesis, see E. E. Ellis, *Paul's Use of the Old Testament* (Grand Rapids, MI: Baker, 1981).

[34] For the most thorough critique of the New Perspective, see D. A. Carson, P. T. O'Brien, and M. A. Seifrid, eds., *Justification and Variegated Nomism*, 2 vols. (Grand Rapids, MI: Baker, 2001, 2004).

[35] See C. Brown, "Scholasticism," in *Eerdmans' Handbook to the History of Christianity*, ed. T. Dowley (Grand Rapids, MI: Eerdmans, 1985), 278–79.

was Thomas Aquinas. Aquinas devoted many years to writing an enormous work called the *Summa Theologica,* in which he scrutinized the classic themes of Christian theology in light of the teachings of Aristotle.[36]

Aquinas taught that humans can receive eternal life only when God graciously transforms their nature. Human nature is sinful and so qualitatively different from God's nature that humans are incapable of pleasing God.[37] The OT law was incapable of producing the conduct necessary to satisfy God because it was hampered by this fallen human nature.[38] God graciously gave the new law (the gospel message and the law written on the heart) and sent the Holy Spirit to transform individuals.[39] This transformation enabled people to do what was right and good not out of fear of punishment but from their own desire to love and please the Lord, resulting in eternal life.[40] Aquinas emphasized that individuals did not merit the grace that transformed them. He insisted, however, that once they were transformed by that grace, they truly merited eternal life for the good deeds they performed. He also taught that one person's good works might merit eternal life for someone else.[41]

The Lutheran Perspective

Martin Luther, an Augustinian monk of the early sixteenth century, lived a miserable existence under the influence of scholastic theology. Luther was tormented by the growing dread that neither his own good works nor the merits of his monastic order were sufficient to save him from the wrath of the heavenly Judge. However, while Luther was lecturing on Paul's Letters at the University of Wittenberg, he became captivated by the missives to the Romans and Galatians and the concept of the "righteousness of God" portrayed there. Luther eventually concluded that an individual's "active righteousness" was utterly incapable of saving him from eternal punishment.

Instead, salvation came through "passive righteousness," a righteousness provided by God that was imputed to the sinner through faith in Jesus Christ. Luther argued that the law was never intended to be a means of salvation. Its role was to terrify the sinner so that he despaired of his own self-righteousness and trusted the atoning death of Jesus Christ alone for salvation. Luther saw the law as having little significance for the believer since whatever remained useful in the law was written on the Christian's heart in fulfillment of the new covenant promise.[42]

Luther closely associated the dependence on good works for salvation in medieval Catholicism with an assumed works-righteousness in the Judaism of Paul's day. He read

---

[36] For a brief biography of Aquinas, see R. G. Clouse, "Thomas Aquinas," in *Eerdmans' Handbook*, 288.

[37] *Summa Theologica*, 1a2ae.109.2.

[38] *Summa Theologica*, 1a2ae.98.1.

[39] *Summa Theologica*, 1a2ae.98.3.

[40] *Summa Theologica*, 1a2ae.108.1.

[41] For an excellent summary of the Thomist view of salvation and the Protestant reaction, see F. Thielman, *Paul and the Law: A Contextual Approach* (Downers Grove, IL: InterVarsity, 1994), 15–24.

[42] See Thielman, *Paul and the Law*, 18–20.

references in Romans and Galatians as if he and Paul contended with opponents who affirmed essentially the same view of the relationship of the law to salvation. The hermeneutic that confused the Catholicism of Luther's day with the Judaism of Paul's day dominated Protestant exegesis of Paul's Letters and discussions of Paul's theology for the next 400 years until it was challenged by a number of Jewish and Protestant scholars in the twentieth century.

Few Protestant scholars undertook an extensive study of ancient Judaism in order to determine whether the equation of medieval Catholic theology with Judaism was accurate. F. Weber produced a handbook titled *Jewish Theology on the Basis of the Talmud and Related Writings*, the German version of which was published in 1880. Weber asserted that legalism, the study and quest to obey the law, was the essence of Talmudic Judaism.[43] Weber described Jewish theology as depicting God as a great shopkeeper who carefully recorded the good and bad deeds of individuals in an enormous ledger and who punished or rewarded individuals with eternal life or eternal torment based on these deeds. Interpreters of the NT often relied on Weber's handbook as an aid in understanding the Judaism of Paul's time, even though the Talmud postdated the Pauline era by several hundred years.

The New Perspective

Weber's description of rabbinic Judaism (and, at least implicitly, Luther's) met with several forceful challenges. In 1900, C. G. Montefiore labeled Weber's work a gross caricature of rabbinic Judaism since the Jews viewed the law as a blessing and a delight rather than an oppressive burden.[44] In 1921, G. F. Moore offered a more devastating critique of Weber's portrayal of legalistic Judaism.[45] Despite these objections from rabbinic scholars, both Jewish and non-Jewish interpreters of Paul continued to portray first-century Judaism as a more ancient version of the legalistic view of salvation by works that Luther encountered in Roman Catholicism.

Luther's portrayal of Judaism reigned until the publication of E. P. Sanders's *Paul and Palestinian Judaism* in 1977. The stated purpose of the book was to destroy the view held and propagated by Weber and others (particularly Bousset and Billerbeck) that first-century Judaism was based on legalistic works-righteousness. Although Sanders admitted that Weber's view was held by the majority of NT scholars, he argued that the view "is based upon a massive perversion and misunderstanding of the material."[46] Sanders argued that the essence of ancient Judaism was what he termed "covenantal nomism." He initially defined the idea this way: "Covenantal nomism is the view that one's place in God's plan is established on the basis of the covenant and that the covenant requires as the proper response of man his obedience to its commandments, while providing means of atonement

[43] F. Weber, *Jüdische Theologie auf Grund des Talmud und verwandter Schriften*, ed. F. Delitzsch and G. Schnedermann, 2nd ed. (Leipzig, Germany: Dörffling Franke, 1987), 25.

[44] C. G. Montefiore, "Rabbinic Judaism and the Epistles of St. Paul," *JQR* 13 (1900–1901): 161–217.

[45] G. F. Moore, "Christian Writers on Judaism," *HTR* 14 (1921): 197–254.

[46] E. P. Sanders, *Paul and Palestinian Judaism: A Comparison of Patterns of Religion* (Philadelphia, PA: Fortress, 1977), 59.

for transgression."[47] Sanders clearly stated that the required response to the covenant was man's obedience to its commandments. He later clarified that the obedience required by the covenant was merely intended but not actual obedience. Consequently, as long as the Israelite did not renounce God's right to command, he need not fear an eschatological judgment in which God would closely scrutinize his individual deeds. Such a judgment would not occur.[48]

Sanders admitted that some ancient Jewish texts seem to affirm a view in which salvation is dependent on personal acts of righteousness. However, Sanders insisted that statements seeming to imply that salvation was accomplished by human effort must somehow be reconciled with other statements emphasizing divine grace and mercy.

He appealed to three important pieces of evidence to argue that covenantal nomism was not legalistic but was dominated by an emphasis on divine grace. First, God established his covenant with the Jews due to his own gracious election. Second, God required only the intention to obey his law rather than actual obedience, and Israelites need not fear a strict judgment that would evaluate individual deeds. Third, God provided means of atonement for failure to obey.[49]

Sanders acknowledged that the Judaism challenged by Paul in his Letters seemed different from his covenantal nomism. He suggested that this distinction resulted from the fact that Paul developed his view of the law "from solution to plight" rather than "from plight to solution." Rather than recognizing a problem within Judaism that Christ answered, Paul first concluded that Christ was the answer and then created a need for Christ by developing a view of the function of the law in salvation that no other first-century Jew shared, that is, a person must fulfill the law perfectly in order to be saved by it.

Sanders's portrayal of ancient Judaism has been so widely accepted by NT scholars that it has virtually become the consensus view. In his 1982 Manson Memorial lecture, J. D. G. Dunn coined the phrase "New Perspective" to describe the view of Second Temple Judaism espoused by Sanders and his followers.[50]

Variations of the New Perspective

The views Sanders posited have been significantly modified even by those who embrace the essentials of his portrait of Judaism. N. T. Wright has often remarked that "there are as many versions of the New Perspective as there are people writing in it."[51] Wright and

---

[47] Ibid., 75.

[48] See esp. ibid., 234.

[49] Ibid., 75.

[50] J. D. G. Dunn, "The New Perspective on Paul," *BJRL* 65 (1983): 95–122. The article is reprinted in *Jesus, Paul, and the Law: Studies in Mark and Galatians* (Louisville, KY: Westminster John Knox, 1990), 183–214.

[51] R. A. Streett, "An Interview with N. T. Wright," *CTR* 2 (2005): 9. Compare N. T. Wright, "New Perspectives on Paul" (paper presented at the 10th Annual Edinburgh Dogmatics Conference, Rutherford House, Edinburgh, Scotland August 28, 2003), n. p.; online at http://www.ntwrightpage.com/Wright_New Perspectives.htm.

J. D. G. Dunn are two important scholars who have adapted elements of Sanders's position and added their own unique contributions.

Dunn accepted Sanders's conviction that the Lutheran view, which assumes first-century Judaism was a religion depending on works-righteousness for salvation, is inaccurate. But Dunn disputed Sanders's theory that the view of the law that Paul attacked was his own creation and was shared by no one in ancient Judaism.[52] According to Dunn, Paul's real opponent was not legalism but Jewish exclusivism. The Jews believed that they alone had been chosen by God as his covenant people. They further saw the law as a badge, an identity marker that distinguished them from those of other nations and identified them as recipients of God's grace and special blessing. Although the phrase "works of the law" in texts such as Romans 4:4–5 included obedience to the entirety of the Torah, the phrase more particularly denoted fidelity to those aspects of the law that functioned socially to separate Jews from Gentiles.

These aspects included especially the law of circumcision, the law of the Sabbath, and the laws of clean and unclean.[53] Dunn reasoned, "To affirm justification by the works of the law is to affirm that justification is for Jews only, is to require that Gentile believers take on the persona and practices of the Jewish people."[54] Paul distinguished "works of the law" (acts that distinguished Jew from Gentile) from "good works" (acts of righteousness). For this reason, Paul could rail against dependence on works of the law for salvation and still affirm a judgment according to works (Rom 2:6–11). Dunn concluded,

> It is difficult to sustain the claim that Paul was polemicizing against "self-achieved righteousness." Of course the texts just reviewed can be read that way. The only question is whether those who read them that way have shifted the issue from one of Israel's works of the law *vis-à-vis* Gentile acceptability to the more fundamental one of the terms of human acceptability by God. That may have happened already in Eph. 2.8–9, where the issue does seem to have moved from one of works of law to one of human effort. But when the texts in the undisputed Pauline Letters are read within the context of Paul's mission emerging from its Jewish matrix, the resulting picture is rather different. Within that context we gain a clear picture of Paul fiercely resisting his own earlier pre-Christian assumption that God's righteousness was only for Israel, and only for Gentiles if they became Jews and took on the distinctive obligations of God's covenant with Israel.[55]

---

[52] J. D. G. Dunn, *Romans 1–8*, WBC 38A (Dallas, TX: Word, 1988), lxix–lxxii.

[53] J. D. G. Dunn, *The Theology of Paul the Apostle* (Grand Rapids, MI: Eerdmans, 1998), 356.

[54] Ibid., 364.

[55] Ibid., 370–71. Like most proponents of the New Perspective, Dunn considered Ephesians (as well as the Pastorals) to be Deutero-Pauline, that is, written by someone other than Paul.

N. T. Wright independently arrived at a view similar to Dunn's. He acknowledged that Paul challenged Jewish exclusivism rather than a self-dependent moralism that sought to please God through good works. Wright made his own unique contribution to the New Perspective by insisting that Protestant scholars have missed the mark by identifying the "righteousness of God" as imputed righteousness. Although Wright admits that the phrase "the righteousness from God" (*hē ek theou dikaiosynē*) in Philippians 3:9 looks back to the Hebrew law court and refers to the righteousness that is "the status, which the vindicated party possesses as a result of the court's decision," he insists that the phrase "the righteousness of God" refers to God's covenant faithfulness.[56] Wright denied that the righteous status of the believer is the result of the imputation of God's or Christ's own righteousness. The believer is declared righteous by God before his judgment bar, but the NT never speaks of a transfer of God's personal righteousness to the believer.

Moreover, this "justification" is essentially an eschatological declaration that occurs in final judgment and will be based on the evaluation of the totality of one's life, a judgment according to works.[57] This in no way implies that an individual earns or achieves salvation by his own moral efforts. Rather, good works are the inevitable expression of the activity of the Spirit in the believer so that one's life demonstrates whether an individual is truly "in Christ." Justification is a projection of eschatological justification into the present, an anticipation of God's final verdict.[58]

A Critique of the New Perspective

Although the majority of scholars today appear to have accepted the major tenets of Sanders's portrait of Judaism, many believe that some of Sanders's claims were imbalanced and that NT scholarship is moving toward a more balanced position. Several have argued that NT scholarship has already moved beyond the New Perspective toward what might be termed the "post-New Perspective perspective."[59] Although scholars may be grateful for some of the contributions of the New Perspective, several criticisms are in order. Since the New Perspective is not a clearly defined school of thought with established parameters but more of a movement with serious disagreement among even its strongest advocates, these criticisms do not apply to all representatives of the New Perspective. They primarily respond to the groundbreaking research of Sanders in *Paul and Palestinian Judaism* that spawned the movement.

---

[56] See N. T. Wright, *What Saint Paul Really Said: Was Saul of Tarsus the Real Founder of Christianity?* (Grand Rapids, MI: Eerdmans, 1997), 100–11.

[57] Dunn essentially agreed, but this detail has been especially emphasized by Wright. For Dunn's agreement, see *Theology*, 365–66.

[58] For the most recent articulations of Wright's perspective, see N. T. Wright, *Justification: God's Plan and Paul's Vision* (Downers Grove, IL: InterVarsity, 2009) and *Paul and the Faithfulness of God* Christian Origins and the Question of God 4 (Minneapolis, MN: Fortress Press, 2013), 925–1042.

[59] See B. Byrne, "Interpreting Romans Theologically in a Post-'New Perspective' Perspective," *HTR* 94 (2001): 227–41; and M. F. Bird, "When the Dust Finally Settles: Coming to a Post-New Perspective Perspective," *CTR* 2 (2005): 57–69.

Sanders's attempt to find a single "pattern of religion" in first-century Judaism sometimes led him to downplay the vast differences between various sects and theological perspectives within Judaism.[60] Although one may affirm that Sanders discovered *a* pattern of religion in Second Temple Judaism, Sanders was incautious to claim that he had discovered *the* pattern. Scholars of the NT are increasingly aware that Second Temple Judaism was not theologically uniform. Precision demands that one speak of Second Temple Judaism*s* (in the plural), rather than assuming that all Jews of the period shared a single soteriological system.

Sanders appealed to three important lines of evidence to argue that covenantal nomism was not legalistic but was dominated by an emphasis on divine grace. However, all three of these arguments are problematic. First, Sanders argued that God established his covenant with the Jews due to his own gracious election. God demanded obedience to the covenant not so people could "get in" a covenant relationship with him, but only so they could "stay in" such a covenant relationship.[61] But Sanders's portrayal of the pattern of religion in Second Temple Judaism still makes human effort the determining factor in eschatological judgment and easily degenerates into legalism.

Second, according to Sanders, God required only the intention to obey his law rather than actual obedience, so Israelites need not fear a strict judgment that would evaluate individual deeds. Sanders's dismissal of a requirement of actual obedience in Second Temple Judaism is at odds with *m. Avot* 3:16, which is perhaps the most systematic statement of soteriology in the Mishnah.[62] Rabbi Akiba taught that the "world is judged according to righteousness but all is according to the majority of works that be good or evil." Although Sanders dismissed the text from consideration in his composition of a pattern of religion by claiming that the text is "enigmatic," a parable that immediately follows the statement makes its meaning clear. The parable describes God as a great shopkeeper who carefully records moral debits in his ledger. The shopkeeper will eventually send out his collectors to exact payment from the debtors, whether or not they like it, based on the record of their debts. The parable concludes: "the judgment is a judgment of truth and all is ready for the banquet." The conclusion demonstrates that eschatological judgment is the focus of the parable and confirms that the parable illustrates the judgment according to the majority of works described by Akiba.

---

[60] See J. Neusner, *Mishnah, Midrash, Siddur*, vol. 1 of *The Study of Ancient Judaism* (n.p.: Ktav, 1981), 21–22. Neusner's cautions against the application of a harmonizing approach to the study of rabbinic literature applies equally well to the study of Second Temple literature.

[61] Sanders, *Paul*, 427; idem, "The Covenant as a Soteriological Category and the Nature of Salvation in Palestinian and Hellenistic Judaism," in *Jews, Greeks and Christians: Studies in Honor of W. D. Davies*, ed. R. G. Hamerton-Kelly and R. Scroggs, vol. 2 of *Studies in Judaism in Late Antiquity* (Leiden, Netherlands: Brill, 1976), 11–44; and idem, *Judaism: Practice and Belief 63 BCE–66 CE* (London, England: SCM, 1992), 262–78.

[62] See C. L. Quarles, "The Soteriology of Rabbi Akiba and E. P. Sanders's *Paul and Palestinian Judaism*," *NTS* 42 (1996): 185–95.

Rabbi Akiba thus taught that one's eternal fate was determined by the preponderance of one's deeds. If an individual did more bad than good, he could expect punishment in the afterlife. If an individual did more good than bad, he could expect a reward. The concept of judging according to the majority of deeds is affirmed in other statements of the Tannaim[63] such as *m. Qiddushin* 1:10 and *m. Avot* 4:22. The interpretations of these mishnaic references in the Tosefta[64] and by later Amoraic[65] rabbis confirm that Akiba's view was shared.[66] Through a carefully crafted paradoxical statement, Akiba contrasted this judgment according to the majority of deeds with a judgment according to divine righteousness, implying that he recognized that God's unmitigated holiness demanded total perfection rather than a mere majority of good deeds. This more extreme standard of eschatological judgment was affirmed by Gamaliel II in *b. Sanhedrin* 81a. The great rabbi wept as he read Ezekiel 18:5–9, because he interpreted the text as demanding total and perfect obedience, of which he was incapable.

Although Sanders appealed at length to the apocryphal book of *Jubilees* to confirm that covenantal nomism was the pattern of religion for first-century Judaism, even *Jubilees* frequently refers to great ledgers like that of Akiba's parable to describe the basis for final judgment. Sanders appealed to *Jubilees* 30:22 and 36:10 to argue that the "heavenly tablets" are the books of life and destruction rather than a ledger of deeds. Actually, the heavenly tablets have a variety of functions throughout *Jubilees*. In *Jubilees* 6:17 and 16:29–30, the tablets appear to be records of God's laws. But at least in *Jubilees* 39:6 the heavenly tablets appear to be ledgers of deeds. The text explains that Joseph refrained from committing adultery with Potiphar's wife because Jacob had taught him the words of Abraham that those who committed adultery would receive a judgment of death in heaven before the Most High and that "the sin is written (on high) concerning him in the heavenly books always before the Lord." Despite the evidence of *Jubilees* 5:13; 28:6; 30:19; 39:6, Sanders referred to two passages that refer to the Books of Life and Destruction *and* the heavenly tablets and mistakenly concluded they are one and the same. The book of *Jubilees* confirms that God kept a careful record of the deeds of Israelites in preparation for just eternal judgment. Several recent scholars, such as A. Das, S. Kim, and S. Westerholm, have regarded the above evidence as seriously undermining the portrait of Jewish soteriology affirmed by the New Perspective.[67]

---

[63] From Aram. *tanna*, "to repeat, learn"; masters of teaching transmitted by oral repetition.

[64] From Aram. *tosefta*, "addition, supplement"; additional teachings supplementing the Mishnah.

[65] From Aram. *amar*, "to say, comment"; commentators of Tannaitic teachings.

[66] See A. Das, *Paul, the Law, and the Covenant* (Peabody, MA: Hendrickson, 2001), 32–33. The definitions are adapted from H. L. Strack and G. Stemberger, *Introduction to the Talmud and Midrash*, trans. M. Bockmuehl (Minneapolis, MN: Fortress, 1992), 7, 168.

[67] Das, *Paul*, 32–36; S. Kim, *Paul and the New Perspective: Second Thoughts on the Origin of Paul's Thought* (Grand Rapids, MI: Eerdmans, 2002), 146–52. Cf. S. Westerholm, *Perspectives Old and New on Paul: The "Lutheran" Paul and His Critics* (Grand Rapids, MI: Eerdmans, 2004), 343.

SIDEBAR 9.1: 4QMMT, THE "WORKS OF THE LAW," AND THE "NEW PERSPECTIVE" ON PAUL

The piece of evidence that has become the subject of considerable scholarly discussion is a passage in one of the Dead Sea Scrolls, in a document called 4QMMT. As C. Evans noted, 4QMMT "has offered dramatic proof that the position that Paul attacked was indeed held in his time. According to 4QMMT, if the faithful observe the law properly, especially with respect to 'the works of the law,' about which the author(s) of this letter wrote, they 'will rejoice in the end time,' when they discover that their obedience 'will be reckoned to (them) as righteousness" (4Q398 frags. 14–17 ii 7 = 4Q399 frag. 1 ii 4)."[1]

Evans rightly contended that the Qumran writers referred to Ps 106:30–31 where Phinehas is reckoned righteous because of his righteous act. Paul, of course, argued from Gen 15:6 that Abraham's faith was the source of imputed righteousness.[2] Clearly, covenantal nomism did not serve as a monolithic paradigm for all of Second Temple Judaism. J. D. G. Dunn, on behalf of those who affirm the New Perspective, responded that the "works of the law" required the covenanters to separate from the rest of Judaism, though this may represent a case of special pleading.[3]

[1] C. A. Evans, "The Old Testament in the New," in *The Face of New Testament Studies: A Survey of Recent Research*, ed. S. McKnight and G. R. Osborne (Grand Rapids, MI: Baker, 2004), 142–43.

[2] Ibid., 143.

[3] J. D. G. Dunn, "Paul's Theology," in *Face of New Testament Studies*, 345; idem, "4QMMT and Galatians," *NTS* 43 (1997): 147–53.

Finally, Sanders argued that Second Temple Judaism was not dependent on legalistic works-righteousness for salvation because God provided means of atonement for failure to obey.[68] But a detailed examination of Second Temple Jewish literature demonstrates that many Jews viewed legalistic works-righteousness as the means of atonement for sin.[69] The book of Tobit shows that Jews of the Diaspora who had no access to the temple substituted the so-called "pillars of Judaism"—prayer, fasting, and almsgiving—for temple sacrifice as the means of atonement (Tobit 4:9–11; 12:8–10). Likewise, the community documents of the Dead Sea Scrolls demonstrate that sectarian Jews who had temporarily abandoned the temple sought atonement for sin through personal acts of righteousness rather than temple sacrifice (1QS 3.6–10; 8.1–4; 9.5). Motifs in Sirach suggest that approximately 250 years before the destruction of the temple even a leading scribe of Jerusalem substituted acts of righteousness for the atoning rituals of the temple (Sir 3:14, 30; 20:28; 35:1–5; 45:23). Consequently, Sanders's appeal to the means of atonement as precluding Judaism from degenerating into various forms of legalistic works-righteousness falls short of convincing.

[68] Sanders, *Paul*, 75.

[69] See C. L. Quarles, "The New Perspective and Means of Atonement in Jewish Literature of the Second Temple Period," *CTR* 2 (2005): 39–56.

When atonement for failure to observe the law is accomplished by compensatory acts of obedience to the law, works-righteousness, at least to some degree, seems unavoidable.

Conclusion

The New Perspective correctly emphasizes the Jewish context of early Christianity and the need to study the NT documents against the background of Second Temple Jewish literature. It rightly warns of presumptive and misleading caricatures of Judaism that are ungrounded in careful study of the primary documents. Representatives of the New Perspective are correct that not all, probably not even most, first-century Jews depended on legalistic works-righteousness for salvation. However, the evidence demonstrates that many did. Paul's Letters do challenge Jewish exclusivism as Dunn and Wright contend, but they also clearly confront efforts to attain salvation by keeping the law. The "works of the law" on which some Jews depended for their salvation included efforts to keep all the prescriptions of the law and not just those that distinguished Jews from Gentiles.[70]

THE LIFE OF PAUL

Introduction

The NT does not only preserve the letters of Paul, though these alone grant insight into the theological thought and ethical views of the great apostle to the Gentiles. The book of Acts in particular gives special attention to the life and ministry of this influential servant of Christ as well. The details about Paul's life in Acts often enable those who study his letters to identify the occasion in Paul's ministry in which specific missives were written. Such background data often illuminate specific statements in Paul's Letters and give them richer meaning. Thus, this section will give a brief overview of the life and travels of Paul.[71]

Early Life and Training (AD 1–33)

Birth and Family Background Paul was born in a Jewish family in Tarsus of Cilicia (Acts 22:3), probably early in the first decade of the first century. According to a tradition recorded by Jerome (ca. AD 345–420), Paul's family had moved to Tarsus from Gischala in Galilee.[72] Paul's family was of the tribe of Benjamin (Phil 3:5). His parents named him Saul in honor of the most prominent member of the tribe in Jewish history—King Saul. Paul came from a family of tent makers or leatherworkers and, according to Jewish

---

[70] See J. A. Fitzmyer, "Paul's Jewish Background and the Deeds of the Law," in *According to Paul: Studies in the Theology of the Apostle* (New York, NY: Paulist, 1993), 18–35; D. J. Moo, "'Law,' 'Works of the Law,' and Legalism in Paul," *WTJ* 45 (1983): 73–100; and T. R. Schreiner, "Works of Law in Paul," *NovT* 33 (1991): 217–44.

[71] For a more extensive discussion of Paul's life and ministry, see C. L. Quarles, *An Illustrated Life of Paul* (Nashville, TN: B&H Academic, 2013). On Paul as a missionary, see especially A. J. Köstenberger and P. T. O'Brien, *Salvation to the Ends of the Earth: A Biblical Theology of Mission*, NSBT 11 (Downers Grove, IL: InterVarsity, 2001), chap. 7. Cf. E. J. Schnabel, *Early Christian Mission*, vol. 2: *Paul and the Early Church* (Downers Grove, IL: InterVarsity, 2004), 923–1485; and R. L. Plummer, *Paul's Understanding of the Church's Mission*, Paternoster Biblical Monographs (Milton Keynes, UK: Paternoster, 2006).

[72] Jerome, *Commentary on the Epistle to the Philippians*, on v. 23; *De Viris Illustribus* 5.

custom, was taught this trade by his father.[73] Apparently, the business thrived, and Paul's family became moderately wealthy. Paul was a citizen of the city of Tarsus, "an important city" (Acts 21:39). According to one ancient writer, the monetary requirement for Tarsian citizenship was 500 drachmae, a year and a half's wages.[74]

Roman Citizenship Importantly, Paul was *born* a Roman citizen. Many interpreters speculate that Paul's father or grandfather was honored with citizenship because of some special service rendered to a military proconsul.[75] However, early Christian tradition preserved by Jerome (see also Photius, ninth century) states that Paul's parents had been carried as prisoners of war from Gischala to Tarsus, enslaved to a Roman citizen, and then freed and granted citizenship.[76] Regardless of how Paul's parents received their citizenship, Acts states three times that Paul possessed Roman citizenship; this privilege was accompanied by important rights that would benefit him in his missionary labors.[77] The Roman citizen had the right of appeal after a trial, exemption from imperial service, the right to choose between a local or Roman trial, and protection from degrading forms of punishment such as scourging and crucifixion. Paul might have carried a wax tablet that functioned as a birth certificate or certificate of citizenship in order to prove his Roman citizenship. However, most people who claimed citizenship were trusted since the penalty for impersonating a Roman citizen was death.[78]

Paul's Name In official documents, ancient Romans were formally designated by a *praenomen* (first name), *nomen,* or *nomen gentile* (family name), father's *praenomen,* Roman tribe, and *cognomen* (extra name like the modern middle name). Roman citizens had to register with the government using the *tria nomina* consisting of the *praenomen, nomen gentile,* and *cognomen.* The NT refers to the apostle only informally as "Paul" or "Saul." Paul was the apostle's cognomen; Saul was his Hebrew name. The name "Paul" was common in the Roman world (Acts 13:7) and meant "small" in Latin. Later traditions probably inferred that Paul was short from the meaning of his Latin name, but one cannot determine Paul's stature from the name since it was given to him at his birth.[79]

---

[73] See Acts 18:3. Although Paul's Letters make many references to his working at a trade in order to support himself (1 Cor 4:12; 9:1–18; 2 Cor 6:5; 11:23, 27; 1 Thess 2:9; 2 Thess 3:8), only Acts mentions the specific trade. Paul probably made tents from leather. He was likely skilled in making and repairing a wide range of leather and woven goods. See R. F. Hock, *The Social Context of Paul's Mission* (Philadelphia, PA: Fortress, 1980), 20–21; and W. Michaelis, "σκευοποιος," *TDNT* 7:393–94.

[74] Dio Chrysostom, *Orations* 34.1–23.

[75] E.g., F. F. Bruce, *Paul: Apostle of the Heart Set Free* (Grand Rapids, MI: Eerdmans, 1977), 37.

[76] Jerome, *Commentary on the Epistle to the Philippians,* on v. 23; *De viris illustribus* 5; Photius, *Quaest. Amphil.* 116.

[77] The testimony in Acts regarding Paul's Roman citizenship is affirmed by most scholars. The most serious recent challenge to Paul's citizenship has been W. Stegemann, "War der Apostel Paulus ein römischer Bürger?" *ZNW* 78 (1987): 200–29. For a compelling defense of Paul's Roman citizenship, see M. Hengel, *The Pre-Christian Paul* (Philadelphia, PA: Trinity Press International, 1991), 6–15.

[78] For a thorough discussion of Roman citizenship, see A. N. Sherwin-White, *The Roman Citizenship* (Oxford, UK: Clarendon, 1973). Compare B. M. Rapske, "Citizenship, Roman," in *Dictionary of New Testament Background,* ed. C. A. Evans and S. E. Porter (Downers Grove, IL: InterVarsity, 2000), 215–18.

[79] For a detailed discussion of Paul's name, see C. Hemer, "The Name of Paul," *TynB* 36 (1985): 179–83.

SIDEBAR 9.2: WHO WAS GAMALIEL?

Due to Gamaliel's significant influence on Saul, a brief examination of the famed teacher is appropriate. The Mishnah mentions Gamaliel I frequently and expresses many of his opinions. Gamaliel is listed among thirteen great rabbis whose deaths marked the decline of Judaism: "When Rabbi Gamaliel the Elder died, the glory of the Law ceased and purity and abstinence died" (*m. Sotah* 9:15). The passage implies that Gamaliel was as renowned for his high moral standards as for his interpretation of the Scriptures. Gamaliel's students were known for presenting their Shekel offerings for the Terumah in such a way as to ensure that it would be used only for the designated purpose (*m. Sheq.* 3:3). Another text identifies Gamaliel and his students as those who guarded the secret of the location of the ark of the covenant that was hidden in the temple (*m. Sheq.* 6:1).

Several texts that describe Gamaliel's teachings are related to issues of marriage, divorce, and remarriage, suggesting that Gamaliel was particularly concerned about issues related to the family. Gamaliel relaxed the stricter law that required multiple witnesses of a man's death for the wife to remarry by requiring only one (*m. Yeb.* 16:7). Gamaliel prevented a husband from canceling a certificate of divorce without the wife or messenger of the certificate being present to witness the cancellation "as a precaution for the general good." Otherwise, the wife might remarry without realizing the divorce had been annulled (*m. Git.* 4:2, 3). He also prohibited the use of pseudonyms in divorce certificates. Perhaps Gamaliel's work as a champion for the family resulted in the celebration of his "purity and abstinence" mentioned earlier. Although he was zealous for the law, Gamaliel was known to loosen strict standards that were unnecessarily burdensome. For example, Gamaliel relaxed certain legislation (*m. Rosh HaSh.* 2.5).

On other issues, such as tithing, Gamaliel could be far more demanding and meticulous, as is clear from his renowned statement: "Provide yourself with a teacher and remove yourself from doubt, and tithe not overmuch by guesswork" (*m. Avot* 1:16).[1] The statement is related to the rabbinic discussion over whether one should count, measure, or weigh fruit in order to determine the correct tithe. Gamaliel viewed counting and measuring as too imprecise and only weighing as appropriate for a matter as important as the tithe.[2]

[1] In this case, "Rabban Gamaliel" clearly refers to Gamaliel I, since he is identified in the context as the father of Simeon.

[2] See the references to Gamaliel in *m. Peah* 2:6 and *m. Orlah* 2:12.

Rabbinic Training Acts 22:3 shows that Paul was "brought up" in Jerusalem "at the feet of Gamaliel." Although the verb "brought up" *(anatrephō)* may refer to being raised from the time of infancy (Acts 7:21), in this context it probably means nothing more than that Paul received his rabbinic training under Gamaliel after moving to Jerusalem, probably some time in his teenage years.[80] Paul used this fact to prove that he was not one of the Diaspora Jews, those who were more influenced by Gentile culture than Jewish ways. In

[80] See J. McRay, *Paul: His Life and Teaching* (Grand Rapids, MI: Baker, 2003), 44.

Jerusalem Paul was educated in the Jewish religion according to the traditions of his ancestors (Acts 22:3). A century and a half after Paul, Rabbi Judah ben Tema taught, "At five years old [one is fit] for the Scripture, at ten years for the Mishnah, at thirteen [for the fulfilling of] the commandments, at fifteen for the Talmud, at eighteen for the bride-chamber, at twenty for pursuing a calling, at thirty for authority" (*m. Avot* 5:21). Although Judaism may have changed considerably in the period between Paul and this rabbi, Judah's words are probably an accurate description of the regimen of training Paul experienced.

Acts 22:3 says that Paul was trained by Rabbi Gamaliel I, the member of the Sanhedrin mentioned in Acts 5:33–39.[81] Gamaliel was a leading Jewish teacher in Paul's day. Later traditions say that Gamaliel was Hillel's successor in the leadership of the rabbinic school founded by Hillel in about 10 BC. Some suggest that Gamaliel was a member of Hillel's family, but the earliest traditions describe him as the founder of his own school. Others have argued that Paul could not have been a student of Gamaliel since his teachings (Gal 5:3) suggest that he held to the stricter interpretation of the law espoused by Shammai, Hillel's rival. Certainly Paul was more radical than Gamaliel as he is depicted in Acts 5:34–39, but students are often more radical than their teachers.

Paul quickly excelled as a Jewish rabbinical student. Paul said, "I advanced in Judaism beyond many contemporaries among my people, because I was extremely zealous for the traditions of my ancestors" (Gal 1:14). He went on to describe himself as "circumcised the eighth day; of the nation of Israel, of the tribe of Benjamin, a Hebrew born of Hebrews; regarding the law, a Pharisee; regarding zeal, persecuting the church; regarding the righteousness that is in the law, blameless" (Phil 3:5–6). He also identified himself with the sect of the Pharisees, which he described as the "strictest sect of our religion" (Acts 26:5). Paul's father had also been a Pharisee (Acts 23:6).[82]

Persecution of Christians As an ideal Pharisee, Paul may have been active as a Jewish missionary, winning Gentiles as proselytes to the Jewish faith. He may have been like the Pharisees Jesus described who "travel over land and sea to make one convert" (Matt 23:15). Paul's words, "If I still preach circumcision," may allude to his past as a Jewish missionary (Gal 5:11). Paul, more than his mentor Gamaliel (Acts 5:34–39), recognized the serious threat Christianity posed to the Jewish religion and was eager to stamp out this new faith. The Mishnah taught that a Jewish male was ready for a position of authority at age thirty (*m. Avot* 5:21). Thus, Paul was probably in his thirties when he, with authorization from

---

[81] The Mishnah ordinarily refers to Gamaliel I as "Gamaliel the Elder." The person referred to as "Rabban Gamaliel" in the Mishnah was the grandson of Gamaliel the Elder. Gamaliel's counsel to the Sanhedrin is similar to the rabbinic view in *m. Avot* 4:11.

[82] Some scholars deny that Pharisees lived in Tarsus, since faithful Pharisees needed to be near the Jerusalem temple. See B. Rapske, *The Book of Acts and Paul in Roman Custody*, The Book of Acts in Its First Century Setting 3 (Grand Rapids, MI: Eerdmans, 1994), 90–108. For the opposing view, see C. K. Barrett, *Acts 15–28*, ICC (London, England: T&T Clark, 1998), 1063. Some scholars suggest that "son of Pharisees" refers not to Paul's biological ancestry but identifies him as a disciple of Pharisees or the quintessential Pharisee. See Barrett, *Acts 15–28*, 1063; and B. Chilton, *Rabbi Paul: An Intellectual Biography* (New York, NY: Doubleday, 2004), 19.

the chief priest, began to imprison Christians first in the synagogues of Jerusalem and then later in more remote areas like Damascus.

One cannot underestimate Paul's aggression and viciousness in persecuting the church that was inspired by his misguided zeal. When Paul described his efforts to persecute the church, he used the language of warfare and made clear that his intention was to obliterate the church completely (Gal 1:13). In Acts 8:3, Luke described Paul's destruction using the Greek verb *lumainomai,* a verb used in the Septuagint (Greek OT) to speak of a wild animal such as a lion, bear, or leopard tearing at raw flesh.[83] Paul's zeal in persecuting the church, then, was like the savage rage of a hungry predator frenzied by the taste of blood.

Perhaps Paul's clearest description of his activities as a persecutor is found in Acts 26:9–11: "In fact, I myself was convinced that it was necessary to do many things in opposition to the name of Jesus of Nazareth. I actually did this in Jerusalem, and I locked up many of the saints in prison, since I had received authority for that from the chief priests. When they were put to death, I was in agreement against them. In all the synagogues I often punished them and tried to make them blaspheme. Since I was terribly enraged at them, I pursued them even to foreign cities."

Some believe this reference to "casting a vote" (lit. "casting a pebble"—black for "no" or white for "yes") implies that Paul was a member of the Sanhedrin. But it is difficult to imagine that Paul would not have explicitly stated this, especially on those occasions in which he highlighted his devout Jewish pedigree. Thus, the statement is probably a metaphor implying that Paul consented to the execution of Christians, or it suggests that he was a member of a committee appointed by the Sanhedrin and vested with this authority.[84] Paul's initial and adamant rejection of Jesus Christ as the Messiah may have been motivated largely by Christ's ignoble death. Paul knew that death by crucifixion was indicative of a divine curse (Deut 21:23). It was inconceivable to him that the Messiah could die under the curse of God. But when Paul wrote his first letter, he had come to recognize this death curse as the grounds for substitutionary atonement (Gal 3:10–14). In 1 Corinthians, Paul explained that the idea of a crucified Messiah was a stumbling block to the Jews (see 1:23); he was likely speaking from his own past experience.

Paul's Conversion (AD 34)

While Saul was on his way to Damascus to arrest and imprison Christians, the resurrected and glorified Jesus appeared to him with blinding radiance. Christ's words, "It is hard for you to kick against the goads" (Acts 26:14), indicate that God had already begun to prompt Saul to follow Jesus as Messiah. Like an ox kicking against a sharpened prod in the hand of the ox driver, Paul had been resisting divine guidance and leadership; this resulted in his own harm and pain. At the appearance of Christ, Saul immediately surrendered to his authority and went into the city to await further orders from his Master.

---

[83] See Isa 65:25; Sir 28:23; and Theodotion's rendering of Dan 6:23.

[84] J. B. Polhill, *Acts*, NAC 26 (Nashville, TN: B&H, 1992), 501.

There his blindness was healed, he received the Holy Spirit, and he accepted believer's baptism. No doubt Ananias shared with Saul the message that the Lord had given him in a vision: "For this man is my chosen instrument to take my name to Gentiles, kings, and the Israelites. I will show him how much he must suffer for my name" (Acts 9:15). After this Saul spent a few days with the disciples in Damascus.

Paul's Missionary Travels (AD 34–58)

Early Travels (ca. AD 34–47) Soon after his conversion, Paul traveled to Arabia where he began evangelizing the Nabatean Arabs (Gal 1:17; 2 Cor 11:32–33) and probably experienced his first opposition to the gospel from political authorities. He then returned to Damascus where he began to go into the synagogues to preach the message that had been revealed to him on the Damascus road: Jesus is the Son of God and the promised Messiah. The governor in Damascus had the city gates guarded in order to arrest Paul, who was forced to escape through a window in the wall by being lowered in a basket.

Paul then traveled to Jerusalem where he spent fifteen days visiting with Peter and James, the Lord's brother, and doubtless heard them describe Jesus's life and teachings, though Paul's gospel was already clearly defined even before this visit. Church leaders were initially suspicious of Paul, but Barnabas intervened on his behalf (Acts 9:26–30; Gal 1:18). After fifteen days in Jerusalem, Paul returned to Tarsus, evangelizing Syria and Cilicia for several years. While in Syria, Barnabas contacted Paul and invited him to become involved in the outreach of the Antioch church where large numbers of Gentiles were responding to the gospel. The church at Antioch collected money to carry to the Christians who suffered in Judea during a period of famine. Barnabas and Paul were chosen by the church to carry the gift to Jerusalem (Acts 11:27–30). This probably was the occasion of the conference described by Paul in Galatians 2:1–10. Some equate this with the Jerusalem Council, but this is unlikely.[85] If Galatians were written after an official ruling at the Jerusalem Council, Paul could have just displayed the letter from the apostles to discredit the Judaizers. Moreover, the encounter described in Galatians 2:1–10 appears to have been a private meeting rather than a public affair. The pillars of the Jerusalem church,

---

[85] For a detailed defense of the view that the Jerusalem Council of Acts 15 is the event described by Paul in Gal 2:1–10, see C. Keener, *Acts 15:1–23:35* (Grand Rapids, MI: Baker Academic, 2014), 2194–202.

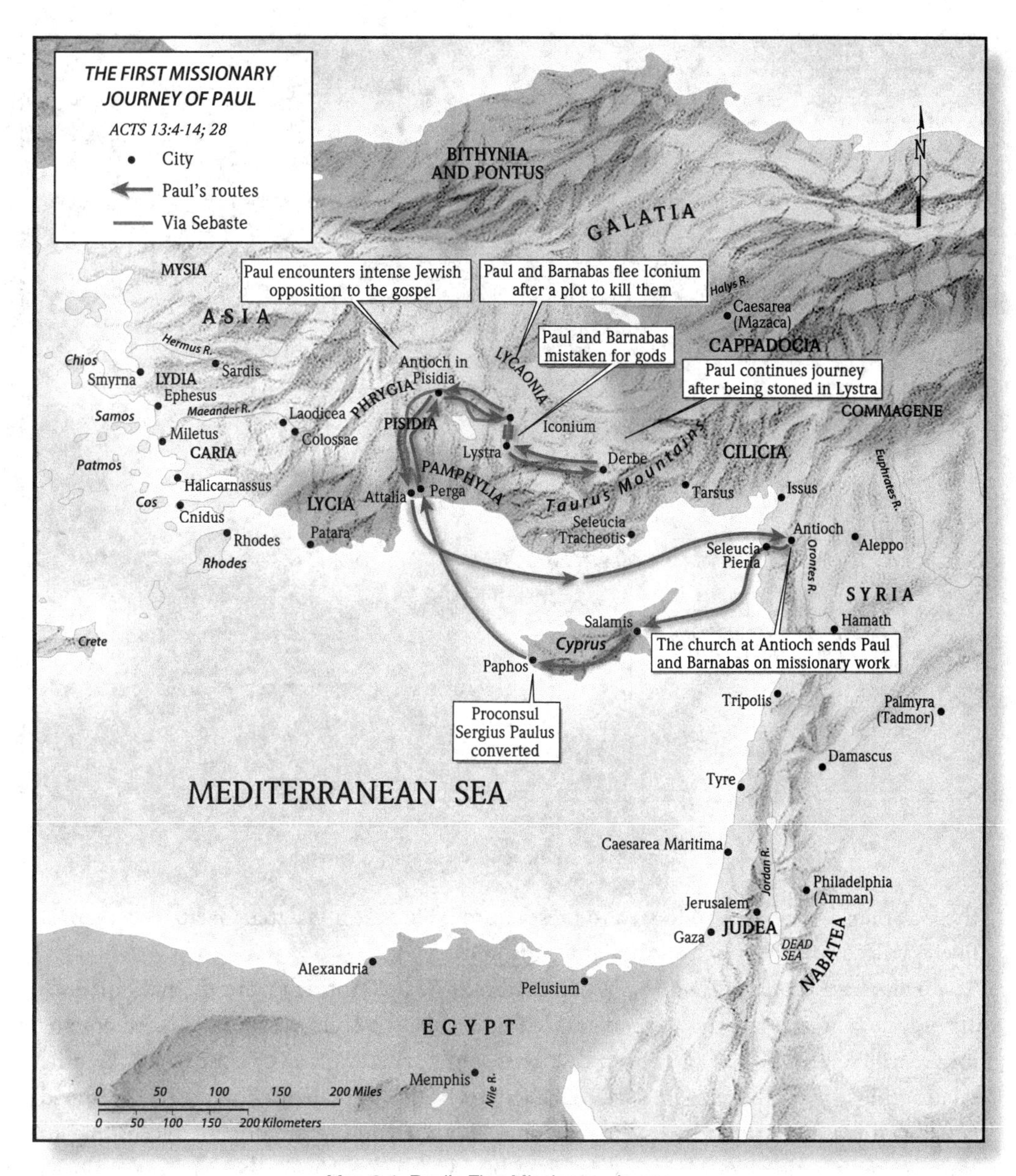

Map 9.1: Paul's First Missionary Journey

Peter, John, and James the brother of Jesus, approved the no-law gospel preached by Paul and his focus on Gentile evangelism.

First Missionary Journey (AD 47–48) Paul and Barnabas soon began their first missionary journey, traveling through Cyprus and Anatolia probably during the years 47–48. The missionary team carried the gospel to the cities of Pisidian Antioch, Iconium, Lystra, and Derbe. These cities were located in the Roman province of Galatia, and the letter to

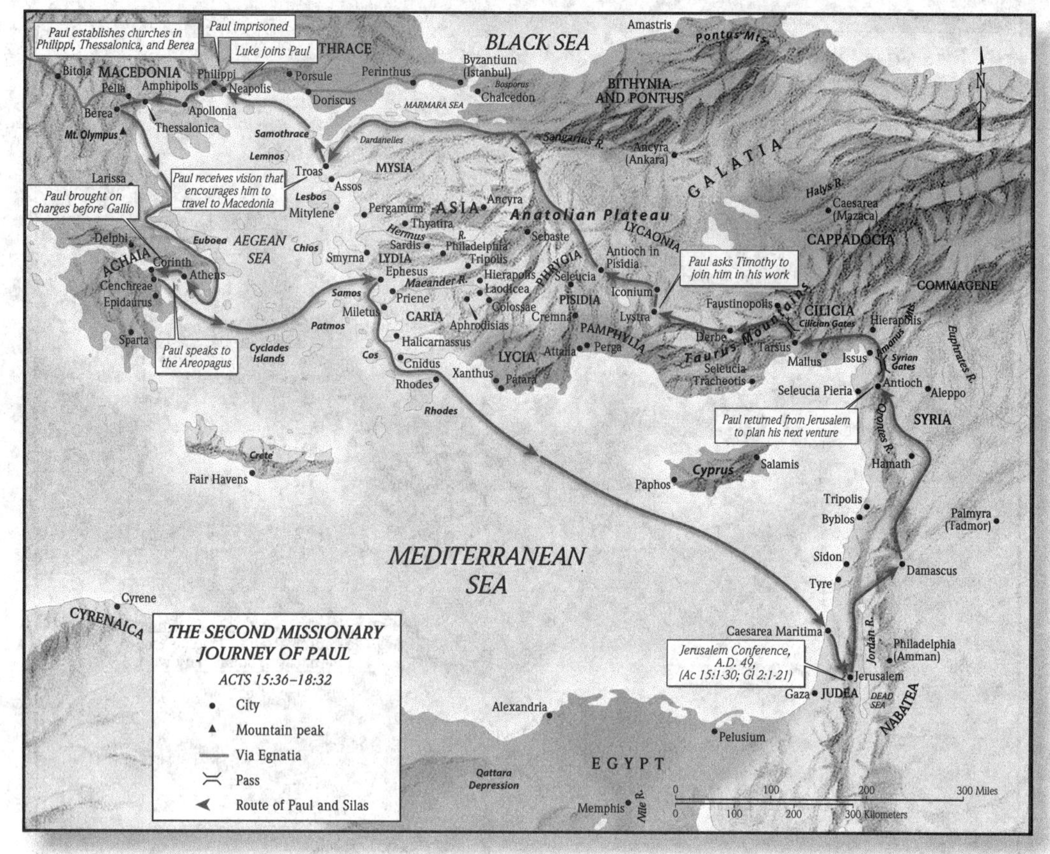

Map 9.1: Paul's Second Missionary Journey

the Galatians is probably addressed to these churches in South Galatia. Galatians was most likely written from Antioch shortly after this journey.

Jerusalem Council (AD 49) When Paul returned to Antioch from the first missionary journey, he immediately found himself embroiled in controversy over requirements for Gentile salvation. Peter and even Barnabas were vacillating on the issue of Jew-Gentile relationships. Even worse, some false teachers from the Jerusalem church had infiltrated congregations in Antioch and were teaching, "Unless you are circumcised according to the custom prescribed by Moses, you cannot be saved" (Acts 15:1). The church appointed Paul and Barnabas to go to Jerusalem and settle the matter. A council was convened in the year 49 that included the missionary team, those who insisted on circumcision as a requirement for salvation, and the apostles. Peter and James the brother of Jesus spoke in defense of Paul's law-free gospel, and a letter was sent to the Gentile churches confirming the official Christian view. Paul returned to Antioch.

Second Missionary Journey (AD 49–51) The second missionary journey carried Paul through Anatolia, Macedonia, and Achaia in 49–51. Paul and Barnabas parted company at this point in a disagreement about the role of Barnabas's nephew John Mark in the second missionary journey. Mark had abandoned the team on the first journey (Acts 15:38). Paul took Silas along instead and established churches in Philippi, Thessalonica, and Berea. Paul also spent eighteen months in Corinth, strengthening a fledgling church there. Four of Paul's Letters are addressed to churches known from this second journey. Most scholars believe that 1 and 2 Thessalonians were written during this trip.

Third Missionary Journey (AD 51–54) Paul's third missionary journey focused on the city of Ephesus where Paul spent the better part of three years (51–54). Toward the end of this, Paul worked hard to collect another relief offering for the Jerusalem Christians. Paul wrote 1 and 2 Corinthians and Romans during this trip.

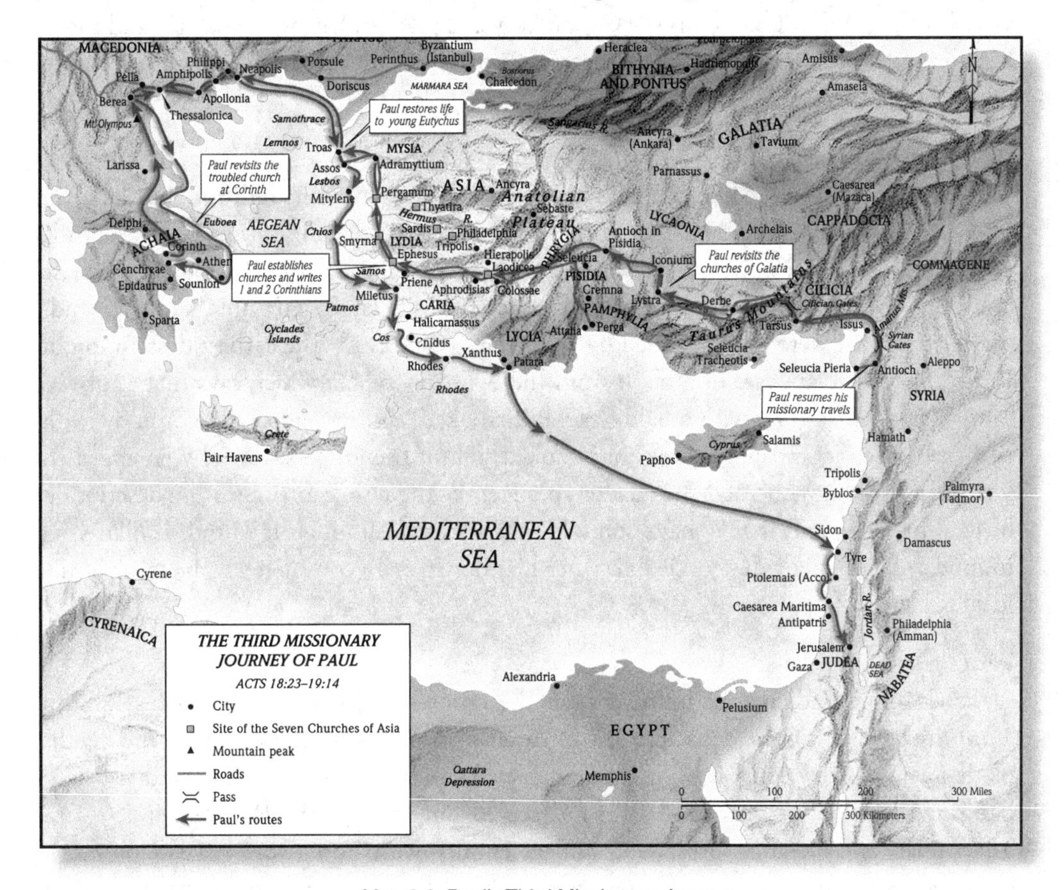

Map 9.2: Paul's Third Missionary Journey

Final Years (AD 55–65/66) Paul carried the relief offering to Jerusalem. While he was in the temple, performing a ritual to demonstrate his Jewish identity to some of the Jerusalem Christians, Jewish opponents incited a riot, and Paul was arrested (55). He was sent to Caesarea to stand trial before the procurator Felix. After two years of procrastination on the part of his detainers, Paul finally appealed to the Roman emperor for trial. After arriving in Rome, Paul spent two years under house arrest awaiting his trial. Paul wrote Ephesians, Philippians, Colossians, and Philemon during this first Roman imprisonment (ca. 58–60).[86]

The record of Acts ends at this point, so information as to the outcome of the trial is sketchy. Early church tradition suggests that Paul was acquitted (ca. 60) or exiled and may possibly have fulfilled the dream expressed in Romans 15:23–29 of carrying the gospel to Spain (60–66).[87] Paul wrote 1 Timothy and Titus during the period between his acquittal and a second Roman imprisonment. According to church tradition, Paul was arrested again and subjected to a harsher imprisonment. Paul wrote 2 Timothy during this second Roman incarceration. He was condemned by the Emperor Nero and beheaded with the sword at the third milestone on the Ostian Way at a place called Aquae Salviae and today lies buried on the site covered by the Basilica of St. Paul Outside the Walls. His execution probably occurred in AD 66 or 67.

Paul's Appearance

There is no biblical record of Paul's appearance or his physical condition, but he must have been a hearty individual to endure the abuses and trials he suffered as an apostle (2 Cor 11:23–29). He was, however, evidently the victim of some serious eye disease (Gal 4:12–16). This may account for his characteristically large signature that he appended to letters that were likely penned by a secretary (Gal 6:11). The earliest description of Paul's appearance appears in a book from the NT Apocrypha, which says that Paul was "a man small of stature, with a bald head and crooked legs, in a good state of body, with eyebrows meeting and nose somewhat hooked, full of friendliness; for now he appeared like a man, and now he had the face of an angel."[88] The writer attributes the description of Paul to Titus, and it may have some historical basis. Although it sounds unflattering to moderns, several of the physical features mentioned were considered to be traits of the ideal Roman.

Paul's Gospel

Paul's gospel indicted all humanity for the crime of rejecting God and his rightful authority.[89] Suffering the consequences of Adam's sin, mankind plunged into the depths of depravity so that they were utterly unable to fulfill the righteous demands of God (Rom 1:18–32; 3:9–20; 9:12–19) and deserved only his wrath (Rom 1:18; 2:5–16). The sinner was alienated from God and at enmity with him (Rom 5:10; Col 1:21). Consequently, the sinner's only hope was the gospel that embodied God's power to save those who had faith in Christ (Rom 1:16).

---

[86] The order in which these four epistles were written is unknown.

[87] For a thorough discussion of Paul's possible missionary work in Spain, see Schnabel, *Early Christian Mission*, 1271–83.

[88] *Acts of Paul* 3:3 in E. Hennecke and W. Schneemelcher, *Writings Relating to the Apostles, Apocalypses and Related Subjects*, vol. 2 of *New Testament Apocrypha*, trans. and ed. R. M. Wilson (Philadelphia, PA: Westminster, 1964), 354.

[89] See the discussion of "The Gospel Paul Preached" in Köstenberger and O'Brien, *Salvation to the Ends of the Earth*, 173–84.

The focus of Paul's gospel was Jesus Christ (Rom 1:3–4). Paul affirmed Jesus's humanity and his deity. Christ was a physical descendent from the line of David (Rom 1:2) and came in the likeness of sinful man (Rom 8:3), assuming the form of a humble, obedient servant (Phil 2:7–8).Yet he was the visible form of the invisible God (Col 1:15), all the fullness of deity living in him in bodily form (Col 2:9), in very nature God (Phil 1:6), and possessed the title "Lord" (Greek title for the God of the OT), the name above all names (Phil 2:9–11). Paul believed that by virtue of his sinlessness, Jesus was qualified to be the sacrifice that made sinners right with God (2 Cor 5:21). In his death on the cross, Jesus had become the curse for sin (Gal 3:10–14), and the righteous had died for the unrighteous (Rom 5:6–8).

Salvation is a free gift granted to believers and grounded solely in God's grace. It is not dependent on human merit, activity, or effort but only on God's undeserved love (Rom 6:23; Eph 2:8–10). Those who trust Jesus for their salvation, confess him as Lord, and believe that God raised him from the dead (Rom 10:9) will be saved from God's wrath, become righteous in God's sight (Rom 5:9), are adopted as God's children (Rom 8:15–17; Eph 1:5), and are transformed by the Spirit's power (Gal 5:22–24). At the second coming of Christ, believers will be resurrected (1 Cor 15:12–57), partake fully of the Son's righteous character (Phil 3:20–21), and live forever with their Lord (1 Thess 4:17).

By their union with Christ through faith, believers participate spiritually in Christ's death, resurrection, and ascension (Rom 6:1–7:6; Eph 2:4–5; Col 3:1–4). Consequently, the believer has been liberated from the power of sin, death, and the law. He is a new, though imperfect, creation that is continually being made more like Christ (2 Cor 5:17; Col 3:9–10). Although the believer is no longer under the authority of the written law, the Holy Spirit functions as a new internal law leading him naturally and spontaneously to fulfill the law's righteous demands (Rom 8:1–4). As a result, the law-free gospel does not encourage unrighteous behavior in believers. Such behavior is contrary to their new identity in Christ.

The union of believers with Christ brings them into union with other believers in the body of Christ, the church. Believers exercise their spiritual gifts in order to help each other mature, to serve Christ and glorify him, which is the church's highest purpose (Eph 3:21; 4:11–13). Christ now rules over the church as its head, its highest authority (Eph 1:22). When Christ comes again, his reign over the world will be consummated, and all that exists will be placed under his absolute authority (Eph 1:10; Phil 4:20). He will raise the dead, unbelievers for judgment and punishment, believers for glorification and reward (2 Thess 1:5–10).

PAULINE CHRONOLOGY

Introduction

One scholar has correctly described efforts to establish the sequence and dates for the events of Paul's life as "one of the most baffling problems of New Testament study."[90] In 1979, R. Jewett carefully compared and contrasted the chronologies of Paul's life suggested by numerous scholars.[91] He discovered a frustrating number of significant differences among these suggested chronologies and lamented the failure of NT scholars to move toward a consensus on Pauline chronology. The failure to reach a consensus was not due to any lack of effort on the part of NT scholars, however. In the thirty years prior to Jewett's work, several scholars (including J. J. Gunther, J. Knox, G. Lüdemann, and G. Ogg) dedicated entire monographs to the perplexing issues of Pauline chronology.[92]

The differences in the chronologies proposed by scholars are largely the result of the different approaches to the issue and the different presuppositions that guide the research. Some scholars rely more heavily on Acts than on the Pauline Letters in developing their chronologies. Others prefer Paul's Letters to Acts. Some use a more subjective approach in which they attempt to develop a chronology of Paul's Letters based on perceived theological development from one letter to another. This more subjective approach often unnecessarily introduces tensions between the chronologies in Paul's Letters and Acts. The most sensible approach relies primarily on Paul's Letters for the chronology of Paul's life and supplements that chronology with data from Acts. When tensions between the chronologies suggested by the Pauline Letters and Acts arise, this approach allows for the possibility that Luke may have arranged some of the material in Acts topically rather than chronologically, much like the Gospel writers sometimes did.[93]

The complexity of combining data from Paul's Letters with data from Acts, ancient histories, and inscriptions is perplexing. Detailed chronologies must be viewed as tentative proposals that may not be confirmed until new evidence arises. However, attempts to pinpoint dates for the events of Paul's life are worth the effort since knowledge of the political climate and current events can often shed important light on the meaning of Paul's Letters.

---

[90] J. McRay, *Paul: His Life and Teaching* (Grand Rapids, MI: Baker, 2003), 60.

[91] R. Jewett, *A Chronology of Paul's Life* (Philadelphia, PA: Fortress, 1979), 1–2. The scholars that he discussed include H. Braun, F. Hahn, E. Haenchen, A. Suhl, C. H. Buck, G. Taylor, J. Hurd, G. Lüdemann, W. G. Kümmel, W. Marxsen, D. Guthrie, W. Michaelis, L. Goppelt, and D. Georgi.

[92] J. J. Gunther, *Paul: Messenger and Exile: A Study in the Chronology of His Life and Letters* (Valley Forge, VA: Judson, 1972); J. Knox, *Chapters in a Life of Paul* (Nashville, TN: Abingdon, 1950); G. Lüdemann, *Paul, Apostle to the Gentiles: Studies in Chronology* (Philadelphia, PA: Fortress, 1984; German original 1977); G. Ogg, *The Chronology of the Life of Paul* (London, England: Epworth, 1968).

[93] A good example of this approach is L. C. A. Alexander, "Chronology of Paul," in *Dictionary of Paul and His Letters*, ed. G. F. Hawthorne, R. P. Martin, and D. G. Reid (Downers Grove, IL: InterVarsity, 1993), 115–23.

Paul's Preconversion Life

The descriptions of Paul's preconversion life in both Acts and his letters lack specific references that enable one to establish firm dates for key events. In Philemon 9, Paul referred to himself as an "elderly man" (*presbytēs*). J. Murphy-O'Connor has demonstrated that ancient Greek texts normally used this term to refer to males in their late fifties or early sixties.[94] Since Philemon was probably written while Paul was in Rome in the late 50s or early 60s, Paul was likely born early in the first decade of the first century.

Acts 22:3 states that Paul was trained at the feet of Gamaliel who taught in Jerusalem from AD 25 to 50. Paul's activity as a zealous persecutor of Jesus's followers naturally postdates Pentecost, following the crucifixion of Jesus. Although scholars still debate whether Jesus's crucifixion occurred on April 7, AD 30, or April 3, AD 33, the later date seems best supported by the evidence in the Gospels.[95]

Paul's Conversion

Statements in two second-century apocryphal works, the Ascension of Isaiah and the Apocryphon of James, suggest that Paul's Damascus road experience may have occurred either 545 or 550 days after the resurrection, that is, on either October third or the eighth in the year 34. More reliable evidence for dating Paul's conversion comes from his statement in 2 Corinthians 11:32–33 concerning his escape from the ethnarch of the Nabateans, Aretas IV (Acts 9:23–35). Aretas IV died in the forty-eighth year of his reign, probably 39. He likely did not begin to exercise control over the city of Damascus until the summer of 37. This dates Paul's narrow escape from Damascus to AD 37–39.[96]

According to Galatians 1:17–18, Paul was in Damascus twice, at the beginning and at the end of the three-year period immediately following his conversion. If the escape from Damascus occurred immediately after Paul's conversion, his conversion took place between 37 and 39. But if it happened during Paul's stay in Damascus after his time in Arabia, his conversion occurred between 34 and 36. The words "after many days" in Acts 9:23 seem to suggest that the dramatic escape occurred during the second stay. Thus, Paul probably encountered the resurrected Jesus on the road to Damascus in the mid-30s. Later aspects of Pauline chronology best fit with a conversion early in this temporal range, most likely AD 34.

Early Visits to Jerusalem

After Paul's second visit to Damascus, three years after his conversion, he traveled to Jerusalem where he stayed for fifteen days visiting with both Peter and James (Gal 1:18–19). Paul then traveled to Syria and Cilicia. He remained there from eleven to fourteen years, depending on whether the words "after 14 years" in Galatians 2:1 begin with Paul's

---

[94] J. Murphy-O'Connor, *Paul: A Critical Life* (Oxford, UK: Clarendon, 1996), 1–4.

[95] H. W. Hoehner, "Chronological Aspects of the Life of Christ. Part IV: The Day of Christ's Crucifixion," *BSac* 131 (1974): 241–64; idem, "Chronological Aspects of the Life of Christ. Part V: The Year of Christ's Crucifixion," *BSac* 131 (1974): 332–48.

[96] Jewett, *Chronology*, 30–33.

conversion and thus include the three years in Arabia or begin with Paul's departure from Jerusalem. Perhaps the most natural reading of Galatians 2:1 sees the fourteen-year period as following the three years in Arabia consecutively rather than as overlapping. But this interpretation suggests the year 51 as the date of the visit, which creates conflicts with other firmly established dates in the chronology. This may be resolved in one of several ways.

First, the two time periods may overlap; that is, this second visit to Jerusalem probably occurred eleven years after the first. Second, time was often calculated inclusively in the ancient world. Thus, the "three years" might include one complete year with any portion of a preceding and following year, and the "14 years" might include twelve complete years with any portion of a preceding and following year. Third, combining the two approaches would mean that the fourteen years denotes a period of twelve years, including portions of the year in which Paul was converted and the year in which he visited Jerusalem the second time. Thus, the second Jerusalem visit may have occurred between the years 46 and 51. Again, other aspects of Pauline chronology best fit with a date early in this range, most likely the year 47.

The visit to Jerusalem is probably the famine relief visit described in Acts 11:27–30. Although some scholars equate Paul's second Jerusalem visit described in Galatians 2:1–10 with the Jerusalem Council of Acts 15, this equation is inconsistent with Paul's claim that he had visited Jerusalem only once before. Moreover, some of the details in Galatians 2:1–10 appear rather unlike the events of the Jerusalem Council.[97] Peter's convictions regarding the inclusion of the Gentiles were already settled before that event, so Peter would have spoken in defense of Paul's law-free gospel before the Jerusalem Council occurred. But Paul described Peter as wavering on the issue of relations between Jewish Christian and Gentile Christian even after the meeting mentioned in Galatians 2 (see vv. 11–14). Moreover, the Jerusalem church leaders' request that Paul "remember the poor" (Gal 2:10) seems to fit best in the context of the famine relief visit. This is especially true if the present tense in Galatians 2:10 has the nuance of continuation of a work already in progress, that is, "keep on remembering the poor." This would imply that the Gentile converts had already begun to display their generosity to the less fortunate through their relief offering.

First Missionary Journey

After the famine relief visit, Paul and Barnabas returned to Antioch. Soon after their return, the Spirit commanded the church to commission Paul and Barnabas for their first missionary journey. Although the account of this journey contains no references that allow one to date the travels, the travel log in Acts contains an itinerary that would have required approximately one year. This missionary journey probably occurred in the years 47–48.

Jerusalem Council

At the conclusion of the first missionary tour, Paul and Barnabas went to Antioch of Syria where they stayed for a prolonged period. During this stay in Antioch, controversy

---

[97] See Introduction to Galatians below.

erupted when some teachers from Jerusalem began to insist that salvation required circumcision. The controversy led the church in Antioch to send Paul and Barnabas to Jerusalem to seek the opinion of the apostles and elders regarding the matter. The resulting Jerusalem conference probably convened in 49.[98]

Second Missionary Journey

Paul's second missionary journey, during which he delivered the report from the Jerusalem Council to Gentile churches, commenced soon after the leaders reached their decision. The journey probably began in late 49. Paul's itinerary was aggressive. Jewett has calculated that if Paul averaged twenty-five miles per day while traveling and stayed very briefly at each ministry site, his journey from Jerusalem to Corinth—of which only about one-fifth would have been by sea—would have taken 640 days.[99] But many scholars doubt that Paul could have maintained such a marathon pace. Jewett suggested that the trip from Jerusalem to Corinth more likely required three or even four years.

Acts 18:2 states that Paul encountered Aquila and Priscilla while in Corinth during this second missionary journey. The couple had recently been expelled from Rome by order of Emperor Claudius. The expulsion of the Jews from Rome is mentioned in other ancient sources such as the writings of Suetonius (early second century), Dio Cassius (third century), and Orosius (ca. 385–420), and can be dated to the year 49.[100] The probable date for the second missionary journey is 49–51.

The suggested dates are corroborated by the famous Gallio Inscription. Acts 18:12 reports that Corinthian Jews brought Paul before the tribunal in Corinth while Gallio was proconsul of Achaia at the end of the second missionary journey. This historical note is particularly helpful since Roman custom dictated that Roman officials in the senatorial provinces should hold office for only one year and the terms of proconsuls typically extended from July 1 to the same day of the following year.[101] At the turn of the last century, an inscription in Delphi was discovered that dated to the period of Claudius's twenty-sixth Acclamation as Imperator and identified Gallio as proconsul of Corinth. Based on other imperial data, scholars have determined that this twenty-sixth acclamation occurred between January 25 and August 1, AD 52.

From this evidence, A. Deissmann concluded that the letter of Claudius to Delphi was written between January and August of the year 52. This strongly suggests that Gallio served as proconsul from July 1, AD 51, to July 1, AD 52, and that Paul appeared before

---

[98] Not only does this date fit well with the date of the Gallio Inscription, but it also comports with the Sabbath year cycle. J. Finegan noted that the year immediately following a sabbatical year was a year of greatest food scarcity, and this may explain the special concern for the poor at the Jerusalem Council as described in Gal 2:10. See J. Finegan, *Handbook of Biblical Chronology*, rev. ed. (Peabody, MA: Hendrickson, 1998), 394.

[99] Jewett, *Chronology*, 58–61.

[100] Suetonius, *Claudius* 25.4; Dio Cassius, *History of Rome* 60.6.6; and Orosius, *Seven Books of History against the Romans* 7.6.15–16.

[101] See Dio Cassius, *History of Rome* 57.14.5. For a thorough description of the inscription and its significance, see Jewett, *Chronology*, 38–40.

him in Corinth during this period.[102] Paul's appearance before Gallio seems to have occurred toward the end of his eighteen months in Corinth. Today most scholars recognize the Gallio Inscription as providing the most secure date by which historians may anchor the chronology of Paul. But scholars such as John Knox, who rely largely on the Letters and reject the reliability of Acts, dismiss the Gallio Inscription since its value for establishing a Pauline chronology is dependent on the accuracy of the account in Acts 18:12–17.[103]

Third Missionary Journey

After returning to Antioch, Paul began his third missionary journey. He traveled through Galatia and Achaia until he reached Ephesus, where he spent two and a half to three years. This journey probably extended from around 51 to 54.[104] At the conclusion of his stay in Ephesus, Paul traveled to Jerusalem. He likely arrived in Jerusalem in the early summer of the year 55.[105] Soon after arriving in Jerusalem, Paul was arrested.

Paul's Arrest

After Paul was arrested, the Roman tribune asked if he was "the Egyptian who started a revolt some time ago and led four thousand Assassins into the wilderness" (Acts 21:38). Josephus discussed this event immediately after his treatment of the death of Claudius, which occurred in October 54 (Josephus, *Ant.* 20.169–72). Assuming that Josephus's arrangement of his material is chronologically accurate, the question of the Roman tribune to Paul was probably not posed before early 55.

After Paul's arrest, he was imprisoned for two years in Caesarea (55–57) before Festus succeeded Felix as procurator. Josephus does not clearly indicate when Festus replaced Felix.[106] Felix was reconfirmed as procurator by Nero and continued to serve under the new emperor for some time.[107] Since Nero began his rule in the year 54, it is unlikely that Festus succeeded Felix before 55. In Jerome's version of Eusebius's Chronicle, Festus's succession occurred in the second year of Nero's reign and the twelfth year of the reign of Herod Agrippa II. This would date the beginning of Festus's rule to the fall of 56. According to imperial policy, Festus would have been required to arrive at his post by late spring or early summer. Paul appeared before Festus soon after his arrival in Caesarea. Thus, Paul likely appeared before Festus in the summer of 57.[108]

---

[102] For the history and early translation of this significant find, see A. Deissmann, *Paul. A Study in Social and Religious History*, trans. W. E. Wilson (London, England: Hodder & Stoughton, 1926), 261–79.

[103] See J. Knox, *Chapters in a Life of Paul* (Nashville, TN: Abingdon, 1950), 81–83. For Knox's view of the testimony of Acts, see pp. 61–73.

[104] So also D. Moody, "A New Chronology for the Life and Letters of Paul," in *Chronos, Kairos, Christos: Nativity and Chronological Studies Presented to Jack Finegan*, ed. J. Vardaman and E. M. Yamauchi (Winona Lake, IN: Eisenbrauns, 1989), 231–33.

[105] So also Moody, "New Chronology," 233; and Finegan, *Biblical Chronology*, 397.

[106] Josephus, *Ant.* 20.182; *Jewish War* 2.271.

[107] Josephus, *Jewish War* 2.252; *Ant.* 20.160–72.

[108] For the possibility that numismatic evidence may confirm this date, see McRay, *Paul*, 66; and J. Finegan, *The Archaeology of the New Testament: The Mediterranean World of the Early Christian Apostles* (Boulder, CO: Westview, 1981), 14, 36,

Paul's Final Years

Paul appealed to Caesar, traveled to Rome, and spent another two years under house arrest as he awaited trial before Nero (AD 58–60). According to Eusebius (ca. AD 260–340), Paul was released from prison after his defense before Nero.[109] After his release Paul traveled to Crete, Asia, Greece, and perhaps Spain.[110] He was arrested again in Troas in the mid-60s, and soon afterward he was martyred in the second half of that same decade—no later than 68 (the year of Nero's death).[111] Paul's martyrdom likely postdates the great fire of Rome in the year 64, which sparked Nero's persecution of Christians.[112]

INTERPRETING PAUL'S LETTERS

Compared to the challenges of correctly interpreting the parables, the historical narratives in the Gospels and Acts, or apocalyptic literature like Revelation, interpreting the NT letters may seem simple. Despite a few differences between ancient and modern letters in form and style, modern readers are familiar with the letter genre and basic principles of interpretation for letters. Thus, one might wonder why a brief section on the interpretation of NT letters is necessary.

Unfortunately, however, it cannot be taken for granted that the familiarity with the epistolary genre prevents interpreters from fallacies in interpreting the NT letters. In fact, these Letters are often misinterpreted because of a failure to observe several simple hermeneutical principles. This brief section will introduce a few of them in hopes that modern readers will fulfill Paul's charge to be faithful workers "correctly teaching the word of truth" (2 Tim 2:15).[113]

---

39. However, this evidence remains in question until photographs of the supposed micrographs are published.

[109] Eusebius, *Eccl. Hist.* 2.22.2; 2.25.5; 3.2.30.1.

[110] See Rom 15:24, 28; *1 Clement* 5–6; Muratorian Fragment; and the Pastoral Epistles. Regarding Paul's possible missionary work in Spain, see esp. the discussion in Schnabel, *Early Christian Mission*, 1271–83.

[111] For a good discussion of the issues, see McRay, *Paul: His Life and Teaching*, 60–84.

[112] The Chronicle of Eusebius, as preserved by Jerome, dates the deaths of both Peter and Paul to the fourteenth year of Nero's reign, which would be AD 68 (or 67 since 54 is Nero's first year and the thirteenth year could be 67). However, a clue in *1 Clement*, which states that Paul suffered "under the rulers" (plural), suggests that Paul's death was between September 66 and March 68. During this time, Nero was traveling in Greece, and Rome was ruled by Helius and Tigellinus, an imperial freedman and a captain of the Praetorian Guard. The plural in Clement is best explained as referring to these two temporary rulers. See Finegan, *Biblical Chronology*, 387.

[113] For more thorough introductions to interpreting the NT letters, see A. J. Köstenberger and R. D. Patterson, *Invitation to Biblical Interpretation: Exploring the Hermeneutical Triad of History, Literature, and Theology* (Grand Rapids, MI: Kregel Academic, 2012), 453–516; W. C. Kaiser and M. Silva, *An Introduction to Biblical Hermeneutics: The Search for Meaning* (Grand Rapids, MI: Zondervan, 1994), 121–38; D. A. Black and D. Dockery, *Interpreting the New Testament: Essays on Methods and Issues* (Nashville, TN: Broadman & Holman, 2001), 412–56; and J. S. Duvall and J. D. Hays, *Grasping God's Word: A Hands-On Approach to Reading, Interpreting, and Applying the Bible* 3rd ed. (Grand Rapids, MI: Zondervan, 2012), 251–68. For an extensive treatment, see T. Schreiner, *Interpreting the Pauline Epistles*, 2nd ed. (Grand Rapids, MI: Baker Academic, 2011). For a general introduction to the NT letters, see D. A. Carson and D. J. Moo, *An Introduction to the New Testament,* 2nd ed. (Grand Rapids, MI: Zondervan, 2005), 331–53.

Table 9.2: A Chronology of Paul's Life and Letters

Event	Approximate Date	Scripture Reference
Paul's Birth	ca. AD 1	
Jesus's Crucifixion, Resurrection, Ascension, and Pentecost	Spring 33	Acts 1–2
Paul's Conversion	34	Acts 9:1–19
First Missionary Journey	47–48	Acts 13–14
Authorship of Galatians	48	
Jerusalem Conference	49	Acts 15
Second Missionary Journey	49–51	Acts 16–18
Antioch to Corinth		
Thessalonian Letters from Corinth		Acts 18:11
Appearance Before Gallio		Acts 18:12
Third Missionary Journey	51–54	Acts 19–21
Stay in Ephesus		Acts 20:31
Corinthians A		1 Cor 5:9, 11
1 Corinthians		Acts 19:10
Corinthians C		2 Cor 2:4; 7:8
2 Corinthians		Acts 20:1–2
Stay in Corinth		2 Cor 13:1–2
Romans		Rom 16:1–2, 23
Jerusalem	55	Acts 21–23
Arrest		Acts 21:27–40
Imprisonment in Caesarea	55–57	Acts 24–27
Journey to Rome	57–58	Acts 27
Voyage and Shipwreck		Acts 27:27–40
Winter in Malta		
First Roman Imprisonment	58–60	Acts 28
Prison Epistles: Ephesians, Philippians, Colossians, Philemon		
Paul's Release	60	
Fourth Missionary Journey	60–66	
Titus		
1 Timothy		
Great Fire in Rome	64	
Paul's Arrest and Second Roman Imprisonment	66	
2 Timothy		
Paul's Death	66 or 67	

1. Interpret Paul's Letters with Historical Sensitivity

One problem in the interpretation of the NT letters often results from the failure to interpret them as *historical documents*. Rather than reading Paul's Letters as correspondence written to churches facing specific challenges and threats in Italy, Greece, and Asia Minor nearly 2,000 years ago, some today read them as letters written from God directly to them. Although the NT letters certainly communicate God's revelation for modern readers, they must first seek to understand what the letter was intended to communicate to the original audience before they can understand what the letter means to believers today.

That said, modern readers can apply many statements in the Letters fairly directly to themselves. Statements such as Galatians 5:14 require little historical study and obviously apply to the present-day church: "For the whole law is fulfilled in one statement: Love your neighbor as yourself. But if you bite and devour one another, watch out, or you will be consumed by one another." The truths of this text are quite clear to nearly anyone. Correctly interpreting the text is not the problem; actually obeying the text is the greater challenge.

However, correct interpretation of texts such as Galatians 5:2 requires greater sensitivity to the original historical context: "Take note! I, Paul, am telling you that if you get yourselves circumcised, Christ will not benefit you at all." Does this text teach that modern Westerners who are circumcised for hygienic purposes or for cultural reasons forfeit salvation and will not receive forgiveness through Christ's atoning death? If one reads the text as if it were written directly to modern readers, this would seem to be the natural interpretation. However, Paul meant something quite different. He was countering the Judaizers' view that Gentiles must become Jewish proselytes by receiving ceremonial circumcision in order to be saved. For Paul's opponents in Galatia, Christ's death, resurrection, exaltation, and granting of the Spirit were not sufficient for salvation. Circumcision, they insisted, was required as well. Paul vigorously dismissed this view as a false gospel. In Galatians 5:2, Paul argues that professing believers who sought to be circumcised in order to secure or complete their salvation were showing that they did not fully trust in Christ for salvation. Paul insists that they could not trust in Christ *and* in circumcision for their salvation. They must trust in Christ alone.[114]

Scholars often refer to the NT letters as "occasional" documents. By this they mean that the Letters were written to address particular sets of circumstances. In other words, they deal with the particular needs of specific churches and individuals in certain times and places. Thus, readers who desire to interpret the NT letters accurately should seek to understand the original historical context of each letter as fully as possible.

Scholars often employ a practice called "mirror-reading" in their quest to understand the historical content. Mirror-reading uses the responses of the authors of the NT letters

---

[114] See the discussions in S. McKnight, *Galatians,* NIVAC (Grand Rapids, MI: Zondervan, 1995), 247–48; T. Schreiner, *Galatians,* ZECNT (Grand Rapids, MI: Zondervan, 2010), 312–13.

to reconstruct the problems in the churches they were addressing. Just as a person can often listen to the words of one participant in a phone conversation and accurately reconstruct much of what the other participant said even though he did not directly hear that portion of the conversation, readers can often reconstruct the problems in the churches based on a careful reading of the responses to those problems. A clearer understanding of these problems then assists in interpreting the response in the Letters. This procedure is admittedly circular. But if the reconstruction of the problem prioritizes explicit descriptions in the Letters above mere inferences, the results are often reliable. The descriptions of the circumstances prompting Paul's Letters later in this book use this approach. They are helpful guides to understanding the historical contexts in which Paul's Letters were written and the specific situations they addressed.[115]

2. Interpret Paul's Letters with Literary Sensitivity

Although modern readers are familiar with the letter genre, they often read the NT letters very differently than they read other letters. Few people receive a letter and read only a paragraph at a time. If their reading of the letter were to be interrupted, they would likely pick back up where they left off in their reading rather than jumping here and there, back and forth to various portions of the letter. They recognize that if they are going to understand the letter, they must read it in a single sitting and appreciate the flow and progression of the argument. Yet many read the NT letters haphazardly and miss the development of thought within them as a result.

For example, if read without an awareness of the preceding context, Galatians 5:12 seems bizarre: "I wish those who are disturbing you might also let themselves be mutilated!" Is Paul wishing sexual tortures on anyone who might upset the readers of his epistle? Earlier statements in Galatians make Paul's point here quite clear. Beginning in chapter 2, Paul shows that the false gospel of the Judaizers involved requiring male Gentile believers to receive circumcision. In 2:3 Paul mentions that Titus, though a Greek, was not "compelled to be circumcised" by the apostles and leaders of the Jerusalem church. Galatians 2:12 refers to the "circumcision party (group)." As mentioned, Galatians 5:2–11 strongly protests the notion that circumcision contributes to the salvation of those who have faith in Christ. Consequently, Galatians 5:12 is a *reductio ad absurdum* (carrying an argument to its logical extreme to make a rhetorical point). If the removal of the foreskin was necessary for salvation, then the Judaizers ought to emasculate themselves completely just to make doubly sure that they would be saved! Yet the OT law, which the Judaizers sought to honor, explicitly warned that those who had been emasculated were banned from the assembly of God's people (Deut 23:1). Paul's mocking statement highlights one of the fallacies of the Judaizers' view of salvation.[116] Reading the letter in full and in order easily clarifies an otherwise puzzling text.

---

[115] For a more thorough discussion of the historical study of the NT letters, see Kaiser and Silva, *Introduction to Biblical Hermeneutics,*124–29; and Black and Dockery, *Interpreting the New Testament,* 415–21.

[116] See R. Longenecker, *Galatians*, WBC 41 (Dallas, TX: Word, 1990), 234–35; McKnight, *Galatians*, 252–53.

As one reads through the letter from start to finish, he should pay attention to the introduction and conclusion which often summarize major themes. He should highlight instances of repetition or heavy concentrations of specific words that identify the author's emphases. Greek letter writers sometimes organized the thoughts in their works using the conventions of Greco-Roman rhetoric. An understanding of the various types of rhetoric and the major components of the different forms may help readers trace the argument of the letter. Discussions of the structure of the biblical letters in this text will mention various views of the organization of the letters based on the study of ancient rhetoric.[117]

3. Interpret Paul's Letters with Theological and Hermeneutical Sophistication

Sometimes statements in the NT letters are culturally conditioned. They were written assuming the conditions of first-century Jewish or Gentile culture in various parts of the world. They may not, therefore, apply to readers in a different culture or era in precisely the same way that they applied to the original readers.

For example, Paul instructs Timothy this way: "No widow is to be enrolled on the list for support unless she is at least sixty years old" (1 Tim 5:9). Should the church today apply this statement directly, or should it seek to determine any underlying principles and then apply these with a measure of theological and hermeneutical sophistication?

In order to interpret and apply the NT letters, readers must appreciate the differences between then and now, there and here. The differences are sometimes vast and influence interpretation and application greatly. Most evangelical scholars recognize that prudent application of texts that address cultural situations quite different from those of the modern reader requires principlization. This involves an attempt to discover "the spiritual, moral, or theological principles that have relevance for the contemporary believer."[118] Klein, Blomberg, and Hubbard have proposed a four-step process for deriving and applying such principles:

1. Determine the original application(s) intended by the passage.
2. Evaluate the level of specificity of those applications. Are they transferable across time and space to other audiences?
3. If not, identify one or more broader cross-cultural principles that the specific elements of the text reflect.
4. Find appropriate applications for today that embody those principles.[119]

---

[117] For more thorough treatments of the literary study of the NT letters, see Kaiser and Silva, *Introduction to Biblical Hermeneutics*, 130–33; and Klein, Blomberg, and Hubbard, *Introduction to Biblical Interpretation*, 355–58. For a helpful introduction to rhetorical criticism, see Köstenberger and Patterson, *Invitation to Biblical Interpretation*, 464–68. For a thorough introduction, see G. A. Kennedy, *New Testament Interpretation through Rhetorical Criticism* (Chapel Hill, NC: University of North Carolina Press, 1984).

[118] H. A. Virkler, *Hermeneutics* (Grand Rapids, MI: Baker, 1981), 212.

[119] Klein, Blomberg, and Hubbard, *Introduction to Biblical Hermeneutics*, 407. See also the discussion in Köstenberger and Patterson, *Invitation to Biblical Interpretation*, 780–97 (esp. the guidelines for application on pp. 790–97).

This process will help readers interpret and apply passages such as 1 Timothy 5:9 within the context of verses 3–16.[120]

Step 1: Determine original application. What does Paul mean when he instructs Timothy, "No widow is to be enrolled on the list for support unless she is at least sixty years old" (1 Tim 5:9)? Rather than taking the statement at face value and applying it straightforwardly to our contemporary context, this calls for theological and hermeneutical sophistication. Historically, widows were a needy group in the first century, so the church bore a special responsibility to care for widows in need who had no relatives to provide for them. To regulate this situation, and to prevent abuse, Paul established a series of criteria in the present passage to stipulate which widows were worthy of church support. He also established sixty years as a minimum age limit. If a widow met these requirements, she qualified for such support and was put on a list.

Step 2: Evaluate the level of specificity of those applications. Certainly the church still has a responsibility to care for widows who need help today. However, the status of widows is very different in twenty-first-century North America than it was in first-century Greco-Roman culture. The original age restriction may relate to the health and strength of the average sixty-year-old woman of this era and the age to which a woman might reasonably be expected to work to provide for herself. If so, the general health and the ability of the widow to work would be factors to consider in contemporary application. Today widows generally live longer, and many have retirement plans; thus, the specific qualifications, including the age limit, may need to be adjusted. At the same time, the general principle continues to apply that the church should care for widows who are godly and truly in need.

Step 3: Identify one or more broad cross-cultural principles. In keeping with our findings in the previous step, a given local church or group of churches should establish guidelines and criteria for providing financial or other support for widows in their congregation. This should be based on factors such as the Christian character and proven track record of a widow's service in the church, on her specific needs, and on the resources available.

Step 4: Find appropriate applications for today. Once a church has committed itself to the care of widows and established proper guidelines for identifying them, it may designate special funds for the financial assistance of widows in the church. It may also send out teams to widows and other needy individuals in the church and in the community, visiting their homes and helping with house repairs and other needs. In addition, widows may be held accountable to serve in the church and to take an active part in the church's ministry to the extent that they are able.

---

[120] For an exposition of this passage, see A. J. Köstenberger, "1 Timothy," in *Expositor's Bible Commentary*, vol. 12: *Ephesians–Philemon*, ed. T. Longman III and D. E. Garland (Grand Rapids, MI: Zondervan, 2005), 540–49.

Interpreting the NT letters with historical sensitivity, literary sensitivity, and theological and hermeneutical cultural sophistication will help ensure that modern readers handle these texts responsibly.

STUDY QUESTIONS

1. How many letters of Paul are included in the NT?
2. How are the Quests for the Historical Jesus and the idea that Paul created Christianity related?
3. What kind of evidence did Wenham advance to support his claim that Paul was a follower of Jesus?
4. What is the main passage advanced by Bultmann to prove that Paul was not interested in details about Jesus's life?
5. Who sparked the "New Perspective" on Paul, and what is the title of his major work?
6. What is the label this scholar affixes to first-century Judaism?
7. What has the "New Perspective" correctly emphasized, and how should it be critiqued?
8. Which legal status enabled Paul to appeal to the Roman emperor?
9. Where was Paul born and raised?
10. Who was Paul's teacher?
11. What does the name *Paul* mean?
12. When Paul was converted, what central tenet in his belief system had to change?
13. What was the focus of Paul's gospel?
14. What difficulties are faced by someone who seeks to construct a chronology of Paul?
15. Why should the writing of Galatians be placed before the Jerusalem Council?

FOR FURTHER STUDY

Barnett, P. *Paul: Missionary of Jesus.* After Jesus, vol. 2. Grand Rapids, MI: Eerdmans, 2008.

Barrett, C. K. *Paul: An Introduction to His Thought.* Louisville, KY: Westminster John Knox, 1994.

Bird, M. F. *The Saving Righteousness of God: Studies on Paul, Justification, and the New Perspective.* Paternoster Biblical Monographs. Milton Keynes, UK: Paternoster, 2007.

Bruce, F. F. *Paul: Apostle of the Heart Set Free.* Grand Rapids, MI: Eerdmans, 1977.

Capes, D., R. Reeves, and E. Richards. *Rediscovering Paul: An Introduction to his World, Letters and Theology.* Downers Grove, IL: InterVarsity, 2011.

Carson, D. A., P. T. O'Brien, and M. A. Seifrid, eds. *Justification and Variegated Nomism.* 2 vols. Grand Rapids, MI: Baker, 2001, 2004.

Dunn, J. D. G. *The Theology of Paul the Apostle.* Grand Rapids, MI: Eerdmans, 1998.

Gundry, Stanley N., et al. *Four Views on the Apostle Paul.* Grand Rapids, MI: Zondervan, 2012.

Hawthorne, G. F., R. P. Martin, and D. G. Reid, eds. *Dictionary of Paul and His Letters*. Downers Grove, IL: InterVarsity, 1993.

Hengel, M., and A. M. Schwemer. *Paul Between Damascus and Antioch: The Unknown Years*. London, England: SCM, 1997.

Kim, S. Y. *The Origin of Paul's Gospel*. Grand Rapids, MI: Eerdmans, 1982.

Köstenberger, A. J., and P. T. O'Brien. *Salvation to the Ends of the Earth: A Biblical Theology of Mission*. NSBT 11. Downers Grove, IL: InterVarsity, 2001.

Ladd, G. E. *A Theology of the New Testament*. Rev. ed. Grand Rapids, MI: Eerdmans, 1993.

Longenecker, R. N. *Biblical Exegesis in the Apostolic Period*. 2nd ed. Grand Rapids, MI: Eerdmans, 1999.

_________. *The Ministry and Message of Paul*. Grand Rapids, MI: Zondervan, 1971.

Marchal, J. A. *Studying Paul's Letters: Contemporary Perspectives and Methods*. Minneapolis, MN: Fortress Press, 2012.

Piper, J. *The Future of Justification: A Response to N. T. Wright*. Wheaton, IL: Crossway, 2007.

Plummer, R. L. *Paul's Understanding of the Church's Mission*. Paternoster Biblical Monographs. Milton Keynes, UK: Paternoster, 2006.

Polhill, J. B. *Paul and His Letters*. Nashville, TN: B&H, 1999.

Ridderbos, H. *Paul: An Outline of His Theology*. Translated by J. R. De Witt. Grand Rapids, MI: Eerdmans, 1975.

Riesner, R. *Paul's Early Period: Chronology, Mission Strategy, Theology*. Grand Rapids, MI: Eerdmans, 1998.

Sanders, E. P. *Paul and Palestinian Judaism: A Comparison of Patterns of Religion*. Philadelphia, PA: Fortress, 1977.

Schnabel, E. *Early Christian Mission*. 2 vols. Downers Grove, IL: InterVarsity, 2004.

_________. *Paul the Missionary: Realities, Strategies, and Methods*. Downers Grove, IL: InterVarsity, 2008.

Schreiner, T. R. *Paul: Apostle of God's Glory in Christ: A Pauline Theology*. Downers Grove, IL: InterVarsity, 2001.

Thielman, F. *Paul and the Law: A Contextual Approach*. Downers Grove, IL: InterVarsity, 1994.

Wenham, D. *Paul: Follower of Jesus or Founder of Christianity?* Grand Rapids, MI: Eerdmans, 1995.

Witherington, B., III. *The Paul Quest: The Renewed Search for the Jew of Tarsus*. Grand Rapids, MI: Eerdmans, 1998.

_________. "'Almost Thou Persuadest Me . . .': The Importance of Greco-Roman Rhetoric for the Understanding of the Text and Context of the NT." *Journal of the Evangelical Theological Society* 58 (2015): 63–88.

Wright, N. T. *Justification: God's Plan and Paul's Vision*. Downers Grove, IL: InterVarsity, 2009.

________. *Paul and the Faithfulness of God*. Christian Origins and the Question of God 4. Minneapolis, MN: Fortress, 2013.

Yinger, Kent L. *The New Perspective on Paul: An Introduction*. Eugene, OR: Cascade Books, 2011.

Chapter 10

Paul's Letter to the Galatians

CORE KNOWLEDGE

Basic Knowledge: Students should know the key facts of Galatians. With regard to history, students should be able to identify the letter's author, date, provenance, destination, and purpose. With regard to literature, they should be able to provide a basic outline of the book and identify core elements of the book's content found in the Unit-by-Unit discussion. With regard to theology, students should be able to identify the major theological themes in Galatians.

Intermediate Knowledge: Students should be able to present the arguments for historical, literary, and theological conclusions. With regard to history, students should be able to discuss the evidence for Pauline authorship, date, provenance, destination, and purpose. With regard to literature, they should be able to provide a detailed outline of the book. With regard to theology, students should be able to discuss the major theological themes in Galatians and the ways in which they uniquely contribute to the NT canon.

Advanced Knowledge: Students should be able to argue for the literary integrity of Galatians. They should also be able to evaluate critically the North Galatian and the South Galatian theories of destination and to assess how each affects the dating of Galatians.

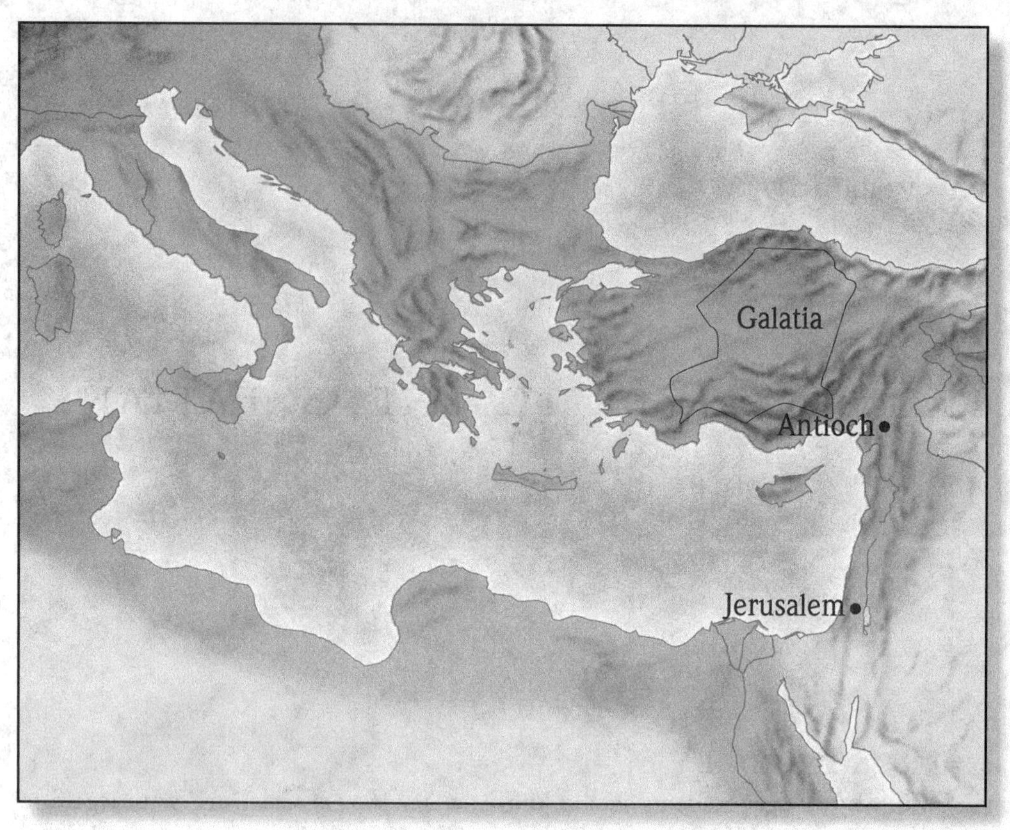

Map 10.1: Provenance and Destination of Galatians

KEY FACTS

Author:	Paul
Date:	AD 48 or 49
Provenance:	Possibly Antioch, Jerusalem, or along the route between the two cities
Destination:	Churches of South Galatia visited by Paul during first missionary journey
Occasion:	False teaching (Judaizing heresy)
Purpose:	To defend the one true gospel
Theme:	Both Jews and Gentiles are saved through faith in Jesus Christ, not by works of the law
Key Verses:	3:10–14

INTRODUCTION

THE LETTER TO the Galatians is in all likelihood the first letter Paul wrote that is included in the NT. Since this introduction follows a chronological approach with regard to Paul's Letters, treating them in the order in which they were written rather than in canonical order, Galatians is the place to start. Although the letter is relatively short, it has exerted enormous influence on Christianity. The early church fathers wrote more commentaries on Galatians than on any other NT book.[1] The letter was a favorite of the Protestant Reformer Martin Luther, who described it as being as dear to him as his own precious wife and called it "my own epistle, to which I have plighted my troth [i.e. pledged my truthfulness]."[2]

As a tribute to the foundational nature of Galatians for understanding the Christian gospel, G. Duncan described the letter as the "magna carta of Evangelical Christianity."[3] R. Longenecker elaborated: "Historically, Galatians has been foundational for many forms of Christian doctrine, proclamation, and practice. And it remains true today to say that how one understands the issues and teachings of Galatians determines in large measure what kind of theology is espoused, what kind of message is proclaimed, and what kind of lifestyle is practiced."[4]

Indeed, Galatians makes numerous and significant contributions to NT theology and ethics. The most important contribution of the letter is its exposition of the doctrine of justification. This brief missive attacks all notions, both ancient and modern, that one's eternal destiny is dependent on one's personal actions, participation in rituals, or conformity to group norms. Instead, the letter liberates the believer from slavery to the law and expounds a higher righteousness that is prompted and empowered by the indwelling Spirit.[5] The letter addresses the Spirit's transforming work in the believer as well as the nature of Christ's substitutionary atonement; it expresses an early but high Christology.

The importance of Galatians for Christian doctrine cannot be overstated. In clarifying the nature of the gospel, in teaching salvation as offered entirely by God's grace and as appropriated exclusively through faith, the letter clarified and fortified the true Christian message at a time when some even within the church sought to subvert the gospel. Thus, A. Cole was correct in his assessment of Galatians as "a theological refutation of a heresy that, if accepted, would have destroyed the whole church."[6] Galatians remains the fiercest and clearest dismissal of salvation through human effort from the pen of the apostle Paul.

---

[1] CA. B. Cousar, *Galatians*, Interpretation (Atlanta, GA: John Knox, 1982), 1.

[2] G. W. Hansen, "Galatians, Letter to the," in *Dictionary of Paul and His Letters*, ed. G. F. Hawthorne, R. P. Martin, and D. G. Reid (Downers Grove, IL: InterVarsity, 1993), 323.

[3] G. Duncan, *The Epistle of Paul to the Galatians* (London, England: Hodder & Stoughton, 1934), xvii.

[4] R. N. Longenecker, *Galatians*, WBC 41 (Dallas, TX: Word, 1990), xliii.

[5] L. Morris's description of Galatians is apt when he called the letter "Paul's charter of Christian freedom" (the subtitle of *Galatians: Paul's Charter of Christian Freedom* [Downers Grove, IL: InterVarsity, 1996]).

[6] A. Cole, *The Epistle of St. Paul to the Galatians* (Grand Rapids, MI: Eerdmans, 1965), 57.

In recent years, however, the letter has been the focus of much debate as NT scholars and theologians have begun to question traditional understandings of justification by faith.[7]

HISTORY

Author

Authenticity The letter to the Galatians is regarded as an authentic letter of the apostle Paul by all but the most radical critics. Acceptance of Paul's authorship is so widespread that extended discussion of the issue is unnecessary. In the late eighteenth century, however, several Dutch scholars rejected Paul's authorship.[8] In the nineteenth century, B. Bauer denied the authenticity of the letter and influenced a number of other scholars to do the same.[9] In the twentieth century, L. G. Rylands and F. R. McGuire rejected Pauline authorship of Galatians.[10] However, the arguments against Paul's authorship have been deemed unpersuasive by a large majority of scholars.

The consensus of NT scholarship views the alternate authorship theories espoused by Bauer and McGuire as excessively skeptical. F. C. Baur categorized Galatians, 1 and 2 Corinthians, and Romans as the "major letters" (German *Hauptbriefe*), letters whose authorship was indisputable.[11] And many other critics are so convinced of Paul's authorship of Galatians that they use the book as the standard by which to test the authenticity of other Pauline Letters.

Importantly, the early church unanimously accepted Paul's authorship of Galatians. Allusions to Galatians appear in the works of Clement of Rome (ca. AD 96), Ignatius (ca. AD 35–110), Polycarp (ca. AD 69–155), and Justin Martyr (ca. AD 100–165). Galatians was included in the ancient canonical lists and in the ancient versions. It was quoted directly and was explicitly ascribed to Paul by Irenaeus (ca. AD 130–200), Clement of Alexandria (ca. AD 150–215), Origen (ca. AD 185–254), and Tertullian (ca. AD 160–225).[12] The author identified himself as Paul in Galatians 1:1 and appealed to his personal signature in 6:11 as confirmation of the authenticity of the letter. Paul's authorship of the epistle, then, may be accepted with great confidence. As R. Longenecker noted, "If Galatians is not by Paul, no NT letter is by him, for none has any better claim."[13]

---

[7] The issues of the authorship of Galatians and its provenance, destination, and date are significantly interrelated, as will become clear in the following integrated discussion below.

[8] H. Ridderbos, *St. Paul's Epistle to the Churches of Galatia* (Grand Rapids, MI: Eerdmans, 1953), 35.

[9] B. Bauer, *Kritik der paulinischen Briefe* (Berlin, Germany: Hempel, 1852).

[10] L. G. Rylands, *A Critical Analysis of the Four Chief Pauline Epistles* (London, England: Watts, 1929), 273–367; F. R. McGuire, "Did Paul Write Galatians?" *Hibbert Journal* 66 (1967–68): 52–57. See the discussions in D. Guthrie, *New Testament Introduction* (Downers Grove, IL: InterVarsity, 1990), 485; W. G. Kümmel, *Introduction to the New Testament*, rev. ed., trans. H. C. Kee (Nashville, TN: Abingdon, 1975), 304.

[11] F. C. Baur, *Paul: His Life and Works* (London, England: Williams and Norgate, 1875), 1.246.

[12] J. B. Lightfoot, *St. Paul's Epistle to the Galatians,* 10th ed. (London, England: Macmillan, 1921), 57–62. Cf. E. De Witt Burton, *A Critical and Exegetical Commentary on the Epistle to the Galatians*, ICC (Edinburgh, Scotland: T&T Clark, 1921), lxviii–lxix.

[13] Longenecker, *Galatians*, lviii.

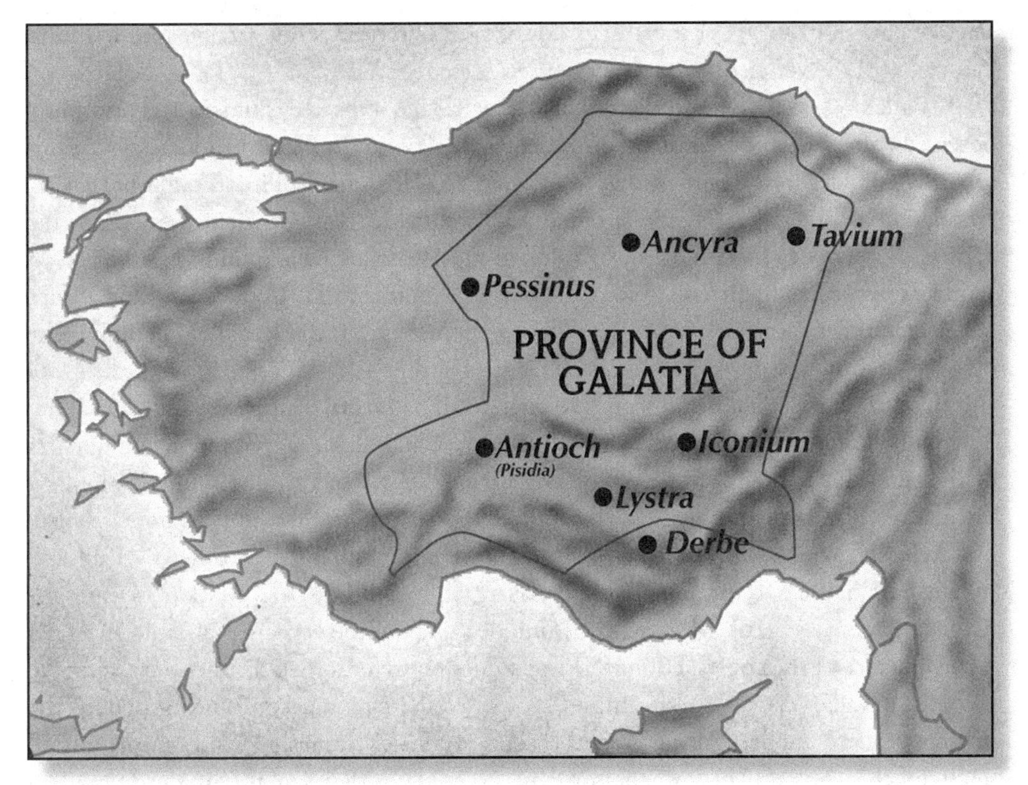

Map 10.2: The Province of Galatia

Literary Integrity More serious challenges have been raised against the integrity of the letter. Especially in the last two centuries, a considerable number of scholars have questioned whether Galatians was originally written in the form that appears in the NT. In the last half of the twentieth century, J. C. O'Neill revived a theory from the nineteenth century which suggested that Paul wrote the majority of the letter, although it contains numerous glosses. In other words, he suggested early scribes inserted some words and passages in the letter.[14]

More recently, W. Walker has suggested that Galatians 2:7b–8 is a non-Pauline interpolation.[15] Walker appealed to six factors in the text as evidence against Paul's authorship of these verses: (1) Paul did not elsewhere use the name "Peter"; (2) he did not elsewhere use the verb *energein* in the same syntactical construction that is used in Galatians; (3) he did not elsewhere distinguish between two legitimate gospels; (4) the presentation of Peter and Paul as the two great missionaries of the Christian movement seems to reflect a later

[14] J. C. O'Neill, *The Recovery of Paul's Letter to the Galatians* (London, England: SPCK, 1972). For a good summary of the book, see Longenecker, *Galatians*, lviii–lix.

[15] W. O. Walker Jr., "Galatians 2:7b–8 as a Non-Pauline Interpolation," *CBQ* 65 (2003): 568–87.

stage of church history; (5) this discussion of apostleship does not ascribe apostleship to Paul; and (6) the verses sit awkwardly in their present context.

To date, no extensive response to Walker's article has appeared, but scholars previously observed some of the phenomena discussed by Walker and offered various explanations for it. E. Dinkler has suggested that Galatians 2:7b–8 is non-Pauline though not an interpolation. The text, he asserts, is a quotation by Paul from a written decree from the apostolic conference in Jerusalem.[16] Although most scholars have found some aspects of Dinkler's proposal unpersuasive, some such as O. Cullmann, H. D. Betz, and F. F. Bruce have argued that some allusion to an official document from the Jerusalem church is the best explanation for some of the unusual features of the Galatians text.[17]

Still, reasonable explanations can be offered for the unusual features of Galatians 2:7b–8 without adopting Dinkler's theory. For instance, Walker has exaggerated the uniqueness of the text. U. Wilckens has demonstrated that the text is permeated with terminology distinctively Pauline.[18] Although Walker correctly pointed out that Paul did not elsewhere use the verb *energein* with the bare dative, the verb is used eighteen times by Paul and only by him in the NT, except for a single saying of Jesus (Matt 14:2; Mark 6:14) and one usage in James (Jas 5:16). Moreover, the unique syntax of the verse is explicable given the special nuance of the construction.[19] The text does not refer to two distinct but legitimate gospels as Walker claimed. The phrases "gospel of the circumcision" and "gospel of the uncircumcision" are better translated as "gospel for the circumcision" and "gospel for the uncircumcision."[20] Many commentators have pointed out that Paul is not referring to two

---

[16] E. Dinkler, "Der Brief an die Galater: Zum Kommentar von Heinrich Schlier," *Verkündigung und Forschung* 1–3 (1953–55): 175–83, especially 182–83, reprinted with "Nachtrag" in his *Signum Crucis: Aufsätze zum Neuen Testament und zur christlichen Archäologie* (Tübingen, Germany: Mohr [Siebeck], 1967), 270–82, esp. 278–80.

[17] R. Hays ("The Letter to the Galatians: Introduction, Commentary, and Reflections," *NIB* 11:226) rejected the theory completely. O. Cullmann (*Peter: Disciple-Apostle-Martyr: A Historical and Theological Study*, trans. F. V. Filson [London, England: SCM, 1953], 18) supported the theory, and H. D. Betz (*Galatians*, Hermeneia [Philadelphia, PA: Fortress, 1979], 97) accepted the theory with some modifications. Compare F. F. Bruce, *The Epistle to the Galatians*, NIGTC (Grand Rapids, MI: Eerdmans, 1982), 120–21.

[18] The verb *pepisteumai* ("entrusted") with the accusative case appears only in Pauline literature (1 Cor 9:17; 1 Thess 2:4; 1 Tim 1:11; Titus 1:3). The contrast between "circumcision" and "uncircumcision" is characteristically Pauline, appearing outside Paul's Letters only in Acts 11:2–3. The noun *apostolē* ("apostolate") appears only in Pauline literature, except for Acts 1:25. See U. Wilkens, "Der Ursprung der Überlieferung der Erscheinungen des Auferstandenen: Zur traditionsgeschichtlichen Analyse von 1 Kor 15, 1–11," in *Dogma und Denkstrukturen. Edmund Schlink in Verehrung und Dankbarkeit zum sechzigsten Geburtstag dargebracht*, ed. W. Joest and W. Pannenberg (Göttingen, Germany: Vandenhoeck & Ruprecht, 1963), 72n41.

[19] Most likely, the bare dative in Gal 2:8 is a dative of advantage that indicates God worked for the advantage of Peter and Paul. See *BDAG*, s.v. "*energeō*."

[20] As J. L. Martyn (*Galatians*, AB 32A [New York, NY: Doubleday, 1997], 202) has explained, the two genitives are objective genitives that identify the persons who are being evangelized. Martyn suggested the translation "the gospel as it is directed to those who are not circumcised." He added, "In these parallel clauses, then, Paul in no way suggests that there are two gospels. There are, rather, two missions in which the one gospel is making its way into the whole of the cosmos."

different gospels with distinct content but to the two different audiences or recipients for the gospel in the church's mission (cf. Rom 4:9–12).[21]

B. Ehrman has argued that "the only real exception to the Pauline character of these verses is the name 'Peter' itself."[22] Paul may here use the Greek name *Peter* rather than the Aramaic name *Cephas* as he otherwise did because the meaning of the name ("rock") is significant, either due to an allusion to the saying of Jesus preserved in Matthew 16:16–20[23] or to the identification of Peter as "those recognized as pillars," since pillars were typically carved from stone.

In addition, E. R. Richards has argued that suspected interpolations in Paul's Letters that are not indicated by variants in the ancient manuscripts may well be interpolations by the amanuensis which were inserted between Paul's original draft and the final copy and that were approved by Paul.[24]

Galatians 2:7b–8 is fully explicable without suggesting that it is an interpolation. None of the extant manuscripts of Galatians lack the text or express any suspicion that the verses are a later scribal addition. Thus, the large majority of scholars affirm the integrity of the letter as well as its authenticity.

Provenance

The provenance of Galatians is inextricably related to the identity of the addressees and the date of authorship. Most NT introductions and commentaries do not even venture a guess as to the place of authorship. However, if one affirms the South Galatian theory (see below) and accepts a date of authorship between the first missionary journey and the Jerusalem Conference, Paul probably wrote the letter either from Antioch, Jerusalem, or some location en route.[25]

Destination

While Paul's authorship of Galatians is widely accepted, scholars differ in their opinions regarding those to whom it was addressed. It is clear that the letter was addressed to the Galatians (1:2; 3:1), but precise identification of the Galatians is difficult. The term *Galatia* could be used in the first century in either an ethnic sense or a provincial one. The issue is complicated, but the study is worthwhile. Pinpointing the precise location of the Galatian churches addressed in the letter is crucial for determining its date.

---

[21] See Longenecker, *Galatians*, 55; Bruce, *Galatians*, 120; Morris, *Galatians*, 75; T. George, *Galatians*, NAC (Nashville, TN: B&H, 1994), 160–61; Lightfoot, *Galatians*, 109.

[22] B. Ehrman, "Cephas and Peter," *JBL* 109 (1990): 463–74, esp. 469. Ehrman argued that Cephas is another figure distinct from the apostle Peter.

[23] The theory that associates Galatians 2 with Matt 16:16–19 was first advanced by J. Chapman, "St. Paul and Revelation to St. Peter, Matthew XVI.17," *Revue Bénédictine* 29 (1912): 133–47. The theory was revived by D. Wenham, *Paul: Follower of Jesus or Founder of Christianity?* (Grand Rapids, MI: Eerdmans, 1995), 200–5.

[24] E. R. Richards, *Paul and First-Century Letter Writing: Secretaries, Composition and Collection* (Downers Grove, IL: InterVarsity, 2004), 94–121.

[25] Cole, *Galatians*, 23.

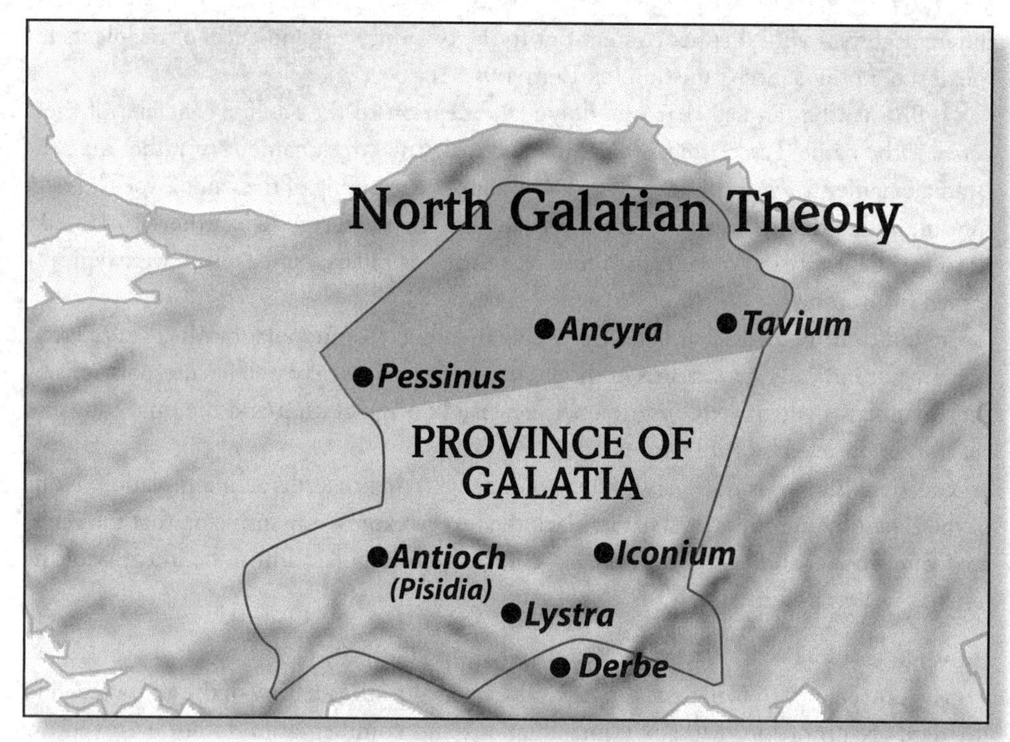

Map 10.3: North Galatian Theory

In the ethnic sense, the term *Galatia* could be used to describe the area inhabited by the Gauls or Celts who invaded north central Asia Minor from Central Europe in 278 BC and were of the same ethnic origin as the Celts of France and Britain. If this is the sense Paul intended, he was writing to churches in northern Galatia, possibly in such cities as Ancyra, Pessinus, and Tavium. The theory that Paul addressed his letter to churches in these northern cities is called the North Galatian theory.

If, on the other hand, Paul's address refers to the Roman province of Galatia, he could be writing to churches in southern Galatia. In 64 BC, the Roman general Pompey rewarded the Galatians for their support in his battle against Mithradates V by making them a client kingdom. Over the next several decades, the kingdom was enlarged toward the south and the east. In 25 BC, Augustus reorganized the area into a Roman province. During Paul's time, the province extended from Pontus on the Black Sea to Pamphylia on the Mediterranean. The Roman province included cities such as Antioch of Pisidia, Iconium, Lystra, and Derbe. Paul visited these cities during his first missionary journey. The theory that he addressed the letter to the churches in these cities is called the South Galatian theory.

Evidence for the North Galatian Theory The North Galatian theory was the view of the early church fathers, medieval commentators, and the Protestant reformers. It was championed by J. B. Lightfoot in the nineteenth century, by J. Moffatt in the early twentieth century, and most recently by H. D. Betz.[26] While the evidence from the early church fathers is impressive, they may have imposed their own contemporary geography on Paul's address. In the year 74, Vespasian detached most of Pisidia from the Galatian province. In 137, the Lyconian portion of the province was transferred to Cilicia, and in about 297, the remaining southern portions were transferred to a new province of Pisidia. By the time the early church fathers read the word *Galatia,* geographical boundaries had changed; therefore, the prominent Galatian cities that Paul visited during his first missionary journey were no longer considered Galatia.[27] Reading the geography of their day back into the NT would have been an easy mistake. This would be much like interpreting "Louisiana" in the Louisiana Purchase to refer only to the small area contained in the present state rather than to the vast lands that comprised Louisiana in 1803.

Some argue that Luke's usage of the term *Galatia* in Acts suits the North Galatian theory. In Acts 16:6 and 18:23, Luke wrote of the region of Phrygia and Galatia. Since Galatia is distinguished from Phrygia (a regional district but not a province), one might conclude that Luke was referring to the Galatian district excluding the districts of Pisidia and Lycaonia.[28] But in Acts 16:6 Luke used a grammatical construction that appears to mean "the Phrygio-Galatic territory." F. F. Bruce has argued convincingly that Luke was referring to the section of the Galatian province that was inhabited by Phrygians,[29] and Acts 18:23 speaks of the same area even though slightly different terminology is used.

Scholars who affirm the North Galatian theory have also appealed to Acts 13:13–14 and 14:6. In these passages Luke identified locations based on geographical regions rather than Roman provinces.[30] Antioch is described as in Pisidia rather than Galatia, and Lystra and Derbe are described as cities of Lycaonia rather than Galatia. Thus, the terms in Acts 16:6 are *regional* rather than *provincial.* While Luke often used regional rather than provincial descriptions, Paul, when he described the location of the churches he founded, normally did so by province: "the churches of Asia" (1 Cor 16:19); "churches of Macedonia" (2 Cor 8:1); "Achaia" (2 Cor 9:2). Moreover, the reference to "Galatia" in 1 Peter 1:1 appears to support the provincial use since Galatia is named along with Anatolian provinces.[31]

Some scholars have argued that there is no hint in Galatians of the strong opposition Paul faced when he preached in the churches of South Galatia. But there are some hints

---

[26] J. Moffatt, *An Introduction to the Literature of the New Testament,* 3rd ed. (Edinburgh, Scotland: T&T Clark, 1918), 90–101; Betz, *Galatians.*

[27] Hansen, "Galatians," 323. One ancient writer, Asterius (d. 340), did affirm the South Galatian theory. See the discussion in W. Ramsay, "The 'Galatia' of St. Paul and the 'Galatic Territory' of Acts," in *Studia Biblica et Ecclesiastica IV* (Oxford, UK: Clarendon, 1896), 16.

[28] Moffatt, *Introduction,* 93.

[29] F. F. Bruce, "Galatian Problems. 2. North or South Galatians?" *BJRL* 52 (1970) 258; and idem, *Commentary on Galatians* (Grand Rapids, MI: Eerdmans, 1982), 10–13.

[30] Moffatt, *Introduction,* 93.

[31] Bruce, *Galatians,* 14–15.

in Galatians 5:11; 6:17, and in Paul's reference to the suffering of the Galatians in 3:4. Moreover, since Paul was persecuted in virtually every city he visited, mention of persecution does not appear a helpful means to narrow the possible parameters of what is meant by "Galatia."

Evidence for the South Galatian Theory W. Ramsay popularized the South Galatian theory in his *Historical Commentary on Galatians,* which was published in 1899. More recently, the view has been championed by F. F. Bruce and R. Longenecker. Scholars point to the following evidence to support this view.

First, Paul obviously knew the Galatian readers personally (Gal 1:8; 4:11–15, 19). Acts contains large amounts of information about Paul's work among the churches of South Galatia, yet no information exists about his work in North Galatia (unless Acts 16:6 and 18:23 are exceptions). Some scholars insist that this argument is weakened by the fact that Acts does not record the founding of the Colossian church either.[32] But the circumstances with Colossians are different since the Colossian church was apparently founded by Epaphras (Col 1:7–8; 4:12–13), a coworker of Paul, rather than Paul himself. Thus, the silence of Acts regarding a Pauline ministry in North Galatia does seem significant.

Second, the route described in Acts 16:6 and 18:23 seems to be a South Galatian route as discussed above.

Third, "Galatia" was the only word that would have encompassed Antioch, Lystra, Iconium, and Derbe. Antioch was in the region of Pisidia; Lystra and Iconium were in Lycaonia. Moreover, Paul normally used Roman imperial names for provinces.[33]

Fourth, in 1 Corinthians 16:1 Paul referred to the Galatian churches as being among the contributors to the collection for Jerusalem. Acts 20:4 mentions a Berean, two Thessalonians, two south Galatians, and two Asians who appear to represent the churches presenting the gift. This suggests that the Galatian churches Paul mentioned in 1 Corinthians were South Galatian churches. If Paul used the term *Galatia* consistently, then the letter to the Galatians was addressed to South Galatians. The argument is weakened by the fact that the list may be incomplete. No Corinthian representatives are mentioned either.[34]

Fifth, Barnabas is mentioned three times in Galatians (2:1, 9, 13). Barnabas accompanied Paul only on the first missionary journey through cities in South Galatia. He did not accompany Paul on the second or third journeys, the supposed occasion of a visit to North Galatia. This evidence is not conclusive, however, since Barnabas is referred to in 1 Corinthians 9:6, though no evidence exists that he was known by the church.[35] Still, the prominence of Barnabas in Galatians seems to imply that he was known by the Galatian churches.

---

[32] D. A. Carson and D. J. Moo, *Introduction to the New Testament,* 2nd ed. (Grand Rapids, MI: Zondervan, 2005), 458.

[33] Bruce, *Galatians,* 15.

[34] Ibid., 13–14.

[35] Ibid., 9.

Conclusion Both theories have their strengths and weaknesses. Neither can be proven or disproven conclusively. The balance of the evidence weighs in favor of the South Galatian theory.[36] Perhaps most importantly, there is no biblical evidence that Paul ever visited the North Galatian cities, while Acts records Paul planting churches in South Galatia. Also, as discussed, the reference to the Galatian churches in 1 Corinthians 16:1 and the repeated mentions of Barnabas in Galatians (2: 1, 9, 13) also seem to favor a South Galatian destination.

Date

The date for Galatians depends largely on three factors: (1) the question of destination; (2) the relationship of Paul's two visits to Jerusalem mentioned in Galatians (1:18; 2:1–10) with the four visits to Jerusalem mentioned in Acts (9:26–30; 11:30; 15:1–30; 21:15–17); and (3) the number of visits to the Galatian churches made before the letter was written as implied in Galatians 4:13. The determination of destination makes the greatest difference in date. Those who espouse the South Galatian theory normally affirm a relatively early date for the letter: either shortly after Paul's first missionary journey or just before or shortly after the Jerusalem Council. Those who accept the North Galatian theory typically affirm a later date, usually during Paul's third missionary journey.[37]

Evidence for a Late Date (North Galatian Theory) Those who espouse the North Galatian theory normally date Galatians during Paul's third missionary journey (ca. 53–57).[38] A date at least as late as the second missionary journey is necessary since the letter must have been written after Paul's first visit to Galatia described in Acts 16:6 and possibly the second visit described in Acts 18:23 (depending on how one treats Gal 4:13). Some interpreters argue from the use of the word *quickly* in Galatians 1:6 that Galatians was written soon after the Acts 18:23 visit and probably during the early stages of Paul's three-year ministry in Ephesus. J. B. Lightfoot argued that similarities among Galatians, Romans, and 1 and 2 Corinthians suggest that they were written in the same period of the apostle's life. He argued that one could trace the development of an increasingly sober and mature response to Jewish legalism through 1 Corinthians, 2 Corinthians, Galatians, and Romans. This

---

[36] Betz (*Galatians*, 4) rather casually dismissed the South Galatian theory, stating, "The arguments in favor of the 'province hypothesis,' . . . , depend upon another hypothesis, the historical reliability of the itineraries in Acts, and upon the argument from silence. . . . There is no real need to think that the author of Acts always had reliable or complete information."

[37] Betz (*Galatians*, 11–12) is an interesting exception. Although he accepted the North Galatian theory, he argued based on internal evidence that Paul wrote Galatians between 50 and 55. On the other side of the spectrum is M. Silva, *Explorations in Exegetical Method: Galatians as a Test Case* (Grand Rapids, MI: Baker, 1996), 129–39, esp. 131–32, who favored the South Galatian theory but argued for a late date.

[38] Calvin (*Galatians, Ephesians, Philippians and Colossians*, vol. 11 of *Calvin's New Testament Commentaries*, trans. T. H. L. Parker [Grand Rapids, MI: Eerdmans, 1965], 24–25) was an exception since he assumed the North Galatian theory but argued that Galatians was written before the Jerusalem Council. The chronology assumed by most who affirm the North Galatian theory differs by several years from the chronology suggested in this text (see "Pauline Chronology" in chap. 9 above).

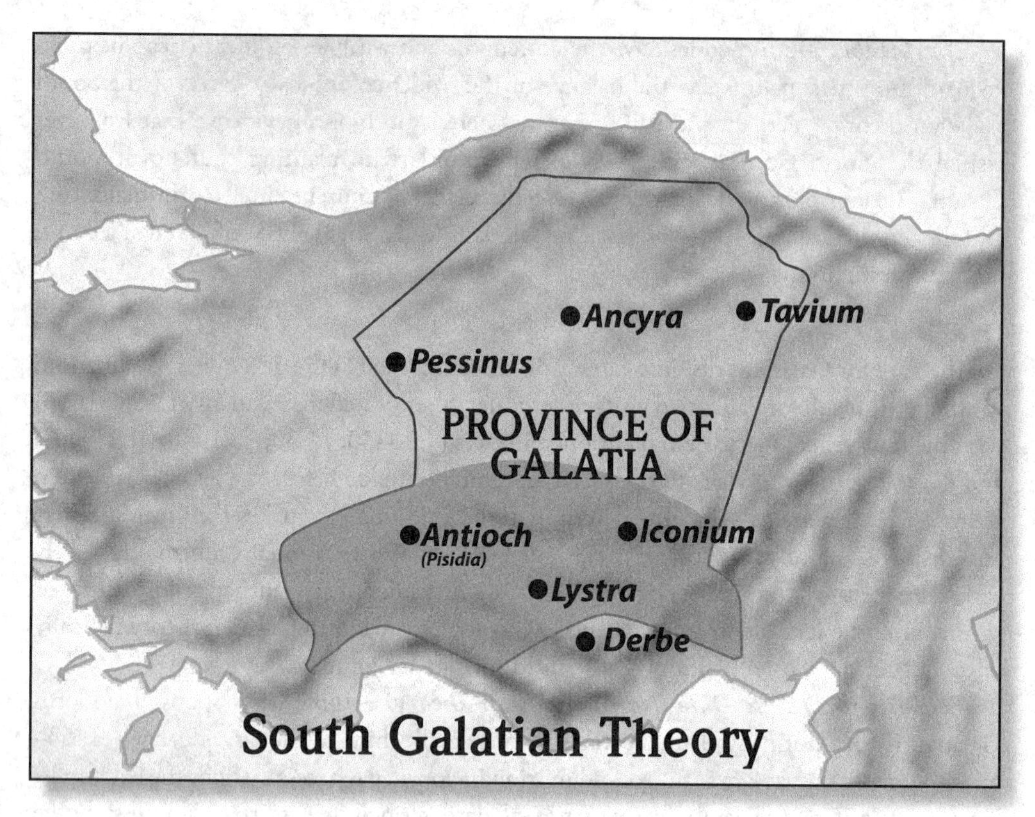

Map 10.4: South Galatian Theory

development placed the authorship of Galatians between 1 and 2 Corinthians and Romans. Thus, Paul wrote Galatians from Macedonia or Achaia in late 57 or early 58.[39]

Evidence for an Early Date (South Galatian Theory) Paul lists two visits to Jerusalem in the first two chapters of Galatians. The visit mentioned in Galatians 1:18 corresponds with Acts 9:26. The visit described in Galatians 2:1–10 could correspond either with Acts 11:28–30 or Acts 15:1–20. If Galatians 2:1–10 corresponds with Acts 11:28–30, then the letter was written before the Jerusalem Council. If Galatians 2:1–10 corresponds with Acts 15:1–20, Galatians was written after the Jerusalem Council.

Post-Jerusalem Council Date Some who espouse the South Galatian theory identify the Jerusalem visit of Galatians 2:1–10 with the Jerusalem Council in Acts 15:1–20. If this is so, the date of composition for Galatians is likely sometime between the years 50 and 57. Scholars appeal to several pieces of evidence to support this equation.[40]

---

[39] Lightfoot, *Galatians*, 36–56.

[40] C. A. Keener lists six possible views of the relationship of Gal 2:1–10 to Acts but describes the equation of Acts 15 and Gal 2:1–10 as the "majority view." He later states, "That Gal 2:1–10 refers to the same meeting as Acts 15 seems to many scholars, including me, to be obvious." See Keener, *Acts*, 3:2195 and 2200.

First, the conference in Galatians 2:1–10 and the council in Acts 15:1–20 involve the same participants: Paul, Barnabas, Peter, and James. They address the same issue: the obligation of Christians to keep Jewish law. They lead to the same outcome: circumcision is not imposed on Gentile converts, but the converts must remember the poor. E. De Witt Burton, an early proponent of the South Galatian theory, argued that this evidence was unequivocal: "The points of coincidence between this narrative [Galatians 2] and that of Acts, chapter 15, are so many and of such character as practically to establish the identity of the two events."[41]

Advocates of a post-Jerusalem Council date for Galatians also point out that there is no mention of any conference with the apostles during the famine relief visit described in Acts. Thus, any equation of Galatians 2:1–10 and Acts 11:30 is based on an argument from silence.

Equating the visits of Galatians 2:1–10 and Acts 15:1–20 means that Paul does not mention the Acts 11:30 visit at all. But proponents of the hypothesis offer several possible explanations for this silence. First, Acts 11:30 says that Paul and Barnabas delivered the relief offering to the "elders," which may not have included the apostles. Since Galatians 2:1–10 concerns Paul's interaction with the apostles, the Acts 11:30 visit was irrelevant to the discussion. Second, many modern scholars doubt the historical reliability of Acts and particularly Luke's description of several of Paul's Jerusalem visits.[42] They argue that either the famine relief visit never occurred or that the visit actually took place after the Jerusalem Council and that Luke transposed it. Paul's failure to mention the apostolic decrees does not require a date before the Jerusalem Council since Paul never appealed to the decrees in any of his letters.

Pre-Jerusalem Council Date The visit in Galatians 2:1–10 seems to correspond with Acts 11:28–30. The latter describes a visit for the purpose of providing famine relief to the Christian Jews in Jerusalem and does not mention the apostle's discussion of Paul's Gentile mission. However, part of the purpose for the relief offering sent from the Gentile mission to the Jerusalem church later in Paul's ministry seems to be to demonstrate the Gentiles' authentic confession of the gospel and to inspire the Jerusalem church's love for and acceptance of the Gentile converts (2 Cor 9:12–14). This may also have been a factor motivating this earlier relief offering. It would be natural for discussion of Paul's gospel and the Gentile mission to arise in such a context.

Equating the Galatians 2:1–10 visit with the Jerusalem Council would mean that Paul neglected to mention one of his visits to Jerusalem in his letter to the Galatians. Such an omission is highly improbable. Paul was demonstrating that his apostleship was of purely divine origin and not derived from the apostolic leaders in Jerusalem. For Paul's theological argument to be valid, all of his visits needed to be accounted for. Paul's insistence on

---

[41] Burton, *Galatians*, xliv.

[42] E.g., J. Knox (*Chapters in a Life of Paul: Explorations into Paul's Career and His Religious Experiences as Revealed in the Personal Passages in His Letters* [New York, NY: Abingdon, 1950], 61–73) argued that Paul actually made only three of the five Jerusalem visits described in Acts and that the famine relief visit of Acts 11:28–30 was actually the last Jerusalem visit.

his absolute integrity in reporting the Jerusalem visits demanded nothing less (Gal 1:20). Thus, the two visits of Paul to Jerusalem described in Galatians correspond to the first two visits described in Acts.

An appeal to the decree of the Jerusalem Council could have strengthened Paul's challenge to the Judaizers. No appeal was made, presumably because the decree had not yet been given. Peter's hesitancy about table fellowship with Gentiles (Gal 2:12) would also fit better with a pre-Council date. Efforts to equate the Galatians 2 visit with the Jerusalem Council described in Acts 15 face serious difficulties. Most importantly, Galatians 2 describes a private conference; the one in Acts 15 is a public event.

Paul referred to visiting Syria and Cilicia between his visits to Jerusalem. If the second visit is the Jerusalem Council, then Galatia should be added to Syria and Cilicia. But since Paul visited Syria and Cilicia before the famine relief visit and only after that visit began his first missionary journey, the specific mention of Syria and Cilicia supports the correspondence between Galatians 2:1–10 and Acts 11:28–30 rather than Acts 15.

Galatians 4:13 refers to when Paul "first preached the gospel" (NIV) to the Galatians, possibly implying that Paul visited the Galatian churches twice before he penned his letter.[43] Some scholars identify the second visit as the one described in Acts 16:6, requiring the letter to have been written after the beginning of Paul's second missionary journey and thus after the Jerusalem Council. However, the Greek adverb can mean "previously" (CSB) rather than "on the former of two visits." Usage in classical literature would require "former," but in the NT era the sense "previously" was common.[44] Even if one insists on the classical usage here, the second visit can be identified as the visit to South Galatian cities in Acts 14:21 and thus took place before the Council. Consequently, a pre-49 date for the letter may still be maintained.

Conclusion The preponderance of evidence favors the equation of the famine relief visit in Acts 11:30 with the visit recounted in Galatians 2:1–10. Although superficial similarities between Acts 15:1–20 and Galatians 2:1–10 exist, close examination of the data suggests the Galatians 2:1–10 visit holds more in common with the famine relief visit of Acts 11:30. Hence Galatians was most likely written in AD 48 or 49.

Table 10.1: Events Surrounding the Writing of Galatians

Event	Likely Date	NT Passage
1. Famine relief visit to Jerusalem	AD 47	Acts 11:30 = Gal 2:1–10
2. First missionary journey	AD 47–48	Acts 13:4–14:28
3. Paul wrote Galatians	AD 48/49	Galatians
4. Jerusalem Council	AD 49	Acts 15:1–20

[43] The Greek construction translated "first" in the NIV can function as a comparative adjective meaning the earlier of two.

[44] K. Lake, *The Earlier Epistles of Paul: Their Motive and Origin* (London, England: Rivington's, 1927), 266.

Occasion and Purpose

Assuming the South Galatian theory, Acts 13–14 combined with scattered references in Galatians charts Paul's church-starting work in the churches of South Galatia. Paul's initial evangelistic work among the Galatians was complicated by an illness that harmed his vision (Gal 4:13–16). Yet the Galatians gave Paul a warm reception, recognized that his message was of divine origin, and welcomed Paul as if he were an angel or even Christ himself. Many believed Paul's gospel, thereby demonstrating their divine appointment for eternal life (Acts 13:48; 14:4, 21). The Galatians loved Paul so powerfully that they would have sacrificed their eyes to restore Paul's vision if that had been possible (Gal 4:15).

Paul clearly proclaimed the gospel of grace from the very beginning of his Galatian ministry. According to Acts 13:38–39, Paul offered the Jews and the Gentiles who worshipped God in the synagogue of Pisidian Antioch forgiveness of sins through Jesus: "Everyone who believes is justified through him from everything that you could not be justified from through the law of Moses." Paul's work met with heavy opposition from the Jews of the area. This was initially motivated by jealousy over Paul's success and popularity with the people (Acts 13:45). But personal rivalry was quickly overwhelmed by religious disputes. The statement in Acts 14:3 that the Lord "testified to the message of his grace" through miraculous signs and wonders implies that the Jewish opposition had focused their campaign against Paul's teaching about grace. Thus, the issue of salvation by grace versus the law of Moses permeated Paul's Galatian ministry and was the crux that divided Christian disciples from Galatian Jews.

Soon after Paul left the area, false teachers infiltrated the church and preached a different gospel—a gospel that insisted that keeping the law of Moses, in particular receiving circumcision, rather than faith in the gospel of grace alone was essential to salvation. The false teachers were probably Jews who considered themselves Christians, but Paul was emphatic that imposition of the law as a requirement for salvation was inconsistent with genuine Christianity (Gal 1:6–9). Scholars typically label these false teachers as "Judaizers" since they sought to impose Judaism on new Christian converts. The Judaizers proclaimed a message akin to the one expressed in Acts 15:1: "Unless you are circumcised according to the custom prescribed by Moses, you cannot be saved." The Judaizers may not have insisted that the Galatians keep the entire law. Circumcision was their main focus. But Paul warned that requiring circumcision for salvation ultimately made the entire OT law obligatory (Gal 5:3). Thus, Paul often defended the gospel against the necessity of observing the law in general (Gal 1:16, 21; 2:2, 5, 10).

Paul's proclamation of the gospel of grace had been so clear that insistence on circumcision and the observance of the law could not be made without rejection of Paul's apostleship. This led to the Judaizers' charge that Paul's apostleship was somehow inferior to that of the other apostles. These opponents twisted Scripture and claimed that their doctrines were imbued with true authority—the authority of the original apostles in the

Something to Think About: No Other Gospel

In the ancient world it was customary to start letters with some kind of special opening—a wish for the recipient's well-being, or a reminder of good times from the past. Most of Paul's Letters, correspondingly, open with a thanksgiving, or a prayer, for the recipients. But this is not the case in his letter to the Galatians. This is a measure of the apostle's exasperation. "I am amazed," he jumped right into the heart of the matter, "that you are so quickly turning away from him who called you by the grace of Christ, and are turning to a different gospel—not that there is another gospel!" (Gal 1:6–7)

In first-century Galatia, as in our day, there are those who would change the gospel of God's grace into a message of human effort. But, as Paul aptly noted, if our salvation depends on our own contribution or ability, this message is no longer "the gospel"—the good news—because we are sinners! If our salvation depends on something we do, we are doomed! This is why Paul said in Romans, "I am not ashamed of the gospel, because it is the power of God for salvation to everyone who believes. . . . For in it the righteousness of God is revealed from faith to faith" (Rom 1:16–17).

The adherents of virtually all world religions, except for Christianity, seek to attain communion with God—or Nirvana or some other form of final state—through self-effort. Ultimately, these people are without hope. True hope comes not through what man may do but only through faith in what another man has already done—Jesus, the Lamb of God and the Savior of the world, who died on the cross for the sins of the world. This is the salvation that is both the power of God and the righteousness of God, and thus truly "good news."

Jerusalem church. The members of the Galatian church defected from the true gospel and began to resent Paul and his teaching and to reject the apostle's authority.

Paul wrote Galatians to defend the gospel of justification by faith alone against the false gospel of the Judaizers. In the process he had to defend his apostolic authority against the Judaizers' attack. Finally, since some readers might interpret Paul's defense of the gospel of grace as justification for immoral or unethical behavior, Paul wrote to defend the consistency of the Spirit-led life with the law's righteous demands.

LITERATURE

Literary Plan

Although some scholars have suggested that Galatians is an impassioned letter composed in the heat of controversy and thus lacking a clear and planned structure, recent research suggests that the letter was much more carefully composed.[45] Like most letters

[45] Betz (*Galatians*, 312) pointed out that Paul's use of a personal secretary or professional letter writer implies a careful process of composition: "It is apparent that the very employment of an amanuensis [secretary] rules out a haphazard writing

from the period, Galatians has an obvious introduction (1:1–9), body (1:10–6:10), and conclusion (6:11–18). Earlier commentators generally saw the body of the letter as breaking down into three major parts: a historical section (1:10–2:21), a theological section (3:1–5:1), and an ethical section (5:2–6:10).[46] The historical section demonstrates the divine origin of Paul's gospel—his encounter with the risen Christ on the road to Damascus. The theological section defends the gospel of justification by faith apart from the works of the law. The ethical section describes the lifestyle prompted by the Spirit in those justified by faith.

Since H. D. Betz's groundbreaking application of rhetorical criticism to Galatians in his 1979 commentary, numerous scholars have sought to compare Paul's Letters to the various categories of speeches and letters described by the ancient rhetoricians.[47] According to the rhetoricians, speeches written for various purposes should contain specific elements in a specific arrangement. But after nearly thirty years of debate over whether Galatians should be classified as forensic (Betz), deliberative (Kennedy), or epideictic (Hester) rhetoric, scholars still seem far from any consensus on the matter.[48] This suggests that the methods of rhetorical criticism are frustratingly subjective. Moreover, many scholars have protested against applying categories devised for public orations to personal letters.[49] Still others have expressed grave doubt that rhetorical classifications of Paul's Letters shed much light on their meaning.[50]

---

of the letter and suggests the existence of Paul's draft and the copy by an amanuensis, or a sequence of draft, composition, and copy."

[46] E.g., Lightfoot, *Galatians*, 5–6; Cole, *Galatians*, 27.

[47] The three major types of rhetoric are (1) forensic or judicial rhetoric (accusation or defense); (2) deliberative rhetoric (persuasion or dissuasion); and (3) epideictic rhetoric (praise or blame). Major parts of an author's or speaker's argument are (1) the *exordium* (introduction); (2) the *narratio* (exposition of facts); (3) the *partitio* (listing of propositions); (4) the *probatio* (support for propositions); (5) the *refutatio* (refutation of opposing arguments); and (6) the *peroratio* (summary and emotional appeal). For a helpful resource on rhetorical criticism, see D. F. Watson, "Rhetorical Criticism," in *Dictionary of Jesus and the Gospels*, 699.

[48] See Betz, *Galatians*; G. A. Kennedy, *New Testament Interpretation Through Rhetorical Criticism* (Chapel Hill, NC: University of North Carolina, 1980), 144–52; and J. D. Hester, "Epideictic Rhetoric and Persona in Galatians 1 and 2," in *The Galatians Debate: Contemporary Issues in Rhetorical and Historical Interpretation*, ed. M. Nanos (Peabody, MA: Hendrickson, 2002), 181–90. The latter volume introduces students to major rhetorical approaches.

[49] See especially Longenecker, *Galatians*, civ–cv; Martyn, *Galatians*, 20–23.

[50] See especially Dunn, *Theology*, 12: "Rhetorical analysis can beget its own scholasticism. In particular it seems to me fairly pointless to argue about whether Paul's Letters are 'epideictic' or 'deliberative' or something else, when most are agreed that Paul's creative genius has adapted to his own ends whatever model he may have borrowed and has done so to such an extent that the parallels are as likely to be misleading as helpful. And as for some of the elaborate structures which have been proposed for Paul's Letters, one might simply observe that there seems to be an inverse ratio between the length of proposed chiasms in an individual letter and the light they shed on either the argument or its point. The vigour of Paul's theology evidently did not allow it to be easily contained within regular grammatical and compositional structures!" Recently, however, B. Witherington ("'Almost Thou Persuadest Me…': The Importance of Greco-Roman Rhetoric for the Understanding of the Text and Context of the NT," *JETS* 58 [2015]: 63–88) has pointed out that scholars utilizing epistolary analysis are no closer to reaching a consensus on the forms than those applying rhetorical analysis. He has also noted that epistolary analysis is sometimes anachronistic since the major handbooks on epistolary forms postdate the Pauline era.

Rather than comparing Galatians to speeches, Longenecker has sought to compare Galatians to the various kinds of letters written in the ancient world. Demetrius's handbook *On Style* describes twenty-one different kinds of letters. Some letters combine two or more of these categories. Based on epistolary formulas in Galatians, Longenecker suggested that Galatians was a letter of rebuke and request. The outline below represents an adaptation of Longenecker's proposed structure of Galatians.[51]

OUTLINE

I. OPENING (1:1–5)
II. REBUKE: PAUL'S GOSPEL AND THE "OTHER GOSPEL" (1:6–4:11)
  A. Historical Section (1:6–2:21)
    1. No Other Gospel (1:6–10)
    2. Paul's Conversion, Visits to Jerusalem, and Encounter with Peter (1:11–2:14)
    3. No Justification by Works of the Law (2:15–21)
  B. Theological Section (3:1–4:11)
    1. Justification by Faith: The Example of Abraham (3:1–18)
    2. The Purpose of the Law (3:19–4:7)
  3. Don't Turn Back (4:8–11)
III. APPEAL: CHOOSE THE LIBERTY OF LIFE IN THE SPIRIT (4:12–6:10)
  A. Children of the Free Woman (4:12–31)
    1. Paul's Exasperation (4:12–20)
    2. An Illustration: Sarah and Hagar and the Two Covenants (4:21–31)
  B. Living a Life of Liberty (5:1–6:10)
    1. Stand Firm: The Freedom of the Christian (5:1–15)
    2. Walk by the Spirit, Not Under the Law (5:16–26)
    3. Fulfill the Law of Christ and Sow to the Spirit (6:1–10)
IV. CONCLUSION (6:11–18)

UNIT-BY-UNIT DISCUSSION

I. Opening (1:1–5)

The need of the Galatian churches was so urgent that Paul did not wait until the body of his letter to begin to address their confusion. Even as he identified the sender and addressees of the letter and greeted his readers, he touched on the key issues that he would address more fully later. First, Paul defends his genuine apostleship. An "apostle" is one who is commissioned for a task by another and entrusted with authority to carry out that task. Paul stresses that his commissioning for service did not come from a body of people, nor was his commissioning communicated through a human who acted on God's behalf. Paul was commissioned for ministry by Jesus Christ and the Father.

---

[51] Longenecker, *Galatians*, c–cix.

By contrasting Jesus with humans and by placing Jesus Christ beside the Father as the two sources of his commission, Paul implies the deity of Christ as well as affirming his own divine commission. Paul's mention of the resurrection should have led readers to recall that his commissioning came from the glorified and resurrected Jesus so that his own apostleship was in no way inferior to that of the Twelve. Paul also refers to his co-laborers who accompanied him on his travels to demonstrate that his gospel was not an idiosyncrasy affirmed only by him but that it was also embraced by other devout men.

Paul identifies Jesus Christ from whom grace and peace come by appealing to his sacrificial death. Christ gave himself for our sins, bearing in our place the curse that our sins deserved so that we might escape that curse (see 3:13). Paul's opponents might have argued that the view that forgiveness is based on Christ's substitutionary atonement alone fosters reckless and immoral behavior. Paul anticipates the objection even before it was raised and insisted that Jesus's sacrificial death was not only intended to grant the believer forgiveness but also to rescue him from the corrupting influences of a depraved age.

This and nothing less fulfilled God's will for the believer. The believer is rescued from the present evil age when he recognizes that he belongs to the coming age and begins to live in light of this awareness (see Col 3:1–17). The coming age is the resurrection age in which the believer will be fully delivered from his corruption and is the age in which Christ will bring all things into subjection. Paul's brief summary of the gospel prompts him to burst into doxology, and rightly so. The gospel with its message about forgiveness and transformation displays God's eternal glory and urges his creatures to praise him as nothing else does.

II. Rebuke: Paul's Gospel and the "Other Gospel" (1:6–4:11)

Paul rebukes the Galatians for abandoning the one true gospel by accepting the Judaizers' claim that circumcision is necessary for salvation.

A. Historical Section (1:6–2:21) Because the Judaizers dismissed the gospel that Paul preached, Paul demonstrates that his gospel was of divine, not human, origin. Jesus Christ had himself revealed this gospel to Paul. Paul's gospel clearly was not derived from his Jewish background. His loyalty to Jewish tradition only prompted him to seek to destroy the church and the faith. Likewise, Paul's gospel was not derived from the other apostles or the leaders of the Jerusalem church (1:11–12). In fact, he did not consult with these prominent Christian believers until years after his conversion.

When he did finally consult with the apostles and the leaders of the Jerusalem church, they heartily approved Paul's gospel and encouraged his continued ministry to the Gentiles. Moreover, Paul discovered that some of these prominent church leaders did not behave in a manner that was consistent with the gospel they all proclaimed. Paul had been forced to challenge the church leaders for this hypocrisy (2:11–14). Paul's challenge demonstrated that his apostolic authority was in no way inferior to theirs.

Paul reminded these Christian Jews that even they were saved by faith in Jesus Christ and not by obedience to the law. If even Jews were not saved by the law, surely the law was not the means of Gentile salvation. By their union with Christ, believers have participated in Jesus's death. They have died to the law, and the law no longer exercises authority over them. But Christ indwells believers, which enables them to live righteously. The believer's gratitude for Christ's great love and enormous sacrifice motivates his or her righteous living.

B. Theological Section (3:1–4:11) Paul continues his assault on the false gospel of the Judaizers with a series of theological arguments. First, the Galatians' own religious experience confirmed the centrality of faith rather than the law (3:1–5). The Holy Spirit was conferred on the believers when they believed the gospel. His presence in them was proven by the occurrence of miracles. This implies that faith, not the law, was the real basis for salvation. Second, the law's description of Abraham demonstrated that faith was the means by which a person was declared righteous by God (3:6–9). Although Abraham was known as the father of the Jews, the OT foretold that people of all nations would share the blessing of justification by faith.

Third, salvation by the works of the law requires complete and absolute obedience. A person who does not keep all of the law all of the time is actually cursed by the law. In his substitutionary death, Jesus bore this curse for sinners in order to free them from the law's curse. Fourth, God's covenant with Abraham, which was based on faith, preceded the giving of the law by 430 years (3:15–16). The covenant based on faith still takes precedence.

Fifth, the law was not given in the first place to provide salvation but to lead sinners to Christ (3:19–26). The law brought about knowledge of sin and condemned all humanity for that sin; thus, the law was intended to drive sinners to look to Christ for salvation. Sixth, Gentile believers are not second-class citizens of God's family (3:27–4:7). Christ has abolished spiritual distinctions among believers. God has adopted believers, both Jews and Gentiles, as his children, and they have equal status. Seventh, observing the Jewish ritual calendar as a means of salvation was nothing more than a lapse back into the paganism from which the Galatians had been delivered (4:8–11).

III. Appeal: Choose the Liberty of Life in the Spirit (4:12–6:10)

After explaining the faults of the Judaizing heresy, Paul appeals to the Galatians to return to the true gospel (4:12–20). He begins his appeal by reminding the Galatians of the intimate relationship that he had shared with them, warning them that the Judaizers did not care for them the way Paul did. In fact, the Judaizers' ministry to the Galatians had selfish ulterior motives.

The apostle uses an allegory about Sarah and Hagar to teach that the true children of Abraham were free, not enslaved to the law, and that they had always been persecuted by the false children of Abraham who lived in slavery (4:21–31). He urges the Galatians to expel the Judaizers from their congregations, warning that circumcision could not be separated from the other demands of the law. If circumcision were required for salvation, the entire law became obligatory.

The apostle thwarts suspicions that faith without law led to immoral living by appealing to three sources of righteousness for the believer: the Spirit, faith, and the influence of the church (5:15–26). The righteousness that the law demanded was produced by the Spirit through faith. Faith working through love is what pleases God and fulfills the law. The life that the Spirit produces is characterized by love, joy, peace, patience, kindness, goodness, faith, gentleness, and self-control. This lifestyle was fully consistent with the law's moral demands. Moreover, if a believer lived sinfully, fellow believers in the church had the responsibility to restore him or her to righteous living.

IV. Conclusion (6:11–18)

Paul concludes the letter with his characteristic signature. His closing remarks reminded the Galatians again of the selfish motives of the Judaizers, humanity's inability to keep the law, and the necessity of experiencing the new creation (transformation through the Spirit's activity) in order to belong to the true Israel. Finally, Paul pointed to the scars that he had received in his ministry for Christ as marks proving his identity as a true servant of the Lord.

THEOLOGY

Theological Themes

Justification by Faith Versus Works of the Law Paul stresses that a person is justified by faith apart from the works of the law. Since the Protestant Reformation, texts such as Galatians 2:15–16 and 3:6–14 have been interpreted as teaching that because of Jesus's sacrificial death, sinners are declared righteous by the heavenly Judge through faith in Christ rather than by personal acts of obedience. Recent scholarly discussions have questioned this traditional understanding at several levels. Scholars have suggested new interpretations of the meaning of justification, the identity of the "works of the law," and the nature of faith. N. T. Wright has argued that "justification" is not the imputation of God's righteousness or Christ's righteousness to the believer but is actually an anticipation of God's final judgment of the individual. Final judgment involves an examination of the totality of the believer's life and is not dependent upon a mere profession of faith.[52]

Wright's explanation of justification is a helpful corrective to views that completely ignore the role of works in eschatological judgment. Galatians 5:19–21 makes clear that a life characterized by the "works of the flesh" excludes a person from the kingdom of God. Thus, one's life and deeds have a definite role in final judgment. But the premise that the works of the flesh disqualify a person from kingdom entrance does not lead to

---

[52] Dunn (*Theology*, 365–66) essentially agrees, but this detail has been especially emphasized by Wright.

the implication that the fruit of the Spirit qualifies a person.[53] Paul did not assert that the believer's actual righteousness qualifies him to inherit the kingdom, even though a clear statement to that effect would have nicely balanced his contrast of the fruit of the Spirit and the works of the flesh. Paul's silence at this point confirms the message that permeates the entire letter: the righteousness that qualifies an individual to pass the scrutiny of divine judgment is an alien righteousness imputed to the believer on the basis of his or her faith. Although imputed righteousness (justification) and imparted righteousness (sanctification) are inseparable, they are distinguishable. Ultimately, it is the former rather than the latter that makes the believer acceptable to God.[54]

J. D. G. Dunn has argued that although "works of the law" refers in general to the deeds prescribed by the Torah, the term primarily referred to the rituals and activities such as circumcision, Sabbath keeping, and the observance of purity laws that distinguished Jews from Gentiles Thus, Paul's insistence on justification by faith apart from the works of the law was not addressed to people who attempted to earn salvation through moral achievement; it was meant for those who mistakenly believed that one had to become a Jew in order to be saved. However, a large amount of evidence suggests that the "works of the law" on which some Jews depended for their salvation included efforts to keep all the prescriptions of the law and not just those that distinguished Jews from Gentiles.[55] Paul's free citation of Deuteronomy 27:26 in Galatians 3:10 stresses the necessity of fulfilling every element of the law in order to evade the curse of the law. This suggests that the totality of the law—and not just Jewish "boundary markers"—was in view in the phrase "works of the law." Moreover, Paul's insistence that "even the circumcised don't keep the law themselves" (6:13) suggests that his opponents were concerned with more than circumcision, Sabbath, and purity issues.[56]

Finally, some scholars argue that the phrase normally translated "faith in Jesus Christ" *(pistis Christou*; e.g., 2:16) should actually be translated "Christ's faith/faithfulness" and refers to Christ's faithfulness to God, particularly as expressed through his obedient death.[57] However, the statement "we have believed in Christ Jesus" (2:16); the references to "hearing with faith" (3:2, 5); the example of Abraham's faith (3:6–9); and the reference to Christ as the object of faith (3:26) all support the traditional interpretation.[58]

---

[53] Wright also denied that the life of the believer in any way earns God's favor or eternal blessing. Although the believer's righteous life is insufficient to merit eternal life, it does demonstrate whether an individual truly is "in Christ."

[54] See the discussion of "Justification" in chap. 13.

[55] See J. A. Fitzmyer, "Paul's Jewish Background and the Deeds of the Law," in *According to Paul: Studies in the Theology of the Apostle* (New York, NY: Paulist, 1993), 18–35; D. J. Moo, "'Law,' 'Works of the Law,' and Legalism in Paul," *WTJ* 45 (1983): 73–100; and T. R. Schreiner, "'Works of Law in Paul,'" *NovT* 33 (1991): 217–44.

[56] See Gal 2:15–16, 19; 3:10–14; 5:3.

[57] R. B. Hays, *The Faith of Jesus Christ: An Investigation of the Narrative Substructure of Galatians 3.1–4.11* (Chico, CA: Scholars Press, 1983), 139–91; M. Hooker, "*Pistis Christou,*" in *From Adam to Christ: Essays on Paul* (Cambridge, UK: Cambridge University Press, 1990), 165–86.

[58] For a compelling defense of the objective interpretation of *pistis Christou* ("faith in Christ"), see Dunn (*Theology*, 379–85), who noted that Paul's consistent contrast is between "works of the law" and faith in Christ (see Rom 3:22, 26;

In Galatians Paul teaches that believers are declared righteous by God, both now and in eschatological judgment, based on Christ's sacrifice and in response to their faith in Jesus and not through obedience to the OT law.

The Nature of the Atonement Galatians 3:10–14 is one of the clearest statements in the NT on the substitutionary nature of Jesus's death. Those who rely on the works of the law for salvation are under a divine curse. In order to be deemed righteous through one's fidelity to the law, a person has to fulfill all of the law all of the time. Interpreted in light of Deuteronomy 27:26, the fact that Jesus died by crucifixion demonstrates that he bore the curse of believing sinners in their place. Thus, Jesus granted forgiveness to sinners by suffering the penalty for their sins so that they might escape God's wrath.

The Transformation of the Believer Paul's Jewish opponents in Galatia likely argued that the law was necessary to restrain the sinful conduct of believers. His libertine opponents argued that since believers are saved through faith alone, their personal lifestyles do not matter to God. Paul counters both errors in Galatians by stressing the dramatic change that takes place in the life of the believer. Paul reminded his audience that God had granted his Spirit to them when they placed their faith in Christ (3:2). The Spirit had manifested his presence among them through amazing miracles (3:5). The indwelling Spirit was the source of the personal righteousness to which true believers aspire (5:5). The Spirit leads the believer to live a life characterized by spiritual fruit, which satisfies and even exceeds the law's moral demands (5:22). The fact that love is the primary expression of the Spirit is significant because love is the essence of the law (5:13–15; see Lev 19:18). This transformation produced by the Spirit is so dramatic and radical that Paul described it as "a new creation" (6:15), echoing the new covenant promises of Ezekiel 11:19–20; 36:26–27. The new creation effected by the Spirit in the believer serves as the standard, the rule, according to which the believer lives (Gal 6:16).[59] Consequently, the gospel that Paul preached was not a license for sinful behavior but the impetus for true righteous living.

The Identity of Jesus Galatians reflects a high Christology. The unique identity of Jesus appears even in the first verse of the letter when Paul insists that he was made an apostle "not by man, but by Jesus Christ." The contrast has the effect of identifying Jesus as someone far greater than a mere man, great prophet, or divine spokesman, and it hints at both his supremacy and deity. Four times the letter calls Jesus God's "Son" (1:16; 2:20; 4:4, 6). It also repeatedly assigns to Jesus the title "Lord," a title of deity that was the preferred substitute for the name Yahweh in Jewish Greek texts as well as in Paul's Letters.[60]

If Galatians is indeed the earliest of Paul's Letters and perhaps even the earliest NT document, this high Christology is even more significant. Galatians clearly demonstrates that

---

Gal 2:16 [twice], 20, 22; Phil 3:9).

[59] Martyn, *Galatians*, 567. See also A. J. Köstenberger, "The Identity of the Ἰσραὴλ τοῦ θεοῦ (Israel of God) in Galatians 6:16," *Faith and Mission* 19/1 (2001): 3–24.

[60] L. W. Hurtado, "Jesus as Lord," in *Lord Jesus Christ: Devotion to Jesus in Earliest Christianity* (Grand Rapids, MI: Eerdmans, 2003), 108–17.

a high Christology was not a product of theological evolution in which Jesus grew from a mere man to semi divine to divine as stories about him were embellished and descriptions of him were exaggerated. Rather, the earliest Christology is a high Christology because Jesus himself claimed and demonstrated his deity before his earliest followers.

CONTRIBUTION TO THE CANON

- Gentiles included in the church on equal terms with the Jews (3:28); circumcision not required, contrary to the "false gospel" of the Judaizers (1:6–9; 6:15)
- Paul's confrontation of Peter regarding the inclusion of the Gentiles, most likely prior to the Jerusalem Council (2:11–14; see Acts 15)
- Justification by faith apart from works of the law (see 2:15; 3:24); demonstration from Scripture that Abraham was also justified by faith apart from works (3:1–4:7, esp. 3:6 citing Gen 15:6)
- Defense of Christian freedom from the demands of the law (5:1–15)
- Teaching on life in the Spirit and the fruit of the Spirit (5:16–26)

STUDY QUESTIONS

1. What are some indications that Galatians has exerted enormous influence on Christianity?
2. What are the two possible destinations for Galatians?
3. What is the support for each of these possibilities?
4. How are the destination and the dating of Galatians interrelated?
5. What are the two major theories regarding the destination of Galatians?
6. According to the authors, was Galatians written before or after the Jerusalem Council? What evidence supports this claim?
7. What was Paul's primary purpose in writing Galatians?
8. Who were the Judaizers?
9. What was their message?
10. Why did Paul rebuke the Galatians?
11. What did Paul teach in Galatians concerning justification by faith versus works of the law?
12. What contributions to the canon does Galatians make?

FOR FURTHER STUDY

Betz, H. D. *Galatians.* Hermeneia. Philadelphia, PA: Fortress, 1979.

Bruce, F. F. *The Epistle to the Galatians.* New International Greek Testament Commentary. Grand Rapids, MI: Eerdmans, 1982.

Das, A. A. *Galatians.* Concordia Commentary. St. Louis, MO: Concordia, 2014.

Dunn, J. D. G. *The Epistle to the Galatians.* Black's New Testament Commentary. Peabody, MA: Hendrickson, 1993.

__________. *The Theology of Paul's Letter to the Galatians.* Cambridge, UK: Cambridge University Press, 1993.

Fung, R. Y. K. *The Epistle to the Galatians.* New International Commentary on the New Testament. Grand Rapids, MI: Eerdmans, 1988.

George, T. *Galatians.* New American Commentary. Nashville, TN: B&H, 1994.

Hansen, G. W. "Galatians, Letter to the." Pages 323–34 in *Dictionary of Paul and His Letters.* Edited by G. F. Hawthorne, R. P. Martin, and D. G. Reid. Downers Grove, IL: InterVarsity, 1993.

Hays, R. B. *The Faith of Jesus Christ: The Narrative Substructure of Galatians 3:1–4:11.* 2nd ed. Grand Rapids, MI: Eerdmans, 2002.

Hove, R. *Equality in Christ? Galatians 3:28 and the Gender Dispute.* Wheaton, IL: Crossway, 1999.

Longenecker, B. W. *The Triumph of Abraham's God: The Transformation of Identity in Galatians.* Edinburgh, Scotland: T&T Clark, 1998.

Longenecker, R. N. *Galatians.* Word Biblical Commentary 41. Dallas, TX: Word, 1990.

Martyn, J. L. *Galatians: A New Translation with Introduction and Commentary.* Anchor Bible 33A. New York, NY: Doubleday, 1997.

McKnight, S. *Galatians.* The NIV Application Commentary. Grand Rapids, MI: Zondervan, 1995.

Moo, D. J. *Galatians.* Baker Exegetical Commentary on the New Testament. Grand Rapids, MI: Baker Academic, 2013.

Morris, L. *Galatians: Paul's Charter of Christian Freedom.* Downers Grove, IL: InterVarsity, 1996.

Nanos, M., ed. *The Galatians Debate: Contemporary Issues in Rhetorical and Historical Interpretation.* Peabody, MA: Hendrickson, 2002.

Richards, E. R. *Paul and First-Century Letter Writing: Secretaries, Composition and Collection.* Downers Grove, IL: InterVarsity, 2004.

Schreiner, T. R. *Galatians.* Zondervan Exegetical Commentary on the New Testament. Grand Rapids, MI: Zondervan, 2011.

Silva, M. *Interpreting Galatians: Explorations in Exegetical Method.* 2nd ed. Grand Rapids, MI: Baker, 2001.

__________. "Galatians." Pages 785–812 in *Commentary on the New Testament Use of the Old Testament.* Edited by G. K. Beale and D. A. Carson. Grand Rapids, MI: Baker, 2007.

Thielman, F. *From Plight to Solution: A Jewish Framework for Understanding Paul's View of the Law in Galatians and Romans.* Novum Testamentum Supplement 61. Leiden, Netherlands: Brill, 1989.

Witherington, B., III. *Grace in Galatia: A Commentary on Paul's Letter to the Galatians.* Grand Rapids, MI: Eerdmans, 1998.

Chapter 11

Paul's Thessalonian Correspondence: 1–2 Thessalonians

CORE KNOWLEDGE

Basic Knowledge: Students should know the key facts of 1 and 2 Thessalonians. With regard to history, students should be able to identify each book's author, date, provenance, destination, and purpose. With regard to literature, they should be able to provide a basic outline of each book and identify core elements of each book's content found in the Unit-by-Unit discussion. With regard to theology, students should be able to identify the major theological themes in 1 and 2 Thessalonians.

Intermediate Knowledge: Students should be able to present the arguments for historical, literary, and theological conclusions. With regard to history, students should be able to discuss the evidence for Pauline authorship, date, provenance, destination, and purpose. With regard to literature, they should be able to provide a detailed outline of each book. With regard to theology, students should be able to discuss the major theological themes in 1 and 2 Thessalonians and the ways in which they uniquely contribute to the NT canon.

Advanced Knowledge: Students should be able to assess the role that language, style, form criticism, and theology play in attributing Pauline authorship to 1 and 2 Thessalonians. In addition, they should be able to defend the traditional chronological order of the letters and determine the influence of rhetorical criticism on the documents.

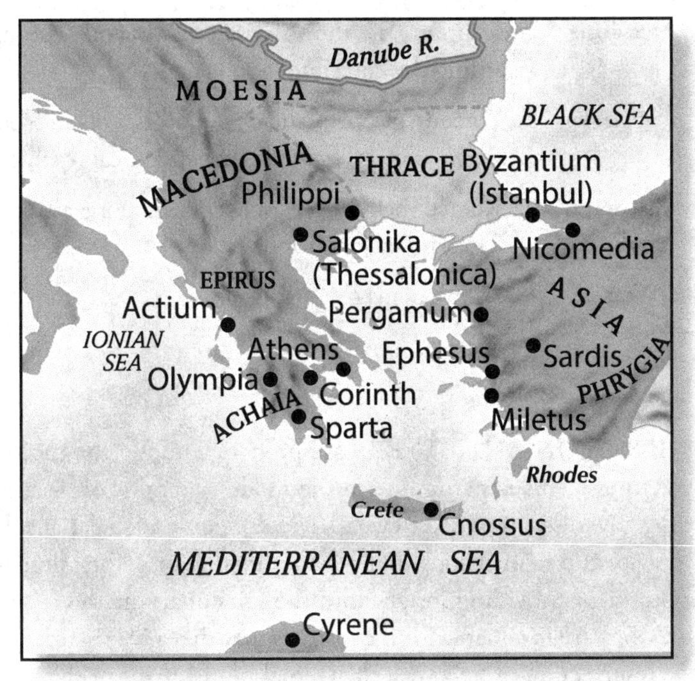

Map 11.1: Provenance and destination of 1–2 Thessalonians

KEY FACTS

Author:	Paul
Date:	50
Provenance:	Corinth
Destination:	Church at Thessalonica in Macedonia
Occasion:	Persecution of the Thessalonians and confusion regarding the end time
Purpose:	To encourage persecuted believers, defend Paul's integrity, and clarify Paul's eschatological teaching
Theme:	Persecuted believers should be encouraged by the anticipation of Jesus's return
Key Verses:	1 Thessalonians 4:13–18

INTRODUCTION

THE THESSALONIAN LETTERS are probably among the more neglected of Paul's writings. This is partly due to the modest amount of discussion in them regarding salvation compared to works like Romans and Galatians. It is also partly due to their brevity and to questions about the authorship of 2 Thessalonians. But these letters are significant for providing insight into the missionary methods and message of the great apostle. They are invaluable for the insights that they give regarding the return of Jesus Christ, the resurrection of believers, the eternal punishment of the wicked, and the events immediately preceding Jesus's return. They also offer helpful instructions regarding sanctification, election, and the Christian work ethic.

Paul's Letters to the Thessalonians are also among the earliest missives written by Paul. Those who affirm the North Galatian theory of provenance for Galatians typically view the Thessalonian correspondence as the earliest samples of Pauline literature. Most who hold to the South Galatian theory place 1 and 2 Thessalonians after Galatians. Since Paul's Letters are treated here in likely chronological order, and since the South Galatian theory has been established as more plausible than the North Galatian one, Paul's Thessalonian correspondence is discussed subsequent to Galatians. In any event, 1 and 2 Thessalonians offer important information about the foundational truths of the apostle's theology.

HISTORY

Author

Modern NT scholars generally recognize 1 Thessalonians as an authentic letter of Paul. The Pauline authorship of the letters attributed to him in the NT is of considerable importance since these documents tie this correspondence to this important figure in the history of the early church, the one who was commissioned by the risen Christ himself to his apostolic ministry. At least from the time of Irenaeus (ca. AD 130–200), the early church unanimously accepted 1 Thessalonians as both Pauline and canonical. Irenaeus quoted 1 Thessalonians 5:23 and identified that quotation as the words of the "apostle" in "his first epistle to the Thessalonians" (*Against Heresies* 6.5.1). Clement of Alexandria (ca. 150–215; *Paedagogus* 5) and Tertullian (ca. 160–225; *Against Marcion* 5.15) also acknowledged that the letter was Paul's own composition.[1]

The first scholar to challenge Paul's authorship of the letter was K. Schrader in 1836.[2] A decade later F. C. Baur argued that the letter was spurious, and his arguments were deemed persuasive by a number of other scholars.[3] But a century later, Frame painstakingly compiled the statistics necessary to demonstrate that the vocabulary, phrases, and concepts are so thoroughly Pauline as to "establish the Pauline authorship of I [Thessalonians], unless one is prepared to assert that Paul never lived or that no letter from him has survived."[4] By the end of the twentieth century, one commentator could accurately state "no contemporary scholars of repute seem to doubt the authentic Pauline character of the letter."[5]

Despite the near unanimous acceptance of 1 Thessalonians, the majority of modern scholars reject the Pauline authorship of 2 Thessalonians. However, external evidence for the authenticity and acceptance of 2 Thessalonians is slightly better than that for the first letter. Like 1 Thessalonians, the letter was included in the Canon of Marcion (ca. 150), the Muratorian Canon (likely late second century), and was mentioned by Irenaeus (ca. 130–200) by name.[6] In addition, Justin Martyr (ca. 100–165) alluded to the letter, and Polycarp (ca. 69–155) twice quoted from it.[7] Although 2 Thessalonians is now completely missing from 𝔓[46], an early manuscript of the Pauline corpus produced around the year

---

[1] See D. Guthrie, *New Testament Introduction*, 2nd ed. (Downers Grove, IL: InterVarsity, 1990), 589.

[2] K. Schrader, *Der Apostel Paulus*, (Leipzig, Germany: Kollmann, 1836), 5:23ff., cited by J. E. Frame, *Epistles of St. Paul to the Thessalonians*, ICC (Edinburgh, Scottland: T&T Clark, 1953), 37.

[3] F. C. Baur, *Paulus, der Apostel Jesu Christi: Sein Leben und Wirken, seine Briefe und seine Lehre* (Osnabruck, Germany: Otto Zeller, 1968 [1845]), 2:94–107.

[4] J. E. Frame, *A Critical and Exegetical Commentary on the Epistles of St. Paul to the Thessalonians*, ICC (New York, NY: Charles Scribner's Sons, 1912), 37.

[5] C. A. Wanamaker, *Commentary on 1 and 2 Thessalonians*, NIGTC (Grand Rapids, MI: Eerdmans, 1990), 17.

[6] See the discussion in G. Milligan, *St. Paul's Epistles to the Thessalonians* (London, England: Macmillan, 1908), lxxvii. Irenaeus referred to 2 Thessalonians by name in *Against Heresies* 3.7.2.

[7] Justin's allusion appears in *Dialogue with Trypho* 110. Polycarp (*Philippians* 11:3, 4) quoted 2 Thess 1:4; 3:13. He identified the source of his first quote as Paul's letter to the Philippians, though the words appear only in 2 Thessalonians. But Philippi and Thessalonica were both important cities in Macedonia, and Polycarp may have viewed them as a single community.

200, it clearly belonged to the final pages that were later lost from the book. No one appears to have challenged Pauline authorship of the letter until J. E. C. Schmidt (1801) cast doubt on it.[8] He argued that 2 Thessalonians 2:1–12 contradicted the eschatology depicted in 1 Thessalonians 4:13–5:11. The former text describes a sequence of events that would precede the Second Coming, but the latter text emphasizes the immediacy of the Second Coming. Schmidt initially argued that 2 Thessalonians 2:1–12 was an interpolation in an otherwise authentic letter of Paul.[9] Three years later Schmidt denied the authenticity of the letter as a whole.[10]

More influential was the work of Kern, who argued that 2 Thessalonians 2:1–2 assumed the preexistence of the belief that Nero would rise to power again *(Nero Redivivus).* This would require a date of composition after 68–70 for the letter, a date too late to allow for Pauline authorship.[11] Kern's arguments were widely accepted throughout most of the nineteenth century.

At the beginning of the twentieth century, T. Zahn vigorously defended the authenticity of 2 Thessalonians in his *Introduction to the New Testament.* So many scholars were persuaded by Zahn's arguments that by 1908, G. Milligan could accurately state that the great majority of commentators in Germany and the general consensus of NT scholarship in Britain and America treated the letter as genuine.[12] J. E. Frame's work defending the authenticity of the letter inspired a trend toward acceptance of the book throughout most of the twentieth century. However, the consensus of opinion shifted again with the 1972 publication of W. Trilling's research on 2 Thessalonians. Trilling raised three arguments against Paul's authorship of 2 Thessalonians: (1) the style of the letter is unlike Paul's normal style; (2) form-critical features suggest that the letter is a forgery; and (3) the theology is incompatible with Pauline tradition.[13] However, as the following interaction will seek to demonstrate, none of the concerns advanced by Trilling needs to lessen the modern reader's confidence in Pauline authorship.

Language and Style Scholars such as W. Wrede have argued that the vocabulary of 2 Thessalonians is so similar to that of 1 Thessalonians that it must be a forgery based on the earlier letter.[14] But Frame showed that the vocabulary of 2 Thessalonians is nearly as similar to Paul's other letters as it is to 1 Thessalonians. For example, of the 146 words

---

[8] Milligan, *Thessalonians*, lxxviii.

[9] J. E. C. Schmidt, *Vermutungen über die beiden Briefe an die Thessalonicher*, Bibliothek für Kritik und Exegese des Neuen Testaments und der ältesten Christengeschichte 2/3 (Hadamar, Germany: Gelehrtenbuchhandlung, 1801).

[10] Frame, *Thessalonians*, 40.

[11] F. H. Kern, "Über 2. Thess 2,1–12. Nebst Andeutungen über den Ursprung des zweiten Briefs an die Thessalonicher," *Tübinger Zeitschrift für Theologie* 2 (1839): 145–214.

[12] Milligan, *Thessalonians*, lxxviii.

[13] W. Trilling, *Untersuchungen zum zweiten Thessalonicherbrief* (Leipzig, Germany: St. Benno, 1972). Form criticism gives special attention to the forms of biblical literature, that is, typical genres of verbal discourse. See K. L. Sparks, "Form Criticism," in *Dictionary of Biblical Criticism and Interpretation*, ed. S. E. Porter (London, England: Routledge, 2007), 111–14.

[14] W. Wrede, *Die Echtheit des zweiten Thessalonicherbriefes*, TU 9/2 (Leipzig, Germany: J. CA. Henrich, 1903).

shared by 1 and 2 Thessalonians, all but four also appear in Paul's major letters (Galatians, Romans, 1 and 2 Corinthians). Two of these four appear in the Prison Letters. The only two words shared by 1 and 2 Thessalonians alone are the words "Thessalonica" (which one would expect in two letters addressed to the same audience) and the word "direct" (*kateuthynō*; used seventy-two times in the LXX and once in Luke). This is hardly compelling evidence for a forgery based on 1 Thessalonians!

Trilling argued that forty expressions unique to 2 Thessalonians suggest that it was written by someone other than Paul. But many of the unique expressions in 2 Thessalonians were required by the unusual problem that the author was addressing in the church of Thessalonica, a problem that Paul did not encounter elsewhere. Moreover, the actual number of *hapax legomena* (words used only once in a document) in 2 Thessalonians is ten, which is half the number of *hapax legomena* in 1 Thessalonians, a letter scholars regard as authentic.[15] Significantly, Menken, who argued that 2 Thessalonians is pseudonymous, admitted that the vocabulary of the letter is no less Paul's than that of the recognized letters.[16]

Arguments based on stylistic features are equally unpersuasive. For example, some scholars point out that the sentences in 2 Thessalonians tend to be significantly longer than sentences in 1 Thessalonians. But they overlook the fact that the short sentences in 1 Thessalonians are due to its many exhortations. Moreover, many sentences in Paul's accepted letters are quite long (1 Cor 1:4–8; Phil 1:3–11; 1 Thess 1:2–5, perhaps 2–7).[17]

Form-Critical Features In the second part of his argument, Trilling attempted to use a form-critical investigation of 2 Thessalonians to dismiss Paul's authorship.[18] Trilling pointed out that the prescripts in 1 and 2 Thessalonians are more similar than any other prescripts. This suggested to him that the prescript of 2 Thessalonians was forged by someone other than Paul using 1 Thessalonians as a model. But one would expect a greater similarity between the two prescripts if Paul wrote both letters since the letters were written closer in time to one another than any other two extant letters written by Paul—especially since they were written to the same audience.

Trilling also examined the thanksgiving, apocalyptic material, prayers, ethical material, and conclusion of 2 Thessalonians and argued that various features of these sections suggest the letter is not Paul's. In particular, Trilling asserted that the greater stress on apostolic authority and the impersonal nature of the letter precludes Pauline authorship. But these same criteria could be used to determine that Romans and Galatians, letters almost universally recognized as authored by Paul, were not written by him. Romans is largely impersonal in nature. Galatians, though much more personal than Romans, greatly stresses

[15] Milligan, *Thessalonians*, li–liii.

[16] M. J. J. Menken, *2 Thessalonians* (London, England: Routledge, 1994), 32.

[17] A. Malherbe (*The Letters to the Thessalonians*, AB [New York, NY: Doubleday, 2000], 366) pointed out that the lengthy sentences typically appear early in the epistle. This corresponds to 2 Thess 1:3–12, the lengthiest sentence in the letter. It appears that not only the long sentence but even its placement is characteristically Pauline.

[18] Trilling, *Untersuchungen*, 23. Form criticism looks at the various types of writing present in examining a given document.

Paul's apostolic authority. Although the impersonal nature of Romans can be explained as a result of the fact that Paul had not previously visited Rome, the impersonal nature of 2 Thessalonians is also easily explained since Paul had recently written a more personal letter to the Thessalonians that freed him to write his second letter more expeditiously.

Wanamaker correctly argued that Trilling was wrong to assume that Paul's Letters are "a homogenous set of writings holding to a standard pattern." Although 2 Thessalonians, for example, may have a thanksgiving section that differs from Paul's other letters, Galatians completely lacks a thanksgiving section; nevertheless, no one has argued that the absence of the section precludes Paul's authorship. Scholars generally recognize that Paul's Letters are highly situational, that is, they were written to address particular needs and to respond to specific issues in a local congregation. The unique needs and issues of various congregations significantly influenced the form, style, and tone of Paul's communication.[19]

Theology Trilling argued that certain theological themes in 2 Thessalonians stand in tension with Paul's theology elsewhere. His most important arguments relate to the themes of Christ's return and divine judgment and the image of God and Christ. Trilling argued that the discussion of Christ's return in 2 Thessalonians placed an emphasis on divine judgment and retribution that found no parallel in Paul's undisputed writings.[20] This emphasis, Trilling claimed, reflected the point of view of later NT writers and did not seem to fit in one of Paul's early Letters. Paul never elsewhere referred to God's judgment of the wicked to comfort believers who are being persecuted.

Trilling's objections are easily answered. First, he seems to have overlooked the specific situation that the author was addressing, which is that 2 Thessalonians seeks to comfort believers who are suffering intense persecution. This setting of persecution that is presupposed in 2 Thessalonians is confirmed by 1 Thessalonians and the book of Acts. The promise of vindication of suffering believers through the punishment of their oppressors served to encourage the believers to remain faithful and to discourage them from withdrawing from the Christian community. Second, although the emphasis on retribution is unusual for Paul, it has parallels in Jewish literature that either predated or was contemporary with the apostle Paul.[21] These Jewish texts seriously undermine the claim that any Christian appeal to retribution must belong to the late first century.

Other interpreters have objected to Paul's authorship of 2 Thessalonians because it says that certain events must precede the Second Coming (2:3–12), though Paul elsewhere expected an imminent return of Christ (1 Thess 4:15–17; 5:1–5; Rom 13:11–12; 1 Cor 7:29, 31; Phil 4:5). But, although other Pauline texts stress the suddenness of the Second Coming and imply the expectation that Christ would return soon, they do not preclude the necessity of certain events leading up to the return of Christ. Interpreters should not

---

[19] Wanamaker, *Thessalonians*, 24–25.

[20] Trilling, *Untersuchungen*, 27.

[21] E.g., 2 Macc 6:12–18; *2 Bar* 13:3–10; 78:5; *Pss Sol* 13:9–10.

confuse imminence with immediacy. No real tension exists between the eschatology of 2 Thessalonians and that of Paul's other writings.

Trilling also viewed 2 Thessalonians' portrayal of Jesus as "Lord" as evidence of post-Pauline authorship since 2 Thessalonians 1:9 applies the description of the activity of Yahweh in Isaiah 2:10 to Jesus. Trilling claimed that this reflected the progressive imposition of OT attributes of God to Christ and fits best with a late first-century date for the letter. This argument is puzzling since the title *Lord* is not typically applied to Jesus in the Pastoral Letters, which Trilling regarded as Deutero-Pauline and to which he appealed to explain this feature. More importantly, Paul's undisputed letters frequently describe Jesus as Lord and do so in contexts that clearly portray Jesus as Yahweh.[22] For example, 1 Thessalonians, widely regarded as Pauline, describes the Second Coming as the "Day of the Lord," a phrase drawn from the OT prophets in which the title *Lord* translates the divine name Yahweh. This use of the title *Lord* as a substitute for Yahweh appears in a context that is saturated with references to Jesus as Lord. Consequently, the use of the title *Lord* in 2 Thessalonians neither suggests a late date nor non-Pauline authorship of the letter. The usage of the title *Lord* and the application of Yahweh texts to Jesus in 2 Thessalonians are consistent with the high Christology of Paul's undisputed letters.

The letter claims to have been written by Paul (2 Thess 1:1), describes letters falsely ascribed to the apostle as deception (2 Thess 2:2–3), and confirms Paul's own authorship with a distinctive autograph (2 Thess 3:17). The letter cannot be accepted as written by a person of integrity who writes in the name of Paul to express what he believed to be Pauline doctrine as some scholars have claimed. Either the letter is a genuine document written by the apostle Paul, or it is a forgery written by someone who intentionally deceived his readers. As R. Jewett noted, "The improbability of a forgery is extremely high."[23] Both the external and internal evidence affirm Paul's authorship of the letter. E. Best has pointed out that arguments against Paul's authorship have generally come from scholars who have studied the letter superficially: "It is curious how the vast majority of the commentators accept the letter as genuine while its rejecters are found among those who approach the letter more cursorily from the outset."[24] Those who study the letter in greatest detail typically affirm its authenticity. Modern readers may be confident that the early church was correct in ascribing this letter to Paul.

---

[22] E.g., compare Rom 10:9, 13 and Phil 2:9, 11 with Joel 2:32. In Romans 10, an OT Yahweh text is applied to Jesus. In Philippians 2, the identification of the title *Lord* as the "name that is above every name" demonstrates that *Lord* is functioning like it typically did in Jewish Greek texts as a reverent substitution for the name Yahweh.

[23] R. Jewett, *The Thessalonian Correspondence: Pauline Rhetoric and Millenarian Piety* (Philadelphia, PA: Fortress, 1986), 18.

[24] E. Best, *A Commentary on the First and Second Epistles to the Thessalonians* (London, England: A. and C. Black, 1977), 52.

Order of the Letters

Before the date of the Thessalonian letters may be established, one must first determine the order in which the two letters were written. Although readers may automatically assume that the canonical order of the two letters is the chronological order, the books of the Pauline corpus were arranged according to the length (beginning with the longest and ending with the shortest) rather than according to the date of their composition, and 1 Thessalonians (1,481 words) is significantly longer than 2 Thessalonians (823 words).[25] Thus, it is possible that 2 Thessalonians was actually written before 1 Thessalonians.

A handful of twentieth-century NT scholars defended the priority of 2 Thessalonians,[26] though only a relatively small number of scholars have accepted this view. To date, the first and only commentary to argue for the priority of 2 Thessalonians was the commentary on the Greek text of the letter by C. Wanamaker in 1990. Wanamaker appealed to the five principal reasons for the priority of 2 Thessalonians discussed by Manson and Weiss to support his conclusion.[27] The following section explains these five principal reasons and offers a response.

1. The persecution referred to in 2 Thessalonians 1:4–7 seems to be already past in 1 Thessalonians 2:14. Indeed, 2 Thessalonians 1:4 uses the present tense to describe the Thessalonians' experience of persecution, while 1 Thessalonians 2:14 uses the aorist, a past tense. But this would make sense also if the persecution the Thessalonians suffered in association with Paul's visit ended soon after his departure but recurred with new intensity when the citizens of Thessalonica realized that Paul's absence did not ensure the demise of the Christian movement in that city. In addition, other texts in 1 Thessalonians seem to imply that the Thessalonians were in fact suffering persecution at the time the letter was written (e.g., 3:3–10).

2. The disorder in the church appears to be a new problem in 2 Thessalonians 3:11–15, while being treated as though it were a known difficulty in 1 Thessalonians 4:10–12. The

---

[25] D. Trobisch, *Paul's Letter Collection: Tracing the Origins* (Minneapolis, MN: Fortress, 1994), 19–24. The normal order in the early manuscripts was Romans, 1 Corinthians, 2 Corinthians, Galatians, Ephesians, 1 Thessalonians, 2 Thessalonians, Hebrews, 1 Timothy, 2 Timothy, and Titus (Vaticanus, Sinaiticus, Alexandrinus, and Ephraemi Rescriptus). The only deviation in the order from longer to shorter is Ephesians (2,894 words in the Greek text), which is longer than Galatians (2,771 words in the Greek text), but follows Galatians in the canonical order. 𝔓[46] (the earliest extant collection of Paul's Letters; ca. AD 200) places Hebrews after Romans and Galatians after Ephesians, thus following a strict descending order in length. J. M. O'Connor points out that determiners of length such as *stichoi* and Euthalian numbers indicate very similar lengths for Galatians and Ephesians (*Paul the Letter-Writer: His World, His Options, His Skills* [Collegeville, MN: Liturgical Press, 1995], 120–30).

[26] J. C. West, "The Order of 1 and 2 Thessalonians," *JTS* 15 (1914): 66–74; J. Weiss, *Earliest Christianity: A History of the Period A.D. 30–150*, trans. and ed. F. C. Grant (New York, NY: Harper, 1959), 1:286–91; T. W. Manson, "St. Paul in Greece: The Letters to the Thessalonians," *BJRL* 35 (1952–53): 428–47; R. Gregson, "A Solution to the Problem of the Thessalonian Epistles," *EvQ* 38 (1966): 76–80; C. Buck and G. Taylor, *St. Paul: A Study of the Development of His Thought* (New York, NY: Scribner's, 1969), 140–45; and R. W. Thurston, "The Relationship Between the Thessalonian Epistles," *ExpTim* 85 (1973–74): 52–56. F. F. Bruce (*1 and 2 Thessalonians*, WBC 45 [Waco, TX: Word, 1982], xli) suggested that Hugo Grotius (1641) was the first scholar to suggest the priority of 2 Thessalonians.

[27] Wanamaker, *Thessalonians*, 38–39.

evidence here is inconclusive. It is true that Paul dealt with the issue of disorderly conduct more extensively and forcefully in 2 Thessalonians 3:6–15. But most likely 1 Thessalonians 4:10b–12 reminded the readers of his earlier oral teaching. Then rumors, or perhaps a personal report from Timothy on his return from delivering the first letter (2 Thess 3:11), may have required Paul to address the issue again more specifically in 2 Thessalonians 3:6–15.

3. The closing in 2 Thessalonians 3:17 seems to suggest that 2 Thessalonians is the first letter. To the contrary, the explanation of Paul's signature in 2 Thessalonians 3:17 does not require or imply the priority of 2 Thessalonians. Most of Paul's Letters in the NT are the first letters Paul wrote to a specific congregation, but they contain no such explanation. The explanation was more likely motivated by Paul's concern that someone had forged a letter in his name and confused the Thessalonians regarding the coming of Christ (2 Thess 2:2). The pseudonymous letter prompted Paul to highlight the hallmark that identified his authentic writings.

4. The remark in 1 Thessalonians 5:1 that the readers did not need instruction regarding the end time seems to presuppose 2 Thessalonians 2:1–12. Yet Paul's confidence in the Thessalonians' understanding of "times and seasons" could as easily result from his emphasis on eschatology in his oral teaching in Thessalonica as from a prior letter. In fact, 1 Thessalonians 4:6 implies that Paul had discussed eschatological judgment during his visit.

5. The expression "now concerning" in 1 Thessalonians 4:9; 5:1 appears to be a common formula introducing answers to questions raised previously by the readers (see 1 Cor 7:1). In each case, the subject introduced in 1 Thessalonians can be shown to arise from a question raised by the Thessalonians regarding a subject addressed in 2 Thessalonians.[28] The construction "now concerning" *(peri de)* appears only twice in 1 Thessalonians. Although 1 Thessalonians 5:1 introduces a topic discussed at length in 2 Thessalonians, 1 Thessalonians 4:9 introduces the subject of brotherly love, which Paul does not specifically treat in 2 Thessalonians. This makes it doubtful that 1 Thessalonians was written to address questions raised by 2 Thessalonians.

The reasons listed by Wanamaker do not suggest the priority of 2 Thessalonians. To the contrary, several factors support the traditional order of the two letters. Most importantly, 2 Thessalonians 2:15, "So then, brothers and sisters, stand firm and hold to the traditions you were taught, whether by what we said or what we wrote," seems to refer to a prior letter from Paul to the Thessalonians.[29] When Paul referred to such a tradition later in 2 Thessalonians 3:6, it has parallels with 1 Thessalonians (4:11–12; 5:14) but not with earlier

---

[28] Ibid., 39.

[29] Wanamaker (*Thessalonians*, 41) suggested that the reference may be to another letter no longer known. If so, Paul's first letter to the Thessalonians is no longer extant; 2 Thessalonians is the second letter of Paul to the congregation, and 1 Thessalonians is the third letter. But positing the existence of an otherwise unknown letter when other explanations are plausible results in a strained argument. Alternatively, Wanamaker suggested that "you were taught . . . by our letter" refers to the immediately preceding section of 2 Thessalonians itself. This would require the word *edidachthēte* ("you were taught") to be an "epistolary aorist," which is unlikely. For a brief discussion of Paul's possible use of the epistolary aorist elsewhere,

material in 2 Thessalonians. Also, Paul's reference to a letter falsely ascribed to him (2 Thess 2:2) is most plausible if the Thessalonians had received an earlier letter from Paul that made a later written communication seem less suspicious. Paul's notice that his autograph marked "all" his authentic letters (2 Thess 3:17) likewise seems to imply that he had sent an earlier letter to the Thessalonians. If 2 Thessalonians were the first letter Paul had written to the church, he could have more easily dismissed the suspected forgery by indicating that he had not previously written the church. Paul's failure to deny previous written correspondence implies an earlier letter.

Also, Paul's lengthy description of his personal visit to Thessalonica in 1 Thessalonians 1:4–2:12 makes more sense if 1 Thessalonians was Paul's first correspondence with the Thessalonians after his departure from Thessalonica.[30] Admittedly, 2 Thessalonians also refers to this visit (2 Thess 2:5, 15; 3:6–10) but not as extensively as 1 Thessalonians does.

Therefore, although the balance of internal evidence seems to favor the priority of 1 Thessalonians, M. Martin wisely reminded interpreters that the issue of the sequence of the Thessalonian letters remained unsettled. He cautioned, "As long as this ambiguity remains, the interpreter is wise to avoid leaning heavily on any interpretation that is dependent for its validity on a particular chronological sequence for the letters."[31]

Date

First Thessalonians was written by Paul during his second missionary journey soon after he fled the city of Thessalonica in the face of severe persecution (Acts 17:5–10). If Paul wrote the letter from Corinth, he probably did so in the year 50. Paul's eighteen months in Corinth can be dated in light of the Gallio Inscription that indicates Gallio served as proconsul from July 1, AD 51 to July 1, AD 52. Paul probably appeared before Gallio shortly after he assumed power. Most scholars suspect that Paul's opponents would have brought their charges to a new and untested proconsul in hopes that he might be influenced to rule in their favor. Thus, Paul's appearance before Gallio probably occurred in the late summer or early fall of the year 51. Moreover, Paul seems to have appeared before Gallio toward the end of his eighteen months in Corinth.[32] Timothy remained in Berea while Paul was escorted to Athens (Acts 17:13–14). Paul apparently used these escorts, who returned to Berea as Paul was entering Athens, to deliver his instructions for Timothy to return to Thessalonica. The journey from Athens back to Berea probably took the couriers several weeks. One must then allow several weeks for Timothy's journey from Berea

---

see K. L. McKay, "Observations on the Epistolary Aorist in 2 Corinthians," *NovT* 37 (1995): 154–58; cf. D. B. Wallace, *Greek Grammar Beyond the Basics* (Grand Rapids, MI: Zondervan, 1996), 562.

[30] M. W. Holmes, *1 and 2 Thessalonians*, NIVAC (Grand Rapids, MI: Zondervan, 1998), 28.

[31] D. M. Martin, *1, 2 Thessalonians*, NAC 33 (Nashville, TN: B&H, 1995), 33. See J. W. Simpson Jr., "Letters to the Thessalonians," in *Dictionary of Paul and His Letters*, ed. G. F. Hawthorne, R. P. Martin, and D. G. Reid (Downers Grove, IL: InterVarsity, 1993), 937.

[32] Both assumptions are supported by C. J. Hemer, *The Book of Acts in the Setting of Hellenistic History* (Tübingen, Germany: Mohr Siebeck, 1989), 119.

Something to Think About: Radiant Faith

When Paul came to Thessalonica and tried to establish a church there, he was faced with vehement opposition—so much so that he had to cut his time there short after a few weeks and leave town by night (see Acts 17:1–10). But a wonderful thing happened: the believers in Thessalonica imitated Paul's Christlike attitude in persecution and thus became examples to others in their entire region. This is the way Paul put it in his first letter to the Thessalonians:

> *You know what kind of men we were among you for your benefit, and you yourselves became imitators of us and of the Lord when, in spite of severe persecution, you welcomed the message with joy from the Holy Spirit. As a result, you became an example to all the believers in Macedonia and Achaia. For the word of the Lord rang out from you, not only in Macedonia and Achaia, but in every place that your faith in God has gone out. Therefore, we don't need to say anything (1 Thess 1:5b–8).*

This is truly remarkable. Because these new believers embraced the gospel whole-heartedly and their faith radiated all around them, Paul, the missionary who had planted the church, didn't need to say anything! This shows that we should not leave sharing and spreading our faith to a few God-called evangelists or those with the gift of evangelism (though God certainly uses these individuals; see Eph 4:11; 2 Tim 4:5). Instead, biblical evangelism is first and foremost a corporate affair, something to be done by the entire church.

Unconvinced? Here is what Jesus said in his final prayer:

> *I pray not only for these, but also for those who believe in me through their word. May they all be one, as you, Father, are in me and I am in you.* May they also be one in us, so the world may believe you sent me. *I have given them the glory you have given me, so that they may be one as we are one. I am in them and you are in me,* so that they may be made completely one, so the world may know you have sent me and have loved them as you have loved me *(John 17:20–23, emphasis added).*

Do we have radiant faith? Do we have faith that radiates beyond our local church to the world around us? Do we have the faith that inspires others to "love and good works" (Heb 10:24)? Many can attest to the fact that we were attracted to the gospel message at least in part by observing the love Christians had for one another. This is the biblical model: for the body of Christ to represent Christ to the world, in love and unity, "so the world may believe" and know God's love for them.

This is what they said about the first Christians: "See how they love one another!" (Tertullian, Apology 39.7). Can they say the same about us?

to Thessalonica and his stay in Thessalonica.[33] His travel from there back to Paul, who had now proceeded from Athens to Corinth, probably took about one month. A period of two and a half to three months likely transpired between the time of Paul's entrance into Athens and Timothy's return to Paul. Paul probably wrote 1 Thessalonians soon after Timothy's arrival in Corinth. This suggests that Paul wrote 1 Thessalonians several months after arriving in Corinth. Thus, he could have composed the letter anytime between mid-spring and midsummer AD 50. If Paul appeared before Gallio later in his proconsulate, a date of composition up to one year later is possible. A date within this range—or a few months later—is also compatible with the theory of the priority of 2 Thessalonians.

Second Thessalonians was probably composed several months after the earlier letter, perhaps in the winter of 50. Interpreters who accept the priority of 2 Thessalonians generally suggest that Timothy served as the courier for the letter and that it accompanied him on his trip from Athens to Thessalonica, in which case the letter was composed while Paul was in Athens early in the spring of 50.

Provenance

Two theories regarding the place of composition of the Thessalonian letters emerged in the ancient church. The Marcionite Prologues and introductions and subscriptions in some early manuscripts of the letter claim that 1 Thessalonians was written from Athens.[34] A few later manuscripts claim the letter was written from Corinth.[35] Although the antiquity of the identification of Athens as the place of authorship must be appreciated, the internal evidence of the letter and the account of Paul's second missionary journey in Acts suggest that Corinth is a much more likely provenance. First Thessalonians 3:1–10 explains that Paul decided to remain in Athens alone and to send Timothy to Thessalonica to encourage the church and to find out how the church was faring in Paul's absence. A comparison of 1 Thessalonians 3 and Acts 17 suggests that although Paul was in Athens, he sent instructions through his escorts to Timothy in Berea. Timothy was to travel to Thessalonica and then reconnect with Paul in Athens. But by the time Timothy returned from Thessalonica, Paul had already moved on to Corinth (Acts 17:14–16; 18:5) where Timothy eventually rejoined Paul with his report of the situation in Thessalonica that prompted Paul to write

---

[33] Malherbe added nearly a month to the chronology because he assumed that Timothy had to travel from Berea to Athens (a three-week journey) and then from Athens back to Thessalonica (six weeks). This is possible, but Acts implies that Paul and Timothy did not reconnect until after Paul had begun his ministry in Corinth (Acts 18:5). See M. Dibelius, *Die Briefe des Apostels Paulus. II. Die Neun Kleine Briefe* (Tübingen, Germany: Mohr, 1913), 12; I. H. Marshall, *1 and 2 Thessalonians*, NCBC (London, England: Marshall, Morgan, and Scott, 1983), 89; and Wanamaker, *Thessalonians*, 126–27.

[34] Both Alexandrinus (fifth c.) and the first corrector of Vaticanus (fourth c.) identify the letters as "from Athens." The first corrector of Vaticanus was probably a contemporary of the original scribe. See K. Aland and B. Aland, *The Text of the New Testament* (Grand Rapids, MI: Eerdmans, 1989), 108.

[35] Manuscript 81 (AD 1044) and a few others indicate that 1 Thessalonians was "written from Corinth by Paul and Silas and Timothy."

1 Thessalonians. It appears that Paul and Timothy were not in Athens at the same time.[36] Even if Timothy were sent from Athens by Paul to the Thessalonians, Paul had almost certainly moved on to Corinth before they rejoined. Since 1 Thessalonians names Timothy as a coauthor of the letter, the letter was likely from Corinth.[37]

Subscriptions in some early manuscripts state that 2 Thessalonians was written from Athens;[38] subscriptions in some later manuscripts indicate it was written from Rome.[39] But the large majority of contemporary scholars who affirm Paul's authorship of the letter argue that 2 Thessalonians was written from Corinth several months after the first letter. Second Thessalonians 1:1 identifies Paul, Timothy, and Silas as coauthors. According to the testimony of Acts, these three men traveled together only during the second missionary journey. Second Corinthians 1:9 confirms that Paul and Timothy resided together in Corinth, and Silas is probably also among the "brothers who came from Macedonia" mentioned in 2 Corinthians 11:7–11. Paul was probably not in Athens long enough to have written 1 Thessalonians there. It is even less likely that he composed his second letter in Athens. So 2 Thessalonians was probably written within a few months of the first letter, and Paul's eighteen months in Corinth affords more than enough time for the letter to have been penned there.

Destination

Both 1 and 2 Thessalonians were addressed to believers in the recently planted church in Thessalonica. Thessalonica, modern Thessaloniki or Salonica, was strategically located. It was situated at the head of the Gulf of Therme on the finest natural harbor on the Aegean Sea and became the chief port city for Macedonia. It also lay on the Via Egnatia, the main Roman road between Asia Minor and Dyrrachium, a port on the coast of the Adriatic Sea from which one could sail across the Adriatic to the port at Brundisium and then follow the Via Appia directly to Rome. Thessalonica was thus the largest and most important city in Macedonia during the time of the apostle Paul.[40]

Thessalonica was a cosmopolitan city inhabited by both Greeks and Romans, and a significant Jewish population lived there (Acts 17). Most of Paul's readers had been pagan

---

[36] This reconstruction was affirmed earlier by E. von Dobschütz, *Die Thessalonicherbriefe*, 7th ed., KEK (Göttingen, Germany: Vandenhoeck & Ruprecht, 1909), 130. Best (*Thessalonians*, 131) rejected von Dobschütz's reconstruction on the grounds that the interpretation "deprives his willing determination to remain behind alone in Athens of meaning." This protest is incorrect since in this reconstruction Paul was left alone by his escorts who had to carry instructions back to Timothy in Berea. Some commentators make no attempt to integrate the statements in 1 Thessalonians with the account in Acts. D. A. deSilva (*An Introduction to the New Testament: Contexts, Methods and Ministry Formation* [Downers Grove, IL: InterVarsity, 2004], 529) argued, "In such cases it is probably better to rely on Paul's firsthand account of the events rather than Luke's second-hand, later and often incomplete account."

[37] Malherbe (*Thessalonians*, 71–72) treated the issue of an Athenian versus a Corinthian provenance more extensively than most commentators.

[38] This provenance is supported by subscriptions in Alexandrinus (fifth c.), the revision of Vaticanus (fourth c.), and a number of later mss.

[39] See the subscriptions in mss. 6 (13th c.), 614 (13th c.), and the margin of 1739 (10th c.).

[40] Wanamaker, *Thessalonians*, 3.

idolaters before their conversion to Christianity (1 Thess 1:9). They may have worshipped a number of the various gods of Thessalonica, including Dionysius, Sarapis, Kabiros, and Caesar.[41] The congregation in Thessalonica was a mixed one that included new believers from both Jewish and pagan backgrounds.

Occasion

Acts 17:1–10 records Paul's founding of the church at Thessalonica. After Paul was expelled from Philippi, he continued westward on the Via Egnatia to Thessalonica.[42] There, for three consecutive Sabbaths, he spoke in the Jewish synagogue and sought to convince the Jews that Jesus is the Messiah and that he had "to suffer and rise from the dead" (Acts 17:3). Some of the hearers embraced the gospel, not because of the persuasiveness of Paul's arguments but because of God's own mysterious activity among the Thessalonians. Paul had no doubt that God had chosen them because his gospel "did not come to you in word only, but also in power, in the Holy Spirit, and with complete certainty" (1 Thess 1:5). Although Paul's ministry in the synagogue only lasted a few weeks, evidence from the Thessalonian letters suggests that he may have continued his ministry in his workshop (1 Thess 2:9). Paul mentioned receiving financial support from the Philippians at least twice during his stay in Thessalonica (Phil 4:16), thus implying a longer stay in the city than a superficial reading of Acts 17 might suggest. While Paul was in Thessalonica, persecution against the missionary team and the new believers erupted. Some interpreters pit Acts and the Thessalonian letters against one another by claiming that Acts describes the Jews as persecutors while 1 Thessalonians 2:14 identifies the persecutors as Gentiles. A careful reading of Acts 17:5, however, suggests that Jews incited the persecution but that the entire city was quickly caught up with anti-Christian sentiments. The Jews stirred the anger of "scoundrels from the marketplace" who formed a mob and "started a riot in the city." Their complaints against the Christians were brought to the city magistrates and invoked Caesar's decrees. The magistrates viewed the matter as serious enough to require them to take a security bond from some of the new believers.

Recognizing that Paul's presence would only continue to inflame the animosity against Christians in the city, the Thessalonians urged Paul and Silas to depart for Berea. Paul later departed for Athens where he preached his famous sermon before the Areopagus. While Paul was in that city, he sent Timothy back to Thessalonica to inspect the state of the church there. Timothy met up with Paul again in Corinth. He gave Paul a report concerning the church and may have even delivered a letter from the Thessalonians to Paul. The phrase "now concerning" *(peri de)* may imply that Paul was answering questions raised by the Thessalonians in their correspondence to him.[43] Paul wrote his first letter to

---

[41] See especially C. Edson, "Cults of Thessalonica," *HTR* 41 (1948): 153–204; and K. P. Donfried, "The Cults of Thessalonica and the Thessalonian Correspondence," *NTS* 31 (1985): 336–56.

[42] See Destination above.

[43] Compare 1 Thess 4:9; 5:1 with 1 Cor 7:1, 25; 8:1. Some argue that this is especially likely since two of the issues that Paul addressed, brotherly love and the Day of the Lord, are issues he personally did not feel needed to be addressed.

the Thessalonians in response to Timothy's report and, possibly, correspondence from the Thessalonians that Timothy delivered.

Paul apparently learned from Timothy that some opponents of the church were challenging the motives of Paul's ministry. He discovered that the believers continued to suffer persecution. Perhaps he found out that some of them were struggling with sexual temptations, that they were confused about the sequence of events related to Jesus's return, that some were living irresponsibly and not seeking to support themselves financially, and that some were not properly respecting their spiritual leaders and were practicing their spiritual gifts in a disorderly manner.

Second Thessalonians deals with some of the same problems. Paul did not find it necessary to defend himself in the second letter as he had in the first. Evidently he knew that his first letter had succeeded in convincing the Thessalonians of the purity of his motives. But Paul was alert to another influence on the church which had succeeded in confusing them about the end time. He also seems to have learned more about the problem of the "idle" in the church.

Purpose

Both 1 and 2 Thessalonians are letters by the apostle who planted the church of Thessalonica written to address the specific needs of this particular congregation. First Thessalonians was written to (1) encourage the church during a time of persecution; (2) defend the purity of Paul's motives behind his mission to the Thessalonians; (3) urge the church to live holy lives characterized by sexual purity; (4) define a Christian work ethic; (5) correct confusion about the return of Christ; and (6) prompt the church to respect its leaders.

Second Thessalonians was written to address issues in the church about which Paul appears to have learned through an oral report (2 Thess 3:11). He wrote the letter to (1) encourage a persecuted church with the promise of final vindication; (2) correct confused views about the end time caused by misrepresentations of Paul's teaching; and (3) give the church more extensive directions for dealing with the "idle."

LITERATURE

Literary Plan

Although commentators of past generations have generally outlined Paul's Letters based on the topics treated in their various sections, rhetorical criticism has sought new insights into the purpose and organization of the NT letters. Modern-day letter writers use certain literary conventions like the greeting "Dear" or the closing "Sincerely." The format of a modern letter is dependent to some degree upon its purpose. A personal letter typically assumes one format and a business letter another. Similarly, ancient speeches and

---

But Paul's statements in 1 Thess 4:9 ("you don't need me to write you") and 5:1 ("you do not need anything to be written to you") are examples of a common rhetorical device called paralipsis and do not provide any real support for theories of written correspondence from the Thessalonians to Paul. See *BDF* 495.1. For other Pauline examples, see 2 Cor 9:1; Phlm 19.

Something to Think About: How Is Your Work Ethic?

Apparently, when Paul wrote 2 Thessalonians, there were those who believed Christ's Second Coming was so imminent that all they had to do was quit their jobs and wait around for his arrival. Paul had no tolerance for such laziness. In fact, he commanded believers to "keep away" from those who lived "idle" (2 Thess 3:6, 11), reminding them of his own example when he was with them: "We did not eat anyone's food free of charge; instead we labored and toiled, working night and day, so that we would not be a burden to any of you" (2 Thess 3:8). So even when he was with them, Paul established this maxim: "If anyone isn't willing to work, he should not eat" (2 Thess 3:10).

Many of us have quoted this verse in jest to our children, but the implications of Paul's words are serious and profound. Whether people misunderstood or misrepresented his teaching of salvation by grace apart from works, or were confused about the time of Christ's Second Coming, Paul frequently combated the notion that Christians had certain liberties that exempted them from the normal responsibilities of life—including work. Surely this is not the case. Already the ancient preacher had said, "Whatever your hands find to do, do with all your strength" (Eccl 9:10), and both Jesus and Paul worked as craftsman and tentmaker, respectively, for many years. Paul often chose to forego his right to be supported by the congregations he served. Instead, he worked for his sustenance so he could offer the gospel "free of charge."

This is an attitude that should be emulated by all Christians, especially by those in Christian service, including pastors and missionaries. We should not easily take the hard-earned money of those who would support us while refraining from work ourselves. Certainly, we should not listen to those cults who, as Jesus predicted, claim to know the exact timing of Christ's coming and seek to confuse and distract us from doing our work today:

> *Many false prophets will rise up and deceive many. Because lawlessness will multiply, the love of many will grow cold. But the one who endures to the end will be saved. This good news of the kingdom will be proclaimed in all the world as a testimony to all nations, and then the end will come (Matt 24:11–14).*

letters used particular conventions and formats. Understanding these can help the interpreter better grasp ancient communication. Rhetorical criticism compares particular features of Paul's Letters with various patterns and purposes for speeches and letters in the ancient world in order to yield new insights about their literary plan.

Of the three major genres of rhetoric described by Aristotle, 1 Thessalonians is best classified as epideictic (praise or blame) rhetoric, a genre in which an author reinforces and celebrates values or ideas shared with his audience. Such rhetoric could be either positive or negative. On the one hand, it might use praise to persuade the audience to continue present behavior. On the other, it might use blame to dissuade the audience from continuing present behavior. Most scholars classify 1 Thessalonians as epideictic because Paul's praise and thanksgiving for the Thessalonians are so dominant throughout the letter.[44]

First Thessalonians may be seen as consisting of five major rhetorical components: (1) *exordium* (1:1–5); (2) *narratio* (1:6–3:10); (3) *transitus* (3:11–13); (4) *probatio* (4:1–5:22); and (5) *peroratio* (5:23–28).[45] The *exordium,* or introduction, typically establishes rapport with the audience by praising them or giving thanks for them. It also states the main themes of the letter. In this case, the *exordium* addresses the themes of the Thessalonians' endurance in the face of persecution, Paul's selfless service to the Thessalonians, and the Christian's eschatological hope.

The *narratio,* or narrative, states the facts of the writer's case. In 1 Thessalonians, the *narratio* states facts supporting the purity of Paul's life and motives for ministry that he introduced in the previous section.

The *transitus* provides a smooth transition from one section of the work to another, in the present instance from Timothy's encouraging report to other matters.

The *probatio,* or proofs, establishes the writer's position through a series of arguments. In 1 Thessalonians, the section seeks to strengthen and clarify the beliefs of the Thessalonians regarding purity, love, and the end time.[46]

The *peroratio,* or closing, of the letter restates the principal theme of the letter, which in 1 Thessalonians is that the anticipated return of Christ requires godly living.

Second Thessalonians is best described as deliberative rhetoric. This genre sought to persuade people to follow a particular course of action in the future, so 2 Thessalonians is classified as deliberative because Paul sought to persuade the Thessalonians to adopt a different understanding of the Day of the Lord and to abandon their idleness.[47]

R. Jewett offered the following rhetorical analysis of 2 Thessalonians.[48] The *exordium* or introduction (1:1–12) contains the prescript, a prayer of thanksgiving, and an intercessory prayer. These elements are typical in introductions to Paul's Letters.[49]

The *partitio,* or outline (2:1–2), functions much like a thesis statement and announces the two main arguments of the letter: (1) the second coming of Christ has not occurred;

---

[44] Jewett, *Thessalonian Correspondence,* 71–72; G. Lyons, *Pauline Autobiography: Toward a New Understanding,* SBLDS 73 (Atlanta, GA: Scholars Press, 1985), 219–21; Wanamaker, *Thessalonians,* 47.

[45] See Wanamaker, *Thessalonians,* viii. Jewett (*Thessalonian Correspondence,* 72–76) suggested that the *exordium* ended at 1 Thess 1:5 and the *narratio* began in 1:6. Jewett compared his own analysis to other rhetorical analyses on pp. 76–78.

[46] The classification of this section as *probatio* is somewhat problematic. The section is more devoted to exhortations than to proofs or arguments to support the author's case. The analyses by F. W. Hughes, G. Kennedy, and H. Koester recognize this section as devoted to exhortations, injunctions, or admonitions. For a chart that conveniently compares various topical and rhetorical outlines of the book, see Jewett, *Thessalonian Correspondence,* 216–21.

[47] F. W. Hughes, *Early Christian Rhetoric and 2 Thessalonians,* JSNTSup 30 (Sheffield, UK: JSOT, 1989), 55; Jewett, *Thessalonian Correspondence,* 82; G. A. Kennedy, *New Testament Interpretation Through Rhetorical Criticism* (Chapel Hill, NC: University of North Carolina, 1984), 144; Wanamaker, *Thessalonians,* 48.

[48] Jewett, *Thessalonian Correspondence,* 82–84.

[49] For a good introduction to the basic format of Paul's Letters, see P. T. O'Brien, "Letters, Letter Forms," in *Dictionary of Paul and His Letters,* 550–53.

and (2) believers can be confident in their anticipation of Christ's return if they remain faithful to Paul's teaching and example.

The *probatio,* or proof section (2:3–3:5), then offers evidence to support these two main theses of the letter. In 2 Thessalonians, 2:3–12 refutes the claim of the false teachers that the coming of Christ had already occurred, and 2:13–3:5 offers believers assurance.

The *exhortatio,* or exhortation section of the letter (3:6–15), offers a series of three exhortations: (1) an exhortation to discipline the idle; (2) an exhortation to abandon idleness; and (3) an exhortation to exclude the idle from the fellowship.

The *peroratio,* or conclusion (3:16–18), included a benediction, Paul's signature, and a final greeting. According to Jewett, this rhetorical analysis suggests that the eschatological confusion in the church and the behavior of the idle or disorderly were interrelated.[50]

As explained in regard to the letter to the Galatians, caution should be exercised in attempting to interpret Paul's Letters in terms of rhetorical categories. These are letters, not speeches, and an analysis of ancient epistolary patterns is generally more helpful in understanding Paul's correspondence.[51]

OUTLINES

1 Thessalonians

I. INTRODUCTION (1:1)

II. EXPRESSIONS OF THANKS AND LOVE FOR THE THESSALONIANS (1:2–3:13)
   A. First Prayer of Thanksgiving for the Thessalonians (1:2–10)
   B. Paul's Relationship with the Thessalonians During His Visit, Demonstrating the Purity of His Motives for the Thessalonian Ministry (2:1–12)
   C. Second Prayer of Thanksgiving for the Thessalonians (2:13–16)
   D. Paul's Relationship with the Thessalonians After His Departure (2:17–3:10)
   E. Third Prayer of Thanksgiving Introducing the Three Major Topics of the Next Section: Personal Holiness, Christian Love, and the Second Coming (3:11–13)

III. EXHORTATIONS AND INSTRUCTIONS (4:1–5:22)
   A. Introduction to Exhortations (4:1–2)
   B. Exhortation to Personal Holiness and Sexual Purity (4:3–8)
   C. Exhortation to Christian Love and Responsible Living (4:9–12)
   D. Instructions about the Second Coming (4:13–18)
   E. Exhortations Related to the Second Coming (5:1–11)
   F. General Exhortations (5:12–22)

---

[50] Jewett, *Thessalonian Correspondence*, 87.

[51] See H. Boers, "The Form Critical Study of Paul's Letters. I Thessalonians as a Case Study," *NTS* 22 (1975–76): 140–58; I. H. Marshall, *1 and 2 Thessalonians: A Commentary* (Vancouver, Canada Regent College, 1983), 6–11, 23–24. That being said, B. Witherington ("'Almost Thou Persuadest Me . . .': The Importance of Greco-Roman Rhetoric for the Understanding of the Text and Context of the NT," *JETS* 58 [2015]: 63–88) has recently argued persuasively that some first-century writers viewed letters as forms of speech in absentia. Thus, distinctions between speeches and letters should not be overemphasized.

IV. CONCLUSION (5:23–28)

2 Thessalonians

I. INTRODUCTION (1:1–12)
II. THESIS STATEMENT: THE DAY OF THE LORD HAS NOT OCCURRED AND TRUE BELIEVERS NEED NOT FEAR IT (2:1–2)
III. PROOFS SUPPORTING PAUL'S THESIS (2:3–19)
  A. First Proof: The Day of the Lord Has Not Occurred (2:3–12)
  B. Second Proof: Christians Can Have Hope and Confidence as They Anticipate the End Time (2:13–17)
IV. EXHORTATIONS (3:1–15)
  A. Exhortation to Pray (3:1–5)
  B. Exhortations Related to the Idle (3:6–15)
V. CONCLUSION (3:16–18)

UNIT-BY-UNIT DISCUSSIONS

1 THESSALONIANS

I. Introduction (1:1)

II. Expressions of Thanks and Love for the Thessalonians (1:2–3:13)

In his first major section, Paul assured the Thessalonians of his love for them and the purity of his motives for his mission in Thessalonica. He apparently did so in response to claims by his opponents that his mission was driven by selfish motives and that he had abandoned the church when it needed him most. The criticism was, of course, untrue. Luke clearly indicated that Paul fled Thessalonica at the church's request (Acts 17:10). The new church evidently thought that Paul's departure would defuse the growing anti-Christian sentiments in the city. But now that Paul was gone, his opponents probably argued that he had incited the wrath of the city and then conveniently disappeared at the first sign of trouble.

A. First Prayer of Thanksgiving for the Thessalonians (1:2–10) Paul's first letter to the Thessalonians is peppered with prayers of thanksgiving that demonstrate Paul's love for the congregation. In this first prayer, Paul thanked God for the evidences of his gracious election of the believers (1:2–4). Their election and authentic conversion were evidenced by the miracles that accompanied Paul's message and had confirmed the truthfulness of the gospel and the Holy Spirit's activity in persuading them to embrace the truth (1:5–7). The Thessalonians had abandoned their idols to serve God and were an example to other believers in their Christian service, evangelistic zeal, and faithfulness in the face of persecution (1:8–10). The prayer introduces the major themes of the letter by reminding the Thessalonians of (1) the effects of Paul's ministry that confirmed God's approval of Paul;

(2) the Thessalonians' perseverance in the face of persecution; and (3) the believers' eager anticipation of Christ's return.

B. Paul's Relationship with the Thessalonians during His Visit, Demonstrating the Purity of His Motives for the Thessalonian Ministry (2:1–12) Paul responded to his opponents' attack by reminding the Thessalonians of the characteristics of his ministry (2:1–4). He had preached at great risk with integrity and sincerity and without receiving any financial support from the new believers (2:5–9). Paul appealed to both the Thessalonians and to God as witnesses who testified to his devotion and blamelessness (2:10–12).

C. Second Prayer of Thanksgiving for the Thessalonians (2:13–16) Paul's second prayer of thanksgiving confirmed the divine origin of Paul's gospel. It reminded the Thessalonians that they were not alone in their sufferings for Christ. It encouraged them to persevere with the assurance that God would judge their persecutors.

D. Paul's Relationship with the Thessalonians after His Departure (2:17–3:10) Paul's love for the Thessalonian church had been displayed by his efforts to return to Thessalonica (2:17–20) and by sending Timothy to strengthen and encourage the church while he remained in Athens (3:1–5; cf. Acts 17). Paul expresses gratitude for Timothy's positive report about the Thessalonians' faith and love and assures them of his earnest and constant prayers for them (3:6–10).

E. Third Prayer of Thanksgiving Introducing the Three Major Topics of the Next Section: Personal Holiness, Christian Love, and the Second Coming (3:11–13) Paul's third prayer of thanksgiving and petition for the church introduced the three main topics of the next main section. The prayer "may the Lord cause you to increase and overflow with love for one another and for everyone" (v. 12) anticipates the discussion of brotherly love in 4:9–12. The petition "May he make your hearts blameless in holiness before our God and Father" (v. 13) anticipates the discussion of personal holiness in 4:1–8. The reference to the "coming of our Lord Jesus with all his saints" (v. 13) introduces the eschatological discussion in 4:13–5:11 and hints that deceased believers will accompany Christ at the time of his return.

III. Exhortations and Instructions (4:1–5:22)

This major section is permeated by numerous commands to the church, along with supporting arguments.

A. Introduction to Exhortations (4:1–2) Paul urged the church to pursue a moral and ethical lifestyle that was pleasing to God. He reminded the Thessalonians that the commands that he gave ultimately came from Christ himself.

B. Exhortation to Personal Holiness and Sexual Purity (4:3–8) Paul urged the church to abstain from sexual immorality (4:3). He went so far as to define sexual purity as the essence of God's will for the believer and a goal of the process of sanctification. Sexual immorality was pagan behavior and inappropriate for followers of Jesus. After earlier insisting that his moral teaching came from Christ (4: 2), Paul now insisted that it came from God through the Holy Spirit (4:8). Consequently, a lifestyle of immorality defied the commands of the triune God and invited his holy vengeance.

C. Exhortation to Christian Love and Responsible Living (4:9–12) The Thessalonians naturally and spontaneously expressed love to each other as a by-product of the Spirit's transforming work in them (4:9). Paul urged them to do so even more (4:10). Love for others demanded that one live responsibly and work for a living rather than depending on the generosity of other believers (4:11). This insistence was aimed at the idle who were mentioned again in 5:14 and would be addressed in greater detail in Paul's second letter. Paul warned that failure to live compassionately and responsibly would thwart the church's witness to outsiders (4:12).

D. Instructions about the Second Coming (4:13–18) Paul prepared his audience for exhortations related to the Second Coming by first clearing up some confusion about events accompanying Christ's return. The church was apparently concerned about the fate of believers who died before the Second Coming and feared that the deceased believers might not be able to enjoy the dramatic and exciting events related to Jesus's return (4:13). Paul encouraged the church by assuring them that believers who had died would be raised as Jesus descended to consummate his reign over the earth (4:14–16). Those alive at Christ's return would be "caught up" together with them in the clouds to meet the Lord in the air and so forever be with the Lord (4:17).

E. Exhortations Related to the Second Coming (5:1–11) Paul urged the Thessalonians to be alert and vigilant because Jesus's return would be sudden (5:1–8). He comforted the church with the assurance that God's people would escape God's wrath because of Jesus's sacrificial death. Thus, they could anticipate Jesus's return with joy rather than dread (5:9–11).

F. General Exhortations (5:12–22) Paul urged the church to support and respect spiritual leaders, to show love and forgiveness to others, and to be faithful in prayer (5:12–18). He also commanded the church to value the gift of prophecy by which God revealed his truth through gifted individuals in the church but to test prophetic pronouncements and to accept only those that were "good," that is, consistent with the truth Christ revealed through Paul (5:19–22).

IV. Conclusion (5:23–28)

Paul's final prayer encapsulates the two greatest concerns of the letter by focusing on the purity of God's people in anticipation of the Second Coming. The letter ends on the confident note that the congregation would be found blameless at the time of Jesus's return because of God's faithfulness to those whom he called. God called his people to sanctification (see 4:7), and he would accomplish it (5:24).

2 THESSALONIANS

I. Introduction (1:1–12)

Following his customary greeting (1:1–2), Paul sought to encourage the Thessalonians to remain faithful as they endured persecution (1:3–4). In an act of talionic justice, God would torment those who tormented his people and give rest to those who were suffering (1:5–7a). This judgment would occur in conjunction with the Second Coming when sinners would confront the same glorious divine presence that would slay the Antichrist (1:7b–10; cf. 2:8).[52] As Paul anticipated that great event, he prayed that the believers would be characterized by goodness and thus bring glory to Christ (1:11–12).

II. Thesis Statement: The Day of the Lord Has Not Occurred and True Believers Need Not Fear It (2:1–2)

Paul announced two topics that dominate the second chapter of his letter: Christ's return and the gathering of believers. Somehow, whether by a spirit or a spoken word or a letter seeming to be from Paul and his associates, the Thessalonians had begun to suspect that the Day of the Lord had already occurred or that it was presently occurring.

III. Proofs Supporting Paul's Thesis (2:3–19)

Paul wrote to insist that the Day of the Lord had not yet taken place and to describe events that must transpire prior to Christ's return.

A. First Proof: The Day of the Lord Has Not Occurred (2:3–12) The Day of the Lord, which encompasses such important eschatological events as the Second Coming, the resurrection of the dead, and the final judgment, would be preceded by widespread apostasy inspired by the "man of lawlessness" (i.e., the Antichrist; 2:3). This figure would enthrone himself in the place of God in the Jerusalem temple and would deceive unbelievers with amazing counterfeit miracles (2:4, 9–12). Ultimately, the man of lawlessness would be destroyed by Christ at his return. Some unnamed person and power were restraining lawlessness, and the man of lawlessness would not appear until the restrainer was removed (2:5–8).[53]

B. Second Proof: Christians Can Have Hope and Confidence as They Anticipate the End Time (2:13–17) Paul recognized that his warning about the great delusion that would accompany the coming of the man of lawlessness might have frightened his readers. Paul encouraged the believers to stand firm by reminding them that God had chosen them for salvation and that he had called them for final glorification (2:13–15). This gracious election and powerful call assured them that God would strengthen and protect them until his plan for them was fulfilled (2:16–17). Paul repeated this assurance in 3:3–5.

---

[52] For the view that divine judgment consists of confrontation with Christ's glorious presence rather than separation from it, see C. L. Quarles, "The *Apo* of 2 Thessalonians 1:9 and the Nature of Eternal Punishment," *WTJ* 59 (1997): 201–11.

[53] See the discussion of the man of lawlessness and the sidebar on the "one who restrains" in the Theological Themes section below.

IV. Exhortations (3:1–15)

Paul concluded his letter by tackling some of the practical problems in the church at Thessalonica.

A. Exhortation to Pray (3:1–5) First, Paul exhorted the church to pray for the spread and positive reception of the gospel. Paul was convinced that the effectiveness of his ministry was dependent on the exercise of God's gracious power and not his own skills or abilities. Paul also asked the church to pray for the protection of the missionary team.

B. Exhortations Related to the Idle (3:6–15) Second, Paul instructed the church on how to handle the idle. These individuals were living irresponsibly by refusing to work and depending on the generosity of other members of the church for their survival (3:6). This lifestyle might somehow be linked to the confused eschatology of the church or represent a separate issue. Paul appealed to both Christian tradition and his own example to argue that believers must work for a living (3:7–13). Church members should disassociate themselves from the idle and no longer support them financially in hopes that they will repent and begin to live responsibly (3:14–15).

V. Conclusion (3:16–18) Paul prayed that the church would experience both the peace and grace of the Lord Jesus. He also explained how he authenticated his letters so that the church could now distinguish letters actually authored by him from those fraudulently ascribed to him.

THEOLOGY

Theological Themes

The Second Coming Both letters to the Thessalonians were written to address questions or false assumptions about the end time. These letters provide Paul's most explicit teaching about the events surrounding the Second Coming. Paul's teaching regarding the Second Coming in 1 Thessalonians 4:13–18 was derived from "a word from the Lord" (lit. "the word of the Lord"). This may refer either to Jesus's eschatological teachings during his earthly ministry (see Matthew 24–25; Mark 13) or to revelation from Christian prophets in the early church. Although Jesus's teaching preserved in the Gospels did not directly address the issue of whether deceased believers would be resurrected before the transformation of living believers, Paul's discussion reverberates with so many themes of the Olivet Discourse that one must suspect that Paul was alluding to Jesus's teaching.[54]

At the Second Coming, the Lord Jesus will descend from heaven. The accompanying shout of the Messiah (John 5:25) will raise the dead. The voice of the archangel and the blast of a trumpet (Matt 24:29–31; 1 Cor 15:52) serve as signals to the angels to gather God's people, both dead and alive, for final transformation. The newly resurrected believers and the believers who had not experienced death will be caught up together in the

[54] E.g., G. K. Beale, *1–2 Thessalonians* (Downers Grove, IL: InterVarsity, 2003), 136–38; Wanamaker, *Thessalonians*, 170–71; and Marshall, *Thessalonians*, 125–27.

clouds to meet the Lord in the air. The clouds serve to portray Christ's appearance as a manifestation of God (Exod 16:10;19:16; Dan 7:13; Mark 13:26).

The noun "meet" (*apantesis*) was often used to speak of a group who went out to meet an approaching dignitary and then turned around and escorted him or her into their city or home (Matt 25:6; Acts 28:15). The approach of the dignitary was sometimes called the *parousia*, the word used here to describe the coming of Christ. Several commentators argue that the interplay of the noun "coming" that could speak of the approach of the King and the noun "meet" imply that believers meet Christ in the heavens and then escort him back to earth in royal procession.[55] Such language may imply that Paul intended for his readers to envision living forever with the Lord in a transformed earth over which Christ rules with absolute authority.

Some interpreters regard 1 Thessalonians 4:13–18 as a discussion of a pretribulational rapture rather than the Second Coming. But the close connection of the passage to Jesus's descriptions of the Second Coming (see esp. Matt 24:30–31 and parallels) and the possible technical use of the terms "coming" and "meeting" make this interpretation unlikely. First Thessalonians 5:1–11 describes the Second Coming as belonging to the Day of the Lord predicted by the OT prophets (e.g., Amos 5:18–20; Obadiah 15; Zeph 1:2–18; see also 2 Thess 2:1–3). The fact that Paul associated Jesus's coming with the Day of the Lord and utilized the imagery of OT theophanies to describe Jesus's coming expresses a high Christology that recognizes Jesus as divine.

Paul insisted that the Day of the Lord would come suddenly. It would take unbelievers, though not God's people, by surprise. Paul characterized the Day of the Lord as a time of destruction and intense pain for the wicked. He assured believers, however, that they would escape this frightening outpouring of divine wrath. Paul urged believers to prepare themselves for Jesus's return by clothing themselves with Christian character.

Second Thessalonians adds some detail to Paul's early description of the Second Coming. Although 1 Thessalonians 4 stresses the joy believers will know by participating in the events of the Second Coming, 2 Thessalonians 1:3–12 stresses the horrors experienced by unbelievers when Jesus returns. As in OT theophanies, the glory of Christ at his coming will destroy unbelievers. Eternal punishment will be the sinners' penalty for their rebellion against God and their rejection of the gospel. Believers, however, will glorify Christ at his return and be glorified by him.

The Antichrist and Mystery of Lawlessness In 2 Thessalonians 2, Paul introduced the issue of the coming of the Lord Jesus Christ and the gathering of the believers. Paul had taught on these subjects in 1 Thessalonians 4:13–18, in which Christ's return and the gathering of the believers appear to be two concurrent events that constitute the Day of the

---

[55] E.g., Bruce, *Thessalonians*, 102–3; and Marshall, *Thessalonians*, 130–31; see J. Chrysostom, *Homilies on 1 Thessalonians* 8, in P. Schaff, ed., *Saint Chrysostom: Homilies on Galatians, Ephesians, Philippians, Colossians, Thessalonians, Timothy, Titus, and Philemon*, vol. 13 of *A Select Library of the Nicene and Post-Nicene Fathers of the Christian Church* (Grand Rapids, MI: Eerdmans, 1956), 554–61.

Lord. Paul's concern in this text is not to offer a detailed description of the Day of the Lord, but to identify precursors to it. Although Paul had earlier encouraged the Thessalonians to live in a constant state of preparation for Christ's return, the Thessalonians had wrongly concluded that the Day of the Lord had come.

By describing the precursors to the Day of the Lord, Paul hoped to persuade his readers that those climactic events still lay in the future. Paul insisted they would be preceded by a great apostasy and by the coming of an Antichrist figure. The figure is identified as "the man of lawlessness" because he will lead a great rebellion against God's authority. He is further identified as the "son of destruction" because he is destined for destruction by Christ. The Antichrist figure will arrogantly claim to be divine and will enthrone himself in the holy of holies in the temple of Yahweh in Jerusalem.

SIDEBAR 11.1: WHO IS THE ONE WHO RESTRAINS? (2 THESS 2:6–7)

Paul explained that the manifestation of "the man of lawlessness" was being temporarily thwarted by an unidentified restrainer ("the one now restraining," 2 Thess 2:7). Interpreters continue to debate the identity of this restrainer. Various theories identify the restrainer as (1) the Roman government; (2) an angel, such as the archangel Michael; (3) an agent of Satan; (4) the Holy Spirit; or (5) the pretribulation church.

Perhaps the most important clue for identifying the restrainer is a grammatical feature in the text. Paul used both a neuter and a masculine participle to describe the restrainer. This may imply that the restrainer is an impersonal force that is personified by a human being. Thus many commentators have argued that the restrainer is the principle of law and order or the Roman government embodied by the emperor and now other officials or have given an alternative scenario that fits both masculine and neuter forms.

Whatever his identity, when the restrainer is "out of the way," the "lawless one" will perform counterfeit miracles that delude those who have rejected the gospel (2 Thess 2:9). Their veneration of the man of lawlessness will heighten their guilt and intensify their condemnation. Jesus will ultimately destroy the man of lawlessness by the breath of his mouth and the brightness of his coming (2 Thess 2:8). Jesus's powerful command and intense glory will ruin the Antichrist and end the great apostasy.

While the identity of the "restrainer" was most likely known to Paul's original readers, students of Scripture today should exercise restraint and humility in their efforts to pinpoint the exact interpretation of this puzzling passage.[1]

[1] See Morris, *Thessalonians*, 213, 227.

Some commentators have argued that Paul's prophecy regarding the coming Antichrist has failed. For example, Wanamaker claimed, "The passage can no longer be understood as valid, since the temple was destroyed in A.D. 70 without the manifestation of the person of lawlessness or the return of Christ occurring."[56] Evangelical scholars with a high view of Scripture argue that the passage remains valid. The emerging consensus does so by arguing that Paul's apocalyptic language should be interpreted symbolically rather than literally and is "a graphic way of saying that he [the man of lawlessness] plans to usurp the authority of God."[57] Other interpreters affirm the interpretation that may be traced to Hippolytus (ca. AD 170–236) and possibly to Irenaeus (ca. AD 130–200), which holds that the temple in Jerusalem will be rebuilt in the last days.[58]

Although one should not construct an eschatological view from the Thessalonian letters in isolation from other eschatological texts, Paul's discussion seems most consistent with the notion of a premillennial return of Christ that acknowledges that the church will experience the persecution associated with the mystery of lawlessness.[59] Jesus's return will end this period of tribulation and usher in his earthly reign. Paul's argument that the Day of the Lord had not come and that the church would recognize its approach because of the appearance of the man of lawlessness implies that believers who are alive at the time will be present when the man of lawlessness appears. Moreover, in 1 Thessalonians 4:17, the catching up and the Second Coming are contemporaneous. The text does not seem to allow for a seven-year interval between the two events, nor does Paul's discussion of the Second Coming in 2 Thessalonians 2:1–10.[60]

If Paul had affirmed a pretribulational rapture, his most powerful argument against the notion that the Day of the Lord had already come would have been to point out that the church had not yet been raptured. But Paul did not use this potentially powerful argument, apparently because he saw the Second Coming and the catching up as concurrent. The royal terminology "meet" and "coming" seem to imply that an earthly reign follows the Second Coming. However, the precise nature or duration of this earthly reign is not defined. Many legitimate questions still surround this text. Whatever view one adopts, one must affirm the view with humility and be willing to reexamine one's position as new evidence surfaces.

The Eternal State of Believers The Thessalonian letters offer important descriptions of the eternal state of believers and unbelievers after the Second Coming. Paul comforted

---

[56] Wanamaker, *Thessalonians*, 248.

[57] Bruce, *Thessalonians*, 169. The symbolic view is pressed further by Marshall, *Thessalonians*, 191–92.

[58] R. L. Thomas, "2 Thessalonians," EBC 11 (Grand Rapids, MI: Zondervan, 1978), 322; and apparently Martin, *1, 2 Thessalonians*, 236–37.

[59] See Beale, *Thessalonians*, 136; Bruce, *Thessalonians*, 163; Wilkins, *Thessalonians*, 238–39; R. Gundry, *First the Antichrist* (Grand Rapids, MI: Baker, 1997); G. E. Ladd, *The Blessed Hope: A Biblical Study of the Second Advent and the Rapture* (Grand Rapids, MI: Eerdmans, 1956).

[60] T. R. Schreiner, *Paul, Apostle of God's Glory in Christ: A Pauline Theology* (Downers Grove, IL: InterVarsity, 2001), 460–61.

believers in 1 Thessalonians 4:13–18 with the assurance that after the Second Coming and the accompanying resurrection of the dead "we will always be with the Lord." Paul did not specifically refer in this text to the resurrection and glorification of living believers. But the adverb "first" in the clause "the dead in Christ will rise first" implies that the resurrection of believers soon follows. First Corinthians 15:51–57 supports this assumption by associating the bodily transformation of living believers with the "last trumpet," which is probably to be identified as a trumpet blast related to the Second Coming as described in 1 Thessalonians 4:16.

Paul did not clearly identify the place where believers will spend eternity in this text. The "air" is the place where believers meet Christ but not necessarily where they remain.[61] "So we will always be with the Lord" is not equivalent to "there [i.e., in the air] we will always be with the Lord." What matters for Paul is that believers eternally experience the joys and blessings of the Lord's glorious and comforting presence. For this reason Paul repeated in 1 Thessalonians 5:10 that believers "may live together with him."

The Everlasting Destruction of Unbelievers In 2 Thessalonians 1:4–12, Paul turned his attention to the consequences of the Second Coming for unbelievers. He emphasized that the return of Christ would initiate the righteous judgment of the wicked. The characterization of God's judgment as "righteous" counters claims that God's judgment is unjust. Paul emphasizes the righteous nature of divine judgment further by portraying divine judgment as an act of talionic justice in which the wicked receive a punishment appropriate to their crimes: "It is just for God to repay with affliction those who afflict you" (2 Thess 1:6). Unbelievers are fully deserving of judgment because they have rejected the only means of salvation, obedience to the gospel's commands to repent and believe in Christ. Eternal punishment is thus an act of "vengeance" against those who "don't know God and . . . who don't obey the gospel of our Lord Jesus" (2 Thess 1:8).

Paul described the result of divine condemnation as "everlasting destruction." This is not an annihilation in which the sinner ceases to exist and thus finds escape from God's eternal wrath. It is rather a state of continual misery and ruin that results from a confrontation with the glorious divine Christ. Although many interpreters regard the phrase "away from the Lord's presence and from his glorious strength" as an indication that eternal punishment consists of separation from God, the phrase more likely identifies the source or cause of eternal destruction.[62] Due to the verse divisions of the modern NT, English readers naturally assume that Paul described the instrument of divine punishment as "flaming fire." However, this interpretation has been contested by interpreters who suggest that the phrase "with flaming fire" modifies the noun "revelation" and portrays Jesus's coming as a theophany.

Although the description of Jesus's coming is clearly theophanic (i.e., a manifestation of God's presence), "with flaming fire" more likely modifies "taking vengeance" as the CSB

---

[61] Marshall, *Thessalonians*, 131.

[62] Quarles, "The *Apo* of 2 Thessalonians 1:9," 201–11.

suggests. Second Thessalonians 1:8 appears to be a paraphrase of the Greek translation (LXX) of Isaiah 66:15. The Greek texts of these two passages share the word "vengeance" and the phrase "in flaming fire." Isaiah 66:15–16 warns, "Look, the LORD will come with fire—his chariots are like the whirlwind—to execute his anger with fury, and his rebuke with flames of fire. For the LORD will execute judgment on all people with his fiery sword, and many will be slain by the LORD."[63] Paul thus "uses the image of the flaming fire to portray the frightening experience awaiting the enemies of God when God inflicts vengeance on the Thessalonians' oppressors" and on those who reject the good news.[64] The Greek word order places special emphasis on the phrase "with flaming fire" and intensifies Paul's warning about the horrific nature of eschatological punishment.

A Christian Work Ethic Because of the unique challenge posed by the presence of the "idle" (1 Thess 5:14) who lived irresponsibly (2 Thess 3:6–15), Paul emphasized the importance of a Christian work ethic in these letters.[65] The "idle" were apparently refusing to work and were taking advantage of the generosity of other members of the church. This lifestyle of idleness may have been adopted by some members of the church because of their confused eschatology. Perhaps, like some end-time enthusiasts today, they quit their jobs and climbed on their rooftops to sit and wait for Christ's return. Whatever the motivations for their behavior, Paul insisted that such inaction was contrary to Christian teaching and to the apostle's own example. He had forfeited his right as an apostle to live at the church's expense and had instead labored and toiled night and day to make a living.

Paul listed several damaging consequences of the behavior of the idle. First, because the idle were not occupied with work, they used their free time to interfere with the work of others (2 Thess 3:11). Second, their refusal to work was placing an undue financial burden on generous brothers and sisters. Third, their behavior earned the disrespect of unbelievers or "outsiders" (1 Thess 4:10–12). Paul insisted that the church must not support the idle. A few pangs of hunger would be just the motivation needed to inspire productivity in those unwilling to earn. Paul even urged the church to initiate a process of compassionate church discipline in order to encourage the idle to change their behavior.

Paul's teaching demonstrates the importance of believers working diligently to provide for themselves and their families through wholesome work. It also reminds believers that their faithfulness on the job can become either a positive or negative testimony to unbelievers.

Election and Perseverance Although the Thessalonian letters do not give a lengthy or detailed explanation of the doctrines of election and perseverance, they offer the clearest succinct treatment of those doctrines in Pauline literature. In 2 Thessalonians 2:13–15, Paul expressed his conviction that God had chosen the members of the church at Thessalonica

---

[63] By applying this text about the coming of Yahweh to describe the coming of Jesus, Paul identified Jesus as Yahweh and clearly expressed the doctrine of Jesus's deity.

[64] Wanamaker, *Thessalonians*, 227; cf. Marshall, *Thessalonians*, 177.

[65] Cf. the section above, "Something to Think About: How Is Your Work Ethic?"

for salvation. God had determined to save these believers "from the beginning," in eternity past. Since God had made his choice before the Thessalonians were even born, it was clear that his decision was motivated by his own mysterious grace and not by the merit of the Thessalonians (Rom 9:11). Paul hinted at the gracious nature of election by describing the elect as "brothers and sisters loved by the Lord" (2 Thess 2:13). This identification of believers occurs only twice in Paul's Letters (see 1 Thess 1:4). In both texts, the phrase is connected to a discussion of divine election.

The salvation planned for the elect is experienced by them through "sanctification by the Spirit and belief in the truth." The fact that "sanctification" precedes "belief" in the word order of this clause probably implies that it does so chronologically as well. Thus, the "sanctification" of which Paul speaks here refers to God's gracious work of liberating the sinner from his bondage to his sinful nature and moving him to repent and believe. Paul also implied this in 1 Thessalonians 1:4–5, where evidence of the Thessalonians' election was demonstrated by the fact that the apostle's gospel proclamation "did not come to you in word only, but also in power, in the Holy Spirit, and with complete certainty." The powerful activity of the Spirit in assuring the Thessalonians of the truth of the gospel appears to be equivalent to the sanctifying work of the Spirit in connection with faith in 2 Thessalonians 2:13 as well.

For Paul, divine election clearly did not eradicate the necessity of human choice. He affirmed both divine sovereignty and human responsibility. He placed responsibility for the sinner's rejection of the gospel in the lap of the sinner and not on God, arguing that sinners perish "because they did not accept the love of the truth and so be saved" and characterizing the condemned as "those who did not believe the truth but delighted in unrighteousness" (2 Thess 2:12). Paul stated that God confirms and even heightens the unbelief of those who are perishing, but—importantly—he did not view God as the original source of their unbelief.

In 2 Thessalonians, Paul's appeal to the doctrine of election serves a practical purpose. It functioned to comfort and encourage believers who may have been frightened by anticipations of the great delusion that would accompany the work of the Antichrist discussed in the immediately preceding context. Paul assured the believers that although many would be misled by the "unrighteous deception" of the man of lawlessness, by his "false miracles," and by the "strong delusion," the believers would be guarded from deception. The doctrine of election demonstrated that their faith in Christ was no accident, nor was it merely a product of their own whim. Their salvation was grounded in God's eternal purpose and dependent on his own faithfulness. Because of God's powerful call, they would obtain the glory that he planned for them (1 Thess 5:23–24; 2 Thess 2:14; 3:3). Paul viewed the believer's eternal security as a by-product of the doctrine of election. His appeal to the doctrine of election to comfort Christians anticipating the great delusion probably demonstrates his awareness of and dependence on the eschatological teachings of Jesus. Christ also appealed to the doctrine of election to encourage his followers as they anticipated the deceptions that would occur in the great tribulation (Mark 13:21–24).

CONTRIBUTION TO THE CANON

- Teaching regarding the events immediately preceding the second coming of Christ, including the rapture (1 Thess 4:13–18)
- Teaching on the "man of lawlessness," the Antichrist (2 Thess 2:3–4), and "the one now restraining," whose identity is disputed (2 Thess 2:7)
- Believers' election and calling by God (1 Thess 1:4; 2 Thess 2:13–15)
- The importance of a Christian work ethic (1 Thess 5:12–14; 2 Thess 3:6–13)
- Teaching on how to live expectantly in the light of Christ's return (e.g., 1 Thess 5:1–22)

STUDY QUESTIONS

1. Why are the Thessalonian letters often neglected? Why are they significant?
2. Which one of the letters do many modern scholars reject as Paul's? Why?
3. What role does theology play in assigning authorship to 2 Thessalonians?
4. When was 1 Thessalonians likely written? How much time passed between the penning of 2 Thessalonians and 1 Thessalonians?
5. What are some of the primary reasons Paul wrote the Thessalonian letters?
6. What was the cause of the Thessalonians' deficient work ethic?
7. How does rhetorical criticism help the modern reader better understand the Thessalonian letters?
8. What is the most likely genre of the Thessalonian letters?
9. What are the five major rhetorical components of 1 Thessalonians, and how do they function?
10. Who is "the man of lawlessness" in 2 Thessalonians 2? Who has been identified as "the restrainer"?
11. Which position regarding the rapture finds most support in 1 Thessalonians and why?
12. What is the most significant contribution of the Thessalonian letters to the NT canon?

FOR FURTHER STUDY

Beale, G. K. *1–2 Thessalonians*. IVP New Testament Commentary. Downers Grove, IL: InterVarsity, 2003.

Best, E. *A Commentary on the First and Second Epistles to the Thessalonians*. New York, NY: Harper & Row, 1972.

Bruce, F. F. *1 and 2 Thessalonians*. Word Biblical Commentary 45. Waco, TX: Word, 1982.

Collins, R. F., ed. *The Thessalonian Correspondence*. Bibliotheca ephemeridum theologicarum lovaniensium 87. Leuven, Belgium: University Press, 1990.

Donfried, K. P. "The Cults of Thessalonica and the Thessalonian Correspondence." *New Testament Studies* 31 (1985): 336–56.

_________, and J. Beutler, eds. *The Thessalonians Debate: Methodological Discord or Methodological Synthesis?* Grand Rapids, MI: Eerdmans, 2000.

Frame, J. E. *A Critical and Exegetical Commentary on the Epistles of St. Paul to the Thessalonians.* International Critical Commentary. New York, NY: Charles Scribner's Sons, 1912.

Fee, G. *The First and Second Letters to the Thessalonians.* New International Commentary on the New Testament. Grand Rapids, MI: Eerdmans, 2009.

Green, G. *The Letters to the Thessalonians.* Pillar New Testament Commentary. Grand Rapids, MI: Eerdmans, 2002.

Harrison, J. R. "Paul and the Imperial Cult at Thessaloniki." *Journal for the Study of the New Testament* 25 (2002): 71–96.

Holmes, M. W. *1 and 2 Thessalonians.* NIV Application Commentary. Grand Rapids, MI: Zondervan, 1998.

Jewett, R. *The Thessalonian Correspondence: Pauline Rhetoric and Millenarian Piety.* Foundations and Facets: New Testament. Philadelphia, PA: Fortress, 1986.

Malherbe, A. J. *The Letters to the Thessalonians.* Anchor Bible 32B. New York, NY: Doubleday, 2000.

_________. *Paul and the Thessalonians: The Philosophical Tradition of Pastoral Care.* Philadelphia, PA: Fortress, 1987.

Marshall, I. H. *I and II Thessalonians.* New Century Bible. Grand Rapids, MI: Eerdmans, 1983.

Martin, D. M. *1, 2 Thessalonians.* New American Commentary 33. Nashville, TN: B&H, 1995.

Nicholl, C. R. *From Hope to Despair in Thessalonica: Situating 1 and 2 Thessalonians.* Society for New Testament Studies Monograph Series 126. Cambridge, UK: Cambridge University Press, 2004.

Richards, E., E. Krentz, R. Jewett, and J. M. Bassler. "The Theology of the Thessalonian Correspondence." Pages 37–85 in *Pauline Theology.* Vol. 1: *Thessalonians, Philippians, Galatians, Philemon.* Edited by J. M. Bassler. Minneapolis, MN: Fortress, 1991.

Shogren, G. and C. E. Arnold. *1–2 Thessalonians.* Zondervan Exegetical Commentary on the New Testament. Grand Rapids, MI: Zondervan, 2012.

Still, T. D. *Conflict at Thessalonica: A Pauline Church and Its Neighbours.* Journal for the Study of the New Testament Supplement 183. Sheffield: Sheffield Academic Press, 1999.

Wanamaker, C. A. *Commentary on 1 and 2 Thessalonians.* New International Greek Testament Commentary. Grand Rapids, MI: Eerdmans, 1990.

Weima, J. A. D. *1–2 Thessalonians.* Baker Exegetical Commentary on the New Testament. Grand Rapids, MI: Baker Academic, 2014.

_________. "1–2 Thessalonians." Pages 871–90 in *Commentary on the New Testament Use of the Old Testament.* Edited by G. K. Beale and D. A. Carson. Grand Rapids, MI: Baker, 2007.

_________, and S. E. Porter. *An Annotated Bibliography of 1 and 2 Thessalonians.* Leiden, Netherlands: Brill, 1998.

Chapter 12

Paul's Corinthian Correspondence: 1–2 Corinthians

CORE KNOWLEDGE

Basic Knowledge: Students should know the key facts of 1 and 2 Corinthians. With regard to history, students should be able to identify the author, date, provenance, destination, and purpose for each book. With regard to literature, they should be able to provide a basic outline of each book and identify core elements of the book's content found in the Unit-by-Unit discussion. With regard to theology, students should be able to identify the major theological themes in 1 and 2 Corinthians.

Intermediate Knowledge: Students should be able to present the arguments for historical, literary, and theological conclusions. With regard to history, students should be able to discuss the evidence for Paul's authorship, date, provenance, destination, and purpose. With regard to literature, they should be able to provide a detailed outline of the book. With regard to theology, students should be able to discuss the major theological themes in 1 and 2 Corinthians and the ways in which they uniquely contribute to the NT canon.

Advanced Knowledge: Students should be able to assess the literary integrity and unity of 2 Corinthians in relation to interpolation theories. In addition, students should be able to discuss the theories concerning the identity of Paul's opponents in 2 Corinthians.

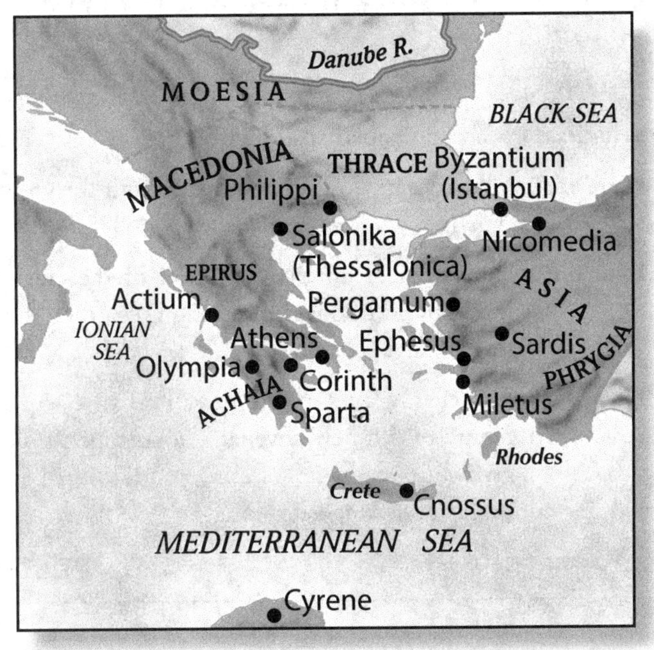

Map 12.1: Provenance and Destination of 1–2 Corinthians

KEY FACTS

1 Corinthians

Author:	Paul
Date:	53 or 54
Provenance:	Ephesus
Destination:	The church at Corinth
Occasion:	Oral reports and a letter from the Corinthians
Purpose:	To address practical issues such as schisms in the church, lawsuits in local courts, the exercise of church discipline, questions related to idolatry, Christian marriage, the ordinances, spiritual gifts, and theological issues such as the nature of salvation and the doctrine of resurrection
Key Verses:	13:1–3

KEY FACTS

2 Corinthians

Author: Paul

Date: 54 or 55

Provenance: Macedonia, perhaps Philippi

Destination: Churches in Corinth and throughout the province of Achaia

Occasion: Titus's report on the condition of the church, followed by additional information regarding the intrusion of false apostles

Purpose: To defend Paul's apostolic authority, to explain the nature of the new covenant, to encourage sacrificial giving to the relief offering, and to challenge the claims of false apostles

Key Verses: 5:16–21

INTRODUCTION

PAUL'S LETTERS TO the church at Corinth are among the most theologically rich and most practically helpful books in the NT. They are most likely next in chronological sequence after Galatians and the Thessalonian letters. In his Corinthian correspondence Paul addressed numerous problems in a church plagued by many troubles. His response to these problems applies his thoughtful theology to very practical issues and demonstrates that for Paul theology was not static. It was dynamic and made a practical difference in daily living. The Corinthian letters show Paul's remarkable integration of faith and practice.

First Corinthians contains Paul's most extensive discussion of topics such as Christian unity, Christian morality, the ordinances of the church, spiritual gifts, and the resurrection of believers. It challenges the development of personality cliques in the church, guides church leaders in the exercise of church discipline, and explains ways to conduct worship decently and in order. It also addresses issues of importance in contemporary society, such as the abiding distinction between the genders and the limits of personal freedom.

Although 2 Corinthians is perhaps the most difficult letter of Paul in many ways, its contribution to the NT is considerable as well. The letter is invaluable in guiding interpreters to understand Paul's theology of the new covenant that forms the foundation for much of his thought. It also guides students of the Bible in constructing a theology of suffering like no other NT book does. Just as importantly, the Corinthian letters, especially 2 Corinthians, aid in developing a theology of ministry that emphasizes compassion, sacrifice, humility, and dependence on God. One never peers as deeply into the heart of the apostle as one does when scouring the pages of this letter.[1]

In an era in which spiritual leaders are being turned into celebrities and humility is viewed as an undesirable trait, 2 Corinthians may be more important than ever.[2] Perhaps more than any other NT document, 2 Corinthians calls the church to repent of making super apostles out of jars of clay, eschewing suffering, depending on mere human resources, veiling the glory of God, and depreciating divine grace. As C. K. Barrett noted, "Writing 2 Corinthians must have come near to breaking Paul, and . . . a church that is prepared to read it with him, and understand it, may find itself broken too."[3]

Paul's response to the Corinthians' problems offers modern students of the NT a powerful guide for addressing the problems of the local church today. But attempting to understand these letters and to mine the principles which are so important to the contemporary church is not for the lazy reader. The exegesis and application of the Corinthian letters demand hard work and serious study.[4] This chapter is designed to be a first step in the difficult but rewarding study of the Corinthian letters.

HISTORY

Author

1 Corinthians Paul's authorship of 1 Corinthians is so widely accepted that some prominent commentaries on the letter do not even treat the issue of authorship.[5] The ancient external evidence for the authenticity of the letter is also compelling. Clement of Rome quoted from 1 Corinthians and ascribed the quote to "the epistle of the blessed apostle Paul" around AD 96. He did so, remarkably, in a letter also addressed to the church at Corinth.[6] There are also frequent echoes of 1 Corinthians in the letters of Ignatius that were composed prior to AD 110.[7]

Some scholars have suggested that although 1 Corinthians was written by Paul, portions of the letter as it is presently known were non-Pauline interpolations. Weiss argued

---

[1] See R. V. G. Tasker, *The Second Epistle to the Corinthians: Introduction and Commentary*, TNTC (Grand Rapids, MI: Eerdmans, 1958), 9.

[2] Ibid., 12–13.

[3] C. K. Barrett, *A Commentary on the Second Epistle to the Corinthians*, HNTC (New York, NY: Harper & Row, 1973), vii.

[4] See L. Morris, *The First Epistle of Paul to the Corinthians*, TNTC (Grand Rapids, MI: Eerdmans, 1960), 9; P. Hughes, *Paul's Second Epistle to the Corinthians*, NICNT (Grand Rapids, MI: Eerdmans, 1962), xi.

[5] E.g., G. D. Fee, *The First Epistle to the Corinthians*, NICNT (Grand Rapids, MI: Eerdmans, 1987); D. E. Garland, *1 Corinthians*, BECNT (Grand Rapids, MI: Baker, 2003); and C. K. Barrett, *The First Epistle to the Corinthians*, HNTC (Peabody, MA: Hendrickson, 1968), 11.

[6] *1 Clement* 47:1–3 alludes to the discussion of factions in 1 Cor 1:10–17 and in chap. 3; *1 Clement* 49 contains a hymn about love based on 1 Corinthians 13.

[7] *To the Ephesians* 16:1; 18:1; *To the Romans* 4:3; 5:1; 9:2; and *To the Philadelphians* 3:3.

that 1 Corinthians 1:2b, "with all those in every place who call on the name of Jesus Christ our Lord—both their Lord and ours," was added by a later editor who wanted to give the letter universal application.[8] Others have suggested that the prohibition of women speaking in church in 1 Corinthians 14:34b–35 is a non-Pauline gloss added by a Jewish Christian.[9] But such theories have failed to convince most interpreters since the suspected texts are present in all extant manuscripts of 1 Corinthians. Moreover, objections to the authenticity of 1 Corinthians 14: 34b–35 seem to be driven largely by modern sensitivity to gender issues.

Since H. Hagge first raised questions about the integrity of 1 Corinthians in 1876, dozens of scholars have suggested that 1 Corinthians is a composite letter in which portions of other Pauline correspondence have been inserted into another letter. Since the Corinthian letters clearly refer to at least four letters Paul sent to Corinth, some interpreters suggested that the lack of an orderly arrangement of the letter and tensions between sections of the letter were best explained by regarding 1 Corinthians as a pastiche of Pauline fragments.[10]

Although many different proposals for reconstructing the original documents assembled by the alleged editor of 1 Corinthians have been and continue to be set forth, no proposal has won the favor of NT scholars. Most recognize that the fragmentary nature of the letter is due largely to the fact that Paul's letter responds point by point to issues raised by oral reports and a letter from Corinth. Moreover, good exegetical solutions exist for supposed tensions within the book without resorting to a composite document theory. Finally, changes in tone throughout the letter are probably the result of Paul's writing the letter over a period of time during which he received new information regarding the state of the Corinthian church.[11]

2 Corinthians Paul's authorship of 2 Corinthians has not been seriously contested, though the external attestation of 2 Corinthians is not as strong as that for 1 Corinthians. Echoes of 2 Corinthians may appear in the letters of Ignatius (prior to 110) and the *Epistle of Barnabas* (ca. AD 135).[12] But the possible parallels are not close enough to demonstrate dependence on 2 Corinthians.[13] Polycarp's letter to the Philippians almost certainly

---

[8] J. Weiss, *Der erste Korintherbrief*, KEK (Göttingen, Germany: Vandenhoeck & Ruprecht, 1910), 4.

[9] One of the most detailed discussions appears in Fee (*1 Corinthians*, 699–708), who challenged the authenticity of the text largely because (1) some ancient manuscripts place the verses at the end of the chapter, which suggests to Fee that the text was originally a marginal note later incorporated into the text; (2) the text does not appear to fit with Paul's present topic; and (3) the text seems to contradict Paul's statement in 1 Cor 11:2–16 that women may pray and prophesy. For a convincing reply to Fee that supports the authenticity of the text, see Garland, *1 Corinthians*, 664–77, esp. 675–77.

[10] See esp. J. C. Hurd (*The Origin of 1 Corinthians*, 2nd ed. [Macon, GA: Mercer University Press, 1983]), who introduced some of the major proposals and offered compelling arguments for the integrity of the letters. Other important defenses of the integrity of the letter include H. Merklein, "Die Einheitlichkeit des ersten Korintherbriefes," *ZNW* 75 (1984): 153–83; and M. M. Mitchell, *Paul and the Rhetoric of Reconciliation: An Exegetical Investigation of the Language and Composition of 1 Corinthians* (Louisville, KY: Westminster John Knox, 1992).

[11] Barrett, *1 Corinthians*, 11; M. C. de Boer, "The Composition of 1 Corinthians," *NTS* 40 (1994): 229–45.

[12] See Ignatius, *To the Ephesians* 15:3 (2 Cor 6:16); *To the Trallians* 9:2 (2 Cor 4:14); *To the Philadelphians* 6:3 (2 Cor 1:12; 2:5; 11:9–10; 12:16); *To Barnabas* 4:11–13 (2 Cor 5:10); 6:11–12 (2 Cor 5:17).

[13] V. P. Furnish, *II Corinthians*, AB (Garden City, NY: Doubleday, 1984), 29–30.

contains a loose paraphrase of 2 Corinthians 5:10, and other statements in the letter imply Polycarp's familiarity with 2 Corinthians.[14] Polycarp wrote this letter some time near the death of Ignatius, which is typically dated during the reign of Trajan (98–117).[15] Thus, Polycarp showed an awareness of the existence and authority of 2 Corinthians in the early second century.[16] According to Tertullian (ca. AD 160–225; *Against Marcion* 5.11–12), Marcion also included 2 Corinthians in his canon in the same general time period. By the late second century, 2 Corinthians was listed in the Muratorian Canon (ca. later second century) and widely quoted and ascribed to Paul. The weaker external attestation for 2 Corinthians is not sufficient to raise suspicions regarding its authenticity. The letter is so thoroughly Pauline in form, style, and content that Paul's authorship of 2 Corinthians is practically indisputable.

Despite this evidence, many scholars suspect that 2 Corinthians is a composite document consisting of several pieces of Pauline correspondence addressed to Corinth and elsewhere and possibly including some non-Pauline material as well. The integrity of the letter has been challenged at four points. First, many scholars believe that the change in tone from chapters 1–9 to 10–13 suggests that chapters 10–13 belong to an originally separate letter written either before or after chapters 1–9. Second, some scholars believe that the transition from chapter 8 to chapter 9 is unusually abrupt and that chapter 9 may have been pasted to chapter 8 by a later editor. Third, 2:14–7:4 is recognized by some as a unit distinct from the rest of the letter that interrupts Paul's discussion of Titus and his travel to Macedonia in 2:12–13 and 7:5–16. Fourth, some scholars see 6:14–7:1 as out of place and out of character for Paul. Moreover, affinities between this text and some Qumran documents suggest that the section may be a non-Pauline interpolation.

2 Corinthians 10–13 A bewildering array of theories exists that attempt to demonstrate that 2 Corinthians 10–13 was originally a separate piece of correspondence appended to chapters 1–9. Some scholars have argued that chapters 10–13 are an earlier "painful letter" mentioned in 2 Corinthians 7:8.[17] However, it is clear that the painful letter demanded that an offender in the church be punished (2 Cor 2:5–6; 7:12), and chapters 10–13 make no reference to such an offender. Moreover, no satisfactory reasons have been offered to explain why a redactor would fuse two separate letters together and ignore their chronological order.

---

[14] Polycarp (*Phil.* 4:1) may have quoted 2 Cor 6:7 ("weapons of righteousness") and Phil 2:2, and he probably alluded to 2 Cor 4:14. M. J. Harris (*Second Epistle to the Corinthians*, NIGTC [Grand Rapids, MI: Eerdmans, 2005], 3) sees "three or four clearer allusions" to 2 Corinthians in Polycarp's letter.

[15] See the discussion in M. W. Holmes, *The Apostolic Fathers: Greek Texts and English Translations*, 3rd ed. (Grand Rapids, MI: Baker, 2007), 170, 276.

[16] H. Koester, *History and Literature of Early Christianity*, vol. 2 of *Introduction to the New Testament* (Philadelphia, PA: Fortress, 1982), 306.

[17] A. Plummer, *A Critical and Exegetical Commentary on the Second Epistle of St. Paul to the Corinthians*, ICC (Edinburgh, Scotland: T&T Clark, 1915), xxvii–xxxvi; R. Bultmann, *The Second Letter to the Corinthians* (Minneapolis, MN: Augsburg, 1985), 18.

The majority of recent commentators argue that Paul wrote chapters 10–13 sometime after chapters 1–9.[18] After Titus delivered chapters 1–9 to the Corinthians, Paul received further information about their situation, which demanded another stern response.[19] He wrote chapters 10–13 as his final letter to the Corinthians. The major difficulty with the theory is that it requires a later editor to have excised both the original conclusion of the letter containing chapters 1–9 and the original introduction of the letter comprised of chapters 10–13 in order to combine the two. One wonders why, if an editor were willing to make such changes in order to join two letters seamlessly, he would not take additional steps to smooth out the transition from one section to another. This theory is also complicated by references to Paul's upcoming visit to Corinth in the two sections. As L. Belleville has noted,

> While Paul obliquely speaks of his upcoming visit in 9:4 ("if any Macedonians come with me"), it is only in chapters 10–13 that an explicit announcement is made and details are given. Indeed, it would have been a breach of epistolary etiquette for Paul to have written without formally announcing a forthcoming visit.[20]

In light of these difficulties with theories that 2 Corinthians is a composite document, many continue to affirm the original unity of the letter. The shift in tone between the earlier and later sections can be easily explained without requiring an interpolation. Chapters 1–9 may be addressed to the congregation at large, while chapters 10–13 are directed primarily to Paul's opponents. More likely Paul received new information about the situation in Corinth after a lengthy dictation pause. Depending on the schedules of authors and their secretaries, periods of days or even weeks might pass between the dictations of various sections of a letter. This was more than an adequate amount of time for Paul to receive new information that might require a fresh approach in the final chapters of the letter.

2 Corinthians 9 Several scholars have noted that 2 Corinthians 9 sits rather awkwardly in its present context. After discussing the collection of the relief offering in chapter 8 at length, the writer begins chapter 9 with what many deem to be an introductory formula ("Now concerning the ministry to the saints, it is unnecessary for me to write to you") and discusses the relief offering all over again. J. S. Semler advanced the theory that chapter 9 was originally a separate letter addressed to Christians in Achaian cities other than Corinth. But recent research has demonstrated that the so-called introductory formula in 2 Corinthians 9:1 was used for a variety of purposes,[21] and one of the most common uses

---

[18] This theory was first proposed by J. S. Semler in 1776.

[19] F. F. Bruce, *1 and 2 Corinthians* (London, England: Oliphants, 1971), 166–70; Furnish, *II Corinthians*, 30–41; R. P. Martin, *2 Corinthians*, WBC 40 (Waco, TX: Word, 1986), xl; C. G. Kruse, *The Second Epistle of Paul to the Corinthians*, TNTC (Grand Rapids, MI: Eerdmans, 1987), 29–35.

[20] L. L. Belleville, *2 Corinthians* (Downers Grove, IL: InterVarsity, 1996), 32.

[21] The construction *peri men gar* in 2 Cor 9:1 is not to be confused with *peri de* that Paul used frequently as an introductory formula in 1 Corinthians (7:1, 25, 37; 8:1; 12:1; 16:1, 12).

was to give an explanation of preceding material.[22] Moreover, chapter 9 refers repeatedly to "the brothers," known only by their previous identification in 8:16–24. Both of these features strongly imply the original unity of chapters 8 and 9.

2 Corinthians 6:14–7:1 Initially, 2 Corinthians 6:14–7:1 does appear to be positioned somewhat awkwardly. In 6:11–13 Paul spoke of his heart being open to the Corinthians and urged them to open their hearts to him. This closely matches 7:2: "Make room for us in your hearts." The intervening text appears to disrupt this connection.

But Paul may have viewed 6:14–7:1 as a necessary qualification for his plea to the Corinthians to "be open" in 6:13. Paul insists that this desired openness does not mean forsaking all discretion and embracing all people regardless of their lifestyles. The prohibition of idolatry in 6:16 seems to confirm this. In Deuteronomy 6:11 (LXX), the open or widened heart is associated with involvement in idolatry. Perhaps after urging the Corinthians to open their hearts, Paul sensed that he must clarify his intentions so as not to encourage the Corinthians' predisposition toward idolatry. The text does parallel texts from Qumran, but these parallels do not require it to be an interpolation since Paul may have incorporated a preformed text into the letter. Moreover, commentators have observed several Pauline features in the text: (1) the description of the church as God's temple; (2) the emphasis on righteousness; (3) the contrast between light and darkness; and (4) the tension between the "already" and the "not yet."[23]

The letter also expresses concerns virtually identical to those expressed in 1 Corinthians. For example, 2 Corinthians 6:14, "Don't become partners with those who do not believe," closely parallels 1 Corinthians 6:15–17 and the command to marry "only in the Lord" (1 Cor 7:39). Moreover, Paul's command in 2 Corinthians 6:14 clearly interprets OT animal laws (here Deut 32:10), allegorically applying a hermeneutic identical to the one he utilized in 1 Corinthians 8:8–11. Also, 2 Corinthians 6:15–16 seems closely related to concerns Paul expressed in 1 Corinthians 10:20–22. Numerous commentators believe that the disruption in thought was caused by a lapse of time between Paul's composition of the preceding text and this section.[24]

2 Corinthians 2:14–7:4 Paul broke off his discussion of Titus and Macedonia in 2:14 and did not return to that discussion until 7:5. But a rather tight connection exists between 2:13 and 2:14 that makes it unlikely that 2:14 begins a completely different document. In 2:13 Paul explained that despite his evangelistic opportunities in Troas, he felt compelled to leave the city and travel to Macedonia out of concern for Titus— who had apparently left Troas for Macedonia shortly before Paul's arrival. In verse 14 Paul further stated that Titus's, and later Paul's, journeys to Macedonia fulfilled God's gracious plan to spread "the aroma of the knowledge of him in every place." This naturally flowed into a discussion of the purpose and motives for Paul's missionary work. H. Lietzmann demonstrated that

---

[22] S. K. Stowers, "*Peri men gar* and the Integrity of 2 Cor. 8 and 9," *NovT* 32 (1990): 340–48.

[23] See Martin, *2 Corinthians*, xliv.

[24] Martin (*2 Corinthians*, xliv) listed Stephenson, Bates, Bruce, Guthrie, Tasker, Hughes, and Kümmel.

7:4 is closely bound to 7:5–6 by three verbal links that strongly suggest the original unity of the sections.[25] Thus, theories that 2:14–7:4 originally constituted a separate document are unconvincing.

In 1 Corinthians 1:1 Paul listed Sosthenes as a cosender. Some have inferred from the use of the first person plural pronoun "we" in the letter that Sosthenes had a greater role in composing the letter than was normally the case for Paul. Sosthenes is not mentioned elsewhere in Paul's Letters, but it is possible that the Sosthenes of 1 Corinthians is the same individual mentioned in Acts 18:17, the ruler of the synagogue who was beaten by bystanders after the Jews accused Paul before Gallio in Corinth. If so, Sosthenes was a follower of Christ at the time of the writing of 1 Corinthians and supported and encouraged the ministry of the apostle he once persecuted.

In 2 Corinthians 1:1 Paul listed Timothy as a cosender. In contrast to Sosthenes, much is known about Timothy and his relationship to Paul. Paul met Timothy on his second missionary journey (Acts 16:1), and the two became life-long friends. Two of Paul's Letters, 1 and 2 Timothy, are personally addressed to the man. Moreover, Timothy was named as cosender of more of Paul's Letters than any other individual. In addition to 2 Corinthians, he was Paul's cosender of five other missives: Philippians, Colossians, 1 and 2 Thessalonians, and Philemon.

Date and Provenance

Paul's history with the Corinthians is complex, but it is possible to reconstruct the course of the apostle's dealings with this difficult congregation from the available evidence in Acts and 1 and 2 Corinthians with a high degree of plausibility. As the following list shows, Paul made at least three visits to Corinth and wrote at least four letters—only two of which have been preserved in the Christian canon. Below is the sequence of these visits and letters:

1. First visit: Paul planted the church in Corinth in AD 50–52 (Acts 18).
2. Paul wrote the "previous letter" (1 Cor 5:9, 11; "Corinthians A").
3. Paul wrote 1 Corinthians from Ephesus in AD 53/54 (1 Cor 16:8; "Corinthians B").
4. Second visit: the "painful visit" (2 Cor 2:1; see 12:14; 13:1–2)
5. Paul wrote the "severe letter" (2 Cor 2:4; 7:8; "Corinthians C").
6. Paul wrote 2 Corinthians from Macedonia in AD 54/55 (2 Cor 7:5; 8:1; 9:2; "Corinthians D").
7. Third visit (Acts 20:2)

1 Corinthians According to 1 Corinthians 16:8, Paul wrote 1 Corinthians during his third missionary journey when he was well into his two-and-a-half-year stay in Ephesus. Based on the Delphi Inscription, Paul's appearance before Gallio in Corinth on the second

[25] See Martin, *2 Corinthians*, xliii.

missionary journey can be dated to late 51. Paul then returned to Antioch and later traveled through Galatia and Achaia to Ephesus, where he remained for two and a half to three years. Paul probably wrote 1 Corinthians shortly before Pentecost either in late AD 53 or early 54.[26]

2 Corinthians Paul wrote 2 Corinthians from Macedonia (2 Cor 7:5; 8:1; 9:2). The subscription in several ancient manuscripts of the letter states more specifically that Paul wrote from Philippi. This is a plausible provenance but remains uncertain unless more evidence becomes available. Second Corinthians 9:2 implies that the Corinthians had been preparing for the Jerusalem relief offering "since last year." This seems to require a date of composition in late AD 54 or perhaps early 55. The letter was delivered to Corinth by Titus and two other church representatives who later accompanied Paul to Jerusalem with the relief offering.[27]

Destination

Paul addressed the Corinthian letters to "the church of God at Corinth, to those sanctified in Christ Jesus, called as saints" (1 Cor 1:2) and to "the church of God at Corinth" (2 Cor 1:1). Although the church at Corinth was Paul's primary intended recipient, he wanted the letters to be read by many congregations, particularly those in Achaia. First Corinthians was co-addressed to "all those in every place who call on the name of Jesus Christ our Lord—both their Lord and ours" (1:2). Similarly, 2 Corinthians was co-addressed to "all the saints who are throughout Achaia" (1:1).

Paul planted the churches in the province of Achaia in cities such as Athens and Corinth during his second missionary journey (Acts 17:16–18:17). He revisited the area during his third missionary journey (Acts 20:1–6). He returned again after his release from his first Roman imprisonment (2 Tim 4:20).

In Paul's day, the population was probably about 200,000, although some scholars and ancient writers suggest it was much larger.[28] Since even conservative estimates make Corinth eight times larger than Athens, the enormous population of Corinth probably explains why Paul left Athens for Corinth after only a brief ministry there during the second missionary journey. It may also explain why Paul felt compelled to serve in that location for an entire eighteen months. Corinth's political importance also exceeded that

---

[26] For similar views on the dating of 1 Corinthians, see Barrett, *First Epistle to the Corinthians*, 5; Fee, *First Epistle to the Corinthians*, 4–5; R. F. Collins, *First Corinthians*, SacPag 7 (Collegeville, MN: Glazier/Liturgical Press, 1999), 24; and B. Witherington, *Conflict and Community in Corinth: A Socio-Rhetorical Commentary on 1 and 2 Corinthians* (Grand Rapids, MI: Eerdmans, 1995), 73.

[27] Many commentators date 2 Corinthians one year later, in AD 56; see the discussion in Harris, *Second Epistle to the Corinthians*, 67. Those accepting this later date typically assume a later date for 1 Corinthians than we think possible. This later date for 2 Corinthians also conflicts with the numismatic evidence that Felix succeeded Festus in AD 56. The late date does appear to allow sufficient time for Paul's travel to Jerusalem, his arrest, and his Caesarean imprisonment.

[28] W. J. Larkin Jr., *Acts*, IVPNTC 5 (Downers Grove, IL: InterVarsity, 1995), 262. Some estimate the population to have been significantly higher. See W. McRay, *Archaeology and the New Testament* (Grand Rapids, MI: Baker, 1991), 312.

of other cities in the region. Since 27 BC, Corinth had been the administrative center for the province of Achaia.[29]

Corinth's prosperity was due in part to its strategic location. The city was located on the isthmus that connected the Peloponnesus, the southern peninsula of Greece, to mainland Greece. At its most narrow point, this land bridge was only about three and a half miles wide. On the western side of the isthmus lay the port of Lechaeum, which gave access to the Adriatic Sea and across the sea to Italy. On the eastern side of the isthmus lay the port of Cenchrea, which gave access to the Aegean Sea and across the sea to Asia. The Greeks paved a stone road known as the *diolkos* across the narrow isthmus between these two important ports in the sixth century BC.[30]

The Greeks portaged cargo from one side of the isthmus to another on the *diolkos* and reloaded it on another vessel. This expedited the shipment of their cargo, shaved hundreds of miles off their journeys, and eliminated the need to sail through the treacherous waters south of the Peloponnesus. According to two ancient writers, some crews even loaded small ships on wagons on the *diolkos* and carried them across the isthmus.[31]

This isthmus was also the location of ancient Isthmia, the site of the famous Isthmian games. These were held every two years, the years both before and after the Olympics, and attracted athletes from all over the ancient world to compete in contests. Several ancient writers note that the games were an important boost to Corinth's economy and enabled the city to prosper when other Greek cities like Athens were languishing.[32]

The events of the Isthmian games were similar to those of the Olympics. Participants could compete in wrestling or boxing matches, the *pankration* (a combination of ancient martial arts that combined special holds, hand strikes, and kicks), footraces, long jumping, discus and javelin throwing, chariot races, and even music contests. First Corinthians is rich with athletic imagery, and Paul may have used it in part because of the prominence of the Isthmian games in Corinth's history. First Corinthians 9:24–28 refers to racing, boxing, and even the "crown that will fade away" made of wilted celery that was awarded to victors in the Isthmian games. Paul's time in Corinth probably overlapped with one season of the games, giving him a strategic opportunity to share the good news with people from all over ancient Greece and much of the civilized world.

Corinth was infamous for its immorality. Because of the numerous vices that characterized the city, an ancient Greek proverb said, "Not for every man is the voyage to Corinth."[33] Aristophanes (450–385 BC) demonstrated the immorality of ancient Corinth when he coined the term "Corinthianize" to describe the act of fornication. Plato used the term

---

[29] D. Bock, *Acts*, BECNT (Grand Rapids, MI: Baker, 2007), 577.

[30] The road was excavated in the late 50s by N. M. Verdelis of the Greek Archaeological Service; see McRay, *Archaeology and the New Testament*, 312.

[31] Thucydides, *History of the Peloponnesian War* 8.7–8; Polybius, *Histories* 5.101.4.

[32] Strabo, *Geography* 8.4; Plutarch, *Quaestiones conviviales* 5.3.1–3; 8.4.1; Pausanias, *Description of Greece* 2.2.

[33] Strabo, *Geography* 8.6.2.

"Corinthian girl" as a euphemism for a prostitute.[34] Strabo, who wrote only a few decades before Paul's visit, claimed that one thousand prostitutes served as slaves for the temple of Aphrodite in Corinth.[35] The Corinthians and the numerous visitors to the city worshipped the goddess of love by engaging in immoral acts with the prostitutes. Similar sexual practices have also been associated with the Sanctuary of Demeter and Kore in Corinth.[36]

Corinth was known for other vices too. A common figure in ancient Greek plays was a drunk who typically wore a Corinthian hat.[37] This implies that the Corinthians were notorious for their tendency to consume too much wine. Thus, it is not surprising that in his letters Paul had to combat heinous immorality including incest, prostitution, and drunkenness among the Corinthians.

Although not as religious as Athens, Corinth's landscape was also dotted with temples and shrines. Looming over the city on the Acrocorinth was the temple of Aphrodite. Worshippers would make the two-hour climb up a long series of steps to the top of the small mountain to express their devotion to the goddess of love, lust, and beauty. Near the Forum in Corinth was a temple of Apollo or Athena, one of the oldest temples in Greece. Just inside the northern city wall stood a sanctuary of Asclepius, the god of healing. This sanctuary was one of the premier medical centers of the day; people came from long and far in hopes of being cured of a wide range of maladies there. A huge structure at the western end of the forum is believed to have been a temple dedicated to the worship of the emperor.[38] Dozens of gods were worshipped, including Apollo, Aphrodite, Asclepius, Athena, Demeter and Kore, Dionysius, Ephesian Artemis, Hera Acraea, Hermes, Isis, Jupiter, Poseidon, Tyche, Fortuna, Zeus, and the emperors.[39] Scores of cults thrived in Corinth.

These centers of pagan religion also figure prominently in the Corinthian letters. The letters discuss at length whether the Corinthian believers should continue to participate in pagan feasts in the temples of the city (1 Cor 8: 1–13; 10:1–22; 2 Cor 6:14–7:1) and whether they should eat the meat leftover from the feasts that was sold in Corinth's markets (1 Cor 10:25–11:1). Many of the theological problems in the church of Corinth were a product of syncretism in which the Corinthians misunderstood resurrection, spiritual gifts, gender roles, baptism, and the Lord's Supper due to the influence of their pagan background.

Although Gentile believers clearly composed the large majority of the membership, the church at Corinth was a mixed congregation with both Jewish and Gentile believers. The city of Corinth did have at least one synagogue, and the Jews that gathered there were the focus of Paul's initial ministry in the city (Acts 18:4). Although Paul abandoned his synagogue ministry due to opposition from the Jews, Paul's outreach to the Jews and God

---

[34] J. Murphy-O'Connor, *St. Paul's Corinth: Texts and Archaeology* (Wilmington, DE: Glazier, 1983), 56.

[35] Strabo, *Geography* 8.6.20.

[36] McRay, *Archaeology and the New Testament*, 315–17.

[37] C. E. Fant and M. G. Reddish, *A Guide to Biblical Sites in Greece and Turkey* (New York, NY: Oxford University Press, 2003), 54.

[38] McRay, *Archaeology and the New Testament*, 322–24.

[39] See Garland, *1 Corinthians*, BECNT, 9.

fearers in the synagogue was effective. Even Crispus, the leader of the synagogue, embraced the gospel and was baptized—together with his entire family (Acts 18:8). After his conversion, he was replaced by Sosthenes as leader of the synagogue (Acts 18:17). Sosthenes may have eventually followed Crispus in his new faith, since this Sosthenes may be the "brother" of the same name whom Paul identified as the cosender of 1 Corinthians (1:1).

The church also included members from different social and economic strata. Some were slaves (1 Cor 7:21–23), while many others were very prosperous (1 Cor 4:6–8). Paul's discussion of the collection for the saints implies that the church in Corinth had few economic worries compared to the financial struggles of the believers in Macedonia (2 Cor 8:1–7, 13–15). Erastus, one of the members of the church at Corinth, was the treasurer for the city (Rom 16:23). This appears to be the city official who was honored in an inscription in front of the ancient Corinthian theater for paving one of the streets of the city at his own expense.[40] Erastus was probably only one of several high-ranking, wealthy, and influential members of the church. The material prosperity of the church, however, would eventually create problems for Paul. Some members of the church questioned Paul's spirituality because of his poverty (1 Cor 4:10–13).[41]

The rampant immorality, the prominence of pagan religion, and the economic, social, and ethnic diversity of the city of Corinth help explain many of the unique challenges that Paul faced there. These factors provide helpful insights that guide the interpretation of the Corinthian letters.

Occasion

Paul had a long and somewhat complicated relationship with the church at Corinth. He established the church there during his second missionary journey. After traveling from Athens to Corinth, Paul met Aquila and Priscilla and worked as their partner in his tent-making trade. He preached each Sabbath in the synagogue until some of the Jews blasphemed Jesus. Paul then continued his missionary work next door to the synagogue in the home of Titus Justus, a Gentile who frequented the synagogue and embraced Paul's gospel. Crispus, the leader of the synagogue, together with his entire family, and many other Corinthians believed the message that Paul preached and received Christian baptism. Some of Paul's Jewish opponents accused Paul before Gallio, the proconsul of Achaia. He dismissed Paul's case as irrelevant to Roman law and drove the accusers away. After spending a total of eighteen months in Corinth, Paul sailed to Syria. After a brief stay in Ephesus, he journeyed to Antioch by way of Caesarea and Jerusalem to report to the church there (see Acts 18:1–22).

Paul then traveled through Galatia and Phrygia until he finally arrived at Ephesus, where he remained for approximately two and a half years (see Acts 18:23–20:1). Perhaps

---

[40] McRay, *Archaeology and the New Testament*, 331–33.

[41] For an excellent summary of the history of Corinth and its religious and cultural background, see Garland, *1 Corinthians*, 1–14. For an almost exhaustive treatment of Corinth, see Murphy-O'Connor, *St. Paul's Corinth: Texts and Archaeology*.

some time early in Paul's stay at Ephesus, he received news of trouble in the church at Corinth. Evidently the church was facing problems with sexual immorality within the fellowship. In response, Paul wrote a letter urging the Corinthians to avoid associating with sexually immoral people who claimed to be Christians. This letter, mentioned in 1 Corinthians 5:9, is generally referred to by scholars as "Corinthians A" since it has not been preserved either in our NT or in any presently known manuscript. According to 1 Corinthians 5:10–13, some of the church members misunderstood the letter and assumed that Paul was demanding that believers retreat from pagan society and isolate themselves from all interaction with immoral people.

Meanwhile, Apollos, a disciple of Aquila and Priscilla, was preaching in Corinth with great effect, and some of the Christians at Corinth began rallying around him. Soon church members began to compare Apollos to Paul. Some felt Apollos was superior to Paul, and others felt he was inferior to the apostle. Soon the church had divided into four major factions: a Paul group, an Apollos group, a Cephas (Peter) group, and a Christ group. Other problems arose. A church member began to live in an incestuous relationship with his stepmother. Some members of the church developed confused ideas about marriage, sexual relationships, and gender roles. They were also practicing a form of the Lord's Supper that was more akin to celebrations in pagan temples than to the ordinance commanded by Christ. Some church members were taking other church members to court to settle disputes. The church became obsessed with the more spectacular spiritual gifts and neglected Christian compassion. Moreover, it had begun to doubt the doctrine of bodily resurrection. On top of all this, some members of the church had challenged Paul's apostolic authority.

Paul received information about the church's condition from at least two sources. First, a group of people identified as "members of Chloe's people" (1 Cor 1:11; lit. "those of Chloe") reported to Paul about the personality cults in the church that were ripping it apart. Second, Stephanus, Fortunatus, and Achaicus (1 Cor 16:15–18), three official delegates from the church, delivered a letter from it to Paul that raised a number of doctrinal and practical questions. No doubt the three delegates supplemented the letter with their own verbal reports on the condition of the church so that Paul had a clear understanding of the church's situation. Paul wrote a second letter to the congregation that answered the questions raised in the Corinthian correspondence and responded to other issues Paul knew about through the verbal reports. This letter is now known as 1 Corinthians and is identified by scholars as "Corinthians B."[42]

According to 1 Corinthians 16:5–11, when Paul wrote Corinthians B, he intended to remain in Ephesus until Pentecost and then travel through Macedonia to Corinth where

[42] D. A. Carson and D. J. Moo, *An Introduction to the New Testament*, 2nd ed. (Grand Rapids, MI: Zondervan, 2005), 420–25. Some use a different scheme borrowed from Paul's own descriptions. Letter 1 is the "previous letter"; Letter 2 is 1 Corinthians; Letter 3 is the "sorrowful letter"; and Letter 4 is 2 Corinthians. See D. Guthrie, *New Testament Introduction*, rev. ed. (Downers Grove, IL: InterVarsity, 1990), 437.

he might spend the entire winter. Paul would then send church representatives chosen by the Corinthians to Jerusalem with the relief offering. In the meantime, Paul sent Timothy to the Corinthians (1 Cor 16:10–11). When Timothy arrived in Corinth, he was unsettled by the severity of their crises. He somehow informed Paul of the situation, and Paul determined to visit the Corinthians as soon as possible. Corinthians B contained a warning that if their problems were not soon corrected, Paul might be forced to "come to you with a rod [of discipline]" (1 Cor 4:21).

When Paul learned of the church's reaction to Corinthians B, he determined that the time for such disciplinary action had arrived. Paul later characterized this personal confrontation with the church as his "painful visit" (2 Cor 2:1). It was painful not only for the Corinthians but also for Paul. He returned to Ephesus doubting that his visit had provided any real remedy to their crises and with "an extremely troubled and anguished heart" (2 Cor 2:2–4).

Paul's abandonment of his earlier plan to spend the winter in Corinth prompted some of his opponents in the church to charge him with vacillation. Paul defended his change of plans and explained his reasons for the change in 2 Corinthians 1:15–24. In short, Paul felt he could handle the situation better by letter than by another face-to-face confrontation with his opponents in the church. His tear-stained letter (2 Cor 2:4) is now lost. It is generally identified by scholars as "Corinthians C." In the absence of the letter, scholars can reconstruct its contents only by a few obscure references in 2 Corinthians. At the very least, the letter called for the church to prove its obedient character by disciplining one of the opponents who had personally maligned Paul (2 Cor 2:3–9; 7:8–12). Titus delivered the letter and worked to encourage the church's contribution to the relief offering that the Gentile churches were collecting for the church in Jerusalem.

In the meantime, the "wide door for effective ministry" in Ephesus (1 Cor 16:9) began to close for Paul. He began to suffer such great affliction that he was "completely overwhelmed" and "even despaired of life." The great affliction could refer to the Demetrius riot (Acts 19:23–20:1) or could indicate that the town clerk's dismissal of the mob in the Ephesian theater did not end the anti-Christian persecution in Ephesus but was only the prelude to more intense persecution. Owing to this great affliction, Paul was forced to flee from Ephesus. He traveled to Troas, where he hoped to preach the gospel and to be reunited with Titus who would report on the situation at Corinth. Paul's ministry in Troas enjoyed encouraging results (2 Cor 2:12). However, Titus was nowhere to be found (2 Cor 2:13). Paul decided to leave Troas and travel throughout Macedonia. As he passed through the cities there, he proclaimed the gospel, encouraged new believers, and organized the collection of the relief offering for the believers in Jerusalem (2 Cor 8:1–4; 9:2). These churches were suffering intense persecution, which Paul described as "a severe trial brought about by by affliction" (2 Cor 8:2). This severe persecution had an economic impact on the believers and left many of them in "extreme poverty." But the Macedonian believers gave eagerly, generously, even "beyond their ability," to aid the believers in Jerusalem.

Paul was disturbed that Titus had still not appeared. When the man finally met up with Paul in Macedonia, he delivered such an encouraging report about the Corinthians' response to Corinthians C that Paul was ecstatic. Paul had feared that his letter might have been too harsh and might have ended all hopes of restoring his relationship with the Corinthians. In the end, it had the desired effect: to produce a godly sorrow in the Corinthians that moved them to repentance (2 Cor 7:10). Paul hurried to write a final letter to the Corinthians that expressed his joy at their change of heart. This letter has been traditionally identified as 2 Corinthians, and scholars refer to it as "Corinthians D."

Unfortunately, during a pause in his dictation of Corinthians D, Paul somehow received disturbing new information about the situation in Corinth. When he dictated the final three chapters of Corinthians D (or possibly took up the pen himself), his writing exhibits a noticeable shift in tone that suggests that Paul's fears for the Corinthians had returned. Paul's concerns related primarily to the influence that a group of false apostles bore over the congregation. These "super-apostles" (2 Cor 12:11) boasted that their apostolic credentials exceeded Paul's and that he was unworthy to exercise leadership over the congregation. They apparently preached "another Jesus" and "a different gospel" than that proclaimed by Paul (2 Cor 11:1–4).

The letters of Paul and the history in Acts do not indicate whether the Corinthians responded to Paul's correction with repentance. *First Clement*, written by Clement of Rome to the Corinthians in about AD 96, implies that the letter was effective and that the church of Corinth became a model congregation for nearly half a century. Interestingly, when problems erupted in the church again at the end of the first century, the threats to the church were very similar to those that Paul had addressed: rejecting legitimate spiritual authority in order to be manipulated by a few headstrong and arrogant leaders and lacking the unity that should characterize the body of Christ.[43]

Paul's Opponents in 2 Corinthians

Scholars still debate the identity of Paul's opponents in 2 Corinthians. Since the 1800s scholars have proposed three major theories concerning their identity.[44] R. Bultmann and W. Schmithals theorized that the opponents were Gnostics. C. K. Barrett suggested that the opponents were legalistic Judaizers similar to those that Paul battled in Galatians.

---

[43] See *1 Clement*, otherwise known as the "Letter of the Romans to the Corinthians." The Greek text with an updated English translation and a helpful introduction is available in M. W. Holmes, *The Apostolic Fathers: Greek Texts and English Translations*, 3rd ed. (Grand Rapids, MI: Baker, 2007), 44–131.

[44] C. Machalet listed eleven different theories of identification of Paul's opponents in 2 Corinthians that scholars affirmed in various works between 1908 and 1940 ("Paulus und seine Gegner. Eine Untersuchung zu den Korintherbriefen," in *Theokratia. Jahrbuch des Institutum Judaicum Delitzschianum, II. Festgabe für Karl Heinrich Rengstorf zum 70. Geburtstag*, ed. W. Dietrich et al. [Leiden, Netherlands: E. J. Brill, 1973], 183–203).

D. Georgi argued that the opponents were Hellenistic Jewish missionaries who held to a mixed theology with both legalistic and gnostic/pneumatic elements and who venerated Moses as a "divine man" or miracle worker.[45]

In his synthesis of various characterizations of the false apostles and their message throughout 2 Corinthians, V. P. Furnish exhibited rare caution in not exceeding clear exegetical evidence in his descriptions. He suggested this reconstruction: (1) The intruders claimed a relationship with Christ and an apostolic authority superior to Paul's. (2) They supported these claims with letters of recommendation and boasts of their Jewish heritage, eloquence, boldness, missionary accomplishments, ecstatic experiences, miracles, and special knowledge gleaned from visionary experiences. (3) They were critical of Paul for being weak, having poor skills in public speaking, being a ne'er-do-well who suffered almost constant hardship, and lacking the confidence to expect financial support from the Corinthians.[46]

The most important texts for identifying these opponents are 2 Corinthians 3:1–18; 11:4, 22–23. Some texts in 2 Corinthians clearly address Paul's opponents. Other texts do not specifically mention Paul's opponents but appear to be part of Paul's apologetic against them. Close examination of Paul's defense enables scholars to reconstruct elements of the theology of the opposition using a process called "mirror-reading." Mirror-reading attempts to reconstruct the theology of Paul's opponents based on Paul's critique of their theology in much the same way one can reconstruct essential elements of an unheard person's telephone conversation by listening carefully to the words of the present party. An application of mirror-reading to 2 Corinthians 3:1–18 suggests that Paul's opponents failed to recognize the temporary nature of the old covenant and the greater glory of the new. They argued that the gospel had in no way changed the obligation to fulfill the law of Moses and that the law was somehow necessary to Christian experience. The emphasis on spiritual gifts in 1 Corinthians is matched in 2 Corinthians by the opponents' apparent claim that they were "superapostles" whose miracles surpassed Paul's (2 Cor 11:5; 12:11–12). The great emphasis on Paul's sufferings as an apostle may imply that the opponents taught that they were superior to Paul since God had supernaturally protected them from such things (2 Cor 1:3–11; 4:7–15; 6:4–10; 11:23–29). From 11:4, it is clear that the opponents preached "another Jesus," "a different spirit," and "another gospel." But determining precisely what this means is difficult. The following chart (Table 12.1) shows some of the popular explanations of the teaching of these false apostles.

---

[45] See the summary of various theories regarding the identification of Paul's opponents in S. J. Hafemann, "Corinthians, Letters to the," *Dictionary of Paul and His Letters*, 164–79, esp. 177–78.

[46] Furnish, *II Corinthians*, 52–53.

Something to Think About: Lost in Affluence

The Corinthians had it all. Many were wealthy in this thriving seaport, and with this affluence came the arrogance that so often accompanies possessions. Jesus warned the rich, saying, "It will be hard for a rich person to enter the kingdom of heaven. Again I tell you, it is easier for a camel to go through the eye of a needle than for a rich person to enter the kingdom of God" (Matt 19:23–24). John counseled, "Do not love the world or the things in the world. If anyone loves the world, love for the Father is not in him. . . . And the world with its lust is passing away, but the one who does the will of God remains forever" (1 John 2:15, 17).

Paul often began his letters with an opening greeting and a thanksgiving section. In 1 Thessalonians, for example, he rejoiced that these believers had become an example in the entire region (1 Thess 1:2–10). In 1 Corinthians, however, the only thing Paul can thank God for is that God has blessed the Corinthians with every spiritual gift (1 Cor 1:5–7)! What he cannot thank God for is the way in which they exercised these gifts. As becomes clear later in the letter, all too often chaos reigned, and the most important ingredient—love—was conspicuously absent in the life of the church (1 Corinthians 13).

So, early in the letter (1:26–31) Paul felt compelled to write,

> *Brothers and sisters, consider your calling: not many were wise from a human perspective, not many powerful, not many of noble birth. Instead, God has chosen what is foolish in the world to shame the wise, and God has chosen what is weak in the world to shame the strong. God has chosen what is insignificant and despised in the world—what is viewed as nothing—to bring to nothing what is viewed as something, so that no one may boast in his presence. It is from him that you are in Christ Jesus, who became wisdom from God for us—our righteousness, sanctification, and redemption, in order that, as it is written: "Let the one who boasts, boast in the Lord."*

Most assuredly, this is a prophetic word that has in no way lost its relevance in the Western church, where affluence has significantly eroded the NT teaching of the church as the body of Christ, where its various members work together for the glory of God. May God help us in our performance orientation and shallow lip service to Christianity. If we keep Christ at arm's length, we will remain "babies in Christ" (1 Cor 3:1) rather than growing up into mature spiritual adulthood. And tragically, we will not be the salt and light of the earth by which people will see our good works and give glory to our Father in heaven (Matt 5:16).

Table 12.1: Teaching of False Apostles in 2 Corinthians

2 Cor 11:4	Judaizing Heresy*	Gnosticism **	Divine-man***
"Another Jesus"	Denial of Jesus's deity and resurrection; Jesus is little more than a model of obedience to the law; he is viewed in a purely human way ("according to the flesh"; 2 Cor 4:10–14)	View that saw the physical body (Jesus) as the wretched dwelling in which the heavenly being (Christ) was temporarily trapped	View that focused on Jesus's powers as a miracle worker, powers that were equally available to "superapostles" who flaunted signs and wonders in a boastful manner
"A different S[s]pirit"	Spirit of bondage to Judaizing teaching	Emphasis on the spiritual as opposed to the material and physical due to gnostic dualism	Spirit of self-centered and abusive authority or emphasis on visionary experiences
"A different gospel"	Teaching demanding obedience to outmoded ordinances	The secrets of Gnosticism	Message that focused on present self-glorification rather than future glorification by God following a life of humility and self-sacrifice

*See Hughes, *The Second Epistle to the Corinthians,* 377–78. A similar view was suggested by R. V. G. Tasket, *The Second Epistle to the Corinthians,* TNTC (Grand Rapids, MI: Eerdmanns, 1960), 147–48

**W. Schmithals, *Gnosticism in Corinth: An Investigation of the Letters to the Corinthians,* trans. J. E. Steely (Nashville: Abingdon, 1971), 134; R. Bultmann, *Der zweite Brief an die Korinther,* ed. E. Dinkler (Göttingen: Vandenhoeck & Ruprecht, 1976), 205.

***See F. T. Fallon, *2 Corinthians* (Wilmington: Glazier, 1980), 94; Martin, *2 Corinthians,* 341.

Although the debate over the identity of Paul's opponents in 2 Corinthians is far from settled, the Divine-man view outlined in the chart is growing in popularity and may eventually emerge as the new consensus. Along those lines, Belleville argued that "Paul's rivals were Palestinian Jews who, claiming the backing of the Jerusalem church, came to Corinth carrying letters of reference."[47] They brandished an impressive array of credentials—including visions, ecstatic experiences, and revelations—and sought to sway their audience through polished oratory, preaching what Paul referred to as "a different gospel" (2 Cor 11:4).

S. Hafemann, in his reconstruction, sought to integrate the various elements of the false teaching into a more coherent system. According to him, Paul's opponents had embraced "a theology of 'over-realized glory,' in which participation in their gospel, with its tie to the old covenant, was said to guarantee freedom from sin and suffering in this world."[48] Likely

---

[47] Belleville, *2 Corinthians,* 274.

[48] Hafemann, "Corinthians," 178. Compare S. J. Hafemann, *Suffering and Ministry in the Spirit: Paul's Defense of His Ministry in II Corinthians* (Grand Rapids, MI: Eerdmans, 1990). A cautious and helpful summary description of the opponents appears in Furnish, *II Corinthians,* 48–54.

at the center of the debate was the relationship between the two covenants as it pertained to the roles of Moses and the law on the one hand and Paul as an apostle of Christ engaged in "the ministry of the Spirit" on the other (see 2 Cor 2:16; 3:4–18).

Precisely identifying Paul's opponents is notoriously difficult. A bewildering array of theories of identification has been proposed. So far, none of these has succeeded in becoming the consensus view. Attempts to reconstruct the teachings of the opponents should proceed with caution and humility. Interpreters must hesitate before using the reconstruction to interpret difficult texts in 2 Corinthians since the dependent interpretation may be no more accurate than their reconstruction.

Purpose

1 Corinthians Paul wrote 1 Corinthians to respond to oral reports he had received from those associated with Chloe (1 Cor 1:11) and elsewhere and to answer questions raised by the Corinthians in a letter that they wrote to him (1 Cor 7:1). The oral report focused primarily on the disunity of the Corinthian church. The congregation had divided into several factions, each of which celebrated a particular Christian leader. Paul wrote 1 Corinthians to urge the church to seek unity and to follow Christ rather than idolizing a human leader such as Paul, Apollos, or Cephas (1 Cor 1:12; see 1:10–4:21). He recognized that the glorification of human leaders indicated that the Corinthians did not understand the nature of divine grace and that they had a flawed view of the nature of human leadership. God's grace uses unlikely people for great purposes to display his power and wisdom. This promotes God's glory and diminishes human pride.

Paul had also heard from several different sources that a member of the church of Corinth was living in an incestuous relationship with his stepmother. He urged the church to repent of its casual acceptance of such immorality. He commanded the church to exercise church discipline in hopes of encouraging the immoral church member to repent and preventing the spread of immorality throughout the congregation (1 Cor 5:1–13). Paul also wrote to clarify the doctrine of Christian liberty and to demonstrate that freedom in Christ was not a license for immoral behavior (1 Cor 6:12–20).

Paul also knew that believers were taking fellow believers to court to settle disputes. He recognized that this was a poor witness to unbelievers in the local court systems and that justice was more likely to be found in decisions made by believers than by unbelievers. Paul thus urged the Corinthians to settle their disputes through arbitrators who were fellow Christ-followers.

Several issues were raised by the Corinthians' letter to Paul, and his reply to these concerns begins in chapter 7 and extends at least through chapter 14 and possibly through chapter 15. These concerns include questions about Christian marital relationships (chap. 7), participation in pagan feasts in various temples in Corinth and eating food formerly sacrificed to idols (chaps. 8–10), proper dress and decorum during worship and the Lord's Supper (chap. 11), and the exercise of spiritual gifts (chaps. 12–14).

Some of the Corinthians had rejected the doctrine of the bodily resurrection of believers. This had a significant impact on their moral as well as their theological views. Paul wrote to defend the doctrine of the resurrection and to show the crucial nature of this doctrine to the Christian gospel (chap. 15).

Finally, Paul gave the church practical instructions for the collection of the relief offering for believers in Jerusalem and informed the Corinthians of his tentative travel plans (chap. 16).

2 Corinthians Although 2 Corinthians constitutes a single letter rather than a composite of several different Pauline Letters, a letter of this length was likely composed over a period of several days or weeks. The needs of the churches to which Paul traveled, the demands of his occupation as a tentmaker, and the limited availability of secretaries with the skills needed to produce such a letter probably required Paul to dictate various portions of it at different times and possibly in different places. This chapter has suggested that when Paul dictated chapters 1–9 he was greatly encouraged by the positive report about the Corinthians that he received from Titus. But, after dictating the first nine chapters, he may have received more news from Corinth that alarmed him again and prompted him to write the final chapters of the letter with a different tone.[49] Some interpreters suggest that a secretary was not available for the last three chapters and that Paul actually penned chapters 10–13 with his own hand.[50]

Paul wrote chapters 1–9 for four major purposes. First, Paul's change in travel plans had made him vulnerable to his opponents' charge that he was inconsistent and unworthy of the Corinthians' trust. Paul wrote to defend his reliability and to explain the reasons for his change of plans. Second, Paul wrote to encourage the Corinthians to restore a church member who had been disciplined by the congregation for vicious attacks on the apostle. Third, Paul wrote to clarify the nature of his apostolic ministry and his qualifications for it. Under the influence of new leaders who boasted that their apostolic qualifications were superior to Paul's, his credentials had been scrutinized and rejected by a growing number of Corinthian believers. Paul attempted to demonstrate that his qualifications for spiritual leadership exceeded those of his opponents in every way. This defense of Paul's apostleship is the primary motivation for the earlier section of the letter, and Paul seems confident that the Corinthians would be convinced by his defense. Fourth, Paul wrote to encourage the Corinthians to fulfill their pledge to contribute generously to the relief offering for the Jerusalem believers.

---

[49] See Carson and Moo, *An Introduction to the New Testament,* 435; T. D. Lea, *The New Testament: Its Background and Message* (Nashville, TN: B&H, 1996), 426–27; Guthrie, *New Testament Introduction*, 456–57 (influenced by W. Ramsey); and Harris, *Second Epistle to the Corinthians*, 50–51. Bruce (*1 and 2 Corinthians*, 170) even suggested that chaps. 10–13 were a separate letter that was dispatched slightly later than chaps. 1–9. Alternatively, R. Gundry, *A Survey of the New Testament*, 3rd ed. (Grand Rapids, MI: Zondervan, 1994), 371, proposed that chaps. 1–9 are addressed to the repentant majority and chaps. 10–13 to a reactionary minority, but few have adopted his view.

[50] Belleville, *2 Corinthians*, 33.

In chapters 10–13, Paul's defense of his apostolic authority becomes much more intense. He was no longer confident that the Corinthians would recognize the false apostles for what they were or that they would reaffirm his own apostolic authority. Paul wrote these chapters to urge the Corinthians to reject the false apostles and their message and to embrace again the gospel that Paul had preached. He also wrote to announce his plans to make a third visit to Corinth. Finally, he wrote to urge the Corinthians to examine their faith to determine whether it was authentic.

LITERATURE

Literary Plan

The literary plan of 1 Corinthians is in some ways much simpler than that of other Pauline Letters. After his introduction and customary prayer of thanksgiving, Paul systematically addressed issues of concern from oral reports relayed to him by those of Chloe and representatives of the Corinthian church. Paul then addressed questions posed to him in a letter from the Corinthians. The responses to questions from the letter begin in 1 Corinthians 7:1 as indicated by the introduction "Now in response to the matters you wrote." New topics culled from the Corinthians' letter are introduced using the construction "now concerning" *(peri de)*, which appears in 1 Corinthians 7:1, 25, 37; 8:1; 12:1; and 16:1, 12. Rather than following an elaborate literary plan based on rhetoric or epistolary conventions, Paul simply addressed one issue after another as they were raised to him. The apostle concluded his letter with his customary greeting and blessing.

Efforts to understand the literary plan of 2 Corinthians are complicated by the many theories of interpolation that regard 2 Corinthians as a composite of several different letters rather than a single literary document. Several scholars have attempted rhetorical classifications of 2 Corinthians and have sought to understand the structure of the letter based on rhetorical analyses. However, no single classification or analysis has won wide support. So many different analyses have been proposed that M. Harris concluded, "The practice of rhetorical criticism seems to be more of an art than a science, with the highly subjective nature of the enterprise reflected in the wide divergence between the findings of the practitioners."[51]

Other scholars have attempted to analyze the chiastic structure of the letter. Again, no single analysis has won the favor of a large number of supporters. Chiastic analyses tend to locate the center of the chiasm, which is typically the climax and emphasis of the construction, in an unlikely place or match elements in the proposed chiasm based on artificial similarities.[52] The majority of commentators prefer to analyze the structure of the

---

[51] Harris (*Second Epistle to the Corinthians*, 110) also presented a brief summary of the analyses by B. Witherington, G. A. Kennedy, H. D. Betz, B. K. Peterson, and H. G. Sundermann (pp. 105–10).

[52] E.g., H. Segalla ("Struttura letteraria e unità della 2 Corinzi," *Teologia* 13 [1988]: 189–218) saw 2 Corinthians 8–9 as the center and climax of the letter.

letter based on content alone. Such a procedure divides the letter into three major sections consisting of chapters 1–7, 8–9, and 10–13.

OUTLINES

1 CORINTHIANS

I. INTRODUCTION (1:1–9)
   A. Salutation (1:1–3)
   B. Prayer of Thanksgiving (1:4–9)
II. RESPONSE TO ORAL REPORTS (1:10–6:20)
   A. A Proper Perspective on Christian Ministers and Ministry (1:10–4:20)
      1. The Problem of Disunity (1:10–17)
      2. The Sin of Dependence on Personal Abilities (1:18–25)
      3. The Sin of Personal Boasting (1:26–31)
      4. Paul, a Model of Dependence on God (2:1–5)
      5. Spiritual Wisdom versus Worldly Wisdom (2:6–16)
      6. The Immaturity of the Corinthians (3:1–9)
      7. God's Evaluation of Christian Ministry (3:10–17)
      8. Final Argument Against Human Boasting (3:18–23)
      9. Paul's Example of Christian Ministry (4:1–20)
   B. Immorality in the Church (5:1–13)
   C. Disputes Between Believers (6:1–11)
   D. Limitations on Freedom in Christ (6:12–20)
III. RESPONSES TO A LETTER FROM THE CORINTHIANS (7:1–16:4)
   A. Matters Related to Sex and Marriage (7:1–40)
      1. To the Married (7:1–7)
      2. To Singles and Widows (7:8–9)
      3. To Those in Difficult Marriages (7:10–24)
      4. To Virgins (7:25–38)
      5. To Widows (7:39–40)
   B. Matters Related to Idol Feasts (8:1–11:1)
      1. Food Offered to Idols (8:1–13)
      2. Paul Foregoes Rights of Apostle (9:1–27)
      3. Food Offered to Idols (continued; 10:1–11:1)
   C. Matters Related to Christian Worship (11:2–34)
      1. Gender Distinctions in Worship (11:2–16)
      2. Behavior During the Lord's Supper (11:17–34)
   D. Matters Related to Spiritual Gifts (12:1–14:40)
      1. Diversity of Gifts, Unity in the Body (12:1–31)
      2. The Supremacy of Love (13:1–13)

3. Prophecy and Tongues (14:1–40)
E. Matters Related to the Resurrection (15:1–58)
F. Matters Related to the Relief Offering (16:1–4)
IV. CONCLUSION (16:5–24)
A. Paul's Travel Plans (16:5–12)
B. Final Exhortations (16:13–18)
C. Closing (16:19–24)

2 CORINTHIANS

I. INTRODUCTION (1:1–11)
A. Salutation (1:1–2)
B. Prayer of Thanksgiving (1:3–7)
C. Explanation of Paul's Thanksgiving (1:8–11)
II. PAUL'S RELATIONSHIP WITH THE CORINTHIANS (1:12–2:11)
A. Paul's Pure Conduct (1:12–14)
B. Paul's Change in Plans (1:15–22)
C. The Reason for the Change in Plans (1:23–2:4)
D. Forgiveness to the Repentant Sinner (2:5–11)
III. PAUL'S DEFENSE OF HIS MINISTRY (2:12–7:16)
A. Paul's Ministry in Troas and Macedonia (2:12–17)
B. Paul's Letters of Recommendation (3:1–3)
C. Paul's Competence (3:4–6)
D. Ministry of the New Covenant (3:7–18)
E. The Unveiled Truth (4:1–6)
F. Treasure in Clay Jars (4:7–18)
G. The Coming Resurrection (5:1–10)
H. The Ministry of Reconciliation (5:11–6:2)
I. Catalog of Paul's Sufferings (6:3–13)
J. Call to Separate from Paul's Opponents (6:14–7:1)
K. Paul's Final Defense (7:2–16)
IV. THE COLLECTION FOR THE BELIEVERS IN JERUSALEM (8:1–9:15)
A. Example of the Churches in Macedonia (8:1–7)
B. Examples of Christ's Sacrifice and the OT (8:8–15)
C. Administration of the Offering (8:16–24)
D. Importance of Having the Offering Ready (9:1–5)
E. Principles Motivating Generous Giving (9:6–15)
V. PAUL'S RENEWED DEFENSE OF HIS APOSTLESHIP (10:1–13:4)
A. The Tone of Paul's Appeal (10:1–11)
B. Divine Commendation of Paul's Ministry (10:12–18)
C. Danger of the False Apostles (11:1–15)

D. Paul's Sufferings (11:16–33)
E. Paul's Visions and Revelations (12:1–10)
F. Paul's Miracles (12:11–13)
G. Paul's Final Defense (12:14–13:4)
VI. FINAL EXHORTATIONS (13:5–12)
VII. CLOSING (13:13)

UNIT-BY-UNIT DISCUSSIONS

1 CORINTHIANS

I. Introduction (1:1–9)

A. Salutation (1:1–3) Paul opens his letter, as was the custom, by identifying the author and intended recipients. His self-description "called as an apostle of Christ Jesus by God's will" confirmed Paul's apostleship to a church that was apparently beginning to question his apostolic authority and would ultimately deny it. The address emphasizes the importance of Jesus Christ to the church. Jesus Christ is both the agent of the church's sanctification and the object of her confession.

B. Prayer of Thanksgiving (1:4–9) Paul's prayer offers thanks to God for the numerous spiritual gifts enjoyed by the Corinthian church. The prayer thus encouraged a significant change in the Corinthians' outlook on these gifts. Rather than being an object of personal pride and an incentive for boasting, the gifts were to be recognized as graciously imparted to the believers by God and thus incentives for thanksgiving and praise to him alone.

Paul's greeting "grace and peace" is his typical greeting.[53] However, it may take on a slightly different significance in this church that had depreciated divine grace through its boasting in human accomplishments and had traded peace for heated conflict.

Paul also expresses his confidence that the gracious God who called the Corinthians to fellowship with his Son would ensure that they passed the scrutiny of final judgment. His reference to the "day of our Lord Jesus Christ" borrows the familiar phrase "day of the LORD/Yahweh" from the OT and applies it to Jesus's second coming. The application of this phrase that describes the coming of Yahweh in judgment to Jesus's return strongly implies the deity of Jesus and confirms that the title "Lord," used of Jesus frequently in 1 Corinthians (six times in the introduction alone: see 1:2–3, 7–10), functions as a title of deity rather than mere authority.

II. Response to Oral Reports (1:10–6:20)

A. A Proper Perspective on Christian Ministers and Ministry (1:10–4:20) Paul indicates that he had received word from people associated with Chloe that the church

[53] See Rom 1:5; 2 Cor 1:2; Gal 1:3; Eph 1:2; Phil 1:2; Col 1:2; 1 Thess 1:1; 2 Thess 1:2; Titus 1:4; Phlm 1:3.

had divided into four major factions (1:10–17). Three of these factions wrongly idolized individuals and gave them a standing dangerously close to that of Jesus himself. This was terribly wrong since Jesus's role in the church was completely unique. Only he had suffered crucifixion for their sake, and only he was the Messiah in whose name believers were baptized. Moreover, the Corinthians' celebration of human skills and abilities emptied the cross of its effect in ways that Paul soon described.

By turning Christian servants into celebrities based on their speaking and intellectual abilities, the Corinthians had shown a complete lack of understanding of the economy of God (1:18–25). God uses weak, foolish, and ignoble people and an apparently foolish and scandalous message to save sinners. This displays the supremacy of God's power and wisdom and reduces human wisdom and power to mere foolishness and weakness. The makeup of the Corinthian church confirmed Paul's description of the divine economy. An understanding of God's ways eliminated human boasting and drove sinners to praise God alone (1:26–31).

Paul's ministry to the Corinthians illustrated the principles that Paul had just explained (2:1–5). He did not seek to impress people with rhetorical abilities or his persona. Instead, a weak man who trembled before God preached a simple message about God's provision of forgiveness through Jesus's sacrificial death. The Corinthians had embraced this message not because Paul's wisdom was on display but because God's power was at work.

The worldly wisdom that the Corinthians prized was no true wisdom at all (2:6–16). Those responsible for Jesus's crucifixion touted themselves as wise men, but they did not even recognize who Jesus was. True wisdom was granted only through the revealing work of God's Spirit. Paul's ministry was an expression of this revelatory work. However, only those indwelled and influenced by God's Spirit could understand spiritual matters.

Paul had been forced to explain only the most elementary truths of the Christian faith to the Corinthians because they lacked the spiritual maturity to understand more difficult truths (3:1–9). Their disunity confirmed their immaturity. If they had been mature, they would have understood that the Christian servants they celebrated were only instruments in the hands of God and that God alone was to be glorified for the harvest produced through their ministries.

God gave Paul the resources needed to lay the foundation for the Corinthian church, and another person was building on that foundation (3:10–17). Those involved in the ministries of the church needed to make sure that Jesus Christ remained the focal point of those ministries. Those who served needed to be mindful that their service would be evaluated by God, and unworthy contributions to the ministry would be destroyed. The church is God's holy temple, and God will justly punish those who desecrate it.

True wisdom came only through embracing the message that the world viewed as foolishness (3:18–23). But God viewed the world's wisdom as foolishness. God's evaluation of the worldly wisdom that prompted boasting and stirred dissension should silence all human boasting at last.

Paul's own ministry exemplified the principles he had just explained (4:1–20). He desired others to view him as a servant and a manager, not as a celebrity. His only aim was to be faithful to the Master he served. It mattered little to him whether he passed the judgment of others, but it was of supreme importance that he pleased God. Consequently, no room remained for personal pride and arrogance based on one's giftedness or the results of his ministry. With biting sarcasm, Paul contrasts the experience of the apostles with the Corinthians' own arrogant self-appraisal. He presents the humility, self-sacrifice, and obeisance of the apostles as a model fit for all believers to follow.

Paul's earlier sarcasm was not intended to shame the Corinthians. He loved them like a father loves his children. Indeed, they were his spiritual children since he had first preached the gospel to them. Now they should seek to imitate him like a little boy imitates his father. Timothy, who would soon visit the Corinthians, was also Paul's spiritual son who exemplified the love and faithfulness to the Lord that was appropriate for one of Paul's children. He would remind the Corinthians of Paul's example. Paul would eventually come to Corinth and was prepared to use the rod of discipline on the arrogant and divisive members of the family as a father must sometimes do.

B. Immorality in the Church (5:1–13) Paul heard reports that a member of the church in Corinth was committing incest with his stepmother. This sin was so deplorable that not even pagans tolerated it. Yet the church celebrated this sin in a confused attempt to flaunt its freedom in Christ. Paul calls the church to repent and to expel this person from the church. This expulsion had two major purposes. First, it would hopefully lead to the sinner's repentance and restoration. Second, it would protect the church from an immoral influence that might corrupt the entire congregation.

Although it was impractical for believers to attempt to dissociate themselves from unbelievers who lived sinfully, believers should break fellowship with so-called believers who live immorally. As OT Israel expelled certain individuals from the congregation for particularly heinous sins (5:13 quotes Deut 17:7), so the Christian church must expel those who sin with impudence.

C. Disputes Between Believers (6:1–11) Paul scolds believers in Corinth for attempting to settle disputes between one another in the civil courts. Fellow Christ-followers were far better qualified to make just and righteous decisions in such disputes than unbelievers were. Moreover, taking Christian disputes to the civil courts flaunted Christian disunity in a way that damaged Christian witness. In such cases everyone lost. Believers should therefore prefer being wronged or defrauded to triumphing over fellow believers in court. But Paul warns those who wronged and defrauded their brothers and sisters that such actions were completely inconsistent with genuine Christianity. Those who practiced particularly heinous sins would not inherit the kingdom of God. Though the Corinthians had once practiced such sins, they had been dramatically transformed by Christ and rescued from these wicked lifestyles.

D. Limitations on Freedom in Christ (6:12–20) The Corinthians' toleration of incest and fraud among members of the church indicated that they had a perverted view of Christian liberty. Paul insists that freedom in Christ is not absolute. Christians should not engage in any behavior unbeneficial for others or that has the potential of dominating their lives. They should recognize that their bodies were created to glorify God. His intention to resurrect their bodies demonstrated that the body, and what one does with it, is important to him. Believers should also recognize that their connection with Christ necessarily involved him in all of their activities. The body of the believer was now God's temple and should be regarded as holy. Finally, all notions of Christian freedom should be tempered by the consideration that believers are slaves of the Lord Jesus; they have been bought with the redemptive price of his blood.

III. Responses to a Letter from the Corinthians (7:1–16:4)

A. Matters Related to Sex and Marriage (7:1–40) Perhaps because of a confused eschatology, some Corinthian believers were seeking to practice abstinence within marriage (7:1–7). Paul critiques this practice on both theological and practical grounds. First, a married person's body belongs to his or her spouse. Withholding the body defrauds the spouse of what rightfully belongs to him or her. Second, such abstinence is risky business because it makes the spouse more vulnerable to sexual temptation.

Believers who had no sexual compulsion for marriage should remain single (7:8). Believers should not divorce unbelieving spouses on religious grounds as if a believer were corrupted by the relationship (7:10–16). If the unbeliever decided to leave the believer, the believer should permit him or her to do so. But a believer married to an unbeliever should seek to preserve the marriage in the hope of having a positive spiritual influence on the unbelieving spouse.

Paul's general advice was for Christ-followers to remain in the situation in which they lived at the time of their conversion, particularly with regard to slavery and circumcision (7:17–24). Because of the nearness of Jesus's return and the distress believers would experience as that time approached, unmarried believers should remain unmarried. This would enable believers to focus their concerns on the things of the Lord and prevent them from being distracted from their devotion to him. However, when two unmarried believers felt passionately for each other and struggled to control themselves, marriage remains the best option.

Marriage is a lifelong covenant, which means that widows are no longer bound to their deceased spouses. Widows may be happier if they remain single, but they are free to marry another believer if they so desire (7:25–40).

B. Matters Related to Idol Feasts (8:1–11:1) Many of the Corinthian believers had formerly worshipped in idolatrous temples. Some of these believers had now sworn off any association with pagan idolatry. They refused to participate in the idol feasts or even to eat meat formally sacrificed to idols that was later sold in Corinthian markets. Others avoided the idol feasts but felt free to purchase and enjoy the food that had been devoted to the idol. Still others felt free to participate even in the feasts based on their conviction that the idol gods did not really exist anyway.

Paul confirms the theological premise of those who felt free to attend the idol feasts but challenges the conclusion that they drew from that premise. Paul agrees that there is only one true God, quoting the Shema of Deuteronomy 6:4: "The Lord our God, the Lord is one." Strikingly, he interpreted this confession as an expression of a high Christology in which the Father is the one true God and Jesus is the one true Lord who created all that exists. This Christological interpretation of the Shema is one of the clearest and most stunning affirmations of the deity of Jesus in Paul's Letters.

However, Christian rejection of polytheism and the existence of idol gods did not necessarily lead to unqualified approval of eating food formerly sacrificed to idols. Believers needed to be aware that others might follow their example of eating such food, only to suffer a tormented conscience. They ought to be sensitive to how other believers perceived their actions and the potential impact of others following their example (8:1–13).

Although some believers might resent this limitation on their Christian liberty, Paul himself willingly sacrificed some of his liberties as an apostle. He relinquished his right to financial support from the churches that he served—even though secular examples, OT law, and the teaching of Jesus confirmed his right to that support. Paul also sacrificed other freedoms in order to relate better to the people whom he was attempting to reach. Paul was concerned that some Corinthians viewed Christian liberty as a throwing off of all restraints on their behavior. He used several athletic examples familiar to them from the nearby Isthmian Games to remind them that self-control and personal restraint are practical necessities in all areas of life (9:1–27).

Paul suspected that the Corinthian view of Christian liberty was related to what we might call sacramental theology. The Corinthians apparently believed that reception of baptism and participation in the Lord's Supper guaranteed salvation, as if those who received those ordinances were free to live in any way they wanted without fear of divine judgment. Paul attacks this sacramental theology by arguing that the Israelites had participated in events analogous to baptism and a spiritual meal. However, all but two of the Israelites died in the wilderness wanderings as a result of divine judgment. Moreover, they fell under divine judgment because they had committed the very same sins in which the Corinthians were now engaged: idolatry, sexual immorality, and rejection of the authority of divinely appointed leaders. The example of the Israelites functioned as a warning to the Corinthians. They must not presume that the ordinances guaranteed salvation, and they must beware falling into temptation (10:1–13).

Although the idol gods did not actually exist, those who participated in the idol feasts thus became partners with demons (10:14–22). This was inconsistent with the Corinthians' Christian commitment and could only provoke the Lord's jealousy as the second commandment warned (Exod 20:4). Because believers should only do what is helpful, edifying, and beneficial for other believers, they ought to limit their freedom to eat idol meat for the sake of those with weaker consciences. In the privacy of their own homes, they were free to eat the meat. However, in public settings where people were present who might be disturbed by the consumption of idol meat, believers should refrain from eating it. The believer's primary concern is to glorify God rather than exercise his own freedom. Thus, he should avoid giving unnecessary offense to others by his actions. This was in keeping with the examples of both Paul and Christ, who lived for the benefit of others rather than their own pleasure (10:23–11:1).

C. Matters Related to Christian Worship (11:2–34) Paul addresses two important issues related to worship. First, some believers in the church at Corinth were apparently practicing gender role reversal and seeking to abolish distinctions between the sexes in worship (11:2–16). This practice probably resulted from their confused eschatology, the influence of their pagan backgrounds, and misunderstandings of Paul's own teaching. Women in the church began to dress in a masculine fashion, and some men possibly dressed in a feminine manner. In response, Paul argues that the distinction between men and women had been ordained by God. These distinctions and the biblical roles of men and women should be reflected in the dress and hairstyles of believers.

Second, Paul expresses concern about abuses of the sacred ordinance of the Lord's Supper (11:17–34). During the Supper, the church was divided by personality cliques. Some members overindulged in both food and wine, while others, particularly the poorer members of the congregation, remained hungry and thirsty. In this, the congregation desecrated the Supper that should have been a celebration of the new covenant, a remembrance of Jesus's sacrifice, and an anticipation of his return. Paul urges the Corinthians to examine themselves to ensure that they partook of the Supper in a worthy manner. In their observance of the Supper, they should gratefully reflect on the body and blood of the Lord that had been sacrificed for them. Paul warns that sickness or even death might result (and in fact already had resulted) from the sacrilege of the Corinthians with regard to the Lord's Supper.

D. Matters Related to Spiritual Gifts (12:1–14:40) The Corinthians evidently had confused notions about the nature, importance, and proper exercise of spiritual gifts. Apparently, some in the congregation who thought that they were exercising the gift of prophecy had actually cursed Jesus in corporate worship (12:1–3). Paul saw the need to correct the Corinthians' confused views. He explains that the same Spirit had bestowed different gifts to different people for the benefit of the church (12:4–11). The fact that the different gifts all came from the same source implied that the gifts were all equally "spiritual" and no gift was unimportant. Paul confirms this by comparing the different gifts to the various abilities of different parts of the human body (12:12–31). All gifts, like all physical abilities, were necessary and important. No individual would have all the gifts. However, he should exercise whatever gift God granted him without comparing his gift to someone else's.

Paul urges the Corinthians to cultivate the attribute of love, which is more important than the exercise of any spiritual gift (13:1–13). Love is more important than the gifts of human or heavenly speech, miracle-working faith, liberal generosity, or even the faithfulness that motivated a person to embrace martyrdom. Paul's prose soared into poetry as he beautifully described this patient, kind, humble, forgiving, and virtuous love. This kind of love exceeded all spiritual gifts, even the gifts of tongues, prophecy, and faith, because only the gift of love would endure after Jesus's return and would continue to be exercised throughout eternity.

Paul encourages the Corinthians to aspire to the gift of prophecy and demonstrated that prophecy was superior to the gift of languages in many ways (14:1–6). Evidence suggests that the Corinthians had confused the true gift of languages given at Pentecost with ecstatic utterances common in the pagan religions of Corinth (14:6–12). The gift of languages described here seems different from the gift exhibited in Acts 2 since the spoken languages were not intelligible to others or apparently even to the speaker himself without an added gift of interpretation. Because the utterances communicated no message to the hearer, they were like shrill notes from a flute that lacked a clear melody or blasts from a bugle that communicated no meaningful message to the troops (14:8–10). Whereas the Acts 2 display of languages transformed foreigners who could not communicate with one another into friends and brothers who spoke the same language, this gift of languages turned friends and brothers who spoke the same language into foreigners who could not communicate.

Paul also expresses concern that the Corinthian view of the gift of languages involved utterances that were unintelligible to the speaker himself (14:13–19). He urged the Corinthians to exercise the gift only when the utterance was intelligible to the speaker and when someone could interpret the message in an intelligible manner to the others who were present. Paul preferred five intelligible words understood by the speaker that instructed others to 10,000 words that no one understood. Paul quoted Isaiah 28:11–12 to argue that unintelligible utterances were actually a sign of divine judgment on unbelievers (14:21). Moreover, the Corinthian practice of languages might give visitors to the church the impression that believers had lost their minds. However, prophecy revealed the secret sins of the unbeliever, drove him to his knees in repentance, and displayed to him the presence of God (14:20–25).

Finally, Paul offers instructions about maintaining order in corporate worship (14:26–33a). Worship services should be organized. Those who prophesied should maintain their composure and self-control rather than attempting to work themselves into a frenzy like pagan prophets in idolatrous temples. The congregation should evaluate the prophets and silence those departing from the truth.

Paul also silences women in the church whose speech in the setting of corporate worship somehow undermined the authority of their husbands and publicly embarrassed them (14:33b–36). Possibly, some wives were questioning or challenging the legitimacy of the prophecies of their husbands or other leaders of the church, thereby seizing a role that Paul recognized as inconsistent with the wife's role of submission. Paul's general guideline for the conduct of public worship was that all things should be done "decently and in order" (14:37–40).

E. Matters Related to the Resurrection (15:1–58) Against attacks on the historicity and reality of Jesus's resurrection, Paul affirms that the gospel he received testified to Christ's death, burial, and resurrection "according to the Scriptures," that is, in fulfillment of OT prophecy (15:3–4). He also cites numerous appearances of the resurrected Jesus to various audiences (including "over five hundred brothers at one time," v. 6), many of whom were still living at the time of his writing (15:5–8), and last but not least to Paul himself on the road to Damascus.[54]

Under the influence of the dualism that pervaded much of the ancient pagan world, some Corinthians denied the doctrine of bodily resurrection (15:1–2, 9–11). This was probably accompanied by an eschatological view which said that believers experienced a spiritual resurrection at the moment they believed or were baptized. But in the Corinthians' view, Christ-followers were to expect no future bodily resurrection.

So Paul writes at length to defend the doctrine of bodily resurrection. He demonstrates that Jesus's bodily resurrection was intrinsic to the gospel (15:12–19). Denial of bodily resurrection required denial of Jesus's resurrection. And without a resurrected Jesus, the entire Christian faith collapsed. Moreover, Jesus's resurrection was the prelude to the resurrection of believers, which would occur at the Second Coming when Jesus would conquer death once and for all (15:20–28). Paul's willingness to risk his own life on an hourly basis to proclaim the gospel demonstrates the depth of his own belief in a coming bodily resurrection.

He clarifies that the body Jesus raised from the dead would be dramatically transformed and significantly different from the believer's present body (15:35–49). It would be incorruptible, glorious, powerful, and perfectly adapted for a life controlled by the Spirit in which the old battle between flesh and Spirit ceased at last. Through the dramatic transformation that Christ brought about through the resurrection, believers would have complete and final victory over both sin and death (15:50–58). The doctrine of resurrection serves as a reminder to believers that their work for the Lord is not in vain but will be rewarded in eternity.

F. Matters Related to the Relief Offering (16:1–4) Paul gives the Corinthians practical instructions about the collection of the relief offering for believers in Jerusalem. These ensured that the Corinthian offering would be ready when Paul arrived and that it would be handled with integrity.

---

[54] For a defense of the historicity of this passage, see K. R. MacGregor, "1 Corinthians 15:3b–6a, 7 and the Bodily Resurrection of Jesus," *JETS* 49 (2006): 225–34.

IV. Conclusion (16:5–24)

A. Paul's Travel Plans (16:5–12) Paul announces his intentions to remain in Ephesus until Pentecost and to then travel to Corinth by way of Macedonia. He also urges the Corinthians to treat Timothy respectfully since he would arrive in Corinth ahead of Paul.

B. Final Exhortations (16:13–18) Paul concludes the letter by urging the Corinthians to stand firm in their faith and to do all things with the love he described in chapter 13. He urges the Corinthians to acknowledge the authority of their spiritual leaders.

C. Closing (16:19–24) Paul sends greetings from those with him and pronounces a blessing on the church.

2 CORINTHIANS

I. Introduction (1:1–11)

A. Salutation (1:1–2) In addition to features typical of Paul's greetings, Paul identifies Timothy as co-sender of this letter. He also addressed the letter not only to believers in Corinth but to those scattered throughout the entire province of Achaia.

B. Prayer of Thanksgiving (1:3–7) Paul's opponents in Corinth probably argued that the great difficulties Paul experienced in his ministry proved that he did not enjoy God's blessing on his ministry. But Paul viewed his sufferings as essential to his ministry and as an authentication of his divine call. He thanked God for comforting him in his afflictions so that he could use his experiences of suffering to bring comfort to others. Thus, Paul viewed his suffering as a continuation of the suffering endured by Christ. He also anticipated sharing in Christ's comfort through resurrection.

C. Explanation of Paul's Thanksgiving (1:8–11) Paul recounts the suffering and brush with death he had experienced in Asia, which strengthened his trust in the coming resurrection. Paul knew that the God who had delivered him from death by sparing his life in Asia would ultimately deliver him from death by raising him. Paul urges the Corinthians to thank God for sparing his life.

II. Paul's Relationship with the Corinthians (1:12–2:11)

A. Paul's Pure Conduct (1:12–14) Despite attacks on Paul's ministry by his opponents, Paul's conscience was clear. In his ministry toward the Corinthians, he had conducted himself with sincerity and purity that came from God. He wrote clearly and plainly to the Corinthians because he had nothing to hide from them. He also had nothing to hide from God. Thus, he looked confidently to the day that Christ would evaluate his ministry to the Corinthians.

B. Paul's Change in Plans (1:15–22) Paul's opponents in Corinth evidently argued that he could not be trusted since he had not followed through with the travel plans he had announced earlier. Paul argues that the Corinthians must distinguish the gospel that he preached from his travel plans. The latter were subject to change, but his gospel was consistent. Paul had not vacillated in the least with regard to his message.

C. The Reason for the Change in Plans (1:23–2:4) Paul had not changed his travel plans on a mere whim. He had refrained from visiting the Corinthians to avoid hurting them and being hurt by them. He decided that he could best address the problems in Corinth by a letter rather than by another personal visit.

Something to Think About: The Difference Christ Makes

When Paul wrote his second letter to the Corinthians—which was at least his fourth letter, though it appears two have not survived—he was beleaguered and hard-pressed on many fronts. He had been beaten, stoned, shipwrecked, in danger from rivers, robbers, Jews and Gentiles, and many other sources (2 Cor 11:23–36). He had suffered "toil and hardship, many sleepless nights, hunger and thirst, [was] often without food, [was] cold, and [was] without clothing" (11:27). He also carried daily concern for the churches he had planted.

Yet was Paul discouraged? No. This is how he described his situation:

> *we are afflicted in every way but not crushed;*
> *we are perplexed but not in despair;*
> *we are persecuted but not abandoned;*
> *we are struck down but not destroyed (4:8–10)*

—and all this for the sake of Christ and his body, the church.

Why was Paul not discouraged when all those bad things were happening to him? For most of us it would take only a small fraction of the misfortunes that befell Paul to get us down. The reason Paul could keep up his spirits was that he knew he was in the center of God's will, and he suffered not for wrongs he had done but in order for God's church to be built up.

The difference, then, is just a matter of perspective. For Paul, his sufferings brought him closer to "the God of all comfort" (1:3). Persecution reinforced the notion that Paul was called to a glorious new covenant ministry far superior to the administration of the old one through Moses (chap. 3). His weaknesses reminded him that he carried the treasure of the gospel in a "clay jar," an earthly body. The frailty of it made him look forward to the time when his "earthly tent" would be transformed into a glorious heavenly existence.

When things go wrong in our lives, do we have Paul's perspective? Do we count it all joy when we face various trials, as James urged us (Jas 1:2)? Do we "do everything without grumbling and arguing," as Paul exhorted the Philippians (Phil 2:14)? If so, the peace of God, which surpasses all understanding, will guard our hearts and our minds in Christ Jesus. Then we will know the presence of the God of peace in every situation—just as Paul did (Phil 4:6,8).

D. Forgiveness to the Repentant Sinner (2:5–11) Paul demonstrates that his change in plans had produced the desired result. In response to his tearful letter, the Corinthians had disciplined the church member who led the congregation to reject Paul's apostolic authority. That member had now repented, and Paul urged the church to forgive and restore him in a display of Christian love.

III. Paul's Defense of His Ministry (2:12–7:16)

A. Paul's Ministry in Troas and Macedonia (2:12–17) God's guidance in changing Paul's travel plans was further confirmed by the fruits of his ministry in Troas where God opened a door for effective ministry. But Paul's concern to find Titus and to hear his report about the situation at Corinth quickly prompted him to travel to Macedonia.

To describe God's work in his own life, Paul uses the analogy of the Roman triumph in which a victorious general marched his conquered enemy through the streets of the capital and ultimately to his death. God had conquered his enemy, Saul of Tarsus, on the road to Damascus. Paul was now God's prisoner in chains, driven wherever God willed. Just as the defeat of the conquered enemy brought the victorious general great glory, Paul's defeat and subjection glorified God.

Paul's ministry was like the OT incense offering (see Exod 29:18). Whether Paul's ministry was an attractive scent or repulsive odor to others, it was a pleasing fragrance to God. Paul's ministry was pleasing to God because it was prompted by sincere motives, was empowered by God, and was performed in anticipation of divine judgment. Through Paul's ministry, the world had the opportunity to know God.

B. Paul's Letters of Recommendation (3:1–3) Paul's opponents evidently appealed to letters of recommendation from impressive church leaders, perhaps leaders of the church in Jerusalem, for their authority. They criticized Paul's lack of such letters. Paul countered that the Corinthian believers themselves functioned as his letters of recommendation that confirmed the legitimacy of his apostleship. Paul's contrast between letters written with ink on tablets of stone (see Exod 24:12; 31:18; 32:15; 34:1; Deut 9:10) and those written by the Spirit on the tablets of the human heart (see Ezek 11:19; 36:26–27) recalls OT descriptions of the old covenant and new covenant respectively. It paves the way for Paul's description of his role as a minister of the new covenant.

C. Paul's Competence (3:4–6) God made Paul competent to serve as a minister of the new covenant. Although the old covenant, the law, could only produce death because it demanded a righteousness from sinners that they could not achieve, the new covenant grants the Holy Spirit to believers. This Spirit imparts life to them.

D. Ministry of the New Covenant (3:7–18) Although the old covenant was glorious, the glory of the new covenant greatly surpasses that of the old. The old covenant only produced condemnation of sinners since it was incapable of making them righteous. But the new covenant actually makes sinners righteous. Moreover, the old covenant was only temporary; the new covenant is eternal.

After Moses received the old covenant, he veiled his face to prevent the Israelites from gazing on the reflection of God's glory that frightened them. That demonstrated that the old covenant only condemned sinners and sentenced them to death. Moses also veiled his face because he did not want the Israelites to see the final glimmers of glory ebb from his countenance when the glory faded.

Although the sons of Israel had a veil over their hearts that prevented them from understanding the writings of Moses, the veil was removed for those who turned to the Lord. Those who did and thus received the promises of the new covenant would be transformed by the Spirit so that the image of God is restored in them with an ever-increasing glory.

E. The Unveiled Truth (4:1–6) Because of the glorious ministry entrusted to Paul, he had no reason to adopt the underhanded techniques of his opponents. His legitimate apostleship was confirmed by his "open display of the truth." If his gospel appeared to be veiled, it was only because Satan had blinded the minds of unbelievers. The glory of God shone from the face of Jesus in the hearts of those who believed.

F. Treasure in Clay Jars (4:7–18) The great treasure of the message about Jesus Christ was housed in a suffering apostle, a vessel made of clay—weak, fragile, and vulnerable. By using so weak a vessel as Paul to bear the glorious good news, God put his great power on display. Although the gospel ministry constantly exposed the apostle to the threat of death, he pressed on, assured that God would resurrect his body and that his sufferings were only the prelude to an "absolutely incomparable eternal weight of glory."

G. The Coming Resurrection (5:1–10) Paul knew that when his body was destroyed, he would be given a new resurrection body. The indwelling Spirit was a down payment that guaranteed that final transformation and glorification. Paul's aim was to please God in all things because he knew that the deeds of all people will one day be judged by God.

H. The Ministry of Reconciliation (5:11–6:2) Driven by anticipation of this judgment and by Christian love, Paul sought to persuade others that Jesus died for them and that they died together with him so that they were liberated from their old selfish way of life to live for the crucified and resurrected Jesus.

Paul had abandoned his pre-Christian view of Jesus, which saw him as a mere human sufferer and nothing more. He now saw Christ as the One who initiated the new creation. Christ both radically transformed believers and was the One through whom God reconciled to himself those alienated from him by sin.[55]

---

[55] Translations such as the NIV render 2 Cor 5:20 this way: "We implore *you* on Christ's behalf: Be reconciled to God." But there is no equivalent for the word rendered "you" in the Greek original. Nor would it make sense for Paul to implore *the Corinthians* to be reconciled to God since, for all their failings, Paul addressed the Corinthians generally as believers (see 2 Cor 1:1). For this reason it is preferable to understand 2 Cor 5:20 as a description of Paul's message of reconciliation in his evangelistic preaching in general: "Therefore, we are ambassadors for Christ, since God is making his appeal through us. We plead on Christ's behalf, 'Be reconciled to God'" (CSB). See A. J. Köstenberger, "'We Plead on Christ's Behalf: "Be Reconciled to God"': Correcting the Common Mistranslation of 2 Corinthians 5:20," *BT* 48 (1997): 328–31, followed by J. Piper, *The Future of Justification: A Critique of N. T. Wright* (Wheaton, IL: Crossway, 2007), 178n32.

Jesus took the guilt of believers' sins upon himself and endured the penalty for those sins so that believers might be counted righteous by God. In his apostolic preaching, Paul pleads with sinners on Christ's behalf to be reconciled to God and insists that the day of salvation has come at last.

I. Catalog of Paul's Sufferings (6:3–13) Although Paul's opponents probably argued that a true apostle would be divinely protected from suffering, Paul argues that his sufferings actually confirmed the legitimacy of his apostleship. He lists the sacrifices he had endured in the fulfillment of his divine call.

J. Call to Separate from Paul's Opponents (6:14–7:1) Paul addresses the relationship of believers to unbelievers. The unbelievers in this context are Paul's opponents who have rejected his apostleship and his gospel. Paul urges the Corinthians to separate themselves from these lawless, evil, and impure persons so that they might cleanse themselves of every impurity in both flesh and spirit and be the pure sanctuary of the living God.

K. Paul's Final Defense (7:2–16) Paul affirms again his innocence in the face of the ludicrous charges against him. He urged the Corinthians to embrace him with their hearts. He expresses his joy at the report from Titus concerning the repentance of the Corinthians and the renewal of their affection for Paul. He joyfully exclaims that his complete confidence in the Corinthians has been restored.

IV. The Collection for the Believers in Jerusalem (8:1–9:15)

A. Example of the Churches in Macedonia (8:1–7) Paul turns his attention from his opponents in the church at Corinth to the collection of a relief offering for believers in Palestine, a topic he addressed briefly in 1 Corinthians 16. Paul appealed to the example of giving by the impoverished churches in Macedonia to motivate the Corinthians to give more sacrificially.

B. Examples of Christ's Sacrifice and the OT (8:8–15) Gratitude for Jesus's sacrifice should motivate the Corinthians to give sacrificially and joyfully. Paul did not want the Corinthians to relieve the believers in Jerusalem by imposing hardship on themselves. But he did believe that there should be a general equality among believers as illustrated by the gathering of the manna in the OT.

C. Administration of the Offering (8:16–24) Some of Paul's opponents apparently argued that Paul intended to misuse the relief offering the Corinthians were collecting. Paul assures the Corinthians that the funds would be used for their designated purpose. Both Titus and a representative appointed by the churches would oversee the collection and distribution of the gift "so no one will criticize us."

D. Importance of Having the Offering Ready (9:1–5) Paul had already informed the Macedonians that the Corinthians had begun their collection of the offering. This made it especially important to have the offering ready when the church representatives arrived so that the Corinthians would not appear reluctant to give.

E. Principles Motivating Generous Giving (9:6–15) The Corinthians should give generously because God would reward them in proportion to their generosity. They should give cheerfully because God loves a cheerful giver. God would provide for their needs so they could give liberally. Their generosity would not only express their gratitude to God but would also prompt the Jerusalem Christians to glorify God and pray more fervently for Gentile believers.

V. Paul's Renewed Defense of His Apostleship (10:1–13:4)

A. The Tone of Paul's Appeal (10:1–11) Paul concluded the earlier defense of his apostleship by expressing complete confidence that the Corinthians would separate from his opponents and affirm his authority and his gospel. But as Paul wrapped up chapter 9, he evidently received fresh news of problems in Corinth that prompted him to readdress the issue of his apostleship with a much sterner tone.

Paul's opponents argued that he was weak because he was willing to speak sternly only through his letters written from a distance. They evidently used this inconsistency to argue that Paul walked "in a fleshly way." Paul counters that he sought to relate to the Corinthians with the gentleness and graciousness of Christ, but he warned that he could adopt a much sterner posture if necessary.

B. Divine Commendation of Paul's Ministry (10:12–18) Unlike his opponents who sought to commend themselves with competitive comparisons, Paul appeals only to divine commendation of his ministry. God had assigned to Paul a ministry that extended to Corinth and would ultimately extend far beyond it. Paul's appeal to the effectiveness of his ministry to confirm his apostolic authority did not constitute self-commendation. He sought only to glorify God and to be commended by him.

C. Danger of the False Apostles (11:1–15) Paul was concerned that the false apostles were wooing the Corinthians from their devotion to Christ, much like an immoral man might seek to allure a bride from the one to whom she was promised. Like Satan had deceived Eve, the false apostles deceived the Corinthians by preaching another Jesus, a different spirit, and a different gospel.

The false apostles claimed to be "super-apostles" who exceeded Paul in speaking ability, knowledge, and status. Their supposed superiority was demonstrated in that they felt worthy to demand financial support of the Corinthians while Paul did not. Paul argues that he had forfeited his right to financial support to avoid being a burden to the Corinthians and in a display of his love for them. Paul warned the Corinthians that the false apostles were servants of Satan disguised as servants of righteousness.

D. Paul's Sufferings (11:16–33) Paul's opponents argued that they had a more impressive religious background than Paul did. They argued that their own protection from suffering demonstrated that God's blessing was upon them and, conversely, that the suffering Paul endured showed that he did not enjoy divine favor. Paul countered that his religious background was actually more impressive than that of his opponents. Moreover, his suffering for Christ and for the church authenticated—rather than diminished—his apostolic ministry.

E. Paul's Visions and Revelations (12:1–10) Paul's opponents also contended that they had spiritual gifts Paul lacked. In particular, they had experienced visions and revelations that Paul had not. Paul counters that he had spiritual experiences that he did not typically publicize. On one occasion he had been caught up to paradise and heard a revelation that he dared not even repeat. However, God humbled Paul by giving him a thorn in the flesh that prevented him from exalting himself. This "thorn," the identity of which is debated, left Paul weak and forced him to live in dependence on God's great power.

F. Paul's Miracles (12:11–13) Paul also reminds the Corinthians that they had personally witnessed his signs, wonders, and miracles during his stay in Corinth. These were "the signs of an apostle" that confirmed the legitimacy of Paul's apostleship.

G. Paul's Final Defense (12:14–13:4) Paul insists that neither he nor those associated with him had taken advantage of the Corinthians in any way. Although he appeared to be defending himself, his real concern was to build up the church. This required him to confront sin and the false teaching that sought to justify it. Paul warns the Corinthians that his third visit to them might serve as a third witness against them. He alerts the Corinthians that he would sternly confront their sin without leniency in display of the power of Christ.

VI. Final Exhortations (13:5–12)

Paul urges the Corinthians to examine themselves to determine whether they truly possess authentic Christian faith. He prays that the Corinthians would grow toward spiritual maturity and commands them to pursue Christian unity.

VII. Closing (13:13)

Paul's final words in his canonical correspondence with the Corinthians are a concluding blessing, commending these believers to the grace of Christ, the love of God, and the fellowship of the Holy Spirit (a trinitarian formula). This expresses the apostle's hope and confidence that only the triune God was able to do a spiritual work in this congregation.

THEOLOGY

Theological Themes

The Nature of the Resurrection Body (1 Corinthians) The most detailed discussion of the resurrection in Paul's Letters and in the entire NT is in 1 Corinthians 15. Paul wrote this chapter to combat a perverted eschatology that was influenced in part by the Platonic dualism rampant in Greco-Roman culture. Such dualism held that matter was innately evil and only the spiritual was good. At death the spirit of man was liberated from his material prison so he could become pure.

The Corinthian denial of bodily resurrection was probably also influenced by an over-realized eschatology, which teaches that believers experienced at conversion the only resurrection that they should expect: a spiritual resurrection (compare the teaching of Hymeneaus and Philetus; 2 Tim 2:16–19). Some apparently believed, perhaps based on a confused application of Jesus's teaching in Luke 20:34–38, that this spiritual resurrection made them virtually identical to angels. Consequently, they attempted to live a sexless existence (1 Cor 7:1–5), endeavored to abolish distinctions between genders (1 Cor 11:2–6), and ventured to speak in angelic languages (1 Cor 13:1).[56] Paul realized that much of the confused theology and many of the unbiblical practices of the Corinthians were ultimately related to their denial of bodily resurrection. He determined to defend the doctrine of bodily resurrection at length.

First, Paul argues that the resurrection of Jesus had been prophesied in the OT and proclaimed by eyewitnesses of Jesus's ministry. Denying the possibility of bodily resurrection entailed denial of the resurrection of Jesus and a dismissal of the reliability of OT prophecy and apostolic testimony. Such a denial reduced both the apostles and the Scripture to the status of false witnesses.

Second, Paul argues that the Christian faith was worthless without the resurrection of Jesus. Participation in Christ's resurrection effectively ends the sinner's old life and begins a new and different life. Consequently, without the resurrection of Jesus, believers are "still in [their] sins." These first two arguments combine to remind the contemporary church that the resurrection of Christ is an absolutely indispensable element of the Christian faith and that Jesus's resurrection must remain a central focus of the church's apologetic ministry.

Third, Paul argues that Jesus's resurrection was the prelude, the firstfruits, of the resurrection of all believers. He counters the over-realized eschatology of the Corinthians by arguing that the resurrection of the people of Christ occurs "afterward, at his coming" (1 Cor 15:23). He also demonstrates that Corinthian practices such as proxy baptism for the dead (however misguided) and his own willingness to risk martyrdom implied the veracity of the doctrine of bodily resurrection.[57]

After defending the doctrine of bodily resurrection, Paul devotes the second half of his discussion to a treatment of the nature of the resurrection body. His primary point was that the resurrection body will have some continuity with the body that is buried but will also be dramatically different. Both continuity and change are expressed in Paul's seed illustration. A seed dies when it is buried in the ground. This buried seed then produces a living plant that bears little resemblance to the seed itself because the plant is so much greater and more glorious than the seed. In a similar way, the future body produced by

---

[56] See especially the treatment of over-realized eschatology in Corinth in Fee, *First Epistle to the Corinthians*.

[57] See below for the argument that Paul had earlier challenged the sacramental theology that led to the practice of proxy baptism for the dead. Due to this early challenge, Paul saw no need to critique the practice here.

resurrection will bear little resemblance to the body that is buried because it so exceeds the present body in greatness and glory.

At the same time, however, verse 38 stresses continuity between the buried and the resurrected body. Paul points out that the plant that sprouts is of the same kind as the seed that is planted, that is, a wheat kernel produces a stalk of wheat, not a tomato plant. Similarly, the body that is raised corresponds to the body that is buried.[58] As Paul argued earlier, this continuity between the buried body and the resurrected one is sufficient to give eternal significance to the deeds performed by the earthly body in the here and now (1 Cor 6:13).

Paul then moves on to the question as to how an earthly body may be made fit for heavenly existence. He explained that different earthly bodies are composed of different

SIDEBAR 12.1: THE NATURE OF THE RESURRECTION BODY (1 CORINTHIANS 15)

Much confusion exists today over what Paul means by "natural body" and "spiritual body." Some interpreters assume that a spiritual body is a body composed of spirit, that is, an immaterial body.[1] However, the adjectives "natural" *(psychikos)* and "spiritual" *(pneumatikos)* are used frequently in Paul's writings and particularly in 1 Corinthians. In other contexts it is clear that they do not refer to persons or objects as made of either matter or spirit.[2] In 1 Cor 2:14–15, for example, the terms refer respectively to people influenced by human drives versus people under the control of the Spirit.

It is likely, therefore, that Paul's use in 1 Cor 15:44 is related to this earlier use. Moreover, if Paul had wished to state that the resurrected body was made or composed of spirit, he would likely have used another adjective (*pneumatinos*). In light of this evidence, Paul described the resurrection body as a "spiritual body" because it is a body completely under the control of the Holy Spirit. The resurrection body will no longer experience the war that is presently waging between flesh and Spirit described in texts such as Gal 5:16–18. Instead, the resurrection body will be perfectly suited to the Spirit's domination and control and will joyfully comply with his will. Through the resurrection, the restoration of the image of God in the believer will be complete.

[1] See the translation options suggested for this text by Johannes P. Louw and Eugene A. Nida (*Greek-English Lexicon of the New Testament Based on Semantic Domains* [New York: UBS, 1988], 1:694), who interpret the adjective *pneumatikos* here as meaning "not physical" or "not having flesh and bone" (subdomain 79.3). Thiselton (*1 Corinthians*, 1277) referred to the view as startling and astonishing, "since all the exegetical, theological, and lexicographical evidence is against it."

[2] See Michael Licona, "Paul on the Nature of the Resurrection Body," in *Buried Hope or Risen Savior: The Search for the Jesus Tomb*, ed. C. L. Quarles (Nashville: B&H, 2008), 177–98.

[58] See also Garland, *1 Corinthians*, 729.

kinds of flesh, and the point seems to be that the resurrection body can be composed of flesh particularly suited for heavenly existence. Paul also states that different heavenly bodies possess different kinds of glory, meaning that the resurrection body can display its own unique heavenly glory as well.

He then launches into an extended contrast of the earthly body versus the resurrection body. The earthly body is characterized by corruption, shame, and weakness. More importantly, it is a natural body. The resurrection body is incorruptible, glorious, powerful, and spiritual. Importantly, the "spiritual body" does not refer to an immaterial body. Instead, it references a body perfectly adapted to the Spirit's control and in which the battle between flesh and Spirit is finally ended.

Confusion about the doctrine of the resurrection impacted the Corinthians' ethics as much as their eschatology. Their rationale for deeds of the body was expressed in the slogan, "Food for the stomach and the stomach for foods, but God will do away with both of them."[59] They reasoned that since God was going to destroy the stomach in any case, it did not matter what or how much one ate. What is more, the Corinthians likely extended their reasoning to the function of the sexual organs as well. Since God was going to destroy the body, he did not care in which sexual activities the believer engaged nor how or with whom. Hence, the Corinthians reasoned that in order to be sinful, an act had to be "against his own body" (1 Cor 6:18).[60] If the material body was not raised, God must not care about that body or what one did with it. Thus, the thought train went, believers were free to engage in sexual acts with prostitutes without fear of sin. Paul dismantles this argument by contending that "God raised up the Lord and will also raise us up by his power" (1 Cor 6:14). According to Paul, the resurrection demonstrated that the body has enduring significance to God; therefore, God cared about both the body and what one did with it.[61]

Paul's arguments demonstrate that a correct biblical doctrine of the resurrection is a watershed issue. The Corinthian view of the resurrection and its impact on other areas of church life provide an interesting case study that demonstrates the relevance of doctrine to the contemporary church. Theology does not exist in a vacuum; it is not an impractical study that has no significant impact on the daily life of believers. An intrinsic relationship exists between one's doctrines and deeds, and between one's beliefs and behavior. A proper

---

[59] Although many translations punctuate the text so that the Corinthian motto ends after the word "foods," thus making the threat of divine destruction part of Paul's response, the context strongly suggests that the Corinthian motto included the words "God will do away with both of them." See A. Thiselton, "Realized Eschatology at Corinth," *NTS* 24 (1978): 517; J. Murphy-O'Connor, "Corinthian Slogans in 1 Cor. 6:12–20," *CBQ* 40 (1978): 391–96; and Collins, *First Corinthians*, 239.

[60] So correctly the CSB. See especially R. Omanson, "Acknowledging Paul's Quotation," *TBT* 43 (1992): 201–13. For an introduction to the major views, see A. C. Thiselton, *1 Corinthians*, New International Greek Testament Commentary (Grand Rapids, MI: Eerdmans, 1985), 471–73.

[61] For an incisive treatment of this passage against the backdrop of pagan views of sexuality, see P. Jones, "Paul Confronts Paganism in the Church: A Case Study of First Corinthians 15:45," *JETS* 49 (2006): 713–37.

SIDEBAR 12.2: THE OLD TESTAMENT BACKGROUND TO PAUL'S TEACHING ON THE NEW COVENANT

As early as Genesis 15, blood sacrifice functioned to seal and guarantee a covenant. When God made his covenant with Abraham, he had Abraham slaughter a heifer, a goat, and a ram, and cut them in two. This sacrifice sealed the covenant.[1] This background suggests that when Jesus spoke of the new covenant in his blood or the blood of the covenant, he meant that his death would be the sacrifice that established and sealed a new covenant between God and his people. The shedding of Jesus's blood at the initiation of the new covenant paralleled the blood that was sprinkled on the people at the giving of the old covenant in Exod 24:8.[2]

The new covenant was promised by God through OT prophets (Jer 31:31–34; Ezek 36:24–30). The old covenant was ineffective because it imposed demands on God's people but did not effect the transformation necessary for them to fulfill those demands. In this new covenant, God would transform the hearts and wills of his people so that they naturally and spontaneously fulfilled the law's righteous demands. Paul's reference "not on tablets of stone but on tablets of human hearts" (2 Cor 3:3) alludes to the law of Moses (Exod 32:15–16; 34:1–28) and the new covenant (Jer 31:33), respectively.

Paul's description of the new covenant as "not of the letter, but of the Spirit" alludes to the OT promise of the Spirit (Ezek 36:26). The indwelling Spirit compelled believers from within to fulfill the law's righteous demands. Paul's allusions to the new covenant promises of the OT suggest that his description of his apostolic ministry as "the ministry of righteousness" refers primarily—not to imputed righteousness in which the believer is justified before God through Jesus's atoning death—but to the actual righteousness of the believer that is produced by the Spirit's transforming work.

[1] In fact, in Hebrew the words "make a covenant" literally mean "cut a covenant" because the making of a covenant required the slaughter or "cutting" of a sacrificial animal.

[2] See the insightful remarks in F. Thielman, *Paul and the Law* (Downers Grove: InterVarsity, 1994), 105–6.

response to unchristian behavior in the church includes not only moral rebuke and ethical challenge, but instruction in correct doctrine as well.

The New versus the Old Covenant (2 Corinthians) Second Corinthians 3 contains the most explicit discussion of the new covenant in Paul's Letters. The term "covenant" appears nine times in Paul's Letters,[62] but explicit references to the "new covenant" and the "old covenant" appear only in the Corinthian letters. Some scholars have argued that the paucity of references to the new covenant in Paul's writings implies that covenant was not a dominant theme in his theology. However, even when explicit references to the new covenant are absent in Paul's Letters, new covenant theology is pervasive and provides the

[62] Rom 9:4; 11:27; 1 Cor 11:25; 2 Cor 3:6, 14; Gal 3:15, 17; 4:24; Eph 2:12.

foundation for many of Paul's discussions of salvation, the law, new creation, and the role of the Spirit in the believer's life.

The reference to Jesus's utterance regarding the new covenant during the Last Supper in 1 Corinthians 11:25 suggests that Paul's new covenant theology must be traced at least in part to his dependence on Jesus's teachings. Jesus described the cup as a picture of the new covenant in his blood that is poured out for believers (Matt 26:28; Mark 14:24; Luke 22:20). Although casual readers of Jesus's eucharistic statements may assume the reference to Jesus's blood implies that the new covenant consists primarily or even exclusively of atonement for sin, a close examination of biblical teachings regarding the new covenant suggests otherwise.[63]

Paul's description of the impact of the new covenant on the believer climaxes with this statement: "We all, with unveiled faces, are looking as in a mirror at the glory of the Lord and are being transformed into the same image from glory to glory; this is from the Lord who is the Spirit" (2 Cor 3:18). Thus, the result of the new covenant is not merely acquittal before God in eschatological judgment; it is also a radical transformation that restores the image of God to believers and that imparts to them an increasing measure of God's own glory by granting them God's righteous character (see Rom 8:1–4).

Paul contrasts the old and new covenants to highlight the supremacy of the new. The old covenant resulted in death and condemnation because sinners were incapable of fulfilling its demands and were thus destined to be declared guilty by God and punished; the new covenant resulted in life and righteousness. This life produced by the Spirit is probably resurrection life. The statement, "The Spirit produces life," is likely an allusion to Ezekiel 37:13. Finally, Paul pointed out that although the old covenant was being abolished, the new covenant remained forever. Although the old was temporary, the new was eternal. Thus, the glory of the new covenant so outshone the glory of the old covenant as to eclipse that glory completely.

Paul illustrates the fact that the old covenant resulted in death and condemnation by reminding his readers that after Moses received the old covenant, he had to veil his face to prevent the Israelites from being destroyed by the mere reflection of the divine glory (Exod 34:29–35), even though that glory, like the covenant it represented, was already in the process of being abolished.[64] If the Israelites feared the mere reflection of the divine glory, how much more should they fear the divine glory itself? Paul added that even though the glory of Moses's face was so intense that sinners could not look on it, that glory nonetheless was a fading glory.

The old covenant was nullified by God because it resulted in condemnation and death rather than righteousness and life. Not only did it fail to make God's people the partakers

---

[63] The new covenant definitely includes forgiveness of sins, as Matt 26:28; Jer 31:34; and Ezek 36:33 make clear.

[64] This interpretation conflicts with the one suggested by many English translations. For an extensive defense of the interpretation, see Hafemann, *2 Corinthians*, 147–49; Hughes, *2 Corinthians*, 108. For the interpretation suggested by the translations, see Belleville, *2 Corinthians*, 99.

of divine glory, it left them unable even to gaze on the divine glory. Moses veiled his face because he did not want the sons of Israel to gaze on it when God at last abolished the old covenant, an event that would be signaled by the faint and final glimmer of the reflection of the divine glory from Moses's face fading away at last.[1]

The veil that hid the abolishment of the old covenant was still over the eyes of many of Paul's contemporary Jewish hearers when they read the books of Moses. But Christ removed the veil. When a sinner turned to the Lord and came under the power of the new covenant, the veil masking the demise of the old covenant was destroyed. Then the believer was privileged to look on and reflect the glory of the Lord. Unlike Moses, the believer did not reflect a glory that was ever diminishing. He reflected an ever-increasing degree of glory as he was transformed into the image of Jesus.

The Relationship of the Christian Ordinances to Salvation Differing views regarding the meaning and purpose of Christian baptism and the Lord's Supper constitute one of the major disagreements between various Christian groups. Many theologians in the Roman Catholic and Eastern Orthodox churches, for example, insist that baptism and the Supper belong to a group of rituals called "sacraments" that, in some way, impart salvation.[2] Many evangelicals, on the other hand, insist that baptism is a symbol of the believer's union with Christ and his participation by faith in Jesus's death, burial, and resurrection (Rom 6:3–4). Baptism pictures, but does not produce, the washing away of sins; further, forgiveness of sins depends only on genuine personal faith in the crucified, resurrected, and ascended Christ.[3]

The teaching of the apostle Paul in 1 Corinthians 10:1–12 constitutes one of the clearest biblical warrants for the view that baptism and the Lord's Supper are symbolic rituals commanded by Christ rather than sacraments that actually grant salvation. Both 1 Corinthians 9:24–27 and 10:12 suggest that the Corinthians had a false view of eternal security that they presumed granted them the liberty to persist in sinful lifestyles without fear of divine retribution. Since there was nothing they could do to forfeit their salvation, they believed that they had nothing to lose by living in heinous sin.

The Corinthians flaunted their licentiousness with the libertarian motto that Paul quoted, then corrected and qualified: "Everything is permissible for me" (1 Cor 6:12; 10:23). They had relations with prostitutes, engaged in incest, participated in idol worship,

---

[1] 2 Corinthians 3:13 is a notoriously difficult verse. For the various views, compare Harris, *Second Epistle to the Corinthians,* 296–300; Hafemann, *2 Corinthians*, 142–56; and Furnish, *2 Corinthians*, 207, 232. Harris neatly distinguished the major interpretive options. After much wrestling, we independently arrived at a view identical to the interpretation he defended on p. 299.

[2] E.g., L. Ott, *Fundamentals of Catholic Dogma*, ed. J. Bastible, trans. P. Lynch, 4th ed. (Rockford, IL: Tan Books, 1960), 350–54. He further explained (pp. 328–30) that baptism may incorporate into the mystical body of Christ even those who do not believe or repent since the faith of the church can substitute for the faith of the individual and since baptism has an efficacy that is independent of the state of the recipient or of the minister.

[3] E.g., the London Confession of 1644; the Second London Confession of 1677; the Philadelphia Confession of 1742; the New Hampshire Baptist Confession of 1833; and the Baptist Faith and Message 1925, 1963, and 2000.

and turned the Lord's Supper into a pagan orgy, apparently justifying their behavior by claiming, "Once saved, always saved!" or "We can live any way we want!" The fact that Paul interjected a discussion of baptism and the Lord's Supper into his challenge of the Corinthians' distorted view of eternal security suggests that the Corinthian presumption of salvation was grounded in sacramentalism.[4]

This suspicion seems confirmed by the "baptism for the dead" mentioned in 1 Corinthians 15:29.[5] While the reference is obscure and scholars still debate the motivations for this apparently vicarious baptism for the deceased, the most plausible explanation is that the Corinthians viewed baptism as a saving sacrament.[6] Consequently, when believers died before they had an opportunity to be baptized, the church deemed it necessary that another receive baptism on behalf of the deceased believer.[7] By appealing to OT history, Paul showed that a lifestyle of heinous sinfulness was inconsistent with genuine Christianity and that participation in mere outward rituals will not protect a person from the judgment of God.[8]

In 1 Corinthians 10:1–5 Paul compared the events of the Israelites' exodus from Egypt to the ordinances of the Christian faith. He argued that the Israelites were baptized into Moses in the cloud and in the sea. When the Israelites passed through the Red Sea, they were completely surrounded by water. Water was above them in the form of the cloud. The parted waters of the Red Sea surrounded them both to the right and to the left. These

---

[4] Sacramentalism is the belief that sacraments are inherently efficacious and necessary for salvation. Older theologians distinguish sacramentalism from sacramentarianism, which is the belief that sacraments are mere visible symbols. Although modern theologians use the terms *sacramental* and *sacramentarian* interchangeably, historically one term was the opposite of the other. For a good introduction to sacramental theology with further bibliographic references, see S. Ferguson and D. Wright, eds., *New Dictionary of Theology* (Downers Grove, IL: InterVarsity, 1988), 606–8. Cf. W. Grudem, *Systematic Theology: An Introduction to Biblical Doctrine* (Grand Rapids, MI: Zondervan, 1994), 966–87.

[5] Note that Paul did not refer to "baptism for the dead" approvingly. Instead, he was using a series of rhetorical questions to show that the Corinthians' theology was inconsistent with their practice, that is, baptism for the dead was inconsistent with the Corinthians' denial of a bodily resurrection. If the dead are not raised bodily, why baptize them? Paul did not wish to support the practice of baptism for the dead. After having attacked Corinthian sacramentalism in chap. 10, Paul deemed an explicit refutation of baptism for the dead unnecessary in chap. 15 where the focus was resurrection.

[6] Some scholars have counted more than 200 different interpretations of the "baptism for the dead" throughout Christian history. See K. C. Thompson, "1 Corinthians 15, 29 and Baptism for the Dead," *Studia Evangelica*, vol. II, part I, ed. F. L. Cross, TU 87 (Berlin, Germany: Akadamie, 1964), 647.

[7] See T. R. Schreiner, *Paul: Apostle of God's Glory in Christ* (Downers Grove, IL: InterVarsity, 2001), 376; H. Conzelmann, *1 Corinthians,* G. W. MacRae, ed., trans. J. W. Leitch, Hermeneia (Philadelphia, PA: Fortress, 1975), 275. Allusions to such practices in heretical movements within the early church appear in Tertullian, *Against Marcion* 5.10; Chrysostom, *Homily on 1 Corinthians* 40.1; Epiphanius, *Against Heresies* 28; and Philaster, *Heresies* 49.

[8] Garland (*1 Corinthians*, BECNT, 452–54) objected that the context here is Christian idolatry. But Paul was clearly concerned with more than idolatry. The immediately preceding context rebuts the Corinthians' assurance that entering the Christian race guarantees receiving the prize. Paul was concerned with the Corinthians' assumed impunity of engaging in idolatry, sexual immorality, and rejection of spiritual authority—all of which were related to sacramentalism. The interpretation affirmed here is supported by a large number of commentators, including C. K. Barrett, G. Fee, B. Witherington, and C. Blomberg.

devotees to Moses were, in a sense, "immersed" as God began their deliverance, just as disciples of Christ are immersed immediately subsequent to their conversion.

Paul referred to the Israelites' partaking of the manna in Exodus 16 as eating "spiritual food." Similarly, he referred to their enjoyment of the miraculous provision of water in Exodus 17 as "spiritual drink." By calling the manna and water "spiritual food" and "spiritual drink," Paul was purposefully comparing them to the bread and wine of the Lord's Supper. The fact that he designated Christ himself as the source of the miraculous water may imply that drinking it was a form of "communion" with Christ so that the water and manna even more closely paralleled the Supper shared by Christians.

While careful reflection may suggest some other parallels between these OT events and the NT ordinances, Paul did not appeal to the OT images to teach what the ordinances do mean but rather to demonstrate what they do not. Paul was simply demonstrating that God's OT people participated in an "immersion" that was roughly analogous to Christian baptism and a spiritual meal that loosely paralleled the Lord's Supper in order to present a biblical response to sacramentalism.[9]

Despite the fact that "all" were baptized and "all" partook of the "same" spiritual meal, God was not pleased with most of the Israelites, and their bodies were scattered over the desert. Of the thousands baptized into Moses who ate the spiritual meal, only two, Joshua and Caleb, actually entered the Promised Land. Importantly, participation in "baptism" and the "spiritual meal" did not guarantee the salvation of all the Israelites. By analogy, neither did the Corinthians' observance of the NT ordinances guarantee their salvation. This, it appears, was contrary to what the Corinthians believed.[10]

Paul forcefully decried the magical view of the ordinances at Corinth. He insisted that baptism and Communion do not guarantee salvation. Appealing to familiar OT narratives, he demonstrated that all the Hebrews were baptized and took Communion, but God destroyed more than he saved. After establishing the basic premise that baptism and a spiritual meal did not guarantee salvation, Paul warned that the Corinthians had much more in common with the Hebrews than baptism and Communion. They were reenacting the same sins that brought about the destruction of the Israelites in the wilderness.[11]

Although some interpretive questions remain, the primary point of the passage is abundantly clear: baptism and the Lord's Supper do not guarantee salvation or authorize believers to live in a sinful manner, so no one should presume that the ordinances will protect

---

[9] See Conzelmann, *1 Corinthians,* 166.

[10] E.g., Schreiner, *Paul,* 376. In all likelihood, the Corinthians carried this concept into the church from their pagan background. In some pagan religions, initiation into the cult through ceremonial washings or baptisms and communion with the god through food and drink guaranteed salvation through that pagan god. See Conzelmann, *1 Corinthians,* 167. This has been disputed by D. Newton, *Deity and Diet: The Dilemma of Sacrificial Food at Corinth,* JSNTSup 169 (Sheffield: Sheffield Academic Press, 1998), 217.

[11] The grammar of vv. 7, 10 (*mē* + present imperative) suggests the Corinthians were already involved in idolatry and grumbling (see D. B. Wallace, *Greek Grammar Beyond the Basics* [Grand Rapids, MI: Zondervan, 1996], 724–25). Cf. 1 Corinthians 4; 10:14–22.

them from divine wrath.[12] If one follows the basic hermeneutical principle of interpreting more obscure texts in light of clearer ones, 1 Corinthians 10 serves as a guide for interpreting more difficult texts related to baptism and the Lord's Supper and precludes sacramental interpretations of texts such as Romans 6:1–4 or Acts 2:38.

CONTRIBUTION TO THE CANON

- Dealing with division and spiritual immaturity in the church (1 Corinthians 1–4)
- Church discipline (1 Corinthians 5; 2 Cor 2:5–11)
- The respective advantages of singleness and marriage (1 Corinthians 7)
- Principles for NT giving (1 Corinthians 9; 16:1–4; 2 Corinthians 9)
- Spiritual gifts and the supremacy of love (1 Corinthians 12–14)
- The resurrection of Christ and believers and the nature of the resurrection body (1 Corinthians 15)
- The redemptive grace of suffering and the revelation of God's power in human weakness (2 Cor 1:3–11; 4:7–18; 12:1–10)
- Paul's defense of his apostolic ministry (2 Corinthians, esp. chaps. 10–13)

STUDY QUESTIONS

1. Why are the Corinthian letters especially practical for the modern church?
2. Why is the authorship of the Corinthian letters not seriously contested in modern scholarship?
3. How many letters did Paul write to the Corinthian church? How are they designated in this chapter? How do the letters coincide with Paul's visits? List the letters and the visits together in chronological order.
4. From where did Paul receive information about the church's condition?
5. What are the three major theories concerning Paul's opponents in 2 Corinthians?
6. What is the dual purpose of 1 Corinthians, and what is the main purpose of 2 Corinthians?
7. What is the basic literary plan of 1 Corinthians?
8. Why is it so difficult to understand the literary plan of 2 Corinthians?
9. Explain the nature of the believers' resurrection bodies.
10. What is the relationship between the new and old covenants in 2 Corinthians?
11. What is the relationship between the Christian ordinances (baptism and the Lord's Supper) and salvation?
12. What are the Corinthian letters' major contributions to the canon?

---

[12] So Conzelmann, *1 Corinthians,* 167; Fee, *First Epistle to the Corinthians,* 443.

FOR FURTHER STUDY

1 Corinthians

Barrett, C. K. *A Commentary on the First Epistle to the Corinthians*. Harper New Testament Commentary. New York, NY: Harper, 1968.

Blomberg, C. *1 Corinthians*. NIV Application Commentary. Grand Rapids, MI: Zondervan, 1994.

Ciampa, R. E., and B. S. Rosner. *The First Letter to the Corinthians*. Pillar New Testament Commentary. Grand Rapids, MI: Eerdmans, 2010.

__________. "1 Corinthians." Pages 695–752 in *Commentary on the New Testament Use of the Old Testament*. Edited by G. K. Beale and D. A. Carson. Grand Rapids, MI: Baker, 2007.

Clarke, A. D. *Secular and Christian Leadership in Corinth: A Socio-Historical and Exegetical Study of 1 Corinthians 1–6*. Arbeiten zur Geschichte des antiken Judentums und des Urchristentums 18. Leiden, Netherlands: Brill, 1993.

Fee, G. D. *The First Epistle to the Corinthians*. Rev. ed. New International Commentary on the New Testament. Grand Rapids, MI: Eerdmans, 2014.

Garland, D. E. *1 Corinthians*. Baker Exegetical Commentary on the New Testament. Grand Rapids, MI: Baker, 2003.

Hays, R. B. *First Corinthians*. Interpretation. Louisville, KY: Westminster John Knox, 2011.

Litfin, D. *St. Paul's Theology of Proclamation: 1 Cor 1–4 and Greco-Roman Rhetorica*. Society for New Testament Studies Monograph Series 79. Cambridge, UK: Cambridge University Press, 1994.

Mihaila, C. *The Paul-Apollos Relationship and Paul's Stance toward Greco-Roman Rhetoric: An Exegetical and Socio-Historical Study of 1 Corinthians 1–4*. Library of New Testament Studies 402. Edinburgh, Scotland: T&T Clark, 2009.

Morris, L. *The First Epistle of Paul to the Corinthians: An Introduction and Commentary*. 2nd ed. Tyndale New Testament Commentary. Grand Rapids, MI: Eerdmans, 1985.

Taylor, M. *1 Corinthians*. New American Commentary 28. Nashville, TN: B&H Academic, 2014.

Thiselton, A. C. *The First Epistle to the Corinthians*. New International Greek Testament Commentary. Grand Rapids, MI: Eerdmans, 2013.

Winter, B. W. *Philo and Paul among the Sophists*. Society for New Testament Studies Monograph Series 96. Cambridge, UK: Cambridge University Press, 1997.

2 Corinthians

Balla, P. "2 Corinthians." Pages 753-84 in *Commentary on the New Testament Use of the Old Testament*. Edited by G. K. Beale and D. A. Carson. Grand Rapids, MI: Baker, 2007.

Barnett, P. *The Second Epistle to the Corinthians*. New International Commentary on the New Testament. Grand Rapids, MI: Eerdmans, 1997.

Belleville, L. *2 Corinthians*. IVP New Testament Commentary. Downers Grove, IL: InterVarsity, 1996.

Carson, D. A. *From Triumphalism to Maturity: An Exposition of 2 Corinthians 10–13*. Grand Rapids, MI: Baker, 1984.

Furnish, V. P. *II Corinthians*. Anchor Bible. Garden City, NY: Doubleday, 1984.

Garland, D. E. *2 Corinthians*. New American Commentary. Nashville, TN: B&H, 1999.

Guthrie, G. H. *2 Corinthians*. Baker Exegetical Commentary on the New Testament. Grand Rapids, MI: Baker Academic, 2015.

Hafemann, S. J. *2 Corinthians*. NIV Application Commentary. Grand Rapids, MI: Zondervan, 2000.

Harris, M. J. "2 Corinthians." Pages 415–545 in *The Expositor's Bible Commentary*. Rev. ed. Vol. 11: *Romans–Galatians*. Grand Rapids, MI: Zondervan, 2008.

__________. *The Second Epistle to the Corinthians*. New International Greek Testament Commentary. Grand Rapids, MI: Eerdmans, 2005.

Hughes, P. *The Second Epistle to the Corinthians*. New International Commentary on the New Testament. Grand Rapids, MI: Eerdmans, 1962.

Kruse, C. *2 Corinthians*. Tyndale New Testament Commentary. Grand Rapids, MI: Eerdmans, 1987.

Martin, R. P. *2 Corinthians*. Word Biblical Commentary 40. 2nd ed. Grand Rapids, MI: Zondervan, 2014.

Seifrid, M. A. *The Second Letter to the Corinthians*. Pillar New Testament Commentary. Grand Rapids, MI: Eerdmans, 2014.

Tasker, R. V. G. *The Second Epistle of Paul to the Corinthians: An Introduction and Commentary*. Tyndale New Testament Commentary. Grand Rapids, MI: Eerdmans, 1958.

Witherington, B., III. *Conflict and Community in Corinth: A Socio-Rhetorical Commentary on 1 and 2 Corinthians*. Grand Rapids, MI: Eerdmans, 1995.

CHAPTER 13

PAUL'S LETTER TO THE ROMANS

CORE KNOWLEDGE

Basic Knowledge: Students should know the key facts of Paul's letter to the Romans. With regard to history, students should be able to identify the book's author, date, provenance, destination, and purpose. With regard to literature, they should be able to provide a basic outline of the book and identify core elements of the book's content found in the Unit-by-Unit discussion. With regard to theology, students should be able to identify the major theological themes in the book of Romans.

Intermediate Knowledge: Students should be able to present the arguments for historical, literary, and theological conclusions. With regard to history, students should be able to discuss the evidence for Paul's authorship, date, provenance, destination, and purpose. With regard to literature, they should be able to provide a detailed outline of the book. With regard to theology, students should be able to discuss the major theological themes in the book of Romans and the ways in which they uniquely contribute to the NT canon.

Advanced Knowledge: Students should be able to interact critically with alternative proposals concerning the New Perspective on Paul as it relates to Romans and with scholars who suggest that Paul's original letter to the Romans concluded at the end of chapter 14 or 15. In addition, students should be able to assess the genre classification of Romans.

KEY FACTS

Author:	Paul
Date:	Mid- to late AD 50s
Provenance:	Greece, probably Corinth
Destination:	Several congregations in Rome
Occasion:	Preparation for Paul's journey through Rome to Spain
Purpose:	To promote Jewish-Gentile unity in the church by setting forth Paul's gospel
Theme:	The gospel proclaims that God acquits both Jews and Gentiles who believe in Jesus on the basis of Jesus's sacrificial death
Key Verses:	1:16–17; 3:21–26

INTRODUCTION

PAUL WROTE THE letter to the Romans subsequent to the letters to the Galatians, Thessalonians, and Corinthians. It is the product of Paul's mature theological thought and a thorough presentation of his gospel. In fact, the book of Romans may be the most important letter ever penned. Countless multitudes in modern times have confessed faith in Jesus as the risen Savior after being led through a series of texts known as the "Roman Road" and taken from this letter (3:23; 5:8; 6:23; 10:9). Although some of the letter's truths still baffle learned scholars, its basic assertions are clear enough to guide children as well as adults to faith in Christ. Thus, it is no surprise that this is a favorite NT book for many.

Some of the most influential theologians and Christian leaders in church history were converted to Christianity while studying this book. In the summer of 386, Aurelius Augustinus, professor of rhetoric at Milan, was weeping in the garden of his friend Alypius as he struggled with the choice over whether to embrace the Christian faith. He heard a child in a nearby house singing "*Tolle, lege*! *Tolle, lege*!" ("Take up and read! Take up and read!"). He rushed to a bench where there lay a scroll of the letter to the Romans, picked it up, began to read the powerful words of Romans 13:13–14, and immediately resolved to follow Christ. He later noted, "I wanted to read no further, nor did I need to. For instantly, as the sentence ended, there was infused in my heart something like the light of full certainty and all the gloom of doubt vanished away."[1] One commentator aptly stated, "What

[1] Augustine, *Confessions*, 8.29.

the church and the world owe to this influx of light which illuminated Augustine's mind as he read these words of Paul is something beyond our power to compute."[2]

Also while reading Romans, Martin Luther, an Augustinian monk and theology professor at the University of Wittenberg, discovered that the "righteousness of God" was not God's justice that motivated him to punish the wicked. He wrote,

> Finally by the mercy of God, as I mediated day and night, I paid attention to the context of the words, "In it the justice of God is revealed, as it is written, 'He who through faith is just shall live.'" Then I began to understand that the justice of God is that by which the just lives by a gift of God, namely by faith. This, then, is the meaning: the justice of God is revealed by the gospel, viz. the passive justice with which the merciful God justifies us by faith, as it is written, "the just one lives by faith." Here I felt that I was altogether born again and had entered paradise itself through open gates. There a totally other face of all Scripture showed itself to me.[3]

Luther's dramatic discovery would forever change the course of history by sparking the Protestant Reformation.

The book of Romans warrants detailed study both by believers and unbelievers. The latter should study it because of the amazing impact it has had on the course of world history. Believers should study it because, as seventeenth-century English Puritan Thomas Draxe claimed, Romans is "the quintessence and perfection of saving doctrine."[4] All who study the book should be prepared to be changed by it. F. F. Bruce stated it well:

> There is no saying what may happen when people begin to study the letter to the Romans. What happened to Augustine, Luther, Wesley and Barth launched great spiritual movements which have left their mark in world history. But similar things have happened, much more frequently, to very ordinary men and women as the words of this letter came home to them with power. So, let those who have read thus far be prepared for the consequences of reading farther: you have been warned![5]

HISTORY

Author

The letter to the Romans claims to have been written by Paul. Historically, NT scholarship has been so certain of Paul's authorship of the book that it has served as an important

[2] F. F. Bruce, *The Letter of Paul to the Romans: Introduction and Commentary*, rev. ed., TNTC (Grand Rapids, MI: Eerdmans, 1985), 56.

[3] M. Luther, *Luther's Works*, ed. J. Pelikan and H. Lehman (Philadelphia, PA: Fortress, 1958–86), 34:336–37.

[4] Quoted in D. J. Moo, *The Epistle to the Romans*, NICNT (Grand Rapids, MI: Eerdmans, 1996), 1.

[5] Bruce, *Romans*, 58.

standard for evaluating the claim of his authorship in other letters. C. Hodge, a commentator in the mid-nineteenth century, surveyed the strong internal and external evidence for Paul's authorship and concluded, "There is . . . no book in the Bible, and there is no ancient book in the world, of which the authenticity is more certain than that of this epistle."[6]

In the late nineteenth century, some scholars disputed Paul's authorship, but the large majority of scholars deemed their arguments unconvincing. C. E. B. Cranfield rightly commented, "The denial of Paul's authorship of Romans by such critics as E. Evanson, B. Bauer, A. D. Loman and R. Steck is now rightly relegated to a place among the curiosities of NT scholarship. Today no responsible criticism disputes its Pauline origin."[7] Half a century ago, C. H. Dodd confidently stated, "The authenticity of the Epistle to the Romans is a closed question."[8]

The question was closed because the internal evidence for Paul's authorship, particularly the language, style, and theology of the book, was so compelling. Moreover, all ancient sources who mention the author of Romans identify him as the apostle Paul. These include Marcion's *Apostolicon* as quoted by Tertullian (ca. AD 160–225), the Muratorian Canon (later second century), the canons of the Council of Laodicea (363–364), as well as the writings of Athanasius (ca. 296–373) and Amphilochus (ca. 340–395).[9] Although the matter of Paul's authorship has been settled, two related issues are worthy of discussion.

First, some have suggested that Paul's role as author needs to be redefined. Romans 16:22 demonstrates that Paul used Tertius as an amanuensis or personal secretary to pen the letter to the Romans. O. Roller showed that an author who used an amanuensis could approach his task in a number of different ways. Sometimes authors dictated their work to the amanuensis who penned the material *verbatim*, either in longhand or in shorthand in preparation for a final longhand edition. At other times, an author summarized his ideas to the amanuensis, and the latter took responsibility for the wording and form in which the ideas were expressed in writing. Roller argued that Paul used Tertius's services in the latter manner.[10] Roller's work, however, has been heavily criticized by other scholars.[11] Several lines of evidence strongly suggest that Paul dictated the letter to Tertius. The language and style of Romans is similar to Paul's other letters. If Tertius were responsible for the wording of Romans, one could only account for the high degree of similarity

---

[6] C. Hodge, *Commentary on the Epistle to the Romans* (Grand Rapids, MI: Eerdmans, 1976), 9.

[7] C. E. B. Cranfield, "Introduction and Commentary on Romans I–VIII," in *A Critical and Exegetical Commentary on the Epistle to the Romans*, ICC (Edinburgh, Scotland: T&T Clark, 1975), 1. J. Fitzmyer (*Romans: A New Translation with Introduction and Commentary*, AB [Garden City, NY: Doubleday, 1993], 40–42) also mentioned W. C. van Manen and G. Schlaeger as among scholars of the late nineteenth and early twentieth century who challenged Paul's authorship of Romans.

[8] C. H. Dodd, *The Epistle of Paul to the Romans* (London, England: Fontana Books, 1959; repr. of 1932 edition), 9.

[9] Fitzmyer, *Romans*, 40.

[10] O. Roller, *Das Formular der paulinischen Briefe: Ein Beitrag zur Lehre vom antiken Briefe* (Stuttgart, Germany: Kohlhammer, 1933), 14–23, 295–300.

[11] Fitzmyer, *Romans*, 41.

between Paul's Letters by claiming that Tertius was responsible for the wording of Paul's other missives as well. But no evidence exists that Tertius served as Paul's amanuensis for letters other than Romans. The degree of similarity between Romans and Paul's other works is best explained by assuming that Paul dictated Romans. Moreover, some features of the letter to the Romans, such as the frequent use of the conjunction "for" (*gar*), even in contexts in which it appears to be unnecessary, support the claim that Romans was a dictated text.[12] E. R. Richards, who argued that most of Paul's Letters were not transcribed *verbatim* by an amanuensis since Paul rarely had access to a secretary who knew shorthand, acknowledged the possibility that Tertius did know shorthand and that the initial draft of Romans was a product of *verbatim* dictation, since "the book of Romans demonstrates more oratorical features than Paul's other letters."[13]

A second related issue is that some scholars have questioned the unity of the letter, suggesting it is a patchwork of two or three letters or sermons.[14] Few scholars have been convinced of the validity of these theories, however. R. Hays insightfully commented, "Such theories belong in a museum of exegetical curiosities rather than in a serious discussion of the theological coherence of Romans. These hypotheses demonstrate nothing more than the inability of their authors to tolerate dialectical complexity."[15]

More serious are the suggestions that Paul's letter originally concluded at the end of chapter 14 or at the end of chapter 15 and that the final chapters were added some time later, either by Paul or someone else. These suggestions are based in part on manuscript evidence. The papyrus 𝔓[46], dating to around AD 200, places the concluding doxology (Rom 16:25–27) at the end of chapter 15. Although the manuscript contains chapter 16, some scholars believe that the placement of the doxology indicates the letter may have circulated without the final chapter. Some Greek manuscripts, old Latin manuscripts, and early manuscripts of the Vulgate and other texts place the doxology at the end of chapter 14. Tertullian (ca. AD 160–225) referred to chapter 14 as the conclusion of the letter, which may imply that chapters 15–16 were not present in the texts of Romans available to him.[16] These placements of the doxology imply that chapters 15–16 or chapter 16 alone was missing in some early manuscript traditions. This raises two possibilities. Either chapters 15–16 or chapter 16 was added to an original letter containing fourteen or fifteen chapters, or this original material was at some early point deleted from manuscripts of the letter.

---

[12] Ibid., 42; J. H. Michel, "A Phenomenon in the Text of Romans," *JTS* 39 (1938): 150–54.

[13] E. R. Richards, *Paul and First-Century Letter Writing: Secretaries, Composition and Collection* (Downers Grove, IL: InterVarsity, 2004), 59–93, esp. 92–93.

[14] W. Schmithals, *Der Römerbrief: Ein Kommentar* (Gütersloh: G. Mohn, 1988); J. Kinoshita, "Romans—Two Writings Combined: A New Interpretation of the Body of Romans," *NovT* 7 (1965): 258–77; J. C. O'Neill, *Paul's Letter to the Romans* (Harmondsworth, UK: Penguin, 1975).

[15] R. B. Hays, "Adam, Israel, Christ—the Question of Covenant in the Theology of Romans: A Response to Leander E. Keck and N. T. Wright," in *Romans*, vol. 3 of *Pauline Theology*, ed. D. M. Hay and E. E. Johnson (Minneapolis, MN: Fortress, 1995), 76.

[16] H. Gamble, *The Textual History of the Letter to the Romans: A Study in Textual and Literary Criticism*, Studies and Documents (Grand Rapids, MI: Eerdmans, 1977), 21.

K. Lake, largely followed by J. Knox, argued that the fourteen-chapter version was original and was written as a circular letter intended for numerous congregations. Later Paul added the Roman address and chapter 15 for the benefit of the congregation in Rome specifically.[17] Lake thought that chapter 16 was a letter originally addressed to the Ephesians that was later appended to Romans. T. W. Manson suggested that Paul originally addressed chapters 1–15 to the Roman congregation but later added chapter 16 and sent chapters 1–16 to the Ephesian congregation.[18]

The theory that Romans originally consisted of only fourteen chapters has been most decisively refuted by H. Gamble.[19] He pointed out that although a few late manuscripts omit the address to the Romans in 1:7, no manuscript addresses the letter to a place other than Rome. The fourteen-chapter form of the letter also broke the unity of the treatment of the strong and weak and makes the ending unusually abrupt. Gamble offered a strong defense of the Pauline authorship and original Roman destination of chapter 16.[20] He demonstrated that to claim that Romans originally ended with chapter 15 was to deprive the letter of a formal epistolary conclusion, a feature without parallel among Paul's other letters. Gamble's arguments were sufficiently persuasive to convince J. Fitzmyer, who in an earlier commentary adopted Manson's view that chapter 16 was a letter originally addressed to the Ephesians, to abandon that hypothesis and affirm the original unity of Romans 1:1–16:23.[21]

Several scholars have argued that the last chapter or two of an original sixteen-chapter letter were removed either accidentally or intentionally. F. J. A. Hort and M.-J. Lagrange suggested that the last two chapters were removed in order to make the letter more suitable for reading in public worship.[22] C. W. Emmet and H. J. Frede suggested that the final pages of an early codex were lost and that this gave some early scribes the impression that Romans originally ended at that point.[23] H. Gamble argued that the final two chapters were eliminated by some scribes out of a concern for "catholic generalization," a desire to make the letter more directly applicable to a wider audience.[24] W. Sanday and A. C. Headlam, C. E. B. Cranfield, J. D. G. Dunn, D. J. Moo, and T. R. Schreiner have adopted the view of Origen (ca. AD 185–254), who claimed that the shortest form of the letter

---

[17] K. Lake, "Shorter Form of St. Paul's Epistle to the Romans," *ExpTim* 7 (1910): 504–25; J. Knox, "A Note on the Text of Romans," *NTS* 2 (1955–56): 191–93.

[18] T. W. Manson, "St. Paul's Letter to the Romans—and Others," in *The Romans Debate*, ed. K. P. Donfried (Peabody, MA: Hendrickson, 1991), 3–15.

[19] Gamble, *Textual History*, 96–123.

[20] Ibid., 57–95.

[21] Fitzmyer, *Romans*, 60.

[22] F. J. A. Hort, "On the End of the Epistle to the Romans," in *Biblical Essays*, J. B. Lightfoot, repr. 1871 (Grand Rapids, MI: Baker, 1979), 321–51; M.-J. Lagrange, "La Vulgate latine de l'épître aux Romains et le texte grec," *RevBib* 13 (1916): 225–39.

[23] C. W. Emmet, "Romans XV and XVI: A New Theory," *ExpTim* 8 (1916): 275–88; H. J. Frede, *Altlateinische Paulus-Handschriften*, Vetus Latina: Die Reste der Altlateinischen Bibel (Freiburg im Breisgau, Austria: Herder, 1964), 152–58.

[24] Gamble, *Textual History*, 116.

was the result of removal of the two final chapters by Marcion or one of his disciples.[25] Cranfield suggested that Marcion would have objected to the final section's heavy concentration of OT quotations as well as the statements in Romans 15:4, 8 and may have wished to delete references to the church in Rome in retaliation for their rejection of him.[26]

The one difficulty with this increasingly popular explanation is the evidence that Tertullian (ca. AD 160–225) probably only knew the shorter form of the letter. Since Tertullian would not likely have knowingly accepted Marcion's mutilated version, his claim that chapter 14 constitutes the conclusion of the letter suggests that the loss of chapters 15–16 may have predated the time of Marcion (ca. AD 150). If manuscripts before his time lacked the two final chapters, the explanation of Emmet and Frede seems most plausible. The fact that the shorter form of the letter ends the book in the middle of a discussion strongly suggests that the shorter form was more likely the result of an accident than intentional editorial work by one who wished to adapt the letter for public reading or a more general audience.

Compelling evidence confirms the historic claim that the apostle Paul is the true author of all sixteen chapters of the letter to the Romans. Except for a few radical critics in the last two centuries, no one has seriously questioned Paul's authorship of it. A. M. Hunter was correct when he humorously quipped, "No one outside Bedlam [an institution for the mentally ill] seriously doubts that Romans was written by St. Paul."[27]

Date

Romans 15 contains important details about Paul's travel plans that are helpful in dating the composition of the letter. Romans 15:25 indicates that Paul was about to begin or had just begun his journey to Jerusalem to deliver the relief offering to the impoverished believers there. Romans 15:19 and 23 show that Paul viewed his work in the regions between Jerusalem and Illyricum as complete. Paul had determined to carry the gospel to Spain (Rom 15:24, 28) and would pass through Rome on his trip from Jerusalem to Western Europe. Paul had already completed the collection of the relief offering in Macedonia and Achaia (Rom 15:26).

These details readily coalesce with others in Acts 20. Acts 19:21 records that Paul resolved to pass through Macedonia and Achaia on his way to Jerusalem from Ephesus. Paul traveled through Macedonia to Greece where he stayed for three months (Acts 20:1–3). He likely stayed in Corinth during most of this period during which he wrote the letter to the Romans. While there, Paul discovered a plot had been devised by his Jewish opponents

---

[25] W. Sanday and A. C. Headlam, *A Critical and Exegetical Commentary on the Epistle to the Romans*, ICC (New York, NY: Charles Scribner's Sons, 1922), xc; Cranfield, *Introduction and Commentary on Romans I–VIII*, 8; J. D. G. Dunn, *Romans 1–8*, WBC 38A (Dallas, TX: Word, 1988), lx; Moo, *Romans*, 8; T. R. Schreiner, *Romans*, BECNT (Grand Rapids, MI: Baker, 1998), 7–8; G. Bray, *Romans*, ACCS (Downers Grove, IL: InterVarsity, 1998), 379–80. Bray provided an English translation of Origen's important quotation.

[26] Cranfield, *Romans*, 1:8.

[27] A. M. Hunter, *The Epistle to the Romans*, Torch Bible Commentaries (London, England: SCM, 1955), 12.

that led to a change in his travel plans. Rather than sailing from the port in Cenchrea near Corinth to Syria as he originally planned, he reversed course and traveled back through Macedonia, sailed to Troas, Miletus, Cos, Patara, and then to Tyre, Ptolemais, and Caesarea to travel overland to Jerusalem.

Paul's third missionary journey probably extended from around AD 51 to the winter of AD 54–55. The key factors for dating this journey are the dates of Paul's stay in Corinth during the second missionary journey that are established by the Delphi Inscription and the probable date of Paul's arrest in Jerusalem. The latter can be calculated based on the Roman tribune's statement in Acts 21:38 and the ascension of Festus. Paul probably wrote the letter to the Romans in the winter of AD 54–55.[28]

One factor may complicate this date. At the time Paul wrote this letter, Aquila and Priscilla had taken up residence in Rome again, and a church was meeting in their home. They had likely been in Rome long enough to become familiar with the situation of the churches there and to correspond with Paul about it. If Jews were not allowed to return to Rome until after the death of Claudius in the year 54, this date for the composition of Romans is probably too early to allow time for the couple to become aware of Claudius's death, move to Rome, become informed about certain situations, and correspond with Paul. But it is likely that the ban of Jews in Rome began to relax toward the end of Claudius's reign. If so, these factors do not necessarily preclude this early date.[29] After all things are considered, it is wisest to content oneself with a general estimate that Romans was written in the mid- to late AD 50s.

Provenance

Scholars have suggested a variety of cities as the probable location in which the letter to the Romans was written. Suggestions include Corinth, Athens, Ephesus, Philippi, Thessalonica, or the province of Macedonia.[30] Two views of the provenance of the letter were affirmed in the early church. Some versions of the Marcionite Prologue preserved in

---

[28] This date is supported by J. Finegan, *Handbook of Biblical Chronology: Principles of Time-Reckoning in the Ancient World and Problems of Chronology in the Bible*, rev. ed. (Peabody, MA: Hendrickson, 1998), 396–97, §687; L. Morris, *The Epistle to the Romans* (Grand Rapids, MI: Eerdmans, 1988), 6–7; and C. K. Barrett, *A Commentary on the Epistle to the Romans*, HNTC (New York, NY: Harper & Row, 1957), 5. Although J. McRay dated the composition of Romans a year earlier, during the first three months of the year AD 54 (J. McRay, *Paul: His Life and Teaching* [Grand Rapids, MI: Eerdmans, 2003], 77), most recent discussions date the letter a year or two after the date proposed here. Dates affirmed by important recent commentaries are (1) winter of AD 55–56 or AD 56–57 (Cranfield, *Romans*, 1:16); (2) "sometime in the 50s A.D., probably in the middle 50s, and most probably late 55/early 56, or late 56/early 57" (Dunn, *Romans*, xliii); (3) AD 56 (P. Stuhlmacher, *Paul's Letter to the Romans: A Commentary*, trans. S. J. Hafemann [Louisville, KY: Westminster/John Knox, 1994], 8); (4) AD 56–57 (Paul Barnett, "Why Paul Wrote Romans," *RTR* 62 [2003]: 139); (5) AD 57 (Moo, *Romans*, 3; though Moo correctly warned that constructing an absolute chronology of Paul is a "hazardous process"); (6) winter of AD 57–58 (Fitzmyer, *Romans*, 87); and (7) AD 55–58 (Schreiner, *Romans*, 5).

[29] S. Mason suggested that the expulsion of the Jews from Rome was not comprehensive in the first place. See Mason, "'For I am not ashamed of the Gospel' (Rom 1:16): The Gospel and the First Readers of Romans," in *Gospel in Paul*, ed. L. A. Jervis and P. Richardson (Sheffield, UK: Sheffield Academic Press, 1994), 254–87.

[30] Fitzmyer, *Romans*, 85.

a few manuscripts of the Vulgate assign the letter to Athens. But two early subscriptions to the letter in ancient Greek manuscripts stated that Paul wrote Romans from Corinth. An early scribe who corrected Codex Vaticanus added a subscription that reads, "It was written to the Romans from Corinth." Another scribe who corrected Codex Claromontanus added an identical subscription to that manuscript. Several later manuscripts mention a Corinthian provenance as well.[31]

The same clues suggesting Paul wrote Romans at the end of his third missionary journey while en route to Jerusalem also point to Greece as the place where the letter was composed. Paul's three months in Greece (Acts 20:3), during which he stayed in the home of Gaius (Rom 16:23), probably afforded rare opportunities for the careful and prolonged reflection necessary for such an extensive project as well as daily access to an amanuensis to assist in writing the work. Although Acts does not specifically mention where Paul primarily stayed during the three months in Greece, several considerations point to Corinth as the most likely place of composition for Romans.

First, the NT mentions four men by the name of Gaius: (1) one from Derbe (Acts 20:4); (2) one from Macedonia, who was with Paul in Ephesus (Acts 19:29); (3) one from Corinth, who was one of the few persons Paul baptized there (1 Cor 1:14); and (4) the recipient of 3 John, who is not known to be associated with Paul (3 John 1). The Gaius of Romans 16 is likely Gaius of Corinth.

Second, Paul sent greetings from Erastus, the city treasurer or manager, who is probably the person by the same name mentioned in Acts 19:22 and 2 Timothy 4:20. Paul probably mentioned Erastus here because he was a prominent member of the church of Corinth largely due to his authority in the local government. A Latin inscription that dates to the mid-first century AD and that remains in its original location in the paved square near the Corinthian theater refers to an Erastus who paved the square: "Erastus, in return for his aedileship, laid the pavement at his own expense." This Erastus who served as *aedilis coloniae* ("city treasurer") of Corinth is generally recognized to be the same person mentioned in Romans 16:23.[32]

Third, Romans 16:1–2 serves as a letter of recommendation for Phoebe to the church of Rome. According to subscriptions to Romans in some Greek manuscripts, Phoebe also served as the courier for the letter. Paul mentioned that Phoebe was "a servant [*diakonos*] of the church in Cenchreae." Cenchreae was a port city that was located only a few miles from ancient Corinth.

The question of the provenance of the letter is closely connected with the question of the integrity of the letter. If chapter 16 was not part of the original form of the letter as composed by Paul, insufficient evidence exists to determine the provenance. But strong

---

[31] MS P, MS L, and MS 337.

[32] J. Murphy-O'Connor, *St. Paul's Corinth* (Collegeville, MN: Liturgical Press, 2002), 37; J. H. Kent, *Ancient Corinth: A Guide to the Excavations* (Athens, Greece: American School of Classical Studies at Athens, 1954), 74; V. P. Furnish, "Corinth in Paul's Time: What Can Archaeology Tell Us?" *BAR* 14/3 (1988): 14–27.

evidence supports the integrity of the letter. Thus, most scholars today affirm the legitimacy of using clues from chapter 16 to pinpoint the city from which Romans was composed. Phoebe, Erastus, and Gaius were with Paul when he wrote this letter. They are associated with Corinth or a city close by. Thus, Corinth is the most likely provenance of the letter. This evidence is sufficient to allow J. D. G. Dunn to make the confident assertion that there is "scarcely any dispute" today over the Corinthian provenance.[33]

Destination

As the present title of the letter indicates, it was addressed to Christians who lived in Rome, the capital of the Roman Empire. The address of the letter in Romans 1:7, "To all who are in Rome, loved by God, called as saints," and in Romans 1:15, "who are in Rome," clearly identifies the addressees as believers living in Rome. Their home was the capital of the great Roman Empire. During Paul's lifetime, it rivaled Alexandria in Egypt, Corinth in Greece, and Antioch in Syria as the most important city of the Mediterranean world. In the first century, the city of Rome had a population of approximately one million people from every corner of the empire and the strange lands beyond its borders.[34] The population included 40,000 to 50,000 Jews.

The mixture of cultures in the city ensured that it would be home to a great variety of religions, too. Worship of the traditional Roman pantheon and the imperial cult thrived there. But many Romans gave foreign religions like Mithraism, Judaism, and Christianity a warm reception as well. When Christianity first reached Rome, the worship of Jupiter, Juno, and Minerva in the large temple on the Capitolium dominated the city.[35]

Like Corinth and other large population centers of the Mediterranean world, Rome was known for its decadence and immorality. Tacitus described Rome during the reign of Nero as "the City, where all degraded and shameful practices collect from all over and become the vogue."[36] When Paul wrote Romans, Emperor Nero had not yet begun his war of terror against the Christians of the city. Even early in his reign, however, the emperor was known to "practice every kind of obscenity." Suetonius described in vivid detail Nero's sins with mistresses and prostitutes and his unthinkable perversions. Nero raped one of Rome's Vestal Virgins. He emasculated and then publicly wed a boy named Sporus, leading Rome to joke that the world would have been a happier place if Nero's father had married such a wife. Nero also made himself the bride of his freedman Doryphorus. This was Rome's noble leader, and his conduct was undoubtedly a reflection, though perhaps an exaggerated one, of the immoral culture in which he lived.[37]

---

[33] Commentators who affirm a Corinthian provenance include Schreiner, *Romans*, 4; Moo, *Romans*, 2–3; Dunn, *Romans*, 1:xliv; and Fitzmyer, *Romans*, 85–87.

[34] M. Reasoner, "Rome and Roman Christianity," in *Dictionary of Paul and His Letters*, ed. G. F. Hawthorne, R. P. Martin, and D. G. Reid (Downers Grove, IL: InterVarsity, 1993), 850–55, esp. 851.

[35] Ibid., 851.

[36] Tacitus, *Annals* 15.44.

[37] Suetonius, *Nero* 28–29.

Christianity, nevertheless, began to thrive in Rome very early. The origins of the church in Rome are unknown. It is clear that Paul did not found the church. Perhaps it began when Jewish pilgrims from Rome traveled to Jerusalem for one of the major feasts and heard the gospel from Jesus's disciples (possibly as early as Pentecost; Acts 2:10). Perhaps the church began when Christians from other cities migrated to Rome; Christians were clearly present there by the late AD 40s. Suetonius claimed that Claudius expelled the Jews from Rome in AD 49 because of disturbances that arose in the instigation of "Chrestus." Apparently, Jews and Jewish Christians were debating whether Jesus was the Christ, and these debates led to serious conflict that upset the capital.[38]

A few Greek manuscripts, old Latin texts, and manuscripts of the Vulgate omit the phrase "in Rome."[39] But many more manuscripts that are significantly earlier include the phrase, and most scholars are confident that it belonged to the original text of the letter. The omission of the identification of the addressees in later manuscripts was probably intentional and suggests that at some point scribes edited Romans in order to make it a general letter addressed to all of Christendom.[40]

Some scholars have denied that Paul wrote to the Romans and claim that details of chapter 16 point to the church of Ephesus as the original addressee.[41] The most popular version of the Ephesian destination of the letter is by T. W. Manson, who suggested that Paul composed two versions of the letter. One version consisted of chapters 1–15 and was intended for believers at Rome; a second version added chapter 16 and was intended for Ephesus.[42] Those who supported Manson's hypothesis appealed to several features of chapter 16 to support an Ephesian address. First, one would not expect Paul to know and greet personally twenty-six people in Rome, a city he had never visited. Second, Priscilla and Aquila, to whom Paul sent greetings in Romans 16:3–4, had traveled with Paul to Ephesus (Acts 18:18–19) and established a home and a church there (1 Cor 16:19). In fact, they still lived in Ephesus toward the end of Paul's life (2 Tim 4:19). They would not likely have been present in Rome at the time Paul wrote this letter. Third, Paul sent greetings to Epainetus, who was from Asia (Rom 16:5), the province in which Ephesus was located. Fourth, the warning in Romans 16:17–20 regarding false teachers would be puzzling if the letter were sent to Rome since Paul knew little about the situation of the Roman churches and since no evidence suggests that false teachers had infiltrated the churches there.

Although these pieces of evidence initially seem compelling, their force is weakened by several considerations. Contrary to what the above argument assumes, Paul did not typically send personal greetings to individuals in letters addressed to churches with which

---

[38] See Acts 18:1–2.

[39] A few late mss. omit the address to the Romans (see Bray, *Romans*, 13–14). But an overwhelming number of mss., including many early mss. (e.g., $\mathfrak{P}^{10}$,$\mathfrak{P}^{26}$, and the major uncials), include the phrase "in Rome."

[40] So also Gamble, *Textual History*, 116; and Schreiner, *Romans*, 7.

[41] Cranfield (*Romans*, 9) showed that "the suggestion that Romans 16 is a fragment of a Pauline Letter to the church in Ephesus was made as early as 1829 by D. Schulz, in *TSK* 2 (1829), pp. 609ff."

[42] Manson, "St. Paul's Letter to the Romans—and Others," 3–15.

he had a personal relationship. A survey of Paul's Letters shows that Paul sent greetings to named individuals only in Romans and Colossians, both of which were cities Paul had never visited. Apparently he did not wish to single out individuals in churches that he had established or visited, since this might be taken to imply that he loved some there more than others. However, greeting individuals that he knew in a church that he had never visited was a strategic way to build rapport and establish a connection with the congregation.

Moreover, Aquila and Priscilla were among the Jewish Christians expelled from Rome by Claudius in the year AD 49 (Acts 18:2).[43] They later lived in Corinth and Ephesus but may have maintained a residence in Rome during this time in hopes of returning to Rome after the expulsion. Since they owned a home in Ephesus that was large enough to accommodate a church, they were probably persons of some means. Rome may have remained the central hub of their business.

That Epaenetus was Paul's first convert in Asia would likely have been well-known in churches throughout Asia and thus unnecessary to mention in a letter to Ephesus. But Roman Christians might not have been aware of Epaenetus's historic conversion, and the comment would have been of enormous interest to them. The warning in Romans 16:17–20 is probably directed against a potential danger rather than a known one, and the presence of close friends like Aquila and Priscilla in the church suggests that Paul may have known more about the situation of the Roman churches than is generally assumed. He was almost certainly aware of tensions between Jewish and Gentile believers (Romans 14–15), and information about this discord likely came from his associates in Rome.

Overall, the details of Romans 16 more strongly support an address to Rome than to Ephesus. The Ephesian hypothesis should be laid to rest.[44] The address to the Romans that is affirmed in the major uncials and oldest papyri is clearly original. Unlike 1 Corinthians, 2 Corinthians, 1 Thessalonians, and 2 Thessalonians, Romans is addressed generally to all believers throughout the city of Rome rather than to a single congregation. Paul was aware that multiple Christian congregations existed in the city. He later mentioned a church that met in the home of Aquila and Priscilla (Rom 16:5), a group of Christians associated with Asyncritus, Phlegon, Hermes, Patrobas, and Hermas (Rom 16:14), and another group associated with Philologus, Julia, Nereus, and his sister (Rom 16:15). The Christians in the households of Aristobulus and Narcissus may also have met together as a group for worship in these homes. If so, Paul mentioned five congregations of believers in Rome. Other congregations unknown to Paul likely existed there as well.[45]

---

[43] On the event and its probable date, see Suetonius, *Life of Claudius*, 25; and Orosius, *Seven Books of History Against the Pagans*, trans. I. W. Raymond (New York, NY: Columbia University Press, 1936), 332.

[44] In addition to the standard commentaries, see B. N. Kaye, "To the Romans and Others: Revisited," *NovT* 18 (1976): 37–77.

[45] See esp. Dunn, *Romans*, 1:lii.

Scholars debate whether the churches in Rome were predominantly Jewish or Gentile. J. Munck argued that nearly all Christians in Rome were Gentiles.[46] W. Wiefel argued that the churches of Rome were predominantly Jewish.[47] In favor of a Gentile composition is Paul's discussion in Romans 1:5–6 of his witness among Gentiles, and 1:15 clearly includes the addressees in that group. Paul directly addressed Gentiles using the second person in Romans 11:13 and 31 in a rebuke of Gentile pride over their election by God. Paul's discussion of the strong and the weak in Romans 14:1–15:13 is primarily addressed to the strong, almost certainly Gentile believers who had a stronger sense of liberty in Christ than some of their brothers from a Jewish background.

On the other hand, Paul addressed many issues in the letter that would have been of concern primarily to Jewish Christians, such as the role of the law in salvation and the place of Israel in God's redemptive plan. Moreover, Paul's rebuke of Jewish pride and hypocritical self-righteousness in Romans 2 frequently uses the second person and implies that Paul was directly addressing people of Jewish origin. In texts such as Romans 6:14; 7:1, 4, he closely associated his readers with the Mosaic law. He also referred to Abraham as "our forefather according to the flesh" (Rom 4:1) in a manner implying that his original readers included biological descendants of Abraham. These features demonstrate that Christianity in Rome was of mixed composition, including believers from both Jewish and Gentile backgrounds.

The discussion of the occasion of the letter to the Romans in the next section suggests that the Roman churches were dominated by Gentiles during the five years or so preceding the letter. However, a sudden influx of Jewish believers into the Christian community caused such conflict to erupt that it threatened the unity of God's people in Rome. The historical circumstances suggest that the church was of mixed composition, predominantly Gentile but with a growing number of Jewish believers.[48]

Occasion

Paul wrote Romans shortly before his final recorded journey to Jerusalem (Rom 15:25–29). He wanted to travel to Jerusalem in order to present the money collected by the Gentile churches in Macedonia and Achaia to help meet the needs of poor Christians in Jerusalem (15:26). The relief offering was partially motivated by a desire to promote good relations between Jewish Christian and Gentile Christian churches. This concern is related to some of the topics Paul addressed in Romans 9–11 and 14–15.

The apostle planned to travel from Jerusalem through Rome to Spain due to his longing to "preach the gospel where Christ was not known" (Rom 15:20 NIV). This information fits well with Luke's description of Paul's travels at the close of the third missionary

---

[46] J. Munck, *Paul and the Salvation of Mankind* (Richmond, VA: J. Knox, 1959), 201.

[47] W. Wiefel, "The Jewish Community in Ancient Rome and the Origins of Roman Christianity," in *The Romans Debate*, 85–101.

[48] This is the view of most modern commentators (e.g., Moo, *Romans*, 12–13).

journey (Acts 19:21; 20:16). Acts 20:3 shows that Paul spent three months in Greece during his trip from Macedonia and Achaia to Jerusalem. Paul wrote Romans at this time, and it served as a formal introduction of Paul and his gospel to the church in Rome in preparation for his eventual visit.

These circumstances are clear and based on explicit data in Romans and Acts. Additional clues regarding the occasion of the letter can be gleaned from extrabiblical sources. Several sources document Claudius's expulsion of the Jews from Rome around 49. After Jewish Christians evacuated Rome, the leadership of the Roman churches fell entirely to Gentile believers. Gentile congregations developed largely without Jewish influence and thus without sensitivity to Jewish scruples. Some Jews likely began to return to Rome during the final years of Claudius's reign, coming in far greater numbers after Claudius's death when his decree officially expired. They returned to find that the very churches they formerly dominated were now controlled and led by Gentile Christians. They likely felt that Gentile Christian leaders were not appropriately appreciative of and sensitive to their own rich Jewish heritage. Gentile Christians, meanwhile, resented pressure from their Jewish brothers and sisters to adopt Jewish ways and restrict their freedom in Christ. These factors in the historical setting help explain why much of the letter to the Romans addresses issues of importance to the relationship between Jewish and Gentile Christians.[49]

Tacitus recorded a description of the political situation in Rome that may be helpful in explaining some features of this letter. He described political unrest related to the tax burden born by people in the empire.[50] The people of the empire had repeatedly demanded that Nero take actions to prevent greedy revenue collectors from imposing higher taxes on them than the law allowed. Nero considered repealing all custom taxes since these were more commonly abused. The Senate discouraged such an action since it might encourage the people to protest even income taxes without which the empire could not survive. Thus, instead of abolishing the abused taxes, Nero ordered that the laws regarding these taxes be published throughout the empire; thus, people could be properly informed of the amounts due and protest and prosecute excessive taxation. He also ordered judicial officials to give priority to cases in which subjects claimed that they were abused by tax collectors. He repealed the 2 percent and 2.5 percent duties since these were the most notorious examples of taxes that he knew collectors had cleverly invented as a cover for their extortion. These events described by Tacitus occurred in AD 58. The growing unrest throughout the empire concerning the matter of taxation in the years prior to that time is probably the reason Paul concluded his discussion of the Christian's responsibility to the state with a command to pay taxes (Rom 13:6–7).

---

[49] So also Schreiner, *Romans*, 13–14; Stuhlmacher, *Paul's Letter to the Romans*, 6–8; Moo, *Romans*, 4–5; Dunn, *Romans*, 1:liii–liv.

[50] For a helpful English translation, see M. Grant, *Tacitus: The Annals of Imperial Rome* (London, England: Penguin, 1996), 308–9.

Purpose

Some interpreters have felt that Romans is a theological treatise or a compendium of Christian doctrine. The earliest comment on the purpose of Romans appears in the Muratorian Canon, which probably dates to the later second century:

> As for the Epistles of Paul, they themselves make clear to those desiring to understand, which ones [they are], from what place, or for what reason they were sent. First of all, to the Corinthians, prohibiting their heretical schisms; next, to the Galatians, against circumcision; then to the Romans he wrote at length, explaining the order (or, plan) of the Scriptures, and also that Christ is their principle (or, main theme).[51]

Although the author of the fragment viewed 1 Corinthians and Galatians as occasional documents that addressed specific problems in particular congregations, he viewed Romans as a summary of Christocentric biblical doctrine. The view of Romans as a compendium of Christian doctrine was later advanced by Philip Melanchthon in his *Loci Communes* (1521) and his commentary on Romans (1532). The book of Romans has generally been viewed as a summary of Christian theology ever since.[52]

Although Romans is an intensely theological letter, most scholars today see it not as a general treatise but as an occasional document, that is, a letter written to address the particular needs of a specific group of churches. They point out that the letter does not expound some important aspects of Paul's theology, such as his doctrine of the Lord's Supper (1 Cor 11:17–24), the Second Coming (1 Thess 4:13–5:11), or the doctrine of the church that is explicated in far greater detail in Ephesians and 1 Corinthians. This silence is indeed difficult to explain if the letter were written as a general theological treatise.

Moreover, Paul also gives significant attention in this letter to matters such as the wrath of God (Rom 1:18–32) and the Jews' rejection of Jesus (Romans 9–11), which he did not discuss extensively in his other letters. Several aspects of Romans, such as the discussion about how believers should relate to the government (Rom 13:1–7) and the discussion of the weak and the strong (Rom 14:1–15:6), seem to reflect the specific struggles faced by this particular congregation. Thus, Romans should not be viewed as a textbook of systematic theology written to total strangers.

An examination of the entirety of the letter demonstrates that Paul had several reasons for writing this book. First, in fulfillment of his priestly duty of proclaiming the gospel to the Gentiles (Rom 15:14–16), he wanted to remind the Roman believers of some of the gospel's fundamental truths. Paul was well aware of the many ways in which his message might be misunderstood or misapplied. He therefore wrote to clarify important aspects of his message to those who had heard about him and his gospel only indirectly. Moreover,

---

[51] This translation is from B. Metzger, *The Canon of the New Testament* (Oxford, UK: Clarendon, 1987), 305–7.

[52] See Stuhlmacher, *Romans*, 2.

Romans 16:17–20 shows that Paul was concerned about false teachers infiltrating the Roman church.[53] In the face of this danger, a careful articulation of the essentials of Paul's gospel was needed.

Second, the apostle wanted to address several of the problems faced by the Roman church. In particular, he desired to call the churches to unity. He was aware that some of the differences in outlook between the Jewish and Gentile Christians had produced disunity in the congregations at Rome. These differences emerged in arguments about obligations to OT dietary laws and the observance of Jewish holy days. Perhaps at the heart of the debate was the larger question: Did the inclusion of the Gentiles among the people of God mean that God had abandoned his promises to Israel (see esp. Romans 9–11)? In dealing with this question, Paul stresses the equality between Jewish and Gentile believers. He insisted that Jews and Gentiles alike were condemned as sinners (Rom 2:9; 3:9, 23) and that both Jews and Gentiles were saved by grace through faith apart from the works of the law (Rom 3:22, 28–30).[54] He explains the different roles for Jews and Gentiles during different phases of God's redemptive plan (Romans 9–11). He also directly addresses issues such as diet and calendar observances that were apparently the immediate sources of tension between Jewish and Gentile believers (Rom 14:1–15:13).

Third, Paul wanted to formally introduce himself to the Roman churches and solicit their support for his Spanish mission. He had fully proclaimed the gospel through the eastern half of the Roman Empire, "from Jerusalem all the way around to Illyricum" (Rom 15:19). Now he was planning to introduce the gospel in Spain, which lay in the far west of the empire. After Paul left Jerusalem, he would travel to Spain by way of Rome. Paul hoped to receive a material gift from the Roman church to assist him in his new missionary endeavors (Rom 15: 21).

Most scholars affirm these three purposes for the letter at least to some degree. The disagreement among scholars that has led to what J. D. G. Dunn aptly described as "a long and seemingly unending debate" over the purpose of the letter is generally a disagreement over which of the several purposes was primary for Paul. Many commentators claim that the second purpose, that is, encouraging unity between Jewish and Gentile believers, was Paul's main goal. But, they point out, a careful articulation of the gospel was necessary to promote that unity. Paul recognized that the key to unity between all believers was a clear understanding of the Christian message. Other scholars suggest that of the three purposes

---

[53] Scholars debate whether opponents had already infiltrated the churches of Rome or Paul simply assumed they would eventually do so based on his previous experience. Stuhlmacher (*Romans*, 253) represents the former view, while Schreiner (*Romans*, 21) argued that the verses Stuhlmacher believed were explicitly directed against opponents (Rom 3:8; 16:17–20): "Do not relate to actual opponents in Rome but to the enemies Paul faced in the east and whom he feared might reach Rome. He knew that doubts and questions had surfaced in the Roman congregations about his gospel, but he did not yet face full-fledged opponents."

[54] Schreiner (*Romans*, 19) states, "The majority position is now that Paul wrote to resolve the disunity between Jews and Gentiles," citing Marxsen, Minear, Bartsch, W. Campbell, Käsemann, Dunn, Russell, Wedderburn, Crafton, Reasoner, Wiefel, Donfried, Bruce, P. Lampe, Stuhlmacher, Walters, Wright, and Guerra as representatives of this view.

Paul's desire to introduce his gospel to the churches of Rome seems central. Arguments over which purpose was primary will not likely be resolved. The wisest conclusion seems to be to affirm all three purposes.

Two cautions should be heeded in the study of the purpose of Romans. First, the multiple reasons for the book are clearly interrelated. To affirm one and neglect another leads to an impoverished view of the letter. Second, efforts to identify a primary versus a secondary purpose often degenerate into discussions of a sociological or psychological nature that involve a great deal of speculation. M. Seifrid's attempt to integrate the accepted views regarding the purpose of Romans is commendable: Paul wrote to unite the churches of Rome under his gospel.[55]

On the other hand, interpreters must take care not to confuse Paul's purpose with the means by which he sought to accomplish it. Identifying a primary purpose for the book is not the same as identifying the book's central theme. Interpreters of Romans have long searched for a single theme that unifies and gives continuity to the letter. During the Protestant Reformation, the tendency was to focus on the first major section of the book and single out "justification by faith" as the theme of the letter.[56] Later interpreters argued that Romans 6–8 was the heart of the letter and the central theme was the believer's union with Christ and the work of the Spirit.[57] Others replied that Romans 9–11 was the centerpiece of the letter and that the real focus was the relationship of Jews and Gentiles in God's saving plan.[58] Still others insisted that the practical section, Romans 12–15, expressed the central theme of the book.[59] Paul's main intention, then, was to call the church to unity and to promote harmony between Jewish and Gentile Christians. Each of these views tended to emphasize one section of the letter and neglect the rest.

Recent scholars generally agree that the one theme that may encapsulate the entire book is "the righteousness of God." Unfortunately, the precise meaning of this phrase

---

[55] M. A. Seifrid, *Justification by Faith: The Origin and Development of a Central Pauline Theme*, NovTSup (Leiden, Netherlands: Brill, 1992), 182–210.

[56] Bruce (*Letter of Paul to the Romans*, 38–39) correctly observes, "Yet, crucial as the justification of sinners by faith alone is to the Pauline gospel, it does not exhaust that gospel. It is not, as Albert Schweitzer called it, 'a subsidiary crater,' but in itself it is not the centre of Paul's teaching." Moo (*Romans*, 29) writes, "There is too much in Romans that cannot, without distortion, be subsumed under the heading of justification: the assurance and hope of the believers (chaps. 5 and 8); freedom from sin and the law (chaps. 6 and 7); God's purpose for Israel (chaps. 9–11); and the life of obedience (chaps. 12–15). To be sure, we can relate all of these to justification, as its fruits, or implications, or requirements; and Paul makes this connection himself at several points (see 5:1, 9; 8:33; see 9:30–10:8). But he does not do so often enough to make us think that justification, or 'the righteousness of God,' is his constant reference point."

[57] E.g., A. Schweitzer, *The Mysticism of Paul the Apostle* (London, England: A&C Black, 1931), 205–26; and W. Wrede, *Paul* (London, England: P. Green, 1907), 123–25.

[58] This was the view of F. C. Baur and F. J. A. Hort. See the summary of their views in Sanday and Headlam, *Epistle to the Romans*, xlv, li.

[59] E.g., W. S. Campbell, "Why Did Paul Write Romans?" *ExpTim* 85 (1974): 264–69; and K. Donfried, "A Short Note on Romans 16," in *The Romans Debate*, 46–48.

is still disputed. However, by any definition, the concept of "the righteousness of God" seems a bit too narrow to be identified as the central theme of the entire book.[60]

A better approach recognizes "the gospel" or "the gospel of the righteousness of God" as the theme of the whole letter.[61] Several pieces of evidence support this claim. The word "gospel" and related terms appear frequently in the introduction and conclusion to the letter (Rom 1:1, 9, 16; 15:16, 19; 16:25). The word is also most prominent when Paul announces the theme of the book in Romans 1:16–17. Romans 1:16–15:13, then, explains the major facets of Paul's gospel in great detail.

Paul's intention to introduce his good news to churches about which he knew fairly little resulted in a letter that was more general and directly applicable to the Christian church at large and throughout all time. Indeed, one recent commentator has suggested that Melanchthon's classification of the letter as a "treatise" has been too readily dismissed:

> These features show that the main body of Romans is what we may call a "treatise," or "tractate." It addresses key theological issues against the backdrop of middle first-century Christianity rather than within the context of specific local problems. Nevertheless, Romans is no timeless treatise. We must not forget that Romans as a whole is a letter, written on a specific occasion, to a specific community. Romans, then, is a tractate letter and has at its heart a general theological argument, or series of arguments.[62]

Several other scholars who affirm that Romans is an occasional document agree with D. Moo in emphasizing the theological character of the letter. T. W. Manson portrayed Romans as a manifesto of Paul's theology that sums up the apostle's response to the theological controversies he had faced in Galatia, Corinth, and Philippi.[63] Similarly, Bornkamm described Romans as Paul's "last will and testament" through which he bequeathed a summary of his theology to the Roman churches.[64] P. Barnett asserted that "Melanchthon was more or less right in saying that Romans is 'a compendium of Christian doctrine.'"[65]

The general character of the message of Romans makes it directly applicable and particularly helpful to modern believers. D. Moo stated,

---

[60] Those who view the righteousness of God as the central theme of the letter include Schreiner, *Romans*, 25–27 (as is evident from his outline); Stuhlmacher, *Romans*, 10; E. Käsemann, *Commentary on Romans*, trans. G. Bromiley (Grand Rapids, MI: Eerdmans, 1980); U. Wilckens, *Der Brief an die Römer*, EKKNT (Zürich, Germany: Benziger, 1978–82); and A. Schlatter, *Romans: The Righteousness of God*, trans. S. Schatzmann (Peabody, MA: Hendrickson, 1995).

[61] Moo, *Romans*, 27–30.

[62] Ibid., 14.

[63] Manson, "St. Paul's Letter to the Romans—and Others," 14–15.

[64] G. Bornkamm, "The Letter to the Romans as Paul's Last Will and Testament," in *The Romans Debate*, 16–28.

[65] Barnett, "Why Paul Wrote Romans," 141.

> We moderns must beware the tendency to overhistoricize: to focus so much on specific local and personal situations that we miss the larger theological and philosophical concerns of the biblical authors. That Paul was dealing in Romans with immediate concerns in the early church we do not doubt. But, especially in Romans, these issues are ultimately those of the church—and the world—of all ages: the continuity of God's plan of salvation, the sin and need of human beings, God's provision for our sin problem in Christ, the means to a life of holiness, and security in the face of suffering and death.

LITERATURE

Literary Plan

Recent scholars have made numerous attempts to classify the genre of Romans. Several have been convinced by K. P. Donfried's classification of Romans as a "letter-essay."[66] The letter-essay has an epistolary introduction that includes a statement of the letter's theme, a reference to the need or request that inspired the letter, the writer's response to the request with a statement of purpose, and a description of the method of presentation of the material. The transition from this introduction to the body was marked by a specific phrase (*prōton men oun*). The body of the letter was "almost rigidly cast in the objective third person or editorial first person."[67] The arrangement of the body of the letter is flexible. The closings of the letter-essays reveal no consistent pattern.

Although Stirewalt is correct that his category has certain advantages over older terms such as "literary epistle" or *Lehrbrief* (German for "didactic letter"), this new classification offers no new insights into the interpretation of Romans. It tells interpreters nothing that they could not have already inferred from a close examination of the book.

Other scholars have suggested that Romans is best classified according to accepted categories of rhetoric. R. Jewett argued that rhetorical criticism of Romans "allows us to grasp the structure of the argument within the context of the peculiar purpose of the letter, which stands in a communicative context with a specific audience. This may allow us to counterbalance the tendency to follow the argument primarily from the viewpoint of contemporary theology."[68] Several have classified Romans as epideictic or demonstrative

---

[66] This category was suggested and defined by M. L. Stirewalt Jr., "The Form and Function of the Greek Letter-Essay," in *The Romans Debate*, 147–71. Stirewalt pointed to fifteen different documents as examples of the letter-essay. These included the letters of Epicurus, the letters of Dionysius of Halicarnassus, selections of Plutarch's works, 2 Maccabees, and the Martyrdom of Polycarp. Stirewalt did not discuss the classification of Romans. However, the classification of Romans as a "letter-essay" was adopted by K. P. Donfried, "False Presuppositions in the Study of Romans," in *The Romans Debate*, 122–25; and Fitzmyer, *Romans*, 68–69 (though Fitzmyer preferred the term "essay-letter," which better stressed the document's "missive character").

[67] Stirewalt, "Greek Letter-Essay," 163.

[68] R. Jewett, "Following the Argument of Romans," in *The Romans Debate*, 266.

rhetoric, a genre in which a writer reinforces values shared with his audience.[69] Others classify the letter as protreptic rhetoric, a genre in which an author attempts to persuade his audience. D. Aune classified Romans as a "speech of exhortation" (*logos protreptikos*) set in an epistolary framework. In this kind of speech, a philosopher sought to win converts and attract young people to a particular way of life. Similarly, in Romans Paul addressed Roman Christians "to convince them (or remind them) of the truth of *his* version of the gospel (Rom 2:16; see 16:25; Gal 1:6–9; 2:1) and to encourage a commitment to the kind of lifestyle which Paul considered consistent with his gospel."[70] If rhetorical classifications are appropriate for Romans, this evidence may best support classification of the book as protreptic (persuasive) rhetoric.

A growing number of scholars argue that although rhetorical classification can be helpful, no classification fits the letter without significant modification. J. D. G. Dunn observed,

> The key fact here is that the distinctiveness of the letter far outweighs the significance of its conformity with current literary or rhetorical custom. Parallels show chiefly how others wrote at that period; they provide no prescription for Paul's practice and no clear criterion by which to assess Paul; and the fact that no particular suggestion has commanded widespread assent in the current discussion suggests that Paul's style was as much or more eclectic and instinctive than conventional and conformist.[71]

Indeed, it is unlikely that Paul arranged his letter according to rhetorical conventions. Cranfield was correct when he noted, "Once having decided to attempt to compose a summary of the gospel as he had come to understand it, he allowed the inner logic of the gospel as he understood it itself to determine, at any rate for the most part, the structure and contents of what was now going to be the main body of his letter."[72]

Several objective features of the letter aid interpreters in understanding its intended structure, and most scholars agree on its major divisions. The letter opens with an epistolary prescript (1:1–7), which summarizes Paul's gospel, followed by an expression of thanksgiving. Next is the proem containing preliminary comments (1:10–15) that are followed

---

[69] W. Wuellner, "Paul's Rhetoric of Argumentation in Romans: An Alternative to the Donfried-Karris Debate over Romans," in *The Romans Debate*, 128–46, esp. 139. Cf. R. Jewett, "Following the Argument of Romans," in *The Romans Debate*, 266; G. A. Kennedy, *New Testament Interpretation Through Rhetorical Criticism* (Chapel Hill, NC: University of North Carolina, 1984), 152–56; M. L. Reid, "A Rhetorical Analysis of Romans 1:1–5:21 with Attention Given to the Rhetorical Function of 5:1–21," *Perspectives in Religious Studies* 19 (1992): 255–72; B. Byrne, *Romans*, SacPag (Collegeville, PA: Glazier, 1996), 15–18.

[70] D. Aune, "Romans as a Logos Protreptikos," in *The Romans Debate*, 278–96, esp. 278–79. The classification of Romans as protreptic rhetoric has been argued at greatest length by A. J. Guerra, *Romans and the Apologetic Tradition: The Purpose, Genre, and Audience of Paul's Letter*, SNTSMS 81 (Cambridge, UK: University Press, 1995).

[71] Dunn, *Romans*, 1:lix.

[72] Cranfield, *Romans*, 818.

by the programmatic statement that summarizes the message of the letter (1:16–17). This statement begins the doctrinal section of the letter (1:16–11:36), which is followed by a hortatory or ethical section (12:1–15:13). Paul included a summary of his travel plans and some requests for prayer (15:14–33), following them with a letter of recommendation for Phoebe and greetings to various groups and individuals in Rome (16:1–23). The letter concludes with a doxology (16:25–27).[73]

The major debate regarding the structure of Romans concerns the divisions of the doctrinal section. Scholars generally agree that the major divisions are chapters 1–8 and 9–16. They further agree that 1:16–4:25 and 6:1–8:39 constitute major units in the first division, but there is a lot of disagreement on the placement of chapter 5. Many scholars see it as forming the conclusion of 1:16–4:25, but a slight majority thinks it introduces 6:1–8:39.[74] The evidence for 5:1–8:39 as a major section of the letter is based on both the topic of the chapters and important structural markers. After an introductory paragraph (5:1–11), the section addresses three important freedoms for believers: freedom from sin and death (5:12–21), freedom from sin and self (chap. 6), and freedom from the law (chap. 7). The discussion of these areas of freedom naturally flows into a discussion of life in the Spirit. Moreover, the section divisions in chapters 5–8 are marked by a concluding formula that appears at the end of chapters 5, 6, 7, and 8 with only slight variation: "through [*dia*] Jesus Christ our Lord" (5:21; 7:23) and "in [*en*] Christ Jesus our Lord" (6:23; 8:39).[75]

OUTLINE

I. INTRODUCTION (1:1–15)
 A. Jesus Christ Is the Focus of the Gospel, and Paul Is Qualified to Proclaim It (1:1–7).
 B. Paul Thanks God for the Roman Christians and Expresses His Love for Them (1:8–15).
II. THEME: THE GOSPEL REVEALS GOD'S POWER FOR SALVATION AND HIS RIGHTEOUSNESS (1:16–17)
III. THE PROMISE OF THE GOSPEL: JUSTIFICATION BY FAITH IN CHRIST (1:18–4:25)
 A. Man's Need for Justification (1:18–3:20)
  1. All Gentiles Are Sinners (1:18–32).
  2. All Jews Are Sinners (2:1–3:8).
  3. All People Are Sinners (3:9–20).
 B. God's Gift of Justification (3:21–4:25)
  1. God Provides Justification through Christ by Faith (3:21–26).
  2. Justification of Both Jews and Gentiles Is Based on Faith Rather than Works (3:27–4:25).

---

[73] Verse 24 is not in the oldest and best manuscripts of the letter. For a more detailed analysis of the structure of the book that takes into consideration objective features such as word repetition, shifts in person, the use of diatribe, and so on, see Aune, "Romans as a Logos Protreptikos," 290–96.

[74] For a convenient list of scholars supporting each view of the structure, see Fitzmyer, *Romans*, 96–97.

[75] See the more thorough treatment of the structure in Fitzmyer, *Romans*, 96–98; Cranfield, *Romans*, 1:252–54.

IV. THE BENEFITS CONFERRED BY THE GOSPEL (5:1–8:39)
   A. The Believer Has Peace, Righteousness, and Joy (5:1–11).
   B. The Believer Escapes the Consequences of Adam's Transgression, the Reign of Sin in Death (5:12–21).
   C. The Believer Is Liberated from Slavery to Sin (6:1–23).
   D. The Believer Is Liberated from Bondage to the Law (7:1–25).
   E. The Believer Lives a Righteous Life through the Power of the Spirit (8:1–17).
   F. The Believer Will Ultimately Enjoy Complete Victory over Corruption (8:18–39).

V. ISRAEL'S REJECTION OF THE GOSPEL (9:1–11:36)
   A. Israel Has Rejected Christ (9:1–5).
   B. Israel's Temporary Rejection of Christ Is Consistent with God's Eternal Plan (9:6–29).
   C. Israel's Temporary Rejection of Christ Is Due to Her Own Stubborn Pursuit of Self-Righteousness (9:30–10:21).
   D. God Has Chosen a Present Remnant of the Jews for Salvation while Hardening the Rest (11:1–10).
   E. God Will Ultimately Save the Nation of Israel (11:11–32).
   F. God's Plan Is Mysterious and Wise (11:33–36).

VI. THE PRACTICAL IMPLICATIONS OF THE GOSPEL (12:1–15:13)
   A. Christians Should Respond to God's Mercy by Living Transformed Lives (12:1–2).
   B. Transformed Living Will Impact Relationships in the Church (12:3–21).
   C. Transformed Living Will Affect Relationships with Political Authorities (13:1–7).
   D. Transformed Living Is Urgent Because of the Nearness of Christ's Return (13:8–14).
   E. Transformed Living Will Lead to Mutual Acceptance of Stronger and Weaker Christians (14:1–15:13).

VII. CONCLUSION (15:14–16:27)
   A. Paul's Travel Plans: Visiting Rome on the Way to Spain (15:14–33)
   B. Commendation of Phoebe and Greetings to Roman Christians (16:1–16)
   C. Final Warning (16:17–18)
   D. Final Commendation and Greetings (16:19–24)
   E. Concluding Benediction (16:25–27)

UNIT-BY-UNIT DISCUSSION

I. Introduction (1:1–15)

A. Jesus Christ Is the Focus of the Gospel, and Paul Is Qualified to Proclaim It (1:1–7). The introduction of the letter includes a brief summary of the gospel that highlights its foundation in the OT and its focus on Christ. Paul maintains at the outset that the gospel he preached was not his message but "the gospel of God" (1:1) and that God had promised this gospel "beforehand through his prophets in the Holy Scriptures" (1:2).

As Paul notes, Christ's Davidic lineage confirmed his right to rule as Messiah-King. By virtue of his resurrection, Jesus was also "the powerful Son of God" (1:4). Since the next occurrence of "power" in Romans refers to God's saving power (1:16), the title signified that Jesus possessed the power to save because of his resurrection (see 4:25; 1 Cor 15:14, 17, 20). Finally, Jesus was called "our Lord," a title that clearly denoted deity (see 10:9, 13; Joel 2:32). Thus, the introduction to the gospel focused on Jesus's identity, power, and authority as Messiah-King, Savior, and Lord God. In addition, Paul briefly alludes to his Damascus road experience and apostolic call. He explains that Christ appointed him as an apostle in order to produce obedience among the Gentiles to the gospel command to believe the good news.[76] This ministry was motivated by zeal for Jesus's name, a desire to see Christ glorified among all the peoples of the earth.

B. Paul Thanks God for the Roman Christians and Expresses His Love for Them (1:8–15). Paul explains that his failure to visit the churches of Rome did not imply his lack of concern for them. He prayed for them incessantly and thanked God for their faith that was acclaimed throughout the entire Christian world (1:8–10). He longed to preach the gospel in Rome due to a deep sense of obligation to proclaim Christ to all people.

II. Theme: The Gospel Reveals God's Power for Salvation and His Righteousness (1:16–17)

Romans 1:16–17 expresses the theme of the letter. Paul was not ashamed to proclaim the gospel because the gospel is God's saving power that accomplishes salvation for all who believe, whether they are Jews or Gentiles. The gospel reveals God's righteousness in declaring sinners to be righteous despite their misdeeds based on Jesus's sacrificial death—a truth more fully developed in 3:21–26 (see below). Paul reminded his readers that salvation by faith was not a new message but in fact constituted the central message of the OT prophets (1:17, citing Hab 2:4, which is also cited at Gal 3:11; cf. Rom 1:1–2). For both OT and NT believers, the righteousness that resulted in life had always been imputed on the basis of an individual's faith.

III. The Promise of the Gospel: Justification by Faith in Christ (1: 18–4:25)

A. Man's Need for Justification (1:18–3:20) Beginning in 1:18, Paul explains that all individuals need justification since all are sinners justly condemned by God. He first addresses the sinfulness of Gentiles, then that of Jews, and then that of all humankind generally.

Gentiles deserved God's wrath because their sins were not committed in ignorance but involved suppression of the truths about God that were apparent to all (1:18). Man's chief sin is failure to give God the glory he deserves. God expresses his wrath by releasing humanity to the corrupting power of sin so that man's sinful behavior becomes progressively more heinous and repulsive. Gentiles experience a spiritual and moral devolution that

---

[76] Scholars dispute whether the phrase "obedience of faith" refers to faith as an act of obedience to the gospel (appositional genitive) or an obedience that results from faith (genitive of source). Paul's frequent mention of obedience to the gospel message (see 1:8; 10:16; 11:23, 30–31; 15:18; 16:19) strongly suggests the phrase refers to obedience to the gospel that consists primarily of faith. But this does not imply that an obedient lifestyle does not issue from the believer's commitment to Christ.

leads them to idolatry, sexual perversion, and complete moral decadence (1:26–27). They choose to live in rebellion against God despite their clear understanding that sin results in death.

Although the Jews may have felt that their moral superiority to Gentiles would benefit them in judgment, Paul warns that condemning others did not prevent God from noticing one's own guilt (2:1). God's kindness to Israel did not imply that the Jews were righteous in and of themselves so that they had no need to repent. On the contrary, God's kindness to Israel was a summons to repentance (2:4). God would judge each person fairly and give him either the punishment or reward his deeds deserve. He would judge Jews and Gentiles equally and justly because God's judgment was not based on favoritism. Ignorance of the written law did not exempt a person from judgment since God inscribed the requirements of the law on the heart of every person.

Jews as well as Gentiles, then, deserve God's wrath (2:5). Though the Jews preach and teach the law, they fail to obey it and thereby dishonor God and blaspheme his name. Circumcision, likewise, grants no protection against divine judgment and was rendered meaningless by the transgression of the law (2:25). Conversely, an uncircumcised Gentile who keeps the law of God should be viewed as a circumcised Jew and a member of the covenant people (2:27). The true Jew whom God will praise in judgment is one who has been internally transformed (2:28–29).

Jews do possess certain advantages over Gentiles, however. God chose to grant them the OT Scriptures, and he has remained faithful to his promises to Israel (3:1–4). Still, God's justice is not compromised by his punishment of the sins of Jews, but it would be diminished if he failed to punish their sins. Although the innate post-fall sinfulness of humanity accentuates the glorious righteousness, faithfulness, and truthfulness of God, it does not excuse sin, nor does it encourage it (3:7–8).

In fact, the descriptions of the Jews in the OT itself demonstrate their intense sinfulness and show that Jews are no better than Gentiles (3:9). The law Israel possesses is not a means of salvation. Rather, it demonstrates man's sinfulness so that he despairs of saving himself by his own righteousness. All people, Jews and Gentiles, are justly condemned by God as sinners (3:19–20). Grace can come only when people see their desperate need for it; those who are spiritually poor will inherit the kingdom of heaven (Matt 5:3).

B. God's Gift of Justification (3:21–4:25) Having established the universal sinfulness of Jews and Gentiles alike—the "plight" of humanity—Paul goes on to state the solution: justification by faith in Jesus Christ. The present section elaborates more fully on Paul's comments in the introduction. Both the Law (esp. Gen 15:6; see below) and the Prophets (esp. Hab 2:4; see above) testify that God pronounces sinners righteous in his sight if they believe in Jesus Christ (1:1–2, 16–17). In a startling pronouncement, Paul declares, "But now, apart from the law, God's righteousness has been revealed, attested by the law and the prophets. God's righteousness is through faith in Jesus Christ, to all who believe, since there is no distinction. For all have sinned and fall short of the glory of God" (3:21–23).

This righteous standing is granted freely by divine grace and is based on the atoning sacrifice of Jesus Christ. This gracious declaration of righteousness eliminates all human boasting and places both Gentiles and Jews on equal footing. Jesus's sacrificial death displays the justice of God in declaring sinners to be righteous on the basis of faith. If God were to simply overlook the sins of his creatures, it would call his own righteousness into question. However, through Jesus's death, the wonderful righteousness of God is beautifully expressed and God is able to forgive and justify sinners without compromising his own holiness.

At the same time, the gospel that righteousness comes through faith in Christ rather than by keeping the law does not dispense with the law altogether—though it did put its role into proper perspective (see esp. 10:4 below). On the contrary, it affirmed what the law had said about salvation all along (3:31). The law states plainly that Abraham, the father of the Jews, was declared righteous in God's sight through faith (Rom 4:3, citing Gen 15:6; cf. Gal 3:6). This righteousness was not a standing that Abraham achieved through his good works but a gift he received. Psalm 32:1–2 also describes this imputed righteousness. Hence, the OT Scriptures upheld the gospel preached by Paul.

This righteousness was imputed to Abraham before he was circumcised (4:10). Thus, God credited this righteousness to a person based on faith alone, apart from circumcision. This righteousness was also credited to Abraham before the Mosaic law was given, further demonstrating that God granted this righteousness on the basis of faith and not observance of the law (4:13–15). The promises to Abraham's offspring, which included receiving a righteous standing and life in the world to come, were granted to believers—both Jews and Gentiles—in fulfillment of the promise that Abraham would be the father of many nations (4:18).

Abraham's faith paralleled Christian faith. Abraham believed that God could bring "life out of death," a promised son out of aged people as good as dead (4:19; see Heb 11:12). Christians likewise believe that God raised Jesus from the dead, thereby exhibiting Abraham's faith and receiving the promise of imputed righteousness.

IV. The Benefits Conferred by the Gospel (5:1–8:39)

A. The Believer Has Peace, Righteousness, and Joy (5:1–11). In Romans 5:1 Paul begins to describe the benefits conferred on the believer through the gospel. This description of benefits occupied his attention for four entire chapters. To begin with, because of justification, believers are at peace with God and joyfully anticipate their full and final transformation (5:1–5). While sinners were in a wretched spiritual condition—weak, unable to save themselves, ungodly, and prone to wrong—Christ died for them (5:6). Through Jesus's sacrificial and substitutionary death, believers who were formerly God's enemies have been reconciled to him. Those doomed to suffer his eternal wrath have been rescued from condemnation, and those who were judged to be sinners have been declared righteous (5:9–11).

B. The Believer Escapes the Consequences of Adam's Transgression, the Reign of Sin in Death (5:12–21). The impact of Adam's disobedience on the human race offers a negative parallel to the impact of Christ's obedience on believers (5:12). Due to Adam's sin, all people die. Even those who lived before the giving of the law and who had no explicit commandment to defy died (5:13). Clearly, a single act by one person can have a universal and eternal impact. However, the obedience of Jesus Christ had the power to cancel the consequences of Adam's disobedience. If the disobedience of one man could cause the death of many others, Christ's obedience could likewise grant righteousness and life to many (5:15). Just as the effects of Adam's disobedience were universal, the effects of Christ's obedience were also universal in that Christ granted righteousness and life to those who believe, whether Jews or Gentiles. The law did not introduce death into the world. It offered Adam's descendants explicit commandments to defy, just as Adam had done (5:20). This made sin more rampant and more heinous. This pervasive and intense sinfulness, however, magnifies the abundance and greatness of God's grace (5:21).

C. The Believer Is Liberated from Slavery to Sin (6:1–23). One should not conclude from this, as some of Paul's opponents charged him as teaching, that sin serves a positive purpose and should be continued (6:1–2). The believer's union with Christ in his death, burial, and resurrection is inconsistent with a sinful lifestyle. The person the believer had been has died with Christ (6:3). Now the believer has been liberated from sin's mastery. Eventually, the believer's union with Christ will result in his resurrection and complete liberation from sin. In the present, Christ-followers should live in light of the fact that sin's mastery has been broken. They should offer themselves to God as instruments for righteousness (6:11–14). Salvation by grace does not grant license for sinful behavior. The believer has a new spiritual master: righteousness, so he should live as a slave to righteousness (6:8). Slavery to sin grants no benefits to the sinner; it condemns him to die. Slavery to righteousness, on the other hand, produces holiness and results in eternal life.

Table 13.1: Rhetorical Questions and Answers in Romans 6–7

Passage	Rhetorical Question	Answer
6:1–3	"What should we say then? Should we continue in sin in order that grace may multiply?"	"Absolutely not! How can we who died to sin still live in it?
6:15–16	"What then? Should we sin because we are not under law but under grace?"	"Absolutely not! Don't you know that if you offer yourselves to someone as obedient slaves, you are slaves of that one you obey?"

Table 13.1: Rhetorical Questions and Answers in Romans 6–7 (continued)

Passage	Rhetorical Question	Answer
7:7	"What should we say then? Is the law sin?"	"Absolutely not! On the contrary, I would not have known sin if it were not for the law."
7:13	"Therefore, did what is good become death to me?"	"Absolutely not! On the contrary, sin, in order to be recognized as sin, was producing death in me through what is good, so that through the commandment, sin might become sinful beyond measure."

D. The Believer Is Liberated from Bondage to the Law (7:1–25). The Christ-follower has been liberated from the law. Death nullifies the marriage covenant so that it is no longer legally binding (7:1). After a spouse has died, the surviving spouse is liberated from the law of marriage and free to marry someone else. In a similar way, death nullified the power of the law (7:4). By his union with Christ in his death, the believer was liberated from the law and freed to devote himself to God. Liberation from the law, union with God in Christ, and empowerment by the Spirit enabled the believer to live a righteous life—something that the law could not accomplish.

The law actually aggravated and aroused sin in unbelievers, but this did not mean that the law was bad (7:7). The law was holy, righteous, and good, but the sinful nature used the law as a weapon to destroy the sinner. Paul illustrates this truth by presenting the example of a person striving to obey the law perfectly. He shows that the law still served a positive function by demonstrating the person's utter corruption and slavery to sin. At the same time, the law was powerless to save the person from his slavery to sin (7:13). Anyone who tries to fulfill the law's demands apart from the enabling of the Holy Spirit engages in a frustrating exercise of futility. Such a person is caught in a constant tug-of-war between that part of him that delights in God's law and that part of him that is dominated by sin (7:14–25). Only crucifixion and resurrection with Christ and transformation by the Spirit can resolve this desperate struggle.[77]

E. The Believer Lives a Righteous Life Through the Power of the Spirit (8:1–17). Yet the believer enjoys present victory over sin. The Spirit accomplishes for the believer that which the law cannot do. The Spirit, who enables this new life in Christ, thus replaces the old law as a reference point in the life of the believer (8:2; see 10:4). The Spirit liberates the believer from his slavery to sin and moves him to fulfill naturally and spontaneously

---

[77] Alternatively, Paul's question, "Who will rescue me from the this dying body?" (7:24) anticipates both the activity of the Spirit that sets the believer free from the law of sin and death (8:1–17) and the final redemption of the body through resurrection and glorification (8:18–39).

the law's righteous demands (8:9). The Spirit exercises the same power that he used to raise Jesus from the dead in order to produce new life in the believer. Those who live by God's Spirit are God's children and are thus heirs who will share in God's glory (8:17).

F. The Believer Will Ultimately Enjoy Complete Victory over Corruption (8:18–39). The whole creation eagerly awaits the glorification of God's people (8:18). Believers long for the completion of their adoption through the redemption of the body when their transformation will be complete and their struggle with sin comes to an end. In the present, God works through every circumstance to accomplish the spiritual good of believers (8:28). God's eternal purpose will not be thwarted, and he will unfailingly make those whom he loved from eternity past to become like his Son (8:29–30). The completion of the believer's salvation through his justification at the final judgment and at his glorification are absolutely certain because God will make sure all these things occur for the people he loves.

V. Israel's Rejection of the Gospel (9:1–11:36)

A. Israel Has Rejected Christ (9:1–5). While Romans 1–8 is primarily concerned with the justification of man—accomplished through faith in Christ on the basis of his atoning death—chapters 9–11 move on to a more important topic still (anticipated in chaps. 1–8)—the justification of God. This refers to what scholars call "theodicy," the demonstration that, contrary to what some might allege, God was just and righteous in all he did. In the present case, the alleged incongruity in God's purposes was the fact that the majority of Jews had not believed in Jesus as Messiah. Hence, many Jews charged, God had reneged on his covenant promises.

Not so, Paul countered. Despite what could appear as a change in God's mode of operation, God's promises to Israel continue unabated. At the same time, God now includes the Gentiles in the Abrahamic promise that in him "all the peoples on earth will be blessed" (Gen 12:3). Hence, "it is not as though the word of God has failed" (9:6). In this regard, Paul himself, known as the apostle to the Gentiles, was deeply torn within, for he still dearly loved his fellow Israelites. In fact, he says that he could wish that he himself "were cursed and cut off from the Messiah" for the benefit of his fellow Jews (9:3).

B. Israel's Temporary Rejection of Christ Is Consistent with God's Eternal Plan (9:6–29). Although Israel's rejection of Jesus might seem to contradict the infallibility of God's promises and shake the believer's hopes, God's promises to Israel have not failed (9:6). The remainder of chapters 9–11 is devoted to demonstrating the truthfulness of Paul's assertion. To begin with, not all physical descendants of Abraham are true Israelites. God's promises apply only to those whom he has chosen. His choice, in turn, is based, not on human character or behavior but on God's mysterious purpose (9:14–18).

For this reason one must not charge God with injustice (9:19–21) because to do so reverses the roles of creature and Creator (see the book of Job). God is free to show his mercy to whomever he wills because in his utter sovereignty the Creator has complete authority over his creatures. Nor is it proper to challenge God's character if he glorified himself by expressing his wrath against some people while lavishing his mercy on others. God would have been just if he had saved no one. He is certainly just if by sheer grace he chose to save many without saving all.

C. Israel's Temporary Rejection of Christ Is Due to Her Own Stubborn Pursuit of Self-Righteousness (9:30–10:21). Still, Israel was fully responsible for its spiritual condition. Gentiles were declared righteous by God based on their faith. Yet Israel sought righteousness but did not attain it because she attempted to establish her own righteousness through personal obedience to the law rather than through faith in Christ (9:30–32). Paul cites Isaiah 8:14 and 28:16 to demonstrate that salvation comes only through confession of faith in Jesus Christ (9:33). Those who believe in him will not be put to shame in eschatological judgment since they will be vindicated by God.

Christ is "the end of the law for righteousness to everyone who believes." In context, this means that Christ ends the effort to establish one's own righteousness through the law as far as believers are concerned. Unlike Israel, the believer ceases from seeking to establish his own righteousness (10:3). He or she gives up the vain hope of receiving life by doing the things written in the law (10:5).[78]

Paul proceeds to cite additional OT proof texts in order to demonstrate that the salvation of both Jews and Gentiles clearly followed from the OT message. This salvation, in turn, was predicated upon confession that "Jesus is Lord" and upon faith that God raised him from the dead (10:9). This was the essence of faith and fulfilled the premise that "everyone who calls on the name of the Lord will be saved" (10:13, citing Isa 28:16)—Jew as well as Gentile. Moreover, if faith in Christ is required for salvation, then there must be messengers telling people the good news of salvation in Christ (10:14–21; see Isa 52:7; 53:1). In truth, Israel did not fail to confess faith in Christ because of a lack of information. All Israel heard the message about Christ, but most rejected it in stubborn disobedience.

D. God Has Chosen a Present Remnant of the Jews for Salvation While Hardening the Rest (11:1–10). Thus far, Paul's "justification of God" has been largely devoted to the demonstration that God was right to condemn Jews for seeking to establish a righteousness of their own rather than submitting to the way of salvation God has established (10:3). This opened the door for the salvation of a large number of Gentiles who had no such ambition and who had previously been far off (10:20, citing Isa 65:1), perhaps provoking Israel to jealousy (10:19, citing Deut 32:21). Yet, as Paul proceeds to show in

---

[78] The word translated "end" can mean "termination" or "goal." Several commentators are convinced that the term means *both* "termination" and "goal" in this context since Paul has used race imagery in the preceding context (9:30–32), and the finish line is both the end of a race and the goal of the race at the same time. If so, Paul means that Christ brought to an end the effort to establish one's own righteousness through the law and that he is the One that the law anticipated and foreshadowed. See Bruce, *Romans*, 190; Moo, *Romans*, 638–41. For the view that "end" means "termination" exclusively, see Dunn, *Romans*, 1:596-97; Schreiner, *Romans*, 544–48; Stuhlmacher, *Romans*, 155–56; Käsemann, *Romans*, 282–83.

chapter 11, God has not rejected Israel entirely. By his grace he has chosen a portion of Israel for salvation. This remnant will obtain the righteousness Israel had sought.

E. God Will Ultimately Save the Nation of Israel (11:11–32). Thus, God used Israel's rejection of the gospel for his gracious purposes to bring salvation to the Gentiles (11:11–12). Now God uses the Gentiles' reception of the gospel to make the Jews envious and move some of them to faith in Christ. At the same time, Gentiles should not be arrogant toward Jews (11:17–21). Their salvation rests on God's promises to Israel and is predicated on faith. God is ready to accept the rest of Israel when they repent of their unbelief.

Meanwhile, Gentiles, Paul warns, should not assume that they have favored status with God. At the appointed time, God would shift his focus to national Israel again. Great masses of Jews will be saved. This was necessary because God's gifts and call are irrevocable. Hence Paul's argument has come full circle, and he establishes that God's word is true (9:6). God's righteous salvation-historical purposes for both Jews and Gentiles proved coherent and consistent, though ultimately beyond complete human comprehension.

F. God's Plan Is Mysterious and Wise (11:33–36). Appropriately, therefore, Paul concluded his demonstration of the righteousness of God in chapters 9–11 with a doxology, affirming the mystery and wisdom of God's ways. As the apostle explains, God wondrously displayed his mysterious wisdom by using Gentiles and Jews to prompt one another to believe in Christ. This realization should drive all believers to praise the depth of God's wisdom and to acknowledge that God is glorious in all he does—whether or not they presently fully understand all of his purposes.

VI. The Practical Implications of the Gospel (12:1–15:13)

A. Christians Should Respond to God's Mercy by Living Transformed Lives (12:1–2). On the basis of Paul's foregoing arguments ("Therefore," 12:1), he calls on believers to respond to God's mercy by devoting their lives completely to him and by having renewed minds that know God's will. They are to do so, not by bringing a variety of sacrifices as people did in OT times, but by presenting themselves—their very own bodies in their entirety—as a "living sacrifice, holy and pleasing to God." This will be their "true worship," and this is how they will be able to discern "the good, pleasing, and perfect will of God" (12:2).

B. Transformed Living Will Impact Relationships in the Church (12:3–21). The renewed mind is characterized by humility. It recognizes the interdependency of the different members of the church and does not establish a church hierarchy based on spiritual gifts (12:3–8). The renewed mind is also characterized by love. This love expresses itself through forgiveness, sympathy, harmony, humility, and kindness (12:9–21).

C. Transformed Living Will Affect Relationships with Political Authorities (13:1–7). Another important implication of the gospel Paul preached is that all believers should submit themselves to governing authorities. Such authority has been appointed by God, preserves order, and thwarts lawlessness. For this reason, believers should conscientiously pay their taxes and show respect for political leaders. These words take on special significance in light of the fact that they were written during the tenure of Emperor Nero (54–68), whose ignominious reign would be responsible for the martyrdom of numerous Christians, including Paul himself.

D. Transformed Living Is Urgent Because of the Nearness of Christ's Return (13:8–14). Believers should fulfill the law by expressing love for others. Expressing love and living righteously are especially important since Christ's return is fast approaching.

E. Transformed Living Will Lead to Mutual Acceptance of Stronger and Weaker Christians (14:1–15:13). Believers should accept one another in love even when they disagree over issues of conscience, such as diet and the observance of holy days (14:1–8). They should follow their own consciences in this regard while taking care not to allow their behavior to disturb other believers who hold different convictions. What is more, they should make sure not to encourage other believers to do something that they do not believe is right. It is wrong to eat, drink, or do anything that disturbs another's conscience.

Jewish and Gentile Christians, the weak and the strong, should live in unity and seek to build up one another (14:19). They should learn to glorify God with one heart and one voice. Jesus himself came into the world as a servant to the Jews, fulfilling the promises to them and yet including Gentiles in God's plan so that they might glorify God as was foretold in the OT Scriptures.

VII. Conclusion (15:14–16:27)

The conclusion of Paul's Letter to the Romans is longer than those in his other letters, yet it is appropriate in light of the length of the entire piece and in view of the fact that Paul had neither planted the church in Rome nor yet paid a visit to it. Especially noteworthy is the high number of individuals greeted by Paul in 16:1–16.

A. Paul's Travel Plans: Visiting Rome on the Way to Spain (15:14–33) At long last, Paul elaborates on one of the major purposes for writing the letter: his plan to visit Rome on his way to Spain (15:24). Rather than making Rome the final destination of his impending visit, Paul intended for Rome to be merely a stop on his way to the far western frontiers of his European mission. In this Paul serves as a model of a frontier missionary, his aim being "to preach the gospel where Christ has not been named, so that I will not build on someone else's foundation" (15:20). Paul also asks for prayer that he would be rescued from unbelievers in Judea and for a successful delivery of the Gentile offering for the Jerusalem church (15:30–32). But as the book of Acts makes clear, Paul was arrested in Jerusalem and eventually arrived in Rome, though not in the way he had originally envisioned (Acts 21–28).

B. Commendation of Phoebe and Greetings to Roman Christians (16:1–16) At the end of the letter, Paul first commends the likely courier, Phoebe, a servant or deaconess (*diakonos*) of the church in Cenchrea and a benefactress or patroness for many, including him (16:1–2).[79] Paul also greets his trusted coworkers, Priscilla and Aquila (who had apparently returned to Rome), including the church that met in their house (16:3–5; see Acts 18:2). This is followed by a long list of greetings to various individuals and house churches, including a surprisingly high number of women.[80]

C. Final Warning (16:17–18) A final warning is issued against those who cause divisions. Believers are implored to avoid these individuals and not to be deceived by their smooth talk or flattering words.

D. Final Commendation and Greetings (16:19–24) The believers in Rome are commended for their obedience and are urged to be wise about what is good and innocent about what is evil. God will soon crush Satan under his feet. Timothy and others sent greetings, as did Tertius (Paul's amanuensis), Gaius (Paul's host), and Erastus (the city-treasurer), among others.

E. Concluding Benediction (16:25–27) A glorious benediction concludes the letter. It includes Paul's final reference to his gospel and to God's revelation of the "mystery kept silent" anticipated in the prophetic Scriptures, according to which "the obedience of faith among all Gentiles" was now advancing through Paul and his associates to the glory of God in Christ.

THEOLOGY

Theological Themes

The Gospel Paul's Letter to the Romans makes an enormous contribution to the NT canon. It contains the most extensive presentation of Paul's gospel. Romans 1:18–3:20 is Paul's most thorough and sustained treatment of the universal sinfulness of humanity. Paul's portrait of the sinner is a graphic depiction of the creature's rebellion against the Creator, unmasking his deep depravity. Rarely does one see the horrific ugliness of his soul with such shocking clarity as in these riveting verses.

Further, Romans 3:21–4:20 contains Paul's most developed exposition of his doctrine of justification. Paul discussed this doctrine extensively in Galatians. But, as F. F. Bruce stated, "The arguments which are pressed on the churches in an urgent and *ad hoc* manner are set forth more systematically in Romans."[81] J. B. Lightfoot wrote that the treatment of justification in Galatians compared to the treatment in Romans "as the rough model to the

---

[79] See the discussion of Phoebe in A. J. Köstenberger, "Women in the Pauline Mission," in *The Gospel to the Nations: Perspectives on Paul's Mission*, ed. P. Bolt and M. Thompson (Downers Grove, IL: InterVarsity, 2000), 228–29. Cf. Moo, *Romans*, 912–16; and Schreiner, *Romans*, 786–88, both of whom, while also complementarian in their view of gender roles, leaned toward identifying Phoebe as a deacon. Among translations, the CSB has "servant" in the text, with a footnote saying, "Others interpret this term in a technical sense: *deacon*, or *deaconess*, or *minister*." Similarly, both the NASB and the NIV have "servant" in the text and a footnote: "Or *deaconess*"; this is reversed in TNIV: "deacon" in the text, "Or *servant*" in a footnote.

[80] See Köstenberger, "Women in the Pauline Mission," 221–47.

[81] Bruce, *Letter of Paul to the Romans*, 30–31.

finished statue."[82] Romans adds specific details to the discussion of justification that the earlier treatment in Galatians did not include, such as the point that Abraham was justified before he was circumcised; that Abraham's faith closely parallels Christian faith in the God who resurrected Jesus and who justifies sinners; and that all three major sections of the OT affirm justification by faith.

Also, Romans 5:1–8:39 contains Paul's most developed discussion of the believer's new spiritual state, particularly his liberation from death, sin, the law, and corruption. Then in 12:1–15:13, Paul described in vivid detail the practical implications of this new spiritual state. Although Romans is frequently associated with the doctrine of justification by faith alone, it must not be overlooked that Paul sees justification as leading inevitably to sanctification in which the Spirit prompts and empowers the Christ-follower to fulfill God's righteous demands in fulfillment of the new covenant promises (8:1–4).

Finally, Romans contains what is by far Paul's most complete treatment of God's relationship to national Israel. Romans 9–11 discusses in great detail Israel's gracious election, God's faithfulness to his covenant, Israel's rejection of God's grace, the positive purpose of this rejection in redemptive history, and the future salvation of Israel. These chapters express the love of the "apostle of the Gentiles" for the people of Israel more powerfully and passionately than any other text.

The Christian's knowledge of the gospel is far richer and his joy more abundant when he has immersed his soul in the study of this great letter. As Martin Luther wrote nearly 500 years ago in the preface for his commentary on Romans, this letter "is worthy not only that every Christian should know it word for word, by heart, but occupy himself with it every day, as the daily bread of the soul. It can never be read or pondered too much, and the more it is dealt with the more precious it becomes, and the better it tastes."[83]

The "Righteousness of God" A major theme of Romans is the insistence that individuals are viewed by God as righteous only on the basis of faith, rather than by the works of the law. This theme is so prominent that many interpreters since the Protestant Reformation have viewed justification by faith as the primary focus of the letter. Although many now insist that justification cannot be singled out as the central theme of the entire book, most still acknowledge that it is at least the focus of 1:1–4:25 where Paul explained that believers are declared righteous on the basis of Jesus's sacrificial death and that this is the only means of salvation since all have failed to live up to the standard of the law.

The "Righteousness of God" Refers to Righteousness That Is Credited to the Believer by God Paul exclaims that the "righteousness of God" is being revealed through the gospel (1:17). The presence of this phrase in the programmatic statement of the letter demonstrates the importance of God's righteousness in this letter. In fact, a number of scholars have suggested that the central focus of the book of Romans is the righteousness of God.

---

[82] J. B. Lightfoot, *Saint Paul's Epistle to the Galatians* (London, England: Macmillan, 1921), 49.

[83] M. Luther, *Commentary on the Epistle to the Romans*, trans. J. T. Mueller (Grand Rapids, MI: Kregel, 1954), viii.

Something to Think About: Let God Be True and Every Man a Liar

In the course of history, many have devised supposed paths of salvation. Virtually all man-made religions have one thing in common: they are based on human efforts. Among the major religions, Christianity is unique in that it focuses on what one man—Jesus Christ—has already done for all humans. Christianity revolves around what is now available for all on the basis of simple trust in Christ.

Thus, Paul's words ring out in his letter to the Romans:

> *But now, apart from the law, God's righteousness has been revealed, attested by the law and the prophets. God's righteousness is through faith in Jesus Christ, to all who believe, since there is no distinction. For all have sinned and fall short of the glory of God. They are justified freely by his grace through the redemption that is in Christ Jesus (Rom 3:21–24).*

In his day, Jesus was asked by religious Jews, "What can we do to perform the works of God?" (John 6:28). This question encapsulates what has always been, and will always be, the misguided human quest to please or placate God by self-effort. But what was Jesus's response? It was this: "This is the work of God—that you believe in the one he has sent" (John 6:29). Jesus and Paul concurred: faith in Jesus for salvation on the basis of his work on the cross is all that is required.

Glorious gospel! Wonderful news! For if salvation depended on us, we would fail since we could never do enough to overcome our sinful nature or make amends for our sins. Not only did Jesus, the God-man, die a perfect, sin-atoning death, but he lived a perfect, sinless life. In a wonderful exchange, life and death are credited to the account of those who trust Christ: "He made the one who did not know sin to be sin for us, so that in him we might become the righteousness of God" (2 Cor 5:21).

A. Schlatter was so convinced of this that he titled his commentary on this letter, *Romans: The Righteousness of God.*[84] Still, an enormous debate rages over the precise meaning of the phrase "righteousness of God" (*dikaiosynē tou theou*). Grammatically, these are the major options: (1) the righteousness that God produces (subjective genitive); (2) God's own attribute of righteousness (possessive genitive); and (3) the righteousness imputed by God (genitive of source). We briefly examine these options below.

The Righteousness That God Produces An increasing number of scholars sees the righteousness of God as *God's saving activity or power*. Several factors support this interpretation. First, a number of ancient Jewish texts, including several OT passages, use the terms "righteousness" and "salvation" interchangeably. Perhaps the best example is Isaiah 51:5–8:

---

[84] A. Schlatter, *Romans: The Righteousness of God,* trans. S. Schatzmann (Peabody, MA: Hendrickson, 1995).

> My righteousness is near, my salvation appears, and my arms will bring justice to the nations. The coasts and islands will put their hope in me, and they will look to my strength. Look up to the heavens, and look at the earth beneath; for the heavens will vanish like smoke, the earth will wear out like a garment, and its inhabitants will die like gnats. But my salvation will last forever, and my righteousness will never be shattered.
>
> Listen to me, you who know righteousness, the people in whose heart is my instruction: do not fear disgrace by men, and do not be shattered by their taunts. For moths will devour them like a garment, and worms will eat them like wool. But my righteousness will last forever, and my salvation for all generations.

If Paul used the term "righteousness of God" in keeping with this or similar OT texts, "righteousness" would refer to God's saving activity.[85] Second, this interpretation closely associates the terms "righteousness" in 1:17 and "power" in 1:16. Third, God's saving power is a broad category well suited to serve as a summary not only of the first four chapters of Romans but of the contents of the entire letter. It would encompass justification, sanctification, and glorification.

Scholars who see God's righteousness in Paul's writings as meaning God's saving power normally insist that God's righteousness is more than a gift and involves more than the mere imputation of righteousness. Instead, God's saving power actually makes the sinner righteous and transforms and restores the entire fallen cosmos. Käsemann, for example, defined the righteousness of God this way: "It speaks of the God who brings back the fallen world into the sphere of his legitimate claim . . . , whether in promise or demand, in new creation or forgiveness, or in the making possible of our service, and—what must be no less considered according to Gal 5:5—who sets us in the state of confident hope and, according to Phil 3:12, constantly earthly change."[86] Although this interpretation is attractive, it does not seem to fit Paul's usages in specific contexts as well as the two alternative views do. Some scholars who previously endorsed this view have subsequently abandoned it.[87]

God's Own Attribute of Righteousness The identification of the righteousness of God as a *divine attribute* is supported by several considerations. First, the righteousness of God seems to include his divine wrath, since a close connection exists between the righteousness of God in 1:17 and the wrath of God in 1:18. In both verses, a noun with the modifier "of God" serves as the subject of the verb "is revealed." This parallelism seems intentional.

---

[85] Compare Pss 31:1; 36:10; 40:10; 71:2; 88:10–12; 98:2–3; 143:1; Isa 46:13.

[86] Käsemann, *Romans*, 29; cf. Stuhlmacher, *Romans*, 28–32. Käsemann and his student Stuhlmacher were both influenced by the seminal work of Schlatter (*Romans*, 18–22) on the "righteousness of God."

[87] Schreiner hesitantly interpreted the "righteousness of God" as God's saving power in his 1998 commentary on Romans but abandoned the view when writing his Pauline theology published three years later. Compare Schreiner, *Romans*, 63–70; and idem, *Paul: Apostle of God's Glory in Christ* (Downers Grove, IL: InterVarsity, 2001), 192–209.

Moreover, the conjunction "for" that begins 1:18 may imply that the expression of God's wrath is an expression of his righteousness.[88] Second, the righteousness of God seems to refer to a divine attribute: God's righteousness refers to his divine justice in eschatological judgment (3:5); and God's righteousness is his uprightness and justice, which were called into question by his tolerance of sin in the past but which has now been vindicated through Jesus's sacrifice (3:25–26).[89]

The Righteousness Imputed by God to the Believer The identification of the righteousness of God as *a gift that God imputes to the sinner who believes in Christ* is supported by abundant and persuasive evidence in the letter. First, the phrase "from faith to faith" in 1:17 does not seem to fit with the revelation of God's attribute of righteousness. God's righteousness—particularly his wrath, faithfulness, and truthfulness—is in no sense dependent on human faith. The phrase "from faith to faith" seems to imply that the righteousness of God is being revealed only to those who believe, and this qualification makes the most sense if "righteousness of God" refers in some way to God's act of declaring sinners righteous on the basis of their faith.

Second, this interpretation best suits the quotation of Habakkuk 2:4 in the next clause of Romans 1:17. Paul's citation of Habakkuk 2:4 clearly confirms or clarifies the statement that the righteousness of God is revealed "from faith to faith." Paul introduced the OT quotation with an intensive comparative adverb (*kathōs*) that establishes a tight parallel between the first and second halves of v. 17. That tight parallel strongly implies that the noun "righteousness" in v. 17a, the adjective "righteous" in v. 17b (the Hab 2:4 quotation), and the prepositional phrases "from faith" or "by faith" (both are the same phrase in Greek: *ek pisteōs*) are used in the same senses. Paul's understanding of Habakkuk 2:4 is clear from his discussion of that text in Galatians 3:11. He used the text to demonstrate that "no one is justified before God by the law, because 'the righteous will live by faith.'" In Galatians 3:11, the "righteous" is the one who has been justified or declared righteous by God, and "faith" refers to the faith of the believer that is required to receive justifying righteousness. If Paul used Habakkuk 2:4 in Romans 1:17 in a manner consistent with Galatians 3:11, the "righteous" person is the one who has been justified, and "righteousness" is primarily a reference to justifying righteousness.[90] Given the observation that "righteousness" and

---

[88] On the other hand, it could simply demonstrate that the works of humanity only deserve divine wrath, thus confirming the impossibility of salvation by works and the necessity of justification by faith in 1:17.

[89] These interpretations are fiercely contested by commentators defending alternative views, especially when they insist on a single, narrow meaning for the phrase "righteousness of God" throughout the entire letter. For a more detailed defense of the attributive view, see Fitzmyer (*Romans*, 257–63), who demonstrated that the attributive interpretation has a rich history in the church, especially prior to the Reformation.

[90] For a more detailed defense of this handling of Rom 1:17 and Gal 3:11, see C. L. Quarles, "From Faith to Faith: A Fresh Examination of the Prepositional Series in Romans 1:17," *NovT* 45 (2003): 1–21, esp. 16–18. Scholars have long debated whether Paul saw the prepositional phrase "by faith" in Hab 2:4 as adjectival or adverbial, that is, as modifying "righteous" or "live." The issue cannot be settled on grounds of syntax or word order. But throughout Romans and elsewhere in his writings, Paul far more frequently associates faith with righteousness than with life (1:17; 3:22, 25–26, 28, 30; 4:3, 5, 9, 11, 13; 5:1; 9:30; 10:4, 6, 10; see Gal 2:16; 3:6, 8, 11, 24; 5:5; Phil 3:9). This strongly suggests he intended his readers to

"righteous" are parallel and probably share the same sense, "righteousness" most likely refers to the righteousness God grants the believer.

Third, in several other contexts in Romans, the righteousness of God clearly refers to righteousness imputed by God. Although in 3:25–26 the phrase refers to righteousness as a divine attribute, only a few verses earlier in 3:21–22 it refers to righteousness as a divine gift. In 10:3 Paul contrasted the righteousness of God with "their own righteousness," the personal righteousness the Jews attempted to achieve through obedience to the law (9:30–31). In this context, the righteousness of God is most likely the righteousness that God imputes to the believer.[91]

Finally, this interpretation is confirmed by those occasions in the letter where Paul more clearly defined the relationship between God and righteousness. Throughout Romans 4, Paul defined "justification" (*dikaioō*) as the act by which a sinner's faith is considered to be or counted as righteousness. The verb used to describe this new gracious evaluation of the believing sinner is *logizomai*, a mathematical and accounting term that generally referred to crediting (when used positively) or charging (when used negatively) a person's account. Paul's quotations of Genesis 15:6 and Psalm 32:2 show that he borrowed this terminology from the OT. What is more, the expression may have been especially appropriate in Paul's context because of a popular rabbinic view of divine judgment that portrayed God as an omniscient accountant who maintained an enormous accounting book in which he carefully recorded a person's sins on the debit side of the ledger and his good works on the credit side. On judgment day the great accountant would audit each person's account, determine the person's final credit score, and either sentence the sinner to punishment or reward his righteousness (*m. Avot* 3:15–16). Paul used the accounting terminology of the rabbis to promote a very different view of divine judgment in which a person's faith in Jesus Christ was credited to his or her account, and this credit resulted in God's evaluation of the sinner as righteous.[92]

In justification, God refused to charge (the negative sense of *logizomai*) sin to the debit side of the believer's ledger (4:8). He counted (the positive sense of *logizomai*) faith as righteousness on the credit side (4:6). Thus, in the accounting analogy, the believer

---

understand the Habakkuk quote as a reference to people declared righteous on the basis of faith and who enjoyed eschatological life because of that declared righteousness. Commentators who affirm that "by faith" is adjectival include Cranfield, *Romans*, 102; Moo, *Romans*, 78; and Käsemann, *Romans*, 32. A few suggest the prepositional phrase modifies both the subject and the verb: R. M. Moody, "The Habakkuk Quotation in Romans 1:17," *ExpTim* 92 (1981): 205–8; and Dunn, *Romans*, 45–46. Although Schreiner (*Romans*, 74) took the prepositional phrase to modify "will live," the view suggested here seems confirmed by Paul's reasoning in 5:17.

[91] This was the view of the Reformers. It was so popular among Protestant commentators in the late nineteenth century that Charles Hodge could write, "This [the view that the righteousness of God was the righteousness that God imputed in justification] is the interpretation which is given substantially by all the modern commentators of note" (*Romans*, 31). The view was also affirmed in J. Murray, *The Epistle to the Romans* (Grand Rapids, MI: Eerdmans, 1968), 1:30.

[92] Notice also the concentration of the accounting terms "count," "gain," and "loss" in Phil 3:2–11 where Paul also discussed "the righteousness from God based on faith."

was considered perfectly righteous on the basis of Christ's sacrificial death.[93] Thus, God credits a sinner's faith to his account as righteousness.[94] Since God is always the stated or implied agent who credits righteousness, Paul may well have conceived of the "righteousness of God" as the righteousness that God credits in particular contexts rather than the righteousness that God possesses or produces.[95] Paul explicitly identifies righteousness as a "gift" (*dōrea*) in 5:17, and this is also implied by the use of verbal and adverbial forms in 3:24 (see 4:4).

The evidence for both views, that the "righteousness of God" is God's attribute of righteousness, including his faithfulness and justice and that the term refers to the righteousness God credits to the believer, is so strong that neither view should be dismissed lightly. In fact, the evidence for both is so compelling that one must either broaden one's interpretation of the phrase "righteousness of God" to refer to both God's attribute of righteousness and the righteousness credited by God in each context or acknowledge that Paul's use of the phrase throughout the letter is variegated, referring in some contexts to divine righteousness and in others to righteousness imputed or credited by God.

An increasing number of commentators have adopted the first view. This is to a certain extent justified by Paul's statement in 3:26 that through Jesus's sacrificial death God "would be righteous and declare righteous the one who has faith in Jesus."[96] On the other hand, to claim that the genitive "of God" expresses source and possession simultaneously is so grammatically awkward and so unlike Paul's normal usage of similar constructions that it is not likely to have been Paul's intent.[97] Most likely, he used the phrase "the righteousness of God" or "his [God's] righteousness" in the sense of a divine attribute in 3:5, 25–26. But "the righteousness of God" means the righteousness that God credits to the believer in 1:17; 3:21–22; 10:3 (twice) and is roughly equivalent to the phrase "the righteousness from God" (*tēn ek theou dikaosynē*) in Philippians 3:9.[98]

Justification Is a Legal Term That Refers to the Verdict Delivered by the Heavenly Judge Throughout history, scholars have often debated whether the verb "to justify" (*dikaioō*) means "to declare righteous" or "make righteous." In the past, Protestant scholars have generally argued that "to justify" is a term drawn from the law court that refers to a pronouncement of innocence or acquittal by the heavenly Judge. In terms used in modern

---

[93] This verb *logizomai* ("credit" or "charge") was used eleven times in Romans in a soteriological sense; nine times it appeared in the passive voice. These are clearly instances of the divine passive in which God is the unnamed agent who performs the action of the verb.

[94] That God is the one who credits or imputes righteousness is made clear by the two occasions in Romans in which Paul used an active (deponent) form of the verb "credit" and explicitly identified a subject. In 4:6 "God credits righteousness," and in Paul's quotation of Ps 32:2 in Rom 4:8, "the Lord" refuses to charge *(logizomai)* sin to the believer's account.

[95] In other words, even if the modifier in the phrase "righteousness of God" is a subjective genitive rather than a genitive of source, this would not necessarily preclude viewing this righteousness as the righteousness God imputes to the believer.

[96] Commentators such as Sanday and Headlam (*Romans*, 24–25), Moo (*Romans*, 74–75), and Schreiner (*Paul*, 202) opted for the first view.

[97] See the concern expressed by Cranfield, *Romans*, 98–99.

[98] See also 2 Cor 5:21 and the similar construction in Phil 3:9.

Western courts, the heavenly Judge pronounces the sinner "not guilty." Roman Catholic scholars have traditionally argued that "to justify" means "to make righteous" and refers to the moral transformation of the sinner. Today many Roman Catholics blend the two concepts and insist that justification includes both a legal pronouncement and an actual transformation.[99] Certainly Paul viewed the salvation of believers as including both an acquittal before God and moral transformation. Romans 5–8 thoroughly discusses the transformation of the believer through his union with Christ in his death and resurrection, the activity of the Holy Spirit, and the still future final redemption of the body.

However, several important features of Paul's discussion of justification show that he viewed justification as an acquittal and not moral transformation. First, Romans 2:13 and 3:20 show that justification relates not to the moral nature of the individual but to his standing "before God." Second, in 8:33 the verb "justify" is contrasted with the verb "condemn." Since the verb "condemn" means "to declare guilty," the contrast implies that the verb "justify" means "to declare innocent." Moreover, the verb "charge" that immediately precedes the verb "justify" is also a forensic term, which supports the conclusion that Paul's use of "justify" was likewise related to courtroom imagery. Third, the use of "justify" in 3:4 associates "justification" with the courtroom. In this context it appears to refer to God's being declared righteous in a lawsuit in which men accuse him of injustice in his decisions.[100] A similar usage in 1 Corinthians 4:4 confirms that the courtroom scene was prominent in Paul's mind when he used the term. Finally, Romans 4 equates justification with faith being "counted" as righteousness. As will be seen, the verb translated "counting" or "calculating" is related to the activity of the divine Judge. In light of this evidence, the verb "justify" describes the action of the judge who acquits or "declares righteous." God has deemed believers to be "not guilty" because of Christ's sacrificial death.

Justification Is Not Granted Based on the "Works of the Law" Paul insisted that justification is not based on the "works of the law" (3:20) and that God justifies sinners "apart from the law" (3:21, 28). Some recent scholars have claimed that the "works of the law" as well as the abbreviated reference to "works" are primarily the "boundary markers" that clearly distinguish Jews from Gentiles.[101] These markers included circumcision, OT dietary laws, and calendar observances. Thus, Paul's polemic is against Jews who trusted their identity as Israelites in light of God's promises to Israel for their salvation rather than

---

[99] The Council of Trent stated that justification is "not the remission of sins merely, but also the sanctification and renewal of the inward man." See also Fitzmyer (*Romans*, 347), who stated, "The sinful human being is not only 'declared upright,' but is 'made upright' (as in 5:19), for the sinner's condition has changed."

[100] See Cranfield, *Romans*, 1:182n4 and 183n1. For a similar usage, see 1 Cor 4:4. See also use of *tsadaq/tsadiq* (MT) and *dikaioō/dikaios* (LXX) in a court context from the law of Moses in Deut 25:1; and the use of *tsadaq* in Ps 51:4.

[101] E.g., Dunn, *Romans*, 1:153–55. A similar interpretation that equates the "works of the law" with ceremonial law was first advanced by Pelagius. See M. F. Wiles, *The Divine Apostle: The Interpretation of St. Paul's Epistles in the Early Church* (Cambridge, UK: Cambridge University Press, 1968), 67–69.

against those who attempted to earn God's favor through obedience to the law in general as Protestant interpreters have traditionally claimed.[102]

A concern for boundary markers in Romans is evident in numerous texts. Paul treats the issue of circumcision repeatedly (2:25–29; 3:1, 30; see 15:8) and even explores the relationship of circumcision to justification (4:9–12). He later deals with the issues of diet and calendar observance (chap. 14). These texts, especially coupled with explicit references to pride in one's Jewish identity and to boasting in relation to circumcision (2:17; 3:27–30), clearly indicate that Paul was at least partially countering a soteriology that insisted that "all Israelites have a share in the world to come" (*m. Sanh.* 10:1).[103]

But contrary to many recent scholars influenced by the New Perspective, this view was only one of several soteriological views current in Paul's day.[104] Other Jewish teachers insisted that Jewish identity was not enough to ensure salvation and that a righteous life was necessary to satisfy the demands of divine judgment. These teachers basically debated this question: Did divine judgment merely weigh the majority of one's deeds and lead to salvation for those who obeyed more laws than they transgressed, or did it require complete and total obedience to the law? Paul argues that neither one's righteousness before God nor his Jewish identity was established through boundary markers. If the Israelite did not "practice the law," he dishonored the law, and his circumcision was therefore regarded by God as uncircumcision (2:17–29).[105] This affirms that the law demanded obedience to requirements beyond the typical boundary markers. Romans 2:27 demonstrates that obedience to the law involved "the letter" and not merely circumcision. "The letter" included all of the regulations of the law inscribed in the old covenant, not just ritual acts.[106]

What is more, Paul argues that "no one will be justified in his sight by the works of the law" (Rom 3:20) by citing a catena of OT texts (Pss 14:1–3; 53:1–3; 5:9; 140:3; 10:7; Isa 59:7–8; Ps 36:1), which describe the Jews' failure to do good, their dishonest and profane speech, their murderous ways, their violence, and their refusal to reverence God. Paul's argument is that salvation through the law requires fidelity to the moral prescriptions of the law and not just to teachings regarding boundary markers. Yet no one has satisfied the

---

[102] A convenient summary of Dunn's view of the "works of the law" appears in *The Theology of Paul the Apostle* (Grand Rapids, MI: Eerdmans, 1998), 354–71.

[103] Exceptions to this general rule were so few that the Mishnah lists them: those who deny the resurrection; those who deny the heavenly origin of the law; those opposed to rabbinic teaching; three kings (Jeroboam, Ahab, and Manasseh); four commoners (Balaam, Doeg, Ahitophel, and Gehazi); the generations of the flood and the Dispersion; the men of Sodom; the spies; and the wilderness generation.

[104] C. L. Quarles, "The Soteriology of Rabbi Akiba and E. P. Sanders' *Paul and Palestinian Judaism*," *NTS* 42 (1996): 185–95; idem, "The New Perspective and Means of Atonement in Jewish Literature of the Second Temple Period," *CTR* 2 (2005): 39–56.

[105] The verbs used to describe the obedience that the law requires (*prassō*, "practice"; *teleō*, "keep") in 2:17–29 indicate that Paul had the law's moral requirements and not only boundary markers in view. This is even clearer in 2:26 where Paul spoke of Gentiles who were uncircumcised keeping the "law's requirements" so that they were regarded by God as circumcised even though they were uncircumcised.

[106] So also Moo, *Romans*, 173.

law's prescriptions. Thus, justification through "works of the law," which includes both ritual and moral prescriptions, is not possible for anyone.

This interpretation is supported by Paul's remarks in Romans 4:4–5 where works of the law are described in terms of working for a reward. Paul insists that justification was a gift, not a payment. He also maintained that God declared "the ungodly" righteous.[107] God's justification of the "ungodly" in 4:5 suggests that justification "apart from works of law" (3:28) means justification is not granted on the basis of the requirements of the law, including both moral and ritual requirements.

This interpretation is further supported by Paul's argument in 9:11–12 that Isaac was not chosen by God based on "works" since he was chosen before he was born and before he had "done anything good or bad." The context shows that "works" here relates to "good works" as opposed to "bad works."[108] Romans 10:5 also confirms that the law required "doing" the things prescribed in the law, the things Israel had failed to do.

Consequently, when Paul insists that justification is not "by works of the law," he means that all have failed to live up to the standards of the law and that no one can attain righteousness before God by means of obedience to the law. This is precisely the point of Paul's extended description of the sinfulness of Gentiles and the hypocrisy of Jews in 1:18–3:18.

Closely related to the denial that justification is based on "works of the law" is Paul's insistence that justification is a gift. In 3:23–24, Paul explains that due to the universality of sin and humanity's failure to manifest the glory of the divine image as they were created to do, God justified sinners "freely" or "as a gift" (*dōrean*) and that this justification occurred "by his grace."[109] The theme resurfaced in Paul's statement that justification was granted "according to grace" (4:16) and not "as something owed" in 4:4–5. Romans 5:15–17 uses three different Greek terms to describe justification as a "gift of grace" (*charisma*) and a "free gift" (*dōrea; dōrēma*).

The fact that justification was granted as a gift and apart from the works of the law had several practical consequences. First, this completely eliminated any legitimate human boasting about one's righteousness before God. Paul argues that justification by works promoted human boasting rather than divine glory while justification by grace as a gift excluded human boasting and promoted God's glory (3:27). In an abbreviated statement Paul wrote, "If Abraham was justified by works, he has something to brag about—but [he does] not [have anything to brag about] before God" (4:2).

---

[107] The adjective "ungodly" and the related noun "ungodliness" characterize the behavior of both Gentiles (1:18) and Jews (11:26), both the uncircumcised and the circumcised.

[108] Paul's use of the verb *prassō* ("done") in this context confirms that the verb describes actions of a moral nature as argued above.

[109] The dative *tē autou chariti* ("by his grace") is probably a dative of cause as in Eph 2:8. See Wallace, *Greek Grammar Beyond the Basics*, 167–68.

Second, justification by grace apart from the works of the law assured the sinner that his enmity with God had ended. He had been reconciled to God and enjoyed peaceful relations with him. The one once alienated from God now had "peace with God through our Lord Jesus Christ" (5:1), having "obtained access through him by faith into this grace in which we stand" (5:2) so that "therefore, there is now no condemnation for those in Christ Jesus" (8:1).

The Law and the Prophets Bear Witness to the Doctrine of Justification Paul is emphatic that the doctrine of justification by faith is not a novelty of his own invention. God's gracious justification of believers had been clearly attested in the OT. "The law and the prophets" witnessed to "God's righteousness through faith in Jesus Christ" (3:21–22). This theme is also prominent in the programmatic statement of the letter. Romans 1:17 confirms the claim that God's justifying righteousness was revealed "from faith to faith" by citing Habakkuk 2:4 and introducing the quotation with the words "just as it is written."

In chapter 4 Paul adds to this citation from the Prophets a confirmation from the Pentateuch (4:3), to which he referred no less than three times in this single chapter, and a citation from the Writings (Ps 32:1–2). Paul appears to employ a rabbinic method of proving an argument by demonstrating that all three major portions of the OT—the Law, the Prophets, and the Writings—affirm a particular truth (see also 1:2).[110] This same affirmation is probably implied by the perplexing prepositional series "from faith to faith" in 1:17. The phrase may mean that God's revelation of his justifying righteousness through the gospel extends from the OT saint to the NT believer, or that it reached first to the Jews (to whom justification had already been revealed in the Law and the Prophets) and then to the Gentiles (who together with the Jews received the revelation of justification by faith in Christ in the gospel).[111]

Justification Requires Faith After denying that God justifies sinners on the basis of their works, Paul adamantly affirms that justification required faith. In 1:5 Paul presented faith as the essence of obedience to the gospel. This same description appears at the conclusion of the letter (16:26). In the programmatic statement of 1:16–17, Paul argued that

---

[110] E. E. Ellis, *Paul's Use of the Old Testament* (Grand Rapids, MI: Baker, 1981), 46.

[111] Quarles, "From Faith to Faith." Alternatively, "from faith to faith" may refer to the expression of God's covenant-keeping faithfulness (see 3:3) in Christ to believers, "God's righteousness through faith in Jesus Christ, to all who believe" (3:22). See the discussion in Dunn (*Romans*, 1:43–46), whose entire treatment repays careful study. Dunn suggested that the phrase *ek pisteōs eis pistin* represents Paul's interpretation of Hab 2:4 and that this interpretation is to be understood against the background of the tension between the Hebrew original of Hab 2:4 and the rendering of the passage in the Greek Septuagint. Specifically, the question was, "Whose faithfulness was in mind in this passage?" The Hebrew text referred to the righteous man, while the Septuagint referred to God. Paul omitted explicit reference to either the believer or God, yet most likely his way of putting things—"from faith to faith"—represented an effort to hold the roles of God and the believer in proper tension by interpreting Hab 2:4 as indicating that God's righteousness extended "*from* faith" (i.e., God's faithfulness) "*to* faith" (i.e., the faith response of the believer). Thus Paul navigated the Scylla and Charybdis (dangerous extremes) of the history of interpretation of Hab 2:4 by affirming God and his faithfulness as the *source* of salvation and believers' faith as the proper *response* to God's covenant faithfulness expressed in sending Christ. See Quarles, "From Faith to Faith" for a discussion of difficulties with Dunn's view.

the saving power of the gospel was operative specifically and exclusively "to everyone who believes." The prepositional series "from faith to faith" implies that justification had always been granted on the basis of faith throughout every era of salvation history, which Paul demonstrates through his citation of Habakkuk 2:4 that speaks of those made righteous by faith.

The necessity of faith for justification is prominent in chapter 4, where Paul appealed to the example of Abraham based on Genesis 15:6. The OT text clearly demonstrates that Abraham was declared righteous not by working but by "believing on the one who justifies the ungodly" (4:4–5, author translation). Justification thus requires believing from the heart (10:10). In 4:17–25, Paul discussed the nature of Abraham's faith and demonstrated that it parallels the faith required for justification in the Christian gospel. Abraham's faith involved trusting God against all human hopes to fulfill his promise to make Abraham the father of many nations. Since Abraham was 100 years old and, as far as his capacity to produce offspring was concerned, "already dead," and since Sarah was likewise barren, Abraham's belief that God would fulfill his promise entailed believing God "who gives life to the dead." Thus, Abraham's faith correlates to Christian faith that God raised Jesus from the dead, a requirement for justification attested in 4:24 and again in 10:9.

Also, Abraham's faith involved believing in God who "calls things into existence that do not exist" (4:17). Many commentators see this as a reference to God's creation of the universe out of nothing.[112] In this context, it refers to the exercise of God's creative power in producing Isaac through the union of the "dead" Abraham and Sarah.[113] Perhaps this reference is intended to parallel the resurrection of Jesus like the immediately preceding description. However, the grammar of the Greek text suggests that Paul may have had another point in mind. He describes God as One who literally "calls things into existence that do not exist." One would expect Paul to have said that God calls the things that do not exist "into existence" rather than "as existing."[114] The apostle probably used this particular construction to evoke a comparison between the birth of Isaac and justification in which God calls those who are not righteous "righteous," that is, declaring righteous the ungodly.[115] This view seems to be supported by 4:23–24 where Paul explained how Abraham's faith paralleled Christian faith and where he addressed not only faith in Jesus's resurrection but the forgiveness of our trespasses and "our justification."

But the discussion in chapter 4 is not an exhaustive treatment of the faith required for justification. It only discusses those aspects of faith that are closely paralleled in Abraham's experience. Other statements in the letter demonstrate that the faith required

---

[112] E.g., Sanday and Headlam, *Romans*, 113.

[113] So Cranfield, *Romans*, 245; Fitzmyer, *Romans*, 386.

[114] E.g., Philo, *Spec. Leg.* 4.187.

[115] Thus, "call . . . as" functions as the equivalent to "counts" or "considers" *(logizomai)*. According to Käsemann, similar suggestions have been made by Zahn, Kühl, Billerbeck, and entertained by Michel. Moo (*Romans*, 281–82) and Käsemann (*Romans*, 122–24) viewed the construction as an allusion to the creative activity of God in salvation. Fitzmyer (*Romans*, 386) suggested it refers to God's act of creating children of Abraham out of Gentiles.

for justification includes not only belief in Jesus's resurrection and the justification that his death and resurrection accomplished but also belief in important aspects of Jesus's identity as well.

In the introduction to the letter, Paul described the gospel message as one *from* God, mediated *through* the prophets, but a message *about* Jesus specifically (1:1–3). He confirmed this by describing the gospel as "the good news about his Son" (1:9) and in a later passage by describing the message that must be believed for justification (10:10) as the "message about Christ" (10:17). Hearers are called to respond to this gospel with the "obedience of faith" (1:5; 16:26), which means that they obey the Christocentric gospel by believing its claims about him. Not surprisingly, Paul describes the faith required for justification in 3:26 as "faith in Jesus."

Paul articulates fundamental claims of the gospel about Jesus in 1:3–4. It claims that Jesus fulfilled OT prophecies about the coming Messiah by being born of the line of David. Jesus is the Messiah, the Son anointed by the Father to receive the nations as his inheritance and to break the wicked with a rod of iron. He is the One to whom all must pay homage, or else they will perish for their rebellion (Psalm 2). Jesus is also the "powerful Son of God"—literally, the "Son of God with power"—by virtue of his resurrection. Since the next reference to "power" in Romans refers to the power to save (1:16), this title identifies Jesus as the One with the power to save, the Savior of sinners.

The gospel also identifies Jesus Christ as "our Lord" (1:4). Although the title "Lord" can function as a title of authority or a title of deity depending on its context, abundant evidence in this letter demonstrates that "Lord" is used of Jesus in Romans as a title of deity. This is clearest in 10:9–13 where Paul articulated the "message of faith" (10:8). He argues that "if you confess with your mouth, 'Jesus is Lord,' . . . you will be saved." Paul confirmed this with a quotation of Joel 2:32: "Everyone who calls on the name of the Lord will be saved." He derived his statement in 10:9 from this OT text that he quoted in 10:13, and there is a close correlation between the two. Confessing with the mouth "Jesus is Lord" parallels calling on the name of the Lord, and "will be saved" exactly matches "will be saved." In the OT context, "LORD" *(kyrios)* is the Greek translation of the Hebrew name Yahweh and unambiguously refers to the God of Israel. Paul's application of this OT text to clarify and confirm the necessity of confessing "Jesus is Lord" demonstrates that "Lord" functions in Christian confession as the name of the God of the OT. Thus, the gospel insists that Jesus is Yahweh: God in human flesh.[116] This insistence on Jesus's deity also surfaces in 9:5 where the Messiah is described as the One "who is God over all."[117]

---

[116] See the similar treatment in L. W. Hurtado, *Lord Jesus Christ: Devotion to Jesus in Earliest Christianity* (Grand Rapids, MI: Eerdmans, 2003), 111–12.

[117] The original text lacks punctuation, and scholars continue to debate the correct punctuation. The manner in which modern editors and translators punctuate this text significantly impacts its meaning. Paul's theology, style, and the literary context support the punctuation of the text as it appears in the CSB (rather than the margin). Paul clearly affirmed Jesus's

Moreover, Paul asserts in 10:6 that the righteousness that comes by faith says, "Do not say in your heart, 'Who will go up to heaven?' that is, to bring Christ down." Those made righteous by faith affirm Christ's heavenly origin and the fact that he has "come down" to live among sinners through the incarnation.[118] The righteousness that comes by faith does not ask, "Who will go down to the abyss?" to bring Christ up from the dead. Thus, it not only affirms his heavenly origin and incarnation but also his bodily resurrection. The confession related to righteousness that comes by faith in 10:6–7 closely parallels the confession of Jesus as "Lord" and the affirmation of his resurrection in 10:9.

The faith required for justification in Romans is one in which sinners believe in Jesus's identity as the Messiah, the Savior whose sacrificial death secures the believer's acquittal before the eternal and almighty God. Such faith acknowledges both that Jesus died a sacrificial death and that he rose from the dead. Only this Christ-centered faith is sufficient for the gracious acquittal of the sinner.

The Death and Resurrection of Jesus Are the Bases for the Believer's Justification Paul writes that believers "are justified freely by his grace through the redemption that is in Christ Jesus" (3:24). The term "redemption" normally referred to a payment of a ransom that liberated a prisoner of war, a slave, or a condemned criminal. Since "justified" is a forensic term drawn from the legal proceedings of the courtroom, one would expect the noun "redemption" in this context to bear the nuance of the liberation of a condemned criminal, rather than that of a prisoner of war or slave. This interpretation is supported by Paul's equation of redemption and the "forgiveness of sins" in the Prison Epistles (Eph 1:7 NIV; Col 1:14).

Although the noun "redemption" may refer to liberation without reference to the payment of a ransom, allusion to a ransom is expected here based on usage in the Septuagint, Josephus, and Philo.[119] Moreover, in Ephesians 1:7 Paul describes "redemption" as being accomplished "through his blood," which identifies Jesus's death as the ransom price. Paul's claim that believers were "bought at a price" (1 Cor 6:20; 7:23) likewise demonstrates that redemption involved the payment of a ransom.[120] Although the word translated "redeem" in Galatians 3:13–14 is not the same as the one used here, Paul's discussion there confirms that he could speak of redemption as a deliverance from the penalty of sin accomplished

---

deity in texts such as Rom 10:9; Phil 2:6–11; Col 2:9; and Titus 2:13. Paul's doxologies are normally dependent (Rom 1:25; 11:36; 2 Cor 11:31; Gal 1:15; Eph 3:21; Phil 4:20; 1 Tim 1:17; 2 Tim 4:18). All of the instances of the adjective *eulogētos* ("blessed") in the OT, Apocrypha, and NT (98 occurrences) place the adjective before the noun referring to God when independent (Ps 68:19–20 [LXX Ps 67:19–20] is mispunctuated and not an exception). Paul's construction in 9:5 most closely parallels 2 Cor 11:31, which is clearly not independent.

[118] Most church fathers and many modern commentators interpret this passage in this fashion; e.g., Moo, *Romans*, 655; Fitzmyer, *Romans*, 590; Cranfield, *Romans*, 2:525; Schreiner, *Romans*, 558–59.

[119] Morris, *Apostolic Preaching*, 9–26; I. H. Marshall, "The Development of the Concept of Redemption in the New Testament," in *Reconciliation and Hope*, 153.

[120] Moo, *Romans*, 229–30n51. Paul's usage of the concept of redemption to describe the consequences of Jesus's death was likely influenced by his knowledge of the Jesus tradition (see Mark 10:45; Matt 20:28).

through the sufferings and sacrificial death of Jesus. Thus, justification is accomplished by God through the death of Christ.

This is confirmed by Romans 3:25. Although many translations treat verse 25 as a separate sentence detached from verse 24, the verse begins with a relative pronoun that closely connects the two verses. The verse describes Jesus Christ "whom God presented as a propitiation through faith in his blood" (author's translation). The word "propitiation" *(hilastērion)* was used in the LXX to refer to the "mercy seat," the cover of the ark of the covenant on which sacrificial blood was poured on the Day of Atonement to avert the wrath of God and to secure atonement for sins committed during that year. Several clues in the immediate context suggest that Paul intended for this term to evoke the imagery of the OT sacrificial system. First, the phrase "in his blood" compares the blood Jesus shed during his sufferings and death to the blood poured out on the mercy seat. Jesus's blood is mentioned, not as the object of faith but as the means through which God accomplished propitiation. Second, Paul saw this propitiation as necessary for satisfying the demands of God's justice. The argument of verse 26 is that God's justice or righteousness would be compromised if he leniently passed over sin and declared the sinner righteous apart from a substitutionary sacrifice. Only by means of the cross can the heavenly Judge be just and justify believing sinners. Third, Paul's discussion of the just wrath of God that began in 1:18 highlights the need for a means to appease divine wrath.[121] Consequently, Paul not only presents Jesus's death as a ransom that rescued condemned criminals from their deserved sentence; he also portrays Jesus's death as an atoning sacrifice that satisfied the justice of God so that believing sinners may be declared righteous and escape the wrath their sins incited.

At the conclusion of his discussion of justification, Paul describes Jesus as the One who "was delivered up for our trespasses" (Rom 4:25), a description that echoes Isaiah 53:12 (LXX). The verb "delivered up" often functioned as a technical term referring to placing someone in the custody of law enforcement officials or the court for imprisonment, trial, sentencing, and punishment.[122] The idea is that Jesus was handed over to the Judge in order to suffer the penalty for the believer's trespasses. It is on these grounds that the Judge may pronounce the verdict that the sinner is "not guilty." Divine justice has been fully satisfied through the substitutionary suffering of God's Son.

CONTRIBUTION TO THE CANON

- The gospel—promised through the prophets and preached by Paul (1:1–4, 16–17; see Hab 2:4)
- Righteousness and justification by faith apart from works of the law (1:17; 3:21–5:2; see esp. 4:3, 9, 22–23, citing Gen 15:6)

---

[121] Notice also the discussion of divine wrath in 5:9. Believers are justified now through Jesus's sacrificial death and will be saved from God's wrath in eschatological judgment.

[122] This is another of the forensic terms Paul used in Romans to describe God's salvific work.

- Promotion of Jew-Gentile unity on the basis of the universality of sin (1:18–3:20; 3:23); the free gift of salvation through Jesus Christ (6:23); and God's all-encompassing plan of salvation (chaps. 9–11)
- The impossibility of keeping the law and the provision of new life in the Spirit (chaps. 6–8)
- God's salvation-historical plan for Jews and Gentiles past, present, and future (chaps. 9–11)

STUDY QUESTIONS

1. Why is Paul's authorship of Romans so certain?
2. Why are Paul's travel plans so important in dating the book of Romans?
3. What considerations point to a likely Corinthian provenance for Romans?
4. What was the occasion for Paul's letter to the Romans?
5. Why did Paul write Romans?
6. On what major divisions of Romans do most scholars agree?
7. When Paul says in Romans 3:23 that "all have sinned and fall short of the glory of God," whom does he have in mind?
8. What rhetorical questions did Paul pose in Romans 6–7, and what was his succinct answer to each?
9. What role does the "therefore" play in Romans 12:1?
10. How are individuals viewed by God as righteous?
11. What support is given by the authors for the following statement: "The righteousness of God is a gift which God imputes to the sinner who believes in Christ"?

FOR FURTHER STUDY

Bruce, F. F. *The Letter of Paul to the Romans: An Introduction and Commentary*. Tyndale New Testament Commentaries. Rev. ed. Grand Rapids, MI: Eerdmans, 1985.

Cranfield, C. E. B. *A Critical and Exegetical Commentary on the Epistle to the Romans*. International Critical Commentary. 2 vols. Edinburgh, Scotland: T&T Clark, 1975–79.

Donfried, K. P., ed. *The Romans Debate*. Rev. and exp. ed. Peabody, MA: Hendrickson, 1991.

Dunn, J. D. G. *Romans*. Word Biblical Commentary 38A–B. 2 vols. Dallas, TX: Word, 1988.

Fitzmyer, J. *Romans: A New Translation with Introduction and Commentary*. Anchor Bible. Garden City, NY: Doubleday, 1993.

Gamble, H. *The Textual History of the Letter to the Romans: A Study in Textual and Literary Criticism*. Studies and Documents. Grand Rapids, MI: Eerdmans, 1977.

Harrison, E. F., and D. A. Hagner. "Romans." Pages 19–237 in *The Expositor's Bible Commentary*. Rev. ed. Vol. 11: *Romans—Galatians*. Grand Rapids, MI: Zondervan, 2008.

Käsemann, E. *Commentary on Romans*. Translated by G. Bromiley. Grand Rapids, MI: Eerdmans, 1980.

Kruse, C. G. *Paul's Letter to the Romans*. Pillar New Testament Commentary. Grand Rapids, MI: Eerdmans, 2012.

Longenecker, R. N. *The Epistle to the Romans*. New International Greek Testament Commentary. Grand Rapids, MI: Eerdmans, 2015.

Moo, D. J. *Encountering the Book of Romans: A Theological Survey*. Encountering Biblical Studies. Grand Rapids, MI: Baker, 2002.

___________. *The Epistle to the Romans*. The New International Commentary on the New Testament. Grand Rapids, MI: Eerdmans, 1996.

Morris, L. *The Epistle to the Romans*. Grand Rapids, MI: Eerdmans, 1988.

Osborne, G. R. *Romans*. IVP New Testament Commentary. Downers Grove, IL: IVP Academic, 2010.

Sanday, W., and A. C. Headlam. *A Critical and Exegetical Commentary on the Epistle to the Romans*. International Critical Commentary. New York, NY: Charles Scribner's Sons, 1922.

Schlatter, A. *Romans: The Righteousness of God*. Translated by S. Schatzmann. Peabody, MA: Hendrickson, 1995.

Schreiner, T. R. *Romans*. Baker Exegetical Commentary on the New Testament. Grand Rapids, MI: Baker, 1998.

Seifrid, M. A. "Romans." Pages 607–94 in *Commentary on the New Testament Use of the Old Testament*. Edited by G. K. Beale and D. A. Carson. Grand Rapids, MI: Baker, 2007.

Stuhlmacher, P. *Paul's Letter to the Romans: A Commentary*. Translated by S. J. Hafemann. Louisville, KY: Westminster/John Knox Press, 1994.

Wright, N. T. "The Letter to the Romans." Pages 393–770 in *The New Interpreter's Bible*. Vol. 10. Nashville, TN: Abingdon, 2002.

Chapter 14

The Prison Epistles: Philippians, Ephesians, Colossians, and Philemon

CORE KNOWLEDGE

Basic Knowledge: Students should know the key facts of Philippians, Ephesians, Colossians, and Philemon. With regard to history, students should be able to identify each book's author, date, provenance, destination, and purpose. With regard to literature, they should be able to provide a basic outline of each book and identify core elements of each book's content found in the Unit-by-Unit discussions. With regard to theology, students should be able to identify the major theological themes in Philippians, Ephesians, Colossians, and Philemon.

Intermediate Knowledge: Students should be able to present the arguments for historical, literary, and theological conclusions. With regard to history, students should be able to discuss the evidence for Pauline authorship, date, provenance, destination, and purpose. With regard to literature, they should be able to provide a detailed outline of each book. With regard to theology, students should be able to discuss the major theological themes in Philippians, Ephesians, Colossians, and Philemon and the ways in which they uniquely contribute to the NT canon.

Advanced Knowledge: Students should be able to interact with alternative proposals concerning the literary integrity of Philippians, the authorship of Ephesians and Colossians, and the nature of Ephesians as a circular letter. Students should also be able to critically assess proposals concerning the nature of the "Colossian heresy" and its relation to the letter's purpose, discuss the interpretive options with regard to the phrase "the circumcision of Christ" in Colossians 2:11, and be prepared to adjudicate the possible occasions for Paul's letter to Philemon.

INTRODUCTION

AS THE BOOK of Acts makes clear, Paul established several local congregations in major urban centers on at least three missionary journeys. Toward the end of his distinguished apostolic ministry, and after writing Galatians, 1 and 2 Thessalonians, 1 and 2 Corinthians, and Romans, Paul engaged in additional correspondence with several churches and individuals during his first Roman imprisonment (AD 58–60). Paul's Letters to the Philippians, Ephesians, Colossians, and Philemon (commonly called the Prison Epistles) date to this period.

Most likely Philippians was written before the others. In Philemon 22, Paul expected to be released from prison soon, while in Philippians 1:21–25 he inferred what the future held based on spiritual principles, but he had no idea as to the timing of his release.

Ephesians, Colossians, and Philemon were all related to the return of Onesimus and were most likely written roughly at the same time and under similar circumstances. But the precise sequence in which these letters were penned is unknown. Because Ephesians and Colossians are connected via Tychicus (Eph 6:21; Col 4:7), and Colossians and Philemon via Onesimus (Col 4:9; Phlm 10) and Epaphras (Col 1:17; 4:12; Phlm 23), and because Ephesians, Colossians, Philemon is the order in which the books are included in the NT canon, we will discuss these three letters in that same order.

Philippians

KEY FACTS

Author:	Paul
Date:	Around AD 59 (most likely prior to Ephesians, Colossians, and Philemon)
Provenance:	Roman imprisonment
Destination:	The church at Philippi
Occasion:	Thanksgiving for the Philippians' partnership in the gospel and warnings against disunity and false teaching as hindrances to the spread of the gospel
Purpose:	To promote gospel-centered unity for the sake of advancing the gospel
Theme:	Partnership in the gospel and walking worthy of the gospel
Key Verses:	1:27–30

INTRODUCTION

PHILIPPIANS IS A favorite among Paul's Letters because of its inspiring message of joy in the midst of trying circumstances (e.g., imprisonment). Some students may know Philippians in piecemeal fashion because of the numerous memorable phrases or expressions found in the letter. Familiar phrases include, "For me, to live is Christ and to die is gain" (1:21); "so that at the name of Jesus every knee will bow . . . and every tongue will confess that Jesus Christ is Lord" (2:10–11); "I am able to do all things through him who strengthens me" (4:13); and "rejoice in the Lord always. I will say it again: Rejoice!" (4:4). However, this bits-and-pieces approach to Philippians does justice neither to the depth of the letter nor to Paul's overall purpose for writing. One must see how the pieces fit together into a coherent whole in order to appreciate the profound message of the letter.

HISTORY

Author

Authenticity Most scholars regard Philippians as an authentic letter written by Paul. Scholarly acceptance of Paul's authorship is so widespread, in fact, that an extended discussion is unnecessary. The reasons for accepting authenticity include (1) the letter opens with the words "from Paul" (author's translation); (2) the early church accepted Paul as the author without dissent; and (3) the intensely personal nature of the letter. The early church fathers Polycarp (ca. AD 69–155), Irenaeus (ca. AD 130–200), Clement of Alexandria (ca. AD 150–215), and Tertullian (ca. AD 160–225) unanimously accepted Pauline authorship. This consensus was momentarily questioned in the nineteenth century by critics such as F. C. Baur, whose historical reconstructions led him to believe that Paul only wrote Romans, 1 and 2 Corinthians, and Galatians.[1] Baur's case, however, did not garner widespread support, and his arguments have now been largely abandoned—except for an occasional unsuccessful attempt to revive his thesis.

The only major debated element concerning authorship centers on the so-called "Christ hymn"[2] of 2:6–11. Some scholars contend that this passage is pre-Pauline because of (1) the unusual vocabulary; (2) the rhythmic style; (3) the presence of the "servant" theme; and (4) the absence of key Pauline themes such as redemption and resurrection. Those who think Paul wrote 2:6–11 customarily respond by claiming that (1) other Pauline passages contain as many unusual words within a comparable space; (2) other passages convey a rhythmic style; (3) "servant" theology is expressed through the characteristically Pauline expression "death on a cross" (2:8); and (4) Paul need not mention all of his theology in every passage.[3]

Literary Integrity More serious challenges have been raised against the integrity of the letter.[4] The case for a composite letter is sufficiently convincing so that a growing number of scholars have accepted Philippians as a composite document that merged several separate documents into one.[5] Factors commonly cited in favor of this include the following.

1. In terms of external evidence, Polycarp's letter to the Philippians provides possible evidence for a composite interpretation, because he stated that Paul wrote "letters" (plural) to the Philippians (Phil 3:2).

[1] F. C. Baur, *Paul, the Apostle of Jesus Christ* (Peabody, MA: Hendrickson, 2003).

[2] A significant debate exists over whether to call this passage a "hymn" or "exalted prose." P. T. O'Brien, *Philippians*, NIGTC (Grand Rapids, MI: Eerdmans, 1991), 186–202, makes the best case for calling this passage a hymn, while G. D. Fee, "Philippians 2:5–11: Hymn or Exalted Pauline Prose?" *BBR* 2 (1992): 29–46, provides the most forceful account for why the passage is Pauline exalted prose.

[3] Debates rage over the passage's structure (how many strophes or couplets?), theology (does it express preexistence?), and purpose (imitation of Christ's humility or sharing in Christ's death and resurrection in order to secure a place in the church body?). For an excellent guide, see O'Brien, *Philippians*, 186–202.

[4] Space constraints do not permit a detailed analysis of the textual tradition of Philippians. See the excellent work of M. Silva, *Philippians*, BECNT, 2nd ed. (Grand Rapids, MI: Baker, 2005), 22–26.

[5] V. Koperski, "The Early History of the Dissection of Philippians," *JTS* 44 (1993): 599–603, notes that a partition theory for Philippians was first proposed in the nineteenth century but did not come to prominence until the twentieth. Advocates include W. Schenk, "Der Philipperbrief oder die Philipperbriefe des Paulus? Eine Antwort an V. Koperski," *ETL* 70 (1994): 122–31; and W. Harnisch, "Die paulinische Selbstempfehlung als Plädoyer für den Gekreuzigten: Rhetorisch-hermeneutische Erwägungen zu Phil 3," in *Das Urchristentum in seiner literarischen Geschichte: Festschrift für Jürgen Becker zum 65. Geburtstag*, eds. U. Mell and U. B. Müller, BZNW 100 (Berlin, Germany: de Gruyter, 1999), 133–54.

2. With regard to internal evidence, Paul's opponents do not appear to be the same throughout the letter.
3. Also, there seems to be a change in the health of Epaphroditus that assumes a time lapse. Paul stated in 2:25–30 that Epaphroditus was very ill, but Paul does not mention his illness when Epaphroditus's name emerges again in 4:18.
4. What appears to be a concluding remark is found at 3:1 ("finally" ESV) halfway through the letter. This remark occurs immediately after a discussion of the travel plans of Paul and his associates, material that one would expect at the end of the letter.
5. Along similar lines, 3:1 appears to fit together with 4:4, while an abrupt change of tone occurs at 3:2 and continues through 4:3.[6]
6. Surprisingly, Paul waited until the end of the letter to thank the Philippians for their beneficence.

However, despite the strength of some of the arguments advanced in favor of a composite reading of Philippians, the case for the letter's unity is even stronger.

1. Polycarp's citation of Pauline "letters" written to the Philippians does not necessitate that Philippians in its current form is a composite of several letters. J. B. Lightfoot argued at length that the plural *epistolai* in Polycarp had the nuance of the singular. He demonstrated that the use of the plural for the singular of "letter" occurred in the work of a number of classical writers, including Thucydides, Josephus, Euripides, Lucian, Julian, and others.[7] Even if the plural refers to multiple letters, it is possible that Polycarp wrongly inferred that Paul wrote multiple missives to Philippi based on a misinterpretation of 3:1 rather than direct knowledge that the Philippians possessed multiple letters that Paul wrote to the congregation. Perhaps Polycarp wrongly assumed that when Paul referred to writing the "same things" to the Philippians, he had in mind a previous letter rather than earlier discussions from Paul's ministry with the Philippians. But, as O'Brien pointed out, 3:18 appears to confirm that Paul had in mind those things which he had previously taught by mouth.[8]

2. No external evidence exists for taking Philippians as a composite document. Every Greek manuscript preserves Philippians in its current form, including 𝔓[46], a manuscript dating to the late second or early third century. Neither do any of the early church fathers hint at a suspicion that Philippians was a composite document.

---

[6] See esp. E. J. Goodspeed, *An Introduction to the New Testament* (Chicago, IL: University Press, 1937), 90–91: "There is between 3:1 and 3:2 a break so harsh as to defy explanation."

[7] See Lightfoot, *Philippians*, 138–42. But the entry in *BDAG*, s.v. "ἐπιστολή," states, "In all probability the plur. in our lit.—even Ac 9:2; Pol 3:2—always means more than one letter, not a single one."

[8] See O'Brien, *Philippians*, 350–52.

3. The references to Epaphroditus do not necessitate a lapse in time. Carson and Moo provided a fitting response to this line of argument: "There is no reason why the man's illness should be brought up every time he is mentioned."[9]

4. The same terms and themes pervade all the alleged "parts" of the letter. The mere repetition of lexical terms does not offer conclusive evidence, but repeated vocabulary together with thematic similarities offers a substantial case for unity.[10]

5. The personal nature of Philippians accounts for seemingly abrupt shifts and stylistic variance. In fact, the arguments for the letter's abrupt features cut both ways. Why should one assume that any redactor would stitch these various letters together in what, to advocates of a composite document, appears to be such a haphazard way?[11]

6. The Greek phrase translated "finally" in 3:1 (ESV) is most likely a transitional, not a terminal, phrase.[12] Nor does the mention of Paul's travel plans in the middle of the letter indicate that this section was originally at the conclusion of the document. After all, 2 Corinthians and 1 Thessalonians mention travel plans in the body of the letter, and there were good contextual reasons for doing so here as well.[13]

7. Paul may place his acknowledgment of the Philippians' generosity at the end for the sake of emphasis. This structural feature would not betray a lack of gratitude.

Date

The date for Philippians depends on the place of writing. Dates as early as AD 50 or as late as 63 are possible. If Paul wrote during his first Roman imprisonment, he probably wrote the letter in the late 50s (early 60s in the conventional reckoning). If he wrote during his Caesarean imprisonment, the letter should be dated 55–57 (58–60 in the conventional reckoning). If he wrote from Ephesus, Paul wrote the letter between the years 51 and 54 (54 and 57 in the conventional reckoning). Although the issues are complex, the evidence for a Roman provenance is most persuasive. Philippians appears to have been written somewhat earlier than the other Prison Epistles. Paul appears to have written Colossians, Philemon, and Ephesians at about the same time. Philemon implies that Paul's release from prison was imminent (Phlm 21). However, when Paul wrote Philippians, he

---

[9] Carson and Moo, *Introduction to the New Testament*, 510.

[10] See the extensive links proposed by P. Wick, *Der Philipperbrief: Der formale Aufbau des Briefs als Schlüssel zum Verständnis seines Inhalts*, BWA(N)T 7/15 (Stuttgart, Germany: Kohlhammer, 1994); and J. T. Reed, *A Discourse Analysis of Philippians: Method and Rhetoric in the Debate over Literary Integrity*, JSNTSup 136 (Sheffield, UK: Sheffield Academic Press, 1997).

[11] The best summary of the options and case for literary integrity is probably still D. E. Garland, "The Composition and Literary Unity of Philippians: Some Neglected Factors," *NovT* 27 (1985): 141–73.

[12] See M. E. Thrall, *Greek Particles in the New Testament: Linguistic and Exegetical Studies*, New Testament Tools and Studies (Leiden: Brill, 1962), 28: "λοιπόν in post-classical Greek could be used simply as a transitional particle, to introduce either a logical conclusion or a fresh point in the progress of thought" (cf. *BDAG*, s.v. "λοιπός," 602–3). The expression can mean "finally" (2 Cor 13:11), but context must determine if it has a concluding or a transitional nuance. E.g., 1 Thess 4:1 clearly uses the word in a transitional sense, because it is followed by two chapters of material.

[13] See 2 Cor 1:12–2:4; 2:12–13; 8:16–24; 1 Thess 2:17–3:10. On the reasons for including the travelogue here, see O'Brien, *Philippians*, 15.

seemed less certain about the outcome of his trial and was contemplating the possibility that he would be martyred (Phil 1:21–26). On the other hand, Paul's extensive outreach (Phil 1:12–14) and the widespread knowledge of his circumstances suggest that he had been imprisoned in Rome for at least several months at the time he wrote Philippians. These factors suggest the composition of Philippians should be dated to around the midpoint of the Roman imprisonment, in or around the year 59.[14]

Provenance

The question of provenance is one of the most contested issues regarding Philippians. Paul clearly identified himself as a prisoner (1:7, 13, 17), but he did not explicitly state the location of this imprisonment. Presumably, the Philippians knew where he was imprisoned and thus did not need to be told. Three different answers commend themselves as worthy of consideration: (1) Rome,[15] (2) Caesarea, and (3) Ephesus.[16]

The traditional view places Paul's imprisonment in Rome. A Roman imprisonment hypothesis would account for (1) the mention of the Praetorium (1:13) and Caesar's household (4:22); (2) the loose restrictions implied by Paul's activity during his imprisonment (see Acts 28:16, 30–31); (3) references to a seemingly well-established church (1:14); (4) external evidence such as the subscription added by the first corrector of Codex Vaticanus and the comments in the Marcionite Prologue;[17] and (5) the "life or death" nature of the imprisonment (Paul could have appealed to Caesar while under any other incarceration).

Until recently the Roman hypothesis held almost universal sway. But scholars began to note two primary weaknesses in the traditional hypothesis related to geography and Paul's travel plans. First, the distance between Philippi and Rome (about 1,200 miles) renders the number of journeys implied in Philippians (perhaps as many as seven) problematic.[18] Second, the letter to the Romans mentions Paul's intention to travel to Spain (Rom 15:24,

---

[14] See further the discussion below.

[15] M. Bockmuehl, *The Epistle to the Philippians*, BNTC 11 (Peabody, MA: Hendrickson, 1998), 25–32; G. D. Fee, *Paul's Letter to the Philippians*, NICNT (Grand Rapids, MI: Eerdmans, 1995), 34–37; Silva, *Philippians*, 5–7; O'Brien, *Philippians*, 19–26.

[16] F. Thielman, "Ephesus and the Literary Setting of Philippians," in *New Testament Greek and Exegesis, Fs. Gerald F. Hawthorne*, ed. A. M. Donaldson and T. B. Sailors (Grand Rapids, MI: Eerdmans, 2003), 205–23; idem, *Theology of the New Testament* (Grand Rapids, MI: Zondervan, 2005), 307. Kümmel (*Introduction*, 332) also slightly favored the Ephesian hypothesis over the Caesarean one and regarded the Roman theory as the least probable. Carson and Moo (*Introduction to the New Testament*, 506) cautiously said that "there is a little more to be said for Ephesus than for Rome, but we can say no more than this (and many would hold that we are not entitled to say even this)." Finally, some suggest the city of Corinth, but this proposal has not garnered much scholarly support.

[17] "The Philippians are Macedonians. These, having received the word of truth, remained steadfast in the faith. The apostle commends them, writing to them from prison in Rome."

[18] O'Brien (*Philippians*, 25) correctly calculated that as few as three journeys between Rome and Philippi are possible before Paul penned the letter, depending on where Epaphroditus was when he became ill. If Paul wrote Philippians toward the end of his two-year imprisonment in Rome, there is more than adequate time for the required trips. The three one-way trips to Philippi by Epaphroditus, Timothy, and Paul, respectively, do not pose a real problem for a Roman provenance. Concern should focus on the number of trips between the beginning of Paul's incarceration and the penning of the letter.

28), while Philippians states that Paul planned to visit Philippi after his release (Phil 2:24). Beginning in the nineteenth century, these problems led some critics to propose Caesarea as the place of writing for Philippians. Some scholars advocated a Caesarean provenance because (1) Acts records a two-year imprisonment in that location (Acts 24:27); (2) Herod had Praetorian guards there (Acts 23:35); and (3) an early date hypothesis places Paul's Judaizing opponents of 3:2–4 within the same time frame as his earlier letters.

But the Caesarean hypothesis is also problematic because its distance from Philippi leads to many of the same problems raised against the Roman hypothesis, and there is no evidence of a thriving church in Caesarea that would account for the scenario in Philippians 1:12–18. Since 1897, the Caesarean hypothesis has been eclipsed by the Ephesian hypothesis, first proposed by A. Deissmann.[19] This view currently enjoys the strongest advocacy for these reasons: (1) though Acts does not identify an imprisonment in Ephesus, Paul mentioned many imprisonments not recorded in Acts (2 Cor 11:23);[20] (2) the close proximity of Ephesus to Philippi eases the concern over the possibility of the number of trips between Paul's place of imprisonment and Philippi; (3) Philippians bears a close literary affinity to Paul's earlier letters;[21] (4) inscriptions show a section of the Praetorian Guard was stationed at Ephesus;[22] and (5) Philippians fails to mention Luke, who was with Paul in Rome (2 Tim 4:11) but was probably not with him during his Ephesian ministry in Acts (i.e., the Ephesian ministry is not one of the "we" passages in Acts).[23]

Nevertheless, the Ephesian hypothesis also faces some objections from scholars. First, the theory is built on implicit inferences because there is no explicit mention of an imprisonment in Ephesus. Second, the collection for the poor believers in Jerusalem was of central importance during Paul's Ephesian ministry, but there is no hint of it in Philippians. And third, Paul spoke somewhat harshly about those around him except for Timothy (Phil 2:19–21), which would be a strange way of characterizing Ephesus because his friends Priscilla and Aquila were in Ephesus at the same time he was.[24]

The mixed nature of the evidence for provenance precludes a dogmatic position. Caesarea appears the least likely option.[25] The choice between Rome and Ephesus is

---

[19] A. Deissmann, "Zur ephesinischen Gefangenschaft des Apostels Paulus," in *Anatolian Studies Presented to Sir William Ramsay*, ed. W. H. Buckler and W. M. Calder (Manchester, UK: University Press, 1923), 121–27.

[20] Some scholars also point out that 2 Corinthians records a reference to a severe hardship in Ephesus, which could imply imprisonment.

[21] Thielman ("Ephesus and the Literary Setting of Philippians," 205–23) offered the most sustained case for links between Philippians and earlier letters such as Galatians, Corinthians, and Romans. G. W. Beare (*Philippians*, BNTC, 2nd ed. [London, England: A. & C. Black, 1969], 20) adopted the Roman hypothesis but called the literary similarities between Philippians and the earlier letters "perhaps the most weighty *[sic]* part of the argument for Ephesus."

[22] F. F. Bruce (*Philippians*, NIBC [Peabody, MA: Hendrickson, 1989], 12) argued that this inscriptional evidence is irrelevant because the "praetorianus mentioned in three Latin inscriptions was a former member of the praetorian guard who later discharged police duties as a stationarius on a Roman road in the province of Asia."

[23] See esp. G. S. Duncan, "A New Setting for Paul's Epistle to the Philippians," *ExpTim* 43 (1931–32): 7–11.

[24] These criticisms are largely drawn from G. F. Hawthorne, "Philippians, Letter to the," in *Dictionary of Paul and His Letters*, ed. G. F. Hawthorne, R. P. Martin, and D. G. Reid (Downers Grove, IL: InterVarsity, 1993), 710.

[25] Hawthorne ("Philippians, Letter to the," 711) remains a contemporary advocate.

difficult. Scholars weigh the geographical arguments against a Roman imprisonment in various ways. Some treat it as the linchpin issue, while others regard it as irrelevant.[26] Many scholars occupy a middle position and contend that the geographical arguments are somewhat exaggerated. The so-called literary affinities between Philippians and Paul's earlier Letters may not provide any persuasive proof either way for the provenance of this letter.[27]

In the end, although many respectable scholars affirm an Ephesian provenance, the arguments for a Roman imprisonment seem stronger. The hypothesis of the Roman provenance of the Prison Epistles is persuasive because it depends on a known imprisonment, enjoys more abundant external evidence, and has a long-standing tradition behind it.[28] These considerations may force the Ephesian hypothesis to bear a slightly greater burden of proof.

The hypothesis of a Roman provenance for Philippians is even stronger than that for the other Prison Epistles due to the references to the Praetorium (Phil 1:13) and Caesar's household (Phil 4:22). J. B. Lightfoot showed that evidence in ancient inscriptions, Tacitus, Pliny, Suetonius, and Josephus supports the view that the Praetorium was not a place but the group of men who formed the Praetorian Guard. Lightfoot's interpretation seems confirmed by the words "and to all the rest," which appears to be a reference to persons rather than places. Although inscriptions refer to a member of the Praetorian Guard being present in Ephesus, F. F. Bruce is probably correct that the man had previously served as a member of the Guard while living in Rome before relocating to Ephesus. Although one generally found a Praetorium in the capitals of imperial provinces, Ephesus was the capital of a senatorial province (Asia) and was unlikely to have had a contingency of the Praetorian Guard stationed there.[29] Thus, the reference to the Praetorium supports the Roman provenance of the letter.[30]

What is more, although "Caesar's household" might be a reference to the staff that supervised the imperial bank for Asia in Ephesus as some scholars have claimed,[31] the phrase more naturally, and far more commonly, refers to those holding various positions in the imperial court in Rome.[32] The Ephesian provenance theory of the letter appears destined to become the consensus view of NT scholars in the near future,[33] but the Roman

---

26 Silva, *Philippians*, 6.

27 Kümmel (*Introduction*, 329–30) rejected the Roman hypothesis and stated that "the observations concerning linguistic kinship of Phil with I and II Cor and Rom can be matched by observations of linguistic kinship with Col (and Eph), which shows that Phil does not have a unilateral association linguistically with one or the other group of Pauline Letters." He also pointed out that Paul could have faced Judaizing opponents at a later date or feared similar groups.

28 Beare, *Philippians*, 24; Bruce, *Philippians*, 11–16.

29 Bruce, *Philippians*, xxii–xxiv.

30 See the note in J. B. Lightfoot, *Epistle to the Philippians* (London, England: Macmillan, 1913), 99–104. Lightfoot assumed a Roman provenance and used it to define the term in this particular context.

31 R. P. Martin, *Philippians*, NCBC (Grand Rapids, MI: Eerdmans, 1980), 51.

32 For an extensive discussion of "Caesar's household," see the excursus in Lightfoot, *Philippians*, 171–78.

33 Most recent commentaries on Philippians prefer the theory of Ephesian provenance. See G. W. Hansen, *The Letter to the Philippians* PNTC (Grand Rapids, MI: Eerdmans, 2009); J. Reuman, *Philippians: A New Translation with Introduction and Commentary* AB 33B (New Haven, CT: Yale University Press, 2008); B. B. Thurston and J. M. Ryan, *Philippians and Philemon* Sacra Pagina (Collegeville, MN; Liturgical Press, 2005). For a defense of Roman provenance, see D. Fleming, *Phi-*

provenance theory is still favored by the balance of the evidence. Fortunately, questions of provenance do not drastically alter one's interpretation of Philippians' message.

Destination

In Philippians 1:1 Paul addresses the letter to the believers in Christ Jesus "who are in Philippi." The straightforward nature of this declaration has created a consensus among NT scholars that Philippi is indeed the destination of the letter. The Acts narrative reveals that Philippi represents the first church Paul planted in Europe (Acts 16:6–40) on his second missionary journey (ca. AD 49–51).[34]

In the ancient world the city of Philippi was best known as the site of the battle in which Antony and Octavian emerged victorious over Brutus and Cassius (who helped assassinate Julius Caesar) in 42 BC. Octavian later defeated Antony in 31 BC and rebuilt Philippi, giving it the *ius italicum* ("law of Italy"), which was the highest privilege a colony could obtain.[35] The city was a site of historic interest long before these events.[36] It was founded by Philip II of Macedon in 358–57 BC, who named it after himself. It was situated in a fertile region eight miles from the Aegean Sea and enjoyed an abundance of springs and gold.[37] Philippi became part of the Roman Empire in 168 BC and prospered due to its strategic location along the Via Egnatia, the main land route between Rome and the East.

Occasion

The text of Philippians suggests several possible reasons for the writing. It is important to note that Paul addresses both pastoral problems and personal concerns. Two major pastoral problems surface in Philippians. First, Paul had apparently heard a report of disunity among the Philippians, which included a specific conflict between two women in the church, Euodia and Syntyche. Paul urged them to be united and to live in harmony together in the Lord (4:2). Second, he sounded a serious warning against false teachers and their teachings.[38]

---

lippians: A Commentary in the Wesleyan Tradition New Beacon Bible Commentary (Kansas City, MO: Beacon Hill, 2009); S. R. Llewelyn, "Sending Letters in the Ancient World: St. Paul and the Philippians," *TynBul* 46 (1995): 337–56. Llewelyn shows that the amount of travel presupposed by the letter between Rome and Philippi is plausible without resorting to claims of utilizing the imperial postal system. That was normally reserved for official government correspondence.

[34] Acts 16:14 records that Lydia was the first convert. She and her family responded to the gospel and were baptized (Acts 16:15). Her house also functioned as the meeting place for the church. The Acts account also mentions the conversion of the Philippian jailer and his family (16:30–33). G. F. Hawthorne (*Philippians*, WBC 43 [Waco, TX: Word, 1983], xxxv) noted that the names in Philippians (Epaphroditus, Euodia, Syntyche, and Clement) reveal that the church was made up largely of Gentiles.

[35] Colonists were exempt from the poll tax and land tax. They could also purchase, own, or transfer property, and file civil lawsuits (see Hawthorne, *Philippians*, xxxiii).

[36] L. M. McDonald, "Philippi," in *Dictionary of New Testament Background*, ed. C. A. Evans and S. E. Porter (Downers Grove, IL: InterVarsity, 2000), 787–89.

[37] Strabo, *Geography* 7.331.

[38] Debate exists over whether the false teachers were present in Philippi or Paul was warning the church about a potential threat.

Paul also includes numerous personal concerns. To begin with, the apostle sought to provide the Philippians with an update regarding his own circumstances and the advancement of the gospel since he regarded them as partners in it (1:5) who labored in prayer for him (1:19). The evidence also suggests three other personal concerns: (1) a commendation of Timothy in order that the Philippians would welcome him upon his arrival (2:19–23); (2) an announcement of Paul's desire to visit the church in the future (2:24); and (3) a report on Epaphroditus and his illness (2:25–30).

Purpose

Paul's main purpose in Philippians is connected to the main theme of the letter: partnership in the gospel and walking worthy of the gospel. "Partnership" or "fellowship" is the customary rendering here for the Greek word *koinōnia.* The Philippians' partnership in the gospel should be understood in an active, not passive, sense.[39] D. A. Carson captures the sense well when he writes, "Christian fellowship, then, is self-sacrificing conformity to the gospel. There may be overtones of warmth and intimacy, but the heart of the matter is this shared vision of what is of transcendent importance, a vision that calls forth our commitment."[40] This partnership involved, but was not limited to, the Philippians' financial support for Paul's missionary work (4:15–16).

"Live your life worthy of the gospel of Christ" (1:27) is shorthand for living in a manner that befits the greatness of the gospel. This worthy walk involves both Christian unity and a willingness to suffer for the advancement of the good news. This necessary unity was not "peace at any cost" but was instead a unity that was inspired by a shared faith in the gospel message. Paul calls believers to stand together as one in a battle for faith in the gospel. This stand involved resisting false teachings that compromised the message of the gospel, courageous suffering of persecution for the sake of the gospel, and being undaunted in the proclamation of the gospel.

LITERATURE

Literary Plan

Some scholars have analyzed Philippians along rhetorical lines as epideictic[41] or deliberative.[42] In terms of epistolary analysis, greater sensitivity toward literary models and ancient

---

[39] See esp. the excellent discussion in O'Brien (*Philippians*, 61–63), who highlighted the "many-sided activity" of the Philippians in their partnership in the gospel. He said it probably included (1) proclamation of the gospel to outsiders (1:27–28); (2) suffering for the gospel with Paul (1:30; 4:14–15); (3) intercessory prayer (1:19); and (4) their cooperation with Paul in the gospel (1:5), which was demonstrated by their financial assistance in the past (4:15–16) and the present (4:10).

[40] D. A. Carson, *Basics for Believers: An Exposition of Philippians* (Grand Rapids, MI: Baker, 1996), 16.

[41] G. Kennedy, *New Testament Interpretation Through Rhetorical Criticism* (Chapel Hill, NC: University of North Carolina Press, 1984), 77.

[42] D. F. Watson, "A Rhetorical Analysis of Philippians and Its Implications for the Unity Question," *NovT* 30 (1988): 57–88, esp. 59.

letter writing has shown promise in identifying Philippians as a "letter of friendship."[43] Others have compared Philippians to the genre of "family letters."[44] Despite the insights these studies have generated, the "friendship" or "family" letter approach has difficulty accounting for the function of 3:1–4:9 and 4:10–20 in the letter, and some question how much actual light the hypothesis sheds on the document as a whole.[45]

Other scholars argue for a chiastic structure of Philippians. P. Wick identified the structure this way:

A (1:12–26) = A'(3:1–16)
B (1:27–30) = B'(3:17–21)
C (2:1–11) = C'(4:1–3)
D (2:12–18) = D'(4:4–9)
E (2:19–30) = E'(4:10–20).[46]

A. B. Luter and M. V. Lee followed a more traditional chiastic approach.[47] Below is their proposed structure:

(1:1–2) Opening Greetings
  A (1:3–11) Prologue: Partnership in the Gospel
    B (1:12–26) Comfort
      C (1:27–2:4) Challenge
        D (2:5–16) Example
          E (2:17–3:1a) Models of Gospel Partnership
        D'(3:1b–21) Example
      C'(4:1–5) Challenge
    B'(4:6–9) Comfort
  A'(4:10–20) Epilogue
(4:21–23) Closing Greetings

The fact that the proposals of Wick and Luter and Lee only agree on 4:10–20 as a textual unit calls the search for macrochiastic structures into question.[48]

---

[43] See Fee, *Philippians*, 2–7; B. Witherington III, *Friendship and Finances in Philippi* (Valley Forge, PA: Trinity Press International, 1994); S. K. Stowers, "Friends and Enemies in the Politics of Heaven: Reading Theology in Philippians," in *Pauline Theology: Thessalonians, Philippians, Galatians, Philemon*, vol. 1, ed. J. M. Bassler (Minneapolis, MN: Fortress, 1991), 105–21, esp. 107–14.

[44] L. Alexander, "Hellenistic Letter-Forms and the Structure of Philippians," *JSNT* 37 (1989): 87–101.

[45] See, e.g., Silva, *Philippians*, 19.

[46] Wick, *Philipperbrief*.

[47] A. B. Luter and M. V. Lee, "Philippians as Chiasmus: Key to the Structure, Unity, and Theme Questions," *NTS* 41 (1995): 89–101.

[48] The skepticism regarding macrochiastic structures expressed by I. H. Thomson (*Chiasmus in the Pauline Letters*, JSNTSup 111 [Sheffield, UK: Sheffield Academic Press, 1995], 25) seems appropriate.

Many scholars, most notably J. T. Reed, have analyzed Philippians at the discourse level and concluded that the letter is, from start to finish, a unified and coherent composition.[49] The unity and internal coherence of Paul's Letter to the Philippians are further demonstrated in the outline and Unit-by-Unit Discussion below.

OUTLINE

The complexity of the preceding discussion may lead one to conclude that the search for an outline is hopeless. But a simpler structural solution is available: introduction (1:1–2); body (1:3–4:20); and conclusion (4:21–23). The body appears to subdivide into three natural sections: the opening (1:3–11); the body proper (1:12–4:9); and the closing (4:10–20).

I. INTRODUCTION: GREETINGS TO THE PHILIPPIANS (1:1–2)
II. BODY: THE PHILIPPIANS' PARTNERSHIP WITH PAUL IN THE GOSPEL (1:3–4:20)
  A. Opening: Thanksgiving and Prayer for the Philippians (1:3–11)
  B. Body Proper: Exhortation to Unity for the Sake of the Gospel (1:12–4:9)
    1. Positive Examples of Putting the Needs of Others First (1:12–2:30)
      a. The Example of Paul (1:12–30)
      b. The Example of Jesus (2:1–11)
      c. The Example of Timothy (2:19–24)
      d. The Example of Epaphroditus (2:25–30)
    2. Warning Against False Teachers and Internal Disunity (3:1–4:9)
      a. The Threat of the False Teachers and Paul's Example (3:1–21)
      b. The Threat Arising from Internal Disunity (4:1–7)
      c. Final Encouragement (4:8–9)
  C. Closing: Thanksgiving for the Philippians' Present and Previous Gifts (4:10–20)
III. CONCLUSION: FINAL GREETINGS (4:21–23)

UNIT-BY-UNIT DISCUSSION

I. Introduction: Greetings to the Philippians (1:1–2)

Following standard epistolary conventions, Paul identifies himself as the sender and Timothy as a cosender of the letter.[50] He refers to the recipients in Philippi and specifically mentioned the elders and deacons of the church at Philippi (1:1). In the salutation, Paul,

---

[49] Reed, *Discourse Analysis of Philippians*. Hawthorne (*Philippians*, xlviii) took the opposite view that there is no logical progression in the letter, remarking that the "swift changes of topic and even of tone come as no surprise" and casting Philippians as the "antithesis of Romans" in this regard.

[50] Some scholars minimize the importance of Paul's mention of Timothy. Acts portrays Timothy in a significant ministry role throughout Macedonia. Silva (*Philippians*, 39) is probably correct in stating that good reasons exist to believe that "the Philippians had a strong attachment to Timothy." Carson and Moo (*Introduction to the New Testament*, 507) took a different track in saying that Paul's later commendation of Timothy (2:19–24) implies that "the Philippians did not know him well."

as customary, changed the standard greeting *(chairein)* to the theologically pregnant grace-wish (*charis*, 1:2).

II. Body: The Philippians' Partnership with Paul in the Gospel (1:3–4:20)

The body of the letter centers on the theme of gospel partnership. Paul stresses the urgent need for unity in the cause of the gospel. This unity not only arises as a natural outgrowth of the gospel; it also remains necessary for the continued growth of the gospel. Paul urges the Philippians to unite against those things that threatened the progress of the gospel.

A. Opening: Thanksgiving and Prayer for the Philippians (1:3–11) Paul's thanksgiving centers on the Philippians' participation and partnership in the gospel. The apostle rejoices that this partnership, which extended from the past into the present (1:5) would continue to the end because the One who began the work could be trusted to complete it (1:6). He comments on how fitting these feelings were in light of his firm conviction that the Philippians were fellow recipients of divine grace—united with him in his work of defending and confirming the gospel (1:7). Paul also calls God as witness to the sincerity of these affections for the Philippians (1:8). He concludes this section with a prayer for the continued growth of the Philippians in the gospel (1:9–11).

B. Body Proper: Exhortation to Unity for the Sake of the Gospel (1:12–4:9) Paul provides the Philippians with four biographical vignettes in 1:12–2:30. The lives of Paul (1:12–26), Jesus (2:5–11),[51] Timothy (2:19–24), and Epaphroditus (2:25–30) serve a hortatory function because they demonstrated humility by putting the needs of others first, even in the face of potential (1:20–24; 2:27, 30) or actual death (2:8). The testimony of these lives provided examples for the Philippians to emulate as they sought the greater progress of the gospel amid their own hardships. They served to strengthen the Philippians so that they too could endure the suffering (1:29) they faced at the hands of their opponents (1:28). Paul even refers to this hardship as a gracious gift from God (1:29).

The call to emulation continues in 3:17 and 4:9, but in 3:1–4:9 this call differs in that it focuses on two grave threats against the gospel: (1) false teachers; and (2) disunity among the Philippians. Paul's note of urgency throughout this section reads like a call to mobilize in the fight for the gospel.

The threat from the false teachers was much more serious than the threat posed by the evangelists mentioned earlier by Paul (1:15–17). The evangelists preached the right message with the wrong motives. They preached because they envied Paul and wished to increase his suffering. If they had doctrinal differences with the apostle, those were relatively minor so that Paul could still rejoice that they proclaimed the gospel. The present unit

---

[51] Martin (*Philippians*, 76) rejected the traditional interpretation that Paul used Phil 2:5–11 as a lesson in humility. But see the convincing case of N. T. Wright, *The Climax of the Covenant: Christ and the Law in Pauline Theology* (Minneapolis, MN: Fortress, 1996), 82–90.

makes clear that these false teachers got their message very wrong. It contained disturbing departures from the true gospel that Paul had to confront.[52]

Paul rebukes their zeal for a false gospel that apparently viewed circumcision and OT dietary laws as necessary for salvation. In a biting irony, he turns the tables on the false teachers and demonstrates that their indictment of Gentile believers was in fact a self-indictment. Jews would call non-Jews "unclean," partly because they ate a forbidden diet, much like dogs who fed on carrion and garbage.[53] Paul calls the false teachers "dogs" in order to show that they did not belong to the true people of God.

In a play on words, Paul describes the false teachers' circumcision as mutilation, which referred to the kind of pagan, self-inflicted wounds of the prophets of Baal (1 Kgs 18:28) that were forbidden in OT law (Lev 19:28; 21:5; Deut 14:1; Isa 15:2; Hos 7:14). Paul's point is that the false teachers' dependence on circumcision for salvation demonstrated that they did not understand God's grace and were in fact pagans rather than the chosen people of God. Christians are the true circumcision who worship God in the Spirit and forsake confidence in the flesh (3:1–3). In fact, Paul reminded the Philippians that if anyone had reason to put stock in the flesh, it was he (3:4–6).

Yet after his conversion to Christ, Paul came to relegate those former things (3:7), and indeed all things (3:8), to the loss side of the ledger in comparison with the surpassing value of gaining and knowing Christ (3:8) and being found righteous in him by faith (3:9). Paul's passion was now knowing Christ in the power of his resurrection and in the fellowship of his sufferings (3:10), so that he might eventually follow Christ in experiencing resurrection (3:11).

Paul reminds the Philippians that he had not attained the goal of the resurrection or become perfect (3:12). He intentionally forgot about the qualifications he once depended on for salvation and now pressed on in pursuit of the heavenly prize (3:12–14). This perspective represented the mark of mature thinking for Christians (3:15), which God would reveal even to those who disagreed (3:16). The apostle presents himself and those who took the same perspective as examples to emulate in contrast to the behavior of the opponents who were enemies of the cross (3:17–19). He draws a stark contrast between their focus on "earthly things" (3:19) and believers' "citizenship is in heaven" (3:20). Paul then shows that these contrasting focal points would lead to contrasting outcomes: destruction for the opponents (3:19) and glorified bodies for believers (3:20–21). Believers "eagerly wait" for Jesus the Savior[54] (3:20), who will transform them by his almighty power (3:21).

---

[52] See Silva, *Philippians*, 64–65; Fee, *Philippians*, 122–23; and Bockmuehl, *Philippians*, 77–78.

[53] See *m. Sab.* 24:4; *m. Pes.* 2:3; *m. Ned.* 4:3; and *m. Bek.* 5:6.

[54] S. K. Stowers, "Friends and Enemies in the Politics of Heaven: Reading Theology in Philippians," in *Pauline Theology: Thessalonians, Philippians, Galatians, Philemon*, vol. 1, ed. J. M. Bassler (Minneapolis, MN: Fortress, 1991), 105–21. He brought out the political nuances in Paul's language in Philippians. The term *savior* was also commonly used for political rulers, and the Roman emperors were especially associated with "savior" language.

The second threat to the gospel is disunity. Philippians 4 begins with a charge to stand firm in the Lord (4:1). Paul continues this by urging two prominent women in the church to "agree in the Lord" (4:2). Disunity obviously threatened "partnership" in the gospel, so Paul asks the Philippians to help these women who contended for the gospel at Paul's side like Clement and the rest of Paul's coworkers did (4:3). Rejoicing in the Lord (4:4), prayer (4:6), and the heart-guarding power of the peace of God (4:7) represent the cure for disunity. Paul concludes by urging the Philippians to concentrate on excellent things (4:8) and to emulate his own teaching and lifestyle (4:9).

C. Closing: Thanksgiving for the Philippians' Present and Previous Gifts (4:10–20) Paul rejoiced with thanksgiving for the Philippians' present (4:10, 14, 18) and past (4:15–16) financial gifts. He did not rejoice in the gifts themselves so much as in what they represented: the Philippians' partnership with Paul in the gospel. The apostle testifies that Christ's strength enabled him (4:13) to be content in every circumstance (4:11), whether poverty or abundance (4:12). He reminds the Philippians that their gifts to him were in reality sacrifices of praise to God (4:18), who would supply all their needs according to his riches in glory in Christ Jesus (4:19). Therefore, Paul closed with a fitting doxology in which he gave God all the glory (4:20).

III. Conclusion: Final Greetings (4:21–23)

Paul urges the Philippians to greet all the believers in Christ Jesus. He also reminds them that all the believers sent their greetings, including the brothers who were with him. Among those in the category of "all believers," Paul especially highlights "Caesar's household" (4:22). He follows these greetings with the grace benediction: "the grace of our Lord Jesus Christ be with your spirit" (4:23).

THEOLOGY

Theological Themes

The Gospel and Its Implications Paul's theology in Philippians is essentially a gospel-centered theology. This focus on the gospel grounds his concern for the important practical and ethical implications that flow forth from the gospel. This connection is seen in its most comprehensive form in Paul's exhortation in 1:27: "live your life [*politeusthe*] worthy of the gospel of Christ." Christ-followers have become citizens of heaven through the gospel; therefore, their conduct must match their citizenship. The same theme surfaces again in 3:20: "our citizenship is in heaven." The political nuance of these two texts is an important reminder that the believers' heavenly citizenship made Philippi's status as a Roman colony pale in comparison. Acts of personal and practical obedience—unity, humility, rejoicing, not grumbling or being anxious—not only arose *from* the gospel but were also necessary *for* the gospel and its further progress.

Something to Think About: The Uniquely Christian Virtue of Humility

If humility is defined in Paul's terms as "consider[ing] others as more important than" ourselves (2:3), then humility is a uniquely Christian virtue. In this fallen, sinful universe, with its "survival of the fittest" mentality, the immediate prize usually goes to those who are aggressive, assertive, and self-seeking—even if this means stepping over others to get ahead.

Yet considering others as more important than ourselves is exactly what Christians are told to do in Scripture. How can this be? In short, because humility is supremely epitomized in the life of Christ, who, existing in the form of God, did not consider equality with God as something to be used for his own advantage. Instead He emptied Himself by assuming the form of a slave, taking on the likeness of men. And when He had come as a man in His external form, He humbled Himself by becoming obedient to the point of death—even to death on a cross (2:6–8).

Jesus was God, yet he humbled himself—not once, but repeatedly—in an ever-descending sequence: from God to man; from man to slave; from obedient slave to death—a death on an ignominious Roman cross. In this Jesus became a model for his followers to emulate (see John 13:1–20, especially vv. 12–17; Paul may well have had that passage in mind as he wrote). So, rather than arguing over who is the greatest—as Jesus's disciples often did in the first century and still do—Jesus calls on us, as Paul puts it, to "carry one another's burdens" and "in this way . . . [to] fulfill the law of Christ" (Gal 6:2).

In the Philippian church (see 4:2–3) as well as in our churches today, we often find it difficult to get along with one another. Why? According to Paul, the reason may be rivalry, conceit, or selfish ambition—in one word, pride (2:3). So what is the remedy? Again, one word encapsulates Paul's answer: humility: "in humility . . . [e]veryone should look out not only for his own interests, but also for the interests of others" (2:3–4). May God help us to do so. And as we strive for humility, let us contemplate the outcome of Christ's: "For this reason God also highly exalted him, and gave him the name that is above every name, so that at the name of Jesus every knee will bow—in heaven and on earth and under the earth—and every tongue will confess that Jesus Christ is Lord, to the glory of God the Father" (2:9–11).

As noted in the Unit-by-Unit analysis, the whole letter can be understood in its relation to the gospel. Paul's opening thanksgiving centers on the Philippians' partnership in the gospel (1:5). As partakers of grace with Paul in his defense and confirmation of the gospel (1:7), they must not only "fight together for the faith of the gospel" (1:27, author's translation), but also emulate the examples of Paul (1:21–26), Jesus (2:5–11), Timothy (1:19–24), and Epaphroditus (1:25–30): these put the needs of others in front of their own for the sake of the gospel. Likewise, Paul addressed false teachers (3:2–21) and disunity (4:2–3) among the Philippians because they represented threats to the gospel's progress. The letter concludes with a thanksgiving for their partnership in the gospel (4:10–20) in that their financial gifts helped further the progress of the good news.

The Person and Work of Christ This central concern for the gospel of Christ springs from the centrality of Christ in Paul's thought, which is another major theme that characterizes the theology of Philippians. The letter reflects an exalted view of the person and work of Jesus Christ. The most obvious and outstanding passage concerning Christology is the exquisite "Christ hymn" in 2:6–11.[55] The glory of the gospel is seen in (1) the glorious height of Christ's preexistent state (2:6); (2) his humble obedience to the Father in every respect, from taking on the limitations of human flesh to the culminating act of the humiliating and excruciating death on a cross (2:7–8); and (3) the exalted position of the resurrected Christ as the One to whom every knee will bow and whom every tongue will confess as Lord (2:9–11).

In this Christological hymn Paul clearly affirms the deity of Jesus, describing him as having eternally existed in the very form of God, fully equal to God,[56] and yet refusing to use his equality with the Father for his own selfish advantage. Emphasis on Jesus's exalted status is especially prominent in the conclusion of the hymn where Paul insisted that Jesus possessed "the name that is above every name" (Phil 2:9). In the NT era, Jews so reverenced the name of God, Yahweh, that they refused to utter it. It was generally pronounced only by the high priest on the Day of Atonement and by local priests who pronounced the priestly blessing. For any other person at any other time in any other place to speak the divine name was considered blasphemy, a crime punishable by death.

The Jews referred to God using substitutions for the divine name. Approved substitutions were called *kinnuyim*. The common substitutions were "Lord" (*Adonai*); "the Name" (Hb. *Hashem*); "the Separate name"; "God's own name"; and "the name of four letters" (*tetragrammaton*). In Philippians 2:9 Paul used the substitution "the name" (with the definite article in Greek) and further described it as that "above every name." Every Jew in Philippi who heard this phrase would automatically recognize these words as an allusion to the divine name. Paul identified this supreme name in the confession "Jesus Christ is Lord." Since the Greek title "Lord" *(kyrios)* was the translation of the name "Yahweh" in the OT and since the description "name above every other name" is a clear example of *kinnuyim*, Paul explicitly identified Jesus as God who possesses the very name of God.[57]

Paul confirms this identification by also applying the description of worship of Yahweh in Isaiah 45:23 to Jesus. Paul's promise that every knee would bow before Jesus and every tongue would confess that Jesus is Lord clearly alluded to the promise, "Turn to me and

---

[55] See esp. R. P. Martin, *A Hymn of Christ: Philippians 2:5–11 in Recent Interpretation and in the Setting of Early Christian Worship* (Downers Grove, IL: InterVarsity, 1983).

[56] For a good grammatical overview of the articular infinitive construction in 2:6, see D. Burk, *Articular Infinitives in the Greek of the New Testament: On the Exegetical Benefit of Grammatical Precision*, New Testament Monographs 14 (Sheffield, UK: Phoenix, 2006), 139–40.

[57] Geza Vermes, *The Religion of Jesus the Jew* (Minneapolis, MN: Augsburg Fortress, 1993), 34–35; "ὄνομα," *TDNT* 4:268–69; Gordon D. Fee, *Pauline Christology: An Exegetical-Theological Study* (Peabody, MA: Hendrickson, 2007), 396–98.

be saved, all the ends of the earth. For I am God and there is no other. . . . Every knee will bow to me, every tongue will swear allegiance" (Isa 45:22–23). Paul's application to Jesus of a text describing homage to Yahweh demonstrates that he saw Jesus as far more than a mere man or a great religious teacher. He viewed Christ as deity, the One who had come to the earth in the form of a human servant.[58]

However, Paul's depiction of Christ's journey from heaven to earth, earth to grave, and grave to heaven in 2:6–11 must not cause one to neglect the many other passages in Philippians that testify to the centrality of Christ. Few Pauline passages can compare with 1:21–23 and 3:7–11 in terms of expressing Paul's all-consuming passion to honor Jesus and to know Christ more fully in this life and in the life to come.

What is more, references to Christ saturate the entire letter from beginning to end.[59] Further evidence comes from the frequency of phrases such as "in Christ," "in him," or "in the Lord" throughout Philippians. These expressions can convey union with Christ (1:1, 14, 29; 3:9; 4:21) or stress an action that takes place in response to or on the basis of Jesus's person, work, and lordship. This includes confidence abounding in Christ (1:26); encouragement in Christ (2:1); having the mind or attitude as in Christ (2:5); hoping in Christ (2:19, 24); receiving others in the Lord (2:29); rejoicing in the Lord (3:1; 4:4, 10); glorying in Christ (3:3); pressing on toward the call of God in Christ (3:14); standing firm in the Lord (4:2); living in harmony in the Lord (4:3); guarding hearts and minds in Christ (4:7); or supplying needs according to God's riches in Christ (4:19). The letter ends with a benediction concerning the "grace of the Lord Jesus Christ" (4:23).

Christian Unity Paul repeatedly stresses his special relationship with the Philippian church. In 4:15, he wrote that "in the early days of the gospel . . ., no church shared with me in the matter of giving and receiving except you alone." In the opening thanksgiving, he expressed his gratitude for the Philippians' "partnership in the gospel from the first day until now" and noted his confidence "that he who started a good work in you will carry it on to completion until the day of Christ Jesus" (1:5–6).

Yet, not all was well in the Philippian church. Not only were there threats from without in the form of false teachers (see 3:2), but there was also internal disunity that had the potential of dividing the church. This problem was epitomized by Euodia and Syntyche (4:2), and the fact that Paul named them indicates the seriousness of their rift. Interestingly, Paul said that both women "have contended for the gospel at my side," together with "the rest of my coworkers" (4:3).

While they once strove to make the gospel known alongside Paul, united in the common cause of Christian witness, they now were in need of a mediator to work out their differences, whatever they were (4:3). This, most likely, is why Paul wrote earlier in the letter,

---

[58] For a thorough scholarly discussion of the worship of Jesus as God in the early church, see L. W. Hurtado, *Lord Jesus Christ: Devotion to Jesus in Earliest Christianity* (Grand Rapids, MI: Eerdmans, 2003).

[59] I. H. Marshall ("Philippians," in *New Dictionary of Biblical Theology*, ed. T. D. Alexander and B. S. Rosner [Downers Grove, IL: InterVarsity, 2000], 319–22) devoted his entire article on the theology of Philippians to Christology.

"Just one thing: As citizens of heaven, live your life worthy of the gospel of Christ. Then, whether I come and see you or am absent, I will hear about you that you are standing firm in one spirit, in one accord, contending together for the faith of the gospel" (1:27).

Paul also exhorts the Philippians to "[d]o nothing out of selfish ambition or conceit, but in humility consider others as more important than yourselves. Everyone should look out not only for his own interests, but also for the interests of others" (2:3–4). This is followed by a moving and poetic description of Jesus Christ, the supreme example of such humility (2:5–11). He renounced *all* his privileges in order to meet humanity's desperate need for salvation.

Consequently, believers are exhorted to "work out [their] own salvation with fear and trembling. For it is God who is working in [them], both to will and to work according to his good purpose" (2:12–13). Paul's concern was for the unity of believers so that the gospel proclamation would not be hindered. Internal disunity continues to be a major tool of Satan hindering effective Christian ministry. The gospel will go forth, and God will be glorified if only the Euodias and Syntyches in the churches will lay aside their differences and "agree in the Lord" (4:2).

Joy in Christ One must not discount the theological theme of joy merely because it is not the primary theme of the letter. Paul used the "joy" word family sixteen times in this short missive. Thus, Philippians testifies to the deep-rooted reality of joy in the life of a follower of Christ. One should not regard delight in Christ as an "icing on the cake" version of Christianity but as an essential outgrowth of union with Christ in the gospel. Joy is an inevitable overflow of progressively perceiving the "surpassing value" of knowing Christ Jesus as Lord through faith in the gospel of Christ. F. Thielman summarized Philippians as "a sustained attempt to persuade believers to rejoice in what matters (1:10, 18)."[60]

Christian Suffering Suffering is an important, though often neglected, theological theme in Philippians.[61] Paul's trying circumstances had served to advance the gospel (1:12–13). He faced the prospect of death in his imprisonment (1:20–21), and Epaphroditus almost died in the cause of the gospel as well (2:27). In the Philippians' fight for the faith of the gospel (1:27), they would meet suffering as well; but they needed to respond to opposition without being frightened (1:28). They also needed to regard their suffering, like their faith, as a gracious gift from God (1:29). This experience of conflict mirrored Paul's suffering, which they had both witnessed in the past and now heard about in the present (1:30). Paul's use of the suffering theme invited the Philippians to "see their marginalization as a sign of their citizenship in another, heavenly society" because "although the citizenry of Philippi have marginalized them, they are citizens of a heavenly city and . . . one day the ruler of that city will subject all other entities to himself."[62]

---

[60] Thielman, *Theology of the New Testament*, 321.

[61] P. Oakes, *Philippians: From People to Letter*, SNTSMS 110 (Cambridge, UK: University Press, 2001), 59–96. Oakes said that the Philippians suffered economically and physically for their refusal to join in pagan religious rituals.

[62] Thielman, *Theology of the New Testament*, 312.

Paul mentions the suffering of Christ on the cross (2:8) and regarded his own suffering as a fellowship in Christ's sufferings and conformity to his death (3:11). What is more, Paul could endure suffering, such as hunger and poverty (4:12), through the strength that Christ provided (4:13). Joy in the midst of suffering is especially illuminating in the account of Paul and Silas rejoicing at midnight in a Philippian prison after being beaten with rods (Acts 16:16–25).

Justification by Faith Alone Philippians 3:9 is one of the most emphatic statements concerning justification in the entire NT.[63] Philippians 3:3–6 summarizes the thrust of Paul's former pursuit for salvation before his Damascus road encounter. His flawless Jewish credentials (3:5–6) led him to put confidence in the flesh (3:4). Paul's conversion, however, caused a radical reassessment. These former credentials (3:7) and all other things (3:8) were loss compared to knowing and gaining Christ. Paul identifies two contrasting types of righteousness *after* his experience with the risen Christ: a righteousness that came from the law; and a righteousness that came from God (3:9).[64] Therefore, Paul saw a marked contrast between a righteousness that he mustered by obeying the law and a righteousness provided by God and received through faith in Christ.[65] The only hope unrighteous humanity had for acceptance by the divine Judge was the gift of righteousness that came from God and was received by faith.

These verses are saturated with accounting language and probably refer to the image of the heavenly Judge as a great shopkeeper who kept an enormous ledger. Each time a person sinned, the sin was recorded on the debit side of the ledger. Many Jews also believed that good works were recorded on the credit side of the ledger. If a person could remain "in the black," that is, perform more good works than bad, he would receive a reward in judgment. If a person's account was "in the red," he would be sentenced to eternal punishment when the moral account was balanced on the day of judgment.[66] Paul's point is that the very things he once depended on as credits to his account with God were in reality debits. They could in no way contribute to, and were in reality hindrances to, his salvation. He had discovered that Christ was the only credit to his account that would ensure that he

---

[63] A good overview of the role of this passage in the wider justification debate can be found in B. Vickers, *Jesus' Blood and Righteousness: Paul's Theology of Imputation* (Wheaton, IL: Crossway, 2006), 205–11.

[64] The phrase "the righteousness of the law" in 3:9 (author's translation) is also found in Rom 10:5. The parallels between the two passages are striking. See J. A. Fitzmyer, *Romans: A New Translation with Introduction and Commentary*, AB 33 (Garden City, NY: Doubleday, 1993), 582; and P. Stuhlmacher, *Paul's Letter to the Romans: A Commentary* (Louisville, KY: Westminster John Knox, 1994), 154–55.

[65] For the debate surrounding the translation of *pistis Christou*, see the chapter on Romans above. Silva (*Philippians*, 161) is probably correct in his argument that ambiguous grammatical forms should be read in the light of unambiguous ones, and while Paul never spoke unambiguously about "the faithfulness of Christ" (subjective genitive), he did speak elsewhere of "faith in Christ" (objective genitive; e.g., Gal 2:16). Cf. idem, "Faith Versus Works of Law in Galatians," in *Justification and Variegated Nomism*, vol. 2, ed. D. A. Carson, P. T. O'Brien, and M. A. Seifrid (Tübingen, Germany: Mohr Siebeck, 2004), 217–48. For the subjective genitive interpretation, see R. B. Hays, "Salvation History: The Theological Structure of Paul's Thought (1 Thessalonians, Philippians and Galatians)," in *Pauline Theology: Thessalonians, Philippians, Galatians, Philemon*, vol. 1, ed. J. M. Bassler (Minneapolis, MN: Fortress, 1991), 232–33.

[66] *m. Avot* 3:15–16.

could pass God's scrutinizing examination on judgment day. Paul now depends not on his own personal attempts at righteousness for his salvation; instead, he relies completely on the righteousness that God imputed to him through his faith in Jesus.

This text is an important part of a wider debate concerning the New Perspective on Paul.[67] The New Perspective's understanding of this verse, which views righteousness in a nationalistic sense, does not cohere well with the passage itself. Paul's own righteousness cannot be restricted to Jewish nationalism and exclusivism (Jews as opposed to Gentiles) because he distinguished his own personal righteousness from that of other Jews in his day. In other words, he distinguished his own personal righteousness by distancing himself from the lower attainments of some of his countrymen—not from Gentiles outside the confines of Israel.

Ephesians

KEY FACTS

Author:	Paul
Date:	Around 60
Provenance:	Roman imprisonment
Destination:	Circular letter or Ephesus
Occasion:	Not clearly identifiable
Purpose:	To declare and promote cosmic reconciliation and unity in Christ
Theme:	The summing up of all things in Christ
Key Verses:	1:3–14, especially 1:9–10

[67] F. Thielman (*Philippians*, NIVAC [Grand Rapids, MI: Zondervan, 1995], 171) called this text a "hornet's nest" in the current debate. On the law/gospel debate in Paul, the best overview is S. Westerholm, *Perspectives Old and New on Paul: The "Lutheran" Paul and His Critics* (Grand Rapids, MI: Eerdmans, 2004). On the New Perspective, see the discussion in the chapter on Romans above.

INTRODUCTION

EPHESIANS IS A magisterial summary of Paul's teaching and was Calvin's personal favorite.[68] R. Brown claimed that only Romans has exercised more influence on Christian thought throughout church history.[69] The letter continues to encourage Christians today with the cosmic scale of Christ's reconciling work and to challenge believers to maintain the unity of the church that Christ purchased and that the Spirit produced.

Ephesians makes numerous and significant contributions to the canon. First, Paul presents the theme of subjecting all things to Christ's lordship most clearly and articulately in Ephesians. He develops this cosmic realignment of proper submission to God's authority along the lines of the reconciling work of Christ in two spheres: the heavens and the earth. Paul's focus on trinitarian-based soteriology, gospel-centered ecclesiology, Spirit-empowered ethics, and spiritual warfare are all encompassed by this overarching theme.

Second, perhaps only Colossians can compare with Ephesians' emphasis on the staggering aspects of Christ's victory that believers already enjoy in Christ. He is exalted above all other powers to the point that they will all serve as the footstool for his feet. A unified church consisting of Jews and Gentiles shares that victory as the church sits and reigns with Christ.

Third, Ephesians contains perhaps the most developed discussion of and vision for the church. This same church that already shares in Christ's victory serves as a herald or foreshadowing of God's great plan to "bring all things back together under one head," the Lord Jesus Christ (1:10, author's translation). Therefore, the unified church testifies to the unified universe in God's new creation when he will place all hostile forces under the feet of his Son.[70] This same church possesses a moral identity apart from ethnicity that proclaims the character of God. The church consisting of God's adopted sons and daughters bears a family resemblance to their Creator and Redeemer.

Fourth, Ephesians also contains the most developed discussion of spiritual warfare in the NT (6:10–18; see 2 Cor 10:3–6). The church plays a crucial role in these times as all things are being subjected to the authority of Christ. The two realms clash in warfare as the hostile heavenly powers wage war against the redeemed forces of humanity upon the earth. Believers advance by standing united in God's armor. This unity heralds God's manifold wisdom to the rulers and authorities in the heavenly realms. Standing against their

---

[68] For an excellent survey of accolades ascribed to Ephesians (including the Calvin reference), see H. W. Hoehner, *Ephesians: An Exegetical Commentary* (Grand Rapids, MI: Baker, 2003), 1–2.

[69] R. E. Brown, *An Introduction to the New Testament* (New York, NY: Doubleday, 1997), 620. For an extensive look at the influence exercised by Ephesians, see R. Schnackenburg, *Ephesians: A Commentary* (Edinburgh, Scotland: T&T Clark, 1996), 311–42.

[70] So also Thielman, *Theology of the New Testament*, 407: "The church plays a critical role, therefore, in God's plan to bring the times to their fulfillment by summing up everything in Christ. They are the new humanity that replaces the old, disintegrated humanity, and they are the evidence that God's plan to sum up everything in Christ is rapidly coming to its end."

ungodly onslaught shows that God's work in Christ has crushed their feeble attempt to frustrate God's plan for his creation.

HISTORY

Author

Authenticity It has become fashionable to speak of three tiers within the "Pauline" corpus: (1) undisputed Letters (Romans, 1 and 2 Corinthians, Galatians, Philippians, 1 Thessalonians, Philemon); (2) Deutero-Pauline Letters (Ephesians, Colossians, 2 Thessalonians); and (3) pseudonymous Letters (1 and 2 Timothy, Titus). Many modern scholars reject the traditional view that Ephesians is an authentic Pauline Letter.

This denial began in the nineteenth century when F. C. Baur argued that Ephesians employed gnostic terms and ideas. The late date of Gnosticism effectively precluded Paul's authorship. R. Bultmann and his disciples followed Baur, which led to an escalating loss of confidence that Paul wrote Ephesians. Though many have rightly abandoned the idea of a gnostic background to Ephesians, literary and theological issues continue to call Paul's authorship into question. Scholars who dismiss Paul's authorship of Ephesians point to five lines of evidence: (1) theology, (2) vocabulary, (3) literary style, (4) the relationship to Colossians, and (5) the impersonal nature of Ephesians.

In terms of theology, three themes dominate the debate: cosmic Christology, developed ecclesiology, and realized eschatology. The cosmic Christology of Ephesians raises red flags for some exegetes because they argue that Ephesians emphasizes Christ's status as Lord over the cosmos and thus focuses more on his exaltation than his death. Advocates of authenticity respond by pointing out that (1) there are four references to the death of Christ (1:7; 2:16; 5:2, 25) in Ephesians; (2) other Pauline texts emphasize exaltation (1 Cor 15:3–28; Phil 2:5–11); and (3) the cross and exaltation go together in Paul's thought.[71]

The ecclesiology of Ephesians has given many scholars pause since it deviates from Paul's customary use of the term for "church" (*ekklēsia*). The apostle normally used the term to refer to the local church, but every usage in Ephesians has the universal church as the referent (1:22; 3:10, 21; 5:23–25, 27, 29, 32). Ephesians also makes the claim that Christ is the head of the church, which is his body (1:23; 4:15–16; cf. Col 1:18). Moreover, whereas Christ is the foundation of the church in the undisputed letter 1 Corinthians (3:11), Ephesians states that the church is built on the foundation of the apostles and prophets (2:20). R. Schnackenburg read the letter as occupying a later stage of tradition that looked back at Paul's establishment of the church and the apostolic tradition.[72] E. Käsemann interpreted the ecclesiology of Ephesians as an example of early Catholicism.[73]

---

[71] Hoehner, *Ephesians*, 50: "There is no hint that the exaltation could come without the death of Christ."

[72] R. Schnackenburg, *The Epistle to the Ephesians* (Edinburgh, Scotland: T&T Clark, 1991), 28.

[73] E. Käsemann, "The Theological Problem Presented by the Motif of the Body of Christ," in *Perspectives on Paul*, trans. M. Kohl (Philadelphia, PA: Fortress, 1971), 102–21; esp. 120–21.

Advocates of authenticity argue that other Pauline texts also refer to the universal church as the church of God (1 Cor 10:32; 15:9; Gal 1:13; Phil 3:6). Therefore, Paul addressed not only "the church of God at Corinth," but also "all those . . . who call on the name of Jesus Christ our Lord—both their Lord and ours" (1 Cor 1:2). Moreover, the portrayal of Christ as the head of the body also appears in Colossians 1:18 and is a natural extension of Paul's earlier metaphor of the church as the body of Christ in the undisputed letters. Thus, it represents a development of, not a departure from, his thought. Likewise, although Ephesians presents the apostles and prophets as the foundation of the church, this claim does not contradict the earlier one that the foundation is Christ because the apostles and prophets establish this foundation through their witness to the life, death, and resurrection of Christ, so that Jesus remains the "cornerstone" (Eph 2:20–22). Ephesians does not read like it belongs to a later time in ecclesiastical tradition, which looks back to the time of the apostles and prophets who have passed from the scene. Instead, Ephesians shows that the risen Christ continued to give the gifts of apostles and prophets to the church at the time the letter was written (4:11–12).

In terms of eschatology, some scholars hold that the "realized" eschatology of Ephesians makes a clean break with Paul's typical eschatological approach.[74] Ephesians portrays the believer as presently seated with Christ (2:6) and emphasizes one's relationship to Christ in the heavenly realms (1:3, 20–21). Those who believe that Paul wrote Ephesians attempt to show that the letter presents a future dimension to salvation. It includes references to future redemption (1:13–14; 4:30), "the [age] to come" (1:21; 2:7), and the future presentation of the church to Christ (5:27). Ephesians also clearly speaks of eschatology in terms of uniting all creation under Christ's headship in the future "fullness of the times" (1:10 NASB).[75] As Hoehner said, Ephesians does not present "a realized eschatology with no future realization but a present realization of what we are in Christ with a future consummation. Thus, it is not an either/or but a both/and situation."[76] A. T. Lincoln, who argued against authenticity, has made a sustained case for seeing a futurist eschatology in Ephesians.[77]

Therefore, opponents of authenticity claim that these three theological themes do not represent developments of the undisputed Pauline Letters but departures from these.[78]

---

[74] J. C. Beker, *Paul the Apostle: The Triumph of God in Life and Thought* (Minneapolis, MN: Fortress, 1990).

[75] A. Lindemann (*Die Aufhebung der Zeit: Geschichtsverständnis und Eschatologie im Epheserbrief*, SNT 12 [Gütersloh, Germany: Mohn, 1975], 98–99) believed that this "summing up" has already been accomplished. But this understanding does not own up to Paul's own assessment. Paul conceived of his own apostolic ministry as one of bringing this goal to a future fulfillment (3:8–10). All things will not be summed up until the future redemption of humanity (1:14) and the consummation in the coming age (2:7).

[76] Hoehner, *Ephesians*, 56.

[77] Lincoln, *Ephesians*, lxxxix–xc.

[78] See esp. A. T. Lincoln and A. J. M. Wedderburn, *The Theology of the Later Pauline Letters*, New Testament Theology (Cambridge, UK: University Press, 1993), 91–166. W. G. Kümmel (*Introduction to the New Testament*, rev. ed., trans. H. C. Kee [Nashville, TN: Abingdon, 1975], 360) went so far as to say that the theology of Ephesians "makes the Pauline composition of the letter completely impossible."

Proponents of Paul's authorship respond by pointing out texts in the undisputed Pauline Letters that parallel the thought of Ephesians. These resemblances are close enough to represent an organic relationship between the theology of Ephesians and the undisputed Pauline Letters.[79] One must also remember that pastoral factors may also play a role in these theological emphases. C. E. Arnold argued strongly that the emphasis on cosmic Christology and realized eschatology is intended to strengthen believers in the cosmic conflict against the "principalities and powers."[80]

In terms of vocabulary, those who reject Paul's authorship point out that Ephesians uses unique language not found elsewhere in his writings, and they contend that the letter has too many *hapax legomena* (words that only occur once in the Pauline corpus) to be considered Pauline.[81] Proponents of Paul's authorship generally protest by pointing out that Paul's undisputed letters also contain a high number of *hapax legomena*, so that Ephesians is not unique in the Pauline corpus in this regard.[82] Hoehner highlighted the comparison between Ephesians (forty-one words not found elsewhere in the NT and eighty-four words not found elsewhere in Paul) and Galatians (thirty-five words not found elsewhere in the NT and ninety words not found elsewhere in Paul). No one doubts the authenticity of Galatians, even though Galatians contains six more words than Ephesians that are not found elsewhere in Paul *and* Galatians is ten percent shorter than Ephesians.[83] In other words, assessing authorship must not rest solely on a statistical analysis of vocabulary.

In terms of literary style, opponents of authenticity cite the high percentage of pleonastic elements such as prepositions and participles, the compound use of the genitive, unusually long sentences, and elevated diction.[84] Proponents of Paul's authorship counter with the claim that many of these features are not unusual for Paul, especially in light of the doxologies and prayers in chapters 1–3.[85] They also add that many significant vocabulary words and literary examples in Ephesians resemble material found only in his writings.[86]

---

[79] P. T. O'Brien, *The Epistle to the Ephesians*, PNTC (Grand Rapids, MI: Eerdmans, 1999), 21–33.

[80] C. E. Arnold, *Ephesians: Power and Magic. The Concept of Power in Ephesians in Light of Its Historical Setting*, SNTSMS 63 (Cambridge:, UK University Press, 1989), 124–29.

[81] R. F. Collins, *Letters That Paul Did Not Write: The Epistle to the Hebrews and the Pauline Pseudepigrapha*, Good News Studies 28 (Wilmington, DE: Michael Glazier, 1988), 142.

[82] P. N. Harrison, *Paulines and Pastorals* (London, England: Villiers, 1964), 48.

[83] Hoehner, *Ephesians*, 24.

[84] Pleonasm is the use of more words than necessary to express an idea. See esp. A. T. Lincoln, *Ephesians*, WBC 42 (Dallas, TX: Word, 1990), xlv–xlvi.

[85] A. van Roon, *The Authenticity of Ephesians*, trans. S. Prescod-Jokel, NovTSup 39 (Leiden, Netherlands: Brill, 1974), 105–11; D. A. Carson and D. J. Moo, *An Introduction to the New Testament*, 2nd ed. (Grand Rapids, MI: Zondervan, 2005), 484.

[86] N. Turner, *Style*, vol. 4 of *A Grammar of New Testament Greek*, ed. J. H. Moulton (Edinburgh, Scotland: T&T Clark, 1976), 84–85.

In terms of the relation to Colossians, many opponents of authenticity claim Ephesian dependence upon Colossians,[87] though others argue for Colossian dependence[88] or no interdependence.[89] Some scholars say that Ephesians represents the "actualization of authoritative tradition" as the author updated Paul's gospel.[90] Advocates of authenticity claim the conceptual closeness between the two letters does not call common authorship into question.[91]

In terms of the impersonal nature of Ephesians, some scholars observe that the letter lacks any personal greetings and ends with an impersonal farewell. Moreover, the author apparently knew the readers only on a general level. These observations seem out of place in light of the fact that Paul spent three years in Ephesus (Acts 20:31). Many advocates of authenticity are quick to point out that the letter is a circular letter because of the probability on text-critical grounds that the words "at Ephesus" (1:1) are not part of the original text.[92] The impersonal nature of the letter would fit well with the theory that it is a general letter written to believers in Asia Minor. But advocates of authenticity who doubt the circular letter hypothesis point out that Paul does not give personal greetings in 2 Corinthians, Galatians, 1 and 2 Thessalonians, or Philippians either.[93]

In the face of so many challenges to authenticity, some scholars are willing to concede that Ephesians contains genuine Pauline material because the author was a disciple of Paul.[94] Others see serious social consequences arising from the Deutero-Pauline distortion of Paul's message in the genuine letters.[95]

---

[87] V. P. Furnish, "Ephesians, Epistle to the," in *ABD* 2:536–37; Lincoln, *Ephesians*, xlvii–lviii.

[88] van Roon, *The Authenticity of Ephesians*, 413–37. He also theorized that both Colossians and Ephesians borrowed from an *Ur*-text (original text common to both).

[89] E. Best, *A Critical and Exegetical Commentary on Ephesians*, ICC (Edinburgh, Scotland: T&T Clark, 1998), 36–40.

[90] Lincoln *Ephesians*, lviii. Lincoln also claimed that Ephesian dependence on Colossians and its use of Romans is the "most decisive" argument against authenticity (Lincoln and Wedderburn, *Theology*, 84).

[91] C. E. Arnold, "Ephesians, Letter to the," in *Dictionary of Paul and His Letters*, ed. G. F. Hawthorne, R. P. Martin, and D. G. Reid (Downers Grove, IL: InterVarsity, 1993), 242–43.

[92] O'Brien, *Ephesians*, 5.

[93] Hoehner (*Ephesians*, 22) noted that the lack of personal greetings in 2 Corinthians is striking because Paul spent eighteen months in Corinth. He also observed that the letter is not completely impersonal because Paul prayed for the recipients of the letter (1:16) and asked for their prayers (6:19–20; ibid., 23).

[94] D. Trobisch (*Paul's Letter Collection: Tracing the Origins* [Minneapolis, MN: Fortress, 2000], 53–54) said that Ephesians is "the beginning of an appendix" to Paul's own collection of his letters. F. F. Bruce (*Paul: Apostle of the Heart Set Free* [Grand Rapids, MI: Eerdmans, 1977], 424) and L. T. Johnson (*The Writings of the New Testament: An Interpretation* [Philadelphia, PA: Fortress, 1986], 372) stressed that even if a disciple of Paul wrote Ephesians, it should be regarded as a masterful summary of Paul's theology.

[95] The most notable is N. Elliott, *Liberating Paul: The Justice of God and the Politics of the Apostle* (Maryknoll, NY: Orbis, 1994), esp. 25–54; idem, "Paul and the Politics of Empire: Problems and Prospects," in *Paul and Politics: Ekklesia, Israel, Imperium, Interpretation*, ed. R. A. Horsley (Harrisburg, PA: Trinity, 2000), 26–27. Elliott asserted that the Deutero-Paulines arose in order to "hijack" and "distort" Paul's liberating social legacy. He also argued that the "domestic codes" are contaminated at 1 Cor 14:34–35 with regard to women and 1 Thess 2:14–16 with regard to Jews. This fact demonstrates that Elliott approached Paul's Letters with a preconceived notion of what Paul was or was not allowed to say. This bias—not the undisputed Pauline corpus—functions as the adjudicating factor for authenticity.

One is left wondering how to respond. The reader may say that the point-counterpoint nature of the case renders the decision difficult. However, when all arguments are weighed, the Pauline authorship of Ephesians rests on a firm foundation. The arguments that the proponents of authenticity set forward appear more formidable. Despite complicated disagreements among scholars over how to weigh statistical analysis,[96] Hoehner convincingly showed that the use of unique vocabulary in Ephesians is not unusual for Paul, especially in comparison with Galatians. Though the stylistic and theological differences are real, there is no clear conflict between Ephesians and Paul's other writings. The stylistic features of the letter are not unusual for Paul, especially the elevated diction in the doxologies and prayers. The theological emphases can be traced out in other Pauline writings, and Paul's emphasis on the principalities and powers accounts for the cosmic Christology, realized eschatology, and the focus on the church.

Conversely, the counter response that the proponents of authenticity have made against the opponents of authenticity does not constitute the strongest case for authenticity. Paul's authorship of Ephesians rests most securely on two early and influential claims for authenticity: (1) that of the letter, and (2) the testimony of the early church.[97] The case against authenticity is further plagued by questions surrounding the practice and validity of pseudonymity.[98]

Therefore, the sheer number of modern scholars who discount Paul's authorship need not dictate a decision in favor of inauthenticity.[99] The student should interact with the arguments of critical scholarship instead of uncritically accepting their conclusions. When one weighs the evidence and does not merely count the opinions, the totality of the data favors Pauline authorship.

Literary Integrity In terms of literary integrity, there are no significant partition theories for Ephesians. In terms of textual integrity, the textual tradition is well preserved except for the debated phrase "in Ephesus" (1:1). Therefore, apart from the question of

---

[96] See S. Michaelson and A. Q. Morton, "Last Words: A Test of Authorship for Greek Writers," *NTS* 18 (1972): 192–208. They argued that the Pauline Letters do not meet the minimum requirement of 10,000 words similar in length and substance that are necessary to make proper comparisons. Cf. the severe critique of this proposal by P. F. Johnson, "The Use of Statistics in the Analysis of the Characteristics of Pauline Writing," *NTS* 20 (1973): 92–100.

[97] C. L. Mitton (*Ephesians*, NCB [London, England: Oliphants, 1976], 15–16) wrote, "The external evidence is wholly on the side of those who maintain Pauline authorship. Among all the early writers of the Christian Church there is never the slightest hint that questions it." Clement of Rome (ca. 95) appears to be the first church father to allude to Ephesians (*1 Clem.* 46:6). It appears that Ignatius (died ca. 110), Irenaeus (ca. 180), Polycarp (ca. 155), Clement of Alexandria (ca. 200), and Tertullian (d. 225) knew Ephesians and confirmed its authenticity. The book can also be found in Marcion's canon and the Muratorian canon. See Hoehner's excellent survey of Ephesians in the early church (*Ephesians*, 2–6).

[98] See the excellent discussion on pseudonymity and pseudepigraphy in Carson and Moo, *Introduction to the New Testament*, 337–53.

[99] In 1984 R. E. Brown, *The Churches the Apostles Left Behind* (New York, NY: Paulist, 1984), 47; idem (*Introduction*, 620) estimated that "at the present moment about 80 percent of critical scholarship holds that Paul did not write Eph." The extensive chart in Hoehner (*Ephesians*, 9–20) shows that this estimate was overstated at best and irresponsible at worst.

destination, the textual variants do not create any substantial cause for doubting the literary integrity of the letter.[100]

Date

The date for Ephesians depends on complex questions concerning authorship and provenance. If the letter was written during Paul's Roman imprisonment, then it dates to 58–60 (60–62 in the conventional reckoning).[101] Since Ephesians, Colossians, and Philemon appear to have been written at approximately the same time and since Philemon belongs to the final phase of Paul's imprisonment, a date around the year 60 is reasonable. If one places Ephesians earlier in Paul's ministry, then it dates to the early or mid-50s. Most who see the letter as Deutero-Pauline or post-Pauline date the document somewhere between 70 and 90.[102]

Provenance

The provenance of Ephesians is inextricably related to issues such as authorship, the identity of the addressees, and the date. Many hold that Ephesians was written from the same place as Colossians, Philemon, and possibly Philippians.[103]

Destination

The fact that some important manuscripts do not include "at Ephesus" (1:1) poses problems for identifying a destination.[104] Prominent textual critics such as B. Metzger doubt the integrity of the phrase "at Ephesus."[105] Therefore, some scholars have theorized that Ephesians was a circular letter.[106] As mentioned above, this assumption coheres with some of the letter's internal evidence. The impersonal tone throughout Ephesians is

---

[100] T. K. Abbott (*A Critical and Exegetical Commentary on the Epistles to the Ephesians and to the Colossians*, ICC [Edinburgh, Scotland: T&T Clark, 1897], xl–xlv) provided a list of the most important readings for certain key manuscripts. Cf. B. M. Metzger, *Textual Commentary on the Greek New Testament*, 2nd ed. (New York, NY: American Bible Society, 1994), 532–43.

[101] O'Brien (*Ephesians*, 57) opted for 61–62.

[102] A. T. Lincoln (*Ephesians*, lxxiii) proposed a range of 80–90. Carson and Moo (*Introduction to the New Testament*, 487) noted that the latest possible date appears to be approximately 90 because it seems that Clement of Rome referred to Ephesians in his letter, which is usually dated to the year 96. But Lincoln (*Ephesians*, lxxii–lxxiii) joined J. Gnilka (*Der Epheserbrief* [Freiburg, Germany: Herder, 1971], 18) in rejecting this conclusion, arguing that Ignatius, who died about 110, is the first early church father to show an awareness of Ephesians while Tertullian was the first to make the attribution explicit.

[103] See the discussion below.

[104] "At Ephesus" is omitted by key early Alexandrian texts such as 𝔓[46] ℵ B 424[c] 1739. Early church fathers such as Basil, Origen, and Gregory the Great also omit the phrase. Some scholars say Marcion was not familiar with the phrase because he named the letter "The Epistle to the Laodiceans." Tertullian has the phrase "to the saints who are also believers in Christ Jesus." See M. Barth, *Ephesians 1–3*, 67. The Western (D, F, G) and the Byzantine (K, L, P) mss. traditions, along with some Alexandrian texts (ℵ[2]) A B[2] miniscule 33, 81, 104, 1175, 1881), support the inclusion of "at Ephesus."

[105] Metzger, *Textual Commentary*, 532.

[106] Ibid.; Bruce, *Colossians and Ephesians*, 250; O'Brien, *Ephesians*, 5, 86–87; M. Barth, *Ephesians 1–3*, 67. For further investigation, see M. Santer, "The Text of Ephesians 1:1," *NTS* 15 (1969): 247–48; E. Best, "Ephesians i.1," in *Text and Interpretation: Studies in the New Testament Presented to Matthew Black*, ed. E. Best and R. M. Wilson (Cambridge, UK: University Press, 1979), 29–41; idem, "Ephesians 1.1 Again," in *Paul and Paulinism: Essays in Honour of C. K. Barrett*, ed. M. D. Hooker and S. G. Wilson (London, England: SPCK, 1982), 276–78; and "Excursus 1: Textual Problem in Ephesians 1:1," in Hoehner, *Ephesians*, 144–48.

surprising in light of the considerable amount of time Paul spent in Ephesus (Acts 19:8, 10; 20:31). Moreover, some texts seem to imply that the author did not even know the readers (Eph 3:2; 4:21).

However, one should also note that the circular letter hypothesis is not without problems in that even the manuscripts not containing the phrase "at Ephesus" have "Ephesus" in the title.[107] What is more, even those who adhere to the circular letter hypothesis admit that the omission of "at Ephesus" creates an awkward grammatical construction: "to the saints and believers in Christ Jesus."[108] This debate seems somewhat inconsequential because some scholars who think that "at Ephesus" is part of the original text still believe that the letter circulated to the churches in Asia Minor as well.[109]

Occasion

Paul's letters are not expressions of merely theoretical theology. They are letters written by a compassionate spiritual leader to address specific congregational circumstances. But Ephesians appears to break this mold; thus, it is difficult to detect a clear occasion for it.[110] Most agree that Gentile readers are the primary audience, but the consensus quickly crumbles after that observation. In contrast to the tone and content of Colossians, Ephesians does not read like a response to false teaching. Some have questioned the search for an occasion to the extent that they doubt whether Ephesians is a letter at all. These scholars prefer to describe it as a homily or a speech.[111]

If one assumes the circular nature of the letter, Ephesians represents a careful summary and exposition of Paul's thought. If the original document was addressed to the Ephesians, then questions concerning the occasion of the letter largely become educated guesses culled from the content of Ephesians. Views regarding the occasion also vary according to whether scholars adhere to authenticity or inauthenticity. Among those who argue for inauthenticity, N. A. Dahl detects a baptismal setting for the letter as a pseudonymous

---

[107] Hoehner, *Ephesians*, 147.

[108] Bruce (*Ephesians*, 250) theorized that the space after the verb "are" was left blank in order for Tychicus to insert the appropriate geographical name to each locale in which he delivered a copy of the circular letter. Bruce made this assertion while admitting that this device is difficult to find in the first century. Bruce cited G. Zuntz (*The Text of the Epistles* [London, England: British Academy, 1954], 228n1), who pointed to multiple copies of royal letters in the Hellenistic period that were based on a master copy "with the address left blank, and it is most probable that the blank in the address of Ephesians goes back to such an original." M. Barth has an excellent discussion that traces the historical development of this approach. He identified T. Beza and H. Grotius as the first to suggest this line of thinking. Barth said that J. Ussher defended this solution in his *Annales Veteris et Novi Testamenti* (London, England: Crook, 1650–54) and also cited Lightfoot, Hort, Haupt, Robinson, Percy, and Schlier as proponents. D. N. Freedman (by letter, cited in M. Barth, *Ephesians 1–3*, 67) compared this text-critical problem with 2 Sam 4:1 and offered a similar solution. But there are significant problems with this approach. Kümmel (*Introduction*, 355) strongly asserted that "there is no parallel in antiquity" to this practice. O'Brien (*Ephesians*, 85–86) rightly pointed out that this practice does not fit in an age when each copy had to be handwritten. He also reminds the readers that no copies have survived that were addressed to a place other than Ephesus.

[109] Arnold, "Ephesians," 244–45; Hoehner, *Ephesians*, 79.

[110] So also Carson and Moo, *Introduction to the New Testament*, 490.

[111] Best, *Ephesians*, 61–63.

writing intended for new believers that stresses the implications of their baptism.[112] A. T. Lincoln believed that many of the issues in Ephesians arise out of a context in which Paul had just passed from the scene and thus the readers lack a sense of unity because of the loss of Paul as their unifying source of authority.[113] R. Schnackenburg argued that Ephesians confronts a group of churches in Asia Minor around the year 90 with the need for unity and a Christian lifestyle distinct from that of their pagan neighbors.[114] C. L. Mitton identified a gnostic threat as the occasion.[115]

Among those who argue for Pauline authenticity, most stress that there is no specific crisis in view. Paul simply had time to write a positive exposition of his theology while under house arrest in Rome.[116] Others identify specific needs that Christians in Asia Minor would have had. F. Thielman argued that Christians possibly facing suffering in Asia Minor would have needed an encouraging reminder of all that God had done for them in Christ and a challenge to live in a manner consistent with God's purposes for the church in summing up all things in Christ.[117] C. E. Arnold stated that Christians in Asia Minor would have required positive grounding in the gospel because they were converts from a pagan past saturated with magic, astrology, and mystery religions. Their past also necessitated moral guidance for living a life consistent with the lordship of Christ. Arnold also noted that the flood of Gentile converts into the church required Paul to address the Jew-Gentile tensions that customarily would come to the surface. He therefore argued that Paul wrote a genuine Pastoral Letter for "a multiplicity of needs shared by the readership."[118]

Purpose

Despite the variegated proposals for the life setting of the letter, most scholars agree on the main themes in Ephesians. They see it emphasizing cosmic reconciliation in Christ and stressing the need for (1) unity in the church, (2) a distinctive Christian ethic, and (3) vigilance in spiritual warfare.[119] As noted above, various exegetes take these emphases and then attempt to develop points of contact with possible concrete needs.

The attempt to ascertain a specific purpose may engender a variety of proposals, but most would acknowledge, as Carson and Moo pointed out, that Ephesians is "an important statement of the gospel that may have been greatly needed in more than one first-century situation."[120] The general nature of Ephesians renders it particularly suitable for application by present-day believers, too.

---

[112] N. A. Dahl, "Gentiles, Christians, and Israelites in the Epistle to the Ephesians," *HTR* 79 (1986): 38.
[113] Lincoln, *Ephesians*, lxxv–lxxxvii.
[114] Schnackenburg, *Ephesians*, 22–35.
[115] Mitton, *Ephesians*, 30–31.
[116] J. A. Robinson, *St. Paul's Epistle to the Ephesians*, 2nd ed. (London, England: Macmillan, 1907), 10–11.
[117] Thielman, *Theology of the New Testament*, 394.
[118] Arnold, "Ephesians, Letter to the," 246.
[119] O'Brien, *Ephesians*, 58–65.
[120] Carson and Moo, *Introduction to the New Testament*, 491.

LITERATURE

Literary Plan

Recent works have set forth a variety of proposals regarding the literary plan of Ephesians. In terms of rhetorical analysis, N. A. Dahl proposed that Ephesians is a variant of epideictic or demonstrative rhetoric.[121] A. T. Lincoln[122] and A. C. Mayer[123] came to the same conclusion, although they admit that the letter does not fit the conventional ancient Greco-Roman rhetorical handbooks with precision and resists generic classification. P. S. Cameron discovered a chiastic structure for Ephesians, though he favored the term *palinstrophe* over *chiasm*.[124] Mayer advocated two chiastic sections (1:3–3:21; 4:1–6:9). J. P. Heil proposed another chiasm for the letter.[125] This proliferation of proposals is problematic for rhetorical and chiastic analysis. Though these studies are insightful and thought provoking, many rightly remain unpersuaded by macrochiastic[126] and rhetorical analyses[127] because of the ever-present danger of pressing Paul's Letters into preconceived models.

OUTLINE

I. OPENING (1:1–2)

II. BODY: SEATED WITH CHRIST, WALKING WITH CHRIST, STANDING FOR CHRIST (1:3–6:20)

- A. Shared Spiritual Blessings in Union with Christ and Unity in Christ (1:3–3:21)
    1. Spiritual Blessings in Christ (1:3–14)
    2. Thanksgiving and Prayer (1:15–23)
    3. Believers' Past and Present Life (2:1–10)
    4. Jews and Gentiles One in Christ (2:11–22)
    5. Paul's Ministry and the "Mystery" (3:1–13)
    6. Prayer for Unity in Christ (3:14–21)
- B. Walk with Christ and Stand for Christ (4:1–6:20)
    1. The Church's Sevenfold Unity (4:1–16)
    2. Living as Children of Light (4:17–5:17)

---

[121] N. A. Dahl, "Ephesians," in *Harper's Bible Commentary*, ed. J. L. Mays (San Francisco, CA: Harper & Row, 1988), 1212.

[122] Lincoln, *Ephesians*, 46.

[123] A. C. Mayer, *Sprache der Einheit im Epheserbrief*, WUNT 150 (Tübingen, Germany: Mohr Siebeck, 2002), 20.

[124] P. S. Cameron ("The Structure of Ephesians," *Filologia Neotestamentaria* 3 [1990]: 3–17) proposed that eight parallel panels demonstrate linguistic links (excluding 6:18–22).

[125] J. P. Heil, *Ephesians: Empowerment to Walk in Love for the Unity of All in Christ*, Studies in Biblical Literature 13 (Leiden, Netherlands: Brill, 2007).

[126] The sheer complexity of Cameron's proposal casts doubt on its viability and usefulness. Mayer's two-chiasm proposal is marginally better, though still problematic and implausible at points. In particular, one wonders how the readers or hearers could have possibly detected the kind of chiasm proposed by Mayer.

[127] See the critique of Lincoln's rhetorical outline by D. E. Aune, *The Westminster Dictionary of New Testament and Early Christian Literature and Rhetoric* (Louisville, KY: Westminster John Knox, 2003), 159.

3. Spirit-Filled Living in the Home and at Work (5:18–6:9)
4. Putting on the Armor of God (6:10–20)

III. CLOSING (6:21–24)

UNIT-BY-UNIT DISCUSSION

I. Opening (1:1–2)

Ephesians begins with the three customary elements that introduce a letter: (1) author, (2) recipient, and (3) greeting.

II. Body: Seated with Christ, Walking with Christ, Standing for Christ (1:3–6:20)

The body of the letter naturally subdivides into an indicative section conveying general theological truths regarding its recipients (1:15–3:21) and an imperative section (4:1–6:20) that issues a series of commands and exhortations on the basis of these realities. The key terms of Ephesians appear to be "sit," "walk," and "stand."[128] The first half of the letter lays the proper foundation by defining believers' identity in Christ. On the basis of their spiritual status, they are exhorted in the second half to attain to the unity and maturity in the Spirit that are already theirs in Christ. In this way, as the key verse of the entire letter states (1:10), Christ, the centerpiece of God's salvation-historical purposes, will be restored to his rightful place of supremacy and preeminence in all things in the church and the cosmos.

A. Shared Spiritual Blessings in Union with Christ and Unity in Christ (1:3–3:21) In this section Paul (1) unpacks the spiritual blessings believers have in the heavenly realms in Christ (1:3–14); (2) prays for his readers (1:15–23); (3) describes conversion as a change from spiritual death to spiritual life (2:1–10); (4) portrays the gospel-centered unity of the church (2:11–22); (5) highlights his own role in this unity as the minister to the Gentiles entrusted with the mystery of the gospel (3:1–13); and (6) ends with a concluding prayer and doxology (3:14–21).

The letter's lengthy eulogy (1:3–14) is one sentence in the Greek text, and in it Paul explains the spiritual blessings believers possess in Christ (1:3). These center on the work of the Trinity in the salvation of believers and elicit the praise of God's glory. God the Father plans salvation (1:4–5) for his glory (1:6). God the Son procures salvation (1:7–12) for the praise of God's glory (1:12). God the Spirit seals salvation (1:13) and serves as the down payment of the believer's inheritance for the praise of God's glory (1:14).

Paul follows the eulogy with an opening prayer for his readers (1:15–23) and concludes the section with a closing prayer (3:14–21). The opening prayer pleads that God would give believers a spirit of wisdom and revelation and open the eyes of hearers' hearts so that they would be enabled fully to grasp their hope in the glorious riches of Christ's

---

[128] "Sit"/"seat" (*kathizō*; 1:20); "walk" (*peripateō*; 2:2, 10; 4:1, 17 [twice]; 5:2, 8, 15); "stand" (*histēmi*; 6:11, 13–14). See B. Weber, "'Setzen'-'Wandeln'-'Stehen' im Epheserbrief," *NTS* 41 (1995): 478–80.

inheritance and his immeasurably great power at work in believers. Paul compares this power with the power that raised Christ from the dead and seated him at God's right hand above all rule and authority (1:20–23).

The next three sections portray the unity God has created through the gospel from three different angles: (1) the heavenly angle where God gives life to the spiritually dead and raises them up so they are spiritually seated together with Christ in the heavenly realms (2:1–10); (2) the cross-centered angle that depicts the cross of Christ demolishing old barriers in order to create the church as the one new man and the one new building (2:11–22); and (3) Paul's apostolic ministry angle that highlights his role in bringing to light the mystery of the spiritual equality of Gentiles with Jews in the body of Christ (3:1–13). The apostle's closing prayer and doxology again stress unity as he prayed for believers to be able to grasp the love of Christ "with all the saints" (3:18) and as he exulted in the God who is glorified "in the church" (3:21).

Ephesians 2:1–10 and 2:11–22 both use the "once-now" schema,[129] which rehearses the readers' condition before and after conversion to Christ. Verses 1–10 speak of the spiritual separation between God and men in soteriological terms, while 11–22 portray this separation in the context of salvation history.

Ephesians 2:1–10 moves from the sphere of spiritual death and the status of unbelievers as "children under wrath" to the realm of spiritual life and the state of salvation. This ultimate "rags to riches" experience rests on God's amazing grace apart from any human works (2:4–5). Paul links his earlier description of the experience of Christ (1:20–23) with the experience of the believer in Christ (2:6). The believers' union with Christ means that just as he was raised up and seated at God's right hand (1:20), so believers are made alive with Christ, raised up with him, and seated with him in the heavenly places (2:6). The joy of this present experience can only be exceeded by that in the ages to come when God will "show the surpassing riches of His grace in kindness" to believers in Christ (2:7 NASB). Paul also stresses the unmerited nature of salvation as a gift of God's grace, which is received by faith (2:8). This salvation precludes human boasting because it is based on the work of God and not the works of man (2:8–9). Though salvation does not result from good works, good works flow from salvation (2:10).

In 2:11–12 Paul described the plight of his readers' past. Paul calls them to remember their former condition as Gentiles.[130] Specifically, Paul stated that they were formerly separated from (1) Christ, (2) citizenship in Israel, (3) covenants of promise, (4) hope, and (5) God. But Christ has established peace and unity between Jews and Gentiles by abolishing the dividing wall through the cross (2:14–15) and by creating in himself one new

---

[129] J. Pfammatter (*Epheserbrief; Kolosserbrief*, Neue Echter Bibel [Würzburg, Germany: Echter, 1987], 22) believed that the author alludes to Isa 57:19 with the use of this schema.

[130] This text resembles Rom 9:4–5 but fulfills a different purpose: Rom 9:4–5 lists the advantages of being an Israelite, while Eph 2:11–12 describes the disadvantages of being a Gentile. See R. Schnackenburg, *Der Brief an die Epheser* (Zürich, Germany: Benziger, 1982), 108–9.

man, the church (2:15), which is a united building or sanctuary for God's dwelling place in the Spirit (2:21–22).

Paul highlights his apostolic ministry to the Gentiles and as the "mystery" of the gospel (3:1–13). God's "mystery," formerly hidden and now revealed to the apostles and prophets, is the spiritual equality of Gentiles with Jews in the body of Christ through the gospel (3:5–6). God empowered Paul to bring his plan to pass (3:8–9) so that through the church God's wisdom will be revealed "to the rulers and authorities in the heavens" (3:10; see 1:21).

Paul's closing prayer (3:14–21) petitions God to empower believers so they will be able "to comprehend with all the saints what is the length and width, height and depth of God's love, and to know Christ's love that surpasses knowledge, so you may be filled with all the fullness of God" (3:18–19). Paul closed with a doxology to God as the One who works with power beyond all we could ask or imagine (3:20–21).

B. Walk with Christ and Stand for Christ (4:1–6:20) The indicative section (chaps. 1–3) provides the basis ("therefore"; 4:1) for the imperative section. The two key words in this section appear to be "walk" (4:1, 17 [twice]; 5:2, 8, 15) and "stand" (6:11, 13–14). Hoehner's proposed structure of the "walk" section is pedagogically helpful. Paul called the church to walk in (1) unity (4:1–16), (2) holiness (4:17–32), (3) love (5:1–6), (4) light (5:7–14), and (5) wisdom (5:15–6:9).[131] Ephesians 6:10–20 constitutes a call for Christ-followers to stand in spiritual warfare against the dark forces of wickedness by accessing God's power in God's armor (6:10–17) and in prayer (6:18–20).

Ephesians 4:1–16 highlights diversity in unity (4:1–13) in the church for the maturity (4:13), stability (4:14), and growth (4:15–16) of the body of Christ. Ephesians 4:1–6 specifically outlines *what* Christians are called to do (walk worthy of their calling as Christians). It tells *how* they are to do it (with humility, gentleness, patience, and loving forbearance, maintaining the unity of the Spirit). It gives the *why* (because of the sevenfold "oneness" of the faith). Ephesians 4:7–13 adds the observation that "oneness" does not imply "sameness." Believers are not called to be "cookie-cutter" Christians, because Christ graciously gives a variety of gifts as the spoils of his victory (4:7–10) for the sake of the church (4:11–12). He does this so that the body will be built up and will attain unity, maturity, and fullness in the faith (4:12–13).[132]

This unity and maturity will guard the body not only from false teaching (4:14) but also from false living (4:17–19). Christians must not walk in darkness like the Gentiles (4:17–19; 5:6–7), but must "live as children of light" (5:8–10) and remain separate from

---

[131] See the outline in Hoehner, *Ephesians*, 66–68.

[132] Scholars have wrestled with the apparent verb change ("he received gifts") in Ps 68:8 (LXX 67:19; MT 68:19) to "he gave gifts" in Eph 4:8. Some believe Paul drew upon a later targumic reading found in the Peshitta. See E. Nestle, "Zum Zitat in Eph 4,8," *ZNW* 4 (1903): 344–45. Bruce (*Ephesians*, 342) argued that the reading is earlier than the written targum because the readings "often had a long oral prehistory." For an extensive survey of approaches to this text, see W. Hall Harris III, *The Descent of Christ: Ephesians 4:7–11 and Traditional Hebrew Imagery*, AGJU 32 (Leiden, Netherlands: Brill, 1996), 64–122.

dark deeds and expose them by bringing them into the light (5:11–14). Christ's followers walk in light (5:6–14) and in wisdom (5:15–17).

Paul commands Christians to be continually filled by the Spirit,[133] which is contrasted with drunkenness (5:18). A series of dependent participles[134] follows the command to be filled by the Spirit in order that the reader will see that "being filled" by the Spirit has effects such as whole-hearted praise (v. 19), thanksgiving (v. 20), and submission (v. 21). Paul developed the specifics of this submission in the form of a domestic code, which delineates the various roles and responsibilities of the members of the household (5:22–6:9).[135]

As a result of "being filled by the Spirit," wives are enjoined to submit to their husbands (5:22), children to obey their parents (6:1), and slaves to obey their masters (6:5). Paul also stresses what Spirit-filled behavior entails for those in positions of authority: husbands are called to love their wives as Christ loves his bride, the church (5:28); fathers ought not provoke their children to anger but should bring them up in the training and instruction of the Lord (6:4); and masters should treat those under their authority fairly and without making threats (6:9).

The last clarion call is for believers to stand firm for Christ (6:10–20). The text consists of three parts: (1) verses 10–13 provide an introductory admonition for believers to be strong in the Lord and to put on the full armor of God in light of the hostile forces arrayed against them; (2) verses 14–17 build upon ("therefore") and reinforce the introductory admonition and further specify the pieces that constitute the "full armor"; and (3) verses 18–20 call on Christ's followers to access God's power in prayer for all their fellow believers (6:18), including Paul (6:19–20). The word for "stand" occurs three times (6:11, 13–14) as a call to stand strong in God's power (i.e., the full armor of God) against the Devil and the spiritual powers of wickedness.

---

[133] Paul wanted to see the distinctively Christian solution of "being filled *by* the Spirit." Greek grammarians note that this specific construction never refers to the content of the filling, so translations such as "filled *with* the Spirit" are grammatically suspect. Most likely, the Spirit here is not the *content* but the *agent* of the filling. With what does the Spirit fill believers? An examination of the use of the Greek word for "fill" in Ephesians reveals that believers are filled by Christ (1:23) and the Spirit (5:18) with the fullness of God (3:19). See esp. D. B. Wallace, *Greek Grammar Beyond the Basics* (Grand Rapids, MI: Zondervan, 1996), 375. So also O'Brien, *Ephesians*, 391–92; Hoehner, *Ephesians*, 702–4. Cf. G. D. Fee, *God's Empowering Presence: The Holy Spirit in the Letters of Paul* (Peabody, MA: Hendrickson, 1994), 721n196. Fee argued that while the Greek construction signifies the means of filling, "it is but a short step to seeing the Spirit as that substance as well." J. P. Heil ("Ephesians 5:18b: 'But Be Filled in the Spirit,'" *CBQ* 69 [2007]: 506) contended for the translation "be filled *in* the Spirit," conveying the sense of "being within the dynamic realm or sphere established and characterized by having been given the Spirit." For a survey of various proposals, see A. J. Köstenberger, "What Does It Mean to Be Filled with the Spirit? A Biblical Investigation," *JETS* 40 (1997): 231–35; and Heil, "Ephesians 5:18b."

[134] The five participles convey result. So also Lincoln, *Ephesians*, 345; Wallace, *Greek Grammar Beyond the Basics*, 639. Paul's grammar highlights the cause-and-effect relationship between "being filled by the Spirit" (5:18) and the godly characteristics that follow (5:19–21). These are not independent realities believers are called to create by their own willpower; instead, they are dependent on the Spirit's work (cf. the fruit of the Spirit in Gal 5:22–23).

[135] See T. G. Gombis, "A Radically New Humanity: The Function of the *Haustafel* in Ephesians," *JETS* 48 (2005): 317–30.

Ephesians 6:10–20 serves as a climax for the letter.[136] Therefore, the reader finds many earlier themes repeated and made more emphatic. The list of armor pieces that believers use in spiritual warfare (6:14–17) were already prominent in Ephesians: truth (1:13, 4:15, 21, 24–25; 5:9), righteousness (4:24; 5:9), peace (1:2; 2:14–18; 4:3), the gospel (1:13; 3:6), the word of God (1:13; 5:26), salvation (1:13; 2:5, 8; 5:23), and faith (1:1, 13, 15, 19; 2:8; 3:12, 17; 4:5, 13). The lexical and conceptual links between 1:3–14 and 6:10–20 are also pronounced, especially the cluster of key theological terms between 1:13 and 6:14–17. Importantly, as in the case of the command to be "filled by the Spirit" (5:18), the Ephesian "spiritual warfare" passage has important corporate as well as individual dimensions. Both individual believers and the church *as a whole* must be spiritually equipped to engage in spiritual warfare.[137]

III. Closing (6:21–24)

Paul concludes the letter with some brief references regarding his travel plans and a standard closing formula. He states that he is sending Tychicus to inform the readers regarding Paul's personal affairs (6:21–22) and to encourage them (6:22). Paul closed the letter with a wish for peace and love from God the Father and the Lord Jesus Christ (6:23) and with the grace benediction (6:24).

THEOLOGY

Theological Themes

The Lordship of Christ The "[bringing back of] all things . . . together again under one head" (*anakephalaioō*, 1:10 NIV), the Lord Jesus Christ, is the central theme of the whole letter. God progressively brings about this realignment of proper authority and submission in two spheres: the heavens (1:3, 10, 20; 2:6; 3:10; 6:12) and the earth (1:10; 3:15; 4:9; 6:3).[138] Each realm has its own representative: the powers in the heavens and the church upon the earth.[139] Therefore, God's subjection of all things to Christ becomes a progressive reality through Christ's supremacy over and defeat of the evil powers

---

[136] Moritz, *Profound Mystery*, 181–83; O'Brien, *Ephesians*, 457; Lincoln, *Ephesians*, 438–39. Lincoln ("'Stand, Therefore . . .': Ephesians 6:10–20 as *Peroratio*," *BibInt* 3 [1995]: 99–114) identified the climax in rhetorical terms as the *peroratio*. This category was used at the end of the speech, and it sought to sum up the main themes and move the listener to action. O'Brien (*Ephesians*, 459–60) rightly noted that this passage fulfills the function of a *peroratio*, but this does not necessarily justify the use of the rhetorical category since any good writing would attempt to summarize the argument and conclude with a passionate plea for action.

[137] See D. R. Reinhard, "Ephesians 6:10–18: A Call to Personal Piety or Another Way of Describing Union with Christ?" *JETS* 48 (2005): 521–32.

[138] This theological theme and the division of the two spheres is becoming somewhat of a consensus viewpoint. See O'Brien, *Ephesians*, 58; Lincoln and Wedderburn, *Theology*, 96–97; M. Turner, "Mission and Meaning in Terms of 'Unity' in Ephesians," in *Mission and Meaning: Essays Presented to Peter Cotterell*, ed. A. Billington, T. Lane, and M. Turner (Carlisle, UK: Paternoster, 1995), 138–66; Thielman, *Theology of the New Testament*, 394.

[139] See the excellent treatment by C. C. Caragounis, *The Ephesian* Mysterion*: Meaning and Content* (Lund, Sweden: Gleerup, 1977), 144–46.

Something to Think About: All Things under Christ's Lordship

In the opening section of his letter to the Ephesians, Paul admirably encompasses the purpose of God's plan for the ages: to bring all things back together under one head, namely Christ (1:10). The rebellion against God started in the angelic realm with the fall of Satan and his demons. It infected the human race when Satan incited Eve to eat of the forbidden fruit and Adam followed suit. In fact, the entire universe is groaning and awaiting redemption (Rom 8:22).

But God is still the sovereign ruler and King of the universe. And he has chosen his Son, the Messiah, to be the designated Lord. Thus, in keeping with Isaiah's vision, "at the name of Jesus every knee will bow . . . and every tongue will confess that Jesus Christ is Lord, to the glory of God the Father" (Phil 2:10–11). As Paul points out in Ephesians, God showed that this was his will by Christ's resurrection:

> *He exercised this power in Christ by raising him from the dead and seating him at his right hand in the heavens—far above every ruler and authority, power and dominion, and every title given, not only in this age but also in the one to come. And he subjected everything under his feet [alluding to Ps 8:6] and appointed him as head over everything for the church, which is his body, the fullness of the one who fills all things in every way (1:20–23).*

If Christ, then, has already been exalted and every knee will one day bow to him, how should we then live? The answer: we should submit to his lordship in every area of life already in the here and now "to the praise of his glory" (1:12,14). We should submit in the church (4:1–16); in our personal lives and relationships with one another (4:17–5:21); in our marriages and families, as wives and husbands (5:22–33), children and parents (6:1–4), and at work (6:5–9). Not that we are "making him Lord"—he already is. He created us and bought us by dying on the cross for our sins, so we are doubly his. So let us live our lives fully submitted to his lordship, and let us do so in a manner worthy of the immeasurably great calling we received.

(1:19–22) and his gathering together of both Jews and Gentiles into one body (2:11–22).

Though the theme is the subjection of all things to the lordship of *Christ*, Paul stressed the unified work of all three members of the Trinity in bringing this goal to fulfillment. This thematic theological center is expressed through four theological themes: soteriology, ecclesiology, ethics, and spiritual warfare. References to the united work of the Trinity emerge in eight passages: 1:4–14; 1:17; 2:18; 2:22; 3:4–5; 3:14–17; 4:4–6; and

5:18–20.[140] The first two passages (1:4–14, 17) are related to soteriology; the next five (2:18, 22; 3:4–5, 14–19; 4:4–6) to ecclesiology; and the last (5:18–20) to ethics.

The Nature of Salvation Ephesians 1:1–14 describes the salvific blessings in the heavenly realms that belong to all those who are in Christ. Paul unpacked these blessings in terms of the role that each member of the Trinity plays in the salvation of believers and bursts into doxology each time. God the Father *plans* salvation (1:4–6); God the Son *purchases* salvation (1:7–12); God the Spirit *applies* and *seals* salvation (1:13–14). Paul's prayer in 1:17 also involves the three persons of the Trinity, as the God and Father of our Lord Jesus Christ gives the Spirit of wisdom and revelation to believers.

Paul also stresses the amazing power of grace in salvation. Ephesians 2:1–3 sets the stage for this remarkable work of God by painting the pre-Christian state of his readers in strokes both broad and black. They were spiritually dead in transgressions and sins, and this death involved walking to the enslaving tune of the world (2:2), the Devil (2:2), and the flesh (2:3). They by nature rested under the terrible wrath of God, just like the rest of unbelievers (2:3).

The dawning of hope began with two simple words: "But God" (2:4).[141] God gave life to Paul's readers even when they were spiritually dead because of his rich mercy and great love. Paul briefly interrupts his discussion with a statement about God's grace: "You are saved by grace!" Paul said almost the same thing three verses later (2:8), so why did he interrupt his flow of thought at this point? There appears to be a doxological rationale behind this intrusion. This act of God's amazing grace greatly amazed Paul because it is not merely the offer of life but is also the giving of life. One should stand amazed that God gave this spiritual life even to the spiritually dead (2:5).[142]

The believers' union with Christ means that just as Christ was raised up and seated at God's right hand (1:20), so believers are made alive and raised up with Christ and seated with him in heaven (2:6).[143] The joy of this present experience can only be exceeded by that in the ages to come when God will "show the surpassing riches of His grace in kindness" to believers in Christ (2:7 NASB).

This incredibly great salvation is a gift of God, not an achievement of man, because it is by grace through faith (2:8) and thus precludes human boasting (2:9). Salvation does

[140] Hoehner (*Ephesians*, 106–7) said that "Ephesians is known as the Trinitarian letter."

[141] See esp. the excellent sermon on this two-word text by D. M. Lloyd-Jones, *God's Way of Reconciliation* (Grand Rapids, MI: Baker, 1972), 59–69.

[142] See T. R. Schreiner (*Paul, Apostle of God's Glory in Christ* [Downers Grove, IL: InterVarsity, 2001], 246): "Grace is not merely unmerited favor in the sense that one may choose to receive or reject a gift. Grace is the impartation of new life. Grace is a power that raises someone from the dead, that lifts those in the grave into new life. Grace is not merely an undeserved gift, though it is such; it is also a transforming power. Grace imparted life when we were dead, and grace also raises us and seats us with Christ in the heavenlies (Eph 2:6)."

[143] On the meaning of being "seated with Christ," see esp. H. N. Ridderbos, *Paul: An Outline of His Theology*, trans. J. R. de Witt (Grand Rapids, MI: Eerdmans, 1975), 347; Lincoln, *Ephesians*, 105–7, and his more sustained exposition of inaugurated eschatology in *Paradise Now and Not Yet: Studies in the Role of the Heavenly Dimension in Paul's Thought with Special Reference to His Eschatology*, SNTSMS 43 (Cambridge, UK: University Press, 1981).

not result from good works; rather, good works result from salvation (2:10).[144] The role of Christ in salvation is also stressed in 2:11–22. In his flesh Christ abolished "the law consisting of commands and expressed in regulations" (2:15) and "proclaimed the good news of peace" to Gentiles and Jews (2:17).

The Church Ephesians places a marked emphasis on the nature of the church. Discussions of ecclesiology must follow after soteriology because the trinitarian work of salvation has massive implications for the church. This dynamic comes across succinctly in 2:18: "*through him* [Christ] we both have access *in one spirit to the Father*" (emphasis added). Christ has broken down the dividing wall through the cross and created the church as one new man (2:13–22). This redeeming work of Christ reconciles believers to the Father (2:16). Christ-followers are "fellow citizens with the saints, and members of God's household" (2:19).

Trinitarian ecclesiology emerges again in 2:22: in Christ, the church becomes God's dwelling place in the Spirit. Paul expresses the work of the Trinity in ecclesiology again in 3:4–5: God the Father reveals the mystery of Christ—believing Gentiles and Jews are one in Christ—through his apostles and prophets by the Spirit. Paul's prayer in 3:14–19 also reflects his trinitarian theology. He prays to God the Father that Christ would dwell with the Ephesians by faith through the power of the Spirit, so that they would be able to grasp with all believers the unfathomable love of Christ. Paul also called believers to maintain—not create—unity because the Spirit has produced unity (4:3).[145] Oneness in the church is a top priority because of the oneness of the Trinity and other dimensions of the concept (4:4–6). If the unity of the body is based on the unity of the Godhead, then dividing the church is as unthinkable and heinous as dividing the Trinity.[146]

Paul's teaching on spiritual gifts also addresses the theme of ecclesiology. He stresses that spiritual gifts are connected to the work of Christ as the spoils of his victory. Christ bestowed these gifts on individual believers for the sake of the growth of the corporate body, not just the individual. The building up of the body of Christ is essential for attaining unity in the faith (4:13).

Proper Christian Conduct (Ethics) Ethics also has a trinitarian dimension as Paul calls on believers to give thanks to God the Father in the name of Jesus Christ our Lord as a result of being filled by the Spirit (5:18–20). One of Paul's ultimate concerns in Ephesians

---

[144] I. H. Marshall, "Salvation, Grace and Works in the Later Writings in the Pauline Corpus," *NTS* 42 (1996): 339–58, esp. 342–45.

[145] Genitive of the producer (i.e., "unity of the Spirit"="unity produced by the Spirit"). See Wallace, *Greek Grammar Beyond the Basics*, 105.

[146] J. R. W. Stott (*The Message of Ephesians: God's New Society*, BST [Downers Grove, IL: InterVarsity, 1979], 151) agreed with this assessment. "Is there only one God? Then He has only one church. Is the unity of God inviolable? Then so is the unity of the church. The unity of the church is as indestructible as the unity of God Himself. It is no more possible to split the church than it is possible to split the Godhead."

is that believers would learn to walk with Christ as children of light.[147] The new humanity may not possess a specific ethnic identity, but it certainly manifests a moral identity that reflects the character of God. The moral witness of the church is a central part of the re-alignment of all things under Christ's lordship because it is tied so closely to the Christian calling of which believers should walk in a worthy manner in every way (4:1).

Paul's ethical approach is not divorced from his soteriology. Because believers are chosen to be "holy and blameless in love before him" (1:4), they will imitate their loving Father (5:1), forgive as Christ forgave them (4:32), and love as Christ loved them (5:2). Ephesians 2:8–10 also highlights the link between soteriology and ethics in that believers reflect the character of God as his "workmanship" (2:10 NASB). Though they are saved by grace and not by works (2:8–9), they are enjoined to walk in the good works God has prepared for them (2:10). Paul's ethics also echo his emphasis on ecclesiology because he focused on the virtues necessary for building community. These virtues include humility, gentleness, patience, love (4:2–3), and forgiveness (4:32).

Divine enablement's role in ethics occurs in various ways. First, at the structural level Paul clearly based the imperative (chaps. 4–6) on the indicative (chaps. 1–3); that is, he grounds his commands in the spiritual reality engendered by Christ. The order of Paul's key words is important: being seated with Christ in the past must precede walking with Christ (4:1–6:9) or standing for Christ (6:10–20) in the present. Second, at the grammatical level Paul placed worship (5:19), thankfulness (5:20), and submission (5:21–6:9) in subordinate relationships to the phrase "be filled by the Spirit" (5:18). This shows that godliness is an effect caused by God's power.

Spiritual Warfare C. E. Arnold appropriately noted the importance of spiritual warfare in Ephesians: "More than any other Pauline Letter, Ephesians stresses the hostile role of the principalities and powers against the church."[148] One can see this emphasis by examining the terms Paul used in Ephesians.

Paul speaks of specific groups such as "powers" (*dynameis*, 1:21); "dominions" (*kyriotēs*, 1:21); "principalities" (*archai*, 1:21; 3:10; 6:12); and "authorities" (*exousiai*, 1:21; 2:2; 3:10; 6:12). The apostle also identified hostile powers in an inclusive sense as "cosmic powers of this darkness against evil" (*kosmokratores tou skotous toutou*, 6:12). Ephesians 1:21 asserts that Christ's rule is over not only the four specific groups of evil powers listed there, but also over "every name that is named, not only in this age but in the age to come" (NASB).

D. G. Reid summarized the significance of this inclusive phrase: "Against a cultural background in which successful magical manipulation of evil powers was commonly believed to be predicated on the knowledge of the power's name, Ephesians emphasizes the

---

[147] T. Moritz, "Ephesians," in *New Dictionary of Biblical Theology*, ed. T. D. Alexander and B. S. Rosner (Downers Grove, IL: InterVarsity, 2000), 317.

[148] Arnold, "Ephesians," 247.

triumph and sovereignty of Christ over every power—known or unknown, real or imagined, present or future."[149]

This focus on spiritual warfare is connected to Paul's earlier discussion of soteriology and the work of Christ.[150] Christ has already won the victory over the evil heavenly powers and is seated at God's right hand above "every ruler and authority, power and dominion, and every title given" (1:21). God put everything under the feet of Christ and appointed him as head over everything for the church (1:22). In their pre-Christian state, believers lived under the power of the "ruler of the power of the air" (2:2). Moreover, the church is the vehicle that conveys God's wisdom "to the rulers and authorities in the heavens" (3:10).

Spiritual warfare is also connected to Paul's earlier discussion of ecclesiology and ethics. In terms of ecclesiology, the fact that the injunctions are plural throughout 6:10–14 shows that Paul addresses the whole church in the need to fight and stand against the hostile forces of the evil one.[151] In terms of ethics, the same Devil who attacks with insidious methods (6:11) and flaming arrows (6:16) has already been described as attempting to gain a foothold through anger (4:26) and other conduct that reflects the old man and the old way of life. Therefore, putting on the full armor of God (6:10–20) is connected to putting off the old (4:22) and putting on the new (4:24).

Ephesians 6:10–20 stands out as one of the clearest passages on spiritual warfare in Scripture. The key theme of verses 10–17 is the exhortation to stand in God's strength against the powers arrayed against the believer. The battle lines are drawn between God and the armored believer on one side (6:10–11) and the Devil, the rulers, authorities, world powers of this darkness, and spiritual forces of evil in the heavens on the other (6:11–12). Christ-followers need the spiritual armor of God because the battle is not against flesh and blood but against spiritual foes (6:12). Paul further heightened the intensity and closeness of the conflict by using the word for "wrestling" instead of more customary terms for warfare.[152]

Believers can overcome these forces only in God's strength. They receive this (6:10) by putting on his armor (6:11).[153] The various pieces of armor at the believer's disposal reflect

---

[149] D. G. Reid, "Principalities and Powers," in *Dictionary of Paul and His Letters*, 749.

[150] The church militant "advances from a position of power founded on the 'already' of the defeat of the devil and his forces" (ibid., 751).

[151] O'Brien (*Ephesians*, 460n84) rightly corrected Neufeld's (*Put on the Armour of God*, 111) false dichotomy. Neufeld took the plural as proof that Paul gave a corporate call, which should not be understood "in individualistic terms." Yet O'Brien noted that the plural conveys "common action"; believers individually and corporately must stand "together as one" against the Devil.

[152] M. E. Gurdorf ("The Use of *palē* in Ephesians 6:12," *JBL* 117 [1998]: 334) made the same point when claiming that Paul used the picture of a fully armed soldier and wrestler to portray "close-quarter struggling." Cf. Arnold, *Ephesians: Power and Magic*, 116–17, for background information drawn from inscriptions.

[153] The armor "of God" refers to God's armor that he gives to the believer. Gnilka (*Epheserbrief*, 305) is probably correct in identifying "of God" as a genitive of origin.

the arsenal of a fully armed Roman foot soldier.[154] The OT also serves as a backdrop.[155] In particular, Paul's description of the armor of God draws on imagery in Isaiah (see esp. 11:5; 52:7; 57:19). These texts portray God and his Messiah as warriors dressed in armor, going out to fight for God's people. Hence, the armor God gives *to* his people is the armor God himself has already used to gain the victory *for* his people. The indicative of what God has done in Christ and the imperative of what believers are called to do in Christ converge.

Prayer should be seen as a further weapon in spiritual warfare. The battle advances as the gospel progresses (6:18–20). Again, Paul emphasized ecclesiology as he urged intercession for all believers (6:18).

Colossians

KEY FACTS

Author:	Paul
Date:	Around AD 60
Provenance:	Imprisonment in Rome
Destination:	Colossae
Occasion:	False teaching
Purpose:	Combat false teaching with the supremacy and sufficiency of Christ.
Theme:	Christ is complete in every way; thus, believers are complete in Christ.
Key Verses:	2:6–10

INTRODUCTION

PAUL'S LETTER TO the Colossians is perhaps the most Christocentric letter in the NT. Colossians offers a strong corrective to the false teachings in the Lycus Valley that minimized the importance of the person and work of Christ. Paul firmly places the emphasis back on the centrality of Christ in all things. The letter clearly and passionately argues for the supremacy of Christ, the sufficiency of his work for the believer, and the application of Christ's lordship to every aspect of the Christian life. Colossians

[154] O'Brien, *Ephesians*, 462. The Greek term *panoplia* ("armor") emphasizes the idea of a complete set of armor so as to highlight the danger of the battle and the need for total dependence on God. See Arnold, *Ephesians: Power and Magic*, 118.

[155] Reid ("Principalities and Powers," 751) agreed: "While the terminology of military paraphernalia is taken from the Roman world, the archetype of warfare is clearly Israelite." O'Brien (*Ephesians*, 472–82) also has a discussion of the OT imagery behind the armor of God.

thus serves as a stringent reminder of the serious problems that arise when one's focus is taken off Christ and he is displaced from the center of the Christian life.

The letter also demonstrates that gratitude to Christ for the great salvation he provided serves as a principal motivation for the Christian life. Although Colossian legalists may have pursued righteousness out of a sense of obligation and fear, Paul stresses that the believer lives his life in a manner worthy of his calling and motivated by joyful thanksgiving to the Father who adopted him, rescued him from Satan's dominion, delivered him from punishment, and forgave his sins.[156] Perhaps more than any other Pauline Letter, Colossians presents the Christian life as an unrestrainable outburst of joy, praise, and thanksgiving, in which all that the believer says and does is an expression of grateful worship of an all-supreme Lord who has provided an all-sufficient salvation.

HISTORY

Author

Authenticity The following discussion bears many striking similarities to the debate over the authorship of Ephesians, so it is not necessary to tread all of the same terrain again. The letter opens with a claim that Paul was the author (1:1) and contains two further expressions of personal identification in 1:23 ("I, Paul") and 4:18 ("I, Paul, write this greeting in my own hand" NIV). The letter also refers to Timothy, Epaphras, John Mark, and Barnabas, who were companions of Paul as documented in the book of Acts. The closing of the letter makes many personal references unexpected in a pseudepigraphical writing. Paul's authorship was also affirmed by the unbroken testimony of the early church.

Once again, however, despite strong evidence for authenticity, the letter's authorship is heavily debated. Objections did not begin until the nineteenth century,[157] but they steadily increased in the twentieth.[158] Today, three recurring factors dominate the case for inauthenticity: (1) language and literary style, (2) theology, and (3) the close relationship of Colossians to Ephesians.

---

[156] Every chapter of Colossians mentions thanksgiving: it is the motivation for the life that pleases God (1:9–12); the programmatic statement of the letter stresses that walking in Christ Jesus is prompted by overflowing thanksgiving (2:6–7); Christian thanksgiving motivates all that the believer says and does (3:17); Paul urged the Colossians to make sure that their prayers, like his (1:3–8), were permeated with a spirit of thanksgiving (4:2).

[157] E. T. Mayerhoff asserted in 1838 that Colossians was dependent on Ephesians, reflected a second-century polemic against Gnosticism, and contained some other ideas foreign to Paul. E. T. Mayerhoff, *Der Brief an die Colosser, mit vornehmlicher Berücksichtigung der drei Pastoralbriefe kritisch geprüft*, ed. J. L. Mayer (Berlin, Germany: Hermann Schultze, 1838). R. Bultmann and his followers subsequently attached the influential label "deutero-Pauline" to Colossians.

[158] R. E. Brown (*An Introduction to the New Testament* [New York, NY: Doubleday, 1997], 600) estimated that about 60 percent of critical scholarship believes the letter is pseudonymous. D. A. deSilva (*An Introduction to the New Testament: Contexts, Methods, and Ministry Formation* [Downers Grove, IL: InterVarsity, 2004], 696) argued that "[s]cholarship is fairly evenly divided on this question." Cf. the useful summary in R. F. Collins, *Letters That Paul Did Not Write: The Epistle to the Hebrews and the Pauline Pseudepigrapha*, Good News Studies 28 (Wilmington, DE: Michael Glazier, 1988).

Colossians contains thirty-four *hapax legomena*, words that do not appear elsewhere in the NT. The letter also contains twenty-eight that do not appear in Paul's other letters.[159] Some scholars argue that this fact favors non-Pauline authorship. W. Bujard examined the use of connectives and the structure of sentences in Colossians and concluded that the style of this letter was too different for Paul to have been the author.[160] J. D. G. Dunn approached the question of authorship from a literary standpoint and claimed that the flow and rhetorical features of the letter "confirm the strong likelihood that the letter comes from a hand other than Paul's."[161]

In terms of theology, some scholars object to additions to and departures from the undisputed letters in the areas of Christology,[162] eschatology,[163] and ecclesiology.[164] Others focus not only on departures and additions but also on the absence of key Pauline theological terms such as "law," "justification," "salvation," and others. Concerning the close relationship between Colossians and Ephesians, some scholars assert that one writer would never produce two such similar letters.

Scholars who favor Pauline authorship typically reply with four points. First, some arguments against authenticity reflect a strong bias against the authenticity of the letter and are better viewed as positive evidence for Paul's authorship of Colossians. For example, the close relationship of Colossians and Ephesians does not logically lead to the denial of Paul's authorship of Colossians. Carson and Moo questioned the logic behind such an argument when they quipped, "It is a curious argument that we should reject a writing as Pauline because of its resemblances to another writing in the Pauline corpus."[165] Especially if Ephesians was a circular letter addressed to churches in Asia Minor in the

---

[159] See O'Brien, *Colossians and Philemon*, xlii.

[160] E. Percy's stylistic assessment led him to argue for authenticity: *Die Probleme der Kolosser-und Epheserbriefe* (Lund, Sweden: C. W. K. Gleerup, 1946). However, the stylistic study of W. Bujard challenged Percy's analysis and conclusions: *Stilanalytische Untersuchungen zum Kolosserbrief als Beitrag zur Methodik von Sprachvergleichen*, SUNT 11 (Göttingen, Germany: Vandenhoeck & Ruprecht, 1973). E. Lohse (*Colossians and Philemon*, ed. W. R. Poehlmann and R. J. Karris, Hermeneia [Philadelphia, PA: Fortress, 1971], 84–91) provided an extensive survey of the language and style of Colossians. Lohse concluded that linguistic and stylistic considerations could not serve as the basis for reaching any final decisions regarding the question of Paul's authorship of Colossians (ibid., 91).

[161] J. D. G. Dunn, *The Epistles to the Colossians and to Philemon*, NIGTC (Grand Rapids, MI: Eerdmans, 1996), 35.

[162] Some claim that Colossians goes beyond the undisputed Pauline Letters in focusing on the cosmic dimensions of Christ. J. D. G. Dunn (*Colossians and Philemon*, 36) offered a similar recent assessment: "The Christology expressed in 1:15–20 and 2:9–10 and 15 looks to be further along the trajectory than that of the undisputed Paulines." He concluded that the theological content is thus "significantly different from what we are accustomed to in all the undisputed Paulines."

[163] They detect a realized eschatology instead of the already/not yet eschatology characteristic of the undisputed Paulines. E.g., Colossians says the believer is already raised with Christ (2:12; 3:1) and is already in the kingdom of Christ (1:13).

[164] Colossians is unique in its imagery of Christ as the head of his body, the church (1:18; 2:17, 19; 3:15) when compared with undisputed Paulines (but see Eph 4:15; 5:23). Colossians also focuses more on the "universal" church than the "local" church. Lohse (*Colossians and Philemon*, 177–83) stated that these theological differences are too great to conclude that Paul wrote the letter.

[165] Carson and Moo, *Introduction to the New Testament*, 520. There are links between Colossians and other Pauline Letters. The work of A. R. Bevere highlights one such line in the parallels between Galatians and Colossians: *Sharing the Inheritance: Identity and Moral Life in Colossians*, JSNTSup 226 (Sheffield, UK: Sheffield Academic Press, 2003), 59–121.

vicinity of Colossae and was written in the same place and at approximately the same time as Colossians, the similarities between the two documents are not surprising.

Second, those who reject Paul's authorship are hard pressed to provide a rationale for the personal references in the letter and the choice of this particular church. Why would an imitator go to such great lengths to fake personal references or write to a city as unimportant as Colossae?[166]

Third, the theological differences between Colossians and the undisputed Pauline Letters have been exaggerated.[167] For example, several influential scholars such as E. Lohse have argued that the Christology of Colossians is too high for Paul to have written it. Such arguments assume that the high Christology of Colossians that identifies Jesus as the incarnation of deity and the agent and sustainer of creation evolved from a significantly lower Christology in the undisputed Pauline Letters.[168]

However, the Christology of the undisputed Pauline Letters is much higher than some scholars acknowledge. Romans 10:6–13 not only identifies Jesus as the Lord Yahweh but also insists that the confession of Jesus's deity is necessary for salvation. If the great Christological hymn of Philippians 2:6–11 is pre-Pauline, this high Christology was shared by others in the church very early in Christian history and had become an established element of the church's worship by the mid-first century. Christ's identity as the agent and sustainer of creation is a natural conclusion required by his identity as Yahweh. In 1 Corinthians 8:4–6 Paul had already laid the foundation for these assertions by identifying Jesus as the one Lord of the Shema (Deut 6:4–5) and by insisting that Jesus was the One through whom all things came into existence, including humanity itself. The incarnational theology of Colossians 1:19 and 2:9 is not, as Dunn claimed, "a step beyond any of those passages,"[169] but is wholly consistent with them. Colossians uses new expressions to articulate this high Christology, but the Christology is not significantly more developed.

The claims that the ecclesiology of the letter is too highly developed to allow for Paul's authorship also falter. Though Paul does not elsewhere in his undisputed letters refer to Jesus as the "head of the body, the church" (Col 1:18), this is easily explained as a natural development of Paul's imagery of the church as a body in which individual believers constitute its members (Rom 12:4–8; 1 Cor 6:15; 12:12–21) and his insistence that Jesus is Messiah, the divinely appointed ruler of God's people (Rom 1:1–4) and the new master of believers (1 Cor 7:22). Regarding eschatology, no one doubts that Paul stressed the

---

[166] J. B. Lightfoot (*Saint Paul's Epistles to the Colossians and to Philemon*, 9th ed. [London, England: Macmillan, 1890], 16) commented, "Without doubt Colossae was the least important church to which any epistle of Paul is addressed."

[167] Even R. Brown (*Introduction*, 613), who cautiously rejected Pauline authorship, conceded that the theological differences are "overstated." DeSilva (*Introduction to the New Testament*, 698) recognized that these theological differences are "major objections," but he concluded that they were "explicable in terms of the challenges posed by a philosophy that stresses the authority of powers, angels and principalities over human life."

[168] See Lohse, *Colossians and Philemon*, 77–83.

[169] Dunn, *Epistles to the Colossians and Philemon*, 36.

"already" aspect of eschatology more than the "not yet" aspect in Colossians, but both are found in this letter and in his undisputed letters.[170]

Fourth, the arguments from language and style are unpersuasive. P. N. Harrison, who used word statistics to refute Paul's authorship of the Pastorals, found that Colossians falls within the normal range of *hapax legomena* in comparison with Paul's other letters.[171] Moreover, G. U. Yule argued that samples of at least 10,000 words similar in length and subject matter are necessary to determine authorship based on vocabulary.[172] Colossians is simply too short for word statistics to determine the identity of the author with any degree of confidence. Many of the words in Colossians that appear nowhere else in Paul's undisputed letters do appear either in the LXX or in other NT books, showing that the vocabulary would have been known to a Greek speaker in the first century who was familiar with the LXX and widely used Christian vocabulary. Most of the terms unusual for Paul appear either in the hymn in Colossians 1:15–20, which is possibly pre-Pauline, or in his treatment of the Colossian heresy, which is exactly what one would expect.[173] Many of the unusual words may be accounted for by the occasion of the letter. Paul probably used some of the distinct vocabulary of the Colossian heretics in his effort to combat their heresy.

One weakness of rejections of Paul's authorship based on vocabulary and style is that such dismissals tend to examine only the differences between Colossians and other Pauline Letters while ignoring the significant number of similarities between them. On the other hand, W. G. Kümmel found several features of the style of Colossians that appear only in Paul's Letters in the NT.[174] Finally, such dismissals often fail to consider the degree of influence that a coauthor like Timothy might have on the vocabulary and style of the letter.[175] Thus, the vocabulary and style of Colossians are not valid grounds for the rejection of Paul's authorship.

---

[170] A. Lincoln (*Paradise Now and Not Yet: Studies in the Role of the Heavenly Dimension in Paul's Thought with Special Reference to His Eschatology*, SNTSMS 43 [Cambridge, UK: University Press, 1981], 122–23) asserted that the believer's present resurrection with Christ in Col 2:12 and the believer's future resurrection with Christ in Rom 6:5 occupy two poles in Paul's eschatological theology of the already and the not yet. He said, "Believers enter this resurrection life when they are joined to Christ," while the consummation of this reality "still lies in the future."

[171] P. N. Harrison, *The Problem of the Pastoral Epistles* (London, England: Oxford University Press, 1921), 20–22.

[172] G. U. Yule, *The Statistical Study of Literary Vocabulary* (Cambridge, UK: University Press, 1944), 281.

[173] D. E. Garland (*Colossians and Philemon*, NIVAC [Grand Rapids, MI: Zondervan, 1998], 19) pointed out the significant fact that "much of the supposedly 'unpauline' vocabulary occurs in the section dealing with the 'philosophy.'" G. E. Cannon (*The Use of Traditional Materials in Colossians* [Macon, GA: Mercer University Press, 1983]), conceded that Colossians contains passages that deviate from Paul's customary vocabulary and style, but he argued for Pauline authorship because the high percentage of pre-Pauline material in Colossians accounts for the divergence. Readers should especially note the summary argument on p. 229.

[174] Kümmel, *Introduction*, 241.

[175] See Dunn, *Epistles to the Colossians and Philemon*, 44; E. R. Richards, *The Secretary in the Letters of Paul*, WUNT 2/42 (Tübingen, Germany; J. C. B. Mohr, 1991); and Garland, *Colossians/Philemon*, 20–21. D. Guthrie (*New Testament Introduction* [Downers Grove, IL: InterVarsity, 1970], 554) ably summarized this case: "There is no shred of evidence that the Pauline authorship of the whole or any part of this Epistle was ever disputed until the 19th century. It formed part of the Pauline corpus as far back as can be traced, and evidence of such a character cannot lightly be swept aside. This strong

Conclusion The case for authenticity is customarily crafted as a response to the rejection of Paul's authorship. While such responses are important points to make, one must not adopt a merely defensive approach without advancing the case in positive terms. Paul's authorship primarily rests on the strength of four pillars: (1) the letter's own claim to authenticity; (2) the unbroken tradition throughout church history; (3) the close connections between Colossians and Philemon, a letter which almost all accept as authentic;[176] and (4) the questions surrounding the practice and acceptance of pseudonymity.

Date

The date for Colossians is difficult to determine with precision, especially because it depends on the letter's authorship and provenance. If written by Paul from Caesarea or Ephesus, then the letter has a date sometime in the AD 50s. If written by Paul from Rome, then the letter's composition must be placed at around 58–60 according to the chronology of Paul suggested in this text.[177] If one rejects the authenticity of Colossians, then the book should be dated about 70–100. However, this late date is problematic because of the earthquake that presumably destroyed Colossae in 60–61.[178]

Provenance

Many difficulties surround the provenance of the letter as well.[179] Debate about it began in ancient times. Although subscriptions in many manuscripts, including Alexandrinus (fifth century) and the first corrector of Vaticanus, assign the letter to Rome, and no subscriptions suggest any other provenance, the Marcionite Prologue (ca. 160–180) stated that the letter was written in Ephesus.

The presence of Luke, Aristarchus, Timothy, and other coworkers with Paul at the time of writing are important clues for the provenance of Colossians.[180] Luke's presence, for example, appears to support a Roman hypothesis because Acts places Luke with Paul in Rome, while Paul's Ephesian ministry is not one of the "we" passages in Acts.[181] Acts 27:2 also indicates that Aristarchus accompanied Paul to Italy and most likely all the way to Rome. Although Acts does not mention the presence of Timothy in Rome, the Acts

---

external attestation is further supported by the close link between the Epistle and Philemon, whose authenticity has been challenged only by the most extreme negative critics."

[176] Dunn (*Epistles to the Colossians and Philemon*, 37–38) listed some of the similarities between Colossians and Philemon.

[177] Many scholars date the first Roman imprisonment to the early 60s.

[178] This argument is especially emphatic in the case of B. Reicke (*Re-Examining Paul's Letters: The History of the Pauline Correspondence* [Harrisburg, PA: Trinity Press International, 2001], 76): "All attempts to make Colossians a deutero-Pauline composition of the period A.D. 70–100 are rendered null and void by documents that demonstrate that Colossae lost its cultural importance through an earthquake in 61." The earthquake in Colossae may also pose problems for the date of authorship of Colossians in the conventional dating of the Roman imprisonment.

[179] See the details covered in the discussion of Philippians above.

[180] Dunn (*Epistles to the Colossians and Philemon*, 41) and P. T. O'Brien (*Colossians, Philemon*, WBC 44 [Dallas, TX: Word, 1982], xlix–liv) favored the Roman hypothesis for Colossians.

[181] Guthrie, *New Testament Introduction*, 557.

narrative closes without identifying by name any persons who visited Paul there during his house arrest. In light of the close relationship shared by Paul and Timothy, one would expect Timothy to visit Paul sometime during the two-year Roman incarceration. Although good arguments can be made for Ephesus, the balance of the evidence favors a Roman provenance.

Destination

The destination is not in question. J. D. G. Dunn could say that there is "no dispute regarding where and to whom the letter was addressed: 'to the saints in Colossae.'"[182] J. B. Lightfoot provided a wealth of information about Colossae.[183] The city enjoyed a mixed population of Phrygians, Romans involved in political affairs, and Jews of the Diaspora. Though no one knows when the city was established, Herodotus called Colossae a "great city of Phrygia" as early as 480 BC. The greatness of the city was due to its location in the Lycus Valley (modern-day Turkey) on the main east-west road from Ephesus to the east.[184] The lush Lycus Valley provided plenty of food for grazing sheep, and the wool from these flocks supported a large clothing industry.[185]

Two neighboring towns, Laodicea and Hierapolis, eclipsed Colossae in importance by the time of Paul. The Romans made Laodicea the *conventus* (capital in a district of twenty-five towns) and changed the road system so that Laodicea was located on the junction between four other roads and the east-west highway. While Laodicea prospered as a commercial center, Hierapolis increased as a place of luxury and pleasure because of its mineral baths. Strabo, writing about twenty years before Paul, testified to the diminished importance of Colossae when he described it as a "small town." As mentioned above, the demise of all three cities came in the form of a mighty earthquake in AD 60–61 (though Laodicea was rebuilt; see Rev 3:14–22).

Occasion

The occasion of the letter is the most complex introductory issue. Paul addressed a false teaching some have called the "Colossian heresy." J. D. G. Dunn objected to this nomenclature and suggested that it may amount "to little more than cheap and unworthy name

---

[182] Dunn, *Epistles to the Colossians and Philemon*, 20.

[183] Lightfoot, *Colossians and Philemon*, 1–72; cf. L. M. McDonald, "Colossae," in *Dictionary of New Testament Background*, 225–26.

[184] Travelers would journey on the main route from Antioch to Tarsus, through the Cilician Gates to Derbe, Lystra, Iconium, and then to Colossae and its neighboring towns, Laodicea and Hierapolis. One would then journey about one hundred miles to Ephesus and between 1,000 to 1,200 land miles to Rome.

[185] One branch of the Lycus River also left chalk deposits used in the dyeing of cloth.

calling."[186] I. K. Smith rightly responded that Dunn's approach to this question is out of step with the world Paul occupied, where teaching was dubbed as either truth or error.[187]

An even more debated issue than nomenclature is the identity of the teachers and their teachings. Scholars have noted some of the distinguishing marks of the teaching through a mirror reading of Colossians. At the formal level, it is identified as a "philosophy" that has a longstanding pedigree of support in "human tradition" (2:8). It is more difficult to detect certain catchwords of this philosophy in Colossians, but a few phrases stand out: "the entire fullness" (2:9); "with delight in ascetic practices and the worship of angels" (2:18); "claiming access to a visionary realm" (2:18); "don't handle, don't taste, don't touch" (2:21); and "self-made religion, false humility, and severe treatment of the body" (2:23). There also seems to be an emphasis on circumcision, food laws, Sabbaths, and purity regulations (2:11, 13, 16, 20–21).

Scholars have studied these strands and attempted to locate a group or movement in the first century that matches all the criteria. Paul's opponents were notoriously difficult to identify with precision, so the sheer multitude of scholarly proposals should not surprise the reader. In 1973 J. J. Gunther catalogued forty-four different reconstructions of the Colossian heresy, and dozens of new reconstructions have been proposed since Gunther's work.[188] M. D. Hooker called this whole enterprise into question at the outset by denying the existence of attacks from false teachers. She suggested the problem came from within the congregation as the Colossians were in danger of conforming to the beliefs and practices of their pagan and Jewish neighbors.[189] This proposal has not been well received because it ignores key pronouns (2:8, 16, 18), fails to explain Paul's use of the term "philosophy" (2:8), and minimizes some clear catchwords of the philosophy.[190]

The most up-to-date work offering an overview of scholarship is that by I. K. Smith. Smith surveyed four main proposals: (1) Essene Judaism and Gnosticism, (2) Hellenism, (3) paganism, and (4) Judaism. This arrangement is pedagogically instructive, but the categories are not watertight since many reconstructions blend themes from two or more of them.

J. B. Lightfoot is an advocate of the first proposal. He argued for a line of development from Judaism to second-century Gnosticism and located the Colossian philosophy within that stream. Lightfoot saw the Colossian emphasis on mysticism and rigid asceticism as

---

[186] Dunn, *Epistles to the Colossians and Philemon*, 25. Dunn wanted to remain sensitive to two considerations: (1) orthodoxy was not fully developed, and the boundaries were not fully defined; and (2) Paul's tone is much more relaxed in Colossians than in Galatians. Dunn is sympathetic to M. D. Hooker's theory that the Colossians simply faced the danger of conforming to the beliefs around them (ibid., 24–26).

[187] I. K. Smith, *Heavenly Perspective: A Study of Paul's Response to a Jewish Mystical Movement at Colossae*, LNTS 326 (Edinburgh, Scotland: T&T Clark, 2007), 19.

[188] J. J. Gunther, *St. Paul's Opponents and Their Background*, NovTSup 35 (Leiden, Netherlands: Brill, 1973), 2–4.

[189] M. D. Hooker, "Were There False Teachers in Colossae?," in *Christ and Spirit in the New Testament*, ed. B. Lindars and S. S. Smalley (Cambridge, UK: University Press, 1973), 315–31.

[190] J. Gnilka (*Der Kolosserbrief*, HTKNT 10 [Freiburg, Germany: Herder, 1980], 164n4) rejected Hooker's view as an oversimplification because it does not reflect on the connection between the belief in the powers and the ritual prohibitions.

stemming from Essene Judaism, while Gnosticism contributed to the Colossians' focus on wisdom, intermediate beings, and cosmological speculation. The discovery of the Dead Sea Scrolls led more scholars to conclude that the Colossian philosophy shared links with Essene Judaism.

The second broad category is that of Hellenism. The proposals in this category are variegated and include (1) Hellenistic mystery cults (M. Dibelius), (2) Jewish Gnosticism and paganism (G. Bornkamm), (3) Middle Platonism (R. E. DeMaris), and (4) Cynic philosophy (T. Martin). M. Dibelius saw a syncretism between Christianity and the Isis Mystery cult with a practice of initiation into a cosmic mystery associated with "the elements." While Dibelius was criticized for underplaying the clear Jewish features of the Colossian error, G. Bornkamm saw a syncretism of Jewish Gnosticism and paganism.[191] Specifically, Bornkamm theorized that the Colossian philosophy promised redemption and deification along gnostic lines, which are stated in the Mithras Liturgy and the Isis Mystery found in Apuleius and Corpus Hermeticum.

R. E. DeMaris proposed a syncretism of Middle Platonic, Jewish, and Christian elements.[192] DeMaris stated that the proponents of the philosophy were "philosophically-inclined Gentiles" who pursued divine knowledge or wisdom and thus were drawn to the congenial answers of Judaism and then Christianity. He pointed to similarities between Hellenistic philosophy and the Colossian philosophy[193] but did not give due attention to the distinctive Jewish elements of circumcision and Sabbath. T. Martin offered a novel interpretation of the situation at Colossae. He detected an approach that resembled a Cynic critique of certain practices such as the Eucharist and the ritual calendar. Thus, the Cynics did not pressure the Colossians to join another religious group; they merely mocked the views the Colossians already held.[194]

C. E. Arnold offered the most persuasive case for the third proposal. He identified the Colossian philosophy as a syncretism of Phrygian folk belief, local folk Judaism, and Christianity.[195] Arnold's attention to local background evidence, especially folk religion and the magical papyri, sets his proposal apart from others.[196]

---

[191] G. Bornkamm, "The Heresy of Colossians," in *Conflict at Colossae*, 2nd ed., ed. F. O. Francis and W. A. Meeks, SBLSBS 4 (Missoula, MO: Scholars Press, 1975), 123–45.

[192] R. E. DeMaris, *The Colossian Controversy: Wisdom in Dispute at Colossae*, JSNTSup 96 (Sheffield, UK: Sheffield Academic Press, 1994).

[193] DeMaris built on the work of E. Schweitzer and his understanding of the "elements of the world." See E. Schweitzer, *Colossians* (Minneapolis, MN: Augsburg, 1982), 136–38. A. Wedderburn ("The Theology of Colossians," in *The Theology of the Later Pauline Letters*, ed. J. D. G. Dunn [Cambridge, UK: University Press, 1993], 3–12) took a similar approach to the Colossian error and also shared an indebtedness to Schweitzer.

[194] T. Martin, *By Philosophy and Empty Deceit: Colossians as a Response to Cynic Critique*, JSNTSup 118 (Sheffield, UK: Sheffield Academic, 1996), 15–16.

[195] C. E. Arnold, *The Colossian Syncretism: The Interface Between Christianity and Folk Belief at Colossae*, WUNT 2/77 (Tübingen, Germany: Mohr Siebeck, 1995).

[196] C. E. Arnold (ibid., 90–194) interpreted "worship of angels" (2:18) as an objective genitive, which refers to the invoking of angels for protection against evil spirits; "claiming access to a visionary realm" (2:18) as a reference to a mystery cult; and "elemental forces of the world" (2:8) as personalized evil spiritual powers related to the stars and fate.

The fourth proposal differs from the other three in holding that every aspect of the philosophy fits with certain forms of Judaism.[197] S. Lyonnet challenged the assumption of pagan backgrounds and pointed out that all aspects of the philosophy may have a Jewish provenance. F. O. Francis proposed that the modifier in the phrase "worship of angels" is a subjective genitive denoting the angelic worship of God. This interpretation made a Jewish background for the philosophy a tenable position because the worshipping of angels (objective genitive) seemed to compromise Jewish monotheism. The philosophy encouraged practice of an imaginary journey to heaven where mystics witnessed the angelic worship of God. Ascetic practices prepared these visionaries for their mystical journey. T. J. Sappington identified the error as the ascetic-mystical piety of Jewish apocalypticism.

F. F. Bruce further narrowed this Jewish apocalyptic group to a particular strand: *Merkabah* mysticism.[198] This is associated with the vision of God's throne and the heavenly chariot beneath it (Ezek 1:4–28). The mystic's ascent through the heavens to participate in the angelic liturgy and to view the throne chariot of God required the meticulous observance of the minutiae of the Mosaic law, asceticism, and appeasement of angelic mediators.[199]

I. K. Smith's assessment is attractive because it seems to strike the right balance. Smith offered reasons that some proposals are "dead ends." The first approach is a temporal and geographical dead end. For example, full-fledged Gnosticism postdates Colossians, and Essene Judaism at Qumran is geographically far removed from the Lycus Valley.[200] The second group of proposals either devalues the distinctive Jewish elements in the philosophy (e.g., circumcision and Sabbath) or draws again from gnostic ideas that postdate Colossians (e.g., Bornkamm).

According to Smith, category three is plausible but proves to be a dead end as well for three main reasons: (1) Colossae has never been excavated;[201] (2) Arnold's proposal is based more on background information than exegesis;[202] and (3) much of Arnold's material post-

---

197 The commentaries of J. D. G. Dunn (*Epistles to the Colossians and Philemon*, 29–33) and N. T. Wright (*Colossians and Philemon*, TNTC [Grand Rapids, MI: Eerdmans, 1987], 24–27) also argued for a Jewish source. Cf. T. J. Sappington, *Revelation and Redemption at Colossae*, JSNTSup 53 (Sheffield, UK: JSOT, 1991), 19–21. Sappington differed from Wright and Dunn in that he believed the threat of false teaching was coming from within the church, not outside from the synagogue (ibid., 15).

198 Bruce, "The Colossian Heresy," 202.

199 J. M. Scott, "Throne-Chariot Mysticism in Qumran and in Paul," in *Eschatology, Messianism and the Dead Sea Scrolls*, ed. C. A. Evans and P. W. Flint (Grand Rapids, MI: Eerdmans, 1997), 101–19, esp. 103.

200 Lightfoot (*Colossians and Philemon*, 91–96) himself recognized the latter of these two difficulties and defended the plausibility of his claim that Essene Judaism was known in Asia Minor during Paul's time.

201 Smith, *Heavenly Perspective*, 32.

202 Smith (ibid.) claimed that Arnold did not explain why Colossians did not even mention magic, amulets, spells, and charms. What is more, Arnold's link between wisdom and magic did not fit Colossians, where Paul associated wisdom with behavior (1:9–14; 3:16; 4:5). Smith also found fault with Arnold for being too selective in that he did not deal with 1:15–20; 2:9–15; and 3:1–4.

dates Colossians.[203] While the proposals in category four are closer to the mark, Smith says that some fall short because they tend to treat the *stoicheia* as impersonal principles or laws instead of personal beings.[204]

Smith's proposal locates the philosophy firmly within the stream of apocalyptic Judaism. He claimed strong affinities exist between the philosophy and *Merkabah* mysticism, though *Merkabah* mysticism as a system probably postdates Colossians. Smith pointed to written evidence like the Enochic literature, Revelation, and Jewish mystical ascents to show the contemporary significance of mystical ascents, arguing that the existence of written evidence both predating and contemporaneous with Colossians shows that the Colossian error was influenced by Jewish mystical movements. He also claimed that the *stoicheia* were fallen angels and their domain was the world. The errorists did not placate them or invoke them; they sought to escape their domain through a heavenly ascent.[205]

Smith's proposal is probably the most satisfactory option today, but it fails to account for the distinction between voluntary and involuntary ascents. While some texts demonstrate a fascination by some of Paul's contemporaries with heavenly ascent, descriptions of involuntary ascents by Enoch, the seer of Revelation, or even Paul himself do not demonstrate that contemporary mystics sought to experience such things themselves through self-induced trances as one finds in developed *Merkabah* mysticism.[206] Perhaps all one can conclude at this point is that Paul faced some form of Jewish mysticism. This mystical approach could be called incipient or proto-*Merkabah* mysticism, much in the same way that NT scholars identify strands of incipient or proto-Gnosticism.

Purpose

Although Smith's discussion of the occasion for Colossians is the most satisfactory, he overestimated the importance of having a definitive view of the occasion for the correct interpretation of the letter. Smith insisted that knowing the situation is essential to understanding Paul's response, but many scholars who disagree over the occasion still agree on the main lines of Paul's response. One can easily see that Colossians serves as a Christ-centered correction to the Colossian errorists, whether one knows all the details of their errors or not.

In other words, we may be able to interpret the text with greater precision when equipped with a clear understanding of the background of the letter, but we can still understand the overall response regardless of background. For example, most would acknowledge that

---

[203] Smith (ibid.) highlighted Arnold's concession that much of his papyrological evidence dates from the third and fourth centuries. But Arnold would also argue that the nature of the magical papyri would lead one to anticipate only minimal changes over time.

[204] Smith (ibid., 206) said that those who interpreted the *stoicheia* as laws or principles "disregard a first-century Jewish mind-set which saw the cosmic realm as determinative for human affairs."

[205] Ibid.

[206] For a discussion of the origins of *Merkabah* mysticism, see C. L. Quarles, "Jesus as *Merkabah* Mystic," *Journal for the Study of the Historical Jesus* 3, no. 1 (2005): 5–22, esp. 8–15. The concern that Smith expressed over the date of many of Arnold's sources impacts Smith's theory as well.

Paul made at least three main points in Colossians: (1) all the fullness dwells in the preeminent Christ (1:15–20); (2) believers are complete in Christ (2:10); and thus (3) they should seek to know more of Christ in his fullness by seeking the things above where he dwells, not the things on the earth (3:1–2). Background questions may help clarify Paul's rebuke. For example, if he was responding to mystical ascents in Colossians, the irony is that "their desire to witness the worship rendered by angels is not a heavenly pursuit, but worldly, as it focuses on regulations that are destined to perish."[207] It is also fleshly in that these ascents and the visions associated with them do not offer help in overcoming the flesh because they lead to spiritual elitism and divisions.

LITERATURE

Literary Plan

W. Bujard classified Colossians as a letter written for the purpose of exhortation and encouragement.[208] M. Wolter has examined the letter along epistolary lines. His proposed structure consists of five parts:

1. Prescript (1:1–2)
2. *Proömium* (1:3–23)
3. Self-conception of the apostle (1:24–2:5)
4. Body of the letter (2:6–4:6)
5. Epistolary conclusion (4:7–18)

Wolter also analyzed the body of the letter along rhetorical lines in four parts: (1) *partitio* (2:6–8); (2) *argumentatio* (2:9–23), which includes (2a) *probatio* (2:9–15) and (2b) *refutatio* (2:16–23); (3) *peroratio* (3:1–4); and (4) *exhortatio* (3:5–4:6).[209]

Wolter's analysis is somewhat artificial and arbitrary. This is true especially of his division of 2:8 and 2:9. Commentators almost universally view these two verses as part of the same textual unit. Therefore, it seems far better to divide the text along epistolary lines that conform to the common Pauline tendency to begin with a doctrinal section and end with a paraenetic (hortatory) section.

OUTLINE

I. INTRODUCTION (1:1–8)
  A. Opening (1:1–2)
  B. Thanksgiving (1:3–8)
II. BODY: THE SUPREMACY AND ALL-SUFFICIENCY OF CHRIST (1:9–4:6)
  A. The Centrality of Christ and the Colossian Heresy (1:9–2:23)

---

[207] Smith, *Heavenly Perspective*, 207.

[208] Bujard, *Stilanalytische Untersuchungen*, 129, 229.

[209] M. Wolter, *Der Brief an die Kolosser; Der Brief an Philemon* (Gütersloh, Germany: G. Mohn, 1993).

1. Opening Prayer (1:9–14)
2. The Supremacy of Christ (1:15–20)
3. The Reconciliation of Believers to God Through Christ (1:21–23)
4. Paul as a Minister of the Mystery of Reconciliation (1:24–2:5)
5. Warning Against Succumbing to the Colossian Heresy (2:6–23)

B. Believers' New Life in Christ (3:1–4:6)
1. Pursuing the Things Above (3:1–4)
2. Putting Earthly Things to Death (3:5–8)
3. Putting off the Old Self and Putting on the New Self (3:9–11)
4. Extending Grace and Forgiveness to Others (3:12–17)
5. Bringing the Christian Household Under the Realm of Christ's Lordship (3:18–4:1)
6. Encouragement to Prayer and Circumspect Interaction with Unbelievers (4:2–6)

III. CLOSING (4:7–18)
A. Commendation of Tychicus and Onesimus (4:7–9)
B. Greetings from Paul's Coworkers (4:10–14)
C. Final Instructions (4:15–17)
D. Final Greetings and Benediction (4:18)

UNIT-BY-UNIT DISCUSSION

I. Introduction (1:1–8)

The introduction to Paul's Letter to the Colossians consists of an opening statement (1:1–2) and a thanksgiving section (1:3–8).

A. Opening (1:1–2) Paul opens the letter with the customary identification of the author, recipients, and the grace salutation.

B. Thanksgiving (1:3–8) Paul offers a thanksgiving for the Colossians' faith, love, and hope (1:4–5), which he had heard about from Epaphras, who apparently founded the Colossian church (1:7). Paul also rejoiced in the spread of the gospel among the Colossians (1:5–6) and beyond them to the entire world (1:6).

III. Body: The Supremacy and All-Sufficiency of Christ (1:9–4:6)

A. The Centrality of Christ and the Colossian Heresy (1:9–2:23) Paul begins the letter body with a prayer that God would fill the Colossians with the knowledge of God's will (1:9) and that the overflow of this knowledge would result in a worthy way of life, that is, a moral and ethical lifestyle pleasing to the Lord. Such is characterized by bearing the fruit of good works, continuing to grow in the knowledge of God, being strengthened by his power for perseverance, and joyfully giving thanks to the Father (1:10–12). God is worthy of thanksgiving because he qualified Christians to share in the heavenly inheritance, rescued them from the dominion of darkness, and transferred them into the kingdom of his dearly loved Son (1:12–13), in whom they have the forgiveness of sins (1:14).

Paul highlights the supremacy of Christ in 1:15–20.[210] The structure of the passage is debated, but most scholars recognize two central structural points: (1) Christ as head over creation (1:15–17); and (2) Christ as head over the church (1:18–20).[211] This staggering supremacy of Jesus is seen not only in his lordship over creation and the church but also in his equality with God: he is the image of the invisible God (1:15), and all the fullness of deity dwells in him (1:19; 2:9). Because Jesus is over everything, he has first place in everything (1:18); thus, God effects the cosmic reconciliation of all things to himself through Christ (1:20).

Paul moves from the sweeping reconciliation of all things in Christ to the specific reconciliation of believers to God through Christ (1:21–23). His readers were formerly alienated from and hostile to God, yet now God had reconciled them through his body of flesh through death in order that believers might stand holy and blameless before God (1:21–22). This glorious work of salvation is a reality only in those who persevere until the end in the faith and in the hope of the gospel that they heard and that Paul proclaimed as a minister (1:23).

Paul then expands on his own unique contribution as a minister of the mystery of reconciliation (1:24–2:5). He emphasizes his unique role as a sufferer for (1:24) and a steward of (1:25) the formerly hidden but now manifest mystery (1:26) of God's good news to the Gentiles: "Christ in you, the hope of glory" (1:27). Paul proclaims Christ to everyone so that everyone might be presented complete in Christ (1:28), a task that God empowered Paul to perform (1:29).

The apostle also informs his readers of his struggle on their behalf so that they and others (2:1) would have full assurance in the knowledge of God's mystery, namely Christ (2:2), in whom are all the treasures of wisdom and knowledge (2:3). This reminder served as a safeguard against the deluding force of false teaching (2:4), and Paul rejoiced to see their stability in the faith (2:5).

Colossians 2:6–23 builds on this teaching by laying out its implications for the readers. Verses 6–7 show that they must walk in the Christ they have received and in whom they have become rooted and established. Verse 8 directly warns against captivity to the errorists' philosophy and empty deception. Accordingly, Paul repeats his earlier argument: all the fullness of deity dwells bodily in Christ (2:9; see 1:19). Paul applies this point to the

---

[210] The elevated diction and extensive parallelism throughout the passage has prompted many scholars to label this passage a "hymn." Scholars then debate whether it is a Pauline or pre-Pauline composition. Other scholars doubt that 1:15–20 is a hymn because of a widespread failure to identify a metrical pattern. See the discussions in Lohse, *Colossians and Philemon*, 41–46; and O'Brien, *Colossians, Philemon*, 32–37.

[211] E.g., M. J. Harris, *Colossians and Philemon*, Exegetical Guide to the Greek New Testament (Grand Rapids, MI: Eerdmans, 1991), 42. M. Dübbers (*Christologie und Existenz im Kolosserbrief: Exegetische und semantische Untersuchungen zur Intention des Kolosserbriefes*, WUNT 2/191 [Tübingen, Germany: Mohr Siebeck, 2005], 91) recently argued for two strophes (1:15–16 and 1:18–20), with 1:17–18a functioning as an in-between strophe. N. T. Wright (*The Climax of the Covenant: Christ and the Law in Pauline Theology* [Minneapolis, MN: Fortress, 1996], 112) argued for a chiasm consisting of A (vv. 15–16), B (v. 17), and C (v. 18c–d).

Something to Think About: Presenting Everyone Mature in Christ

What was Paul's ministry goal? He tells us in Colossians: "We proclaim him, warning and teaching everyone with all wisdom, so that we may present everyone mature in Christ. *I labor for this, striving with his strength that works powerfully in me" (1:28–29, emphasis added). This is what Jesus said should be the goal of his followers. We find it in the Great Commission: "Go, therefore, and make disciples of all nations, baptizing them . . . [and] teaching them to observe* everything I have commanded you*" (Matt 28:19–20,* emphasis added*). Likewise, when some apparently believed in Jesus, he was unimpressed and challenged them: "If you continue in my word, you really are my disciples" (John 8:31), and later Jesus elaborated on what it means to "remain" in him (John 15:1–8).*

Are you and I followers of Jesus Christ—close followers, that is—or are we following him only from a distance? Are our lives profoundly transformed so that we can say with Paul that "I have been crucified with Christ and I no longer live, but Christ lives in me. The life I now live in the body, I live by faith in the Son of God, who loved me and gave himself for me" (Gal 2:19–20)? Are we taking our cues typically and habitually from the indwelling Holy Spirit as guided by God's Word or from other people, even Christians, or from the world around us? Are we driven by deep inner convictions and commitments instilled by our allegiance to Christ, or are we, in Paul's words, "tossed by the waves and blown around by every wind of teaching" (Eph 4:14; similarly, Jas 1:6)?

Again, Paul's words in Colossians are wonderfully comforting and reassuring: "So then, just as you have received Christ Jesus as Lord, continue to live in him, being rooted and built up in him and established in the faith, *just as you were taught, and overflowing with gratitude" (2:6–7,* emphasis added*). What is more, our focus should not merely be inward on our own maturation as believers but also outward as we lead others to true Christian discipleship and help them mature in Christ. Are you and I engaged in several committed, nurturing mentoring relationships with several specific fellow believers? This was clearly both Jesus's and Paul's practice. Jesus had the Twelve, and Paul had his circle of close associates, including Timothy. With Paul, let us therefore strive to "present everyone mature in Christ" (1:28).*

believer in 2:10: therefore those who are in Christ "have been made complete" (NASB). In other words, if *all* the fullness dwells in Christ, and the believer is in Christ, then the believer is complete in Christ and does not need any supplements. Just as in the mathematical realm one cannot add anything to infinity, so in the spiritual realm nothing can be added to Christ. He is infinite.

Paul focuses on the great spiritual change that Christ's cross had effected for believers in their union with him in his crucifixion, burial, and resurrection (2:11–12). God granted them new life even when they were dead in transgressions (2:13), which he forgave and canceled by nailing each sinner's IOU to the cross (2:14). Christ's cross also thoroughly and publicly spelled the defeat of the evil forces aligned against believers (2:15). The supremacy of Christ's person and work severely undercuts the false teachers and their message. Believers did not, therefore, need to worry about supplementing their Christian faith with the ceremonial law (2:16–17), self-abasement, angelic worship, boasting in visions (2:18–19), or man-made decrees (2:20–23).

B. Believers' New Life in Christ (3:1–4:6). Paul builds on the foundational indicative concerning the person and work of Christ by adding the imperative call for bringing every area of life under that lordship. The cosmic scope of Christ's lordship must now be applied to the individual believer as he or she pursues the things above (3:1–4), and puts earthly things to death (3:5–8). Believers should put to death their old deeds because they have put off the old self and put on the new self (3:9–11). What is more, because they have experienced the forgiving grace of Christ, they can now express this same grace to others (3:12–17). Paul also exhorts his readers to bring the Christian household under the realm of Christ's lordship (3:18–4:1). He concludes the imperative section by focusing on prayer (4:2–4) and interaction with outsiders (4:5–6).

IV. Closing (4:7–18)

Paul concludes the letter in four ways.

A. Commendation of Tychicus and Onesimus (4:7–9) First, Paul informs the Colossians that Tychicus and Onesimus (the converted runaway slave featured in the book of Philemon), who were charged with carrying the letter back to the church at Colossae, would fill them in on his current situation.

B. Greetings from Paul's Coworkers (4:10–14) Second, he passes along some personal greetings from his coworkers, including Aristarchus, Mark, Jesus Justus, Epaphras, Luke, and Demas. Notably, two of the four evangelists are with Paul at this point in his ministry, visiting him in prison.

C. Final Instructions (4:15–17) Third, he issues final instructions regarding the church at Laodicea, a church meeting at the house of a lady named Nympha, and a certain Archippus (see Phlm 2).

D. Final Greeting and Benediction (4:18) Fourth, Paul greets the Colossians, signing the letter with his own hand and offering a concluding grace benediction.

THEOLOGY

Theological Themes

The Supremacy of Christ The theology of Colossians is Christ centered in that Paul especially focused on both the person and work of Jesus. Colossians insists on the absolute supremacy of Christ over all things. This especially comes to the forefront in 1:15–20, which contains one of the most exalted depictions of Christ in the NT.

Most scholars recognize 1:15–20 as a pre-Pauline Christian hymn.[212] The structure of the hymn is still heavily debated.[213] The best analysis suggests that the hymn breaks into two major strophes beginning with the words "who is" (*hos estin*; translated "He is" in the CSB in vv. 15, 18) and containing the word "firstborn" *(prōtotokos)* in the second line. These two major strophes also parallel each other in the phrases "because by Him" and "For . . . in Him" (*hoti en autō*; vv. 16, 19); and "all things . . . through Him" and "through Him . . . everything" (*ta panta di' autou*; vv. 16, 20).[214] Thus, the hymn probably has two major sections, portraying Christ as Lord in creation and Lord in the new creation.

It also seems to adapt and develop descriptions of personified wisdom, the divine *Logos* ("Word"), and the Spirit that appear in several ancient Jewish texts in a fresh way. These descriptions portray wisdom, the *Logos,* or the Spirit as the "fashioner of all things" who "pervades and penetrates all things," an "emanation of the glory of the Almighty," an "image of his goodness" who "renews all things" and "orders all things well," and "that which holds all things together."[215] The hymn borrows elements of this imagery to present Jesus as the incarnation of deity.

Paul first describes Jesus as the "image of the invisible God" (1:15). Although Paul elsewhere describes humans as "the image and glory of God" (1 Cor 11:7) against the backdrop of Genesis 1, his language here implies far more than that Jesus was merely a perfect man who manifested the image of God that had been marred through the fall. Colossians 3:10 further develops the affirmation in 1:16 by describing Jesus as the Creator in whose image believers are being renewed. This hints that Jesus was the image of God, in keeping with God's original creation of humanity in Genesis 1:26–27.

Although a few scholars have attempted to explain the phrase "the image of God" solely against the background of Genesis 1, most recognize that the phrase was derived from wisdom literature that adapted themes from Genesis 1 to describe personified wisdom.[216] In Wisdom literature the word *image* refers to a visible manifestation or tangible expression of God's attributes. For example, the intertestamental work Wisdom describes wisdom as "a reflection of eternal light, a spotless mirror of the working of God, and an image of his

---

[212] See esp. R. Martin, *Colossians: The Church's Lord and the Christian's Liberty* (Grand Rapids, MI: Zondervan, 1972), 40–55; Dunn, *Colossians and Philemon,* 83–87; and O'Brien, *Colossians, Philemon,* 32–37. V. A. Pizzuto (*A Cosmic Leap of Faith: An Authorial, Structural, and Theological Investigation of the Cosmic Christology in Col 1:15–20* [Leuven, Belgium: Peters, 2006]) argued that the Deutero-Pauline author of Colossians also composed the hymn.

[213] O'Brien (*Colossians and Philemon,* 35–36) noted that despite extensive efforts by scholars to resolve the issue of the structure of the hymn, no consensus has emerged. He suggested that "[n]o single reconstruction is completely convincing" and stated that the wisest course is simply to speak of parallels in the text.

[214] The word order is slightly altered in the second appearance of the latter construction.

[215] See esp. Prov 8:22–31; Wis 1:7; 7:21–8:1. Dunn incorrectly stated that Wis 1:7 portrayed wisdom as the one who "holds all things together." But the neuter gender of the substantive participle *to synechon* makes clear that the One being described is the Spirit of God mentioned in the preceding clause.

[216] C. F. Burney ("Christ as the APXH of Creation," *JTS 27* [1926]: 160–77) argued that Genesis 1 alone was sufficient to explain the language of the Christological hymn.

goodness" (Wis 7:26). Against this background, Paul's language presents Jesus as *the* visible form of the invisible God.

The description of Jesus as the image of God is rare in Paul's Letters, occurring elsewhere only in 2 Corinthians 4:4. There the description of Jesus as "the image of God" appears along with a reference to Jesus's identity as "Lord," the "glory" of Christ, the creation of light in Genesis 1, and the glory of God shining in the face of Jesus. Paul was probably reflecting on the appearance of Jesus during his encounter with Christ on the Damascus road. Acts 9:3 says that as Paul approached Damascus, "a light from heaven suddenly flashed around him." Paul recognized this brilliant light as the resurrected and exalted Christ. He fell on his face to shield his eyes from this intense and consuming radiance just in time to spare his life but not quickly enough to save his eyesight. To his surprise the voice that spoke to him from the divine glory was the voice of Christ: "I am Jesus, the one you are persecuting" (Acts 9:5). This was likely the moment that defined many aspects of both Paul's soteriology and his Christology—Jesus was the visible form of the invisible God who radiated the divine glory.[217]

If the Colossian heresy was influenced by incipient *Merkabah* mysticism as the clues of the letter suggest, this description of Jesus may directly address the heresy. One of the motivations for the mystic's ascent was the desire to see God and to know what he looked like. J. H. Laenen wrote,

> After the person who descended to the Merkavah had passed all the tests after a long and difficult journey through the heavenly realms, he finally reached the goal of his journey: the vision of the Holy One on his throne of glory. Here in the seventh palace of the seventh heaven God, the holy king, who had come down from an area unknown to humankind, had taken his place on his throne of glory. The traveler is completely overwhelmed by the sight of the mysteries of the divine throne. The Holy One was clothed in dazzling heavenly raiment, radiant with white light, and wore a crown which shimmered with rays of light.[218]

Paul's point may be that believers need not ascend through the heavens to see God in his visible form. God revealed his glory to believers already in the face of Christ, the visible manifestation of the invisible God.

After identifying Jesus as the image of God in keeping with God's original creation of humanity in his image, Paul continues with an explanation of Jesus's involvement in creation. Jesus is the "firstborn over all creation" (1:15). The genitive modifier "over all creation" generated an enormous controversy in the early church. Arius interpreted the phrase as a wholative genitive and viewed Jesus as a part of creation and thus himself a created

---

[217] For the significance of Paul's Damascus road experience for his theology, see especially S. Kim, *The Origin of Paul's Gospel* (Grand Rapids, MI: Eerdmans, 1982).

[218] J. H. Laenen, *Jewish Mysticism: An Introduction*, trans. D. Orton (Louisville, KY: Westminster John Knox, 2001), 31.

being. Some modern Arian cults such as the Jehovah's Witnesses still use this passage to argue that Christ was a created being rather than the eternal Son of God.

This analysis, however, is sadly mistaken. When a genitive noun modifies a title of authority, the genitive is typically a genitive of subordination that identifies the realm over which the authority figure rules. Because of the principle of primogeniture (right of the firstborn), the title "firstborn" is such a title of authority. The title "firstborn" typically described someone who had supremacy in rank because of his priority in time.[219] The full title means that since Jesus existed before creation, he has authority over creation and is greater than it.[220] Paul described Jesus as existing before creation explicitly in 1:17: "He is before [in time] all things."[221] Jesus existed before the first beam of light, the first drop of water, the first grain of sand, the first blade of grass, and the first man and woman. Because he existed before all things, he has authority over all things.

The word "firstborn" was used to speak of supremacy in rank throughout the OT. Israel was called God's firstborn, which means that the nation of Israel was God's favored and exalted nation. David is called God's "firstborn": "I will also make him my firstborn, greatest of the kings of the earth" (Ps 89:27). Thus, when Jesus is called the "firstborn over creation," this means that he existed before the act of creation and that he is the exalted King over all creation. All that exists must answer to him.

Paul then explains why Christ is supreme over creation. First, Jesus is the agent of creation. He is the One through whom the Father made all that exists. He not only created the material universe, the visible world, he also created the spiritual world, including angelic beings of all kinds, four of which are thrones, dominions, rulers, and authorities (1:16).[222] Thrones are apparently the angels that attend to the throne of God in the highest heaven. If the Colossian heresy was influenced by incipient *Merkabah* mysticism as abundant evidence suggests, it is probably significant that this is the only reference in Pauline literature to the "thrones," a special category of angels who have access to the heavenly throne room, the coveted destination of the *Merkabah* ascent. In the ascent to God, the angels served as guardians to prevent intruders. One had to present seals to these angels in

---

[219] For evidence that the etymological sense of *tokos* in *prōtotokos* dropped out, see *TDNT* 6:871–81; O'Brien, *Colossians, Philemon*, 44–45; Bruce, *Colossians, Philemon, Ephesians*, 58–61; and R. R. Melick Jr., *Philippians, Colossians, Philemon*, NAC (Nashville, TN: B&H, 1991), 215–17. These two themes, priority in time and rank, permeate this hymn in the words *prōtotokos* (twice), *pro pantōn*, and *archē*.

[220] Elsewhere Paul used the argument from priority in time to demonstrate man's authority over the woman (see 1 Cor 11:8–9).

[221] The use of *eimi* in the present tense rather than the imperfect may allude to Jesus's eternality in this context. Lightfoot linked the use of *eimi* in vv. 17–18 to John's *egō eimi*.

[222] In the *Testaments of the Twelve Patriarchs* (*T. Levi* 3), archangels are mentioned as the angelic class that resides in the uppermost heaven "with the Great Glory in the Holy of Holies." They offer propitiatory sacrifices for the sins of ignorance of the saints. In the heaven just below them, the messenger angels, along with the thrones and authorities, continually offer praises to God. This source is dated to the second century BC. In 2 (Slavic) Enoch 20 (J: longer recension), archangels, dominions, authorities, and thrones are described as present in the seventh heaven. Thrones are described as many eyed and grouped together with cherubim and seraphim.

order to gain access to the next heavenly level. Some of these seals were Hebrew gibberish or angelic names. Since these angels granted access to God, they essentially fulfilled the function of a mediator, a role reserved for Christ alone. Thus, the status of the angels in Jewish mysticism rivaled the role of Christ as the one mediator between God and man. Paul, however, demonstrated Jesus's supremacy to the angelic mediators, who supposedly had to be appeased in the process of the mystic's ascent, by insisting that Jesus created all angelic beings. He is Lord over all because he is Creator of all.

Paul adds that Jesus is the purpose of creation: "All things were created for him" (1:16, author's translation). Every created thing exists for the pleasure of Christ and for his glory. Jesus is also the sustainer of creation: "by him all things hold together" (1:17). Unlike the Creator portrayed by the deists, Jesus did not simply wind up the universe and then sit back and watch it run, refusing ever to intervene with the mechanical and automatic processes he set in motion. Instead, the Creator, who contrived the physical laws that govern the universe, sustains those principles by the active exercise of his power. If ever he withdrew his powerful hand from the universe, planets would stray from their courses to be incinerated by the sun. Celestial bodies would collide and crumble. People and objects would be flung from the spinning planet into the darkness of outer space. Apart from his powerful intervention, the cosmos would be reduced to chaos. The Greeks once glorified the giant Titan Atlas as one who stood on the edge of the earth, supporting the sky on his shoulders lest it fall and crush the world's inhabitants. But the power ascribed to Christ here dwarfs even Atlas's mythical strength. He is not merely One who suspends the sky above the earth; he orders and preserves the entire universe.

Paul demonstrates Christ's preeminence in all matters by exclaiming that Jesus was not only the Lord of creation; he is also the Lord of the new creation. He is the head of the church by virtue of his resurrection from the dead (1:18). Jesus's resurrection is the key to the transformation of rebellious sinners into the holy people of God and the promise of final redemption. Jesus's qualification as the "firstborn from the dead" serves to identify him as the beginning of the church, the founder of a new humanity.

Paul's description of Jesus's supremacy climaxed with an amazing statement: "For God was pleased to have all his fullness dwell in him" (1:19). The word "fullness" *(plērōma)* means "the sum total" or "completeness." Thus, Paul asserts that the sum total or completeness of God dwelled in Christ. This statement was later clarified by Paul in 2:9: "For the entire fullness of God's nature dwells bodily in Christ." Not just a part of God, but God in his completeness made his home in the body of Jesus. Jesus is not partially but completely God. Everything that makes God God has made its home in the body of Jesus Christ.

This certainly was an amazing statement to the readers of this letter who were familiar with the OT. The OT often spoke of how tremendous the fullness of God is. Solomon said God is too vast for the temple to contain his fullness. When Solomon dedicated the magnificent temple he had built for Yahweh, he prayed and said, "But will God indeed live on

SIDEBAR 14.1: WHAT IS "THE CIRCUMCISION OF CHRIST" IN COL 2:12?

The meaning of the phrase "the circumcision of Christ" is debated. Is the genitive (1) objective (the circumcision that Christ received), (2) subjective (the circumcision that Christ performs), or (3) possessive (the circumcision that belongs to Christ, that is, Christian circumcision)?

On the whole, the first of these options (objective genitive) appears to be the most defensible reading. This approach understands circumcision as the act of death, when Christ stripped off his physical body. P. T. O'Brien argued for the objective genitive because the phrases "putting off the body of flesh" and "the circumcision of Christ" are parallel expressions.[1] This reading would render both of the genitives in an objective sense so that Paul effectively says, "The body of the flesh was stripped off when Christ was circumcised, that is, when he died." O'Brien cited the earlier reference to the death of Christ in 1:22 as a parallel expression to 2:11. He also stated that this meaning results in a familiar Pauline theme (see Rom 6:3–4; 1 Cor 15:3–4) of death (circumcision), burial, and resurrection.

T. R. Schreiner also understood the "circumcision of Christ" as the death of Christ.[2] He asserted that the passage fits with the argument of Galatians in which Paul said that the cross replaced circumcision as the new point of entrance into the people of God. Therefore, "the new circumcision for believers is accomplished in the cross."[3]

The second option (subjective genitive), while less likely, has received some support because of the parallelism with "uncircumcision of your flesh" in verse 13. Paul identified "uncircumcision of your flesh" as something people possess who are dead in transgressions, so the "circumcision performed by Christ" must be something believers possess. But the text does not require this meaning for the parallel to work. The text only says that the "circumcision of Christ" removes the "uncircumcision of your flesh."

The third alternative (genitive as possessive), while yielding a straightforward reading, has also the most difficulties. The reading demands that "of Christ" equals "Christian," which is far from normative in the literature of the NT. It also begs the question of identity: What does Paul mean by "Christian" circumcision?

---

[1] O'Brien, *Colossians, Philemon*, 117.

[2] T. R. Schreiner, "Circumcision," in *Dictionary of Paul and His Letters*, ed. G. F. Hawthorne, R. P. Martin, and D. G. Reid (Downers Grove: InterVarsity, 1993), 139.

[3] See also P. Borgen, "Paul Preaches Circumcision and Pleases Men," in *Paul and Paulinism: Essays in Honour of C. K. Barrett*, ed. M. D. Hooker and S. G. Wilson (London: SPCK, 1982), 85–102.

earth with humans? Even heaven, the highest heaven, cannot contain you, much less this house I have built" (2 Chr 6:18). But now Paul reveals that the wonder of all wonders, the fullness of God that the temple, and the earth, and the very universe could not contain, gladly resided in the body of Jesus Christ. One can hardly imagine a Christology any higher than this.

The Work of Christ in Salvation Christ's status as Lord over the church introduces a question regarding his work. How does Paul describe the work of Christ in Colossians?

In a word, Christ's work is sufficient. He is the One who provides redemption, that is, the forgiveness of sins (1:14). Redemption refers to an act of paying a price in order to liberate a slave or prisoner of war from captivity or to rescue a criminal from punishment. Since Paul equated redemption with the forgiveness of sins, he apparently had the rescue of condemned criminals in mind.

Jesus is the One who provides reconciliation through the blood of his cross (1:20, 22). This reconciliation is cosmic in scope and includes all created things. Paul's point is not that all created beings will enter into a joyful fellowship with God but that God acted through Jesus's death to restore all of creation to its prefall submission to the authority of the Creator (1:20). The believer's former enmity with God has been replaced with submission to and fellowship with God through his own voluntary surrender. Others who live in rebellion against God will ultimately submit to his authority through forced subjugation, much like the authorities and powers described in 2:15.

The flow of thought in 2:8–10 gloriously conveys the believer's completeness in Christ. Believers should not be held captive by a "philosophy" that commends certain supplements to faith in Christ (2:8) because *all* the fullness of deity is found in Christ (2:9); and, because Christ possesses all the fullness, believers are also complete in him (2:10). Despite being dead in transgressions and uncircumcision, humanity receives new life in union with Christ in his death, burial, and resurrection (2:11–13). This new life results in a radical transformation of the Christian's character and behavior.

Believers experience forgiveness of all transgressions. The spiritual certificate of debt that lists the transgressor's sins and demands his punishment was nailed to the top of Jesus's cross in the very spot where the crimes of the victim of crucifixion were normally listed (2:14). This demonstrated that Christ himself bore the punishment for the believer's sins in his place, so that the believer could escape the condemnation that he rightly deserved. Because of Jesus's substitutionary death, the believer's sin list has been erased so that he will be declared innocent in eschatological judgment. This "glorious thought" makes all well within the Christ-follower's soul because, in the words of hymn writer Horatio Spafford, "My sin . . . not in part but the whole, is nailed to the cross and I bear it no more, praise the Lord, praise the Lord, O my soul!"

Christ's sufficient work allows believers to stand complete even against evil forces (2:15).[223] Christ has conquered the demonic spirits that rebelled against the authority of the Almighty. "He stripped them of their malevolent abilities, just as captured soldiers are stripped of their weapons, and he led them in a triumphal procession, just as a victorious general leads defeated soldiers to their execution."[224]

---

[223] The principalities, powers, and "elemental spirits" are evil spiritual forces aligned against believers. See esp. the helpful history of interpretation and persuasive study of P. T. O'Brien, "Principalities and Powers: Opponents of the Church," in *Biblical Interpretation and the Church*, ed. D. A. Carson (Grand Rapids MI: Baker, 1984), 110–50.

[224] Thielman, *Theology of the New Testament*, 351. So also M. J. Harris, "Colossians," in *New Dictionary of Biblical Theology*, ed. T. D. Alexander and B. S. Rosner (Downers Grove, IL: InterVarsity, 2000), 324–25.

The supremacy of Christ and the sufficiency of his work shatter any false notion that one must supplement Christian faith. Nothing can be added to the infinite fullness of Christ, and therefore nothing can be added to faith in him. Christ's lordship is so complete that Paul called believers to live in the light of it by bringing every aspect of their lives under it (chaps. 3–4). Thus, the theological theme of ethics flows out of Paul's focus on Christology.

Proper Christian Conduct (Ethics) The indicative explanations in Colossians 1–2 of who Christ is and what he has done leads to the imperative proclamation in chapters 3–4 of who believers are and what they are to do. E. Lohse said it well: "Christ is Lord over everything—over powers and principalities, but also over the Christian's daily life."[225] Paul established the cosmic scope of Christ's lordship and the complete scope of the believer's salvation in him (chaps. 1–2); he applied these two points in three broad ways (chaps. 3–4).

First, the complete scope of Christ's sufficient work and believers' spiritual union with him means that they can keep pursuing the things above where Christ dwells (3:1–2). But though believers are complete in Jesus, the Christian life is not static. Believers should have a passion to pursue Christ, and that pursuit necessitates looking away from earthly things and putting to death earthly passions and deeds that belong to the old way of life (3:5).

Second, union with Christ means that the believer is a new creature and acts accordingly. He or she has "put off the old self with its practices" (3:9) and has "put on the new self" (3:10). Paul stated earlier that Christ is the image of God (1:15) and the Creator (1:16), and now in union with Christ the believer is made anew according to the image of the Creator (3:10). Thus, the believer is being transformed so that he becomes more and more like Christ.

Third, the cosmic scope of Christ's lordship has staggering implications for his lordship over every aspect of the believer's life, which is especially emphasized in the household code of 3:18–4:1.[226] A. Kuyper made the sweeping claim that "there is not a square inch in the whole domain of our human existence over which Christ, who is Sovereign over all, does not cry: 'Mine!'"[227] Christ's lordship extends to one's personal holiness, family life, work life, and everything in between ("whatever you do, in word or in deed," 3:17).

---

[225] Lohse, *Colossians and Philemon*, 178.

[226] See the analysis of Bevere (*Sharing in the Inheritance*, 225–54, esp. 240), who argued that the household code is an integral piece of the entire letter in light of the lordship of Christ.

[227] These words were spoken as part of his inaugural address at the founding of the Free University on October 20, 1880. J. D. Bratt, ed., *Abraham Kuyper: A Centennial Reader* (Grand Rapids, MI: Eerdmans, 1988), 488.

Philemon

KEY FACTS

Author:	Paul
Date:	Around AD 60
Provenance:	Roman imprisonment
Destination:	Philemon
Occasion:	Philemon's slave escapes, meets Paul, becomes a believer, and is sent back to his owner.
Purpose:	To encourage Philemon to accept Onesimus as a brother and to send him back to Paul and possibly grant him his freedom
Theme:	Love and reconciliation in the body of Christ
Key Verses:	17–20

INTRODUCTION

EVEN THOUGH IN the NT canon Philemon is separated from the book of Colossians, it shares with Colossians its likely destination and its presumed date of writing during Paul's first Roman imprisonment. For this reason it is appropriate to group Philemon with the other Prison Epistles (Philippians, Ephesians, and Colossians) and to discuss the letter under the present rubric.

Philemon bears the distinction of being the shortest Pauline Letter with its 335 words in the Greek text.[228] Carson and Moo also characterized Philemon as the "most personal" letter of Paul.[229] The issue of slavery is probably the first thought that comes to mind when the average Christian thinks about Philemon, but Paul's Letter is not a position paper on slavery. Rather, it makes a much more multifaceted contribution to the canon than a one-dimensional reading of the document might suggest.

While Philemon may be the briefest Pauline Letter, it still makes a significant contribution to NT theology. It effectively takes Colossians' concept of cosmic reconciliation through the cross of Christ and translates it into a specific setting of reconciliation between two individuals. The gospel message does not stand alone; it includes an important message on how to deal with real-life issues. In a very real sense, relationships in the body of Christ are gospel relationships, and social issues such as slavery are gospel issues.

---

[228] A. G. Patzia, "Philemon, Letter to," in *Dictionary of Paul and His Letters*, 703.

[229] Carson and Moo, *Introduction to the New Testament*, 589.

HISTORY

Author

Authenticity Philemon is almost universally recognized as an authentic letter of the apostle Paul. The only sustained case against Pauline authorship was made by the Tübingen School in the nineteenth century. As mentioned previously, F. C. Baur affirmed the authenticity of only four letters ascribed to Paul—Romans, 1–2 Corinthians, and Galatians—which he categorically called the *Hauptbriefe* (German for "major epistles").[230] His arguments against authenticity are now dismissed by virtually all Pauline scholars.[231]

Literary Integrity No serious challenges to the integrity of Philemon have arisen. Both the letter's brevity and its personal nature provide obstacles for those who would contend against its literary integrity.

Date

The date for Philemon depends largely on the date assigned to Colossians. The evidence for the close relationship between the two includes (1) Colossians refers to Onesimus (Col 4:9); (2) both letters have Timothy as the cosender (Phlm 1:1; Col 1:1); (3) both letters refer to Epaphras (Phlm 23; Col 1:7) and Archippus (Phlm 2; Col 4:17); and (4) both letters include Mark, Aristarchus, Demas, and Luke among Paul's companions (Phlm 24; Col 4:10, 14). Assuming the Roman provenance of Colossians, the letter should be dated to around the year 60.

Destination

Paul addressed the letter to Philemon, whom Paul called his "dear friend and coworker" (v. 1). Virtually everyone accepts this destination. John Knox suggested that Philemon was the initial recipient of the letter, while Archippus was the ultimate recipient, but his view has generated little acceptance.[232]

Philemon was the master of a slave named Onesimus. The letter provides a number of possible biographical details concerning Philemon. First, Paul presents Philemon in glowing terms as a cherished coworker (v. 1) and a model of love and faith toward Jesus (v. 5). Philemon's love and faith had also overflowed to all the believers (v. 5), whom he had often refreshed (v. 7). Second, it is likely the apostle Paul played a significant role in Philemon's conversion (v. 19) because Paul parenthetically commented that Philemon owed his "very self" to the apostle.[233] Third, Philemon was probably wealthy since he hosted the church (v. 2) in Colossae (see Col 4:9) and was able to provide a guest room for Paul (v. 22).[234]

---

[230] F. C. Baur, *Paul: His Life and Works* (London, England: Williams and Norgate, 1875), 1:246.

[231] E.g., O'Brien, *Colossians, Philemon*, xli–liv.

[232] J. Knox, *Philemon Among the Letters of Paul*, 2nd ed. (New York, NY: Abingdon, 1959).

[233] From early times (e.g., Theodoret), it has been conjectured that Apphia was Philemon's wife since her name appears beside his own (v. 2). See O'Brien, *Colossians, Philemon*, 273 ("probably correctly"). Some theorized further that Archippus was Philemon's and Apphia's son, though this is impossible to verify (ibid.: "possibly").

[234] Dunn, *Colossians and Philemon*, 300–1.

Provenance

Questions concerning the provenance of Philemon are dependent on the provenance of Colossians. Paul was in prison when he wrote both letters. In addition to the other similarities sketched above, Colossians indicates that Onesimus was a resident of Colossae (Col 4:9). Thus, one may safely infer that Philemon resided in the same place as his slave. Many scholars conclude that these similarities between the two letters suggest that they were written at the same time and place and were sent together to Colossae.[235] The time and place, however, continue to be vigorously contested.

The three major proposals regarding the provenance of Philemon are Rome, Ephesus, and Caesarea, with Rome and Ephesus being the most seriously debated.[236] In favor of Rome, external evidence dating to the fourth and fifth centuries "uniformly attributes" the provenance of Philemon to Rome.[237] Other scholars believe that two factors in Philemon favor an Ephesian imprisonment: (1) it is more likely that Onesimus would flee to Ephesus as the nearest metropolis, not the distant city of Rome; and (2) Paul's request to Philemon for a room in the near future (Phlm 22) fits more readily with the shorter distance between Ephesus and Colossae.[238]

Those who hold to a Roman imprisonment make two points in response. First, the proximity of Ephesus to Colossae cuts both ways. It may be that Onesimus would seek the anonymity found within the capital of the Roman Empire because a place like Ephesus was too close for comfort. Second, Paul's request for lodging does not preclude a Roman imprisonment because he could still make the trip in about five weeks. Carson and Moo argued that the reference to an imminent arrival could have been a way to put further pressure on Philemon and to obtain a favorable decision from him.[239]

Occasion

Scholars have suggested five possible scenarios for the letter's occasion: (1) traditional hypothesis, (2) sanctuary hypothesis, (3) mediation hypothesis, (4) "sent" hypothesis, and (5) Knox hypothesis. The traditional hypothesis regarding the letter's occasion posits that Philemon had a runaway slave named Onesimus, who may have added to his crime of desertion by stealing from his master (v. 18). Subsequent to his escape, Onesimus encountered Paul in prison (or house arrest). The apostle befriended Onesimus and eventually led him to Christ. Paul now faced a difficult decision. Should he send his valued helper Onesimus back to his master Philemon? Though Paul desired to keep Philemon with him,

---

[235] Kümmel, *Introduction*, 349.

[236] The proposal of Corinth has found little scholarly support.

[237] Dunn, *Colossians and Philemon*, 308; cf. B. M. Metzger, *A Textual Commentary on the Greek New Testament*, 2nd ed. (New York, NY: United Bible Societies, 1994), 589–90.

[238] deSilva, *Introduction to the New Testament*, 668.

[239] Carson and Moo, *Introduction to the New Testament*, 592. Dunn (*Colossians and Philemon*, 308) also claimed that one should observe the note of uncertainty in v. 22. He said that one cannot exclude the possibility that Paul was simply saying, "Keep a room ready for me; you never know when I might turn up."

he knew that he must send Onesimus back. But he did so with the expressed expectation that Philemon would return Onesimus to Paul in order to provide him with further assistance, perhaps with the additional hope that Philemon would grant freedom to his slave, who was now a fellow slave of Christ with Philemon and thus a fellow Christian brother.[240] This portrayal has come under fire recently because of the improbability that Onesimus just happened to stumble on Philemon's close friend, Paul. Carson and Moo capture this attitude well in saying that "[s]uch a coincidence seems more in keeping with a Dickens novel than with sober history."[241]

Therefore, other views have been proposed in lieu of the traditional view. The sanctuary hypothesis suggests that the fugitive Onesimus fled to Paul's home for protection in keeping with the Roman statute that considered the home a place of sanctuary. The mediation hypothesis offers a different construal of the events by claiming that Onesimus was not a *fugitivus* (Lat. for "fugitive") in legal terms but rather a slave who had somehow wronged his master and thus sought out Paul for mediation as the *amicus domini* (Lat. for "friend of the master").[242] The "sent" hypothesis simply states that the Colossian congregation sent Onesimus to minister to some of Paul's physical needs while in prison.[243]

The Knox hypothesis refers to the view championed by John Knox, who offered the earliest (1935) and most elaborate revision of the traditional view. Knox's theory essentially consists of five parts. First, he argued that Archippus was the owner of Onesimus and thus the ultimate addressee of the letter. Second, he theorized that Paul actually sent the letter to Philemon, the overseer of the churches in that region, in order that it might be read aloud in the Colossian church. Third, Paul devised this strategy in order that the added pressure on Archippus would cause him to release Onesimus for Christian service. Fourth, the mysterious letter to Laodicea (Col 4:16) is really a reference to this letter to Philemon. Fifth, this request to release Onesimus represents the "ministry" that Paul called upon Archippus to complete (Col 4:17).[244]

How should the reader evaluate these various proposals? In the case of the "sent" hypothesis, the exegesis is questionable at times.[245] Knox's reconstruction is sometimes insightful and always ingenious but ultimately founders upon the rocks of speculation and

---

[240] J. G. Nordling, "Onesimus Fugitivus: A Defense of the Runaway Slave Hypothesis in Philemon," *JSNT* 41 (1999): 97–119.

[241] Carson and Moo, *Introduction to the New Testament*, 590.

[242] Bruce, *Colossians, Philemon, and Ephesians*, 197; P. Lampe, "Keine Sklavenflucht des Onesimus," *ZNW* 76 (1985): 135–37; J. M. G. Barclay, *Colossians and Philemon* (Sheffield, UK: Sheffield Academic Press, 1997), 101.

[243] S. Winter, "Paul's Letter to Philemon," *NTS* 33 (1987): 1–15.

[244] Knox brought the story full circle by proposing that Onesimus became the bishop of Ephesus who used his influence to ensure that the letter made it into the canon.

[245] Winter ("Philemon," 3–4) read the "hearing" of Philemon's faith (v. 5) as a report from Onesimus and the "sharing of your faith" as Paul's response to Philemon's sending of Onesimus (v. 6). While this reading is possible, it is by no means the most straightforward interpretation of the text.

improbability.[246] For example, almost all Pauline scholars reject Knox's public reading theory because it is simply incompatible with the internal evidence of the letter. The full frontal assault of a public reading would completely negate Paul's deft and delicate handling of this sensitive issue.

It is much more difficult to adjudicate between the traditional, sanctuary, and mediator hypotheses since none of these views is free from difficulty. These points of critique and evaluation have been raised:

1. The sanctuary and mediation proposals have difficulty answering why Onesimus would seek Paul for sanctuary or mediation if he were in the distant capital. Could Onesimus not have found a closer place of sanctuary or a closer person to serve as mediator?
2. The traditional view does not require a "coincidental" meeting between Paul and Onesimus. Even if a proposed scenario involves a chance encounter, it is not inconsistent with the providential activity of God evidenced elsewhere in Scripture.[247]
3. The traditional view that considers Onesimus a fugitive is problematic because Paul does not use the customary legal terms or verbs of flight.[248]
4. Pliny's letter to Sabinianus (*Ep.* 9.21) is an impressive literary and historical parallel for the mediation hypothesis.[249]
5. The runaway slave hypothesis has difficulty explaining the letter's absence of any echoes of Onesimus's regret or repentance for this criminal act.[250]

Paul left the reader to wrestle with these questions because he did not explicitly state the reasons behind Onesimus's flight. Therefore, dogmatism should be avoided. The practice of appealing to precedents in the ancient world is problematic because plentiful examples exist of runaway slaves and mediation. Carson and Moo rightly noted a further caveat in that the traditional view allows for other possibilities. Perhaps, for example, Onesimus fled to Rome and then subsequently had second thoughts about his escape, so he sought out Paul for refuge or mediation.[251] In any case, questions such as these do not materially affect the understanding and appreciation of the overall message of the book.

---

[246] Many scholars, however, acknowledge the possibility that the Onesimus of Philemon and the Onesimus of Ignatius might refer to the same person (e.g., O'Brien, *Colossians, Philemon*, 268).

[247] The claim that a coincidental meeting between Paul and Onesimus in Rome is likely unhistorical may unduly diminish scriptural teaching on God's gracious providence (e.g., Matt 2:1–12; Luke 2:25–38; Acts 8:26–40).

[248] J. A. Fitzmyer, *The Letter to Philemon: A New Translation with Introduction and Commentary*, AB 34C (New York, NY: Doubleday, 2000), 17–18.

[249] Aune, *Westminster Dictionary*, 356.

[250] Dunn (*Colossians and Philemon*, 303) contrasted this state of affairs with Pliny's letter to Sabinianus. He also claimed that this contrast is what led to widespread dissatisfaction with the runaway slave hypothesis. According to Dunn, the failure to explain this contrast is the "principal weakness" of Nordling's recent defense of the hypothesis (n. 11).

[251] Carson and Moo, *Introduction to the New Testament*, 592.

LITERATURE

Literary Plan

Recent research on Philemon focuses on rhetorical criticism. F. F. Church read Philemon through the lens of deliberative rhetoric as the prescript (vv. 1–3); the *exordium* (vv. 4–7); *probatio* (vv. 8–16); and *peroratio* (vv. 17–22). This rhetorical device aims "to demonstrate love or friendship and to induce sympathy or goodwill, in order to dispose the hearer favorably to the merits of one's case."[252] Others have argued along epistolary lines that Philemon is a letter of mediation or intercession.[253] J. P. Heil and J. W. Welch independently advocated a chiastic structure for Philemon in which verse 14 is the central point.[254]

The hardest decision for the outline of the letter is where the body ends and the closing begins. Many think the body extends from verses 8 to 22 and the final greetings begin in verse 23.[255] Though certainty is nearly impossible, it may be preferable to read verse 20 as the end of the letter body, with verses 21–25 forming the closing.

OUTLINE

I. OPENING (1–7)
  A. Salutation (1–3)
  B. Thanksgiving and Prayer (4–7)
II. BODY: THREE APPEALS FOR ONESIMUS (8–20)
  A. Initial Appeal: He is Useful for Both You and Me (8–11).
  B. Second Appeal: Accept Him as a Brother in Christ (12–16).
  C. Third Appeal: Refresh My Heart by Sending Onesimus Back (17–20).
III. CLOSING (21–25)

UNIT-BY-UNIT DISCUSSION

I. Opening (1–7)

A. Salutation (1–3) The letter opens with the customary identification of the senders (Paul and Timothy; v. 1) and the recipients (Philemon, Apphia, Archippus, and the house church; v. 2) as well as the grace salutation (v. 3).

B. Thanksgiving and Prayer (4–7) Paul offers a thanksgiving (v. 4) for the report of Philemon's love and faith (v. 5). He also prays that Philemon's participation in the faith

---

[252] F. F. Church, "Rhetorical Structure and Design in Paul's Letter to Philemon," *HTR* 71 (1978): 19–20.

[253] S. K. Stowers, *Letter Writing in Greco-Roman Antiquity* (Philadelphia, PA: Westminster, 1986), 153–65.

[254] J. P. Heil, "The Chiastic Structure and Meaning of Paul's Letter to Philemon," *Bib* 82 (2001): 178–206. J. W. Welch ("Chiasmus in the New Testament," in *Chiasmus in Antiquity: Structures, Analyses, Exegesis*, ed. J. W. Welch [Hildesheim, Germany: Gerstenberg, 1981], 225–26) identified a similar chiastic arrangement, but his proposal is problematic because of the sheer complexity of identifying twenty chiastically paired units.

[255] Patzia, "Philemon," 703.

Something to Think About: Faith Changes Everything

Paul was in prison when he wrote his letter to Philemon, the Christian master of the runaway slave Onesimus. Yet in his opening words he identified himself, not as a prisoner of Rome, but as "a prisoner of Christ Jesus" (v. 1). The way Paul saw it, he was in prison by the will of God. While others may have been slaves of their earthly masters, by faith Paul was God's slave (see Titus 1:1, "Paul, a slave of God"). That kind of faith changes everything.

Faith also changed everything in the life of Paul's new protégé, Onesimus. Apparently, the slave had run away from his master Philemon and then met Paul in prison in Rome. There, it appears, Paul shared the gospel with this desperate man, and he was converted to Christ. Accordingly, Paul refers to Onesimus as "my son. . . . I became his father while I was in chains" (v. 10). Onesimus, whose name means "useful," would have been "useful" for Paul, but the apostle chose to send him back to his earthly master so that he would be "useful"—truly useful to him—now that he had become a Christian.

In his letter to Philemon, Paul appeals to his friend to receive Onesimus back "no longer regarded as a slave, but more than a slave—as a dearly loved brother" (v. 16). Onesimus was a changed man, and Paul urges Philemon to recognize that his relationship with Onesimus had changed as well: they were now brothers in Christ. This is a wonderful example of how Paul envisioned Christianity as transforming not only individuals but also social structures such as slavery.

At the conclusion of his letter, Paul has one more personal request that he saved for last: "Meanwhile, also prepare a guest room for me, for I hope that through your prayers I will be restored to you" (v. 22). At the time of writing, Paul was still in prison, but he was hopeful that he would be released soon, so hopeful, in fact, that he had already begun to make preparations to visit Philemon and Onesimus—including reserving a guest room! That's faith.

would be effective through knowledge (v. 6). Philemon's act of refreshing the hearts of the believers brought joy and encouragement to Paul (v. 7).

II. Body: Three Appeals for Onesimus (8–20)

A. First Appeal: He Is Useful for Both You and Me (8–11). Paul lovingly issues a series of fatherly pleas to Philemon on behalf of Onesimus as Paul's "son" (v. 10). To Philemon Paul appeals as an aged and imprisoned man, not as an authoritarian apostle (vv. 8–9). The first appeal focuses on the current usefulness of Onesimus to both Philemon and Paul, which is contrasted with the former uselessness of Onesimus to Philemon alone (v. 11). The expression involves a pun of Onesimus's name, which means "profitable" or "useful." Previously, he had been "useless" *(achrēston)*, but he had become "useful" *(euchrēston)* to Philemon as well as to Paul.[256]

B. Second Appeal: Accept Him as a Brother in Christ (12–16). The second appeal (vv. 12–16) petitions Philemon to accept Onesimus back as a beloved brother, not as a slave (vv. 15–16). Paul sent Onesimus back for this purpose, though Paul would have preferred to keep Onesimus, who could take Philemon's place in ministering to Paul in prison (v. 13). The apostle did not act according to this desire because he wanted Philemon's free and heartfelt consent to this good deed (v. 14).

C. Third Appeal: Refresh My Heart by Sending Onesimus Back (17–20). The third appeal (vv. 17–20) again asks for the acceptance of Onesimus (v. 17) in light of the partnership between Paul and Philemon. The apostle assumed a fatherly role in that anything that Onesimus owed to Philemon could be charged to Paul, even though Philemon was already a debtor who owed Paul everything (vv. 18–19). Paul expresses confidence that Philemon would refresh his heart (v. 20), just as Philemon had previously refreshed the hearts of the believers (v. 7).

III. Closing (21–25)

Paul concludes the letter with the confident expectation that Philemon would exceed his expectant appeals (v. 21), which many take as veiled reference to granting Onesimus his freedom.[257] He also urged Philemon to prepare a place for him in light of his hope that Philemon's own prayers for Paul's release would be answered (v. 22). Paul also extends greetings to Philemon from others (vv. 23–24), ending the letter with the familiar grace benediction (v. 25).

THEOLOGY

Theological Themes

Mutual Love and Brotherhood in the Body of Christ Paul not only asks for Philemon's brotherly acceptance of Onesimus in the gospel, he also models brotherly love in the act of asking for it. The aged apostle could command Philemon and easily attain forced or feigned obedience, but Paul opted for a fatherly approach in the form of a series of tender appeals. He also highlighted the mutuality of Christian relationships. Philemon had refreshed the believers in the past (v. 7), and now he had a chance to refresh the heart of another fellow believer (Paul) by accepting Onesimus as a fellow Christian (v. 20). Paul willingly assumed all of Onesimus's possible debts to Philemon (v. 18), but he also asks Philemon to remember his own indebtedness to Paul (v. 19). The family ethos of the letter stems from the fact that the author saw Onesimus not only as his child (v. 10) but also as a

---

[256] See O'Brien (*Colossians, Philemon*, 291–92) who noted that there are many extrabiblical instances of the play on words involving "useless" and "useful."

[257] Kümmel (*Introduction*, 349) regarded the idea that Paul expected Philemon to set Onesimus free as "unlikely," though he never gave a rationale for this assertion.

part of himself—"his very heart" (v. 12 NASB). Patzia rightly called Paul's overall request a "masterpiece of pastoral diplomacy."[258]

A Christian Approach to Slavery and Other Social Issues Though Paul did not *directly* tackle social issues such as slavery in Philemon, he did suggest that the gospel had important implications for such matters. Paul asked Philemon to accept Onesimus as a fellow brother in Christ.[259] Equality before God through the gospel challenges the very heart and soul of slavery: one human's ownership of another.[260]

This approach closely coheres with Paul's teaching in Colossians. Colossians 4:1 urges Christian masters to pay their slaves that which was right and fair and to treat their slaves as they wished to be treated by their master, Jesus Christ. If masters heeded Paul's words, the institution of slavery within the church would have been transformed from a master-slave relationship to an employer-employee relationship or, even better, to a brother-brother relationship.

Relationships at the social level (masters and slaves) look much different in the redefining light of those enjoyed at the spiritual level (fellow brothers and slaves of Christ). The social convention can only wilt and die when the gospel uproots the concept that grounds it and establishes its growth. Carson and Moo said it well: "That it took so long for this to happen is a sad chapter in Christian blindness to the implications of the gospel."[261]

CONTRIBUTION TO THE CANON[262]

- The centrality of the gospel of Christ and partnership in the gospel (Phil 1:5; 4:15)
- Christ's self-humiliation *(kenōsis)* and subsequent exaltation (Phil 2:5–12)
- The supremacy of Christ, the cosmic reconciling work of Christ, and spiritual warfare (Eph 1:10, 20–23; 6:10–18; Col 1:15–20)
- The subjection of all things to Christ's lordship and the present implications of Christ's victory for believers (Eph 1:10; 4:1–6:9; Col 3:1–4:1)
- The unity of the church as the body of Christ consisting of Jews and Gentiles (Eph 2:11–22; 3:1–13; 4:1–6; Col 1:24–2:3; 3:12–17)
- Christian joy and thanksgiving (Phil 1:12–20; 4:4; Col 1:9–12; 2:6–7; 3:17; 4:2)
- The Christian transformation of socio-economic structures such as slavery (Philemon)

---

[258] Patzia, "Philemon," 706.

[259] N. R. Petersen (*Rediscovering Paul: Philemon and the Sociology of Paul's Narrative World* [Philadelphia, PA: Fortress, 1985]) argued along sociological lines that the letter of Philemon is a narrative drama in which Paul confronted Philemon to choose between kinship with the church or the world.

[260] For excellent treatments of slavery in the ancient Near East, the OT, and the Greco-Roman world, see the entries by M. A. Dandamayev and S. S. Bartchy in *ABD* 6:56–73.

[261] Carson and Moo, *Introduction to the New Testament*, 594.

[262] Note that the Contribution to the Canon, Study Questions, and For Further Study sections cover all four Prison Epistles.

- Social relationships (Eph 5:22–6:9; Col 3:18–4:1)

STUDY QUESTIONS

1. What five evidences are usually used to dismiss Paul's authorship of Ephesians?
2. What are the probable date, provenance, destination, occasion, and purpose of each of the four Prison Epistles?
3. What is the central theological theme in Ephesians?
4. Why is the question of provenance one of the most contested issues in Philippians?
5. What is the foremost contribution of Ephesians to the canon?
6. What is the "Colossian heresy," and how does it relate to the occasion of Colossians?
7. What are the three main points that Paul made in Colossians?
8. What are three major contributions that Colossians makes to the canon?
9. Why is Philemon included with the discussions of Ephesians, Philippians, and Colossians when it is canonically separated from them?
10. What are five possible occasions for Philemon?
11. What are two theological themes in Philemon?

FOR FURTHER STUDY

Abbott, T. K. *A Critical and Exegetical Commentary on the Epistles to the Ephesians and to the Colossians.* International Critical Commentary. Edinburgh Scotland: T&T Clark, 1897.

Alexander, L. C. A. "Hellenistic Letter-Forms and the Structure of Philippians." *Journal for the Study of the New Testament* 37 (1989): 87–110.

Arnold, C. E. *The Colossian Syncretism: The Interface Between Christianity and Folk Belief at Colosse.* Wissenschaftliche Untersuchungen zum Neuen Testament 77. Tübingen, Germany: Mohr Siebeck, 1995. Repr. ed., Grand Rapids, MI: Baker, 1996.

________. *Ephesians.* Zondervan Exegetical Commentary on the New Testament. Grand Rapids, MI: Zondervan, 2010.

________. "Ephesians, Letter to the." Pages 238–49 in *Dictionary of Paul and His Letters.* Edited by G. F. Hawthorne, R. P. Martin, and D. G. Reid. Downers Grove, IL: InterVarsity, 1993.

________. *Ephesians: Power and Magic. The Concept of Power in Ephesians in Light of Its Historical Setting.* Society for New Testament Studies Monograph Series 63. Cambridge, UK: University Press, 1989.

Barth, M. *Ephesians: A New Translation with Introduction and Commentary.* 2 vols. Anchor Bible 34–34A. Garden City, NY: Doubleday, 1974.

________. *Colossians.* Anchor Bible Commentary 34B. Garden City, NY: Doubleday, 1994.

________. "Colossians." Pages 841–70 in *Commentary on the New Testament Use of the Old Testament.* Edited by G. K. Beale and D. A. Carson. Grand Rapids, MI: Baker, 2007.

Best, E. *A Critical and Exegetical Commentary on Ephesians.* International Critical Commentary. Edinburgh, Scotland: T&T Clark, 1998.

Bevere, A. R. *Sharing in the Inheritance: Identity and the Moral Life in Colossians.* Journal for the Study of the New Testament Supplement 226. London, England: Sheffield Academic Press, 2003.

Black, D. A. "The Discourse Structure of Philippians: A Study in Textlinguistics." *Novum Testamentum* 37 (1995): 16–49.

Bockmuehl, M. *The Epistle to the Philippians.* Black's New Testament Commentaries 11. Peabody, MA: Hendrickson, 1998. New York, NY: Continuum, 2006.

Bruce, F. F. *The Epistles to the Colossians, to Philemon, and to the Ephesians.* New International Commentary on the New Testament. Grand Rapids, MI: Eerdmans, 1984.

__________. *Philippians.* New International Bible Commentary. Peabody, MA: Hendrickson, 1989.

Caragounis, C. C. *The Ephesian* Mysterion*: Meaning and Content.* Lund, Sweden: Gleerup, 1977.

Carson, D. A. *Basics for Believers: An Exposition of Philippians.* Grand Rapids, MI: Baker, 1996.

Dahl, N. A. *Studies in Ephesians: Introductory Questions, Text- and Edition-Critical Issues, Interpretation of Texts and Themes.* Wissenschaftliche Untersuchungen zum Neuen Testament 131. Tübingen, Germany: Mohr Siebeck, 2000.

Dübbers, M. *Christologie und Existenz im Kolosserbrief: Exegetische und semantische Untersuchungen zur Intention des Kolosserbriefes.* Wissenschaftliche Untersuchungen zum Neuen Testament 2/191. Tübingen, Germany: Mohr Siebeck, 2005.

Dunn, J. D. G. *The Epistles to the Colossians and to Philemon.* The New International Greek Testament Commentary. Grand Rapids, MI: Eerdmans, 1996.

Fee, G. D. *Paul's Letter to the Philippians.* New International Commentary on the New Testament. Grand Rapids, MI: Eerdmans, 1995.

________. "Philippians 2:5–11: Hymn or Exalted Pauline Prose?" *Bulletin of Biblical Research* 2 (1992): 29–46.

Fitzmyer, J. A. *The Letter to Philemon: A New Translation with Introduction and Commentary.* Anchor Bible 34C. New York, NY: Doubleday, 2000.

Furnish, V. P. "Ephesians, Epistle to the." Pages 536–37 in *The Anchor Bible Dictionary.* Edited by D. N. Freedman. New York, NY: Doubleday, 1992.

Garland, D. E. *Colossians and Philemon.* NIV Application Commentary. Grand Rapids, MI: Zondervan, 1998.

________. "The Composition and Unity of Philippians: Some Neglected Literary Factors." *Novum Testamentum* 27 (1985): 141–73.

________. "Philippians." Pages 175–261 in *The Expositor's Bible Commentary.* Rev. ed. Vol. 12: *Ephesians–Philemon.* Grand Rapids, MI: Zondervan, 2005.

Garlington, D. *2 Corinthians.* Exegetical Guide to the Greek New Testament. Nashville, TN: B&H Academic, forthcoming.

Hansen, G. W. *The Letter to the Philippians.* Pillar New Testament Commentary. Grand Rapids, MI: Eerdmans, 2009.

Harris, M. J. *Colossians and Philemon.* Exegetical Guide to the Greek New Testament. Grand Rapids, MI: Eerdmans, 1991.

Hawthorne, G. F. *Philippians*. Word Biblical Commentary 43. Rev. and exp. by R. P. Martin. Nashville, TN: Nelson, 2004.

Heil, J. P. *Ephesians: Empowerment to Walk in Love for the Unity of All in Christ*. Studies in Biblical Literature 13. Leiden, Netherlands: Brill, 2007.

Hellerman, J. *Philippians*. Exegetical Guide to the Greek New Testament. Nashville, TN: B&H Academic, 2015.

Hoehner, H. W. *Ephesians: An Exegetical Commentary*. Grand Rapids, MI: Baker, 2003.

Klein, W. W. "Ephesians." Pages 19–173 in *The Expositor's Bible Commentary*. Rev. ed. Vol. 12: *Ephesians–Philemon*. Grand Rapids, MI: Zondervan, 2005.

Lightfoot, J. B. *Saint Paul's Epistles to the Colossians and to Philemon*. 9th ed. London, England: Macmillan, 1890.

Lincoln, A. T. *Ephesians*. Word Biblical Commentary 42. Dallas, TX: Word, 1990.

________. *Paradise Now and Not Yet: Studies in the Role of the Heavenly Dimension in Paul's Thought with Special Reference to His Eschatology*. Society for New Testament Studies Monograph Series 43. Cambridge, UK: University Press, 1981.

________. "The Use of the OT in Ephesians." *Journal for the Study of the New Testament* 14 (1982): 16–57.

Lincoln, A. T., and A. J. M. Wedderburn. *The Theology of the Later Pauline Letters*. New Testament Theology. Cambridge, UK: University Press, 1993.

Lohse, E. *Colossians and Philemon*. Hermeneia. Edited by W. R. Poehlmann and R. J. Karris. Philadelphia, PA: Fortress, 1971.

Marshall, I. H. "Philippians." Pages 319–22 in *New Dictionary of Biblical Theology*. Edited by T. D. Alexander, B. S. Rosner, D. A. Carson, and G. Goldsworthy. Downers Grove, IL: InterVarsity, 2000.

Martin, R. P. *Colossians and Philemon*. New Century Bible. Grand Rapids, MI: Eerdmans, 1973.

________. *A Hymn of Christ: Philippians 2:5–11 in Recent Interpretation and in the Setting of Early Christian Worship*. Downers Grove, IL: InterVarsity, 1983.

________. *Philippians*. New Century Bible. Greenwood: Attic, 1976.

Mayer, A. C. *Sprache der Einheit in Epheserbrief*. Wissenschaftliche Untersuchungen zum Neuen Testament 150. Tübingen, Germany: Mohr Siebeck, 2002.

Melick, R. R. *Philippians, Colossians, Philemon*. New American Commentary. Nashville, TN: Broadman, 1991.

Merkle, B. *Ephesians*. Exegetical Guide to the Greek New Testament. Nashville, TN: B&H Academic, forthcoming 2016.

Moo, D. J. *The Letters to the Colossians and to Philemon*. Pillar New Testament Commentary. Grand Rapids, MI: Eerdmans, 2008.

Moritz, T. "Ephesians." Pages 315–19 in *New Dictionary of Biblical Theology*. Edited by T. D. Alexander, B. S. Rosner, D. A. Carson, and G. Goldsworthy. Downers Grove, IL: InterVarsity, 2000.

________. *A Profound Mystery: The Use of the Old Testament in Ephesians*. Novum Testamentum Supplement 85. Leiden, Netherlands: Brill, 1996.

Oakes, P. *Philippians: From People to Letter*. Society for New Testament Studies Monograph Series 110. Cambridge, UK: University Press, 2001.

O'Brien, P. T. *Colossians, Philemon.* Word Biblical Commentary 44. Dallas, TX: Word, 1982.

________. *The Epistle to the Ephesians.* The Pillar New Testament Commentary. Grand Rapids, MI: Eerdmans, 1999.

________. *Philippians.* New International Greek Testament Commentary. Grand Rapids, MI: Eerdmans, 1991.

Pao, D. W. *Colossians and Philemon.* Zondervan Exegetical Commentary on the New Testament. Edited by Clinton E. Arnold. Grand Rapids, MI: Zondervan, 2012.

Patzia, A. G. "Philemon, Letter to." Pages 703–7 in *Dictionary of Paul and His Letters.* Edited by G. F. Hawthorne, R. P. Martin, and D. G. Reid. Downers Grove, IL: InterVarsity, 1993.

Peterman, G. W. *Paul's Gift from Philippi: Conventions of Gift-Exchange and Christian Giving.* Society for New Testament Studies Monograph Series 92. Cambridge, UK: University Press, 1997.

Reed, J. T. *A Discourse Analysis of Philippians: Method and Rhetoric in the Debate over Literary Integrity.* Journal for the Study of the New Testament Supplement 136. Sheffield, UK: Sheffield Academic Press, 1997.

Reumann, John. *Philippians.* Anchor Yale Bible Commentaries. New Haven, CT: Yale University Press, 2008.

Roon, A. van. *The Authenticity of Ephesians.* Translated by S. Prescod-Jokel. Novum Testamentum Supplement 39. Leiden, Netherlands: Brill, 1974.

Sampley, J. P. *"And the Two Shall Become One Flesh." A Study of Traditions in Ephesians.* Society for New Testament Studies Monograph Series 16. Cambridge, UK: University Press, 1971.

Schnackenburg, R. *Ephesians: A Commentary.* Edinburgh, Scotland: T&T Clark, 1996.

Silva, M. *Philippians.* 2nd ed. Baker Exegetical Commentary on the New Testament. Grand Rapids, MI: Baker, 2005.

________. "Philippians." Pages 835–40 in *Commentary on the New Testament Use of the Old Testament.* Edited by G. K. Beale and D. A. Carson. Grand Rapids, MI: Baker, 2007.

Smith, I. K. *Heavenly Perspective: A Study of Paul's Response to a Jewish Mystical Movement at Colossae.* Library of New Testament Studies 326. Edinburgh, Scotland: T&T Clark, 2007.

Thielman, F. "Ephesus and the Literary Setting of Philippians." Pages 205–23 in *New Testament Greek and Exegesis, Fs. Gerald F. Hawthorne.* Edited by A. M. Donaldson and T. B. Sailors. Grand Rapids, MI: Eerdmans, 2003.

________. *Philippians.* NIV Application Commentary. Grand Rapids, MI: Zondervan, 1995.

________. "Ephesians." Pages 813–34 in *Commentary on the New Testament Use of the Old Testament.* Edited by G. K. Beale and D. A. Carson. Grand Rapids, MI: Baker, 2007.

________. *Ephesians.* Baker Exegetical Commentary on the New Testament. Grand Rapids, MI: Baker, 2010.

Thompson, M. M. *Colossians and Philemon.* Two Horizons New Testament Commentary. Grand Rapids, MI: Eerdmans, 2005.

Turner, M. "Ephesians." Pages 1222–44 in *New Bible Commentary.* Edited by D. A. Carson, R. T. France, J. A. Motyer, and G. J. Wenham. Downers Grove, IL: InterVarsity, 1994.

________. "Mission and Meaning in Terms of 'Unity' in Ephesians." Pages 138–66 in *Mission and Meaning: Essays Presented to Peter Cotterell.* Edited by A. Billington, T. Lane, and M. Turner. Carlisle, UK: Paternoster, 1995.

Ware, J. *The Mission of the Church in Paul's Letter to the Philippians in the Context of Ancient Judaism*. Novum Testamentum Supplement 120. Leiden, Netherlands: Brill, 2005.

Watson, D. F. "A Rhetorical Analysis of Philippians and Its Implications for the Unity Question." *Novum Testamentum* 30 (1988): 57–88.

Wilson, R. McL. *A Critical and Exegetical Commentary on Colossians and Philemon*. London, England: T&T Clark, 2005.

Winter, S. "Paul's Letter to Philemon." *New Testament Studies* 33 (1987): 1–15.

Witherington, B., III. *Friendship and Finances in Philippi*. Valley Forge, PA: Trinity Press International, 1994.

__________. *The Letters to Philemon, the Colossians, and the Ephesians: A Socio-Rhetorical Commentary on the Captivity Epistles*. Grand Rapids, MI: Eerdmans, 2007.

__________. *Paul's Letter to the Philippians: A Socio-Rhetorical Commentary*. Grand Rapids, MI: Eerdmans, 2011.

Wright, N. T. *The Epistles of Paul to the Colossians and to Philemon*. Tyndale New Testament Commentary. Grand Rapids, MI: Eerdmans, 1986.

Yoder Neufeld, T. R. *"Put on the Armour of God": The Divine Warrior from Isaiah to Ephesians*. Journal for the Study of the New Testament Supplement 144. Sheffield, UK: Sheffield Academic Press, 1997.

Chapter 15

The Letters to Timothy and Titus: 1–2 Timothy, Titus

CORE KNOWLEDGE

Basic Knowledge: Students should know the key facts of 1 and 2 Timothy and Titus. With regard to history, students should be able to identify each book's author, date, provenance, destination, and purpose. With regard to literature, they should be able to provide a basic outline of each book and identify core elements of each book's content found in the Unit-by-Unit Discussion. With regard to theology, students should be able to identify the major theological themes found in the letters to Timothy and Titus.

Intermediate Knowledge: Students should be able to present the arguments for historical, literary, and theological conclusions. With regard to history, students should be able to discuss the evidence for Pauline authorship, date, provenance, destination, and purpose. With regard to literature, they should be able to provide a detailed outline of each book. With regard to theology, students should be able to discuss the major theological themes in the letters to Timothy and Titus and the ways in which they uniquely contribute to the NT canon.

Advanced Knowledge: Students should be able to discuss the genre of the letters to Timothy and Titus and to discuss how ancient pseudonymous literature relates to the authorship of the letters to Timothy and Titus. In addition, students should be able to assess critically the alternative structural proposals for 1 and 2 Timothy and Titus, and should be able to discuss the differences between viewing the three letters individually or as a cluster.

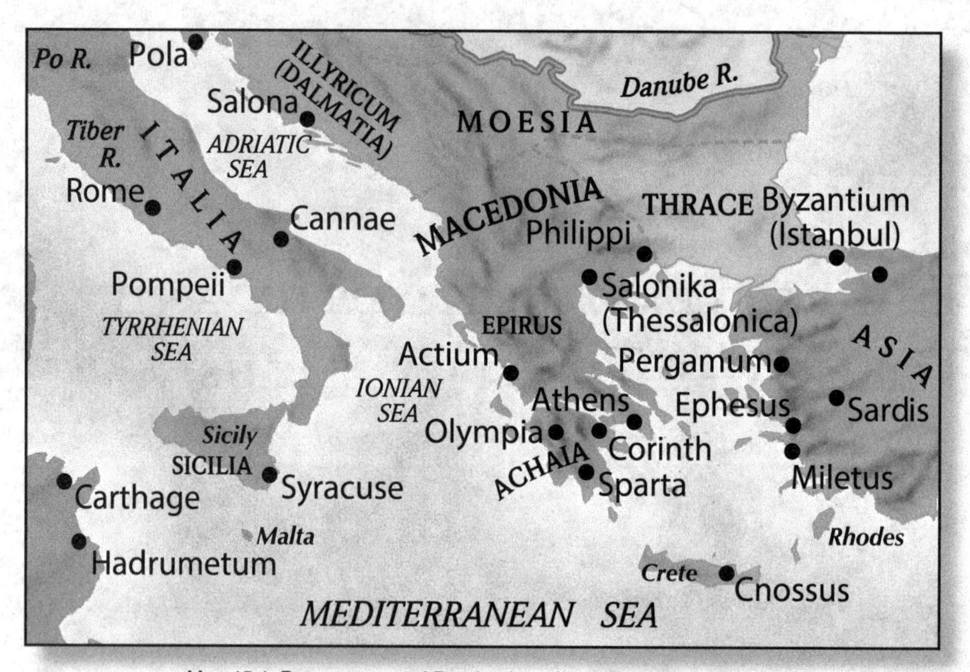

Map 15.1: Provenance and Destination of 1–2 Timothy and Titus

KEY FACTS

Author:	Paul
Date:	Early to mid-AD 60s
Provenance:	Macedonia (1 Timothy); Rome (2 Timothy); unknown (Titus)
Destination:	Ephesus (1 Timothy; 2 Timothy); Crete (Titus)
Occasion:	Instructions for apostolic delegates on how to deal with various issues in the church
Purpose:	To instruct and equip Timothy and Titus in their role as apostolic delegates
Theme:	Establishing the church for the postapostolic period
Key Verses:	2 Tim 4:1–2

INTRODUCTION

THE LETTERS TO Timothy and Titus make a unique and indispensable contribution to the writings of the NT.[1] Supplementing Acts, they provide vital instructions regarding qualifications for church leaders and other important matters for governing and administering the church. Most likely, they were the last letters Paul wrote during his long missionary career and were penned toward the end of his apostolic ministry. As early as in the Muratorian Fragment (later second century), the special character of the letters to Timothy and Titus was acknowledged, and they were designated as having to do with "the regulation of ecclesiastical discipline."[2] The designation "Pastoral Epistles" apparently dates back to D. N. Berdot, who called Titus a "Pastoral Epistle" in 1703, and P. Anton of Halle, who in 1726 delivered a series of lectures on 1 and 2 Timothy and Titus entitled "The Pastoral Epistles."[3]

In spite of these three letters being traditionally known as the Pastoral Epistles, a trend away from this designation has emerged in scholarship, and rightly so.[4] While Timothy and Titus are often viewed as paradigmatic (lead/senior) pastors of local congregations, it should be noted that the role of these two men was not technically that of a permanent, resident pastor of a church. Rather, Timothy and Titus were Paul's apostolic delegates who were temporarily assigned to their present locations in order to deal with particular problems that had arisen and needed special attention.[5] For this reason the letters to Timothy and Titus are not merely letters giving advice to younger ministers or manuals of church order. They are Paul's instructions to his special delegates, set toward the closing of the apostolic era at a time when the aging apostle would have felt a keen responsibility to ensure the orderly transition from the apostolic to the postapostolic period. As such, they contain relevant and authoritative apostolic instruction for the governance of the church at any time and place.

As discussed below, it appears that Paul wrote 1 Timothy and Titus after his release from his first Roman imprisonment (see chap. 14 on the Prison Epistles above) but before a second, considerably more severe, Roman imprisonment. During this second imprisonment

---

[1] Parts of this chapter draw on A. J. Köstenberger, "1–2 Timothy, Titus," in *Expositor's Bible Commentary*, vol. 12: *Ephesians—Philemon*, rev. ed. (Grand Rapids, MI: Zondervan, 2005), 487–625; and idem, *Commentary on 1-2 Timothy and Titus*, BTCP (Nashville, TN: B&H Academic, 2017). Note the most recent update on research on the letters: I. H. Marshall, "The Pastoral Epistles in Recent Study," in *Entrusted with the Gospel: Paul's Theology in the Pastoral Epistles*, ed. A. J. Köstenberger and T. L. Wilder (Nashville, TN: B&H Academic, 2010), 268–324. Ongoing updates on newly published works are posted at www.pastoralepistles.com.

[2] L. T. Johnson, *Letters to Paul's Delegates: 1 Timothy, 2 Timothy, Titus*, The New Testament in Context (Valley Forge, PA: Trinity Press International, 1996), 3; G. W. Knight, *Commentary on the Pastoral Epistles*, NIGTC (Grand Rapids, MI: Eerdmans, 1992), 3.

[3] D. Guthrie, *The Pastoral Epistles*, TNTC, 2nd ed. (Grand Rapids, MI: Eerdmans, 1990), 11.

[4] Note P. H. Towner (*The Letters to Timothy and Titus*, NICNT [Grand Rapids, MI: Eerdmans, 2006], 88–89), who believes it is time to bid "farewell to 'the Pastoral Epistles'" due to the restraining nature of the nomenclature. He prefers to speak of Paul's "letters to his coworkers."

[5] See G. D. Fee, *1 and 2 Timothy, Titus*, NIBCNT 13 (Peabody, MA: Hendrickson, 1988), 21 (though see the interaction with Fee's *ad hoc* hermeneutic further below).

in Rome, Paul wrote 2 Timothy, which turned out to be the last of his letters included in the canon. It is not known whether 1 Timothy or Titus was written first.[6] In the canon, the order is "1 Timothy, 2 Timothy, Titus," even though the actual chronological order of writing was almost certainly "1 Timothy, Titus, 2 Timothy" or "Titus, 1 Timothy, 2 Timothy."[7] For our present purposes, we follow the canonical order, treating 2 Timothy prior to Titus and in conjunction with 1 Timothy, since 1 and 2 Timothy are addressed to the same individual and the same church; thus, both letters entail a similar set of introductory issues best discussed jointly.[8]

A significant question for biblical-theological research in the letters to Timothy and Titus is the extent to which the three ought to be treated as a unit. Recent NT scholarship has rightly cautioned against referencing the three letters as an indivisible corpus and thus placing them into an interrelationship that hinders each letter from being read on its own merits.[9] Given a stance of pseudonymous authorship, of course, it is common to propose that the three were indeed meant to be read together,[10] but on the assumption of Pauline authorship the letters should be taken at face value as three distinct compositions written to two distinct recipients in two distinct locales. At the same time, certain characteristics of the three missives do bind them together over against other Pauline Epistles (e.g., the "trustworthy sayings" and the status of the recipients as apostolic delegates). In the end, it

---

[6] See W. D. Mounce, *The Pastoral Epistles*, WBC 46 (Nashville, TN: Nelson, 2000), lxi. He adds, "It is not possible to determine whether Paul wrote 1 Timothy or Titus first. All that I am comfortable saying is that the similarity of language between 1 Timothy and Titus may suggest that they were written at approximately the same time" (p. lxii).

[7] The Muratorian Fragment (later second century) has the order Titus, 1 Timothy, 2 Timothy, presumably both to place 2 Timothy last as Paul's final letter and to keep the letters to Timothy together; J. D. Quinn (*The Letter to Titus*, AB 35 [Garden City, NY: Doubleday, 1990], 3) adopts this order in his work in that it is the oldest attested. I. H. Marshall hypothesizes that 2 Timothy was written first, and 1 Timothy and Titus were written by someone other than Paul after his death (*Pastoral Epistles*, 92), and so addresses the three letters in that order. Similarly, Johnson (*Letters to Paul's Delegates*) deals first with 2 Timothy and then 1 Timothy and Titus.

[8] The sections on Authorship, Date and Provenance, and Occasion integrate a discussion of all three letters to Timothy and Titus under a single heading due to the interrelated nature of the questions addressed by these particular introductory issues.

[9] See the survey in J. Herzer, "Abschied vom Konsens? Die Pseudepigraphie der Pastoralbriefe als Herausforderung an die neutestamentliche Wissenschaft," *TLZ* 129 (2004): 1267–82. Herzer has objected to treating the three letters as a corpus, fleshing out this objection in the realm of the letters' opponents ("Juden–Christen–Gnostiker: Zur Gegnerproblematik der Pastoralbriefe," *BTZ* 25 [2008]: 162–66), the letters' ecclesiology ("Rearranging the 'House of God': A New Perspective on the Pastoral Epistles," in Empsychoi Logoi—*Religious Innovations in Antiquity: Studies in Honour of Pieter Willem van der Horst* [ed. A. Houtman, et al.; Leiden, Netherlands: Brill, 2008]), and the letters' portrayal of piety ("'Das Geheimnis der Frömmigkeit'—Sprache und Stil der Pastoralbriefe im Kontext hellenistisch-römischer Popularphilosophie—eine methodische Problemanzeige," *TQ* 187 [2007]: 309–29). For other recent works questioning the corpus-reading of the three letters, note M. Engelmann, *Unzertrennliche Drillinge? Motivsemantische Untersuchungen zum literarischen Verhältnis der Pastoralbriefe*, BZNW (Berlin, Germany: Walter de Gruyter, 2012), 192; R. Fuchs, *Unerwartete Unterschiede. Müssen wir unsere Ansichten über die Pastoralbriefe revidieren?* Bibelwissenschaftliche Monographien 12 (Wuppertal: R. Brockhaus, 2003); L. T. Johnson, *Letters to Paul's Delegates: 1 Timothy, 2 Timothy, Titus,* The New Testament in Context (Valley Forge, PA: Trinity Press International, 1996), 7–9; idem, *Letters*, 63–64; P. H. Towner, *The Letters to Timothy and Titus,* NICNT (Grand Rapids, MI: Eerdmans, 2006), 88–89.

[10] Some, of course, affirm Pauline authorship for at least one of the letters, but not all three. Others deny Pauline authorship for all three letters, but see the missives as variously authored.

seems best to engage the three letters not as a corpus but as a "cluster," being sensitive to both the things that bind them together and the things that make them distinct. Listening to each letter on its own merits is always important, but for certain issues that are more directly tied to the situation of a particular letter, it is more necessary to allow each one to have its own voice. The letters' common authorship and the common status of their recipients arguably allows a treatment that collectively considers the contribution of the entire cluster.

HISTORY

Author

External Evidence The authenticity of Paul's correspondence with Timothy and Titus went unchallenged until the nineteenth century.[11] In all probability Paul's Letters to Timothy were known to Polycarp (ca. AD 117), who almost certainly quoted from 1 Tim 6:7 and 10 (Pol., *Phil.* 4.1).[12] The first unmistakable attestations are found in Athenagoras (*Supplication* 37.1; ca. 180) and Theophilus (*Autol.* 3.14; later second century), both of whom cite 1 Timothy 2:1–2 and allude to other passages in the letters to Timothy and Titus. Irenaeus (ca. AD 130–200), in several passages in his work *Against Heresies* (see 1.pref.; 1.23.4; 2.14.7; 3.1.1), cited each of the letters and identified their author as the apostle Paul. Clement of Alexandria (ca. AD 150–215; *Strom.* 2.11) noted that some Gnostics who perceived themselves to be the targets of the denunciation of 1 Timothy 6:20–21 rejected Paul's Letters to Timothy. In the later second century, the Muratorian Fragment included all three letters in the Pauline corpus.[13]

Marshall's overall assessment of the patristic evidence regarding the letters to Timothy and Titus is especially noteworthy since he does not hold to Paul's authorship: "It can be concluded that the PE [Pastoral Epistles] were known to Christian writers from early in the second century and that there is no evidence of rejection of them by any writers except for Marcion."[14] Consequently, the letters to Timothy and Titus became part of the

---

[11] For a brief survey, see R. F. Collins, *Letters That Paul Did Not Write* (Wilmington, DE: Michael Glazier, 1988), 89–90. Collins discusses the earliest challengers of the authenticity of the letters to Timothy and Titus, naming Schmidt (1804), Schleiermacher (1807), Eichhorn (1812), Baur (1835), and Holtzmann (1885). For more detail, see the history of interpretation provided by L. T. Johnson, *The First and Second Letters to Timothy*, AB 35A (New Haven, CT: Yale University Press, 2001), who discusses the nineteenth-century debate over authorship on pp. 42–54.

[12] See the discussion in Marshall, *Pastoral Epistles*, 3–8 (including the tables on pp. 4–5).

[13] For recent discussion of this important document, including a defense of its second-century dating, see E. J. Schnabel, "The Muratorian Fragment: The State of Research," *JETS* 57 (2014): 231–64.

[14] Marshall, *Pastoral Epistles*, 8. Marshall discusses the evidence from the early church on pp. 2–8; other surveys of the evidence include that of J. H. Bernard, *The Pastoral Epistles*, CGTC (Cambridge, UK: University Press, 1899), xi–xxi; J. D. James, *The Genuineness and Authorship of the Pastoral Epistles* (London, England: Longmans, 1906); Mounce, *Pastoral Epistles*, lxiv–lxix. A helpful resource for the student is found in C. Looks, *Das Anvertraute bewahren: Die Rezeption der Pastoralbriefe im 2. Jahrhundert*, Münchner theologische Beiträge (Munich, Germany: Herbert Utz, 1999); on pp. 481–90, Looks works through the letters to Timothy and Titus verse by verse, listing for each verse the places it is referred to in second-century Christian writings, along with an evaluation of how certain it is that the writer is actually referring to that verse.

established NT canon of the church, and Paul's authorship of these was not seriously questioned for a millennium and a half.[15]

Pseudonymity and Internal Evidence It was only in the nineteenth century that an increasing number of commentators began to allege that the letters to Timothy and Titus constituted an instance of pseudonymous writing in which a later follower attributed his own work to his revered teacher in order to perpetuate that person's teaching and influence.[16] At first, this view may seem surprising since all three letters to Timothy and Titus open with the unequivocal attribution, "Paul, an apostle of Christ Jesus," or a similar phrase (1 Tim 1:1; 2 Tim 1:1; Titus 1:1). It seems difficult to fathom that these letters could have been falsely attributed to the apostle Paul by their author(s) and subsequently accepted into the NT canon as Pauline by the church—both of which supposedly took place without any error or intent to deceive on the church's part.[17]

Indeed, as will be seen, Paul's authorship of the letters to Timothy and Titus is by far the best conclusion based on all the available evidence and in light of several major problems attached to any pseudonymity position, which are here addressed by answering several questions.[18] First, was pseudonymous letter writing an acceptable first-century practice; if so, was this practice devoid of deceptive intent?[19] Second, would the church knowingly have accepted pseudonymous letters into the canon? Third, is pseudonymity more plausible than authenticity?[20]

---

[15] Mounce helpfully points out, "The authenticity of the PE [Pastoral Epistles] was not questioned until the nineteenth century. This does not make the raising of this question wrong; but it must be admitted that it is a modern concern" (lxix).

[16] A recent example of this position is found in B. D. Ehrman, *Forgery and Counterforgery: The Use of Literary Deceit in Early Christian Polemics* (Oxford, UK: Oxford University Press, 2012). Ehrman discusses the letters to Timothy and Titus at length in his chapters on "Later Forgeries Dealing with Eschatology" (esp. pp. 191–222) and "Forgeries Involving Church Organization and Leadership" (esp. pp. 367–84). Ehrman's position is that "the real, but unknown, author lied about his own identity in order to bring the apostolic voice to bear on a set of issues that were very much a matter of intense debate in his own day" (p. 384).

[17] Marshall (*Pastoral Epistles*, 83–84) holds a variation of the pseudonymity view which he terms "allonymity" or "allepigraphy," the view that the letters to Timothy and Titus were written "under another name" without intent to deceive.

[18] See more extended recent responses to the theory of pseudonymous authorship of the letters to Timothy and Titus in E. J. Schnabel, "Paul, Timothy, and Titus: The Assumption of a Pseudonymous Author and of Pseudonymous Recipients in the Light of Literary, Theological, and Historical Evidence," in *Do Historical Matters Matter to Faith? A Critical Appraisal of Modern and Postmodern Approaches to Scripture*, ed. J. K. Hoffmeier and D. R. Magary (Wheaton, IL: Crossway, 2012); T. L. Wilder, "Pseudonymity, the New Testament, and the Pastoral Epistles," in *Entrusted with the Gospel: Paul's Theology in the Pastoral Epistles* (Nashville, TN: B&H, 2010), 28–51; idem, "Does the Bible Contain Forgeries?," in *In Defense of the Bible: A Comprehensive Apologetic for the Authority of Scripture*, ed. S. B. Cowan and T. L. Wilder (Nashville, TN: B&H, 2013), 166–81. Cf. D. A. Carson, "Pseudonymity and Pseudepigraphy," in *DNTB*, 856–64.

[19] For a forceful argument against this contention, see E. E. Ellis, "Pseudonymity and Canonicity of New Testament Documents," in *Worship, Theology and Ministry in the Early Church: Essays in Honor of Ralph P. Martin*, ed. M. J. Wilkins and T. Page, JSNTSup 87 (Sheffield, UK: JSOT, 1992), 212–24; see also T. L. Wilder, *Pseudonymity, the New Testament, and Deception: An Inquiry into Intention and Deception* (Lanham, MD: University Press of America, 2004; rev. ed. forthcoming).

[20] For a thorough discussion of these issues in connection with the letters to Timothy and Titus, a still-helpful resource is D. Guthrie, *New Testament Introduction*, 4th rev. ed. (Downers Grove, IL: InterVarsity, 1990), 607–49, 1011–28. Helpful for further research is A. D. Baum, "Authorship and Pseudepigraphy in Early Christian Literature: A Translation of the Most

Regarding the first two questions, the evidence suggests pseudonymity was exceedingly rare in the case of ancient letters,[21] a genre which by its very nature entails interpersonal communication.[22] Not only is there little evidence for the common acceptance of pseudonymous letters during the apostolic period, there seems to have been considerable concern that letters might have been forged (2 Thess 2:2: "a letter as if from us").[23] Consequently, Paul in his earlier letters repeatedly refers to his own distinctive hand (1 Cor 16:21; Gal 6:11; Col 4:18; 2 Thess 3:17; Phlm 19), though admittedly the letters to Timothy and Titus do not include such an *autographon*. Both *3 Corinthians* and the *Epistle to the Laodiceans* are transparent attempts to fill in a perceived gap in canonical revelation (see 1 Cor 5:9; 2 Cor 2:4; 7:8; Col 4:16).[24] Serapion, bishop of Antioch (died AD 211), pointedly distinguishes between apostolic writings and those that "falsely bear their names" (*pseudepigrapha*; cited in Eusebius, *Hist. eccl.* 6.12.3). In light of this evidence, it is unlikely that the early church would have knowingly accepted pseudonymous letters into the Christian canon.[25]

Important Source Texts and an Annotated Bibliography," in *Paul and Pseudepigraphy*, ed. S. E. Porter and G. P. Fewster, Pauline Studies 8 (Leiden, Netherlands: Brill, 2013), 11–63.

[21] R. Bauckham ("Pseudo-Apostolic Letters," JBL 107 [1988]: 487) notes the rarity of apocryphal or pseudepigraphical apostolic letters in relation to other genres and conjectures that the reason for this "may well have been the sheer difficulty of using a pseudepigraphical letter to perform the same functions as an authentic letter."

[22] The labels "epistle" and "letter" for the *Epistle of Jeremy* and the *Letter of Aristeas* are misleading because neither writing is properly a letter: the former is a homily, the latter an account of the circumstances surrounding the translation of the Hebrew Scriptures into Greek (Bauckham ["Pseudo-Apostolic Letters," 478] considers it "misclassified" and a "dedicated treatise"). Bauckham also discusses several didactic letters such as 1 Enoch 92–105; *Epistle of Jeremiah*; *Baruch*; and *2 Baruch* 78–87. See Wilder, "Does the Bible Contain Forgeries?," 167.

[23] Wilder, "Does the Bible Contain Forgeries?," 170.

[24] Bauckham ("Pseudo-Apostolic Letters," 485) calls *Laodiceans* "a remarkably incompetent attempt to fill the gap. . . . nothing but a patchwork of Pauline sentences and phrases from other letters, mainly Philippians." *Third Corinthians* is part of the late second-century *Acts of Paul*.

[25] See, e.g., T. D. Lea, "The Early Christian View of Pseudepigraphic Writings," *JETS* 27 (1984): 65–75. This is true despite Metzger's conclusion that "since the use of the literary form of pseudepigraphy need not be regarded as necessarily involving fraudulent intent, it cannot be argued that the character of inspiration excludes the possibility of pseudepigraphy among the canonical writings" ("Literary Forgeries and Canonical Pseudepigrapha," *JBL* 91 [1972]: 22). L. R. Donelson, himself a proponent of pseudonymous authorship of the letters to Timothy and Titus, categorically states, "No one ever seems to have accepted a document as religiously and philosophically prescriptive which was known to be forged. I do not know of a single example" (*Pseudepigraphy and Ethical Arguments in the Pastorals*, HUT 22 [Tübingen, Germany: Mohr Siebeck, 1986], 11). See esp. J. Duff, "A Reconsideration of Pseudepigraphy in Early Christianity" (Ph.D. thesis, Oxford University, 1998), who concludes (1) that the value of a text was closely linked to its true authorship; (2) that pseudonymity was generally viewed as a deceitful practice; and (3) that texts thought to be pseudonymous were marginalized. Duff also points out that the question of pseudonymity is important for interpretation because one will interpret the letters to Timothy and Titus differently if one views them as second-century forgeries rather than first-century authentic compositions. This is against J. D. G. Dunn, "The Problem of Pseudonymity," in *The Living Word* (Philadelphia, PA: Fortress, 1988), 65–85, who claims that authoritative tradition was not regarded as fixed and static but as living tradition continued to be reworked. According to Dunn, the criterion for acceptability was not authorship by the author of record but continuity and coherence of the newer expression of a living tradition with preceding ones (Dunn cites Matthew's and Luke's use of Mark and the Chronicler's use of Samuel-Kings as canonical examples). In this vein, Dunn views the letters to Timothy and Titus as "appropriate and authentic re-expression of the Pauline heritage and tradition," which the church acknowledged as

Regarding the third question ("Is pseudonymity more plausible than authenticity?"), the first important issue to consider is the significant number of *historical particularities* featured in these letters. While it is possible that a later imitator of Paul fabricated these pieces of information to lend greater verisimilitude to a given piece of writing, it seems more likely that these references reflect actual circumstances in Paul's life and ministry.[26] Some object that the historical details in 1–2 Timothy and Titus cannot be easily fitted into the chronology in Acts. This is true, but these details can be accommodated without much difficulty at a later time toward the end of Paul's career.[27] In fact, the notion of pseudonymous authorship is rendered less plausible because it would likely entail a pseudonymous readership as well (double pseudonymity), not to mention lack of historicity of the plethora of historical details in these letters. Consistency would seem to demand that pseudonymity envelop a given letter in its totality (which seems difficult to sustain in the case of letters such as those to Timothy and Titus).[28]

The second piece of evidence often offered by those questioning the Pauline authorship of 1–2 Timothy and Titus is *differences in style and vocabulary when compared with other Pauline letters*.[29] Paul's letters to Timothy and Titus feature words not used elsewhere in Paul's undisputed writings,[30] while characteristic Pauline terminology is lacking.[31] What

---

such based on the "Jewish understanding and practice of tradition of a living force" (p. 84). However, one looks in vain for confirmation of this understanding of the letters to Timothy and Titus in the patristic writings.

[26] Against Bauckham ("Pseudo-Apostolic Letters," 492), who believes that the author of the letters to Timothy and Titus "has thought himself into situations in Paul's ministry and . . . has filled out whatever historical information was available to him with historical fiction." Bauckham even ventures the conjecture that Timothy might have written 1–2 Timothy himself (p. 494). Also against N. Brox ("Zu den persönlichen Notizen der Pastoralbriefe," *BZ* 13 [1969]: 76–94), who believes the personal references constitute "typical situations in the ecclesiastical office, which are historicized and attributed to Paul." Also against L. R. Donelson, who straightforwardly argues that in the letters to Timothy and Titus, a pseudonymous author "is trying to deceive," and does so by employing verisimilitude as a standard pseudepigraphical technique; "he is writing fiction, and it is not difficult to include a few life-like moments" (*Pseudepigraphy and Ethical Arguments in the Pastorals*, 54).

[27] Wilder, "Does the Bible Contain Forgeries?," 176.

[28] See on this Schnabel, "Paul, Timothy, and Titus," 396–97.

[29] See Mounce, *Pastoral Epistles*, xcix–cxviii; Marshall, *Pastoral Epistles*, 60–61; Johnson, *First and Second Letters to Timothy*, 60, 68–72; and Schnabel, "Paul, Timothy, and Titus," 386–91, who points out that "the notion that an author has a consistent style is a romantic notion of the modern Western world" and asserts that "it is the occasion that determines the style adopted" (p. 389). See also A. D. Baum, "Semantic Variation within the Corpus Paulinum: Linguistic Considerations Concerning the Richer Vocabulary of the Pastoral Epistles." *TynBul* 51 (2008): 271–92; and A. W. Pitts, "Style and Pseudonymity in Pauline Scholarship: A Register Based Configuration," in *Paul and Pseudepigraphy*, ed. S. E. Porter and G. P. Fewster; Pauline Studies 8 (Leiden, Netherlands: Brill, 2013), 113–52. Pitts notes that "studies in the Pastoral letters famously employ several (mainly) linguistic criteria to detect shifts in style on the typically unargued assumption that a shift in style necessarily entails a shift in authorship" and proceeds to bring this assumption into question "based on theoretical and field research in sociolinguistics" (p. 113). For a comparison of lexical similarities among the letters to Timothy and Titus, see chart 71: "Similarities between the Pastoral Epistles," in L. Kierspel, *Charts on the Life, Letters, and Theology of Paul* (Grand Rapids, MI: Kregel, 2012), 133–35, 234–35.

[30] E.g., εὐσεβεία ("godliness"), σώφρων ("self-controlled"), or ἐπιφάνεια in the place of παρουσία ("coming," referring to Christ's return).

[31] E.g., ἐλευθερία ("freedom"), σάρξ ("flesh," in contrast to "Spirit"), σταυρός ("cross"), and δικαιοσύνη θεοῦ ("righteousness of God"). Cf. the list in Marshall, *Pastoral Epistles*, 104–6, who cites as missing from 1–2 Timothy and Titus (1) the fatherhood of God; (2) the power and witness of the Spirit; (3) union with Jesus Christ and spiritual resurrection

is more, the letters to Timothy and Titus include a high number of unique words (*hapax legomena*) not found elsewhere in the NT.[32] There are also differences in sentence length, word order, and the use of conjunctions and particles.[33] However, establishing authorship on the basis of stylistic differences is fraught with difficulty and remains notoriously inconclusive.[34] Not only is there a difference between public letters sent to congregations and personal correspondence addressed to individuals,[35] Paul's desire to preserve his apostolic legacy, which likely stands behind the letters to Timothy and Titus, would adequately account for the emphasis on church leadership and the faithful passing on of apostolic tradition found in these letters.[36] What is more, while Paul's earlier letters owe more to conceptual orality, regularly featuring parentheses and anacolutha, the letters to Timothy and Titus are closer to conceptual writing. This suggests that "their author has expressed himself more carefully and probably had more time at his disposal than the author . . . of the other ten Paulines."[37]

Third, it is often claimed that the *church structure* in the letters to Timothy and Titus reflects the church in the early second century rather than the first, most notably as set forth by Ignatius of Antioch (ca. 35–110), who advocates a monarchial episcopate and

---

from death in sin; and (4) freedom from the law; and the discussion in Mounce, *Pastoral Epistles*, lxxxviii–xcvii (including the chart on p. xc).

[32] E.g., ἀνδραποδιστής ("slave-trader") and ἐπιόρκος ("perjurer," both in 1 Tim 1:12); and ἀφθορία ("integrity," Titus 2:7). See Guthrie, *New Testament Introduction*, 619, who puts the number at 175; Harrison, *Problem of the Pastoral Epistles*, whose count is 176; and Mounce, *Pastoral Epistles*, xcix–cxviii, who provides an extensive analysis of the data as well as a critique of Harrison's work. Kierspel, *Charts on the Life, Letters, and Theology of Paul*, 156, says there are 175 NT *hapax legomena* and 131 additional words not found in the other Pauline Letters. See also the lexical data (including special vocabulary) provided in A. J. Köstenberger and R. P. Bouchoc, *The Book Study Concordance* (Nashville, TN: B&H Academic, 2003), 1172–1234.

[33] See the literature cited in Schnabel, "Paul, Timothy, and Titus," 387, nn. 14–15.

[34] For an incisive treatment, see the still-relevant B. M. Metzger, "A Reconsideration of Certain Arguments against the Pauline Authorship of the Pastoral Epistles," *ExpTim* 70 (1958): 91–94 (see esp. the four questions on p. 93). See also Wilder, "Does the Bible Contain Forgeries?," 173: "Stylistic arguments tend to be quite subjective and unimpressive. . . . Furthermore, the Pastoral Epistles are simply too brief to determine with accuracy the writing habits of a particular author"; and the similar assessment by Schnabel, "Paul, Timothy, and Titus," 387–88. See also Baum, "Semantic Variation within the *Corpus Paulinum*," 271–92 (including an extensive word list), who shows that 1–2 Timothy and Titus feature "a much higher percentage of distinctive words than the rest of the Pauline Letters" (p. 277).

[35] See esp. M. Prior, *Paul the Letter-Writer and the Second Letter to Timothy*, JSNTSup 23 (Sheffield, UK: JSOT, 1989); idem, "Revisiting the Pastoral Epistles," *ScrB* 31 (2001): 2–19, who points out that most of Paul's Letters appear to be co-authored ("Revisiting," 14); and Johnson, *First and Second Letters to Timothy*, 55–99.

[36] In addition, Paul may have employed amanuenses, as he did at other occasions. See E. R. Richards, *The Secretary in the Letters of Paul*, WUNT 2/42 (Tübingen, Germany: Mohr Siebeck, 1991); idem, *Paul and First-Century Letter Writing*; Ellis, "Pastoral Letters," 663–64; and Schnabel, "Paul, Timothy, and Titus," 390.

[37] Baum, "Semantic Variation," 290, with reference to M. Reiser, "Paulus als Stilist," *SEÅ* 66 (2001): 151–65. But see the summary and critique by Marshall, "Pastoral Epistles in Recent Study," 291–92, who objects that the synonyms advanced by Baum are not close enough and that the vocabulary in the letters to Timothy and Titus "indicates a process of thought different from that of the other letters" (p. 292). Marshall also notes that Baum's hypothesis does not account for the smaller number of particles in the letters to Timothy and Titus when compared with the undisputed Pauline Letters (ibid.).

a three-tiered ecclesiastical hierarchy (see *Eph.* 2.2; *Magn.* 3.1; *Trall.* 2.2; 3.1).[38] But this second-century model is markedly different from that in the letters to Timothy and Titus, where the terms "overseer" (*episkopos*) and "elder" (*presbyteros*) refer to one and the same office (Titus 1:5, 7; see Acts 20:17, 28).[39] As far as an interest in proper congregational leadership is concerned, Paul and Barnabas appointed elders in the churches they had established prior to the year 50 (Acts 14:23; see 11:30; 15:2; 20:28–31; 21:18), so there is nothing novel in Paul's instruction to Titus to "appoint elders in every town" (Titus 1:5). Subsequent to the reference in Acts 14:23, in a letter only slightly earlier than those to Timothy and Titus, Paul addressed one of his Prison Epistles to the "overseers and deacons" at Philippi (Phil 1:1). This coheres precisely with the two-tiered structure presupposed in the letters to Timothy and Titus (see 1 Timothy 3).[40] Also, the hierarchy is different from the first century to the second century, and one detects development from 1 Timothy to Ignatius.

Fourth, proponents of pseudonymity maintain that there are insurmountable *theological and conceptual differences* between Paul's earlier letters and the letters to Timothy and Titus.[41] Some argue that references to the gospel as "sound teaching," "the faith," or "the truth" (1 Tim 1:10, 19; 3:9, 13; 4:1, 6; 6:3, 10; 2 Tim 1:13; 4:3; Titus 1:9, 13; 2:1) reflect a later point in time when the body of Christian teaching was viewed as a fixed set of creedal beliefs. However, there is no reason why Paul toward the end of his life should not look at the gospel as a precious stewardship to be passed on to the next generation of leaders. What is more, there are some indications that Paul even earlier viewed the gospel in similar terms (e.g., Rom 16:7; 1 Cor 11:2; 4:17; 15:1–3). Others contend that the references to "godliness" (εὐσεβεία) in the letters to Timothy and Titus indicate a more advanced stage subsequent to Paul's martyrdom. However, it is certainly possible that Paul here upholds a virtue that was highly valued in the surrounding Greco-Roman culture in the belief that it was "truly attainable only in Christ."[42] Similar arguments can be made with regard to the references to the church as "God's household," "epiphany" (ἐπιφανεία) language, and references to both God and Christ as Savior.[43]

---

[38] See Mounce (*Pastoral Epistles*, lxxxvi–lxxxviii, 186–92), who cites Polycarp, Clement, Clement of Alexandria, and Irenaeus as referring to a two-tiered structure, using ἐπίσκοπος and πρεσβύτερος interchangeably.

[39] See B. L. Merkle, *The Elder and Overseer: One Office in the Early Church*, Studies in Biblical Literature 57 (New York, NY: Peter Lang, 2003). F. M. Young ventured the "admittedly tentative" hypothesis that the origins of the *episkopos* and the *presbuteros* are distinct. But Young's interpretation of the letters to Timothy and Titus in light of Ignatius (died ca. 110) rather than vice versa seems precarious if not methodologically fallacious ("On *Episkopos* and *Presbyteros*," *JTS* 45 [1994]: 142–48).

[40] See A. J. Köstenberger, "Church Government," in *Encyclopedia of Christian Civilization*, ed. G. T. Kurian (Malden, MA: Wiley-Blackwell, 2011), 1:543–51.

[41] See the discussion in Schnabel, "Paul, Timothy, and Titus," 391–96.

[42] Towner, *Letters to Timothy and Titus*, 174, cited in Schnabel, "Paul, Timothy, and Titus," 394.

[43] Schnabel, "Paul, Timothy, and Titus," 393–95. See, e.g., D. C. Verner, *The Household of God: The Social World of the Pastoral Epistles*, SBLDS 71 (Chico, CA: Scholars Press, 1983), who argues that the metaphor of the "household of God" is used to enforce the traditional patriarchal structure of the household within the church in response to the charge that the church is subverting the political structures of the state; and D. G. Horrell, "From ἀδελφοί to οἶκος θεοῦ: Social Transforma-

The theology of the letters to Timothy and Titus is not identical in form to that of Paul's other letters, but it can plausibly be viewed as complementary, not contradictory, and as no less Pauline than the earlier undisputed letters. As E. Schnabel contends,

> The absence of Pauline theological themes from the Pastoral Epistles (e.g., the cross, the Holy Spirit, the flesh/spirit dichotomy) does not prove inauthenticity. There is no reason why Paul should mention the whole range of basic theological topics in all of his letters, particularly in letters to coworkers who know his theology. It is only if it could be shown that the theology of the Pastoral Epistles *contradicts* Paul's undisputed letters that we would have a serious problem.[44]

In light of this set of historical, literary, and theological considerations, the conclusion seems reasonable that the letters to Timothy and Titus "are much more akin to the accepted letters of Paul than they are to the known pseudonymous documents that circulated in the early church."[45] This is not to deny that there are legitimate differences between Paul's earlier undisputed letters and the letters to Timothy and Titus. Clearly, 1 and 2 Timothy and Titus were written at a later juncture in the history and mission of the early church and aim to contextualize the Christian message in the midst of a unique set of circumstances. This is the genuine insight underlying pseudonymity proposals. However, there seems no compelling evidence to push the letters to Timothy and Titus beyond Paul's lifetime into the post-Pauline period. Historically, literarily, and theologically, these three fit at least as comfortably toward the end of Paul's ministry as they do in the period following his death.[46]

If Paul, then, was the author of the letters to Timothy and Titus, it is necessary to remember some of the major biographical details in his life prior to his writing them. Paul came from "the thriving commercial and intellectual center"[47] of Tarsus (Acts 9:11; 21:39;

---

tion in Pauline Christianity," *JBL* 120 (2001): 293–311, who contends that whereas Paul addresses believers as "brothers," the pseudo-Pauline Letters use the model of a hierarchically structured household.

[44] Schnabel, "Paul, Timothy, and Titus," 392.

[45] D. A. Carson and D. J. Moo, *An Introduction to the New Testament*, 2nd ed. (Grand Rapids, MI: Zondervan, 2005), 563. Similarly, D. Guthrie, "The Development of the Idea of Canonical Pseudepigrapha in New Testament Criticism," *VE* 1 (1962): 43–59. One further argument is mentioned by G. D. Fee ("Reflections on Church Order in the Pastoral Epistles, with Further Reflection on the Hermeneutics of *Ad Hoc* Documents," *JETS* 28 [1985]: 141): the lack of a satisfactory answer to the question, "Why three letters? That is, given 1 Timothy, why did a pseudepigrapher write Titus, and given 1 Timothy and Titus and their concerns, why 2 Timothy at all?" Similarly, T. Manabu, "Der zweite Timotheus als letzter Gefangenschaftsbrief," *Kwansei Gakuin University Humanities Review* 11 (2006): 2. Manabu also draws attention to the fact that 2 Timothy never refers to 1 Timothy, which would be curious if the three letters were intended as a letter collection (he cites 1–2 Peter and 1–2 Thessalonians as contrasting examples; cf. 2 Pet 3:1; 2 Thess 2:2). In response to "Why three letters?," J. D. Quinn and W. C. Wacker, *The First and Second Letters to Timothy*, ECC (Grand Rapids, MI: Eerdmans, 2000), 20, point to the genre of letter collections, maintaining that the Pastorals "as a collection would have been received and read not as individual letters from the Paul of history but as a 'characterization' of the great apostle and his teaching for the new generation"; and R. I. Pervo (*The Making of Paul: Constructions of the Apostle in Early Christianity* [Minneapolis, MN: Fortress, 2010], 84) simply states that three letters is "a satisfactory and symbolic number, implying a true collection."

[46] Cf. P. H. Towner, "Pauline Theology or Pauline Tradition in the Pastoral Epistles: The Question of Method," *TynBul* 46 (1995): 287–314.

[47] R. N. Longenecker, *The Ministry and Message of Paul* (Grand Rapids, MI: Zondervan, 1971), 24.

22:3), "the greatest of all the cities of Cilicia"[48] about which the first-century geographer Strabo stated, "It not only has a flourishing population but also is most powerful, thus keeping up the reputation of the mother-city."[49] Paul studied under the eminent first-century Jewish rabbi Gamaliel I (Acts 22:3; see 5:34–39) and zealously persecuted the early Christians (Acts 7:56–8:3; 9:1–2; 1 Cor 15:9; Phil 3:6). One encounter with the risen Christ on the road to Damascus (Acts 9:1–9; 22:6–10; 26:12–18), however, caused a paradigm shift in Paul's thinking and a radical reorientation of the course of his life. He who had assumed Jesus to be a messianic pretender accursed by God now recognized him as God's Messiah (Gal 3:10–14; 2 Cor 5:21). And he who had been the church's most committed nemesis (see 1 Tim 1:15–17) now became its most fervent champion. After several years of relative quiet as well as possible missionary work (Gal 1:17–24),[50] Paul was recruited to participate in the early church's Gentile mission (Acts 11:25–26). He quickly became the leader of this mission and gathered around himself a group of coworkers that included Timothy and Titus.

While the apostle himself assumed ultimate responsibility for the churches he established, he delegated certain tasks to his trusted associates.[51] This became a necessity, especially toward the end of Paul's life, which was characterized by several imprisonments (Acts 24:22–27; 28:11–31; 2 Cor 11:23; Eph 6:20; Phil 1:14; 2 Tim 1:8), various ailments (Gal 4:13–15; 2 Cor 12:7–10), and advancing age.[52] Hence, as shown below, if Paul is affirmed as the author of the letters to Timothy and Titus, the life setting of these writings was most likely Paul's desire to provide continuity between the apostolic period and the subapostolic period (the time subsequent to the apostolic era), to pass on the orthodox message of the Christian faith, and to provide sound principles for church government. While addressed to specific situations, these instructions transcend their original context and apply also to the church of all ages.[53]

Destination

1–2 Timothy Paul writes in 1 Timothy 1:3, "As I urged you when I went to Macedonia, remain in Ephesus." This indicates that Timothy had been put in charge of

---

[48] Dio Chrysostom, *Or.* 34.7–8; cf. *Or.* 33.17; 34.37.

[49] *Geogr.* 14.5.13.

[50] See Schnabel: "Paul did not go to Arabia to work through the theological and practical consequences of his conversion. He went to Arabia in order to engage in missionary work." E. J. Schnabel, *Paul the Missionary: Realities, Strategies and Methods* (Downers Grove, IL: InterVarsity, 2008), 60. See also idem, *Early Christian Mission* (2004), 2:1032–45; J. Murphy-O'Connor, "Paul in Arabia," *CBQ* 55 (1993): 732–37; M. Hengel and A. M. Schwemer, *Paul between Damascus and Antioch: The Unknown Years* (Louisville, KY: Westminster John Knox, 1997), 196–26; M. Hengel, "Paul in Arabia," *BBR* 12 (2002): 47–66.

[51] See the excellent treatment by E. E. Ellis: "Paul and His Co-Workers," *DPL*, 183; note also M. M. Mitchell, "New Testament Envoys in the Context of Greco-Roman Diplomatic and Epistolary Conventions: The Example of Timothy and Titus," *JBL* 111 (1992): 641–62.

[52] See A. J. Malherbe, "*Paulus Senex*," *ResQ* 36 (1994): 197–207.

[53] This thesis is argued in G. W. Knight, "The Scriptures Were Written for Our Instruction," *JETS* 39 (1996): 3–13.

the church in this important city.[54] Ephesus was situated on the west coast of Asia Minor (modern Turkey). Josephus calls Ephesus "the chief city of Asia" (*Ant.* 14.224). Similar to Corinth, the city's location along a major trade route made it a primary prospect for planting a church that could serve as a beachhead for other congregations throughout the Roman Empire. The city was famous for its cult and temple dedicated to the Greek goddess Artemis (see Acts 19:28–41).[55] As a center of pagan worship, Ephesus presented a considerable challenge for the Christian mission. It is also likely that Ephesus boasted a considerable Jewish population.[56] The Ephesian church was started during Paul's three years in the city (Acts 19:8; see 20:31) and probably consisted of several house churches (see 1 Cor 16:19).[57] There is no indication in 2 Timothy of any difference of location with regard to Timothy's ministry, and there is every reason to assume that Timothy and the church in Ephesus are also the destination of Paul's second letter to Timothy.

This man occupied a special place in Paul's heart and mission (1 Cor 4:17; Phil 2:20, 22; 1 Tim 1:2; 2 Tim 1:2). Paul first met him in Lystra, which at that time was part of the Roman province of Galatia (modern Turkey). It is possible, but not certain, that their paths crossed during Paul's previous visit to Lystra (Acts 14:8–20; see 2 Tim 3:10–11). Timothy was the product of a mixed marriage of a Gentile father and a Jewish mother. He was a "believer" (Acts 16:1–2), having been taught the Scriptures from his youth (2 Tim 1:5; 3:15). Recommended by his local church, Timothy joined Paul on his second missionary journey and shared in the evangelization of Macedonia and Achaia (Acts 16:2; 17:14–15; 18:5). He was associated with Paul during much of his extended ministry in Ephesus (Acts 19:22), traveled with him from Ephesus to Macedonia, to Corinth, back to Macedonia, and to Asia Minor (Acts 20:1–6), and was with Paul during his first Roman imprisonment (Phil 1:1; Col 1:1; Phlm 1).

Timothy also served as Paul's emissary on at least three occasions prior to his current assignment in Ephesus: to Thessalonica (ca. 50), to Corinth (ca. 53–54), and to Philippi (ca. 60–62). Paul frequently called him "coworker" (Rom 16:21; 1 Cor 16:10; Phil 2:22; 1 Thess 3:2) and referred to him as coauthor of six of his apostolic letters (1 and 2 Thessalonians, 2 Corinthians, Philippians, Colossians, Philemon; see esp. Phil 2:19–22; cf. 1 Cor 16:10). The author of Hebrews mentioned Timothy's release from an otherwise unknown imprisonment (Heb 13:23). Due to his mixed Jewish-Gentile heritage (Acts 16:1), Timothy was an ideal choice for ministering in a Hellenistic-Jewish environment and for dealing with a Jewish proto-gnostic heresy. Even at the time 1 Timothy was

---

[54] For an overview of the city of Ephesus, see C. E. Arnold, "Ephesus," in *DPL*, 249–53. For a more thorough treatment, see two important and recent general studies: P. Trebilco, *The Early Christians in Ephesus from Paul to Ignatius* (Grand Rapids, MI: Eerdmans, 2007); and Jerome Murphy-O'Connor, *St. Paul's Ephesus: Texts and Archaeology* (Collegeville, MN: Liturgical Press, 2008).

[55] See the recent work on Artemis in S. L. Glahn, "The Identity of Artemis in First-Century Ephesus," *BSac* 172/688 (2016). Also note Trebilco, *The Early Christians in Ephesus*, 19–30.

[56] See the thorough discussion in Trebilco, *The Early Christians in Ephesus*, 37–51.

[57] See ibid., 94–99.

written, Timothy was still fairly young by the standard of the ancient world (1 Tim 4:12), though he had met Paul about ten years earlier (Acts 16:1; ca. AD 49), if not earlier yet.[58] Timothy was therefore probably in his late thirties when he received 1 and 2 Timothy.

Titus As Paul's letter to Titus indicates, Titus had been left on Crete, a Mediterranean island Paul had previously passed on his sea voyage to Rome (Titus 1:5; see Acts 27:7–13).[59] Paul indicates that the inhabitants of Crete were proverbial in that day for their dishonesty, immorality, and laziness (Titus 1:12). Paul's statement that he left Titus in Crete seems to imply that Paul had been there with him, presumably subsequent to the events in Acts. Titus had been directed by Paul to straighten out unfinished business and to appoint elders in every town (Paul's pattern—see Acts 14:21–23). Compared with Timothy's task, Titus's may have been a bit easier since Crete was no Ephesus—though it had been known for its many cities ever since Homer (*Il.* 2.649). And, while Timothy found himself in a situation where there were already elders (at least some of whom seem to have been in need of rebuke, 1 Tim 5:19–20), Paul tells Titus to appoint elders in every town. Thus, it is possible that Paul and Titus planted these churches after Paul's first Roman imprisonment, having no time left to establish leadership before Paul decided to leave. Nevertheless Titus, like Timothy, faced the challenge of false teachers, "especially those from the circumcision party" (Titus 1:10).

While Titus was not as close to Paul as Timothy was, Titus was also a trusted associate. When Paul went to discuss his gospel with the leaders of the Jerusalem church, he took Titus with him (Gal 2:1–3). Titus, a Gentile, was not compelled to be circumcised upon his conversion to Christianity, which served to illustrate the nature of Paul's gospel (Gal 2:3–5). While not mentioned in Acts, Titus surfaces repeatedly in Paul's Letters as a member of the Pauline circle.[60] His commission by Paul found him on the island of Crete, where he was to take care of "what was left undone" (Titus 1:5). Cretan culture was known for its moral decay; hence, Titus's task was not an easy one. Similar to 1 Timothy, Paul's letter to Titus was written to encourage his delegate to complete the assignment given to him in Crete by his apostolic mentor. Later, Titus was to meet Paul in Nicopolis (Titus 3:12), and after being with Paul for what was likely the last time, Titus departed for Dalmatia (2 Tim 4:10).

---

[58] On Timothy's age, see D. W. Pao, "Let No One Despise Your Youth: Church and World in the Pastoral Epistles," *JETS* 57 (2014). See also J. M. G. Barclay, "There Is Neither Old Nor Young? Early Christianity and Ancient Ideologies of Age," *NTS* 53 (2007): 225–41.

[59] On Crete, see D. W. J. Gill, "A Saviour for the Cities of Crete: The Roman Background to the Epistle to Titus," in *The New Testament in Its First Century Setting: Essays on Context and Background in Honour of B. W. Winter on His 65th Birthday*, ed. P. J. Williams et al. (Grand Rapids, MI: Eerdmans, 2004), 220–30; and G. M. Wieland, "Roman Crete and the Letter to Titus," *NTS* 55 (2009): 338–54.

[60] 2 Cor 2:12–13; 7:5–6, 13–14; 8:6, 16, 23; 12:18; Gal 2:1–5; 2 Tim 4:10; Titus 1:4.

Date and Provenance

At what point in his ministry did Paul write the letters to Timothy and Titus? A brief survey of Pauline chronology helps set the stage for adjudicating this question.[61] Paul hails from "the thriving commercial and intellectual center" of Tarsus of Cilicia (Acts 9:11; 21:39; 22:3).[62] He studies under the eminent first-century Jewish rabbi Gamaliel I (Acts 22:3; see 5:34–39) and zealously persecutes the early Christians (Acts 7:56–8:3; 9:1–2; 1 Cor 15:9; Phil 3:6). An encounter with the risen Christ on the road to Damascus (Acts 9:1–9; 22:6–10; 26:12–18) causes a radical reorientation of Paul's life and a paradigm shift in his thinking. Up until that moment Paul had considered Jesus to be a messianic pretender cursed by God; now he recognizes him as the Messiah sent by God (Gal 3:10–14; 2 Cor 5:21). With this, the church's most committed nemesis (see 1 Tim 1:15–17) becomes its most fervent propagator.

After a few quiet years of preparation (Gal 1:21–24), Barnabas recruits Paul to participate in the early church's mission to the Gentiles (Acts 11:25–26). Paul quickly rises to assume a leadership role and gathers a group of coworkers that includes Timothy and Titus. While assuming responsibility for the churches he establishes, Paul delegates certain tasks to his trusted associates.[63] This becomes a necessity, especially toward the end of Paul's life which is characterized by imprisonments (Acts 24:22–27; 28:11–31; 2 Cor 11:23; Eph 6:20; Phil 1:14; 2 Tim 1:8), ailments (Gal 4:13–15; 2 Cor 12:7–10), and advancing age.[64] If Paul is the author of the letters to Timothy and Titus, the setting of these writings, as mentioned, is most likely his desire to ensure continuity between the apostolic and the post-apostolic period, to pass on the message of the Christian faith, and to provide sound principles for church governance.[65]

---

[61] For helpful discussion setting the general framework, see C. L. Quarles, *Illustrated Life of Paul* (Nashville, TN: B&H, 2014).

[62] R. N. Longenecker, *The Ministry and Message of Paul* (Grand Rapids, MI: Zondervan, 1971), 24.

[63] See M. M. Mitchell, "New Testament Envoys," 641–62, who focuses on 1 Thessalonians 3 and 2 Corinthians 7; and "The Role of Paul's Delegates" in Towner, *First and Second Letters to Timothy*, 94–96.

[64] See Malherbe, "*Paulus Senex*."

[65] Regarding the appropriateness of speaking of first-century "orthodoxy," see A. J. Köstenberger and M. J. Kruger, *The Heresy of Orthodoxy: How Contemporary Culture's Fascination with Diversity Has Reshaped Our Understanding of Early Christianity* (Wheaton, IL: Crossway, 2010).

There are essentially three possibilities as to when the letters to Timothy and Titus were written:[66] (1) during Acts;[67] (2) after the end of Acts;[68] and (3) after Paul's death.[69] A date during Acts was commonly accepted in the early centuries of the church and until the nineteenth century. The view was rejected not on the basis of contrary evidence but in favor of inauthenticity and non-Pauline authorship (pseudonymity). In light of the difficulties of accommodating the information contained in the letters to Timothy and Titus within the Acts chronology, postulating a date after the end of Acts may be the "simplest solution,"[70] but it, too, is not without its difficulties.

First, the ministry locations mentioned in 1–2 Timothy and Titus may presuppose ministry in the East, such as in Ephesus (1 Tim 3:14–15), Troas (2 Tim 4:13), and Miletus (2 Tim 4:20), a region Paul left after the third missionary journey and did not expect to revisit (cf. Acts 20:25). Second, Paul, in 1 Timothy 4:12, speaks of Timothy's "youth," which may point to an earlier date. Third, the detailed instructions regarding church order and qualifications for church leaders in 1 Timothy and Titus suggests a time when the church was still being established. In addition, it is possible to accommodate the information included in the letters to Timothy and Titus within the Acts chronology. J. Van Brugge, followed by R. Fuchs and P. Towner, suggests that Paul may have interrupted his three-year ministry in Ephesus on his third missionary journey (Acts 19; cf. 20:31) and embarked on an "interim journey" to Macedonia (1 Tim 1:3) and Crete (Titus 1:5) during that time.[71]

---

[66] For a survey, see S. E. Porter, "Pauline Chronology and the Question of Pseudonymity of the Pastoral Epistles," in *Paul and Pseudepigraphy*, 65–88, who concludes that "there is and can be no final and definitive solution to the issue of Pauline authorship and pseudepigraphy of the Pastoral Epistles on the basis of Pauline chronology" (p. 88). Porter believes that 2 Timothy was probably written from a Roman imprisonment, most likely during one of the missionary journeys recorded in Acts. For a tentative reconstruction, see Ellis, "Pastoral Letters," 661–62; cf. Köstenberger, "1–2 Timothy, Titus," 596–98. For a comparison chart, see chart 73, "Locating the Pastoral Epistles within Paul's Ministry," in Kierspel, *Charts on the Life, Letters, and Theology of Paul*, 137.

[67] See, e.g., J. van Bruggen, *Die geschichtliche Einordnung der Pastoralbriefe* (Wuppertal: R. Brockhaus, 1981); R. Fuchs, "Eine vierte Missionsreise des Paulus im Osten? Zur Datierung des ersten Timotheosbriefs und des Titusbriefs," *JET* 25 (2011): 33–58; idem, Unerwartette *Unterschiede*, 5–30; Towner, *Letters to Timothy and Titus*, 10–15; idem, *1–2 Timothy & Titus*, 14–20; B. Reicke, "Chronologie der Pastoralbriefe," *TLZ* 101 (1976): 81–96; D. A. deSilva, *An Introduction to the New Testament: Contexts, Methods & Ministry Formation* (Downers Grove, IL: InterVarsity, 2004), 734–35.

[68] See, e.g., J. B. Lightfoot, "The Date of the Pastoral Epistles," in *Biblical Essays* (London, England: Macmillan, 1893), 399–410; Ellis, "Pastoral Letters," 661–62; Fee, *1 and 2 Timothy, Titus*, 3–4; J. B. Polhill, *Paul and His Letters* (Nashville, TN: B&H, 1999).

[69] See, e.g., Quinn and Wacker, *First and Second Letters to Timothy*, 1–23; Pervo, *The Making of Paul*; and the discussion of pseudonymity above.

[70] Polhill, *Paul and His Letters*, 405, cited in Kierspel, *Charts on the Life, Letters, and Theology of Paul*, 255.

[71] Van Bruggen, *Geschichtliche Einordnung der Pastoralbriefe*, 91–96 *et passim*; Fuchs, "Vierte Missionsreise des Paulus im Osten?," 33–58; idem, *Unerwartete Unterschiede*, 5–30; Towner, *Letters to Timothy and Titus*, 10–15; idem, *1–2 Timothy & Titus*, 14–20. See also P. Walker, "Revisiting the Pastoral Epistles: Part I," *EuroJTh* 21 (2012): 4–16; and idem, "Revisiting the Pastoral Epistles: Part II," *EuroJTh* 21 (2012): 120–32, who proposes that Paul wrote 1 Timothy and Titus in the period between September AD 55 and January AD 57 when Paul left Ephesus and went into Macedonia and Illyricum before wintering in Corinth (Acts 20:1–3; Rom 15:19). He also suggests that Paul wrote 2 Timothy when arriving in Rome in March AD 60 (Acts 28:14) prior to writing his other "Prison Epistles," Colossians, Ephesians, Philemon, and Philippians.

Nevertheless, on balance it seems a date after the end of Acts is preferred. Any reconstruction within Acts is essentially an argument from silence, and it is far from certain that Luke would have omitted reference to such an "interim journey" to Macedonia and Crete in his account of Paul's whereabouts in Acts. On the other hand, if such a journey took place after Acts, its non-inclusion in Acts would be plausible if Luke chose to end his account with Paul's arrival in Rome. While it is true that in Romans Paul envisioned traveling west, not east (Rom 15:28), and while Acts reports that Paul did not expect to visit Ephesus again following his "Ephesian farewell" (Acts 20:25), this does not rule out subsequent travels to the Aegean region.

Most likely, therefore, Paul engages in a second Aegean ministry after his release from his first Roman imprisonment (Acts 28). He writes the first letter to Timothy from Macedonia (1 Tim 1:3) sometime after the year 60 (the most likely date of Paul's release from his first Roman imprisonment) but before 66 (the likely date of his second Roman imprisonment, issuing in his martyrdom under Nero who died in 68). Timothy, at that time stationed in Ephesus, needs counsel on how to deal with false teachers in the Ephesian church. To this end Paul interwove personal instructions with those on community life, so Timothy received public apostolic support while it was acknowledged that he also had certain standards to meet.[72] Paul likely writes the letter to Titus either between 1 and 2 Timothy or prior to 1 Timothy from an unknown location (possibly Macedonia or Achaia).[73] He probably writes 2 Timothy from Rome subsequent to 1 Timothy and Titus during his second, more severe imprisonment in 65 or 66.

Occasion

Paul's primary concern was not to describe the respective heresy in question but to refute it. The nature of the false teachings combated in the letters to Timothy and Titus must therefore be deduced from the apostle's responses.[74] Moreover, while there are doubtless similarities between the heresies confronted in the letters to Timothy and Titus, one must not assume that the opponents are precisely the same in each case.[75] The teaching seems to have arisen from within the churches rather than having invaded from the outside

---

[72] While 1 Timothy is addressed to Timothy, it was likely meant to be "overheard" by the Ephesian congregation(s). See further in the discussion of genre below.

[73] So Quarles, *Illustrated Life of Paul*, 259.

[74] Essays directly addressing the nature of the false teachers include B. J. Oropeza, "1, 2 Timothy and Titus: The Influence of False Teachers in the Pastoral Letters," in *Jews, Gentiles, and the Opponents of Paul: The Pauline Letters,* Apostasy in the New Testament Communities 2 (Eugene, OR: Cascade, 2012), 260–308; O. Skarsaune, "Heresy and the Pastoral Epistles," *Them* 20 (1994): 9–14. Note also J. L. Sumney, "Studying Paul's Opponents: Advances and Challenges," in *Paul and His Opponents*, ed. S. E. Porter, Pauline Studies 2 (Leiden, Netherlands: Brill, 2005), 7–58. See D. T. Thornton, *Hostility in the House of God: An Investigation of the Opponents in 1 and 2 Timothy,* BBR Supplement 15 (Winona Lake, IN: Eisenbrauns, 2016), noteworthy for its rigorous methodology in handling the textual evidence.

[75] Towner, *1–2 Timothy and Titus*, 22; Mounce, *Pastoral Epistles*, lxi. Cf. Herzer, "Juden," 143–68, who approaches the letters as pseudonymous and argues, over against the tendency to blend the various heretical elements into some kind of Jewish-Christian Gnosticism, that a specific, distinctive group of opponents stands behind each letter.

(1 Tim1:3; 6:2; 2 Tim 2:14; 4:2; Titus 1:13; 3:10; cf. 1 Tim 1:20; 2 Tim 2:17–18),[76] which was in keeping with Paul's prediction (Acts 20:28–31). Some even suggest that the heretics were elders in the church, but this is uncertain.[77] Thornton demonstrates that the textual description of the opponents—at least in Ephesus—emphasizes their initial repudiation of apostolic teaching followed by an ensuing erosion of their moral character.[78] There may be a connection with problems in Corinth (see 1 Cor 15:12, 34)[79] and especially in the Lycus Valley (compare 1 Tim 4:3 with Col 2:8, 16–23).

Materially, the heresy involves an interest in "myths" and "genealogies" (1 Tim 1:4; 4:7; 2 Tim 4:4; Titus 1:14; 3:9)[80] and a concern with the law (1 Tim 1:7; Titus 1:10, 14; 3:9; see Col 2:16–17), which suggests that the false teachers were (Hellenistic) Jews.[81] In Ephesus at least, one finds ascetic elements such as the prohibition of marriage or the eating of certain foods (1 Tim 4:1–5; see Titus 1:15; Col 2:18–23) and the teaching that the resurrection had already taken place (2 Tim 2:17–18; see 1 Cor 15:12; 1 Tim 1:19–20),[82] which may point to a distortion of Paul's teaching, particularly that regarding eschatology. As is the case with many forms of false teaching, the heretics displayed a tendency toward acrimony and speculation (1 Tim 1:4, 6; 6:4, 20; 2 Tim 2:14, 16, 23; Titus 1:10; 3:9), deceptiveness (1 Tim 4:1–3; 2 Tim 3:6–9, 13; Titus 1:10–13; see Col 2:8), immorality (1 Tim 1:19–20; 2 Tim 2:22; 3:3–4; Titus 1:15), and greed (1 Tim 6:5; 2 Tim 3:2, 4; Titus 1:11; contrast 1 Tim 3:3).[83]

---

[76] See the thorough case made in Thornton, *Hostility in the House of God*, 237–40.

[77] Fee, *1 and 2 Timothy, Titus*, 7–9. Support would include the careful setting forth of qualifications for elders (1 Tim 3:2–7; Titus 1:7–9) and the instruction on discipline for elders (1 Tim 5:19–20). The careful investigation of Thornton (*Hostility in the House of God*, 36, 239–40) leads to his opinion that it is possible but not probable that the opponents were elders.

[78] Thornton, *Hostility in the House of God*, 240–49.

[79] See P. H. Towner, "Gnosis and Realized Eschatology in Ephesus (of the Pastoral Epistles) and the Corinthian Enthusiasm," *JSNT* 31 (1987): 95–124.

[80] The "Jewish myths" in view may have reference to Second Temple Jewish works related to the Law, including things such as *Jubilees*, Pseudo-Philo, and the Genesis Apocryphon. The first-century Greek geographer Strabo writes that "the things that are ancient and false and monstrous are called myths, but history wishes for the truth" (*Geog.* 11.5.3). Philo frequently contrasts myths and truth (see the discussion and source references in Spicq, *Les épîtres pastorales*, 93–96; idem, "μύθος," *TLNT* 2.529–30). "Myth" thus stands in contrast with the Christian message which is grounded in historical reality (cf. Titus 1:3). "Genealogies" is probably broader than OT examples such as Genesis 5 or 1 Chr 1:1–9:44. See F. J. A. Hort, *Judaistic Christianity: A Course of Lectures* (New York, NY: Macmillan, 1894), 135–38, with reference to Polybius, *Histories* 9.1.1–5; 9.2.1–2, who speaks of "myths and genealogies" and writes that in his day many "historians . . . attract a variety of readers by entering upon all the various branches of history" and that the "curious reader is attracted by the genealogical style"; see also Philo, *Mos.* 2.8.

[81] Ignatius, who died ca. 110, likewise warned his readers not to be "led astray by strange doctrines or by old fables which are profitless" (see *Pol.* 3.1; *Smyrn.* 6.2), linking these teachings with Judaism (*Magn.* 8.1; see 9.1; 10.3; *Phld.* 6.1) involving the proper interpretation of the OT Scriptures (*Phld.* 8.2). See S. Westerholm, "The Law and the 'Just Man' (1 Tim 1,3–11)," *ST* 36 (1982): 82. Although the identification of the opponents as Jewish is commonly made and likely correct, see the objections of Thornton, *Hostility in the House of God*, 26, 65–66, 258–59.

[82] See Towner, "Gnosis and Realized Eschatology"; Thornton, *Hostility in the House of God*, 250–54.

[83] On the polemic employed by Paul in 1–2 Timothy and Titus, see esp. R. J. Karris, "The Background and Significance of the Polemic of the Pastoral Epistles," *JBL* 92 (1973): 549–64; L. T. Johnson, "II Timothy and the Polemic against False

The practice of forbidding marriage was evident in both Judaism (especially among the Essenes; see Philo, *Hypoth.* 380 [11.14]) and later Gnosticism (Irenaeus, *Haer.* 1.24.2). Even Paul himself at times extolled the advantages of celibacy (1 Cor 7:1–7).[84] Fee suggests that the problem may have been"the reflection of the influence of Hellenistic-Jewish speculation on Christian thought."[85] Knight calls it a "Gnosticizing form of Jewish Christianity" (see 1 Tim 6:20); others term it "a form of aberrant Judaism with Hellenistic/Gnostic tendencies," "Jewish proto-Gnosticism," or "Judaism crossed with Gnosticism."[86] Perhaps there was a "growing suspicion that marriage belonged to the old order which had passed away, or that the model for living in the resurrection age was to be found in descriptions of life before the fall into sin."[87] In any case, what Paul apparently opposed here was an appeal to the Mosaic law in support of ascetic practices that at the root may have been motivated by a distortion of Paul's teaching on eschatology.[88]

Paul denounced the various permutations of heresy in strong language as "fruitless discussion" (1 Tim 1:6), "godless myths and old wives' tales" (1 Tim 4:7 NIV), "irreverent, empty speech" (1 Tim 6:20), "foolish and stupid arguments" (2 Tim 2:23 NIV), and "foolish debates" (Titus 3:9). This would have engaged an already-existing stereotype in believers' minds, cautioning them against associating with these false teachers.[89] To some extent, Paul may have viewed the heresy as more irrelevant than false ("myths," "quarrels about words"), indicating that the "main stock-in-trade of these teachers was empty platitudes which Paul did not even consider it worthwhile to refute."[90]

Purpose

1 Timothy Paul states the occasion for 1 Timothy this way: "As I urged you when I went to Macedonia, remain in Ephesus so that you may instruct certain people not to teach false doctrine" (1 Tim 1:3–4; see vv. 18–20). The question is whether this occasion constituted the purpose for 1 Timothy in its entirety or whether Paul had other purposes besides instructing Timothy on how to deal with these false teachers. Contrary to those

---

Teachers: A Reexamination," *JRS* 6–7 (1978): 1–26; and L. K. Pietersen, *The Polemic of the Pastorals: A Sociological Examination of the Development of Pauline Christianity*, JSNTSup 264 (New York, NY: T&T Clark), 2004. As these works show, Paul appears in these letters to be appropriating polemical language from his Greco-Roman milieu. Some argue from this that much of Paul's language is *merely* conventional, and thus we can know little about the opponents and their teaching. This is not necessarily the case, however, in that Paul was perfectly capable of choosing from stock polemical language what he needed to accurately describe his opponents.

[84] Towner, *1–2 Timothy and Titus*, 25.

[85] Fee, *1 and 2 Timothy, Titus*, 8–9.

[86] Knight, *Pastoral Epistles*, 27–28; Mounce, *Pastoral Epistles*, lxix–lxxvi; Collins, *Letters That Paul Did Not Write*, 100, referring to A. Hanson as well as M. Dibelius and H. Conzelmann; and Ellis, "Pastoral Letters," 663, with reference to Lightfoot (see Ignatius [died ca. 110], *Magn.* 8–11; *Trall.* 9). See the objections to using the term "gnostic" or even "proto-gnostic" to describe the opponents in Thornton, *Hostility in the House of God*, 25, 257–59.

[87] Towner, *1–2 Timothy and Titus*, 25.

[88] So Westerholm, "The Law and the 'Just Man,'" 82.

[89] See the above note on the polemical language of 1–2 Timothy and Titus.

[90] Guthrie, *New Testament Introduction*, 628.

who emphasize the *ad hoc* nature of the letters to Timothy and Titus,[91] it is likely that Paul's purpose was broader than merely dealing with false teachers.[92]

Specifically, 1 Timothy 1 and 4–6 are concerned primarily with the challenge of the false teachers, while chapters 2–3 focus more constructively on general organizational matters. This is suggested, first, by the phrase "First of all, then" (1 Tim 2:1) that introduces 2:1–3:16, which suggests the beginning of a new section;[93] and, second, the closing words of the same section in 3:15: "But if I should be delayed, *I have written so that you will know how people ought to act in God's household, which is the church of the living God, the pillar and foundation of the truth.*" This solemn affirmation, plus the following hymn in 1 Timothy 3:16, indicates that Paul conceived of 1 Timothy not merely as occasional (i.e., as limited to this specific occasion) but as applicable to the church more broadly. That said, it is reasonable to suppose that the false teaching is still lurking in the background and informs to some degree the instructions on organizational matters Paul gives.

Third, Paul's office of apostle (1 Tim 1:1; 2 Tim 1:1; Titus 1:1) would mean that his letters transcend the scope of any one local congregation. As Paul wrote elsewhere, the church is "God's household, built on the foundation of the apostles and prophets, with Christ Jesus himself as the cornerstone" (Eph 2:19–20). Hence, the letters to Timothy and Titus are foundational documents for the church, not just *ad hoc* instructions dealing with merely local circumstances that had no lasting implications for the church overall.[94]

In 1 Timothy 4:1, Paul returns to the matter of false teachers. What is more, even if the apostle addressed local circumstances requiring resolution, such as principles for the care of needy widows (1 Tim 5:3–16) or sinning elders (1 Tim 5:17–25), the truths and principles Paul teaches as an apostle are true and therefore binding—not merely for Timothy and the church of Ephesus at the time of writing—but also for every church, "the church of the living God, the pillar and foundation of the truth" (1 Tim 3:15).[95] Hence, Paul's purpose for writing 1 Timothy was both to instruct him on how to deal with false teachers and to provide guidelines on a variety of matters of perennial significance for the church.[96]

---

[91] "*Ad hoc*" is Latin for "to this," i.e., addressed to a given circumstance only.

[92] See Fee, "Reflections on Church Order," 141–51; idem, *1 and 2 Timothy, Titus*, 5–14 and throughout. Fee claims that "the whole of 1 Timothy . . . is dominated by this singular concern" of refuting the false teachers and that "the whole of chs. 2–3 is best understood as instruction vis-à-vis the behavior and attitudes of the FT [false teachers]" ("Reflections," 142–43). But see the critique of Fee in G. Knight, "The Scriptures Were Written for Our Instruction"; and in Köstenberger ("1–2 Timothy, Titus," 514), who notes that Fee unduly diminishes the structural markers in 2:1 and 3:15–16 that set off chaps. 2 and 3 from chaps. 1 and 4–6, respectively. Cf. the further interaction under the heading "Reflections" (ibid., 520).

[93] See Köstenberger ("1–2 Timothy, Titus," 510), who notes that the verb *parakaleō* ("I urge"), which is found in 1 Tim 2:1, is used regularly by Paul in transitioning to the "business portion" of a letter (1 Cor 1:19; 2 Cor 2:8; 6:1; Eph 4:1; 1 Thess 4:1; Phlm 10).

[94] See the discussion of genre below.

[95] See A. J. Köstenberger, "Women in the Church: A Response to Kevin Giles," *EvQ* 73 (2001): 205–24; in response to K. Giles, "A Critique of the 'Novel' Contemporary Interpretation of 1 Timothy 2:9–15 Given in the Book, *Women in the Church*. Parts I and II," *EvQ* 72 (2000): 151–67, 195–215.

[96] This raises the issue of hermeneutical consistency. If an interpreter were to relativize Paul's instructions regarding women in church leadership in 1 Tim 2:11–15, he or she, to be consistent, would need to view Paul's instructions on

2 Timothy The most personal of Paul's Letters is clearly 2 Timothy. With Paul in prison again (2 Tim 1:8) and nearing the end of his life (2 Tim 4:6–8), this book contains his final charge to Timothy to "preach the word" of the Christian gospel (2 Tim 4:1–2) as Paul passed on his mantle to his foremost disciple. In terms of salvation history, this book marks the transition from the apostolic to the subapostolic period, during which believers were charged to build on the foundation of the apostles and to guard the "good deposit" made by them (2 Tim 1:12, 14 NIV). But the apostle touches on many topics of perennial significance in this letter that are not limited to the original circumstance to which they were addressed.[97]

Titus Paul's letter to Titus was most likely written around the same time as 1 Timothy and for similar reasons. In Titus's case, the occasion is stated in Titus 1:5: "The reason I left you in Crete was to set right what was left undone and, as I directed you, to appoint elders in every town." This is followed by a set of qualifications for elders in Titus 1:6–9. While initially given to provide guidance for Titus, this passage is hardly limited to the original occasion but continues to have relevance for the church today as it ensures that its leaders meet biblical requirements. Beyond this immediate purpose, Paul provides a variety of other instructions for Titus in overseeing the life of the church. He articulated a series of important and abiding Christian doctrinal truths, such as salvation not by works, the regeneration of believers by the Holy Spirit, justification by grace, and so on (see Titus 3:4–7).

LITERATURE

Genre

In general terms, Paul's missives to Timothy and Titus conform to the standard format of the ancient letter, including an opening salutation, a body with features such as a thanksgiving and the main content, and a closing greeting. Beyond this, 1 Timothy and Titus (as well as 2 Timothy, though see further below), are often identified as exemplars of the paraenetic or hortatory letter, which contains a series of moral exhortations to its recipients.[98] More specifically, 1 Timothy and Titus are often compared with ancient letters known as "mandate" or "administrative" documents, in which an official sets forth instructions for a newly appointed delegate regarding his administrative duties.[99]

---

qualifications for church leaders in 1 Tim 3:1–12 as relative and nonbinding for the church as well. See Mounce, *Pastoral Epistles*, 185.

[97] E.g., the affirmation in 2 Tim 1:9–10; the "trustworthy saying" in 2:11–13; and the "inscription" in 2 Tim 2:19. On the "trustworthy sayings" in the letters to Timothy and Titus, see the discussion under Theological Themes below.

[98] See M. Harding, "The Pastoral Epistles," in *All Things to All Cultures: Paul among Jews, Greeks, and Romans*, ed. M. Harding and A. Nobbs (Grand Rapids, MI: Eerdmans, 2013), 333–34.

[99] See the excellent overview in Towner, *Letters to Timothy and Titus*, 33–35. Johnson (*Letters to Paul's Delegates*, 106–7, 168; idem, *First and Second Letters to Timothy*, 96–97) relies heavily upon a particular papyrus, Tebtunis 703, in support of his identification of 1 Timothy and Titus as examples of what he calls "*mandata principis*" ("commandments of the ruler") letters, and it should be noted that his use of this papyrus has come under heavy critique in M. M. Mitchell, "PTebt 703

While the letters to Timothy and Titus are each addressed to an individual, it is important to recognize that they were evidently meant for a larger audience, as indicated by the plural pronoun which closes each epistle: "Grace be with you (plural: ὑμῶν)."[100] This understanding coheres with Witherington's more general observation:

> What we have in the NT, almost without exception, are communications composed *for groups of people* meant to be read out loud to groups of people. . . . They are not documents meant for private individuals to quietly read at their leisure, and as such they are not much like the vast majority of ancient letters on papyri we know about.[101]

Typically, 2 Timothy is considered a special case. Since 2 Timothy is Paul's last recorded letter—written from a second and much more severe Roman imprisonment with Paul's martyrdom apparently imminent—it takes on the character of a last testament, similar to 2 Peter.[102] S. Martin, regarding 2 Timothy as pseudonymous, argues that the letter is Paul's testament much like Deuteronomy is the testament of Moses, in the sense that both books present a prominent figure as passing on his authority to a successor and summarizing his own teaching. Martin draws attention to the references to Moses in 2 Timothy 2:19 and 3:8–9, in both cases in the context of Moses's authority being challenged (similar to

---

and the Genre of 1 Timothy: The Curious Career of a Ptolemaic Papyrus in Pauline Scholarship," *NovT* 44 (2002): 344–70. Seminal work on the letters to Timothy and Titus in comparison with mandate documents was done by M. Wolter, *Die Pastoralbriefe als Paulustradition*, FRLANT 146 (Göttingen, Germany: Vandenhoeck & Ruprecht, 1988), 156–80, with examples of the form on pp. 164–70. On 1 Timothy and Titus as "mandate" or "administrative" letters, see also E. R. Richards, *Paul and First-Century Letter Writing: Secretaries, Composition, and Collection* (Downers Grove, IL: InterVarsity, 2004), 203–4; B. Witherington, *Letters and Homilies for Hellenized Christians*, vol. 1: *A Socio-Rhetorical Commentary on Titus, 1–2 Timothy and 1–3 John* (Downers Grove, IL: InterVarsity, 2006), 90–94, 177–80; L. Kidson, "1 Timothy: An Administrative Letter," *Early Christianity* 5 (2014): 97–116.

While acknowledging their character as mandate letters, R. W. Wall (*1 & 2 Timothy and Titus*, THNTC [Grand Rapids, MI: Eerdmans, 2012], 9–10) suggests the "literary form" or "species" of the letters to Timothy and Titus is that of "letters of succession" in that "they are written in response to a particular theological crisis when the leader departs and his work must be succeeded and continued by others." The notion of 2 Timothy in particular as a "succession letter" is developed at length in J. Barentsen, *Emerging Leadership in the Pauline Mission: A Social Identity Perspective on Local Leadership Development in Corinth and Ephesus*, Princeton Theological Monograph Series 168 (Eugene, OR: Wipf & Stock, 2011), 252–89.

[100] This farewell closes both 1 and 2 Timothy (1 Tim 6:21; 2 Tim 4:22), with the wording of Titus being even more explicit: "Grace be with you all" (Titus 3:15). Knight (*Pastoral Epistles*, 277) contends that the use of plural pronouns "indicates that Paul expected this letter to be read to the believers, and it further indicates that all along he has had them, not just Timothy, in view." J. Ellington ("Problem Pronouns in Private Letters," *BT* 50 [1999]: 222–23) similarly concludes these plural pronouns indicate the letters "were, at least at some point, meant for the Church as a whole." M. M. Yarbrough (*Paul's Utilization of Preformed Traditions in 1 Timothy: An Evaluation of the Apostle's Literary, Rhetorical, and Theological Tactics*; LNTS 417 [London, England: T&T Clark, 2009], 173–74) examines 1 Timothy and distinguishes between Timothy as the "primary recipient" and the church at Ephesus as the "primary audience," arguing that although the letter was directly addressed to Timothy, it "extends through Timothy to the church at Ephesus. . . . It is community instruction."

[101] B. Witherington, "'Almost Thou Persuadest Me . . .': The Importance of Greco-Roman Rhetoric for the Understanding of the Text and Context of the NT," *JETS* 58 (2015): 72. Witherington lists "the Pastorals and 2–3 John" as "possible exceptions," but the balance of evidence indicates that the letters to Timothy and Titus, at least, are indeed no exceptions.

[102] See the discussion in Marshall, *Pastoral Epistles*, 12–13.

Timothy's). He also compares Moses's laying hands on Joshua with Paul's laying hands on Timothy (Num 27:18–23; Deut 34:9; 2 Tim 1:6; cf. 1 Tim 4:14). He then adduces the designations of "servant of the Lord" and "man of God," both used for Timothy, as evocative of Moses and views the exhortation to "be strong" (2 Tim 2:1) in the light of Deuteronomy 31. The parallels noted by Martin are highly suggestive, even though they do not necessarily prove pseudonymous authorship.

Yet the letters to Timothy and Titus are much more than mere notes written by one individual to another for the purpose of conveying exhortation and information. As T. D. Gordon observed, "The Pastoral Epistles are the only New Testament writings that are expressly written with the purpose of providing instructions for ordering churches at the close of the apostolic era."[103] He continued,

> The very apostle who had established churches and provided for their continued oversight, doctrinal purity, and worship, now gives instructions to his co-workers regarding the organization of churches in subsequent generations. The norms and principles he himself had observed in the ordering of his churches, Paul makes explicit to his colleagues so that they, too, might order their churches correctly.[104]

Hence, the genre of the letters to Timothy and Titus is inextricably bound to the historical life-setting of Paul's ministry as set forth in Acts and Paul's Letters.

Hermeneutically, the important implication from this understanding of the genre of the letters to Timothy and Titus is that "these letters contain norms that are especially germane to the issues of life in the church, the 'household of God'" (see 1 Tim 3:14–15).[105] As Gordon noted, "The instructions in these letters, far from being primarily of local significance, are significant wherever there is concern for the proper ordering of God's house. Indeed, as instructions given to postapostolic ministers, the instructions contained in the Pastoral Epistles are particularly germane to other postapostolic churches."[106]

Literary Integrity

R. van Neste summarized the state of scholarship on the letters to Timothy and Titus: "Until recently, one of the widely accepted tenets of modern scholarship regarding the Pastoral Epistles was that they lacked any significant, careful order or structure."[107] This assertion was not confined to liberal critics; even an otherwise conservative commentator, D. Guthrie, wrote, "There is a lack of studied order, some subjects being treated more than

---

[103] T. D. Gordon, "A Certain Kind of Letter: The Genre of 1 Timothy," in *Women in the Church: A Fresh Analysis of 1 Timothy 2:9–15*, ed. A. J. Köstenberger, T. R. Schreiner, and H. S. Baldwin (Grand Rapids, MI: Baker, 1995), 59.

[104] Ibid. Gordon provides a specific list of such instructions on pp. 59–60.

[105] Ibid., 60.

[106] Ibid.

[107] R. van Neste, *Cohesion and Structure in the Pastoral Epistles*, JSNTSup 280 (New York, NY: T&T Clark, 2004), 1.

once in the same letter without apparent premeditation. . . . These letters are, therefore, far removed from literary exercises."[108] A. T. Hanson, an opponent of the Pauline authorship of the letters to Timothy and Titus, maintained, "The Pastorals are made up of a miscellaneous collection of material. They have no unifying theme; there is no development of thought."[109]

But in the last decade the pendulum has swung away from such assessments. Against those who have argued against the literary unity and integrity of the letters to Timothy and Titus, van Neste demonstrated, in the most careful study of the topic to date, that there is "evidence of a high level of cohesion in each of the Pastoral Epistles" and that "all three letters show evidence of care in their design."[110] I. H. Marshall also noted, "There is a growing body of evidence that the Pastoral Epistles are not a conglomerate of miscellaneous ideas roughly thrown together with no clear plan, purpose or structure. On the contrary, they demonstrate signs of a coherent structure and of theological competence."[111]

In light of assessments such as these, it appears the literary integrity and coherence of the letters to Timothy and Titus has been amply rehabilitated against charges of incoherence. In what follows, the literary plan for each of the letters to Timothy and Titus is briefly discussed. As the above quotes demonstrate, the question of the literary unity of the letters and their theological coherence are closely intertwined. For this reason the discussion of major theological themes following the study of the literary dimension of the letters to Timothy and Titus will contribute to a further adjudication of the topic as well.

Literary Plan

1 Timothy

W. D. Mounce divides the structure of 1 Timothy this way:

I. SALUTATION (1:1–2)
II. THE EPHESIAN PROBLEM (1:3–20)
III. CORRECTION OF IMPROPER CONDUCT IN THE EPHESIAN CHURCH (2:1–4:5)
IV. PERSONAL NOTES TO TIMOTHY (4:6–16)
V. HOW TIMOTHY IS TO RELATE TO DIFFERENT GROUPS IN THE CHURCH (5:1–6:2A)
VI. FINAL INSTRUCTIONS (6:2B–21)[112]

---

[108] Guthrie, *Pastoral Epistles*, 18.

[109] A. T. Hanson, *The Pastoral Epistles* (Grand Rapids, MI: Eerdmans, 1982), 42.

[110] Van Neste, *Cohesion and Structure*, 285; against J. D. Miller, *The Pastoral Letters as Composite Documents*, SNTSMS 93 (Cambridge, UK: Cambridge University Press, 1997).

[111] I. H. Marshall, "The Christology of Luke-Acts and the Pastoral Epistles," in *Crossing Boundaries: Essays in Biblical Interpretation in Honor of Michael D. Goulder*, ed. S. E. Porter, P. Joyce, and D. E. Orton (Leiden, Netherlands: Brill, 1994), 171.

[112] Mounce, *Pastoral Epistles*, cxxxv (note that the numbering is off in that Mounce has two II.s and two IV.s). Similarly, Guthrie (*Pastoral Epistles*, 63–64) has these major divisions: I. 1:1–20; II. 2:1–4:16; III. 5:1–6:2; and IV. 6:3–21. Even less

On the whole, this outline is sound, especially in drawing a line of demarcation between 1:20 and 2:1[113] and in identifying 5:1–6:2a as a separate literary unit. However, it seems preferable to see 3:16 as concluding Paul's instructions that began in 2:1[114] and to see him as starting a new major unit in 4:1 with reference to the last days.[115] If so, the discussion of the literary plan of 1 Timothy may proceed as discussed below.[116]

Paul's first letter to Timothy immediately turns to the subject at hand: the need for Timothy to "instruct certain people not to teach false doctrine" in the church at Ephesus (1:3–4). Paul's customary thanksgiving follows after his initial comments regarding these false teachers, which is in fact a thanksgiving to God for Paul's own conversion since he himself at one point persecuted the church of God (1:12–17). At the end of the first chapter, Paul mentions two of these false teachers by name: Hymenaeus and Alexander (1:20).

After this, Paul transitions ("First of all, then," 2:1) to a section where he sets forth instructions for the church, in keeping with his purpose: "I write these things to you, hoping to come to you soon. But if I should be delayed, I have written so that you will know how people ought to act in God's household, which is the church of the living God, the pillar and foundation of the truth" (3:14–15). This makes clear that 2:1–3:16 constitutes a section apart from chapter 1 on the one hand and chapters 4–6 on the other, both of which are dominated by Paul's concern with the false teachers. While that concern is not completely absent from chapters 2–3, these chapters are taken up with Paul's more positive instructions to Timothy on how to govern the church. This includes instructions on prayer (2:1–8), the roles of women in the congregation (2:9–15), and qualifications for church leadership, both overseers (3:1–7) and deacons (3:8–13). The section concludes with a presentation of the "mystery of godliness," possibly drawing on a piece of liturgy (3:16).

Chapter 4 opens with the dramatic phrase, "Now the Spirit explicitly says" (4:1), setting the work of the false teachers squarely in the context of the end time, during which things would go from bad to worse. In this context, Timothy was to set himself apart by giving close attention both to his personal life and to his doctrine, thus preserving both himself and his hearers (4:11–16). Additional instructions are given regarding the care of widows (5:3–16); dealing with elders, including those who had sinned (5:17–25); the proper conduct of Christian slaves (6:1–2); and the rich (6:3–10, 17–19). Timothy, on

---

structure is discerned by Lea and Griffin (*1, 2 Timothy, Titus*, 17), who divide the letter into I. 1:1–2; II. 1:3–20; and III. 2:1–6:21.

113 Against Towner (*Letters to Timothy and Titus*, ix), who kept 1:3–3:16 as a single unit and gave insufficient attention to the markers "first of all" and "then" at 2:1. But Towner (unlike Mounce) rightly discerns a break between 3:16 and 4:1 (ibid., x).

114 See the interaction with G. D. Fee, "Reflections on Church Order in the Pastoral Epistles," *JETS* 28 (1985): 145, in Köstenberger, "1 Timothy," 504, 509–10.

115 This critique pertains to Mounce as well as Guthrie and Lea/Griffin.

116 See Köstenberger, "1 Timothy," 497. Cf. the proposed structure by Marshall (*Pastoral Epistles*, 30), who divided the letter between 1:3–3:16 and 4:1–6:21a.

the other hand, is to guard what has been entrusted to him, as Paul's final charge makes clear (6:11–16, 20–21).

2 Timothy

P. H. Towner's structure of 2 Timothy is below:

I. OPENING GREETING (1:1–2)
II. BODY OF THE LETTER (1:3–4:8)
   A. Call to Personal Commitment (1:3–18)
   B. Call to Dedication and Faithfulness (2:1–13)
   C. The Challenge of Opposition (2:14–26)
   D. Prophecy, Commitment, and Call (3:1–4:8)
III. FINAL INSTRUCTIONS (4:9–18)
IV. CLOSING GREETINGS (4:19–22)[117]

This structure is far preferable to that of Mounce, who rather idiosyncratically provides this breakdown:

I. SALUTATION (1:1–2)
II. THANKSGIVING (1:3–5)
III. ENCOURAGEMENT TO TIMOTHY (1:6–2:13)
IV. INSTRUCTIONS FOR TIMOTHY AND OPPONENTS (2:14–4:8)
V. FINAL WORDS TO TIMOTHY (4:9–22)[118]

Recently, C. L. Westfall has proposed this structure for the letter:

I. EPISTOLARY OPENING AND THANKSGIVING (1:1–5)
II. BODY OF THE LETTER: PAUL'S MORAL EXHORTATION TO TIMOTHY (1:6–4:8)
   A. Body Opening: Paul Is Timothy's Spiritual Father and Model (1:6–18)
   B. Body Middle (2:1–3:17)
      1. Timothy Is Entrusted with a Gospel of Suffering (2:1–13)
      2. Timothy's Conduct in Teaching and Speech (2:14–21)
      3. Timothy's Conduct in Conflict with His Opponents (2:22–26)
      4. Paul Is Timothy's Ultimate Model (3:1–17)
   C. Body Closing: Paul's Charge and Timothy's Commission (4:1–8)
III. EPISTOLARY CLOSING (4:9–22)[119]

---

[117] Towner, *Letters to Timothy and Titus*, xi. Marshall's proposal is identical (*Pastoral Epistles*, 38).

[118] Mounce, *Pastoral Epistles*, cxxxvi.

[119] C. L. Westfall, "A Moral Dilemma: The Epistolary Body of 2 Timothy," in *Paul and the Ancient Letter Form*, Pauline Studies 6, ed. S. E. Porter and S. A. Adams (Leiden, Netherlands: Brill, 2010), 251.

The forthcoming discussion of the literary plan for 2 Timothy proceeds with a modified version of Westfall's outline.

Paul's second letter to Timothy opens with the customary greeting and thanksgiving (1:1–7), followed by an exhortation for Timothy not to be ashamed of Paul who is now in prison (1:8–12). After contrasting various coworkers, Paul instructs Timothy on the nature of Christian ministry by way of three metaphors: the soldier, the athlete, and the farmer. Each one has important lessons to teach regarding the proper disposition of the Lord's servant (2:1–7). Paul uses three additional metaphors for Christian ministry: the workman, various instruments, and the servant (2:14–26). Further charges, recent news, and a concluding greeting round out the letter (chaps. 3–4).

Titus

Once again, the various proposals regarding the structure of Titus reveal a certain amount of consensus as well as differences in the details. Towner proposed this outline:

I. OPENING GREETING (1:1–4)
II. BODY OF LETTER (1:5–3:11)
  A. Instructions to Titus (1:5–16)
  B. Instructions for the Church (2:1–3:11)
III. PERSONAL NOTES AND INSTRUCTIONS (3:12–14)
IV. FINAL GREETINGS AND BENEDICTION (3:15).[120]

Towner's outline is similar to that of Mounce, who breaks down 1:5–16 further into 1:5–9 and 1:6–16 but keeps 3:12–15 together as a unit.[121] The structural proposal set forth below differs only slightly from those of these two major commentators.[122]

Similar to 1 Timothy, Paul goes straight to the point by reminding Titus why Paul left him in Crete: "to set right what was left undone and . . . to appoint elders in every town" (1:5). Also similar to 1 Timothy, Titus receives various instructions on how to correct the enemies of the gospel while himself staying above the fray. Christians are to "adorn the teaching of God our Savior in everything" (2:10) and to devote themselves to "every good work" (3:1). In keeping with the personal nature of the letter, Paul concludes with some final instructions and a closing greeting (3:12–15).

OUTLINE

1 Timothy

I. OPENING (1:1–2)
II. PERSONAL CHARGE (1:3–20)
  A. The Challenge of the False Teachers (1:3–11)
  B. Paul's Testimony (1:12–17)

[120] Towner, *Letters to Timothy and Titus*, xii.

[121] Mounce, *Pastoral Epistles*, cxxxvi.

[122] Köstenberger, "Titus," 603. Cf. Marshall (*Pastoral Epistles*, 24).

C. Exhortation to Timothy (1:18–20)

III. CONGREGATIONAL MATTERS (2:1–3:16)
  A. On Prayer (2:1–8)
  B. Regarding Women (2:9–15)
  C. Qualifications for Leaders (3:1–13)
    1. Overseers (3:1–7)
    2. Deacons (3:8–13)
  D. Purpose of Paul's Letter and Concluding Confession (3:14–16)

IV. FURTHER CHARGES (4:1–6:2A)
  A. Latter-day Apostasy (4:1–5)
  B. Being a Good Servant of Jesus Christ (4:6–16)
  C. Further Congregational Matters
    1. Relating to Older and Younger Men, Older and Younger Women (5:1–2)
    2. Ministering to Widows (5:3–16)
    3. Dealing with Elders (5:17–25)
    4. Instructions for Slaves (6:1–2a)

V. EXTENDED FINAL EXHORTATION (6:2B–19)

VI. CLOSING (6:20–21)

2 Timothy

I. LETTER OPENING (1:1–5)
  A. Greeting (1:1–2)
  B. Thanksgiving (1:3–5)

II. BODY OPENING: PERSONAL EXHORTATION (1:6–18)
  A. Call to Suffering and Faithfulness (1:6–14)
  B. Faithless and Faithful Coworkers (1:15–18)

III. BODY MIDDLE: MINISTRY METAPHORS AND ADDITIONAL EXHORTATIONS (2:1–3:17)
  A. Ministry Metaphors, Paul's Gospel, and a Trustworthy Saying (2:1–26)
    1. Three Ministry Metaphors: Soldier, Athlete, Farmer (2:1–7)
    2. Paul's Gospel and a Trustworthy Saying (2:8–13)
    3. Three Additional Ministry Roles: Workman, Instrument, Servant (2:14–26)
  B. Additional Exhortations (3:1–17)
    1. Latter-Day Apostasy (3:1–9)
    2. Stay the Course (3:10–17)

IV. BODY CLOSING: PREACH THE WORD (4:1–8)

V. LETTER CLOSING (4:9–22)
  A. Recent News (4:9–18)
  B. Farewell and Greeting (4:19–22)

Something to Think About: Remember His Mercy

When Paul wrote his first letter to Timothy, he had planted dozens of churches, masterminded the early Christian mission almost single-handedly, and orchestrated the astonishing growth of a worldwide movement spawned by a humble Galilean who met an ignominious death on a Roman cross. If ever anyone were entitled to a dose of self-congratulatory satisfaction or legitimately could have rested on his laurels, it was the apostle to the Gentiles. But Paul remembered his roots; he recalled his former pride and sin. Do you and I remember that if it were not for the mercy and grace of God, we would still be in our sins?

In the first chapter of 1 Timothy, Paul devotes the customary thanksgiving section to an acknowledgment of his blasphemous past—how he had persecuted God's people until on the road to Damascus he met the risen Christ. Humbly, he acknowledges that he was the worst of sinners, so that he might serve as an example to other believers. So when Paul goes on shortly thereafter in the letter to expose the false teachers Hymenaeus and Alexander (1 Tim 1:20), he is cognizant of the fact that in himself he was no better than them or anyone else. It was only by the grace of God that he was who he was. The same is true for you and me.

UNIT-BY-UNIT DISCUSSIONS

1 TIMOTHY

I. Opening (1:1–2)

The standard epistolary opening names Paul as the author and Timothy, his "true son in the faith," as the recipient. "Mercy" is added to the traditional greeting of "grace and peace."

II. Personal Charge (1:3–20)

At the outset, Paul states the occasion for writing, the challenge of the false teachers (1:6–11). Paul's testimony shows that God's grace alone separated him from the false teachers (1:12–17). The opening section concludes with an exhortation to Timothy and an identification by name of two false teachers, Hymenaeus and Alexander (1:18–20).

III. Congregational Matters (2:1–3:16)

With the transition, "First of all, then, I urge," Paul turns to some of the major business at hand. He addresses various issues related to congregational prayer (2:1–8) before turning to matters related to leadership in the church. Women are to dress modestly and must not teach or exercise authority over men (2:8–15). Male candidates for overseer must meet certain qualifications (3:1–7), as must candidates for deacon, male or female (3:8–13).[123]

[123] See the discussion of qualifications for church leaders under Theological Themes below.

The section ends with a statement of the purpose of Paul's letter and a concluding confession (3:14–16).

IV. Further Charges (4:1–6:2a)

Returning to the challenge of the false teachers, Paul sets this phenomenon in the larger context of latter-day apostasy (4:1–5). He instructs Timothy on being a good servant of Jesus Christ (4:6–16) and addresses several additional congregational matters, such as relating to older and younger men as well as to older and younger women (5:1–2); ministering to widows who are truly in need (5:3–16); appointing or disciplining elders (5:17–25); and providing instructions for slaves (6:1–2a).

V. Extended Final Exhortation and Closing (6:2b–21)

The first part of Paul's final exhortation is taken up with a closing indictment of the false teachers (6:2b–10). This is followed by a final charge for Timothy in the sight of God to discharge his ministry in keeping with his "good confession" made in the presence of many witnesses (his ordination service?) and in light of the hope of Christ's return. A doxology (6:15–16) is followed by an exhortation to the rich (6:17–19) and one last exhortation for Timothy to oppose what is falsely called "knowledge" (perhaps incipient Gnosticism; 6:20–21).

2 TIMOTHY

I. Opening and Thanksgiving (1:1–5)

The opening of 2 Timothy closely resembles that of 1 Timothy. Again, Paul identifies himself as the writer, calls Timothy his "dearly loved son," and greets Timothy with "Grace, mercy, and peace" (1:1–2). This is followed with an opening thanksgiving (1:3–5).

II. Body Opening: Personal Exhortation (1:6–18)

A brief opening challenge to Timothy and a general call to suffering and faithfulness (1:6–14) replace the more urgent appeal found at the beginning of Paul's first letter to his co-laborer. Paul closes the introduction with a contrast between faithless and faithful coworkers (1:15–18).

III. Body Middle: Ministry Metaphors and Additional Exhortations (2:1–3:17)

In his exhortation of Timothy his "son," Paul draws on three metaphors illustrating the nature of Christian ministry: soldier, athlete, and farmer (2:1–7). Each conveys a key characteristic Paul wanted Timothy to cultivate. At the heart of this section is a carefully arranged mini-doxology (one of the several "trustworthy sayings" featured in the letters to Timothy and Titus), which focuses on Christ's work of salvation and its implications for God's workers (2:8–13). Three additional ministry roles are set forth: workman, instrument, and servant (2:14–26). As in 1 Timothy, about halfway through the letter Paul

Something to Think About: 2–2–2

Paul's plan of discipleship was as simple as 2–2–2, that is, as simple as what is explained in 2 Timothy 2:2! In this, his final letter to his foremost disciple, the apostle wrote about his mentoring strategy: "And what you have heard from me in the presence of many witnesses, commit to faithful men who will be able to teach others also." In this short sentence Paul lists as many as four generations of those who safeguard the faithful passing on of the Christian tradition:

Generation 1: Paul the apostle

Generation 2: Timothy

Generation 3: Faithful men

Generation 4: Others

When Jesus spoke his final prayer as recorded in John's Gospel, he prayed first for himself (17:1–5), then for his immediate followers (17:6–19), and then for those who would become disciples through their ministry (17:20–25). For both Jesus and Paul, therefore, the key to the successful spread of the Christian faith lay in multiplying faithful generations of Christian witnesses. This places a premium on faithfulness, for if any one generation is unfaithful, the chain of witnesses is broken and the tradition is distorted.

Paul wrote elsewhere, "A person should think of us in this way: as servants of Christ and managers of the mysteries of God. In this regard, it is required that managers be found faithful" (1 Cor 4:1–2). In Jesus's parable of the Talents, the master commends his servant: "Well done, good and faithful servant! You were faithful over a few things; I will put you in charge of many things. Share your master's joy!" (Matt 25:21).

In today's culture faithfulness is a largely overlooked virtue. Flashiness typically triumphs over solid character; self-promotion over quiet, steady faithfulness; and "Christian celebrities" garner the lion's share of attention while those who pastor small rural or inner-city churches or who labor in tucked-away assignments on the mission field go unheralded. Be that as it may, let us be comforted and spurred on by the fact that, in heaven one day, it will be faithfulness, not flashiness, that will be rewarded for those who have run the race with endurance.

refers to the latter-day apostasy at work in the false teachers (3:1–9); in response to this, he encourages Timothy to stay the course (3:10–17).

IV. Body Closing: Preach the Word (4:1–8)

Paul encourages Timothy to preach the Word (4:1–8). The charge to preach the Word marks the solemn, climactic concluding exhortation of Paul's two letters to Timothy, in that it is given "before God and Christ Jesus, who is going to judge the living and the dead, and because of his appearing and his kingdom."

V. Letter Closing (4:9–22)

The letter concludes with some recent news from the apostle's busy life, even while in prison as he coordinated the mission of the early church (4:9–18), and with final greetings (4:19–22). Paul urged Timothy to come to him quickly, and if possible before winter. Only Luke was with Paul, and the apostle wanted Timothy to bring Mark with him as well, once he was relieved by Tychicus, who would stay in Ephesus and take Timothy's place after delivering the present letter to him. Closing greetings are sent to Priscilla and Aquila and to the household of Onesiphorus.

OUTLINE

Titus

I. OPENING (1:1–4)
II. OCCASION FOR WRITING (1:5–16)
  A. The Need to Appoint Qualified Elders (1:5–9)
  B. The Cretan Opposition (1:10–16)
III. INSTRUCTIONS CONCERNING DIFFERENT GROUPS IN THE CHURCH (2:1–15)
  A. Introduction (2:1)
  B. Household Code (2:2–10)
    1. Older Men (2:2)
    2. Older and Young Women (2:3–5)
    3. Younger Men (2:6–8)
    4. Slaves (2:9–10)
  C. The Manifestation of the Grace of God in Christ and the Expectation of Christ's Return (2:11–14)
  D. Conclusion (2:15)
IV. INSTRUCTIONS ON DOING WHAT IS GOOD IN THE CONTEXT OF THE GENERAL CULTURE (3:1–11)
  A. On Keeping the Peace (3:1–2)
  B. The Manifestation of God's Kindness and Love in Christ and Regeneration by the Spirit (3:3–8a)
  C. On Dealing with Divisive Persons (3:8b–11)
V. CONCLUSION (3:12–15)
  A. Final instructions (3:12–14)
  B. Closing (3:15)

UNIT-BY-UNIT DISCUSSION

TITUS

I. Opening (1:1–4)

Paul's rather lengthy opening greeting to Titus bears considerable resemblance to the greeting in 1 Timothy. In addition, Paul provides an extended statement on the purpose of his apostleship.

II. Occasion for Writing (1:5–16)

The occasion is described in terms of the need to appoint qualified elders (1:5–9), which is set in the context of Titus's Cretan opposition (1:10–16). The list of qualifications for church leaders in Titus 1:6–9 is roughly equivalent to the one in 1 Timothy 3:1–7, though there is no equivalent list of qualification for deacons (1 Tim 3:8–12).

Something to Think About: Can a Liar Tell the Truth?

Here's a question. When someone who is a liar says all people are liars, is he telling the truth? This has been called the "liar paradox," and it is raised by a statement in Titus 1:12–13, where Paul states, "One of their very own prophets said, 'Cretans are always liars, evil beasts, lazy gluttons.' This testimony is true." So, then, there is one exception to Cretans always being liars: when they say of themselves that they are always liars, at least that statement is true! This is the solution to the puzzle of "liar paradox."

In Titus's case, of course, this sad statement highlights the difficulty of his assignment: to bring the truth of the gospel to an island not known for its virtue, just as first-century Rome and Corinth were known for their decadence and immorality. It was difficult for the gospel to make inroads in such depraved cultures; and even if some were converted, where was one to find leadership material among those converts?

This brings into sharper focus the transforming power of Christ and of his Spirit and of the gospel. As Paul wrote later in Titus, "He [Jesus Christ] gave himself for us to redeem us from all lawlessness and to cleanse for himself a people for his own possession, eager to do good works" (2:14). And again, "But when the goodness and love for man appeared from God our Savior, He saved us—not by works of righteousness that we had done, but according to His mercy, through the washing of regeneration and renewal by the Holy Spirit" (3:4–5).

Can a Cretan tell the truth? Well, according to one of their own, the answer is "no." But the same can be said about all of us in our unregenerate state: "To the pure, everything is pure, but to those who are defiled and unbelieving nothing is pure; in fact, both their mind and conscience are defiled. . . . They are detestable, disobedient, and unfit for any good work" (1:15–16). I thank God that he still reaches down into the depths of depravity and saves wretched sinners such as me, transforming them to serve him.

III. Instructions Concerning Different Groups in the Church (2:1–15)

Similar to his instructions to Timothy (1 Tim 5:1–2), Paul summarizes how Titus should treat older men (2:1–2), older and younger women (2:3–5), and younger men (2:6–8); and he provides instructions for slaves in the church (2:9–10). Paul proceeds to identify two major incentives for Titus as he discharged his ministry: the grace of God and the return of Christ, "the appearing of the glory of our great God and Savior, Jesus Christ," which Paul calls "the blessed hope" (2:11–14). The section concludes with an affirmation of Titus's authority (2:15).

IV. Instructions on Doing What Is Good in the Context of the General Culture (3:1–11)

The closing general instructions focus on being "ready for every good work." This involves comments on keeping the peace (3:1–2) and remarks on salvation in Christ and on the renewal by the Spirit, plus a final warning (3:3–11). At the outset of this section Paul describes the state of non-Christians by way of seven characteristics, making clear that it is only by God's grace that he, Titus, and other believers are any different.

V. Conclusion (3:12–15)

The customary closing comments conclude the letter (3:12–15).

THEOLOGY

Theological Themes

Qualifications of Church Leaders One of the major contributions the letters to Timothy and Titus make to the Christian canon relates to qualifications for church leaders.[124] The threat of the false teachers provided the backdrop for Paul's stipulations in this area. Since church leaders are charged with doctrinal oversight of local congregations, it is absolutely essential that they are chosen carefully in conformity to clearly articulated standards of character and integrity. For this reason it is fitting that a considerable portion of the letters to Timothy and Titus is given to instructions on qualifications for church leaders.[125]

---

[124] For helpful materials on the subject, see esp. P. A. Newton, *Elders in Congregational Life: Rediscovering the Biblical Model for Church Leadership* (Grand Rapids, MI: Kregel, 2005); Merkle, *Elder and Overseer*; idem, *40 Questions About Elders and Deacons* (Grand Rapids, MI: Kregel, 2008); Köstenberger, "Church Government"; idem, "1 Timothy," 521–30. For presentations of different views, see S. B. Cowan, gen. ed., *Who Runs the Church? 4 Views on Church Government* (Grand Rapids, MI: Zondervan, 2004); and C. O. Brand and R. S. Norman, eds., *Perspectives on Church Government: Five Views of Church Polity* (Nashville, TN: B&H, 2004).

[125] For a helpful survey, see D. A. Mappes, "Moral Virtues Associated with Eldership," *BSac* 160 (2003): 202–18, who argues that some of the qualifications are designed to contrast true and false teachers and discusses these qualifications within the larger context of the power of the personal example in Paul's Letters to Timothy and Titus. Mappes also compares elder qualifications in 1 Tim 3:1–6 with Greco-Roman lists of virtues and vices (pp. 207–12). See also B. A. Paschke, "The *cura morum* of the Roman Censors as Historical Background for the Bishop and Deacon Lists of the Pastoral Epistles," *ZNW* 98 (2007): 105–19, who investigates the *cura morum* ("care of manners") practiced by Roman censors investigating the private life of candidates for the Roman senate; and J. K. Goodrich, "Overseers as Stewards and the Qualifications for Leadership

These leaders, variously called "overseers" or "elders," are to meet the following qualifications (1 Tim 3:1–7).[126] They are to be above reproach, faithful husbands,[127] self-controlled, sensible, respectable, hospitable, able to teach, not addicted to wine, not violent but gentle, not quarrelsome, not greedy, good managers of their own households with their children in submission, not new converts, and of good reputation with those outside the church (a similar list is given in Titus 1:6–9).[128]

The second office regulated in the letters to Timothy and Titus is that of deacon. That Paul provides qualifications for deacons in 1 Timothy but not in Titus may be accounted for by the fact that the church in Ephesus to which 1 Timothy was addressed was more developed (with existing elders) than that in Crete (the church under Titus's charge), where elders had not yet been appointed. Qualifications for deacons include: being worthy of respect, not hypocritical, not drinking a lot of wine, not greedy for money, holding the mystery of the faith with a clear conscience, faithfulness in marriage, and competent management of their own children and households (1 Tim 3:8–10,12). To this is added the requirement that these deacons first be tested (v. 10) and that serving well as deacons brings a good standing and great eternal rewards (v. 13).

An interesting question is raised with regard to the presence of qualifications for "women" *(gynaikes)* in 1 Timothy 3:11, referring either to women married to deacons (deacons' wives) or to women who are themselves serving as deacons (deaconesses). Both interpretations are possible and have advocates in major commentators and translations.[129] Some fear that appointing women as deacons would compromise the NT (and Pauline) principle of reserving leadership roles in the church and ordination to the ministry for men (see esp. 1 Tim 2:12; and the husband of one wife requirement for overseers in 1 Tim 3:2 and Titus 1:6). However, such concern is unnecessary if it is kept in mind that "deacon" *(diakonos)* means "servant," and that, unlike the role of elder or overseer (1 Tim 3:2; Titus 1:9), the role of deacon does not entail the exercise of teaching or governing authority over the church.[130] Most likely, they engaged in various forms of practical service in the church. In

---

in the Pastoral Epistles," *ZNW* 14 (2013): 77–97. Note also B. L. Merkle, "Are the Qualifications for Elders or Overseers Negotiable?," *BSac* 171 (2014): 172–88.

[126] See the comparative chart in Köstenberger, "1–2 Timothy, Titus," 523–24.

[127] See A. J. Köstenberger (with D. W. Jones), *God, Marriage, and Family: Rebuilding the Biblical Foundation,* 2nd ed. (Wheaton, IL: Crossway, 2010), 239–44 (see esp. the chart listing the different views on p. 243).

[128] Separate lists of qualifications are provided for deacons and women (whether female deacons or deacons' wives; 1 Tim 3:8–13; see Acts 6:1–6; Rom 16:1–2). For a discussion of these qualifications, see Köstenberger, "1–2 Timothy, Titus," 522–30, 606–8.

[129] See the discussion and literature cited in Köstenberger, "1–2 Timothy, Titus," 529–30. Among translations, the CSB has "wives"; the NASB "women" (fn "i.e. either deacons' wives or deaconesses"); the NIV "their wives" (fn: "Or deaconesses"); and the TNIV: "the women" (fn: "Probably women who are deacons, or possibly deacons' wives").

[130] Contrary to J. N. Collins, *Diakonia: Re-interpreting the Ancient Sources* (Oxford, UK: Oxford University Press, 2009), who argues that the word *diakonos* meant "messenger" or "emissary" and did not have any connotation of service or helping the needy; and A. Hentschel, *Diakonia Im Neuen Testament: Studien zur Semantik unter besonderer Berücksichtigung der Rolle von Frauen* (WUNT 2/226; Tübingen, Germany: Mohr Siebeck, 2007), who contends that the focus of the activity of

any case, these women are to be "worthy of respect, not slanderers, self-controlled, faithful in everything" (1 Tim 3:11).

In addition to providing qualifications for church leaders, 1 Timothy and the other letters to Timothy and Titus provide insight into many areas of congregational life, such as the role of women (1 Tim 2:9–15),[131] caring for widows (1 Tim 5:1–16),[132] dealing with sinning elders (1 Tim 5:17–25),[133] and exhorting wealthy church members (1 Tim 6:2–10, 17–19). All in all, the letters to Timothy and Titus are a treasure trove for the training of church leaders for the ministry. The men serve as representative figures for any aspiring pastor who would enter into the venerable tradition of those who over the centuries have served Christ in local church ministry.

Salvation P. H. Towner rightly observes that "at the centre of the theology of the Pastoral Epistles is the theme of salvation."[134] Frequent reference is made in the letters to Timothy and Titus to God (or Christ) as Savior and to the salvation he provides in Christ.[135] Paul identifies himself immediately as "an apostle of Christ Jesus by the command of God our Savior" (1 Tim 1:1). He uses the phrase "God our Savior" later on

---

diakonoi is in the leadership function of preaching and teaching (see esp. 397–402). But see the review of Hentschel's work by E. J. Schnabel in *BBR* 18 (2008): 179–81.

[131] See A. J. Köstenberger and T. R. Schreiner, eds., *Women in the Church: An Analysis and Application of 1 Timothy 2:9–15*, 3rd ed. (Wheaton, IL: Crossway, 2016).

[132] Many argue that the discussion of widows in 1 Timothy 5 regulates (or at least recognizes) a formal office of widows, parallel in at least some regards to that of overseer or deacon. Others see the passage as focusing simply on the support of needy widows. For discussion, see in addition to the commentaries, J. M. Bassler, "Limits and Differentiation: The Calculus of Widows in 1 Timot5.3–16," in *A Feminist Companion to the Deutero-Pauline Epistles*, ed. A.-J. Levine with M. Blickenstaff (Cleveland, OH: Pilgrim, 2003), 122–46; D. G. Horrell, "Disciplining Performance and 'Placing' the Church: Widows, Elders and Slaves in the Household of God (1 Tim 5:1—6:2)," in *1 Timothy Reconsidered*, ed. K. P. Donfried (Leuven, Belgium: Peeters, 2008), 109–34; M. D. Moore, "The 'Widows' in 1 Tim. 5:3–16," in *Essays on Women in Earliest Christianity*, ed. C. D. Osburn (Eugene, OR: Wipf & Stock, 2007), 321–66; B. Thurston, "1 Timothy 5.3–16 and the Leadership of Women in the Early Church," in *A Feminist Companion to the Deutero-Pauline Epistles*, 159–74; B. Winter, "Providentia for the Widows of 1 Timothy 5:3–16." *TynBul* 39 (1988): 83–99. Note that Mounce (*Pastoral Epistles*, 300–302) has an excellent summary discussion on widows in the postapostolic church.

[133] See D. A. Mappes, "The Discipline of a Sinning Elder," *BSac* 154 (1997): 333–43; W. Kowalski, "The Reward, Discipline, and Installation of Church Leaders: An Examination of 1 Timothy 5:17–22" (Ph.D. diss., University of Gloucestershire, 2005).

[134] P. H. Towner, "The Pastoral Epistles," in *New Dictionary of Biblical Theology*, ed. T. D. Alexander and B. S. Rosner (Downers Grove, IL: InterVarsity, 2000), 332.

[135] E.g., Mounce, *Pastoral Epistles*, cxxxii–cxxxv. Note the important recent treatment by G. M. Wieland, *The Significance of Salvation: A Study of Salvation Language in the Pastoral Epistles*, Paternoster Biblical Monographs (Eugene, OR: Wipf & Stock, 2006); his work is summarized as "The Function of Salvation in the Letters to Timothy and Titus," in *Entrusted with the Gospel: Paul's Theology in the Pastoral Epistles*, ed. A. J Köstenberger and T. L. Wilder (Nashville, TN: B&H: 2010), 153–72. Other focused contributions include I. H. Marshall, "Salvation in the Pastoral Epistles," in *Geschichte—Tradition—Reflexion: Festschrift für Martin Hengel zum 70. Geburtstag*, vol 3: *Frühes Christentum*, ed. H. Lichtenberger (Tübingen, Germany: J. C. B. Mohr (Paul Siebeck), 1996), 449–69; C. H. Talbert, "Between Two Epiphanies: Clarifying One Aspect of Soteriology in the Pastoral Epistles," in *Getting "Saved": The Whole Story of Salvation in the New Testament*, ed. C. H. Talbert and J. A. Whitlark (Grand Rapids, MI: Eerdmans, 2011), 58–71.

On the question of the extent of the atonement, see on the one hand I. H. Marshall, "Universal Grace and Atonement in the Pastoral Epistles," in *The Grace of God and the Will of Man*, ed. C. H. Pinnock (Minneapolis, MN: Bethany House, 1989), 51–70; and on the other, T. S. Schreiner, "'Problematic Texts' for Definite Atonement in the Pastoral and General

when he speaks of "God our Savior who wants everyone to be saved and to come to the knowledge of the truth" (1 Tim 2:3–4). A third time in 1 Timothy, Paul refers to God, "the Savior of everyone, especially of those who believe" (1 Tim 4:10). In addition, in one of the trustworthy sayings in the letters to Timothy and Titus, he asserts that "Christ Jesus came into the world to save sinners" (1 Tim 1:15).[136]

In 2 Timothy, Paul speaks of "God, who has saved us" (2 Tim 1:8–9), and in the same context he refers to "the appearing of our Savior Christ Jesus" (2 Tim 1:10). He also asserts that "salvation is in Christ Jesus," a salvation that, while secured in the past, will be consummated in the future, necessitating faithfulness and perseverance in the faith (2 Tim 2:10). The source of knowledge regarding this salvation through faith in Christ Jesus is the Holy Scripture, that is, the OT, which spoke prophetically of him (2 Tim 3:15). Several passages also speak of believers' safe preservation in this life and their safe passage into the next (1 Tim 2:15; 4:16; 2 Tim 4:18).[137]

In the introduction of his letter to Titus, Paul refers to both "God our Savior" (1:3) and "Christ Jesus our Savior" (1:4), putting God the Father and Jesus Christ on par with regard to their role as Savior of humanity. This teaching is further developed in the body of the letter, where Paul speaks of "the teaching of God our Savior," according to which "the grace of God has appeared, with salvation for all people," teaching them to live righteous and godly lives in the present while waiting for the return of "our great God and Savior, Jesus Christ" (Titus 2:10–13).

Also, in a remarkable trinitarian passage, Paul asserts that

> when the kindness of God our Savior and his love for mankind appeared, he saved us—not by works of righteousness that we had done, but according to his mercy, through the washing of regeneration and renewal by the Holy Spirit. He poured out this Spirit on us abundantly through Jesus Christ our Savior so that, having been justified by his grace, we may become heirs with the hope of eternal life (Titus 3:4–7).

Again, it is evident that Paul considered God the Father and Jesus Christ on par as to their role as Savior of humanity, for he understood the triune Godhead as integrally involved in providing and applying this salvation.

How are we to account for the frequency of the "Savior/salvation" word group in the letters to Timothy and Titus? Most likely, the reason is that Paul sought to present Jesus as Savior in contrast to other gods or the emperor. Evidence is strong that especially in Ephesus the title "Savior" *(sōter)* was used as "a title of description of gods, emperors,

---

Epistles," in *He Came and Sought Her: Definite Atonement in Historical, Biblical, Theological, and Pastoral Perspective*, ed. D. Gibson and J. Gibson (Wheaton, IL: Crossway, 2013), 375–97.

[136] It is of note that most of the "faithful sayings" in the letters to Timothy and Titus are salvation-oriented.

[137] See the discussion on the preservation of believers below.

provincial proconsuls, and local patrons,"[138] so it is possible Paul was responding to that false teaching perpetrated in Ephesus. Rather than salvation being found by adhering to various myths and genealogies, Paul contended that it was for "everyone" (1 Tim 2:4) and came through Christ the Savior (1 Tim 1:15; 2:3–4; 4:10; Titus 2:10–11; cf. Titus 3:2, 4).

The Preservation of Believers The letters to Timothy and Titus exhibit a consistent concern for believers' preservation from Satan or demonic forces.[139] In 1 Timothy 1:20, Paul says that he has delivered two false teachers over to Satan so that they might learn not to blaspheme.[140] He mentions that Eve was deceived at the fall, providing instructions for women on how to escape a similar fate (1 Tim 2:14–15; cf. 5:14–15 with reference to young widows). He warns against appointing new converts to positions of church leadership, lest they become conceited and fall into the condemnation incurred by the Devil (1 Tim 3:6). He also requires that candidates for ecclesiastical office be above reproach and enjoy a good reputation with those outside the church (1 Tim 3:7).

Paul also denounces those who teach others to refrain from marriage or to abstain from certain foods because of a false dichotomy between material and spiritual things, a dichotomy described as "teachings of demons" (1 Tim 4:1–3). Another area from which believers need to be preserved spiritually is the desire to grow wealthy (1 Tim 6:9–10; see 2 Tim 2:26). Paul warns Timothy to guard himself against "irreverent, empty speech and contradictions from what is falsely called "knowledge" (1 Tim 6:20). This apparently relates to an early form of Gnosticism, which taught a dualism between matter and spirit, disparaging all things created (see 1 Tim 2:14–15; 4:1–3).

Paul explains that the false teachers have been ensnared by the Devil and held captive to do his will (2 Tim 2:26). In contrast to these heretics, Timothy is repeatedly exhorted to guard what had been entrusted to him (1 Tim 6:12; 2 Tim 1:12, 14; 4:7, 15, 18) so that he may "escape" (author's translation) the grasp of the errorists and "pursue" Christian virtue (1 Tim 6:11; 2 Tim 2:22). As Paul's apostolic delegate, he is to be conscientious about himself and his teaching and to persevere in these things, for by doing so he would "preserve" (NASB) both himself and his hearers (1 Tim 4:16). By contrast, the false teachers have "wandered away from the faith," having "strayed" or "turned aside," so that their faith suffered "shipwreck" (see 1 Tim 1:6, 19; 5:13, 15; 6:9, 10, 21).

The Trustworthy Sayings Five statements in the letters to Timothy and Titus (at least one in each letter) are designated by the author as "trustworthy sayings" (*pistos ho logos*, lit.

---

[138] S. M. Baugh, "'Savior of All People': 1 Tim 4:10 in Context," *WTJ* 54 (1992): 335. Baugh mentions, and Glahn ("The Identity of Artemis") highlights, the fact that the term "savior" was applied in particular to Artemis of the Ephesians.

[139] See A. J. Köstenberger, "Ascertaining Women's God-Ordained Roles: An Interpretation of 1 Timothy 2:15," *BBR* 7 (1997): 107–44, esp. 130–33. Cf. E. Schlarb, *Die gesunde Lehre: Häresie und Wahrheit im Spiegel der Pastoralbriefe* (Marburg, Germany: N. G. Elwert, 1990).

[140] "Delivering to Satan" is a way of referring to exclusion of an unrepentant professing Christian from the congregation of believers; see 1 Cor 5:5.

"trustworthy [is] the saying"; see the chart below).[141] This interesting feature, together with other linguistic, literary, and theological elements, provides a degree of coherence for this cluster of letters. Beyond this, there is considerable variety among these five "trustworthy sayings." The first such saying (1 Tim 1:15) is reminiscent of Jesus's statement in Luke 19:10 and is accompanied by the phrase that is "deserving of full acceptance" (as in 1 Tim 4:9), which is also attested in Hellenistic literature.[142]

In the second "trustworthy saying" (1 Tim 3:1), Paul underscores the propriety of aspiring to the office of overseer and the nobility of the task, similar to Jesus's solemn affirmation, "Truly I tell you" (*amēn, amēn*; see John 1:51). The third saying (1 Tim 4:8) is surrounded by scholarly controversy. Some claim that the "trustworthy saying" occurs in verse 10, not in verse 8.[143] On balance, however, verse 8 is to be preferred for these reasons: (1) verse 8 has the form of a proverbial saying; (2) *gymnasia* ("training"; once in the NT) and *sōmatikē* ("of the body"; twice in the NT) are rare words, which makes adaptation as a "trustworthy saying" more likely; (3) verse 8 (but not v. 10) speaks of an action that verse 9 seems to call for; and (4) verse 8a can be better explained as part of a saying.

The fourth saying (2 Tim 2:11–13) focuses on the rewards of suffering while affirming that God remains faithful even if his servants are not. In light of the numerous Pauline parallels (see esp. Rom 8:28–39), the saying was most likely coined by Paul himself. The statement consists of four conditional clauses, the first two on faithful service, the final two on denying Christ. The last clause features an added reason: "For he cannot deny himself." The cadence makes for an interesting dynamic, especially the breaking of the pattern in the last element where an expected negative statement is replaced by a positive one. The fifth saying (Titus 3:4–7) constitutes a summary of Paul's soteriology in highly condensed form and in trinitarian import, centering on God's salvation of believers through Christ and his regenerating work through the Holy Spirit.

Hence, the range of "trustworthy sayings" in the letters to Timothy and Titus includes (1) a possible adaptation of a saying of Christ (1 Tim 1:15); (2) a solemn apostolic affirmation about church leadership (1 Tim 3:1); (3) an apostolic pronouncement about the value of godliness (1 Tim 4:8); (4) a hymn-like, artistically crafted affirmation of God's

---

[141] The seminal monograph is G. W. Knight, *The Faithful Sayings in the Pastoral Letters* (Grand Rapids, MI: Baker, 1979); see also R. A. Campbell, "Identifying the Faithful Sayings in the Pastoral Epistles," *JSNT* 54 (1994): 73–86; Marshall, *Pastoral Epistles*, 326–39; Mounce, *Pastoral Epistles*, 48–49; Towner, *Letters to Timothy and Titus*, 143–53; and Yarbrough, *Paul's Utilization of Preformed Traditions*.

On the (related) theme of "faith" (*pistis*) in the letters to Timothy and Titus, see Mounce (*Pastoral Epistles*, cxxx–cxxxii), who noted that the noun *pistis* ("faith") occurs thirty-three times and the adjective *pistos* ("trustworthy") seventeen times in the letters to Timothy and Titus. Mounce found that "there is no *one* single concept of πίστις" in the PE [Pastoral Epistles]," but that "no new use of πίστις is introduced in the PE. Although the creedal use is more evident here than in other Pauline writings, it is still present in the earliest of Paul's writings" (ibid., cxxxii). The fact that the opponents were attacking the body of belief that comprised "the faith" (understood as the embodiment of orthodox Christian doctrine) explains the frequency of this kind of usage in the letters to Timothy and Titus.

[142] Philo, *Flight* 129; *Rewards* 13.

[143] Interestingly, verse 8 is favored as the "trustworthy saying" by a vast majority of commentators but not translations.

faithfulness in the face of human faithlessness (2 Tim 2:11–13); and (5) a summary of Paul's soteriology in trinitarian terms (Titus 3:4–7). Also, two of the five have the formula after the referent (1 Tim 4:8; Titus 3:4–7).

Table 15.1: The "Trustworthy Sayings" in the Letters to Timothy and Titus

	Trustworthy Saying
1 Tim 1:15	This saying is trustworthy and deserving of full acceptance: "Christ Jesus came into the world to save sinners."
1 Tim 3:1	This saying is trustworthy: "If anyone aspires to be an overseer, he desires a noble work."
1 Tim 4:8–9	"For the training of the body has a limited benefit, but godliness is beneficial in every way, since it holds promise for the present life and also for the life to come." This saying is trustworthy.
2 Tim 2:11–13	This saying is trustworthy: "For if we have died with him, we will also live with him; if we endure, we will also reign with him; if we deny him, he will also deny us; if we are faithless, he remains faithful, for he cannot deny himself."
Titus 3:4–8	"But when the goodness and love for man appeared from God our Savior, He saved us—not by works of righteousness that we had done, but according to His mercy, through the washing of regeneration and renewal by the Holy Spirit. This Spirit He poured out on us abundantly through Jesus Christ our Savior, so that having been justified by His grace, we may become heirs with the hope of eternal life." This saying is trustworthy.

CONTRIBUTION TO THE CANON

- God our Savior and salvation in Christ (1 Tim 2:3–4; 4:10; 2 Tim 1:10; Titus 1:3–4)
- Qualifications for church leaders (1 Tim 3:1–12; Titus 1:6–9) and the role of women in the church (1 Tim 2:9–15)
- Preservation of sound doctrine and refutation of false teachers (see 1 Tim 4:16)
- The importance of pursuing godliness, self-control, and Christian virtues (see 1 Tim 4:11–16; 6:6; 2 Tim 2:22)
- Trustworthy sayings (see Table 15.1 above)

STUDY QUESTIONS

1. Is it proper to call 1 and 2 Timothy and Titus "Pastoral Epistles"? Explain.
2. Which of the three letters was written from prison?
3. When did scholars begin to question Paul's authorship of these letters?
4. What is the genre of the letters to Timothy and Titus, and what implications does this have?
5. How many church offices are prescribed in the letters to Timothy and Titus?

6. What is the likely meaning of the phrases "the husband of one wife" (1 Tim 3:2) and "husbands of one wife" (1 Tim 3:12; Titus 1:6)?
7. What is the best description of Timothy's and Titus's ministry assignments?
8. Which important theme in the letters to Timothy and Titus helps the reader understand Paul's reference to women being "saved through childbearing" (1 Tim 2:15)?
9. What are the qualifications of church leaders (1 Tim 3:1–7; Titus 1:6–9)?
10. What is meant by the authors' designation "trustworthy sayings"?
11. What contributions do 1–2 Timothy and Titus make to the canon?

FOR FURTHER STUDY

Aageson, J. W. *Paul, the Pastoral Epistles, and the Early Church*. Peabody, MA: Hendrickson, 2008.

Baugh, S. M. "1, 2 Timothy, Titus." Pages 444–511 in vol. 3 of *Zondervan Illustrated Bible Background Commentary*. Edited by C. E. Arnold. Grand Rapids, MI: Zondervan, 2001.

Belleville, L. "Introduction to the Pastoral Epistles" and "1 Timothy." Pages 3–123 in *1 Timothy, 2 Timothy, Titus, Hebrews*. Cornerstone Biblical Commentary 17. Carol Stream, IL: Tyndale, 2009.

Blight, R. C. *An Exegetical Summary of 1 Timothy*. Dallas, TX: SIL International, 2009.

Carson, D. A. "Pseudonymity and Pseudepigraphy." Pages 856–64 in *Dictionary of New Testament Background*. Edited by C. A. Evans and S. E. Porter. Downers Grove, IL: InterVarsity, 2000.

Collins, R. F. *1 and 2 Timothy and Titus: A Commentary*. New Testament Library. Louisville, KY: Westminster John Knox, 2002.

Dibelius, M., and H. Conzelmann. *A Commentary on the Pastoral Epistles*. Hermeneia. Philadelphia, PA: Fortress, 1972.

Ellis, E. E. "Pastoral Letters." Pages 658–66 in *Dictionary of Paul and His Letters*. Edited by G. F. Hawthorne and R. P. Martin. Downers Grove, IL: InterVarsity, 1993.

Fee, G. D. *1 and 2 Timothy, Titus*. New International Biblical Commentary on the New Testament 13. Peabody, MA: Hendrickson, 1988.

Fiore, B. *The Function of Personal Example in the Socratic and Pastoral Epistles*. Analecta biblica 105. Rome, Italy: Biblical Institute Press, 1986.

___________. *The Pastoral Epistles*, Sacra Pagina. Collegeville, MN: Liturgical Press, 2007.

Gorday, J. *Colossians, 1–2 Thessalonians, 1–2 Timothy, Titus, Philemon*. Ancient Christian Commentary on Scripture, New Testament 9. Downers Grove, IL: InterVarsity, 2000.

Harding, M. *Tradition and Rhetoric in the Pastoral Epistles*. Studies in Biblical Literature 3. New York, NY: Peter Lang, 1998.

___________. *What Are They Saying about the Pastoral Epistles?* Mahwah, NJ: Paulist, 2001.

Johnson, L. T. *The First and Second Letters to Timothy: A New Translation with Introduction and Commentary*. Anchor Bible 35A. New York, NY: Doubleday, 2001.

___________. *Letters to Paul's Delegates: 1 Timothy, 2 Timothy, Titus*. Valley Forge, PA: Trinity International, 1996.

Kelly, J. N. D. *A Commentary on the Pastoral Epistles*. Black's New Testament Commentaries. London, England: A&C Black, 1963.

Kidd, R. M. *Wealth and Beneficence in the Pastoral Epistles: A "Bourgeois" Form of Early Christianity?* SBL Dissertation Series 122. Atlanta, GA: Scholars, 1990.

Knight, G. W. *The Faithful Sayings in the Pastoral Epistles*. Grand Rapids, MI: Baker, 1979

__________. *The Pastoral Epistles*. New International Greek Testament Commentary. Grand Rapids, MI: Eerdmans, 1992.

Köstenberger, A. J. "Church Government." Pages 543–51 in vol. 1 of *Encyclopedia of Christian Civilization*. Edited by G. T. Kurian. Malden, MA: Wiley-Blackwell, 2011.

__________. "1–2 Timothy, Titus." Pages 487–625 in *Expositor's Bible Commentary*. Rev. ed. Vol. 12: *Ephesians–Philemon*. Grand Rapids, MI: Zondervan, 2005.

__________. *Commentary on 1-2 Timothy and Titus*. Biblical Theology for Christian Proclamation. Nashville, TN: B&H, 2017.

__________. "The New Testament Pattern of Church Government." *Midwestern Journal of Theology* 4/2 (2006): 24–42.

__________, and T. R. Schreiner, eds. *Women in the Church: An Analysis and Application of 1 Timothy 2:9–15*. 3rd ed. Wheaton, IL: Crossway, 2016.

__________, and T. L. Wilder, eds. *Entrusted with the Gospel: Paul's Theology in the Pastoral Epistles*. Nashville, TN: B&H Academic, 2010.

Laansma, J. C. "2 Timothy" and "Titus." Pages 124–302 in *1 Timothy, 2 Timothy, Titus, Hebrews*. Cornerstone Biblical Commentary 17. Carol Stream, IL: Tyndale, 2009.

Laniak, T. S. *Shepherds After My Own Heart: Pastoral Traditions and Leadership in the Bible*. New Studies in Biblical Theology 20. Downers Grove, IL: InterVarsity, 2006.

Lau, A. Y. *Manifest in the Flesh: The Epiphany Christology of the Pastoral Epistles*. Tübingen, Germany: Mohr Siebeck, 1996.

Malherbe, A. J. *Light from the Gentiles: Hellenistic Philosophy and Early Christianity. Collected Essays, 1959–2012*. Edited by C. R. Holladay, J. T. Fitzgerald, G. E. Sterling, and J. W. Thompson. 2 vols. Supplements to Novum Testamentum 150. Leiden, Netherlands: Brill, 2014.

Marshall, I. H. *A Critical and Exegetical Commentary on the Pastoral Epistles*. International Critical Commentary. Edinburgh, Scotland: T&T Clark, 1999.

__________. "The Pastoral Epistles in Recent Study." Pages 268–324 in *Entrusted with the Gospel: Paul's Theology in the Pastoral Epistles*. Edited by A. J. Köstenberger and T. L. Wilder. Nashville, TN: B&H Academic, 2010.

Merkle, B. L. *The Elder and Overseer: One Office in the Early Church*. Studies in Biblical Literature 57. New York, NY: Peter Lang, 2003.

__________. *40 Questions About Elders and Deacons*. Grand Rapids, MI: Kregel, 2008.

Mills, W. E. *Pastoral Epistles*. Bibliographies for Biblical Research 14. Lewiston, NY: Mellen Biblical Press, 2000.

Mounce, W. D. *The Pastoral Epistles*. Word Biblical Commentary 46. Waco, TX: Word, 2000.

Prior, M. *Paul the Letter-Writer and the Second Letter to Timothy*. Journal for the Study of the New Testament Supplement 23. Sheffield, UK: JSOT, 1989.

Quinn, J. D. *The Letter to Titus*. Anchor Bible 35. Garden City, NY: Doubleday, 1990.

Quinn, J. D., and W. C. Wacker. *The First and Second Letters to Timothy*. Eerdmans Critical Commentary. Grand Rapids, MI/Cambridge, UK: Eerdmans, 2000.

Schnabel, E. J. "Paul, Timothy, and Titus: The Assumption of a Pseudonymous Author and of Pseudonymous Recipients in the Light of Literary, Theological, and Historical Evidence." Pages 383–403 in *Do Historical Matters Matter to Faith? A Critical Appraisal of Modern and Postmodern Approaches to Scripture*. Edited by J. K. Hoffmeier and D. R. Magary. Wheaton, IL: Crossway, 2012.

Smith, C. *Pauline Communities as "Scholastic Communities": A Study of the Vocabulary of "Teaching" in 1 Corinthians, 1 and 2 Timothy and Titus*. Wissenschaftliche Untersuchungen zum Neuen Testament 2:335. Tübingen, Germany: Mohr Siebeck, 2012.

Spencer, A. B. *1 Timothy*. New Covenant Commentary Series. Eugene, OR: Wipf & Stock, 2013.

___________. *2 Timothy and Titus*. New Covenant Commentary Series. Eugene, OR: Wipf & Stock, 2014.

Stepp, P. L. *Leadership Succession in the World of the Pauline Circle*. New Testament Monographs 5. Sheffield, UK: Sheffield Phoenix, 2005.

Swinson, L. T. *What Is Scripture? Paul's Use of* Graphe *in the Letters to Timothy*. Eugene, OR: Wipf & Stock, 2014.

Thornton, D. T. *Hostility in the House of God: An Investigation of the Opponents in 1 and 2 Timothy*, BBR Supplement 15 (Winona Lake, IN: Eisenbrauns, 2016).

Towner, P. H. "1–2 Timothy and Titus." Pages 891–918 in *Commentary on the New Testament Use of the Old Testament*. Edited by D. A. Carson and G. K. Beale. Grand Rapids, MI: Baker, 2007.

___________. *1–2 Timothy and Titus*. IVP New Testament Commentary. Downers Grove, IL: InterVarsity, 1994.

___________. *The Goal of Our Instruction: The Structure of Theology and Ethics in the Pastoral Epistles*. Journal for the Study of the New Testament Supplement 34. Sheffield, UK: Sheffield Academic, 1989.

___________. *The Letters to Timothy and Titus*. New International Commentary on the New Testament. Grand Rapids, MI: Eerdmans, 2006.

Trebilco, P. *The Early Christians in Ephesus from Paul to Ignatius*. Wissenschaftliche Untersuchungen zum Neuen Testament 166. Tübingen, Germany: Mohr Siebeck, 2004.

Twomey, J. *The Pastoral Epistles through the Centuries*. Blackwell Bible Commentaries. Malden, MA: Wiley-Blackwell, 2009.

Van Neste, R. *Cohesion and Structure in the Pastoral Epistles*. Journal for the Study of the New Testament Supplement Series 280. London, England: T&T Clark, 2004.

Verner, D. C. *The Household of God: The Social World of the Pastoral Epistles*. SBL Dissertation Series 71. Chico, CA: Scholars, 1983.

Wall, R. W. *1 and 2 Timothy and Titus*. Two Horizons New Testament Commentary. Grand Rapids, MI: Eerdmans, 2012.

Wieland, G. M. *The Significance of Salvation: A Study of Salvation Language in the Pastoral Epistles*. Paternoster Biblical Monographs. Carlisle, PA: Paternoster, 2006

Wilder, T. L. "Pseudonymity and the New Testament." Pages 296–335 in *Interpreting the New Testament: Essays on Methods and Issues*. Ed. D. A. Black and D. S. Dockery. Nashville, TN: B&H, 2001.

__________. *Pseudonymity, the New Testament, and Deception: An Inquiry into Intention and Reception*. Lanham, MD: University Press of America, 2004.

Witherington, B., III. *Letters and Homilies for Hellenized Christians: A Socio-Rhetorical Commentary on Titus, 1–2 Timothy and 1–3 John*. Downers Grove, IL: InterVarsity, 2006.

Yarbrough, M. M. *Paul's Utilization of Preformed Traditions in 1 Timothy: An Evaluation of the Apostle's Literary, Rhetorical, and Theological Tactics*. Library of New Testament Studies 417. London, England: T&T Clark, 2009.

Zamfir, K. *Men and Women in the Household of God: A Contextual Approach to Roles and Ministries in the Pastoral Epistles*. Novum Testamentum et Orbis Antiquus / Studien zur Umwelt des Neuen Testaments 103. Göttingen, Germany: Vandenhoeck & Ruprecht, 2013.

Part Four

THE GENERAL EPISTLES AND REVELATION

THIS COMPREHENSIVE INTRODUCTION to the NT has provided treatments of the four Gospels, the book of Acts, and the thirteen letters of Paul. Nine additional books remain to be discussed: eight letters conventionally grouped together under the rubric General Epistles and then the book of Revelation. While often not considered as central to the canon of the NT as the Pauline correspondence, these letters make an indispensable contribution to the biblical canon; their study should in no way be neglected. With one minor change, the treatment of these books follows the canonical order. Chapter 16 considers the book of Hebrews; chapter 17, the book of James; chapter 18, 1 and 2 Peter and Jude; chapter 19, 1 and 2 and 3 John; and chapter 20, the book of Revelation.

Each of these documents raises a unique set of questions that are discussed as appropriate. In the case of Hebrews, a difficulty pertains to the unknown identity of the author. James is a unique writing representing early Jewish Christianity in the NT. The relationship between 2 Peter and Jude and the authorship of 2 Peter also raise interesting questions that are considered. Both James and 1 John are notoriously difficult to outline, so this problem also receives attention. The relationship between the Johannine Letters, John's Gospel, and Revelation is treated as well. A discussion of the historical, literary, and theological issues raised by the book of Revelation concludes Part Four.

CHAPTER 16

THE LETTER TO THE HEBREWS

CORE KNOWLEDGE

Basic Knowledge: Students should know the key facts of the book of Hebrews. With regard to history, students should be able to identify the book's author, date, provenance, destination, and purpose. With regard to literature, they should be able to provide a basic outline of the book and identify core elements of the book's content found in the Unit-by-Unit Discussion. With regard to theology, students should be able to identify the major theological themes in the book of Hebrews.

Intermediate Knowledge: Students should be able to present the arguments for historical, literary, and theological conclusions. With regard to history, students should be able to discuss the evidence for authorship, date, provenance, destination, and purpose. With regard to literature, they should be able to provide a detailed outline of the book. With regard to theology, students should be able to discuss the major theological themes in the book of Hebrews and the ways in which they uniquely contribute to the NT canon.

Advanced Knowledge: Students should be able to assess critically the authorship of Hebrews and how it relates to canonicity. They should be able to discuss the genre of Hebrews, the use of the OT, and rhetorical devices used in the book. They should be able to adjudicate the warning passages in light of the hermeneutic employed by the author and in view of the spiritual condition of the original readers and interact critically with the major structural proposals for the book.

KEY FACTS

Author:	Unknown
Date:	ca. AD 65
Provenance:	Unknown
Destination:	Jewish-Christian congregation(s) in Rome
Occasion:	Persecution of Christians causing some to revert back to Judaism
Purpose:	To warn people in these Jewish-Christian congregations against reverting back to Judaism in order to avoid being persecuted as Christians
Theme:	The supremacy of Christ over OT antecedent figures and other intermediaries
Key Verses:	12:1–2

INTRODUCTION

THE EVENTS OF AD 410 created a crisis for the church in the West. Rome had fallen to Alaric's Goths. The Roman pagans blamed the Christians, who had been in favor since the conversion of Constantine a century earlier. "Your soft and weak philosophy is incapable of providing a stable and secure society" was the essence of the complaint. The accusation led to the production of what is perhaps one of the greatest works of theology in the West, Augustine's *City of God*. Augustine's thesis is that there are two "cities." The city of man stands in contrast to the city of God, and the two cannot be wedded completely, although they are intermingled today. Ironically, the basis for such a teaching that laid the foundation for Western theology is found most clearly in a book the West had difficulty receiving, the book of Hebrews.[1] According to the author of Hebrews, Abraham was looking forward to the city that has foundations, whose architect and builder is God (11:10). In fact, all OT believers were aspiring to enter the city God had built for them (11:16). Zion is our heavenly city (12:22), and there is no enduring city here: "we seek the one to come" (13:14).

One studying the book of Hebrews becomes accustomed to such things. It is a book of profound contrasts and irony. Hebrews is written in the most classical style of Greek in the NT, yet it reflects distinctly Jewish hermeneutics. The book has traditionally been known

---

[1] Augustine begins his exposition of the concept of the city of God (book XII) by acknowledging the idea comes from Scripture (citing several Psalms) and noting the idea is common in Scripture. He describes God's relationship to the city as its "Founder" (Lat. *conditor*). This is at least an echo of Heb 11:10 where the Vulgate describes God as the city's *conditor*. Since Augustine affirms and cites Hebrews often, it is plausible to suggest it played a formative part in his thinking.

as "the letter of Paul to the Hebrews," but, as will be seen, scholars dispute almost every word of this description. The author calls the document a brief "message of exhortation" (13:22), though it is in fact one of the longest letters in the NT. While Hebrews has been acknowledged as one of the greatest works of theology in the NT, it struggled for full canonical acceptance longer than any other NT book.

Indeed, the student of Hebrews encounters a rather daunting series of unknowns, which have consistently defied consensus over the centuries.[2] What is more, studying Hebrews is taxing because understanding it requires considerable familiarity with OT teaching. Yet anyone who immerses himself in the book and its message will be richly rewarded, for, as L. T. Johnson aptly noted, "Hebrews is one of the most beautifully written, powerfully argued, and theologically profound writings in the NT. Its anonymous author summons readers to a vision of reality and a commitment of faith that is at once distinctive, attractive, and disturbing."[3]

With its emphasis on the unmatched, eternal high priesthood of Jesus Christ, the once-for-all character of his substitutionary sacrifice, and particularly the inauguration of the new covenant, Hebrews makes a vital and indispensable contribution to the canon. Against religions that claim God has revealed himself through various prophets and revelations, Hebrews affirms that in these last days God has revealed himself definitively "by his Son" (*en huiō*; 1:2). This Son, after dying on the cross as a substitutionary sacrifice, "sat down" to rest from his work (1:3) and is in heaven as a "forerunner" (6:20) of those who have faith in him for eternal salvation.[4]

HISTORY

Author

It has been suggested that the author of Hebrews is "one of the three great theologians of the New Testament."[5] Unfortunately, the authorship of the letter is the first in the list of mysteries regarding this book. The debate most familiar to evangelical Christians is whether Paul was its author, but it is unlikely that he was (see below). Few scholars today

---

[2] L. D. Hurst (*The Epistle to the Hebrews: Its Background of Thought*, SNTSMS 65 [New York, NY: Cambridge University Press, 1990], 1) even described the book as "something of a joke—a joke played upon a church obsessed with finding complete certainty about its origins." D. A. Black ("The Problem of the Literary Structure of Hebrews," *Grace Theological Journal* 7 [1986]: 164) noted that today the book frequently becomes a collection of proof texts and memory verses.

[3] Preparation for reading Hebrews involves, among other things, reading about the wilderness wanderings of the Israelites (esp. Numbers 13–14) and the OT sacrificial system and accessories (e.g., Exodus 25–30; 35–40). L. T. Johnson, *Hebrews: A Commentary*, NTL (Louisville, KY: Westminster John Knox, 2006), 1.

[4] In this decidedly Christological focus, the book of Hebrews has major soteriological and missiological implications in a pluralistic world that seeks to be inclusive while Scripture teaches that salvation is found only in Jesus and his once-for-all sacrifice. See C. W. Morgan and R. A. Peterson, ed., *Faith Comes by Hearing: A Response to Inclusivism* (Downers Grove, IL: InterVarsity, 2008).

[5] B. Lindars, *The Theology of the Letter to the Hebrews*, New Testament Theology (Cambridge, UK: Cambridge University Press, 1991), 25. Lindars did not specify the other two theologians; one surmises that one of them is Paul.

believe Paul wrote Hebrews.[6] Two major factors, in particular, support the near-unanimous consensus in this regard. First, the language of the book is different from that in Paul's Letters. These differences extend beyond its vocabulary and style to the book's imagery and theological motifs, such as the high priesthood of Christ. Second, and perhaps most damaging, is that the writer says he heard the gospel from those who received it from Christ (see 2:3)—something Paul vehemently denied about himself elsewhere (Gal 1:11–16; see 1 Cor 15:8).

In lieu of Pauline authorship, a long parade of candidates has been proposed as the possible writer of Hebrews. These include Clement of Rome, Barnabas, Apollos, Luke, Silas, Priscilla, Philip, and even Mary the mother of Jesus.[7] Each of these, excluding Luke, has the same problem: we have no known documents by these authors to compare with Hebrews. Lukan authorship has been vigorously defended by D. L. Allen.[8] However, linguistic and rhetorical differences make it difficult to sustain high confidence in that view.[9] It is nonetheless more possible than many other suggestions. Given the circumstances, therefore, it is best to admit that the authorship of Hebrews is unknown.[10]

The good news is that not one point of exegesis is dependent on knowing the identity of the person responsible for the letter. The document itself is formally anonymous; that is, the author does not name himself. At the same time it is apparent that the book was likely never intended to be an anonymous letter to its first readers. The author fully expected the recipients of his letter to know who he was, given the nature of the personal references to his readers (see 13:19–23). He may even have been part of their congregation at some point in the past, and he expected to see them again in the future.

---

[6] But see D. A. Black, "Who Wrote Hebrews? The Internal and External Evidence Re-examined," *Faith and Mission* 18 (Spring 2002): 57–69.

[7] Clement (as Paul's amanuensis) is supported by Eusebius, *Eccl. Hist.* 3.38; Barnabas by the church father Tertullian and more recently E. Riggenbach, *Der Brief an die Hebräer: Kommentar zum Neuen Testament*, ed. T. Zahn (Wuppertal, Germany: R. Brockhaus, 1987 [1922]). Apollos was proposed by M. Luther, first in his *Commentary on Genesis* in 1545 (Luther's Works 8:178); as early as 1522, Luther qualified this opinion with "some say." Luke is favored by D. L. Allen, *Lukan Authorship of Hebrews*, New American Commentary Studies in Bible and Theology (Nashville, TN: B&H, 2010); idem, *Hebrews*, NAC 35 (Nashville, TN: B&H, 2010). Silas was suggested by T. Hewitt, *The Epistle to the Hebrews* (Grand Rapids, MI: Eerdmans, 1960), 26–32. Priscilla is the choice of A. von Harnack, "Probabilia über die Addresse und den Verfasser des Hebräerbriefes," *ZNW* 1 (1900): 16–41; and R. Hoppins, "The Epistle to the Hebrews Is Priscilla's Letter," in *A Feminist Companion to the Catholic Epistles and Hebrews*, ed. A. J. Levine with M. M. Robbins, Feminist Companion to the New Testament and Early Christian Writings 8 (London, England: T&T Clark, 2004), 147–70. The suggestion of Philip is noted by J. Moffatt, *The Epistle to the Hebrews*, ICC (Edinburgh, Scotland: T&T Clark, 1924), xx; cf. W. Ramsay, *Luke the Physician and Other Studies in the History of Religion* (New York, NY: Hodder & Stoughton, 1908), 301–8. D. A. Hagner (*Encountering the Book of Hebrews: An Exposition*, EBS [Grand Rapids, MI: Baker, 2002], 22) mentioned the suggestion of both Philip and Mary the mother of Jesus.

[8] D. L. Allen, *Lukan Authorship*; idem, *Hebrews*, NAC 35 (Nashville, TN: B&H, 2010); and idem, "The Authorship of Hebrews: Historical Survey of the Lukan Theory," *CTR* 8 (2011): 3–18.

[9] See the critiques of G. L. Cockerill, *Hebrews*, 9; and T. Schreiner, *Hebrews*, 4 who states it is intriguing.

[10] This was the judgment of Origen: "But who wrote the epistle, in truth God knows" (cited in Eusebius, *Eccl. Hist.* 6.25.14).

The difficulty is not just that the book is anonymous but that the early church struggled with identifying its author when they had no such struggle with other formally anonymous works in the NT (e.g., the Gospels and Acts).[11] The book first appears in the canon among the handwritten manuscripts in Paul's Letters, usually between 2 Thessalonians and 1 Timothy.[12] This phenomenon is best accounted for by the tradition that Paul was the source of the letter in the letter collection.[13] If so, it is possible that Paul was not the author of the document but that he included it in a collection of his letters on the basis that it was penned by one of his close associates, though this must of necessity remain in the realm of conjecture.[14] Ultimately, the West accepted the book as Scripture without completely embracing Pauline authorship. It was enough that the author was connected to Paul.[15] After the sixth century the placement of Hebrews is usually in its current position after Philemon, signifying canonicity, connection to Paul, and likely hesitancy concerning authorship.[16]

If the book is put in the Pauline corpus without Paul's being the author, what is its connection to the apostle? The first piece of evidence is in the letter's conclusion. Some, however, have asserted that the connection is fabricated. For them, the ending (chap. 13, in part or as a whole) is a forgery intended to pass the letter off as Paul's.[17] However, one must ask why the culprit would not also add an epistolary beginning while he was inserting material.[18] What is more, the ending, at best, can be said to have a Pauline flavor since

---

[11] The Eastern part of the church (represented by Alexandria, Egypt) affirmed the Pauline authorship of Hebrews, while recognizing the difficulty of this position. The best example is Athanasius's festal letter of AD 326 that refers to fourteen letters of Paul (including Hebrews). The Western part of the church rejected Pauline authorship. This is represented by such luminaries as Irenaeus and Hippolytus (according to Photius), who are said to have rejected it, as well as its absence in the Muratorian Canon that is careful to mention thirteen letters of Paul.

[12] The oldest extant collection of Paul's Letters (𝔓[46]; ca. AD 200) has Hebrews immediately after Romans.

[13] The point is complicated by the position of Hebrews within the mss. Metzger notes that the book is in eight different places within the Pauline Letter collection mss. (B. M. Metzger, *A Textual Commentary on the Greek New Testament*, 2nd ed. [Stuttgart, Germany: UBS, 1994], 591–92). Recently a fragment of Hebrews (13:12–13/recto and 13:19-20/verso) dated to the beginning of the fourth century was identified and given the identification 𝔓[126]. Perhaps the most interesting feature of this fragment is that it bears the page numbers 161 and 162. This suggests a ninth position for Hebrews in the mss. of Paul. Clearly, just how Hebrews fits with Paul was uncertain among the scribes. See, C. Clivaz, "A New NT Papyrus: 𝔓[126] (PSI 1497)," *Early Christianity* 1 (2010), 158–62.

[14] Many think it likely the writer was a close associate of Paul. See, e.g., C. Koester "Hebrews" in *The Blackwell Companion to the New Testament*, ed. D. Aune (West Sussex, UK: Blackwell, 2010), 614.

[15] P. T. O'Brien, *The Letter to the Hebrews*, PTNC (Grand Rapids, MI: Eerdmans, 2010), 3.

[16] G. L. Cockerill, *The Epistle to the Hebrews*, NICNT (Grand Rapids, MI: Eerdmans, 2012), 6.

[17] It is assumed to be inserted by either the author of chaps. 1–12 or another person. W. Wrede, (*Die literarische Rätsel des Hebräerbriefs* [Göttingen, Germany: Vandenhoeck & Ruprecht, 1906]) first suggested the culprit was the author who, as an afterthought, attempted to pass off his work as Paul's. This line of reasoning has been revived by C. K. Rothschild, who suggests it is no mere afterthought but the intention all along. C. K. Rothschild, *Hebrews as Pseudepigraphon: The History and Significance of the Pauline Attribution of Hebrews*, WUNT 235 (Tübingen, Germany: Mohr Siebeck, 2009). See also G. J. Steyn, "The Ending of Hebrews Reconsidered," *ZNW* 103 (2012): 235–53, who argues that 13:22–25 is a forgery; A. J. M. Wedderburn, "The 'Letter' to the Hebrews and Its Thirteenth Chapter," *NTS* 50 (2004): 390–405.

[18] Koester, "Hebrews," 623.

SIDEBAR 16.1: THE CANONICITY OF HEBREWS

Hebrews struggled for full acceptance in the early church longer than any other book (including 2 Peter). Many have asserted that those who accepted Paul's authorship (as did the East) honored its place in the canon, while those who did not (the West) rejected it. As usual, the truth is more complex.

The concern over its authorship was equally matched by its use among the heretics in the West that led the Western church to exclude the book from its canon. One particular item of contention was the interpretation and application of Heb 6:4–6 by Montanus and Novatian, both of whom denied the possibility of readmission into the church by those who recanted their faith when confronted with persecution.[1]

Thus, in the Western churches the problem of heresy was easily handled by canonical surgery,[2] while the churches in the East defended apostolic authorship. The Council of Hippo (AD 393) recognized Hebrews as canonical, and the Council of Carthage (AD 397) followed suit.[3]

[1] See J. Calvin, *Commentaries on the Epistle to the Hebrews*, trans. J. Owen (Grand Rapids, MI: Eerdmans, 1949), xxvi; and S. Kistemaker, *Hebrews*, Baker New Testament Commentary (Grand Rapids, MI: Baker, 1984), 13.

[2] Gaius of Rome, described as "a very learned man" by Eusebius (*Eccl. Hist.* 6.20.3), denied that Paul wrote Hebrews. Most likely this was a response against the Montanists who rejected postbaptismal repentance. He also did something similar regarding the Johannine literature. Eusebius recorded that Gaius rejected Revelation (*Eccl. Hist.* 3.28.1–2), and apparently he rejected John's authorship of the Gospel as well. Hippolytus wrote a book against Gaius defending John's authorship of the Gospel, which is preserved in the works of Dionysius bar Salibi (twelfth century). The main difference is that the move to oust Hebrews seems to have been more successful.

[3] Kistemaker, *Hebrews*, 14.

there is no direct statement of authorship. One, then, would have to think the forger is using subtle suggestion to cast the letter as from Paul. Such subtlety is not normally the style of pseudepigraphers. As argued elsewhere in this book, such individuals normally wrote to promote false doctrine or to fill in historical gaps. The book of Hebrews does neither. The assumption that it was to grant acceptance of the letter further flounders on the lack of any manuscript evidence and lack of any known patristic reference to it while the Fathers debated the book. It is not likely a forgery.

The conclusion points out connections to Paul. Primarily the mention of Timothy in 13:23 recalls a prominent member of the Pauline circle, although the imprisonment mentioned there is not attested elsewhere in the NT. Also, the thematic connections in the rest of the epistle are vast.[19] L. D. Hurst sketched the possible points of contact between Paul and the author of Hebrews:[20] (1) Hebrews does not reflect literary borrowing from Paul

[19] Building on the fifteen parallels noted by H. Windisch (*Hebräerbrief* [Tübingen, Germany: Mohr, 1913], 128), Hurst (*Hebrews*, 108) located at least twenty-five strong points of theological connection.

[20] Hurst, *Hebrews*, 124.

by one of his followers. At the same time, one detects certain thematic similarities. (2) If these ideas were originally Pauline, the author could at some point have been a disciple of Paul. (3) Personal Pauline influence other than direct literary dependence is likely. Along similar lines the church father Origen (ca. AD 185–254) wrote, "If I were to venture my own opinion, I would say that the thoughts are the apostle's but the style and construction reflect someone who recalled the apostle's teachings and interpreted them."[21]

What is more, while the author's precise identity remains elusive, it is possible to infer a few pieces of information regarding the writer from the letter itself. First, the author was male. The masculine participle "tell" *(diēgeomai)* at 11:32 removes Priscilla, Mary, and any other female from consideration.[22] Second, the author was obviously a gifted and eloquent writer, displaying an impressive command of ancient rhetoric. This points to the third characteristic, which is that the author was well educated. Fourth, he is most likely Jewish, showing familial relations with his readers. While his rhetoric was Greek, his hermeneutic was consistent with early Jewish and Christian principles of interpretation. Fifth, the writer was familiar with the Greek OT (the LXX).[23] He was an accomplished preacher and pastoral in his concern for both admonition and encouragement. He is both firm and tender with this flock facing many perils.[24] Finally, as previously mentioned, the author was a second-generation believer (see 2:3).[25] This is all that can be confidently said about the author.

Date

The second element of uncertainty regarding Hebrews is its date. Scholars have proposed a fairly narrow range of possibilities, spanning from the mid-60s AD just years prior

---

[21] Cited in Eusebius, *Eccl. Hist.* 6.25.

[22] R. Hoppin ("Priscilla and Plausibility: Responding to Questions About Priscilla as Author of Hebrews," *Priscilla Papers* 25 [2011]: 26–28) attempts to answer the question regarding the participle. She suggests first that the participle may be neuter and may express that individuality is not in force. Second, it may be a "fossilized" masculine used by either gender (ibid., 27). By way of response, because it is a word of speaking and modifies the pronoun, it must be masculine. Second, the fossilization of the idiom is theoretically possible but yet to be proved in this case. At the end of the day, if Priscilla did write the letter, she disguised her femininity with even a generic "he" (Allen, *Hebrews*, 564). The other characteristics that supposedly point to Priscilla ("a gifted teacher, catechist, and evangelist; a colleague of Paul with a career along the Rome/Ephesus axis; a towering figure in the early church" [ibid.]) point also to almost all of the usual suspects. It is not that we know she lacked giftedness to write the book. We simply have no grounds to insist on her above other candidates and evidence to exclude a female writer.

[23] G. Guthrie (*Hebrews*, NIVAC [Grand Rapids, MI: Zondervan, 1998], 19) noted that there are thirty-five direct quotes, thirty-four clear allusions, nineteen summaries of OT materials, and thirteen times when the author mentioned an OT name or topic, often without reference to a specific context. For the difficulty in assessing a strict number, see W. L. Lane (*Hebrews 1–8*, WBC 47A [Dallas, TX: Word, 1991], cxvi), who located thirty-one quotations and four implicit quotations, thirty-seven allusions, nineteen summaries, and thirteen references of names or topics that are introduced without a reference. The exact form of the LXX employed by the author is also the subject of scholarly debate.

[24] O'Brien, *Hebrews*, 8–9.

[25] Defined as a convert of the disciples rather than a hearer of Jesus.

to the destruction of the Jerusalem temple in AD 70 to about 90.[26] R. Brown, for example, cautiously opted for a date in the 80s based on comparative theology.[27]

The earliest possible date, of course, is subsequent to the death, resurrection, and ascension of Jesus since Hebrews makes repeated references to Jesus's earthly life and ministry (see esp. 2:10–18; 5:7–10). At the same time, the author's claim that he and his readers were second-generation Christians (2:3) must be taken into account. Moreover, the author indicated that some time had elapsed after his readers' conversion (5:12) and after they had been persecuted for their faith in the past (10:32; 12:4), urging them to remember their leaders and to follow their example, observing "the outcome of their conduct" (13:7).

From these observations it is safe to assume that a date prior to AD 45 is unlikely.[28] The latest possible date is near the end of the first century since Clement of Rome (ca. AD 96) was clearly influenced by the letter (indisputably *1 Clem.* 36:1–6).[29] If one adds to this the fact that the letter must have been written in Timothy's lifetime (13:23) and during the life span of a second-generation Christian (2:3), this places the upper limit of the letter at about the time of Clement.[30] Hence, the letter must have been written between the years AD 45 and 95.

But it is possible to narrow the range still further. The letter was in all probability written before the Jewish War, including the destruction of the Jewish temple in the year 70, since the writer speaks of the sacerdotal ministry in the present tense (9:6–10). Lane rejected this use of the present tense as altogether irrelevant for dating Hebrews on the grounds that reference is made to the tabernacle rather than the temple.[31] But it is more likely that the references are to the temple.[32] Lane further cautioned that since other writers subsequent to the Jewish War referred to the temple and its worship in the present tense, one should not read too much into the verb tenses associated with the temple throughout Hebrews.[33] Lindars responded: "It would have been an irresistible impulse to point out that the temple, sacrifices and priesthood had all ceased to exist, if that had already

---

[26] L. Gaston, *No Stone on Another: Studies in the Significance of the Fall of Jerusalem in the Synoptic Gospels*, NovTSup 23 (Leiden, Netherlands: Brill, 1970), 467; and T. Zahn, *Introduction to the New Testament*, trans. J. M. Trout et al. (New York, NY: Scribner's, 1909), 315–23. Zahn based his arguments on the interpretation of Heb 3:7–4:11: "Your fathers tested me, tried me, and saw my works for forty years," as the years 30–70.

[27] R. E. Brown, *An Introduction to the New Testament*, ABRL (New York, NY: Doubleday, 1997), 696–97.

[28] Johnson, *Hebrews*, 39.

[29] See esp. *1 Clem.* 36:2–5.

[30] See D. A. Carson and D. J. Moo, *An Introduction to the New Testament*, 2nd ed. (Grand Rapids, MI: Zondervan, 2005), 605.

[31] Lane, *Hebrews*, lxiii. So also Brown, *Introduction to the New Testament*, 696.

[32] G. A. Barton, "The Date of the Epistle to the Hebrews," *JBL* 57 (1938): 199–200. Barton noted nine different verbs used "to describe the performance of parts of the ritual and in every instance he employs the present tense." The verbs are in 9:6 *eiseimi* ("to enter"); in 9:7 and 9 *prospherō* ("to offer"); in 9:22 *katharizō* ("to cleanse") and *ginomai* ("to become"); in 9:25 *eiserchomai* ("to enter"); in 10:1 and 8 *prospherō* ("to offer"); and in 13:11 *katakaiō* ("to burn").

[33] Lane (*Hebrews*, lxiii) cited Josephus (*Ant.* 4.224–57); *1 Clem.* 41:2; *Barn.* 7–8; and *Diogn.* 3.

happened. What better sign could there be that the old covenant was 'becoming obsolete'?"[34] The present-tense references to the temple and the lack of references to its razing point to a date prior to the destruction of Jerusalem in AD 70.

As will be seen below, Hebrews was most likely written to a group of churches in Rome. If so, the experience of believers mentioned in the book is entirely congruent with the time period subsequent to the edict of Claudius (ca. AD 49) and the beginning of the persecution of Christians under Nero (AD 64–66). Since these believers seem to be undergoing persecution at the time of writing, a date of composition toward the end of this time period seems most likely, yet not at the very end, for the author noted that the recipients had not yet shed any blood (12:4). On balance, therefore, a date in the mid-60s seems most likely.

Provenance

The provenance of Hebrews is unknown. The only possible internal piece of evidence is 13:24, which states, "Those who are from Italy send you greetings." But, as is argued below, most likely this indicates a Roman destination while leaving the question of the letter's provenance open. If so, perhaps the only safe conclusion is that wherever the letter was written, it was not penned in Rome since this was its probable intended destination. Especially since the author's identity is unknown, it is even more difficult to establish where that unknown author was at the time he wrote Hebrews. For this reason, to reappropriate Origen, "The provenance of Hebrews, only God knows."[35]

Destination

The third unknown is the destination of the letter. The question of the letter's destination encompasses several factors. One is the ethnic makeup of the congregation(s) being addressed. Another is the geographical location of the recipients. Yet another is any other characteristic of the original recipients or their situation at the time of writing.

The first question is about the recipients' ethnic makeup. This is the most important of our considerations. As G. L. Cockerill states, "One can understand Hebrews without identifying either the name of the author or the location of the recipients. One cannot, however, interpret Hebrews without taking a position as to whether the recipients were Jewish or Gentile believers."[36] At first glance this issue seems to be settled by the designation of the letter as "To the Hebrews." Yet while this title suggests the recipients were Jewish Christians, scholars do not all agree that the book was written to a Jewish audience. Some contend that they were Gentiles, and they view the title as vague and

---

[34] B. Lindars, "Hebrews and the Second Temple," in *Templum Amicitiae: Essays on the Second Temple Presented to Ernst Bammel*, ed. W. Horbury (Sheffield, UK: JSOT, 1991), 416.

[35] It is, of course, true that presumably the first recipients of Hebrews knew who the author was, but the point of Origen's remark (which is still true today) is that this knowledge of the author was soon lost in subsequent generations.

[36] Cockerill, *Hebrews*, 19. However, C. Koester does remain agnostic about the recipients. Koester, "Hebrews," 614. The interpretive impact is well illustrated in the recent work of J. A. Whitlark (*Resisting Empire: Rethinking the Purpose of the Letter to "the Hebrews,"* LNTS [JSNTS] 484 [New York, NY: Bloomsbury, 2014]), whose operating assumption that the first audience was Gentile (ibid., 12–16) enables him to defend the thesis that the pressure on them is to revert to paganism.

misleading—something added after the knowledge of the recipients was lost.[37] Nevertheless, while some factors are congruent with a Gentile audience, none override the cumulative impression that the original readers were Hebrew Christians.[38]

The first major argument in favor of a Jewish Christian audience of Hebrews is bound up with the title of the book. This title, the only title that is extant, most likely dates to the book's inclusion in the Pauline corpus. If so, it is so close chronologically to Paul's time that any appeal to the recipients being forgotten becomes untenable. Thus, the title "To the Hebrews" should be taken seriously, and it unequivocally points to Jewish readers. The question of whether these Jews lived in Palestine or the Diaspora is not addressed by the title. Some have tried to identify the recipients with the Qumran covenanters[39] or Jewish priests in Jerusalem (such as those converted in Acts 6:7),[40] but these views have not generated a great following. The fact that the readers had not heard Jesus personally (2:3), the author's exclusive use of the LXX, and the presence of linguistic features characteristic of the Hellenistic synagogue all point to readers outside of Palestine.

The second major argument for a Jewish Christian audience is related to the pervasive use of the OT in the book. The author presupposed that his readers were thoroughly familiar with OT teaching, including the Levitical ritual, the priesthood, and the pattern of the tabernacle. Achtemeier, Green, and Thompson correctly stated, "It is difficult not to see Hebrews as directed toward Jewish Christians, to whom the exhortations and arguments

---

[37] Twentieth-century scholars include Moffatt, *Epistle to the Hebrews*, xvi–xvii; H. Windisch, *Der Hebräerbrief*, HNT (Tübingen, Germany: Mohr, 1931), 31; and E. Käsemann, *The Wandering People of God: An Investigation of the Letter to the Hebrews* (Minneapolis, MN: Augsburg, 1984). More recently, a growing number deny a Jewish audience: D. A. deSilva, *An Introduction to the New Testament* (Downers Grove, IL: InterVarsity, 2005), 778; idem, *Perseverance in Gratitude: A Socio-Rhetorical Commentary on the Epistle "to the Hebrews"* (Grand Rapids, MI: Eerdmans, 2000), 2–7; B. D. Ehrman, *The New Testament: A Historical Introduction to the Early Christian Writings*, 2nd ed. (New York, NY: Oxford University Press, 2000), 378; H. W. Attridge, *Hebrews*, Hermeneia (Philadelphia, PA: Fortress, 1989), 10–13. deSilva (*Introduction*, 777) suggested that the title "to the Hebrews" was added as a "canonical 'response' to the parent religion that had rejected them." But in response—to borrow a phrase from Moffatt (*Hebrews*, xvii), referring to the suggestion that Barnabas wrote the letter—it may be said, "But all this is guessing in the dark about a guess in the dark." A. C. Mitchell (*Hebrews*, SacPag 13 [Collegeville, MN: Liturgical Press, 2007], 12) and C. R. Koester (*Hebrews*, AB 36 [New York, NY: Doubleday, 2001], 48) hold the recipients of the letter to be of indeterminate social background.

[38] Most who disagree begin with the assumption that the title was added after the recipients had been lost to history. Then the argument from silence is made that the writer never called them Jews or mentioned the temple in Jerusalem (not completely true; see 8:9). Further supposed evidence is that the author used the LXX (i.e., a Greek Bible) and that Gentile Christians were indeed interested in the OT (e.g., Moffatt, *Hebrews*, xvi). Ehrman (*New Testament*, 378) also argued that the letter was written to Gentiles, for the only explicit reason that the foundational matters at 6:1–2 (faith in God, resurrection, eternal judgment) were already adhered to by Jews. O'Brien points out, however, that the writer never specifically mentions circumcision. So then, the problem is not a "Jewish propaganda" in order to convert Gentiles. He states, "The failure to mention circumcision makes sense if Hebrews was sent to a Jewish Christian community but would be surprising if the listeners are Gentile believers who were in danger of being seduced by so-called Judaizers." (O'Brien, *Hebrews*, 11).

[39] See P. E. Hughes, *A Commentary on the Epistle to the Hebrews* (Grand Rapids, MI: Eerdmans, 1977), 10–15.

[40] C. Spicq, *L'Épître aux Hébreux* (Paris, France: J. Gabalda, 1952), 1:226–31; D. Allen, "Argument for the Lucan Authorship of Hebrews," 29.

from the exposition of so many OT passages, especially those regarding the wandering Israelites looking for the Promised Land, would have a particularly strong appeal."[41]

The next question regarding the letter's destination relates to the audience's geographic location. The only possible clue in this regard is found in 13:24, which states, "Those who are from Italy send you greetings." This passage evidently establishes a connection between the readers and Italy. But is the reference to the location of the readers or to that of the writer? In other words, does the reference indicate that Italian expatriates are sending greetings back home or that the writer was in Italy at the time of writing?

It is possible that the recipients were Jewish Christians living in Palestine.[42] The threat of reverting to Judaism to escape persecution was quite real in the area. However, a few points give pause. First, in addressing the audience, the preacher affirms, "You have not yet resisted to the point of shedding your blood" (Heb 12:4). The Jerusalem community certainly experienced their own suffering unto death for the sake of Christ (e.g., James and Stephen).[43] Second, the community as well as the author are considered second-generation Christians at Hebrews 2:3. It is unlikely, therefore, that the author could say this to a Jerusalem audience. Finally, the cultic references to things like the temple and priesthood are appropriate for Jewish believers no matter where they live. On the whole another destination seems more likely.

Guthrie advocates a Roman destination based on the following arguments: (1) "from Italy" is used in Acts 18:2 for Aquila and Priscilla, who were Italian expatriates; (2) the reference to pastors as "leaders" (Gk. *hēgoumenoi*) in Hebrews (13:7, 17, 24) is paralleled outside the NT only in *1 Clement* (ca. 95) and the *Shepherd of Hermas* (early second century?), both of which are of Roman origin; (3) *1 Clement* (written in Rome) made extensive use of Hebrews, so the earliest evidence of the book's existence comes from Rome.[44] At Hebrews 13:14 the preacher may make a veiled reference to Rome. He states, "For we do not have an enduring city here." J. A. Whitlark suggests this is a veiled reference to the Roman propaganda of "the eternal city." If so, it is likely another indication of Roman recipients.[45] On the basis of this type of evidence, a Roman destination for Hebrews is indeed plausible, if not probable.

Beyond this a few other audience characteristics may be inferred from the letter. For instance, the author of the letter referred to the fact that the recipients, as well as the author, are second-generation Christians (2:3); that is, the author looked back to the apostles as belonging to the preceding spiritual generation. While the recipients had been believers for

---

[41] P. J. Achtemeier, J. B. Green, and M. M. Thompson, *Introducing the New Testament* (Grand Rapids, MI: Eerdmans, 2001), 471.

[42] See, C. Mosser, "No Lasting City: Rome, Jerusalem and the Place of Hebrews in the History of Earliest Christianity'" (Ph.D. diss., St. Andrews University, 2004).

[43] Noted by Koester, "Hebrews," 617.

[44] Guthrie, *Hebrews*, 20–21.

[45] J. A. Whitlark, "'Here We Do Not Have a City That Remains': A Figured Critique of Roman Imperial Propaganda in Hebrews 13:14," *JBL* 131 (2012):161–79.

some time, they had regressed in their growth in Christ (5:11–6:3), and some had stopped attending the weekly assembly (10:25). On the whole, however, the author was confident in his readers' salvation because of their labor of love (6:10), which includes supporting fellow Christians in need (10:34). These believers were not only under doctrinal pressure, but they also seem to have been well acquainted with persecution. They had endured "a hard struggle with sufferings" at their conversion (10:32), had their property seized, and had endured this ill treatment joyfully (10:34). Moreover, they were currently under pressure (12:3–13), though they had yet to suffer to the point of martyrdom (12:4), but there was an expectation of more severe suffering in the future (13:12–14).

All this evidence fits well with the audience being Hebrew Christians in Rome in the mid-60s. If the discussion above is accurate, the most likely date would be shortly before Nero's persecution as the last half of the AD 60s reached its climax. The community, having existed for some time, had previously undergone persecution. Their property had been confiscated, and they had endured shame from outside their group (12:4; 13:13). All of this matches the situation in Rome from the time subsequent to the edict of Claudius in the year 49—at which time the confiscation of property was experienced when the Jews were temporarily expelled from Rome[46]—to the latter half of Nero's reign (AD 54–68). The warning passages and the repeated exhortations to endure, as well as the author's effort to prevent a reverting back to Judaism, indicate that this was a serious temptation for his readers. Also, by the time of Nero's persecution (ca. AD 65–68), the state recognized the distinction between Judaism, a tolerated religion (Lat. *religio licita*) with certain leniencies, and Christianity, which was oppressed. Thus, a Jewish Christian tempted to escape persecution may have found it appealing to retreat back under the protective umbrella of Judaism.[47]

Purpose and Occasion

The book of Hebrews is certainly a marvel of rhetoric and a joy to behold. Yet the rhetoric is not merely aesthetic; the preacher has a real and pressing reason to write his audience.[48] The occasion and purpose of the letter are closely connected to the judgments

---

[46] Suetonius (*Claudius*, 25.4) stated that "[Claudius] banished from Rome all the Jews, who were continually making disturbances at the instigation of one Chrestus," which suggests that a disturbance over Christ among the synagogues had spilled out into the streets of Rome. See O'Brien, *Hebrews*, 17.

[47] The same scenario would also obtain if the author were writing to a Greek-speaking church in Palestine. These converts certainly existed in Palestine (see Acts 6–7), and a retreat to Judaism would have provided them with an escape from Jewish persecution and ridicule.

[48] T. Schreiner, *Commentary on Hebrews*, BTCP (Nashville, TN: Holman Reference, 2015), 13. Schreiner states, "We may become dazzled and dazed by Melchizedek, angels, and the contrast between heaven and earth so that we fail to see why the letter was penned. The author isn't attempting to amaze us with his theological sophistication, his understanding of the relationship between the old covenant and the new, his reading of the Levitical and Melchizedekian priesthoods, and his construal of old and new covenant sacrifices. He writes for a practical reason, which become evident when we observe the warning passages that permeate the letter" (ibid.).

made about the recipients.[49] As argued, Hebrews was most likely written to a congregation of Jewish Christians who were urged to move on to maturity (see 5:11–6:8) in the face of looming persecution. Whether the letter was written to one or several Jewish Christian congregations in Rome, two things seem certain: first, the recipients were facing continued pressure, whether social or physical; and, second, a retreat back into Judaism was viewed, at least by some, as an appealing solution that offered relief. As suggested above, a Jewish Christian in mid-60s Rome might be tempted to flee back to his or her ancestral religion to avoid persecution. Whether this is the specific temptation, the issue addressed by the preacher involves something along these lines.

The author described his writing as a "message of exhortation" (13:22), a phrase found elsewhere in the NT only in Acts 13:15, where it refers to a synagogue homily (sermon). This makes it likely that the genre of Hebrews is that of a written series of oral messages. Lane argued that this means the author identified his work as "an earnest passionate and personal appeal."[50] As the book unfolds, this appeal turns into a series of arguments designed to encourage the readers to move on to maturity, holding on to their Christian confession (see 6:1; 10:23).

The basis of this series of appeals is the utter superiority of the Son to all previous intermediary figures, whether human or angelic, who spoke for God. Moreover, the recent revelation of God's Son, the Lord Jesus Christ, ushered in the new covenant that had been announced by the OT prophets (see 8:8–13, citing Jer 31:31–34), so that now the old Mosaic covenant had become obsolete.

The essence of the appeal can be found in the three exhortations at 10:19–25 (marked in English by "let us"). The first is, "Let us draw near with a true heart in full assurance of faith, our hearts sprinkled clean from an evil conscience and our bodies washed in pure water" (v. 22). The author invited his readers to draw near and approach God in trust, based on the assumption that they were believers. His primary concern was the actual conversion of his hearers and their orientation toward God. The second injunction is in verse 23: "Let us hold on to the confession of our hope without wavering, for he who promised is faithful." Thus, the related concern subsequent to salvation was an authentic confession of faith in Jesus Christ. The third exhortation, appearing in verse 24, further enjoins believers to express that faith to one another: "Let us watch out for one another to provoke love and good works."[51]

This triad of concerns climaxes at 12:1–2, where believers are encouraged to "run with endurance the race that lies before us." Thus, the purpose of Hebrews is not merely to maintain believers' confession in the face of persecution but also to spur them on to full maturity in Christ by holding fast to their confession.

---

[49] See the discussion under "Destination" above.

[50] W. Lane, "Hebrews," in *Dictionary of the Later New Testament and Its Developments*, ed. R. P. Martin and P. H. Davids (Downers Grove, IL: InterVarsity, 1997), 453.

[51] On the structural implications of these injunctions, see the discussion under "Literary Plan" below.

LITERATURE

Genre

In literary matters the genre and structure of Hebrews have dominated the modern discussion related to the book. The genre of Hebrews, while complicated, is actually the simpler of these issues. It is simple, though, only in comparison. A. C. Mitchell rightly states, "It is easier to describe Hebrews than to classify it."[52] Thus, Hebrews's genre has been the subject of considerable debate. The generic mystery can be easily seen by the fact that it opens and proceeds like a work of rhetoric but closes like a letter.[53] Schreiner rightly notes, "It is like nothing else in the New Testament."[54] So what is it?

Since the author describes his piece of writing as a "message of exhortation" (13:22), many have made the questionable assumption that the letter is an example of a Hellenistic-Jewish synagogue sermon based on the usage of the same phrase in Acts 13:15, following H. Thyen.[55] Several writers have attempted to advance Thyen's work.[56] For the most part these proposals suffer from exceeding the available evidence since there is an insufficient number of examples contemporaneous to Hebrews to derive a set style of the "synagogue sermon," Hellenistic or otherwise.

Whether a specific type of sermon can be identified, the description "homily" or "sermon" certainly seems to fit the book. Johnson located four phenomena that support the notion that this work derived from an oral original.[57] First, the author refers to himself in the first person (both singular and plural, asserting authority and identifying with his hearers). Second, he casts his activity as an act of speaking, not writing. When making such a self-reference, he generally used verbs of speaking rather than words of writing.[58] He also prefers "hearing" to "reading" in reference to his audience. Thus, he created a sense of personal presence with his audience.[59] Third, he alternates exposition and exhortation, which "allows an orator to drive home points immediately without losing the hearers' attention."[60] Fourth, the author introduces a theme only to explain it later in his work. Thus, Jesus's priesthood is introduced at

---

[52] Mitchell, *Hebrews*, 13.

[53] In this regard only 1 John is similar in its opening. James is the exact opposite, opening like a letter but ending differently.

[54] Schreiner, *Hebrews*, 13.

[55] E.g., H. Thyen, *Der Stil der Jüdisch-Hellenistischen Homilie* (Göttingen, Germany: Vandenhoeck & Ruprecht, 1955). The same phrase, "word of exhortation," is used in 1 Macc 10:24 and 2 Macc 15:11 without reference to an actual sermon.

[56] L. Wills, "The Form of the Sermon in Hellenistic Judaism and Early Christianity," *HTR* 77 (1984): 277–99; and G. Gelardini, "Hebrews, an Ancient Synagogue Homily for Tisha be-Av: Its Function, Its Basis, Its Theological Interpretation," in *Hebrews: Contemporary Methods, New Insights*, ed. H. W. Attridge (Boston, MA: Brill, 2005), 107–27.

[57] The following comes from Johnson, *Hebrews*, 10.

[58] E.g., 2:5; 5:11; 6:9; 8:1; 9:5; 11:32. The only exception is 13:22, where the author used the verb translated "to write a letter" *(epesteila)*, though even this is not a real exception since 13:22 is part of the epistolary framework provided for the body of the document.

[59] Lane, *Hebrews*, lxxiv.

[60] Johnson, *Hebrews*, 10.

4:14 but not developed until 7:1–9:28, and his connection with Melchizedek is mentioned in 5:10 but not taken up in detail until 7:1.

For these reasons it may be concluded that Hebrews was in all probability first delivered as a series of oral messages and subsequently compiled and edited for publication as a letter, which included attaching an epistolary ending. Also, in keeping with the ancient notion that the written form of the letter served as a substitute for the author's presence, the missive was aimed at moving the audience persuasively to adopt the author's argument that reverting back to Judaism would be a serious mistake with disastrous spiritual consequences. Most likely, Hebrews would have been read to the congregation aloud; thus, the writer used several devices that enhanced the material's memorability: alliteration, repetition, and arguments from the lesser to the greater. Indeed, the identification of the letter as originating in a homily or sermon calls attention to a host of rhetorical devices and matters in the book. Table 16.1 contains just a sample.

Table 16.1: Rhetorical Devices in the Letter to the Hebrews

- *alliteration* (repetition of letters; 1:1)
- *anaphora* (repetition for effect; chap. 11)
- *antithesis* (a use of words or phrases that contrast with each other to create a balanced effect; 7:18–20)
- *assonance* (resemblance of sound; 1:1–3)
- *asyndeton* (linking sentences without conjunctions; 6:3)
- *chiasm* (reflexive parallelism; 2:8–9)
- *ellipsis* (the omission of one or more words of a sentence; 7:19)
- *hendiadys* (two nouns representing a single concept; 5:7)
- *hook words* (word at beginning of paragraph repeated from end of preceding paragraph; see "angels" in 1:4 and 1:5).
- *hyberbaton* (departure from normal word order; 12:25)
- *inclusio* (bracketing words/phrases; see 5:10 and 7:1)
- *isocolon* (succession of phrases of approximately equal length and corresponding structure; 1:3)
- *litotes* (denying the opposite word which would otherwise be used; 4:15)
- *paronomasia* (puns exploiting confusion between similar-sounding words; 9:16–18)*

*For a more extensive list see Spicq, *L'Epître aux Hébreux*, 2:252–78. For a chart on hook words in Hebrews, see D. J. MacLeod, "The Literary Structure of the Book of Hebrews," *BSac* 146 (1989): 188.

Literary Plan

The structure of Hebrews continues to be a major point of discussion among scholarship. Without question the book has proven difficult to outline. Scholars have suggested many different divisions of the text, some based on traditional exegesis,[61] others based on the newest literary methods. In spite of the prolonged interest, no consensus is on the horizon. The intricate structure that makes it difficult to outline the book is due to a variety of factors, including the rhetorical style and hermeneutical principles employed by the writer, but most of all it is due to the fact that the author of Hebrews employed some of the smoothest transitions in the entire NT.[62]

At present three proposals are the most popular. First, some are influenced by A. Vanhoye and understand the book to be arranged into five parts, plus an introduction and conclusion. These parts are generally arranged chiastically (in an ABB′A′ pattern), with Christ's high priesthood taking center stage. But these divisions often seem contrived, and it is unlikely that any hearer could follow an extended series of macro-chiasms for an extended period of time.[63]

Second, some see in the letter a rhetorical structure following the conventions of ancient rhetoric that basically arranges the text in five sections.[64] The problem is that Hebrews resists such a structure. Westfall's conclusion seems cogent: "Therefore, though Hebrews is riddled with rhetorical devices, the organization of Hebrews does not fit the template of typical classical Hellenistic structure."[65]

Third, many divide Hebrews into three major literary units. These scholars organize the material around the major exhortations in the letter while viewing any intervening paraenetic (hortatory) material as subordinate.[66] Refined by W. Nauck, the divisions are (1) 1:1–4:13 (marked by hymnic portions); (2) 4:14–10:31 (marked by parallel hortatory subjunctives); and (3) 10:32–13:17 (marked by parallel imperatives).[67]

Whole monographs have been written on this subject.[68] In short, the tripartite proposal by Nauck, which was refined by the discourse analysis of Westfall (see below), seems to unlock the structure of the text most successfully. What follows is a slight adaptation of that scheme. One of the strengths of Westfall's approach is that it recognizes the importance of transitional phrases in Hebrews, which properly belong to both of the sections they span.

---

[61] See F. F. Bruce, *The Epistle to the Hebrews* (Grand Rapids, MI: Eerdmans, 1984).

[62] Lane, *Hebrews*, xc.

[63] Scholars who follow this pattern are Attridge, *Hebrews*, xx; Lane, *Hebrews*; and, to a lesser extent, P. Ellingworth, *The Epistle to the Hebrews*, NIGTC (Grand Rapids, MI: Eerdmans, 1993), 58. One of the more recent and intricate proposals comes from J. P. Heil *Hebrews: Chiastic Structures and Audience Response*, CBQMS 46 (Washington, DC: Catholic Biblical Association of America, 2010).

[64] E.g., Koester, *Hebrews*, 84–85.

[65] C. L. Westfall, *A Discourse Analysis of the Letter to the Hebrews: The Relationship Between Form and Meaning*, Library of New Testament Studies, Studies in New Testament Greek 11 (New York, NY: T&T Clark, 2005), 6–7.

[66] W. G. Kümmel, *Introduction to the New Testament*, rev. ed., trans. H. C. Kee (Nashville, TN: Abingdon, 1975), 390.

[67] W. Nauck, "Zum Aufbau des Hebräerbriefes," in *Judentum Urchristentum Kirche:* BZNW 26 *Festschrift für Joachim Jeremias*, ed. J. Jeremias and W. Eltester (Berlin, Germany: A. Töpelmann, 1960), cited in Westfall, *Discourse Analysis*, 12–13.

[68] E.g., in English, A. Vanhoye, *Structure and Message of the Epistle to the Hebrews*, Subsidia Biblica 12 (Rome, Italy: Editrice Pontificio Istituto Biblico, 1989); G. H. Guthrie, *The Structure of Hebrews: A Text-Linguistic Analysis* (New York, NY: Brill, 1994); and Westfall, *Discourse Analysis*.

For example, the perennial difficulty about whether 4:14 concludes the previous section or begins a new unit is thus solved: the verse belongs to both sections at once.[69]

Two thematic discourse peaks appear at 4:11–16 and 10:19–25, marked by triads of hortatory subjunctives (see 4:11, "Let us then make every effort"; 4:14, "Let us hold fast to the confession"; 4:16, "Let us approach"). These mark the end of the first division and the beginning of the third. This creates a central section dominated by the theme of Christ's high priesthood. While the beginning and ending sections feature a whole series of exhortations, only one appears in the main text of the central section, and only one imperative occurs as well. This is because the central section is a sustained exposition of the high priesthood of Jesus.

Table 16.2: Major Structural Proposals for Hebrews

Westfall		Guthrie	
I. 1:1–4:16	Jesus Apostle of Confession	I. 1:1–3	Better than the Prophets
II. 4:11–10:25	Jesus High Priest of Confession	II. 1:1–2:18	Better than the Angels
III. 10:19–13:16	Partners with Jesus	III. 3:1–4:13	Better than Moses and Joshua
IV. 13:17–25	Closing	IV. 4:14–7:28	Better than OT Priesthood
[Note: overlapping verses between I., II., and III. are deliberate]		V. 8:1–10:18	Better than Old Covenant
		VI. 10:19–12:29	Call to Follow Jesus
		VII. 13:1–25	Concluding Exhortations

Vanhoye	
1:1–4	Introduction
I. 1:5–2:18	The Name Certainly Different than that of the Angels
II. 3:1–5:10	Jesus, Faithful and Compassionate High Priest
III. 5:11–10:39	Jesus, High Priest According to Melchizedek and Author of Eternal Salvation
IV. 11:1–12:13	The Faith of the Men of Old and the Necessary Endurance
V. 12:14–13:19	The Peaceful Fruit of Justice
13:20–21	Conclusion*

*The structure proposed by A. Vanhoye in his monograph *La Structure Littéraire de l'Épître aux Hébreux,* 2nd ed. (Paris: Desclée de Brouwer, 1976; ET 1989) and various other works on the structure of Hebrews is reproduced in Guthrie, *Structure of Hebrews,* 14–17 (it is here condensed; for subheads, see ibid., 16). As Guthrie noted, Vanhoye's work represents the most influential work ever written on the structure of Hebrews. Major commentators who follow Vanhoye include Attridge, Ellingworth, and Lane.

[69] Westfall, *Discourse Analysis,* 297, to whom the following paragraph is indebted.

OUTLINE

I. JESUS THE APOSTLE OF OUR CONFESSION (1:1–4:16)
- A. Jesus as the Heir of the Universe (1:1–3:2)
  - 1. God's Ultimate Messenger (1:1–2:4)
    - a. God Has Spoken Through His Son (1:1–4).
    - b. "Son" Is a Better Name (1:5–14).
    - c. Warning: Do Not Drift (2:1–4)
  - 2. Jesus as a Faithful High Priest (2:5–18).
    - a. God's Intention for Humanity (2:5–9)
    - b. Jesus Is Superior Because of His Humanity (2:10–18).
    - c. Partners in the Heavenly Calling (3:1–2)
- B. Enter the Remaining Sabbath Rest (3:1–4:16)
  - 1. Jesus Is Better than Moses (3:1–6).
  - 2. A Call to Endurance (3:7–19)
  - 3. Enter the Remaining Rest (4:1–16)

II. JESUS OUR HIGH PRIEST (4:11–10:25)
- A. Carry on to Maturity (4:11–5:14)
  - 1. Draw Near to the Throne of Grace (4:11–16).
  - 2. A High Priest like Melchizedek (5:1–10)
  - 3. The Fact of Sluggishness (5:11–14)
- B. Maturity Enables Hope (6:1–7:3)
  - 1. Let Us Be Carried on to Maturity (6:1–3).
  - 2. Warning: Do Not Languish (6:4–12).
  - 3. The Basis of Hope (6:13–7:3)
- C. Drawing Near to God (7:4–10:25)
  - 1. The Fact of Jesus's High Priesthood: He Is the High Priest like Melchizedek (7:4–28).
    - a. The Superiority of Melchizedek (7:4–10)
    - b. Changing to an Eternal High Priest (7:11–19)
    - c. Jesus's Priesthood Is Initiated by an Oath and Held Forever (7:20–25).
    - d. Conclusion: Jesus Is Our Fitting High Priest (7:26–28).
  - 2. The Results of Jesus's Priesthood: Cleansing and Qualification (8:1–10:18)
    - a. Jesus's Priesthood, Covenant, Tabernacle, and Sacrifice (8:1–13)
    - b. Cleansing the Conscience of the Believer (9:1–14)
    - c. The Mediator of the New Covenant (9:15–28)
    - d. The End of Sacrifice (10:1–18)
  - 3. The Response to Jesus's Priesthood: Draw Near to God (10:19–25).

III. JESUS, THE ONE WHO RAN THE RACE BEFORE US (10:19–13:16).
- A. Run the Race (10:19–11:40).
  - 1. Move One Another Forward (10:19–25).
  - 2. Warning: No Other Sacrifice for Sin (10:26–39)
  - 3. Faith and Endurance (11:1–40)
- B. The Course Set Before Us (12:1–29)
  - 1. Endure the Discipline of God (12:1–13).

2. Hold on to Grace (12:14–29).

C. Go with Jesus Outside the Camp (13:1–16).

IV. CONCLUSION (13:17–25)

UNIT-BY-UNIT DISCUSSION

I. Jesus the Apostle of Our Confession (1:1–4:16)

Hebrews begins in a rather abrupt manner. Some have identified 1:1–4 as the introduction to the book. If so, the mention of angels at both 1:4 and 5 is an example of how the author elegantly transitions from one section to another.

A. Jesus as the Heir of the Universe (1:1–3:2) Without a formal prescript, the book opens like a rhetorical presentation rather than a letter (1:1–4). Immediately the author draws a sharp contrast between the prophets of old who spoke and the Son through whom God speaks in the present. This smoothly transitions into the first major section of the book.

Hebrews 1:4 introduces the idea that "Son" is a better name than the angels enjoy, and verses 5–18 adduce seven OT quotations to prove this point (1:5–14). These are organized in the form of a pair of three quotations with a concluding quote, a common rabbinical rhetorical device called "pearl stringing."[70]

The three pairs of quotations are as follows. (1) In 1:5–6 the author contrasts the position of the Son and of the angels: he is the Son, and the angels worship him (citing Ps 2:7; 2 Sam 7:14; Deut 32:43, LXX). (2) In 1:7–12 the author contrasts the work of the Son and the angels: angels are his servants, but he is the sovereign ruler of the universe (citing Pss 104:4; 45:6; 102:25–27). (3) In 1:13–14 the author concludes the string of citations with a quote of Psalm 110:1, reemphasizing that the Son is the ruler while the angels are "ministering spirits."

The first of several warning passages follows on the heels of the exposition (2:1–4). The argument follows a lesser to greater pattern.[71] If just punishment was meted out for violations of the OT law (mediated through angels), how much more would this be the case for those who rejected the Son, who was manifestly greater than the angels? (This points back to 1:1–4.) Thus, the readers should pay close attention to what God says today through the Son.

The author then cites two reasons the recipients ought to pay close attention to his message: (1) lest they "drift away" (a constant danger for believers; notice that this does not necessarily imply apostasy); and (2) lest they fall under the discipline of the Lord.

Citing Psalm 8:4–6, the author continues to demonstrate his thesis that Jesus is superior to the angels (2:5–9). "The world to come" will not be under the dominion of angels but subject to One who had become human, the Lord Jesus Christ. Through the

---

[70] Hb. *haraz.* See Lane, *Hebrews,* cxxii.

[71] Hb. *qal wahomer.* Ibid., cxx.

OT citation, the author recalls that God's original intent was for humans to subdue the earth (Gen 1:28) but this intent went unfulfilled. Humanity had not fully subdued the earth. Yet God's purpose would be fulfilled in Jesus (the first time the humanity of Jesus is stressed), who had been "crowned with glory and honor because he suffered death" (2:9).

The author notes that it was fitting for God to perfect the source or author (Gk. *archēgos*) of humanity's salvation through suffering (as a human) because both Christ and believers are united in their relationship to the Father as sons of God (v. 11). Christ even calls believers his brothers (vv. 12–13 set the OT foundation for this identification). The ultimate intent is that since humans and Christ share "flesh and blood," in his death on the cross Christ was able to break the power of the one who held humans in bondage through fear of death, that is, the Devil (vv. 14–15). In 2:16–18 the author explains that Jesus had to be made truly human so he could serve as an effective high priest for God's people.

The argument proceeds smoothly into the next section (3:1–2; note the conjunction "therefore"), where Jesus, the superior messenger or "apostle" (Gk. *apostolos*) is contrasted with Moses, who was a servant in God's house.

B. Enter the Remaining Sabbath Rest (3:1–4:13) At the end of the previous section, the author introduces the fact that Jesus became a human to serve as an effective high priest for God's people. The entirety of the present section functions as preparation for the development of this theme later on in the letter.

The movement from angels to Moses is best understood against the common notion in ancient Judaism that Moses was considered superior to the angels (3:1–6). The author, however, points his readers toward Jesus so they would consider him. The basis for this appeal is that Jesus is worthy of greater glory than Moses (3:3–4) and that he was faithful as a Son over the household rather than having been faithful only as a servant (an allusion to Num 12:7). The essence of "considering Jesus" is fleshed out in 3:6b. The readers must hold on to their public confession of Jesus in order to retain unhindered access to him and to attain the object of their hope. This leads directly to the next section, which represents a call to endurance and challenges the readers to be faithful as Jesus was.

Hebrews 3:7–19 begins with a quotation of Psalm 95:7–11 that was used weekly in the synagogue. Every week worshippers were reminded of the tragic consequences of the rebellion recorded in Numbers 13–14. The injunction in verses 12–13 is to "watch out" and to "encourage each other daily," lest the readers grow "hardened by the deceit of sin" (v. 13, author's translation). The example from Numbers refers to a group of people (the Israelites) who were about to receive God's blessings but did not because they would not trust God. The author warns his readers to endure to the end and trust God.

The present section (4:1–13) is made up of two paragraphs. The first describes the remaining rest and encourages the recipients of the letter to enter it. The unit is followed by a second warning passage concerning the necessity of heeding the Word of God. The author shifted from a discussion of those who failed to enter the rest to a discussion of the continuing validity of a rest from God. He cited Genesis 2:2 as the foundation of the Sabbath rest (which would have been the second scriptural citation given in the synagogues each Sabbath) to explain that God had invited the Israelites into his rest, but through unbelief and disobedience they had failed. Since later through David God issued another offer of rest (Ps 95:7–11), surely this "rest" was not merely the rest of conquering Canaan but a real Sabbath-type rest from God that remained for the people of God (see 4:8: "For if Joshua had given them rest, God would not have spoken later about another day"). The encouragement, then, was to make sure the readers had entered this remaining rest, that is, a rest from their own labors, salvation by grace. The final exhortation is to "make every effort to enter that rest, so that no one will fall into the same pattern of disobedience" (4:11).

According to the common pattern, the exhortation is followed by a warning not to drift away (4:11–16). The people of God are to heed his voice as he calls out to them "today" (see Psalm 95). The author compares God's Word to a double-edged sword that pierces through all human excuses, exposing the innermost portions of the heart, painting a picture of the hearer of the Word as being naked so that his thoughts are laid bare. People are indeed defenseless before God when they disobey his Word. Hebrews 4:11–16 forms what Westfall called a "discourse peak," concluding the first section of the letter with three inseparable exhortations: "Let us then make every effort" (4:11); "Let us hold fast to the confession" (4:14); and "Let us approach the throne of grace" (4:16).[72]

Typical of the author's transitions, the movement between the major sections is seamless. The warning not to drift away (4:11–16) is both the conclusion to the present section and the introduction to the next. In cinematic terms the author preferred a fade to a hard cut.

II. Jesus Our High Priest (4:11–10:25)

Prior to 4:13 the author refers to Jesus as "high priest" (2:17; 3:1), but now a sustained defense of the meaning and implications of his priesthood is presented. Just as the previous section was an exposition of Psalm 95:7–11, so this section is an exposition of Psalm 110:4, which is not cited in any other NT book: "The Lord has sworn an oath and will not take it back: 'Forever, You are a priest according to the pattern of Melchizedek.'"

A. Carry on to Maturity (4:11–5:14) Hebrews 4:14–16 draws a conclusion based on the humanity of Christ (mentioned in chap. 2). The readers should "hold fast" to their "confession" because they have a high priest familiar with their sinful condition without having succumbed to it. For this reason they are able to go before God's throne to receive mercy and find grace to help.

Having declared Christ's high priesthood, the author describes the perfection of this high priest through his earthly life and sufferings (5:1–10). He begins by noting God's intent for the Levitical high priest, who was appointed to serve God by offering gifts and

[72] Westfall, *Discourse Analysis*, 142.

sacrifices for sins on behalf of his people. It was God's intent that a human serve in this role since he would be familiar with people's weakness, and the high priest himself is included in the sin offering. Finally, he was not self-appointed but designated by God.

Similarly, Christ was appointed by God, though not in the likeness of Aaron but according to the order of Melchizedek (5:5–6). Verses 7–8 most likely refer to Jesus's prayer in Gethsemane where his ultimate request was for God's will to be done. Thus, "he learned obedience from what he suffered" (5:8).[73] From 5:11 to 6:12 the author took a temporary reprieve from his explication of the high priesthood of Christ. The reason for this is that his hearers had become slow to understand (Gk. *nōthroi*; "sluggish, lazy"). The reason they could not understand the author's teaching on Melchizedek was not that the nature of his priesthood was impossible to grasp but that they had ceased paying attention to the teaching of God's Word and needed to go back to the ABCs of the Christian faith.

B. Maturity Enables Hope (6:1–7:3) The "elementary doctrine of Christ" (ESV) is spelled out in 6:1–2 (another transitional passage). Instead of languishing at these elementary things, the author wanted his readers to press on to maturity. The exhortation—the only one in this entire unit—is in the passive (most likely, a "divine passive" with God as the agent of the action), conveying the sense "let us be carried on [by God]" to full maturity. This was important because it was impossible to renew those to repentance who were "recrucifying the Son of God" (6:4–12).

If it is kept in mind that the author envisioned his hearers in a similar situation as Israel in the wilderness, then the description of those who fell—"once enlightened" (v. 4), "tasted the heavenly gift" (v. 4), "partakers of the Holy Spirit" (v. 4 NASB), "tasted God's good word" (v. 5)—does not necessarily refer to legitimate believers. Just as the whole nation of Israel in the wilderness saw the pillar of fire, ate the manna, witnessed the manifestation of God's power in Moses's mighty miracles, and received the divine promises of deliverance from their enemies, the readers had seen manifestations of God's reality, presence, and power all around them in the congregation of which they were, at least nominally, a part (6:4–6). Yet as is still true today, external association with a given congregation does not guarantee salvation; what is required is a heart that trusts in God and in the provision he made in Christ.

The author contrasts his hearers as following either in the footsteps of Joshua and Caleb or in those of the disobedient generation of Israelites who perished in the desert. Those who fell away repudiated Christ in a way similar to those who rejected him in Jerusalem—thus, "recrucifying" (6:6) him does not have an atoning significance but emphasizes the rejection of Christ—and openly casts aspersions on him. Thus, the illustration in 6:7–8 describes believers as those producing fruit and unbelievers as producing thorns.

---

[73] Learning obedience and attaining to perfection do not imply any imperfection on Jesus's part; instead, the reference implies that Jesus had completed his course to be installed as high priest. The term *teleioō* ("to perfect") was used in the LXX to describe the installation of a priest (e.g., Exod 29:9, 33).

This reinforces the previous affirmation that true believers persevere to the end (see 3:14). Nevertheless, the author had confidence in the salvation of most of his readers (6:9–10).

The Christ follower has assurance of enduring faith because the oath made to Abraham has application also for believers today (6:13–7:3). By two immovable realities—God's oath and his word—God established the covenant with Abraham that his seed would be innumerable. This covenant implies the endurance of the believer. Christians thus have encouragement to seize this immovable hope secured for them because Jesus entered the inner sanctuary for them as an eternal high priest like Melchizedek.

Hebrews 7:1–3 establishes who Melchizedek was and how Christ resembled him in certain respects. Melchizedek was the priest of the Most High God who received tithes from Abraham. The name *Melchizedek* means "king of righteousness," and he was the "King of Salem" (i.e., king of the city of "Salem," meaning "peace"). The author also skillfully exploits the silence of the OT and noted that Melchizedek had "neither beginning of days nor end of life" because the Genesis narrative where he is introduced mentions neither his birth nor his death.

C. Drawing Near to God (7:4–10:25) In the prominent central section of the letter, the author develops (1) the arguments for Christ's high priesthood (7:4–28); (2) the accomplishment of Jesus's priesthood (8:1–10:18); and (3) the proper response to Jesus's priesthood (10:19–25).

Hebrews 7:4–10 establishes the greatness of Melchizedek's priesthood over the sons of Aaron for three reasons. First, the sons of Aaron collected tithes from their brothers, but Melchizedek blessed Abraham—the possessor of the promise of God—proving that he was Abraham's superior. Second, the sons of Aaron died, but there is no mention of Melchizedek's death; thus in a sense he still lives. Third, Levi himself, while still in Abraham's loins, paid tithes to Melchizedek prior to Levi's birth.

Having established the superiority of Melchizedek, the author moves on to the changing of the priesthood—implying that the old covenant deals with Aaron, and the new with Melchizedek—and its superiority (7:11–19). He begins by asking the question, If perfection came through the law, why was there the need for another priest not of the Aaronic order? The answer is that there must be a change of law as well. Jesus became high priest not by a command of the law and physical descent—after all, he was from Judah's line—but based on the power of an indestructible life (a priest forever like Melchizedek).[74]

The words "not without an oath" (v. 20 NIV) form a litotes and emphasize two important points (7:20–25): (1) Jesus's priesthood was confirmed by the oath of God; and (2) the Aaronic priesthood possessed no such oath. Because Jesus's priesthood was sworn by God as a permanent oath, it will never be taken away. This could not be said of the old Levitical order. The emphasis on the duration of the two sets of priests continues throughout this

---

[74] Melchizedek actually drops off the scene at 7:17, having served the purpose of demonstrating that the OT made allowance for a priest not after Aaron's lineage.

section. The Levites were prevented from being permanent priests through their own deaths, but not Jesus. The great benefit, of course, is that because Jesus lives forever, he is able to save forever those who come to him on account of his priesthood. Jesus is qualified to be believers' high priest in every way. He is "holy, innocent, undefiled, separated from sinners, and exalted above the heavens" (7:26); he offers a better sacrifice and serves for a better, eternal term.

Hebrews 8:1–6, the main assertion of the chapter, is supported by 8:7–13. In the former unit the author highlighted the main point that Jesus is a superior high priest, serving in a superior (i.e., heavenly) tabernacle.[75] Levitical priests only served in a faint copy of the heavenly tabernacle. The upshot is stated in 8:6: "But Jesus has now obtained a superior ministry, and to that degree he is the mediator of a better covenant, which has been established on better promises." At 8:7–13, the author provides scriptural support for his assertion, calling attention to the promise of the new covenant in Jeremiah 31:31–34 and noting that the fault was not with the old covenant itself but with the old covenant community, that is, the people (8:8). Because people were unable to keep the old covenant, God promised a new covenant, indicating that the old was about to disappear.

Hebrews 9:1–14 further explicates the assertions made in 8:1–6. In 9:1–10, the author described two main limitations of the old covenant. First, there were serious barricades separating the worshipper from God under the old covenant. The purpose of the separation of the holy place and the holy of holies was to show that the way to God's presence was not yet open (see 9:8). Thus, the setup of the earthly tabernacle pointed forward to a new day. The second limitation of the old covenant was that no one was perfected by the sacrifices it required. Hence, the old covenant was ultimately ineffective because the worshipper was required to repeat the same sacrifices year after year.

In 9:11–14 the contrast with the inefficacy of the old covenant is completed by showing the accomplishment of Christ in cleansing the believer. He entered the holy of holies in the more perfect tabernacle once for all, not once a year; offering his own blood, not representative animals; obtaining eternal redemption, not a temporary covering. The author then summed up his argument with an appeal from the lesser to the greater (animals versus Christ) to declare the actual cleansing of the people of God.

By his perfect sacrifice Jesus became the mediator of the new covenant (9:15–28). The reason Jesus had to die was rooted in the ancient Near Eastern practice (see Gen 15:1–18; Jer 34:18–20), where in permanent covenants animals representative of the two parties making the covenant were slain and divided between the parties establishing the agreement. The blood of the new covenant—the blood from the death of Jesus as believers' representative—insured the permanent arrangement. As in the old covenant where the instruments of the tabernacle were cleansed by blood, so Jesus's blood effected cleansing

[75] Some have asserted that the heavenly tabernacle is proof of an Alexandrian neo-Platonizing theology (see Moffatt, *Hebrews*, 106), but it seems better to understand the reference simply as a straightforward extrapolation from the cited passage of Exod 25:40 (see Lane, *Hebrews*, 1:207).

for believers as they appeared in the heavenly tabernacle. Jesus's death was so powerful that it removed sins once for all, obtaining an eternal salvation. The next action of Jesus that believers awaited was the ultimate salvation to be effected at his (second) coming.

In 10:1–4 the author summarizes his previous arguments. The old sacrifices made no one perfect; annual sacrifices were a reminder of sin; and the blood of animals did not truly remove it. In 10:5–10 the result was stated that these symbolic and repeated sacrifices were replaced by the all-sufficient sacrifice of Christ. The next paragraph pictures the futility of the old covenant after the advent of the new covenant was announced (10:11–14). The author pictures the Levitical priests perennially performing the obsolete offerings that could never permanently remove sins. The contrast was between the standing priests of the old order and the seated priest of the new order, according to Melchizedek. Jesus completed the course of Psalm 110:1–4 and was seated, awaiting the subjugation of all his enemies. As Bruce stated, "A *seated* priest is the guarantee of a finished work and an accepted sacrifice."[76]

Finally, 10:15–18 refers again to the text of the new covenant. When God said, "I will never again remember their sins and their lawless acts," this implied a completed payment for sins. There was thus no other offering for sin; the temple sacrifices achieved *nothing*, while Jesus's sacrifice accomplished *everything* necessary for salvation.

The capstone of the previous teaching is found in 10:19–25.[77] Three exhortations to the readers ("let us") mark this section as a thematic peak that both concludes this section and introduces the next section through the third exhortation.[78] There are also several links back to the previous trio of exhortations (4:14–16). Because of what Jesus accomplished, there was no longer a series of boundaries between the believer and God since the veil had indeed been torn down. The proper response of believers is to draw near to God with confidence, knowing their sins are forgiven; to hold on to their confession without wavering because God is faithful; and to exercise genuine care for other believers, spurring them on to love, good works, and faithful fellowship.

III. Jesus, the One Who Ran the Race Before Us (10:19–13:16)

The dominant thought throughout this section is that believers are pilgrims in this life, looking forward to the life to come. Lane called this the concept of "committed pilgrimage."[79] The author began by describing the life of faith as a race.

A. Run the Race (10:19–11:40) The entire passage is so tightly knit structurally that the discussion of "divisions" is problematic. Having given the thematic commands, the author suggested a course of action: move forward rather than drawing back. The declaration

---

[76] Bruce, *Hebrews*, 239.

[77] See Westfall, *Discourse Analysis*, 235.

[78] This is almost the same pattern as with 4:11–16. The three hortatory subjunctives are inseparable, but the transition to the next section is introduced by the third hortatory subjunctive "let us watch out" (10:24), which is developed through the following warning.

[79] See W. Lane, *Hebrews: A Call to Commitment* (Peabody, MA: Hendrickson, 1998), 162.

that a believer, by definition, does not draw back elicits the discussion of faith in chapter 11, which in turn is predicated on the encouragement to run the race with endurance.

The last exhortation, "And let us watch out for one another to provoke love and good works" (10:24), introduces the final section of the letter. It is dominated by an increased ratio of second person plural verbs ("you"), as the application of the sermon is now fully in view.[80]

The unit 10:26–39 is made up of two paragraphs: the first warns (10:26–31); the second encourages (10:32–39). Perhaps drawing on Numbers 15:27–31, this warning is probably the most urgent. The distinction between "unintentional" and "defiant" sins does not seem to be in view here but rather the rejection of Christ (in Num 15:30, the sinner "blasphemes the LORD"). The person who rejects Christ after hearing the gospel "has trampled on the Son of God, who has regarded as profane the blood of the covenant by which he was sanctified, and who has insulted the Spirit of grace" (10:29). The point is simply that if one rejects the sacrifice of Christ, no other sacrifice remains. The terrifying prospect is that of falling into the hands of the living, Almighty God without having proper covering for one's sin.

The second paragraph (10:32–39) softens the blow with an encouragement to those who have not rejected Christ. The author called them to remember the former days when they were treated harshly but responded in joy, and he encourages them not to throw away their confidence. Instead, they had need of endurance, which the author connected to faith (see chap. 11). Hence, the writer did not put the majority of his readers in the category of those who drew back: "But we are not those who draw back and are destroyed, but those who have faith and are saved" (10:39).

Beginning with the definition of faith (11:1), the author recounts the faithful endurance of believers in the past in five movements.[81] The chapter includes an introduction (11:1–3); preliminary examples from the patriarchs to Abraham (11:4–12); a description of their pilgrim status (11:13–16); more examples from the patriarchs from Abraham forward (11:17–31); and finally the continuation of the faithful up to the time of the writer (11:32–40). The pivot seems to be Abraham, who is the prime example of the one who overcame "by faith" (a phrase used eighteen times in this chapter). By faith, Abraham looked beyond the earthly to the heavenly city; all believers, like him, do the same.

The exhortation that flows from having such a "large cloud of witnesses" (12:1) is to follow their example and to run the race with endurance, looking to Jesus who also endured great suffering. Importantly, the kind of faith required of the readers was the same faith exhibited by OT believers, a powerful point to make if the recipients were Jewish Christians. Thus, the author argues that having the same faith Abraham had means to believe in Jesus, who had already come to make perfect atonement for sin. Reverting back

---

[80] See Westfall (*Discourse Analysis*, 242), who noted fourteen pronouns, twenty-six finite verbs, and eighteen imperatives—almost twice the number of the first two sections combined (thirty/fifty-eight).

[81] See Guthrie, *Hebrews*, 373.

to Judaism, therefore, is not a legitimate option because this would not only mean drawing back from Christ but also falling short of the type of faith displayed by Abraham. To be a true descendant of Abraham, subsequent to God's revelation "by his Son" (1:2), means to believe in Jesus.

B. The Course Set Before Us (12:1–29) Hebrews 12:1–2 describes running the race set before believers. The rest of this major section describes running that race. This involves enduring the discipline of God in everyday life and making every effort to hold on to his grace. The author describes the Christian life as a marathon (12:1–13) in which one does not compete against the other runners but encourages them to run the race as well (the idea of the competition is resumed in 12:12–13). This paragraph describes the significance of, the purpose of, and the response to divine discipline.[82] The significance of discipline is that being subjected to it proves one is the child of God (12:4–10). The purpose of discipline is that, in due course, it yields the fruit of peace and righteousness (12:11). The proper response to the Lord's discipline is to encourage one another to persevere and endure (12:12–13).

The final section of this unit contains three paragraphs. The first is made up of three commands pertaining to the stability of the community (12:14–17). The first command is to pursue peace and holiness (12:14). The second is to encourage others (12:15), realizing that falling short of the grace of God as a believer means not using the grace given by God to believers to pursue peace and holiness. Thus, the resulting bitterness causes trouble and defiles many. The third one is to remember those who did not possess true faith, such as Esau, who was the antithesis of those who endured, having sold his birthright for a single meal.

The second paragraph in this section (12:18–24) builds on the previous one by giving the grounds for the exhortations found there: believers have not come to the Mount of Terror (Sinai) but to the Mount of Joy (Zion) where Jesus works in believers to accomplish his will. The final illustration is that Abel's blood cried out for vengeance, while Christ's blood cries out for grace. The third paragraph in this section (12:25–29) contains the last warning passage of the book. The warning is not to reject Christ, the One who speaks. In essence, since believers have received an unshakable kingdom, they must hold on to grace.

C. Go with Jesus Outside the Camp (13:1–16) The first paragraph of this section (13:1–4) is an exhortation to remember brotherly love. This is spelled out as (1) remembering strangers; (2) remembering prisoners; and (3) remembering spouses, that is, marital fidelity. The second paragraph (13:5–16) revolves around commands relating to matters of doctrine. The first command (13:5–6) urges believers to forsake the love of money. The second (13:7–8) encourages them to esteem their leaders and to imitate their lives because Jesus does not change. The third injunction (13:9–15) is to hold fast to correct doctrine. Finally, the author encourages believers to continue in good works (13:16).

---

[82] Lane, *Call to Commitment*, 163.

IV. Conclusion (13:17–25)

The conclusion of the book makes two requests. First, the writer enjoins his readers to obey their leaders (13:17). Second, they are to pray for "us," whoever the intended beneficiaries of these requested prayers may be (13:18–19). Finally, the author ends with concluding exhortations and pieces of information (13:20–25), asking his readers to receive his "message of exhortation" (describing the nature and purpose of the work) and giving notice that Timothy was out of prison and on his way to them. Final greetings and benediction close out the book.

THEOLOGY

Theological Themes

The God Who Speaks in Scripture The major source of the theology of Hebrews is clearly the OT Scriptures as interpreted in light of Christ's coming.[83] The use of the OT in Hebrews proceeds from the assumption of its enduring validity as the Word of God (see 1:1; 3:7; 4:12; 13:7). In most cases an OT quotation is cited as God or the Holy Spirit "speaking," so that it is ultimately not the human authors of a given book of the OT that are speaking in and through the text but God, who still speaks to his people (including the readers) today.[84] This striking feature affirms that the OT is God speaking.

On the basis of this premise, the author also hints at revelation beyond the OT, for God is said to speak in the present economy of salvation "by his Son" (1:2; see 2:1–3). Thus, it is both the word mediated by angels—the law—and the word spoken by God through the Son that are to be obeyed, with serious repercussions in the case of disobedience. The speaking God must be heeded. However, since the author makes no reference to specific words of Christ, only to the gospel message in general, the written Word of God in the Hebrew Scriptures seems to take precedence.

Frequently, the author's use of the OT represents a straightforward interpretation of the text (e.g., the application of Jer 31:31–34 in Heb 8:8–13). At other points the Christological significance is elusive to modern Western readers (e.g., 2:13), and it is not always clear which passage is being cited (e.g., 1:6).[85]

---

[83] Käsemann (*Wandering People of God*) tried to make the case for a pre-Christian Gnosticism as the conceptual background of Hebrews. But since full-fledged Gnosticism postdates Christianity, these theories are now fading (see Hurst, *Hebrews*, 74).

[84] More often he said that it is God who speaks; once he named David (4:7); and once an ambiguous "someone" (2:6 NIV). His favorite phrase is "saying" (*legōn*), vividly reinforcing the idea of the enduring validity of the OT (Lane, *Hebrews* cxvii). A. H. Trotter Jr. (*Interpreting the Epistle to the Hebrews*, Guides to New Testament Exegesis [Grand Rapids, MI: Baker, 1997], 191) stated, "Probably no book of Scripture gives a clearer and more forceful proof that the NT authors regarded the OT as the very Word of God." On the "God who speaks" in the book of Hebrews, see A. J. Köstenberger, "Mission in the General Epistles," in *Mission in the New Testament: An Evangelical Approach*, ed. W. J. Larkin Jr. and J. F. Williams (Maryknoll, NY: Orbis, 1998), 194–95.

[85] The author never disclosed to his readers the source of his quotation. Twice he located a passage only as "somewhere" (2:6; 4:4).

SIDEBAR 16.2:
THE USE OF THE OLD TESTAMENT IN THE BOOK OF HEBREWS

Hebrews is unmatched in its rich diversity of methods for appropriating the OT Scriptures. Characteristically, the author did not simply quote a text but used the OT in a variety of ways to make his point. The following nine types of approaches can be identified:

1. Dispelling confusion (2:8–9)
2. Reinforcement using an OT text to support an exhortation (10:19–39)
3. Drawing implications (8:8–13)
4. Employing the literal sense of a word or phrase (7:11)
5. Early rabbinic rules of interpretation, including
   a. *Qal wāhômer,* an argument from lesser to the greater (2:2–4)
   b. *Gĕzērâ šāwâ,* the use of verbally analogous words to draw attention to the relationship between two passages (4:1–11)
6. Chain quotations or "pearl stringing" (Hb. *haraz*) of several passages (1:5–13)
7. Example lists (11:32–38)
8. Typology, when historical entities correspond in redemptive plan of God (8:1–5)
9 Homiletical midrash, interpreting a biblical text in preaching (6:13–20).[1]

[1] Lane, *Hebrews,* cxxi.

Some have tried to link the author's use of the OT to an underlying background of thought similar to that of Philo of Alexandria, a highly educated Jewish writer of the first century (20 BC–AD 50). Specifically, Philo's appropriation of Platonic philosophy has often been seen as having influenced the writer of Hebrews.[86] However, Barrett seemed to speak for many when he suggested that the background of thought was not Platonism but mainstream Christian tradition closer to Jewish apocalypticism.[87] The use of the OT in Hebrews reflects its early Greek translation and shares commonalities with Jewish and early Christian usage.[88]

[86] Platonism held that physical entities have a heavenly archetype or pattern. The archetypes are the eternal and better form, while the earthly entities are merely a material copy. Some see the description of the tabernacle in Hebrews 8 and the references to the sacrifices of the old covenant (referred to as "shadows" and "examples" in Hebrews) as predicated on Platonic dualism. From the late nineteenth century until the 1950s, this view was widely popular. E.g., C. Spicq, *L'Épître aux Hébreux*; and Moffatt, *Hebrews,* xxxi. For a rebuttal, see R. Williamson, *Philo and the Epistle to the Hebrews* (Leiden, Netherlands: Brill, 1970). The idea that Hebrews is Platonic in its outlook is all but dead today.

[87] C. K. Barrett, "The Eschatology of the Epistle to the Hebrews," in *The Background of the New Testament and Its Eschatology,* ed. W. D. Davies and D. Daube (Cambridge, UK: Cambridge University Press, 1964), 363, 366. Barrett went on to suggest that the philosophical language was intentionally appropriated by the author as an appropriate tool to communicate Christian truth (ibid., 393).

[88] The exact version of the LXX text form is an unsettled question. For most of his quotations, the author's text looks similar to the one found in the fifth-century manuscripts Alexandrinus and Vaticanus. But there are quotations that defy a

The Superiority of the Person and Work of Christ and His High Priesthood The first major theme of the letter is the supremacy of the person and work of Christ. Christ is the eternal, preexistent Son of God, who created the world and was made human to provide atonement for his people. He then sat down in order to return at the end of time for judgment and salvation. The book opens with a series of contrasts demonstrating the superiority of Christ. Jesus is not merely a servant like the prophets; he is the unique Son of God. While God spoke in the past through various prophets, in these last days he spoke by his Son. As the maker of the universe, Christ is also its heir. The angels are merely ministering servants who worship the Son. Moses was a servant in God's house; Christ was the Son over the house.

On the basis of his uniqueness as a person, Christ also rendered a unique work, described in Hebrews against the larger backdrop of the high priesthood of Christ.[89] While this emphasis is virtually unparalleled in the NT, it does not represent an innovation by the author. To the contrary, the author's use of Psalm 110:4 in his argument finds support in Jesus's own application of the figure mentioned in Psalm 110:1 to himself (see Matt 22:41–45 and parallels). From this it was only a small step to conclude that the oath of God to this figure also pertained to Christ. Hence, Jesus is a priest forever like Melchizedek, as the author of Hebrews argued on the basis of the two major OT passages dealing with this priest-king (Gen 14:18–20; Ps 110:4).

The first reference to Christ's priesthood involved his sacrifice. Christ redeemed his "brothers" (i.e., humans) in that he tasted death for everyone; thus, he functioned as their high priest in making the sacrifice (see 2:17). That Jesus was a high priest like Melchizedek means that he was superior to the Levitical priesthood. The author argued that the Melchizedek of the Genesis account was a superior priest because in a sense Levi paid tithes to Melchizedek through Abram and Melchizedek blessed Abram; thus, the greater blessed the lesser (7:7).

Christ was a priest like Melchizedek in that he did not descend from Levi, but even more so because of his eternal existence—he will never die again. As an eternal priest, he represents a far superior priesthood. The Levitical priests had to offer sacrifices for their own sins; Christ did not. Their sacrifices made no one perfect; they had to keep making them year after year; Christ's priesthood was once for all. The Levitical priests had to be continually replaced because of death; Christ lives forever. Finally, the Levites served in the midst of "shadows" under a covenant that had become obsolete; Christ is the fulfillment of OT typology, the minister of the new covenant, which is far superior to the old.

Jesus was prepared for his priesthood (and qualified for it) by becoming human and by suffering in this life like all other humans do.[90] He was also installed by the oath of

---

simple solution as to the source. See J. C. McCollough, "The Old Testament in Hebrews," *NTS* 26 (1980): 363–79.

[89] Nowhere else in the NT is there such a clear affirmation of the high priesthood of Jesus.

[90] See 2:17 and esp. 5:9, where "perfected" is most likely a term used to describe the completion of a priest's preparation and his installation as a priest.

God (stated in 5:5 and 7:20; clearly the implication of Psalm 110) as a permanent, that is, eternal priest (7:24, 28). His offering is presented in terms of fulfilling the OT typology of the Day of Atonement. Jesus brought his sacrifice outside the camp and carried his blood into the holy of holies (13:12–13; see Lev 16:27). As a high priest he sat down at the right hand of the throne of God and lives forever to make intercession for his people.

Table 16.3: Jesus in Hebrews*

Actions
Created the World (1:2, 7, 10–12)
Sustains/Bears All Things (1:3)
Entered the World (9:26; 10:5, 10)
Made like Humans (2:9, 14, 17)
The Agent of God's Revelation/Shared the Message of Salvation (1:1–2; 2:3; 6:1)
Proclaimed God's Name (2:12)
Trusted in/Obeyed God (2:13, 10:7, 9)
Experienced Temptation (2:18; 4:15; 7:26–27)
Cried Out to God (5:7)
Suffered (2:9–10, 18; 5:8; 9:26; 13:12)
Was Made Perfect (2:10; 5:8–9; 7:28)
Learned Obedience (5:8)
Experienced Death (1:9, 14; 13:12; 12:2–3, 12, 14)
Saved/Redeemed Humanity (5:9; 7:25; 9:12, 15)
Bore and Removed Sins (9:26, 28)
Offered/Sacrificed Himself (7:27; 9:14, 25, 28; 9:12, 14, 26; 10:10, 12; 12:24; 13:12)
Cleansed Sins and Consciences (1:3; 9:14; 4:15; 7:26; 9:14)
Atoned for Sins (1:3; 2:17)
Destroyed the Power of the Devil (2:14)
Freed Humanity from the Fear of Death (2:15)
Takes Hold of Humanity (2:16, 18)
Leads Humanity to Glory (2:10)
Inaugurates a New and Living Way (10:20)
Perfects and Sanctifies (10:14; 13:12)
Raised from the Dead (13:20)
Entered the Heavenly Realm (4:14; 6:19–20; 9:11–12, 24)
Crowned King/Seated at the Right Hand of God (1:3, 13; 2:9; 8:1; 10:12; 12:2)
Anointed (1:9)
Made Heir of All Things (1:2, 4)
Worshipped by Angels (1:6)

Jesus in Hebrews* (continued)

Actions
Victorious over His Enemies/Subdues All Things (1:13; 2:8; 10:13)
Appointed High Priest (3:1–2; 5:5–6, 10; 6:19–20; 7:16, 21; 9:11–12, 24)
He Helps/Sympathizes with/ Intercedes for Humanity (2:18; 4:16; 7:25–26; 8:2; 9:11–12, 24, 26; 10:19, 22)
He will Come Again (9:28; 10:37–38)
Titles and Descriptions
The Eternal God (1:3, 8–9; 7:3, 16, 24)
Lord (1:10; 2:3; 7:14; 13:20)
Son of God (1:2, 5–6, 8, 3:6; 4:14; 5:5, 8; 6:6; 7:3, 28; 10:29)
Heir (1:12)
High Priest (2:17; 3:1; 4:14–15; 5:5, 10; 6:20; 7:26; 8:1; 9:11)
King (i.e., royal status) (1:3, 5, 8–9; 7:1; 8:1; 10:12)
Pioneer and Perfecter of Faith (12:2)
Apostle (3:1)
Forerunner (6:20)
Guarantee and Mediator of the New Covenant (7:20; 12:24)
Minister (7:22)
Shepherd of the Sheep (13:20)

* Adapted from B. C. Small, *The Characterization of Jesus in the Book of Hebrews*, Biblical Interpretation Series (Leiden, Netherlands: Brill, 2014), 159–256.

Perseverance and Christian Assurance As the author desired to encourage believers to adhere to their confession and progress to maturity, it is necessary to address the nature of salvation. A key component of his argument is to warn his hearers of the dangers of not heeding his call. The author accomplished this in alternating blocks of exposition and exhortation.[91] Within the exhortations of Hebrews are a group of passages that sternly warn the hearers about the dangers of not heeding God's Word.[92] These warnings are deemed so strong that they become a common thread in the age-old debate over the preservation of believers.[93] Most likely, the writer did not warn Christians about the possibility of apostasy

---

[91] Guthrie, *Structure of Hebrews*.

[92] The five "warning passages" are 2:1–4; 3:7–4:13; 5:11–6:12; 10:19–39; and 12:14–29.

[93] H. W. Bateman IV, gen. ed., *Four Views on the Warning Passages in Hebrews* (Grand Rapids, MI: Kregel, 2006), describes the four main views: (1) the classical Arminian view, which holds that these passages indicate that believers can lose their salvation; (2) the classical Reformed view, which believes that these passages encourage believers to maintain their confession and that those who repudiate Christ were never really saved in the first place; (3) the Wesleyan Arminian view, which contends that these passages teach that one can lose one's salvation and never regain it; and (4) a moderate Reformed view, which argues that these passages merely warn against not reaching maturity.

but rather enjoined them to examine the condition of their faith and to consider the repercussions of not moving on to maturity. Two critical considerations point in this direction.

First, the author affirms the teaching of Jesus that, by definition, all true believers endure to the end (Matt 10:22 and parallel). The author states, "For we have become participants in Christ if we hold firmly until the end the reality that we had at the start" (3:14). Hebrews 6:9 affirms that apostasy is not connected to salvation, that is, those who possess salvation are not those who fall away. The author asserted that Christ is able to save his own eternally because of his eternal intercession (7:25) and that Christ-followers are not among those who draw back to destruction but are instead among those who believe, resulting in the salvation of their souls (10:39). Clearly, the author of Hebrews affirms the perseverance and eternal preservation of believers.[94]

Second, the author acknowledges that some are related to Christ only superficially. He likens these kinds of people to the wilderness generation who rebelled at Kadesh Barnea (Numbers 13–14), noting that they heard the word but that their exposure did not meet with faith (4:2). In fact, the author describes their actions in terms of rebellion (as does Psalm 95, which he quoted), and to be like these disobedient individuals is to have "an evil, unbelieving heart that turns away from the living God" (3:12). Thus, he portrays his hearers as falling either in the category of those who perished in the wilderness or under the rubric of those who believed and were allowed to enter God's rest, namely Joshua and Caleb. The all-important contrast, then, is between those who trusted in God and his promise and those who were connected to God only nominally—those who in truth resembled a fruitless field good only for burning (6:8).

The Benefits of the Sacrificial Death of Christ Hebrews depicts the death of Christ as the superior ultimate sacrifice, offered once for all (7:27; 8:26), and sealed by Jesus's ascension to the right hand of the heavenly throne (1:3; 8:1; 10:12; 12:2). His sacrifice is the blood of the new covenant (9:15–17; see Jer 31:31–34).[95] Now that the promised new covenant has been enacted, the old covenant—intended to be temporary from the beginning, only a shadow of the good things to come—has been made obsolete (8:13).

The description of the new covenant is vitally connected to the purpose of the letter in at least two ways. First, because of the inauguration of the new covenant in Christ, reverting back to the old covenant is an invalid option. Since there is no sacrifice for sins other than the one made by Christ, it is vital to hold fast to one's Christian confession (4:14; 10:23). Second, because the stipulations of the new covenant are unconditional,

---

[94] Against I. H. Marshall (*New Testament Theology* [Downers Grove, IL: InterVarsity, 2005], 619–20), who so strongly insisted on the possibility of apostasy that he contended that passages elsewhere in the NT that appear to teach the perseverance of believers ought to be reevaluated in light of the "warning passages" in Hebrews. The reverse is considerably more likely.

[95] Some translations render the word *diathēkē* in 9:13 as "will," which is probated at the death of the one making it. But this is foreign to the context. It is better to understand 9:13 and the following verses as describing the process of making a permanent covenant. This involved the slaying of animals and walking between the bodies as a representation of the death of the testators. In the case of the new covenant, there is no representative body; instead, the body is Christ's.

Something to Think About: Turn Your Eyes upon Jesus

For Jewish people who related to God through the Mosaic law and satisfied its requirements by offering sacrifices through their priests, trusting in Christ for salvation demanded a major paradigm shift. How could that which was once so right (trying to keep the law) suddenly be wrong, now that Christ has come? It is challenging for us—most of who are Gentiles—to understand the difficulty Jews faced in this regard.

Yet change they must—understanding, as Paul pointed out, that the function of the law was limited to the time before Christ. The law was a reflection of God's righteous demands, upholding a standard of holiness; in itself, however, it was unable to save a person. Accomplishing salvation is something only Christ could do, and that is what he did. For this reason it is imperative that we not "neglect such a great salvation," as the author of Hebrews exhorted (2:3).

To make his case, the author built a powerful defense, showing Jesus's superiority to the angels (who had mediated the law at Sinai), to Moses (through whom God had given the law), and to the OT priesthood (who had administered the sacrificial system prescribed in the law). The author showed how Jesus mediated a new covenant by serving as a priest of a different order than the Levites. Christ is a priest of the order of Melchizedek—a priest who will never die again.

As the author's point neared its climax, he launched a most daring proposal. In chapter 11, the "Hall of Faith," the author stated that it is Jesus in whom he exhorted his readers to place their trust—it was, in fact, this same Jesus on whom the greatest OT believers already had fixed their eyes, including Abel, Enoch, Noah, Abraham, and even Moses himself!

How can this be? It is so because all these people chose to live not by sight but by faith—faith in the God who could raise the dead (11:19), faith in the God who would lead his people to the land he would show them (11:10), faith in the God who would save those who believed in him apart from works through faith. This is how even an OT believer such as Noah "became an heir of the righteousness that comes by faith" (11:7).

If even OT saints, then, rightly understood, were believers, not only in God but, in a sense, already also in Jesus, how much more must people—now that Jesus has come and died and sat down to rest from his work at the right hand of God—fix their eyes on Jesus, "the source and perfecter of our faith, who for the joy that lay before him endured a cross and despised the shame" (12:2)?

"Therefore, since we also have such a large cloud of witnesses surrounding us, let us lay aside every hindrance and the sin that so easily ensnares us. Let us run with endurance the race that lies before us, keeping our eyes on Jesus, the source and perfecter of our faith. . . . For consider him who endured such hostility from sinners against himself, so that you won't grow weary and give up" (12:1–3).

believers have unprecedented access to God and should take advantage of this to move on to maturity (3:16; 10:19–22).

Hebrews pictures the death of Christ with its "soteriological, psychological, and social benefits."[96] The author refers to Christ's death in terms of its typological fulfillment of the Day of Atonement. The sacrifice includes not only his death on the cross but also his ascension into heaven to present the blood of his sacrifice before the Father in the heavenly tabernacle (4:14; 7:26), and ultimately his intercession for believers is an ongoing reality (7:25). What is more, psychologically, the death of Christ also cleanses the conscience of those who come to him (9:14) on the basis of the actual cleansing of human sins accomplished at the cross (10:14).

Finally, there are social benefits to the death of Christ as well. Since the sacrifice is the blood of the new covenant, all the benefits of that covenant are available to participants, including knowing God: "For all will know me, from the least to the greatest of them" (8:11 NASB). What is more, on the basis of believers' access to God through the blood of Christ, they are encouraged to assemble together to spur each on to love and good works (10:23–25). Because of their response of faith, they are in direct continuity with believers of all time (see chap. 11). In essence, their story is not complete until our story is finished (11:40).

The Nature of Discipleship In Christian circles discipleship is often treated as a series of disciplines practiced by the believer. The author does mention several Christian disciplines (e.g., 13:15–19), yet not as the means but as the result of progressing toward maturity. At the conclusion of the letter, the author petitions God to equip his readers "with everything good to do his will, working in us what is pleasing in his sight" (13:21). The last phrase suggests that accomplishing the will of God is a matter of God providing believers the ability to accomplish his will.[97] This is reminiscent of 6:1, which properly reads, "Let us be carried on to perfection" (author's translation), a divine passive indicating that God will move his children on to maturity on the premise that they have not become sluggish (5:11).

This seems to build on the nature of the new covenant, in which God does all the foundational work. He writes the law on believers' hearts and reveals himself to those who have entered into covenant with him. In this covenant those who participate are equipped to do God's will. Christians, above all, need endurance, which they are already promised (3:14). Thus, the exhortations in chapters 10–12 construe the nature of discipleship as running a long-distance race with endurance. Believers are to be like Abraham, who was "looking forward to the city that has foundations, whose architect and builder is God" (11:10). They must look to Jesus for their supreme encouragement (12:1), for the call to follow him is a call to follow him in suffering. Thus, in the midst of all the pressures faced by believers,

---

[96] R. N. Perkins, "He Offered Himself: Sacrifice in Hebrews," *Int* 53 (2003): 251–65.

[97] Johnson, *Hebrews*, 57.

they are admonished to "go to him outside the camp, bearing his disgrace. For here we do not have an enduring city; instead, we seek the one to come" (13:13–14).

CONTRIBUTION TO THE CANON

- The definitive revelation and redemption brought by Christ (1:1–4; 7:27; 8:26)
- Christian perseverance and the warning passages (e.g., 2:1–4)
- The eternal high priesthood of Christ (4:14–5:10; 7:1–28)
- The inauguration of the new covenant (8:1–9:25)
- The example of faith by OT believers (chap. 11)

STUDY QUESTIONS

1. What is the evidence against the Pauline authorship of Hebrews?
2. What do we know about the author?
3. What seems the latest possible date for Hebrews, and why?
4. What are the likely destination and audience of Hebrews?
5. What is the purpose of the book of Hebrews?
6. Why were the early church fathers in the West slow to receive Hebrews into the canon?
7. What are two major issues that have dominated the modern discussion of literary matters in Hebrews?
8. Are the hermeneutics of Hebrews Jewish or Greek? Explain.
9. What devices of Greek rhetoric does the author employ?
10. Why is it difficult to ascertain the structure of Hebrews?
11. What is the major source of theology for the author of Hebrews, and how was it interpreted?
12. What is the major role attributed to angels in Hebrews 1 and 2?

FOR FURTHER STUDY

Allen, D. L. *Hebrews* NAC 35. Nashville, TN: B&H, 2010.

Attridge, H. W. *The Epistle to the Hebrews*. Hermeneia. Philadelphia, PA: Fortress, 1989.

Bateman, H. W., IV, gen. ed. *Four Views on the Warning Passages in Hebrews*. Grand Rapids, MI: Kregel, 2006.

Black, D. A. "The Problem of the Literary Structure of Hebrews: An Evaluation and Proposal." *Grace Theological Journal* 7 (1986): 163–77.

Bruce, F. F. *The Epistle to the Hebrews*. New International Commentary on the New Testament. Rev. ed. Grand Rapids, MI: Eerdmans, 1990.

Cockerill, G. L. *The Epistle to the* Hebrews. NICNT. Grand Rapids, MI: Eerdmans, 2012.

Ellingworth, P. *The Epistle to the Hebrews*. New International Greek New Testament Commentary. Grand Rapids, MI: Eerdmans, 1993.

France, R. T. "Hebrews." Pages 17–195 in *The Expositor's Bible Commentary*. Rev. ed. Vol. 13: *Hebrews–Revelation*. Grand Rapids, MI: Zondervan, 2005.

Guthrie, G. *Hebrews*. "Hebrews." Pages 919–96 in *Commentary on the New Testament Use of the Old Testament*. Edited by G. K. Beale and D. A. Carson. Grand Rapids, MI: Zondervan, 2007.

________. *Hebrews*. NIV Application Commentary. Grand Rapids, MI: Zondervan, 1998.

________. *The Structure of Hebrews: A Text-Linguistic Analysis*. New York, NY: Brill, 1994. Paperback edition, Grand Rapids, MI: Baker, 1998.

Hagner, D. A. *Encountering the Book of Hebrews: An Exposition*. Encountering Biblical Studies. Grand Rapids, MI: Baker, 2002.

________. *Hebrews*. New International Biblical Commentary. Peabody, MA: Hendrickson, 1990.

Hughes, G. *Hebrews and Hermeneutics: The Epistle to the Hebrews as a New Testament Example of Biblical Interpretation*. Society of New Testament Studies Monograph Series 36. Cambridge, UK: Cambridge University Press, 1979.

Hughes, P. E. *A Commentary on the Epistle to the Hebrews*. Grand Rapids, MI: Eerdmans, 1977.

Hurst, L. D. *The Epistle to the Hebrews: Its Background and Thought*. Society for New Testament Studies Monograph Series 65. Cambridge, UK: Cambridge University Press, 1990.

Isaacs, M. E. *Sacred Space: An Approach to the Theology of the Epistle to the Hebrews*. Journal for the Study of the New Testament Supplement 73. Sheffield, UK: JSOT, 1992.

Johnson, L. T. *Hebrews: A Commentary*. New Testament Library. Louisville, KY: Westminster John Knox, 2006.

Käsemann, E. *The Wandering People of God: An Investigation of the Letter to the Hebrews*. Translated by R. A. Harrisville and I. L. Sandberg. Minneapolis, MN: Augsburg, 1984 [1957].

Lane, W. *Hebrews*. Word Biblical Commentary 47A–B. 2 vols. Dallas, TX: Word, 1991.

________. *Hebrews: A Call to Commitment*. Peabody, MA: Hendrickson, 1998.

Lehne, S. *The New Covenant in Hebrews*. Journal for the Study of the New Testament Supplement 44. Sheffield, UK: JSOT, 1990.

Lindars, B. *The Theology of the Letter to the Hebrews*. New Testament Theology. Cambridge, UK: Cambridge University Press, 1991.

O'Brien, P. T. *The Letter to the Hebrews*. PNTC. Grand Rapids, MI: Eerdmans, 2010.

Peterson, D. *Hebrews and Perfection: An Examination of the Concept of Perfection in the "Epistle to the Hebrews."* Society for New Testament Studies Monograph Series 47. Cambridge, UK: Cambridge University Press, 1982.

Schreiner, T. R. *Commentary on Hebrews*. BTCP. Nashville, TN: B&H, 2015.

Trotter, A. H., Jr. *Interpreting the Epistle to the Hebrews*. Guides to New Testament Exegesis. Grand Rapids, MI: Baker, 1997.

Vanhoye, A. *Structure and Message of the Epistle to the Hebrews*. Subsidia Biblica 12. Rome, Italy: Editrice Pontificio Istituto Biblico, 1989.

Westfall, C. L. *A Discourse Analysis of the Letter to the Hebrews: The Relationship Between Form and Meaning*. Library of New Testament Studies. Studies in New Testament Greek 11. New York, NY: T&T Clark, 2005.

Chapter 17

The Letter of James

CORE KNOWLEDGE

Basic Knowledge: Students should know the key facts of the book of James. With regard to history, students should be able to identify the book's author, date, provenance, destination, and purpose. With regard to literature, they should be able to provide a basic outline of the book and identify core elements of the book's content found in the Unit-by-Unit Discussion. With regard to theology, students should be able to identify the major theological themes in the book of James.

Intermediate Knowledge: Students should be able to present the arguments for historical, literary, and theological conclusions. With regard to history, students should be able to discuss the evidence for Jacobean authorship, date, provenance, destination, and purpose. With regard to literature, they should be able to provide a detailed outline of the book. With regard to theology, students should be able to discuss the major theological themes in the book of James and the ways in which they uniquely contribute to the NT canon.

Advanced Knowledge: Students should be able to assess critically which James wrote the book of James. They should be able to discuss the genre of James and adjudicate the various proposals concerning the structure of the letter. They should also be able to evaluate the relationship between faith and works in James and critically compare the teachings of James and Paul in this regard.

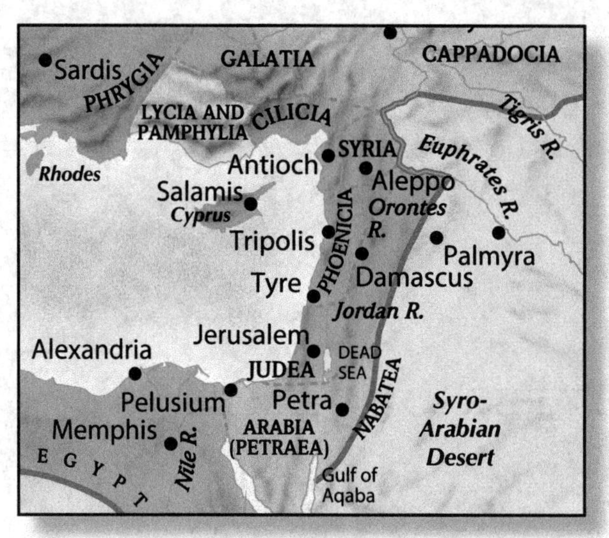

Map 17.1: Provenance and Destination of James

KEY FACTS

Author:	James, son of Joseph, half brother of Jesus
Date:	ca. AD 45
Provenance:	Jerusalem?
Destination:	Diaspora Jewish Christians outside Jerusalem
Occasion:	A circular letter to believers who had fled Jerusalem because of Agrippa's persecution
Purpose:	To exhort Jewish Christians to live in keeping with wisdom, to act on their faith, and not to show preferential treatment to the rich
Theme:	Faith that works
Key Verses:	2:21–22

INTRODUCTION

FREDERICK DOUGLASS, THE famed African-American abolitionist of pre-civil war Maryland, is often said to have left his Christianity behind when he joined the abolitionist movement.[1] This does not seem to be the case. Instead, Douglass chose to read and cherish the Bible in spite of the abusive reading of some. He states concerning the Bible: "Do you declare that a thing is bad because it has been misused, abused, and made a bad use of? Do you throw it away on that account? No! You press it to your bosom all the more closely; you read it all the more diligently; and prove from its pages that it is on the side of liberty—not on the side of slavery."[2] One of the most precious and foundational passages to Douglass was James 3:17: "But the wisdom from above is first pure, then peace-loving, gentle, compliant, full of mercy and good fruits, unwavering, without pretense." Douglass incorporated this verse into ten extant speeches from 1845 to 1860.[3] Clearly James's demand for impartial Christianity played an integral part in changing the lives and status of millions in America.

A much earlier Reformer had a different view of James that was born of his own struggles. Martin Luther, in the midst of controversies with the medieval Catholic Church, repeatedly dealt with the issue of the relationship between faith and works (in James 2) in debates with his opponents. He subsequently sought to relegate the book to the margins of Scripture. Luther remarked that the book of James was "a right strawy epistle" (i.e., a lightweight epistle, one made of straw). In this case Douglass's approach is to be preferred to Luther's.[4] If anything is made of chaff, it is the effort to minimize the book of James. We should rightly deem the effort "strawy."[5]

James makes an important contribution to the NT, and we would be poorer without it.[6] The book represents an early form of Jewish Christianity that is firmly grounded in Jewish Wisdom literature while having embraced Jesus as Messiah. This can be easily seen from his sources. James quotes at least three Proverbs (3:34/4:6; 9:30/3:18; 10:12/5:20) and exhibits similarities to Sirach (see Sir. 15:11–20/1:12–18).[7] Yet James also has ingested the sayings of Jesus (especially as found in Matthew's Sermon on the Mount) and expresses

---

[1] M. P. Aymer, *First Pure, Then Peaceable: Frederick Douglass Reads James*, LNTS (JSNTS) 379 (London, England: T &T Clark, 2008), 23.

[2] F. Douglass, "The American Constitution and the Slave," in G. T. Thomson and F. Douglass, Constitution of the United States (London Emancipation Committee: Tract no. 5; London, 1860), 16–34; cited in Aymer, *First Pure, Then Peaceable*, 25.

[3] Ibid., 27.

[4] We must be fair to note that the Reformation was one of the greatest movements of God since the first century. We choose to give Luther some slack but do not follow his example in this matter.

[5] D. G. McCartney (*James*, BECNT [Grand Rapids, MI: Baker, 2009], 1) notes that most of the Reformers did not follow Luther on the matter, including Luther's immediate successor, Melanchthon (citing *Loci Communes* 9.5.12).

[6] L. T. Johnson (*The Writings of the New Testament*, 3rd ed. [Minneapolis, MN: Fortress, 2010], 449) states, "Those who have managed to read James on its own terms discover in it a writing of rare vigor and life, which interprets the 'faith of our Lord Jesus Christ of glory' (2:1) in a distinctive and compelling manner."

[7] B. Witherington, III, *Invitation to the New Testament: First Things* (Oxford, UK: Oxford University Press, 2013), 264.

them frequently.[8] The wisdom ethic is thus congruent with the demands of faith in Jesus. Thus, James promotes a new covenant faith that is faith in action.

Since the late 1990s, James has become a popular figure as an object of historical research, much of which has come in response to a Tel Aviv antiquities collector's claim to have found the man's ossuary on the Israeli antiquities market.[9] While the academy has often found James controversial, many regular students of Scripture have found comfort in the book. James's ethical admonitions render the letter as applicable today as it was when it was first written.

HISTORY

Author

The book of James, from a modern reader's perspective, begins with the name of the author. It claims to be from a certain *Iakōbus*, Greek for the Hebrew *Ia'acov* (Jacob), translated into English as "James."[10] Although the name was extremely common,[11] and several figures in the NT carry the name "James," it is virtually certain that the "James" referred to at 1:1 is the half brother of the Lord.[12] The question mainly debated by scholars is not which James is mentioned but whether the letter could actually be from James the Just, the half brother of Jesus.

Arguments against James's authorship are essentially fourfold. First, the writer of the letter is skilled in Greek. His style is described by R. Martin as "fluent and elegant" and rich in the Hellenistic linguistic virtues.[13] Moreover, the writer often used the LXX. Some deem it impossible for a Galilean peasant to pen such elegant Greek and unlikely that he

---

[8] See the chart below.

[9] E.g., P.-A. Bernheim, *James Brother of Jesus*, trans. J. Bowden (London, England: SCM, 1997); J. Painter, *Just James: The Brother of Jesus in History and Tradition* (Columbia, SC: University of South Carolina Press, 1997); R. Eisenman, *James the Brother of Jesus: The Key to Unlocking the Secrets of Early Christianity and the Dead Sea Scrolls* (New York, NY: Viking, 1997); B. Chilton and C. A. Evans, eds., *James the Just and Christian Origins* (Leiden, Netherlands: Brill, 1999); B. Chilton and J. Neusner, eds., *The Brother of Jesus: James the Just and His Mission* (Louisville, KY: Westminster John Knox, 2001); and H. Shanks and B. Witherington III, *The Brother of Jesus: The Dramatic Story and Meaning of the First Archaeological Link to Jesus and His Family* (New York, NY: HarperCollins, 2003). The story of the ossuary of James is one full of political intrigue, historical curiosity, and religious import. O. Golan (the ossuary's owner) was accused of forgery by the Israeli antiquities department. The seven-year trial ended in March 2012 with Golan's acquittal (see Matti Friedman, "Oded Golan Is Not Guilty of Forgery. So Is the 'James Ossuary' for Real?" *Times of Israel*, March 14, 2012). However, the ossuary itself was not authenticated, so the debate continues. That Jesus had a brother named James is neither proved nor falsified by the ossuary's legitimacy.

[10] Often the first question asked by American students is, "How do we get 'James' from *Ia'acov*?'" The answer requires a long trek through both translations and geopolitical entities. Suffice it to say that the name *Ia'acov* becomes *Iacomus* in Latin, *Giacomo* in Italian, *Gemmes* or *Jaimmes* in French, and "James" in English as a result of the Norman conquest at the Battle of Hastings in AD 1066.

[11] According to R. Bauckham (*Jesus and the Eyewitnesses: The Gospels as Eyewitness Testimony* [Grand Rapids, MI: Eerdmans, 2006], 85), the name "Jacob" ranked as the eleventh most popular male name among Palestinian Jews from 330 BC to AD 200.

[12] L. T. Johnson, *The Letter of James*, AB 37A (New York, NY: Doubleday, 1995), 93.

[13] R. P. Martin, *James*, WBC 48 (Waco, TX: Word, 1988), lxx.

would use the LXX.[14] This can be countered on two fronts. (1) The Greek in James is, as D. Moo stated, "Far from literary Greek." (2) The use of the words and concepts in James are within mainstream use.[15]

SIDEBAR 17.1: WHICH "JAMES" WROTE THE LETTER OF JAMES?

Several figures in the NT are known as "James":

1. James, the son of Zebedee (brother of John, one of the Twelve, Mark 1:19; 5:37; 9:2; 10:35; Acts 12:2); he was martyred too early to be the author of James.
2. James, the son of Alphaeus (another member of the Twelve, possibly also James the younger; Mark 15:40; see 3:18); although an apostle (and Calvin's choice for the writer of this letter[1]), he is an unlikely candidate because (a) the writer was not called an apostle; and (b) this James was not well known enough to sign a circular letter only as "James."
3. James the father of Judas (Luke 6:16; Acts 1:13); he was far too obscure to be this well-known James.
4. James, the Lord's half brother (Matt 13:55); this James is the only viable candidate: (a) he was sufficiently well known to have written this letter; (b) he was known to be an authoritative voice in the Jerusalem church (Acts 12:17; 15:13; 21:18; Gal 1:19).

[1] J. Calvin, "Commentary on the Epistle of James," in *Commentaries on the Catholic Epistles*, trans. J. Owen (Grand Rapids, MI: Eerdmans, 1948), 227. Calvin conjectured that it was unlikely that a nonapostle would be considered a "pillar" of the church (Gal 2:9).

What is more, as the leader of the church in Jerusalem, James dealt with many Hellenists (see Acts 6), and a great number of them, by definition, would be dependent on Greek.[16] In fact, the Greek language had penetrated deeply into the area, especially into Jerusalem. Herod the Great had made Greek the official language of the government.[17]

The classic refutation is J. N. Sevenster's work *Do You Know Greek?* Sevenster investigated how deeply Greek had penetrated Palestinian Judaism, specifically regarding James, and has concluded that the letter is certainly not beyond the ability of a Palestinian Jew. He stated, "[T]he possibility can no longer be precluded that a Palestinian Jewish Christian of

[14] E.g., M. Dibelius, *James: A Commentary on the Epistle of James*, trans. M. A. Williams, Hermeneia (Philadelphia, PA: Fortress, 1976), 17; W. G. Kümmel, *Introduction to the New Testament*, rev. ed., trans. H. C. Kee (Nashville, TN: Abingdon, 1975), 411; and J. H. Ropes, *St. James*, ICC (Edinburgh, Scotland: T&T Clark, 1916), 50.

[15] D. J. Moo, *The Letter of James*, PNTC (Grand Rapids, MI: Eerdmans, 2000), 14. Ropes (*St. James*, 25) stated, "There is nothing to suggest acquaintance with the higher styles of Greek literature."

[16] See R. Bauckham, *James: Wisdom of James, Disciple of Jesus the Sage, New Testament Readings* (London, England: Routledge, 1999), 24. He noted that Greek was the native language for 10–20 percent of Jerusalem's residents.

[17] J. S. Jeffers, *The Greco-Roman World of the New Testament Era: Exploring the Background of Early Christianity* (Downers Grove, IL: InterVarsity, 123.

the first century A.D. wrote an epistle in good Greek."[18] S. McKnight has recently weighed in and concluded, "This argument against the brother of Jesus should be laid to rest."[19]

The related issue is the letter's use of the LXX. As it turns out, the question is complicated. James does not use simple strings of exact citations from the LXX.[20] The text forms are mixed at best and difficult to isolate. Davids concluded that only one citation in the letter is clearly from the LXX.[21] The most that can be said, therefore, is that James knew the LXX but was not limited to it.[22] This is not at odds with what one would expect from any Palestinian Jew living in cosmopolitan Jerusalem, including James the Just.

Second, the letter lacks specifics expected from this particular figure. Some propose that this James, had he been the author, would certainly have mentioned his relationship to Jesus. In contrast, the letter only mentions the Lord Jesus two times (1:1; 2:1). This is said to be evidence of a further problem: the lack of specifically Christian material. These objections, however, turn out to be invalid upon closer scrutiny. The veneration of the biological family of the Lord is clearly a phenomenon beyond the lifetime of James.[23] In fact, if James had made direct claims about his physical relationship to the Lord, there is no doubt that many in the academy would see this as proof of pseudepigrapha.[24] The restraint exercised in the letter is best explained by its authenticity.

Regarding the objection that there is little overt Christian content in James, it should be noted that he is demonstrably immersed in the teachings of Jesus.[25] Adamson suggests that James echoes the sayings of Jesus in such a way that it can only be accounted for in two ways. First, James knows an early written form of the sermon. Second, he remembers the teachings of Jesus.[26] Both suggest close Christian connections. Moreover, P. Davids noted that references to salvation (1:18) and church structure (5:14) and oblique references to Jesus as "judge," "Lord," and "the name" lead to the conclusion that "only with great

---

[18] J. N. Sevenster, *Do You Know Greek? How Much Greek Could the First Jewish Christians Have Known?* (Leiden, Netherlands: Brill, 1968), 191. Sevenster's conclusions have been reached by others as well. See e.g., S. E. Porter, *The Criteria for Authenticity in Historical-Jesus Research: Previous Discussion and New Proposals*, JSNTSup 191 (Sheffield, UK: Sheffield Academic, 2000). Cf. G. Kittel, *Die Probleme des palästinischen Spätjudentums und das Urchristentum* (Stuttgart, Germany: W. Kohlhammer, 1926), 38. Kümmel (*Introduction*, 290) said, "The cultured language of James is not that of a Palestinian," and B. Reicke ("James," in *The Epistles of James, Peter and Jude*, AB 37 [New York, NY: Doubleday, 1964], 4) agreed: "It is highly improbable that James could write Greek." Such statements are no longer tenable.

[19] McKnight, *James*, 34.

[20] This is contrary to S. Laws, "Does Scripture Speak in Vain?," *NTS* 20 (1974): 211–12.

[21] P. Davids, *Commentary on James*, NIGTC (Grand Rapids, MI: Eerdmans, 1982), 10.

[22] Ibid., 11.

[23] See R. Bauckham, *Jude and the Relatives of Jesus in the Early Church* (Edinburgh, Scotland: T&T Clark, 1990), 125–30.

[24] One need only look at how the references at 2 Pet 1:16–18 are treated.

[25] See Table 17.1 for a catalog. Several monographs have been written on the subject; e.g., P. J. Hartin, *James and the Q Sayings of Jesus*, JSNTSup 47 (Sheffield, UK: Sheffield Academic, 1991). Moo states, "James depends more than any other NT author on the teaching of Jesus" (Moo, *James* [2000], 7).

[26] J. B. Adamson, *The Epistle of James*, NICNT (Grand Rapids, MI: Eerdmans, 1976), 22.

difficulty can one fit these examples—and the larger whole of which they are example—into a purely Jewish context."[27]

Table 17.1: The Teachings of Jesus in James

Teaching	James	Gospels
Joy in trials	1:2	Matt 5:11–12; Luke 6:23
Endurance, maturity, and perfection	1:4	Matt 5:48
Asking and receiving	1:5, 17; 4:2–3	Matt 7:7–11; Luke 11:9–13
God as Father	1:17, 27; 3:9	Matt 6:6, ff., pars.
Endurance and salvation	1:12	Matt 10:22; 24:13
Anger and righteousness	1:20	Matt 5:20–22
Doers of the Word	1:22–23	Matt 7:24, 26
The poor inherit God's kingdom	2:5	Matt 5:3, 5; Luke 6:20
The law and love for the neighbor	2:8–12	Matt 22:36–40; Luke 10:25–28
The unity of the law	2:10	Matt 5:19
The merciless are judged	2:13	Matt 7:1
Care for the poor related to salvation	2:14–16	Matt 25:34–35
A tree is known by its fruit	3:12	Matt 7:16–18; Luke 6:43–44
The call to peace	3:18	Matt 5:9
One cannot love God and the world	4:4	Matt 6:24; 16:13
God is close to the pure in heart	4:8	Matt 5:8
The great reversal	4:10	Matt 23:12; Luke 14:11; 18:14
Prohibition against judging	4:11–12	Matt 7:1–5
The danger of wealth	5:1–6	Matt 6:19–21; Luke 12:33–34
Judge standing at the door	5:9	Matt 24:33
The prophet's example	5:10	Matt 5:11–12; Luke 6:23
Oaths forbidden	5:12	Matt 5:33–37
Restoring a sinner	5:19–20	Matt 18:15*

* For similar lists, see Witherington, *Invitation*, 265; McKnight, *James*, 25–26; Johnson, *Writings*, 453; for a lengthier treatment see Bauckham, *James*, 93–108.

The third objection to Jacobean authorship is that the church fathers were late in canonizing the book. By the fourth century, both the Eastern and Western churches recognized the letter.[28] However, before then the book endured a somewhat uneven history.[29] Rather

[27] Davids, *James*, 15.

[28] Moo, *James* (2000), 2.

[29] Johnson (*James*, 124–61) compiled perhaps the most extensive catalog of the reception of James to date.

than questions of authorship or the orthodoxy of the book, the pressing issue among a few of the church fathers of the third and fourth centuries was the lack of citation by the earlier fathers. It is not the case, however, that it was never cited. The *Shepherd of Hermas* likely refers to James (mid-second century),[30] and *1 Clement* (ca. AD 96) apparently cites James.[31] Origen (ca. AD 185–254) is the first known father to cite the book as being from James the Just, although it is said that Clement (ca. AD 150–215), Origen's predecessor at Alexandria, wrote a commentary on the book.[32] Eusebius (ca. AD 260–340) placed James among the *antilegomena* (the disputed works), although he himself had no doubts about the book.[33] Those who dispute its authenticity included some in the Syrian church. This is mainly because Theodore of Mopsuestia (ca. AD 350–428) rejected James as part of his rejection of all the General Epistles.[34] The Western church of the fourth century was somewhat ambiguous about the book but eventually embraced it under the influence of Jerome (ca. AD 345–420).[35] The way Jerome put it, James gained acceptance "little by little."[36] Most likely owing to the influence of Augustine, the West, as evidenced by the Councils of Carthage and Hippo, dropped all discussion.[37]

The book, then, has a curious history of a pronounced neglect in the writings of the church fathers up until the late fourth century. Martin may be correct in noting that the gnostics venerated James as the receptor of true knowledge, thus creating a mistrust of the letter.[38] Yet, as Moo observed, the evidence is that the book was "not so much *rejected* as *neglected*."[39] Apparently, this neglect did not stem from a belief that the book was spurious; rather, it appears that a combination of factors led to the state of affairs in the third and fourth centuries. Most likely, the book was first neglected in the second century, due to the nature of second-century debates surrounding Gnosticism and the nature of Christ.[40] Subsequently, the book became suspect in the minds of a few because of this lack of reference.

---

[30] Both Davids (*James*, 8) and Johnson (*James*, 75–79) believed the earliest extant reference to James is in the *Shepherd of Hermas* (early second century?).

[31] Johnson, *James*, 72–75.

[32] See Eusebius, *Eccl. Hist.* 6.13.2; and Cassiodorus, *De Institutione Divinarum Litterarum* (PL 70:1120).

[33] Eusebius, *Eccl. Hist.* 3.23.3.

[34] Moo (*James* [2000], 3); he further noted that the Syrian church eventually included the General Epistles in the canon and that such Syrian luminaries as Chrysostom (d. AD 407) and Theodoret (d. AD 458) quoted James with approval.

[35] Jerome is admittedly dependent on Origen in many instances. Origen's views may come from his teacher Didymus the Blind, a successor to Origen in Alexandria.

[36] Jerome, *De Viris Illustribus* 2 (PL 23, Col. 639).

[37] See Johnson, *James*, 138. On our estimation of the councils' role in recognizing the canon, see chap. 1.

[38] Martin, *James*, lv.

[39] Moo, *James* (2000), 4.

[40] D. Guthrie (*New Testament Introduction*, rev. ed. [Downers Grove, IL: InterVarsity, 1990], 521) stated, "It is the kind of letter which could easily be neglected as, in fact, the treatment of it in the modern church abundantly shows and, once neglected, a fertile soil was provided for future doubts, especially at a time when spurious productions were being attributed to apostolic names."

We should be careful not to overstate the canonical problem. Witherington puts it into perspective well: "Although the early church had a few questions about this document, real suspicions about James largely arose in a much later era of church history."[41] In other words, the debate was not really heated until after Luther, in the days of the form critics.

The fourth argument against James's authorship is that some suggest the book's outlook concerning the Torah is in contrast with what is otherwise known about James and his commitment to Jewish tradition. For Dibelius, this is the "decisive argument."[42] That the law is "the royal law" (2:8) and the "law of freedom" (1:25; 2:12) suggests a downplaying of the ritual matters of the law in favor of its ethical demands.[43] The author of James does not mention food laws, circumcision, Sabbath observance, or Gentile inclusion, making it impossible, it is argued, for James the Just to have written the book. Scholars such as Dibelius have alleged that this is problematic on two fronts. First, since James was placed in the canon after Paul's Letters were included, the fact that no particularly Jewish matters such as food laws or circumcision are mentioned in the book points to a late time of composition beyond James's lifetime when these matters were no longer an issue. Second, the NT elsewhere depicts James as an advocate of legalistic piety and of a ritualistic preference for Jewish tradition over innovation (see Gal 2:12), which would have been incompatible with the ethics of the letter.[44]

This line of reasoning, however, is built on questionable interpretations regarding James and equally questionable judgments concerning the date of the document. Regarding the latter, an early date for James has long been suggested, and the issues related to the law are arguments from silence that are easier to explain from the standpoint of an early rather than a later one.[45] Lack of mention of food laws, circumcision, and other similar issues is more likely from a date before these practices became controversial; in other words, these matters were assumed rather than forgotten. Second, the picture of James that is presented is more developed from tradition than from the NT. James (especially in Acts) certainly practiced a Jewish form of Christianity. But in the NT he settled the issue of Gentile inclusion (Acts 15:13–21), rejoiced in Paul's ministry (Acts 21:18–20), and seems to be more concerned about Jewish evangelism than about preserving rituals (Acts 21:20–25).[46] James is certainly no pure ritualist.

Finally, the most persistent complaint against James's authorship is the thorny issue that 2:14–26 creates in connection with justification by faith as taught by Paul. Paul, in fact, has been seen as the stimulus to which James is the response.[47] Generally today James's response is seen not as a direct response to Paul but, at the most, a response to a

---

[41] Witherington, *Invitation*, 260.

[42] Dibelius, *James*, 17.

[43] Moo, *James* (2000), 16.

[44] Dibelius, *James*, 18.

[45] See below under "Date."

[46] For an excellent discussion, see Moo, *James* (2000), 17–18.

[47] Johnson, *James*, 110.

misunderstanding of Paul. The author is therefore said to respond to Paul's Letters and to presuppose a clear understanding of Paul. Chronologically, this puts the letter beyond the lifetime of James the Just, who died in the year 63.[48]

But this assessment is based on some questionable presuppositions about James, Paul, and early Christianity.[49] Johnson was right in noting that "where they [James and Paul] appear (from our perspective) to disagree (Jas 2:14–26), the disagreement is at least partially due to the presupposition we bring that they are debating a single issue."[50] As shown below, the "James versus Paul" view is neither necessary nor compelling.[51]

If the book is not from James the Just, then who wrote it? Many think the letter is merely a pseudepigraphical document penned by someone other than James who then attached the document to him for some unknown reason.[52] Some who hold this view consider the book of James an intentional forgery. Others believe the letter was originally an anonymous work only later attributed to James. Perhaps, they conjecture, James was originally a Jewish document to which Christian references were added at a later point.[53]

However, apart from the problems noted above, the austerity of the author's description at 1:1 deflates any notion of intentional pseudepigraphy. The author described himself merely as "a servant of God and of the Lord Jesus Christ." It is more than unlikely that a pseudepigrapher would be so bland in his personal description. Most of the pseudepigraphical works attributed to James (and one addressed to him) cannot resist the descriptions "brother of the Lord" and "Bishop of Jerusalem."[54] The description in the canonical sources is inexplicable if a forgery. J. A. T. Robinson was no doubt correct when he wrote that "the argument for pseudonymity is weaker here than with any other of the New Testament epistles."[55]

---

[48] See Kümmel, *Introduction*, 414.

[49] In the minds of most of these interpreters, Acts is dismissed as a valuable historical source for either James or Paul; the pseudo-Clementine literature is a valued source for early Christianity; and Paul is understood solely on the basis of *Hauptbriefe* (his "major letters," i.e., Romans, 1 and 2 Corinthians, and Galatians). These views are addressed elsewhere in this volume.

[50] Johnson, *James*, 114.

[51] See the section on "The Relationship Between Faith and Works" under "Theological Themes" below.

[52] E.g., S. Laws, *A Commentary on the Epistle of James* (San Francisco, CA: Harper & Row, 1980), 40.

[53] See Moo, *James* (2000) 12, citing L. Massebieau, "L'Épître de Jacques, est-elle l'œuvre d'un Chrétien?," *RHR* 32 (1895): 249–83; F. Spitta, "Der Brief des Jakobus," in *Zur Geschichte und Literatur des Urchristentums*, vol. 2 (Göttingen, Germany: Vandenhoeck & Ruprecht, 1896), 1–239.

[54] Most of the apocryphal works clearly identify the intended James either by context or direct statement. E.g., the *Protevangelium of James* 9.2 and 20.5; the *Apocryphon of James*, which refers to a former letter, now lost, that probably identified the James in view; and the *Gnostic Apocalypses of James*, the first of which has Jesus address James as "my brother" while the second identifies James as "James the just." See J. M. Robinson, ed., *The Nag Hammadi Library in English*, 3rd rev. ed. (San Francisco, CA: Harper & Row, 1988), 262, 270. W. O. E. Oesterly ("A Coptic Fragment Attributed to James the Brother of the Lord," *JTS* 8 [1907]: 240–48) contends that James may be a document Hippolytus ascribed to Naassene Gnostics. But the brief, humble description found in this letter is unlike that found in the pseudepigraphical works.

[55] J. A. T. Robinson, *Redating the New Testament* (London, England: SCM, 1976), 129. This is essentially the view of McKnight regarding the objections against James writing the letter. He states, "The arguments against it are not as conclusive or decisive as is often made out" (McKnight, *James*, 37). The same difficulties arise with those who conjecture that the letter

A mediating position understands that the letter has its origins in James the Just but has been edited and presented by one of his (presumably Hellenistic) disciples. Martin defended this view since he found the idiomatic difficulties compelling and noted (regarding Jerome's statement) that "some say" the letter was "published [Lat. *edita*] by another under his name."[56] But Jerome in no way endorsed the idea, and the theory that James the Just could not have employed this level of Greek is doubtful as well. Guthrie rightly noted that this view cannot explain the shaping of the material in James into a letter rather than another literary form.[57] Finally, similar to a pseudepigrapher, an editor who added material late in the first century surely would have identified the author more clearly.

Yet another view posits a different James as the author. In the past James the son of Alphaeus was a candidate.[58] Both Luther and Erasmus suggested a now unknown "James."[59] Until recently this view has not been commonly suggested. However, R. Metzner revived the view in 2013. Metzner denies that the letter is pseudepigrapha, advocates the not-connected-to-Jesus argument, and finds the early doubts question the validity that James the brother of Jesus wrote it. He suggests the connection to Jesus's brother comes from the association of the "pillars" of Galatians 2:9 (James, Cephas, and John) with the collection of the General Epistles corpus. It is, however, more likely that convictions over authorship is why James shows up in the General Epistles collection.[60] As the arguments for pseudepigrapha are less and less convincing in the academy, this view will likely become a more popular option. The major problem with the "some other James" view is the authority that the author of the letter wields. Any other candidate must be so well known and wield enough authority to be simply identified as "James."

In the vacuum of convincing arguments against the Lord's half-brother James as writer, evidence for his authorship should bear more weight. Several arguments can be made in

---

was originally anonymous but that the name "James" was added later. E.g., A. C. McGiffert, *A History of Christianity in the Apostolic Age* (New York, NY: Scribner, 1897), 585.

[56] Martin (*James*, lxxii) enlisted the apocryphal *Second Apocalypse of James* 44.13–17 (NHS 5), which states, "This is [the] discourse that James [the] Just spoke in Jerusalem, [which] Mareim, one [of] the priests wrote." Cf. Davids, *James*, 22, recently repeated this in P. Davids, *A Theology of James, Peter, and Jude*, BTNT (Grand Rapids, MI: Zondervan, 2014), 41. Davids proposes that the book of James was the product of an editor, using an amanuensis, revisioning the sermons of James (and/or Jesus) shortly after the death of James the Just. He does note that it "would be presumptuous to argue that the work could not have been produced during the lifetime of James or that James would never have put his own sermons and sayings together" (ibid.). Only the assumption that James the Just could not have written in Greek, or employ an amanuensis, make this theory more probable than direct authorship (see below).

[57] Guthrie, *Introduction*, 536. Guthrie's further comments are worth repeating: "If the editor was working under the supervision of James himself, this would amount almost to the traditional view. But if he is editing some time later than James's lifetime, the problem of motive becomes acute, for why a later editor should suddenly have conceived such a publication plan when the great majority of the intended readers must have known that James was already dead is difficult to see, and it is even more difficult to understand how the letter came to be received. If some real connection with James would have been generally recognized, why the need for this theory at all, since it would possess no advantage over the traditional view? It would furnish no better explanation for the tardiness of recognition among the church's orthodox writers."

[58] Calvin, "Commentary on the Epistle of James," 227.

[59] Moo, *James* (2000), 12.

[60] R. Metzner, "Der Lehrer Jakobus: Überlegungen zur Verfasserfrage des Jakobusbriefes," *ZNW* 104 (2013): 238–67.

defense of James the Just. First, the reference to "James, a servant of God and of the Lord Jesus Christ" at the beginning of the letter (1:1) suggests that this James was a person with considerable name recognition and equally great authority. Otherwise, it would have been necessary for the author to provide additional information and distinguishing characteristics about himself. James the Just, as the leader of the church in Jerusalem, fits both of these descriptions unlike any other person by that name in the first century. For another James to be so important but quickly to fade into obscurity is highly unlikely. As R. Bauckham stated, "Only one James was so uniquely prominent in the early Christian movement that he could be identified purely by the phrase: 'James, a servant of God and of the Lord Jesus Christ' . . . . This 'James' was the eldest of the four brothers of Jesus (Mark 6:3)."[61]

Second, despite claims to the contrary, the writer showed some evidence of being a Palestinian Jew. He mentioned "early and late rains" (5:7), which was demonstrably a weather phenomenon in Palestine. More significantly, the author's language is immersed in the OT Scriptures.[62]

Third, there are striking verbal similarities to Acts 15. "Greetings" (Gk. *chairein*) occurs in James 1:1 and Acts 15:23 (and elsewhere in Acts only in 23:16). Strikingly, Acts 15:23 is part of the Jerusalem decree, in which James had a leading role. In both James 2:7 and Acts 15:17, believers are called by God's name. The exhortation for the "brothers and sisters" to "listen" occurs in James 2:5 and Acts 15:13. Uncommon words are found in both James and Acts in conjunction with James: "to look after" (Gk. *episkeptomai*) in James 1:27 and Acts 15:14; "to turn" (Gk. *epistrephō*) in James 5:19 and Acts 15:19; and "to keep oneself" (Gk. *tēreō* + *heautou*) in James 1:27 and Acts 15:29. While not constituting conclusive proof, these linguistic parallels corroborate James's authorship.[63]

Finally, the man reflected in the letter comports well with James the half brother of Jesus as he is portrayed in the rest of the NT. This James is identified as the leader of the Jerusalem church and viewed as the guarantor of a Jewish expression of Christianity (Acts 12:17; 21:18–25; Gal 1:19).

For these reasons recent years have witnessed a trend among scholars to recognize that the internal evidence from the letter is not incompatible with James's authorship. Even many scholars who are otherwise critical of traditional views now see this letter as indeed from James the Just.[64] Without compelling evidence to the contrary, the best understand-

---

[61] Bauckham, *James*, 16. Bauckham's ultimate opinion on authorship is, "The letter can be read as what it purports to be: an encyclical from James of Jerusalem to the Diaspora" (ibid., 25).

[62] Although James only quoted the OT explicitly in five verses (1:11; 2:8, 11, 23; 4:6), Guthrie (*Introduction*, 521) noted that "indirect allusions are innumerable (cf., e.g., 1:10; 2:21, 23, 25; 3:9; 4:6; 5:2, 11, 17–18)."

[63] D. Moo, *James*, rev. ed., TNTC (Downers Grove, IL: InterVarsity, 2015), 35.

[64] F. Mussner, *Der Jakobusbrief*, HTKNT 13/1 (Freiburg, Germany: Herder, 1964), 1–59; Johnson, *James*, 108–21; R. Bauckham, *James*, 11–25; idem, *Jude and the Relatives of Jesus* (Edinburgh, Scotland: T&T Clark, 1990), 128; M. Hengel, *Paulus und Jakobus*, WUNT 141 (Tübingen, Germany: Mohr Siebeck, 2002), 511–48; P. J. Hartin, *James*, SacPag 14 (Collegeville, MN: Liturgical Press, 2003), 24–25; and T. C. Penner, *The Epistle of James and Eschatology: Re-reading an Ancient Christian Letter* (Sheffield, UK: Sheffield Academic, 1996), 35–103.

ing of the author of James is that in fact he is James the son of Joseph, the half brother of the Lord Jesus.

Date

Given the absence of conventional indications of time such as references to specific individuals, places, or events, the letter is not simple to date. J. A. T. Robinson noted a wide spectrum of suggested dates offered in the scholarly literature, anywhere from AD 50 to 150.[65] However, more recently scholars have been advocating an early date. In truth, everything about James shouts, "I am early." If the above discussion of authorship is correct, the book was written during the lifetime of James the Just, that is, sometime before AD 62 or 63 (Josephus, *Ant.* 20.200).[66] On the other end of the spectrum, the letter must have been written subsequent to James's conversion (see 1 Cor 15:7), that is, no earlier than approximately AD 33. This provides a range of possible dates spanning about thirty years.

To narrow the range yet further, the letter must have been written after James became the prominent leader in the Jerusalem church. This can be dated to around AD 41 or 42 (see Acts 12:17). Several factors suggest a date of composition subsequent to this time frame, such as that some economic difficulties suggested in the letter match the time of the famine in Palestine mentioned in Acts 11:28–30. Possibly, the recipients were dispersed because of the persecution of Herod Agrippa I mentioned in Acts 12:1–4 (ca. AD 43).[67] At the same time, the letter shows an acquaintance with the teaching of Jesus that does not seem a result of mere literary knowledge,[68] suggesting that the letter was most likely written prior to the canonical Gospels (and thus prior to the mid-50s).[69] This narrows the most likely date of composition to between AD 42 and the mid-50s.

In addition, the letter does not seem to address any of the issues that arose subsequent to AD 48 or 49. There is no discussion or even acknowledgement of the question of Gentile inclusion in the church (e.g., Acts 11:1–18) or the controversy spawned by the Judaizers (e.g., Acts 15:5; Gal 2:11–13), much less the resolution of these issues at the Jerusalem Council in the year 49 (Acts 15:1–21). Thus, it seems the letter was most likely written prior to the Jerusalem Council and therefore prior to Paul's Letters and perhaps even prior to the Gentile mission.[70] So the most likely range during which the letter was

---

[65] Robinson, *Redating*, 118–19.

[66] According to Josephus (*Ant.* 20.9.1), James's death occurred after that of the procurator Porcius Festus and before his successor Lucceius Albinus took office. The Jewish high priest Ananus took advantage of the power vacuum and assembled the Sanhedrin. There, "a man named James, the brother of Jesus who was called the Christ," and certain others were accused of having transgressed the law and were delivered up to be stoned. Apparently, this offended some of the fair-minded, law-observant Jews who petitioned Albinus on the matter when he entered the province and king Agrippa had Ananus replaced with Jesus, the son of Damnaeus, as high priest.

[67] See below under "Occasion."

[68] See Table 17.1 on "The Teachings of Jesus in James" above.

[69] See deSilva, *Introduction*, 816.

[70] E.g., in the book of James, the meeting place of Christians is still called a "synagogue" (2:2), which may indicate a time of writing prior to the launch of the Gentile mission.

composed spans from AD 42 until 49. For this reason J. A. T. Robinson was probably correct in stating that James's letter "can take its natural place, alongside other literature in the process of formation in the second decade of the Christian mission, as the first surviving finished document of the church."[71]

Provenance

Those proposing a different author than James the Just have offered various locations for the source of the letter, including Rome. If our views of authorship, date, destination, and occasion are correct, then Jerusalem is the most likely place of writing—in particular since it is not known if James spent significant time outside of Palestine during the early years of the church. The provenance is unknown. Fortunately, little rests on this identification.

Destination

The letter is addressed to "the twelve tribes dispersed abroad" (1:1). Most understand these recipients to be Jewish Christians.[72] The term "twelve tribes," while elsewhere used figuratively of all the people of God (see 1 Pet 1:1), in the present case most likely refers to a specifically Jewish Christian audience. Several features point to a Jewish setting: (1) the reference to meeting in a synagogue (2:2 CSB "meeting"); (2) the reference to "Abraham our father" (2:21); (3) the use of the OT in both direct quotations and allusions; (4) the letter's resemblance to Jewish Wisdom literature; and (5) the prophetic tone.

This view is also confirmed by clear indications from the letter that the readers were expected to be familiar with conditions in Palestine. Johnson noted seven factors that point to this conclusion: (1) the effect of burning wind on vegetation (1:11); (2) proximity to a dangerous sea (1:6; 4:13); (3) salt and bitter springs (3:11); (4) agriculture featuring figs, olives, and grapes (3:12); (5) a specific Palestinian weather pattern, the early and latter rains (5:7); (6) daily workers deprived of pay (5:4); and (7) the use of the term *gehenna* (hell) in 3:6, a term found elsewhere in the NT only in the Gospels.[73]

But where are these Jewish believers? The term "dispersed" (1:1) usually refers to Jews living outside of Palestine (e.g., John 7:35), describing the people of God who were scattered due to divine judgment but who carried with them the hope of restoration (see 1 Pet 1:1, 17; 2:11, with reference to believers in general).[74] The fact that this is a letter demands a congregation at some distance from the author. Hence, it is possible that the recipients were Jewish Christians somewhere in the area known as the Diaspora, perhaps in Syrian Antioch.

---

[71] Robinson, *Redating*, 139.

[72] See, e.g., Moo, *James* (2015), 46.

[73] Johnson, *James*, 120–21.

[74] Moo (*James* [2015], 46) notes that the NT elsewhere can use the term to apply to Gentile believers. Therefore, the term itself doesn't necessarily mean Jewish Christians.

Occasion

The missive seems to address specific individuals but not one specific situation. It is best to see James as a general letter (warranting its inclusion among the General Epistles in the NT canon) written to give pastoral advice to the recipients, whatever their specific circumstances. There were precedents for such a letter among Jews and early Christians (see Jeremiah 29; 2 Macc 1:1–9; Acts 15:23–29). Bauckham notes that letters from Jerusalem authorities to Jews in the Dispersion on "cultic and other legal matters, is evidenced as early as the late fifth century BCE [BC]."[75]

Given the likely date of the letter, we do know of a group of recently scattered Jewish Christians. After the stoning of Stephen, the Jerusalem believers (quite a large number by this time) fled from Jerusalem (Acts 8:1; 11:19). A little later the persecution is continuing through Herod Agrippa I, who noted that the death of James, the son of Zebedee, pleased the Jews (Acts 12:1–4; ca. AD 43). Clearly this was a difficult time for the church. Acts tells us the apostles stayed in Jerusalem.[76] Thus, this time period accounts for both the "Dispersion" and the separation between the writer and the audience. The injunctions in the letter seem appropriate for both wealthy and poor, and in particular portray wealthy landowners as oppressing poor laborers. Those displaced by persecution would certainly find themselves working essentially as migrant workers (though some might flourish). The encouragement to live out their lives fully committed to Christ's lordship would certainly be appropriate for such a group. This, like all reconstructions, cannot be proven, but seems likely.[77]

LITERATURE

Genre

Given the epistolary opening of the work, the intent for the letter to serve as a substitute for the writer's presence, and the document's hortatory nature, it is best to consider James a letter of some kind.[78] While most do consider James a letter, this category does not adequately describe it in every respect. While the book opens like a letter, no occasion behind the correspondence is discernible, no individuals are mentioned, and there is no

---

[75] Bauckham, *James*, 19. Bauckham cites the examples above as well as a letter to the Jewish colony at Elephantine in Egypt and Gamaliel the elder having penned a letter "to our brethren, belonging to the exile in Babylonia . . . Media . . . Greece . . . and all the rest of the exiles of Israel" (ibid., 19–20).

[76] See Provenance above. Antioch is the tentative preference of A. Chester, "The Theology of James," in A. Chester and R. P. Martin, *The Theology of the Letters to James, Peter, and Jude*, New Testament Theology (Cambridge, UK: Cambridge University Press, 1994), 13–15.

[77] Moo, *James* (2015), 46.

[78] This is disputed by writers such as Dibelius (*James*, 2), who noticed the lack of epistolary features and stated, "It [is] impossible to consider James an actual letter."

epistolary ending (cf. Phil 4:10–23). The book is purposefully general and intended for a wide audience (the twelve tribes in the Dispersion).[79]

Is it possible to identify more precisely what kind of letter James represents? From looking at other NT letters, it appears that the genre of James is much like that of Hebrews and 1 John, namely, an essay addressing a widely dispersed group of readers. J. H. Ropes labeled the letter a "diatribe" (i.e., a series of rhetorical arguments).[80] Indeed, James displays several characteristics of this genre. He frequently addresses the readers directly (1:2, 16, 19; 2:1, 5, 14; 3:1, 10, 12; 5:12, 19); employs an imaginary interlocutor (e.g., 2:18–22); poses short questions that are answered immediately (e.g., 3:13; 4:14; 5:13–14); and frequently uses comparisons (1:6, 10–11; 2:26; 3:5–6, 11–12; 4:14; 5:2, 3, 18).[81] Yet despite these similarities, James does not neatly fit the scheme of a diatribe.[82] First, properly defined, a diatribe is "a form of argumentation in which a clear thesis is argued within the (fictive or real) setting of a school."[83] Clearly James does not fit this narrow definition. The author did not state an explicit thesis that he then argued, and his audience cannot be thought of as a "school." Second, not everything in James fits even a broader definition of diatribe. The various literary subunits do not cohere as a series of demonstrations of a central thesis but are connected much more loosely.

Another popular understanding of the genre of James is to classify the letter as an exemplar of Wisdom literature. This has in its favor the fact that "wisdom" is a major theme in the letter (1:5; 3:13, 15, 17). In addition, certain topics commonly found in Wisdom literature are also found in James, such as controlling one's speech (3:1–12) and issues related to wealth and poverty (5:1–6). However, the book does resemble the list of sayings in OT wisdom works such as the book of Proverbs. Although recent discussion about the connection of James to Wisdom literature, investigating the connection between James and the type of wisdom found in Sirach and the Wisdom of Solomon, may account for the movement from topic to topic in James,[84] only a broad definition of "Wisdom literature" allows James to be identified within this genre category.[85]

Yet another proposal came from M. Dibelius, who described the book of James as a series of exhortations (paraenesis). More than including mere teaching, Dibelius contended, James presented material "in the form of unconnected sayings which have no real

---

[79] Deissmann classified James as a literary letter, similar to other writings included in the General Epistles. See A. Deissmann, *Light from the Ancient East*, 2nd ed., trans. L. R. M. Strachan (London, England: Hodder & Stoughton, 1911), 235.

[80] Ropes, *James*, 17.

[81] Johnson, *James*, 9–10.

[82] Ibid., 17–18.

[83] Ibid., 17.

[84] D. W. Watson, "An Assessment of the Rhetoric and Rhetorical Analysis of the Letter of James," in *Reading James with New Eyes: Methodological Reassessments of the Letter of James*, LNTS 342 (London, England: T&T Clark, 2007), 118–19. Cf. L. L. Cheung, *The Genre, Composition and Hermeneutics of the Epistle of James*, Paternoster Biblical and Theological Monographs (Carlisle, UK: Paternoster, 2003), 40.

[85] Moo, *James* (2000) 8.

relationship to one another."[86] But more recent research has abandoned the identification of James in these terms.[87] Especially since paraenesis can be employed within other types of literature, a book does not necessarily qualify as paraenesis merely because it includes exhortations directed to its readers.[88] Thus, Watson critiqued the idea that James displays the formal characteristics of paraenesis, noting that certain elements are missing: "The paraenesis in the Epistle of James in not a dominant, organizing feature, but is subsumed to the needs of broader argumentation and rhetorical strategy."[89] Others go even further, questioning whether paraenesis should even be considered a genre category.[90]

A growing preference among scholars is to classify James as an example of protreptic literature.[91] This kind of writing advocates what is true over against what is false, rather than expressing preference for one thing over another for other reasons. A commitment to a specific lifestyle with urgency and conviction within the broad category of paraenesis is one of the more obvious hallmarks of protreptic literature. In this sense James certainly qualifies.[92] However, it is probably unwise to be unduly specific in identifying the genre of James.[93] It may be best to understand James as a literary circular letter with affinities to protreptic literature influenced by Jewish Wisdom literature.

Literary Plan

There is little consensus on the structure of James. Opinions today vary from the minimalist to the maximalist end of the spectrum. Minimalists see no apparent literary structure in James,[94] a view promoted primarily by the publication of M. Dibelius's commentary on James in 1921.[95] While Dibelius denied even a loosely structured text, others suggest that James intended a loosely constructed composition. For example, D. Moo described James as an only somewhat connected text, centered on certain key motifs.[96] Bauckham affirmed that James's thought was coherent but conceded that the letter lacked

---

[86] Dibelius, *James*, 3.

[87] For a thorough discussion, see Johnson, *James*, 17–20.

[88] Ibid., citing A. J. Malherbe, "Ancient Epistolary Theorists," *Ohio Journal of Religious Studies* 5 (1977): 71.

[89] Watson, "Rhetorical Analysis," 109.

[90] Moo, *James* (2000) 8, citing L. J. Perdue, "Paraenesis and the Epistle of James," *ZNW* 72 (1981): 241–56.

[91] For a thorough treatment, see Hartin, *James*, 10–16.

[92] See Johnson, *James*, 20–21.

[93] Against Johnson, *James*; and Hartin, *James*.

[94] Among these are Dibelius, *James*, 1–11 (see further below); and S. Stowers, *Letter Writing in Greek Antiquity*, LEC 5 (Philadelphia, PA: Westminster, 1986), 97. Preceding Dibelius and agreeing on the lack of structure are Mayor, *James*, cxxi; Ropes, *James*, 2–4; and A. Jülicher, *An Introduction to the New Testament*, trans. J. P. Ward (London, England: Smith-Elder, 1904), 215.

[95] Dibelius, *James*, 2, 11. In this Dibelius is similar to Luther, whose "epistle of straw" statement, among other things, alleged chaotic arrangement (M. Luther, "Preface to the Epistles of St. James and St. Jude," in *Luther's Works*, vol. 35, trans. C. M. Jacobs [Philadelphia, PA: Muhlenberg, 1960], 397). But in contrast to Luther, Dibelius viewed the lack of cohesion as a function of paraenesis rather than a matter diminishing the value of the letter (*James*, 5n21).

[96] Moo, *James* (2000) 45.

a tight logical structure.[97] Both detected a basic epistolary structure but noted that within the body (chaps. 2–5) the development of thought is not obvious.

On the other end of the spectrum, maximalists identify a discernible structure. Often this structure is identified as chiasm (a reflexive parallel pattern–e.g., ABB′A′). F. O. Francis pioneered this proposal by positing that James introduced his topics in chapter 1 (joy, blessing, and testing) and then proceeded in the body to expand the first two topics while discussing the third topic throughout the letter.[98] P. Davids agreed partially with Francis but saw the topics introduced in the introduction in chapter 1 (testing, wisdom, and wealth) and treated in reverse order in three subsequent sections (wealth: 2:1–26; wisdom: 3:1–4:12; and testing: 4:13–5:6), with 5:7–20 serving as the "closing statement."[99]

Probably the most densely defended and well thought-out chiastic proposal is made by M. E. Taylor.[100] However, like Davids, Taylor's proposal is unlikely. For example, it breaks down in the details since he finds a twofold introduction in chapter 1 and a chiastic development in chapters 2–5. His least likely argument is that 2:12–13 constitutes an inclusion with 4:11–12. This is problematic in two ways. First, it is artificial to separate passages such as 2:12–13 or 4:11–12 from their surrounding context. Second, the connections between the two passages are superficial at best. All chiastic arrangements proposed to date have similar weaknesses.[101] These are further complicated by the fact that proponents of chiastic structure rarely agree on the parallels.[102]

The most likely proposal views James in terms of a more linear structure in which chapter 1 serves as an introduction of major themes but demurs from identifying a chiasm therein. Instead, the structure is viewed as reflecting three stages. First, following the introduction of major themes in chapter 1, the first major unit in the body of the letter (2:1–26) describes the nature of saving faith. Second, 3:1–4:10 contains an appeal to repentance in view of God's opposition to pride. Third, 4:11–5:11 constitutes an

---

[97] Bauckham, *James*, 61–63.

[98] F. O. Francis, "Form and Function of the Opening and Closing Paragraphs of James and 1 John," *ZNW* 61 (1970): 118.

[99] Davids, *James*, 25–26. The effect is a chiasm. But the notion of a double introduction of themes in chap. 1 is doubtful. Davids's unit 3:1–4:12 includes 4:11–12, which perhaps more likely belongs to the next unit, while the unit 4:13–5:6 unduly excludes 5:7–11. J. P. Heil (*The Letter of James: Worship to Live By* [Eugene, OR: Wipf & Stock, 2012]) suggests the letter features eleven micro-chiasms that form a five-point macro-chiasm with a central "F" section. Heil is to be commended for more than usual rigor in discerning parallels in his text. However, the results are unconvincing. For the sake of space, the segmentation of Heil's proposals will suffice as illustrations of the issues. It is unlikely that the first unit ends at 1:16 (ending a unit with a vocative is unlikely). Also, 3:1–10 is an unlikely segmentation, and 3:11–12 more likely belongs with 3:1–10 than the subsequent passage. Although admittedly short, 4:11–12 is more likely a stand-alone unit than verses that form a unit with 4:13–17 (there is no parallel otherwise for Heil unless these are together).

[100] M. E. Taylor, *A Text-Linguistic Investigation into the Discourse Structure of James*, LNTS 311 (London, England: T&T Clark, 2006).

[101] E.g., J. M. Reese, "The Exegete as Sage: Hearing the Message of James," *BTB* 12 (1982): 82–85; R. B. Crotty, "The Literary Structure of the Letter of James," *ABR* 40 (1992): 45–57; C. L. Blomberg (*From Pentecost to Patmos: An Introduction to Acts Through Revelation* [Nashville, TN: B&H, 2006], 391), who followed Davids to a degree; and G. H. Guthrie, "James," in *Expositor's Bible Commentary*, rev. ed., vol. 13: *Hebrews–Revelation* (Grand Rapids, MI: Zondervan, 2006), 206.

[102] A. J. Batten, *What Are They Saying About the Letter of James?* (Mahwah, NJ: Paulist, 2009), 6.

exhortation to patience and endurance in light of God's judgment.[103] The book concludes without a formal epistolary closing.

OUTLINE

I. OPENING (1:1)
II. INTRODUCTION: THE PATH TO TRUE CHRISTIAN MATURITY (1:2–27)
  A. Introduction of Major Themes: Trials and Temptations (1:2–18)
  B. Obedience to the "Law of Liberty" as the Mark of True Piety (1:19–27)
III. BODY: THE NATURE OF TRUE FAITH AND EXHORTATIONS TO REPENTANCE AND PATIENCE (2:1–5:11)
  A. Thesis: Genuine Faith Results in Works (2:1–26).
    1. Genuine Faith Is Incompatible with Partiality (2:1–13).
    2. Genuine Faith Is Shown by Works (2:14–26).
  B. Exhortation to Repentance in View of God's Opposition to Pride (3:1–4:10)
    1. The Proper or Improper Use of the Tongue (3:1–12)
    2. The Proper or Improper Use of Wisdom (3:13–18)
    3. The Results of an Improper Use of Wisdom (4:1–10)
  C. Exhortation to Patience in View of God's Judgment (4:11–5:11)
    1. God's Judgment of Slanderers (4:11–12)
    2. God's Judgment of Arrogant Merchants (4:13–17)
    3. God's Judgment of Wealthy Landowners Exploiting the Poor (5:1–6)
    4. Exhortation to Patience (5:7–11)
IV. CONCLUSION (5:12–20)
  A. The Matter of Oaths (5:12)
  B. Faithful Prayer (5:13–18)
  C. Rescue the Perishing (5:19–20)

UNIT-BY-UNIT DISCUSSION

I. Opening (1:1)

The writer introduced himself as "James, a servant of God and of the Lord Jesus Christ." As mentioned, this seems to indicate that the author was a well-known figure. If he was Jesus's half brother, identifying himself as his slave and God's is an exceedingly humble self-identification. The letter is addressed to the twelve tribes in the Dispersion, which may refer to Jewish believers scattered through the persecution of Herod Agrippa I in about AD 43 (Acts 12:1–4).

II. Introduction: The Path to True Christian Maturity (1:2–27)

A. Introduction of Major Themes: Trials and Temptations (1:2–18) James 1:2–12 is best understood as a play on the Greek word *peirasmos*, which, depending on the context,

[103] This is similar to R. Bauckham's organization. He defends, prescript, 1:1; Introduction, 1:2–27; and Exposition, 2–5. Bauckham, *James*, 63.

can mean either "trial" or "temptation." James first assures those experiencing "trials" that these serve to test and refine their faith (1:2–4). Asking for wisdom refers to wisdom needed in dealing with trying situations (1:5–8). James briefly digresses to deal with the rich and the poor (1:9–11), an issue to which he returns later (5:1–6). In verse 12 the word *peirasmos* occurs again, but the context makes clear that the meaning has now changed from "trials" to "temptations." James's major burden here is to exonerate God from any connection with this kind of *peirasmos* (see 1:2–4). God is not the source of temptation; instead, he is the giver of "every good and perfect gift . . . from above" (1:17). As will be shown later, this also includes "the wisdom from above" (3:17). The direct address "my dear brothers and sisters" (1:16) introduces the transition to the next section, taking its point of departure from the trials/temptations of the previous unit and signaling the topic of the next section, true religion, by introducing its source: the election of God (1: 18).

B. Obedience to the "Law of Liberty" as the Mark of True Piety (1:19–27) The direct address "My dear brothers and sisters" (1:19; see 1:16) marks the beginning of the next section and introduces one of the letter's major themes: true piety cannot be separated from obedience. James 1:19–20 states the general principle: "Everyone should be quick to listen, slow to speak, and slow to anger, for human anger does not accomplish God's righteousness." Thus, verse 21 draws the proper inference: believers are to rid themselves of all moral filth and evil excess and to receive the "implanted word," which is able to save them.[104]

The thesis statement of this unit is in verse 22: "But be doers of the word and not hearers only, deceiving yourselves." A person who is a mere hearer of the word is compared to a man who briefly looks at a mirror and then forgets what he saw; he heard the word but forgot it. The section ends with a summary of the nature of "pure and undefiled religion" (1:26–27). Such piety involves controlling one's tongue (a subject developed more fully in 3:1–12) as well as helping orphans and widows and avoiding spiritual defilement by the world (see 4:1–5, esp. v. 4).

III. Body: The Nature of True Faith and Exhortations to Repentance and Patience (2:1–5:11)

The body of the letter consists of three major units. The first (2:1–26) sets forth James's thesis concerning the nature of true saving faith: it is the kind of faith that inexorably issues in specific works that give concrete evidence of this faith. This thesis is followed by two major exhortations that echo significant components of the thesis. Of these the first (3:1–4:10) is an exhortation to repentance and humility in light of the fact that all human pride sets itself in opposition to God. What follows (4:11–5:11) is an exhortation to patience and endurance in view of God's judgment addressed to various groups of offenders.

A. Thesis: Genuine Faith Results in Works (2:1–26) The general thrust of 2:1–26 is the nature of true saving faith. In essence, the first two paragraphs insist that true faith

---

[104] "Word" is the hook word, occurring in both 1:21 and 22, which connects 1:19–21 with 1:22–27.

does not distinguish between people in the church based on their socioeconomic standing (2:1–13). It does not give preferential treatment to the wealthy in the church (2:1–7) since this represents a violation of the commands of God (2:8–13) and exposes those who do so as lawbreakers. This leads to James's second major point that true faith is shown by believers' actions rather than their mere words (2:14–26).

The topic of faith is introduced in 2:1 by way of a warning against showing favoritism in the church. Those partial toward the wealthy have become "judges with evil thoughts" (2:4), and, even more disturbingly, they are acting contrary to God's own actions; he has not chosen the rich in this world but the poor (2:5). Moreover, partiality exposes people as lawbreakers because they do not love their neighbors as themselves. Thus, they fail to fulfill their obligations toward others as stipulated in the law (2:8–13; see Lev 19:18).

Hence, James insists that faith is useless without accompanying works, just as telling a hungry and ill-clothed man to "stay warm, and be well fed" is inadequate (2:15–17). Faith without works is dead, and works are a natural outflow of faith. James substantiates this dual thesis with three illustrations. The first is negative: even the demons believe in God, but they shudder (2:19). The reader is left to draw the obvious inference in this case: the "faith" of the demons is not accompanied by works; hence, their bare confession is insufficient.The second and third illustrations are positive: Abraham was justified by his willingness to offer Isaac on the altar (2:21; see Genesis 22; cf. the citation of Gen 15:6 in v. 23), as was Rahab the prostitute (2:25; see Joshua 2; cf. the commendation of Rahab's faith in Heb 11:31). Each of these three illustrations concludes with a declaration reiterating the basic premise: faith without works is useless (v. 20); faith is the partner of works (v. 24); and faith is dead apart from works (v. 26).[105]

B. Exhortation to Repentance in View of God's Opposition to Pride (3:1–4:10) Although 3:1–12 may be a self-contained essay on the tongue, the connection between the teacher (3:1) and the sage (3:13) seems to provide cohesion with the surrounding contexts. By contrast the section on the tongue ends with completely negative results (see esp. 3:8: "no one can tame the tongue"), while wisdom from above has positive results (see 3:17–18). James then affirms the central truth that authentic faith results in good works since it flows out of God's work in the believer's life.

The warning about desiring to be a teacher is predicated on the dangers of the tongue (see 1:26). Although small the tongue can accomplish great things, illustrated by the bit of a horse, the rudder of a ship, and a spark that starts a forest fire (3:3–5). Regarding the latter, the human tongue "sets the course of life on fire, and is itself on fire by hell" (3:6). The untamed tongue may inconsistently bless the Lord and curse a fellow human. Just as a spring cannot produce both fresh and salt water, or a fig tree olives, or a grapevine figs, the untamed tongue cannot be expected to produce any fruit contrary to its own nature; "it is

---

[105] See also the comparison between faith and works in James and Paul under Theological Themes below.

a restless evil, full of deadly poison" (3:8). Thus James, echoing the teachings of Jesus (Matt 7:16–20; 12:33–37), made clear that a person's speech exposes the contents of his heart.

In contrast to the untamed tongue, wise and understanding church members are to be marked by good conduct and the gentleness of wisdom (3:13).[106] The worldly-wise person is characterized by bitter envy and ambition that is willing to boast and lie in promoting what James called "truth" (3:14). James identified the source of such worldly "wisdom" as demonic. By contrast, "the wisdom from above is first pure, then peace-loving, gentle, compliant, full of mercy and good fruits, unwavering, without pretense" (3:17).[107] James affirmed that the end result of this "wisdom from above" is peace (3:17–18).

The call to humility in 4:1–10 flows directly from the section on wisdom in 3:1–18. Thus, in 3:1–4:10 James establishes the need for a humble, God-centered ministry, and offered an appeal to repentance. If the "wisdom from above" produces people who are peace-loving, gentle, compliant, full of mercy and good fruits, and unwavering, without pretense, one might ask, "What is the source of disputes among believers?" The answer is that dissension stems from a sinful human heart. Covetousness (4:2), selfishness (4:3), and worldliness (4:4) place us in a hostile position toward God and others. But the good news is that while God resists the proud, he gives grace to the humble (4:6). The final three verses of this section constitute a call to repentance, urging people to abandon pride and arrogance and to humble themselves before God.

C. Exhortation to Patience in View of God's Judgment (4:11–5:11) This final major section of James features three examples of arrogance—slanderers, arrogant merchants, and wealthy landowners exploiting the poor—and issues a stern warning to each group. Like the previous section, the present unit concludes with an exhortation—in the present case, to patience and endurance in a sinful world—based on the exposure of sinful behavior (5:7–11). In essence, this constitutes a call for believers to approach the world by faith.

Taking the discussion into a new direction by the vocative "brothers and sisters," James warned against slandering one's neighbor (4:11–12). Those who act as judges and criticize the law are guilty of the ultimate arrogance. The next warning is introduced by the address "come now." Merchants presume upon the grace of God by making great plans without submitting them to the will of God. Again James rebukes these people for their arrogance and presumption (4:16–17).

Finally, he describes wealthy landowners who, while amassing a large number of possessions on earth, have heaped up a storehouse of condemnation for themselves. Speaking in end-time terms, he says moths ate those people's expensive clothes, and their gold and silver rusted. By gaining riches in an unrighteous manner, those wealthy landowners "fattened [their] hearts in a day of slaughter" (5:5 NASB). By this sharp denunciation, James

---

[106] The section on righteous versus worldly wisdom in 3:13–18 is at the heart of the macro-chiasm proposed by Guthrie, "James," 206.

[107] CSB slightly altered. The rendering "submissive" (NIV) is preferable to "compliant" (CSB).

took the stance of an OT prophet, which leads naturally into his commendation of the prophets in his ensuing call to repentance.

Closely related to the previous section by the conjunction "therefore," 5:7–11 represents an exhortation for believers to display patience and endurance. The examples of both the prophets and Job are models for Christians who live in the hostile world. The prophets were patient, Job endured, and both received great blessings from God (5:11). Rather than seeking to beat the world at its own game or playing by its rules, Christ followers must commit themselves and all their ways to him and look to Jesus to give them grace. If they are arrogant, they will be judged like the world.

IV. Conclusion (5:12–20)

In staccato fashion James concludes the letter with a series of short commands. This is marked off by the prominent vocative, "Above all, my brothers and sisters." There is no proper epistolary ending (cf. Heb 13:20–25).

A. The Matter of Oaths (5:12) Rather than making pledges or vows, whether by heaven or by earth, the believer's yes or no should suffice. Like other pronouncements, this statement echoes Jesus's teaching (see Matt 5:33–37).[108]

B. Faithful Prayer (5:13–18) Connected, perhaps, to the previous verse by addressing situations that might lead one to make an oath, 5:13–18 cites scenarios involving prayer. Specifically, a call to prayer is issued to the suffering, cheerful, and sick. The teachings in 5:14–16 do not have exact NT parallels, calling for the elders of the church to come and anoint a sick member of the church and enjoining believers to confess their sins and to pray for one another. This passage led to the Roman Catholic sacraments of confession and the "last unction"—a person being anointing with oil on his deathbed. By contrast both teachings are widely ignored in evangelical churches today. In keeping with the Jewish character of the book, the biblical example cited for persistent prayer is the OT prophet Elijah. Believers today likewise are called to fervent, righteous prayer.

C. Rescue the Perishing (5:19–20) James concludes his letter with an exhortation for believers to rescue straying sinners, resulting in salvation. The phrase "cover a multitude of sins" in verse 20 closely resembles 1 Peter 4:8, which echoes Proverbs 10:12. Most likely, James's point is that such a rescue operation is prompted by love. Here the letter comes to a rather abrupt halt. The customary closing features for a letter (such as greetings and benediction) are absent. It is unclear what accounts for this departure from the standard format for ancient letters.

---

[108] See Table 17.1 on The Teachings of Jesus in James above.

THEOLOGY

Theological Themes

The Nature of James's Theology James's theology is often described as "primitive." For instance, S. McKnight, discussing James's Christology, sees a high Christology, but "not what it will be with Paul, Hebrews, John, or Peter, but it is in the chrysalis awaiting reformation."[109] Similar to McKnight, McCartney sees a primitive stage of theological development in James. Most of the evidence is the lack of certain topics (e.g., no concern for ecclesial authority or no mention of substitutionary atonement). He goes on to note that James, on the topic of suffering, employs "simple exhortations to endure because it pleases God, produces maturity, and will someday be over."[110] This is deemed to be less sophisticated than Paul's connection of suffering to our union with Christ. Thus, in the continuum of theological development, James is said to be on the underdeveloped end.

In one respect this opinion can be affirmed but caution is warranted on this topic in two aspects. First, how should we weigh the sophistication of James's theology? Should we, for example, deem it primitive because he does not advocate understanding suffering through the lens of identification with Christ's suffering? Probably not. Such a conclusion is based on a rather modern value judgment that concrete expressions are less sophisticated than abstract. This is not a necessary conclusion. So then, the label "simple" is better than "primitive."

Second, if we say the letter of James contains a simple expression of theology, it says nothing about the nature of the author's beliefs (simple or otherwise). Complex and sophisticated men may express themselves in a simple manner. The need of the hour may not call for refined theological exposition. What we can say is that the letter does not deeply delve into the more abstract areas of theology. To say anything more is to critique the letter (and to some extent, the man) for not being what we want.

Finally, if we affirm a simple expression of theology, we should be careful not to employ these matters in a way that would suggest an evolutionary model for Christian theology. To be clear, neither McKnight nor McCartney is overtly defending such a model, but many have.[111] The suggestion that an uncomplicated expression is an indication that orthodox Christian theology develops and morphs over time is a misreading of the evidence. Instead, to borrow McKnight's "chrysalis" allusion, in James we find a high Christology

---

[109] S. McKnight, *The Letter of James*, NICNT (Grand Rapids, MI: Eerdmans, 2011), 43.

[110] McCartney, *James*, 8.

[111] This is part of the so-called Bauer Thesis that suggests Christianity was fractured from the beginning (multiple evolutionary branches) and the orthodox merely won the battle of ideas. It was most recently espoused by B. Ehrman, *Lost Christianities: The Battles for Scripture and the Faiths We Never Knew* (Oxford: Oxford University Press), 2003, or the less hostile J. D. G. Dunn, *Christology in the Making: A New Testament Inquiry into the Origins of the Doctrine of the Incarnation*, 2nd ed. (Grand Rapids, MI: Eerdmans, 1996). Dunn is careful to separate reality of Christ from the understanding of the church; Ehrman, not so much. For a description and rebuttal see, A. J. Köstenberger and M. Kruger, *The Heresy of Orthodoxy: How Contemporary Culture's Fascination with Diversity Has Reshaped Our Understanding of Early Christianity* (Wheaton, IL: Crossway, 2010).

(see below) congruent with the elements expressed in the later expression of orthodox Christology. It is proper to say the doctrine is refined in expression through later reflection but improper in reference to the content of the doctrine itself.

The source of James's doctrine is germane to this discussion. So where would James, the brother of Jesus, get such teaching? Likely from the same place the teachings of Jesus came from—from Jesus Himself. Thus, James is more accurately evidence of a body of doctrine stemming from Jesus than the front end of an evolutionary stream that results in orthodox teaching.

Theology, Christology, and Eschatology James begins his book with the nature of God. God is the gracious giver of wisdom (1:5) who responds to those who ask of him (1:6–7). The Father will test his children, and he rewards endurance (1:12). He never tempts us to sin (1:13). If a gift is generous and perfect, it is from the unchanging God (1:17). It is by the sovereign choice of God that we are born again (1:18). God expects us to endure (1:12), resist temptation (1:14–15), control our tongues (1:19, 26), cleanse our lives of moral filth (1:21), receive and do his word (1:21, 24), and look after the weakest of society (1:27). These themes are repeated throughout the rest of the book (as chapter 1 is an introduction to the whole).

As the book unfolds, James continues to describe God. God is again stated as the one sovereign in salvation (2:5). He is one (2:19) and the object of our faith (2:19, 23). He makes humankind in his likeness (3:9). He resists the proud but gives grace to the humble (4:6). He may be experienced by his people (4:8). He exalts the humble (4:10). He is the only Judge and Lawgiver (4:12). All of these are in concord with the OT's teaching about God.

Two items are not common usages in the OT. First, James describes God as "Father" three times (1:17, 27; 3:9). While it is not unheard of in either the OT (see e.g., Ps 103:13) or Second Temple literature (Wis. 14:3), it is exceedingly rare.[112] McCartney suggests that two passages in James refer to God as the Father of creation (1:17) and humanity (3:9). But at 1:27, God's care for the poor and widows is in light of the eschatological and redemptive dimension of the people of God. Because God cares for the weakest of society, so should those who are related to him in redemption. To be sure, this usage of "Father" is more like the teachings of Jesus than OT concepts.[113] This suggests yet another connection to Jesus in James.

The second item is the use of "Lord" (Gk.: *kurios*) in the book of James. *Kurios* is highly significant in this context. It was the word used in the LXX to translate the *tetragrammaton* (YHWH, "LORD"). James, as expected, employs the term to refer to the Father (as at 1:7; 3:9; 5:4). Yet his use is not limited to references to God. Importantly, he employed the term to refer to Jesus as well (1:1; 2:1; 5:7–8). Given the early production of the letter

[112] McCartney, *James*, 68.

[113] Ibid., 68–69, citing E. Ng, "Father-God Language and Old Testament Allusions in James,' *TynBul* 54 (2003): 41–54.

and the author's clear expression of monotheism (see 2:19; 4:11), the use is notable. One could suggest that James is simply employing different semantic domains of *kurios* (as in "lord—one possessing authority"). However, on occasion it is not at all certain whom James is referencing (see 4:10, 15; 5:14). This flexible use is also seen in the fact that while the Father is the only Judge (4:11), Christ is also the eschatological Judge at 5:7, 10.[114] Such flexibility suggests a high Christology.[115]

Some would object to this line of reasoning, noting that James only mentions the name of Christ twice (1:1; 2:1).[116] While admittedly infrequent, these references are also highly significant. This is borne out by James's clear Hebrew milieu. Thus, the term "Christ" is not merely a stereotyped title (fossilized in Christian tradition) but a translation of the Hebrew "Messiah." Hence, James identifies Jesus as the embodiment of the hope of Israel, as the Son of David, the eschatological messianic King.

This eschatological dimension is borne out in James's further descriptions. To be clear, his Christology is not merely suggestive of eschatology—it is strongly eschatological. Jesus is not only Lord; he is the *coming* Lord (5:7). This is consistent with James's teaching regarding the end time throughout the letter. In particular, he made clear that there will be a future day of reckoning and judgment (1:10–11; 2:12–13; 3:1; 5:1–6, 9, 12) and warned his readers that this life will inevitably culminate with Jesus's glorious return. Thus, believers must conduct their lives in the light of Christ's coming.

One further matter gives the reader insight into James's Christology. Not only is Jesus "Lord" as mentioned above; he is "our *glorious* Lord Jesus Christ" (2:1). In a Jewish context the adjective "glorious" immediately recalls the heavy presence of God in the OT (e.g., Exod 33:18–19; 1 Kgs 8:11). God is clearly jealous of his glory in the OT. For example, he refuses to share his glory with another in Isaiah 42:8. That Jesus is described in this way reflects an exceedingly high Christology on James's part.

Thus, in summary, James applies titles, attributes, and roles to Jesus that belong indisputably to God. James's pattern of reference to Jesus is clearly expressive of a firm commitment to his deity. What is more, not only did James hold to Jesus's messianic identity and divine nature; he also evinced the expectation of Jesus's return at the end of time. Although James does not expressly develop his theology and Christology, the way he references both God and Christ fit squarely within the orthodox tradition.

The Relationship Between Faith and Works Perhaps the most prominent theme running throughout James is the relationship between what we believe and what we do. At the core of this idea is James 2:14–26. As briefly touched on above, it is often interpreted

---

[114] See Moo, *James* (2000), 29.

[115] Ibid. Moo states, "We find in the juxtaposition of these points an incipient trinitarianism. Without in any way modifying his inherited monotheistic profession, James attributes titles and functions to Jesus that are properly God's alone" (ibid.). Bauckham, on the foundation of similar arguments, likewise suggests, "Christology, though presumed rather than expounded, is more prominent and considerably higher than is often allowed" (Bauckham, *James*, 138).

[116] E.g., Ehrman, *Introduction*, 331–32.

Something to Think About: Do You and I Walk Our Talk?

There are, in the end, only two kinds of people: people who do what they say and those who don't. Do you and I walk our talk? Jesus called the latter group of people "hypocrites," playactors who wore a mask that hid the true self underneath. God desires that we be genuine, unhypocritical, and real—the same on the inside as we are on the outside.

This is easier said than done. Only by the grace of God can we be the kinds of people God wants us to be. Yet follow-through is of critical importance, as James, the half brother of Jesus, told his readers:

> *But be doers of the word and not hearers only, deceiving yourselves. Because if anyone is a hearer of the word and not a doer, he is like someone looking at his own face in a mirror. For he looks at himself, goes away, and immediately forgets what kind of person he was. But the one who looks intently into the perfect law of freedom and perseveres in it, and is not a forgetful hearer but a doer who works—this person will be blessed in what he does (1:22–25).*

As far as we know, James did not become a believer in Jesus until after the resurrection. But doubtless he was familiar with Jesus's similar words in the Sermon on the Mount: "Not everyone who says to me, 'Lord, Lord!' will enter the kingdom of heaven, but only the one who does the will of my Father in heaven" *(Matt 7:21, emphasis added). Let us be careful, therefore, to be doers of the word and not hearers only. Let us not merely* study *the Bible but* do what it says.

As an example of one whose life did not match his words, consider Karl Marx. Marx, the founder of communism, was born into a Jewish family, but his family later became Lutheran. Marx was baptized at age six and confirmed at fifteen. But Marx showed absolutely no fruit of the Christian faith. To the contrary Marx's life abounded with hypocrisy and self-contradiction. He, the self-proclaimed advocate of the working class, knew virtually no workers personally and did not pay the one servant that he had. Rather than work with his own hands, he lived off his inheritance and family money. His mother lamented that perhaps he should accrue some capital of his own by working rather than simply writing about it. How pitiful!

When contemplating the outcome of Karl Marx's life and of others like him, we should say, "There, but by the grace of God, go I." But we should also aim to thrust ourselves upon Christ and exclaim with Paul, "What a wretched man I am!" (Rom 7:24). Then we can live our lives fully in the strength supplied by God—"I am able to do all things through him who strengthens me" (Phil 4:13)—and do our best to "walk our talk," to the glory and praise of God.

as in conflict with Paul's doctrine of salvation through faith alone (see Rom 3:28; Gal 2:15–16; Eph 2:8–9). Three views have appeared in the scholarly literature: (1) James disagreed with Paul and was seeking to correct him (or vice versa);[117] (2) James corrected a misunderstanding of Paul;[118] or (3) James and Paul addressed two related but distinct issues.[119]

Historically, the picture of James and Paul gives no indication of any friction, theologically or otherwise. Theologically, Paul affirmed that the pillars in Jerusalem, including James, gave him "the right hand of fellowship" (Gal 2:9). That is, their doctrine was not at odds. Personally, James and Paul seem well acquainted and friendly (Acts 21:18–25). James "solves" the problem of Gentile inclusion in Acts (Acts 15:13–20). In Galatians 2:12 Paul notes that Peter withdrew after "certain men came from James." The text does not tell us James or even the men themselves were the problem but that Peter withdrew. It is not known whether James approved the action. Clearly friction with James is not the characterization with the rest of the NT.

The text itself does not mention Paul. Nor does it address the doctrine of justification by faith directly. In *koinē* Greek, when a noun is introduced into a text, it is normally without the article; after that, subsequent appearances of that noun appear with the article that is essentially pointing back to the aforementioned noun. This is known as "the article of previous reference."[120] In our text faith (Gk. *pistis*) is introduced without the article in 2:14. James asks, "What good is it, my brothers and sisters, if someone claims to have faith but does not have works?" The appearance of the word in the next clause appears with the article. It is pointing back to a specific kind of faith, the aforementioned faith: faith without works. So, then, the NASB and ESV translate it best as, "Can *that* faith save him?"

In this light the surrounding context makes more sense. James compared faith without works (not faith itself) to words without action. Mere words do not help alleviate the situation of hunger and nakedness. Thus, a needy brother who is offered only a platitude has not been helped. But one who has his needs met has had his situation changed. Likewise, faith apart from works is like a platitude—it is merely empty words.

James rather insists that faith accompanied by works is actually saving faith.[121] Saving faith is like the faith of Abraham, proven through our actions.[122] As James says, "I will show you faith by my works" (2:18). One should notice the sequence: faith then works. This is in exact agreement with the rest of the NT (not just Paul) regarding justification by faith (see Table 17.2).

---

[117] See Hengel, *Paulus und Jakobus*, 526–29; and P. A. Holloway, "James" in *The Blackwell Companion to the New Testament*, ed. D. E. Aune (Malden, MA: Blackwell, 2010), 573.

[118] See Ropes, *James*, 204–6.

[119] See Guthrie, *James*, 241.

[120] The alternate designation is "anaphoric." See chap. 5 in A. J. Köstenberger, B. L. Merkle, and R. L. Plummer, *Going Deeper with New Testament Greek: An Intermediate Study of the Grammar and Syntax of the New Testament* (Nashville, TN: B&H Academic, 2016).

[121] In 2:24 James did not say that a man is justified by works and not by faith—he added by faith *alone* (i.e., without works).

[122] In another sense, of course, it was Abraham's faith that was credited to him as righteousness; see Gen 15:6, cited in Jas 2:23; Gal 3:6; and Rom 4:3, in likely chronological order of writing.

Table 17.2: Faith and Works: Comparing James and Paul

Doctrine	James	Paul
Faith is necessary for salvation.	2:18	Eph 2:8–9
Faith without works is not saving faith.	2:17, 24	1 Cor 15:2
Saving faith is accompanied by works.	2:24	Rom 3:31; Eph 2:8–10

The person James describes in 2:14 is all too familiar. That person claims to have faith, and to an extent he believes all the right things about God, Jesus, and salvation. But his faith is not lived out in his daily life. James condemns this kind of faith; faith without works is useless. It neither sanctifies nor saves. Saving faith—or, as James put it, faith accompanied by works—is "faith that works" in that it radically affects the way a person lives.

Wisdom and Ethics Apart from his treatment of faith and works, James is perhaps best known for his strong ethical teaching in keeping with Jewish Wisdom literature. James's entire letter is saturated in an emphasis on the need to deal with practical aspects of the Christian life in a godly and wise manner. Thus, James features a striking number of imperatives (fifty-nine all together—nearly twelve per chapter!). Clearly a course of action given the circumstances is a priority to the author.

These commands include dealing with trials and temptations (1:2–18); helping those in need, such as widows and orphans, as an expression of a practical form of Christianity that refuses to divorce faith from works (1:19–27; see 2:14–26); avoiding preferential treatment of those of a higher socioeconomic status in society (2:1–13); controlling one's speech (3:1–12); cultivating wisdom and understanding in a variety of good works (3:13–18); adopting an attitude of humility in one's dealings with others and in the way one goes about one's business (4:1–17); and many other practical, ethical matters (chap. 5).[123]

We should be careful to note that the works James advocates find foundation in true faith. So then, James's ethical admonitions are the result of being in a covenantal relationship with God through Jesus Christ. The goal is to be "mature and complete" (1:4) and to practice "pure and undefiled religion" (1:27). We live, however, in a fallen world, awaiting the eschatological Judge (5:7). The believer, then, must struggle with not being perfected yet.[124] In the meantime our goal is to approach life with a godly point of view. Thus, the commands previously mentioned are the rational natural response of those who are the people of God. Unfortunately, we all have to be reminded of this.

---

[123] For a fuller discussion of James's ethical teaching, including aspects such as speech control, the rich and the poor, testing and suffering, and love, mercy, and humility, see Chester, "Theology of James," 16–45.

[124] Moo, *James* (2000) 37.

CONTRIBUTION TO THE CANON

- An exemplar of early Jewish Christianity written by James, the half brother of Jesus (1:1)
- The relationship between faith and works (2:14–26)
- The need for wisdom in the Christian life (1:5; 3:13–18)
- Practical exhortations related to dealing with the rich (1:9–11; 2:1–13; 5:1–6), controlling one's tongue (3:1–12), humility in planning (4:13–17), and other matters
- The abiding examples of OT men of faith, such as Job and Elijah (5:11, 17)

STUDY QUESTIONS

1. Which James authored the book of James, and which other persons named James are less likely candidates?
2. Between what two dates was James likely written, and why?
3. Where was James most likely written and to whom?
4. What is the likely occasion for James?
5. What is the genre of James?
6. In what ways is the genre of James similar to that of Hebrews and 1 John?
7. Why do you think there is little consensus today about the structure of James?
8. According to the authors, what is the most likely structure of James?
9. Why is James 2:14–26 controversial?
10. What are three scholarly views of James 2:14–26?
11. In what ways do Paul and James agree on faith and works?
12. How does James contribute to the canon?

FOR FURTHER STUDY

Bauckham, R. *James: Wisdom of James, Disciple of Jesus the Sage*. New Testament Readings. New York, NY/London, England: Routledge, 1999.

________. *Jude and the Relatives of Jesus in the Early Church*. Edinburgh, Scotland: T&T Clark, 1990.

Carson, D. A. "James." Pages 997–1,013 in *Commentary on the New Testament Use of the Old Testament*. Edited by G. K. Beale and D. A. Carson. Grand Rapids, MI: Baker, 2007.

Chilton, B., and C. A. Evans, eds. *James the Just and Christian Origins*. Novum Testamentum Supplement 98. Leiden, Netherlands: Brill, 1999.

Chilton, B., and J. Neusner, eds. *The Brother of Jesus: James the Just and His Mission*. Louisville, KY: Westminster John Knox, 2001.

Davids, P. H. *The Epistle of James: A Commentary on the Greek Text*. New International Greek Testament Commentary. Grand Rapids, MI: Eerdmans, 1982.

________. *A Theology of James, Peter and Jude: Living in the Light of the Coming King*. BTNT. Grand Rapids, MI: Zondervan, 2014.

Deppe, D. B. *The Sayings of Jesus in the Epistle of James*. Chelsea, MI: Bookcrafters, 1989.

Guthrie, G. H. "James." Pages 197–273 in *The Expositor's Bible Commentary*. Rev. ed. Vol. 13: *Hebrews–Revelation*. Grand Rapids, MI: Zondervan, 2005.

Johnson, L. T. *The Letter of James*. Anchor Bible 37A. New York, NY: Doubleday, 1995.

Laato, T. "Justification According to James: A Comparison with Paul." *Trinity Journal* 18 (1997): 47–61.

Laws, S. *A Commentary on the Epistle of James*. Harper's New Testament Commentary. San Francisco, CA: Harper & Row, 1980.

Martin, R. P. *James*. Word Biblical Commentary 48. Waco, TX: Word, 1988.

Maynard-Reid, P. V. *Poverty and Wealth in James*. Maryknoll, NY: Orbis, 1987.

McCartney, Dan G., and and Robert Yarbrough. *James*. BECNT. Grand Rapids, MI: Baker, 2009.

McKnight, S. *The Letter of James*. NICNT. Grand Rapids, MI: Eerdmans, 2011.

Moo, D. J. *The Letter of James*. Pillar New Testament Commentary. Grand Rapids, MI: Eerdmans, 2000.

__________. *The Letter of James*. Tyndale New Testament Commentary. Grand Rapids, MI: Eerdmans, 1985.

Painter, J. *Just James: The Brother of Jesus in History and Tradition*. Columbia, SC: University of South Carolina Press, 1997.

Shanks, H., and B. Witherington III. *The Brother of Jesus: The Dramatic Story and Meaning of the First Archaeological Link to Jesus and His Family*. New York, NY: HarperCollins, 2003.

Chapter 18

The Petrine Epistles (1–2 Peter) and the Letter of Jude

CORE KNOWLEDGE

Basic Knowledge: Students should know the key facts of 1 and 2 Peter and Jude. With regard to history, students should be able to identify each book's author, date, provenance, destination, and purpose. With regard to literature, they should be able to provide a basic outline of each book and identify core elements of the book's content found in the Unit-by-Unit Discussion. With regard to theology, students should be able to identify the major theological themes in the Petrine Epistles and the book of Jude.

Intermediate Knowledge: Students should be able to present the arguments for historical, literary, and theological conclusions. With regard to history, students should be able to discuss the evidence for Peter's and Jude's authorship, date, provenance, destination, and purpose. With regard to literature, they should be able to provide a detailed outline of each book. With regard to theology, students should be able to discuss the major theological themes in the Petrine Epistles and the book of Jude and the ways they uniquely contribute to the NT canon.

Advanced Knowledge: Students should be able to critically engage modern scholarship concerning the supposed pseudonymity of 2 Peter and how this affects the dating of the letter. They should be able to discuss the different interpretations of 1 Peter 3:18–22 and to assess the genre of Jude. They should also be prepared to evaluate critically the relationship between the book of Jude and 2 Peter, explaining how this affects the dating of these letters.

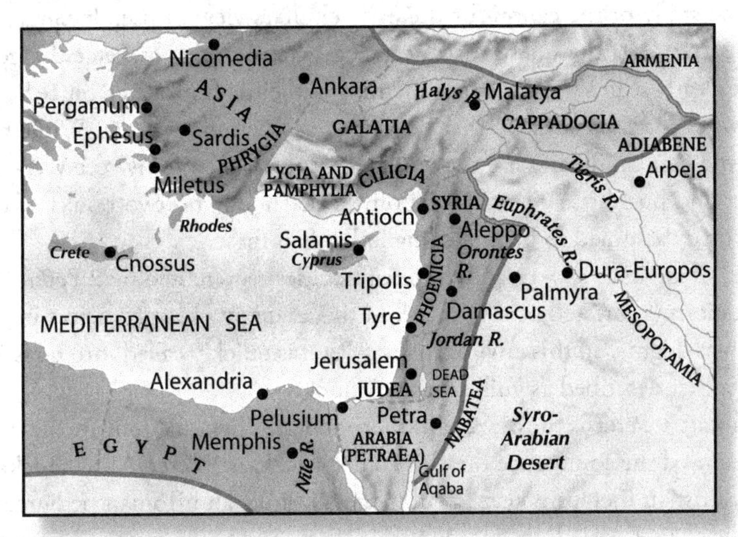

Map 18.1 Provenance and destination of 1 and 2 Peter

1 Peter

KEY FACTS

Author:	Simon Peter
Date:	ca. AD 62–63
Provenance:	Rome
Destination:	Christians in Northern Asia Minor
Occasion:	Persecution of the church
Purpose:	To encourage these Christians to stay the course
Theme:	Christians living in a hostile world
Key Verses:	3:15–17

INTRODUCTION

"WE, DEAR brothers, receive both Peter and the other apostles as Christ, but writings falsely attributed to them we reject, knowing that such were not handed down to us."[1] This was the response of Serapion, a Syrian Bishop from about AD 189 to 211 whom we met in chapter 1, as he responded to the church at Rhossus regarding a forged "Gospel of Peter." Serapion's reproof is well known in the study of the canon for the early church's view of pseudepigrapha. What is not discussed much is the question concerning what writings of Peter the good bishop receives. He clearly seems to allude to something authentic from Peter. Since he is referring to written works, it is most likely that he refers to something written. While he does not identify it, the best candidates are the letters the church manifestly received—at the very least 1 Peter and possibly 2 Peter.[2] The irony is that today no two books of the NT are more confidently assumed to be pseudepigrapha than these.

This state of affairs is largely due to the difficulties represented by 2 Peter. Of the two, it raises questions (addressed below) that lead the academy to largely reject it and then fix the rejection as dogma. In this environment 1 Peter is quickly called into question as well. It is a verdict best described as guilt by association.

Doubt about 1 Peter is, however, a rather modern phenomenon. In the early church few books enjoyed the confidence the church displayed for 1 Peter. As M. Bockmuehl stated, "Early Christian literature never doubts the apostolic and Roman pedigree of 1 Peter. And from the earliest period, the words of this letter were heard as unambiguously authoritative and speaking the voice of Peter."[3] The letter enjoyed a long recognition as one of the high points of NT literature and theology. For example, Martin Luther recognized 1 Peter (along with the Gospel of John and Paul's Letters) as "the true kernel and marrow of all the NT Books. For in them you . . . find depicted in masterly fashion how faith in Christ overcomes sin, death, and hell, and gives life, righteousness, and salvation."[4] It is safe to say the message of 1 Peter was confidently woven into the fabric of Christian theology and identity.

Scholarly confidence of the Petrine origins of 1 Peter waned as commentators in the nineteenth and twentieth centuries began expressing doubt. Those with the most enduring complaints saw the author as a Paulinist (a Christian "standing in the tradition of

---

[1] P. Maier, *Eusebius: The Church History: A New Translation with Commentary* (Grand Rapids, MI: Kregel, 1999), 216.

[2] M. Bockmuehl (*Simon Peter in Scripture and Memory: The New Testament Apostle in the Early Church* [Grand Rapids, MI: Baker, 2012], 44) makes every attempt to ascribe the reference to the memory of the apostle. It is highly unlikely, however, that any reliable memory could survive so late that was directly connected to Peter.

[3] Bockmuehl, *Simon Peter in Scripture and Memory*, 126. He goes on to note, "Indeed, in the face of 1 Peter's effective de-canonization in much recent NT scholarship, it is worth recalling that the apostolicity of 1 Peter was one of the first to be attested in antiquity and one of the last to be widely discounted in the heyday of historical criticism." (Ibid.) Ironically, Bockmuehl can only affirm the possibility that Peter penned the book.

[4] M. Luther, *Prefaces to the New Testament*, 1,522, cited by J. H. Elliott, "Peter, First Epistle of," *ABD* 5:270.

Paul").[5] Largely due to the Hegelian philosophy of F. C. Baur and the Tübingen School, any concordance between Peter and Paul was unthinkable.[6] According to this thought, the apostles were at odds and held to different streams of Christianity: Peter supposedly clung to the old Jewish form, Paul to a new Hellenizing form. While much of Baur's program fell into disfavor rather quickly, the dichotomy between Paul and Peter was entrenched in the continental mind.[7] Thus, the letter was assumed a forgery. And if it were a forgery, its authority was potentially compromised.

Owing mostly to the work of J. H. Elliott, more modern scholars are rejecting direct connection to Paul, and 1 Peter has been rehabilitated in recent years as a dependable source of Christian theology. However, this is not a return to Peter directly. Instead of being considered the work of a Paulinist, the book is now thought of by some as the result of the "Petrine tradition transmitted by Petrine tradents of a Petrine circle."[8] For these the "Paulinist" flavor of the letter has been overstated. In its place the suggestion is that the particularly Pauline items (household codes, spiritual gifts, obligation to the state, etc.) are more likely a tradition shared with Paul.[9] The benefit of such a view is that it gives validity to the use of Peter's name without affirming he was directly responsible. The results are that the authority of 1 Peter is not as deeply challenged.

Yet Peter has not been so comfortably reattached to the letter in the minds of all. Another group of scholars likewise reject the idea of dependence on Paul, but they also deny connections to Peter are discernable. For these the letter is better understood as a "product of a synthesizing and proto-orthodox form of early Christianity."[10] Peter's name, they feel, was added simply to give the letter the authority of a leading figure of Christianity.[11] These are, self-admittedly, returning to F. C. Baur's thesis that 1 Peter is the result of a synthesizing tendency. Thus, the question of authority is still the 800-pound gorilla in the room.[12]

---

[5] One of the first was W. Seufert, "Das Verwandtschaftsverhältnis des ersten Petrusbriefs und Epheserbriefs," *ZWT* (1881): 178–97, 332–80. See also O. D. Foster, "The Literary Relations of 'the First Epistle of Peter' with Their Bearing on Date and Place of Authorship," *Transactions of the Connecticut Academy of Arts and Sciences* 17 (1913): 363–538 and A. E. Barnett, *Paul Becomes a Literary Influence* (Chicago, IL: University of Chicago Press, 1941), 51–69.

[6] Baur suggested that early Catholicism was the result of the synthesis that occurred when early Jewish Christianity clashed with Hellenistic Christianity. Thus, it follows Hegel's philosophy of "Thesis→Antithesis→Synthesis." See H. Harris, *The Tübingen School: A Historical and Theological Investigation of the School of F. C. Baur* (Grand Rapids, MI: Baker, 1990); and W. Baird, *History of New Testament Research*, vol. 1: *From Deism to Tübingen* (Philadelphia, PA: Fortress, 1992).

[7] See, e.g., W. G. Kümmel, *Introduction to the New Testament*, Revised & Enlarged English Edition, trans. H. C. Kee (Nashville, TN: Abingdon, 1975), 423.

[8] J. Elliott, "The Rehabilitation of an Exegetical Step-Child: 1 Peter in Recent Research," *JBL* 95 (1976): 248.

[9] Ibid., 247.

[10] D. G. Horrell, "The Product of a Petrine Circle? Challenging an Emerging Consensus," in *Becoming Christian: Essays on 1 Peter and the Making of Christian Identity* (London, England: Bloomsbury T&T Clark, 2013), 43.

[11] Ibid., 39–40.

[12] To be sure, a number of evangelical scholars have defended the view that pseudepigraphy should not invalidate the authority of a given book. See e.g., A. Schlatter, *The Theology of the Apostles: The Development of New Testament Theology*, trans. A. J. Köstenberger (Grand Rapids, MI: Baker, 1999), 356. More recently D. A. deSilva (*An Introduction to the New Testament: Contexts, Methods, & Ministry Formation* [Downers Grove, IL: InterVarsity, 2004], 846) states, "Pseudonymity

When examined on its own merits, however, little reason emerges to doubt the authenticity of 1 Peter except the caution associated with facing an entrenched position. Thus, a second irony emerges. In a letter that addresses persecution in every chapter, those who hold to its authenticity may face the persecution of scholarly dismissal. As seen in recent years, however, cracks in the façade of the ivory tower are appearing due to weak foundations in these matters. The case for authenticity (and a more solid authority) is much stronger than usually admitted.

HISTORY

Author

External Evidence The early tradition of the church was thoroughly acquainted with 1 Peter and attributed authorship of the book to the apostle Peter in an impressive way. The first clear evidence for the knowledge of the letter comes from 2 Peter; it states, "this is now the second letter I have written to you" (2 Pet 3:1). However one views the authorship of 2 Peter (see below), its date is particularly early: it must be dated at the latest to the late first century (see below). Few would claim that the author is not referring to the first letter.[13] There have been attempts to show allusions to 1 Peter in other first-century documents such as *1 Clement* (ca. AD 96) and the *Didache* (second half of the first or early second century), but the evidence, while likely, is inconclusive.[14] Polycarp—a resident of Asia Minor, which was the destination of 1 Peter—cited 1 Peter repeatedly in his letter to the Philippians (ca. AD 108).[15] According to Eusebius (ca. AD 260–340), both Papias (ca. AD 60–130) and Clement of Alexandria (ca. AD 150–215) cited the book as well.[16]

The first extant citation naming Peter as the author comes from Irenaeus (ca. AD 130–200). He not only named Peter as the author but also referred to 1 Peter often.[17] Both Clement of Alexandria and Tertullian (ca. AD 160–225) cited 1 Peter and attributed the verses to the apostle.[18] Eusebius, in fact, listed 1 Peter as the only "undisputed" book of all the General Epistles.[19] The letter is not listed in the Muratorian Canon (later second century?); however, that manuscript is fragmentary and incomplete for all the General Epistles.[20] Thus, Peter's authorship of the letter is well attested in the early church tradi-

---

does not automatically preclude apostolicity." In the early church, however, it was a given that pseudepigrapha should not be received.

[13] J. R. Michaels, *1 Peter*, WBC 49 (Waco, TX: Word, 1988), xxxii.

[14] T. R. Schreiner, *1, 2 Peter, Jude*, NAC 37 (Nashville, TN: B&H, 2003), 22.

[15] E.g., *Phil.* 1:3; 2:1–2; 6:3; 7:2; 8:1–2; 10:2–3. Polycarp does not name Peter as the author, but such mechanical citations are not his style in the letter. There is no doubt he is citing 1 Peter. He weaves most of his biblical material into the fabric of his letter.

[16] Eusebius, *Eccl. Hist.* 2.15; 3.1.2, 39.

[17] Eusebius, *Eccl. Hist.* 4.9.2; 16.5; 5.7.2.

[18] For Tertullian, see *Scorp.* 12 and 14, as well as *Orat.* 20; For Clement, see *Stromata* 3.11 and 17.

[19] Eusebius, *Eccl. Hist.* 3.3.25.

[20] Schreiner, *1, 2 Peter, Jude*, 22.

tion. As Bigg stated regarding 1 Peter, "There is no book in the New Testament which has earlier, better, or stronger attestation."[21]

Internal Evidence The objections to Peter as the source of this letter cannot appeal to external evidence, so a host of internal objections have been levied against it. Beginning in 1784, some schools of thought deemed 1 Peter a forgery.[22] This rather recent view has become the majority position today, in spite of vigorous protests.[23] Four general matters of contention have been raised against Peter's authorship of 1 Peter. First, the Greek is better than expected of a Galilean fisherman.[24] Second, the contents of the book suggest to some a milieu more suited to a time later than Peter's lifetime.[25] Third, critics see a dependence on the "Deutero-Pauline" Letters, thus requiring a date for 1 Peter in the early second century. Fourth, geographical regions addressed (including remote regions of Asia Minor) were not part of Peter's apostolic jurisdiction and—the criticism goes—could not have been evangelized or have suffered persecution in Peter's lifetime.[26]

These objections, however, are unconvincing. That the letter is written too well to be from Peter raises three immediate questions. First, how well written is it? Recent studies have shown that 1 Peter is certainly not beyond the skills of someone writing in a second language and that the book displays Semitic influence.[27] Second, how deeply had Greek

---

[21] C. Bigg, *A Critical and Exegetical Commentary on the Epistles of St. Peter and St. Jude*, ICC (Edinburgh, Scotland: T&T Clark, 1901), 7. Cf. D. Guthrie's conclusion on the matter: "This Epistle not only exerted a wide influence on early Christian writings, but it also possessed for them apostolic authority. This makes clear that the primitive Church, as far back as any evidence exists, regarded it as a genuine Epistle of Peter, and thus any discussion of objections to Petrine authorship must sufficiently take account of this fact" (*New Testament Introduction*, 2nd ed. [Downers Grove, IL: InterVarsity, 1990], 762).

[22] H. J. Holtzmann (*Lehrbuch der historisch-kritischen Einleitung in das neue Testament* [Freiburg, Germany: J. C. B. Mohr, 1885], 490–91) lists Semler (1784) and Eichhorn (1818) as the first to deny direct Petrine authorship, as did Cludius (1808) and de Wette (1813) and Reuss (1852, 1864). The Tübingen School followed suit, beginning with F. C. Baur (1856).

[23] E. Boring, "First Peter in Recent Study," *WW* 24 (2004): 359–60. E.g., J. H. Elliott, *1 Peter: A New Translation with Introduction and Commentary*, AB (New York, NY: Doubleday, 2000), 127–30.

[24] E.g., E. G. Selwyn, *The First Epistle of St. Peter: The Greek Text with Introduction, Notes and Essays* (London, England: Macmillan, 1955), 10. The axiomatic status can be seen in the statement of the late M. Hengel (*Saint Peter: The Underestimated Apostle*, trans. T. H. Trapp [Grand Rapids, MI: Eerdmans, 2010], 11). He notes, "In reality, we do not even know whether we can say for sure that Peter, who was once a Galilean fisherman, even knew how to write decently. The ability to read, already on the level of being able to know the Holy Scriptures, was more important and more widespread." With this brief dismissal, Hengel goes on to write a 134-page book on the apostle with only twenty references to 1 Peter (five to 2 Peter).

[25] R. E. Brown (*An Introduction to the New Testament*, ABRL [New York, NY: Doubleday, 1997], 719) considers this the weightiest argument against Peter's authorship.

[26] K. H. Jobes, *1 Peter*, BECNT (Grand Rapids, MI: Baker, 2005), 6. D. P. Senior (*1 Peter, Jude, and 2 Peter*, SacPag 15 [Collegeville, MN: Liturgical Press, 2003], 4) mentions five similar objections, adding the fact that the author did not mention anything from the life of Jesus in the first letter. Most scholars recognize a lack of consistency in rejecting Peter's authorship for 1 Peter for this reason while also rejecting the authenticity of 2 Peter, which includes one such major reference (2 Pet 1:16–19) (e.g., Michaels, *1 Peter*, lxvi). The same can be said for the view that if Peter wrote 1 Peter, he would have mentioned Paul (who presumably was with him in Rome at that time) while still rejecting 2 Peter, which does include such a citation. See, e.g., G. Krodel, "The First Letter of Peter," in *Hebrews, James, 1 and 2 Peter, Jude and Revelation*, Proclamation Commentaries (Minneapolis, MN: Augsburg Fortress, 1995), 64.

[27] Ibid., 332. Against Achtemeier (*1 Peter*, 7), who believes the author was linguistically at home in a Greek environment rather than a Semitic one. Jobes (*1 Peter*, 337–38) applies a methodology she devised in her dissertation on Esther to track

penetrated into Palestine? Again, recent studies have shown that Palestine had experienced considerable Hellenization. The Greek language was common, and Peter could be expected to be familiar with it.[28] Moreover, Peter's own brother has a decidedly Greek name, *Andreas* (Andrew), showing at least some degree of Hellenization within Peter's family.[29] Third, did Peter employ a secretary (an amanuensis) to polish his Greek or interpret for him? If so, an obvious candidate is Silvanus (Silas). The writer describes him as the one "through" whom the letter was written (1 Pet 5:12). It is unlikely that means he used Silas as an amanuensis.[30] Most likely, he is simply the letter carrier.[31] However, even if Silas were not an amanuensis, it would not preclude the possibility that Peter employed someone else to fill that role. If Peter did use an amanuensis, it could explain the polished Greek of the letter.[32]

The other objections to Peter's authorship fare no better. The view that the letter appears to address a later situation was originally based on the notion that the persecution mentioned (e.g., 1:6) was sanctioned by the state.[33] Virtually no one holds this position today.[34] Typically, the current consensus is "that the persecution of 1 Peter is local, sporadic and unofficial, stemming from the antagonism and discrimination of the general populace."[35] The only injunctions in 1 Peter regarding the state do not mention any

---

Aramaic influence in 1 Peter. She tracks the use of various syntactical markers, statistically weighted, and finds that it was unlikely "that the author of 1 Peter was a native speaker of Greek" (p. 337) and that "Josephus had a much better mastery of Greek than did the author of 1 Peter, which is consistent with historical information about him" (pp. 337–38). See idem, "The Syntax of 1 Peter: Just How Good is the Greek?," *BBR* 13 (2003): 159–73.

[28] See comments on Sevenster's work in chap. 17. Also see, e.g., J. A. Fitzmyer, "Did Jesus Speak Greek?" *BAR* 18 (1992): 58–63; idem, "Languages of Palestine in the First Century AD," *CBQ* 32 (1970): 501–31 (esp. 507–18). Fitzmyer notes the discovery of a Greek letter from Simon Bar Kokhba to two of his lieutenants. It was written in Greek, to the effect that "a desire has not been found to write in Hebrew" (ibid., 514).

[29] Jobes, *1 Peter*, 326.

[30] See E. R. Richards, "Silvanus Was Not Peter's Secretary: Theological Bias in Interpreting *dia Silvanou . . . egrapsa* in 1 Peter 5:12," *JETS* 43 (2000): 417–32.

[31] See the helpful discussion in D. A. Carson and D. J. Moo (*An Introduction to the New Testament*, 2nd ed. [Grand Rapids, MI: Zondervan, 2005], 645), who note that the Greek preposition *dia* ("through") could convey either notion: that Silas carried the letter or that he served as an amanuensis. While the former seems more likely, this does not mean Silas (or someone else) could not also have had a part in writing the letter.

[32] An appeal to an amanuensis should not be regarded as an act of desperation but more of a frank realization of how letter writing worked in antiquity.

[33] E.g., F. G. Downing, "Pliny's Persecutions of Christians: Revelation and 1 Peter," *JSNT* 34 (1988): 105–23. The connection is often made to a letter from Pliny the Younger (Governor of Bithynia) to the emperor Trajan, that outlines Pliny's (mis)treatment of believers in his province (Pliny, *Letters* 10.96.6; see, e.g., R. B. Vinson, R. F. Wilson, and W. E. Mills, *1 2 Peter, Jude*, Smyth & Helwys Bible Commentary [Macon, GA: Smyth & Helwys, 2010], 17–19). Since it is not at all necessary for the persecution in 1 Peter to be state sanctioned, the connection is rather proof of a thriving Christian community in the area. See D. Warden, "Imperial Persecution and the Dating of 1 Peter and Revelation," *JETS* 34 (1991): 203–12.

[34] L. T. Johnson (*The Writings of the New Testament: An Interpretation* [Minneapolis, MN: Fortress, 2010], 426) states, "Taken as a whole, however, the letter does not support the hypothesis of a state persecution." But see Kümmel, *Introduction*, 424, as one of the last holdouts of this position. On this shift in understanding, see the thorough treatment of T. B. Williams, *Persecution in 1 Peter: Differentiating and Contextualizing Early Christian Suffering*, NovTSup 145 (Leiden, Netherlands: Brill, 2012), 4–15.

[35] M. Dubis, *"Research on 1 Peter: A Survey of Scholarly Literature Since 1985,"* CBR 4 (2006): 203.

persecution. In fact, believers are told to "submit to every human authority," including "the emperor as the supreme authority" and his governors (2:13–14).[36] Schreiner correctly notes that Christians, even in the midst of state-sanctioned persecution, have always been urged to be good, obedient citizens. Thus, Peter's injunctions by themselves do not rule out persecution by the state.[37] But Peter included no mention of threat and little of the urgency one would expect from a church leader writing to Christians under duress from the government. J. N. D. Kelly summarizes the state of affairs well, suggesting the more likely source of hostility comes from the bottom up rather than the top down. He stated, that it was "an atmosphere of suspicion, hostility and brutality on the part of the local population which may easily land Christians in trouble with the police."[38]

Others object that the reference to Rome as "Babylon" makes a post-70 date necessary, and thus beyond Peter's lifetime.[39] T. B. Williams suggests this issue to be a decisive point against Petrine authorship. In his view the question why the reference is employed is necessary, "especially given the fact that 1 Peter would then be the first to make such an association."[40] But the available evidence suggests that this was an entirely intelligible allusion, including the fact that the allusion predates Peter.[41]

The ecclesiology of the church is another contention. It is said to be more developed than was the case during Peter's lifetime. Brown suggests the reference at 5:1 to "elders" describes a church organization "with established presbyters, seemingly appointed and salaried."[42] Nothing in the text, however, demands the professional structure Brown sees. The term "elder" is modified by the participle "overseeing" in 5:2. The cognate noun (Gk. *episkopos*) was the preferred term for the second-century office of bishop. The use describing one office, rather than two (as in Titus 1:5, 7) hardly speaks of a late ecclesiology; instead, it indicates one that is rather early.[43]

---

[36] W. Grudem, *The First Epistle of Peter: An Introduction and Commentary*, TNTC (Grand Rapids, MI: Eerdmans, 1997), 31.

[37] Schreiner, *1, 2 Peter, Jude*, 36.

[38] J. N. D. Kelly, *The Epistles of Peter and of Jude*, HNTC (New York, NY: Harper & Row, 1969), 29. Williams (*Persecution in 1 Peter*) suggests in a detailed study that the threat could include verbal and physical abuse that could lead to legal action as Christianity ran afoul of the customs and mores of first-century Anatolia (summarized at ibid., 331–35).

[39] E.g., Michaels, *1 Peter*, lxiii; B. H. Gregg, "1 Peter," in *The Blackwell Companion to the New Testament*, ed. D. E. Aune (Malden, MA: Blackwell, 2010), 583.

[40] Williams, *Persecution in 1 Peter*, 31. Williams is fair in his assessment and, in his opinion, "probability does tend to favor pseudonymity (if only slightly)" (ibid.). His other complaint is that Silvanus (Silas) is not identified as the amanuensis (see above). Neither objection rises to the level of overturning traditional opinion.

[41] See I. H. Marshall, *1 Peter*, IVPNTC (Downers Grove, IL: InterVarsity, 1991), 175. The commentary on Habakkuk in the Dead Sea Scrolls (1QpHab) interprets Habakkuk's prophecies about Babylon as being fulfilled in Rome. Moreover, a Roman writer, Petronius, compared Roman decadence with that of Babylon (*Satyricon*, AD 60s). Papias, in the early second century, placed 1 Peter in Rome, viewing the "Babylon" metaphor as a reference to Rome (cited in Eusebius, *Eccl. Hist.* 2.15.2).

[42] Brown, *Introduction to the New Testament*, 719.

[43] Jobes, *1 Peter*, 303.

As stated above, the supposed connections to Paul have been an issue in the last couple of centuries. The idea is generally recognized in scholarship as highly questionable but still should be addressed. The typical comparison is to Romans and Ephesians. The similarities lead to the suggestion that theological (if not literary) dependence is necessary. Consequently, the theory has frequently been proposed that the writer was a student of Paul.[44]

Kümmel considers these parallels to be one of many "decisive arguments . . . against the Petrine authorship of I Pet."[45] Chiefly, the comportment with Paul showed that the writer of 1 Peter had departed from the historical Peter theologically. The apostle's understanding of fulfilling the law is replaced by the Pauline concept of freedom from the law.[46] Among other complaints it is unclear why the letter would not have been, then, attributed to Paul rather than Peter if it was so dependent on Pauline theology. We would further note that this argument assumes a disparity between the theologies of Peter and Paul, based largely on the confrontation recorded in Galatians 2:11–14, but there is insufficient scriptural basis for such a divide.[47]

So what about the supposed parallels? Bigg examined them in depth and found that the parallels to Ephesians are not strong, that the resemblances to Romans are superficial, and that the same is true regarding the rest of Paul's Letters.[48] In fact, the work in which he finds the most intriguing parallels are to the book of James.[49] Thus, one finds that the nature of the so-called parallels is not of the sort that demands a literary dependence on Paul.[50]

Most are moving away from such a cut-and-paste approach to the letter. They rightly object to maximizing the parallels to Paul and minimizing parallels to Jesus and James.[51] Thus, the idea that the writer was a follower of Paul is waning among scholars, often being replaced with the assumption of a "Petrine school" in Rome[52] or a synthesizer of early Christian tradition.[53]

---

[44] So N. Brox, *Der Erste Petrusbrief*, EKKNT XXI (Neukirchen-Vluyn, Germany: Neukirchener, 1979), 43–51.

[45] Kümmel, *Introduction*, 423. He values it so much that it is his second "proof" listed.

[46] Ibid.

[47] See, e.g., the critique of M. Bockmuehl (*Seeing the Word: Refocusing New Testament Study, Studies in Theological Interpretation* [Grand Rapids, MI: Baker, 2006], 135): "Even at the more basic level of the historical Peter and Paul, it is possible to show that the evidence supports a rather more nuanced and symbiotic view than the received bipolar paradigm would have us believe: ironically, it shows that paradigm to be insufficiently historical and insufficiently critical."

[48] Bigg, *1 Peter*, 15–23.

[49] The most striking being "love covers a multitude of sins" (Jas 5:20 and 1 Pet 4:8; ibid., 23). This is a quote from Prov 10:20; however, it does not represent the LXX reading but an independent translation or paraphrase. That the quotes are identical is therefore striking. See also the comments of Horrell (*Becoming Christian*, 12–26).

[50] See J. Herzer, *Petrus oder Paulus? Studien über das Verhältnis des ersten Petrusbriefes zur paulinischen Tradition*, WUNT 103 (Tübingen, Germany: Mohr, 1998).

[51] Horrell, *Becoming Christian*, 12–26.

[52] E.g., J. H. Elliott, *A Home for the Homeless* (Philadelphia, PA: Fortress, 1988), 270–80.

[53] Horrell, *Becoming Christian*, 7–44. In some respects this is the merging of the opinions of F. C. Baur and W. Bauer. The former suggested 1 Peter as the result of synthesizing competing streams of tradition; the latter (in modern versions)

Yet even these opinions are unnecessary conclusions. Nothing precludes the apostle Peter from having read (or heard) and appreciated the book of James, or Paul's Letters for that matter.[54] Any continuity can best be explained by a common Christian tradition and perhaps Peter's familiarity with early Christian epistolary literature.[55]

Last in the line of complaints, some doubt Peter's authorship of 1 Peter on account of the addressees of the letter. The assumption is that the remote areas of Asia Minor could not have been evangelized and a well-defined ecclesiological structure put in place (see 5:1) until decades after Peter and Paul.[56] This is an assumption based on a "what must have been" logic rather than on direct evidence. Christianity was commonly recognized as a thorn in the flesh of the Roman Empire in Bithynia around the year 112, according to the letters of Pliny the Younger to Trajan. Pliny interviewed those who claimed to have been Christians, some "as many as 20 years" ago, which was about AD 92. Moreover, Eusebius notes the tradition that Peter ministered in the area (based on 1 Pet 1:1) but also that his brother Andrew was in Scythia nearby (just north of the Black Sea).[57]

K. Jobes has noted several factors that could explain the presence of a well-organized church in the remote areas of Asia Minor. In Acts 2, Pentecost pilgrims from Pontus, Cappadocia, and Asia were among those who heard Peter's sermon. Some may have been among the 3,000 saved who then migrated back to northern Asia Minor and began evangelizing (note that Aquila was a Jew from Pontus; cf. Acts 2:9). The edict of Claudius evicted the Jews from Rome due to disturbances at the instigation of one "Chrestus." Some Jewish Christians may have been forced to flee to the region. Jobes also conjectures that aggressive Roman colonization would have brought many Christians into the area.[58] Furthermore, both Acts and Paul's Letters indicate that aggressive evangelism in Asia Minor was carried out in Paul's lifetime. The expansion of Christianity into these areas more quickly than commonly assumed is entirely conceivable.[59]

---

identifies these streams as "proto-orthodox" rather than Jew vs. Gentile.

[54] The Tübingen theory that Peter and Paul were rivals should be viewed as obsolete. Against M. Goulder, *St. Peter vs. St. Paul: A Tale of Two Missions* (Louisville, KY: Westminster John Knox, 1994).

[55] See Jobes, *1 Peter*, 11–12; and Selwyn, *1 Peter*, 461–66. Even those denying Peter's authorship have abandoned this line of argument; see L. Goppelt, *A Commentary on 1 Peter*, trans. J. E. Alsup (Grand Rapids, MI: Eerdmans, 1993), 28–30; Achtemeier, *1 Peter*, 15–23; and Elliott, *1 Peter*, 20–39. First Peter's knowledge of Paul makes the reference to his letter collection in 2 Pet 3:16 all the more plausible. Moreover, it makes a stronger connection between the two missives, suggesting common authorship.

[56] E.g., Goppelt, *1 Peter*, 46; Brown, *Introduction to the New Testament*, 719–22; and F. Lapham, *Peter: The Myth, the Man and the Writings: A Study of Early Petrine Text and Tradition*, JSNTSup 239 (New York, NY: Sheffield Academic Press, 2003), 141–42.

[57] Eusebius, *Hist. eccl.* 3.1.1–2.

[58] Jobes, *1 Peter*, 27–32.

[59] At the riot in Ephesus, Demetrius the silversmith noted that Paul's mission had been successful "not only in Ephesus, but in almost the whole province of Asia" (Acts 19:26). Evidence of missionary activity beyond Paul can be found in Colossians: though the people had not seen Paul at all (Col 2:1), Luke could confidently proclaim that all of Asia "heard the word of the Lord" (Acts 19:10).

Finally, rather than simply responding to complaints, it should be noted that a few matters positively point to Peter as the author. The self-portrait of the writer is reserved and not characteristic of a pseudepigrapher.[60] The author drew an apparent contrast with his readers, noting that they have not seen Christ, likely implying that he had (1:8). He also claimed to be a "witness of the sufferings of Christ" (5:1). Again, one notes the uncharacteristic reserve with which the author staked this claim to firsthand testimony. It would fit with the apostle but not one employing his name.

Because there is no undisputed sample of Peter's speech and writing, little linguistic evidence exists to analyze the letter(s). But some internal evidence does point to the apostle Peter as the author of 1 Peter. For example, R. Gundry believes there is an almost unconscious "Petrine pattern" in the letter. In 1958, Selwyn listed thirty allusions to the words of Jesus in 1 Peter, calling these the *verba Christi* ("words of Christ").[61] Gundry examined these parallels and found that they were more organic, rather than quotes, and showing no real literary dependence. Many of them occur in contexts in the Gospels associated with Peter.[62] Moreover, there are clear affinities to the speeches of Peter in Acts.[63] In addition, Acts 5:29–30 ("Peter and the other apostles"), Acts 10:39 ("Peter"), and 1 Peter 2:24 employ the phrase "on the tree" (Gk. *epi xylou*) to describe the cross of Christ—as Paul did obliquely in Galatians 3:13, citing Deuteronomy 21:23.

The book of 1 Peter includes no indication of late origins. It contains no references to Gnosticism (flowering only in the second century), no depreciation of the state, no glowing honors given to Peter, "and none of the developed apparatus of pseudonymity."[64] Thus, there are no substantial grounds to resort to pseudepigraphy. Conversely, what is known of Peter does fit the letter, and the confidence of the early church—especially noteworthy since there were hosts of pseudepigraphical writings that claimed Peter as the author—should be given full weight.[65] Thus Robinson rightly affirmed Peter's authorship of 1 Peter, noting that "whatever the intention, [pseudepigraphy] in this case [is] a particularly motiveless exercise which in fact (unlike II Peter) deceived everyone until the 19th century."[66]

---

[60] See esp. T. L. Wilder, *Pseudonymity, the New Testament, and Deception*; Guthrie, "Appendix C: Epistolary Pseudepigraphy," in *New Testament Introduction*, 1,011–28.

[61] Selwyn (*1 Peter*, 23–24) attributed these affinities to the author's knowledge of Q.

[62] R. Gundry, "*Verba Christi* in 1 Peter: Their Implications Concerning the Authorship of 1 Peter and the Authenticity of the Gospel Tradition," *NTS* 13 (1966–67): 336–50; cf. idem, "Further *Verba* on *Verba Christi* in First Peter," *Bib* 55 (1974): 211–32.

[63] E.g., Acts 2:23 and 1 Pet 1:2, 20; 2:4–5; Acts 2:33 and 1 Pet 1:12; 3:22; 4:1; Acts 2:36 and 1 Pet 1:11; 3:14; 4:12; Acts 2:38 and 1 Pet 3:22; and Acts 10:42 and 1 Pet 4:2.

[64] Marshall, *1 Peter*, 24.

[65] J. A. T. Robinson, *Redating the New Testament* (Philadelphia, PA: Westminster, 1976), 164; cf. Marshall (no foe of pseudepigraphy), who rightly states of 1 Peter, "If ever there was a weak case for pseudonymity, surely it is in respect to this letter" (*1 Peter*, 21).

[66] Robinson, *Redating*, 164.

Date

The date of the letter and its authorship are tightly intertwined. Scholars who reject Peter's authorship usually posit a date in the reign of Domitian (AD 81–96).[67] As shown above, the arguments for a late date are neither necessary nor convincing. Since the letter was composed during Peter's lifetime, the question arises concerning its exact date of composition.

There are some indications of an early date regardless of authorship. Many point to a primitive theological expression that includes the Suffering Servant of Isaiah 53, the expectation of Jesus's imminent return, and undeveloped Trinitarian formulation.[68] Any assessment of date should also include the reference to elders at 1 Peter 5:1 as the office of oversight in the church. It was demonstrated above that the mention of elders alone suggests an early date.

The best indicator as to the date of the letter, given Peter's authorship, is the reference to Rome at 1 Peter 5:13. Most agree that "Babylon" refers to Rome here. If so, Peter most likely was in Rome in the mid- to late 60s. The letter gives no hint that there is ongoing persecution, by the state or otherwise, in the environment of the author. This indicates a date prior to the persecution of Nero, which began in approximately AD 64. Most likely, 1 Peter was written slightly before then, around AD 62–63, when the harbingers of this persecution were already on the horizon.[69]

Provenance

First Peter specifically mentions "Babylon" in 5:13 as the place from which the letter was sent. Three options arise from this description. First, the location could be Mesopotamian Babylon. However, at this time the city was all but deserted.[70] Second, there was a Babylon in Egypt, but it was an insignificant military outpost, and there is no evidence of any Christian mission there until much later.[71] The third and best option is Rome. In this case the term is metaphorical, designating the center of Gentile power. Even most of those who do not hold to Peter's authorship and espouse a later date still consider Rome to be the geographical source of 1 Peter.[72]

---

[67] State-sponsored persecution of Christians is only attested for the reigns of Nero, Domitian, and Trajan. Robinson (*Redating*, 155–56) notes that Domitian was chosen as a compromise for those who can tolerate neither Nero nor Trajan. He humorously goes on to say that Revelation, Hebrews, *1 Clement*, *Barnabas*, the *Didache*, Ephesians, Luke, Acts, Matthew, John, the Johannine Letters, James, Jude, and the Pastorals have all been conveniently relegated by some to the reign of Domitian—not because so much is known about it but because we know so little. He states, "Hence its attractiveness as a depository: it can accommodate almost anything."

[68] See Robinson (ibid., 162–63), who also names Kelly, *Epistles of Peter and of Jude*, 30; F. L. Cross, *I Peter: A Paschal Liturgy* (London, England: A. R. Mowbray, 1954), 43–44; and C. F. D. Moule, "The Nature and Purpose of I Peter," *NTS* 3 (1956–57): 11. Although, see the cautions under "Theology" in chapter 17.

[69] For a more detailed discussion of persecution in 1 Peter, see Schreiner, *1, 2 Peter and Jude*, 28–31.

[70] See Achtemeier, *1 Peter*, 353. Strabo (ca. AD 19) noted that the city "is so deserted that one would not hesitate to say . . . 'the Great City is a great desert'" (*Geog.* 16.1.5).

[71] Grudem, *1 Peter*, 33.

[72] See J. H. Elliott, "Peter, First Epistle of," *ABD* 5:277.

Destination

First Peter 1:1 identifies where the recipients of the letter lived: northern Asia Minor (modern Turkey). Peter listed a series of Roman provinces in an unusual order, "to those chosen, living as exiles dispersed abroad in Pontus, Galatia, Cappadocia, Asia, and Bithynia" (1:1). This would include a crescent-shaped region of northern Asia Minor.[73]

The more difficult question is, Who were the recipients of the letter? Earlier commentators claimed that the original readers were Jewish converts in these towns.[74] This is primarily based on taking literally Peter's opening address, "To those chosen, living as exiles dispersed abroad" (1:1). In this sense both "living as exiles" and "dispersed abroad" (Gk. *parepidēmos* and *diaspora*) would indicate Jewish believers, as would the term "strangers" (Gk. *paroikos*) in 2:11 (see also *paroikia*, "time living as strangers," in 1:17). A few today still advocate a Jewish audience for 1 Peter.[75]

Most modern interpreters understand these terms to be metaphorical in light of 1:18: "For you know that you were redeemed from your empty way of life inherited from the fathers"; and 4:3, "For there has already been enough time spent in doing what the Gentiles choose to do: carrying on in unrestrained behavior, evil desires, drunkenness, orgies, carousing, and lawless idolatry." It is improbable that Peter would have referred to Judaism in this way. More likely he was referring to Gentiles as part of the newly constituted people of God in continuity with the old covenant community.[76]

Occasion

Persecution is a common theme in 1 Peter and serves as the occasion for the writing of this letter. While Peter may have been anticipating the persecution of Nero in Rome, his readers were most likely already experiencing private persecution or some localized state persecution. They suffered from various trials (1:6); endured grief from suffering unjustly (2:19); were accused and their Christian life denounced (3:16); were slandered (4:4); suffered fiery ordeals (4:12); shared in the sufferings of the Messiah (4:13); were ridiculed for the name of Christ (4:14); and suffered according to God's will (4:19). But they were not (yet) being executed as criminals.[77]

---

[73] Brown, *Introduction to the New Testament*, 708.

[74] So Augustine, Jerome, and Calvin. This is a plausible understanding, given that Antiochus III in the third century BC sent 2,000 Jews from Babylon to colonize Lydia and Phrygia (Jobes, *1 Peter*, 23).

[75] See, e.g., J. D. G. Dunn, *Beginning from Jerusalem: Christianity in the Making*, vol. 2 (Grand Rapids, MI: Eerdmans, 2009), 1,158–60.

[76] See the solid case for a largely Gentile readership in P. H. Davids, *A Theology of James, Peter, and Jude: Living in the Light of the Coming King*, BTNT (Grand Rapids, MI: Zondervan, 2014), 102–6.

[77] Davids (ibid., 112–20) provides excellent social-historical background to explain why Christians would have been persecuted in a Greco-Roman context.

Purpose

Persecution was not an abstract notion for the believers in Asia Minor; they were undergoing fierce repercussions for their faith. Peter encouraged Christians to endure in the face of difficult times. He did this by promoting a biblical worldview among the believers. They needed to understand who (or whose) they were and then face their situation from this vantage point. The essence of this exhortation is in 1:5–6: "[You] are being guarded by God's power through faith for a salvation that is ready to be revealed in the last time. You rejoice in this, even though now for a short time, if necessary, you experience grief in various trials."

LITERATURE

Literary Plan

Remarkably, there is a rather large consensus regarding the structure of 1 Peter in the recent scholarly literature.[78] The literary plan of 1 Peter is marked by the presence of the direct address "dear friends" (Gk. *agapētoi*), in 2:11 and 4:12, which divides the letter into three parts: 1:1–2:10; 2:11–4:11; and 4:12–5:14; 1:1–2 constitutes the opening greeting and 5:12–14 the final greeting and benediction. The major topic of the first part is believers' identity as God's chosen people due to their salvation through Christ and their rebirth by the Holy Spirit. The address in 2:11 shifts the focus from believers' identity to their consequent responsibility as "strangers and exiles" in a world hostile to Christ, which involves proper submission to authorities in the spheres of government, the workplace, and the home. The address in 4:12 (following a doxology in 4:11) introduces an appeal to submission in yet another context, the church.

Peter addresses "exiles" in parts of the Diaspora (1:1–2). The letter opens with a thanksgiving to God for his spiritual blessings bestowed on the recipients (1:3–12), followed by an exhortation to holy conduct (note esp. the quote of Lev 11:44–45; 19:2; 20:7 in 1:16). In keeping with this continuity with OT Israel, Peter elaborates on the similarity of identity between Israel and the recipients, many of whom would have been Gentile believers, in a series of OT references applied to the readers (2:4–10).

A new section begins in 2:11 with a renewed address to the readers as "exiles and strangers" (see 1:1, 17). In the form of a modified "house table" or "household code," Peter urges his readers to engage in proper submission to those in positions of authority, whether in government (2:13–17), the workplace (2:18–25), or the home (3:1–7). The remainder of this section contains exhortations to righteous suffering in the context of persecution in light of the fact that "the end of all things is near" (4:7; see 3:8–4:11).

---

[78] See the virtually identical outlines in Michaels, *1 Peter*, xxxiv–xxxvii; Jobes, *1 Peter*, vii, 56–57; Davids, *First Epistle of Peter*, 28–29; and Schreiner, *1, 2 Peter, Jude*, 46–48. Grudem (*1 Peter*, 44–46) sees no major break in 4:12 and divides the letter into two major units, 1:1–2:10 and 2:11–5:14. Marshall (*1 Peter*, 28) has a major break at 3:13 rather than 4:12. For a discussion and critique of alternative proposals, see Schreiner, *1, 2 Peter, Jude*, 47–48. For further discussion, see Dubis, "Research on 1 Peter," 208–9.

Another new section begins in 4:12 with a similar address as in 2:11. Peter's readers must not be surprised "when the fiery ordeal comes among you to test you." Also in this section are further instructions on proper submission to those in authority, in the present case to the elders of the church (5:1–7), and on resisting the Devil. Peter includes a doxology (5:8–11) and a brief conclusion (5:12–14). The latter acknowledges the help of Silvanus in writing (or delivering) the letter; refers to "Babylon" (i.e., Rome) as the provenance of the letter, and to (John) Mark who was with Peter at this time; and contains a final greeting.

OUTLINE

I. OPENING (1:1–2)

II. THE STATUS OF THE PEOPLE OF GOD (1:3–2:10)
- A. Their Precious Standing (1:3–12)
- B. The Ethics of Their New Life (1:13–25)
- C. The Growth of Their New Life (2:1–10)

III. THE RESPONSIBILITIES OF THE PEOPLE OF GOD (2:11–4:11)
- A. The Conduct of the People of God (2:11–3:12)
    1. Temporary Residents (2:11–12)
    2. Submission to Unbelieving Government (2:13–17)
    3. Submission to Unbelieving Masters and Christ's Example (2:18–25)
    4. Submission to Unbelieving Husbands (3:1–7)
    5. Suffering for Doing What Is Right (3:8–12)
- B. The Promise of Vindication (3:13–4:6)
    1. The Witness of Believers (3:13–17)
    2. The Witness of Christ (3:18–22)
    3. Call to Christlike Suffering (4:1–6)
- C. The Nearness of the End (4:7–11)

IV. THE RESPONSIBILITY OF THE CHURCH AND THE ELDERS (4:12–5:11)
- A. Response to the Fiery Ordeal (4:12–19)
- B. Relationships in the Church (5:1–11)
    1. Submission to Elders (5:1–7)
    2. Resisting the Devil (5:8–9)
    3. Closing Benediction (5:10–11)

V. CONCLUSION (5:12–14)

Something to Think About: Pilgrim's Progress

While in prison, John Bunyan, an English Baptist, wrote one of the most-loved Christian books of all time: Pilgrim's Progress, *which appeared in two parts in 1678 and 1684. Bunyan's allegorical novel, translated into numerous languages, traces the journey of a man named "Pilgrim," changed to "Christian" after his conversion, from the "City of Destruction" to the "Celestial City." Yet the idea of Christians being pilgrims in this world is certainly not original with Bunyan. In fact, it is already found in the pages of the NT, especially in Hebrews and 1 Peter.*

Peter addresses his letter specifically to believers as "exiles" in this world (1:1). He called on his readers to conduct themselves in reverence "during your time living as strangers" (1:17) and urged them "as strangers and exiles to abstain from sinful desires that wage war against" them (2:11). This "resident alien" motif thus lies at the foundation of how Peter conceived of believers' identity in this life: this world is not their home; rather, they are pilgrims, strangers, and resident aliens.

As one who was a resident alien in the United States for many years before becoming an American citizen, this writer can certainly appreciate Peter's potent metaphor. As a resident alien, I lacked certain basic rights and privileges that regular citizens take for granted, such as the ability to vote. I was a temporary resident who could not establish deep roots. In God's providence this prepared me to regard my Christian existence in this world as temporary also: for as Scripture tells us, heaven is our home because that is where God lives.

Does our lifestyle reflect this reality? In the Sermon on the Mount, Jesus warned us against amassing treasures on earth. Materialism is rampant in our culture, especially among many young people. It often appears that their lives depend on whether they are able to get the latest gadget upon its release. To make matters worse, this materialism has crept from the general culture into the church. It is time believers remembered that, according to God's Word, they are mere pilgrims and resident aliens in this world.

UNIT-BY-UNIT DISCUSSION

I. Opening (1:1–2)

Peter identifies himself as "an apostle of Jesus Christ," and he addresses the recipients of the letter as "chosen, living as exiles dispersed abroad" in different provinces (1:1) and as "chosen according to the foreknowledge of God the Father, through the sanctifying work of the Spirit to be obedient and to be sprinkled with the blood of Jesus Christ" (1:2). Thus, the readers' identity is clarified both with regard to the world and to God.

II. The Status of the People of God (1:3–2:10)

The first major section of the letter's body lays the foundation for the remainder of the letter by addressing the identity of believers as the result of their salvation in Christ and their rebirth by the Holy Spirit.

A. Their Precious Standing (1:3–12) Peter wants believers to appreciate fully their standing before God (1:3–12). They had joy because their salvation was protected, even though they endured trials (1:3–6). Peter notes that this was the proof of genuine faith, which was more precious even than gold (1:7–9). He concludes the section by explaining that this salvation put his readers in a unique position that the prophets had predicted and had searched diligently to understand (1:10–12). Peter thus underscores the continuity of these NT believers with the people of God in the OT.

B. The Ethics of Their New Life (1:13–25) Peter highlights the appropriate response to believers' new identity in Christ (1:13–25). First, they are to be holy because God is holy, setting their hope on Christ's return (1:13–16). Second, they are to conduct themselves in reverence to God (1:17) because they had been redeemed from their previous empty way of life at a great price (1:17–21). Finally, they are to love one another earnestly, having joined the family of God through the new birth, knowing that their human existence was transitory (1:22–25; see Isa 40:6–8).

C. The Growth of Their New Life (2:1–10) Similar to Paul's terminology of "putting off" and "putting on" (e.g., Col 3:8), Peter enjoins believers, after putting aside all wickedness,[79] to desire eagerly the "pure milk" of the Word of God that will help them grow in their new life of faith (2:1–3; see Ps 34:8). While elsewhere in the NT believers' need of "milk" is used as an illustration of their immaturity and need for growth in Christ (1 Cor 3:1–3; Heb 5:12–14), in the present passage babies' craving for milk furnishes a positive example of believers' hunger and thirst for the nourishing qualities of God's Word and as a necessary precondition for "tasting" his goodness (see the quotation of Ps 34:8 in 1 Pet 2:3).

Peter develops this in terms of the corporate life of the church (2:4–10). In doing so, he strung together a series of "stone *testimonia*," applying various OT passages to Jesus Christ that include a reference to a "stone."[80] This Christ was the stone that the builders rejected but that had now become the cornerstone in God's new "temple," the community of believers (2:6; see Isa 28:16; cf. further below). While he turned out to be a stumbling stone for many (2:7–8; see Ps 118:22; Isa 8:14), believers were an elect, holy, and priestly nation, God's possession, called to offer spiritual sacrifices to God (2:9–10; see Exod 19:5–6; Deut 4:20; 7:6; Isa 43:21).

Moreover, one important aspect of these "stone" references is Peter's reapplication of "temple" imagery, presenting Christ as the foundation of the new spiritual temple and believers as "living stones" (1 Pet 2:5) in that temple. This is accomplished by (1) the phrase

---

[79] The phrase rendered as a command in 2:1, "rid yourselves," actually denotes the prerequisite action to the main command found in 2:2, "desire." Specifically enumerated are those sins that would destroy fellowship with other believers—the antithesis to the previous imperative (see Jobes, *1 Peter*, 131).

[80] See D. A. Carson, "1 Peter," in *Commentary on the New Testament Use of the Old Testament*, ed. G. K. Beale and D. A. Carson (Grand Rapids, MI: Baker, 2007), 1,023–33; and N. Hillyer, "'Rock-Stone Imagery in 1 Peter," *TynBul* 22 (1971): 58–81. The word "stone" *(lithos)* occurs in 2:4–8. Peter here engaged in a rabbinic practice known as "pearl-stringing," connecting a series of references on a similar topic (also known as *gezerah shawah*). Characteristically, Peter first paraphrased a given reference and then quoted it.

"as you come to him" in 2:4 (see Ps 34:5, LXX), which is used in the LXX with reference to the Israelites "drawing near" to the OT sanctuary (e.g., Exod 12:48; 16:9; Lev 9:7–8; 10:4–5); (2) the use of "house" (Gk. *oikos*) in 2:5 (e.g., 1 Kgs 5:5; Isa 56:7; see Matt 12:4; 21:13; Mark 2:26; Luke 11:51; John 2:16); and (3) the references to "priesthood" and "sacrifices" in 2:5, all of which hark back to OT terminology regarding the temple.[81]

Table 18.1: Stone *Testimonia* in 1 Peter 2:6–8

1 Peter	OT Passage	Stone *Testimonium*	Other NT Passages
2:6	Isa 28:16	Jesus the cornerstone	Rom 9:33; Eph 2:20
2:7	Ps 118:22	Jesus the cornerstone	Matt 21:42; Acts 4:11
2:8	Isa 8:14	Jesus the stumbling stone	Rom 9:33

III. The Responsibilities of the People of God (2:11–4:11)

In this section of the letter, there is an overriding concern for the witness of the people of God. First, they are to conduct their lives in a respectable and God-honoring fashion (2:11–3:12). As temporary residents (2:11–12), they must submit to the world's government (2:13–17) and submit to masters, even unreasonable ones, following Christ's example (2:18–25); wives should submit even to unbelieving husbands (3:1–7); and thus all must be willing to suffer for doing what is right (3:8–12). Second, believers are encouraged that vindication will come in due course (3:13–4:6). Peter discusses the witness of believers (3:13–17); provides a kind of excursus on the witness of Christ (3:18–22; see 2:21–25); and issues a call to Christlike suffering (4:1–6). Third, Peter impresses on the recipients the urgency of proper Christian conduct in the midst of suffering in light of the nearness of the end (4:7–11).

A. The Conduct of the People of God (2:11–3:12) First Peter 2:11–3:12 begins the so-called "household codes" within the book. The dual general command to these "strangers and exiles" is found in 2:11–12: "Abstain from sinful desires that wage war against the soul" and "Conduct yourselves honorably among the Gentiles." This is developed in the passages that follow in terms of their need to submit to "every human authority because of the Lord" (2:13). Christ followers are to submit to human authorities (2:13–15, reiterated in 2:16–17). After this Peter turns to specific groups of individuals, starting with household servants (2:18). These are called to follow Christ's example in suffering and to look to him as the shepherd and guardian of their souls (2:18–25).

Wives, even those of unbelieving spouses, are enjoined to submit to their husbands (3:1–6). They should adorn themselves with Christ, looking to Sarah as a prime example. Husbands must treat their wives "in an understanding way, as with a weaker partner" (v. 7) (Gk. *kata gnōsin hōs asthenesterō skeuei*; lit. "according to knowledge"). The adverbial participle that

[81] See the discussion in Jobes, *1 Peter*, 144–52.

follows unpacks the meaning of what it means to live in an understanding manner ("weaker partner"; see Col 3:19). It is to treat wives as "coheirs of the grace of life" in Christ so that their prayers will not be hindered (3:7).[82] The command to husbands balances Peter's previous commands to wives, making clear that the call to wives to submit to their husbands is in no way a license for the latter to treat their wives in a dominating, oppressive, or abusive manner.

This section concludes with a summary injunction to be like-minded and not to return evil for evil. Instead, in keeping with Jesus's own words, believers ought to bless those who persecute them (see Matt 5:10–11) and thus inherit a blessing, for "the face of the Lord is against those who do evil" (3:10–12; see Ps 34:12–16). This summary smoothly transitions to the next topic, the Lord's vindication of those who suffer for doing what is right.

B. The Promise of Vindication (3:13–4:6) The next section is introduced by a rhetorical question: "Who then will harm you if you are devoted to what is good?" (3:13). Peter was concerned that persecuted Christians be bold witnesses while maintaining full integrity, "so that when you are accused, those who disparage your good conduct in Christ will be put to shame" (3:16b). The example is none other than Christ himself, who suffered while being righteous and was vindicated by God in the end. After proclaiming his victory to the fallen angels (3:19–20), he was enthroned in heaven, vindicated in the life to come (3:22), as will be believers.[83] Thus, the Christian is to have the same resolve (4:1), knowing that God will call those who persecute him to account (4:5) and give life to believers in the spiritual realm (4:6).

C. The Nearness of the End (4:7–11) Peter desired to impress on his recipients the urgency of the call to righteous suffering in light of the nearness of the end, that is, Christ's return and God's judgment. He therefore concludes the unit with an appeal to personal holiness and sincere love for one another. Believers are to express their care for others by exercising hospitality and by using their gifts to speak or to serve in the church (4:10–11). The point is that Christ followers ought to glorify God through Jesus Christ in all things.

IV. The Responsibility of the Church and the Elders (4:12–5:11)

Peter concludes with instructions to those in the church, including church leaders. His final instruction to the church is to trust God while living for him, especially if one is suffering "as a Christian" (4:12–19; see esp. v. 16).[84] The elders of the church should lead humbly and by example (5:1–4), while the younger men should submit to the elders (5:5). All should exercise humility toward one another and humble themselves under God's mighty hand as they await God's vindication (5:6–7), and all should resist the Devil and bear up under suffering (5:8–11).

---

[82] For helpful discussions, see Schreiner, *1, 2 Peter, Jude*, 158–61; Michaels, *1 Peter*, 167–71.

[83] For a treatment of 3:18–22, see the discussion in Table 18.4.

[84] The term "Christian" (Gk. *Christianos*), while common today, is found only two other times in the NT. In Acts 11:26 Luke stated that the disciples were first called "Christians" in Antioch (ca. AD 43/44). In Acts 26:28 King Agrippa used the term "Christian" (ca. AD 58/59). Other names for Christ's followers at the time of the early church were followers of "the Way" (Acts 9:2; 24:14) or of "the name" (i.e., God/Christ; see Acts 2:21; 4:12; Rom 10:13; Phil 2:9–10; Heb 1:4; see 1 Pet 4:16).

A. Response to the Fiery Ordeal (4:12–19) In a solemn exhortation Peter warns believers to expect increased persecution.[85] As they share in the sufferings of the Messiah, their response should be joy, not despair, as they realize their suffering is evidence of salvation and divine blessing. At the same time, believers should be careful not to suffer because of their own stubborn sinfulness. Peter also strikes the ominous note that judgment begins with the house of God, arguing from the greater to the lesser that if judgment begins with the church and it barely escapes (citing Prov 11:31), what will the fate of sinners be? For this reason believers should entrust themselves to God, their "faithful Creator" (4:19).

B. Relationships in the Church (5:1–11) The final section breaks down into three parts: (1) instructions pertaining to elders (5:1–7); (2) a call to alertness regarding, and resistance against, the Devil (5:8–9); and (3) a final benediction to encourage those who suffer for Christ's sake (5:10–11). As an eyewitness of Christ's sufferings, Peter instructs his fellow elders to shepherd the flock.[86] He employed three sets of contrasts to describe how pastoral ministry should be done: (1) not out of compulsion but freely; (2) not for the money but eagerly; (3) not in an authoritarian manner but as an example (5:2–3). Those who lead in such a way will receive a great reward (5:4). Peter instructed the younger men to be subject to the elders (5:5) and all to be humble toward one another (5:6–7) and to resist the Devil (5:8–9). He closes in a benediction (as he began; see 1:2) that focuses on the sovereignty of God and his promise to strengthen and restore suffering believers (5:10–11).

V. Conclusion (5:12–14)

The conclusion of the letter identifies the likely letter carrier, Silvanus, and refers to the content of the missive as a brief exhortation to "take [a] stand in" the true grace of God (5:12). Peter also sent greetings from the church in Rome ("Babylon") and issued a wish for peace in the lives of those who are in Christ (5:14).

THEOLOGY

Theological Themes

Christian Suffering and the End Time A major emphasis and theological achievement of 1 Peter is the pervasive reference to believers' suffering in the context of the end time and in particular the second coming of Christ. From the outset Peter noted that believers are but "exiles" in this world (1:1; see further below). He reminded these suffering Christ followers of their "living hope through the resurrection of Jesus Christ from the

[85] The expression "fiery ordeal" (Gk. *pyrōsis*) in 4:12 refers most likely to the refinement and purification that persecution brings with regard to believers' character and confession of Christ (see 1:6–7; see Ps 66:10; Mal 3:1–4). For a helpful discussion and further bibliographic references, see Schreiner (*1, 2 Peter, Jude*, 219–20), citing D. E. Johnson, "Fire in God's House: Imagery from Malachi 3 in Peter's Theology of Suffering (1 Pet 4:12–19)," *JETS* 29 (1986): 287–89.

[86] Interestingly, in 1 Pet 5:1 Peter referred to himself as a "witness to the sufferings of Christ"; in 2 Pet 1:16, he called himself one of the "eyewitnesses of his [majesty]" at the transfiguration "when [Christ] received honor and glory from God the Father" (2 Pet 1:17). See further the discussion of the eyewitness theme under Theological Themes in 2 Peter below.

dead" (1:3; see 1:13, 20–21) and their "inheritance that is imperishable, undefiled, and unfading, kept in heaven" for them (1:4), noting that their full salvation "is ready to be revealed in the last time" (1:5; Gk. *en kairō eschatō*).

These references to eternal realities serve to put believers' suffering into its proper context. Christ's followers are to rejoice in their expectation of these soon-to-be-realized expectations, "though now for a short time" they may face the distress of various trials, which then refines their faith and makes it more valuable than gold, resulting "in praise, glory, and honor at the revelation of Jesus Christ" (1:6–7). This preamble provides an eschatological framework for believers in their suffering that, if heeded, will render their ordeal more bearable and instill in them joy that transcends their temporary afflictions and circumstances in the hostile world.

In all this Christ serves as the believer's example. After enduring great hostility from sinners as the Suffering Servant referred to in Isaiah 53 (2:21–25), Jesus now "has gone into heaven [and] is at the right hand of God, with angels, authorities, and powers subject to him" (3:22). On the basis of Christ's example, Peter issues this powerful exhortation to his readers: "Therefore, since Christ suffered in the flesh, arm yourselves also with the same understanding—because the one who suffers in the flesh is finished with sin—in order to live the remaining time in the flesh no longer for human desires, but for God's will" (4:1–2).

In light of the fact that "the end of all things is near" (4:7), believers are to be clearheaded and disciplined for the purpose of prayer. They are to love one another, to exercise hospitality, and to use their spiritual gifts for the glory of God in Christ (4:7–11). Peter identifies himself as a fellow "one who shares in the glory about to be revealed" (5:1) and spoke of his expectation of the day "when the chief Shepherd appears" and Peter and his readers "will receive the unfading crown of glory" (5:4). The closing benediction brings the book to a fitting end: "The God of all grace, who called you to his eternal glory in Christ, will himself restore, establish, strengthen, and support you after you have suffered a little while. To him be dominion forever. Amen" (5:10–11).

The Identity of Believers and Their Witness to the World The believers' identity and their witness to the world are thoroughly intertwined in Peter's presentation. His description of the status of believers is twofold: first, he describes NT believers in terms reminiscent of OT Israel, stressing the continuity of the NT church with the OT people of God; second, he emphasizes the fact that believers are pilgrims and temporary residents in this world. Regarding the first aspect, Peter writes, "You are a chosen race, a royal priesthood, a holy nation, a people for his possession, so that you may proclaim the praises of the one who called you out of darkness into his marvelous light" (2:9). All these designations have OT antecedents.

Table 18.2: The New People of God Described in Old Testament Terms (1 Pet 2:9–10)

1 Peter	OT Passage	Description of God's People
2:9	Isa 43:20; Deut 7:6; 10:15	A chosen race
2:9	Exod 19:6; 23:22; Isa 61:6	A royal priesthood
2:9	Exod 19:6; 23:22	A holy nation
2:9	Exod 19:5; 23:22; Deut 4:20; 7:6; Isa 43:21	A people for his possession
2:9	Isa 42:12; 43:21	To proclaim his praises
2:10	Hos 1:10; 2:23	Once not a people, now God's people

Peter addresses the letter to the "exiles dispersed abroad" (1:1) and called on them to conduct themselves in reverence "during your time living as strangers" (1:17), urging them "as strangers and exiles to abstain from sinful desires that wage war against the soul" (2:11).[87] Because they are the people of God who are called to be holy in serving a holy God and because their stay in this world is merely temporary, Christ followers ought to be good citizens of this world without compromising their purity or integrity.

Believers' status as the redeemed people of God brings with it certain expectations as to what it means to be the people of God. As obedient children, they are to be holy because God is holy (1:12–13). They are to conduct themselves honorably in the world, engaging in good works, which also involves submission to every human institution. They must be good citizens (2:13–17), fulfill their roles within the family (3:1–7), humbly love one another (3:8), and be willing to suffer for righteousness's sake (4:16), casting every care upon God (5:6–7) while resisting the Devil (5:9).

Table 18.3: Submission to Authorities in 1 Peter (Gk. *Hypotassō*)

1 Peter	Authority to Be in Submission to	Other OT and NT References
2:13	Government authorities (instituted by God)	Rom 13:1, 5; Titus 3:1
2:18	Authorities in workplace (even cruel ones)	Titus 2:9; see Eph 6:5–9
3:1	Husbands (even unbelieving ones)	Eph 5:21, 24; Col 3:18; Titus 2:5
3:5	Example: Sarah and holy women in OT	Gen 18:12
3:22	Spirit world subjected to Jesus Christ	1 Cor 15:27–28; Eph 1:22; Phil 3:21
5:5	Younger men [and others] subject to elders	1 Cor 16:16; see Heb 13:17

[87] The relevant Greek words are *parepidēmos* ("exiles" in 1:1; 2:11; see Heb 11:13; these are its only three NT occurrences) and *paroikos* ("strangers" or "exiles" in 2:11; see Acts 7:6, 29; Eph 2:19; these are its only four NT occurrences). Another related word not used in 1 Peter that occurs fourteen times in the NT is *xenos* ("foreigner"; e.g., Eph 2:12, 19; Heb 11:13).

Importantly, the reference to believers as "exiles" has a pronounced eschatological element. Their ultimate personal salvation is protected, "ready to be revealed in the last time" (1:5; see 1:20), and Jesus is the ultimate shepherd of their souls (2:25). Believers' salvation will be fully accomplished when Christ returns, and all of their hopes should be focused on him (1:13; see 4:7). Those who suffer should realize that God will call the perpetrators of unrighteousness and persecution to account at the end of time (4:5).

Regarding the believers' witness to the world, Peter was concerned that his readers not capitulate to societal pressure to conform to their mores and norms. At the same time, he did not want believers to antagonize civic authorities, including the emperor, unnecessarily. Instead, Christ followers were to silence those who slandered them by being good citizens. Peter explains it this way: "Honor everyone. Love the brothers and sisters. Fear God. Honor the emperor" (2:17). Hence, Peter did not want his readers to withdraw from the world but to engage it in an active witness. Peter tells Christians to "in your hearts regard Christ the Lord as holy, ready at any time to give a defense to anyone who asks you for a reason for the hope that is in you" (3:15).[88] This requires a particularly Christian understanding of God, believers' identity, the world, and the ultimate adversary, Satan.

God the Father and the Lord Jesus Christ Peter's theology also focused squarely on God the Father, who had accomplished his salvific purposes in and through the Lord Jesus Christ. Yet Peter's theology does not unfold abstractly; to the contrary it is thoroughly set in the context of believers' suffering and their need for pastoral comfort and encouragement. To this end Peter presents both God the Father and the Lord Jesus Christ in a variety of ways that were profoundly relevant for hard-pressed believers. The first indirect reference to God is to him as the one who chose believers from out of this world (1:1). Peter portrays God the Father as the sovereign God who not only saved but also protected, restored, and allowed suffering for his own purposes (1:5; see 5:12). God was also the one who would bring justice to the oppressed as the Judge of the living and the dead (4:5) and the one to whom believers were to entrust themselves as he is the faithful Creator (4:19). His hand is mighty; he exalts the humble while resisting the proud; and he cares for believers (5:6–7). Further, "the God of all grace, who called you to his eternal glory in Christ, will himself restore, establish,strengthen, and support you after you have suffered a little while" (5:10–11).

Peter portrays Christ as chosen by God before the foundation of the world (1:20) in order to redeem humans with his precious blood (1:18–19; see 1:2). He was the Suffering Servant of Isaiah, who not only had died for believers' sins but had set the example in the way he responded to suffering and persecution (2:21–25). In fact, Peter makes clear

---

[88] See F. Thielman, *Theology of the New Testament: A Canonical and Synthetic Approach* (Grand Rapids, MI: Zondervan, 2005), 571–72.

that Jesus fit the portrait painted by the prophet Isaiah in a thoroughgoing comment on Isaiah 53:

> He *did not commit sin, and no deceit was found in his mouth [Isa 53:9];* when he was insulted, he did not insult in return; when he suffered, he did not threaten but entrusted himself to the one who judges justly. He himself bore our sin in his body on the tree; so that, having died to sins, we might live for righteousness; by *his wounds you have been healed [Isa 53:5]*. For you *were like sheep going astray [Isa 53:6]*, but you have now returned to the Shepherd and Overseer of your souls (2:22–25, emphases added; see also 3:18).

Remarkably, in this passage Peter's primary focus is not that Jesus died *on* the cross for the sins of believers but *on the way* Jesus suffered, that is, as an example in suffering.[89] In his submission to the will of God in suffering, he provided a powerful pattern for believers who are enjoined by Peter to walk in Jesus's steps in this regard (2:21). This is a good example of how NT theology in general, and Peter's theology in particular, was not given in the abstract but was spoken into a specific context designed to be pastorally relevant for the recipients of a given piece of instruction.

Christ's Proclamation to the Spirits in Prison (1 Pet 3:19–22) Peter contributes to the theology of the NT a rather curious item, the so-called *descensus*—Christ's descent to "the prison" (3:18–22). This passage is unique in the NT; it is unclear what Peter's source was for this piece of information. The passage was a hot topic in antiquity, debate on it dating all the way to the second century.[90] Christians have held to four major views, with many additional variations, as to where Jesus went, when he went there, to whom he made proclamation, and so on (see the table below). The comments here will be limited to defending the most likely interpretation.

---

[89] The case following the preposition *epi* ("on") in 2:24, an accusative, suggests that Peter was not so much concerned with Jesus's bearing our sins *on* the cross (where one might have expected the dative case in the Greek), but the manner in which Jesus bore our sins *on the way to* the cross.

[90] See C. T. Pierce, *Spirits and the Proclamation of Christ*, WUNT 11/305 (Tübingen, Germany: Mohr Siebeck, 2011), 3–6. The earliest examples are Clement of Alexandria, *Stromateis* 6.6:38–53, *Adumbrationes on 1 Peter* 17:205; the so-called *Jeremiah Logion*, cited in Justin Martyr, *Dialogue with Trypho*, 72 (PG 6:645AB); Hippolytus, *Easter Homily*; and the *Gospel of Peter* 10:1–4.

Table 18.4: Major Interpretations of 1 Peter 3:18–22*

Name of the Interpretation	Interpretation of "Spirits"	Interpretation of "In the Spirit"	Purpose
1. Harrowing of Hell	Humans	Christ before the resurrection	Releasing OT believers
2. Sinful Antedeluvians	Humans	Christ before the resurrection	Giving a second chance to the wicked dead
3. Augustinian	Humans	The Holy Spirit in Noah's preaching	The wicked in Noah's day
4. Fallen Angels	Fallen angels	Christ after the resurrection	Announcing Christ's victory

* Adapted from Pierce, *Spirits and the Proclamation of Christ*, 3–20.

In order to explore the passage in its immediate context, two important observations should be made. First, it seems most likely that the sequence of events depicted in the passage follows a chronological order of presentation, that is, Peter moves from (1) Christ's crucifixion (v. 18) to his resurrection (v. 19) and to his ascension (v. 22; see further below). If so, the elaboration regarding the proclamation made to the spirits in prison in verses 19–21 falls in the interim between Christ's resurrection and ascension. This would settle the question as to the *time* at which Jesus went to make proclamation: it was subsequent to the resurrection but prior to the ascension.[91]

Second, what is Peter's primary purpose in including this passage in this particular letter? How is this relevant for his readers, and what is the fact's inclusion designed to achieve? Most likely, the answer is that as these believers faced ongoing suffering in their lives, Peter sought to encourage them that Jesus had already made proclamation of his victory over death, sin, and the Devil to the "spirits in prison." Satan was therefore a defeated foe, and his minions knew it because they had been told so by the risen Christ. If this was Peter's purpose, it was consistent with his effort in this letter to place Christian suffering in an eschatological perspective. Just as Jesus was vindicated by God, so believers would be vindicated if they persisted in Christlike suffering.

This still leaves several other questions. First, to whom and where did Jesus go? Most likely, the "spirits" were demons (angelic beings are the referent of "spirits" in the vast majority of instances in Scripture), but not just any demons. They were specifically those demons who were in prison (see 2 Pet 2:4: "cast them into hell"; Gk. *tartaroō*) because they had been

---

[91] Most interpretations place the announcement before the resurrection. This is possible by the nature of the phrase, "in which he went" that must modify "Spirit." However, that seems rather imposed on the text.

"disobedient . . . in the days of Noah" (1 Pet 3:20) prior to the flood.[92] The probable background here is Genesis 6:1–6, where it is said that prior to the flood the "sons of God" (most likely fallen angels) went and married women and had children with them (Gen 6:4). To procreate offspring with fallen angels was such an egregious human sin that it triggered the deluge, which would explain—at least to some extent—why these particular demons were the recipients of Jesus's proclamation of his victory subsequent to his resurrection.

Second, where were those demons? According to 1 Peter 3:19, they were "in prison"; that is, they were being held for divine judgment. Jude also states that "the angels who did not keep their own position but abandoned their proper dwelling, [God] has kept in eternal chains in deep darkness for the judgment on the great day" (v. 6). All of this is part of the NT's teaching that Jesus's victory on the cross had major ramifications not only on the human, but also on the angelic realm. Paul explains that when Christ died on the cross, God "disarmed the rulers and authorities and disgraced them publicly; he triumphed over them in him" (Col 2:15). The interpretation that emerges as the best contextual understanding is that Jesus, after the resurrection, went to those demons held in confinement who had procreated offspring with women in the days of Noah prior to the flood and proclaimed his triumph over death and the Devil to them.[93]

---

[92] This interpretation adds yet another connection to 2 Peter as well. Second Peter 2:4–5 also refers to Genesis 6, fallen angels in prison, and Noah.

[93] For a thorough articulation of this position, see Michaels, *1 Peter*, 205–13 and Davids, *Theology of James, Peter, and Jude*, 147–48. For a thorough exposition of the Augustinian view, see Grudem, *1 Peter*, 203–39. For a modification of the "harrowing of Hell" view, see M. F. Bird, *Evangelical Theology: A Biblical and Systematic Introduction* (Grand Rapids, MI: Zondervan, 2013), 317–24. For the "sinful antediluvian view," see C. E. B. Cranfield, "The Interpretation of 1 Peter III.19 and IV.6," *ExpT* 69 (1957/58): 369–72.

2 Peter

KEY FACTS

Author:	Simon Peter
Date:	ca. AD 65–66
Provenance:	Rome
Destination:	Christians in Northern Asia Minor
Occasion:	False teaching
Purpose:	To combat the false teaching
Theme:	The dangers of false teachers
Key Verses:	3:17–18

INTRODUCTION

WHILE 1 PETER HAS been somewhat rehabilitated in the academy, 2 Peter is not so fortunate. It is often said to be the worst attested book in the NT (i.e., least cited by the Fathers). While the assessment is probably true, it should be put in its proper perspective. Any such quantified list will have a "least member." It does not necessarily follow that the "least member" of the set is insignificant. For example, Hall of Famer Wes Unseld may have been the shortest center in NBA history, but at six feet and seven inches in height, he is still a tall man. Likewise, while 2 Peter is "least" among the giants, it is better attested by far than any rejected book.[94] As will be seen, the book is better cited than is often represented, and its value is self-evident.

Not everyone agrees with this assessment. In modern circles the book's theological contribution is often diminished. J. D. G. Dunn has complained that 2 Peter contains "a somewhat hollow 'orthodoxy'" by a man "who has lost all hope of an immediate parousia."[95] The most extreme example may be E. Käsemann, who considered the letter to be of "a stiff and stereotyped character" and alleged that its parts had been assembled by "embarrassment rather than force," representing an early Catholicism in the second century.[96]

---

[94] Robinson, *Redating*, 188.

[95] J. D. G. Dunn, *Unity and Diversity in the New Testament: An Inquiry into the Character of Earliest Christianity*, 3rd ed. (London, UK: SCM Press, 2006), 382–83.

[96] E. Käsemann, "An Apologia for Primitive Christian Eschatology," in *Essays on New Testament Themes*, SBT 41 (London, England: SCM, 1964), 191, 194.

L. T. Johnson points out that the letters (including Jude) are "marginalized in the NT canon, disliked when not disowned."[97]

However, much of this low esteem for 2 Peter comes from a misapprehension of the style of the letter and from the assumption of a late and pseudonymous origin, according to which the book was written by someone other than Peter and merely attributed to him.[98] Understood properly, however, the contents of 2 Peter indicate that the book is worthy of the canonical status it achieved by the force of its arguments, in spite of some early doubts regarding its authenticity.

HISTORY

Author

Today 2 Peter is widely believed to be pseudonymous. R. Brown states, "Indeed, the pseudonymity of II Pet is more certain than that of any other NT work."[99] Even many of those who believe Peter wrote 1 Peter have difficulty with 2 Peter.[100] Unlike in the case of 1 Peter, this opinion is not entirely a recent phenomenon. The difficulties some of the ancients had with the book are noted by those like Eusebius.[101] However, no record of a categorical denial of the authenticity of 2 Peter exists in the early church.[102] Even Eusebius's

---

[97] Johnson, *The Writings of the New Testament*, 437. In this environment investigating a theology of the historical Peter is said to be an impossible exercise. Helyer notes the comments of A. C. Myers (*The Eerdmans Bible Dictionary* [Grand Rapids, MI: Eerdmans, 1987], 818): "A 'theology of Peter' cannot be reconstructed" (L. R. Helyer, *The Life and Witness of Peter* [Downers Grove, IL: InterVarsity, 2012], 14). Lately scholarship is attempting to address the issue. Note that both M. Bockmuehl, *Simon Peter in Scripture and Memory*, and M. Hengel, *St. Peter*, have addressed the question of the historical Peter. Helyer's book, *The Life and Witness of Peter*, has addressed the issue from the viewpoint of the authenticity of 1 and 2 Peter with a much more substantial work.

[98] On the phenomenon of pseudonymity, see T. L. Wilder, *Pseudonymity, the New Testament, and Deception: An Inquiry into Intention and Reception* (Lanham, MD: University Press of America, 2004; rev. ed. forthcoming). The presence of pseudonymous letters in the NT was advocated by R. Bauckham, "Pseudo-Apostolic Letters," *JBL* 107 (1988): 469–94; K. Aland, "The Problem of Anonymity and Pseudonymity in the Christian Literature of the First Two Centuries," *JTS* 12 (1961): 39–49; D. G. Meade, *Pseudonymity and Canon: An Investigation into the Relationship of Authorship and Authority in Jewish and Earliest Christian Tradition* (Grand Rapids, MI: Eerdmans, 1987). In favor of authenticity are D. A. Carson and D. J. Moo, *An Introduction to the New Testament*, 2nd ed. (Grand Rapids, MI: Zondervan, 2005), 337–50; Guthrie, *New Testament Introduction*, 607–49; and E. E. Ellis, "Pseudonymity and Canonicity of New Testament Documents," in *Worship, Theology and Ministry in the Early Church*, ed. M. J. Wilkins and T. Paige, JSNTSup 87 (Sheffield, UK: Sheffield Academic, 1992), 212–24. The notion that forgery was simply an accepted practice in antiquity has been well challenged by B. Ehrman, *Forgery and Counterforgery: The Use of Literary Deceit in Early Christian Polemics* (Oxford, UK: Oxford University Press, 2012). His further argument that forgery exists in the NT is not endorsed here.

[99] Brown, *Introduction to the New Testament*, 767. Similarly, Ehrman, *Forgery and Counterforgery*, 222–29, who lodges one of the most recent cases against authenticity; see also L. R. Donelson, "Gathering Apostolic Voices: Who Wrote 1 and 2 Peter and Jude?," in *Reading 1–2 Peter and Jude: A Resource for Students*, ed. E. F. Mason and T. W. Martin (Atlanta, GA: Society of Biblical Literature, 2014), 18–21.

[100] E.g., Kelly, *Epistles of Peter and of Jude*, 33, 236.

[101] *Eccl. Hist.* 3.3.1. Eusebius places it (with all the General Epistles except 1 Peter and 1 John) among the "disputed books" (with "rejected" being the ones that lack universal acceptance [*Eccl. Hist.* 3.25.3]).

[102] Eusebius says of 2 Peter, "The so-called Second epistle [of Peter] we have not regarded as canonical, yet many have thought it useful and have studied it with the other Scriptures." (Maier, *Eusebius' Church History*, 93 [3.3]). Eusebius places it in another category entirely than, e.g., the Apocalypse of Peter that is specifically stated as rejected.

doubts are repeatedly nuanced. In modern times the letter is widely judged inauthentic for at least three reasons: (1) the external evidence for Petrine authorship is slim; (2) stylistically, the letter is different from 1 Peter; and (3) alleged historical and doctrinal problems. Each of these will be examined in turn.

External Evidence Works in antiquity *stating* Peter's authorship of the letter are rather late. Origen's comments (ca. AD 185–254) are the earliest extant references claiming Peter's authorship of the second NT book bearing his name. Although Origen wrote late, he was not hesitant to attribute 2 Peter to the apostle Peter, implying the letter's antiquity, and was confident enough to cite it without comment.[103] Eusebius (ca. AD 260–340) included the letter in his list of disputed (but not spurious) books and made clear that the majority of churches in his day accepted the book.[104] Jerome (ca. AD 345–420) both affirmed Peter's authorship and noted some contemporaneous doubts, stating that Peter "wrote two epistles which are called Catholic, the second of which, on account of its differences from the first in style, is considered by many not to be by him."[105] After Jerome's era doubts regarding Peter's authorship of 2 Peter faded until the modern era.[106]

While citations *naming* Peter as the author of 2 Peter are rather late and there were some doubts regarding its authenticity, there is good evidence that 2 Peter was widely considered authoritative, which in many cases may imply belief in Peter's authorship. The Epistle of Barnabas (ca. AD 135?) made allusions to 2 Peter 3:8. Clement of Alexandria (ca. AD 150–215) wrote a commentary on 2 Peter, and he alluded to 2 Peter 2:19 in a letter to Theodorus.[107] Strong echoes of 2 Peter can be found in Irenaeus (ca. AD 130–200)[108] and Justin Martyr (ca. AD 100–165). Moreover, *The Apocalypse of Peter* (ca. AD 110) may be dependent on 2 Peter, which would also suggest an early date for 2 Peter.[109] This pushes the date back into the first century, but how early?

In *1 Clement*, written by Clement of Rome about AD 96, a number of likely allusions and a conspicuous pattern of references indicate Clement was familiar with 2 Peter.[110] So allusions to 2 Peter already existed in the first century.

---

[103] See Origen, *Hom. Jes. Nav.* 7.1; *Hom. Num.* 6.676; though note *Comm. Jo.* 5.3.

[104] *Eccl. Hist.* 3.3.1.

[105] Jerome, *Vir. ill.* i.

[106] M. J. Kruger, "The Authenticity of 2 Peter," *JETS* 42 (1999): 651. It is often stated that the Syrian church did not receive the letter into its canon until the sixth century. This is based on the absence of the book in the Peshitta (ca. AD 411) and its subsequent reappearance in the Philoxenian Version (ca. AD 506). Kruger (ibid., 652), citing Warfield, notes that there is some speculation that the Syriac canons actually contained the book early on.

[107] Bauckham, *Jude, 2 Peter*, 276. Kruger ("Authenticity," 654) states, "Not only would someone of Clement's stature not be duped by a forgery that was only a few years old, but he would hardly write a commentary on a book that most of the church rejected as a recently composed imitation of Peter."

[108] E.g., Irenaeus, *Against Heresies* 3.1.1; 5.23.2.

[109] Bauckham, *Jude, 2 Peter*, 162. Bauckham states that this is "sufficient to rule out a late date for 2 Peter" (ibid.).

[110] Kruger ("Authenticity," 655–56), who cites *1 Clem.* 23.3/2 Pet 3:4 as a strong allusion on account of a common pattern of reference in the context. Cf. the following affinities: false teachers (*1 Clem.* 21.5/2 Pet 2:1); future doubts (*1 Clem.* 23/2 Pet 3:4); and the nearness of Christ's return (*1 Clem.* 23.5/2 Pet 3:10). Moreover, both writers used the unusual phrase "the magnificent glory" in reference to God (*1 Clem.* 9.2/2 Pet 1:17), and Christianity is described by both as "the way of

Thus, the external evidence points to an early document, widely believed to be from Peter.[111] But in the period from the second to the fourth centuries, many had doubts about the authenticity of 2 Peter. These doubts do not seem to have come from a work that suddenly appeared on the scene but from the stylistic differences it displayed when compared with the already accepted 1 Peter. Green notes, "Although stylistic issues may not have been the sole reason for the concern about 2 Peter, this is the only explanation offered by any ancient author."[112] One can certainly understand the early concern, since there were a host of forgeries claiming to be from Peter circulating at the time.[113] That 2 Peter was recognized as canonical in the end surely means it stood out from the rest.[114] To sum up, rather than 2 Peter being virtually nonexistent, as is often suggested, we instead see authoritative use of the text that pushes it back to the first century. Thus, the external evidence is stronger than normally recognized (although not overly impressive) and in no way incompatible with Peter's authorship.[115]

Internal Evidence The stylistic differences between 1 Peter and 2 Peter not only constituted the major problem for the latter book in the early church; they remain problematic today. It is more than simply a different style. Second Peter is often said to be an inferior expression than 1 Peter. One writer went as far as to infamously call 2 Peter "baboon Greek."[116] So then, it was thought that it would be impossible for the writer of 1 Peter to regress so much. But these negative assessments do not take into account the different styles of Greek available at the time of writing. T. Callan showed that 2 Peter was written in a style of Greek that was acceptable to him and his readers, a form known as the Asian Style.[117] The Asian Style was an elevation of language that included thought, vocabulary,

---

truth" (*1 Clem.* 35.5/2 Pet 2:2). G. Green notes that the parallels between 2 Pet 3:4, *1 Clem.* 23.3, and *2 Clem.* 11.2 are strengthened in that "1 Clement identifies the written source as 'Scripture,' and 2 Clement calls it 'the prophetic word.' It is unlikely that some otherwise unknown source would be granted such a high place of honor during this period." Green also notes that "the way Clement tells the Lot story (*1 Clem.* 11), placing emphasis on God's ability to save Lot while delivering the unrighteous to punishment, is strikingly similar to 2 Pet. 2:7–10" (G. L. Green, *Jude and 2 Peter*, BECNT [Grand Rapids, MI: Baker, 2008], 141).

[111] See R. E. Picirilli, "Allusions to 2 Peter in the Apostolic Fathers," *JSNT* 33 (1988): 57–83. He concluded that many of the apostolic fathers knew, alluded to, and reflected upon 2 Peter. Picirilli also noted that these fathers did not typically mention Peter by name as the author but that they did identify Paul as the author of the letters commonly attributed to him.

[112] G. Green, *Jude and 2 Peter*, BECNT (Grand Rapids, MI: Baker, 2008), 143.

[113] There existed a *Gospel of Peter*; *Preaching of Peter*; *Acts of Peter*; *Acts of Peter and the Twelve Apostles*; *Epistle of Peter to Philip*; *Coptic Apocalypse of Peter*; and an *Apocalypse of Peter* and a document we call "the Akhmim fragment" that may or may not be the *Gospel of Peter*, does shift to the first-person narration that is presumably Peter.

[114] Kruger, "Authenticity," 662.

[115] After working through the evidence, G. Green (*Jude and 2 Peter*, 144) concludes similarly, "The evidence from the early centuries of the church in favor of the authenticity of 2 Peter is not robust, but neither is it sufficiently weak to preclude the possibility of Petrine authorship. The book was used early and widely and, although doubts did exist, the letter was never classified as spurious and eventually found its way into the major canons."

[116] E. A. Abbott, "On the Second Epistle of St. Peter. I. Had the Author Read Josephus? II. Had the Author Read St. Jude? III. Was the Author St. Peter?" *The Expositor* 2/3 (1882): 204–19.

[117] T. Callan ("The Style of the Second Letter of Peter," *Bib* 84 [2003]: 202–24) found stylistic affinities to the Grand Asian Style of Greek, particularly the bombastic style. Cf. D. F. Watson, *Invention, Arrangement, and Style: Rhetorical*

and syntax. The bombastic variety included long sentences, a marked rhythm, and unusual language usage. This is similar to the style found in 2 Peter.

While it was an appropriate style, it is certainly different from 1 Peter, which was written in a somewhat conventional form more familiar to modern students of Greek. It is possible that Peter, who stopped being a fisherman some thirty years prior to writing 2 Peter, could have learned the Asiatic literary style in order to communicate effectively with his readers.[118] However, it is more likely that the difference in style may be attributed to an amanuensis. Jerome noticed the different style, structure, and vocabulary. His explanation was that "we understand that he used different interpreters (secretaries) as necessary."[119] So then, the style could be a result of a secretary employed for 1 Peter, 2 Peter, or both. This was such a common occurrence that to dismiss it cavalierly is unwarranted.[120]

In spite of these stylistic differences, many subtle correspondences between 1 and 2 Peter in both thought and vocabulary are difficult to account for if a pseudepigrapher wrote the second letter. The salutation in 2 Peter 1:3, "May grace and peace be multiplied to you," is an exact parallel of 1 Peter 1:5. The rare word "goodness" is used with reference to God in both 1 Peter 2:9 and 2 Peter 1:5. The combination of the words "without spot or blemish" is found in the NT only in 1 Peter 1:19 and 2 Peter 3:14.[121]

Since it is unlikely that these subtle coincidences in language are the result of conscious imitation, these parallels provide significant evidence to suggest the authenticity and Petrine authorship of 2 Peter. As Kruger states, "To believe that an author pretending to be Peter would be able to weave such an intricate and subtle literary web is surely gratuitous."[122]

Finally, and rather notably, in 2 Peter 1:1 the author referred to himself as "Simeon Peter" (Gk. *Sumeōn Petros*). It is a spelling that occurs elsewhere in the NT in reference to Peter only in Acts 15:14 (there on the lips of James). Every other occurrence of Peter being called "Simon" in the NT is rendered *Simōn*.[123] This presents a two-pronged difficulty for those advocating forgery. First, it is an archaic, highly Aramaic form. It seems unlikely a Greek forger (employing the Asian Style) would use it. Second, it is not the form used in 1 Peter. It is, again, unlikely that a pseudepigrapher would make such a conscious distinction from the former epistle: they typically used authentic works as templates. Of all the different explanations, a self-reference by Peter is more likely.[124]

Criticism of Jude and 2 Peter, SBLDS 104 (Atlanta, GA: Scholars, 1988).

[118] See Carson and Moo, *Introduction to the New Testament*, 661. The Grand Asian Style would communicate to the readers that the topic was important and that the author was making an emotional appeal (see Callan, "Style," 224). This is an appropriate convention for the situation of 2 Peter since the author was nearing death in the presence of a false teaching.

[119] Jerome, *Epistula CXX* "to Hedibia."

[120] Davids (*Theology of James, Peter, and Jude*, 195) is noncommittal but notes this as a possibility.

[121] For additional examples, see M. Green, *2 Peter Reconsidered* (London, England: Tyndale, 1960), 12–13.

[122] Kruger, "Authenticity," 661.

[123] *Sumeōn* occurs seven times in the NT, only twice referencing Peter.

[124] So C. Blomberg, *From Pentecost to Patmos: An Introduction to Acts Through Revelation* (Nashville, TN: B&H, 2006), 474–75. Bauckham (*Jude, 2 Peter*, 160) argues that this reference merely indicates the author knew Peter personally, while

The third and final major argument against the Petrine authorship of 2 Peter involves several items that suggest the situation of the letter is later than Peter's lifetime. First, in the past some believed Gnosticism was the false doctrine addressed in 2 Peter. Therefore, since Gnosticism flowered in the second century long after Peter died, it negates the possibility that he wrote the letter.[125] But this opinion has been thoroughly refuted.[126] There is no evidence that the false teachers in 2 Peter held to the characteristic gnostic dualism or that their libertinism was based on such a dualism. There is also no evidence that their eschatological skepticism resulted from a gnostic emphasis on realized eschatology. Moreover, 2 Peter provides no hint of controversy regarding the bodily resurrection, which proved unacceptable to gnostics. Conversely, the question of the delay of Christ's return, a major topic in 2 Peter, was not at issue in second-century Gnosticism. Thus, nothing of what is known regarding the opponents of 2 Peter requires a date past the lifetime of Peter.

Second, along these same lines, the argument is often made that the reference to the letters of Paul in 3:15–16 acknowledges a recognized corpus of letters, which would not have been in existence by the time of Peter's death. But the phrase "in all his letters" (3:16) does not necessarily indicate a full corpus; it only has to refer to a few letters known to Peter at the time. To the contrary, the statement in 3:16–17 is inexplicable for a pseudepigrapher. Peter called Paul a "dear brother," which is perfectly natural for an apostle but is not the language of the second century. Moreover, it is inexplicable that a pseudepigrapher would ever attribute slowness to comprehend to Peter as 3:16 does: "There are some matters that are hard to understand" (3:16). Typically, when appropriating another's authority, it is not wise to denigrate his or her intelligence. Thus, the passage does not point to a time after Peter's death.[127]

Another item said to betray a late date is the reference at 3:4: "Ever since our ancestors fell asleep." It is said to be a reference to the death of the original disciples of Jesus.[128] But the reference is more likely to old covenant believers. In fact, the delay of the second

---

Robinson (*Redating*, 194) uses the reference to defend his thesis that Jude was Peter's amanuensis. P. Davids (*The Letters of 2 Peter and Jude*, PNTC [Grand Rapids, MI: Eerdmans, 2006], 160) minimizes it to the author knows what Peter was called in Jewish circles. Kelly thinks it is part of the forgery process, adding a Jewish flavor (Kelly, *Epistles of Peter and Jude*, 296). One major problem for all these is, if so, why is the forger inconsistent, using "Peter" rather than "Cephas" the Aramaic form (as John and Paul did—cf. John 1:42 and 1 Cor 1:12)? Many simply ignore the implications. See, e.g., Watson and Callan, *First and Second Peter*, 148. The lack of consensus points to the fact that the usage and deviation from 1 Peter is rather odd, given a pseudepigraphic origin, but completely understandable given an amanuensis.

[125] E.g., Kümmel, *Introduction*, 432. Bauckham (*Jude, 2 Peter*, 156) cited H. Werdermann (*Die Irrlehrer der Judas- und 2. Petrusbriefe*, BFcT 17/6 [Gütersloh, Berlin: C. Bertelsmann, 1913]) as the first to propose gnostic opponents.

[126] See Bauckham, *Jude, 2 Peter*, 156. His main lines of argument are summarized in the remainder of the paragraph, and he stated categorically: "The opponents in 2 Peter are not Gnostics." Bauckham agreed with the work of Neyrey, who thought the opponents were "Christians" influenced by Epicureans and not gnostics. See J. H. Neyrey, "The Form and Background of the Polemic in 2 Peter," *JBL* 99 (1980): 407–31.

[127] Guthrie, *Introduction*, 827.

[128] E.g., Kelly, *Epistles of Peter and Jude*, 235. Kelly also mentioned the reference in 2 Pet 3:2 to "your apostles," but this need mean no more than the readers' emissaries.

coming was not so much a problem for the church in the second century as it was in the days of the apostles. That the problem is mentioned here is further proof of an apostolic milieu.[129]

Finally, the use of Jude in 2 Peter 2 is said to suggest a late date. It is one of the most common objections to Petrine authorship. Normally this is based on a rather late date for Jude. While the majority view is that Peter used Jude as a source, most suggest Jude was written early in the Christian era.[130] So there was certainly adequate time for Jude to have been written and for Peter to use it during his own lifetime.

Even so, some consider it unthinkable that Peter, an apostle, would draw on the work of a nonapostle, though it is less clear that Peter himself would have viewed matters this way (e.g., in 1 Pet 5:1, he humbly called himself "a fellow elder"). Conversely, if 2 Peter was not from Peter, how does one explain a forger who was unwilling to draw on 1 Peter (though he was surely aware of the letter; see 2 Pet 3:1) while drawing heavily on Jude?[131]

When we look at the dependence through the lens of ancient rhetoric rather than contemporary literary canons, we see further problems in ascribing the book to a forger. Recently G. L. Green has illumined the ancient practice of imitation.[132] *Imitatio* or *mimēsis* was the practice of borrowing material of another, reworking it, and adapting it to the new author's purposes.[133] It was not done surreptitiously to steal the work of another (that was called "theft"), but rather it was seen as somewhat of a *homage* to the earlier author by applying his/her work to the present situation.[134] Ancient sources note such practice was "an open borrowing" with the intent to be noticed.[135] In other words, the writer wants the reader to see the similarity and recognize the honor being paid to the earlier writer. At the same time, the appropriation is applied to the current situation with the intent of improvement.[136]

One can hardly read both 2 Peter and Jude without noticing the similarities. Clearly, however, the author has not simply cut and pasted Jude into his document.[137] He seems, rather, to have followed the practice of *imitatio* in reworking and adapting. The motivation in using Jude, then, was an intentional appropriation that connects the nature of the later writer's "false teachers" to Jude's earlier "false prophets," and affirming the necessity to "contend for the faith."

---

[129] So Kruger, "Authenticity," 667; Guthrie, *Introduction*, 829–30.

[130] See Bauckham (*Jude, 2 Peter*, 13), who dated the letter in the AD 50s.

[131] See the discussion of the relationship between Jude and 2 Peter below.

[132] G. L. Green, "Second Peter's Use of Jude: *Imitatio* and the Sociology of Early Christianity," in *Reading Second Peter with New Eyes: Methodological Reassessments of the Letter of Second Peter*, LNTS 382, ed. R. L. Webb and D. L. Watson (London, England: T&T Clark, 2010).

[133] Ibid., 2.

[134] Green, *Jude and 2 Peter*, 161.

[135] Green, "Imitatio," citing Seneca the Elder, *Suas.* 3.7; Winterbottom, LCL.

[136] Green, *Jude and 2 Peter*, 161.

[137] See below in the essay on Jude.

The transparent adaptation shows honor to Jude either in personal affection, honoring the earthly family of the Lord,[138] or perhaps both. It is entirely understandable for Peter to do so. It is much more difficult to imagine a forger desiring, for whatever reason, to write in Peter's name in part to subtly give a place of honor to Jude. Why not just forge another letter of Jude? Furthermore, given Peter's status in later Christianity, it is more than unlikely that a forger would appropriate Peter to honor Jude and not the other way around.

None of these arguments are decisively in favor of pseudepigraphy. In fact, 2 Peter constantly defies clear categorization as pseudepigraphy. But is there an option between affirming Peter's authorship and attributing 2 Peter to an unknown pseudepigrapher? R. Bauckham posited that 2 Peter should be dated late in the first century as written by an acquaintance of Peter who wrote the apostle's "last testament." He argued that the letter represents a form of testamentary literature, intended for a specific audience and is, therefore, a real letter. He also believed the testamentary genre and date are "entirely conclusive against Petrine authorship."[139] Taking up the name of Peter, he felt, is "not a fraudulent means of claiming apostolic authority but embodies a claim to be a faithful mediator of the apostolic message."[140] Thus, there is no attempt to deceive, for the name is simply a convention of the genre, a "transparent fiction"[141] that Greek Christians in subsequent centuries failed to recognize. If so, those holding to Peter's authorship of 2 Peter in previous centuries as well as today would fall in the same category, for they read a document that exhibits an ancient cultural practice while being unaware of that practice.[142]

T. Schreiner offered three cogent critiques of Bauckham's theory. First, there is a lack of historical awareness of the pseudepigraphical device. The early church either rejected or received the letter based on the belief that it was or was not from Peter.[143] Could the awareness that it was "transparent fiction" really have passed so quickly? Second, Bauckham's theory is that Jews would have readily recognized the device. But, curiously, there is no evidence that the letter was written to Jews; Gentiles are a more likely destination.[144] It is also debatable whether all farewell addresses are necessarily fictional; Moses, Jacob, David, Jesus, and Paul, among others, all gave farewell addresses, but are these all fanciful? Moreover, not a single undisputed exemplar of the testamentary literature was ever recognized as Scripture. Finally, it is doubtful that 2 Peter fits the testamentary category as comfortably

---

[138] Ibid., 24.

[139] Ibid., 159. Bauckham proposed an earliest possible date solely on the basis of his interpretation of 3:4 as referring to the postapostolic era.

[140] Ibid., 161–62.

[141] Ibid., 134.

[142] See Schreiner (*1, 2 Peter, Jude*, 274), to whom part of this paragraph is indebted.

[143] See the survey of the external evidence in ibid., 262–64, with reference to R. E. Picirilli, "Allusions to 2 Peter in the Apostolic Fathers," *JSNT* 33 (1988): 57–83.

[144] Bauckham (*Jude, 2 Peter*, 13) claimed the letter was written to the same audience as 1 Peter (see 2 Pet 3:1).

as Bauckham suggests.[145] Thus, the effort to maintain the acceptability of pseudonymity by positing that 2 Peter is an example of the testamentary genre is unconvincing.

One final consideration remains. M. Green noted that most pseudepigraphical literature promoted heretical teaching, filled in historical gaps, represented the creative exercise of the author's imagination, or answered another generation's "insatiable questions."[146] Second Peter is decisively not about any of these things. Green thus concluded, "As a pseudepigraph [2 Peter] has no satisfactory *raison d'être* [reason for its existence]."[147] The absence of a satisfactory purpose for 2 Peter as a late pseudepigraphical document is yet one more reason that gives pause to embracing any of the alternatives to Peter's authorship.

To sum up, the options for Peter's authorship are that 2 Peter was produced by an unknown pseudepigrapher subsequent to Peter's lifetime (perhaps as Peter's "last testament") or that the letter was written by the apostle Peter, most likely just before his death. In light of the difficulties associated with the former argument, in light of the absence of compelling external or internal evidence against Peter's authorship, and in view of the above-noted convincing connections between 1 and 2 Peter, the view that the apostle Peter wrote 2 Peter is preferable to alternative options.[148]

Table 18.5: Is 2 Peter a Forgery?

Phenomenon	Assessment	Problem for a Forgery	Likely Source
Stylistic differences between 1 and 2 Peter.	The differences do exist. However, many similarities also exist.	Pseudepigrapha regularly copied known sources.	A secretary(-ies) working with Peter.
The use of Greek is said to be "poorer" than in 1 Peter.	It is a form known as the "Grand Asian Style."	"Poorer" Greek is an anachronism.	A (different?) secretary working with Peter.
"Simeon Peter" (2 Pet 1:1) merely suggests a "Jewish flavor" added by a forger.	This old Aramaic form of Simon is rare in the NT.	The difference is far too subtle; it is a conspicuous departure from 1 Peter.	Most likely it came from Peter himself.
Reference to Paul's Letters (2 Pet 3:15) betrays a later time.	Peter does not necessarily know every letter of Paul.	A forger is not likely to call Peter ignorant.	This is more likely to come from Peter himself.

[145] Schreiner, *1, 2 Peter, Jude*, 274–75.

[146] Green, *2 Peter Reconsidered*, 37.

[147] Ibid.

[148] At the very least, humility would seem to require that interpreters recognize the limited evidence available to adjudicate the matter. See Davids, *2 Peter, Jude*, 129, 149. It seems the burden of proof is on those who deny Petrine authorship.

Table 18.5: Is 2 Peter a Forgery? (continued)

Phenomenon	Assessment	Problem for a Forgery	Likely Source
The reference to the transfiguration (2 Pet 1:17) is a transparent tool of a forger.	The statement in 1:17 does not match any of the Gospel accounts.	A forger is more likely to quote a Gospel than create a new saying.	This is more likely to come from Peter's recall.
The use of Jude is said to be unlikely since Jude is a "lesser man."	Second Peter 2 follows the ancient practice of *imitatio* that adopts and adapts a known writing to a new situation.	A forger is highly unlikely to use *imitatio* to honor Jude while appropriating Peter's name for his work.	Understandable from the humble self-references of Peter in the epistle said to be from Peter.
"Peter" is a rhetorical device of testimonial literature.	Second Peter does not comfortably fit the testimonial genre.	No legitimate reason for the early church to accept a forgery exists.	There is no reason Peter would not write a letter as he is about to depart.
Forgeries promoted false doctrine, filled in historical gaps, and answered questions that would be anachronistic to the supposed writer. Since 2 Peter is thoroughly orthodox, fills in no historical gaps, and is void of such anachronisms, there is no reason for it to exist if it is indeed pseudepigraphy.			

Date

Few books are attributed to such diverse dates as 2 Peter. Those who find the arguments for pseudepigraphy compelling place 2 Peter as late as the mid-second century. However, the references to it by *1 Clement* and the *Apocalypse of Peter* (stated above) demand a first-century date. If 2 Peter is from the apostle, then it must have been written late in his life. Since 2 Peter probably comes from the pen of the apostle, and in light of the reference to his impending death in 2 Peter 1:14–15, it should be placed near the end of the apostle's life. Church tradition holds that Peter died during the Neronian persecution (AD 64–66; see *1 Clem.* 5.4).[149] The best date for Peter's death is AD 65 or 66.[150] Thus, the letter was most likely written just prior to Peter's martyrdom.

[149] For an apocryphal account of Peter's martyrdom, see the *Martyrdom of Peter* (ca. AD 200), reproduced in J. K. Elliott, *The Apocryphal New Testament* (Oxford, UK: Clarendon, 1993), 421–26. Cf. Dionysius of Corinth, "Letter to Soter," cited in Eusebius, *Eccl. Hist.* 2.25.8 (original letter dated to ca. AD 170), who spoke of "Peter and Paul, [who] together also taught in Italy in the same place and were martyred at the same time."

[150] See especially the thorough discussion in Robinson, *Redating*, 140–50.

Provenance

Second Peter does not mention a place of origin, but if the discussions of the authorship and the likely date of composition of 2 Peter are correct, the most plausible place of writing is Rome. If 1 Peter is authentic and was written by Peter in Rome ("Babylon"; 1 Pet 5:13) in the early or mid-60s, and if 2 Peter is authentic and was written by Peter as well, it must have been penned a few years after 1 Peter and thus likely originated in the empire's capital as well. Some have tried to adjudicate the origins of the letter based on linguistic evidence, but these attempts are unconvincing.[151] People can exhibit various types of linguistic traits in myriads of places, which renders determining a place of writing on the basis of linguistic use precarious.[152] Rome continues to be by far the best and most common option for the provenance of the letter.

Destination

Unlike 1 Peter, the second letter does not mention its recipients. However, two clues help us identify its destination. Since this was the second letter Peter had written to this audience (2 Pet 3:1) and since he showed knowledge of Paul's Letters (2 Pet 3:15), it seems reasonable to infer that the destination of 2 Peter was the same as that of 1 Peter (see 1 Pet 1:1).

Moreover, the use of the Grand Asian Style of the letter suggests that the author wrote to readers who would appreciate this style of writing. This would have been the case in the eastern part of the empire (but not the western), though not at the eastern end of the Mediterranean.[153] On the whole the evidence points to the same recipients as 1 Peter: Gentile Christians in Asia Minor.

Occasion and Purpose

The occasion for writing 2 Peter was most likely that the apostle was nearing his death (1:15) and needed to address a false teaching that was circulating in the churches to which he wrote (2:1–22). Thus, in 3:17–18, Peter admonishes his readers to "be on your guard, so that you are not led away by the error of lawless people and fall from your own stable position. But grow in the grace and knowledge of our Lord and Savior Jesus Christ."

The opponents in 2 Peter apparently considered themselves Christian teachers and not necessarily prophets (2:1, 13), although Peter groups them with false prophets of old. They gathered disciples (2:2) and attempted to draw true believers into their sphere of

---

[151] See Bauckham, *2 Peter*, 135–38. D. F. Watson ("Comparing Two Related Methods: Rhetorical Criticism and Socio-Rhetorical Interpretation Applied to Second Peter," in *Reading Second Peter with New Eyes: Methodological Reassessments of the Letter of Second Peter*, LNTS 382, ed. R. L. Webb and D. L. Watson [London, England: T&T Clark, 2010], 31) considers the Grand Asian Style to suggest an Anatolian provenance. It, however, may be employed because of the destination rather than the provenance.

[152] Many who do not consider Peter to be the author of the letter still hold Rome to be the place of origin. A case in point is Bauckham (*2 Peter, Jude*, 159), who concluded that the letter was written from Rome on the basis of close affinities to *1 and 2 Clement* and the *Shepherd of Hermas* and the association with 1 Peter.

[153] See Davids, *2 Peter, Jude*, 133.

influence. At the heart of their teaching seems to have been eschatological skepticism.[154] These false teachers apparently denied the second coming and sought to undermine apostolic testimony (see 1:16; 2:18–19; 3:4). Peter's denial that the apostles followed "cleverly contrived myths when we made known to you the power and coming of our Lord Jesus Christ" (1:16) seems to respond to the charge leveled by his opponents that the apostles' teaching of the resurrection was merely a matter of fabrication (for a similar instance, see 2 Tim 2:17–18; cf. 1 Tim 1:20; 2 Tim 4:14).

Moreover, the eschatological skepticism of the opponents doubted any sort of divine retribution. The world, according to them, would always remain as it had been (3:4); hence they promised freedom (2:19) expressed in fleshly fulfillment (2:13; cf. 2:10, 14). In this they may have used Paul's Letters as the foundation for their error, since Peter notes that "the untaught and unstable will twist [Paul's Letters] to their own destruction" (3:16).[155] Finally, there seems to be a strong element of greed as the motivation for their ministry (2:14–16).

Many have attempted to connect the opponents in 2 Peter to gnostic philosophy,[156] but this seems unlikely since the date of the letter is prior to full-fledged Gnosticism that did not emerge until the second century and in light of the character of the opponents. The parallels with Epicurean philosophy are strong, however, and many have suggested it as the source of Peter's opponents.[157] But Schreiner is most likely correct in doubting the wholesale identification of the opponents with Epicurean philosophy.[158]

It is best to view the opponents as advocating a philosophy otherwise unattested in the NT or extrabiblical literature, similar to the "Colossian heresy," which was likewise unique in its local expression. If so, it is best to reconstruct the false teaching on the basis of the internal evidence, which suggests that the opponents' philosophy at the outset precluded God's intervening in the world at any time (3:3–4), whether by sending a flood (thus denying the veracity of the OT Scriptures; see Genesis 6–9) or by having Jesus return at the end of time (a denial of Jesus's own words and of the apostolic and early church's witness).

---

[154] Bauckham, *Jude, 2 Peter*, 154.

[155] It is possible they contended that grace released them from the obligation to obey ethical standards. So Schreiner, *1, 2 Peter, Jude*, 277.

[156] The first was Werdermann, *Irrlehrer*. More recently, see C. Talbert, "2 Peter and the Delay of the Parousia," *VC 20* (1966): 141–43.

[157] So Bauckham, *Jude, 2 Peter*, 156, following Neyrey, "Form and Background," 407–31. For a brief description of Epicureanism, see chap. 2 above.

[158] Schreiner, *1, 2 Peter, Jude*, 280. Davids (*2 Peter, Jude*, 133–36) suggested it was more of an Epicurean influence prevalent in the day; similarly, Thielman, *Theology of the New Testament*, 526.

LITERATURE

Literary Plan

The unity of 2 Peter is not seriously doubted.[159] Some argue that the letter parallels Greco-Roman rhetorical conventions, but this is far from proven.[160] Overall, 2 Peter conforms to the standard epistolary conventions of the day, featuring opening greetings (1:1–2), the body of the letter (1:3–3:13), and concluding remarks (3:14–18). There is wide consensus that 2:1–22 and 3:1–13 constitute literary units. Less agreement exists with regard to the material in chapter 1. T. Schreiner divided the letter at 1:12, while D. Moo discerned a break at 1:16.[161] Most likely, both are right as the below outline indicates: the sections are 1:3–11; 1:12–15; and 1:16–21.[162]

Second Peter 1:3–21 sets forth Peter's challenge to his readers to pursue Christian virtues in light of God's provision of everything required for life and godliness (1:3–11). It states Peter's purpose for writing the letter (1:12–15) and issues a defense and countercharge against allegations by the false teachers regarding Peter's preaching on the *parousia* (1:16–21). As further developed in the discussion of Jude below, chapter 2 incorporates in modified form large portions of Jude, while 3:1–13 presents the specifics of the heresy at issue and calls the readers to holy conduct and godliness as they await the Lord's return. On the whole the letter balances Peter's concern with believers' pursuit of Christian virtues with his desire to refute the false teaching that denied the reality of the second coming.

The important connection between Peter's focus on holiness and the false teaching he combated ought not to be missed. Apparently, the denial of the second coming led directly to antinominianism and licentious behavior. This is confirmed in the references to the judgment of the angels, those in Noah's day, and Sodom and Gomorrah (2:4–9), assuring the readers that God will hold people accountable for their actions. Hence, the example of the false teachers—whose lack of doctrinal orthodoxy led to a denial of the second

---

[159] See the refutation of the challenge to the unity of 2 Peter by M. McNamara ("The Unity of Second Peter: A Reconsideration," *Scr* 12 [1960]: 13–19) in Schreiner, *1, 2 Peter, Jude*, 281.

[160] See Schreiner (*1, 2 Peter, Jude*, 218), who questioned the application of rhetorical criticism to 2 Peter by Watson (*Invention, Arrangement, and Style*), with reference to S. E. Porter and T. H. Olbricht, eds., *Rhetoric and the New Testament: Essays from the 1992 Heidelberg Conference* (Sheffield, UK: JSOT, 1993); and J. A. D. Weima, "What Does Aristotle Have to Do with Paul? An Evaluation of Rhetorical Criticism," *CTJ* 32 (1997): 458–68. See further on the rhetorical style of 2 Peter, B. Witherington, *Letters and Homilies for Hellenized Christians*, vol. 2: *A Socio-Rhetorical Commentary on 1–2 Peter* (Downers Grove, IL: InterVarsity, 2008), 265–66, 272–77; D. F. Watson, "Comparing Two Related Methods: Rhetorical Criticism and Socio-Rhetorical Interpretation Applied to Second Peter," in *Reading Second Peter with New Eyes: Methodological Reassessments of the Letter of Second Peter*, ed. D. F. Watson and R. L. Webb, LNTS 382 (London, England: T&T Clark, 2010), 27–58; idem, "The Epistolary Rhetoric of 1 Peter, 2 Peter, and Jude," in *Reading 1–2 Peter and Jude: A Resource for Students*, ed. E. F. Mason and T. W. Martin (Atlanta, GA: Society of Biblical Literature, 2014), 27–46.

[161] See Schreiner, *1, 2 Peter, Jude*, 282; and D. J. Moo, *2 Peter, Jude*, NIVAC (Grand Rapids, MI: Zondervan, 1996), 26.

[162] A special case is Bauckham (*Jude, 2 Peter*, 135), who posited a fairly complicated outline, with Peter responding to four objections. See also the recent treatment by J. P. Heil, *1 Peter, 2 Peter, and Jude: Worship Matters* (Eugene, OR: Cascade, 2013), 191–202, 291–94, who understands 2 Peter to be comprised of "five ['text-centered, linguistically-based'] microchiastic units arranged in a cohesive and coherent macrochiastic framework" (1:1–15; 1:16–21; 2:1–16; 2:17–22; 3:1–18).

Something to Think About: Cultivating Christian Virtues

Peter did not write his second letter to tell his readers something new. Instead, he wrote to remind them of things they already knew (3:1). In this Peter's audience was like many of us who basically know what we should be doing in our Christian lives but who need occasional (or frequent) reminders to help us stay on course or to get back on track.

Most distinctive is the "staircase of Christian virtues" Peter lists in the opening chapter of his letter. After assuring his readers that God had given them everything they needed to live a godly life, including his "very great and precious promises" (1:4), he urges his readers to supplement their faith with

goodness
goodness with knowledge
knowledge with self-control
self-control with endurance
endurance with godliness
godliness with brotherly affection and
brotherly affection with love (1:5–7).

There does not appear to be any reason for the order of these virtues that suggests we must cultivate one before progressing to the next, except that it is probably no coincidence that love is the primary virtue as in other similar lists (see 1 Cor 13:13; Gal 5:22–23). While many of these virtues are standard fare and are found also in Paul's writings (e.g., goodness and self-control are in Gal 5:22–23), one word catches our attention: "godliness" (eusebeia). *This word occurs three times in 2 Peter 1 (vv. 3, 6–7) and once in 3:11, which is four out of fifteen NT occurrences (see Acts 3:12; 1 Tim 2:2; 3:16; 4:7–8; 6:3, 5–6, 11; 2 Tim 3:5; Titus 1:1). Related forms occur seven times in the NT: the verb* eusebeō *(Acts 17:23; 1 Tim 5:4); the adjective* eusebēs *(Acts 10:2, 7; 2 Pet 2:9); and the adverb* eusebōs *(2 Tim 3:12; Titus 2:12). Interestingly, therefore, the word group only occurs in Acts, the Pastoral Epistles, and 2 Peter.*

This likely means eusebeia *was a term used in the larger Greco-Roman world of the first century, denoting a person's religious piety or devotion, though not necessarily in a Christian sense. Initially Christians may have been reluctant to incorporate this term into their vocabulary, but at some point they apparently decided to Christianize it. Hence, in Acts 10 we find the word characterizing the Gentile centurion Cornelius (10:2) and one of his devout soldiers (10:7).*

So it is only in the Pastorals and in 2 Peter that believers are urged to "live peaceful . . . lives in all godliness and holiness" (1 Tim 2:2 NIV); and that Timothy is exhorted to "train yourself to be godly," for "godliness has value for all things" (1 Tim 4:7–8 NIV; see 1 Tim 6:11), while false teachers are excoriated for their lack of true godliness (1 Tim 6:5; 2 Tim 3:5). In Titus 1:1, Paul expressed his conviction that the knowledge of the truth leads to godliness. Peter told his readers to engage in holy conduct and godliness in light of the Second Coming (2 Pet 3:11).

There is, therefore, nothing wrong with Christians cultivating Christian virtues. To the contrary, this is strongly encouraged as long as they remember their quest for godliness is not to be done in self-effort. Engaging in spiritual disciplines such as the regular study of and meditation on God's Word (Col 3:16; 2 Tim 3:14–17) or continual prayer (1 Thess 5:17; Phil 4:6–7) is indeed vital. Yet, as Peter reminded us, God's divine power has given us everything required for living a godly life (1:3), so the power for advancing in Christian virtues comes not from ourselves but from God.

coming, resulting in an immoral lifestyle—taught the important lesson that believers who affirm the second coming must cultivate holiness as they await Christ's return.

OUTLINE

I. GREETINGS (1:1–2)
II. ENCOURAGEMENT TO GROWTH IN GODLINESS (1:3–21)
  A. The Pursuit of Christian Virtues (1:3–11)
  B. The Nature of Peter's Letter (1:12–15)
  C. Defense of Peter's and the Prophets' Testimony (1:16–21)
III. CONDEMNATION OF THE FALSE TEACHERS (2:1–22)
  A. The Danger and Nature of the False Teachers (2:1–3)
  B. God's Judgment in the Past (2:4–10a)
  C. The False Teachers' Godless Character (2:10b–16)
  D. The False Teachers Described (2:17–22)
IV. REFUTATION AND RESPONSE TO THE FALSE TEACHERS (3:1–13)
V. CLOSING (3:14–18)

UNIT-BY-UNIT DISCUSSION

I. Greetings (1:1–2)

Second Peter opens with a standard prescript found in first-century letters, including a "well-wish" of a spiritual nature: "May grace and peace be multiplied to you through the knowledge of God and of Jesus our Lord" (1:2). The dual reference to "grace" and "knowledge" also concludes the letter, possibly forming a literary *inclusio* (3:18).[163]

II. Encouragement to Growth in Godliness (1:3–21)

A. The Pursuit of Christian Virtues (1:3–11) Peter made the previous "well-wish" because Christ has given believers everything they need for eternal life and godliness through their knowledge of him and through God's election of believers, having called them by his own glory and goodness. By virtue of this calling, the Christian participates in the divine nature and is able to escape the corruption brought on by evil desires.

The list that follows is not mere moralism, for Peter has already stressed that the foundation that allows the effort to be effectually extended has been laid in salvation, here epitomized in the word *faith*. In this faith the believer is to supply certain things. The verb translated "supply" or "add" (Gk. *epichoregeō*) usually means "to provide at one's own expense," but here it is a linking verb, as if someone made an effort at gaining goodness to obtain a supply of faith, and so on.[164]

Peter follows this encouragement to pursue Christian virtues with references to the negative and positive outcomes of such an effort. If a person did not engage in the pursuit

---

[163] A pattern also found in 1 Peter.

[164] So Davids, *2 Peter, Jude*, 179.

of Christian virtues, that person was nearsighted to the point of blindness. If he did, he would be rewarded with a rich entrance into God's kingdom at the appearing of the Lord Jesus Christ (1:8–11).

B. The Nature of Peter's Letter (1:12–15) In 1:12–15, Peter stated the purpose of his letter, namely to remind believers of important spiritual truths, presumably because of the threat of the false teachers, the exact nature of whose teaching is not specified until chapter 3. Peter wrote what turned out to be his final extant letter because he was convinced his death was imminent and because he was confident he was speaking the truth (1:14; see 1:12). Verse 15 specifies the future benefits of the letter for the readers.

C. Defense of Peter's and the Prophets' Message (1:16–21) The reason Peter made this effort to remind his readers of their need to pursue Christian virtues is that he and his fellow apostles were eyewitnesses of Christ's majesty (1:16–18), so that the prophetic word about the coming of Christ was strongly confirmed (1:19). Peter then affirms that both the origin of prophecy and its interpretation came from God himself (1:20–21). This represented a thinly veiled admonition to beware of those who engaged in their own "private interpretation" of Scripture, resulting in false teaching (the subject of chaps. 2–3).

III. Condemnation of the False Teachers (2:1–22)

Peter most likely incorporated nearly the whole of Jude's letter in his condemnation of the false teachers.[165] Thus, the condemnation was applicable to the present opponents but beyond this to all false teachers. It would not be until chapter 3 that the precise nature of the false teaching was addressed.

A. The Danger and Nature of the False Teachers (2:1–3) The existence of false teachers was as inevitable as was that of the false prophets of old. They were clearly unregenerate and led others to destruction with them, blaspheming the truth out of greed, which resulted in the inevitability of God's judgment.

B. God's Judgment in the Past (2:4–10a) The reason God's judgment was inevitable is that God has always judged false teachers and others who failed to submit properly to authority. The fallen angels were condemned to Tartarus and kept in chains (2:4); the people who lived prior to the flood and who had engaged in egregious sin were destroyed; and Sodom and Gomorrah were obliterated as well (2:5–6). In the midst of this strong note of denunciation, however, Peter—in contrast to Jude, whose portrait is entirely negative (see below)—also strikes an encouraging note. He points out that while God destroyed the ancient world by a flood, he had rescued Noah and his family; he also rescued Lot and his family when he destroyed Sodom and Gomorrah. Thus, God could be counted on not only to judge the unrighteous but also to rescue the righteous from the polluted spiritual state of the world (2:7–10a).

C. The False Teachers' Godless Character (2:10b–16) In 2:10b, Peter delves further into the godless character of these false teachers. They were bold, arrogant, profane, and

---

[165] For a defense of Peter's use of Jude, see the treatment of Jude below.

slanderous; they were like the beasts of the field in their blasphemies and were thus fit for destruction (2:10b–12). They had secretly infiltrated the assembly and polluted the pure doctrine of the church. They were ever seeking to seduce and devour the righteous. Peter compared them to Balaam, a prophet for profit (2:15–16).

D. The False Teachers Described (2:17–22) Peter describes these teachers as "springs without water," who seduced those who had barely escaped. It is tempting to understand these as believers who have fallen from grace, for the apostle stated that it would have been better if they had never known the truth than having turned back from the holy commandment. But verse 22 makes clear that they were never true believers, for "a dog returns to its own vomit, and, 'a washed sow returns to wallowing'" (2 Pet 2:22, citing Prov 26:11). Thus, the true nature of these false teachers becomes apparent: their unregenerate nature had only been masked externally, but in the end it will be made clear that they were never spiritually transformed in the first place.[166]

IV. Refutation and Response to the False Teachers (3:1–13)

The specific nature of the heresy, already hinted at in 1:16, is now set forth, and the error of the false teachers is refuted. These scoffers denied the truthfulness of the apostolic teaching regarding the second coming of the Lord Jesus Christ, contending that "all things continue as they have been since the beginning of creation" (3:3–4). In response Peter firmly rejects this teaching by noting that the underlying premise was wrong. Contrary to the false teachers' assumption, the world will not always exist, for God has already judged it once in the past with a flood (3:6) and will destroy it again by fire in the future (3:7).

In fact, from the vantage point of eternity, Peter notes, there is little difference between a day and 1,000 years. Moreover, the Lord was not delaying his return but patiently waiting for the last of the elect to be saved; then judgment will swiftly ensue (3:8–9). Indeed, the Day of the Lord will come on the wicked without warning; the heavens will pass away, and the earth will melt and be dissolved. Thus, the opponents were wrong regarding the earth's continual existence. In light of the world's final judgment, Christians ought to be a sanctified people, waiting expectantly for the promise of the new heavens and the new earth (3:11–13).

V. Closing (3:14–18)

Peter concludes his letter by affirming that believers should view the apparent delay of the Second Coming as an opportunity for salvation. For confirmation, he calls on Paul's Letters (though it is not clear if he had any specific passage in mind). He concludes with a warning against the false teachers and reiterates his desire that his readers "grow in the grace and knowledge of our Lord and Savior Jesus Christ." This he follows with a closing doxology.

---

[166] See Blomberg, *From Pentecost to Patmos*, 481. This interpretation fits well with Peter's previous statements that God knows how to preserve the righteous in the midst of a filthy world.

THEOLOGY

Theological Themes

The Pursuit of Christian Virtues in Light of the End Time The growth of believers in Christian virtues is a major emphasis in 2 Peter. According to Peter, people may travel on one of two paths.[167] The first is that of progressing in the faith, climbing a staircase of Christian virtues, which enables believers to lead spiritually productive lives (1:3–11; see 3:11–18). The second is that of straying from the path, resulting in destruction and condemnation, as in the case of the false teachers (2:1–3:10). Hence, the letter is permeated by a pastoral concern for the well-being of the flock and its protection from the potential harm caused by those who would twist the Word of God (1:12–21).[168]

Peter's teaching on the pursuit of Christian virtue is epitomized by the word "godliness" (Gk. *eusebeia*), which occurs three times in 1:3–7 (vv. 3, 6–7; see 3:11). Peter makes clear that through their knowledge of God in Christ, believers have been given everything they need to live a godly life (1:3). For this reason they are to pursue godliness in conjunction with faith, goodness, knowledge, self-control, endurance, brotherly affection, and love (1:5–7).[169]

Peter's teaching on the need for believers to pursue Christian virtues also has important end-time implications. The false teachers challenged the belief that Christ will return and that God will bring about a consummation to history. Yet Peter affirms that in spite of apparent delays, the Lord will come again at the appointed time. He will judge all people, and the elements of this world will be dissolved and will melt away (3:12). Thus, Christ followers should live in light of the end and pursue the path of Christian virtue in order to reach their final glorious destination (1:11). In this way the coming Day of the Lord (3:12) provides an incentive for moral behavior (3:14).[170]

Conversely, the eschatological skepticism of the false teachers proved that although they identified themselves with Christianity (2:1, 20–21), they had never truly experienced salvation (2:22). Their bold, arrogant words, their attack on apostolic doctrine, and their lack of Christian virtue marked them as those fitted only for destruction (2:3). Again, as in other passages in the NT (e.g., 1 Cor 15:12; 2 Thess 3:6, 11; 2 Tim 2:18),

---

[167] See Kelly, *Epistles of Peter and of Jude*, 328; Thielman, *Theology of the New Testament*, 527. Peter uses the term *hodos* ("way") four times (2:2, 15 [twice], 21) as well as the related expressions *eisodos* ("entrance," 1:11) and *exodus* ("departure," 1:15).

[168] The most unusual element of Peter's instruction is found in 1:4, where believers are said to share in the divine nature. By this Peter did not mean participation in the essence of God but enablement to progress in Christian virtues. See Thielman, *Theology of the New Testament*, 527, citing J. M. Starr, *Sharers in the Divine Nature: 2 Peter 1:4 in Its Hellenistic Context*, ConBNT 33 (Stockholm, Sweden: Almqvist & Wiksell, 2000), 47–48. Against Bauckham (*Jude, 2 Peter*, 182), who saw immortality as the primary reference. Also against S. Hafemann, "'Divine Nature' in 2 Pet 1,4 within Its Eschatological Context," *Bib* 94 (2013): 80–99, who sees taking part in the divine nature as participation in the eschatological realization of the new heavens and the new earth of 3:13.

[169] See further the earlier section on "Something to Think About: Cultivating Christian Virtue."

[170] Thielman, *Theology of the New Testament*, 535.

this shows that deficiencies in doctrine—in the present case, eschatology—have important practical ramifications. Right belief thus is an essential foundation for proper practice, and Christians ought to live in the light of Christ's return.

Apostolic Eyewitness Testimony Versus Heresy Another distinctive emphasis in 2 Peter is the importance of apostolic eyewitness testimony against heresy with its reliance on human reasoning and fabricated arguments. This is borne out by the presence of two particular word groups in 2 Peter. The first is represented by the noun "eyewitness" (Gk. *epoptēs*) in 1:16, which occurs only here in the NT, though see "eyewitness" (Gk.*autoptēs*) in Luke 1:2; the verb "to witness" (Gk. *epopteuō*) occurs only in 1 Peter in the NT (1 Pet 2:12; 3:2). The second is represented by the Greek word *hairesis* (the etymological root for the English word *heresy*), which can mean "sect" or "party," such as Sadducees (Acts 5:17); Pharisees (Acts 15:5; 26:5); "the Nazarenes" or "the Way," that is, Christians (Acts 24:5, 14; 28:22). It can also mean "faction" or "division" (1 Cor 11:19; Gal 5:20), or "heresy" (2 Pet 2:1). Peter's missive revolves around this contrast between eyewitness testimony and destructive heresies.

Against allegations from his opponents, Peter asserts that he (unlike them) did not follow "cleverly contrived myths" in his preaching of the second coming; instead, he says, "We were eyewitnesses of his majesty" (1:16). He proceeds to recount his eyewitness recollection of Jesus's transfiguration, which included hearing the divine voice from heaven utter the words, "This is my beloved Son with whom I am well pleased!" (1:17–18; see Matt 17:5 and parallels). This meant Peter's message was authoritative because it was based on what really happened (similarly, 1 John 1:1–4; see 1 Tim 1:4; 4:7; 2 Tim 4:4; Titus 1:14), which was contrary to the false teachers' message that they fabricated (2:1–3; 3:4).

The point made in 1:19–21 is, therefore, that Peter's witness of the glorified Christ formed a strong basis for his witness to the expectation of the return of Christ in his glory at the end of time. In this the apostle was allied with the OT prophets, and in his testimony "the prophetic word [was] strongly confirmed" (1:19). The witness of the OT prophets had not been self-induced but had been God given and Spirit inspired (1:20–21). Likewise, Peter's witness was based on what God had done, and was going to do, in Christ. This underscores the crucial importance of relying on OT and NT Scripture in one's expectations of the end, especially with regard to Christ's return. It also inspires confidence in the accuracy and trustworthiness of the apostolic witness handed down to us in Scripture. Based on this sure foundation, believers can zealously pursue Christian virtues in order to be ready for Christ when he returns.

The Letter of Jude

KEY FACTS

Author:	Jude, brother of James
Date:	ca. AD 55–62
Provenance:	Unknown
Destination:	Predominantly Jewish Christian congregation (Asia Minor?)
Occasion:	False teaching and/or improper conduct (antinomianism coupled with licentiousness)[171]
Purpose:	To contend for the faith once for all entrusted to believers
Theme:	Jude urges his readers to contend for the faith and to reject the false teaching of the heretics.
Key Verse:	3

Introduction

WHILE A FEW decades ago Jude could still be called "the most neglected book of the New Testament," this short letter, placed in the canon last among the General Epistles and prior to the book of Revelation, has received considerable attention in recent years.[172] In contemporary preaching, however, Jude continues to

[171] Was Jude concerned primarily about false teaching, about improper conduct, or both? See the discussion in Davids (drawing on the work of Reese) who notes that "Jude never refers to those he critiques as teachers; in fact, the few references to their speech . . . do not indicate any teaching role. It is their behavior, including verbal grumbling and the like, that is the issue, not their teaching." While 2 Peter, most likely based on Jude, speaks of false teachers, Davids argues that Peter is adapting Jude to fit his situation. See Davids, *Theology of James, Peter, and Jude*, 260–61.

[172] D. J. Rowston, "The Most Neglected Book in the New Testament," *NTS* 21 (1975): 554–63; see Bauckham, *Jude, 2 Peter*, xi: "No NT books have been more neglected by scholars than Jude and 2 Peter." Bauckham also provides a history of research up until 1988 in R. Bauckham, "The Letter of Jude: An Account of Research," *Aufstieg und Niedergang der Römischen Welt* 2.25.5 (Berlin, Germany: de Gruyter, 1988), 3,791–826. R. Heiligenthal ("Der Judasbrief. Aspekte der Forschung in den letzten Jahrzehnten," *TRu* 51 [1986]: 117–29) speaks of the "shadowy existence" and a "time of general neglect" of Jude.

In the last decade (2005–2015), however, publications on Jude have burgeoned, including these volumes: P. H. Davids, *Peter and Jude: A Handbook on the Greek Text*, BHGNT (Waco, TX: Baylor University Press, 2011); idem, *The Letters of 2 Peter and Jude*, PNTC (Grand Rapids, MI: Eerdmans, 2006); idem, *Theology of James, Peter, and Jude*; C. P. Giese, *2 Peter and Jude*, ConC (St. Louis, MO: Concordia, 2012); G. L. Green, *Jude and 2 Peter*, BECNT (Grand Rapids, MI: Baker, 2008); J. H. Greenlee, *An Exegetical Summary of Jude*, 2nd ed. (Dallas, TX: SIL International, 2008); J. P. Heil, *1 Peter, 2 Peter, and Jude: Worship Matters* (Eugene, OR: Cascade, 2013); E. F. Mason and T. W. Martin, eds., *Reading 1–2 Peter and Jude: A Resource for Students*, SBLRBS (Atlanta, GA: Society of Biblical Literature, 2014); K.-W. Niebuhr and R. W. Wall,

suffer neglect. Apart from the phrase "the faith that was delivered to the saints once for all" (v. 3), it is only the concluding doxology (vv. 24–25), albeit without reference to its context in Jude, that is a regular part of the church's worship.

In an age when Christian faith and moral integrity are in short supply, Jude's message is particularly appropriate. All too commonly local churches fail to confront false teachings or are unwilling to challenge compromises in the way people live. Frequently, tolerance is the order of the day, and church discipline is at an all-time low. Into this malaise Jude issues a clarion call to defend the faith and to confront false teaching, particularly in light of the reality of a holy God who will judge sin unless it is acknowledged and confessed.

HISTORY

Author

The letter begins with a reference to "Jude, a servant of Jesus Christ, and a brother of James" (1). In all probability, the author of Jude is the brother of the James mentioned in Matthew 13:55. The opening self-reference by Jude as "brother" rather than the customary reference to himself as "son of" his father is unusual.[173] With regard to the expression "brother of James," it is noteworthy that only James the half brother of Jesus could be mentioned simply as "James" (Jas 1:1) without a need for further identification.[174]

Jude begins in a way reminiscent of the book of James.[175] James was much better known and had no need to identify himself further, but Jude is hardly mentioned elsewhere and needed to add the epithet "brother of James."[176] What is more, Jude called himself only

---

eds., *The Catholic Epistles and Apostolic Tradition: A New Perspective on James to Jude* (Waco, TX: Baylor University Press, 2009); D. R. Nienhuis and R. W. Wall, *Reading the Epistles of James, Peter, John, and Jude as Scripture: The Shaping and Shape of a Canonical Collection* (Grand Rapids, MI: Eerdmans, 2013); J. Painter and D. A. deSilva, *James and Jude*, Paideia (Grand Rapids, MI: Baker, 2012); R. A. Reese, *2 Peter and Jude*, THNTC (Grand Rapids, MI: Eerdmans, 2007); R. L. Webb and P. H. Davids, eds., *Reading Jude with New Eyes: Methodological Reassessments of the Letter of Jude*, LNTS 383 (London, England: T&T Clark, 2009); B. Witherington III, *Letters and Homilies for Jewish Christians: A Socio-Rhetorical Commentary on Hebrews, James and Jude* (Downers Grove, IL: InterVarsity, 2007). An excellent and recent history of research, along with the most recent bibliography, is found in Davids, *Theology of James, Peter, and Jude*, 249–53.

[173] R. L. Webb, "Jude," in *DLNT*, 611–21.

[174] So Bauckham, *Jude and the Relatives of Jesus*, 172. Bauckham notes that prior to the nineteenth century (including Calvin and the Council of Trent), Jude the apostle was considered to be the author of Jude (see Luke 6:16; Acts 1:13). However, Jude the apostle was identified with the half brother of Jesus, who is mentioned in Matt 13:55 and Mark 6:3. Jessein (1821) was the first to argue against this consensus and to distinguish Jude the half brother of Jesus and author of Jude from Jude the apostle. See the list of alternative identifications of Jude in Bauckham, *Jude and the Relatives of Jesus*, 172–73.

[175] Compare Jude 1: "Jude, a slave of Jesus Christ and a brother of James" with Jas 1:1: "James, a slave of God and of the Lord Jesus Christ."

[176] According to Gal 2:9, James, together with Peter and John, was one of the "pillars" of the Jerusalem church. James had a leading role in the Jerusalem Council (Acts 15:13; see 12:17; 21:18). Paul also mentioned that the resurrected Jesus had appeared to James (1 Cor 15:7) and called James "the Lord's brother" (Gal 1:19; see Acts 1:14; 1 Cor 9:5). Remarkably, James only called himself "a servant of God and of the Lord Jesus Christ" (1:1).

"brother of James"[177] and not "brother of Jesus Christ."[178] The latter designation may have seemed inappropriate in light of Jesus's divine sonship. Rather than identifying themselves in terms of their flesh-and-blood relationship with Jesus, both James and Jude call themselves "slaves of Jesus Christ" who did his will.

The view is common that Jude's letter is pseudonymous, that it was written by someone other than Jude and attributed to him for some reason.[179] This practice was supposedly in keeping with the ancient convention of pseudonymity, according to which a literary work was attributed to a well-known personality in order to lend it credence and to enlarge its potential audience. But the obvious question is why anyone would have wanted to attribute a writing to a person as little known as Jude rather than to other disciples known much more widely.[180] In addition, Bauckham has convincingly argued for the "very considerable importance of the relatives of Jesus in the mission and leadership of the churches of Palestine in the first century," and it should be unsurprising that the early church has preserved a work produced by one of Jesus's relatives.[181]

How and how early was the Letter of Jude received in the early church? It should first be noted that on the assumption of authenticity, and accepting the chronological priority of Jude over against 2 Peter, Peter himself gives tacit indication to the early existence of Jude.

For these reasons there is no serious doubt that Jude, the full brother of James and half brother of Jesus, is the author of the book bearing his name.

Date

The date for Jude depends in part on its relationship with 1 and 2 Peter, particularly the latter. A comparison between Jude's letter and 2 Peter suggests that Jude's letter was

---

[177] Kelly (*Epistles of Peter and of Jude*, 242) believed Jude would have identified himself as "brother of the Lord" and that the designation "brother of James" points to pseudonymity. So H. Windisch, *Die katholischen Briefe*, HNT, 3rd ed., rev. H. Preisker (Tübingen, Germany: J. C. B. Mohr [Paul Siebeck], 1951 [1911]), 38; but see the decisive response by Bauckham, *Jude, 2 Peter*, 24. Ehrman (*Forgery and Counterforgery*, 298–304) provides one of the most recent cases against authenticity (pp. 222–29); see also the discussion in L. R. Donelson, "Gathering Apostolic Voices: Who Wrote 1 and 2 Peter and Jude," in *Reading 1–2 Peter and Jude: A Resource for Students*, 21–27.

[178] This is a convincing argument against the pseudonymity of Jude. As Bauckham (*Jude and the Relatives of Jesus*, 176) observed, "The lack of reference to Jude's relationship to Jesus is much more easily explicable on the assumption of authenticity than on the assumption of pseudepigraphy."

[179] On the phenomenon of pseudonymity, see the bibliographic references listed in fn 4 above.

[180] So rightly Bauckham, *Jude and the Relatives of Jesus*, 175, with reference to Farrar, Weiss, Zahn, Moffat, Wohlenberg, Cranfield, Green, and Guthrie; cf. Bauckham, "Account of Research," 3,817–18. At times it is argued that the author of Jude was not Jude himself but rather a friend, student, or relative of Jude (B. Reicke, *The Epistles of James, Peter and Jude*, AB 37 [Garden City, NY: Doubleday, 1964]; J. Michl, *Die katholischen Briefe*, RNT 8/2, 2nd ed. [Regensburg, Germany: F. Pustet, 1968]; W. Grundmann, *Der Brief des Judas und der Zweite Brief des Petrus*, THNT 15 [Berlin, Germany: de Gruyter, 1974], 15–16) or that he belonged to a "circle of Judas" (G. Hollmann, *Der Brief Judas und der Zweite Brief des Petrus*, in *Die Schriften des Neuen Testaments*, vol. 2, ed. J. Weiss [Göttingen, Germany: Vandenhoeck & Ruprecht, 1907], 572). The argument has also been advanced that the epithet "brother of James" served to lend authority to Jude's letter (W. Schrage, *Der Judasbrief*, in *Die "Katholischen" Briefe: Die Briefe des Jakobus, Petrus, Johannes und Judas*, 11th ed., ed. H. Balz and W. Schrage, NTD 10 [Göttingen, Germany: Vandenhoeck & Ruprecht, 1973], 220). Yet these theories are far less plausible than the simpler assumption that Jude, the brother of James, was himself the author of the letter.

[181] Bauckham, *Jude and the Relatives of Jesus*, 131.

written first and that Peter, in his second letter, adapted Jude for his own purposes and circumstances.[182] In light of the considerable number of parallels between the letters, a literary relationship between the two is more likely than the independent use of a common source by both writers.

A detailed comparison of Jude and 2 Peter will be provided below. For the time being, the probability of Jude's having been written prior to 2 Peter can be illustrated by the way in which these writings used Jewish apocryphal literature. Jude included three such quotations or allusions: (1) to *The Assumption of Moses* in verse 9; (2) to *1 Enoch* in verses 14–15; and (3) to an otherwise unattested saying of the apostles in verse 18. All three quotations are lacking in 2 Peter. It seems more likely that Peter avoided reference to these apocryphal works rather than that Jude added these references on the assumption of Petrine priority.[183]

Estimates of the date of composition of Jude extend from the year 50 (Bauckham) to AD 65–80 (Guthrie) to AD 100 (Kümmel).[184] The critical question here is whether the letter displays the characteristics of early Catholicism.[185] Dunn cited three such characteristics: (1) a decrease in the expectation of the imminent return of Christ; (2) an emphasis on the institutional nature of the church (as in the Pastorals); and (3) the use of liturgical elements (similar to the Pastorals).[186] However, a closer look shows that none of these elements is present in Jude.

1. The expectation of the parousia (the Second Coming) is given clear and repeated expression in Jude 14, 21, 24. The entire argument in verses 5–19 assumes the false teachers will be judged following Christ's return.[187]

---

[182] So many (if not most) contemporary commentators. Others, however, such as D. J. Moo (*2 Peter, Jude*, NIVAC [Grand Rapids, MI: Zondervan, 1996], 18), contended that Jude used parts of 2 Peter. In addition to the commentaries, a recent discussion is found in J. F. Hultin, "The Literary Relationships Among 1 Peter, 2 Peter, and Jude," in *Reading 1–2 Peter and Jude*, 27–46.

On the assumption of authenticity, it may seem unusual for Peter, Jesus's most prominent disciple and the foremost of the twelve apostles, to have taken and adapted the work of Jude, who was not an apostle. But as Davids (*Letters of 2 Peter and Jude*, 3) notes, "This usage . . . should not raise the old smokescreen, 'Why would an apostle use the work of another church leader?' The answer to that would be, 'And why would he not use the work of another church leader?'" Additionally, and interestingly, B. J. Oropeza (*Apostasy in the New Testament Communities*, vol. 3: *Churches Under Siege of Persecution and Assimilation: The General Epistles and Revelation* [Eugene, OR: Cascade, 2012], 154) suggests that "if the letter is pseudonymous it is odd that the author would choose to call himself "Judas" ["Jude" and "Judas" both translate the same Greek word], a name permanently etched in early Christian memory with someone who betrayed Jesus."

[183] Perhaps in order to compensate, Peter supplemented Jude's letter with the biblical examples of Noah (2 Pet 2:5) and Lot (2 Pet 2:7–9) and provided a more thorough presentation of Balaam (2 Pet 2:15–16).

[184] See Bauckham, *Jude and the Relatives of Jesus*, 168–69n237; idem, "Account of Research," 3,812–15. By Davids's reckoning (*Theology of James, Peter, and Jude*, 254–55), Jude was born between AD 7 and AD 10, and thus could have been alive to write this letter as late as the last part of the first century.

[185] Representatives of this theory include Windisch, *Katholischen Briefe*; and K. H. Schelkle, *Die Petrusbriefe, der Judasbrief*, HTKNT 13/2 (Freiburg, Germany: Herder, 1961). But see Bauckham, *Jude and the Relatives of Jesus*, 158–60.

[186] J. D. G. Dunn, *Unity and Diversity in the New Testament*, 2nd ed. (London, England/Philadelphia, PA: Trinity Press International, 1990), 341–66.

[187] See esp. R. L. Webb, "The Eschatology of the Epistle of Jude and Its Rhetorical and Social Functions," *BBR* 6 (1996): 139–51.

2. There is no reference to holders of ecclesiastical offices anywhere in Jude, and the manner in which the heretics are called to account stands in stark contrast to the early Catholic practice of appealing to ecclesiastical office.
3. Jude does not contain any liturgical fragments (the phrase "the faith that was delivered to the saints once for all" in v. 3 constitutes a simple reference to the gospel; see Gal 1:23).

For these reasons the theory that Jude is a product of early Catholicism is untenable, suggesting the possibility, even probability, of an early date, and as shown below, possibly even a very early date in relation to the other NT letters.

Bauckham shows that one finds a comparable antinomianism already in Corinth after the year 50 and in Asia Minor around AD 90. Since in his view Jude is neither early Catholic nor antignostic, Bauckham postulates a possible date of composition for Jude in the early 50s.[188] It seems that Schlatter presupposes the presence of antignostic polemic,[189] but he also finds no traces of early Catholicism in Jude's letter.[190]

Another factor is the question of the likely literary dependence between Jude and 2 Peter. If 2 Peter postdates and is dependent on Jude (a view held by most commentators today), and 2 Peter is authentic (see the introduction to 2 Peter in this volume), the fact that Peter died a martyr's death around AD 65–66 requires the early AD 60s as the latest possible date for the book of Jude.[191]

Since there is no good reason to question the authenticity of 2 Peter and since it is probable that 2 Peter is dependent on Jude rather than vice versa, AD 55–62 as a date of composition is most likely.[192] But the lack of clear internal evidence regarding the date of composition renders this estimate tentative.

Provenance

The provenance of Jude cannot be determined with certainty. Bauckham shows conclusively that Jude is not a product of early Catholicism but an expression of apocalyptic

---

[188] Bauckham, *Jude, 2 Peter*, 13.

[189] Schlatter, *Theology of the Apostles*, 103–8, esp. 103 with the heading, "The Gnostic Threat." Cf. W. G. Kümmel, *Introduction to the New Testament*, rev. ed., trans. H. C. Kee (Nashville, TN: Abingdon, 1975), 426, 432; and E. Käsemann, "An Apologia for Primitive Christian Eschatology," in *Essays on New Testament Themes* (Naperville, IL: Allenson, 1964), 171–72.

[190] At times Jude 17 is cited in support of a late date since this passage appears to view the apostolic period as a thing of the past. But more likely Jude's reference is to the missionary activity of the apostles that led to the establishment of the church. See Bauckham, *Jude and the Relatives of Jesus*, 170–71.

[191] Robinson (*Redating*, 197) proposes that if James had already died by the time of the writing of Jude, Jude would most likely have referred to him as "the blessed," "the good," or "the righteous." Since he did not, James must still have been alive. James died a martyr's death in the year 62, so Robinson suggested that Jude was written before then.

[192] Similarly, G. Green (*2 Peter and Jude*, 18): "sometime in the latter part of the 50s or the first half of the 60s of the first century." If Jude's letter does reveal antignostic tendencies, then 1 Tim 6:21 provides further confirmation that proto-gnostic elements were already at work in Asia Minor in the early 60s (on the assumption of Paul's authorship of the Pastorals).

Palestinian Christianity.[193] This is confirmed by Jude's use of the Jewish books *The Assumption of Moses* and *1 Enoch* and by the *pesher* exegesis in verses 5–19.[194] In light of these observations, Jude has a closer affinity to James than to 2 Peter.[195] Beyond this, it is difficult to pinpoint the provenance of Jude; therefore, it is best to leave this question open.

Destination

The general reference to "those who are the called, loved by God the Father and kept for Jesus Christ" at the beginning of the letter (v. 1b) does not allow an identification of the letter's recipients. Judging from the internal evidence, it is possible that the missive was directed to a predominantly (though not exclusively) Jewish Christian congregation, possibly one in Asia Minor.[196] Itinerant false teachers had infiltrated the church, living licentiously and practicing a form of Christian antinomianism (lawlessness).

According to these heretics, the grace of God liberated believers from all ethical norms so that a Christian was free to choose his own conduct without any moral restraints. These heretics were not only members of the church but also teachers (vv. 11–13). They took part in the church's worship and sought to spread their prophecies and teachings at the occasion of the church's regular "love feasts," that is, communal meals including the celebration of the Lord's Supper. Jude warned his readers against the heretics and urged them to contend for their faith (v. 3).

Occasion and Purpose

The heretics mentioned in Jude cannot be identified with any of the other false teachers mentioned in the NT.[197] In identifying their exact nature, priority should therefore be given to the internal evidence provided by the book itself.[198] According to Jude, the false

---

[193] Bauckham, *Jude and the Relatives of Jesus*, 155, 161; D. A. Hagner, "Jewish Christianity," in *DLNT*, 582. In his more recent treatment, G. Green thoroughly adjudicates the evidence (sparse as it is) at length and concludes that "the Epistle of Jude . . . brings us into contact with early Palestinian Christianity that was in the process of opening up to the gentile mission" (*Jude and 2 Peter*, 16).

[194] Bauckham, *Jude and the Relatives of Jesus*, 161.

[195] See the interesting parallels cited in Schlatter, *Theology of the Apostles*, 103–6.

[196] See Bauckham, *Jude, 2 Peter*, 26; F. Spitta, *Der zweite Brief des Petrus und der Brief des Judas: Eine geschichtliche Untersuchung* (Halle, Germany: Verlag der Buchhandlung des Waisenhauses, 1885), 301: "If Jude appeals to the authority of James, it seems likely that the readers were such for whom James in fact constituted an authority" (our translation).

[197] See the survey by Bauckham, "Account of Research," 3,809–12; the thorough treatment by G. Sellin, "Die Häretiker des Judasbriefes," *ZNW* 76–77 (1985–86): 206–25; and Werdermann, *Irrlehrer*, who identifies the heretics as libertine proto-gnostics and dates Jude's letter to ca. AD 80. More recently, note the treatments by P. H. Davids, "Are the Others Too Other? The Issue of 'Others' in Jude and 2 Peter," in *Reading 1–2 Peter and Jude: A Resource for Students*, 201–14; and Oropeza, *Churches Under Siege of Persecution and Assimilation*, 155–74.

[198] It is commonly suggested that the author of this letter engages in "vilification" of the opponents by the use of stock terminology connected with conventional villain stereotypes. See, e.g., A. B. du Toit, "Vilification as a Pragmatic Device in Early Christian Epistolography, in *Focusing on Paul: Persuasion and Theological Design in Romans and Galatians*, ed. C. Breytenbach and D. S. du Toit (Berlin, Germany: de Gruyter, 2007), 45–56, who speaks of the "widespread convention of vilifying opponents which obtained throughout the Mediterranean world" (46), and argues that an interpreter must distinguish between stock characterizations and historical information when seeking to describe the opponents in a given NT epistle. See also L. Thurén, "Hey Jude! Asking for the Original Situation and Message of a Catholic Epistle," *JSNT* 43

teachers "have come in[to the church] by stealth" (v. 4; see Gal 2:4). Most likely, they were itinerant teachers or preachers who went from church to church and depended on the hospitality of local Christians (see 1 Cor 9:5; 2 John 10; 3 John 5–10). In their unbelief, these godless individuals denied "Jesus Christ our only Sovereign and Lord" (v. 4 NIV). Their motto was "freedom," in the sense of complete ethical autonomy (vv. 4, 8; see v. 7). Possibly, these false teachers held to an overrealized eschatology, focusing on their present enjoyment of the benefits of salvation while apocalyptic elements were given short shrift (see 2 Tim 2:17–18).

Jude calls the false teachers "dreamers" (v. 8), mystics who boasted of privileged access to esoteric knowledge. This may indicate the charismatic character of these itinerant preachers.[199] These claims of visionary experiences appear to have resulted also in lack of respect toward angels (vv. 9–10). It is possible that people were said to have an angelic nature and thus the distinction between humans and angels was blurred. Jude accounted for this by reference to the lack of spiritual insight on the part of the heretics: "These people blaspheme anything they do not understand" (v. 10). In truth they do not possess the Spirit (v. 19).

These teachers are "blemishes" (v. 12 NIV) at the church's "love feasts," in which they participate without the slightest qualm (v. 12; see vv. 8, 23). Their status as teachers is hinted at in verse 12, where they are called shepherds "who only look after themselves." Like Balaam or the false shepherds in Ezekiel 34, these heretics sought nothing but their own advantage (v. 11). They are as unreliable as waterless clouds or fruitless autumn trees and as unstable as the restless ocean (vv. 12–13; see Isa 57:20; Eph 4:14), leading people astray so they are similar to stars that do not keep their course (see v. 6).

The heretics were highly critical and deeply discontent with their own fate (v. 16).[200] They utter "harsh things" (v. 15) similar to the godless mentioned in the previous quotation from *1 Enoch* (see also vv. 8, 10); they were "scoffers" who displayed a mocking spirit (v. 18). They caused divisions (v. 19; see 1 Cor 1:10–4:7; Jas 3:14) and were earthly minded (v. 19; the word is *psychikoi*; see 1 Cor 2:14; Jas 3:15; 4:5). Although these charismatic itinerant preachers boasted of their visionary experiences, they were devoid of the Spirit (v. 19), thus proving their unregenerate nature (see Rom 8:9). This was impressively demonstrated by their licentious lifestyle.

(1997): 451–65. Oropeza (*Churches Under Siege of Persecution and Assimilation*, 156) contends regarding Jude that "once the author's words are stripped away of denunciations and negative stereotypes, little is left to ascertain about the situation behind the letter or the aberrant doctrines promulgated by the opponents." Davids ("Are the Others Too Other?," 207–8) wisely treads a *via media* by noting that "while vilification language is stereotyped in all literature of this period and thus one must be careful how much information one draws from it, it is too extreme to say that it carries no information about those critiqued."

[199] See G. Theissen, *The First Followers of Jesus* (London, England: SCM, 1978).

[200] Possibly they considered themselves fatalistically—as if they were slaves of their own destiny—and shifted the responsibility for their own licentious conduct to others. So R. P. Martin, *The Theology of Jude, 1 Peter, and 2 Peter*, in *The Theology of the Letters of James, Peter, and Jude* by A. Chester and R. P. Martin (Cambridge, UK: Cambridge University Press, 1994), 71.

These were the false teachers Jude opposed in his letter. While he had intended to write a general and encouraging letter "about the salvation we share," he instead "found it necessary to write, appealing" his readers to contend for the faith once for all entrusted to believers (v. 3). This remarkable change of plans was occasioned by the covert and subversive presence of the false teachers in the congregation to which Jude addressed his letter. Rather than acquiesce to their teachings, the believers in that congregation needed to oppose these heretics, knowing that God's judgment of such individuals is sure.

Just as God severely punished people who did such things in the past—the demonstration of which is the burden underlying Jude's reference to several OT examples in verses 5–19—he will most certainly judge these false teachers. Jude's message for his recipients is given clear expression in verses 20–23, where he called on his readers to build themselves up in their most holy faith, to pray in the Holy Spirit, and to keep themselves in God's love as they await Christ's return (one of the proto-trinitarian references in the NT, vv. 20–21). They were to show mercy toward those who doubted; save others by snatching them from the fire; and to conduct themselves with holy fear, knowing that even the clothing of the false teachers was "defiled by the flesh" (vv. 22–23).

It is difficult to exaggerate the utmost seriousness with which the church, according to Jude, must deal with heretics while acting redemptively toward those who may still be wrenched from the demonic grasp of these wicked, self-seeking individuals.

Something to Think About: Caring Enough to Confront

In the third verse of his short letter, Jude tells his readers that the correspondence they received was not the letter he actually set out to write. Jude intended to write an encouraging letter "about the salvation we share" (v. 3), but when false teachers threatened the church, he instead wrote a scathing denunciation of the false teachers in order to protect the congregation from harm. Rather than glossing over the difficulty, or hoping it would go away on its own, Jude took drastic action. In this he serves as an example for today's churches in which materialism, convenience, and consumerism are too often the rule and radical discipleship and God-centeredness the exception.

For Jude, the false teachers were a spiritual menace that had to be confronted with utmost seriousness and urgency. Their immorality needed exposure, their appeal had to be curtailed, and a rescue operation for those swayed needed to be launched: "Have mercy on those who waver; save others by snatching them from the fire; have mercy on others but with fear, hating even the garment defiled by the flesh" (v. 23). It may be inconvenient to change our plans and (as Jude did) to shift gears from encouragement to exhortation, but if we care enough to confront, we will not let false teachings in our churches go unchecked but will contend for the faith once for all delivered to believers.

LITERATURE

Genre

The letter is addressed to a particular group of people (vv. 1–4). It is therefore not a "Catholic" (i.e., "General") Epistle. Nevertheless, the main body of the letter and the concluding blessing read more like a sermon composed of a midrash on various texts (vv. 5–19), a paraenesis (exhortation; vv. 20–23), and a doxology (vv. 24–25).[201] It may be best to characterize Jude as a "sermon in [the] form of an epistle."[202]

Beyond this, Charles has shown that Jude in its entirety should be viewed as a "word of exhortation," in which references to the OT are used to address a contemporary situation.[203] Presumably, the concluding doxology signals that Jude intended for his letter to be read in the context of the church's worship service.[204] A similar genre can be detected in Hebrews, James, and 1 John.

With regard to Jude's vocabulary, Origen (ca. AD 185–254) noted that he commanded a "strong vocabulary."[205] Jude features no fewer than fifteen NT *hapax legomena* (words used only once), only four of which are found in a Greek translation of the OT. In addition, three words occur elsewhere only in 2 Peter 2, which is most likely dependent on Jude. To this may be added twenty-two words that are rare in the rest of the NT.

As Neyrey observed, Jude's rich vocabulary suggests that the author operated in a literary environment considerably broader than merely the Hebrew and Christian Scriptures. The frequent use of triplets (e.g., "Jude," "servant," "brother"; "loved," "kept," "called"; and "mercy," "peace," "love" in vv. 1–2), by the principle of "amplification by accumulation," is designed to add gravity to the author's argument.[206]

---

[201] See C. A. Evans, "Midrash," in *Dictionary of Jesus and the Gospels*, ed. J. B. Green, S. McKnight, and I. H. Marshall (Downers Grove, IL: InterVarsity, 1992), 544–48.

[202] Bauckham, *Jude, 2 Peter*, 1; D. F. Watson, "Letter, Letter Form," in *DLNT*, 653; B. Witherington (*Hebrews, James and Jude*, 560), avers, "Jude offers us a sermon in rhetorical form that has only an epistolary opening to indicate that it came to the audience in a written form, though it was likely delivered orally at the point of destination."

On the rhetoric of Jude, see J. D. Charles, "Polemic and Persuasion: Typological and Rhetorical Perspectives on the Letter of Jude," in *Reading Jude with New Eyes*, 81–108; D. F. Watson, *Invention, Arrangement and Style: Rhetorical Criticism of Jude and 2 Peter*, SBLDS 104 (Atlanta, GA: Scholars Press, 1988); idem, "The Epistolary Rhetoric of 1 Peter, 2 Peter, and Jude," in *Reading 2 Peter and Jude: A Resource for Students*, 27–46; E. R. Wendland, "A Comparative Study of 'Rhetorical Criticism', Ancient and Modern—with Special Reference to the Larger Structure and Function of the Epistle of Jude," *Neot* 28 (1994): 193–228; Witherington, *Hebrews, James, Jude*, 559–60, 575–76.

[203] J. D. Charles, "Jude's Use of Pseudepigraphical Source-Material as Part of a Literary Strategy," *NTS* 37 (1991): 130–45.

[204] So Webb, "Jude," 612.

[205] Origen, *Comm. Matt. 10.17*; *GCS* 10.22; cited in J. H. Neyrey (*2 Peter, Jude*, AB 37C [New York, NY: Doubleday, 1993], 27), who provides further details.

[206] For an extended list of triplets in Jude—twenty sets in twenty-five verses!—see Charles, "'Those' and 'These': The Use of the Old Testament in the Epistle of Jude," *JSNT* 38 (1990): 109–24. Regarding the rhetorical effect of triplets as "amplification by accumulation," see Watson, *Invention, Arrangement, and Style*; E. von Dobschütz, "Zwei- und dreigliedrige Formeln," *JBL* 50 (1931): 118–32.

One conspicuous feature of Jude's letter is his use of apocryphal material, particularly *1 Enoch*.[207] As noted, this stands in marked contrast to 2 Peter and the rest of the NT—including Jesus's use according to the canonical Gospels. In addition, Jewish traditions, including the OT, provide Jude with the bulk of his sources.[208] Affinities with the *pesher* exegesis at Qumran have already been noted under the previous heading. As mentioned, the book of Jude likely served as a source for 2 Peter.

Relationship with 2 Peter 2

It has already been noted above that 2 Peter 2 likely depends literarily on the book of Jude. Here the relationship between them is given in greater detail. A comparison between Jude 4–19 and 2 Peter 2:1–3:3 yields the following parallels, with identical or synonymous words in the original in boldface.

Jude 4–19

> For some people, who were designated for this judgment long ago, **have come in by stealth;** they are ungodly, turning the grace of our God into **sensuality** and **denying Jesus Christ our only Master and Lord**. Now I want to remind you, although you came to know all these things once and for all, that Jesus: saved a people out of Egypt and later destroyed those who did not believe; and the **angels** who did not keep their own position but abandoned their proper dwelling, he has kept in eternal chains in deep **darkness** for the **judgment** on the great day. Likewise, **Sodom and Gomorrah** and the surrounding towns committed sexual immorality and perversions, and serve **as an example** by undergoing the punishment of eternal fire.
>
> In the same way these people—relying on their dreams—**defile their flesh, reject authority, and slander glorious ones.** Yet when Michael the archangel was disputing with the devil in an argument about Moses's body, he did not dare utter a slanderous condemnation against him but said, "The Lord rebuke you!" But these people **blaspheme anything they do not understand.** What they do understand **by instinct—like irrational**

[207] An excellent survey of Jude's sources is found in Bauckham, "Account of Research," 3,793–800; cf. Rowston, "Most Neglected Book," 557–59; Charles, "Literary Strategy," 130–45. On Jude's use of *1 Enoch* 1:9 in Jude 14–15, see M. Black, "The Maranatha Invocation and Jude 14,15 (1 Enoch 1:9)," in *Christ and Spirit in the New Testament. Fs. C. F. D. Moule*, ed. B. Lindars and S. S. Smalley (Cambridge, UK: Cambridge University Press, 1973), 189–96; G. Green, *Jude and 2 Peter*, 26–33, 101–8; N. J. Moore, "Is Enoch Also Among the Prophets? The Impact of Jude's Citation of *1 Enoch* on the Reception of Both Texts in the Early Church," *JTS* 41 (2013): 498–515; C. D. Osburn, "The Christological Use of 1 Enoch 1:9 in Jude 14,15," *NTS* 23 (1976–77): 334–41.

[208] See D. A. Carson, "Jude," in *Commentary on the New Testament Use of the Old Testament*, ed. G. K. Beale and D. A. Carson (Grand Rapids, MI: Baker, 2007), 1,069–79; J. D. Charles, "'Those' and 'These': The Use of the Old Testament in the Epistle of Jude," *JSNT* 38 (1990): 109–24; T. R. Wolthuis, "Jude and Jewish Traditions," *CTJ* 22 (1987): 21–41; Bauckham, *Jude, 2 Peter*, passim; and P. H. Davids, "The Use of Second Temple Traditions in 1 and 2 Peter and Jude," in *The Catholic Epistles and the Tradition*, ed. J. Schlosser, BETL 176 (Leuven, Belgium: Peeters, 2004), 409–31, who argues that Jude is not necessarily reading the OT directly but via other Second Temple literature such as the pseudepigraphical book of *Jubilees*.

animals—they are destroyed by these things. Woe to them! For they have gone the way of Cain, have plunged into **Balaam's error** for profit, and have perished in Korah's rebellion. These people are **dangerous reefs** at your love feasts as they eat with you without reverence. They are shepherds who only look after themselves. They are **waterless** clouds carried along **by winds**; trees in late autumn—fruitless, twice dead and uprooted. They are wild waves of the sea, foaming up their shameful deeds; wandering stars for whom the **blackness of darkness** is reserved **forever!**

It was about these that Enoch, in the seventh generation from Adam, prophesied:

> Look! The Lord comes with tens of thousands of his holy ones to execute judgment on all and to convict all the ungodly concerning all the ungodly acts that they have done in an ungodly way, and concerning all the harsh things ungodly sinners have said against him.

These people are discontented grumblers, **living according to their desires;** their mouths utter arrogant words, flattering people for their own advantage.

But you, dear friends, remember what was predicted by the apostles of our Lord Jesus Christ. They told you, "**In the end time there will be scoffers living according to their own** ungodly **desires.**" These people create divisions and are worldly, not having the Spirit.

In addition to these remarkable verbal similarities, the two texts display a rather striking commonality in terms of the sequential development of the argument:

Table 18.6: References to OT Figures in Jude and 2 Peter 2

Jude		2 Peter 2	
v. 5	Israel in the wilderness		
v. 6	Angels	v. 4	Angels
		v. 5	Noah
v. 7	Sodom and Gomorrah	v. 6	Sodom and Gomorrah
		v. 7	Lot
v. 9	Archangel Michael	v. 11	[Archangel Michael, not named]
v. 11	Cain		
v. 11	Balaam	v. 15	Balaam
v. 11	Korah		

Jude and Peter concur in their basic structure: angels—Sodom and Gomorrah—[archangel Michael]—Balaam. Beyond this, Peter (on the assumption that Jude served as his source) replaced the two negative examples, Cain and Korah, with two positive figures, Noah and Lot. While the similarity in structure could also be accounted for on the basis of a common source, it seems more likely that Peter used Jude directly and adapted his letter to his own situation.[209] If so, it is particularly conspicuous that Peter reworked Jude's letter in such a way that the sequence of his examples is in proper OT chronological order, while Jude uses a topical arrangement.

Literary Plan

The Letter of Jude displays this concentric chiastic structure:[210]

Section	**Introductory Formula**
A Greeting (1–2)	Jude to those . . .
B Occasion (3–4)	Beloved
C Reminder (5–7)	I want to remind you
D The Heretics (8–13)	In the same way, these people
D′ *1 Enoch* (14–16)	Enoch prophesied about them
C′ Reminder (17–19)	But you, beloved, remember the words
B′ Exhortation (20–23)	But you, beloved
A′ Doxology (24–25)	But to him who is able to keep you . . .

This structure contains correspondence between greeting and doxology and between occasion and exhortation, two reminders, and the two units at the heart of the letter, the section on the false teachers and the quotation from *1 Enoch*. The body of the letter (vv. 5–19) contains an extended exegetical treatment of types and prophecies for the purpose of showing "that the false teachers are people whose behavior is condemned and whose judgment is prophesied in OT types and in prophecy from the time of Enoch to the time of the apostles."[211]

Despite the length of verses 5–19, the actual purpose of the letter is Jude's exhortation that his readers contend for the faith (vv. 20–23; see v. 3). Thus, verses 20–23 are not merely a concluding exhortation or a postscript; they are the climax to which the entire

---

[209] So rightly Rowston, "Most Neglected Book," 563: "It is much easier to assume that Jude is the original." Among those proposing a common source for Jude and 2 Peter are Reicke, *James, Peter, Jude*, 189–90; and M. Green, *2 Peter and Jude*, TNTC, rev. ed. (Downers Grove, IL: InterVarsity, 1987), 58–64.

[210] A slightly different chiastic structure is proposed by Bauckham (*Jude, 2 Peter*, 5–6), and Webb ("Jude," 612), who follows Bauckham:

A Appeal: need to contend for the faith (v. 3)

B Occasion for appeal: false teachers identified and condemned (v. 4)

B′ Occasion for appeal: false teachers identified and condemned (vv. 5–19)

A′ Appeal: how to contend for the faith (vv. 20–23).

On the structure of Jude, see the survey in Bauckham, "Account of Research," 3,800–3,804. See also the recent treatments in J. T. Dennison, "The Structure of the Epistle of Jude," *Kerux* 29 (2014): 3–7; and J. P. Heil, *1 Peter, 2 Peter, and Jude*, 295–302, 340–42.

[211] Bauckham, *Jude, 2 Peter*, 4.

letter builds. Verses 5–19 provide the necessary background and foundation for this paraenesis (exhortation). The message of the letter is therefore a call for the readers to contend for the faith against God's adversaries, who are condemned already in Scripture and who will be held accountable on the last day.

Ellis shows that verses 5–19 represent a midrash, an exegesis of selected passages of Scripture, with a view toward pointing out their contemporary relevance.[212] Four texts are used:

- Texts 1 and 2 each refer to three OT types (vv. 5–7, 11).
- Text 3 is *1 Enoch* 1:9 (vv. 14–15).
- Text 4 is a prophecy of the apostles (vv. 17–18).

Each of these texts is first cited and then interpreted in midrashic fashion:

Table 18.7: Midrashic Elements in Jude 5–18

Verse(s)	Text	Verse	Midrash
5–7	Hebrew Scripture	8–10	In the same way, these people
11	Hebrew Scripture	12–13	These people are
14–15	Apocrypha (1 Enoch)	16	These people are
17–18	Apostolic prophecy	19	These people are

Verses 5–7 and 17–19 are introduced as reminders, while verses 8–13 and 14–16 correspond to each other at the heart of the letter's argument. The transitions between the cited texts and the midrashic portions are characterized by two stylistic elements: verb tenses and the phrase "these people." All verb tenses in the source texts are in the past or the future, while the tense in the commentary portions is consistently in the present. In addition, the quotes of Scripture are linked with the midrashic materials through corresponding transitional phrases:

- "ungodly"/ "ungodly acts"/ "ungodly" (vv. 4, 15, 18)
- "blaspheme"/ "blasphemy" (vv. 8–10)
- "error" (*planē*)/ "wandering" (*planētēs*; vv. 11, 13)
- "keep . . . darkness" (vv. 6, 13)

The purpose served by the midrashim (commentary sections) is transparent and compelling. The argument essentially runs this way:

1. The sin of the false teachers corresponds to the sin of the OT types.
2. The OT types were severely punished by God for their sinful behavior.

---

[212] E. E. Ellis, "Prophecy and Hermeneutic in Jude," in *Prophecy and Hermeneutic in Early Christianity: New Testament Essays*, WUNT 18 (Tübingen, Germany: J. C. B. Mohr [Paul Siebeck], 1978), 221–36.

3. Since the false teachers' sins correspond to those of the OT types and since the OT types were severely punished by God for their sin, the future judgment of the false teachers is equally certain (though still future).

On the basis of this exhortatory message, Jude's readers must cast their lot with the "faith that was delivered to the saints once for all" (v. 3) and separate from the false teachers, seeking to salvage any doubters or others under the spell of the heretics while applying all necessary caution (vv. 20–23). Otherwise, they will share in the false teachers' sins and incur the same judgment.

Jude's interpretive technique of midrash is roughly akin to the pesher exegesis at Qumran.[213] Both are predicated on the conviction that the OT texts represent end-time prophecy that is to be applied by the contemporary interpreter (be it at Qumran or in Jude's day) to a corresponding pattern or situation in his own day (understood as the time of eschatological fulfillment). Several texts among the Dead Sea Scrolls (e.g., 4QFlorilegium and 11QMelchizedek) feature a commentary-style format, which features expositions of related texts ("thematic pesharim"). By way of contrast, Qumran does not use apocryphal texts or oral Christian prophecies, nor does one find typological exegesis. "Jude," on the other hand, "applies Scripture to the last days not only as prophecy, but also as typology, in which the events of redemptive history are seen to foreshadow the eschatological events."[214]

OUTLINE

I. SALUTATION (1–2)
II. OCCASION (3–4)
III. EXPOSITION: GOD'S JUDGMENT ON SINNERS (5–19)
   A. Reminder from the Hebrew Scriptures (5–7)
   B. The False Teachers (8–13)
   C. The Quotation from Enoch (14–16)
   D. Reminder from Apostolic Prophecy (17–19)
IV. EXHORTATION (20–23)
V. DOXOLOGY (24–25)

UNIT-BY-UNIT DISCUSSION

I. Salutation (1–2)

The customary salutation identifies Jude, the brother of James, as the author; includes an address of the recipients as "those who are the called, loved by God the Father and kept for Jesus Christ"; and a greeting of mercy, peace, and love.

---

[213] Bauckham (*Jude and the Relatives of Jesus*, 233) avers that Jude "contains probably the most elaborate passage of formal exegesis in the manner of the Qumran pesharim to be found in the New Testament."

[214] Bauckham, *Jude, 2 Peter*, 5.

II. Occasion (3–4)

In refreshing candor, Jude explains why the letter he actually wrote was different from the one he had intended to write. Rather than penning an encouraging note regarding "the salvation we share," Jude writes a scathing rebuke of the false teachers and urges believers to "contend for the faith that was delivered to the saints once for all."

III. Exposition: God's Judgment on Sinners (5–19)

Jude set his denunciation of the false teachers within the framework of reminders from the Hebrew Scriptures (vv. 5–7) and from apostolic prophecy (vv. 17–19). The false teachers shared several essential characteristics with those who had sinned conspicuously in OT times and subsequently were severely judged by God (vv. 8–16). While still future from Jude's perspective, the judgment of God on the false teachers in his day was nonetheless certain.

A. Reminder from the Hebrew Scriptures (5–7) Jude's denunciation of the false teachers takes on the form of a "reminder" of how God dealt with similar offenders and rebels in the past. Exhibit 1 is God's judgment of the rebellious generation in the wilderness during the exodus from Egypt. Exhibit 2 concerns God's judgment of the fallen angels who were not content with their assigned place in God's creation but rebelled against it. Exhibit 3 is Sodom and Gomorrah, who rebelled against God's creation order by engaging in perverse sexual acts (homosexuality) and consequently were destroyed by divine judgment. These three scriptural examples make clear that those who rebel against God will certainly not escape divine judgment, even if, as in the case of the false teachers in the book of Jude, this judgment is yet future.

B. The False Teachers (8–13) This section, together with verses 14–16, is at the heart of the chiasm of the letter, focusing squarely on the false teachers. Their root sin is defiance of God's authority. The archangel Michael is cited as a positive example, contrasted with three negative predecessors of the false teachers: Cain, who murdered his brother out of jealousy; Balaam, whose error was the result of greed; and Korah, who rebelled in the wilderness. The false teachers are placed in this terrible trajectory of past rebels against God's authority who were severely judged by God. As Jude makes clear, the false teachers' punishment is likewise assured.

C. The Quotation from Enoch (14–16) Jude cites as proof text a passage from the apocryphal book of *Enoch*, attesting to the certainty of divine judgment on the ungodly. The teachers are charged with discontent, sensuality, arrogance, and flattery.

D. Reminder from Apostolic Prophecy (17–19) The reminder from apostolic prophecy corresponds in the chiastic structure to the opening reminder from the Hebrew Scriptures in verses 5–7. With this Jude turns to his audience ("dear friends," v. 17), reminding them that the false teachers were fulfilling end-time prophecy. The heretics are divisive, merely natural, and devoid of the Spirit.

IV. Exhortation (20–23)

On the basis of Jude's exposition regarding God's impending judgment of the false teachers in verses 5–19, the purpose of the letter, stated in verse 3, is now fleshed out in the form of a full-fledged exhortation. In this climactic section Jude dramatically urges his readers to keep themselves pure while attempting to "snatch" some who doubt "from the fire," that is, from eternal judgment by God.

V. Doxology (24–25)

The concluding doxology affirms God's ability to keep believers from stumbling and celebrates the glory, majesty, and power of the only God and Savior through Jesus Christ now and forever.

THEOLOGY

Theological Theme[215]

Contending for the Faith Jude issues an urgent appeal for believers to contend for the Christian faith over against false teaching that accentuates believers' alleged unfettered freedom in Christ, which leads to an immoral lifestyle. In this form of antinomianism, people appealed to God's grace as setting believers free to live any way they chose. Paul elsewhere defended from possible abuse the Christian teaching of grace apart from the "works of the law" (see, e.g., Gal 2:16).

Jude notes that the false teachers persisted in rebellion against authority and did not possess the Spirit. For this reason their activities failed to bear fruit. In essence Jude's letter represents a wake-up call to a church that sat dormant when major doctrinal challenges called them to stand in urgent response. This is not dissimilar to our own day in which much of the church is languishing in moral and spiritual complacency and indifference, where the prosperity gospel is alive and well, and where teaching sound Christian doctrine is often less important than meeting felt needs.

The message of Jude's letter is therefore perennially relevant. Believers must be reminded of the holiness and righteousness of God, which will not allow sin to go unpunished and which requires a holy lifestyle in response to God's grace in Christ. Jude also provided diagnostic tools for spotting false teachers: an immoral lifestyle, a self-serving and self-seeking disposition, and a primarily monetary motivation. In contrast, believers ought to conduct themselves in holy fear, being circumspect and grateful. Similar to the false teachers in Jude's day, there is now the danger that some are "turning the grace of our God into sensuality" (v. 4).

Many a convert wrongly concludes that the gospel of God's grace renders unnecessary a lifestyle characterized by trust in God and obedience to biblical morality and teaching.

---

[215] For recent work regarding the theology of Jude, see Davids, *Theology of James, Peter, and Jude*, 282–92; D. Lockett, "Purity and Polemic: A Reassessment of Jude's Theological World," in *Reading Jude with New Eyes*, 5–31.

After all, God is a God of grace, love, and forgiveness. As Jude made clear, however, the decision to trust Christ must not issue in a life of unfettered freedom and immorality. To the contrary, the believer becomes "a servant of Jesus Christ" (v. 1). There is, therefore, a great need for the church and individual believers to rediscover the important contribution Jude made to the life and practice of the church.[216]

CONTRIBUTION TO THE CANON

- Believers as "exiles" in this world (1 Pet 1:1, 17; 2:11)
- The continuity between OT Israel and the Christian church (1 Pet 2:1–10)
- The importance of submission to authorities (1 Pet 2:13–3:7)
- The importance of Christlike suffering (1 Pet 2:21–25; 3:13–18)
- The need to cultivate godliness and Christian virtues (2 Pet 1:3–11)
- The divine inspiration of the prophetic Scriptures (2 Pet 1:21)
- The need for perseverance and watchfulness in view of Jesus's return (2 Pet 3:1–13)
- The need to contend for the faith once for all delivered to the saints (Jude 3)

STUDY QUESTIONS

1. According to the authors, which was written first: 1 Peter, 2 Peter, or Jude? Why?
2. What is the most likely date for 1 Peter? Why?
3. Why did Peter write 1 Peter, and what is the major example he cites in his exhortation?
4. Why do you think there is virtual unanimity in recent scholarship regarding the structure of 1 Peter?
5. What are four views of 1 Peter 3:18–22?
6. What are three reasons many modern scholars believe Peter did not write 2 Peter?
7. Why are so many diverse dates offered for 2 Peter?
8. What heresy is addressed in 2 Peter?
9. How does Peter's teaching to pursue Christian virtues have important end-time implications?
10. Why is Jude probably not pseudonymous?
11. Who were most likely the "false teachers" mentioned in Jude?
12. Succinctly, what contributions do 1 and 2 Peter and Jude make to the canon?

FOR FURTHER STUDY

Abernathy, D. *An Exegetical Summary of 1 Peter*. 2nd ed. Dallas, TX: SIL International, 2008.

Achtemeier, P. J. *1 Peter*. Hermeneia. Philadelphia, PA: Fortress, 1996.

---

[216] As J. D. Charles noted some years ago ("The Use of Tradition-Material in Jude," *BBR* 4 [1994], 14), "It is perhaps no exaggeration to suggest that there have been periods of church history in which 'the most neglected book in the New Testament' was in fact the most relevant book of all."

Batten, A. J., and J. S. Kloppenborg, eds. *James, 1 and 2 Peter, and Early Jesus Traditions.* Library of New Testament Studies 478. London, England: Bloomsbury T&T Clark, 2014.

Bauckham, R. *Jude, 2 Peter.* Word Biblical Commentary 50. Waco, TX: Word, 1983.

_________. *Jude and the Relatives of Jesus in the Early Church.* Edinburgh, Scotland: T&T Clark, 1990.

Beare, F. W. *The First Epistle of Peter.* 2nd ed. Oxford, UK: Blackwell, 1958.

Bockmuehl, M. *Simon Peter in Scripture and Memory: The New Testament Apostle in the Early Church* (Grand Rapids, MI: Baker, 2012).

Boring, E. M. "First Peter in Recent Study." *Word & World* 24 (Fall 2004): 358–67.

Callan, T. "Use of the Letter of Jude by the Second Letter of Peter." *Bib* 85 (2004): 42–64.

Campbell, B. L. *Honor, Shame, and the Rhetoric of 1 Peter.* Society of Biblical Literature Dissertation Series 160. Atlanta, GA: Scholars Press, 1998.

Carson, D. A. "1 Peter," "2 Peter," and "Jude." Pages 1,015–61, 1,069–79 in *Commentary on the New Testament Use of the Old Testament.* Ed. by G. K. Beale and D. A. Carson. Grand Rapids, MI: Baker, 2007.

Casurella, A. *A Bibliography of Literature on First Peter.* New Testament Tools and Studies 16. Leiden, Netherlands: Brill, 1996.

Charles, J. D. "1, 2 Peter." Pages 275–411 in *The Expositor's Bible Commentary.* Rev. ed. Vol. 13: *Hebrews–Revelation.* Grand Rapids, MI: Zondervan, 2005.

_________. "Jude." Pages 539–69 in *The Expositor's Bible Commentary.* Rev. ed. Vol. 13: *Hebrews–Revelation.* Grand Rapids, MI: Zondervan, 2005.

_________. *Literary Strategy in the Epistle of Jude.* Scranton, PA: University Press, 1993.

_________. *Virtue Amidst Vice: The Catalog of Virtues in 2 Peter 1.* Journal for the Study of the New Testament Supplement 150. Sheffield, UK: Sheffield Academic Press, 1997.

Davids, P. H. *2 Peter and Jude: A Handbook on the Greek Text.* Baylor Handbook on the Greek New Testament. Waco, TX: Baylor University Press, 2011.

_________. *The First Epistle of Peter.* New International Commentary on the New Testament. Grand Rapids, MI: Eerdmans, 1990.

_________. *The Letters of 2 Peter and Jude.* Pillar New Testament Commentary. Grand Rapids, MI: Eerdmans, 2006.

_________. *A Theology of James, Peter, and Jude: Living in the Light of the Coming King.* Biblical Theology of the New Testament. Grand Rapids, MI: Zondervan, 2014.

_________. "The Use of Second Temple Traditions in 1 and 2 Peter and Jude." Pages 409–31 in *The Catholic Epistles and the Tradition.* Edited by J. Schlosser. Bibliotheca Ephemeridum Theologicarum Lovaniensium 176. Leuven, Belgium: Peeters, 2004.

DeSilva, D. A. *The Jewish Teachers of Jesus, James, and Jude: What Earliest Christianity Learned from the Apocrypha and Pseudepigrapha.* Oxford, UK: Oxford University Press, 2012.

Dryden, J. *Theology and Ethics in 1 Peter: Paraenetic Strategies for Christian Character Formation.* Wissenschaftliche Untersuchungen zum Neuen Testament, 2/209. Tübingen, Germany: Mohr Siebeck, 2006.

Dubis, M. *1 Peter: A Handbook on the Greek Text.* Baylor Handbook on the Greek New Testament. Waco, TX: Baylor University Press, 2010.

________. "Research on 1 Peter: A Survey of Scholarly Literature Since 1985." *Currents in Biblical Research* 4 (2006): 199–239.

Elliott, J. H. *1 Peter: A New Translation with Introduction and Commentary*. Anchor Bible 37B. New York, NY: Doubleday, 2000.

________. *A Home for the Homeless: A Social-Scientific Criticism of 1 Peter, Its Situation and Strategy, with a New Introduction*. 2nd ed. Philadelphia, PA: Fortress, 1990.

Ellis, E. E. "Prophecy and Hermeneutic in Jude." Pages 221–36 in *Prophecy and Hermeneutic in Early Christianity: New Testament Essays*. Wissenschaftliche Untersuchungen zum Neuen Testament 18. Tübingen, Germany: Mohr Siebeck/Grand Rapids, MI: Eerdmans, 1978.

Feldmeier, R. *The First Letter of Peter: A Commentary on the Greek Text*. Translated by P. H. Davids. Waco, TX: Baylor University Press, 2008. Translation of *Der erste Brief des Petrus*. Theologischer Handkommentar 15/I. Leipzig, Germany: Evangelische Verlagsanstalt, 2005.

Forbes, G. W. *1 Peter*. Exegetical Guide to the Greek New Testament. Nashville, TN: B&H, 2014.

Giese, C. P. *2 Peter and Jude*. Concordia. St. Louis, MO: Concordia, 2012.

Gilmour, M. J. *The Significance of Parallels Between 2 Peter and Other Early Christian Literature*. Academia Biblica 10. Atlanta, GA: Society of Biblical Literature, 2002.

Goppelt, L. *A Commentary on 1 Peter*. Translated by J. E. Alsup. Grand Rapids, MI: Eerdmans, 1993.

Green, E. M. B. *2 Peter Reconsidered*. London, England: Tyndale, 1961.

Green, G. L. *Jude and 2 Peter*. Baker Exegetical Commentary on the New Testament. Grand Rapids, MI: Baker, 2008.

Green, J. B. *1 Peter*. Two Horizons New Testament Commentary. Grand Rapids, MI: Eerdmans, 2007.

________. "Narrating the Gospel in 1 and 2 Peter." *Interpretation* 60 (2006): 262–77.

Green, M. *The Second Epistle General of Peter and the General Epistle of Jude*. 2nd ed. Grand Rapids, MI: Eerdmans, 1987.

Greenlee, J. H. *An Exegetical Summary of Jude*. 2nd ed. Dallas, TX: SIL International, 2008.

Grudem, W. A. *The First Epistle of Peter: An Introduction and Commentary*. Tyndale New Testament Commentary. Grand Rapids, MI: Eerdmans, 1997.

Harink, D. *1 and 2 Peter*. Brazos Theological Commentary on the Bible. Grand Rapids, MI: Brazos, 2009.

Harner, P. B. *What Are They Saying About the Catholic Epistles?* Mahwah, NJ: Paulist, 2004.

Heil, J. P. *1 Peter, 2 Peter, and Jude: Worship Matters*. Eugene, OR: Cascade, 2013.

Helyer, L. R. *The Life and Witness of Peter*. Downers Grove, IL: InterVarsity, 2012.

Horrell, D. G. *1 Peter*. New Testament Guides. London, England: T&T Clark, 2008.

________. *Becoming Christian: Essays on 1 Peter and the Making of Christian Identity*. Library of New Testament Studies 394. London, England: Bloomsbury T&T Clark, 2013.

Jobes, K. H. *1 Peter*. Baker Exegetical Commentary on the New Testament. Grand Rapids, MI: Baker, 2005.

________. *Letters to the Church: A Survey of Hebrews and the General Epistles*. Grand Rapids, MI: Zondervan, 2011.

________. "The Syntax of 1 Peter. Just How Good Is the Greek?" *Bulletin for Biblical Research* 13 (2003): 159–73.

Kelly, J. N. D. *A Commentary on the Epistles of Peter and of Jude*. Harper's New Testament Commentaries. New York, NY: Harper & Row, 1969.

Kruger, M. J. "The Authenticity of 2 Peter." *Journal of the Evangelical Theological Society* 42 (1999): 645–71.

Marshall, I. H. *1 Peter*. IVP New Testament Commentary. Downers Grove, IL: InterVarsity, 1991.

Martin, R. P. "The Theology of Jude, 1 Peter, and 2 Peter." Pages 63–163 in *The Theology of the Letters of James, Peter, and Jude* by A. Chester and R. P. Martin. Cambridge, UK: Cambridge University Press, 1994.

Martin, T. *Metaphor and Composition in 1 Peter*. Society of Biblical Literature Dissertation Series 131. Atlanta, GA: Scholars, 1992.

Mason, E. F., and T. W. Martin, eds. *Reading 1–2 Peter and Jude: A Resource for Students*. Society of Biblical Literature Resources for Biblical Study. Atlanta, GA: Society of Biblical Literature, 2014.

Mbuvi, A. M. *Temple, Exile and Identity in 1 Peter*. Library of New Testament Studies 345. London, England: T&T Clark, 2007.

McKnight, S. *1 Peter*. NIV Application Commentary. Grand Rapids, MI: Zondervan, 1996.

Michaels, J. R. *1 Peter*. Word Biblical Commentary 49. Waco, TX: Word, 1988.

Moo, D. J. *2 Peter, Jude*. NIV Application Commentary. Grand Rapids, MI: Zondervan, 1996.

Neyrey, J. H. *2 Peter, Jude: A New Translation with Introduction and Commentary*. Anchor Bible 37C. New York, NY: Doubleday, 1993.

Niebuhr, K.-W., and R. W. Wall, eds. *The Catholic Epistles and Apostolic Tradition: A New Perspective on James to Jude*. Waco, TX: Baylor University Press, 2009.

Nienhuis, D. R., and R. W. Wall. *Reading the Epistles of James, Peter, John, and Jude as Scripture: The Shaping and Shape of a Canonical Collection*. Grand Rapids, MI: Eerdmans, 2013.

Osburn, C. D. "Discourse Analysis and Jewish Apocalyptic in the Epistle of Jude." Pages 287–319 in *Linguistics and New Testament Interpretation*. Edited by D. A. Black. Nashville, TN: B&H, 1992.

Painter, J., and D. A. deSilva. *James and Jude*. Paideia. Grand Rapids, MI: Baker, 2012.

Picirilli, R. E. "Allusions to 2 Peter in the Apostolic Fathers." *Journal for the Study of the New Testament* 33 (1988): 57–83.

Reese, R. A. *2 Peter and Jude*. Two Horizons New Testament Commentary. Grand Rapids, MI: Eerdmans, 2007.

____________. *Writing Jude: The Reader, the Text, and the Author in Constructs of Power and Desire*. Biblical Interpretation Series 51. Leiden, Netherlands: Brill, 2000.

Richard, E. J. *Reading 1 Peter, Jude, and 2 Peter: A Literary and Theological Commentary*. Macon, GA: Smyth & Helwys, 2000.

Sargent, B. *Written to Serve: The Use of Scripture in 1 Peter*. Library of New Testament Studies. London, England: Bloomsbury T&T Clark, 2015.

Schreiner, T. R. *1, 2 Peter, Jude*. New American Commentary 37. Nashville, TN: B&H, 2003.

Schutter, W. L. *Hermeneutics and Composition in First Peter*. Wissenschaftliche Untersuchungen zum Neuen Testament 30. Tübingen, Germany: Mohr Siebeck, 1989.

Selwyn, E. G. *The First Epistle of St. Peter: The Greek Text with Introduction, Notes and Essays*. London, England: Macmillan, 1955.

Senior, D. P. *1 Peter, Jude, and 2 Peter*. Sacra Pagina 15. Collegeville, MN: Liturgical Press, 2003.

Strange, D. *An Exegetical Summary of 2 Peter.* 2nd ed. Dallas, TX: SIL International, 2008.

Talbert, C. H., ed. *Perspectives on First Peter.* Macon, GA: Mercer University Press, 1986.

Thurén, L. *Argument and Theology in 1 Peter: The Origins of Christian Paraenesis.* Journal for the Study of the New Testament Supplement Series 114. Sheffield, UK: Sheffield Academic Press, 1995.

____________. "Hey Jude! Asking for the Original Situation and Message of a Catholic Epistle." *Journal for the Study of the New Testament* 43 (1997): 451–65.

Watson, D. F. *Invention, Arrangement and Style: Rhetorical Criticism of Jude and 2 Peter.* SBL Dissertation Series 104. Atlanta, GA: Society of Biblical Literature, 1988.

____________, and T. Callan. *First and Second Peter.* Paideia. Grand Rapids, MI: Baker, 2012.

____________, and R. L. Webb, eds. *Reading Second Peter with New Eyes: Methodological Reassessments of the Letter of Second Peter.* Library of New Testament Studies 382. London, England: T&T Clark, 2010.

Webb, R. L. *The Letters of Jude and Second Peter.* New International Commentary on the New Testament. Grand Rapids, MI: Eerdmans, forthcoming.

____________. "The Petrine Epistles: Recent Developments and Trends." Pages 373–90 in *The Face of New Testament Studies: A Survey of Recent Research.* Edited by S. McKnight and G. R. Osborne. Grand Rapids, MI: Baker, 2004.

____________, and B. Bauman-Martin, eds. *Reading First Peter with New Eyes: Methodological Reassessments of the Letter of First Peter.* Library of New Testament Studies 364. London, England: T&T Clark, 2007.

____________, and P. H. Davids, eds. *Reading Jude with New Eyes: Methodological Reassessments of the Letter of Jude.* Library of New Testament Studies 383. London, England: T&T Clark, 2009.

Williams, M. *The Doctrine of Salvation in the First Letter of Peter.* Society for New Testament Studies Monograph Series 149. Cambridge, UK: Cambridge University Press, 2011.

Williams, T. B. *Good Works in 1 Peter: Negotiating Social Conflict and Christian Identity in the Greco-Roman World.* Wissenschaftliche Untersuchungen zum Neuen Testament 337. Tübingen, Germany: Mohr Siebeck, 2014.

____________. *Persecution in 1 Peter: Differentiating and Contextualizing Early Christian Suffering,* Supplements to Novum Testamentum 145. Leiden, Netherlands: Brill, 2012.

Witherington, B., III. *Letters and Homilies for Hellenized Christians,* vol. 2: *A Socio-Rhetorical Commentary on 1–2 Peter.* Downers Grove, IL: InterVarsity, 2008.

____________. *Letters and Homilies for Jewish Christians: A Socio-Rhetorical Commentary on Hebrews, James and Jude.* Downers Grove, IL: InterVarsity, 2007.

Chapter 19

The Johannine Epistles: 1–3 John

CORE KNOWLEDGE

Basic Knowledge: Students should know the key facts of 1, 2, and 3 John. With regard to history, students should be able to identify each book's author, date, provenance, destination, and purpose. With regard to literature, they should be able to provide a basic outline of each book and identify core elements of each book's content found in the Unit-by-Unit Discussion. With regard to theology, students should be able to identify the major theological themes in 1, 2, and 3 John.

Intermediate Knowledge: Students should be able to present the arguments for historical, literary, and theological conclusions. With regard to history, students should be able to discuss the evidence for Johannine authorship, date, provenance, destination, and purpose. With regard to literature, they should be able to provide a detailed outline of the book. With regard to theology, students should be able to discuss the major theological themes in the Johannine Epistles and the ways in which they uniquely contribute to the NT canon.

Advanced Knowledge: Students should be able to interact cogently with modern critics who jettison the opinion of the ancient church's adherence to John's authorship of

1–3 John. They should also be able to discuss the identity of the "elect lady" in 2 John 1, explain the genre of 1 John, and discuss the various structural proposals for 1 John.

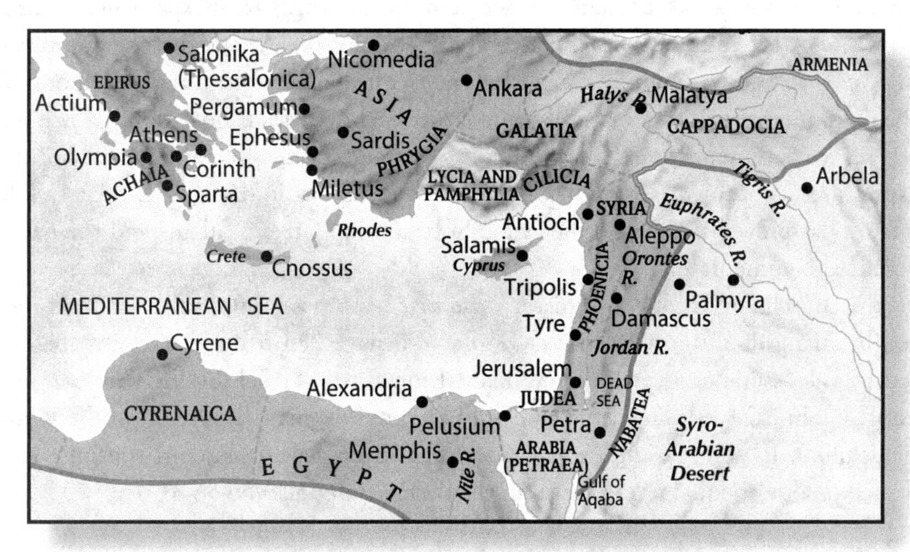

Map 19.1 Provenance and destination of 1–3 John

KEY FACTS

Author:	John the son of Zebedee
Date:	ca. 90–95
Provenance:	Asia Minor
Destination:	Churches in and around Ephesus
Occasion:	The recent departure of false teachers from the Ephesian church (1 John); itinerant false teachers (2 John); an autocratic despot named Diotrephes (3 John)
Purpose:	John encourages believers to love God and one another and reassures them that they are in the Son (1 John). He instructs them not to extend hospitality to false teachers (2 John), and he helps Gaius deal with the autocratic Diotrephes (3 John).
Theme:	Christian reassurance and continuing to walk in love and truth
Key Verses:	1 John 5:11–12; 2 John 9–11; 3 John 4

INTRODUCTION

IN HIS LECTURES on 1 John, Martin Luther declared, "I have never read a book written in simpler words than this one, and yet the words are inexpressible."[1] His fellow Reformer John Calvin remarked about the author, "At one time he admonishes us in general to a godly and holy life; and at another he gives express directions about love. Yet he does none of this systematically, but varies teaching with exhortation."[2]

These two comments reveal a measure of the paradox of the Johannine Letters: simple in expression (a vocabulary of only 303 words) but complex in thought. Especially John's first letter has proved to be both the staple of beginning Greek students and the bane of experienced commentators.

In the church and throughout history, the first letter has been read, loved, and memorized by many doubting Christians, people who have fled to its contents to be comforted by the assurance it provides. William Penn was so struck by the new command given in 1 John that he named the chief city of Pennsylvania "the city of brotherly love" (Philadelphia). In contrast, the second and third letters have been, and continue to be, neglected in almost equal proportions, to the detriment of all who do so.

HISTORY

Author

External Evidence Early church tradition unanimously held that the author of 1 John was the apostle John, the son of Zebedee, but 2 John and 3 John were not as strongly attested. Origen (ca. AD 185–254) noted that some did not receive these letters, though he himself did.[3] In spite of the wavering of a few, 2 and 3 John were received into the canon on the strength of the conviction that John the apostle was their author.

More recently, however, confidence in the tradition has frequently been undermined by the claim that no explicit attribution to John as the author occurs until Irenaeus (ca. AD 130–200). Statements such as this one by R. Brown are common: "[T]here is no certain evidence among Christian writers of a knowledge of any of the Johannine Epistles before the middle of the second century [and] the lack of early attestation makes us cautious about assuming that there was a solid tradition throughout the second century attributing them to a known figure named John."[4] This skepticism is often used to support

---

[1] M. Luther, *D. Martin Luthers Werke: Kritische Gesamtausgabe, Weimarer Lutherausgabe*, vol. 28 (Cologne, Germany: Böhlau, 1903), 183.

[2] J. Calvin, *The Gospel According to St. John 11–21 and the First Epistle of John*, trans. T. H. L. Parker (Grand Rapids, MI: Eerdmans, 1959), 231.

[3] Cited in Eusebius, *Eccl. Hist.* 6.25.10.

[4] R. E. Brown, *The Epistles of John*, AB 30 (Garden City, NY: Doubleday, 1982), 6; cf. J. Painter, *1, 2, and 3 John*, SacPag (Collegeville, MN: Liturgical Press, 2002), 40.

a theory that the orthodox were initially apprehensive of the Johannine Letters until their rehabilitation by Irenaeus.[5]

In response, it should be noted that these kinds of statements arise from the overly rigid demand that a text must be mentioned as "from John" before it can be used in support of John's authorship. But this is an illegitimate burden imposed on the source quotation. If this is kept in mind, it becomes relevant that solid evidence of the authoritative use of these letters, likely implying the assumption and acceptance of John's authorship, exists well before Irenaeus.[6] Polycarp (ca. AD 69–155),[7] Ignatius (ca. AD 35–110), Papias (ca. AD 60–130), the *Epistula Apostolorum* (ca. AD 140), and the Epistle to Diognetus (second or third century), among others, all show at least a great appreciation for the Johannine Letters prior to Irenaeus. If we are correct about the date (late first century) for the epistles, these authoritative citations are beyond impressive. The recognition of the letters happened at a tremendous velocity. Much of this evidence, then, instills confidence that the apostle John wrote them.[8]

From Irenaeus's time forward, there is a steady stream of citations that continues to express the confidence evidenced in the earliest literature. A brief inventory of the more germane evidence since Irenaeus includes the following: the Muratorian Canon (later second century?) refers to the letters (in the plural) as coming from John; Tertullian (ca. AD 160–225) cited 1 John at least forty times as the work of John; Clement of Alexandria (ca. AD 150–215) referred to 1 John as the "greater epistle" (*Stromateis* 2.15.66), and he also wrote a short commentary on 2 John. Third John is first mentioned in the extant patristic works by Origen (ca. AD 185–254). Dionysius of Alexandria (Origen's successor, who died AD 265) held to John's authorship of 1 John but knew there was a "reputed" 2 and 3 John (Eusebius, *Eccl. Hist.* 7.25.7–8.11).

---

[5] See the comments on the external evidence for authorship in the chapter on John's Gospel for a defense against the commonly held opinion that there was a "Johannophobia" among the orthodox (a.k.a. the orthodox "Johannophobia" [OJP] theory), a term coined by C. E. Hill, *The Johannine Corpus in the Early Church* (Oxford, UK: Oxford University Press, 2004), 63–67.

[6] Irenaeus's quote of 2 John 7–8 occurs in a context that refers to 1 John and cites 2 John as if it were in the same letter (*Against Heresies* 3.16.8). Instead of claiming that Irenaeus was mistaken, it is more commonly held that this is evidence that at least 1 and 2 John circulated together. See Brown, *Epistles*, 10.

[7] Brown (*An Introduction to the New Testament*, ABRL [New York, NY: Doubleday, 1997], 389) stated that the letter must have been written prior to AD 150, but it is possible to be more specific. Since the letter, which was sent as a cover letter for the Ignatian Epistles, inquires about the fate of Ignatius (13.2), one can surmise that it was composed soon after his martyrdom, between ca. AD 107 and 110. M. W. Holmes (*The Apostolic Fathers: Greek Texts and English Translations*, 3rd ed. [Grand Rapids, MI: Baker, 2007], 275–76) said that the letter is customarily dated within a few weeks (or at most months) afterward. Thus, many date the letter to the Philippians as early as AD 108 (e.g., S. L. Peterson, *Timeline Charts of the Western Church* [Grand Rapids, MI: Zondervan, 1999], 19). Polycarp showed not only knowledge of 1 John but also affinities with John's language and thought, especially chaps. 9–10; compare 10.1 ("joined together in truth") with 3 John 8 ("co-workers with the truth").

[8] See the impressive study by C. E. Hill, *The Johannine Corpus in the Early Church*, for a thorough catalogue of early Johannine citations.

The external data point quite early to 1 and 2 John as coming from the apostle. John's authorship of 3 John, most likely due to the letter's brevity, its direct address to an individual (Gaius), and the lack of extant patristic works, makes it less widely supported. Even so, C. E. Hill suggests that *The Epistula Apostolorum* 38 (ca. AD 115–140) likely cites 2 John 4 or 3 John 3–4 when it employs the phrase "walking in truth."[9] Nevertheless, since there is evidence to assume that the letters circulated together, it is likely that 3 John was included as well. This would be consistent with what is known of published letter collections in antiquity.[10] So the letters are cited consistently as authoritative without a single source proposing a different author. This assumption of John's authorship held sway until the 1800s.

In modern circles it is common to jettison the opinion of the ancient church and to propose sometimes radically different answers to the questions of authorship and origins. Alternative proposals include: (1) an unknown elder in the so-called "Johannine community"; (2) a follower of the apostle John (or the "one Jesus loved"; 13:23; etc.); or (3) the legendary "John the elder" in Asia Minor.[11] Much of this is based on prior convictions pertaining to the authorship and origins of John's Gospel. The prevailing theory of the last generation of scholarship is that a sectarian community on the fringe of orthodoxy, one related to the beloved disciple, is responsible for John's Gospel. A series of events produced the Gospel in stages in interaction with the "Johannine community's" parent synagogue, and later the letters were generated in response to a painful split in the community.[12] On the assumption that John's Gospel and the Johannine Letters come from two different hands, the theory posits that (1) the stylistic uniformity of John's Gospel and the Johannine Letters is reflective of a "house style" but not common authorship; and (2) that the linguistic and thematic divergences suggest separate authors.

While the vast number of stylistic similarities between John's Gospel and the Johannine Letters is undeniable, some point to several alleged divergences to support the theory of separate authorship. One of the most influential early proponents of separate authorship in the first half of the twentieth century was British scholar C. H. Dodd.[13] Dodd argued that in matters of style, John's Gospel has rich subtlety, "which the Epistle cannot pretend."[14]

---

[9] Ibid., 369. Further, Irenaeus may echo 3 John 9 when he refers to an elder "puffed up in pride of holding the chief seat" (A.H. 4.26.3), ibid., 99.

[10] See "Appendix A: The Collection of Paul's Letters," in D. Guthrie, *New Testament Introduction*, rev. ed. (Downers Grove, IL: InterVarsity, 1990), 986–1,000; D. Trobisch, *Paul's Letter Collection: Tracing the Origins* (Minneapolis, MN: Fortress, 2000 [1994]); and S. E. Porter, ed., *The Pauline Canon*, Pauline Studies 1 (Leiden, Netherlands: Brill, 2004).

[11] This was a popular decision among nineteenth-century theologians that has been reopened by M. Hengel, *The Johannine Question* (London, England: SCM, 1989). See the discussions of Papias's statement in Eusebius, *Eccl. Hist.* 3.39.4.

[12] On the status of the Johannine community theory, see the comments in chapter 7.

[13] C. H. Dodd, *The Johannine Epistles*, MNTC (New York, NY: Harper, 1946); idem, "The First Epistle of John and the Fourth Gospel," *BJRL* 21 (1937): 129–56. This is in spite of able works countering Dodd such as W. G. Wilson, "An Examination of the Linguistic Evidence Adduced Against the Unity of Authorship of the First Epistle of John and the Fourth Gospel," *JTS* 49 (1947): 147–56; W. F. Howard, "The Common Authorship of the Johannine Gospel and Epistles," *JTS* 48 (1947): 12–25.

[14] Dodd, *Epistles*, xlix. According to Dodd, the writer of the letters overworked certain grammatical constructions and used a smaller set of compound verbs. Moreover, he was "immoderately addicted" to conditional sentences. Following

He alleged that these linguistic phenomena pointed to a different writer: (1) a lack of Aramaic influences; (2) a high rate of *hapax legomena* (1 John has forty words that do not appear in the Gospel); and (3) different language used for subjects relating to salvation. Thematically, Dodd argued that 1 John has no OT quotation and only one explicit OT reference (1 John 3:12), while John's Gospel is filled with OT quotes and allusions. Dodd also noted that unlike John's Gospel, 1 John shows few Jewish characteristics. Instead, the letter appears to reflect gnostic thought (e.g., "anointing," 2:20; "divine seed," 3:9, author's translation), which is foreign to John's Gospel.[15]

R. Brown, on the other hand, rightly dismissed most of Dodd's stylistic arguments as easily answered with reference to the respective genres of Gospel and Letter.[16] Nevertheless, Brown took up and expanded several of the thematic issues raised by Dodd, arguing against common authorship on the basis of clarity, thematic issues, and the life situation of the letters. These are the foundations for most who advance separate authorship for the epistles today.[17] According to Brown, the Gospel writer was relatively simple and clear in his expression, while the author of the Johannine Letters wrote with "infuriating" obscurity.[18] But obscurity is itself a subjective phenomenon; what may be obscure for some (such as Brown) may be clear to others (especially the original readers of the Johannine Letters).

Brown cites five major differences in thought between John's Gospel and the Johannine Letters that he found especially damaging to the notion of common authorship:

- The prologue of 1 John does not emphasize the incarnation of the personified Word, as does the prologue of John. Rather, it testifies to the *word (message) of life* which was seen, heard, and felt—the human career of Jesus.
- First John assigns to God features that the Gospel assigns to Jesus; for example, in 1 John 1:5 "God is light" (see John 8:12; 9:5); in 1 John 4:21 and 2 John 5 God gives the command to love one another (see John 13:34).

Dodd, there was a marked readiness on the part of some to disparage the author of the letters in the effort to prove that the Gospel could not have been written by John. E.g., K. Grayston (*The Johannine Epistles*, New Century Bible Commentary [Grand Rapids, MI: Eerdmans, 1984], 7–9) described a hierarchy of ability within the Johannine literature. While the Gospel is the high-water mark of intelligence and expression, the writer of 1 John pedantically transformed the existentialism of the Gospel into a historical expression and "thereby degraded it." Even further down the scale is the "less adept" author of 2 and 3 John, who preferred speaking to writing, simply repeated the tradition, renounced deviation, and on the whole was more limited than the writer of 1 John.

[15] Dodd, *Epistles*, xlix. Dodd considered "God is love" to be Hellenistic thought hammered out on a Christian anvil. The abstract "love" would not be found in Semitic thought. The Fourth Gospel instead declares that "God is spirit" (John 4:24).

[16] Brown (*Epistles*, 24) stated, "Overall, then, it seems that the variation of minute stylistic features between GJohn and 1 John is not much different from the variation that one can find if one compares one part of GJohn to another part. In particular, the Johannine Jesus speaks as the author of the Johannine Epistles writes."

[17] See, e.g., J. Lieu (*I, II, III John: A Commentary*, NTL [Louisville, KY: Westminster John Knox, 2008], 17), who lists similar complaints to suggest, instead of common authorship or knowledge of the Gospel, that the letters and the Gospel draw independently on earlier formulations.

[18] Brown, *Epistles*, 24–25; see Painter, *1, 2, and 3 John*, 60.

- There is less epistolary emphasis on the Spirit as a person, and the Gospel term *paraklētos* is never used of the Spirit; Christ is the *paraklētos* or advocate in 1 John 2:1. In 1 John there is a simple warning that not every spirit is the Spirit of truth or the Spirit of God, and so spirits must be tested (4:1, 6).
- Final eschatology is stronger in 1 John than in John, where realized eschatology dominates. There is more emphasis on the parousia as the moment of accountability for the Christian life (1 John 2:28–3:3).
- Especially as to vocabulary, the Dead Sea Scroll parallels are even closer in 1 John than in John.[19]

In order, we contend that (1) many scholars hold that the referent in the epistolary prologue is indeed the person of Jesus; (2) Johannine Christology clearly would have no problem with Jesus and God being referred to interchangeably (e.g., 1:1–2; 5:17; 10:30; 14:9–11); (3) the reference to the Paraclete in the Gospel obliquely names Jesus as a Paraclete as well (the Holy Spirit is "another Paraclete"; *allos paraklētos*); (4) true, final eschatology is more pronounced in Johannine Letters but is certainly not lacking in John's Gospel (e.g., John 14:2); finally, (5) most of the parallels between Qumran and 1 John are found in the *Community Rule* (1QS),[20] which is not a narrative and may have similar language due to similar emphases (e.g., love for fellow believers). Moreover, the distance Brown suggests between the Gospel and Qumran is not a conceded point in scholarship. E. Mburu contends that something more than a shared milieu (Brown's opinion) is going on between John and Qumran.[21] None of these alleged differences conclusively proves separate authorship for John's Gospel and Johannine Letters, as Brown himself concedes.

For Brown and his followers, it is clearly the historical reconstruction of the "Johannine community" that points to a different author for the Johannine Letters. Yet theories like this have an ebb and flow in academia. For example, Bultmann, in his time, strode across the theological landscape of two continents but is now relegated to chapters in history-of-interpretation works. The Johannine community theory is fast packing up to move to the same location.[22]

---

[19] Brown, *Introduction*, 389.

[20] For a description of the parallels, see T. A. Hoffman, "1 John and the Qumran Scrolls," *BTB* 8 (1978): 117–25; and M.-É. Boismard, "The First Epistle of John and the Writings of Qumran," in *John and the Dead Sea Scrolls*, ed. J. C. Charlesworth (London, England: J. Chapman, 1972), 156–65.

[21] She states, "The implication therefore, is that the author of the Fourth Gospel may well have been exposed to these ideas, whether in Jerusalem or Ephesus. Moreover, the close semantic similarities, particularly with the Rule, make it likely that he was familiar with their mode of thought and followed their model in articulating his ideas in certain parts of his Gospel. The position of this work is that while this does not require a direct literary dependence on the scrolls, the close semantic continuity calls for a closer familiarity with their ideas and terminology than would be provided for merely by a shared milieu." E. M. Mburu, *Qumran and the Origins of Johannine Language and Symbolism*, Jewish and Christian Texts: Contexts and Related Studies 8 (London, England: T&T Clark, 2010), 192.

[22] For a description of the possible demise of the theory and a sociolinguistic investigation of it, see D. A. Lamb, *Text, Context and the Johannine Community: A Sociolinguistic Analysis of the Johannine Writings*, LNTS (JNTS) 477 (London, England: Bloomsbury T&T Clark, 2014). More and more writers do tend to stand at a distance from the theory. See, e.g.,

With regard to Johannine Letters, even if Brown's reconstruction (or the many other varieties) were substantially correct, this still would not *necessarily* demonstrate separate authorship.[23] If common authorship is rejected, this is often done not on the grounds of the available evidence but on *a priori* grounds.

To sum up, none of the objections raised by Dodd, Brown, and others actually prove, or even plausibly suggest, separate authorship of John's Gospel and Johannine Letters. The occasional differences in style can be accounted for by the respective genres and other factors (such as differing document lengths). The alleged thematic divergences often depend on antecedent judgments that are likewise highly questionable or do not necessarily point to a different author. It seems reasonable to conclude that even the cumulative effect of these supposed difficulties does not bear sufficient weight to establish separate authorship.

Internal Evidence B. H. Streeter's dictum is often repeated: "The three Epistles and the Gospel of John are so closely allied in diction, style, and general outlook that the burden of proof lies with the person who would deny their common authorship."[24] The similarities are so numerous and multifaceted that they dwarf any perceived differences by comparison. While admitted by all, these similarities are often attributed to either a "house style" within the Johannine community or a conscious imitation. So it is important not simply to note the similarities but to look for those congruities that suggest a writer was naturally expressing himself in ways other than conscious imitation. The below observations can be made.

1. The same author would be expected to use similar vocabulary in similar ways. This occurs at an overwhelming rate when John's Letters are compared to the Gospel bearing

---

B. Witherington III (*Invitation to the New Testament: First Things* [Oxford, UK: Oxford University Press, 2013], 342) who suggests as many as three different writers for the Johannine corpus but is quick to point out, "None of these conclusions, however, call for the supposition that we are dealing with a Johannine *school* of some sort." L. T. Johnson (*The New Testament Writings*, 3rd ed. [Minneapolis, MN: Fortress, 2010], 463) affirms separation from the synagogue at some point (John 9); a Samaritan connection (John 4); Greek-speaking Jews (e.g., John 12:20); but "what this information amounts to, however, is less than clear." Obviously, the theory no longer holds the hegemony over Johannine scholarship it once did. This is not to say that no one holds to the theory (or some version of it) today. See, e.g., the first volume of the three-volume work by U. von Wahlde, *The Gospel and Letters of John*, Vol. 1: *Introduction, Analysis, and Reference* (Grand Rapids, MI: Eerdmans, 2010). Von Wahlde suggests a theory featuring three editions of the Gospel of John, with the production of the first epistle in AD 65–70 (ibid., 50–56).

[23] Brown (*Epistles*, 30) himself admitted this: "They could have been written at the same time by different men . . . or, and this is more probable, at a different time by either the same man (sadder and wiser as he faces a new battle, now from within the movement) or by different men." Brown, for his part, posited a theory that during the production of John's Gospel there were various struggles with outside groups. What he finds startling is that Johannine Letters show no struggle with those outside but only with insiders. Also, the issue at stake in the debate was not whether Jesus was the Christ but whether he came in the flesh (i.e., whether Jesus was fully human). According to Brown, this points to a period of development and divergence within the "Johannine community." Brown asserted that two rival groups were interpreting the Gospel in different ways. One, the orthodox, was swallowed up by the great church; the other, the opponents of 1 John, was funneled into the gnostic movement. His classic treatment of the issues is R. E. Brown, ***Community of the Beloved Disciple: The Life, Loves and Hates of an Individual Church in the New Testament Times*** (Mahwah, NJ: Paulist, 1978). See also idem, "'Other Sheep Not of This Fold': The *Johannine* Perspective on Christian Diversity in the Late First Century," *JBL* 97 (1978): 5–22.

[24] B. H. Streeter, *The Four Gospels*, rev. ed. (London, England: Macmillan, 1930), 460.

his name. A small sample will give the general contours of the phenomenon.[25] Jesus as the "one and only" (1 John 4:9; John 1:14, 18; 3:16, 18 KJV); "Word" referring to Christ (1 John 1:1; John 1:1, 14); "eternal life" (1 John 1:2; 2:25; 3:15; 5:11, 13, 20; John 3:15, 16, 36); "the Spirit of truth" (1 John 4:6; John 14:17; 16:13); "to practice the truth" (1 John 1:6; John 3:21); "from the world" (1 John 2:16; 4:5; John 8:23); "remain in Him/Me" (1 John 2:27; 4:13; John 15:4, 6–7); and a host of others.[26] There are marked contrasts in both documents: love and hate (1 John 3:11–15; John 3:19–21; 15:18–25); life and death (1 John 3:14; John 5:24); light and darkness (1 John 1:5; John 1:5); truth and falsehood (1 John 1:6, 8; 2:4, 21; John 8:44–45); and children of God and children of the Devil (1 John 3:10; John 8:33–47). This phenomenon is remarkable given the brevity of John's Letters.[27]

2. The same author would be expected to use his stock of phrases and themes in a nimble fashion and not like an imitator. In other words, if all that were found were exact correspondences to the Gospel usage, this might point to imitation. But this is not the case. For example, the "Counselor" (*paraklētos*) in John's Gospel (the Holy Spirit) is "another Counselor" (John 14:16); Jesus is the "atoning sacrifice" (*paraklētos*) in 1 John (2:2). The statement that "God is spirit" (John 4:24; cf. 3:33, "God is true") is similar in form to "God is love" (1 John 4:8, 16) and "God is light" (1 John 1:5). Brooke points out that the author of 1 John frequently filled up the basic outline of a thought in John's Gospel in a distinct yet closely related manner. He cited the following instances, among others: 1 John 5:10//John 3:18; 1 John 1:2//John 1:1; 1 John 3:8//John 8:41.[28] As Brooke observed, "This suggests a writer who varies his own phrases, rather than a mere copyist."[29]

3. The same author would be expected to compose his works with a similar style. This is exactly what characterizes John's Letters. The relatively simple syntax is the norm for both John's Gospel and his letters, and the same stock of Greek words and constructions can be seen in both.[30] A peculiar example of this is the use of intersentence conjunctions. Poythress has demonstrated that sentences are frequently connected by asyndeton, that is,

---

[25] H. J. Holtzmann wrote the foundational work on Johannine vocabulary: "Das Problem des ersten johanneischen Briefes in seinem Verhältnis zum Evangelium," *Jahrbuch für Protestantische Theologie* 7 (1881): 690–712; 8 (1882): 128–52, 316–42, 460–85. These were later included and adapted in English by A. E. Brooke, *A Critical and Exegetical Commentary on the Johannine Epistles* (New York, NY: Scribner, 1912), i–xix.

[26] Brooke (*Epistles*, ii–iv) listed fifty-two separate items, not including fifteen occurrences of "in this/this" followed by an explanatory clause.

[27] Only two words are unique to 1 John and John's Gospel, but these are significant: the words *paraklētos* ("Comforter"/"advocate"; or "Paraclete") and *anthrōpoktonos* ("murderer"). The latter is used in John 8:44, where the Devil is described as a "murderer from the beginning." It is striking that in 1 John 3:8 the word occurs in a section detailing the differences between the children of God and the children of the Devil.

[28] Brooke (*Epistles*, v) noted that one could make the list quite long.

[29] Ibid.

[30] Examples include *ekeinos* ("that one") used as a pronoun; "everyone who is -ing" (*pas ho* + participle instead of *pantes*; 1 John 3:4//John 3:16; similarly, *pan* + participle where *pantes* might be used; 1 John 5:4//John 6: 37); repetition of emphatic words; *kai* + *de* combinations; *kathōs* + *kai* combinations; elliptic use of *ou kathōs* (1 John 3:11–12//John 6:58); and *hina* used like an infinitive.

without coordinating conjunctions. He also noted the infrequent use of "therefore" *(oun)* and other connectors in expository discourse in both John's Gospel and his letters.[31]

4. Another notable piece of evidence is the failure on the part of the proponents of the various forms of the Johannine-community hypothesis to demonstrate Johannine style outside the Johannine literature. If there were "Johannine patterns" or a "house style," would one not expect it to be found also in extrabiblical literature? Indeed, some writings might resemble the "house style" of the "Johannine community." The number of Papias's extant works does not allow one to draw definitive conclusions (though these works do not conform to Johannine style), but there is a larger sample from John's disciple Polycarp. Yet when his *Letter to the Philippians* is examined, it does not display evidence of Johannine style.[32] Kümmel's conclusion is doubtless correct: "[T]here are no cogent reasons for assuming that I John is to be attributed to another author than J[oh]n."[33]

5. The author's self-references indicate that he considered himself an eyewitness to Jesus (see esp. 1 John 1:1–4). There is general agreement, even among those supporting the theory of a "Johannine school," that the writer is one person rather than a community. This is evidenced by his use of the first-person singular thirty-two times throughout the Johannine Letters. However, what is contested is what the writer meant when he used a first-person plural. While the writer did refer to himself several times in the first-person plural in solidarity with his readers, in at least nine instances he referred to himself in distinction from his hearers.[34] Those convinced of the presence of a "Johannine school" find support for their theory in these references.[35]

But this is not necessarily the best way to account for this phenomenon. First, especially in the references in the prologue, the writer used sensory language best understood as the speech of an eyewitness. He claims to have "heard," "seen," and touched with his "hands" "the word of life" (1 John 1:1). The latter expression, using his hands to touch the Word of life, leads us to understand that "word of life" does not refer to the *message* of life but to the Word who *is* life—Jesus Christ (see John 1:1, 14). It is difficult to imagine that such language would have been used by someone not claiming physical contact with Jesus.

6. The author assumed an authoritative tone consistent with an apostle. Although he calls himself an "elder" in 2 and 3 John, this is not inconsistent with being an apostle as

---

[31] V. S. Poythress, "Testing for Johannine Authorship by Examining the Use of Conjunctions," *WTJ* 46 (1984): 350–69. Poythress's test has its flaws, but the general premise is well founded and still holds up to scrutiny. See L. S. Kellum, *The Unity of the Farewell Discourse: The Literary Integrity of John 13.31–16.33*, JSNTSup 256 (New York, NY: T&T Clark, 2004), 113–21.

[32] Polycarp's letter, dated to the first decade of the second century (see above), has a decidedly non-Johannine linguistic stamp. Polycarp does not use *hina* ("in order that") in the same way as the Johannine Epistles; his letter employs *oun* ("therefore") far more frequently in expository genres; it does not use the word *kosmos* ("world") but features *aiōna* ("age") instead; and the Johannine terms *ekeinos* ("that one") and *menō* ("remain") are not used at all. Yet Polycarp was familiar with John's Gospel and the Johannine Epistles and considered them authoritative.

[33] W. G. Kümmel, *Introduction to the New Testament*, rev. ed., trans. H. C. Kee (Nashville, TN: Abingdon, 1975), 445.

[34] 1 John 1:1, 2, 3, 4, 5; 4:6, 14; 3 John 10, 12.

[35] E.g., Brown, *Epistles*, 94–95; and Painter, *1, 2, 3 John*, 45–46.

1 Peter 1:1 shows (cf. 5:1). Papias similarly referred to the apostles as "elders."[36] Thus, there is ample reason to believe John could simultaneously occupy the status of both an apostle and an elder—a prophet also since he wrote Revelation. Thus, in his function as an apostle, he wrote a Gospel; and in his role as an elder, he wrote letters to various congregations.

7. There is also an indication that the author was advanced in years. If the Johannine Letters date from the end of the first century, then any eyewitness would have reached old age by that time. In keeping with this, the author referred to the congregations addressed in John's Letters as "little children," including even those he called "fathers" (1 John 2:12–14).

In the final analysis, although there are recent objections to the apostle John's authorship of the Gospel and of the letters, no evidence has surfaced that is inconsistent with identifying the author of the Gospel with that of the letters.[37] Coupled with the conclusions concerning the authorship of John's Gospel reached above, the apostle John remains the best candidate for author of the letters.

Date

Reliable historical tradition strongly suggests John spent his latter years in Asia Minor in and around Ephesus (see Irenaeus, *Against Heresies* 3.1.2; Eusebius, *Eccl. Hist.* 3.1.1). The apostle's move from Palestine to Asia Minor reportedly took place sometime subsequent to the Jewish rebellion in the year 66. We concluded that John's Gospel was most likely written in the early to mid-80s (see chap. 7). So the question concerning the date of John's Letters is, were they written before or after John's Gospel was penned?

On balance the latter seems more likely. While it is possible that some of the connections with John's Gospel in 1 John are based on a common tradition,[38] in a few places the Gospel seems to be assumed. For example, 1 John 2:7–8 refers to and explicates the meaning of the new commandment of John 13:34–35 without naming it. In 1 John 5:6, reference is made to Jesus's coming by "water and blood," most likely referring to Jesus's baptism and crucifixion respectively (see the verbal parallel with John 19:34).

The idea that the Johannine Letters were written to combat heretical misinterpretations of the Gospel is fairly common.[39] If so, this would require a date after the Gospel. While possible, this is far from settled opinion. Yet even if the purpose for the letters were construed differently, the conclusion that they postdate the Gospel would still appear the most probable in light of the parallels mentioned. The best date, given the death of John

---

[36] Cited in Eusebius, *Eccl. Hist.* 3.39.5–7.

[37] C. S. Keener (*The Gospel of John: A Commentary* [Grand Rapids, MI: Baker, 2012], 1:126) substantially agrees: "The burden of proof remains on those who challenge common authorship, even if more scholars, who often work from minimalist assumptions (i.e., starting from the most skeptical point defensible), hold to different authors than agree with our view here."

[38] See Brooke, *Epistles*, xix–xxii; and Grayston, *Johannine Epistles*, 12–14; Lieu, *I, II, III John*, 17.

[39] D. A. Carson and D. J. Moo, *An Introduction to the New Testament*, 2nd ed. (Grand Rapids, MI: Zondervan, 2005), 676.

at around the turn of the century[40] and the dating of the Gospel in the early to mid-80s, is somewhere in the early to mid-90s.

Provenance

The ancient tradition is uniform that John spent his latter years in Ephesus in Asia Minor. Polycrates, in a letter to Victor of Rome, called John one of the "luminaries" buried in Ephesus.[41] Irenaeus said that John stayed in Ephesus permanently until the reign of Trajan (AD 98–117)[42] and included specific accounts of John's ministry in that city. Without solid evidence to the contrary, most scholars assume the accuracy of the Ephesus tradition.[43]

Destination

In 1 John, John addressed various groups in the congregation as "little children," "fathers," "young men," and "friends" (e.g., 2:12–14; 4:1, 7). These ways of addressing his audience indicate a closely established relationship between John and his readers. Since 1 John does not refer to specific names and places, contains little mention of specific events, and is general in its teaching, it seems that John focused on important truths of broad relevance to address as many believers as possible. This lends credence to the view that 1 John was a circular letter sent to predominantly Gentile churches in and around Ephesus.[44]

Both 2 and 3 John are personal letters. The former was written to an "elect lady and her children" (v. 1), which most likely refers to several local congregations; the latter was written to an individual named Gaius (v. 1), but we know nothing about him.[45]

---

[40] Irenaeus (*Against Heresies* 22.22.5; 3.3.4; quoted by Eusebius, *Eccl. Hist.* 3.23.3–4), placed John's death during the reign of Trajan (98–117); Jerome (*Vir. Ill.* 9) said that John died in the sixty-eighth year after Jesus's passion (98 or 101).

[41] Eusebius, *Eccl. Hist.* 3.31.3; 5.24.2.

[42] Irenaeus, *Against Heresies* 3.1.1.

[43] A minority does posit other provenances. E.g., Kümmel (*Introduction*, 445) advocated a Syrian provenance for John's Gospel on the grounds of "substantive contacts" with the *Odes of Solomon* (which presumably came from Syria) and with Ignatius of Antioch (died ca. AD 110; see ibid., 247, with further bibliographic references in n. 224), and he conjectured that the letters were also written there. Regarding theories that point to linguistic similarities to Gnosticism in Palestine, R. Schnackenburg (*The Johannine Epistles*, trans. R. and I. Fuller [New York: Crossroad, 1992], 40) is undoubtedly correct: "All it means is that the author was born in Palestine."

[44] Augustine's ascription of the letter *ad Parthos*, "to the Parthians," is almost certainly incorrect and may be a corruption of *tou parthenou* ("of the virgin"), a possible reference to John who was frequently regarded as celibate. See P. Schaff, ed., *Nicene and Post-Nicene Fathers*, vol. 7: *Augustin* [sic]: *Homilies on the Gospel of John, Homilies on the First Epistle of John, Soliloquies*, First Series (Peabody, MA: Hendrickson, 1994), 459n1. The title of Augustine's manuscripts is "Ten Homilies on the Epistle of John to the Parthians."

[45] Second and 3 John are more readily recognizable as examples of the first-century personal letter. Both are rather brief (245 and 219 words, respectively) and would easily fit on one papyrus sheet (typical of first-century letters). For a helpful treatment, see the chapter on "New Testament Letters" in Carson and Moo, *Introduction to the New Testament*, 331–53, esp. 332–33 (including further bibliographic references).

Occasion and Purpose

The situation that spawned the letters is an important factor in the interpretation of the letters. In pinpointing the setting of 1–3 John, the historical reconstructions proposed by interpreters have dominated the theological landscape. This is especially the case as it affects how one adjudicates the origins of Johannine literature. Given the importance of the matter and the ripples such decisions generate regarding the interpretation of the Gospel and the letters, a close look at the occasion of each letter is warranted. Below we will survey the options and suggest a methodology that is best suited for interpreting these letters.

Clearly the churches to whom 1–3 John were written are under doctrinal and emotional duress. Three or four specific passages outline the contours of the upheaval: 1 John 2:18–27; 4:1–6; perhaps 5:6–7; and 2 John 7–11.[46] While there was clearly conflict among John's readers, its precise nature is difficult to determine because of the lack of straightforward descriptions of the problem. Schnackenburg aptly observed, "The meager hints and the formulas used in the letter are all we have to go on."[47] Moreover, as Griffin showed, these may be interpreted in different ways.[48]

This, however, has not kept modern scholarship from making a number of attempts to identify the secessionists and their doctrine. At least five views are current, with some degree of variation within the views. The opponents are said to be Gnostics, Docetists, Cerinthian adoptionists, those who downplayed the role of Jesus's death, and Jewish/Judaizing opponents.[49]

Many scholars who confidently reconstruct the history of these churches employ an aggressive "mirror reading" of all the statements in 1 John. The practice takes an expression like "If we say, 'We have no sin'. . ." (1 John 1:8, 10) and confidently promotes it to a slogan by the secessionists that John rebukes by way of oblique reference.[50] K. Jobes is more likely correct to suggest they (and other such "inferences") are "ideas that needed correction regardless of their origin."[51] So that, instead of a sustained polemic, the letter is better characterized as pastoral. Thus, it is best to address the occasion of the letter from a minimum point of view (i.e., from its obvious pastoral nature, not a proposed polemic). We must interpret from what we *know*, not what we guess.

Since the second century it has been proposed that the opponents were Gnostics in one form or another. Since Gnosticism, Docetism, and Cerinthian adoptionism are all related,

---

[46] D. R. Streett, *They Went Out from Us: The Identity of the Opponents in First John*, BZNW 177 (Berlin, Germany: De Gruyter, 2011), 130.

[47] Ibid., 17.

[48] T. Griffith (*Keep Yourselves from Idols: A New Look at 1 John* [London, England: Sheffield Academic Press, 2002]) asserted that the secessionists were reverting back to Judaism and that "in the flesh" does not refer to a docetic theology but merely represents a way of expressing the incarnation. Another nonpolemical argument is found in J. M. Lieu, "'Authority to Become Children of God': A Study of 1 John," *NovT* (1981): 210–28.

[49] Streett, *They Went Out from Us*, 7–8.

[50] Ibid., 113–18.

[51] K. H. Jobes, *1, 2, and 3 John*, ECNT (Grand Rapids, MI: Zondervan, 2013), 68.

they are treated together here.[52] Irenaeus claimed that John wrote his Gospel to refute Cerinthus—an early gnostic teacher who held that the "Christ spirit" descended on Jesus at his baptism and left him at the cross—adoptionism. Irenaeus, however, does not make the same claim for John's Letters.[53] More recently, some drawing upon Irenaeus, claim the letters were written to combat the same or similar gnostic opponent.[54] Thus, it has been fairly common to assert that the problem facing the churches in 1 John is the opposite of the emphasis in the Gospel of John. The Gospel clearly emphasizes the deity of Christ. In contrast, the letters refer to Christ ("come in the flesh," 4:2). Thus, the theory is that a new front in the battle of ideas has emerged: an emphasis on an overly high Christology (e.g., Docetists claimed Christ only appeared to be human).[55] For many the source of this is a misreading of the Fourth Gospel's Christology that in combination with outside forces or developing in isolation produce the schism reported in 1 John.[56]

Nascent Gnosticism of this sort was certainly afoot, and some form of it may have influenced the secession.[57] But wholesale identification of the Ephesian secessionists with Cerinthus's followers, or, for that matter, Gnosticism, is unwarranted.[58]

---

[52] In one sense this is an oversimplification. For the most part, these all find their origins in Greek philosophy. There are, however, a number of non-gnostics who held to a docetic understanding of Christ. Likewise, a number of groups held to a form of adoptionism that are not specifically gnostic.

[53] Irenaeus (*Against Heresies* 3.11.1) also related a confrontation between Cerinthus and John. He noted that John refused to stay in a bath house occupied by Cerinthus and advised the people to flee, "lest even the bath house fall down." Irenaeus (ibid., 3.3.4) named Polycarp as the source of this tradition.

[54] E.g., R. Gundry (*A Survey of the New Testament*, 3rd ed. [Grand Rapids, MI: Zondervan, 1994], 448–49) proposed that Cerinthus is the culprit. But Schnackenburg (*Epistles*, 21–23) noted several differences between the secessionists in 1 John and both Cerinthus and Ignatius's opponents mentioned below.

[55] Not all proponents of a docetic opponent are so specific to name Cerinthus, but this kind of opponent represents a vastly popular stance. See, e.g., Akin, *1, 2, 3 John*, 172–73; M. Hengel, *The Johannine Question* (London, England: SCM, 1989), 59–63; Law, *Tests*, 32; Brooke, *Johannine Epistles*, xliv, xlvi; Schnackenburg, *The Johannine Epistles*, 17–24, and Carson and Moo, *NT Introduction*, 680, to name but a few.

[56] Streett, *They Went Out from Us*, 10–11.

[57] It has been pointed out that Ignatius's letter to the Smyrneans and to the Trallians (in southwest Asia Minor) both show a docetic-type heresy that denies that Christ was actually human (from *dokeō*, "seem," the teaching that Jesus only *appeared* to be human). This is also addressed in his letter to the Ephesians (Ignatius, *To the Smyrnaeans* 2.1, 5.2; *To the Trallians* 10.1; and *To the Ephesians* 7.1). See Marshall, *Epistles*, xx; P. J. Achtemeier, J. B. Green, and M. M. Thompson, *Introducing the New Testament: Its Literature and Theology* (Grand Rapids, MI: Eerdmans, 2001), 539; and F. Thielman, *Theology of the New Testament: A Canonical and Synthetic Approach* (Grand Rapids, MI: Zondervan, 2005), 539–40. Since Ignatius addressed all his letters to churches in Asia Minor, it is likely that something like the docetic doctrines flourished in John's time as well.

[58] So Schnackenburg, *Epistles*, 21–23.

Something to Think About: Speaking the Truth in Love

Interesting, isn't it, that the apostle of love—the apostle John—is also the man who wrote several stern passages warning believers against false teachers. I once attended a church undergoing a nasty split. It had divided into two parties: the "love party" and the "truth party." Those in the "love party" focused on God's love and forbearance with sinners, while the "truth party" emphasized God's righteous demands. Silly, isn't it? I say "silly" because both stances are true if held in proper balance. God is a God of love—in fact, as John tells us, God is love (1 John 4:8)—but he is also most decidedly a God of truth (see John 17:17). Paul rightly said, therefore, that Christians must "speak the truth in love" (see Eph 4:15).

As far as we are able to determine with regard to the background of 1 John, some in the church taught that their confession of Christ was either not enough or invalid. This created all kinds of insecurity and second-guessing among John's "little children" who were no longer sure whether they were Christians at all—when in fact those self-appointed teachers turned out not to be believers in the first place. This seems to follow from 1 John 2:19: "They went out from us, but they did not belong to us; for if they had belonged to us, they would have remained with us. However, they went out so that it might be made clear that none of them belongs to us."

Some in the church might look mighty good for a while. They are the stars, but after a brief time on the ascendancy, they come crashing down like meteorites. This, incidentally, is one of the reasons Paul cautioned his associates not to appoint new converts to positions of church leadership. This also is why John told believers to "test the spirits to see if they are from God, because many false prophets have gone out into the world" (1 John 4:1). So we find that John, the apostle who basked in divine love more than any other NT writer, is also the one who stressed the need for careful discernment of truth in the church. Like Jesus, and like Paul and the other NT authors, John struck a proper balance between truth and love. We, too, should speak the truth in love.

The key passage for this understanding is 1 John 4:2–3 (the Antichrists deny that Jesus has "come in the flesh"; cf. 2 John 7). Thus, it is proposed that the secessionists have some difficulty with the incarnation (whether Gnostic/docetists or adoptionists). It should first be noted that while this passage clearly alludes to the secessionists, it is not certain that it is solely about them. It is more likely that John referred more generally to all false prophets and that the secessionists—whatever their particular manifestation—belonged to this group. The phrase may well be purposefully lacking strict contours.

Moreover, it may not necessarily refer to the incarnation. To be sure, this is possible. However, similar phrasing occurs elsewhere in the NT simply to indicate the standard confession of Christ (see, e.g., 1 Tim 3:16: "He was manifested in the flesh").[59] What is

[59] Streett, *They Went Out from Us*, 204–17. See also 1 Pet 4:1: "Therefore, since Christ suffered *in the flesh*, arm yourselves also with the same understanding—because the one who suffers in the flesh is finished with sin."

more, in what follows, rather than repeating the statement about coming in the flesh, the author simply defined the denial as the failure to confess Jesus. The same pattern continues later in the letter (see 4:15; 5:1, 5). It seems the emphasis lays not so much on refuting a defective fine point of Christology but on the rejection or confession of Jesus as the Messiah.[60] If there is anything else beyond this, it is pure guesswork.[61]

Some, in reference to a theory of origins in the so-called Johannine community, propose the opponents in the Johannine Letters are those former members who downplayed the role of Jesus's death. In this thought, 1 John 4:2 does not describe gnostic Docetism but addresses a denial that Jesus's humanity was important. Moreover, 1 John 5:6 "not by water only, but by water and by blood," is a correction to the belief that Jesus's water baptism, not his conception, is the moment of incarnation. Thus, they deny salvific meaning to the life and death of Christ, suggesting only the pre-existent Christ was important.[62]

However, it has already been noted that 1 John 4:2 is best understood as a rather static expression regarding the church's confession of Christ. The latter passage (5:6) is interpreted by these proponents based on the belief that the phrase "not only . . . but . . ." emphasizes the second element. However, as Streett has pointed out, the same phrase is used at 2:2 ("not only for ours, but also . . .") and cannot be interpreted in this way.[63] Watson is undoubtedly correct to refer to it as the ancient rhetorical device of *amplificatio*.[64] In other words, it is a highlighting method that 2:2 stresses the scope of the atonement to the ultimate degree. Likely a similar use is found at 5:6.[65] Here it could be simply understood as a way of stressing the importance of Jesus's death.[66] It *may* suggest a comment on false doctrine, maybe even the secessionists' doctrine, but there is no indication that it *must*. What is more, we can in no way be as specific as the proponents of this theory. It would apply to all who make Jesus a good teacher, a prophet, or merely a historical figure but deny the Christian meaning of his death. Like the other passages discussed, the text is unable to bear the weight.

The last view proposed for the opponents of 1 John—one that is gaining momentum—is that they are apostate Jews or Judaizing "Christians."[67] In this view they must

---

[60] For this reason the reference to Jesus's having "come in the flesh" in 1 John 4:2 may resemble the affirmation that God "was revealed in the flesh" in 1 Tim 3:16 (NASB).

[61] Many are not nearly so cautious. See, e.g., Achtemeier, Green, and Thompson, *Introducing the New Testament*, 539–42.

[62] See Brown, *Epistles*, 368.

[63] Streett (*They Went Out from Us*, 301) states, "It is almost certainly a rhetorical device and not a polemical refutation."

[64] D. F. Watson, "Amplification Techniques in 1 John: The Interaction of Rhetorical Style and Invention," *JSNT* 51 (1993): 102.

[65] Watson disagrees, identifying 5:6 as *regressio* (a form of amplification that is a repetition that reiterates things already said and draws distinctions between them). He states, "The point is reiterated to emphasize the dual nature of Jesus's coming in opposition to the secessionist stress on him coming only with water" (ibid., 109). Yet there is no restatement in the text other than that of both water and blood. There is no distinction being made but an appeal to the solidarity between the two.

[66] R. Yarbrough, *1–3 John*, BECNT (Grand Rapids, MI: Baker, 2008), 283.

[67] From a gospel point of view, even Judaizers would be considered apostate for they have added to the gospel by creating another errant gospel (see Gal 1:7).

be apostates from the community for they were once a part of it (2:19). This departure consists mainly of a denial of the confession of Jesus as the Messiah (2:22). John identifies the secessionists as Antichrists and false prophets (4:1–6). Thus, according to some who advocate this view, the similarities to the Olivet discourse (Mark 13:22) place them in a Jewish milieu.[68] The last point, however, is rather uncertain that it applies so neatly to the opponents. It just as well could be the result of the author's Jewishness rather than the opponents'. The major feature that makes this position more likely is that it is the same "discussion partners" as in the Gospel of John, where tensions with the synagogue may be discerned.

So, what can we say about these matters? First, we should rightly reject overly specific historical reconstructions dependent on mirror reading texts. We have no idea that such an interpretive enterprise is justified, and the result is inherently circular. That is, it reconstructs the history from less-than-sure interpretations and then uses that reconstruction to return to and interpret the text. Instead, we should confine ourselves to a more sure foundation.

Our choice must be made from what we can actually infer from the text regarding the secessionists. Without a great deal of mirror reading, we can distill a few facts about them. Clearly the churches experienced a recent dispute with false teachers from within the church that apparently was both painful and unpleasant (2:18–27). Their disagreement with the orthodox was so sharp that they departed from the churches (2:19).[69] John identifies the false teachers' departure as a rejection of Christ (4:1–6). Finally, the controversy is ongoing and likely features itinerate "evangelization" on the part of the deceivers (2 John 7–11). This may be echoed in John's plain statements that the opponents went out from the orthodox (2:19) and are trying to deceive the recipients (2:26; 3:7).

A number of opponents could fit the meager allusions in the letters. We should limit the options, however, to those who deny that Jesus is the Messiah (whether gnostic, Jewish, or otherwise). This makes a retreat to Judaism more likely, but a number of scenarios can fit the evidence.[70]

In light of the recent upheaval (5:13; see 2:19), the Christians to whom John wrote were in need of instruction. More importantly, they needed to be reassured and comforted. John does this more by defining orthodoxy rather than minutely defining and rejecting the opponents.[71] Brooke's statement is undoubtedly correct (and therefore often cited): "It is probably true that the writer never loses sight altogether of the views of his opponents in any part of the Epistle. But it is important to emphasize the fact that, in spite of this,

---

[68] B. Witherington, III, *Letters and Homilies for Hellenized Christians, Vol I: A Socio-Rhetorical Commentary on Titus, 1–2 Timothy and 1–3 John* (Downers Grove, IL: InterVarsity, 2010), 430.

[69] Kruse, *Letters of John*, 2.

[70] Jobes (*1, 2, and 3 John*, 24), e.g., suggests some source rooted in Greek philosophical speculation.

[71] Ibid.

the real aim of the Epistle is not exclusively, or even primarily, polemical."[72] Instead, the letter is fundamentally pastoral. Because of this, we have little difficulty applying the letter to modern life.

First John is similar to John's Gospel in that the purpose statement occurs near, but not at the end of, the book (see John 20:30–31).[73] In 1 John, the purpose statement occurs at 5:13: "I have written these things to you who believe in the name of the Son of God, so that you may know that you have eternal life." While two other passages declare John's purpose for writing (2:1; 12–14), they do not carry the same global weight as 5:13. Thus, the reassurance of all genuine Christians in the church(es) addressed is the primary purpose of the book.

Nevertheless, reassurance is only part of John's goal. The book also displays a pronounced emphasis on exhortation, indicated by the fact that many verbs are either formal or implied imperatives.[74] D. Guthrie noted, "Nowhere else in the New Testament is the combination of faith and love so clearly brought out, and it seems probable that this is emphasized because the behaviour of the readers leaves much to be desired."[75] While Guthrie may have overstated his point, there is little doubt that exhortation is an important part of John's purpose for writing his first letter.[76]

Introductory Matters Unique to 2 John and 3 John

The prescripts of 2 and 3 John differ from 1 John in that the recipients and sender are named, albeit imprecisely. The sender is identified in both letters simply as "the elder." The similarity in language and themes to 1 John makes it virtually certain they are from the same person, although this is debated.[77] The use of the term "elder" here is similar to the prologue in 1 John 1:1–4 in that the writer is so well known that the simplest of ascriptions is sufficient to identify him to the readers.[78]

The designation of the recipients in 2 John as "the elect lady and her children" (2 John 1; cf. v. 13) is also imprecise. These recipients have been variously interpreted as an actual woman and her offspring or as a figurative reference to a (series of) local congregation(s),[79]

---

[72] Brooke, *Johannine Epistles*, xxvii.

[73] Thielman, *Theology of the New Testament*, 536.

[74] R. Longacre ("Towards an Exegesis of 1 John," in *Linguistics and New Testament Interpretation*, ed. D. A. Black [Nashville, TN: B&H, 1992], 278–79) observed that while only about 9 percent of the verbs are imperative in form, they dominate the passages in which they occur.

[75] Guthrie, *New Testament Introduction*, 867.

[76] See 1 John 2:4–5, 12–15 and the repeated exhortations to "remain" in Christ (1 John 2:24, 27–28; 3:17; 4:13; 2 John 1:9; see 1 John 3:14).

[77] E.g., G. Strecker (*The Johannine Letters: A Commentary on 1, 2, and 3 John*, Hermeneia, trans. L. M. Maloney [Minneapolis, MN: Fortress, 1996], 3) argued that both 2 and 3 John are earlier than 1 John. The usage of the term "elder" in no way lends credibility to the myth of a "John the elder" mentioned earlier.

[78] Schnackenburg, *Epistles*, 270.

[79] Brown (*Epistles*, 652–53) noted a host of contrary opinions all revolving around a single individual: (1) a lady named "Electa"; (2) "a noble Kyria" (Alford, Bengel, de Wette, Ebrard, Lücke, and Neander); (3) "a Dear Lady" (i.e., a woman of some importance; Plummer, Ross); and (4) the universal church (Schmiedel).

with the latter of these being preferable.[80] John's language is not appropriate in referring to a real person (e.g., v. 5: "So now I ask you, dear lady . . . that we love one another"). Also, the scenario underlying verses 7–11 was more appropriate to a local congregation than to a single home in it. The conspicuous absence of personal names in 2 John—compared to the references to Gaius, Demetrius, and Diotrephes in 3 John—suggests that the intended recipient is a local congregation rather than an individual woman and her children. It is unclear why John chose not to name the location of the church. The omission may have been motivated by John's desire to lend his letter universal application or to protect the specific identity of the church.[81]

The occasion of 2 John may have been the return of a delegation sent by the church to the apostle. In verse 4, John commended "some" as "walking in truth." If related to 1 John (see esp. 2:19), the author may have intended to warn the church against welcoming the secessionists into their homes (see 2 John 8–11).

Third John is specifically written "to my dear friend Gaius" (v. 1), an otherwise unknown individual.[82] John did not specifically mention the secession or problems associated with it. Instead, he commended Gaius for receiving the brothers sent from the apostle (apparently itinerant preachers) and commended Demetrius as one of them (3 John 12). Diotrephes, on the other hand, opposed "fellow believers" and did not support the apostolic missionaries (vv. 9–10).[83] Thus, it is safe to conclude that one of the major purposes of 3 John was to provide a letter of recommendation for the elder's emissaries in general and for Demetrius in particular, as well as to put Diotrephes in his place prior to John's anticipated visit. So, then, if 2 John is a warning to reject false missionaries, 3 John is an affirmation to receive the true ones.

But there is more that we can propose about the relationship among the three letters. First John seems to be a circular letter that is general in appeal and application. Second John is written to an individual church (the "elect lady"). Third John is written to an individual leader in a church (an otherwise unknown "Gaius"). It is possible that the three are connected by more than common authorship. L. T. Johnson suggests they were originally packaged together and sent to an individual church.[84] He suggests 3 John is a letter of recommendation of Demetrius (which it certainly is), thus certifying the other two letters that he carries (although the elder does not specifically say this). Second John, then, was to be read to the whole church, introducing 1 John as a cover letter of sorts. This

---

[80] So Carson and Moo, *Introduction to the New Testament*, 677; Brown, *Epistles*, 655; C. G. Kruse, *The Letters of John*, PNTC (Grand Rapids, MI: Eerdmans, 2000), 38; Marshall, *Epistles*, 60; Brooke, *Epistles*, 167–70.

[81] For a judicious treatment, see J. R. W. Stott, *Letters of John*, TNTC, rev. ed. (Grand Rapids, MI: Eerdmans, 1988), 203–5.

[82] As Carson and Moo (*Introduction to the New Testament*, 677) observed, this Gaius is likely neither the Gaius of Corinth (Rom 16:23; 1 Cor 1:14) nor the Gaius of Macedonia (Acts 19:29) nor the Gaius of Derbe (Acts 20:4; against the fourth-century *Apostolic Constitutions* 7.46.9).

[83] Nothing is known about Demetrius or Diotrephes apart from the references to these individuals in 2 John.

[84] L. T. Johnson, *Writings of the New Testament*, 497.

is necessary because the latter is not really a letter but more of an exhortation/sermon.[85] Others have conceived the relationship a bit differently.[86] For instance, K. Jobes essentially follows Johnson for 1 and 2 John but thinks 3 John exists as a follow-up on the triumphalism of Diotrephes refusing the elders' emissaries.[87] Perhaps the most appealing part of Johnson's theory (and those like it) is that it explains the preservation of both 2 and 3 John. There is virtually no possibility that they could be transmitted to us apart from being collected and published together. As stated elsewhere, the practice of publishing from retained copies by the author was the known practice of published letter collections in antiquity.

LITERATURE

Genre

Both 2 and 3 John are prototypical examples of the first-century letter and may be some of the most situational in the NT.[88] There is an opening prescript featuring sender and recipient (in the dative) without benefit of a verb (assuming some form of "I write"), a health wish, a body, closing greeting, and a formulaic farewell. Moreover, unlike most Christian letters, and like most Greco-Roman letters, the two books are quite brief.[89] Third John may even be classified further as a letter of recommendation for Demetrius. Thus, there is wide consensus for identifying the genre of 2 John and 3 John as simple, straightforward *letters*.

But the genre of 1 John is a different matter. Brown noted that "of the twenty-one NT works normally classified as epistles, I John is the least letterlike in format."[90] The closest parallels in the canon are Hebrews and James, both of which lack some of the formal features of a Greco-Roman letter. A wide variety of proposals has been suggested for the work. Smalley called it "a paper,"[91] Windisch a "tractate."[92] and Grayston an "enchiridion, an instruction booklet."[93] Brown noted that "circular epistle," "homily," and "encyclical" have all been used to describe 1 John. Brown himself declined to settle on a specific genre

---

[85] Ibid., 497.

[86] Achtemeier, Green, and Thompson (*Introducing the New Testament*, 548), see a more isolated occasion for 2 John: "If in 1 John we see the problem from the vantage point of the church from which the false prophets 'went out,' in 2 John we see the problem with the eyes of the church in which they may then have showed up to preach and teach."

[87] Jobes, *1, 2, and 3 John*, 29.

[88] J. L. White, "Ancient Greek Letters," in *Greco-Roman Literature and the New Testament*, ed. D. E. Aune, SBLSBS 21 (Atlanta, GA: Scholars Press, 1988), 100; cf. J. A. D. Weima, "Letters, Greco-Roman," in *Dictionary of New Testament Background*, ed. C. A. Evans and S. E. Porter (Downers Grove, IL: InterVarsity, 2000), 640–44.

[89] D. Aune, *The New Testament in Its Literary Environment* (Philadelphia, PA: Westminster, 1987), 163–64.

[90] Brown, *Epistles*, 87.

[91] S. S. Smalley, *1, 2, 3 John*, WBC 51 rev. ed.; (Nashville, TN: Nelson, 2007), xxx.

[92] Windisch, *Die Katholischen Briefe*, HNT 15, 3rd rev. ed. (Tübingen, Germany: Mohr, 1951), 136, cited in Brown, *Epistles*, 87.

[93] K. Grayston, *The Johannine Epistles*, New Century Bible (Grand Rapids, MI: Eerdmans, 1984), 4.

designation and called the document a "comment patterned on" John's Gospel.[94] Taking his point of departure from Brown's penchant for interpreting the letter based on the historical reconstruction of the community, J. V. Hills suggested that it should be considered a "community rule" document.[95] None of these solutions is particularly convincing, and some border on being contrived.

The unusual situation with regard to 1 John is that the document contains few formal characteristics that would classify it as a letter. There is no prescript, well-wish/prayer, closing, or formulaic farewell. In fact, both the opening, "What was from the beginning," and the closing, "guard yourselves from idols," are highly unconventional. In between the preface and the concluding statement, the elder teaches in a somewhat cyclical manner, frequently returning to a topic he already addressed only to discuss it in somewhat similar though not identical terms. In this regard, 1 John is similar to Hebrews, which likewise opens with a kind of preface rather than an epistolary opening. First John is also like James, which also concludes without a formal epistolary closing. By comparison, 1 John conforms even less to the standard first-century epistolary format than either Hebrews or James, for the former features at least an epistolary closing and the latter an epistolary opening, while 1 John has neither.

So what is the genre of 1 John? Quite a number of scholars describe it as a homily or sermon because of its lack of standard formal epistolary features.[96] It is best to understand it in broad terms as a letter since Greco-Roman letters exhibited a considerable degree of diversity.[97] The work is from a single authoritative source (an apostle), but the recipients are identified only in general (and figurative) terms as "little children." There is some specific, albeit vague, information regarding the secessionists. The act of communicating to the readers is referred to as writing. Finally, it seems the letter was designed to address a situation germane to a number of congregations in the area. It might have begun as a spoken homily or sermon, but it was clearly sent as a letter.

Without imposing external categories on the letter, it is probably best to understand 1 John in terms of a circular letter similar to Ephesians or James. Abundant evidence for this type of letter in antiquity exists, especially among the Jews. Jeremiah 29:4–13; Acts 15:23–29; James; and Revelation 2–3 contain exemplars of this type of genre. If so, 1 John is a situational letter written to instruct and encourage the apostolic Christians in and around Ephesus regarding the nature of the gospel and their part in it.

---

[94] Brown (*Epistles*, 90) admitted that this is a choice not to make a choice, so he simply described the contents.

[95] J. V. Hills, "A Genre for 1 John," in *The Future of Early Christianity: Essays in Honor of Helmut Koester* (Minneapolis, MN: Fortress, 1991), 367.

[96] Johnson, *Writing*, 492; Jobes, *1, 2, and 3 John*, 29. G. L. Parsenios (*First, Second, and Third John*, Paideia Commentaries on the New Testament [Grand Rapids, MI: Baker, 2014], 28) strikes a balance concerning the issue: "The safest conclusion is to recognize that the epistolary quality of 1 John is not at all clear. This commentary will call 1 John a letter, but with the recognition that this label is more convenient than certain."

[97] See Aune, *Literary Environment*, 203.

Literary Plan

The outline of 2 and 3 John is predictable and easily discernible. As typical first-century letters, both follow the simple pattern: "introduction—body—conclusion." But the outline of 1 John has generated much debate,[98] and to date no scholarly consensus has been reached. The options range from those who see an intricate macro-chiasm to those who reject any coherent structure.[99] The lack of consensus in scholarship has led several to posit various theories using source or redaction criticism.[100] Most scholars dismiss such theories as unproven, unlikely, or not particularly helpful.

What makes the structure of 1 John so difficult to discern? In a word, the answer is *subtlety*. The topical transitions are virtually seamless, and the various subjects recur in cyclical intervals throughout the letter. Nevertheless, given the clear structure of John's Gospel and Revelation, as well as the careful nuances displayed within the various paragraphs, it seems unlikely that the author had no plan in mind when writing the letter.[101] With regard to the structure of 1 John, there is wide agreement only with regard to the preface (1:1–4) and the epilogue (5:13–21).

The structural proposals for 1 John fall into three major categories: divisions into two, three, or multiple parts.[102] Among those who hold to a division into two parts, the main item of discussion is whether the break should be placed toward the end of chapter 2 or at 3:11. Among those who hold to a three-part structure, the debate centers on whether the first major break is at 2:17; 2:28; or 2:29, and whether the second major break is at 4:1 or 4:7. Among those who see multiple divisions, one finds a plethora of proposals.[103]

---

[98] For a survey of recent options, see B. Olsson, "First John: Discourse Analyses and Interpretations," in *Discourse Analysis and the New Testament: Approaches and Results*, ed. S. E. Porter and J. T. Reed, JSNTSup 170, Studies in New Testament Greek 4 (Sheffield, UK: Sheffield Academic, 1999), 369–91.

[99] E.g., P. J. van Staden ("The Debate on the Structure of 1 John," *Hervormde Teologiese Studies* 47 [1991]: 487–502) argued for a macro-chiasm. Marshall (*Epistles*, 26) suggested there is no coherent structure, and Kruse (*Letters of John*, 32) said his analysis of the letter does not "trace any developing argument through the letter because there isn't one."

[100] The most recent to propose a series of sources edited into one document is J. C. O'Neill, *The Puzzle of 1 John: A New Examination of Origins* (London, England: SPCK, 1966); yet Marshall (*Epistles*, 30) noted that his theory is "completely speculative, and has won no adherents." For other source theories, see E. von Dobschütz, "Johanneische Studien I," *ZNW* 8 (1907): 1–8; R. Bultmann, *The Johannine Epistles*, Hermeneia, trans. R. P. O'Hara et al. (Philadelphia, PA: Fortress, 1973); and W. Nauck, *Die Tradition und der Charakter des ersten Johannesbriefes*, WUNT 3 (Tübingen, Germany: Mohr, 1953). For a rearrangement theory, see K. Tomoi, "The Plan of the First Epistle of John," *ExpTim* 52 (1940–41): 117–19.

[101] Schnackenburg (*Epistles*, 12–13) is doubtless correct when he said the author "does not merely sail along without any particular plan."

[102] Brown, *Epistles of John*, 116–29.

[103] The presentation of structural proposals for 1 John below is adapted from the chart in Brown, *Epistles*, 764; see also L. S. Kellum, "On the Semantic Structure of 1 John: A Modest Proposal," *Faith and Mission* 23 (2008): 36–38. The works cited are J. Chaine, *Les Epîtres Catholiques*, EB, 2nd ed. (Paris, France: Gabalda, 1939), 97–260; Longacre, "Exegesis of 1 John"; G. M. Burge, *The Letters of John*, NIVAC (Grand Rapids, MI: Zondervan, 1996); Schnackenburg, *Epistles*; M. M. Thompson, in Achtemeier, Green, and Thompson, *Introducing the New Testament*; F.-M. Braun, "Les Epîtres de Saint Jean," in *L'Evangile de Saint Jean*, SBJ 3rd rev. ed.; (Paris: Cerf, 1973), 231–77; Guthrie, *New Testament Introduction*; F. F. Bruce, *The Epistles of John* (Grand Rapids, MI: Eerdmans, 1979); and Stott, *Letters of John*.

Table 19.1: Structural Proposals for 1 John

I. *Division into Two Parts*		
Chaine	**Longacre**	**Burge**
1:5–2:28	1:5–2:29	1:5–3:10
2:29–5:13	3:1–5:12	3:11–5:12
II. *Division into Three Parts*		
Schnackenburg	**Thompson**	**Braun**
1:5–2:17	1:5–2:27	1:5–2:28
2:18–3:24	2:28–3:24	2:29–4:6
4:1–5:12	4:1–5:12	4:7–5:12
III. *Division into Multiple Parts*		
D. Guthrie	**Bruce**	**Stott**
1:5–2:29	1:5–2:2	1:5–2:2
3:1–24	2:3–17	2:3–27
4:1–6	2:18–27	2:28–4:6
4:7–21	2:28–3:24	4:7–5:5
5:1–5	4:1–6	5:6–17
5:6–12	4:7–21	5:18–21
	5:6–12	
	5:13–21	

The following outline for 1 John concurs with those who see a three-part structure to the book and more specifically with those who suggest the following major units: 1:5–2:27; 2:28–3:24; and 4:1–5:12. Within this overall structure, it is possible to discern interrelated paragraphs that provide a further breakdown of the flow of the letter's argument. It is best to understand 1:5–2:27 as an extended overview of the rest of the letter, with 2:28–3:24 elaborating on the ethical and 4:1–5:12 on the doctrinal dimensions of believers' lives.[104]

OUTLINES

1 John

I. PROLOGUE (1:1–4)

II. OVERVIEW (1:5–2:27)

   A. True Believers Walk in the Light (1:5–2:2).

   B. True Believers Keep Jesus's Commandments (2:3–11).

   C. Grow in Christ and Do Not Love the World (2:12–17).

---

[104] For a thorough analysis of the structure of 1 John, see Kellum, "Semantic Structure of 1 John," 34–82.

D. Abiding and Departing (2:18–27)

III. ETHICS (2:28–3:24)

A. Children of God Sanctify Themselves (2:28–3:10).

B. Children of God Keep His Commandments (3:11–24).

IV. DOCTRINE (4:1–5:12)

A. Test the Spirits (4:1–6).

B. The Theological Basis of Brotherly Love (4:7–12)

C. Confidence from Correct Doctrine (4:13–21)

D. Testimony and Proof (5:1–12)

V. EPILOGUE (5:13–21)

2 John

I. INTRODUCTION (1–3)

II. BODY: "WALKING IN THE TRUTH" (4–11)

A. "Walking in the Truth" Requires Brotherly Love (4–6).

B. "Walking in the Truth" Requires Guarding the Truth About the Son (7–11).

III. CONCLUSION (12–13)

3 John

I. INTRODUCTION (1–4)

II. BODY: COMMENDATION OF GAIUS AND DEMETRIUS, CONDEMNATION OF DIOTREPHES (5–12)

A. Gaius's Godly Behavior Toward Other Believers (5–8)

B. The Ungodly Behavior of Diotrephes (9–10)

C. Commendation of Demetrius (11–12)

III. CONCLUSION (13–14)

UNIT-BY-UNIT DISCUSSIONS

1 JOHN

I. Prologue (1:1–4)

Like John's Gospel, 1 John begins with a prologue. The author claimed to be an eyewitness of Jesus and asserted that he was proclaiming to his recipients the message he and the apostles had heard from Jesus.

II. Overview (1:5–2:27)

By way of introduction, this section features an ethical and doctrinal preview of the rest of the letter, sounding many major themes such as the need for believers to remain in Christ and the importance of brotherly love.[105]

---

[105] Interestingly, the verb *graphō* ("to write") is used nine times in chaps. 1–2 and not again until the conclusion in 5:13. See Longacre, "Toward an Exegesis of 1 John," 276–77.

A. True Believers Walk in the Light (1:5–2:2) The text is developed in terms of two implications of the principle that God is light (1:5), which may imply his holiness or the revelation provided by him or both. The first implication (1:6–7) is that if God is light, his children will "walk in the light," that is, conduct their lives in the sphere of righteousness. The second implication is that those who "walk in the light" confess their sins (1:9; cf. 2:1).[106]

B. True Believers Keep Jesus's Commandments (2:3–11) In 2:3 John elaborates on the previous unit.[107] Those who claim to be Christians either keep Jesus's commandments or they turn out to be liars. The principle described in 2:3–6 (those who remain in him keep his commandments) is illustrated in 2:7–11 by the explication of the necessity to keep the most prominent of Jesus's commands, the "new commandment" of love (see John 13:34–35; 15:9–17). The present and the previous sections form the basis for the extended two-part appeal made in the next two units.

C. Grow in Christ and Do Not Love the World (2:12–17) John proceeds to issue instructions to the shaken believers.[108] The apostle did not doubt their salvation but sought to reassure them in light of the false teachers' recent departure. John's comments to three groups at different levels of maturity move, somewhat curiously, from "little children" to "fathers" and then to "young men," whereby the instructions to young men are the most detailed.[109] Apparently, "little children" become "fathers" by following John's instructions for young men.

John then instructs the recipients of his letter not to love the world (2:15–17). This relates to the need for believers to remain in Christ, which constitutes the subject of the following section.[110] John reminds his readers that the things of this world will pass away, while those who do the will of God will remain forever.

D. Abiding and Departing (2:18–27) John opens this section with a contrast between the secessionists who had left the church and the believers who remained. The former, whom he called "antichrists," departed both theologically and physically, which demonstrated that they were not "of God." By contrast, true believers have an "anointing" from God and need no further instruction because the Holy Spirit is their teacher.[111] This

---

[106] Most likely, 2:2 concludes this section. For a detailed defense, see J. Callow, "Where Does 1 John 1 End?," in *Discourse Analysis and the New Testament,* 392–406.

[107] This is indicated by the continued subject matter, the walk of true Christians, and the continued use of the metaphor of walking in light and darkness in 2:9.

[108] This is what Longacre ("Toward an Exegesis of 1 John," 279) called the "ethical peak" of this introductory division.

[109] For a striking parallel, see Josh 1:8. There Joshua is told to be strong and to meditate on the Word so he would have success.

[110] The present passage is, in all probability, commenting on Gen 3:6, where the woman "saw that the tree was good for food and delightful to look at, and that it was desirable for obtaining wisdom."

[111] The phrase "all of you know the truth" (2:20) may constitute a thinly veiled polemic against an early gnostic element among John's opponents. The statement "you don't need anyone to teach you" (2:27) does not imply that believers are without need of instruction subsequent to salvation (see Eph 4:11; 1 Tim 2:7; 3:2; 4:11; 6:2; 2 Tim 1:11; 2:2) but merely warns the readers not to listen to the false teachers.

contrast forms the foundation for the command in 2:24: "What you have heard from the beginning is to remain in you" (see v. 27).

III. Ethics (2:28–3:24)

In the first major unit (1:5–2:27) John underscores the ethical and doctrinal necessities for believers. In the second major unit (2:28–3:24), he highlights the first of these—the ethical dimension. His thesis seems to be that the children of God and the children of the Devil are recognized by their deeds.

A. Children of God Sanctify Themselves (2:28–3:10) In this section John elaborates on the differences between the children of God and those of the Devil. God's children, because Jesus was revealed to destroy sin, do not persist in a sinful lifestyle; in other words, they "do not [characteristically] sin" (see 3:6). John frankly acknowledges that Christians still sinned (2:1: "If anyone does sin"), but he made clear that for believers, sin is neither characteristic of nor compatible with, their true nature as God's children. Conversely, children of the Devil are controlled by their sinful nature (3:8).

B. Children of God Keep His Commandments (3:11–24) John transitions from the negative (not practicing sin) to the positive (keeping God's commandments, especially the "new commandment" of love). John uses the biblical illustration of Cain (the only OT character mentioned in the letter). This son of Adam and Eve murdered his brother because Abel's works condemned his own. In essence John's message is that words by themselves are empty; true love is expressed "in action and in truth" (3:18). The essence of remaining in Christ, therefore, is keeping his commands.

IV. Doctrine (4:1–5:12)

The issue of proper doctrine controls the present section. In 4:1–6, John cautions Christians to be discerning about which spirits to believe. This judgment requires a correct Christology. Brotherly love, likewise, presupposes right doctrine (4:13–21). Finally, in 5:1–12 the author contended that only "the one who has the Son has life."

A. Test the Spirits (4:1–6) John cautions believers to exercise discernment. Since there were many false prophets, they should not "believe every spirit" (4:1) but should test the spirits to see if they are from God. This plainly echoes Jesus's warnings, especially in the Sermon on the Mount and in the Olivet Discourse (Matt 7:15–20; 24:4–5, 23–26 and parallels). Only the Spirit that confesses Jesus is the Spirit of God. The words "come in the flesh" could refer to a variety of Christological errors (e.g., Docetism or Adoptionism—see above), but more likely it is the standard confession of Jesus in the church. If so, the issue at hand is that *Jesus* is the Messiah.[112] In any case, one's Christology identifies the spirit behind one's message. Those who receive the apostolic preaching regarding Jesus and remain in it can be victorious over the spirit of the world.

---

[112] This is the same emphasis as in John's Gospel. See the comments on John 20:31 in A. J. Köstenberger, *John*, BECNT (Grand Rapids, MI: Baker, 2004), 582.

B. The Theological Basis of Brotherly Love (4:7–12) Although it may appear that the command to love one another is a return to the ethics of the previous section, the basis for the command is not ethical (because this is morally right) but theological (because God is love). In fact, John makes a theological point: believers love others because the God who is love indwells them. This is how "his love is made complete in us" (4:12).

C. Confidence from Correct Doctrine (4:13–21) Possession of the Holy Spirit is proof that a person is a believer (4:13), and confession of Jesus as the Son of God results in God's remaining in him or her (4:15). In 4:15–16 John took both elements of the previous sections and applied them to the believer: "Whoever confesses that Jesus is the Son of God—God remains in him and he in God. . . . God is love, and the one who remains in love remains in God, and God remains in him." God's love is manifested in believers so they may have confidence on the day of judgment (4:17).

D. Testimony and Proof (5:1–12) By restatement John clarifies the previous section's main points: "Everyone who believes that Jesus is the Christ has been born of God, and everyone who loves the Father also loves the one born of him" (5:1). John proceeds to note that the essence of loving God is keeping his commandments, and this is not an impossible task because believers have been born of God. Thus, faith in Jesus has overcome the world.

The evidence for John's confidence is stated in 5:6–12. The burden of proof (two or three witnesses) demanded in the OT is met by the testimony of the Spirit, the water, and the blood, a probable reference to Jesus's baptism, Jesus's death, and to the inner testimony of the Spirit of God.[113] The content of the testimony is identified in 5:11: "God has given us eternal life, and this life is in his Son."

V. Epilogue (5:13–21)

The conclusion states the purpose of the letter: "I have written these things to you who believe in the name of the Son of God so that you may know that you have eternal life" (5:13). John elaborates on this purpose in three ways, each of which includes the phrase "we know." First, 5:14–17 describes the confidence in prayer that believers possess when they ask according to God's will, including prayer for "those who commit sin that doesn't lead to death" (5:16).[114] Second, those who belong to God do not practice sin (5:18). Third, believers know the truth and are in the truth (5:19–20). John's final comment,

---

[113] Many editions of the NT include what is known as the "Johannine Comma," which divides the witnesses between those in heaven and those on earth: "For there are three that testify *in heaven, the Father, the Word, and the Holy Spirit, and these three are One. And there are three who bear witness on earth:* the Spirit, the water, and the blood—and these three are in agreement" (5:7–8; the "Johannine Comma" is in italics). Today this is nearly universally understood to be a later addition. It appears in Erasmus's third edition of the NT (commonly known as the *Textus Receptus*), because a sixteenth-century Greek mss., the Codex Montfortianus (Britanicus), included it. This mss. was produced for the purpose of getting Erasmus to include it in the text (see Brown, *Epistles*, 776, 780). Most rightly reject it on the grounds that it is impossibly late.

[114] There is no scholarly consensus on the exact identification of this sin. For a judicious discussion, see Stott, *Letters of John*, 189–93. Stott argued that John here used the term "brother" in a broad sense to refer to another person, not necessarily a fellow Christian (see 1 John 2:9, 11; 3:16–17), and he identified the "sin unto death" as "a deliberate, open-eyed rejection of known truth" akin to the "blasphemy against the Holy Spirit" committed by the Pharisees, who ascribed Jesus's miracles,

"Guard yourselves from idols," provides an abrupt and unconventional ending to the letter, but one that is appropriate for the occasion. It warns believers to accept no substitute for God.

2 JOHN

I. Introduction (1–3)

John employs a standard prescript to this letter, including an identification of sender and recipients and a Christian "well-wish."

II. Body: "Walking in the Truth" (4–11)

The body of the letter consists of a sustained instruction to the church defining "walking in the truth." John instructs his readers to keep the "new commandment" and to guard themselves from antichrists.

A. "Walking in the Truth" Requires Brotherly Love (4–6)

The return of the group to the church (v. 4) provides the occasion for John to remind his readers to be diligent about "walking in the truth." This is defined as keeping the "new commandment" to love one another.

B. "Walking in the Truth" Requires Guarding the Truth About the Son (7–11)

John insists that the church must guard itself against deceivers. This is done in two ways. First, believers must recognize imposters who do not abide by the apostolic teaching and thus have neither the Son nor the Father (v. 9). Second, once the false teachers have been identified, believers must not offer any help to them (v. 10).

III. Conclusion (12–13)

John closes with a standard postscript that features plans to visit soon as well as greetings from mutual friends (the "elect sister" and "her children").

3 JOHN

I. Introduction (1–4)

Again, John employs a standard prescript, featuring sender, recipients, and a Christian well-wish. As in 2 John, it appears that the elder had received a delegation from the church led by Gaius, and he commends this group of believers for "walking in the truth."

II. Body: Commendation of Gaius and Demetrius, Condemnation of Diotrephes (5–12)

In the body of the letter, John requests support for Demetrius. Gaius is commended for his past exposure of the sin of Diotrephes, and the church is urged to support Demetrius.

---

done in the power of the Holy Spirit, to Satan (Matt 12:28 and parallels). Other possibilities listed by Stott include a specific sin (a "mortal" sin) or apostasy.

A. Gaius's Godly Behavior Toward Other Believers (5–8) John begins by commending Gaius's past behavior. Gaius displayed his faith by being hospitable to "the brothers and sisters," who most likely were emissaries from John. The apostle encourages Gaius not only to receive this group but also to send them on with ample provisions. The future tense "you will do well" (v. 6) indicates that this implies support of Demetrius, who is introduced later.

B. The Ungodly Behavior of Diotrephes (9–10) Verses 9–10 outline John's charges against Diotrephes, who did not recognize the authority of the elder and his emissaries and who slandered the apostolic group. What is more, he censors those who received them, all because he "love[d] to have first place among them," in blatant contradiction of Jesus's words that "whoever wants to be first among you let him be your slave" (Matt 20:27).

C. Commendation of Demetrius (11–12) The commendation of Demetrius is set in contrast to the reprehensible conduct of Diotrephes. John instructs Gaius not to "imitate what is evil" (i.e., Diotrephes). He concludes with a brief commendation of Demetrius, who had the respect of his peers, who spoke the truth itself (probably a commendation of his doctrine), and who had the respect of the apostle also (whom Gaius knew declared the truthful testimony).

III. Conclusion (13–14)

The conclusion, similar to that of 2 John, is a standard postscript that contains John's desire to meet Gaius face-to-face, a brief greeting from John's friends, and an instruction to "greet the friends by name."

THEOLOGY

Theological Themes

Ethical Conduct and Christian Discipleship Grounded in Proper Christian Doctrine John's first letter is dominated by his concern for believers to find assurance of their salvation and to continue in the truth. He first affirms the trustworthiness of the message through his status as an eyewitness (1:1–4). Then, in the overview (1:5–2:27), he introduces the concern that believers act in keeping with their beliefs, that is, their ethics must match their doctrine. At the heart of this is the assurance that coming to Christ is a life-changing experience.

Therefore, what believers do serves as an indicator of whether they have had that experience (3:9). Thus, the second division of 1 John (2:28–3:24) explores the ramifications of what believers do. If they have the hope of his return, they purify themselves. Those who remain in him do not practice sin (which he came to destroy). The children of God and the children of the Devil are manifested by their righteous or unrighteous lives. Keeping the new commandment is a matter of obedience. The source of all obedience is love for the Father (2:15–17). So love and obedience go hand in hand and constitute the essence of remaining (abiding) in Christ. These two elements should be considered inseparable; they are somewhat like the two sides of a coin.

The language employed is reminiscent of the contours of the covenant relationship in the OT. In the OT, love for God is the foundation for obedience. See, for example, Deuteronomy 7:9: "Know that the LORD your God is God, the faithful God who keeps his gracious covenant loyalty for a thousand generations with those who love him and keep his commands."[115]As Chennattu notes, "The very idea of giving a commandment . . . carries covenant overtones."[116] Chennattu goes on to describe Johannine discipleship in terms of a covenant relationship.[117]

The best description of this is found in 1 John 2:5: "Whoever keeps his word, truly in him the love of God is made complete. This is how we know we are in him." The phrase "love of God" should be interpreted as the believer's love for God, otherwise it would suggest that God's love for the believer is merit based. Thus, lovers of God keep his word (i.e., obedience). At 2:6, then, John describes the one who loves and obeys as one who "remains in Him." So then, Johannine discipleship and sanctification are wrapped up in one command: to love the Triune God. Practically, this vantage point, based on what it is to participate in a covenant with God, transforms the effort to please God into one overarching ambition to love Him. John refers to this as "remaining (abiding) in him."

Although the second division is doctrinally grounded, in the third division (4:1–5:12) John made a subtle shift that focuses on doctrinal issues, especially the nature of Christ and God. Only the Spirit that confesses Jesus is from God. This idea "from God" (*ek tou theou*) dominates 4:1–6. Those who love do so because the nature of God is love, and the absence of love reveals one who does not know God (vv. 7–9). That the children of God have victory over the world is the result of being "from God." The command to love one another is repeated—this time with a doctrinal rather than an ethical rationale. Believers are to love because God is love. Likewise, they are to keep his commandments, but this time the reason is grounded in the nature of God's redemption (5:4).

Assurance of Salvation The Johannine Letters give insight into the basic theological commitments of believers. Christians are not called on to develop a new theology but to cling to that which they received "from the beginning" (1 John 1:1). It turns out that even in the first century there were "progressives" who, ironically, advanced in the wrong direction (2 John 9). Both 2 and 3 John develop the appropriate Christian response to these individuals in further detail, calling on believers to reject aid to the "progressives" (2 John 9) and to provide aid to those associated with the apostle (3 John 6–8). Believers are challenged to love Christ and one another, not "in word or speech, but in action and in truth" (1 John 3:18), and to grow spiritually by remaining in his word (1 John 2:12–14).

---

[115] See also Exod 20:6 and Deut 5:10, among others.

[116] R. M. Chennattu, *Johannine Discipleship as a Covenant Relationship* (Peabody, MA: Hendrikson, 2006), 96.

[117] Ibid.

The major contribution, however, comes from the grounds for assurance given in these letters.[118] They are so prominent that some have seen these letters as supplying "tests of life."[119] Indeed, nowhere else in the canon is there a sustained discussion laying out such objective grounds for the believer's assurance of salvation. Kruse described the nature of these grounds: "The readers' assurance is to be grounded on God's testimony about his Son, their own godly living, loving action and concern for fellow believers, their obedience to the love command, and the Spirit's testimony to Christ."[120] But just as prominent is the fact that some claim to have fellowship with Christ, to know him, to abide in him, and to be in the light, while being deluded.

Therefore, the point of 1 John is to instill confidence in true believers that their salvation is assured, coupling this with exhortations to persevere (see esp. 1 John 5:13). John wanted his Christian readers to be sure of their salvation, but he also wanted them to remain in Jesus and his word; by contrast, he was not satisfied with believers continuing in sin. Thus, John paints a picture of the ideal believers: (1) they are confident of their standing in Christ because of the life-transforming regeneration they experienced through the Holy Spirit; (2) they are obedient because of their love for Christ; (3) they grow in maturity because of their steadfastness; (4) they love because of the nature of the God who changed their lives; and (5) they are victorious because of their faith in Christ.

Love While not unique to the Johannine Letters, John's emphasis on love is pronounced.[121] Marshall noted that "love is thematized in a way that is unparalleled elsewhere in the New Testament. . . . The indications are that for all the emphasis on right doctrine, the author's main concern is with the Christian behavior of his readers."[122] While the last phrase may be overstated (the author does not separate love from doctrine), it cannot be overstated that love is a major theme in 1 John. (*Agapē* and verbal cognates occur forty-eight times.) Marshall listed six dimensions of love in 1 John: (1) the source of love is God; (2) we love in response to God's love; (3) those who love demonstrate their birth from God; (4) love is expressed in obedience (especially the command to love one another); (5) it is possible for love to be only a claim; and (6) one can argue proof of our new birth from the presence or absence of love.[123]

CONTRIBUTION TO THE CANON

- Jesus Christ as the propitiation for the sins of the entire world (1 John 2:2)

---

[118] For an excellent treatment of this topic in 1 John and the rest of the NT, see D. A. Carson, "Reflections on Christian Assurance," *WTJ* 54 (1992): 1–29.

[119] See R. Law, *The Tests of Life: A Study of the First Epistle of St. John*, 3rd ed. (Edinburgh, Scotland: T&T Clark, 1914; repr. Grand Rapids, MI: Baker, 1979).

[120] Kruse, *Letters of John*, 33.

[121] See esp. A. J. Köstenberger, *A Theology of John's Gospel and Letters: The Word, the Christ, the Son of God*, BTNT (Grand Rapids, MI: Zondervan, 2009), chap. 13.

[122] I. H. Marshall, *New Testament Theology: Many Witnesses, One Gospel* (Downers Grove, IL: InterVarsity, 2004), 539.

[123] Ibid.

- God is love (e.g., 1 John 4:16).
- Christian assurance (1 John 5:11–13)
- Prohibition against extending hospitality to false teachers (2 John)
- Warning against autocratic church leadership (3 John)

STUDY QUESTIONS

1. What are three alternative proposals to John's authorship of the Johannine Letters?
2. How would you summarize the internal and external evidence for John's authorship?
3. Which of these was probably written first: John's Gospel or John's Letters? Explain.
4. What is the major occasion for John's writing of 1 John? What specific reference backs up your point?
5. Which major heresy is combated in 1 John?
6. What are three major heresies perpetrated by the false teachers?
7. What are two major purposes for John's writing of 1 John?
8. What are the purposes for John's writing of 2 John and 3 John?
9. Who is the "chosen lady"?
10. What typical literary pattern do 2 and 3 John follow? What makes the structure of 1 John so difficult to discern?
11. What are several dimensions of love noted in 1 John?
12. What is the "sin that brings death"?

FOR FURTHER STUDY

Akin, D. L. *1, 2, 3 John*. New American Commentary 38. Nashville, TN: B&H, 2001.

Brown, R. E. *The Epistles of John*. Anchor Bible 30. Garden City, NY: Doubleday, 1982.

Bruce, F. F. *The Epistles of John*. Grand Rapids, MI: Eerdmans, 1979.

Bultmann, R. *The Johannine Epistles*. Hermeneia. Translated by R. P. O'Hara et al. Philadelphia, PA: Fortress, 1973.

Carson, "1-3 John." Pages 1,063–68 in *Commentary on the New Testament Use of the Old Testament*. Edited by G. K. Beale and D. A. Carson. Grand Rapids, MI: Zondervan, 2007.

Griffith, T. *Keep Yourselves from Idols: A New Look at 1 John*. Journal for the Study of the New Testament Supplement 233. London, England: Sheffield Academic, 2002.

Hill, C. E. *The Johannine Corpus in the Early Church*. Oxford, UK: Oxford University Press, 2004.

Jobes, K. H. *1, 2, and 3 John*. Zondervan Exegetical Commentary on the New Testament. Grand Rapids, MI: Zondervan, 2013.

Köstenberger, A. J. *A Theology of John's Gospel and Letters: The Word, the Christ, the Son of God*. Biblical Theology of the New Testament. Grand Rapids, MI: Zondervan, 2009.

Kruse, C. G. *The Letters of John*. Pillar New Testament Commentary. Grand Rapids, MI: Eerdmans, 2000.

Law, R. *The Tests of Life: A Study of the First Epistle of St. John*. 3rd ed. Edinburgh, Scotland: T&T Clark, 1914; repr., Grand Rapids, MI: Baker, 1979.

Lieu, J. M. *I, II, III John: A Commentary*. NTL. Louisville, KY: Westminster John Knox, 2008.

________. *The Theology of the Johannine Epistles*. Cambridge, UK: Cambridge University Press, 1991.

Longacre, R. "Towards an Exegesis of 1 John Based on the Discourse Analysis of the Greek Text." Pages 271–86 in *Linguistics and New Testament Interpretation*. Edited by D. A. Black. Nashville, TN: B&H, 1992.

Marshall, I. H. *The Epistles of John*. New International Commentary on the New Testament. Grand Rapids, MI: Eerdmans, 1978.

O'Neill, J. C. *The Puzzle of 1 John: A New Examination of Origins*. London, England: SPCK, 1966.

Painter, J. *1, 2, and 3 John*. Sacra Pagina 18. Collegeville, MN: Liturgical Press, 2002.

Parsenios, G. L. *First, Second, and Third John*. Paideia Commentaries on the New Testament. Grand Rapids, MI: Baker, 2014.

Poythress, V. S. "Testing for Johannine Authorship by Examining the Use of Conjunctions." *Westminster Theological Journal* 46 (1984): 350–69.

Schnackenburg, R. *The Johannine Epistles: A Commentary*. New York, NY: Crossroad, 1992.

Smalley, S. S. *1, 2, 3 John*. Word Biblical Commentary 51. Waco, TX: Word, 1984.

Stott, J. R. W. *The Letters of John*. Tyndale New Testament Commentary. Rev. ed. Grand Rapids, MI: Eerdmans, 1988.

Strecker, G. *The Johannine Letters: A Commentary on 1, 2, and 3 John*. Hermeneia. Translated by L. M. Maloney. Minneapolis, MN: Fortress, 1996.

Streett, D. R. *They Went Out from Us: The Identity of the Opponents in First John*. BZNW 177. Berlin, Germany: de Gruyter, 2011.

Thompson, M. M. *1–3 John*. IVP New Testament Commentary. Downers Grove, IL: InterVarsity, 1992.

von Wahlde, U. *The Gospel and Letters of John*. 3 vols. Grand Rapids, MI: Eerdmans, 2010.

Yarbrough, R. W. *1–3 John*. Baker Exegetical Commentary on the New Testament. Grand Rapids, MI: Baker, 2008.

Chapter 20

The Book of Revelation

CORE KNOWLEDGE

Basic Knowledge: Students should know the key facts of the book of Revelation. With regard to history, students should be able to identify the book's author, date, provenance, destination, and purpose. With regard to literature, they should be able to provide a basic outline of the book and identify core elements of the book's content found in the Unit-by-Unit Discussion. With regard to theology, students should be able to identify the major theological themes in the book of Revelation.

Intermediate Knowledge: Students should be able to present the arguments for historical, literary, and theological conclusions. With regard to history, students should be able to discuss the evidence for John's authorship, date, provenance, destination, and purpose. With regard to literature, they should be able to provide a detailed outline of the book. With regard to theology, students should be able to discuss the major theological themes in the book of Revelation and the ways in which they uniquely contribute to the NT canon.

Advanced Knowledge: Students should be able to assess critically the internal and external evidence for the authorship and date of Revelation. They should be able to explain the genre of the book and be prepared to discuss the literary structure of Revelation in relation to the four visions, the seals, trumpets, and bowls, and the final two visions. They should also be able to discuss the five major approaches to the study of the book of Revelation.

KEY FACTS

Author: John

Date: AD 95–96

Provenance: Patmos

Destination: Ephesus, Smyrna, Pergamum, Thyatira, Sardis, Philadelphia, and Laodicea

Occasion: Persecution of Christians in Asia Minor, John's visions

Purpose: To encourage Christians to faithful endurance by depicting the final judgment and the establishment of Christ's kingdom on earth

Theme: Jesus the slain and resurrected Lamb is coming again as the eschatological King and Judge.

Key Verses: 1:7; 19:11–16

INTRODUCTION

THROUGHOUT THE HISTORY of its interpretation, the book of Revelation has captured imaginations. Scholars have produced a myriad of interpretations and theological schemas in an effort to understand the difficult yet fascinating teachings of the book.[1] Despite the multitude of challenges confronting the interpreter, interest in the book of Revelation continues unabated.[2]

---

[1] On the history of interpretation of Revelation, see A. W. Wainwright, *Mysterious Apocalypse: Interpreting the Book of Revelation* (Nashville, TN: Abingdon, 1993), and more recently, G. L. Stevens, *Revelation: The Past and Future of John's Apocalypse* (Eugene, OR: Pickwick, 2014), 3–142; Koester, *Revelation*, 29-64; and the first chapter of A. S. Bandy, *A Theology of Revelation*, BTNT (Grand Rapids, MI: Zondervan, forthcoming). From a "reception history" perspective, note B. Chilton, *Visions of the Apocalypse: Receptions of John's Revelation in Western Imagination* (Waco, TX: Baylor University Press, 2013); J. Kovacs and C. Rowland, *Revelation: The Apocalypse of Jesus Christ*, BBC (Oxford, UK: Blackwell, 2004).

[2] Important commentaries include D. E. Aune, *Revelation*, 3 vols., WBC 52 (Nashville, TN: Nelson, 1997, 1998); G. K. Beale, *The Book of Revelation*, NIGTC (Grand Rapids, MI: Eerdmans, 1999); H. Giesen, *Die Offenbarung des Johannes*, RNT (Regensburg, Germany: F. Pustet, 1997); C. R. Koester, *Revelation: A New Translation with Introduction and Commentary*, AYB 38A (New Haven, CT: Yale University Press, 2014); G. R. Osborne, *Revelation*, BECNT (Grand Rapids, MI: Baker, 2002); and S. S. Smalley, *The Revelation to John* (Downers Grove, IL: InterVarsity, 2005). Older but still valuable are R. H. Charles, *A Critical and Exegetical Commentary on the Revelation of St. John*, 2 vols., ICC (Edinburgh, Scotland: T&T Clark, 1920); H. B. Swete, *The Apocalypse of St. John*, 3rd ed. (London, England: Macmillan, 1909). Currently the key bibliographic resource is S. E. Porter and A. K. Gabriel, *Johannine Writings and Apocalyptic: An Annotated Bibliography*, Johannine Studies 1 (Leiden, Netherlands: Brill, 2013); slightly newer and robust is the bibliography in Koester, *Revelation*, 151–206. For "state of research" treatments, see S. M. Lewis, *What Are They Saying About New Testament Apocalyptic?* (New York, NY: Paulist, 2004); G. R. Osborne, "Recent Trends in the Study of the Apocalypse," in *The Face of New Testament Studies: A Survey of Recent Research*, ed. S. McKnight and G. R. Osborne (Grand Rapids, MI: Baker, 2004), 473–504; P. Prigent, *Commentary on the Apocalypse of St. John*, trans. W. Pradels (Tübingen, Germany: Mohr Siebeck, 2004), 1–84;

HISTORY

Author

Since the author identified himself as "John," and since most scholars accept that the name was not a pseudonym,[3] the focus of discussion has been on answering the question, *Which* John is the author of the book? Most scholars recognize three major candidates: (1) John the apostle and son of Zebedee;[4] (2) John the elder;[5] and (3) some other unknown John who was a prophet.[6] In addition, John Mark[7] and John the Baptist[8] have been proposed as candidates but have failed to gain serious support.

Internal Evidence Revelation is the only book in the Johannine corpus with an explicit declaration of authorship. The author identifies himself as "John" three times at the beginning and once at the end (1:1, 4, 9; 22:8). The first-person references indicate that the author was an eyewitness and participant in the events narrated in the book.[9] At the outset, the text says that John "testified" as an eyewitness to the veracity of the message directly handed down to him by God (1:2; see 1 John 1:1–3). In the other two opening self-references, it seems John stated his name for the official record (1:4, 9).[10] Hence, he fulfilled the role of a witness to Christ and to the churches by submitting his testimony in writing.

The author refers to himself simply as "John," suggesting he was a well-known figure in Asia Minor. Although he does not explicitly call himself a prophet, he did present himself as such. This is demonstrated by the simple self-designation "I, John" (1:9; 22:8), which conforms to the standard convention used in prophetic and apocalyptic writings.[11] He also

---

F. Tóth, "Erträge und Tendenzen in der gegenwärtigen Forschung zur Johannesapokalypse," in *Die Johannesapokalypse: Kontexte—Konzepte—Rezeption*, ed. J. Frey, J. A. Kelhoffer, and F. Tóth, WUNT 287 (Tübingen, Germany: Mohr Siebeck, 2012), 1–39.

[3] See D. A. deSilva, *An Introduction to the New Testament* (Downers Grove, IL: InterVarsity, 2004), 894; Charles, *Revelation*, 1.xxxix; S. S. Smalley, *Thunder and Love: John's Revelation and John's Community* (Milton Keynes, UK: Word, 1994), 39–40.

[4] Irenaeus, *Haer.* 4.20.11; Tertullian, *Marc.* 3.14.3; 3.24.4; Clement of Alexandria, *Paed.* 2.119; *Quis div.* 42; *Strom.* 6.106; Hippolytus, *Antich.* 36; Origen, *Comm. Jo.* 2.4.

[5] Eusebius, *Hist. eccl.* 3.39.3–7; J. J. Gunther, "The Elder John, Author of Revelation," *JSNT* 11 (1981): 3–20. Apparently, Papias made a distinction between John the apostle and John the elder (see chap. 7 above). With reference to the two tombs of John in Ephesus, Eusebius conjectured that Papias attributed the Gospel to the apostle and Revelation to the elder.

[6] B. K. Blount, *Revelation: A Commentary*, NTL (Louisville, KY: Westminster John Knox, 2009), 5–8; Charles, *Revelation of St. John*, 1.xxxviii; Koester, *Revelation*, 68–69; F. Tóth, "Von der Vision zur Redaktion: Untersuchungen zur Komposition, Redaktion und Intention der Johannesapokalypse," in *Die Johannesapokalypse: Kontexte—Konzepte—Rezeption*, ed. J. Frey, J. A. Kelhoffer, and F. Tóth, WUNT 287 (Tübingen, Germany: Mohr Siebeck, 2012), 319–411.

[7] Eusebius, *Hist. eccl.* 7.25.15. This was suggested but quickly dismissed by Dionysius of Alexandria (d. 265) as a possible alternative, since Mark's name also was John.

[8] J. M. Ford, *Revelation*, AB 38 (New York, NY: Doubleday, 1975), 28–46.

[9] F. Bovon, "John's Self-Presentation in Revelation 1:9–10," *CBQ* 62 (2000): 695.

[10] Beale, *Book of Revelation*, 1127–28.

[11] E.g., "I, Daniel" (Dan 7:15; 8:15, 27; 9:2; 10:2, 7; 12:5); "I, Baruch" (*2 Apoc. Bar.* 8:3; 9:1; 10:5; 11:1; 13:1; 32:8; 44:1); "I, Enoch" (*1 Enoch* 12:3); "I, Ezra" (*4 Ezra* 2:33). See also Swete, *Revelation*, 11; Aune, *Revelation 1–5*, 75.

designates his book as a "prophecy" (1:3; 22:7, 11, 18–19).[12] The inaugural vision includes John's commission in a manner reminiscent of OT prophets (1:9–20).[13] Later in the book John participates in the vision like a prophet when he eats a bittersweet scroll and is told that "it is necessary for [him] to prophesy again" (10:8–11, author's translation; see Ezek 3:1–3). He exhibited a special concern for Christian prophets (10:7; 11:10, 18; 16:6; 18:20, 24; 22:6, 9) and condemned all false prophets (16:13; 19:20; 20:10). This suggests that John regarded himself as a prophet in the tradition of the OT prophets.

When John spoke of himself, he did so with humility, preferring to call himself a "servant" (*doulos*) of God or Christ (1:1; see 2:20; 6:15; 7:3; etc.) and a "brother" (*adelphos*; 1:9). While John was an authoritative figure in the Christian community, he presented himself as one of the believers, a "partner" (*synkoinōnos*) with his readers in hardships, the kingdom, and patient endurance (1:9; see 6:11; 12:10; 19:10; 22:9).

What is more, linguistic and stylistic clues within the text strongly suggest that John was a Jewish Christian originally from Palestine.[14] On the basis of his painstaking analysis, R. H. Charles affirms that the one certainty regarding the author was that he was a Palestinian Jew from the region of Galilee, based on two observations.[15] First, John's mother tongue was Hebrew, as evidenced by the "vast multitude of solecisms [an apparent grammatical incongruity] and unparalleled idiosyncrasies" of his Greek that reflect Semitic syntax.[16] Second, John was a prophet who wrote an apocalypse.[17] John's Palestinian roots

---

[12] See M. E. Boring, "The Apocalypse as Christian Prophecy: A Discussion of the Issues Raised by the Book of Revelation for the Study of Early Christian Prophecy," *SBL Seminar Papers* 2 (1974): 26–27.

[13] See F. D. Mazzaferri, *The Genre of the Book of Revelation from a Source-critical Perspective*, BZNW 54 (Berlin, Germany: W. de Gruyter, 1989), 259–378. On the OT prophetic call narratives, see ibid., 88–102. See also the seminal work in both W. Zimmerli, *Ezekiel 1*, Hermeneia (Philadelphia, PA: Fortress, 1979), 97–100; and N. C. Habel, "The Form and Significance of the Call Narratives," *ZAW* 77 (1965): 297–323. See also the outstanding recent essay of D. N. Phinney, "Call/Commission Narratives," in *Dictionary of the Old Testament Prophets*, ed. M. J. Boda and J. G. McConville (Downers Grove, IL: InterVarsity, 2012), 65–71.

[14] This view is held by a majority of scholars, including Aune, *Revelation 1–5*, l; G. R. Beasley-Murray, *Revelation*, NCBC (London, England: Oliphants, 1974), 35–37; I. Boxall, *Revelation: Vision and Insight* (London, England: SPCK, 2002), 7; Charles, *Revelation of St. John*, 1.xliv; A. Y. Collins, *Crisis and Catharsis: The Power of the Apocalypse* (Philadelphia, PA: Westminster, 1984), 50; W. G. Kümmel, *Introduction to the New Testament*, rev. ed., trans. H. C. Kee (Nashville, TN: Abingdon, 1975), 472; P. A. Rainbow, *Johannine Theology: The Gospels, the Epistles and the Apocalypse* (Downers Grove, IL: InterVarsity, 2014), 42; Smalley, *Thunder and Love*, 39; Swete, *Revelation*, 39. Cf. R. K. MacKenzie (*The Author of the Apocalypse: A Review of the Prevailing Hypothesis of Jewish-Christian Authorship*, MBPS 51 [Lewiston, NY: Mellen, 1997], 3), who posited that John was a Gentile-Christian from Asia Minor.

[15] Charles, *Revelation of St. John*, 1.xliv; H. B. Swete, *The Apocalypse of St. John* (London, England: Macmillan, 1911), cxxv.

[16] Most (if not all) of these solecisms are intentional, such as *apo* ("from," 1:4) followed by the nominative rather than the genitive, pointing to God's self-identification as "I am" in Exod 3:14. On the Semitic syntax of Revelation, see Swete, *Apocalypse of St. John*, cxxv; G. Mussies, *The Morphology of Koine Greek as Used in the Apocalypse of St. John: A Study in Bilingualism*, NovTSup 27 (Leiden, Netherlands: Brill, 1971), 352–53; S. Thompson, *The Apocalypse and Semitic Syntax*, SNTSMS 52 (Cambridge, UK: Cambridge University Press, 1985); S. E. Porter, "The Language of the Apocalypse in Recent Discussion," *NTS* 35 (1989): 582–603; D. D. Schmidt, "Semitisms and Septuagintalisms in the Book of Revelation," *NTS* 37 (1991): 592–603; Beale, *Book of Revelation*, 100–107.

[17] See Aune (*Revelation 1–5*, l): "No known examples of Jewish apocalypses originated in the eastern or western Diaspora, nor did the genre survive long in early Christianity once it had moved outside the boundaries of Palestine."

are also exposed by his awareness of and interest in the temple (11:1–2) and other locations in Palestine (11:8; 16:16; 20:9; 21:2).[18] Even the name "John" is of Jewish origin and did not appear in Gentile settings until much later.[19]

In light of these observations, there is good reason to believe the author of Revelation was John the apostle, the son of Zebedee. But several objections have been raised that dispute this identification—especially in recent decades.

The first possible objection is that John the son of Zebedee was not a prophet but an apostle. Indeed, nowhere in the book does the author claim apostolic authority or personal acquaintance with Jesus during his earthly ministry, and he is identified as a brother with the prophets, not the apostles (22:9).[20] But claiming John was *only* a prophet constitutes an undue inference. It is certainly possible, if not plausible, that one man could function in both roles at the same time.[21] Thus, John's identity as a prophet does not necessarily obviate his status as an apostle.

Another objection is that when John describes the foundations of the new Jerusalem bearing the names of the twelve apostles (21:14; see 18:20; Eph 2:20), he speaks of the apostles as an apparent outsider by referring to them as founding figures of the past.[22] But again, especially in light of the symbolic nature of John's vision, nothing seems to preclude that he was one of them.[23] In reporting such a vision, it would be entirely out of place for the author to interject that he himself was one of the apostles. Thus, 21:14 does not indicate that the author was someone other than the apostle John.

External Evidence Early church tradition unanimously ascribes Revelation to John the apostle. Few other NT books enjoy such clear and unambiguous attribution of authorship.[24] Explicit early and uncontested testimony asserting Johannine apostolic authorship is found in the writings of Justin Martyr (ca. AD 100–165), Irenaeus (ca. AD 130–200), Clement of Alexandria (ca. AD 150–215), Hippolytus (ca. AD 170–236), Origen (ca. AD 185–254), and Tertullian (ca. AD 160–225).[25] In the second century (ca. AD 100–165), Justin Martyr provided the earliest extant evidence that John the apostle wrote Revelation.[26]

---

[18] Ibid.

[19] A. Farrer, *The Revelation of St. John the Divine* (Oxford, UK: Oxford University Press, 1964), 37. The name "John" *(Iōannēs)* occurs frequently in Jewish writings (e.g., 1 Esd 9:29; 1 Macc 2:1–2; 8:17; 9:36, 38; 16:1, 9, 19, 21, 23; 2 Macc 4:11; 11:17; and 188 times in Josephus) but rarely in Greek texts. See also MacKenzie, *The Author of the Apocalypse*, 8n2.

[20] deSilva, *Introduction*, 894.

[21] See Boxall, *Revelation*, 7. Cf. the arguments by D. Guthrie, *New Testament Introduction*, 4th rev. ed. (Downers Grove, IL: InterVarsity, 1990), 936; and D. A. Carson and D. J. Moo, *An Introduction to the New Testament*, 2nd ed. (Grand Rapids, MI: Zondervan, 2005), 702.

[22] Charles, *Revelation of St. John*, 1.xliii–xliv; Aune, *Revelation 1–5*, li; deSilva, *Introduction*, 894.

[23] See Beale, *Book of Revelation*, 1070.

[24] See Charles, *Revelation of St. John*, 1.c; Guthrie, *Introduction*, 933; G. Maier, *Die Johannesoffenbarung und die Kirche*, WUNT 25 (Tübingen, Germany: Mohr Siebeck, 1981), 107; Carson and Moo, *Introduction to the New Testament*, 701.

[25] Irenaeus, *Haer.* 4.20.11; Clement of Alexandria, *Paed.* 2.119; *Quis div.* 42; *Strom.* 6.106; Hippolytus, *Antich.* 36; Origen, *Comm. Jo.* 2.4; Tertullian, *Marc.* 3.14.3; 3.24.4.

[26] Justin, *Dial.* 81.4; see Eusebius, *Hist. eccl.* 4.18.8.

This tradition was not only echoed and affirmed by later church fathers; there is absolutely no hint of any competing views to Johannine apostolic authorship. So strong is this evidence that Guthrie observes that those who deny it suppose the early church fathers were simply ignorant of the true origins of the book and erroneously assumed that the author must have been the son of Zebedee.[27] Thus, these early traditions make a solid case for John the son of Zebedee as the author of Revelation.

Other testimony may provide additional early attestation of Johannine apostolic authorship, such as the writings of Papias of Hierapolis (ca. AD 110), the gnostic *Apocryphon of John*, and the Muratorian Fragment (later second century?), but these sources are less conclusive.[28] Papias of Hierapolis, in particular, continues to be a controversial figure (see Eusebius, *Hist. eccl.* 3.39.1). According to Eusebius (ca. AD 260–340), Papias distinguished between a "John" among the apostles and a "John the elder" (*Hist. eccl.* 3.39.5). But there is evidence that Papias regarded Revelation as from the hand of John the apostle.[29]

The widespread testimony for Johannine apostolic authorship began to be questioned by some fringe groups in the second century. Marcion (ca. AD 150) was the first to reject the book because of its strong Jewish characteristics,[30] but this rejection has had virtually no impact since Marcion repudiated most of the NT.[31] The second challenge came from anti-Montanists. The *Alogi*, a group of Christian heretics that flourished in Asia Minor around AD 170, rejected John's Gospel and Revelation as from the apostle John and believed the book was the product of the heretic Cerinthus, as did Gaius, who detested the earthly nature of Christ's kingdom after the resurrection.[32] Interestingly, these second-century dissenting voices cast aspersions on Revelation not on historical grounds but because its message conflicted with their theology.

The critical analysis of Revelation and the Fourth Gospel by a third-century bishop of Alexandria named Dionysius (ca. AD 247–65) established a tradition maintaining that the two books could not possibly have come from the same hand. In his work *On Promises*, preserved by Eusebius, Dionysius resolutely denied *chiliasm* (the belief in the millennial reign of Christ), faulting it for its alleged emphasis on carnal indulgence and its basis in a literal interpretation of Revelation.[33] While Dionysius affirmed Revelation as inspired Scripture, he denied that it was written by the apostle John.[34]

---

[27] Guthrie, *Introduction*, 935.

[28] In both cases the date of these documents is in question. On the *Apocryphon of John*, see M. Waldstein and F. Wisse, *The Apocryphon of John*, NHMS 33 (Leiden, Netherlands: Brill, 1995), 1–8. On the Muratorian Fragment, see E. J. Schnabel, "The Muratorian Fragment: The State of Research," *JETS* 57 (2014): 231–64.

[29] See especially Maier (*Johannesoffenbarung*, 62–63), who concluded that Papias personally knew John the apostle, referred to as "the elder" in Asia Minor, and regarded Revelation as his writing. Note Maier's list of scholars who argue that Papias knew Revelation and attributed it to the apostle (ibid., 62n243).

[30] Tertullian, *Marc.* 4.5; see Charles, *Revelation of St. John*, 1.c.

[31] Carson and Moo, *Introduction to the New Testament*, 701.

[32] Charles, *Revelation of St. John*, 1.c; cf. Irenaeus, *Haer.* 3.2.9; Epiphanius, *Pan.* 51.3; Eusebius, *Hist. eccl.* 3.28.1–2.

[33] *Hist. eccl.* 7.24.4–6; 7.25.1–2.

[34] *Hist. eccl.* 7.25.1–27.

To this day Dionysius serves as a point of reference for those who deny the Johannine apostolic authorship of Revelation. But none of the arguments used by opponents of the Johannine apostolic authorship of the book have overturned the substantial and unanimous earliest tradition that the author of Revelation is John the apostle, the son of Zebedee.[35]

Date

Scholarly opinion concerning the date of Revelation's composition is divided between an early date (AD 64–69) and a late date (AD 95–96).[36] In addition, some opt for a middle ground, conjecturing that composition began in the 60s and was completed in the late 90s.[37] Although certainty continues to be elusive, the late date, during the reign of Domitian, has considerably stronger support.

Internal Evidence The book of Revelation provides some internal clues regarding its date of composition: (1) the persecution experienced by the churches of Asia Minor; (2) the spiritual condition of these churches; (3) the emperor cult; (4) the reference to the Jerusalem temple in 11:1–2; (5) the "Nero *redivivus* myth" (though not explicitly mentioned in the book); (6) the references to "Babylon" in Revelation; and (7) the seven "heads" mentioned in 17:9–11.

Type of Persecution One of the most common arguments for dating Revelation pertains to the notion that at the time of composition Christians were experiencing fierce persecution. Throughout church history Domitian has been viewed as a great persecutor of the church.[38] But in recent decades this assumption has been increasingly questioned because of the paucity of evidence supporting an empire-wide persecution instigated by him.[39] Therefore, proponents of an early date contend that the persecution of Christians reflected in Revelation best corresponds to Nero's reign. Others speak of the persecution only as a "perceived crisis."[40] Yet recent research suggests that supporting arguments for the Domitianic dating of Revelation may be found in the parallel between Nero's and Domitian's leadership, to the point that Domitian appears as a second Nero.[41]

---

[35] For a discussion of the relationship between John's Gospel and Revelation, see chap. 7.

[36] More recently, a Hadrianic date in the first part of the second century has been advocated by T. Witulski, "Der römische Kaiser Hadrian und die neutestamentliche Johannesapokalypse," and S. Witetschek, "Ein weit geöffnetes Zeitfenster? Überlegungen zur Datierung der Johannesapokalypse," in *Die Johannesapokalypse: Kontexte—Konzepte—Rezeption*, ed. J. Frey, J. A. Kelhoffer, and F. Tóth, WUNT 287 (Tübingen, Germany: Mohr Siebeck, 2012), 79–115, 117–48; this approach, of course, necessarily denies authorship by the apostle John.

[37] Aune, *Revelation 1–5*, lxix–lxx.

[38] Eusebius, *Hist. eccl.* 4.26.9.

[39] See J. G. Cook, *Roman Attitudes Toward the Christians: From Claudius to Hadrian*, WUNT 261 (Tübingen, Germany: Mohr Siebeck, 2010), who discusses the stance that Claudius, Nero, Domitian, Trajan, and Hadrian took vis-à-vis Christians, looking at both primary source material and later Christian reflection. He addresses the question of a Domitianic persecution on pp. 117–37, concluding that the evidence for such a persecution is lacking.

[40] Collins, *Crisis and Catharsis*, 32, 84–110; see W. Schmithals, *The Apocalyptic Movement*, trans. J. E. Steely (Nashville, TN: Abingdon, 1975), 141–50.

[41] See R. Mucha, "Ein flavischer Nero: Zur Domitian-Darstellung und Datierung der Johannesoffenbarung," *NTS* 60 (2014): 83–105, who contends that though current research discounts a wide-ranging persecution of Christians under

The book of Revelation indicates various degrees of persecution and anticipates persecution on a much grander scale in the near future. John addressed the persecution experienced by Christians at the time of composition or in the recent past. John's banishment to Patmos came about because of hostility toward the exclusive claims of the gospel (1:9). The letters to the churches in Asia Minor also demonstrate local persecution. The diverse situations reflected in the letters indicate that each church faced challenges unique to its particular locale. Nevertheless, the persecution experienced by Christians in Asia Minor did not result in death, except for in the case of Antipas in the city of Pergamum (2:13).

The beheaded souls under the heavenly altar provide a final indication of persecution against Christians in the recent past (6:9). The breaking of the fifth seal reveals the souls of believers who were executed for their faith and were crying out for justice (6:10).[42] This cry represents a plea for public justice, not private revenge.[43] The reason they demand justice is because they were unjustly condemned on the grounds of their testimony to the Word of God and to Jesus. Although these souls may include all the martyrs since the time of Abel (Gen 4:10; Matt 23:29–35), more likely they are Christians slain since the time of Stephen (Acts 7:55–60; 12:2; Rev 2:13).[44] The reference does not address a current persecution because Antipas is the only one specifically mentioned to have been executed for his faith. The only well-documented case of widespread persecution occurred during the reign of Nero.[45] Christians in Asia Minor certainly remembered the excessive cruelty and injustice inflicted on believers during Nero's persecution. This piece of evidence thus favors a later date, allowing some time to have transpired since Nero's reign.

At the time of composition, the churches in Asia Minor were experiencing some persecution but nowhere near the extent of what Nero inflicted on Christians. Although they were not currently facing severe persecution, John fully anticipated such in the near future. This is explicitly stated in the answer to the question, "Lord, the One who is holy and true, how long until You judge and avenge our blood from those who live on the earth?" (6:10; see *4 Ezra* 4:33–37). In response believers are told to wait until the full number of their fellow servants and brothers are killed (6:11).

Chapters 12–13 graphically portray the completion of this number as the outcome of a holy war between God and Satan played out on earth. Once expelled from heaven, Satan, the accuser, proceeds to make war against those who obey God's commands and hold to

---

Domitian, this need not necessarily result in a redating of Revelation if Domitian was remembered as a persecutor of Christians, pointing to typological parallels (literary memory, political life, inscriptions, and visual images) between Nero and Domitian.

[42] See 16:7; 20:4. See J. P. Heil, "The Fifth Seal (Rev 6,9–11) as a Key to the Book of Revelation," *Bib* 74 (1993): 220–43.

[43] G. B. Caird, *A Commentary on the Revelation of St. John the Divine* (New York, NY: Harper & Row, 1966), 85.

[44] Beale, *Book of Revelation*, 390.

[45] Tacitus, *Ann.* 15.44; Suetonius, *Nero* 16.2; Tertullian, *Apol.* 5.3; *Nat.* 1.7.8; P. Keresztes, "Law and Arbitrariness in the Persecution of the Christians and Justin's First Apology," *VC* 18 (1964): 204; J. W. P. Borleffs, "Institutum Neronianum," *VC* 6 (1952): 9–145; Cook, *Roman Attitudes Toward the Christians*, 29–111.

the testimony of Jesus (12:17). In 13:1–8, the dragon endows the beast with authority to mandate the worship of his statue and to wage war against believers. This depicts the forced participation in the imperial cult by a future emperor who, like Nero, would savagely persecute the church. Believers are exhorted to persevere and wait for the time when God would vindicate them (13:9–10; see 17:6; 18:24; 19:2; 20:4).

If these examples accurately reflect the situation of Christians in Asia Minor at the time of writing, the evidence favors the time of Domitian. First, the persecution is not severe enough to be that associated with Nero. Second, while the notion that Domitian instituted an empire-wide persecution has been exaggerated,[46] the fact that he did not systematically persecute Christians does not mean he was favorably disposed toward them. To the contrary believers were despised throughout the empire. But not all believers in Asia Minor faced the same level of antagonism; it seems that persecution was more intense in cities competing for Rome's favor. This also suggests the time of Domitian.[47]

The State of the Churches in Asia Minor Many of the Asia Minor churches described in Revelation were clearly in a deteriorated moral and spiritual condition. The Christians in Ephesus had forsaken their "first love" (2:4 KJV). The churches in Pergamum and Thyatira had permitted, and even succumbed to, false teaching (2:14–15, 20–24). Believers in Sardis had become spiritually lethargic (3:1–2). The Laodiceans had indulged in "lukewarm" and arrogant self-sufficiency (3:15–17).[48] While it may be argued in support of a late date that developing this kind of spiritual apathy would have taken some time, this piece of evidence is inconclusive by itself—especially since some of Paul's churches had developed comparable problems already in the AD 50s and 60s.[49]

The Emperor Cult The emperor cult is significant since many have suggested a Domitianic date because of the anti-imperial rhetoric in the book.[50] The phrase "our Lord and God" (4:11; see 19:6), in particular, parallels the Latin *dominus et deus noster*, a title Suetonius said was applied to Domitian during his reign (*Dom.* 13.2). Faithfulness to the one true God in the midst of an idolatrous society is one of the major themes in the book.

---

[46] Bell, "Date of John's Apocalypse," 93–97; Wilson, "Problem of the Domitianic Date," 588–96; L. L. Thompson, *The Book of Revelation: Apocalypse and Empire* (New York: Oxford University Press, 1990), 116; Cook, *Roman Attitudes Toward the Christians*, 117–37.

[47] P. Trebilco, *The Early Christians in Ephesus from Paul to Ignatius* (Grand Rapids, MI: Eerdmans, 2004), 342–47.

[48] Some also point to the reference to wealth in Laodicea as evidence for a later date since the city was destroyed by an earthquake about 61 and was rebuilt without the financial assistance of Rome (Tacitus, *Ann.* 14.27.1). If the city had been destroyed, one would naturally expect a much later date for the composition of the letter. See C. J. Hemer, *The Letters to the Seven Churches of Asia in Their Local Setting*, JSNTSup 11 (Sheffield, UK: JSOT, 1986), 193–96; Mounce, *Book of Revelation*, 35; L. Morris, *The Revelation of St. John*, TNTC (Grand Rapids, MI: Eerdmans, 1969), 37.

[49] See C. H. H. Scobie, "Local References in the Letters to the Seven Churches," *NTS* 39 (1993): 606–24.

[50] L. Mowry, "Revelation 4–5 and Early Christian Liturgical Usage," *JBL* 71 (1952): 80; Mounce, *Book of Revelation*, 140; Beasley-Murray, *Book of Revelation*, 119; H.-J. Klauck, "Das Sendschreiben nach Pergamon und der Kaiserkult in der Johannesoffenbarung," *Bib* 73 (1992): 172; Beale, *Book of Revelation*, 335; C. S. Keener, *Revelation*, NIVAC (Grand Rapids, MI: Zondervan, 2000), 176; J. Roloff, *The Revelation of John: A Continental Commentary*, trans. J. E. Alsup (Minneapolis, MN: Fortress, 1993), 72; Osborne, *Revelation*, 240; Aune, *Revelation 1–5*, 310; idem, "The Influence of Roman Imperial Court Ceremony on the Apocalypse of John," *BibRes* 28 (1983): 20–22.

Thus, 4:11 likely contrasts the imperial claim of divinity with the only true God who is seated on the heavenly throne.

Evidence abounds from Domitian's critics and supporters that he arrogated titles of divinity beyond what was culturally acceptable. In 42 BC, after the death of Julius Caesar, the senate officially declared him *divius Iulius* ("divine Julius"). Soon thereafter Octavian, Caesar's nephew and successor, was called *divi filius* ("son of a divine being").[51] At most, an emperor, usually after death, could attain the status of *divius* ("divine") but not *deus* ("god").[52] Aside from Caligula's excessive claims to divinity,[53] Domitian was the first Roman emperor to adopt and even mandate the title *deus*,[54] a claim his critics found repulsive.[55]

While the reference to "our Lord and God" in 4:11 does not conclusively pinpoint the emperor at the time of composition, of all the emperors Domitian is the most likely candidate. To be sure, all the emperors were afforded some measure of divinity, but this practice seems to have reached a new level under Domitian. What is more, in the accounts of Nero's conflict with Christians there is no evidence that Nero claimed to be divine. The same is true for all other emperors prior to Domitian. If 4:11 represents two competing claims for "our Lord and God," the evidence favors the time of Domitian for the date of the book.

The State of Temple Worship The reference to the Jerusalem temple in 11:1–2 has been taken by some to support a pre-70 date since it appears to suggest that the temple was still standing at the time Revelation was written. If Revelation represents a prophecy against Jerusalem, as preterists hold, 11:1–2 must refer to the literal temple. Yet two plausible alternative interpretations exist, supporting a date subsequent to the destruction of the second temple in the year AD 70.

One alternative is to interpret 11:1–2 as a reference to a literal reconstituted temple in Jerusalem to be built in the future, prior to the return of Christ, in fulfillment of Ezekiel 40–48.[56] According to this view, the reference must be to a literal temple because its location is said to be in Jerusalem, "the holy city" (11:2) where the Lord was crucified (11:8). What John envisions is a future rebuilt temple in Jerusalem which will serve as the locus of events surrounding the tribulation. This temple will be the place where the Antichrist

---

[51] Aune, *Revelation 1–5*, 310.

[52] The deification of the emperor was called the rite of apotheosis. See S. R. F. Price, *Rituals and Power: The Roman Imperial Cult in Asia Minor* (Cambridge, UK: Cambridge University Press, 1984), 75.

[53] Philo, *Legat.* 353; P. Borgen, "Emperor Worship and Persecution in Philo's *In Flaccum* and *De Legatione ad Gaium* and the Revelation of John," in *Geschichte—Tradition—Reflexion: Festschrift für Martin Hengel zum 70. Geburstag*, ed. H. Lichtenberger, vol. 3: *Frühes Christentum* (Tübingen, Germany: Mohr Siebeck, 1996), 498–503; J. S. McLaren, "Jews and the Imperial Cult: From Augustus to Domitian," *JSNT* 27 (2005): 266–69.

[54] T. B. Slater, "On the Social Setting of the Revelation to John," *NTS* 44 (1998): 236.

[55] Suetonius, *Dom.* 13.2; Dio Cassius, *Hist.* 67.4.7; 67.13.4; see Dio Chrysostom, *Def.* 45.1; Juvenal, *Sat.* 4.69–71. See also Parker, "'Our Lord and God' in Rev 4,11," 209.

[56] J. A. Seiss, *The Apocalypse: Lectures on the Book of Revelation*, ZCS (Grand Rapids, MI: Zondervan, 1979), 235–41; J. F. Walvoord, *The Revelation of Jesus Christ: A Commentary* (Chicago, IL: Moody, 1966), 175–77.

pretentiously claims divine prerogatives (Matt 24:15; 1 Thess 2:4). If so, Revelation may have been written either prior or subsequent to the destruction of the second temple.

Another alternative is to interpret the reference to the temple as symbolic.[57] Since Revelation frequently employs symbolic language, this would be in keeping with the general nature of the book. According to this view, the reference to the temple in 11:1–2 is symbolic of the people of God. Thus, K. H. Easley relates 11:1–2 to 21:9–10 where "the holy city," the new Jerusalem, represents the people of God fully glorified and maintains that "the holy city" in 11:2 represents the people of God not fully glorified during their earthly pilgrimage.[58]

If so, the purpose of measurement would be to demonstrate that believers are divinely protected from the judgment of God depicted throughout the vision. The casting out from the outer court to be trampled by the Gentiles would indicate that while the people of God are not subject to God's wrath, they are not immune to the reality of persecution. The purpose of 11:1–2 would be to encourage believers to faithful endurance in the midst of the extreme persecution described in chapter 13. Again the reference to the temple in 11:1–2 would not be a conclusive internal datum regarding the date of composition because the temple could either have been still standing or already have been destroyed at the time of writing. For these reasons 11:1–2 does not provide clear evidence for a particular date of composition.

The "Nero Redivivus Myth" Another fascinating piece of evidence is the "*Nero redivivus* myth" (*redivivus* is Lat. for "revived"). Shortly after Nero committed suicide on June 9, AD 68, Roman historians recount how a belief emerged throughout the empire that Nero had not actually died but was going to return with the Parthian army.[59] The fact that few saw Nero's corpse, coupled with uncertainty regarding the location of his tomb, gave credence to this belief.[60]

The Nero *redivivus* myth surfaced in several apocalyptic Jewish and Christian writings toward the end of the first century, equating him with Belair.[61] The Christian apocalypses

---

[57] Swete, *Revelation*, 132–33; Caird, *Revelation of St. John*, 131–32; Mounce, *Book of Revelation*, 218–20; R. Bauckham, *The Climax of Prophecy: Studies on the Book of Revelation* (Edinburgh, Scotland: T&T Clark, 1993), 272; Beale, *Book of Revelation*, 557–71; Keener, *Revelation*, 287–89; M. Jauhiainen, "The Measuring of the Sanctuary Reconsidered (Rev 11,1–2)," *Bib* 83 (2002): 507n2; Osborne, *Revelation*, 408–15.

[58] K. H. Easley, *Revelation*, HNTC (Nashville, TN: Holman Reference, 1998), 188–89.

[59] Suetonius, *Nero* 49.3; see 57.1.

[60] Bauckham, *Climax of Prophecy*, 412–13; Aune, *Revelation 6–16*, 738. This belief was nourished and reinforced by at least three pretenders. The first, in the year 69, a slave from Pontus or a freedman from Italy, gathered a small army and sailed from Greece, only to experience shipwreck on an island where he was soon executed (Tacitus, *Hist.* 2.8; Dio Cassius, *Hist.* 63.9.3). The second, Terentius Maximus, in the year 80, appeared in the province of Asia, where he gathered a few followers and marched to the Euphrates River, where he eventually sought refuge with the Parthians (Dio Cassius, *Hist.* 66.19.3). The third appeared twenty years after Nero's death in the year 88 (Suetonius, *Nero* 57.2; see Tacitus, *Hist.* 2.8.1). See Bauckham, *Climax of Prophecy*, 412–14; P. A. Gallivan, "The False Neros: A Reexamination," *Historia* 22 (1973): 364–65; A. E. Pappano, "The False Neros," *CJ* 32 (1937): 385–92; and Aune, *Revelation 6–16*, 738–39.

[61] See *Sib. Or.* 3.63–74, where Nero is identified as Beliar, the archenemy of God's people; *Sib. Or.* 4.119–24, 138–39, the earliest known source containing a prophetic expectation of Nero's return from Parthia (most likely dated after the year

also associate Nero with Beliar and cast him as the paradigmatic persecutor of the church.[62] Toward the end of the first century, two distinct traditions developed regarding Nero's supposed return.[63] One stems from the idea that Nero never died and was going to return with the Parthian army to conquer Rome. The other envisions a demonically empowered Nero figure that would attack God's people.[64]

Revelation appears to reflect an awareness of the return of Nero legend.[65] Chapter 13 describes how the dragon gives rise to the beast and endows him with authority.[66] In 13:3 one of the beast's heads receives a fatal wound but is miraculously resuscitated. As a result the entire world worships him as he proceeds to slaughter faithful Christians (13:4–10). Although Nero is not mentioned by name, the language in 13:1–7 suggests that John may have adapted the form of the Nero myth that alludes to the enemy of God's people in Daniel 7:2–25,[67] though it is possible the reference here is not to an individual but to an empire.

In addition, 17:10–12 may reflect parallels with the other form of the Nero *redux* ("never died") myth depicting Nero's attack on Rome.[68] John's portrayal radically differs from other expectations of Nero's return because in Revelation the beast actually rises from the dead (*redivivus*), whereas elsewhere it is assumed that Nero never died (*redux*) in the first place.[69] The reason John departs from the tradition is that in his vision the beast mimics Christ, who died and rose again and will return to conquer the world's kingdoms.[70]

This piece of evidence would seem to favor a Domitianic date. If Revelation reflects the return of the Nero myth, it could not have been written until the year 69 at the earliest. The historical sources all attest that the return of Nero legend continued and increased

---

70 because of the reference to the eruption of Mount Vesuvius, which occurred in the year 79; *Sib. Or.* 1.30–35); and *Sib. Or.* 5.28–34, 93–110, 137–54, 214–27, 361–80, referring to Nero's return from his supposed flight to Parthia and the expectation that he would destroy Rome. See Bauckham, *Climax of Prophecy*, 415–20; Aune, *Revelation 6–16*, 739.

[62] The *Ascen. Isa.* 4:2–4, most likely dated around the end of the first century, expected the coming of a demonically inspired king who would persecute the church. Cf. *Apoc. Pet.* 14:11; see Bauckham, *Climax of Prophecy*, 411–12.

[63] Bauckham, *Climax of Prophecy*, 423.

[64] Ibid., 424–28. Bauckham demonstrates that this apocalyptic tradition is rooted in a reading of Daniel 7.

[65] W. H. C. Frend, *Rise of Christianity* (Philadelphia, PA: Fortress, 1984), 331n8; I. T. Beckwith, *The Apocalypse of John: Studies in Introduction with a Critical and Exegetical Commentary* (London, England: Macmillan, 1919; repr. Grand Rapids, MI: Baker, 1967), 635–36; Collins, *Crisis and Catharsis*, 59; Bauckham, *Climax of Prophecy*, 407–50; Beale, *Book of Revelation*, 17–18; Aune, *Revelation 6–16*, 737–40; Osborne, *Revelation*, 496; Klauck, "Do They Never Come Back?," 683–98.

[66] Philostratus referred to Nero as a beast due to his tyranny (*Vit. Apoll.* 4.38).

[67] Bauckham, *Climax of Prophecy*, 424–29. Cf. G. K. Beale, *The Use of Daniel in Jewish Apocalyptic Literature and in the Revelation of John* (Lanham, MD: University Press of America, 1984), 229–39; and J. Fekkes, *Isaiah and Prophetic Traditions in the Book of Revelation*, JSNTSup 93 (Sheffield, UK: JSOT, 1994), 82–85.

[68] Bauckham, *Climax of Prophecy*, 430.

[69] Ibid., 421.

[70] The language used to describe the beast's resurrection (or that of one of its heads) in 13:3 mimics the same words used to describe Christ in 5:6. The return of the beast in 17:11 also parallels the language used for God in 1:4, 8; 4:8. See Beale, *Book of Revelation*, 875–77; Bauckham, *Climax of Prophecy*, 432, 435; Osborne, *Revelation*, 620–21; A. Farrer, *The Revelation of St. John the Divine* (Oxford, UK: Oxford University Press, 1964), 184; A. Y. Collins, *The Combat Myth in the Book of Revelation* (Missoula, MT: Scholars, 1976), 185; Swete, *Revelation*, 255–58.

in popularity toward the end of the first century. The accounts of Domitian's savagery warranted a reputation similar to that of Nero beyond any of his predecessors. Hence, Domitian gained a reputation as a second Nero.[71] This suggests Nero came to epitomize any tyrant.[72] In light of this, a date at the time of Domitian seems more probable than a pre-70 date.

The City "Babylon" The references to the city "Babylon" in the latter half of the book (14:8; 16:19; 17:5; 18:2, 10, 21) are intriguing. In 17:9, when explaining the vision of the prostitute riding atop a scarlet beast that has seven heads, the interpreting angel explains that "the seven heads are seven mountains on which the woman is seated." Since Rome was known throughout the ancient world as the city on seven hills, "Babylon" should be equated with Rome.[73] This represents a weighty piece of evidence supporting a post-AD 70 date.[74] The reason "Babylon" became a fitting code name for Rome is that both empires, Babylon and Rome, destroyed the temple in Jerusalem. Two post-70 Jewish apocalypses use "Babylon" as a cipher for Rome (4 Ezra 3:1–2, 28–31; 2 Bar 10:1–3; 11:1; 67:7).[75] The fifth Sibylline oracle (post-AD 70) also refers to Rome as "Babylon" in the context of the return of Nero myth (*Sib. Or.* 5.143, 159–60).[76] This constitutes compelling evidence for identifying "Babylon" as Rome in Revelation, which suggests a post-70 date of composition.

The "Seven Heads" Finally, there is the possible identification of the reigning emperor at the time of writing in 17:9–11. The seven heads represent seven kings, which some suggest corresponds to a series of Roman emperors since the beast is associated with "Babylon"/Rome. In 17:10 the interpreting angel remarks that five of these kings have already fallen; one is currently on the throne; and another has not yet come.[77] The sixth king who "is" represents the current reigning Roman emperor at the time of composition.

If the list of seven kings corresponds to a series of Roman emperors, the one who "is" is either Nero or Galba. Julius Caesar marks the foundation of the empire and therefore is the first emperor.[78] The sixth emperor in chronological order is Nero (AD 54–68). But Tacitus regarded Augustus as the first official emperor by distinguishing him as *princeps*

---

[71] Martial, *Epig.* 11.33.1–3; Juvenal, *Sat.* 4.37–38; Pliny, *Pan.* 48.3; 53.4.

[72] Klauck, "Do They Never Come Back," 686.

[73] Virgil, *Georg.* 2.535; *Aen.* 6.738; Horace, *Carm.* 7; Cicero, *Att.* 6.5; Suetonius, *Dom.* 4; *Sib. Or.* 2.18; 13.45; 14.108; Caird, *Revelation of St. John*, 216; Keener, *Revelation*, 408n21.

[74] Collins, *Crisis and Catharsis*, 57–58; J. N. Kraybill, *Imperial Cult and Commerce in John's Apocalypse*, JSNTSup 127 (Sheffield, UK: Sheffield Academic, 1996), 142–47; H. Giesen, *Studien zur Johannesapokalypse*, SBAB 29 (Stuttgart, Germany: Katholisches Bibelwerk, 2000), 238–40; S. J. Friesen, *Imperial Cults and the Apocalypse of John: Reading Revelation in the Ruins* (Oxford, UK: Oxford University Press, 2001), 138–40.

[75] See J. J. Collins, *The Apocalyptic Imagination*, 2nd ed. (Grand Rapids, MI: Eerdmans, 1998), 196.

[76] Ibid., 234.

[77] The use of the term "fallen" may suggest those who have died a violent death. See Aune, *Revelation 17–22*, 949; E. Schüssler Fiorenza, *Revelation: Vision of a Just World* (Minneapolis, MN: Fortress, 1991), 97.

[78] Suetonius, *Jul.* 1.1; Dio Chrysostom *Or. 34.7*; Josephus, *Ant.* 18.32, 225; 4 Ezra 11–12; *Sib. Or.* 5.12; cf. Bell, "Date of John's Apocalypse," 98.

(*Hist.* 1.1; *Ann.* 1.1). In this situation Galba (June AD 68–January 69) was the sixth emperor. In either case John would have written prior to 70. Proponents of an early date see this as conclusive evidence.[79] But these are not the only possible reconstructions.[80]

An alternative attempt omits the interregnum of Galba, Otho, and Vitellius.[81] Although they were declared emperors and chronicled in the respective histories (*Sib. Or.* 5.35; 4 Ezra 12:20), Suetonius viewed them as usurpers (*Vesp.* 1.1). If Augustus is the first emperor and these three rulers are omitted, the five who have fallen are Augustus to Nero, and the current emperor is Vespasian. This makes Titus the seventh ruler and Domitian the Antichrist, the eighth who belongs to the seven.[82] But neither this alternative reconstruction nor other proposals related to a succession of individual Roman emperors have proven satisfactory.

Some reject the notion that John was following a historical chronology in favor of a symbolic one.[83] The number seven may convey the idea of perfection or completion (1:4, 11–12, 16, 20; 2:1; 3:1; 4:5; etc.).[84] Hence, the reference to the seven heads as both "hills" and "kings" could be symbolic,[85] with the seven hills representing seven kingdoms rather than individual kings.[86] Alternatively, "hills" could be translated as "mountains," representing an OT metaphor for kingdom or empire. In this case, then, the "head" in question would not be an individual but a future kingdom.[87] In light of these different historical and symbolic interpretations of the passage, dating Revelation based on 17:9–11 remains inconclusive.

External Evidence The earliest traditions located Revelation in the reigns of Claudius, Nero, Domitian, or Trajan. Starting with the least likely date, Epiphanius (ca. AD 375) placed Revelation in the reign of Claudius. He also remarked that John was compelled by

---

[79] Robinson, *Redating*, 242–53; Bell, "Date of John's Apocalypse," 97–100; C. Rowland, *The Open Heaven: A Study of Apocalyptic in Judaism and Early Christianity* (New York, NY: Crossroad, 1982), 404–7; Gentry, *Before Jerusalem Fell*, 146–65; Wilson, "Problem of the Domitianic Date," 599–602; T. B. Slater, "Dating the Apocalypse to John," *Bib* 84 (2003): 255–56.

[80] See Aune, *Revelation 17–22*, 947–48; Beale, *Book of Revelation*, 874.

[81] Swete, *Revelation*, 220–21; Charles, *Revelation of St. John*, 2.69–70; Ford, *Revelation*, 290; Smalley, *Thunder and Love*, 47–48; Prigent, *Commentary on the Apocalypse*, 493.

[82] Smalley, *Thunder and Love*, 47–48. Another attempt came from Strobel, "Abfassung und Geschichtstheologie," 437–39.

[83] Beckwith, *Apocalypse of John*, 704–8; Beasley-Murray, *Book of Revelation*, 256–57; Caird, *Revelation of St. John*, 218–19; Mounce, *Book of Revelation*, 315; Swete, *Revelation*, 257; Aune, *Revelation 17–22*, 948–49; Beale, *Book of Revelation*, 867–80.

[84] See Caird, *Revelation of St. John*, 218.

[85] Keener, *Revelation*, 409; Aune, *Revelation 17–22*, 948; Beale, *Book of Revelation*, 868.

[86] See Isa 2:2; Jer 51:25; Ezek 35:3; Dan 2:35, 45; Zech 4:7; *1 Enoch* 52; *Tg. Isa.* 41:15; cf. esp. Beale, *Book of Revelation*, 868–69.

[87] One possible reconstruction of the seven "heads" along these lines would be that the first five heads represent the five empires that have fallen, that is, Egypt, Assyria, Babylon, Persia, and Greece; that the "one that is" (17:10) is Rome; and that the head that came to life and is still future is a revived Roman Empire.

the Holy Spirit to write in his old age.[88] But Claudius died in the year 54, and it is highly unlikely that he banished John to Patmos.[89]

The external testimony supporting a date during Nero's reign is equally problematic. Apart from two late Syriac versions,[90] the only testimony asserting Nero as the emperor at the time of composition comes from tenuous statements by Theophylact of Bulgaria in the twelfth century.[91] Most likely, this author misunderstood Irenaeus's assertion that John lived until the time of Trajan.[92]

By far the bulk of early church tradition supports the time of Domitian.[93] Irenaeus's testimony constitutes the earliest available evidence regarding the date of the Apocalypse (ca. AD 130–200).[94] Irenaeus, a native of Smyrna, may have received his information directly from Polycarp, a disciple of John,[95] and his pronouncement gained broad acceptance in the early church.[96]

Irenaeus's testimony was affirmed by Clement of Alexandria (ca. AD 150–215), Origen (ca. AD 185–254), Victorinus (died ca. AD 304), Eusebius (ca. AD 260–340), and Jerome (ca. AD 354–420). Clement and Origen stated that John wrote from Patmos but did not name the emperor. Clement, writing around the end of the first century,[97] remarked that John was released from exile on Patmos after the death of the "tyrant."[98] Although he did not provide the name, Eusebius assumed it was Domitian.[99] After Domitian died, Nerva

---

[88] Epiphanius, *Pan.* 51.12, 33.

[89] F. J. A. Hort, *The Apocalypse of St. John* (London, England: Macmillan, 1908), xviii. Hort suggests that Epiphanius may have been depending on Hippolytus (ca. AD 170–236) and meant Claudius Nero. Cf. J. A. T. Robinson, *Redating the New Testament* (Philadelphia, PA: Westminster, 1976), 224; K. L. Gentry, *Before Jerusalem Fell: Dating the Book of Revelation*, rev. ed. (Powder Springs, GA: American Vision, 1998), 104–5.

[90] See B. M. Metzger and B. D. Ehrman, *The Text of the New Testament: Its Transmission, Corruption, and Restoration*, 4th ed. (New York, NY/Oxford, UK: Oxford University Press, 2005), 99–100; Swete, *Revelation*, cxciii–cxciv.

[91] Theophylact, *Praef. in Ioann.* Elsewhere, Theophylact indicated that John wrote during the reign of Trajan (*On Matt 20:22*).

[92] Irenaeus, *Against Heresies* 2.22.5. See Charles, *Revelation of St. John*, 1.xcii; R. H. Mounce, *The Book of Revelation*, NICNT (Grand Rapids, MI: Eerdmans, 1977), 31n37.

[93] Irenaeus, *Against Heresies* 5.30.3; Clement of Alexandria, *Quis dives salvetur* 42; Origen, *Homily on Matthew* 16.6; Victorinus, *Apocalypse* 10.11; Eusebius, *Hist. eccl.* 3.18; 3.20; Jerome, *De viris illustribus* 9.

[94] Melito of Sardis (died ca. AD 190) also supported a Domitianic dating as recorded by Eusebius (*Hist. eccl.* 4.26.9). He wrote a commentary on Revelation and in his protest against Marcus Aurelius argued that Nero and Domitian unjustly persecuted Christians. See Charles, *Revelation of St. John*, 1.xcii.

[95] Irenaeus, *Against Heresies* 3.3.4.

[96] See Gentry, *Before Jerusalem Fell*, 45–46.

[97] Against J. C. Wilson, "The Problem of the Domitianic Date of Revelation," *NTS* 39 (1993): 592; L. L. Welborn, "On the Date of First Clement," *BibRes* 29 (1984): 35–54. Despite these two authors who question the Domitianic date for *1 Clement*, the scholarly consensus favors a mid-90s date. See Beale, *Book of Revelation*, 16; T. J. Herron, "The Most Probable Date of the First Epistle of Clement to the Corinthians," in *Studia Patristica: Tertullian to Nicaea in the West, Clement of Alexandria and Origen, Athanasius*, ed. E. A. Livingstone (Louvain, Belgium: Peeters, 1989), 106–21.

[98] Clement, *Quis div. salv.* 42; cf. Eusebius, *Hist. eccl.* 3.23.5–19.

[99] Eusebius, *Hist. eccl.* 3.23.1; cf. Aune, *Revelation 1–5*, lix. On the release of those banished under Domitian, see Pliny, *Ep.* 1.5.10; 9.13.5; Dio Chrysostom, *Or.* 13.

promised a "new era" of liberty and justice.[100] The tyrant in question could very well be Domitian, which would corroborate the date indicated by Irenaeus.[101]

Eusebius accepted Irenaeus's testimony, asserting that Revelation was written in the fourteenth year of Domitian's reign (ca. AD 95; *Hist. eccl.* 3.18.1–3 citing Irenaeus, *Haer.* 5.30.3).[102] He depicted Domitian, the successor of Nero, as a cruel tyrant in his hostility toward God and in his persecution of Christians.[103] He also affirmed the tradition that after John was released from Patmos, he took up residence in Ephesus subsequent to Domitian's death.[104] If his sources were in error and no such persecution took place, his dating becomes suspect.[105] In any case Eusebius's testimony preserved a tradition ascribing to Revelation a late date that was widely accepted in the early church.

The strength of a given witness depends on one's confidence in that source.[106] Although it is not without some difficulties, the testimony of Irenaeus should be afforded the most merit. It represents the earliest tradition with possible connections back to Polycarp (first half of second century), one of John's disciples. Testimony supporting any other date came about much later and is not widely attested. The arguments against Irenaeus's dating do not successfully dislodge its validity.[107] Even proponents of an early date must concede that based on external evidence, the Domitian date is the only fully viable possibility. As Hort maintained, "If external evidence alone could decide, there would be a clear preponderance for Domitian."[108]

Conclusion On the whole, the preponderance of the internal and external evidence suggests the mid-90s during the reign of Domitian as the most probable date of composition for Revelation. The external testimony overwhelmingly favors the late date, which became the established tradition throughout church history. The internal testimony, while less than conclusive, also tends to support a later date. Though some passages may reflect historical circumstances prior to AD 70, most of the evidence seems to point to a later

---

[100] Tacitus, *Agr.* 3; cf. Thompson, *Book of Revelation*, 110–11.

[101] For a detailed argument positing Nero as the tyrant, see Gentry, *Before Jerusalem Fell*, 69–83. He shows that Nero was frequently labeled "tyrant" by Roman historians, but he fails to be convincing because those same historians also malign Domitian as a tyrant.

[102] Eusebius, *Chron.* PG 19.551–52; Aune, *Revelation 1–5*, lix.

[103] Eusebius, *Hist. eccl.* 3.17.1; 3.18.4; he also (ibid., 3.20.7) cited Tertullian (*Apol.* 5) who stated, "Domitian also tried to do the same as he, for he was a Nero in cruelty, but, I believe, in as much as he had some sense, he stopped at once and recalled those whom he had banished."

[104] Eusebius, *Hist. eccl.* 3.20.8–9; see Clement, *Quis div. salv.* 42; Jerome, *Vir. ill.* 9.

[105] Robinson, *Redating*, 222–23; Gentry, *Before Jerusalem Fell*, 102–4; B. Newman, "The Fallacy of the Domitian Hypothesis," *NTS* 10 (1963): 135–36; A. A. Bell, "The Date of John's Apocalypse: The Evidence of Some Roman Historians Reconsidered," *NTS* 25 (1978): 93–102; Wilson, "Problem of the Domitianic Date," 587–605.

[106] Robinson, *Redating*, 221.

[107] Swete, *Revelation*, xcix; Charles, *Revelation of St. John*, 1:xci; Collins, *Crisis and Catharsis*, 56; Thompson, *Book of Revelation*, 15.

[108] Hort, *Apocalypse of St. John*, xx; see Robinson, *Redating*, 221.

date. The book of Revelation was penned around AD 95–96 by John the apostle, writing in obedient submission to the vision he received while in exile on Patmos.[109]

Provenance

John identifies the location of his vision as the little isle of Patmos in the Aegean Sea (1:9b).[110] Pliny and Strabo briefly mention Patmos as included among the Sporades islands.[111] It was situated about forty miles west of Miletus and almost sixty miles southwest of Ephesus.[112] This close proximity to the mainland of Asia Minor demonstrates its inclusion in the provincial boundaries. Patmos could have functioned as a place of exile, but no records exist identifying it as such.[113] Although not uninhabited, Patmos's small size and rocky terrain made it an ideal spot for banishment.[114] John indicates that the reason he was there was "the word of God and the testimony of Jesus,"[115] most likely indicating some form of persecution.[116] This is supported by John's self-identification as a fellow participant with the churches in their hardships (1:9; see 2:9–10, 22; 7:14).[117] Therefore, John's presence on Patmos was the result of official opposition to his message.[118]

Exile or banishment to an isolated island constituted a relatively common form of punishment in the Roman Empire.[119] Those condemned to banishment faced either a perpetual sentence (Lat. *deportatio*), which might have resulted in loss of citizenship and property, or a less severe temporary sentence (Lat. *relegatio*).[120] These sanctions were often used instead of the death penalty.[121] The emperor, city prefect, or provincial governor could determine the punishment as he deemed necessary.[122] This included the punishment

---

[109] See Collins, *Crisis and Catharsis*, 54.

[110] The island was about thirty miles in circumference according to Pliny the Elder, *Nat.* 4.12.23, 69; Strabo, *Geog.* 10.5.13; see Thucydides, *Peloponnesian War* 3.33.3.

[111] Pliny the Elder, *Nat.* 4.12.69; Strabo, *Geog.* 10.5.14.

[112] Aune, *Revelation 1–5*, 77; Smalley, *Revelation to John*, 50; Boxall, *Revelation*, 86.

[113] Boxall, *Revelation*, 85. Against Keener, *Revelation*, 83; C. H. Talbert, *The Apocalypse: A Reading of the Revelation of John* (Louisville, KY: Westminster John Knox, 1994), 3; J. N. Sanders, "St. John on Patmos," *NTS* 9 (1963): 75–85; Swete, *Revelation*, 12; Charles, *Revelation of St. John*, vols. 1, 2.

[114] See Aune, *Revelation 1–5*, 77–78; Boxall, *Revelation*, 86.

[115] Every occurrence of *dia* in the accusative case in Revelation expresses cause or reason (1:9; 2:3; 4:11; 6:9; 7:15; 12:11–12; 13:14; 17:7; 18:8, 10, 15; 20:4).

[116] See 6:9; 12:17; 20:4. Against Beckwith, *Apocalypse of John*, 434; Charles, *Revelation of St. John*, 1.22; Aune, *Revelation 1–5*, 81–82.

[117] BDAG, s.v. "θλιψις," 457.

[118] The inference is that John was there as a result of judicial condemnation. Smalley, *Revelation to John*, 50; Swete, *Revelation*, 50.

[119] Plutarch, *Exil.* 12; Juvenal, *Sat.* 1.73; 4.563; 10.170; Tacitus, *Ann.* 1.53; 3.68–59; 4.13, 30; 13.43; Suetonius, *Aug.* 19; *Cal.* 14–15; *Galb.* 10.

[120] *Dig.* 48.13.3; 48.14.1; 48.22.6; 48.22.14.3; 48.22.15; 48.22.7.2; Tacitus, *Ann.* 14.50; 15.71; Pliny, *Ep.* 10.56. See J. Crook, *Law and Life of Rome* (Ithaca, NY: Cornell University Press, 1967), 272–73; Aune, *Revelation 1–5*, 79.

[121] A. N. Sherwin-White, *Roman Society and the Roman Law in the New Testament* (London, England: Oxford University Press, 1963; repr. Eugene, OR: Wipf & Stock, 2004), 21n1.

[122] Crook, *Law and Life of Rome*, 272.

of Christians.[123] Provincial governors had the authority to try cases without direct intervention from the emperor and to sentence the accused to *relegatio ad insulam* (banishment to an island).[124] Cases that warranted *deportatio*, however, required a verdict from the emperor.[125] According to Tertullian (ca. 160–225), John was exiled to Patmos as an *insulam relegatur*.[126] Thus, it seems likely that John was banished from Ephesus in Asia Minor by a provincial governor.[127]

Destination, Occasion, and Purpose

The book of Revelation is addressed to seven churches that existed at the end of the first century (95–96). John addressed Christians living in cities dotted along a postal route in the Roman province of Asia Minor.[128] The cities were Ephesus, Smyrna, Pergamum, Thyatira, Sardis, Philadelphia, and Laodicea. John explicitly stated several times that the occasion for writing was a direct command from the Lord (1:11, 19; see 2:1).

John's vision arrived at a time when the churches of Asia Minor needed encouragement to remain faithful to Christ and to endure hardships as they swam against the currents of the surrounding culture (chaps. 2–3). The implicit occasion is that Christians in these cities stood at the crossroads between faith and culture, having to choose between compromise with the world's system and their commitment to Christ.

The Christians in Ephesus were commended for enduring hardships because of the name of Christ (2:3). John indicated that the cause of their hardship was their faithfulness to Jesus's name, but the exact nature of their suffering remains elusive because all that is said is that believers had patiently endured and continued to do so under a burden. Their hardships may have originated from internal conflicts with the Nicolaitans (2:6). Sadly, however, they seemed to have emphasized doctrinal purity to the extent that they neglected the command to love one another (2:4).

While the church in Ephesus successfully resisted these false teachers, the churches of Pergamum and Thyatira apparently opened their doors to them. John denounces the Nicolaitans in both churches as a specifically detestable group, comparing them to Balaam, who led Israel to worship idols and to commit acts of sexual immorality (2:14). The Nicolaitans most likely encouraged believers to participate in pagan religious rituals. Thyatira had allowed a false prophetess to gain a following in the church (2:20–21). John called her "Jezebel" because, like the infamous queen in Israel's history (1 Kgs 16:31–33; 18:4, 13; 19:1–2; 21; 2 Kgs 9:30–37), this heretical female teacher had led the people of

---

[123] See *Dig.* 47.11–22; cf. A. N. Sherwin-White, "The Early Persecutions and Roman Law Again," *JTS* 3 (1952): 205.

[124] *Dig.* 48.22.7.17; cf. Sherwin-White, *Roman Society and the Roman Law*, 2.

[125] *Dig.* 48.19.2.1. Although the governor could not deport a criminal, the city prefect retained that legal right.

[126] Tertullian, *Praescr.* 36; see Jerome, *Vir. ill.* 9. Against W. M. Ramsay, *The Letters to the Seven Churches of Asia and Their Place in the Plan of the Apocalypse* (London, England: Hodder & Stoughton, 1904), 85.

[127] Caird, *Revelation of St. John*, 22–23, affirmed by Hemer, *Letters to the Seven Churches*, 28; Smalley, *Revelation to John*, 50–51; Boxall, *Revelation*, 85.

[128] The road connecting the cities formed a horseshoe-shaped circuit, and each city could be reached by foot within a day or two. See deSilva, *Introduction*, 895.

God into idolatry and immorality and encouraged a syncretistic blend between the pagan religions of the dominant culture and Christianity. The presence of such false teachers indicates that the churches experienced a number of internal crises compromising their fidelity to Christ and impugning their witness.

Believers in Sardis and Laodicea were also experiencing internal spiritual turmoil due to their complacency, materialism, and self-sufficiency. External conflict in Smyrna apparently arose from the Jewish community (2:9).[129] Their suffering related to unspecified tribulations,

---

[129] P. L. Mayo, *"Those Who Call Themselves Jews": The Church and Judaism in the Apocalypse of John*, PTMS 60 (Eugene, OR: Pickwick, 2006), 51–76; A. J. Beagley, *The "Sitz im Leben" of the Apocalypse, with Particular Reference to the Role of the Church's Enemies*, BZNW 50 (Berlin, Germany: de Gruyter, 1987); P. Borgen, "Polemic in the Book of Revelation," in *Anti-Semitism and Early Christianity*, ed. C. A. Evans and D. A. Hagner (Minneapolis, MN: Fortress, 1993), 199–211;

poverty,[130] and slander from Jews *(blasphēmia)*.[131] The forensic nature of this slander is confirmed by the reference to future imprisonment (2:10). Jewish hostilities against Christians in the form of legal denunciation commonly occurred in the early church.[132] As members of a legally sanctioned religion, the Jewish communities benefited from legal sanctions, and pagans may have grouped Christians together with Jews.[133] Consequently, Jewish leaders made a concerted effort, especially after the year 70, to denounce Christians before the magistrates.[134] The situation for Christians in Smyrna paralleled what was happening in Philadelphia (3:8–9). In both cities the Christians were poor, few in number, and faced intentional, religious, and legal opposition from Jews seeking to decimate their existence.

In the city of Pergamum, external opposition against the Christians resulted in the death of Antipas (2:13). At some point in the recent past, this man had been killed because of his faithfulness to Christ. The lack of details about the situation implies it was common knowledge among the believers in that city. The only possible clue to reconstruct what may have happened to Antipas is the reference to Pergamum as the place where Satan ruled and lived.[135] Antipas's death most likely resulted from the unjust verdict of Pergamum's proconsul who condemned him because he refused to deny Christ when on trial.[136]

M. R. J. Bredin, "The Synagogue of Satan Accusation in Revelation 2:9," *BTB* 28/4 (1999): 160–64; Slater, "Social Setting," 240; A. Y. Collins, "Vilification and Self-Definition in the Book of Revelation," *HTR* 79 (1986): 308–20; idem, *Crisis and Catharsis*, 85–87.

[130] On suffering in poverty brought about by their faith, see Hemer, *Letters to the Seven Churches*, 68; Charles, *Revelation of St. John*, 1.56; Caird, *Revelation of St. John*, 35; Roloff, *Revelation*, 48; cf. 4QpPSa 1.1–10; 2.10–11.

[131] J. Lambrecht ("Jewish Slander: A Note on Revelation 2, 9–10," *ETL* 75 [1999]: 421–29) saw this slander from Jews as stemming from legal proceedings in Smyrna. For a discussion of the bringing of a charge by an accuser in Roman jurisprudence, see "Accusatio," *EDRL*, 340.

[132] NT examples of Jews instigating legal action against Christians include Acts 13:5–12, 50; 18:13–17; 22:30; 23:25–30; 24:1–22; 25:1, 7–27; 26:1–7. For examples of general Jewish hostility against Christians, see Acts 7:1–8:3; 9:1–9; Gal 1:13–14; 1 Thess 2:14–16; cf. *The Martyrdom of Polycarp* (12:2–3; 13:1); Justin Martyr (*Dial.* 16.4; 47.4; 93.4; 95.4; 96.2; 108.3; 110.5; 131.2; 133.6; 137.2); Tertullian (*Scorp.* 10.10; *Praescr.* 26.6); and Eusebius (*Hist. eccl.* 5.16.12).

[133] Beale, *Book of Revelation*, 8, 240; Ford, *Revelation*, 393; S. Applebaum, "The Legal Status of the Jewish Communities in the Diaspora," in *The Jewish People in the First Century*, CRINT 1, ed. M. de Jonge and S. Safrai (Assen, Netherlands: Van Gorcum, 1974), 420–63; T. Rajak, *Jewish Rights in the Greek Cities Under Roman Rule: A New Approach*, Approaches to Ancient Judaism 5 (Atlanta, GA: Scholars, 1985), 19–35; P. Trebilco, *Jewish Communities in Asia Minor*, SNTSMS 69 (Cambridge, UK: Cambridge University Press, 1991), 167–85; and Price, *Rituals and Power*, 220–21; cf. Josephus, *Apion* 2.6; Philo, *Legat.* 349–67.

[134] See J. J. O'Rourke, "Roman Law and the Early Church," 179. For more on the relationship between the church and the synagogue, see Aune, *Revelation 1–5*, 168–72; Borgen, "Polemic in the Book of Revelation," 199–211; W. Horn, "Zwischen der Synagoge des Satans und dem neuen Jerusalem: Die christlich-jüdische Standortbestimmung in der Apokalypse des Johannes," *ZRGG* 46 (1994): 143–62. Cf. S. J. Friesen, "Sarcasm in Revelation 2–3: Churches, Christians, True Jews, and Satanic Synagogues," in *The Reality of Apocalypse: Rhetoric and Politics in the Book of Revelation*, SBLSymS 39, ed. D. L. Barr (Atlanta, GA: SBL, 2006), 127–46; P. Duff, "The 'Synagogue of Satan': Crisis Mongering and the Apocalypse of John," in *Reality of the Apocalypse*, 147–68. Cf. Justin, *Dial.* 16.4; 47.4; 93.4; 95.4; 96.2; 108.3; 133.6; 137.2.

[135] S. J. Friesen ("Satan's Throne, Imperial Cults and the Social Settings of Revelation," *JSNT* 27 [2005]: 351–73) implausibly rejects the notion that "Satan's throne" refers to Pergamum as the seat of Roman power or of the imperial cult in the province of Asia.

[136] According to Aune (*Revelation 1–5*, 183), the Roman proconsul resided in Pergamon; cf. Caird, *Revelation of St. John*, 38.

The references to the "double-edged sword" and the "throne" (2:12–13 NIV) may allude to the judicial authority and official seat of the city's magistrate.[137] The Christians at Pergamum were reminded that Christ, not the proconsul, wielded ultimate judicial authority. Since Satan is the chief adversary of the people of God, one wonders how a judicial verdict against a faithful Christian warranted the identification of Pergamum as the location of "Satan's throne." Apparently, Satan wielded so much authority in Pergamum that Christians were denied justice and faced punishment rendered by the proconsul who acted on Satan's behalf.

The dominant culture was steeped in Greco-Roman paganism with its plethora of gods, goddesses, and temples. Christians represented a religious group that penetrated every level of society and consisted of both Jews and Gentiles. They were tenacious monotheists who refused to participate in local trade guilds or any other common pagan ritual, including participation in the imperial cult. The imperial cult had existed as part of Asia Minor's religious climate ever since the time of Augustus.[138] Pergamum hosted the first temple dedicated to Augustus and the goddess Roma for the entire province of Asia beginning in 29 BC, and it remained active well past the reign of Hadrian.[139] During the reign of Tiberius, the cities of Sardis and Smyrna competed for the right to host a second provincial imperial cult in Asia, which was won by Smyrna in AD 26.[140] During the reign of Domitian, the city of Ephesus erected an unprecedented third imperial temple in Asia Minor (AD 89/90).[141] Some estimates attest to more than eighty smaller localized imperial temples in more than sixty cities in Asia Minor.[142] The cult functioned politically to express just how grateful and loyal the provinces were to the emperor, using religious conventions for political purposes.[143] From

---

[137] The term *rhomphaia* ("sword") may refer to the judicial right of *ius gladii*, symbolized as a sword, giving the proconsul the right to inflict capital punishment (Rom 13:4). See *Dig.* 2.1.3; Berger, "Ius gladii," *EDRL* 529; Ramsay, *Letters to the Seven Churches*, 292–93; Caird, *Revelation of St. John*, 38; Mounce, *Book of Revelation*, 96; Hemer, *Letters to the Seven Churches*, 85; Beale, *Book of Revelation*, 247; Keener, *Revelation*, 122. The term *thronos* ("throne"), as used elsewhere in the NT, and denotes an official seat where a king or judge conducted court (Matt 19:28; Luke 1:23, 52; see Smalley, *Revelation to John*, 68; Swete, *Revelation*, 34). Occasionally, *thronos* is used for a judge's bench (Aune, *Revelation 1–5*, 183; see Plutarch, *Praec. ger. rei publ.* 807b).

[138] For more on the rise and history of the imperial cult, see J. Ferguson, *The Religions of the Roman Empire* (London, England: Thames & Hudson, 1970), 88–98; D. L. Jones, "Christianity and the Roman Imperial Cult," *ANRW* II.23.2, *Principat*, ed. H. Temporini and W. Haase (Berlin, Germany: de Gruyter, 1980), 1,024–54; D. Fishwick, "The Development of Provincial Ruler Worship in the Western Roman Empire," *ANRW* II.16.2 (1978): 1,201–53; idem, *The Imperial Cult in the Latin West: Studies in the Ruler Cult of the Western Provinces of the Roman Empire*, EROER 108/2 (Leiden, Netherlands: Brill, 1991); R. M. Novak, *Christianity and the Roman Empire: Background Texts* (Harrisburg, PA: Trinity Press International, 2001), 267–72; P. A. Harland, "Imperial Cults Within Local Cultural Life: Associations in Roman Asia," *ZAG* 17 (2003): 85–107.

[139] Friesen, *Imperial Cults*, 25, 27.

[140] Ibid., 36–38. So Tacitus, *Ann.* 4.15.

[141] Ibid., 44–46.

[142] Price, *Rituals and Power*, 135. For an excellent map locating imperial temples in Asia Minor, see M. Wilson, *Charts on the Book of Revelation: Literary, Historical, and Theological Perspectives* (Grand Rapids, MI: Kregel, 2007), 115.

[143] Price, *Rituals and Power*, 16, 29–31.

its inception, the emperor, along with the goddess Roma, was worshipped and honored for benevolence toward the provinces.

The imperial cult, however, was much more than a mere political tool; participants actually worshipped the emperor as divine.[144] Inscriptional evidence demonstrates that the emperors Augustus and Caligula were considered gods. The use of the term *theos* ("god"), although rare, attests to the fact that worshippers esteemed emperors by elevating them to a status far above that of regular mortals. Often emperors were so closely associated with patron deities that the worshippers made no distinction between them.[145] The cult employed all the trappings and paraphernalia of rituals common to any religious practice. Images of the emperor or his family members greeted worshippers in the form of massive statues.[146] Some of these images included mechanisms to mimic lightning and thunder, reinforcing the emperor's identification with the god Jupiter.[147] Adherents offered prayers to these statues and sometimes carried smaller pocket-sized versions of imperial figures.[148] Scholars who diminish the significance of the imperial cult as something purely political have imposed a modern conception of a separation between the secular and the sacred. Those who lived in a polytheistic culture easily adopted the imperial cult into their pantheon of gods and divine beings.

Conflict with the imperial cult in Revelation can hardly be ignored.[149] There are what appear to be frequent references to the imperial cult in the latter half of the second vision (13:4, 15–16; 14:9–11; 15:2; 16:2; see 20:4). John saw a time when worship of a ruler

---

[144] On the religious nature of the imperial cult, see H. W. Pleket, "An Aspect of the Emperor Cult: Imperial Mysteries," *HTR* 58 (1965): 331–47; F. Millar, "The Imperial Cult and the Persecutions," in *Le Culte des Souverains dans L'Empire Romain* (Genève, Switzerland: Fondation Hardt, 1973), 145–75; Harland, "Imperial Cults Within Local Cultural Life," 87–90, 93–103. For scholars marginalizing the religious nature of the imperial cult, see P. Harland, "Honours and Worship: Emperors, Imperial Cults and Associations at Ephesus," *SR* 25 (1996): 334n4.

[145] Harland, "Honours and Worship," 328–29; S. J. Friesen, *Twice Neokoros: Ephesus, Asia and the Cult of the Flavian Imperial Family* (Leiden, Netherlands: Brill, 1993), 146. Against Price (*Rituals and Power*, 233), who argued for a "clear distinction between human and divine honours" and contended that the emperor might have been slotted into the intermediate category of hero.

[146] Price, *Rituals and Power*, 170–206. Compare Friesen (*Imperial Cults*, 50), who noted that archaeologists have discovered the remains of a colossal statue of either Domitian or Titus. Based on the size of the head, left forearm, and left big toe, this statue must have towered above worshippers.

[147] S. J. Scherrer, "Signs and Wonders in the Imperial Cult: A New Look at a Roman Religious Institution in the Light of Rev 13:13–15," *JBL* 103 (1984): 605. So Suetonius, *Gaius*, 52.

[148] Millar, "Imperial Cult and the Persecutions," 147–48.

[149] See Klauck, "Sendschreiben nach Pergamon," 157–71; D. A. deSilva, "The 'Image of the Beast' and the Christians in Asia Minor: Escalation of Sectarian Tension in Revelation 13," *TrinJ* 12 NS (1991): 185–208; J. W. van Henten, "Dragon Myth and Imperial Ideology in Revelation 12–13," *SBL Seminar Papers* 33 (1994): 496–515; Borgen, "Emperor Worship and Persecution," 493–509; Giesen, *Studien zur Johannesapokalypse*, 100–213; H. J. de Jonge, "The Apocalypse of John and the Imperial Cult," in *KYKEON: Studies in Honour of H. S. Versnel*, ed. H. F. J. Horstmanshoff et al. (Leiden, Netherlands: Brill, 2002), 127–41; L. J. L. Peerbolte, "To Worship the Beast: The Revelation to John and the Imperial Cult in Asia Minor," in *Zwischen den Reichen: Neues Testament und Römische Herrschaft*, TANZ 36, ed. K. Berger (Tübingen, Germany: A. Francke, 2002), 239–59; G. Biguzzi, "Ephesus, Its Artemision, Its Temple to the Flavian Emperors, and Idolatry in Revelation," *NovT* 40 (1998): 276–90; and S. J. Friesen, "Myth and Symbolic Resistance in Revelation 13," *JBL* 123 (2004): 287–311.

would escalate to a point of mandatory participation by all inhabitants of the earth.[150] Significantly, the term *proskyneō* ("worship"), used in direct connection with the beast (13:4, 8, 12, 15), was also a term commonly found in the imperial cult.[151] Thus, Christians abhorred the imperial cult as idolatry, which was doubly evil due to the political ramifications associated with it.[152]

Christ followers refusing to bow down in worship to the beast would incur his wrath and be summarily executed (13:15).[153] Nevertheless, believers are exhorted to remain faithful and true to Christ even if this means death (2:10, 13; 13:10; 14:12; 17:14). God will vindicate them by judging all those who worshipped the beast (14:9, 11; 16:2). The book of Revelation strongly promotes abstinence from all forms of idolatry because God is the only one worthy of worship (4:11; 5:2, 4, 9, 12). He even receives worship from all the heavenly hosts (4:10; 5:14; 7:11; 11:16; 19:4). Exclusive worship of God constitutes the major theological imperative for Christians as well as for all humanity (9:20; 14:7; 15:4; 19:10; 22:9). If believers were accused by a legal adversary and tried for their faith, it was more than likely that obeisance to the emperor became a standard foil by which to determine guilt.

While the local religious and political climate of each city varied, John, as one who experienced unjust exile, wrote to believers facing similar injustices. Believers might succumb to despair over the triumph of a corrupt justice system that condemns the innocent simply because of their Christian faith. But John's vision assuages these fears by depicting the eventual reversal of these travesties of justice. This concern for vindication is voiced by the martyred souls at the altar (6:9–11; 16:7). Revelation describes Jesus as wielding ultimate judicial authority and as the One who is worthy to unleash God's wrath on impenitent humanity (1:12–20; 5:2–4; see John 5:17–29). To be sure, Christ first investigates his churches, holding them accountable for their sins but also promising to reward their faithfulness (chaps. 2–3). Chapters 6–16 present a series of judgments confirming humanity's guilt and the justice of God's verdicts (9:20–21; 16:9–11). In chapters 17–18, the prostitute Babylon, because of her crimes against believers, is declared guilty and summarily executed. Christ will return as the conquering supreme King and Lord, brandishing the sword of God's justice (19:11–15). No matter what fate Christians might have endured under unjust judges, they will one day reign with Christ and help execute the judgment of the nations (20:4).[154] Thus, the intended purpose is to comfort the weary and oppressed, to fortify faithfulness and endurance, and to cleanse the churches from heresy and

---

150 See deSilva, "Image of the Beast," 197–201.

151 Dio Cassius, *Hist.* 59.24.4; Philo, *Leg.* 116; Aune, *Revelation 6–16*, 741.

152 See Jones, "Christianity and the Roman Imperial Cult,"1,024; Biguzzi, "Ephesus," 277–79.

153 See 6:9; 18:24; 20:4. Against Millar ("Imperial Cult and the Persecutions," 164–65), who contends that the imperial cult only played a minor role in the persecution of Christians. For a critique of Millar, see de Jonge, "Apocalypse of John and the Imperial Cult," 127–41.

154 D. A. deSilva, "Honor Discourse and the Rhetorical Strategy of the Apocalypse of John," *JSNT* 71 (1998): 98.

compromise by depicting the heavenly reality of Jesus as the glorified Judge and all the events surrounding his return to establish his kingdom on earth.

LITERATURE

With deep roots in the OT, a striking literary form, and a structure that continues to challenge scholars, the book of Revelation provides much to explore in terms of its literature. Additionally, recent studies have highlighted how John rhetorically shaped the book of Revelation to accomplish his purposes.[155] John is setting forth his visionary experiences; nevertheless, Witherington is right to say the book of Revelation "is not a mere transcript of such experiences but the literary repristination of them. . . . It is neither a purely literary product nor a mere exercise in exegesis of the OT texts, but some combination of revelation, reflection, and literary composition."[156] We are thus justified in examining literary aspects of John's writing.

Revelation and the OT

The book of Revelation is fascinating in its use of the OT: it contains no formal citations of the OT, yet "no other book of the NT is as permeated by the OT as is Revelation"[157] and "virtually every point made comes in some way via an OT allusion."[158] Statistics of OT usage in Revelation differ widely from scholar to scholar, based on different opinions as to what "counts" as a reference to the OT, but at a minimum there are over 200—and perhaps as many as 1,000—discrete references in the 404 verses of the book.[159] John ap-

---

[155] See D. L. Barr, *The Reality of Apocalypse: Rhetoric and Politics in the Book of Revelation*, SBLSymS 39 (Atlanta, GA: Society of Biblical Literature, 2006); D. A. deSilva, *Seeing Things John's Way: the Rhetoric of the Book of Revelation* (Louisville, KY: Westminster John Knox, 2009); idem, "What Has Athens to Do with Patmos? Rhetorical Criticism of the Revelation of John (1980–2005)," *CurBR* 6 (2008): 256–89; K. B. de Waal, *A Socio-Rhetorical Interpretation of the Seven Trumpets of Revelation: The Apocalyptic Challenge to Earthly Empire* (Lewiston, NY: Edwin Mellen, 2012); Koester, *Revelation*, 132–44; M. Labahn and O. Lehtipuu, eds., *Imagery in the Book of Revelation*, Contributions to Biblical Exegesis and Theology 60 (Leuven, Belgium: Peeters, 2011); S. Pattemore, *The People of God in the Apocalypse: Discourse, Structure and Exegesis*, SNTSMS 128 (Cambridge, UK: Cambridge University Press, 2004); P. S. Perry, *The Rhetoric of Digressions: Revelation 7:1–17 and 10:1–11:13 and Ancient Communication*, WUNT 2/268 (Tübingen, Germany: Mohr Siebeck, 2009); J. L. Resseguie, *The Revelation of John: A Narrative Commentary* (Grand Rapids, MI: Baker, 2009), 18–32.

[156] B. Witherington III, *Revelation*, NCBC (Cambridge, UK: Cambridge University Press, 2003), 14.

[157] G. K. Beale and S. M. McDonough, "Revelation," in *Commentary on the New Testament Use of the Old Testament*, ed. G. K. Beale and D. A. Carson (Grand Rapids, MI: Baker, 2007), 1,081. In addition to the excellent specialized bibliography associated with Beale and McDonough's work, note M. Jauhiainen, *The Use of Zechariah in Revelation*, WUNT 2/199 (Tübingen, Germany: Mohr Siebeck, 2005); D. Mathewson, "Assessing Old Testament Allusions in the Book of Revelation," *EQ* 75 (2003): 311–25; J. R. Michaels, "Old Testament in Revelation," *DLNT*, 850–55; S. Moyise, "Genesis in Revelation," in *Genesis in the New Testament*, ed. M. J. J. Menken and S. Moyise, LTNS 466 (London, England: Bloomsbury T&T Clark, 2012), 166–80; J. Paulien, "Elusive Allusions in the Apocalypse: Two Decades of Research into John's Use of the Old Testament," in *The Intertextuality of the Epistles: Explorations of Theory and Practice*, ed. T. L. Brodie et al., NTM 16 (Sheffield, UK: Sheffield Phoenix, 2006), 61–68; M. Tilly, "Deuteronomy in Revelation," in *Deuteronomy in the New Testament*, ed. S. Moyise and M. J. J. Menken, LNTS 358 (London, England: T&T Clark, 2007), 169–88; and the helpful section on the OT in Revelation in G. R. Osborne, "Recent Trends in the Study of the Apocalypse," 491–95.

[158] G. R. Osborne, *Revelation*, BECNT (Grand Rapids, MI: Baker, 2002), 2.

[159] Beale and McDonough, "Revelation," 1082.

pears to allude most often to Isaiah, Ezekiel, Daniel, and Psalms. Genesis, Exodus, and Zechariah are also important influences on his work.[160]

The way in which John uses the OT in Revelation has been the topic of much discussion. He does not typically cite Scripture to support an argument as Paul does or point explicitly to the fulfillment of a prophecy as Matthew would. Some have argued that John merely appropriates language from the OT with no regard to its OT context, in order to communicate his prophetic visions in biblical terms.[161] This may well be the case at times—John's thought was doubtless steeped in the phraseology of Israel's Scriptures—but to suggest that John had no use for OT context is going too far.[162] It is perhaps best to say with Osborne, "John uses the OT with faithfulness to the original context but at the same time with freedom to transform it so as to apply its larger thrust to the new context of his churches."[163]

Genre

The word *apocalypse* conjures up a myriad of images. Scholars typically distinguish between (1) "apocalypse"; (2) "apocalyptic"; and (3) "apocalypticism."[164] *Apocalypse* refers to a particular genre of literature written between approximately 200 BC and AD 200.[165] The adjective *apocalyptic* is used when describing either the literary genre or the worldview.

---

[160] For specialized studies in this regard, note G. K. Beale, *The Use of Daniel in Jewish Apocalyptic Literature and in the Revelation of St. John* (Lanham, MD: University Press of America, 1984); J. Fekkes, *Isaiah and Prophetic Traditions in the Book of Revelation: Visionary Antecedents and Their Development*, JSNTSup 93 (Sheffield, UK: JSOT Press, 1994); Moyise, "Genesis in Revelation"; idem, "The Psalms in the Book of Revelation," in *The Psalms in the New Testament*, ed. S. Moyise and M. J. J. Menken (London, England: T&T Clark, 2004), 231–46; D. Mathewson, "Isaiah in Revelation," in *Isaiah in the New Testament*, ed. S. Moyise and M. J. J. Menken (London, England: T&T Clark, 2005), 289–310; M. Jauhiainen, *The Use of Zechariah in Revelation*; J.-P. Ruiz, *Ezekiel in the Apocalypse*, Europäische Hochschulschriften 23/376 (Frankfurt, Germany: Lang, 1989).

[161] E.g., E. Schüssler Fiorenza, *The Book of Revelation: Justice and Judgment*, 2nd ed. (Philadelphia, PA: Fortress, 1998), 135: "He does not interpret the OT but uses its words, images, phrases, and patterns as a language arsenal in order to make his own theological statement or express his own prophetic vision."

[162] The extent of John's respect for the OT context was debated in several essays: S. Moyise, "The Old Testament in the New: A Reply to Greg Beale," *IBS* 21 (1999): 54–58; G. K. Beale, "Questions of Authorial Intent, Epistemology, and Presuppositions and Their Bearing on the Study of the Old Testament in the New: A Rejoinder to Steve Moyise," *IBS* 21 (1999): 151–80; J. Paulien, "Dreading the Whirlwind: Intertextuality and the Use of the Old Testament in Revelation," *AUSS* 39 (2001): 5–22; G. K. Beale, "A Response to Jon Paulien on the Use of the Old Testament in Revelation," *AUSS* 39 (2001): 23–33.

[163] G. R. Osborne, "Recent Trends in the Study of the Apocalypse," 494. Osborne goes on to provide a summary of the various ways he understands John to use the OT in Revelation (p. 495); a lengthier treatment is provided in Beale and McDonough, "Revelation," 1,084–87.

[164] P. Hanson, *Dawn of Apocalyptic* (Philadelphia, PA: Fortress, 1975), xi; J. J. Collins, *The Apocalyptic Imagination*, 2nd ed. (Grand Rapids, MI: Eerdmans, 1998), 2.

[165] Collins, *Apocalyptic Imagination*, 21; M. Smith, "On the History of *Apokalyptō* and *Apokalypsis*," in *Apocalypticism in the Mediterranean World and the Near East: Proceedings of the International Colloquium on Apocalypticism*, ed. D. Hellholm (Tübingen, Germany: Mohr Siebeck, 1983), 9–20. The first to identify a group of writings as "apocalyptic" was F. Lücke in 1832 in *Versuch einer vollständigen Einleitung in die Offenbarung Johannis und in die gesamte apocalyptische Literatur* (Bonn: Weber, 1832). Cf. Collins, *Apocalyptic Imagination*, 2–3.

Apocalypticism denotes a worldview, ideology, or theology merging the eschatological aims of particular groups into a cosmic and political arena.[166]

The development of the definition for the apocalyptic genre has a long and complex history.[167] Early studies identified formal features such as pseudonymity, visionary accounts, and historical reviews as well as exhibiting a content expressing a doctrine of two ages, pessimism and hope, universalism, and imminent expectation of the end.[168] In 1979, J. J. Collins and other scholars developed the following classic definition:

> "Apocalypse" is a genre of revelatory literature with a narrative framework, in which a revelation is mediated by an otherworldly being to a human recipient, disclosing a transcendent reality which is both temporal, insofar as it envisages eschatological salvation, and spatial, insofar as it involves another, supernatural world.[169]

This definition emphasizes the form as a narrative framework involving an otherworldly mediator and the content as containing both temporal (eschatological salvation) and spatial (supernatural world) elements. But this definition lacks any reference to the *function* of an apocalypse. For this reason a subsequent study group, led by A. Y. Collins, D. Hellholm, and D. E. Aune, added an amendment in 1986, stating that an apocalypse is "intended to interpret present, earthly circumstances in light of the supernatural world and of the future, and to influence the understanding and behavior of the audience by means of divine authority."[170]

This amended definition of the apocalyptic genre pertains to its form, content, and function.[171] The genre exhibits several formal features that include visionary accounts, otherworldly mediators, and symbolic language. It also expresses content depicting temporal and spatial realities as a way to emphasize the heavenly realities while devaluing earthly circumstances. Finally, the apocalyptic genre functions to encourage piety and faithfulness in the midst of suffering or during times of crisis (whether real or perceived).

These definitions broadly encompass all canonical, extrabiblical, rabbinical, and sectarian examples of apocalyptic literature. Not all apocalyptic writings, however, necessarily

---

[166] K. Koch, *The Rediscovery of Apocalyptic*, trans. M. Kohl (Naperville, IL: A. R. Allenson, 1972), 28–33.

[167] See the survey by D. Mathewson, "Revelation in Recent Genre Criticism: Some Implications for Interpretation," *TrinJ* 13 NS (1992): 193–213. For discussion and examples of the apocalyptic genre, in addition to Collins, *Apocalyptic Imagination*, see G. Carey, *Ultimate Things: An Introduction to Jewish and Christian Apocalyptic Literature* (St. Louis, MO: Chalice, 2005); S. L. Cook, *The Apocalyptic Literature*, Interpreting Biblical Texts (Nashville, TN: Abingdon, 2003); M. G. Reddish, *Apocalyptic Literature: A Reader* (Peabody, MA: Hendrickson, 1995).

[168] P. Vielhauer, "Apocalypses and Related Subjects," in *New Testament Apocrypha II*, ed. E. Hennecke and W. Schneemelcher (Philadelphia, PA: Westminster, 1965), 583–94; cf. Koch, *Rediscovery of Apocalyptic*, 23–28.

[169] J. J. Collins, "Introduction: Towards the Morphology of a Genre," *Sem* 14 (1979): 9.

[170] A. Y. Collins, "Introduction: Early Christian Apocalypticism," *Sem* 36 (1986): 7.

[171] L. Hartman, "Survey of the Problem of Apocalyptic Genre," in *Apocalypticism in the Mediterranean World and the Near East*, 332–36. So D. E. Aune, "The Apocalypse of John and the Problem of Genre," *Sem* 36 (1986): 65–96.

exhibit every genre characteristic discussed in the above definition.[172] This warrants the need to posit a scaled-down assessment of essential elements attributed to the apocalyptic genre. The first essential element is that an apocalypse comprises a visionary or revelatory means of communication. Apocalyptic literature must reveal some heavenly or spiritual reality through the agency of a seer or a prophet. Usually the vision is given in the first-person singular and expressed in a narrative framework. In addition, apocalyptic communication frequently employs the use of divine or angelic intermediaries as guides and interpreters. Embedded within this revelatory communication are prophetic exhortations for desired behaviors, choices, and responses from the recipients. Nonessential elements include pseudonymity and historical reviews often written in predictive form.

Second, apocalyptic literature is saturated with symbolic, figurative, and metaphorical language. Symbols and other figures constitute the common stock of apocalyptic writing. Human and angelic beings and animals serve as symbolic representations of spiritual truths. Symbolic imagery may express historical, contemporary, or future events in cosmic terms. By using metaphors when describing cosmic scenarios, the author invested both current and anticipated earthly events with symbolic meaning.[173]

Apocalyptic language may use symbols as metaphors for the purpose of referring to concrete objects or events as well as to abstract ideas. For example, the opening vision of Revelation depicts Jesus standing in the midst of seven lampstands. These golden lampstands most likely resemble the lampstand *(menorah)* in the Jewish temple. In the present case, the lampstands symbolically represent the seven churches of Asia Minor (1:20). In addition, the description of Jesus and his clothing is reminiscent of the Jewish high priest and his garments. Thus, one may reasonably infer that Jesus actively tends to his churches in a manner similar to the high priest ministering in the temple.

A final element essential to the apocalyptic genre is the dualism between earthly and heavenly realities, usually steeped in eschatological significance. Earthly situations are depicted as temporary and transitory in light of the eternal realities of the spiritual world. This heavenly perspective dramatically contrasts the worldly scenarios the recipients face. Although some downplay the eschatological nature of the visions,[174] apocalyptic literature provides a provocative and effective vehicle for communicating end-time expectations.[175] The beliefs that God

---

[172] Collins, *Apocalyptic Imagination*, 5–9.

[173] G. B. Caird, *The Language and Imagery of the Bible* (Grand Rapids, MI: Eerdmans, 1997), 256.

[174] C. Rowland, *The Open Heaven: A Study of Apocalyptic in Judaism and Early Christianity* (London, England: SPCK, 1982; repr. Eugene, OR: Wipf & Stock, 2002), 70–72.

[175] Eschatology constitutes a slippery term with a broad range of meaning. Caird (*Language and Imagery of the Bible*, 243–56) identified seven senses of eschatology; see G. B. Caird, *New Testament Theology*, ed. L. D. Hurst (Oxford, UK: Oxford University Press, 1995), 243–67. Cf. I. H. Marshall, "Slippery Words, 1: Eschatology," *ExpTim* 89 (1978): 264–69; idem, "A New Understanding of the Present and the Future: Paul and Eschatology," in *Road from Damascus: The Impact of Paul's Conversion on His Life, Thought, and Ministry*, ed. R. N. Longenecker (Grand Rapids, MI: Eerdmans, 1997), 43–61; idem, "Is Apocalyptic the Mother of Christian Theology?" in *Tradition and Interpretation in the New Testament: Essays in Honor of E. Earle Ellis for His 60th Birthday*, ed. G. F. Hawthorne and O. Betz (Grand Rapids, MI: Eerdmans, 1987), 33–42. In its most basic sense, eschatology pertains to the future consummation of God's dealings with humanity.

is sovereign over history and will radically intervene in the near future to consummate his plans for all creation permeate most apocalyptic writings.

The arrival of Jesus the Messiah "in the fullness of time" indicated that certain eschatological expectations had come to fruition. Jesus announced the nearness and even (partial) arrival of the kingdom of God (Mark 1:15; Luke 11:20).[176] The presence of God's kingdom suggests the eschatological fulfillment of the prophetic promises regarding the son of David, the restoration of Israel, and the renewal of creation. Jesus inaugurated the *eschaton* (end time) with his resurrection followed by the outpouring of the Holy Spirit, but believers still expect a time of final consummation at the end of the age. This time between the ages is commonly viewed as the "already" and "not yet" of God's eschatological fulfillment. In this regard the NT shares affinities with an apocalyptic worldview.

Table 20.1: Thematic Parallels Between the Olivet Discourse and the Seals in the Book of Revelation

NT Passage	Revelation 6	Matthew 24	Mark 13	Luke 21
False Messiahs and Prophets	v. 2	v. 5	v. 6	v. 8
Wars	vv. 2–4	vv. 6–7	v. 7	v. 9
International Discord	vv. 3–4	v. 7	v. 8	v. 10
Famines	vv. 5–8	v. 7	v. 8	v. 11
Pestilences	v. 8			v. 11
Persecution–Martyrdom	v. 11	v. 9	vv. 9–13	vv. 12–19
Earthquakes	v. 12	v. 7	v. 8	v. 11
Cosmic Phenomena	vv. 12–14			v. 11

For this reason it is unsurprising that apocalyptic portions are found in various places of the NT. The Olivet Discourse (Matthew 24–25; Mark 13; Luke 21:5–32), also known as "the little apocalypse," comprises Jesus's apocalyptic expectations in the Synoptic Gospels. Apocalyptic language and images appear scattered throughout the NT letters. The book of Hebrews exhibits an apocalyptic worldview contrasting the temporary earthly institutions with eternal heavenly realities, and 2 Peter 3 expresses eschatological expectations in terms of apocalyptic imagery—as when it says the earth and all the elements will be consumed by fire.

The book of Revelation constitutes one of the most unique books of the Bible, not only because it represents the pinnacle of inspired revelation but also because it is the only apocalyptic book in the NT. Revelation exhibits elements consistent with the genres of

[176] The phrase "kingdom of God" occurs sixty-six times in the NT, though in the Johannine corpus elsewhere only in John 3:3, 5. In addition, there are also several references to the "kingdom of heaven."

apocalyptic, prophecy, and letter.[177] Some have maintained that the first word of the book, "revelation" *(apokalupsis)*, suggests an immediate genre classification, especially given the use of apocalyptic language and imagery throughout Revelation. But a more accurate genre designation occurs in passages where John identified the book as a "prophecy" (*prophēteia*; see 1:3; 22:7, 10, 18–19; cf. 11:16; 19:10). This close association between apocalypse and prophecy is natural because the apocalyptic genre stems from and remained under the rubric of OT prophecy.[178] Apocalyptic writings derived from prophetic oracles; therefore, the lines of demarcation separating these genres are somewhat fluid. What is more, Revelation is addressed to specific congregations and thus also has certain epistolary features.

Hence, Revelation constitutes a mixed genre. The book falls into the overall genre of prophecy, but it corresponds to apocalyptic writings in many respects.[179] G. E. Ladd correctly argued for the designation of "prophetic-apocalyptic."[180] S. Fiorenza also contended that the dichotomy between apocalyptic and prophecy cannot be sustained with regard to Revelation since the book blends both elements.[181] The best overall assessment regarding the genre of Revelation is that it constitutes "a prophecy cast in an apocalyptic mold [which is] written down in a letter form."[182] G. D. Fee helpfully contrasts the book of Revelation with typical apocalyptic literature in terms of salvation history:

> Other apocalyptic writers wrote in the name of an ancient worthy, because theirs was the age of the "quenched Spirit"; hence prophecy, which comes by the Spirit, had ceased. But John belongs to God's "new era," evidenced by the coming of the Spirit. Thus John says about his book that he "was in the Spirit" (1:10–11), and that what he writes is "this prophecy" (1:3; 22:18–19).[183]

---

[177] Carson and Moo, *Introduction to the New Testament*, 713.

[178] E. Schüssler Fiorenza, *The Book of Revelation: Justice and Judgment*, 2nd ed. (Minneapolis, MN: Fortress, 1998), 138.

[179] Care must be taken not to assume that because apocalypses have certain characteristics, the book of Revelation must also have those characteristics. G. Fee (*Revelation: A New Covenant Commentary* [Eugene, OR: Cascade, 2011], xiii) helpfully argues that as "a Christian *prophet* who is speaking directly to his own generation," John straightforwardly identifies himself as the author of the book as opposed to assuming a pseudonymous identity, as apocalyptists typically did. In keeping with this identification, Fee points out that John "abandons [a] feature of all prior apocalypses, namely, the command to 'seal up' what he has written for it to be read at a 'later time.' This is a literary device the earlier apocalyptists employed so as to give their own document a sense of 'hoary age,' so that what they were writing to their contemporaries appeared to come to them from centuries past. By way of contrast John is explicitly told *not* to 'seal it up' (22:10), precisely because John understands what he has written to be 'the words of the prophecy of this scroll' (22:18)." Note also the discussion on differences between Revelation and other apocalypses in R. Bauckham, *The Theology of the Book of Revelation*, New Testament Theology (Cambridge, UK: Cambridge University Press, 1993), 9–12.

[180] G. E. Ladd, "Why Not Prophetic-Apocalyptic?" *JBL* 76 (1957): 192–200.

[181] Schüssler Fiorenza, *Book of Revelation*, 133–56.

[182] D. A. Carson, D. J. Moo, and L. Morris, *An Introduction to the New Testament* (Grand Rapids, MI: Zondervan, 1992), 479. Similarly, Rainbow (*Johannine Theology*, 38) asserts, "The Apocalypse is a Christian prophecy dressed in the form of a letter but stylistically in the vein of Jewish apocalypses."

[183] Fee, *Revelation*, xiii.

Literary Plan

Like the turning of a kaleidoscope, scenes in Revelation morph before the reader's eyes with a myriad of symbols, colors, numbers, and heavenly beings, leaving many mystified and confused regarding the literary plan of the book. The rapid shifts in scenery with various intercalations, that is, insertions or interpolations, the recapitulations, and the asides have prompted some interpreters to conclude that the book consists of a patchwork of visions composed in various settings over extended periods of time.[184] But these source and compositional critics have failed to recognize that in its present form Revelation represents a literary unity.[185]

The book represents an intricately woven literary masterpiece intended to convey a unified message. A number of critical scholars have strongly argued for the unity of the book. S. Fiorenza rightly states that "the total configuration *(Gestalt)* and composition of a work cannot be derived from its sources or traditions but only from the formal expression and theological intention of the author."[186] Likewise, Barr maintains that while most critical studies have sought to divide the book, "John's concern was to bind it together."[187] Bauckham's seminal essay on the structure of Revelation convincingly demonstrates the assiduous and intricate nature of its composition and literary unity.[188] What is more, narrative critical approaches not only presuppose this unity, but they also help demonstrate how Revelation presents a unified literary composition.[189] As such, Revelation tells a story complete with characters, settings, plot, and climax.

Table 20.2: Major Structural Proposals for Revelation*

I. Arranged into Seven Series of Sevens	
Collins	
1:1–8	Prologue
1:9–3:22	Seven Messages
4:1–8:5	Seven Seals
8:2–11:19	Seven Trumpets

---

[184] Charles, *Revelation of St. John*, 1.lxxxvii–xci; Aune, *Revelation 1–5*, cx–cxxxiv; Ford, *Revelation*, 50–57; Prigent, *Commentary on the Apocalypse*, 84–92.

[185] Roloff, *Revelation of John*, 7. For an excellent summary of arguments concerning Revelation's literary unity, see Smalley, *Thunder and Love*, 97–101.

[186] Schüssler Fiorenza, *Book of Revelation*, 164.

[187] Barr, "The Apocalypse as a Symbolic Transformation," 43.

[188] Bauckham, *Climax of Prophecy*, 3–22.

[189] L. L. Thompson, "The Literary Unity of the Book of Revelation," in *Mappings of the Biblical Terrain: The Bible as Text*, ed. V. L. Tollers and J. Maier (Lewisburg, PA: Bucknell University Press, 1990), 347–63; J. L. Resseguie, *Revelation Unsealed: A Narrative Critical Approach to John's Apocalypse*, Biblical Interpretation Series 32 (Leiden, Netherlands: Brill, 1998); idem, *Revelation of John*; D. Lee, *The Narrative Asides in the Book of Revelation* (Lanham, MD: University Press of America, 2002); J. R. Michaels, "Revelation 1.19 and the Narrative Voices of the Apocalypse," *NTS* 37 (1991): 604–20.

Table 20.2: Major Structural Proposals for Revelation (continued)

12:1–15:4	Seven Unnumbered Visions
15:1–16:20	Seven Bowls
17:1–19:10	Babylon Appendix
19:11–21:8	Seven Unnumbered Visions
21:9–22:5	Jerusalem Appendix
22:6–21	Epilogue
Tavo	
1:1–3	Prologue
1:4–3:22	Seven Messages
4:1–5:14 = transition	
6:1–7:17	Seven Seals
8:1–5 = transition	
8:6–11:14	Seven Trumpets
11:15–19 = transition	
12:1–14:20	Series of Visions I
15:1–8 = transition	
16:1–16	Seven Bowls
16:17–19:10 = transition	
19:11–20:15	Series of Visions II
21:1–8 = transitions	
21:9–22:5	New Jerusalem
22:6–21	Epilogue
II. Arranged as an Extended Chiasm	
Strand	
1:1–11	Prologue
Part 1: Historical Series (1:12–14:20)	
1:12–3:22	A: Church in Present Earth
4:1–8:1	B: Ongoing Activity of God
8:2–11:18	C(a): Trumpet Warnings to the Wayward
11:19–14:20	C(b): Evil Powers Oppose God and His People
Part 2: Eschatological Series (15:1–22:5)	
15:1–16:21	C(a)′: Vial Plagues on the Wicked
17:1–18:24	C(b)′: Evil Powers Judged by God
19:1–21:4	B′: Judgmental Finale by God
21:5–22:5	A′: Church in New Earth
22:6–21	Epilogue

Table 20.2: Major Structural Proposals for Revelation (continued)

Schüssler Fiorenza	
1:1–8	A: Prologue
1:9–3:22	B: The Inaugural Vision and Letter Septet
4:1–9:21; 11:15–19	C: The Seven-Sealed Scroll
10:1–15:4	D: The Small Prophetic Scroll
15:5–19:10	C′: Seven Sealed Scroll
19:11–22:9	B′: The Visions of Judgment and Salvation
22:10–22:21	A′: Epilogue
Lee	
1:1–20	A: Prologue
2:1–3:22	B: Present Situation
4:1–5:14	C: The Fundamental Paradigm
6:1–17	D: Judgment and Defeat of God's Enemies [1]
7:1–17	E: Faithful Believers
8:1–10:11	F: Judgment and Defeat of God's Enemies [2]
11:1–19	G: The False Power of the Beast
12:1–6	H: A Woman
12:7–18	I: Judgment and Defeat of God's Enemies [3]
13:1–18	J: Moment of Decision
14:1–20	J′: Moment of Decision
15:1–16:21	I.′ Judgment and Defeat of God's Enemies [3]
17:1–6	H′: A Woman
17:7–18	G′: The False Power of the Beast
18:1–24	F′: Judgment and Defeat of God's Enemies [2]
19:1–10	E′: The Faithful Believers
19:11–21	D′: Judgment and Defeat of God's Enemies [1]
20:1–10	C′: The Fundamental Paradigm
20:11–22:5	B′: Future Situation
22:6–21	A′: Epilogue
III. Alternative Arrangements	
Threefold Division from Rev 1:19 (Walvoord, Thomas)	
1:9–18	Past: "What you have seen"
2:1–3:22	Present: "What is"
4:1–22:5	Future: "What will take place later"
Twofold Division (Aune)	
1:1–8	Prologue

Table 20.2: Major Structural Proposals for Revelation (continued)

1:9–3:22	Theophany of the Exalted Christ
4:1–22:9	Series of Episodic Vision Narratives
4:1–2a	John's Heavenly Ascent
4:2b–7:17	The Sovereignty of God, Lamb, and Six Seals
8:1–11:14	The Seventh Seal and Six Trumpets
11:15–16:12	The Seventh Trumpet and the Seven Bowls
17:1–19:10	Revelations of Babylon's Judgment
19:11–21:8	The Final Defeat of God's Remaining Foes
21:9–22:9	The Vision of the New Jerusalem
22:10–21	Epilogue
Drama (Smalley)	
1:1–8	**Prologue: The Oracle Is Disclosed**
1:9–11:19	Act 1: Creation, and Salvation Through Judgment
1:9–3:22	Scene 1: Seven Oracles
4:1–5:14	Interval: Adoration in Heaven's Court: God and His Christ
6:1–17	Scene 2: Seven Seals
7:1–17	Interval: The Church Protected
8:1–9:21	Scene 3: Seven Trumpets
10:1–11:19	Interval: God's Sovereignty
12:1–22:17	**Act 2: Salvation Through Judgment, and New Creation**
12:1–14:20	Scene 4: Seven Signs
15:1–8	Interval: A New Exodus
16:1–21	Scene 5: Seven Bowls
17:1–18:24	Interval: The Fall of Babylon
19:1–20:15	Scene 6: Seven Visions
21:1	Interval: Prelude to the Final Scene
21:2–22:17	Scene 7: Seven Prophecies
22:18–21 Epilogue: The Oracle Is Complete	
Three Scrolls (Barr)	
1:1–3:22	The Letter Scroll: Movement One on Patmos (Theophany)
4:1–11:18	The Worship Scroll: Movement Two in Heaven (Throne Room)
11:19–22:21	The War Scroll: Movement Three on Earth (Holy War)
Encompassing Recapitulation: Revelation 4–22 (Lambrecht)	
4:1–5:14	A: Introductory Vision of the Scroll
6:1–7:17	B: First Six Seals
8:1–22:5	C: Seventh Seal and Trumpets
8:1–6	A′: Introduction

Table 20.2: Major Structural Proposals for Revelation (continued)

8:7–11:14	B′: First Six Trumpets
11:15–22:5	C′: Seventh Trumpet and Bowls
11:15–16:1	A″: Seventh Trumpet
16:2–16	B″: First Six Bowls
16:17–22:5	C″: Seventh Bowl and Completion

* Collins, *Combat Myth*, 15–16; F. Tavo, "The Structure of the Apocalypse: Re-examining a Perennial Problem," *NovT* 47 (2005): 47–68; K. A. Strand, "Chiastic Structure and Some Motifs in the Book of Revelation," *AUSS* 16 (1978): 401–8; E. S. Fiorenza, *Book of Revelation*, 172; Lee, "A Call to Martyrdom: Function as Method and Message in Revelation," *NovT* 40 (1998): 164–94; Walvoord, *Revelation of Jesus Christ*, 47–49; R. L. Thomas, *Revelation 1–7: An Exegetical Commentary* (Chicago: Moody, 1992), 113–16; Aune, *Revelation 1–5*, c–cv; Smalley, *Revelation to John*, 19–21; D. L. Barr, *Tales of the End: A Narrative Commentary on the Book of Revelation* (Santa Rosa: Polebridge, 1998), 13–16; J. Lambrecht, "A Structuration of Revelation 4,1–22, 5," in *L'Apocalypse johannique et l'Apocalyptique dans le Nouveau Testament*, ed. J. Lambrecht (Leuven: University Press, 1980), 77–104.

The Four Visions (Overview) Attempts at explaining Revelation's macrostructure are legion, and commentators universally note the diversity of proposals.[190] Although no formal consensus has emerged, scholars have successfully identified numerous structural features. Revelation has a clearly delineated prologue (1:1–8) and an epilogue (22:6–21). John divided the book into four visions marked by the phrase "in the Spirit" (1:10; 4:2; 17:3; 21:10). Although some scholars arrange the structure as a sevenfold series of sevens, there are only four instances of a clearly enumerated series of sevens (2:1–3:22; 6:1–8:1; 8:2–11:19; 15:1–16:21). John included materials that appear to interrupt or link aspects of the narrative, which have been labeled interludes, intercalations,[191] interlocking,[192] or interweaving.[193] Another commonly acknowledged structural feature is the intended contrast between the harlot city of Babylon (chaps. 17–18) and the bride city of the new Jerusalem (chaps. 21–22). These broad areas of agreement suggest that certain features of Revelation's macrostructure receive wide acceptance.

As mentioned, Revelation consists of four separate interrelated visions introduced by the phrase "in the Spirit" (*en pneumati*), all of which occur within a single day (1:10).[194] M. Tenney notes how "each occurrence of this phrase locates the seer in a different

[190] See D. L. Barr, *Tales of the End: A Narrative Commentary on the Book of Revelation* (Santa Rosa, CA: Polebridge, 1998), 10; Collins, *Combat Myth*, 8; Beale, *Book of Revelation*, 108; Mounce, *Book of Revelation*, 46; Bauckham, *Climax of Prophecy*, 21; and Prigent, *Commentary on the Apocalypse*, 93.

[191] R. J. Loenertz, *The Apocalypse of Saint John*, trans. H. Carpenter (New York, NY: Sheed & Ward, 1948), xiv–xix; Schüssler Fiorenza, "Composition and Structure of the Book of Revelation," *CBQ* 39 (1977): 360–61.

[192] Collins, *Combat Myth*, 16–19; M. S. Hall, "The Hook Interlocking Structure of Revelation: The Most Important Verses in the Book and How They May Unify Its Structure," *NovT* 44 (2002): 278–96.

[193] Bauckham, *Climax of Prophecy*, 9.

[194] Ibid., 3; cf. R. Herms, *An Apocalypse for the Church and for the World: The Narrative Function of Universal Language in the Book of Revelation*, BZNW 143 (Berlin, Germany: de Gruyter, 2006), esp. 149–54.

place."[195] The phrase indicates a shift of setting from Patmos (1:9) to the heavenly throne room (4:1–2) into a desert (17:3) and finally to a great high mountain (21:10). Moreover, the phrase "I will show you" *(deixō soi)* occurs three times (4:1; 17:1; 21:9) in close proximity to *en pneumati* (4:2; 17:3; 21:10), suggesting that these two phrases are used in conjunction with each other to signal major structural transitions.[196] Interestingly, 4:1–2 also contains one of the three occurrences of the phrase "what must take place" (*ha dei genesthai*; 1:1; 4:1; 22:6), which stresses the future prophetic nature of 4:1–22:6.[197]

The four major visions of Revelation constitute the major literary divisions: (1) 1:10–3:22 envisions the glorified Christ who investigates his churches; (2) 4:1–16:21 portrays the divine court proceedings and the trial of the nations; (3) 17:1–21:8 describes the sentencing and destruction of Babylon; and (4) 21:9–22:4 presents the vindication and reward of believers in the new heaven and new earth.

Minor visionary transitions within these four visions are often signaled by verbal phrases pertaining to seeing and hearing. The phrase "and I saw" *(kai eidon)* acts as a marker within a vision, signaling a transition and demonstrating a progression within the narrative but not necessarily introducing a new vision episode since the location of the seer does not change.[198] The effect of this narration would be like listening to someone excitedly share what he or she saw while sitting in a theater watching a play or a movie, creating a flow similar to "I saw this and then I saw that, oh, and then I saw and heard such and such."

Another obvious structuring device is a series of sevens specifically enumerated as such. Schemes vary from six,[199] to seven,[200] and even eight septets.[201] Although John demonstrates a proclivity for explicitly arranging his material into groups of sevens, only three[202] or four septets[203] are explicitly numbered. The number seven carries significant symbolic

---

[195] M. C. Tenney, *Interpreting Revelation* (Grand Rapids, MI: Eerdmans, 1957), 33. See also G. E. Ladd, *A Commentary on the Revelation of John* (Grand Rapids, MI: Eerdmans, 1972), 14; Mazzaferri, *Genre*, 338–39; Bauckham, *Climax of Prophecy*, 3; Beale, *Book of Revelation*, 111; C. R. Smith, "The Structure of the Book of Revelation in Light of Apocalyptic Literary Conventions," *NovT* 36 (1994): 384–92; J. A. Filho, "The Apocalypse of John as an Account of a Visionary Experience: Notes on the Book's Structure," *JSNT* 25 (2002): 215.

[196] Beale, *Book of Revelation*, 110. The first vision (1:9) begins without the phrase *deixō soi*, but it could be implied from the prologue (1:1), or it may only have been necessary to introduce the successive visions with a reinstatement of its revelatory nature.

[197] Beale, *Book of Revelation*, 152–70; W. C. van Unnik, "A Formula Describing Prophecy," *NTS* 9 (1963): 92–94.

[198] Osborne, *Revelation*, 223; cf. Lee, *Narrative Asides*, 142–47.

[199] Ford, *Revelation*, 46–50.

[200] R. J. Korner, "'And I Saw . . .': An Apocalyptic Literary Convention for Structural Identification in the Apocalypse," *NovT* 42 (2000): 175.

[201] K. A. Strand, "The Eight Basic Visions in the Book of Revelation," *AUSS* 25 (1987): 401–8; see Beale, *Book of Revelation*, 115.

[202] Bauckham (*Climax of Prophecy*, 9–11) dismissed the seven letters as one of the septets because the churches are named but not numbered and "since they do not form in any other sense a sequence, it is not important that the hearer be made aware of the numerical progression." Another difference between the letters and the other septets is that they form a 3 + 4 structure while the judgments convey a 4 + 3 or 4 + (2 + intercalation + 1) structure.

[203] Revelation 2:1–3:22; 6:1–8:1; 8:2–11:19; 15:1–16:21. See A. E. Steinmann, "The Tripartite Structure of the Sixth Seal, the Sixth Trumpet, and the Sixth Bowl of John's Apocalypse (Rev 6:12–7:17; 9:13–11:14; 16:12–16)," *JETS* 35

weight, indicating perfection or completion. Aside from the explicitly numbered septets, however, an effort at identifying additional unnumbered series of sevens seems contrived.[204]

The Relationship Among the Seals, Trumpets, and Bowls The relationship among the seals, trumpets, and bowls has long plagued interpreters. There are three primary theories: chronological succession,[205] recapitulation,[206] and telescopic progression.[207] Chronological succession argues that the series of septets occur in strict chronological order without any overlap. The strength of this view is its simplicity, but it fails to account for any overlap between the septets. Recapitulation argues that each septet represents an intensification and closer look at the same material. In other words, the trumpets cover the same occurrences as the seals, and the bowls signify the same period as the seals and trumpets. While recapitulation allows for an intensification of severity with each successive septet and offers a viable explanation for the apparent overlap, it does not adequately account for the dissimilarities between each series of septets.

Telescopic progression—also known as "dove-tailing"—maintains that the seventh seal contains the seven trumpets and the seventh trumpet comprises the seven bowls. It attempts to demonstrate the interconnectedness and overlap between the series of septets but also to account for the progression evident in each new septet. A progressive telescopic theory appears to offer the most satisfying explanation for the literary relationship between the septets. But caution against too strict an application of these theories is warranted since Revelation exhibits both repetition and progression in the unfolding series of judgments revealed in the septets and culminating in the consummation of God's judgment and the establishment of his kingdom on earth.[208]

John incorporated several interludes interspersed throughout the seals, trumpets, and bowls. The first two emerge between the breaking of the sixth and seventh seals (7:1–17) and between the blowing of the sixth and seventh trumpets (10:1–11:14). These interludes appear in the narrative for theological reasons. They are bound to the preceding sections and provide answers for questions the audience might be asking. The sixth seal (6:12–16) unleashes devastating catastrophes causing the earth's inhabitants to flee into caves, praying to die. In their terror they cry out concerning the wrath of God and the Lamb asking,

---

(1992): 69–79. See Bauckham, *Climax of Prophecy*, 9–11.

[204] Mazzaferri, *Genre*, 348–56.

[205] Charles, *Revelation of St. John*, 1.xxv; D. Pentecost, *Things to Come* (Grand Rapids, MI: Zondervan, 1958), 187–88.

[206] Victorinus of Pettau, *Victorini episcopi Petavionensis Opera*, Corpus scriptorum ecclesiasticorum latinorum 49, ed. J. Haussleiter (Leipzig, Germany: F. Tempsky, 1916), 86; Collins, *Combat Myth*, 32–44; J. Lambrecht, "A Structuration of Revelation 4,1–22,5," in *L'Apocalypse johannique et l'Apocalyptique dans le Nouveau Testament*, ed. J. Lambrecht (Leuven, Belgium: University Press, 1980), 80–92; C. H. Giblin, "Recapitulation and the Literary Coherence of John's Apocalypse," *CBQ* 56 (1994): 81–95; Aune, *Revelation 1–5*, xci–xciii; Beale, *Book of Revelation*, 116–44.

[207] R. L. Thomas, "The Structure of the Apocalypse: Recapitulation or Progression?" *MSJ* 4 (1993): 45–66; Beckwith, *Commentary on the Apocalypse*, 606–11; J. F. Walvoord, *The Revelation of Jesus Christ* (Chicago, IL: Moody, 1989), 150–51; Ladd, *Revelation*, 122. Cf. J. R. Michaels (*Revelation*, IVPNTC 20 [Downers Grove, IL: InterVarsity, 1997], 27–29), who used the term "reiteration"; his view comports with the telescopic rather than a strict recapitulation theory.

[208] See Beale, *Book of Revelation*, 121–26.

"Who can stand?" The succeeding narrative (7:1–17) answers this question by depicting the protective sealing and salvation of God's people who are standing before the throne.[209]

A similar pattern occurs when the fifth and sixth trumpets unleash horrible and devastating plagues on the earth's inhabitants. Their response is a failure to repent from their sins.[210] The succeeding narrative (10:1–11:14)[211] not only provides justification for the plagues but also depicts the people of God in their role as prophetic witnesses before the nations.[212] These interludes enable the hearers to identify their role within the narrative, first as protected and then as prophetic witnesses.[213] Thus, the purpose of the interludes is to challenge the churches to remain faithful and to endure opposition because God was protecting and using them as witnesses.

The third interlude differs from the first two in that it occurs at the end of the seventh trumpet and precedes the introduction of the seven bowls. Chapter 12 represents a dramatic shift in the flow of John's vision narrative: it is introduced by the phrase "a great sign [*sēmeion*] appeared in heaven" (12:1), followed by "another sign [*sēmeion*] appeared in heaven" (12:3), and again with "I saw another great and marvelous sign [*sēmeion*] in heaven" (15:1, author's translation).[214] These are the only three occurrences of a *sēmeion* that appear in heaven. The other four occurrences are all false miraculous signs performed on earth on behalf of the "beast" (13:13–14; 16:14; 19:20).[215] The regular sense of *sēmeion* in the NT is that of a supernatural sign or miracle that is either authentic or not.[216] As in John's Gospel, *sēmeion* in Revelation most likely points to something more significant than just the sign or miracle itself.[217] Thus this third interlude, the "signs" narrative, occurs prior to the final outpouring of God's punitive judgments.

As with other interludes, the signs narrative focuses on the role of the people of God concomitant with the series of judgments.[218] The first interlude illustrates the protection and ultimate salvation of believers (7:1–17). The second interlude pictures the role of believers as God's final prophetic witnesses (10:1–11:14). This third interlude (12:1–15:4)

---

[209] Beale (*Book of Revelation*, 405) offered the best treatment of the relationship between the question in 6:17 and chap. 7.

[210] This is reminiscent of Amos 4 where God sent a series of plagues on Israel, but they did not repent.

[211] Giblin, "Revelation 11.1–13," 434.

[212] Aune (*Revelation 6–16*, 555) agrees with Giblin and notes the prophetic emphasis evident within this interlude.

[213] See R. Dalrymple, "These Are the Ones," *Bib* 86 (2005): 396–406; Beasley-Murray, *Book of Revelation*, 31.

[214] Ford (*Revelation*, 194–95) suggests that chap. 12 begins a new division of Revelation that she calls the "book of signs." But this epithet is problematic because it may be taken to imply that this section exists independently from the rest of the vision. See Smalley, *Revelation to John*, 310; Beale, *Book of Revelation*, 621.

[215] Aune, *Revelation 6–16*, 679.

[216] Smalley, *Revelation to John*, 313.

[217] Ibid. See Prigent, *Commentary on the Apocalypse*, 376–77; Osborne, *Revelation*, 456. For an analysis of the use of *sēmeion* in John's Gospel, see A. J. Köstenberger, *Studies on John and Gender*, SBL 38 (New York, NY: P. Lang, 2001), 99–116.

[218] Osborne, *Revelation*, 452: "Thus, this is the final of the three interludes and like them details the church's involvement in these end-time events."

portrays believers as engaged in a holy war against Satan.[219] Although the precise microstructure of this interlude proves elusive,[220] the narrative falls into three natural divisions: (1) holy war in heaven (chap. 12), (2) holy war on earth (chap. 13), and (3) vindication of believers followed by the judgment of the wicked (chap. 14). Amid the scenes of this cosmic spiritual warfare, John made the purpose of this interlude explicit by interjecting calls for encouragement (12:10–12), patient endurance (13:9–10), and the ultimate vindication of believers (14:6–13). Revelation 12:1–15:4 also provides the basis and justification for the severity and finality of the judgments rendered on the inhabitants of the earth.

The Final Two Visions The last two visions (17:1–21:8; 21:9–22:5) starkly contrast the prostitute city of Babylon the Great with the holy bride city of the new Jerusalem.[221] In the third vision (17:1–21:8), John sees a prostitute named Babylon (17:15), who represents Rome (17:9) and rules over the nations as well as the kings of the earth (17:15, 18). The rest of the vision depicts all the events associated with her judgment; these include her trial, sentencing, and lament (18:1–24); the return of Christ (19:1–21); his millennial reign (20:1–10); and the resurrection followed by the final judgment (20:11–15).

The fourth vision (21:9–22:5)[222] portrays the beauty and brilliance of the bride city of the new Jerusalem coming down to earth from heaven. This vision falls into two sections that describe the Holy City as an eternal holy of holies (21:9–27) and as a new Eden (22:1–5).[223] Thus, these two final visions serve to contrast the fate of those who worship the beast with the glory awaiting the followers of the Lamb.[224] When viewed together, these two visions form the climax of the prophecy by providing the culmination of everything anticipated in John's vision.[225]

---

[219] Beasley-Murray, *Book of Revelation*, 191; Beale, *Book of Revelation*, 622–24; Mounce, *Book of Revelation*, 234. Barr (*Tales of the End*, 101–31) proposes that 11:19–22:21 comprises a third narrative unit which he calls "The War Scroll."

[220] Some see chaps. 12–15 as consisting of an unnumbered series of sevens (Farrer, Beale); others see a chiastic structure (Strand, Shae). Note with regard to the latter, D. A. deSilva, "X Marks the Spot? A Critique of the Use of Chiasmus in Macro-Structural Analyses of Revelation," *JSNT* 30 (2008): 343–71.

[221] C. H. Giblin, "Structural and Thematic Correlations in the Theology of Revelation 16–22," *Bib* 55 (1974): 488–89. Earlier scholars who have acknowledged the literary parallels include Swete, Lohmeyer, Allo, Wikenhauser, Lohse, and Rissi. Scholars since Giblin who have incorporated his work into their structural outlines include Bauckham, *Climax of Prophecy*, 4; Beale, *Book of Revelation*, 109–10; Aune, *Revelation 17–22*, 1020–21; M. Wilcock, *The Message of Revelation*, BST (Downers Grove, IL: InterVarsity, 2006), 112–15; and Collins, *Combat Myth*, 19. But Collins could not fit these sections into her series of sevens, so she relegated them to appendices.

[222] Revelation 22:6 marks the beginning of the epilogue by alluding to Rev 1:1. Both passages refer to the angel sent to John to show him what must soon take place.

[223] Osborne, *Revelation*, 604.

[224] B. R. Rossing (*The Choice Between Two Cities*, HTS [Harrisburg, PA: Trinity Press International, 1999], 14–15) argues that this was part of John's rhetorical strategy to compel his audience to make a choice between the two cities. So E. M. Räpple, *The Metaphor of the City in the Apocalypse of John*, SBL 67 (New York, NY: P. Lang, 2004).

[225] Bauckham, *Climax of Prophecy*, 5; S. Moyise, *The Old Testament in the Book of Revelation*, JSNTSup 115 (Sheffield, UK: Sheffield Academic Press, 1995), 64; J. Lambrecht, "Final Judgments and Ultimate Blessings: The Climactic Visions of Revelation 20, 11–21, 8," *Bib* 81 (2000): 262–85; M. Jauhiainen, "'Ἀποκάλυψις Ἰησοῦ Χριστοῦ' (Rev. 1:1): The Climax of John's Prophecy?" *TynB* 54 (2003): 99–117.

OUTLINE

I. PROLOGUE (1:1–8)

II. VISION ONE (ON PATMOS): THE GLORIFIED CHRIST WHO INVESTIGATES HIS CHURCHES (1:9–3:22)
   - A. The Inaugural Vision of Jesus Christ (1:9–20)
   - B. The Messages to the Seven Churches of Asia Minor (2:1–3:22)

III. VISION TWO (IN HEAVEN): THE DIVINE COURT PROCEEDINGS AND THE TRIAL OF THE NATIONS (4:1–16:21)
   - A. Transition from Patmos to Heaven (4:1–2)
   - B. Worship Around the Throne (4:3–11)
   - C. The Divine Courtroom (5:1–14)
   - D. Preliminary Investigative Judgments (6:1–17)
     1. Breaking the Seven Seals (6:1–14)
     2. Transition: "Who Can Stand?" (6:15–17)
   - E. First Interlude: The Protective Sealing of God's People (7:1–17)
   - F. Eschatological Investigative Judgments (8:1–9:21)
     1. Sounding the Seven Trumpets (8:1–9:19)
     2. Transition: The Impenitence of Humanity (9:20–21)
   - G. Second Interlude: God's People as Prophetic Witnesses (10:1–11:19)
     1. Angel with the Little Scroll (10:1–7)
     2. John's Prophetic Commission (10:8–11)
     3. The Protective Measuring of the Temple (11:1–2)
     4. The Two Witnesses (11:3–13)
     5. The Seventh Trumpet (11:14–18)
     6. Transition: Heavenly Temple Opened (11:19)
   - H. Third Interlude: The Signs Narrative/God's People in Holy War (12:1–15:8)
     1. First Sign (12:1–2): The Heavenly Woman (Israel Personified)
     2. Second Sign (12:3): The Red Dragon (Satan Identified)
     3. Holy War with Satan in Historical Perspective (12:4–6)
     4. Holy War with Satan in Heaven (12:7–12)
     5. Holy War with Satan Against Believers on Earth (12:13–13:18)
        - a. The Woman Persecuted (12:13–18)
        - b. The Beast from the Sea: Political War Against Believers (13:1–10)
        - c. The Beast from the Earth: Religious War Against Believers (13:11–18)
     6. The Lamb with the 144,000: The Triumph of Believers (14:1–5)
     7. Three Angels Announcing Judgment (14:6–13)
     8. Harvest of Grain: Harvesting the Believers for Reward (14:14–16)
     9. Harvest of Grapes: Harvesting the Sinners for Wrath (14:17–18)
     10. Third Sign: The Victory of Believers (15:1–4)
     11. Transition: Heavenly Temple Opened (15:5–8)
   - I. Final Investigative Judgments: The Seven Bowls (16:1–21)

IV. VISION THREE (IN THE DESERT): THE DESTRUCTION OF BABYLON AND THE RETURN OF CHRIST (17:1–21:8)
   A. Transition: "Come, I Will Show You the Judgment of the Notorious Prostitute" (17:1–2).
   B. The Prostitute City Babylon Described (17:3–6)
   C. The Prostitute City Babylon as Rome (17:7–18)
   D. The Trial and Sentencing of Babylon (18:1–24)
   E. Heavenly Celebration of Babylon's Destruction (19:1–10)
   F. The Divine Warrior and Final Tribunal (19:11–20:15)
   G. The Renewal of Creation and the Arrival of the New Jerusalem (21:1–8)
V. VISION FOUR (ON A MOUNTAIN): BELIEVERS' REWARD AND THE RENEWAL OF CREATION (21:9–22:5)
   A. Transition: "Come, I Will Show You the Bride" (21:9–10)
   B. The Description of the New Jerusalem Descending from Heaven (21:11–27)
   C. The Paradise of God: The Renewal of Creation (22:1–5)
VI. EPILOGUE (22:6–21)

Interpreting the Book of Revelation: Major Approaches

How one reads Revelation largely depends on one's approach to understanding the areas of history, symbolism, and eschatology. Interpreters differ in their view of the relationship between John's vision and history. Does the book of Revelation reflect past events, present events, purely future events, or events future to John but historical to modern readers? The way one answers these questions significantly influences how one interprets the book.

No one doubts that Revelation is saturated with symbolism, but not all agree on what those symbols mean. Do they have literal referents or literary ones? Literal interpretations produce remarkably divergent meanings from those who follow more literary approaches. Finally, one's eschatological perspectives become the theological lenses influencing how one answers the historical questions as well as how one interprets the book's symbols. The history of interpretation has produced four basic schools of thought for interpreting this complex book.

Preterist The preterist position (from the Lat. *praeteritus* meaning "gone by") is also known as "contemporary historical,"[226] which approaches the relationship between history and the book of Revelation from the viewpoint that the events prophesied were fulfilled in the first century. One school of preterism interprets the book as a message of judgment against apostate Israel for rejecting Christ by prophesying the destruction of Jerusalem in the year 70.[227] Other preterist interpreters see the Roman Empire and the situation of Christians as the focus of John's vision prophesying the fall of Rome.[228]

---

[226] Giesen, *Offenbarung des Johannes*, 44; see Mounce, *Book of Revelation*, 41; Carson and Moo, *Introduction to the New Testament*, 719.

[227] See K. L. Gentry, "A Preterist View of Revelation," in *Four Views on the Book of Revelation*, ed. C. M. Pate (Grand Rapids, MI: Zondervan, 1998), 37–92.

[228] On the types of preterist views, see Beale, *Book of Revelation*, 44–45; and Osborne, *Revelation*, 19–20.

This view, in all its variations, represents the most common approach among contemporary scholars.[229] Its primary appeal resides in that it takes seriously the historically conditioned reception of the original audience. Preterists recognize that Revelation would have had a meaning accessible to the first-century readers. Therefore, their interpretation of Revelation reflects the choices they make regarding the date of composition and the historical situation addressed. The view of the preterist is that Revelation is not so much a blueprint for the distant future as it is a commentary on events contemporary to the time of composition.[230]

Since Revelation was not written in a historical vacuum, preterists correctly locate the message in terms of its historical context as something relevant to the original recipients. John addressed real congregations of Christians living in the Roman province of Asia Minor. Thus, one approaches the interpretation of Revelation in a manner similar to that used for NT letters by attempting to understand the meaning in light of the historical circumstances of the individual churches. The symbols and images produce a "spatial interaction between the earthly and the heavenly so as to give new meaning to the present situation."[231]

By not projecting the contents of the book into the far distant future, preterists helpfully emphasize that John's vision immediately addressed the situation and needs of the churches in Asia Minor. No other book in the NT is as frequently divorced from its historical setting as is Revelation. But to neglect the relationship of Revelation to its first-century audience is hermeneutically fallacious in that such an approach wrongly assumes that the original recipients were not the seven churches, but Christians living today. Having said this, however, it is equally fallacious to restrict the message and meaning of Revelation exclusively to the first century.

Revelation conveys a perspective that extends beyond the confines of the first century. The book depicts the final consummation of the kingdom of God on earth with the physical return of Jesus, the resurrection of all humanity, and the final judgment. An approach that implies that these events have already occurred falls prey to overrealized eschatology.[232] The universal scope of Revelation is apparent by the repeated references to the global character of the earth's inhabitants. The people of God are from every nation, tribe, and language (5:9; 7:9; 13:7; 15:4; 21:24), and the objects of God's wrath comprise all earth dwellers instead of only those in Jerusalem or the Roman Empire.[233]

---

[229] R. H. Charles, J. Sweet, J. Roloff, A. Y. Collins, L. L. Thompson, G. Krodel, D. Barr, E. Schüssler Fiorenza, M. Wilson, and N. Kraybill. Popular-level proponents include K. Gentry, D. Chilton, G. DeMar, and H. Hannegraff.

[230] C. Osiek, "Apocalyptic Eschatology," *TBT* 37 (1996): 343–44.

[231] Osborne, *Revelation*, 19.

[232] Mounce, *Book of Revelation*, 42.

[233] The phrase "those who live on the earth" denotes the objects of wrath in Revelation (3:10; 6:10; 8:13; 11:10; 13:8, 14; 17:2, 8). This group is consistently set in juxtaposition to believers. See Herms, *Apocalypse for the Church and for the World*, 185–201.

The allusions to OT prophecies in Revelation are either universalized to include all nations and not just Israel, or they are specifically drawn from judgment oracles against the nations. For this reason the notion that Revelation prophesies the destruction of Jerusalem in the year 70 seems highly unlikely since the frequent allusions to Daniel 2 and 7 depict the nations, rather than Israel, as the object of judgment.[234] What is more, to equate Jerusalem with Babylon seems implausible because Babylon, in Revelation, wields enormous political control over the inhabitants of the earth; this could not apply to historical Jerusalem.[235]

Historicist The historicist approach[236] was the most popular interpretive approach for the book of Revelation during the Middle Ages and throughout the Reformation.[237] The historicists viewed the book as forecasting the course of history in Western Europe with particular emphasis on popes, kings, and wars.[238] It began with the twelfth-century monastic leader Joachim of Fiore who wanted to find meaningful patterns in history.[239] Franciscan interpreters adopted his approach and applied it to their contention with Pope Benedict XI, since the numbers corresponding to the letters of his name transliterated into Greek added up to 666.[240] Martin Luther, John Calvin, and other Reformers followed suit by equating the Vatican with the harlot Babylon that corrupted and persecuted the true church.[241]

This approach has been largely abandoned, but one may detect modern variations of it when dispensational interpreters read Revelation as if it were being fulfilled through current events on the world's stage.[242] Although a historicist approach offers an interesting window on the history of interpretation of the book of Revelation throughout church history, it fails as a legitimate interpretive model. Its failure stems from its inadequate hermeneutic, which narrowly focuses on Western history and insufficiently considers the book's relevance for the first-century churches to which it is addressed.[243]

Idealist The idealist, timeless, or symbolic approach sets aside the historical question altogether by positing that Revelation is not about events in the space-time continuum

---

[234] Beale, *Book of Revelation*, 44–45.

[235] Against D. Chilton, *The Days of Vengeance: An Exposition of the Book of Revelation* (Tyler: Dominion, 1987), 20; Ford, *Revelation*, 282–88; I. Provan, "Foul Spirit, Fornication, and Finance: Revelation 18 and an Old Testament Perspective," *JSNT* 64 (1996): 81–100; D. E. Holwerda, "Ein neuer Schlüssel zum 17. Kapitel der Johanneischen Offenbarung," *EstBib* 53 (1995): 387–96. For Babylon as a cipher for Rome, see Beale, *Book of Revelation*, 775; Osborne, *Revelation*, 608–9; Aune, *Revelation 17–22*, 936–37.

[236] Giesen, *Offenbarung des Johannes*, 44.

[237] Carson and Moo, *Introduction to the New Testament*, 720.

[238] Mounce, *Book of Revelation*, 42.

[239] C. R. Koester, "On the Verge of the Millennium: A History of the Interpretation of Revelation," *WW* 15 (1995): 131.

[240] Ibid., 132.

[241] Ibid; cf. Beckwith, *Apocalypse of John*, 327–29; A. F. Johnson, "Revelation," in *The Expositor's Bible Commentary*, vol. 12: *Hebrews–Revelation*, rev. ed. (Grand Rapids, MI: Zondervan, 2006), 585; Osborne, *Revelation*, 18; I. Backus, *Reformation Readings of the Apocalypse: Geneva, Zurich, and Wittenberg* (Oxford, UK: Oxford University Press, 2000).

[242] Osborne, *Revelation*, 19.

[243] Beale, *Book of Revelation*, 46.

but instead symbolically portrays the spiritual and timeless nature of the battle between good and evil.[244] The famous dictum of W. Milligan epitomizes this approach: "We are not to look in the Apocalypse for special events, but for an exhibition of the principles which govern the history both of the world and the Church."[245] Thus, the vision and its symbolism are loosed from their historical moorings so they represent a universal message to all believers about God's defeat of Satan and the spiritual victory of faith in Christ as the church contends with a world ruled by wicked potentates.

The roots of this view dig deeply into the soil of Christian interpretive history beginning in Alexandria. Origen taught that the spiritual and timeless meaning of the text was superior to the literal sense and applied this viewpoint to Revelation. He had no use for speculations about the time and location of the battle of Armageddon because he understood it to refer to the triumph of God over sin and wickedness.[246] This deeper and symbolic interpretation of Revelation was adopted by Dionysius, Origen's pupil, and made a lasting impact through the influence of Augustine (AD 354–430). The millennium, according to Augustine, was a way of referring to the spiritual reign of believers throughout time and not a literal thousand years on earth.[247] However, some variations of this view do allow for the future fulfillment of end-time prophecies.

The strengths of this approach are that it accounts for the symbolic nature of John's visions, accurately reflects their universal relevance for all Christians throughout history, and offers a thoroughgoing theological reading of the text. But the disregard for any historical connections or future expectations exposes several flaws. John wrote to real churches facing specific circumstances, especially in the seven letters. The allusions to the imperial cult, the Nero *redux* myth, and other particular first-century historical events indicate that the meaning of his visions is tethered to the space-time continuum. What is more, this approach does not adequately explain the eschatological expectations for the consummation of God's plan in human history with the return of Christ to earth.

Futurist The fourth basic approach for interpreting the book of Revelation contends that chapters 4–22 refer to future events.[248] Early Christian writers such as Justin Martyr (ca. AD 100–165), Ireneaus (ca. AD 130–200), Tertullian (ca. AD 160–225), and Hippolytus (ca. AD 170–236) held to a futuristic interpretation known as *chiliasm*.[249] This expression draws from the Greek term for 1,000 (*chilia*), which they believed was the thousand-year reign of Christ on earth at the end of the age.[250] The view comes from

---

[244] Giesen, *Offenbarung des Johannes*, 44.

[245] W. Milligan, *The Revelation of St. John*, 2nd ed. (London, England: Macmillan, 1887), 154–55. Advocates of this approach include R. Calkins, W. Hendriksen, A. A. Hoekema, P. E. Hughes, and S. Hamstra Jr. For an idealist view of Revelation, see S. Hamstra Jr., "An Idealist View of Revelation," in *Four Views*, 95–131.

[246] Koester, "On the Verge of the Millennium," 130.

[247] Augustine, *City of God* 18.53; 20.7.

[248] Giesen, *Offenbarung des Johannes*, 44–45.

[249] Beckwith, *Apocalypse of John*, 318–34; see Mounce, *Book of Revelation*, 39.

[250] Justin, *Dial.* 80.

a literal interpretation of 20:2–7. But this literal interpretation was eclipsed by more allegorical and spiritual approaches emphasizing the timeless and successive fulfillment of these prophecies throughout church history.[251]

The futuristic approach virtually disappeared from the interpretation of Revelation until it was revived through the writing of a late sixteenth-century Spanish Jesuit named Ribeira who posited that John saw events both in his day and in the far future.[252] While he was not a futurist in the strictest sense, he successfully brought futurism back to the table as a viable interpretive option.[253] In modern times the futurist position enjoys pride of place among most evangelical Christians. But not all futurists agree as to how Revelation portrays the unfolding of future events, and two distinct understandings have developed: (1) dispensational futurism; and (2) modified or moderate futurism.[254]

Dispensational futurism, associated with dispensational premillennialism, began with the teachings of J. N. Darby that were popularized in America by C. Larkin, D. L. Moody, C. I. Scofield, and L. S. Chafer. The twentieth century has witnessed the development of dispensationalism into two distinct expressions: (1) *classic* (J. N. Darby, C. I. Scofield, L. S. Chafer)[255] and *revised* dispensationalism (J. Walvoord, C. C. Ryrie, J. D. Pentecost, T. LaHaye, and R. Thomas);[256] and (2) *progressive* dispensationalism (D. Bock, C. Blaising, R. Saucy, and M. Pate).[257]

The distinguishing difference between these two forms of dispensationalism is hermeneutical. The hermeneutical hallmark of classic and revised dispensationalism is a consistent and insistent commitment to the literal interpretation of prophetic Scripture,[258] a principle often expressed with the dictum, "When the plain sense of Scripture makes common sense, seek no other sense."[259] This hermeneutical approach has resulted in a particular theological system that makes a strict and consistent distinction between Israel

[251] Augustine, *Civ.* 18.53; 20.7.

[252] Mounce, *Book of Revelation*, 40. The key work was F. Riberae, *In sacram Beati Ioannis Apostoli & Evangelistae Apocalypsin Commentarij* (Lugduni: Ex Officina Iuntarum, 1593).

[253] Osborne, *Revelation*, 20.

[254] For the title "modified futurism," see Beale, *Book of Revelation*, 47; for the title "moderate futurism," see G. E. Ladd, *A Theology of the New Testament*, rev. ed. (Grand Rapids, MI: Eerdmans, 1993), 673.

[255] C. I. Scofield's work is most accessible through his *Scofield Reference Bible*, first published by Oxford University Press in 1909. For L. S. Chafer, see his *Systematic Theology* (Dallas, TX: Dallas Seminary Press, 1947).

[256] The key work is C. C. Ryrie, *Dispensationalism*, rev. ed. (Chicago, IL: Moody, 2007); see also D. Pentecost, *Things to Come: A Study in Biblical Eschatology* (Grand Rapids, MI: Academie, 1958).

[257] C. A. Blaising and D. L. Bock, *Progressive Dispensationalism* (Grand Rapids, MI: Baker, 1993), 21–22; cf. H. W. Bateman, "Dispensationalism Yesterday and Today," in *Three Central Issues in Contemporary Dispensationalism: A Comparison of Traditional and Progressive Views*, ed. H. W. Bateman (Grand Rapids, MI: Kregel, 1999); R. L. Saucy, *The Case for Progressive Dispensationalism: The Interface Between Dispensational and Non-Dispensational Theology* (Grand Rapids, MI: Zondervan, 1993).

[258] C. M. Pate, "Introduction to Revelation," in *Four Views*, 29.

[259] D. L. Cooper, "An Exposition of the Book of Revelation: The Great Parenthesis," *Biblical Research Monthly* (May 1954): 84; quoted in T. LaHaye, *Revelation Unveiled* (Grand Rapids, MI: Zondervan, 1999), 17.

and the church.[260] The church is merely a parenthesis inserted between God's dealings with Israel; thus, the book of Revelation focuses on the future of ethnic and national Israel.

Since the term "church" (*ekklēsia*) does not occur in the book of Revelation after 3:22 until 22:15, dispensationalists conclude that God raptures the church at the beginning of the tribulation so he may return to dealing with Israel. Thus, the tribulation and Christ's thousand-year reign in Jerusalem have nothing to do with the church. Dispensationalists typically interpret Revelation as chronologically depicting future events occurring over a seven-year period centered on the nation of Israel. While dispensational futurism affirms a high view of Scripture and the future reality it predicts, its excessive literalism tends to impose onto the text an eschatological system based on inadequate hermeneutical principles.

Progressive dispensationalism constitutes a significantly updated form of dispensationalism, bringing it hermeneutically closer to the standard already/not yet schema and greater continuity between Israel and the church, which typically characterizes evangelical interpretation.[261] The term *progressive* refers to the belief that the various dispensations progressively overlap in keeping with the already/not yet tension of inaugurated eschatology. Thus, progressive dispensationalists maintain that Jesus has already commenced his reign as the Davidic King at the resurrection rather than placing this event at the beginning in the millennium.[262] The millennial reign of Christ, then, is the complete fulfillment for Israel.

Progressive dispensationalism also differs from the earlier forms of dispensationalism in that it does not view the church as a separate segment of humanity or as a competing nation alongside Israel and Gentile nations; instead, it is a redeemed humanity of both Jews and Gentiles existing in this dispensation prior to the coming of Christ.[263] C. M. Pate identifies the essential difference between the classic and progressive dispensational interpretations of the book of Revelation as the belief in the overlapping of "this age" and the "age to come":

> John is to write what he has seen (the visions of Revelation as a whole), which divide into two realities: the things that are—the present age; and the things that will be—the age to come. For John the church of his day lives in the present age (chaps. 1–3), but in heaven, by virtue of Jesus's death and resurrection, the age to come has already dawned (chaps. 4–5). In the future the age to come will descend to earth, effecting the defeat of the Antichrist (chaps. 6–19), the establishment of the temporary messianic kingdom on earth (chap. 20), and subsequently the eternal state (chaps 21–22). Thus

---

[260] Ryrie (*Dispensationalism,* 102–3), who asserts that the words "church" and "Israel" are always kept distinct in the NT, maintaining that this distinction is the result of "a consistent use of literal, normal, or plain method of interpretation without the addition of any other principle that will attempt to give respectability to some preconceived conclusions."

[261] Blaising and Bock, *Progressive Dispensationalism*, 22; cf. Saucy, *The Case for Progressive Dispensationalism.*

[262] Blaising and Bock, *Progressive Dispensationalism*, 177–78.

[263] Ibid., 49.

> the overlapping of the two ages accounts for the continual shifting of scenes between earth (this age) and heaven (the age to come) in Revelation.[264]

Although progressive dispensationalists affirm an inaugurated eschatology and view the church as equal members among the people of God, they continue to maintain the classic dispensational tenets of a future for ethnic Israel, the thousand-year reign, and the rapture of the church prior to the tribulation.[265] This view represents a more viable approach than classic dispensationalism, but by maintaining the Israel/church distinction mandating a pretribulational rapture, the approach effectively renders the majority of the book of Revelation irrelevant for Christians today.

A second form of a futurist approach, modified or moderate futurism, is commonly associated with historical premillennialism because of its affinities with the *chiliasm* of the early church.[266] G. E. Ladd is credited as having pioneered the modern articulation of historical premillennialism as an approach for interpreting Revelation, but this approach has been adopted or adapted by a number of scholars that include R. Gundry, R. Mounce, L. Morris, and W. Grudem. The view is similar to dispensationalism in that it affirms a thousand-year reign of Christ on earth, but it departs from the dispensational insistence on a strict literalism, the rigorous distinction between Israel and the church, the chronology of end-time events, and the belief in a pretribulational rapture.

While dispensationalists argue that the second coming of Christ will involve a *secret* return for the church prior to the tribulation followed by his *visible* return after seven years, modified futurists affirm *only one* return of Christ to earth that allows the church to persevere through the tribulation.[267] This is largely due to the inauguration of the new covenant, which makes all believers in Jesus the spiritual descendants of Abraham and therefore covenant members of the people of God—true Israel.[268] What is more, the relationship between the past, present, and future is more flexible among modified futurists. Ladd, for example, interprets chapters 1–3 as pertaining to the first century, chapters 4–6 as recurring throughout church history, and the events beginning in chapter 7 as referring to the future tribulation.[269]

Modified futurism and historical premillennialism are appealing because they enable interpreters to maintain the future orientation of John's visions while avoiding the literalism of dispensationalism that limits the applicability of Revelation to today's church.

---

[264] Pate, "Introduction to Revelation," 33.

[265] Ibid.

[266] W. Grudem, *Systematic Theology: An Introduction to Biblical Doctrine* (Grand Rapids, MI: Zondervan, 2000), 1111.

[267] Osborne, *Revelation*, 21.

[268] Beale, *Book of Revelation*, 47.

[269] Ladd, *Theology of the New Testament*, 675.

Conclusion A recent trend among commentators incorporates elements of all or some of the approaches described into an eclectic blend.[270] An advantage of this strategy is that it does not force an interpreter to subscribe rigidly to any one of the major interpretive approaches.

At the same time, eclectic views are exceedingly diverse. H. Giesen recognizes the futuristic and idealistic nature of John's vision, yet he is leery of their tendency toward abstraction. This led him to prefer the concrete historical nature of preterism coupled with the tradition-historical approach of scholars such as W. Bousset, R. H. Charles, and E. Lohmeyer.[271]

Another commentator, G. Beale, labels his eclectic approach a "redemptive-historical form of modified idealism."[272] His preference for idealism stems from his view that the symbols in John's visions are "transtemporal" in the sense that they apply to events throughout the church age.

Yet another premillennial commentator, G. Osborne, makes the futurist position the dominant aspect of his form of eclecticism because he believes that John's visions "were primarily intended to describe the events that will end world history."[273] This variety of approaches demonstrates the difficulty of assigning every scholar to one of the major approaches to interpreting Revelation.

The relationship between the historical, symbolic, and eschatological aspects represented in the book of Revelation will continue to exercise the minds of interpreters of the Apocalypse.[274] Since the book itself explicitly claims to be about future events surrounding the return of Christ (1:19; 22:18–20), preference should be given to a form of the futurist approach.

UNIT-BY-UNIT DISCUSSION

I. Prologue (1:1–8)

The prologue informs the reader that this is a revelatory book containing a vision of Jesus, which has his return as the content, John as the seer, and the churches as the recipients. God gave this revelation in order that all his servants could know what must happen in the near future. The divine authority of this vision is expressed by a chain of intermediaries:

God → Jesus → angel → John → churches

---

[270] Commentators using an eclectic approach include G. Osborne, C. Keener, G. Beale, H. Giesen, R. Mounce, A. Johnson, and L. Morris.

[271] Giesen, *Offenbarung des Johannes*, 45.

[272] Beale, *Book of Revelation*, 48.

[273] Osborne, *Revelation*, 22.

[274] For a helpful survey of the respective interpretive schemes, see A. F. Johnson, "Revelation," 584–87.

John affirms the veracity of this vision by submitting it as eyewitness testimony regarding everything he saw and heard.

After promising a blessing to the one who reads, hears, and obeys the vision (1:4–6), John sends greetings from each member of the Trinity—the Father, the Son, and the Spirit (symbolized by "the seven spirits"). Revelation 1:7 speaks of the visible and physical return of Christ by fusing Daniel 7:13 with Zechariah 12:10. The prologue ends with an assertion from God the Father that he, as the Eternal and Almighty One, is the beginning and the end of history.

II. Vision One (on Patmos): The Glorified Christ Who Investigates His Churches (1:9–3:22)

A. The Inaugural Vision of Jesus Christ (1:9–20) The first vision opens with an account of John's call to prophesy and the inaugural vision of Jesus in his glory and standing among his churches. John, while on Patmos, was in the Spirit on the Lord's Day and heard a loud voice commanding him to write down the ensuing vision for seven churches in Asia Minor. He turned to see the owner of the voice speaking to him, only to discover the glorified Lord Jesus. The sight of him stretched the boundaries of John's language as he attempted to describe Jesus using similes drawn from OT theophanies.

Overwhelmed, John fell at Jesus's feet as though dead. Christ responded by placing his hand on John and announcing that he, Jesus, is the first and the last, the living Resurrected One, and the One with authority over death and life. Jesus then explained that the seven lampstands are the seven churches of Asia, and the seven stars in his hand are their angels. This identification transitions from the inaugural vision of Christ to the messages intended for the seven churches.

B. The Messages to the Seven Churches of Asia Minor (2:1–3:22) The messages in chapters 2–3 represent the most familiar portion of the book of Revelation and provide the most practical instructions for believers. Although these messages address situations historically and locally confined to the seven churches mentioned, they apply universally to all churches throughout all time. Because these letters diverge from the normal models of Greco-Roman epistolary writing, they are closer to the genre classification of a prophetic oracle.

The messages begin with an address to the angel of a particular church (cf. 1:20),[275] a command to write, and a predication describing a characteristic of Christ drawn from the

---

[275] Some debate exists regarding the identity of the "angels" of the seven churches. The debate is whether the angels are human messengers (i.e., the pastors of the churches) or angelic beings. The word *angelos* is used occasionally in the NT with regard to human messengers (Luke 9:52), including John the Baptist (Matt 11:10; Mark 1:2; Luke 7:27). In the present instance, however, it is more likely that the word refers to angels. By far the most common use of *angelos* in the NT is with reference to angelic beings. Of the sixty-seven occurrences of *angelos* in Revelation, all instances outside of chaps. 2–3 refer to angels. It is unlikely that *angelos* is used differently in chaps. 2–3. Also, the angels are identified in 1:20 as "stars." Although occasionally used in the OT with reference to believers (Gen 37:9; Dan 12:3), "stars" is more commonly an OT metaphor for angels (Job 38:7; Dan 10:13, 20–21). As G. K. Beale (*Book of Revelation*, 217) notes, angels are corporately identified with Christians as their heavenly counterparts in 8:3–4; 19:10; and 22:9. Because the messages are primarily directed to

inaugural vision and relevant to that specific church (2:1, 8, 12, 18; 3:1a, 7, 14). The official body of the message begins with the "I know" (*oida*) speech that includes either commendations, accusations, or both (2:2, 9, 13, 19; 3:1, 8b, 15). Jesus then admonishes the churches by either encouraging them to continue to persevere in a certain kind of conduct or by calling them to repent, the latter accompanied by a warning of negative consequences in case of disobedience. The final two elements of these messages include a prophetic appeal to listen to what the Spirit says to the churches (2:7a, 11a, 17a, 29; 3:6, 13, 22) and a promise of deliverance for those who overcome (2:7b, 11b, 17b, 26; 3:5, 12, 21).

III. Vision Two (in Heaven): The Divine Court Proceedings and the Trial of the Nations (4:1–16:21)

A. Transition from Patmos to Heaven (4:1–2) John's entrance through the threshold of heaven signals a major transition into a new vision that also constitutes a thematic transition from a juridical investigation of the churches to an investigation of the nations (4:1–2).

B. Worship Around the Throne (4:3–11) The scene radically transforms from the barren rocky isle of Patmos into the heavenly throne room. God's throne is in the center of a series of concentric circles, depicting his sovereignty over the cosmos. In describing his vision, John drew from other prophetic visions involving God's throne (e.g., Ezek 1:5, 10, 18, 22). John's vision of the heavenly throne room offers an apocalyptic perspective contrasting imperial pretensions of cosmic sovereignty with the true King and Judge of the universe.[276] The divine council convenes for the purpose of installing an eschatological Judge worthy to prosecute God's judgment on the earth's inhabitants.

C. The Divine Courtroom (5:1–14) The courtroom scene continues in chapter 5 with the introduction of the scroll and the Lamb. The scene depicts the installment of Christ as the Davidic King and his enthronement at the right hand of God as well as his commission as the eschatological Judge who is the only one worthy to unleash God's judgment on humanity. A sealed scroll is brought, and an angel announces the search for one worthy to break the seals and to open them. After an extensive search throughout the created order, only one is found (5:2–4). The Lamb, the conquering Lion of the tribe of Judah, is deemed worthy to take the scroll and to assume his role as King and Judge (5:5–7). The remainder of the chapter is taken up with the adulation of the Lamb. This chapter sets the stage for the judgment of the nations.

D. Preliminary Investigative Judgments (6:1–17) In the same way Revelation 5 focuses on the worthiness of the Lamb to judge, chapters 6–16 demonstrate the justness of his judgment on humanity. The scroll with seven seals rests securely in the hands of the Lamb who proceeds to break open the seals. Since the contents of the scroll cannot be read

---

the angels, the angels most likely function as heavenly representatives of the earthly congregations (Caird, *Revelation of St. John*, 24).

[276] Aune, "Influence of Roman Imperial Court Ceremony," 5–26.

until all the seals are broken, the seals are best understood as preliminary judgments. The trials introduced by the seals represent the "birth pains" occurring prior to coming days of tribulation that will precede the return of Christ (see Mark 13:8, 19).

The four horsemen constitute a pattern of conquest, war, famine, and death (6:1–8; see Matt 24:7). The martyred believers and their appeal for justice (6:9–11) indicate that during this time God's people will continue to endure persecution. The seals also represent a progressive intensification leading up to a time of cosmic upheaval as indicated by the breaking of the sixth seal. The seals initiate the preliminary judgments against the nations and include warnings directed to covenant violators in the respective churches. These judgments precede the seven trumpets constituting the great tribulation.

E. First Interlude: The Protective Sealing of God's People (7:1–17) Prior to the tribulation, the first of several interludes interwoven between the series of septets assures the believers of their protection from divine judgment and their ultimate salvation (7:1–17). John places the interlude between the breaking of the sixth and seventh seals (see 6:12; 8:1). The interlude is divided into two separate but related segments (7:1–8, 9–17). The first unit pertains to the sealing of the 144,000 for protection prior to the tribulation (see 7:1, 14; see Ezek 9:4–6). While some view the 144,000 as symbolic of the multitude of believers who have come out of the great tribulation, others take the reference literally—meaning the twelve tribes of Israel.[277]

Table 20.3: The Letters to the Seven Churches in Revelation

	Ephesus 2:1–7	Smyrna 2:8–11	Pergamum 2:12–17
Characteristic of Christ	Holding seven stars and walking among the lampstands		Sharp double-edged sword out of mouth
Commendation	Works, labor, endurance, examining false apostles, rejecting the teachings of the Nicolaitans	Faithfully endured tribulation, poverty, and slander	Holding on to his name and did not deny faith in Christ
Accusation	Abandoned first love	None	Some hold to the teachings of a false prophet and the Nicolaitans
Admonition	Repent, remember, and return to prior good works	Be faithful unto death	Repent
Warning	Remove lampstand	None	Quickly fights them with his sword from his mouth (i.e. words)

[277] See Sidebar 20.1: Who Are the 144,000 in Revelation 7?

Table 20.3: The Letters to the Seven Churches in Revelation (continued)

Promise to Overcoming Victors	Right to eat from the tree of life in God's paradise	Never be harmed by the second death	Hidden manna and a white stone with new name
Thyatira 2:18–29	**Sardis 3:1–6**	**Philadelphia 3:7–13**	**Laodicea 3:14–22**
Eyes like fire and feet of burnished bronze	Holding the seven spirits and seven stars	The one who is holy and true and holds the keys of David	The "Amen," "faithful and true witness," and "the ruler of God's creation" (NIV)
Increasingly great works, love, faithfulness, service, and endurance	None	Works, little strength, not denied his name, obedient, and endurance	None
Some hold to the teachings of a false prophetess and commit sexual immorality	Reputation of being alive but spiritually dead	None	Lukewarm, self--sufficient, and self-deluded when in reality they are spiritually pitiful, poor, blind, and naked
Repent and do not hold to her teachings	Be alert, strengthen what remains, remember what you heard, and repent	Hold on to what they have	Receive from Christ refined gold, pure clothes, and eye ointment
Cast the prophetess and her followers unto a bed of suffering	Come against them like a thief	None	Christ rebukes those he loves and will restore fellowship with them
Authority over the nations	Dressed in white and name secure in the book of life	Made a pillar in God's sanctuary and the name of God and his city on them	The right to sit on the throne with the Father and Son

The second unit focuses on the salvation of God's people from every nation, tribe, and language (7:9–17). The fact that this group is standing before God's throne answers the question of who can stand during the day of his wrath (see 6:17). This interlude offers two perspectives regarding the same group. Most likely, the 144,000 represent the entire new covenant community of God's people *about to enter* the tribulation, while the multitude from many nations represents the multitude of the redeemed *coming out of* the tribulation. God's people are assured that God will protect them during this time of distress.

F. Eschatological Investigative Judgments (8:1–9:21) After the protective sealing of the servants of God from the coming divine judgments, John returned to the series of septets with the breaking of the seventh seal in 8:1. He used the device of interlocking to transition from the seals to the trumpets, but he also intimately connected the succeeding trumpet judgments with the preceding seals. The breaking of the seventh seal results in immediate silence; this is followed by the introduction of the seven angels and their trumpets. The first four trumpets impact all of life on earth: a third of the earth's vegetation burns up; a third of the saltwater turns to blood; a third of the freshwater turns bitter; and a third of the sun, moon, and stars turn dark.

The last three trumpets are directed specifically against the inhabitants of the earth. The fifth trumpet releases a horde of locust demons to scourge them, and the sixth trumpet releases a demonic cavalry that inflicts even more terror. Believers are exempt from the last three judgments, as the locusts are commanded not to harm those with God's seal on their foreheads (9:4). Although each successive trumpet blast has dire consequences on the earth's inhabitants, they refuse to repent (9:20–21). The last trumpet comprises the consummation of God's wrath in that it contains the seven bowl judgments that destroy life on earth (see 16:1–21).

G. Second Interlude: God's People as Prophetic Witnesses (10:1–11:19) The second interlude appears between the sixth and seventh trumpet blasts (10:1–11:13). It depicts the role of the people of God on earth during the time of the corresponding trumpet judgments. The interlude divides into two separate but interrelated sections. The first unit contains John's second prophetic commission in which he receives a message pertaining to the nations (10:1–11). The second unit describes the ministry of the two prophetic witnesses before the nations (11:1–13). These sections are inextricably bound together because they pertain to the fulfillment of a prophetic ministry to the nations. John's prophetic commission is ultimately completed in the ministry of the faithful witnesses.

When the Spirit-inspired prophetic testimony of the witnesses reaches completion, they are murdered (11:7–10). John states that the beast from the abyss will wage war against the two witnesses (11:7). This anticipates the war against believers instigated by the beast (13:1–18). The inhabitants of the earth revile these two witnesses to such an extent that a global celebration ensues once they have been violently murdered in the streets. That their corpses remain exposed where they lie indicates the level of umbrage and hatred expressed by humanity toward Christ's faithful representatives. After three and a half days, at a time corresponding with the seventh trumpet, God vindicates his witnesses through an awesome public display of resurrection and ascension (11:11–12). The time of testimony is completed, and the time for judgment has arrived.

H. Third Interlude: The Signs Narrative/God's People in Holy War (12:1–15:1) A third interlude appears between the sounding of the seventh trumpet (11:15–19) and the introduction of the seven bowls containing the final judgments (15:5–8). The narrative falls into three natural divisions of holy war in heaven (chap. 12); holy war on earth (chap. 13); and the vindication of the believers followed by the judgment of the wicked (chap. 14). Amid the scenes of this cosmic spiritual warfare, John made the purpose of this

SIDEBAR 20.1: WHO ARE THE 144,000 IN REVELATION 7?

There are two essential positions on the identity of the 144,000 and the relationship of this group with the multitude from many nations in Revelation 7.[1] One view holds that the reference is to be taken literally to refer to ethnic Jews, the twelve tribes of Israel. This is taken to support the notion that God's purposes during the Great Tribulation will be focused on ethnic Israel. This view maintains that the 144,000 are to be distinguished from the multitude from many nations.[2] The other position maintains that the reference to the 144,000 is symbolic and pertains to believers (not merely Jews) who are alive during the great tribulation and that the 144,000 are to be identified with the great multitude.[3]

The resolution of this question is important because it potentially sheds light on whether the church should be expected to be present during and go through the Great Tribulation (the posttribulational view) or believers have been raptured at the beginning of the Great Tribulation while God's purposes during this time period focus on Israel (the pretribulational rapture position). While identifying the 144,000 with ethnic Israel has the merit of a straightforward reading of the text, several considerations favor taking the reference as symbolic.

First, the 144,000 are explicitly called "servants of God," which elsewhere in the Apocalypse refers to believers in general, whether Jew or Gentile.[4] Second, the list of tribes provided (7:5–8) is unlike any other known list of tribes in the OT.[5] This suggests that John intentionally altered the list in order to present the church as the continuation of the true Israel. Third, John here most likely draws on a pattern by which what the prophet hears is portrayed in terms of one image and what he sees is depicted by another.[6] Thus John hears the number of 144,000 but sees an innumerable multitude from many nations. Finally, the number 144,000 most likely conveys the symbolic notion of completeness, which also speaks against taking the reference to the twelve tribes literally (cf. 14:1–5; 21:16–17).

---

[1] For a summary of interpretative views on the 144,000 see Beale, *Book of Revelation*, 416–23.

[2] Representatives of those who contend that the 144,000 are ethnic Israelites or a group of Jewish Christians include Thomas, *Revelation 1–7*, 475–83; and Walvoord, *Revelation of Jesus Christ*, 143.

[3] Osborne, *Revelation*, 302–3; Bauckham, *Climax of Prophecy*, 216, 225–26; Craig L. Blomberg, *From Pentecost to Patmos: An Introduction Through Revelation* (Nashville: B&H, 2006), 529–30.

[4] The term *doulos* occurs a total of fourteen times (1:1; 2:20; 6:15; 7:3; 10:7; 11:18; 13:16; 15:3; 19:2, 5, 18; 22:3, 6). The majority of uses specifically refer to prophets, but the term also denotes Christians in general.

[5] The primary differences include: (1) Judah heads the list, rather than Reuben; (2) the combination of Joseph with Manasseh, rather than Ephraim; (3) the omission of Dan; and (4) the inclusion of Levi. See Bauckham, *Climax of Prophecy*, 220–23; idem, "The List of the Tribes in Revelation 7 Again," *JSNT* 42 (1991): 99–115.

[6] E.g., in 5:5–6 John hears about the Lion of Judah, but he sees the Lamb who was slain.

interlude explicit by interjecting calls for encouragement (12:10–12), patient endurance (13:9–10), and the ultimate vindication of the believers (14:6–13).

The dragon (Satan) enlists the aid of two beasts in order to execute his war against believers (13:1–18). The beast from the sea represents the brute force of the political and military power of Rome (13:1–8). The beast from the land represents the religious institution that enforces the worship of the first beast (i.e., the imperial cult; 13:11–17). Together these three form an unholy trio, whereby the dragon, the sea beast, and the land beast function in a capacity similar to the three persons of the Godhead. Thus, 12:1–15:4 provides the basis and justification for the severity and finality of the judgments rendered on the inhabitants of the earth.

The seventh trumpet, comprising the third woe, signals the final consummation of God's judgment (11:15–19) by introducing the angels with the seven bowls filled with his wrath (15:5–8).

I. Final Investigative Judgments: The Seven Bowls (16:1–21) The seven bowls contain the wine of God's wrath poured out on the inhabitants of the earth. The objects of this wrath are specifically identified as everyone with the mark of the beast that worshipped his image (16:2). The seal judgments impacted a fourth of the earth and its population, the trumpets a third, but the bowls release the full fury of God's wrath in its entirety.

The first bowl inflicts all unbelievers (i.e., those with the mark of the beast) with ugly and painful sores. The second and third bowls transform all the oceans and fresh waters of the earth into putrid blood. The fourth bowl intensifies the power of the sun, scorching all flesh. The fifth and sixth are direct assaults against the beast's kingdom: a plague of darkness and preparation for the final battle of Armageddon. When the last bowl empties, God's retribution is complete (16:19) as affirmed in the judgment doxology (16:5–7).

IV. Vision Three (in the Desert): The Destruction of Babylon and the Return of Christ (17:1–21:8)

A. Transition: "Come, I Will Show You the Judgment of the Notorious Prostitute" (17:1–2) The last bowl completed the total outpouring of God's wrath, so that the third vision comprises an expanded and more detailed look at the final trial and sentencing of the prostitute city of Babylon. Thus, the third vision represents a different perspective on the final events briefly described during the trumpets and bowls. John metaphorically presents Rome as a prostitute seducing kings and nations into committing fornication with her, and he contrasts the destiny of the prostitute city Babylon with the bride city of the new Jerusalem.

The third vision exhibits five distinct movements: (1) Babylon introduced (17:3–18); (2) Babylon judged as the eschatological judgment of the nations (18:1–19:10); (3) the return of Christ as a divine warrior (19:11–21); and (4) the first and second resurrections as the eschatological judgment of individuals (20:1–15). After the final judgment, (5) the believers are introduced to their eternal reward (21:1–8).

B. The Prostitute City Babylon Described (17:3–6) John, once again, was carried away "in the Spirit" to a desert where he saw a great prostitute sitting astride the seven-headed beast and drunk on the blood of believers (17:3–6).

C. The Prostitute City Babylon as Rome (17:7–18) The woman personifies the city of Rome with her military might, opulence, and allurement, and in a broader sense the world system represented by all great earthly civilizations. By depicting her on the back of the beast, John demonstrates her dependence on and relationship with Satan's kingdom. He also underscores her political power, economic extravagance, and religious devotion. She enticed the earth's inhabitants to forsake truth, righteousness, and justice and to instead indulge in her flagrant adulteries consisting of idolatry, greed, and murder. For all of this she deserves judgment.

D. The Trial and Sentencing of Babylon (18:1–24) Having identified Babylon with Rome, John's tour of Babylon's judgment promised by the angel in 17:1 now comes into sharp focus. One salient feature of this entire scene is that John saturates this section with material drawn from OT prophetic oracles pertaining to the judgment of the historical Babylon. This interweaving of allusions creates the effect that Babylon's judgment represents the culmination of God's judgment against all pagan nations by way of military, political, and economic devastation. The verdict against Babylon is pronounced by an angel with great authority (18:1–3). The angel expresses the verdict in terms conveying the certainty of Babylon's destruction, although the judgment is still a future event from John's vantage point.

God holds Babylon responsible for indulging in sins pertaining to wine, wealth, and political power, thereby leading the nations astray from the true God and obedience to his righteous decrees. Once the verdict is announced, another voice from heaven commences with Babylon's sentencing. This is characterized by a series of imperatives that God has decreed for Babylon based on her sins and crimes (18:6–7). God administers justice through rendering judgment warranted by the crimes committed.

As the angels announce heavenly judgment and its causes, the kings, merchants, and mariners express an earthly response. Although Babylon seemed so strong, wealthy, and powerful, God easily brought about her collapse with his judicial verdict. Babylon's sentencing concludes with a symbolic act depicting her complete destruction along with a final reassertion of her indictment (18:21–24).

E. Heavenly Celebration of Babylon's Destruction (19:1–10) Now that God has declared his verdict, believers duly acknowledge him with the appropriate praise for his avenging justice (19:1–10; see 6:10; Deut 32:43).

F. The Divine Warrior and Final Tribunal (19:11–20:15) In 19:11–21 Jesus returns to earth to carry out the sentence against Babylon. He returns as the rightful King and divine Warrior in this Christological culmination of the book. Accompanied by his army of redeemed believers whom he has made to be his kingdom (see 1:6), he comes to dispense justice through judgment and salvation as made explicit by the white horse, multiple diadems, a scepter of iron, his blazing eyes, and the sword protruding from his mouth. One of the most graphic images depicting Jesus as the divine Warrior is his blood-soaked robe (19:13), red from treading the winepress of the fury of God's wrath (19:15).

Jesus is, therefore, the full revelation of the divine warrior from the OT who executes judgment against all the enemies of God and his people. The great and final battle constitutes a slaughter that ends just as soon as it begins (19:17–21). Despite the boasts of the beast and the false prophet, they are quickly captured and tossed immediately into the lake of fire (19:20). The rest of the combatants die instantly at the spoken word of Christ (19:21). Christ effectively conquered all other kingdoms of the earth and subsumed them under his kingdom now established on earth.

The destruction of Babylon pertains to the judgment of the nations corporately as a political entity, but God will also judge all people individually. Having established his kingdom through a military victory (19:20–21), he orders the dragon bound and imprisoned for the duration of a thousand years (20:1–3). The entire scene in 20:4–6 corresponds to Daniel 7:9–10 where the Ancient of Days holds court and books are opened for judgment, and Daniel 7:22–27 where he renders a favorable verdict for believers by giving them the kingdom. The judicial verdict awarded to individual believers includes the right to reign with Christ, which includes judicial authority over the earth during this thousand-year period. At the end of this period, Satan will instigate one final and futile battle where unredeemed humanity stages a coup against the Lord only to fail miserably.

The second resurrection (20:11–15) pertains to the individual judgment of all humanity. It constitutes the final judicial act of God before the complete renewal of the created order (i.e., the eschatological "age to come."). As the Judge enters the courtroom, all the dead must rise to face the accounting of their deeds. Books are opened as the primary evidence consulted during the investigative trial of every individual human all the way back to Adam. These books are the written records of each person's conduct.

G. The Renewal of Creation and the Arrival of the New Jerusalem (21:1–8) Each individual is judged according to his or her works. These works include attitudes of the heart such as cowardice, unbelief, and moral corruption, as well as actions such as murder, sexual immorality, sorcery or witchcraft, idolatry, and lying (21:8). No one will escape the consequences of their guilt, and the lost will subsequently share the same fate as the dragon (Satan), the beast, and the false prophet in the lake of fire (20:14). The only hope for salvation is whether a person's name is written in the Lamb's book of life (20:14).

V. Vision Four (on a Mountain): Believers' Reward and the Renewal of Creation (21:9–22:5)

A. Transition: "Come, I Will Show You the Bride" (21:9–10) The final vision commences in 21:9–10 when another angel holding one of the seven bowls invites John to see the bride of the Lamb and then John is carried away "in the Spirit" to a high mountain. It constitutes an expanded presentation of the new Jerusalem introduced in 21:1–8. This vision functions as the antithesis of the prostitute city Babylon and presents the glorified church as the bride city of the new Jerusalem. The purpose is to contrast the fate of Babylon with the glory of the new Jerusalem in which believers receive their ultimate vindication and eternal reward. This vision falls into two divisions that describe the Holy City as an eternal holy of holies (21:9–27) and then as a new Eden (22:1–5).[278]

B. The Description of the New Jerusalem Descending from Heaven (21:11–27) The bride city descends from heaven, shining with God's glory and bedecked with precious stones. It has twelve gates named after the twelve patriarchs and twelve foundation stones named after the twelve apostles (21:12–14). The city's measurements indicate that it is a perfect cube of immense proportions. Thus, the new Jerusalem resembles the holy of holies where God dwells with his people in absolute splendor and purity.

C. The Paradise of God: The Renewal of Creation (22:1–5) What is more, "the river of the water of life" flows from the throne of the Lamb and waters "the tree of life," lining the streets of the new Jerusalem. In the eternal and Eden-like paradise, God and humanity dwell together in perfect harmony, for the curse is no more.

VI. Epilogue (22:6–21)

The interpreting angel affirms the truthfulness of the words of the prophecy because it has been authorized by God. John continued with a series of testimonies submitted as forensic verification for the churches. First, John testifies that he has presented an eyewitness account of what he has seen and heard (22:8–11). Second, Jesus testifies that he is coming soon to reward the righteous and punish the wicked (22:12–16). The third testimony comes from the Spirit and the bride (22:17), which probably refers to the Holy Spirit through the church as a prophetic witness (see 19:10). John solemnly warns against any tampering with his vision by invoking the legal consequences of altering a covenant document (22:18–19; see Deut 4:2). John concludes with a final testimony by Jesus who affirms that he is coming soon (22:20). These four testimonies constitute the strongest way to validate the truth of his vision by using legal categories.

THEOLOGY

Theological Themes[279]

The Sovereignty of God The prominent depiction of God as the Creator of the universe, who sits enthroned in heaven and reigns over all people, beings, events, and the

---

[278] Osborne, *Revelation*, 604.

[279] For recent work in the theology of Revelation, see Bandy, *Theology of Revelation*; G. K. Beale, "Revelation (Book)," in *NDBT*, 356–63; L. A. Brighton, "Christological Trinitarian Theology in the Book of Revelation," *Concordia Journal* 34 (2008): 292–97; L. R. Helyer, *The Witness of Jesus, Paul and John: An Exploration in Biblical Theology* (Downers Grove, IL: InterVarsity, 2008), 309–77; I. H. Marshall, *New Testament Theology: Many Witnesses, One Gospel* (Downers Grove, IL: InterVarsity, 2004), 548–78; F. J. Matera, *New Testament Theology: Exploring Diversity and Unity* (Louisville, KY: Westminster John Knox, 2007), 400–422; Rainbow, *Johannine Theology*; U. Schnelle, *Theology of the New Testament*, trans. M. E. Boring (Grand Rapids, MI: Baker, 2009), 751–72; F. Thielman, *Theology of the New Testament* (Grand Rapids, MI: Zondervan, 2005), 612–50. Note also R. Bauckham, *The Theology of the Book of Revelation* (Cambridge, UK: Cambridge University Press, 1993); M. E. Boring, "The Theology of Revelation: 'The Lord Our God the Almighty Reigns,'" *Int* 40 (1986): 257–69. From the perspective of theological interpretation, note F. A. Murphy, "Revelation, Book of," in *Dictionary for Theological Interpretation of the Bible*, ed. K. J. Vanhoozer (Grand Rapids, MI: Baker, 2005), 680–87; M. M. Thompson,

cosmos makes his sovereignty a central theme of the book of Revelation. God's sovereignty over creation, events, and history is depicted in three distinct ways throughout: (1) in designations of divine names, titles, and attributions; (2) in depictions of the heavenly throne room and God's throne; and (3) in displays of God's actions through decrees and judgments. The emphasis on God's sovereignty, a common characteristic of prophetic and apocalyptic writings, functions to remind readers that God is in control of all their circumstances and that they may confidently trust him.

From the outset God is unambiguously identified as the ultimate sovereign ruler of the universe (1:8). This verse contains three of the four most significant designations for God in Revelation: "the Alpha and Omega"; "the One who is, who was, and who is coming"; and "the Almighty."[280] "Alpha and Omega" stems from the first letter (alpha) and last letter (omega) of the Greek alphabet; it is equivalent to "I am the A to Z" in English. The title indicates that God is the origin and goal of all history because he precedes all creation and will bring everything to its eschatological fulfillment (see Isa 44:6).[281] It is used interchangeably of God the Father (1:8; 21:6) and of Jesus (22:13; see 1:17), suggesting that they share in the sovereign administration over the affairs of human history.

God as "the one who is, who was, and who is coming" (1:4, 8; 4:8; 11:17; 16:5) constitutes an interpreted expansion of the divine name YHWH (see Exod 3:14) and stresses his eternal presence in relationship to the world.[282] God is now; he has always been; and he will come in the future when he dramatically brings about the consummation of the ages (11:17; 16:5). The third designation for God as "the Almighty" (1:8; 4:8; 11:17; 15:3; 16:7, 14; 19:6, 15; 21:22) associates him with the "Lord of Hosts" in the OT, emphasizing his omnipotent power and unrivaled authority.[283] The fourth designation asserting God's sovereignty is that he is addressed as "the one sitting on the throne" (4:9; 5:1, 7, 13; 6:16; 7:15; 21:5).[284]

The image of God seated on his throne in chapters 4–5 introduces the second way in which God's sovereignty is depicted throughout John's visions.[285] In 4:1–2 the scene is radically transformed from the barren and rocky isle of Patmos into the heavenly throne room. John described God as infinitely majestic and as gloriously enthroned and surrounded by his courtiers. The first thing John saw upon his entrance through the open door is a throne

---

"Reading What Is Written in the Book of Life: Theological Interpretation of the Book of Revelation Today," in *Revelation and the Politics of Apocalyptic Interpretation*, ed. R. B. Hays and S. Alkier (Waco, TX: Baylor University Press, 2012), 155–71.

[280] Bauckham, *Theology of the Book of Revelation*, 25.

[281] Ibid., 27.

[282] Ibid., 28–30.

[283] Boring, "Theology of Revelation," 259–63.

[284] Bauckham, *Theology of the Book of Revelation*, 31.

[285] For the theological significance of the image of the throne, see Beale, "Revelation (Book)," 356–57. Note further L. Gallusz, *The Throne Motif in the Book of Revelation*, LNTS 487 (London, England: Bloomsbury T&T Clark, 2014), who argues that "the throne motif constitutes the major, though not the only, interpretive key to the complex structure and theology" of Revelation (10).

centrally located in heaven (4:2). God's throne occupies the central location in a series of concentric circles, depicting his sovereignty over the cosmos.

In order to describe his visions, John drew from other familiar prophetic visions involving theophanies of the throne of God (e.g., Ezek 1:5, 10, 18, 22). He briefly remarks on how the One on the throne resembles gemstones like jasper, carnelian, and a halo-like emerald rainbow encircling his throne.[286] Once John establishes the fact that God Almighty sits securely enthroned in heaven, the throne shifts into the background throughout the rest of the vision (6:16; 7:9–17; 8:3; 11:16; 14:3; 16:17; 19:4–5) until it descends from heaven when he comes in judgment to establish his dwelling on earth (20:11–12; 21:3–5).[287]

The sovereignty of God over creation, events, and history is also displayed through his decrees and acts of judgment. God as the Creator is the One who decrees the course and timing of all events while he governs from his throne in heaven. His activity is most apparent in the six scenes revolving around the heavenly throne room and followed by ensuing judgments on the earth. The judgments produced on the earth by the seals, trumpets, and bowls represent a direct outworking of the proceedings in the divine courtroom.

God is the One who judges humanity (11:18; 18:8; 19:11; 20:12–13), and his judgment is swift, severe, and just (14:7; 16:7; 18:10; 19:2). God's activity is sometimes passive (as indicated by the frequent use of the divine passive verb *edothē*, "it was given").[288] He commissions some agents for the purpose of rendering judgments (e.g., the four horsemen and angels) and allows forces of evil to perform certain deeds (e.g., the beast). The fact that God is in control of everything, including the woes of both believers and unbelievers, powerfully reinforces the purpose of Revelation: to encourage believers in their faith in the midst of suffering.[289]

The Second Coming of Christ The book of Revelation is about Jesus.[290] It climaxes in its depiction of the second coming of Christ, showing that Jesus, the victorious Lamb of

---

[286] These iridescent stones also adorn the new Jerusalem that is bedecked with all kinds of precious materials, indicating that the entire city radiates with God's glory (21:11–23); see Aune, *Revelation 1–5*, 285.

[287] John's vision of the heavenly throne room offers an apocalyptic perspective contrasting imperial pretensions assuming cosmic sovereignty with the true King and Judge of the universe; see Aune, "Influence of Roman Imperial Court Ceremonial," 5–26.

[288] Osborne, *Revelation*, 32.

[289] Beale, "Revelation," 357.

[290] It makes important contributions to the Christology of the NT. Recent works in this vein include F. Bovon, "Christ in the Book of Revelation," in *New Testament and Christian Apocrypha*, ed. G. E. Snyder (Grand Rapids, MI: Baker, 2011), 76–90; R. B. Hays, "Faithful Witness, Alpha and Omega: The Identity of Jesus in the Apocalypse of John," in *The Reality of Apocalypse: Rhetoric and Politics in the Book of Revelation*, SBLSymS 39, ed. D. L. Barr (Atlanta, GA: SBL, 2006), 69–83; M. R. Hoffmann, *The Destroyer and the Lamb: The Relationship Between Angelomorphic and Lamb Christology in the Book of Revelation*, WUNT 2/203 (Tübingen, Germany: Mohr Siebeck, 2005); K. Huber, "Jesus Christus—der Erste und der Letzte: zur Christologie der Johannesapokalypse," in *Die Johannesapokalypse: Kontexte—Konzepte—Rezeption*, ed. J. Frey, J. A. Kelhoffer, and F. Tóth, WUNT 287 (Tübingen, Germany: Mohr Siebeck, 2012), 435–72; L. J. Johns, *The Lamb Christology of the Apocalypse of John: An Investigation into Its Origins and Rhetorical Force*, WUNT 2/167 (Tübingen, Germany: Mohr Siebeck, 2003). Note also the older but valuable D. Guthrie, "The Christology of Revelation," in *Jesus of Nazareth: Lord*

God and Lion of Judah, will return to earth as the eschatological Judge of all humanity and as the Davidic King. Indeed, Jesus Christ is the primary subject of John's revelation (1:1), and his return to earth as the victorious messianic King is the object (1:7). Revelation 1:7 represents a conflation of Daniel 7:13 and Zechariah 12:10 and provides the thesis statement for the entire book. The conflation of these two OT passages reflects the eschatological expectation that Christ will return, bringing both salvation and judgment.[291]

John identifies Jesus as the glorious Son of Man, who receives judicial authority over all the nations, as well as the pierced Son, whose appearance will strike terror among the enemies of God. The exalted status of Christ and his role as the eschatological Judge is predicated on the titles explicitly applied to him. For example, the title "the First and the Last" designates Christ as the beginning and the end of history (1:17). It closely parallels the title "the Alpha and Omega" used for God the Father (1:8; 21:6).

The title "First and Last," when applied to Christ, resounds with theological significance because it is drawn from Isaiah 44:6 and 48:12 where Yahweh is identified as the Creator and Redeemer. Its application to Christ in this passage suggests a high Christology. What is more, the book of Revelation prophetically portrays the glorified and exalted Christ as the eschatological Judge and King by way of three Christophanies (1:12–18; 5:1–14; 19:11–21).

The Christophany of Revelation 1 presents Jesus as the faithful witness; the proto-martyr; the firstborn from the dead, who is preeminent in his church; and the ruler of the kings of the earth, thus fulfilling Jewish messianic expectations (see 1:5). John's ensuing visionary description of the Son of Man in 1:12–18 highlights certain characteristics of his appearance, borrowing images from a variety of OT texts, all of which emphasize his judicial role.[292]

The Christophany of chapter 5 presents Jesus as the Lion (5:5; see Gen 49:9) turned Lamb (see 1:5–7; 12:11; 13:8; etc.), an image that combines paschal imagery with the notion of the warrior-lamb prominent in apocalyptic literature.[293] The purpose of this scene is to depict the installment of Christ as the Davidic King and eschatological Judge who is the only one worthy to unleash the judgments of God on humanity. This scene

---

and Christ: Essays on the Historical Jesus and New Testament Christology, ed. J. B. Green and M. Turner (Grand Rapids, MI: Eerdmans, 1994), 397–409.

[291] Beale, *Book of Revelation*, 196; see Mounce, *Book of Revelation*, 73.

[292] As Caird (*Revelation of St. John*, 25–26) rightly noted, one must not simply compile a list of allusions so as to "unweave the rainbow" because John painted a composite portrait rather than a piecemeal collage. Against Beale (*Book of Revelation*, 220), who called Rev 1:12–20 a *midrash* (commentary) on Daniel 7 and 10; see the critique by Aune, *Revelation 1–5*, 74.

[293] See, e.g., *1 Enoch* 90:9–12; *T. Jos.* 19:8; *T. Benj.* 3:8. For helpful studies of Jesus as the Lamb in Revelation, see L. L. Johns, *The Lamb Christology of the Apocalypse of John: An Investigation into Its Origins and Rhetorical Force*, WUNT 2/167 (Tübingen, Germany: Mohr Siebeck, 2003); P. Stuhlmacher, "Das Lamm Gottes—eine Skizze," in *Geschichte–Tradition–Reflexion*, 529–42.

represents the inauguration of Jesus's eternal reign at the right hand of God, also known as his enthronement.[294]

Apart from the Christophany of Revelation 1 and the image of the lion turned lamb, perhaps the most powerful depiction of Christ in Revelation is that of the rider on a white horse, the One who is called "faithful" and "true" (chap. 19). In the Christological culmination of the book, Jesus returns as the rightful King and divine warrior.[295] The imagery of riding a white horse was the common Roman symbol of the emperor who triumphed over his enemies.[296] The diadems on his head demonstrate that his cosmic sovereignty surpasses all other pretentious earthly claims to a throne (see 12:3; 13:1).[297]

Christ comes accompanied by an army of redeemed believers whom he has made to be his kingdom (see 1:6).[298] The fact that he will rule over his domain with a scepter of iron indicates that he is the true messianic King (see Ps 2:9; Isa 11:4). The name engraved on his thigh attests that he is the supreme King and Lord over all (19:16; see 1:5; 17:14). Christ comes to wage a just war against the beast's kingdom to exact vengeance for the unjust war waged against believers (13:7). Two images from the inaugural vision of Christ reappear to denote judicial insight (blazing eyes) and pronouncements (sword out of mouth; see *4 Ezra* 13:9–13).

Jesus is also depicted as the divine warrior whose robe is soaked with blood from treading the winepress of the fury of God's wrath.[299] The blood on Jesus's robe is that of his victims (see Isa 63:2–6). The great and final battle constitutes a slaughter that ends just as soon as it begins (19:17–21). The beast and the earth's kings amass their forces in a deluded attempt to attack the coming King (see 16:13–16).[300] Despite the boasts of the beast and the false prophet, they are quickly captured and tossed into the lake of fire (19:20); the rest die instantly at the spoken word of Christ (19:21). Christ thus effectively conquers all the kingdoms of the earth and subjects them to his own rule.

Theodicy Theodicy pertains to the justification of God concerning "the seeming triumph of the wicked and the suffering of the innocent."[301] As J. L. Mangina rightly notes, "Apocalyptic literature is always a theodicy literature, not in the sense of providing a

---

[294] On the enthronement of Christ, see Gallusz, *Throne Motif*, 142–75; Holtz, *Christologie*, 27–54; Swete, *Revelation*, 121–27; Roloff, *Revelation*, 72–73; Aune, *Revelation 1–5*, 332–35; R. Stefanović, *The Background and Meaning of the Sealed Book of Revelation 5*, AUSDDS 22 (Berrien Springs, MI: Andrews University Press, 1996), 206–17.

[295] Osborne, *Revelation*, 678–79.

[296] Aune, *Revelation 17–22*, 1050–51.

[297] Caird, *Revelation to St. John*, 241; G. A. Krodel, *Revelation* (Minneapolis, MN: Augsburg, 1989), 321; Beale, *Book of Revelation*, 954.

[298] Although believers come as a messianic army, Christ alone executes the battle.

[299] Revelation 19:13, 15; cf. 14:19–20. See also Joel 3:12–13; *1 Enoch* 100:3; *4 Ezra* 15:35–36. Cf. Aune, *Revelation 6–16*, 847; Bauckham, *Climax of Prophecy*, 40–48.

[300] See Ps 2:1–3; Ezek 38:14–16; 39:1–6; Joel 3:2; Zech 12:1–9; 14:2; cf. *1 Enoch* 56:5–6; 90:13–19; 99:4; *2 Bar.* 48:37; 70:7; *4 Ezra* 13:33–38; *Jub.* 23:23; *Sib. Or.* 3.663–68; *Pss. Sol.* 2:1–2; 17:22–23; 1QM 1:10–11. Cf. Aune, *Revelation 17–22*, 1064.

[301] G. R. Osborne, "Theodicy in the Apocalypse," *TrinJ* 14 NS (1993): 63.

theoretical explanation for evil, but in the sense of offering a vision that sees beyond the horrors of 'the present evil age.'"[302] The unfolding visions of the book of Revelation, therefore, illustrate the apocalyptic reality that while the righteous indeed suffer unjustly at the hands of the wicked, they will have their day in court when God's verdict results in a grand reversal of this present world's order.[303]

Theodicy represents an important theme in Revelation that conveys the justice and mercy of God.[304] The request of the martyrs directly addresses the question of justice: "Lord, the one who is holy and true, how long until you judge those who live on the earth and avenge our blood?" (6:10). This request for vindication echoes the sentiments of generations of God's servants who suffered unjustly while the wicked appeared unpunished.

The OT features the same inquiry as to when God will take judicial action vindicating the mistreatment of his people (e.g., Pss 79:5–10; 94:1–3).[305] The concern is not why evil exists in the world or why Christians suffer in general but specifically why they are suffering as a consequence of their faithfulness to Christ and their obedience to the righteous requirements of God's law. John's visions seek to answer this query by demonstrating that God will render true justice in a world filled with evil and injustice.

The trial and sentencing of Babylon illustrate how the concern for justice intersects with God's answer to the martyrs' plea for vindication. In 18:6–7a God decreed to judge Babylon based on her sins and crimes.[306] Some undesignated agents of God's vengeance (possibly glorified believers) will carry out the principle of "an eye for an eye, a tooth for a tooth" *(lex talionis)* and divine retribution.[307] The justice of the sentence is demonstrated

---

[302] J. L. Mangina, "God, Israel, and Ecclesia in the Apocalypse," in *Revelation and the Politics of Apocalyptic Interpretation*, ed. R. B. Hays and S. Alkier (Waco, TX: Baylor University Press, 2012), 85.

[303] Note also the recent treatment of G. Stevenson, *A Slaughtered Lamb: Revelation and the Apocalyptic Response to Evil and Suffering* (Abilene, TX: Abilene Christian University Press, 2013). Stevenson highlights the causal connection between faithful witness and suffering in Revelation, emphasizing God's goodness and sovereignty. While evil and suffering are an unavoidable component of life, God's response is found in the slaughtered Lamb, in whom God has joined with his people in their suffering. "The image of the slaughtered Lamb teaches us that life is about more than the body and that the suffering and hardship we may face in no way nullifies the love of God nor his faithful activity on our behalf," and "above all . . . that suffering concludes with resurrection" (p. 267).

[304] Osborne, "Theodicy," 77.

[305] Cf. D. A. Carson, *How Long, O Lord? Reflections on Suffering and Evil*, 2nd ed. (Grand Rapids, MI: Baker, 2006); J. N. Day, *Crying for Justice* (Grand Rapids, MI: Kregel, 2005), 107; E. Nardoni, *Rise Up, O Judge: A Study of Justice in the Biblical World*, trans. S. C. Martin (Peabody, MA: Hendrickson, 2004), 123.

[306] Osborne, *Revelation*, 640.

[307] Mounce, *Book of Revelation*, 325; Prigent, *Commentary on the Apocalypse*, 504. Against Aune (*Revelation 17–22*, 994), who made a strong case for taking "my people" as the most logical subject for the verbs commanding retributive justice, though viewing believers as the agents of this divine judgment seems unlikely. See the OT and Second Temple references in ibid., 993.

in that each command stems as a direct result of Babylon's action.[308] Babylon unjustly condemned believers to death, and now God justly condemns her accordingly.[309]

Witness The concept of "witness" has significant practical implications for the church (e.g., 1:2, 5, 9). Based on early church usage coupled with the close association between witness and execution in Revelation, some have argued that a martyrological connotation is intended in Revelation.[310] But many commentators reject the use of *martus* in the technical sense of a martyr.[311] Since execution is always subsequent to the witness as a penalty, one should separate death from the actual testimony of the witness (1:9; 2:13; 6:9; 11:7; 12:11; 20:4). Thus, the witness terminology of the book is best understood as forensic declarations of what is true.[312]

The book begins and ends with the affirmation that all that is recorded constitutes a testimony (1:2; 22:16, 18, 20). Jesus is twice called a "faithful witness" (1:5; 3:14), and witness terminology is also applied to Antipas, who was executed because of his faith in Christ (2:13).[313] The term *martyria* ("testimony") occurs most often denoting the contents of the witness that was maintained. Many of the instances of "testimony" are followed by persecution (1:9; 6:9; 11:7; 12:11; 20:4). Witness terminology occurs regularly throughout the book, demonstrating that this is a prominent theme—especially as it pertains to the churches.[314]

---

308 See Ps 137:8; Isa 40:2; Jer 50:29. The language of "paying back double" constitutes a metaphor for rendering a full recompense or requital. See Osborne, *Revelation*, 641; Beckwith, *Apocalypse of John*, 715; Mounce, *Book of Revelation*, 325; Prigent, *Commentary on the Apocalypse*, 504. Against Morris, *Revelation*, 217.

309 Caird, *Revelation of St. John*, 227–48.

310 P. Vassiliadis, "The Translation of *Martyria Iēsou* in Revelation," *BT* 36 (1985): 132–33; T. W. Manson, "Martyrs and Martyrdom," *BJRL* 39 (1956–57): 464; E. Lohmeyer, "Die Idee des Martyriums im Judentum und Urchristentum," *ZST* 5 (1928): 232–49; N. Brox, *Zeuge und Märtyrer: Untersuchungen zur frühchristlichen Zeugnis-Terminologie*, SANT 5 (Munich, Germany: Kösel, 1961); A. Satake, *Die Gemeindeordnung in der Johannesapokalypse* (Neukirchen-Vluyn, Germany: Neukirchener, 1966), 97–119; tentatively Ladd, *Revelation*, 47; Aune, *Revelation 1–5*, 37–38; O. K. Peters, *The Mandate of the Church in the Apocalypse of John*, SBL 77 (New York, NY: P. Lang, 2005), 77–118.

311 Beale, *Book of Revelation*, 190; Osborne, *Revelation*, 62; Swete, *Apocalypse of St. John*, 35; Ford, *Revelation*, 374; Mounce, *Book of Revelation*, 70. The best study of "witness" terminology in Revelation is A. A. Trites, "'Μάρτυς' and Martyrdom in the Apocalypse: A Semantic Study," *NovT* 15 (1973): 72–80. Cf. idem, "Witness, Testimony," *NIDNTT* 3:1,038–50; H. Strathmann, "μάρτυς, μαρτυρέω, κτλ.," *TDNT* 4:474–514; Mazzaferri, *Genre*, 306–10; idem, "*Martyria Iēsou* Revisited," 114–22; B. Dehandschutter, "The Meaning of Witness in the Apocalypse," in *L'Apocalypse johannique*, 283–88; P. Ellingworth, "The *Martyria* Debate," *BT* 41 (1990): 138–39.

312 For two recent essays, see J. W. van Henten, "The Concept of Martyrdom in Revelation," and R. Bergmeier, "Zeugnis und Martyrium," in *Die Johannesapokalypse: Kontexte—Konzepte—Rezeption*, ed. J. Frey, J. A. Kelhoffer, and F. Tóth, WUNT 287 (Tübingen, Germany: Mohr Siebeck, 2012), 589–618, 619–47.

313 M. G. Reddish, "Followers of the Lamb: Role Models in the Book of Revelation," *PRSt* 40 (2013): 65–79, shows that John encourages "unyielding allegiance to God"—particularly as shown in witness—by setting forth various "models of obedience and faithfulness," including not only Jesus and Antipas but also John himself, the 144,000 (7:1–8; 14:1–5), the great multitude (7:9), the two witnesses (chap. 11), those who conquer (2:7, 11, 17, 26; 3:5, 12, 21), the bride of the Lamb (chap. 19), and the martyrs who reign with Christ (20:4).

314 Blount (*Revelation*, 13–14) argues that John's readers were largely "passing themselves off as every other emperor-worshipping, meat-sacrificed-to-pagan-gods-eating Greco-Roman," and not maintaining the active witness which allegiance to Christ required. "They had allowed their world to believe that they were as Greco-Roman as everybody else. John wants them to self-declare that they believed not in the lordship of Rome, its gods, its social, political, and economic infrastructure,

Christians should expect persecutions and hardships as a consequence of living for Jesus. The reason believers are rejected is because they are citizens of God's kingdom (1:6; 5:10). Revelation envisions the eschatological consummation of Christ's kingdom (11:15; 12:10), which is placed in juxtaposition to the Satanic kingdom of this world (16:10; 17:12, 17–18). As members of Christ's kingdom, believers are exhorted to endure unjust suffering because their vindication will come when Christ's kingdom is visibly established on earth. Thus, endurance constitutes the chief virtue for believers during times of hardship and oppression (1:9; 2:2–3, 19; 3:10; 13:10; 14:12–13).

The testimony of faithful endurance in the face of unjust suffering also conveys an evangelistic concern, and the witness of believers is the prerequisite for the conversion of the nations.[315] At this climax of prophecy, suffering and martyrdom are placed in an eternal perspective, with Jesus serving as the prime witness and proto-martyr (1:5; 3:14; see 11:3; 14:6; 17:6; 19:11; 22:16, 20). Thus, "witness" terminology involves not mere indifference to the world's fate but the proclamation of a divine message (see 14:6). Exhortations to repent for five of the seven churches, or individuals in them, clearly indicate that the seer still allowed room for conversions (2:5, 16, 21–22; 3:3, 19).[316]

Worship of the One True God Versus Idolatry The book of Revelation is supremely concerned with the difference between true and false worship.[317] One may unequivocally state that, except for Hebrews, Revelation is the most liturgical book of the NT.[318] When dealing with other religions, this book is extremely relevant regarding the nature and proper object of worship as well as regarding the meaning of martyrdom and the believer's future hope. According to the author of Revelation, ultimately Satan himself stands behind the forces conspiring against Christians. Worship resides at the center of the battle between believers and Satan as it is played out in the arena of the imperial cult versus fidelity to Christ.

References to the imperial cult occur frequently in the latter half of the second vision (13:4, 15–16; 14:9–11; 15:2; 16:2; see 20:4).[319] John envisions a time when the imperial

---

nor its emperor, but in the lordship of Jesus Christ"—and John himself was their model, having been exiled to Patmos because of his witness of Christ.

[315] See A. J. Köstenberger, "The Contribution of the General Epistles and Revelation to a Biblical Theology of Religions," in *Christianity and the Religions: A Biblical Theology of World Religions*, ed. E. Rommen and H. Netland, EMS Series 2 (Pasadena, CA: William Carey Library, 1995), 133–35, with reference to Bauckham, *Climax of Prophecy*, 238–337.

[316] See Osborne, "Theodicy," 63–77; A. Y. Collins, "Persecution and Vengeance in the Book of Revelation," in *Apocalypticism in the Mediterranean World and the Near East*, 729–30.

[317] See Köstenberger, "The Contribution of the General Epistles and Revelation," 133–35.

[318] J. M. Ford, "The Christological Function of the Hymns in the Apocalypse of John," *AUSS* 36 (1998): 207.

[319] After evaluating the data vis-à-vis the imperial cult in four of the seven cities of Revelation 2–3 (Ephesus, Smyrna, Pergamum, Laodicea), K. Cukrowski ("The Influence of the Emperor Cult on the Book of Revelation," *ResQ* 45 [2003]: 51–64) concludes, "In general, the threat of death because of the emperor cult seems *overestimated*, while the influence on the emperor cult on the daily life of early Christians is *underestimated*" (emphasis original). For other recent discussion, see J. Frey, "The Relevance of the Roman Imperial Cult for the Book of Revelation: Exegetical and Hermeneutical Reflections on the Relation Between the Seven Letters and the Visionary Main Part of the Book," in *The New Testament and Early*

Something to Think About: What Goes Around Comes Around

Many of us can identify with the experience of the psalmist who wrote, "But as for me, my feet almost slipped; my steps nearly went astray. For I envied the arrogant; I saw the prosperity of the wicked" (Ps 73:2–3). Indeed, when we look at this world where hardworking teachers command only a basic salary—though they are trying to be content and make ends meet as best they can—while celebrity athletes make millions. Who can blame the psalmist for being tempted to envy the arrogant when he saw their prosperity? Does God care about such inequality? How can he reward the arrogant and overlook the plight of those who fear him?

The problem with this analysis, of course, is that it is premature. Only fools arrive at a final determination of a matter without waiting for its ultimate outcome. This is where the book of Revelation comes in. In the sweep of biblical revelation, this book tells us what this final outcome is going to be from God's perspective. Many biblical interpreters believe Revelation contains four visions (indicated by the phrase "in the Spirit" in 1:10; 4:2; 17:3; and 21:10): (1) the risen Christ and his message to the seven churches (chaps. 1–3); (2) the throne room vision (chaps. 4–16); (3) the prostitute Babylon (chaps. 17–20); and (4) the new Jerusalem (chaps. 21–22). It is no coincidence that of these four, the second one, which has to do with the judgment of the world, is by far the most extended. The end is the time of God's judgment when all people will receive their due.

In graphic detail Revelation depicts the vindication of God's righteous purposes (called "theodicy," from theos, *"God," and* dikaios, *"righteous") and of believers, especially those martyred for their faith. This will also be the time when the arrogant and the wicked, those without Christ, will be judged, as well as Satan and his fallen angels. For this reason, as the angel in the last vision told the seer, "Let him who does wrong continue to do wrong; let him who is vile continue to be vile; let him who does right continue to do right; and let him who is holy continue to be holy" (22:11 NIV), for in the end everyone will surely receive his just reward. For this reason, let us not judge a matter before its end; instead, let us entrust ourselves to God who one day soon will make all things right. "'Vengeance belongs to me; I will repay,' says the Lord" (Rom 12:19, citing Deut 32:35).*

cult escalates to a point of mandatory participation by all inhabitants of earth.[320] While not identical in every respect, there will be a future time of persecution that will involve the inappropriate worship of an earthly political ruler in a manner reminiscent of the imperial cult of ancient Rome. The term *proskyneō* ("worship") is used in direct connection with the

Christian Literature in Greco-Roman Context: Studies in Honor of David E. Aune, ed. J. Fotopoulos, NovTSup 122 (Leiden, Netherlands: Brill, 2006), 231–55.

[320] See deSilva, "The 'Image of the Beast' and the Christians in Asia Minor," 197–201.

beast (13:4, 8, 12, 15). It was also a term commonly employed in the imperial cult.[321] Christians refusing to bow down in worship to the beast incur his wrath and are summarily executed (13:15); they are also exhorted to remain faithful and true to Christ even if it results in death (2:10, 13; 13:10; 14:12; 17:14). God will vindicate them by judging all those who worshipped the beast (14:9, 11; 16:2).

The book of Revelation strongly promotes abstinence from all forms of idolatry because God alone is worthy of worship (4:11; 5:2, 4, 9, 12). Exclusive worship of God constitutes the major theological imperatives for Christians as well as for all humanity (9:20; 14:7; 15:4; 19:10; 22:9). Revelation 19:10 is paralleled in 22:8–9 where the angel who refused to be worshipped identified himself as a "fellow servant" with John and with "your brothers the prophets and those who keep the words of this book. Worship God!"[322] In the end the dragon and all his followers will face God's righteous wrath because of their sin, their mistreatment of God's people, and their failure to worship God (18:19–24; 19:1–3; 22:9).

The two final visions serve to contrast the fate of those who worship the beast with the glory awaiting the followers of the Lamb.[323] Christian commitment is not merely a system of beliefs to be upheld but an allegiance to be maintained in the face of constant opportunities for compromise. This is indeed a timely message in the post-Christian West at the beginning of the third millennium where (according to Francis Schaeffer's prophetic words) personal peace and affluence reign—even in segments of the evangelical subculture.

CONTRIBUTION TO THE CANON

- The worship of God and of Jesus Christ (e.g., chap. 4)
- The revelation of the future by the Lamb who was slain, the Lion of Judah (5:1–7)
- The need for uncompromising faithfulness to Christ through patient endurance (e.g., 14:12)
- The vindication of God's righteousness (theodicy) and of believers who suffer persecution by the hands of the unbelieving world (chaps. 6–18)
- The glorious return of Jesus as the supreme King and Lord (19:11–16)
- The millennial reign of Christ, the defeat of Satan, and the Great White Throne judgment (chap. 20)
- The restoration of all things in the new heaven and the new earth (chaps. 21–22)

STUDY QUESTIONS

1. Who are the three major candidates for the authorship of Revelation? Which is most likely?

---

[321] Dio Cassius, *Hist.* 59.24.4; Philo, *Leg.* 116; Aune, *Revelation 6–16*, 741.

[322] Bauckham (*Theology of the Book of Revelation*, 120) noted the parallel with Moses's encounter with Pharaoh and his magicians and Elijah's conflict with Jezebel and the prophets of Baal.

[323] B. R. Rossing, *The Choice Between Two Cities: Whore, Bride, and Empire in the Apocalypse*, HTS (Philadelphia, PA: Trinity Press International, 1999), 14–15.

2. What are the two major alternatives for the time of Revelation's composition?
3. What date is favored by the internal evidence?
4. What date is favored by the external evidence?
5. What are some of the major pieces of internal evidence that have a bearing on the date of Revelation?
6. What were the occasion and purpose of the book of Revelation?
7. Define *apocalypse*. What are some of its accompanying traits?
8. How many visions are recorded in Revelation, and what phrase indicates a new vision?
9. What are the respective locations of these visions, and what is the range of chapters for each vision in the book of Revelation?
10. What are the three primary theories of relating the seals, trumpets, and bowls in Revelation?
11. What are four primary approaches to the study of the book of Revelation? Briefly describe each in one or two sentences.
12. What contributions does Revelation make to the canon?

FOR FURTHER STUDY

Aune, D. E. "The Apocalypse of John and the Problem of Genre." *Semeia* 36 (1986): 65–96.

________. *Revelation.* 3 vols. Word Biblical Commentary 52. Nashville, TN: Thomas Nelson, 1997, 1998.

Bandstra, A. J. "A Kingship and Priests: Inaugurated Eschatology in the Apocalypse." *Calvin Theological Journal* 27 (1992): 10–25.

Bandy, A. S. *A Theology of Revelation.* Biblical Theology of the New Testament. Grand Rapids, MI: Zondervan, forthcoming.

Barr, D. L. *Reading the Book of Revelation: A Resource for Students.* Resources for Biblical Study 44. Atlanta, GA: Society of Biblical Literature, 2003.

Bauckham, R. *The Climax of Prophecy: Studies on the Book of Revelation.* London, England: T&T Clark, 1993.

________. *The Theology of the Book of Revelation.* New Testament Theology. Cambridge, UK: Cambridge University Press, 1993.

Beagley, A. J. *The* "Sitz im Leben" *of the Apocalypse, with Particular Reference to the Role of the Church's Enemies.* Beihefte zur neutestamentlichen Wissenschaft 50. Berlin, Germany: de Gruyter, 1987.

Beale, G. K. *The Book of Revelation.* New International Greek Testament Commentary. Grand Rapids, MI: Eerdmans, 1999.

________. *John's Use of the Old Testament in Revelation.* Journal for the Study of the New Testament Supplement Series 166. Sheffield, UK: Sheffield Academic, 1998.

________, and S. M. McDonough. "Revelation." Pages 1,081–1,161 in *Commentary on the New Testament Use of the Old Testament.* Ed. by G. K. Beale and D. A. Carson. Grand Rapids, MI: Baker, 2007.

Blaising, C. A., and D. L. Bock. *Progressive Dispensationalism.* Grand Rapids, MI: Baker, 1993.

Blount, B. K. *Revelation: A Commentary.* New Testament Library. Louisville, KY: Westminster John Knox, 2009.

Campbell, W. G. *Reading Revelation: A Thematic Approach*. Cambridge, UK: James Clarke, 2012.

Charles, R. H. *The Revelation of St. John*. International Critical Commentary. 2 vols. Edinburgh, Scotland: T&T Clark, 1920.

Chilton, B. *Visions of the Apocalypse: Receptions of John's Revelation in Western Imagination*. Waco, TX: Baylor University Press, 2013.

Collins, A. Y. *Crisis and Catharsis: The Power of the Apocalypse*. Philadelphia, PA: Westminster, 1984.

________. "Introduction: Early Christian Apocalypticism." *Semeia* 36 (1986): 1–11.

Collins, J. J. "Introduction: Towards the Morphology of a Genre." *Semeia* 14 (1979): 1–20.

deSilva, D. A. *Seeing Things John's Way: The Rhetoric of the Book of Revelation*. Louisville, KY: Westminster John Knox, 2009.

Ford, J. M. *Revelation*. Anchor Bible 38. New York, NY: Doubleday, 1975.

Friesen, S. J. *Imperial Cults and the Apocalypse of John: Reading Revelation in the Ruins*. Oxford, UK: Oxford University Press, 2001.

Giesen, H. *Die Offenbarung des Johannes*. Regensburger Studien zur Theologie. Regensburg, Germany: F. Pustet, 1997.

Gorman, M. J. *Reading Revelation Responsibly: Uncivil Worship and Witness: Following the Lamb into the New Creation*. Eugene, OR: Wipf & Stock, 2011.

Harrington, W. J. *Revelation*. Sacra Pagina 16. Collegeville, MN: Liturgical, 2008.

Hays, R. B., and S. Alkier, eds., *Revelation and the Politics of Apocalyptic Interpretation*. Waco, TX: Baylor University Press, 2012.

Hemer, C. J. *The Letters to the Seven Churches of Asia in Their Local Setting*. Journal for the Study of the New Testament Supplement 11. Sheffield, UK: JSOT, 1986.

Herms, R. *An Apocalypse for the Church and for the World: The Narrative Function of Universal Language in the Book of Revelation*. Beihefte zur Zeitschrift für die neutestamentliche Wissenschaft 143. Berlin, Germany: de Gruyter, 2006.

Johnson, A. F. "Revelation." Pages 571–789 in *The Expositor's Bible Commentary*. Rev. ed. Vol. 13: *Hebrews–Revelation*. Grand Rapids, MI: Zondervan, 2005.

Koester, C. R. "The Church and Its Witness in the Apocalypse of John." *Tidsskrift for Teologi og Kirke* 78 (2007): 266–82.

________. "On the Verge of the Millennium: A History of the Interpretation of Revelation." *Word and World* 15 (1995): 128–36.

________. *Revelation: A New Translation with Introduction and Commentary*. Anchor Yale Bible 38A. New Haven, CT: Yale University Press, 2014.

Kovacs, J., and C. Rowland. *Revelation: The Apocalypse of Jesus Christ*. BBC. Oxford, UK: Blackwell, 2004.

Labahn, M., and O. Lehtipuu, eds. *Imagery in the Book of Revelation*. Leuven, Belgium: Peeters, 2011.

Ladd, G. E. *A Commentary on the Revelation of John*. Grand Rapids, MI: Eerdmans, 1972.

Lioy, D. *The Book of Revelation in Christological Focus*. Studies in Biblical Literature 58. New York, NY: Peter Lang, 2003.

Maier, G. *Die Johannesoffenbarung und die Kirche*. Wissenschaftliche Untersuchungen zum Neuen Testament 25. Tübingen, Germany: Mohr Siebeck, 1981.

Mathewson, D. "Assessing Old Testament Allusions in the Book of Revelation." *Evangelical Quarterly* 75 (2003): 311–25.

__________. "Revelation in Recent Genre Criticism: Some Implications for Interpretation." *Trinity Journal* NS 13 (1992): 193–213.

Mayo, P. L. *"Those Who Call Themselves Jews": The Church and Judaism in the Apocalypse of John.* Princeton Theological Monograph Series 60. Eugene, OR: Pickwick, 2006.

Michaels, J. R. *Interpreting the Book of Revelation.* Guides to New Testament Exegesis. Grand Rapids, MI: Baker, 1992.

__________. *Revelation.* IVP New Testament Commentary 20. Downers Grove, IL: InterVarsity, 1997.

Mounce, R. H. *The Book of Revelation.* Rev. ed. New International Commentary on the New Testament. Grand Rapids, MI: Eerdmans, 1997.

Moyise, S. *The Old Testament in the Book of Revelation.* Journal for the Study of the New Testament Supplement Series 115. Sheffield, UK: Sheffield Academic, 1995.

__________., ed. *Studies in the Book of Revelation.* Edinburgh, Scotland: T&T Clark, 2001.

Murphy, F. J. *Apocalypticism in the Bible and Its World: A Comprehensive Introduction.* Grand Rapids, MI: Baker, 2012.

Naylor, M. "The Roman Imperial Cult and Revelation." *Currents in Biblical Research* 8 (2010): 207–39.

Osborne, G. R. *Revelation.* Baker Exegetical Commentary on the New Testament. Grand Rapids, MI: Baker, 2002.

Osiek, C. "Apocalyptic Eschatology." *The Bible Today* 37 (1996): 341–45.

Pate, C. M., ed. *Four Views on the Book of Revelation.* Grand Rapids, MI: Zondervan, 1998.

Pattemore, S. *The People of God in the Apocalypse: Discourse, Structure and Exegesis.* Society for New Testament Studies Monograph Series 128. Cambridge, UK: Cambridge University Press, 2004.

Patterson, P. *Revelation.* New American Commentary. Nashville, TN: B&H, 2012.

Porter, S. E. "The Language of the Apocalypse in Recent Discussion." *New Testament Studies* (1989): 582–603.

__________., and A. K. Gabriel. *Johannine Writings and Apocalyptic: An Annotated Bibliography.* Johannine Studies 1. Leiden, Netherlands: Brill, 2013.

Rainbow, P. A. *Johannine Theology: The Gospel, the Epistles and the Apocalypse.* Downers Grove, IL: InterVarsity, 2014.

__________. *The Pith of the Apocalypse: Essential Message and Principles for Interpretation.* Eugene, OR: Wipf & Stock, 2008.

Resseguie, J. L. *The Revelation of John: A Narrative Commentary.* Grand Rapids, MI: Baker, 2009.

Sandy, D. B., and D. M. O'Hare. *Prophecy and Apocalyptic: An Annotated Bibliography.* IBR Bibliographies. Grand Rapids, MI: Baker, 2007.

Smalley, S. S. *The Revelation to John: A Commentary on the Greek Text of the Apocalypse.* Downers Grove, IL: InterVarsity, 2005.

________. *Thunder and Love: John's Revelation and John's Community.* Milton Keynes, UK: Word, 1994.

Stevens, G. L. *Revelation: The Past and Future of John's Apocalypse.* Eugene, OR: Pickwick, 2014.

Swete, H. B. *The Apocalypse of St. John.* 3rd ed. London, England: Macmillan, 1909.

Tavo, F. *Woman, Mother and Bride: An Exegetical Investigation into the "Ecclesial" Notions of the Apocalypse*. Biblical Tools and Studies 3. Leuven, Belgium: Peeters, 2007.

Trail, R. L. *An Exegetical Summary of Revelation 1–11*. 2nd ed. Dallas, TX: SIL International, 2008.

________. *An Exegetical Summary of Revelation 12–22*. 2nd ed. Dallas, TX: SIL International, 2008.

Wainwright, A. W. *Mysterious Apocalypse: Interpreting the Book of Revelation*. Nashville, TN: Abingdon, 1993.

Wilson, M. *Charts on the Book of Revelation: Literary, Historical, and Theological Perspectives*. Grand Rapids, MI: Kregel, 2007.

Part Five

CONCLUSION

THE PREVIOUS SECTIONS in this volume have treated foundational matters related to the NT canon and NT backgrounds (Part One) and provided discussions of the Gospels (Part Two), the book of Acts and Paul's letters (Part Three), and the General Epistles and Revelation (Part Four). Thus this comprehensive introduction to and survey of the NT is almost complete. It remains to discuss the relationships among the various component parts of the NT canon. Thus chapter 21 deals with unity and diversity in the NT.

CHAPTER 21

UNITY AND DIVERSITY IN THE NEW TESTAMENT

CORE KNOWLEDGE

Basic Knowledge: Students should know the major issues involved in discussing the unity and diversity of the NT. They should have a grasp of the basic relationship among the Gospels, Acts, the Letters, and Revelation and be able to identify major points of integration in NT theology.

Intermediate Knowledge: Students should be able to compare and contrast the relationship between the Synoptics and John; Jesus and Paul; and the characterization of Paul in Acts and the Pauline Letters. They should also be able to provide a thorough discussion of points of integration in NT theology.

Advanced Knowledge: Students should be able to discuss alleged developments in Paul's thought. They also ought to be able to discuss the relationship among the theologies of Paul, Peter, James, and other NT voices.

INTRODUCTION

AT THE END of this introduction to the NT, it is appropriate to reflect briefly on the relationship of the NT books to one another as part of the NT canon. We have discussed the development of the canon and have provided information on introductory matters for every NT book. The purpose of this concluding chapter is to deal with issues arising from the unity and diversity in the NT, that is, the ways in which these various books cohere and yet reveal a certain amount of diversity.

THE RELATIONSHIP AMONG THE GOSPELS, THE BOOK OF ACTS, THE LETTERS, AND THE BOOK OF REVELATION

On a canonical level it may be helpful to start this chapter with a brief exploration of the relationship among the Gospels, the book of Acts, the Letters, and Revelation, respectively. First, a word on the Gospels is in order. There is no evidence that any Gospel other than the four canonical Gospels was ever part of the church's recognized canon (including the Gnostic Gospels).[1] Conversely, there is early and reliable evidence that Matthew, Mark, Luke, and John were considered apostolic and authoritative virtually from the start. For instance, writing around AD 180, Irenaeus clearly indicates his acceptance of only four Gospels: Matthew, Mark, Luke, and John.[2] As well, the Muratorian Fragment, ca. AD 200, speaks only of four Gospels,[3] and Clement of Alexandria, writing around the same time, spoke of "the four gospels that have been handed down to us."[4] Also of significance, the four canonical Gospels were quoted as authoritative Scripture in early patristic writings; other gospels were rarely so cited.[5]

The canonical order of the Gospels—Matthew, Mark, Luke, John—most likely does not reflect the early church's conviction that these books were written in this order chronologically[6] but rather is due to various topical considerations.[7] Matthew apparently was chosen to be first because this Gospel begins with the genealogy of Jesus Christ and thus

---

[1] See C. E. Hill, *Who Chose the Gospels? Probing the Great Gospel Conspiracy* (Oxford, UK: Oxford University Press, 2010). Hill answers the question of his work's title by arguing that no one really "chose" the four Gospels. They imposed themselves on the early church due to their inherent qualities and apostolic connections; "the question, 'Why did you choose these Gospels?' would not have made sense to many Christians in the second century, for the question assumes that the church, or someone in it, had the authority to make the choice. To many, it would be like the question, 'Why did you choose your parents?'" (p. 231). For a similar argument, see A. J. Köstenberger and M. J. Kruger, *The Heresy of Orthodoxy: How Contemporary Culture's Fascination with Diversity Has Reshaped Our Understanding of Early Christianity* (Wheaton, IL: Crossway, 2010), chaps. 4-6; M. J. Kruger, *Canon Revisited: Establishing the Origins and Authority of the New Testament Books* (Wheaton, IL: Crossway, 2012), esp. chap. 3; idem, *The Question of Canon: Challenging the Status Quo in the New Testament Debate* (Downers Grove, IL: InterVarsity, 2013).

[2] *Haer.* 3.11.7–8.

[3] The Muratorian Fragment is missing its original beginning; the surviving portion begins in the middle of a description of the Gospels, speaking of Luke as "the third book of the gospel" (*tertio euangelii librum*). A bit later it notes, "The fourth of the Gospels is that of John" (*quarti euangeliorum iohannis*). Text and translation from E. J. Schnabel, "The Muratorian Fragment: The State of Research," *JETS* 57 (2014): 234–37.

[4] *Strom.* 3.13.93. See also Origen, *Hom. Luc.* 1.1–2, who wrote in the first half of the third century and said regarding various Gospels of which he knew, "In all these questions we approve of nothing but what the Church approves of, namely only four canonical Gospels" (trans. J. T. Lienhard, ed., *Origen: Homilies on Luke*, FC 94 [Washington, DC: Catholic University of America Press, 1996], 6).

[5] See Kruger, *Question of Canon*, chap. 5.

[6] So, e.g., Irenaeus, *Haer.* 3.1.1. See also Augustine, *Cons.* 2.3; Eusebius, *Hist. eccl.* 3.24.

[7] See the helpful discussion in G. Goswell, "The Order of the Books of the New Testament," *JETS* 53 (2010): 227–32.

provides a fitting transition from the end point of OT revelation and a proper entry point into the story of the NT, particularly as regards the coming of Jesus. In addition, for a number of reasons, Matthew was embraced in the early church as "*the* gospel par excellence" and accorded the place of highest respect among the canonical Gospels.[8]

At the same time a chronological consideration does seem to have been in play with regard to the placement of John last among the four Gospels on the basis of the conviction that his Gospel was written at the end of the apostolic era and thus subsequent to the Synoptic Gospels.[9] Nevertheless, due to its Gospel genre, John is interposed between Luke's Gospel and the book of Acts—even though Luke wrote both, documenting the story of Jesus and the early church in a two-volume format (see Acts 1:1).

Moreover, to be precise, while there are four Gospels in the NT, they all bear witness to one and the same gospel.[10] These Gospels—better, "this gospel"—opens the NT canon even though, chronologically speaking, several of the NT letters were almost certainly written prior to at least some of the Gospels (and in some cases prior to any of them). Their placement in the NT reflects the reality that the Gospels (and the teaching of Jesus they contain) constitute the foundation of NT theology.

The book of Acts follows the Gospels in the canon and narrates the history of "what Jesus continued to do" in the days of the early church (Acts 1:1, author's translation).[11] The important implication of this is that there is no biblical and canonical basis for a radical disjunction between the "Jesus of history" and the "Christ of faith," that is, between Jesus as he was born, lived, died, and rose, and Christ as the object of the faith of his first followers subsequent to the resurrection.[12]

To the contrary, the resurrected Jesus became the central focus of the early apostolic proclamation according to the book of Acts. As Peter preached at Pentecost, "God has raised *this Jesus;* we are all witnesses of this. . . . Therefore let all the house of Israel know

---

[8] R. T. France, *Matthew: Evangelist and Teacher* (Exeter, UK: Paternoster, 1989; repr. Eugene, OR: Wipf & Stock, 2004), 17. See also the helpful discussion of the preeminence of Matthew's Gospel in the early church in ibid., 15–20.

[9] Irenaeus, *Haer.* 3.1.1. Moreover, as noted below, John presupposes that those who read and hear his Gospel are already familiar with the Synoptic tradition (if not one or several of the written Gospels, such as Mark), which provides an additional rationale for placing John's Gospel as the last of the four Gospels.

[10] See M. Hengel, "The Titles of the Gospels and the Gospel of Mark," in *Studies in the Gospel of Mark*, ed. J. Bowden (Philadelphia, PA: Fortress, 1985), 64–84; idem, *The Four Gospels and the One Gospel of Jesus* (Valley Forge, PA: Trinity Press International, 2000).

[11] Notice also the overlap between the end of Luke's Gospel and the beginning of Acts; Goswell ("Order of the Books of the New Testament," 233) observes that "the mission ending of each of the four Gospels . . . helps to prepare for the spread of the gospel, which is what is plotted in Acts." Note further the many parallels between the ministry of Jesus as set forth in the Gospel of Luke and the ministry of the apostles as set forth in Acts. For the latter, note the recent discussion in C. S. Keener, *Acts: An Exegetical Commentary*, vol. 1: *Introduction and 1:1–2:47* (Grand Rapids, MI: Baker, 2012), 558–64, with further references and a helpful comparative table on p. 558.

[12] The distinction is often traced back to M. Kähler, *Der sogenannte historische Jesus und der geschichtliche, biblische Christus* (Leipzig, Germany: A. Deichert, 1892; English translation: *The So-Called Historical Jesus and the Historic, Biblical Christ*, Fortress Texts in Modern Theology, trans. C. E. Braaten [Philadelphia, PA: Fortress, 1964]), though the seeds for this distinction which proved to be influential were sown much earlier in German scholarship.

with certainty that God has made *this Jesus*, whom you crucified, both Lord and Messiah!" (Acts 2:32, 36; emphasis added). The One people crucified has now become, by virtue of his resurrection, the vindicated and exalted Lord who is rightly the object of the church's worship.[13]

With its geographical pattern tracing the expansion of Christianity from Jerusalem all the way to Rome, the empire's capital (Acts 1:8), the book of Acts lays the foundation for the next segment of the NT canon, namely the Letters, in that it provides the framework into which many of them can be fitted. The establishment of churches in Galatia, Thessalonica, Corinth, and Ephesus, and the recruitment of Timothy, provide the essential backdrop for most of the Pauline Letters in the NT canon.[14] Importantly, as Goswell notes, Acts portrays a harmony between the Gentile mission of Paul and the Jewish mission of Peter, James, and John, indicated most specifically in the account of the council at Jerusalem (Acts 15). This is significant in that "in its present canonical setting, Acts is a consensus document that provides the context for interpreting the Pauline and non-Pauline corpora, not as competing traditions within the early church, but as compatible and complementary."[15]

The Letters follow Acts,[16] providing a glimpse into the specific issues dealt with in some of the major churches during the apostolic period. These include attacks against the

---

[13] This is the basic premise of M. Bockmuehl, *This Jesus: Martyr, Lord, Messiah* (Edinburgh, Scotland: T&T Clark, 1994).

[14] Goswell, "Order of the Books of the New Testament," 233. Note also in this regard D. E. Smith (*The Canonical Function of Acts: A Comparative Analysis* [Collegeville, MN: Liturgical Press, 2002], 9), who considers the early church fathers to have understood the book of Acts not merely to join the Gospels and Letters but to be "a unifier of the developing biblical canon." Examining the patristic use of Acts, Smith argues a twofold thesis: "[1] that Acts not only linked the Gospels with the Pauline epistles in the judgment of the Fathers, but that it also linked those texts with the Old Testament and the catholic epistles, *and* [2] it provided a basis for the catholics [sic] to claim the exclusive right of biblical interpretation vis-à-vis their opponents by its support of postapostolic ecclesiastical authority" (p. 18, italics in original).

[15] Goswell, "The Order of the Books of the New Testament," 233. The historical reliability of Acts (as discussed above in chap. 8) indicates that this harmony among leaders in the early Christian movement is accurately reported and should not be viewed as a scenario contrived as revisionist history to indicate unity where none existed. That is, it is not the case that the author of Acts needed to smooth over a fractured early Christian leadership and so invented a council that reconciled these leaders.

[16] This general pattern is not without exception; in Sinaiticus, e.g., the Pauline Epistles come after the Gospels but before Acts. It should be noted as well that the order in English Bibles of Acts—Pauline Letters—General Letters reflects the order of the Latin Vulgate, not that of Greek witnesses, where the order is typically Acts—General Letters—Pauline Letters. The Latin ordering connects the dominance of Paul in the last part of Acts with his letters, and it reflects the larger size of the Letter corpus of Paul as opposed to other Letter authors (James, Peter, John, Jude). The Greek ordering, on the other hand, presents Peter's (and other) Letters, then Paul's, and this reflects Peter being highlighted in the first part of Acts, then Paul in the second part.The General Letters, also called the Catholic Letters, bear this designation in that some of them are addressed to general audiences (see esp. Jas 1:1; 1 Pet 1:1; 2 Pet 1:1). Even though the other letters have a narrower original audience, however, as B. S. Childs notes (*The New Testament as Canon: An Introduction* [Valley Forge, PA: Trinity Press International, 1994], 495), the term "catholic" (= "general") as a descriptor of the canonical letters of James, Peter, John, and Jude remains a useful one to designate a collection of NT writings which is distinct from the Gospels and the Pauline corpus. It is neither a precise canonical nor a modern genre classification. Its usage has no great theological significance other than to reflect the church's growing concern that the NT letters be understood as universal, even when, in their original form, they often carry a specific addressee.Within the General Letters, note that the order of James—Peter—John corresponds with the

gospel message itself, as in Galatia (cf. Gal 1:6; see Acts 15); a variety of congregational issues regarding marriage, eating food sacrificed to idols, and the exercise of spiritual gifts in Corinth (cf. 1 Corinthians 7–16); the doctrine of the church (cf. the Prison Epistles); and church structure and qualifications for leadership (the Letters to Timothy and Titus). So, while Acts provides a sweeping, narrative-oriented look at the progress of the gospel "in Jerusalem and in all Judea and Samaria, and to the end of the earth" (Acts 1:8), the Letters give us a more detailed look at the outworking and implications of the gospel at a local level, focusing on teaching and exhortation. Because of these two different perspectives, Acts and the Letters helpfully inform the interpretation of each other.

Revelation provides closure in that it depicts Jesus's glorious return (the Second Coming), his subsequent judgment of the world, and the gathering of his elect (his covenant community) to be with him forever in heaven. Creation and the fall at the beginning of the canon of Scripture find their complement in the new restored creation and the reversal of the effects of the fall in the final chapters of Revelation.[17]

ISSUES RELATED TO THE NEW TESTAMENT'S UNITY AND DIVERSITY

The Synoptics and John

At least since the end of the eighteenth century, critics have alleged that the Synoptic Gospels and John stand in irreconcilable conflict.[18] The solution, adopted by the vast majority of commentators, has been that the Synoptic writers were more interested in history while John was primarily interested in theology. After all, did not Clement of Alexandria call John's a "spiritual Gospel"?[19] After initial doubts arose in the 1790s, it was particularly K. G. Bretschneider and later D. F. Strauss, both of whom discredited John's historical reliability and proposed that his Gospel deals with "myth," who held that John's book was not historical narrative.[20]

---

order in Gal 2:9. Recently, D. R. Nienhuis and R. W. Wall (*Reading the Epistles of James, Peter, John, and Jude as Scripture: The Shaping and Shape of a Canonical Collection* [Grand Rapids, MI: Eerdmans, 2013], 10) have argued that as a canonical collection, these Letters are to "be read together as the interpenetrating parts of a coherent theological whole."

[17] For helpful treatments, see G. Goldsworthy, *According to Plan: The Unfolding Revelation of God in the Bible* (Leicester, UK: InterVarsity, 1991); T. D. Alexander, *From Eden to the New Jerusalem: An Introduction to Biblical Theology* (Grand Rapids, MI: Kregel, 2009). Cf. D. A. Carson, *The Gagging of God: Christianity Confronts Pluralism* (Grand Rapids, MI: Zondervan, 1996), 253–78.

[18] See A. J. Köstenberger, "Diversity and Unity in the New Testament," in *Biblical Theology: Retrospect and Prospect*, ed. S. J. Hafemann (Downers Grove, IL: InterVarsity, 2002), 146–49.

[19] Cited in Eusebius, *Eccl. Hist.* 6.14.

[20] K. G. Bretschneider, *Probabilia de evangelii et epistolarum Joannis, Apostoli, indole et origine eruditorum Judiciis* (Leipzig, Germany: 1820); D. F. Strauss, *The Life of Jesus Critically Examined* (London, England: SCM, 1973 [1835]). See the discussion in A. J. Köstenberger, "Early Doubts of the Apostolic Authorship of the Fourth Gospel in the History of Modern Biblical Criticism," in *Studies on John and Gender: A Decade of Scholarship*, Studies in Biblical Literature 38 (New York, NY: Peter Lang, 2001), 17–47.

In recent years, however, the historical reliability of John's Gospel has witnessed a remarkable rehabilitation.[21] It is now widely recognized that the above-sketched appraisal of the relationship between the Synoptics and John is not only unduly simplistic but inaccurate. There are several reasons for this. First, there are a notable number of what some have called "interlocking connections" between John and the Synoptics, that is, instances where John's Gospel fills in a detail or a connection in the Synoptic Gospels.[22] This includes, in particular, instances where it seems that John presupposed his readers' familiarity with the Synoptic tradition and possibly one or more of the written Gospels (e.g., John 1:40; 3:24; 4:44; 6:67, 71; 11:1–2).[23] This suggests that the Synoptics and John are not in conflict but sustain a complementary relationship.

Second, it has been shown that many historical, geographical, and topographical details in John's Gospel are historically accurate; they can be corroborated by archaeology and extant extrabiblical sources.[24] Archaeological discoveries such as artifacts related to Caiaphas and the high priestly family or the location of the pool of Siloam are cases in point.[25] The critical view that expulsion from the synagogue for following Jesus (cf. John 9:22) could not have happened in Jesus's day has recently been challenged in a full-length monograph.[26] Historian M. Hengel considered John's Gospel an important source for first-century Judaism, crediting its author with an excellent knowledge of Palestinian topography and the Jewish calendar.[27] Hengel also pointed out that several pieces of information occur in John's Gospel for the first time, such as the Samaritan village named Sychar (4:5), the name *ta enkainia* as a designation for the Feast of Tabernacles (10:22), and the

---

[21] See esp. C. L. Blomberg, *The Historical Reliability of John's Gospel: Issues and Commentary* (Downers Grove, IL: InterVarsity, 2001); A. J. Köstenberger, "John," in *Zondervan Illustrated Bible Backgrounds Commentary*, ed. C. E. Arnold (Grand Rapids, MI: Zondervan, 2002), vol. 2: *John, Acts*, 1–216. See also other recent reevaluations of John's historicity in P. N. Anderson, *The Fourth Gospel and the Quest for Jesus: Modern Foundations Reconsidered* (London, England: T&T Clark, 2006); P. N. Anderson, F. Just, and T. Thatcher, eds., *John, Jesus, and History*, vol. 1: *Critical Appraisals of Critical Views*; vol. 2: *Aspects of Historicity in the Fourth Gospel*; and vol. 3: *Glimpses of Jesus Through the Johannine Lens* (Atlanta, GA: Society of Biblical Literature, 2007, 2009, 2016); R. Bauckham, *The Testimony of the Beloved Disciple: Narrative, History, and Theology in the Gospel of John* (Grand Rapids, MI: Baker, 2007), 93–112, 173–89; D. M. Smith, *The Fourth Gospel in Four Dimensions: Judaism and Jesus, the Gospels and Scripture* (Columbia, SC: University of South Carolina Press, 2008).

[22] L. Morris, "The Relationship of the Fourth Gospel to the Synoptics," in *Studies in the Fourth Gospel* (Grand Rapids, MI: Eerdmans, 1969), 15–63; D. A. Carson, *The Gospel According to John*, PNTC (Grand Rapids, MI: Eerdmans, 1991), 49–58, esp. 52–55.

[23] See R. Bauckham, "John for Readers of Mark," in *The Gospels for All Christians: Rethinking the Gospel Audiences*, ed. R. Bauckham (Grand Rapids, MI: Eerdmans, 1997), 147–71.

[24] A. J. Köstenberger, "John," and the literature cited there.

[25] U. C. von Wahlde, "Archaeology and John's Gospel," in J. H. Charlesworth, ed., *Jesus and Archaeology* (Grand Rapids, MI: Eerdmans, 2006), 523–86.

[26] J. Bernier, *Aposynagōgos and the Historical Jesus in John: Rethinking the Historicity of the Johannine Expulsion Passages*, Biblical Interpretation Series 122 (Leiden, Netherlands: Brill, 2013). See also E. W. Klink III, *The Sheep of the Fold: The Audience and Origin of the Gospel of John*, SNTSMS 141 (Cambridge, UK: Cambridge University Press, 2010).

[27] M. Hengel, "Das Johannesevangelium als Quelle für die Geschichte des antiken Judentums," in *Judaica, Hellenistica et Christiana: Kleine Schriften II*, WUNT 109 (Tübingen, Germany: Mohr Siebeck, 1999), 295, 322.

characterization of Annas as Caiaphas's father-in-law (18:13).[28] And John's portrayal of Annas and Caiaphas earned Hengel's highest praise.[29]

In cases where John's Gospel overlaps with the Synoptics, John frequently supplies additional information.[30] He mentions a boy with five barley loaves and two small fish as well as Jesus's words with Philip and Andrew at the feeding of the multitude (6:5–9); he refers to the fragrance of the perfume and identified Judas as the one who objects to Mary of Bethany's anointing of Jesus's feet prior to the crucifixion (12:3–8; Matthew globally refers to "the disciples" in 26:8, and Mark to "some of those present" in 14:4 NIV); and he specifies Malchus as the name of the servant whose ear Peter cut off at Gethsemane (John 18:10).

Perhaps the most commonly noted difficulty in reconciling John's Gospel with the Synoptics is related to the dating of Jesus's final Passover with his disciples.[31] Some claim the reference to "the preparation day for the Passover" (John 19:14) places the Last Supper on Wednesday night with the crucifixion taking place on Thursday afternoon when the Passover lambs were slaughtered in preparation for Passover later that evening. However, a closer look reveals that both John and the Synoptics present Jesus as having eaten a final meal with his disciples, a Passover meal, on Thursday night, with the crucifixion having taken place on Friday afternoon.

Resolution is found in 19:31, where we are told that Jesus's crucifixion took place on "the day of Preparation" with the next day being a "special Sabbath," that is, the Sabbath of Passover week. Thus, even in John the crucifixion takes place on Friday, with "the day of Preparation" in John, as in Mark and Luke, referring not to the day of preparation for the Passover but to the Sabbath (Mark 15:42; Luke 23:54; see Josephus, *Ant.* 16.163–64). Moreover, since Passover lasted an entire week (in conjunction with the associated Feast of Unleavened Bread; see Luke 22:1), it was customary to speak of the day of preparation for the Sabbath as "the day of preparation *of Passover week*," though not of the Passover in a more narrow sense, as a better rendering of the phrase in John 19:14. Other apparent discrepancies between John and the Synoptics are likewise capable of resolution.[32]

Third, the dichotomy between the Synoptics' alleged primary interest in history and John's focus on theology is itself highly suspect, as M. M. Thompson and others have shown.[33] Many aspects of the historical reliability of John's Gospel have been confirmed

---

[28] Ibid., 296, 322 (in general); p. 301 (Sychar), p. 317 (Tabernacles), p. 323 (Annas).

[29] Ibid., 322–33, esp. 333.

[30] A. J. Köstenberger, *John*, BECNT (Grand Rapids, MI: Baker, 2004), 17–18, and the references cited there.

[31] Köstenberger, "Diversity and Unity," 147–48, and the literature cited there.

[32] Ibid., 148–49. This is contrary to M. A. Matson, "The Historical Plausibility of John's Passion Dating," in *Aspects of Historicity in the Fourth Gospel*, 291–312, who argues that John's dating is incompatible with that of the Synoptics but also that John's is more likely to be historically accurate.

[33] M. M. Thompson, "The Historical Jesus and the Johannine Christ," in *Exploring the Gospel of John*, eds. R. A. Culpepper and C. C. Black (Louisville, KY: Westminster John Knox, 1996), 21–42; L. Morris, "History and Theology in the Fourth Gospel," in *Studies in the Fourth Gospel*, 65–138.

by archaeological and extrabiblical sources. Also, scholars have increasingly come to realize that the Synoptics are also interested in theology, in the sense that they reveal the respective theological interests and emphases of the evangelists. As we have seen above, Luke has a special interest in those with low status in society—the poor, Gentiles, women, and children—and he dealt extensively with issues related to wealth and poverty. Matthew presents Jesus's teaching in the form of five extended discourses after the pattern of Moses and the Pentateuch. Examples could be multiplied.

Hence, the conclusion seems warranted that *both* the Synoptics *and* John are interested in *both* history *and* theology. This is also confirmed by the strong emphasis on eyewitness testimony in John's Gospel (e.g., 1:7–8, 15; 5:31–47).[34] It would be difficult to imagine why a Gospel that explicitly and repeatedly stresses the importance of eyewitness testimony would at the same time play fast and loose with the facts. Even the author himself claims to be an eyewitness of the Last Supper (13:23), the crucifixion (19:35), and the rest of the events recorded in the Gospel narrative (21:24–25). For these reasons the dichotomy between history and theology in describing the relationship between the Synoptics and John is false and should be abandoned.

Jesus and Paul

Another alleged point of tension in NT theology is that between the teachings of Jesus and Paul.[35] Some have dichotomized between the Jesus of history and the Christ of faith, and on the basis of this distinction they have proposed that only the latter properly contributes NT theology. What is more, it has been suggested that the apostle Paul, not Jesus, was the founder of Christianity in the sense that he developed a distinct body of teachings that constituted Christianity as a religion on the assumption that Jesus was in fact the Christ and Son of God.[36] Here caution is imperative for several reasons.

First, while it is true that Paul was not a follower of Jesus during his earthly ministry—in fact, he persecuted the early Christians vigorously until his encounter with the

[34] L. Morris, "Was the Author of the Fourth Gospel an Eyewitness?," in *Studies in the Fourth Gospel*, 139–214; cf. R. Bauckham, *Jesus and the Eyewitnesses: The Gospels as Eyewitness Testimony* (Grand Rapids, MI: Eerdmans, 2006).

[35] See on this chap. 9 in "Paul: The Man and His Message" above; cf. Köstenberger, "Diversity and Unity," 145–46. A recent collection of essays is found in T. D. Still, ed., *Jesus and Paul Reconsidered: Fresh Pathways into an Old Debate* (Grand Rapids, MI: Eerdmans, 2007); note also the treatment by D. G. Horrell, "From Jesus to Paul: Pre-Pauline Christianity," chap. 2 in *An Introduction to the Study of Paul*, 3rd ed., T&T Clark Approaches to Biblical Studies (London, England: Bloomsbury T&T Clark, 2015), 17–36. History-of-research treatments on this particular issue can be found in D. E. Aune, "Jesus Tradition and the Pauline Letters," in W. H. Kelber and S. Byrskog, eds., *Jesus in Memory: Traditions in Oral and Scribal Perspectives* (Waco, TX: Baylor University Press, 2009), 63–78; Y. Lee, *Paul, Scribe of Old and New: Intertextual Insights for the Jesus-Paul Debate*, LNTS 512 (London, England: Bloomsbury T&T Clark, 2015), 5–21; A. Lindemann, "Paulus und die Jesustradition," in R. Buitenwerf, H. W. Hollander, and J. Tromp, eds., *Jesus, Paul, and Early Christianity: Studies in Honour of Henk Jan de Jonge*, NovTSup 130 (Leiden, Netherlands: Brill, 2008), 282–86; and the thorough treatment by D. Häusser, *Christusbekenntnis und Jesusüberlieferung bei Paulus*, WUNT 2/210 (Tübingen, Germany: Mohr Siebeck, 2006), 1–38.

[36] To one extent or another, this is argued by, e.g., A. N. Wilson, *Paul: The Mind of the Apostle* (New York, NY: W. W. Norton, 1997); G. Lüdemann, *Paul, the Founder of Christianity* (Amherst, Germany: Prometheus, 2002); J. D. Tabor, *Paul and Jesus: How the Apostle Transformed Christianity* (New York, NY: Simon & Schuster, 2012).

risen Christ on the road to Damascus (Acts 8:1–3; 9:1–19)—there are some *elements of continuity* in his letters with Jesus's teachings.[37] For example, Paul in a few passages appeals to Jesus's teachings as his authority (e.g., 1 Cor 7:10: "Not I, but the Lord"; see vv. 12, 25; cf. Acts 20:35: "It is more blessed to give than to receive"; 1 Cor 9:14; 11:23–26; 1 Thess 4:15). On a more subtle level, Wenham and others have identified a number of allusions to Jesus's teachings in Paul's Letters (e.g., 1 Cor 13:2 NIV: "If I have a faith that can move mountains"; see Matt 17:20 and parallels). Other references to Jesus's ways are also apparent (2 Cor 8:9; Phil 2:5).[38]

Second, Paul did not dichotomize in any way between Christ and Christianity. In fact, Dunn rightly observes that "for Paul Christianity is Christ."[39] Moreover, the early Christians (including Paul) uniformly held as their first and foremost confession that "Jesus is Lord" (Acts 2:36; Rom 10:9; Phil 2:11). That Paul would set himself off as the "founder of Christianity" over against Jesus is therefore unthinkable.

At the same time things are not so simple as to say that Paul was a mere "follower of Jesus."[40] This does not mean Paul stood in an antagonistic or discontinuous relationship with Jesus—far from it. It does mean Paul had significant sources in developing his theology other than direct recourse to Jesus's teachings. S. Kim has correctly suggested that Paul's conversion led him to reread the Hebrew Scriptures in light of his newfound conviction that the resurrected Christ had died as the sinless substitute for sinful humanity and thus did not bear the curse of God for his own sins as he had previously (and erroneously) assumed.[41] In the months and years that followed, Paul's Spirit-led and inspired rereading of Scripture in the light of this new hermeneutical axiom (Jesus = the Christ) led to a body of Pauline teachings that cannot be reduced to direct dependence on Jesus's own teachings.

This is confirmed also by the logic of Paul's ministry that typically took its point of departure in the local synagogue where people believed in the coming of the Messiah but not in Jesus. Hence it would have been inadequate for Paul's purposes to cite Jesus's teaching, at least in the initial phase of his apostolic proclamation. Rather, Paul had to show from the Hebrew Scriptures that the events in Jesus's life fulfilled messianic prophecy and that the Messiah was in fact Jesus, moving from the known (and widely expected) to the unknown (or unproven, namely, that Jesus was the Messiah; e.g., Acts 9:20, 22; 13:32–41). As the book of Acts makes clear, Apollos and others faced the same challenge and adopted the same strategy (Acts 18:28), as did eyewitnesses Matthew and John in their Gospels, and as we see in the book of Hebrews.

---

[37] See esp. S. O. Stout, *The "Man Christ Jesus": The Humanity of Jesus in the Teaching of the Apostle Paul* (Eugene, OR: Wipf & Stock, 2011).

[38] D. Wenham, *Paul: Follower of Jesus or Founder of Christianity?* (Grand Rapids, MI: Eerdmans, 1996).

[39] J. D. G. Dunn, *The Theology of Paul the Apostle* (Grand Rapids, MI: Eerdmans, 1998), 729.

[40] See A. J. Köstenberger, "Review of David Wenham, *Paul: Follower of Jesus or Founder of Christianity?*," *TrinJ* 16 NS (1995): 259–62.

[41] Though he did bear the curse for us; Gal 3:10–13; cf. Deut 21:23. S. Kim, *The Origin of Paul's Gospel* (Grand Rapids, MI: Eerdmans, 1982).

Also, it is clear that at least in some cases Paul was not able to draw on Jesus's teaching on a certain subject. Likely examples include the nature of the resurrection body (1 Cor 15:35–57), the scenario and timing of the rapture (1 Thess 4:13–18; though see v. 15), the Pauline doctrine of the church as the body of Christ (Rom 12:1–8; 1 Cor 12:12–30; Eph 5:25–32), and his teachings on spiritual gifts (e.g., 1 Corinthians 12–14). In these and other cases, whatever Paul's sources were for developing his theology, be it direct revelation or Spirit-inspired extrapolation from the Hebrew Scriptures or other sources, he did not proceed explicitly on the basis of Jesus's recorded teachings.

Again, this in no way means there is an actual conflict between Jesus and Paul. To the contrary, Jesus and Paul sustain a strong and complementary relationship, essentially grounded in the recognition that Jesus is Lord so that their teachings cohere closely. It also means that care must be taken not to construe the Jesus-Paul relationship in too simplistic a manner, no matter how well intentioned one's efforts may be. The fabric of NT theology thus is rich in texture, weaving a colorful garment that displays diversity of expression and theological development on the basis of the underlying conviction that there is one God, that Jesus is Lord and Messiah, and that salvation is only through the gospel of Jesus Christ.

The Paul of Acts and the Paul of the Letters

"Is the Paul of Acts the real Paul?" F. F. Bruce asked in an article published in 1976.[42] His is a question that scholars had been posing for some time and continue to ask to this day.[43] Especially German scholars in the wake of F. C. Baur have frequently argued that Luke's presentation of Paul in the book of Acts is incompatible with the way the apostle portrayed himself in his Letters.[44] Luke's Paul, it is contended, was invincible and moved

---

[42] F. F. Bruce, "Is the Paul of Acts the Real Paul?," *BJRL* 58 (1976): 282–305.

[43] Recent contributions include C. S. Keener, *Acts: An Exegetical Commentary*, vol 1: *Introduction and 1:1–2:47* (Grand Rapids, MI: Baker, 2012), 221–57; A. J. Kuecker and K. D. Liebengood, "The Paul of Acts and the Paul of the Epistles," in *Evangelical Faith and the Challenge of Historical Criticism*, ed. C. M. Hays and C. B. Ansberry (Grand Rapids, MI: Baker, 2013), 182–203, who focus on comparing the chronology and theology of Acts and Paul's Letters; D. Marguerat, *Paul in Acts and Paul in His Letters*, WUNT 310 (Tübingen, Germany: Mohr Siebeck, 2013); T. E. Phillips, *Paul, His Letters, and Acts*, Library of Pauline Studies (Peabody, MA: Hendrickson, 2010), who argues that "the Paul of Acts is indeed a rehabilitated version of the Paul of the letters, a Paul who was recast in terms more attractive to the church of the late first or early second century" (p. 197); and M. Whitlock, "From the Acts of the Apostles to Paul: Shaking Off the Muffled Majesty of Impersonal Authorship," in *Unity and Diversity in the Gospels and Paul: Essays in Honor of Frank J. Matera*, ed. C. W. Skinner and K. R. Iverson (Atlanta, GA: Society of Biblical Literature, 2012), 149–71, who develops the idea of Acts as "a narrative arrangement that builds the context for reading Paul's Letters" (p. 150).

[44] For Baur's position, see F. C. Baur, *Paul, the Apostle of Jesus Christ: His Life and Works, His Epistles and Teaching* (German original, 1845; trans. A. Menzies, 2 vols., London, England: Williams & Norgate, 1873–75; repr. Grand Rapids, MI: Baker, 2011), 4–5, *et passim*. For a general treatment including a taxonomy of views on the issue, see A. J. Mattill Jr., "The Value of Acts as a Source for the Study of Paul," in *Perspectives on Luke-Acts*, ed. C. H. Talbert (Danville, VA: Association of Baptist Professors of Religion, 1978), 76–98. The disjunction between the Paul of Acts and the Paul of the Letters has been most definitively argued by E. Haenchen, *The Acts of the Apostles*, trans. B. Noble and G. Shinn (Philadelphia, PA: Westminster, 1971), 112–16; and P. Vielhauer, "On the 'Paulinism' of Acts," in *Studies in Luke-Acts*, ed. L. E. Keck and

in victorious procession from place to place.[45] But Paul portrayed himself as weak and frequently confounded.[46] For Luke, Paul was a brilliant, persuasive public speaker.[47] But Paul said of himself that he had little room for rhetoric and that others often viewed him as an inferior preacher.[48]

S. Porter summarizes and critiques five major reasons advanced against an identification of the Paul of Acts and the Paul of the Letters:[49] (1) Luke's apparent unawareness of the Pauline solution to the problem of the mission to the Gentiles without the law; (2) the portrayal of Paul as a miracle worker in Acts and the virtual absence of references to any such miracles in the Letters; (3) the depiction of Paul as an impressive orator in Acts and the characterization of Paul as an unimpressive speaker in the Letters; (4) Paul's claim to apostleship in his Letters versus the difficulty of substantiating it in the book of Acts; and (5) the different portrayals of Jewish-Christian relations in Acts and the Pauline Letters.[50] Beyond this, some also believe to have detected discrepancies in the areas of Christology and eschatology.[51]

Space does not permit us to engage each of these arguments in detail, though this has been done successfully in recent scholarship.[52] Once again it can be shown that the present issue is one of different perspectives that can well be integrated into a cohesive overall picture.[53] Luke did not write a biography of Paul.[54] He was interested in Paul primarily as the leading proponent of the early Christian mission, and this mission overcame numerous obstacles—albeit not on account of Paul's strategizing genius or rhetorical brilliance but through the sovereign power of God. By the same token Paul frequently stressed in his Letters that it is not he but Christ in him who was the driving force behind the Christian

---

J. L. Martyn (Philadelphia, PA: Fortress, 1966), 33–50. See the critique in S. E. Porter, *The Paul of Acts: Essays in Literary Criticism, Rhetoric, and Theology*, WUNT 115 (Tübingen, Germany: Mohr Siebeck, 1999), 187–206.

[45] Acts 14:19–20; 16:40; 18:9–10; 19:11; 20:10–11; 23:11, 31–34; 26:28–29; 27:43–44; 28:30–31.

[46] 1 Cor 2:1–5; 2 Cor 11:16–12:10.

[47] Acts 13:9–11, 16–41; 14:15–17; 17:22–31; 20:18–35; 22:1–21; 24:10–21; 26:2–26.

[48] 1 Cor 2:1–5; 2 Cor 10:1, 10–11. But see the cautionary note sounded in Porter, *Paul of Acts*, 101.

[49] See also a list of contrasts between the "Paul of Acts" and the "Paul of the letters" in R. I. Pervo, *The Making of Paul: Constructions of the Apostle in Early Christianity* (Minneapolis, MN: Fortress, 2010), 150.

[50] Porter, *Paul of Acts*, 190–99. Key aspects of Porter's monograph have been summarized and updated in S. E. Porter, "The Portrait of Paul in Acts," in *The Blackwell Companion to Paul*, ed. S. Westerholm (Oxford, UK: Wiley-Blackwell, 2011), 124–38, which includes an excellent, up-to-date focused bibliography on the topic.

[51] Ibid., 200–205.

[52] For a competent and constructive critique, see esp. Porter, *Paul of Acts*, 187–206; cf. Bruce, "Real Paul," 282–305; L. T. Johnson, *The Writings of the New Testament* (Minneapolis, MN: Fortress, 1986), 231–38; and B. Witherington, *The Acts of the Apostles: A Socio-Rhetorical Commentary* (Grand Rapids, MI: Eerdmans, 1998), 430–38.

[53] See D. Wenham, "Unity and Diversity in the New Testament," in G. E. Ladd, *A Theology of the New Testament*, rev. ed., ed. D. A. Hagner (Grand Rapids, MI: Eerdmans, 1993), 687–92.

[54] So rightly Bruce, "Real Paul," 305; Witherington, *Acts*, 438; et al. Keener (*Acts* 1.227–31) rightly warns against several unrealistic expectations when comparing Paul as portrayed in Acts with Paul as seen in his epistles. (1) We should not expect to find in Acts every aspect of Paul's life and ministry that is mentioned in the Letters, or vice versa. (2) We should not expect Luke and Paul to have precisely the same perspective on Paul's ministry. (3) We should not expect Paul and Luke to have exactly the same emphases in speaking of Paul's ministry.

mission and that the message of the cross, not his own persuasive powers, took center stage (e.g., 1 Cor 2:1–5; Gal 2:20).

Bruce lists a whole series of agreements between Acts and Paul's Letters, some of which are in the category of what he called "undesigned coincidences."[55] First, Paul pointed to his impeccable Jewish credentials: he was a "Hebrew of Hebrews" (Phil 3:5 NIV; see 2 Cor 11:22); he advanced in Judaism beyond many of his peers on account of his zeal for his ancestral traditions (Gal 1:14). But only in Acts do we learn that Paul had been educated in the school of Gamaliel, one of the most prominent Pharisaic teachers of his generation (Acts 22:3; see 5:35; cf. Phil 3:5; Acts 23:6; 26:5).

Second, Paul's activity as persecutor of the early church was recounted repeatedly in the book of Acts (Acts 8:3; 9:1). In his letters the apostle regularly acknowledged this ignominious part of his past (1 Cor 15:9; Gal 1:13, 22–23; Phil 3:6; 1 Tim 1:13).

Third, the accounts of Paul's conversion in Acts (9:1–19; 22:6–21; 26:12–23) are paralleled by Paul's statements in his Letters that God "was pleased to reveal his Son in me" (Gal 1:15; see 2 Cor 4:6) and his indignant question to the Corinthians: "Have I not seen Jesus our Lord?" (1 Cor 9:1; see 15:8). The location of Paul's conversion at or near Damascus is consistent with his statement that after his visit to Arabia, he "returned to Damascus" (Gal 1:17 NIV).[56]

Fourth, both Acts and Paul's Letters indicate that he supported himself by his own labor (Acts 20:34; 28:3; 1 Cor 9:18; 1 Thess 2:9; 2 Thess 3:7–8).

Fifth, both Acts and Paul's Letters reveal Paul's pattern of going "to the Jew first and also to the Greek."[57]

Sixth, in Acts Paul adapted himself readily to Jews and Gentiles as well as to a wide variety of audiences, which is consistent with the one who said: "To the Jews I became as a Jew, in order to win Jews. . . . To those who are outside the law, like one outside the law . . . to win those outside the law. . . . I have become all things to all people, so that I might by all means save some. Now I do all this for the gospel" (1 Cor 9:19–23, author's translation).

Seventh, while Luke was perhaps the theologian of salvation history *par excellence*, salvation history was not an alien concept to Paul. Although he stressed the centrality of justification by faith, Paul also viewed the age of law as a parenthesis in salvation history, a mere interlude in the age of promise that was inaugurated with Abraham and consummated in the gospel (Rom 5:20; Gal 3:15–19).

No wonder Bruce concludes at the end of his essay that the Paul of Acts is the "real Paul." What is more, "Without Paul's Letters we should have a very inadequate and one-sided

---

[55] For the interested student, Keener (*Acts* 1.238–50) provides several extensive lists of correspondences between Acts and Paul's Epistles, drawing from the work of A. von Harnack, T. H. Campbell, and M. D. He goes on to discuss additional correspondences at length.

[56] Bruce ("Real Paul," 285–93) listed several additional pages of similar "undesigned coincidences" under this category; see Köstenberger, "Diversity and Unity," 150.

[57] Acts 13:46–48; 28:25–28; cf. Rom 1:16; 2:9–10; 10:12; 1 Cor 1:22, 24; 12:13; Gal 3:28; Col 3:11.

impression of him, but thanks to Luke's portrayal we have a fuller understanding of Paul's place in the world of his day and of the impact he made on others than if we were dependent on his letters alone."[58] Porter concurs: "The differences between the Paul of Acts and of the letters regarding his person and work, once analyzed in detail, . . . do not point to significant and sustainable contradictions. . . . [T]he standard arguments marshaled regarding differences in theology . . . are also inconclusive. While there may be differences of emphasis and focus, 'the evidence is far from substantiating contradictions.'"[59]

Perhaps most importantly, as Porter points out, while the Paul of the Letters was an epistolographer, the Paul of Acts was an orator.[60] "What differences there are seem to be fully explicable in terms of Acts and the letters being written by two different authors, with their commonalities pointing to close contact between the two."[61] We therefore conclude with Witherington, "The Paul we see in Acts is not un-Pauline, much less anti-Pauline, but in some cases a Paul we do not hear about in the letters, and in some cases a familiar Paul, though from a different and fresh perspective. It is a Paul interpreted through the eyes of admiration and respect."[62]

Alleged Developments in Paul's Thought[63]

In certain scholarly circles it has been fashionable to postulate a pronounced development from Paul's earlier correspondence to his later writings.[64] Thus, it has been maintained by some that the apostle regressed from an egalitarian (Gal 3:28) to a traditional-conservative gospel,[65] or that his expectation of Christ's return changed during the course of his career from an imminent to a more distant one.[66] To cite yet another example, Bruce discussed and critiqued J. Drane's volume on *Paul: Libertine or Legalist?* which sees the apostle as moving, in good Hegelian fashion, from libertinism in Galatians to a kind of

---

[58] Bruce, "Real Paul," 305.

[59] Porter, *Paul of Acts*, 205–6.

[60] Ibid., 5, 98–125.

[61] Ibid., 7.

[62] Witherington, *Acts*, 438.

[63] See D. A. Carson, "Unity and Diversity in the New Testament: The Possibility of Systematic Theology," in *Scripture and Truth*, ed. D. A. Carson and J. D. Woodbridge (Grand Rapids, MI: Zondervan, 1983), 84–86. The idea of development in Paul's thought is not at odds with that of the coherence of the NT. This would only be the case if actual contradictions between Paul's earlier and later thought could be demonstrated.

[64] E.g., U. Schnelle, *Wandlungen im paulinischen Denken* (Stuttgart, Germany: Katholisches Bibelwerk, 1989), and the literature cited below.

[65] See H. D. Betz, *Galatians*, Hermeneia (Philadelphia, PA: Fortress, 1979), 200: "In 1 Corinthians Paul has retracted the Galatian position."

[66] It is particularly in the area of Paul's eschatological thought that development is often posited. See, e.g., W. Wiefel, "Die Hauptrichtung des Wandels im eschatologischen Denken des Paulus," *TZ* 30 (1974), 65–81; A. Lindemann, "Paulus und die korinthische Eschatologie: Zur These von einer 'Entwicklung' im paulinischen Denken," *NTS* 37 (1991): 204–20; U. Schnelle, *Theology of the New Testament*, trans. M. E. Boring (Grand Rapids, MI: Baker, 2009), 349; idem, *Wandlungen im paulinischen Denken*, 37–48; G. Strecker, *Theology of the New Testament*, trans. M. E. Boring (New York, NY: de Gruyter, 2000), 209–16. See also the discussion in C. K. Barrett, *Paul: An Introduction to His Thought* (Louisville, KY: Westminster John Knox, 1994), 55–57.

"legalism" in 1 Corinthians and as taking a more balanced approach in 2 Corinthians and Romans.[67] While benevolent assessments speak of perceived changes such as these merely in terms of a further development in Paul's thinking, others consider them to amount to blatant contradictions. Paul, it is alleged, frequently altered his position and was mistaken or confused with regard to the role of the law or other issues.[68]

Paul only began his writing career about fifteen years after his conversion when he was at least forty years of age, whereby little information is available regarding the long span of intervening years. By the time Paul composed his first extant letter, he was by no means a novice: his thoughts are characterized by considerable theological maturity. From his first missionary journey onward, the apostle's ministry again spanned only about fifteen years, which sets further boundaries for developmental hypotheses.[69] Moreover, the content of Paul's Letters depended to a significant extent on his specific missionary circumstances. For these reasons it is imperative to exercise great caution when comparing with one another the thirteen missives Paul wrote, and care must be taken not to read too much into the silences in these letters, as if silence necessarily indicates the nonexistence of a given Pauline category such as justification by faith.

Despite the influential essays by C. H. Dodd on change and development in Paul over half a century ago[70] and similar treatments since, the substantiation of the thesis of a development in Paul's thinking is therefore fraught with considerable difficulty.[71] It is clear that a paradigm shift occurred in Paul's thinking right at the beginning of his career at the time of his conversion;[72] but if some development of thought occurred in the apostle's thought, it probably took place *before* Paul's Letters were written rather than during the comparatively short period during which Paul wrote.[73]

---

[67] See F. F. Bruce, "'All Things to All Men': Diversity in Unity and Other Pauline Tensions," in *Unity and Diversity in New Testament Theology*, ed. R. Guelich (Grand Rapids, MI: Eerdmans, 1978), 82–83, with reference to J. W. Drane, *Paul: Libertine or Legalist?* (London, England: SPCK, 1975).

[68] E.g., H. Räisänen, *Paul and the Law*, 2nd ed. (Tübingen, Germany: Mohr Siebeck, 1987). T. R. Schreiner (*The Law and Its Fulfillment: A Pauline Theology of Law* [Grand Rapids, MI: Baker, 1993], 137–38) offers a critique of the notion of development in Paul's view of the law.

[69] Though, as J. D. G. Dunn rightly notes, "The brevity of the period cannot be counted as a determinative factor in answering the question" (*Theology of Paul the Apostle*, 730).

[70] C. H. Dodd, "The Mind of Paul: A Psychological Approach," *BJRL* 17 (1933): 91–105. Dodd argues for a "change of temper" on Paul's part in his later epistles as a result of a "spiritual crisis" or a "sort of second conversion" (p. 104). In his "The Mind of Paul: Change and Development," *BJRL* 18 (1934): 69–110, Dodd seeks to show that Paul transcended the dualism of "this age" and "the age to come" in favor of what he called a "universalism" that also entailed a revaluation of the natural order (pp. 109–10).

[71] See R. N. Longenecker, "On the Concept of Development in Pauline Thought," in *Perspectives on Evangelical Theology*, ed. K. S. Kantzer and S. N. Gundry (Grand Rapids, MI: Zondervan, 1979), 195–207.

[72] See esp. Kim, *Origin of Paul's Gospel*.

[73] See Dunn, *Theology of Paul*, 21–22 (with further bibliographical references in n. 72); M. Hengel and A. M. Schwemer, *Paul Between Damascus and Antioch: The Unknown Years*, trans. J. Bowden (Louisville, KY: Westminster John Knox, 1997), 279–91; the study by R. Riesner, *Paul's Early Period: Chronology, Mission Strategy, Theology* (Grand Rapids, MI: Eerdmans, 1998); and B. Witherington, *The Paul Quest: The Renewed Search for the Jew of Tarsus* (Downers Grove, IL: InterVarsity, 1998), 280–81.

For reasons such as these, E. Lohse has argued decisively against the notion of changes of thought in Pauline theology. While allowing that Paul may have varied "his way of speaking to the various churches," Lohse contended that "he did not change his fundamental theological thought."[74] Investigating three major areas in which some claim Paul experienced a change of thought, Lohse failed to find evidence for such in each instance: Paul's eschatology did not change materially between the writing of 1 Thessalonians and Romans;[75] in his interpretation of the law, "Paul did not change his thinking from one stage of his missionary work to the other . . . [but] was, on the contrary, an outstanding theologian arguing from a clear theoretical perspective";[76] and Paul's "understanding of the gospel and his doctrine of justification are identical" from Galatians through Romans.[77]

This is not to deny that in the course of Paul's ministry certain issues moved to the forefront that the apostle considered of great importance. One thinks of the conscious formulation of a theology of the church (1 Corinthians; Ephesians; Colossians) and instructions regarding its organization (1–2 Timothy, Titus) in some of Paul's Letters penned during the middle and later years of his career. At the same time, other questions retreated into the background, such as the Pauline version of a law-free gospel in controversy with his Jewish-Christian opponents (Galatians; Romans). While the exact contours of the gospel are still hotly debated in Galatians, for example, the apostle can in the Pastorals assume the existence of a firmly delineated core of faith.[78]

Therefore, Paul's writings must be judged to exhibit a considerable degree of theological coherence and unity in the midst of a certain extent of terminological diversity and thoughtful contextualization.[79] This is evident perhaps most clearly in the centrality of the gospel in Paul's writings.[80] A further example is the conviction that Jesus is the Messiah and the exalted Lord; the term *Christos* alone occurs in Paul's Letters and sermons almost

---

[74] E. Lohse, "Changes of Thought in Pauline Theology? Some Reflections on Paul's Ethical Teaching in the Context of His Theology," in *Theology and Ethics in Paul and His Interpreters. Essays in Honor of Victor Paul Furnish*, ed. E. H. Lovering Jr. and J. L. Sumney (Nashville, TN: Abingdon, 1996), 160; cf. V. P. Furnish, "Development in Paul's Thought," *JAAR* 38 (1970): 289–303.

[75] Lohse, "Changes of Thought," 151–53. Lohse believed 1 Thessalonians was the first and Romans the last authentic Pauline Letter, while relegating 2 Thessalonians, Colossians, Ephesians, and the Pastorals to Deutero-Pauline status. If Galatians is dated earlier than Lohse allowed, this would further speak against a Pauline development with regard to his doctrine of justification by faith.

[76] Ibid., 154, against H. Hübner, *Law in Paul's Thought*, ed. J. Riches (Edinburgh, Scotland: T&T Clark, 1984).

[77] Ibid., 156, with reference to F. Hahn, "Gibt es eine Entwicklung in den Aussagen über die Rechtfertigung bei Paulus?" *EvT* 53 (1993): 342–66; against G. Strecker, "Befreiung und Rechtfertigung. Zur Stellung der Rechtfertigungslehre in der Theologie des Paulus," in *Rechtfertigung. Festschrift für Ernst Käsemann*, ed. J. Friedrich, W. Pöhlmann, and P. Stuhlmacher (Tübingen, Germany: Mohr Siebeck; Göttingen: Vandenhoeck & Ruprecht, 1976), 479–508. Cf. A. Schlatter (*The Theology of the Apostles*, trans. A. J. Köstenberger [Grand Rapids, MI: Baker, 1999], 306), who commented that "nowhere do the later epistles lead the community beyond these norms [i.e., the ethical instructions of 1 and 2 Thessalonians]; they merely reveal more completely Paul's rationale."

[78] This, of course, assumes the Pauline authorship of the Pastoral Epistles. See the discussion of pseudonymity in chap. 15 above.

[79] See the following discussion and Bruce, "All Things to All Men," 82–99.

[80] Rom 1:1, 9, 16; 2:16; 16:25; 1 Cor 4:15; 9:12, 16, 18, 23; 15:1; Gal 1:6–7, 11; 2:2, 5, 7, 14; Eph 1:13; 3:6; 6:19; etc.

400 times (see Acts 17:2–3; 1 Cor 15:20–28; Phil 2:9–11). P. Achtemeier considers Paul's conviction that God raised Jesus from the dead to be the "generative center" of the apostle's theology.[81] In his focus on the gospel and his conviction that Jesus is the Christ and the exalted Lord, Paul was not alone. The entire NT is pervaded by these major motifs.[82]

We therefore conclude with Dunn:

> Allowing for diversity of circumstance and variety of expression, there does seem to be a remarkable continuity and homogeneity bonding all Paul's Letters into a coherent whole.[83] There are different emphases, certainly, but whether we should speak of significant development is doubtful. There is clarification of earlier insights, an unfolding of fuller meaning and implication; but "evolution" would be a less appropriate term. At most we can probably envisage a number of events and experiences which changed the emphases and prompted the elaborations, but did not alter the main elements or overall character of his theology in a significant way.[84]

Diversity of Expression in Paul and Peter, Paul and James, and Other New Testament Voices

Space does not permit detailed comment on other aspects of the diversity of expression in the NT.[85] Interesting comparisons would involve those between Paul's and Peter's theology (e.g., their ecclesiology); between Paul and James (especially with regard to their teaching on the relationship between faith and works); between Paul and Hebrews (assuming non-Pauline authorship of Hebrews); or between John's Gospel and Hebrews (e.g., cf. John 1:1–3 and Heb 1:1–3).

While certain periods of church history have seen certain portions of the NT and biblical canon being awarded a privileged position (such as Paul, and here especially Romans and Galatians, in the Reformation and ever since), it is important to appreciate all the voices finding expression in the NT, major (the Gospels, Paul) as well as minor (Peter, James, Jude). As seen further below, for example, Caird envisions the NT writers participating in

---

[81] P. Achtemeier, "The Continuing Quest for Coherence in St. Paul: An Experiment in Thought," in *Theology and Ethics in Paul and His Interpreters: Essays in Honor of Victor Paul Furnish*, 132–45, esp. p. 138.

[82] See further the discussion below.

[83] Dunn considers Colossians, Ephesians, and the Pastorals to be non-Pauline (*Theology of Paul*, 13n39; see pp. 732–33).

[84] Ibid., 730–31.

[85] For a brief synopsis, see Köstenberger, "Diversity and Unity," 152–53. For an excellent treatment of the relationships among various NT writers, see A. Schlatter, *New Testament Theology*, 2 vols., trans. A. J. Köstenberger (Grand Rapids, MI: Baker, 1997, 1999). More recently, I. H. Marshall, in his *New Testament Theology: Many Witnesses, One Gospel* (Downers Grove, IL: InterVarsity, 2004), provides a theology of each NT book and offers comparisons of the theologies of various sections in turn: the Synoptics and Acts; Paul, the Synoptics, and Acts; John, the Synoptics and Acts, and Paul; and the remainder of the NT in the context already established. He concludes "there is a significant core of agreement and identity within the theologies of the individual constituents of the New Testament" (p. 717).

a roundtable discussion. While no analogy is perfect, this model well illustrates the nature of NT theology.

POINTS OF INTEGRATION IN NEW TESTAMENT THEOLOGY

G. Maier has rightly noted that the unity of the NT is not dependent on identifying one, and only one, center of NT theology.[86] Even if it were impossible to pinpoint such a solitary center, this would not mean the NT's unity would therefore be jettisoned. In other words, there may not be one center of NT theology, but there clearly is an underlying unity to the NT. For this reason it may be preferable to speak of several points of integration that provide coherence and unity to the NT message.

In 1936 C. H. Dodd called on his scholarly colleagues to counteract disintegrative tendencies in NT theology and to accentuate the commonalities of diverse NT perspectives.[87] In the remainder of this chapter, we propose three major points of integration that provide cohesion to NT theology: (1) the one God of Israel as he is revealed in the Hebrew Scriptures; (2) Jesus the Christ, the exalted Lord; and (3) the gospel of forgiveness and salvation in Jesus Christ. This is not to say these are the only integrative motifs found in the NT—far from it. Our treatment of these three major NT themes is simply designed to demonstrate the substantial theological unity underlying the diversity of expression in the NT and, in fact, in all of Scripture.[88]

The One God

Like Judaism, Christianity came to be known for its monotheism.[89] The various NT writers all speak of the same, one God, the God of Israel (Matt 15:31; Luke 1:68) and Abraham (Matt 22:32; Acts 3:13; 7:32), who revealed himself through the OT and who sent Jesus (John 3:16). The more than 1,300 NT references to God *(theos)* provide a telling testimony to the central significance of this God.[90] Thus Jesus, according to the Synoptic

---

[86] G. Maier, *Biblical Hermeneutics*, trans. R. W. Yarbrough (Wheaton, IL: Crossway, 1997), 202, cited in Köstenberger, "Diversity and Unity," 153. This is contrary to J. M. Hamilton, *God's Glory in Salvation Through Judgment: A Biblical Theology* (Wheaton, IL: Crossway, 2010), who posits the theme given in his title as the single center of all Scripture.

[87] C. H. Dodd, *The Present Task in New Testament Studies, An Inaugural Lecture Delivered in the Divinity School, Cambridge on Tuesday, 2 June 1936* (Cambridge, UK: Cambridge University Press, 1936).

[88] For a recent taxonomy of ways in which practitioners of biblical theology have attempted to balance biblical diversity and unity, see A. J. Köstenberger, "The Present and Future of Biblical Theology," *Them* 37/3 (2012): 445–64, who surveys four major approaches: (1) classic; (2) central themes; (3) single center; and (4) story or metanarrative.

[89] See esp. the work by R. Bauckham, *God Crucified: Monotheism and Christology in the New Testament* (Grand Rapids, MI: Eerdmans, 1999), vii. He argued that from the beginning "early Christians included Jesus . . . within the unique identity of the one God of Israel." Note also N. Macdonald, "Monotheism," in *The World of the New Testament: Cultural, Social, and Historical Contexts* (Grand Rapids, MI: Baker, 2013), 77–84, including further bibliography; and a number of the essays in L. T. Stuckenbruck and W. E. Sproston North, eds., *Early Jewish and Christian Monotheism*, JSNTSup 263 (London, England: T&T Clark, 2004), including the helpful J. F. McGrath and J. Truex, "Early Jewish and Christian Monotheism: A Select Bibliography" (pp. 235–42).

[90] See chap. 4, "The Centrality of God in New Testament Theology," in T. R. Schreiner, *New Testament Theology: Magnifying God in Christ* (Grand Rapids, MI: Baker, 2008), 119–67.

Gospels, speaks about the *kingdom* of God;[91] Paul chooses the *righteousness* of God as a central motif;[92] several NT authors refer to the *glory* of God;[93] and numerous voices even call the Christian *gospel* "the gospel of God."[94] Beyond this one reads about the *will* of God, the *knowledge* of God, the *power* of God, the *peace* of God, the *church* of God, the *work* of God, God the *Father*, God the *Redeemer*, the *word* of God, the *judgment* of God, the *Spirit* of God, the *grace* of God, and so on. The entire NT is pervaded by the belief in God, his character, and his salvific work in Christ. God is therefore the foundation not only of the NT but of the entire Bible and in the NT also of the further unifying themes discussed below: Jesus the Messiah and the exalted Lord, and the gospel.

Jesus the Messiah and the Exalted Lord

The connection between the one God and Jesus the Messiah and exalted Lord is nowhere clearer than in the remarkable early confession cited by Paul in 1 Corinthians 8:6: "Yet for us there is one God, the Father. All things are from him, and we exist for him. And there is one Lord, Jesus Christ. All things are through him, and we exist through him."[95] In light of this close connection between the one God and the Lord Jesus Christ drawn by the early church, Bultmann's famous exclusion of the historical Jesus from NT theology is too radical.[96] Jesus's messianic consciousness and the fact that the Easter event could not by itself produce messianic faith underscore the close connection between the so-called historical Jesus and the faith of the first Christians.[97] In fact, the conviction that Jesus is the Messiah foretold in the OT and the exalted Lord represents an important integrative

---

[91] See Acts 1:3; 8:12; 14:22; 19:8; 28:23, 31; Rom 14:17; 1 Cor 4:20; 6:9–10; 15:50; Gal 5:21; Col 4:11; 2 Thess 1:5; Rev 12:10.

[92] Rom 1:18; 3:5, 21–22; 10:3; 2 Cor 5:21; Phil 3:9; see Jas 1:20; 2 Pet 1:1.

[93] John 11:4, 40; 12:43; Acts 7:55; Rom 1:23; 3:7, 23; 5:2; 15:7; 1 Pet 4:14; Rev 15:8; 19:1; 21:11, 23.

[94] Mark 1:14; Acts 20:24; Rom 1:1; 15:16; 2 Cor 11:7; 1 Thess 2:2, 8–9; 1 Tim 1:11; 1 Pet 4:17.

[95] See F. F. Bruce, "All Things to All Men," 92; and L. W. Hurtado, *One God, One Lord: Early Christian Devotion and Ancient Jewish Monotheism* (Philadelphia: Fortress, 1988), esp. pp. 97–99. See also L. W. Hurtado, *Lord Jesus Christ: Devotion to Jesus in Earliest Christianity* (Grand Rapids, MI: Eerdmans, 2003); and R. Bauckham, *Jesus and the God of Israel: God Crucified and Other Studies on the New Testament's Christology of Divine Identity* (Grand Rapids, MI: Eerdmans, 2008).

[96] See R. Bultmann, *Theology of the New Testament*, trans. K. Grobel (New York, NY: Charles Scribner's Sons, 1970), 3, and the discussion above. See also P. Balla, *Challenges to New Testament Theology* (Peabody, MA: Hendrickson, 1998), 170–77; P. Stuhlmacher, *Biblische Theologie des New Testament* (Göttingen, Germany: Vandenhoeck & Ruprecht, 1992), 1:18: "Jesus' proclamation is not a mere 'presupposition,' but the historical foundation of NT theology"; and R. Morgan, "The Historical Jesus and the Theology of the New Testament," in *The Glory of Christ in the New Testament: Studies in Christology in Memory of George Bradford Caird*, ed. L. D. Hurst and N. T. Wright (Oxford, UK: Clarendon, 1987), 187–206. See also the two-volume NT theology by A. Schlatter, who devoted his entire first volume to "the history of the Christ." A. Schlatter, *New Testament Theology*, vol. 1: *The History of the Christ*; vol. 2: *The Theology of the Apostles*, trans. A. J. Köstenberger (Grand Rapids, MI: Baker, 1997, 1999).

[97] See O. Betz, "The Problem of Variety and Unity in the New Testament," *HBT* 21 (1980): 10–11.

center of NT theology.[98] This conviction unites both the OT with the NT, and the four Gospels with the gospel of the first Christians, including Paul.[99]

Paul's conversion at his encounter with the resurrected Christ was brought about by the realization that the same Jesus whom Paul deemed cursed by the law was in fact the God-sent Redeemer (Gal 3:13–14). With this starting point Paul began to read the OT in light of this revolutionary hermeneutical axiom, which led not merely to important Christological interpretations of the OT but also put into perspective the role of the law in the life of the believer (see Rom 10:4).[100] Fulfilling the law was now replaced by a new "law," that of life in the Spirit of Christ (Rom 8:2; Gal 5:16, 18; see 6:2), and this law was—in contrast to the law in the OT—not merely external to the believer but through his Spirit divinely and directly written into a person's heart (see Jer 31:33–34). In this Paul and John agreed (Rom 8:9; Gal 2:20; John 14:16–17; 1 John 2:20, 27). This does not mean there is no more need for further written instructions or commands, as if possession of the Spirit entirely obviated the need for such. To the contrary, the NT is replete with just such hortatory material.

The Gospel

The gospel of Jesus Christ is one of the major integrative glues of Scripture and particularly of the NT.[101] According to Lohse, it is the task of "NT theology to demonstrate how the early Christians proclaimed the gospel, and to show in detail how this *kerygma* was interpreted in the theology of the apostle Paul, the Synoptics, and in the Johannine writings."[102] The term "good news" is already found in the OT (e.g., Isa 40:9; 52:7). Jesus started out his ministry calling people to repentance and faith in the "good news" (Mark 1:15 and parallels). Paul discovered in the gospel the power for salvation of all who accept it by faith, Jews as well as Greeks.[103] Moreover, the gospel did not merely indicate for the first Christians that the historical Jesus was to be identified with the resurrected, exalted

---

[98] See Balla (*Challenges to New Testament Theology*, 173), who contends that Jesus is the origin of the Christology of the first Christians (including the evangelists); and Guthrie, *New Testament Theology*, 54–55.

[99] See J. D. G. Dunn, *Unity and Diversity in the New Testament: An Inquiry into the Character of Earliest Christianity* (London, England: SCM, 1990), 369; idem, *Theology of Paul*, 729 (see Wenham, "Unity and Diversity," 711); and E. P. Sanders (*Paul and Palestinian Judaism* [Minneapolis, MN: Fortress, 1977], 441–42), who identifies the fact "that Jesus Christ is Lord" and "that in him God has provided for the salvation of all who believe" as one of two "primary convictions which governed Paul's Christian life."

[100] See Bruce ("All Things to All Men," 87), who spoke of "the Christ who, from Paul's conversion onward, replaced the law as the center of his life and thought" (with further reference to Rom 10:4).

[101] E. Lohse, *Die Vielfalt des Neuen Testaments* (Göttingen, Germany: Vandenhoeck & Ruprecht, 1982), 227–30. See A. J. Köstenberger, "The Gospel for All Nations," in *Faith Comes by Hearing: A Response to Inclusivism*, ed. R. A. Peterson and C. W. Morgan (Downers Grove, IL: InterVarsity, 2008), 201–19. Note the recent attempt to approach systematic theology self-consciously through the lens of the gospel in M. F. Bird, *Evangelical Theology: A Biblical and Systematic Introduction* (Grand Rapids, MI: Zondervan, 2013).

[102] Lohse, *Vielfalt des Neuen Testaments*, 246.

[103] Rom 1:16; 2:9–10; 10:12; 1 Cor 1:22, 24; 12:13; Gal 3:28; Col 3:11; see Acts 13:46–48; 28:25–28; see Luke 2:32.

Lord and the Messiah who had been predicted in the OT. It was a message of forgiveness of sins on account of the substitutionary work of Christ at the cross.[104]

As Paul and his apostolic colleagues read the OT in light of the Christ's first coming (see Acts 17:2–3; Rom 1:2, 17; 1 Cor 15:3–5), they realized that the Messiah is cast already there as a *suffering* Messiah, whose plight was in the place of others and was followed by his resurrection (e.g., Isaiah 53). This conviction surfaces repeatedly in the teachings of Jesus in all four Gospels (e.g., Mark 8:31; 9:31; 10:33–34, 45), in Paul (e.g., Rom 3:25; 2 Cor 5:21), in Peter (1 Pet 1:2, 10–12, 18–20), in Hebrews (Heb 1:3), and further NT writings (e.g., 1 John 2:2; Rev 5:5–6). Therefore, the gospel of the first Christians (which in turn was rooted in Jesus's messianic consciousness) has as its content the crucified and risen Messiah and Lord—in conscious application of OT passages to the person and work of Jesus. Finally, in the book of Acts, God's Word is frequently invested with personal traits so that it is not Paul and the first Christians who pursue their mission but the gospel itself marches irresistibly and victoriously to the ends of the earth (see Acts 6:7; 12:24; 19:20). Recent research views the gospel as a central motif especially in the programmatic letter to the Romans.[105] Beyond this, the expression "gospel" (or equivalent expressions such as "message" or "the faith") is found frequently in the NT, even though the precise contours of the Christian message depend on the respective circumstances of proclamation.[106]

Not only did Paul insist on a unified gospel, but he also viewed it as safeguarding the unity of the Christian movement (see Gal 1:6–9).[107] The gospel established common ground among the diverse elements within the church: Jews and Gentiles, slave and free, male and female (Gal 3:28; see 1 Cor 12:13; Col 3:11). Thus, while Paul acknowledged the diversity of local congregations and the distinctive roles and spiritual gifts of individual church members, he saw this diversity within the larger framework of the one church as the one body of Christ (1 Cor 12:12; Eph 4:4; 5:30) as well as of the one God, Lord, and Spirit who works in and through the church individually and corporately (1 Cor 12:4–11; Eph 4:3–6).

SUMMARY AND CONCLUSION

The convictions that there is one God, that Jesus is the Messiah and the exalted Lord, and that the Christian community has been entrusted with the proclamation of the gospel of salvation in Jesus Christ, can be found in the subsequent partial listing of NT writings (Table 21.1) given in the general chronological order of composition.

---

[104] So correctly Carson, "Unity and Diversity," 73. See also P. Stuhlmacher, *Biblische Theologie des Neuen Testaments* (Göttingen, Germany: Vandenhoeck & Ruprecht, 1999), 2:310: "The (major) witnesses of the NT teach jointly that Jesus' cross-death is to be understood as an atoning, divinely commissioned death for 'the many.'"

[105] E.g., D. J. Moo, *Romans*, NICNT (Grand Rapids, MI: Eerdmans, 1996), 29–30.

[106] See J. Reumann, *Variety and Unity in New Testament Thought* (Oxford, UK: University Press, 1991), 289.

[107] See Bruce, "All Things to All Men," 96.

Table 21.1: Major Unifying Themes in NT Theology

The One God	Jesus as Messiah and Lord	Gospel, Message, the Faith
1. James		
1:1, 5, 13, 20; 2:5, 19	2:1	1:27
2. Paul		
Gal 1:1, 10, 13, 20, 24; etc.	Gal 1:3; 3:26; 6:4	Gal 1:7–9, 23; 2:1, 5, 7, etc.
1 Thess 2:2, 8–9; 2 Thess 1:5	1 Thess 1:1, 3; 5:9, 23, 28	1 Thess 1:5; 2:2, 4, 8–9; 3:2; 2 Thess 1:8; 2:14; 3:1
1 Cor 4:20; 6:9–10; 8:6; 15:50; 2 Cor 5:21; 11:7	1 Cor 2:2; 8:6	1 Cor 1:17–18; 2:4; 4:15; 9:12, 14, 16, 23; 15:1–4; 2 Cor 2:12; 4:3–4; 5:19; 8:18; 9:13; 10:14; 11:4, 7
Rom 1:1, 18, 23; 3:5, 7, 21–23; 5:2; 10:3; 14:17; 15:7, 16	Rom 1:1–4; 5:1, 11; 6:23	Rom 1:1–2, 9, 16–17; 2:16; 10:15–17; 15:16, 19–20; 16:25
Eph 1:3–6; Phil 1:2–3; 3:9; Col 1:1, 3, 6, 9–10; 4:11	Eph 1:10; 2:20; 4:15; 5:23; Col 2:6; Phlm 1	Eph 1:13; 3:6; 4:5; 6:15, 19; Phil 1:5, 7, 12, 16, 18, 25, 27; 2:22; 4:3, 15; Col 1:5, 23; 2:5; Phlm 6, 13
1 Tim 1:1, 4, 11, 17; 2:3, 5; 3:5, 15; 4:3–5; etc.	1 Tim 1:12, 15; 2 Tim 1:10	1 Tim 1:2, 11; 2:7; 4:1, 6; 6:10, 12, 21; 2 Tim 1:8, 10, 13–14; 2:8; 3:8; 4:7; Titus 1:9
3. Synoptics and Acts		
Mark 1:14–15; 12:26, 29, 32	Mark 1:1; 8:29; 12:35–37	Mark 1:1, 14–15; 8:35; 10:29; 13:10; 14:9
Matt 15:31; 22: 32, 37	Matt 1:1; 16:16; 22:41–46	Matt 4:23; 9:35; 24:14; 26:13; 28:20
Luke 1:68; 20:37; Acts 1:3; 3:13; 7:32, 55; 8:12; 14:22; 19:8; 20:24; 28:23, 31	Luke 2:11; 9:20; 20:41–44; Acts 2:36; 5:42; 9:22; 17:2–3; 18:28	Luke 4:18, 43; 7:22; 8:1; 9:6; 16:16; 20:1; Acts 2:41; 5:20, 42; 8:4, 12, 25, 35, 40; 10:36; 11:20; 15:7, 35; 17:11, 18; 20:24
4. Hebrews		
1:1–3, 5–6, 13; etc.	3:6; 13:8	2:3; 4:2, 6, 14; 12:2
5. Peter		
1 Pet 4:14, 17	1 Pet 1:1–3, 11; 3:15	1 Pet 1:12, 25; 2:8; 4:17; 5:9
2 Pet 1:1	2 Pet 1:1, 16	2 Pet 1:1
6. Jude		
1, 4, 21, 25	1, 4	3, 20
7. John		
John 1:1–2, 6, 12, 18, 36, 51; etc.	John 1:17, 41, 45; 11:27; 20:31; 1 John 2:22; 5:1	John 12:38; 17:20; 1 John 5:4
Rev 12:10; 15:8; 19:1; 21:11, 23	Rev 1:1–2, 5	Rev 10:7; 14:6

Perhaps the best summary of the gospel is found in Acts 10:36: "He sent the message to the Israelites, proclaiming the good news of peace through Jesus Christ—he is Lord of all." Jesus is Christ and Lord, and his followers proclaim the gospel: "They continued teaching and proclaiming the good news that Jesus is the Messiah" (Acts 5:42). This gospel was also proclaimed by Paul (Acts 17:2–3). The expression "the Lord Jesus Christ" likewise sums up the unified Christian conviction of faith.[108]

The joint foundation of faith of the first Christians comprised several further convictions—not just belief in the one God, in Jesus as Messiah and Lord, and in the gospel of forgiveness of sins in Christ. As examples, we may cite the expectation of Jesus's return[109] and the love commandment, especially in Paul and John but also in Peter. The first Christians were also united in the understanding that the NT church was the new messianic community, in continuity with OT Israel.[110] Paul's statement that speaks of a sevenfold unity should also be cited: "One body and one Spirit, . . . one hope . . .; one Lord, one faith, one baptism, one God and Father of all" (Eph 4:4–6).

The diversity and unity of the NT coexist as joint characteristics of the NT and do not constitute a problem—in the sense of unsolvable tensions or contradictions—but present the reader with the rich legacy of the faith of the first Christians, in which various perspectives of the same Jesus Christ and of the same gospel mutually complemented one another. Paul's reference to the "whole plan of God" (Acts 20:27) seems to presuppose a unified perspective.[111] Wenham talks about a "concern for the working out of an orthodoxy (and orthopraxis) defined by the person and teaching of Jesus" and an organic development that can be likened to a tree whose branches have a common origin and are part of a common entity.[112] Betz notes that the successful mission of the first Christians would not have been possible without the fundamental unity of the Christian faith.[113] One also thinks of the readiness to martyrdom, in which regard Pliny, for example, never portrayed the Christians he interrogated as a divided or diversified group.

The first Christians, and here especially Paul and John, concur that Jesus is the God-sent Christ and the exalted Lord. On the basis of this conviction and the resulting gospel message, Paul, John, and other NT authors develop their own theologies depending on a variety of circumstances: the respective requirements of ministry, their own faith experience, and numerous other cultural, historical, and missionary factors. Thus, the NT shows that the first Christians were from the start united in their belief that Jesus was and is the

---

108 E.g., Gal 6:14; 1 Thess 5:9; 2 Thess 2:1, 14; 1 Cor 1:7; 8:6; 15:57; Rom 1:4; 5:1, 11; 6:23; 13:14; Col 2:6; Jas 1:1; 2:1; 1 Tim 1:12; 2 Pet 1:16; Jude 4, 17, 21.

109 See G. E. Ladd, "Eschatology and the Unity of New Testament Theology," *ExpTim* 68 (1956–57): 268–73; cf. Stuhlmacher, *Biblische Theologie des Neuen Testaments*, 2:310: "The NT witnesses . . . also all teach the expectation of parousia and final judgment."

110 See Stuhlmacher, *Biblische Theologie des Neuen Testaments*, 2:310–11.

111 D. P. Fuller, *The Unity of the Bible* (Grand Rapids, MI: Zondervan, 1992), 22–23.

112 Wenham, "Unity and Diversity," 703; see Carson, "Unity and Diversity," 65–95.

113 Betz, "Problem of Variety and Unity," 6.

Messiah. This is indicated already in the earliest apostolic tradition.[114] Only gradually were these fundamental convictions applied to various situations and further relevant theological conclusions drawn. W. Bauer believed there was a movement from diversity to unity, but—importantly—the first Christians actually developed from unity to diversity.[115]

G. B. Caird puts it well:

> The question we must ask is not whether these books all say the same thing, but whether they all bear witness to the same Jesus and through him to the many splendoured wisdom of the one God. If we are persuaded that the second Moses, the son of Man, the friend of sinners, the incarnate *logos*, the firstborn of all creation, the Apostle and High Priest of our calling, the Chief Shepherd, and the Lamb opening the scroll are the same person in whom the one God has achieved and is achieving his mighty work, we shall neither attempt to press all our witnesses into a single mould nor captiously complain that one seems at some points deficient in comparison with another. What we shall do is rejoice that God has seen fit to establish His gospel at the mouth of so many independent witnesses. The music of the New Testament choir is not written to be sung in unison.[116]

The one God, Jesus Christ, and the gospel—these are the major pillars of NT theology.[117] It remains the interpreter's task to exegete individual passages in the respective NT writings and to relate diverse motifs in different NT documents to one another.[118] Yet this may take place in the confidence that the NT is not a disparate collection of ill-fitting parts, which together result in nothing more than a cacophony of voices but is instead a well-composed symphony in which different elements combine into a harmonious work. It echoes to all the world to the glory of God and for the edification of those individuals who respond to the divine revelation not with skepticism but in faith.[119]

---

[114] See I. H. Marshall, "Orthodoxy and Heresy in Earlier Christianity," *Them* 2/1 (1976): 5–14.

[115] W. Bauer, *Orthodoxy and Heresy in Earliest Christianity* (Philadelphia: Fortress, 1979; German original 1934). But see the compelling critique by P. Trebilco, "Christian Communities in Western Asia Minor into the Early Second Century: Ignatius and Others as Witnesses Against Bauer," *JETS* 49 (2006): 17–44; and the extensive refutation by A. J. Köstenberger and M. J. Kruger, *The Heresy of Orthodoxy: How Contemporary Culture's Fascination with Diversity Has Reshaped Our Understanding of Early Christianity* (Wheaton: Crossway, 2010).

[116] G. B. Caird, *New Testament Theology*, ed. L. D. Hurst (Oxford, UK: Clarendon, 1994), 24. See the largely positive assessment of Caird's work in D. A. Carson, "New Testament Theology," in *Dictionary of the Later New Testament and Its Developments*, ed. R. P. Martin and P. H. Davids (Downers Grove, IL: InterVarsity, 1998), 803–4.

[117] Jesus the Messiah and Lord and the gospel are cited by Betz ("Problem of Variety and Unity," 8–9) as establishing the unity of the NT.

[118] See C. L. Blomberg, "The Legitimacy and Limits of Harmonization," in *Hermeneutics, Authority, and Canon*, ed. D. A. Carson and J. D. Woodbridge (Grand Rapids, MI: Zondervan, 1986), 139–74; and H-W. Neudorfer, "Ist Sachkritik nötig? Anmerkungen zu einem Thema der biblischen Hermeneutik am Beispiel des Jakobusbriefs," *KD* 43 (1997): 301. Neudorfer included in his proposed methodology the placing of an individual portion of Scripture into the overall framework of biblical teaching, which also entails the showing of interconnections and the demonstration of Scripture's unity.

[119] For a defense of the existence of God, the deity of Jesus, and the reliability of the Bible, see A. J. Köstenberger, D. L. Bock, and J. D. Chatraw, *Truth Matters: Confident Faith in a Confusing World* (Nashville, TN: B&H, 2014); and the more

STUDY QUESTIONS

1. To what does "unity and diversity in the NT" refer?
2. How would you briefly explain the relationship among the Gospels, the book of Acts, the Letters, and the book of Revelation?
3. Why do many scholars think the Synoptic Gospels and John's Gospel stand in irreconcilable conflict?
4. Why do the Synoptics and John complement instead of conflict with each other?
5. Why should interpreters undertake caution in dichotomizing Jesus's and Paul's teachings and theology?
6. Why did F. C. Baur argue that Luke's presentation of Paul in the book of Acts is incompatible with the way the apostle portrayed himself?
7. What are some reasons the Paul of Acts and the Paul of the Letters differ?
8. What are some of Paul's alleged developments of thought?
9. Concerning these alleged developments, what two examples suggest a considerable degree of Pauline coherence and unity?
10. What are three major points of integration that provide cohesion to the theology of the NT?
11. What further convictions did these three points of integration produce among the first Christians?
12. Why do the diversity and unity present in the NT not produce unsolvable tensions or contradictions?

FOR FURTHER STUDY

Alexander, T. D. *From Eden to the New Jerusalem: An Introduction to Biblical Theology*. Grand Rapids, MI: Kregel, 2009.

Balla, P. *Challenges to New Testament Theology: An Attempt to Justify the Enterprise*. Peabody, MA: Hendrickson, 1998.

Bauer, W. *Orthodoxy and Heresy in Earliest Christianity*. Edited by R. A. Kraft and G. Krodel. Philadelphia, PA: Fortress, 1979 (German original, 1934).

Beale, G. K. *A New Testament Biblical Theology: The Unfolding of the Old Testament in the New*. Grand Rapids, MI: Baker, 2011.

Blomberg, C. L. "The Legitimacy and Limits of Harmonization." Pages 139–74 in *Hermeneutics, Authority, and Canon*. Edited by D. A. Carson and J. D. Woodbridge. Grand Rapids, MI: Zondervan, 1986.

Bockmuehl, M. N. A. *Seeing the Word: Refocusing New Testament Study*. Studies in Theological Interpretation. Grand Rapids, MI: Baker, 2006.

Bruce, F. F. "'All Things to All Men': Diversity in Unity and Other Pauline Tensions." Pages 82–99 in *Unity and Diversity in New Testament Theology*. Edited by R. Guelich. Grand Rapids, MI: Eerdmans, 1978.

___________. "Is the Paul of Acts the Real Paul?" *Bulletin of the John Rylands Library* 58 (1976): 282–305.

---

fully documented work by the same authors, *Truth in a Culture of Doubt: Engaging Skeptical Challenges to the Bible* (Nashville, TN: B&H, 2014).

Caird, G. B. *New Testament Theology*. Edited by L. D. Hurst. Oxford, UK: Clarendon, 1994.

__________. "New Testament Theology." Pages 796–814 in *Dictionary of the Later New Testament and Its Developments*. Edited by R. P. Martin and P. H. Davids. Downers Grove, IL: InterVarsity, 1998.

Carson, D. A. "Unity and Diversity in the New Testament: The Possibility of Systematic Theology." Pages 65–95, 368–75 in *Scripture and Truth*. Edited by D. A. Carson and J. D. Woodbridge. Grand Rapids, MI: Zondervan, 1983.

Dunn, J. D. G. *Unity and Diversity in the New Testament: An Inquiry into the Character of Earliest Christianity*. London, England: SCM, 1990.

Fuller, D. P. *The Unity of the Bible*. Grand Rapids, MI: Zondervan, 1992.

Furnish, V. P. "Development in Paul's Thought." *Journal of the American Academy of Religion* 38 (1970): 289–303.

Goldsworthy, G. *According to Plan: The Unfolding Revelation of God in the Bible*. Leicester, UK: InterVarsity, 1991.

Goswell, G. "The Order of the Books of the New Testament." *Journal of the Evangelical Theological Society* 53 (2010): 225–41.

Guelich. R. A., ed. *Unity and Diversity in New Testament Theology: Essays in Honor of George E. Ladd*. Grand Rapids, MI: Eerdmans, 1978.

Guthrie, D. *New Testament Theology*. Downers Grove, IL: InterVarsity, 1981.

Hengel, M. *The Four Gospels and the One Gospel of Jesus*. Valley Forge, PA: Trinity Press International, 2000.

Hill, C. E. *Who Chose the Gospels? Probing the Great Gospel Conspiracy*. Oxford, UK: Oxford University Press, 2010.

Köstenberger, A. J. "Diversity and Unity in the New Testament." Pages 144–58 in *Biblical Theology: Retrospect and Prospect*. Edited by S. J. Hafemann. Downers Grove, IL: InterVarsity, 2002.

__________. "The Gospel for All Nations." Pages 201–19 in *Faith Comes by Hearing: A Response to Inclusivism*. Edited by R. A. Peterson and C. W. Morgan. Downers Grove, IL: InterVarsity, 2008.

__________. "The Present and Future of Biblical Theology." *Themelios* 37, no. 3 (2012): 445–64. Available online at http://themelios.thegospelcoalition.org/article/the-present-and-future-of-biblical-theology1.

__________, and M. J. Kruger. *The Heresy of Orthodoxy: How Contemporary Culture's Fascination with Diversity Has Reshaped Our Understanding of Early Christianity*. Wheaton, IL: Crossway, 2010.

__________, D. L. Bock, and J. D. Chatraw. *Truth in a Culture of Doubt: Engaging Skeptical Challenges to the Bible*. Nashville, TN: B&H, 2014.

__________, D. L. Bock, and J. D. Chatraw. *Truth Matters: Confident Faith in a Confusing World*. Nashville, TN: B&H, 2014.

Kruger, M. J. *Canon Revisited: Establishing the Origins and Authority of the New Testament Books*. Wheaton, IL: Crossway, 2012.

__________. *The Question of Canon: Challenging the Status Quo in the New Testament Debate*. Downers Grove, IL: InterVarsity, 2013.

Ladd, G. E. *A Theology of the New Testament*. Rev. ed. Edited by D. A. Hagner. Grand Rapids, MI: Eerdmans, 1993.

Lohse, E. "Changes of Thought in Pauline Theology? Some Reflections on Paul's Ethical Teaching in the Context of His Theology." Pages 146–60 in *Theology and Ethics in Paul and His Interpreters: Essays in Honor of Victor Paul Furnish*. Edited by E. H. Lovering Jr. and J. L. Sumney. Nashville, TN: Abingdon, 1996.

Longenecker, R. N. "On the Concept of Development in Pauline Thought." Pages 195–207 in *Perspectives on Evangelical Theology*. Edited by K. S. Kantzer and S. N. Gundry. Grand Rapids, MI: Zondervan, 1979.

Marshall, I. H. *New Testament Theology: Many Witnesses, One Gospel*. Downers Grove, IL: InterVarsity, 2004, esp. chap. 31.

__________. "Orthodoxy and Heresy in Earlier Christianity." *Themelios* 2/1 (1976): 5–14.

Matera, F. J. *New Testament Theology: Exploring Diversity and Unity*. Louisville, KY: Westminster John Knox, 2007.

Morgan, R. "The Historical Jesus and the Theology of the New Testament." Pages 187–206 in *The Glory of Christ in the New Testament: Studies in Christology in Memory of George Bradford Caird*. Edited by L. D. Hurst and N. T. Wright. Oxford, UK: Clarendon, 1987.

Porter, S. E. *The Paul of Acts*. Wissenschaftliche Untersuchungen zum Neuen Testament 115. Tübingen, Germany: Mohr Siebeck, 1999.

Reumann, J. *Variety and Unity in New Testament Thought*. Oxford, UK: University Press, 1991.

Schlatter, A. *New Testament Theology*. Vol. 1: *The History of the Christ*. Vol. 2: *The Theology of the Apostles*. Translated by A. J. Köstenberger. Grand Rapids, MI: Baker, 1997, 1999.

Schreiner, T. R. *New Testament Theology: Magnifying God in Christ*. Grand Rapids, MI: Baker, 2008.

Scobie, C. H. H. *The Ways of Our God: An Approach to Biblical Theology*. Grand Rapids, MI: Eerdmans, 2003.

Stout, S. O. *The "Man Christ Jesus": The Humanity of Jesus in the Teaching of the Apostle Paul*. Eugene, OR: Wipf & Stock, 2011.

Stuhlmacher, P. *Biblische Theologie des New Testament*. 2 vols. Göttingen, Germany: Vandenhoeck & Ruprecht, 1992, 1999.

Thielman, F. *Theology of the New Testament: A Canonical and Synthetic Approach*. Grand Rapids, MI: Zondervan, 2005.

Wenham, D. "Unity and Diversity in the New Testament." Pages 684–719 in *A Theology of the New Testament*. By G. E. Ladd. Rev. ed. Edited by D. A. Hagner. Grand Rapids, MI: Eerdmans, 1993.

Epilogue

The Story Line of Scripture

THE NT IS not a book unto itself. It cannot be understood apart from its predecessor, the OT Scriptures. Just as the OT is incomplete without the NT, the NT is lacking context and foundation without the OT. Together the two contain a story line that stretches from creation to new creation, from promise to fulfillment, from dominion and disaster to renewed dominion. Now that we have surveyed the NT, we can complete our understanding of Scripture as a whole by tracing the entire story line of which the NT is the culmination.[1] In so doing, we will not only trace the main story line but will also highlight significant side plots that illumine that big picture.

The story of the Bible could be told in many ways. And there is not necessarily one, and only one, right way to present it. What we offer here is the story of God's dealings with his people through the lens of the covenants he made with Israel and then with the representatives of the new messianic community, the church. This story line extends from creation through God's covenants with Abraham, Moses, and David, to Jesus's institution of the new covenant with the Twelve. It is explicated particularly in the book of Hebrews and consummated in the book of Revelation.[2]

---

[1] In this way the following treatment, in particular the portion that covers the NT, will provide a capstone for this volume, reiterating many of the themes sounded in the preceding pages.

[2] For other treatments see, e.g., T. D. Alexander, *From Eden to the New Jerusalem: An Introduction to Biblical Theology* (Grand Rapids, MI: Kregel, 2009); G. K. Beale, *A New Testament Biblical Theology: The Unfolding of the Old Testament in the New* (Grand Rapids, MI: Baker, 2011); G. Goldsworthy, *According to Plan: The Unfolding Revelation of God in the Bible* (Downers Grove: InterVarsity, 2002); T. R. Schreiner, *The King and His Beauty: A Biblical Theology of the Old and New Testaments* (Grand Rapids, MI: Baker, 2013); and on a more popular level, J. M. Hamilton Jr., *What Is Biblical Theology? A Guide to the Bible's Story, Symbolism, and Patterns* (Wheaton, IL: Crossway, 2013).

GOD'S PURPOSES IN CREATION

The story begins "in the beginning"—with creation. The creation account in Genesis 1:1–2:3 is the preamble to the history of redemption narrated in the NT. It begins with God's creation of the heavens and the earth. While the creation story does not provide a formal introduction for God, it does furnish a considerable amount of information about the God who created. He is the absolute Ruler over the earth and all its inhabitants. He is extremely powerful. He spoke the entire creation into existence. He has a Spirit who moved upon the waters (Gen 1:2), and he constitutes a plurality, reflected in his creation of humanity as a plurality of male and female (Gen 1:26–28).

The story proceeds at a steady pace through the first five days of creation, ending at verse 25 with the refrain, "And God saw that it was good." At verse 26, both thematically and linguistically, the story slows, indicating emphasis and prominence. P. Gentry and S. Wellum note ten items connected with the sixth day of creation, seven of which are relevant for our purposes.[3] (1) The narrative as a whole contains seven paragraphs corresponding to a chronological week, day by day. (2) The sixth paragraph (creation of humanity) is the longest; in fact, it is twice as long as the lengthiest of the previous paragraphs. (3) The sixth paragraph is marked for prominence in that the previous creation events were mere declarations, while humanity is the result of deliberation ("let us"), among other formulaic deviations from the structure of the preceding paragraphs. (4) In previous days the days are mentioned without an article ("an *x* day") but, strikingly, it is "*the* sixth day."[4] (5) The word "create" (Hebrew *bārā*) is used three times in this paragraph—as many times as it appears in the rest of the narrative. But more noticeably, these appearances "mark important points in the creation work."[5] (6) Significantly, humanity is created and commanded to rule over God's creation (Gen 1:26–27).[6] (7) All of creation is good, but once humanity is created, creation is pronounced "very good" (1:31).

The creation of humans, however, was for a purpose, not necessarily a place of privilege. Man and woman are first told to "be fruitful, multiply, fill the earth, and subdue it" (Gen 1:28). These are best understood as indicating not only procreation but also domestication. That is, humans are not only to be numerous but on mission to inhabit the entirety of the earth. This is integral to the larger mission to subdue the planet.

Ruling, in turn, is intimately connected to being created in the image of God. In Genesis 1:26, "Let us make man in our image" is followed by what is likely a purpose

---

[3] The list is adapted from P. J. Gentry and S. J. Wellum, *Kingdom Through Covenant: A Biblical-Theological Understanding of the Covenants* (Wheaton, IL: Crossway, 2012), 181–84.

[4] The references are as follows: 1:5, *yôm eḥād*; 1:8, *yôm šēnî*; 1:13, *yōm šelîšî*; 1:19, *yôm rěbî'î*; 1:23, *yôm ḥămîšî*; but it is *yôm haššiššî* at 1:31. The seventh day is also articular but does not occur in the same formulaic expression. As Gentry and Wellum (ibid., 184) note, while the exact significance of the article is debated, the fact it is noticeably different is not.

[5] Ibid.

[6] It is also significant that only humanity is made in the image of God; for a defense of the relationship between God's image and humanity's dominion, see further the discussion below.

clause: "They will rule."[7] Scholars have long debated whether the image of God in man is ontological (a matter of being) or functional (a matter of office/activity).[8] It is probably best to think of it as both: ontology (sonship) that is inseparable from function (to rule).[9] In antiquity "image" was related to a king being the divine representative of a deity.[10] Thus, God's intent in making humanity after his own image was to set men and women as his vice-regents over the earth to rule it for him as his earthly representatives (Gen 1:26, 28).

The fall of humankind in the garden is the single most devastating tragedy that ever occurred. Humanity lived in a garden planted by God. God created the man and the woman outside the garden and placed them in it, signifying God's ownership of the garden and indicating that humans were not originally part of it. They were in the garden based on their relationship to God. When they sinned, they forfeited the privilege to be there.[11]

The primordial pair was given access to every tree of the garden except the tree of the knowledge of good and evil.[12] This "knowledge" is best understood as moral discernment and the propensity to be self-legislating.[13] To seek such knowledge is to seek autonomy from God and to be one's own god. They were, as Dumbrell puts it, "snatching at Divinity."[14] The fall, then, was not merely the result of the pair deviating from a (short) list of do's and don'ts; it was the result of their quest to exalt themselves to equality with God. This treasonous attempt inexorably breaks their relationship with the Creator.[15]

The fall's results are immediate and comprehensive, devastating the human race. At once the man and woman recognize their nakedness and experience shame. Previously

---

[7] Alexander notes, "A Hebrew jussive [command] with unconverted *wāw* (*wĕyirdû*, 'and let them rule') that follows a cohortative (*naʿăśeh*, 'let us make') always expresses the intention or aim of the first-person perspective (singular or plural) represented by the cohortative. The syntax, in other words, points to 'rule' as the purpose, not simply the consequence or result, of the *imago Dei*" (Alexander, *From Eden to the New Jerusalem*, 77). See also W. J. Dumbrell, *The Faith of Israel: A Theological Survey of the Old Testament*, 2nd ed. (Grand Rapids, MI: Baker, 2002), 16.

[8] See, e.g., E. H. Merrill, "Image of God," in *Dictionary of the Old Testament: Pentateuch* (Downers Grove, IL: InterVarsity, 2002), 441–45.

[9] Gentry and Wellum, *Kingdom Through Covenant*, 189–202. For a strong case for a functional view, see J. H. Walton, *The Lost World of Adam and Eve: Genesis 2–3 and the Human Origins Debate* (Downers Grove, IL: InterVarsity, 2015). See also G. Ortlund, "Image of Adam, Son of God: Genesis 5:3 and Luke 3:38 in Intercanonical Dialogue," *JETS* 57 (2014): 673–88, for a fascinating exploration of the image of God as conveying a familial, father-child relationship.

[10] T. D. Alexander, *From Paradise to the Promised Land: An Introduction to the Pentateuch*, 3rd ed. (Grand Rapids, MI: Baker, 2012), 125–26. Alexander cites sources from Rameses II in Egypt that explain his own kingship as being in the divine image. This does not necessarily mean Moses is borrowing from Egypt; instead, it might indicate that Egypt was displaying an ancient understanding that had its roots in the creation account (ibid., 126n18).

[11] Dumbrell, *Faith of Israel*, 22.

[12] Dumbrell notes it is only after the fall that access to the tree of life (which is at the center of the garden and thus controls it) is prohibited lest Adam and Eve live forever in a fallen state (ibid.).

[13] Ibid. S. Dempster describes the prohibition as rejecting the quest for moral and epistemological autonomy required when one violates the commandment (*Dominion and Dynasty: A Theology of the Hebrew Bible*, NSBT [Downers Grove, IL: InterVarsity, 2003], 63).

[14] Dumbrell, *Faith of Israel*, 23.

[15] See M. F. Bird's comments in *Evangelical Theology: A Biblical and Systematic Introduction* (Grand Rapids, MI: Zondervan, 2013), 227.

they had no need to feel shame in their nakedness; they had no reason to hide. Now in their shame they want to cover their nakedness and devise a way to do so (Gen 3:7).

Everything has changed for humanity. God pronounces judgment on Adam, Eve, and the serpent in an observable hierarchy. He curses the serpent above all other creatures (an action which suggests the effects of the fall on all creation; cp. Rom 8:20–22) to forever crawl in the dust. Moreover, God's fiat replaces the unholy collaboration between humanity and the serpent with unending enmity (Gen 3:15). God also addresses the woman (although he does not employ the word "curse"). The consequences for the woman are twofold. First, she will experience increased pain in childbirth. But second, she will desire to rule over her husband, to no avail (Gen 3:16). Likewise, God does not specifically "curse" the man, though he indicates that the ground is "cursed" on account of the man's actions. The phrase "sweat of the brow" makes clear that the man will cultivate the ground with difficulty. Nothing will ever be easy again. The statement, "You will eat bread by the sweat of your brow until you return to the ground, since you were taken from it. For you are dust, and you will return to dust" (Gen 3:19), pronounces the original penalty for eating the fruit of the tree: death. God reaffirms the creation order: the serpent is under the woman, the woman under the man, and the man under God.[16]

The Creator then casts his creatures from the garden lest they eat of the tree of life and live forever. Their attempt to better themselves has led to devastating consequences. They can no longer endure the direct presence of God. They are no longer innocent or pure. As V. Hamilton notes, "They have found nothing, and lost everything."[17] This, however, does not mean the story is over, an eternal tragedy. The rest of the Bible's story line shows God's activity in restoring his original purposes for humanity and the earth.

PRIMORDIAL PROMISES

The fall came as no surprise to God. The fact that Christ was crucified from "before the foundation of the world" (1 Pet 1:20; Rev 13:8) reveals that the gospel was not a change in plans or a last resort but the plan from the beginning. It also strongly suggests that God's fundamental attitude toward humanity is one of grace.

The display of grace was immediate. It is initially evident in three events. First, God does not expel the frightened man and woman when they are naked, but he first clothes them (Gen 3:21). Second, he casts them out in order to prevent them from eating from the tree of life and living forever (Gen 3:22–24). This constitutes an act of God's grace in limiting human sin. It would be a disaster for a human to live forever in a fallen state. Third, God will one day crush the serpent who tempted the pair (Gen 3:15, the *protoevangelium* or "first gospel"). We should see here more than just hostility between people and serpents. One of the descendants of the woman will be a threat to the existence of the serpent (and whom it represents). Both Jesus (Luke 10:19) and Paul (Rom 16:20) note the connection

---

16 K. A. Matthews, *Genesis 1–11:26,* NAC 1A (Nashville, TN: B&H, 1996), 251.

17 V. Hamilton, *The Book of Genesis, Chapters 1–17,* NICOT (Grand Rapids, MI: Eerdmans, 1990), 208.

between Genesis 3:15 and Satan's defeat. The implication is that the fall of humanity did not thwart God's ultimate purposes. The NT will later unveil the seed of the woman as the Messiah. For now, however, the promise alone is significant.

Genesis 4–11 chronicles the world's early history through ten generations from Adam to Noah. In chapters 4 and 5, there is an increasing separation between the line of Cain and the line of Seth. For Cain's line it is a time of increasing sin and separation from God. Although Cain communicates with God much like his parents, as the story moves forward, such communication vanishes among his descendants. They are creative but also alienated and violent. In contrast, only some of Seth's descendants are walking with God. However, it does not seem that an ongoing relationship with God happens through descent alone. Only Noah, the tenth from Adam, finds grace in the eyes of the Lord. The Creator thus saves him and his sons, together with their wives, from the flood.

The ultimate expression of the ever-expanding descent into sin is the story of the sons of God and the daughters of humans that precedes the flood at Genesis 6. The NT understands the "angels" here to be fallen angels (1 Pet 3:19–20; 2 Pet 2:4; Jude 6–7). Unprecedented rebellion and violence lead God to wipe out humanity as narrated in the flood account of Genesis 6–9.

The flood story has many connections to the creation account. It seems to depict somewhat of a new creation with certain differences. It is clear that it is not a redo of creation, for there is no resolution of the problem: "I will never again curse the ground because of human beings, even though the inclination of the human heart is evil from youth onward" (Gen 8:21). Instead, it is another act of God's grace to limit human sin.

The Tower of Babel incident also serves God's purposes in two ways. First, in response to human hubris, God confuses people's language. This limits the proliferation of human sinfulness by cutting off easy communication among peoples. Common culture and language enabled the easy trafficking of sin. The goal of the nations of Genesis 11 was to cooperate and consolidate so that they would not scatter and thus have no name for themselves (v. 4). There is not a single clue that God's glory played any part in their thinking. What is more, their aim was in direct disobedience to the command to fill the earth. Second, and more importantly, the confusion of languages dispersed them throughout the world, at least partially fulfilling the command to fill the earth.

At the close of primeval history, humanity has progressed culturally but not spiritually. The depth of human sin is demonstrated in that after an almost complete reset of creation, the human heart is continuously wicked (Gen 8:21). People fill the earth but not with God worshippers. God, however, has a plan. The next step in the story line of Scripture is known as patriarchal history. It chronicles the climb of a few descendants who become a mighty nation, beginning in the tenth generation from Noah with the promise to Abram regarding the nations.

THE PROMISE TO ABRAM

It is difficult to overstate the importance of the promise to Abram made at Genesis 12:1–3. The threefold promise regards descendants, a land, and a blessing to all the families of the earth. The scope of this promise is so expansive that it drives the story from Genesis 12 to Revelation 22. The promise has such ramifications for the whole world that Paul declares it to be the gospel "proclaimed . . . ahead of time" (Gal 3:8). Much of what follows in Genesis and beyond revolves around this promise. At first it centers on Abram. As Dempster notes, Genesis 12–15 focuses (although not exclusively) on the promise of the land, while in chapters 16–22 the focus is on the promise of descendants.[18]

The promise made to Abram was ratified as a covenant in Genesis 15:18. An unconditional "grant covenant" that epitomizes the grace of God. At the same time, Abram is called to obedience (Gen 18:19; 22:16–18; 26:5; cf. 12:1–2; 17:1–2).[19] At this point the "exalted father" (Abram) becomes the "father of multitudes" (Abraham). As Dumbrell states, "We bear in mind that 12:1–3 recovers the ultimate divine purpose, namely, a kingdom of God to establish God's rule and to unite human beings with their world."[20] The Genesis narratives show Abram's and Sarai's struggles with this promise in light of their advanced age and continued barrenness, yet God reasserts his promise five times from Genesis 12 to 17. That promise is unwavering, and Isaac the son of promise comes from Abraham through Sarah.

God sets up a nation through Abraham so that this family, ultimately represented by its royal head, will be the vehicle of blessing for all the nations. There is a twofold implication of this promise regarding the nations. First, Israel is to be a light to the nations; the blessing will be mediated to the nations through God's people Israel (Exod 19:5–6; cf. Isa 49:6). What is more, the promised blessing will ultimately come through a single male offspring of Abraham.[21] Later we also learn that he will be a king in the line of Judah (Gen 49:8, 10). Second, even here the nations are on the heart of God. The ultimate fulfillment, of course, comes through the Messiah (whom Paul interprets as both the "seed of the woman" and the source of this blessing in Gal 3:8–16; cf. Acts 3:25–26). The creation of a holy people was not a matter of separation from the surrounding nations so as to condemn them but the raising up of the means to rescue them.

---

[18] Dempster, *Dominion and Dynasty*, 78–85.

[19] For a concise comparison between a "grant covenant" and a "suzerain-vassal" treaty, see M. Grisanti, "The Davidic Covenant," *Master's Seminary Journal* 10 (1999): 235. Grisanti affirms, "An unconditional covenant is not necessarily without conditions" (240), noting that in a grant the superior places no obligations on the vassal "as it relates to enactment or perpetuation of the covenant" (ibid.) and that any conditions pertain only to the question of whether a given person will enjoy certain benefits of the covenant (240–41). Obedience is mandatory for an individual to enjoy the Promised Land or dynasty; sin can cause him to forfeit his personal enjoyment, but the land or dynasty will never leave the family. This mirrors precisely the pattern in the ancient world.

[20] Dumbrell, *Faith of Israel*, 28.

[21] See the third singular masculine pronominal suffix in Gen 22:17b–18; cf. Ps 72:17.

The rest of Genesis demonstrates the establishment of this family, known as the Hebrews or Israelites, and God's preservation of its descendants in Egypt through Joseph. At the end of the book of Genesis, the promised descendants, in the form of twelve tribes, number about seventy—hardly a great nation.[22] The growth that will expand them into a strong nation takes place in Egypt. With this the first part of the promise of many descendants has come to pass, at least initially (cf. Rom 4:16–18). As Exodus 1:7 states, "And the Israelites were fruitful, increased rapidly, multiplied, and became extremely numerous, so that the land was filled with them." This echoes the command in Genesis 1 to be fruitful and multiply, indicating that God's ultimate purposes have not faded with the passage of time. He intends to fill the earth with God worshippers, extending his kingdom over the face of the planet. The next step in the story line is that God's separate, distinct people become a holy nation living in the land promised to Abraham.

A HOLY NATION

The establishment of Israel as a sovereign nation begins with their liberation through Moses, also a descendant of Abraham. Notably, a great deal of the book of Exodus concerns the Sinai covenant and the tabernacle. Exodus is a book that begins in slavery, chronicles redemption, and ends in worship. Thus, Abraham's descendants leave slavery behind, find deliverance, and worship God in the tabernacle. The redemption from Egypt occupies a central place in Israel's self-understanding from that time onward.[23] The Sinai covenant demands bilateral stipulations along the lines of a suzerain-vassal treaty. This covenant fits within the Abrahamic covenant but does not replace it.[24] It is part of God's constitution of Israel as a nation; they must follow in God's ways.

Once Moses has led the Israelites out of Egypt and to Sinai, God instructs Moses. He explains the purposes of Israel as a nation: "'Now if you will carefully listen to me and keep my covenant, you will be my own possession out of all the peoples, although the whole earth is mine, and you will be my kingdom of priests and my holy nation.' These are the words that you are to say to the Israelites" (Exod 19:5–6). Israel will be God's "own possession," a "kingdom of priests," and a "holy nation."[25]

The latter two terms resonate with the mission in the garden. "Kingdom of priests" and "holy nation" most likely constitute one reference. Israel is to be a priestly, mediatorial nation whose role consists in "attracting the world to her form of government (i.e.,

---

[22] Schreiner, *The King in His Beauty*, 102.

[23] Ibid., 32.

[24] This is essentially Paul's argument in Gal 3:17: "The law, which came 430 years later, does not revoke a covenant that was previously ratified by God and cancel the promise."

[25] As Gentry and Wellum note, the first expression "my own possession" (Hebrew *sĕgullâ*) implies personal property and service, recalling Adam's role in the garden: "We are back, here, to the divine image in Genesis 1:26–28. Israel has inherited an Adamic role, giving the devoted service of a son and honored king in a covenant relationship" (*Kingdom Through Covenant*, 318).

the kingdom of God) by her embodied holiness."[26] The Israelites are not just a priestly kingdom, then, but a royal priesthood: their dominion is one of service in order to attract the nations to YHWH, the Creator who loves them.[27] As in the Abrahamic covenant, the ultimate result will be that all nations are blessed through Israel.[28] The implication is that Israel's role, in continuity with and in further development of Adam's in the garden, is to guard, serve, and bring the world under God's dominion.

Israel in short order enters into a suzerain-vassal treaty with YHWH, whose stipulations are that they keep the Sinai covenant. This covenant is delivered in two sections, the "Ten Words," more commonly known as the Ten Commandments (Exod 20:1–17), and the "Book of the Covenant" (Exod 20:22–23:33).[29] The former is made up of the familiar commands that seem to be general obligations, and the latter consists mainly of something more like case laws.[30] Moses, Aaron, Nadab, Abihu, and the seventy elders ascend the holy mountain to affirm the covenant. There they see God himself (Exod 24:10)—exposing the subsequent golden calf incident, in which the people called an idol their "god," as even more rebellious. Moses stays to receive the instructions for the tabernacle; for once the covenant is ratified, a place of worship is necessary.

What ensues drives the story line of Scripture until the end. Moses cannot get off the mountain before Israel transgresses the first and second of the "Ten Words" in the gross idolatry of the golden calf (among other sins; Exod 32:1–6). Moses's intercession for the nation—based on the promise to Abraham, Isaac, and Jacob/Israel (Exod 32:13), not the covenant at Sinai—saved people's lives.[31] The people break the covenant as previously envisioned, but God (in Exod 34:1–28) makes another covenant that is essentially a restatement of the broken one, albeit with certain changes.[32] God renews the covenant in Deuteronomy for the generation poised in Moab to enter the promised land. People read and reaffirm the covenant at the beginning and end of the conquest of that area (Josh 8:30–35; 24:24). In one sense the rest of the OT is the story of Israel's national failure to obey the covenant. Yet God will not abandon his plan to subdue the earth under his reign. As Dumbrell states, the covenant's "continuance, therefore, would depend upon the

---

[26] Dumbrell, *Faith of Israel*, 38.

[27] Gentry and Wellum, *Kingdom Through Covenant*, 323; Dempster, *Dominion and Dynasty*, 101–2; Alexander, *From Paradise to the Promised Land*, 210.

[28] Gentry and Wellum, *Kingdom Through Covenant*, 323.

[29] The phrase "Book of the Covenant" is used by Moses to refer to this section in Exod 24:7. However, the expression came to be used for the whole Pentateuch in 2 Kgs 23:2, 21 and 2 Chr 34:30. It also seems to be used of the whole OT in 1 Macc 1:57 and Sir 24:23. It is best to see the usage in 2 Kgs 24:7 as referring to the scroll at hand and the rest to a more expansive reference to the whole OT.

[30] P. House, *Old Testament Theology* (Downers Grove, IL: InterVarsity, 1998), 111. Dumbrell refers to them as "descriptive of laws which are contextually tailored to fit the particular needs of an emerging society." W. Dumbrell, *Covenant and Creation: An Old Testament Covenant Theology*, rev. ed. (Milton Keynes, UK: Paternoster, 2013), 121.

[31] Dempster, *Dominion and Dynasty*, 104.

[32] Ibid., 106. E.g., priests will now come from the tribe of Levi.

unchanging character of the divine nature and not upon the indifferent quality of human performance."[33]

Israel's shortcomings came as no surprise to God and are predicted at several occasions. When Israel and its human leader Joshua are faithful, they have success (e.g., Jericho). When they are not, disaster comes upon them (e.g., Ai). But the people quickly forget this lesson. The book of Judges records the events that follow Joshua's death and demonstrates the progressive Canaanization of Israel.[34] Rather than driving out the people of the land as instructed, Israel falls into a pattern of tolerating them, assimilating their ways, and ultimately committing abominations as a result. Twin refrains mark the book and the time period: "The Israelites did what was evil in the LORD's sight" (Judg 2:11; 3:7, 12; 4:1; 6:1; 10:6; 13:1); and "In those days there was no king in Israel; everyone did whatever seemed right to him" (Judg 17:6; 21:25).[35]

After the book of Judges, two-thirds of the promise to Abraham has become a reality—though not perfectly.[36] The Israelites are in the promised land and have grown numerous. However, a Canaanized Israel cannot be a conduit for the blessing of the nations and certainly does not represent God. Things must change. The last judge of Israel, Samuel, demonstrates what judgeship could be through fidelity to God. It is shocking, then, that in the next chapter the nation demands a king (1 Sam 8:5–7).

God's assessment of Israel, spoken to Samuel, is devastating: "They are doing the same thing to you that they have done to me, since the day I brought them out of Egypt until this day, abandoning me and worshiping other gods" (1 Sam 8:8). The demand for a king is predicted and delimited in Deuteronomy 17:14–20. The king is to be one of them, living a relatively austere lifestyle and reading his personal copy of the Torah. The request for a king, therefore, is rebellious not because of the desire for a king but because of the desire that he be like the kings of the other (pagan) nations. This represents "a virtual unilateral withdrawal from the Sinai covenant, which mandated Israel's difference from the world."[37] On the whole the king(s) ruling over Israel look little like the man described in Deuteronomy.

Saul, while starting well, quickly falls out of favor, and God replaces him with David, the man after God's own heart (1 Sam 13:14; cf. Acts 13:22). This, too, comes after previous forebodings. David and his line are the fulfillment of Jacob's expansive prophecy in Genesis 49:8–11,[38] which reaches beyond David himself to the Messiah ("until he whose

---

[33] Dumbrell, *Covenant and Creation*, 142.

[34] D. Block, *Judges, Ruth*, NAC 6 (Nashville, TN: B&H, 1999), 58.

[35] E. H. Merrill, M. F. Rooker, and M. A. Grisanti, *The World and the Word: An Introduction to the Old Testament* (Nashville, TN: B&H, 2011), 292.

[36] See Schreiner's summary in *King in His Beauty*, 127.

[37] Dumbrell, *Faith of Israel*, 83. See also House, *Old Testament Theology*, 233.

[38] The complete reference is, "Judah, your brothers will praise you. Your hand will be on the necks of your enemies; your father's sons will bow down to you. Judah is a young lion—my son, you return from the kill. He crouches; he lies down like

right it is comes," Gen 49:10) and echoes God's promise to Abraham regarding the nations, as the kingdom will witness the obedience of the nations.[39]

THE PROMISE TO DAVID

Under David's leadership, peace, security, and the expansion of borders are the hallmarks of the kingdom of Israel. David finishes the conquest of the land Joshua failed to complete.[40] In the time of rest, David becomes convinced that God deserves a better house. God, however, replies that he never dwelt in a house and never will. Instead, he promises to establish a house, an eternal house, for David. Solomon his son will build the temple, but God will establish David's house as a permanent kingdom: "Your house and kingdom will endure before me forever, and your throne will be established forever" (2 Sam 7:16).[41] Thus, David is promised an eternal house (i.e., descendants), an eternal kingdom, and an eternal dynasty. It is no wonder David's response is an extended time of prayer and worship (2 Sam 7:18–29).

The promise of an eternal Davidic kingdom constitutes a grant covenant like the Abramaic covenant.[42] The promises to Abraham (name, land, inheritance, and descendants) are now funneled through the promise to David. Consequently, Matthew introduces Jesus of Nazareth as "the son of Abraham, the son of David" (Matt 1:1).[43] By instituting a grant covenant with the house of David, God introduces a secure point of reference for Israel's understanding of God's actions and hope for the future. Thus, the legitimacy of the southern kingdom (Judah) is seen in its single Davidic dynasty. In contrast, the northern kingdom (Israel) transitions through ten different dynasties and dissolves into obscurity more than a hundred years before its rival.[44] Even when ruled by apostate kings, the southern kingdom is not eradicated for "David his servant's sake" (1 Kgs 15:5). The breaking of the Sinai covenant, however, demands the people's exile from the land. This is the most likely context of the prophecy of Isaiah 7:14, which is best understood as prophesying a distant future for the house of David.[45]

The rest of the books of Kings narrates the decline and fall of the Israelite kingdom. However, the promise and hope of the eternal dynasty is not destroyed. The book of 2 Kings ends with the heir of David, Jehoiachin, pardoned and provisioned in the Babylonian court for the rest of his days (2 Kgs 25:27–30). Davidic hope is alive and well.

---

a lion or a lioness—who dares to rouse him? The scepter will not depart from Judah or the staff from between his feet until He whose right it is comes and the obedience of the peoples belongs to Him" (Gen 49:8–10).

[39] See K. Matthews, *Genesis 11:27–50:26*, NAC 1B (Nashville, TN: B&H, 2005), 892–96.

[40] Dempster, *Dominion and Dynasty*, 141.

[41] See also 1 Chronicles 17; Psalm 89.

[42] Grisanti, "Davidic Covenant," 234, 240.

[43] Ibid., 248.

[44] Dempster, *Dominion and Dynasty*, 152.

[45] See M. R. Adamthwaite, "Isaiah 7:16: Key to the Immanuel Prophecy," *Reformed Theological Review* 59 (2000): 65–83.

The kingdoms have been destroyed because Israel broke the Sinai covenant. God, however, makes a unilateral perpetual covenant with David.[46] Therefore hope remains. God's people can still anticipate the rule of the greater son of David.[47] However, the nation forged at Sinai, under which the dynasty functioned, is taken into exile.[48]

Looking at the promise to David from a distant vantage point generates some interesting conclusions. The eternal right to sit on the throne is granted to David's descendants alone. The descent is irrevocable, even though individual kings may be removed. In this situation there are only two ways an eternal kingdom and dynasty can exist. The first is that each generation must produce a male heir and then keep the kingdom intact. Obviously, this did not happen. The second is that an heir is born who never dies and rules a kingdom that is not strictly geopolitical. The latter is the only fulfillment of the promise available, and it only comes through the Messiah who lives forever to rule the kingdom from the Father's side.[49]

This eschatological hope is not a NT innovation. This eschatological Davidic hope endures in the remainder of the OT. One of the clearest transitions takes place in Jeremiah 22:30 where Jehoiachin is declared childless and without heir. In one sense the Davidic dynasty is cut off in exile. However, five verses later God promises to "raise up a righteous Branch for David" (Jer 23:5). All doubt is removed in Jeremiah 33:14–15 where God promises, "In those days and at that time I will cause a Righteous Branch to sprout up for David, and he will administer justice and righteousness in the land." Similarly, Haggai 2:25 reverses the declaration against Jehoiachin through Zerubbabel.[50] The coming Davidic ruler appears in texts closely associated with a future restoration.[51]

The result is that after the exile a physical Davidic kingdom is not restored. Nor does this even seem a remote possibility. It is noteworthy that the Israelites who return never even attempt to reinstate the Davidic dynasty. The foundation for such an abandonment of the literal hope for a Davidic descent to ascend to the throne was not just the physical

---

[46] While the Davidic covenant is unilateral, note the numerous conditions stressed (e.g., David: 1 Kgs 2:2–4; Solomon: 1 Kgs 8:25; Yahweh: 1 Kgs 9:4–5; the psalmist: Ps 132:11–12).

[47] This can also be seen in the Psalter. The book contains a number of "royal psalms" that extol the king. Yet the Psalter is clearly compiled after the destruction of the kingdoms. To what king do they refer? They are included because of the hope the Davidic covenant provides.

[48] Essentially the nation is dissolved. Dumbrell, *Creation and Covenant*, 240. Dumbrell disagrees with the assessment that David's wayward but living son still represented hope. His assessment of the dissolution of the nation formed at Sinai is difficult to deny.

[49] Gentry and Wellum, *Kingdom Through Covenant*, 421–22.

[50] The prophecy against Jehoiachin (also called "Coniah" and "Jeconiah") describes him as a signet ring that God has torn off God's finger (Jer 22:24). But in Haggai 2:25, Zerubbabel, Jehoiachin's grandson, is made "my signet ring." Dempster puts it well: "If Yahweh had shaken off his signet ring with Jehoiachin's exile (Jer 22:24) he has now put it on again" (Dempster, *Dominion and Dynasty*, 186). One of the implications is that Jehoiachin's appearance in Matthew's genealogy (Matt 1:11–12) is not affected by the curse in Jer 22:24.

[51] See, e.g., Jer 30:4–11.

dismantling of the kingdom but was, more importantly, the prospect of a new covenant upheld by the exilic and postexilic prophets.[52]

THE PROMISE OF A NEW COVENANT

As Israel realizes the repercussions of breaking the Sinai covenant (losing the land and their identity as a nation), a note of hope sounds through the great writing prophets: God will establish a new covenant. The covenant is mentioned at several places in the OT. It is often referred to in the Prophets under three different names: "new covenant," "permanent covenant" (e.g., Ezek 16:59–63), and "covenant of peace" (e.g., Isa 54:1–10). In Ezekiel several texts describe a new heart and a new spirit against the backdrop of the promise of Jeremiah 31 (e.g., Ezek 11:18–21; 36:24–28).[53] The classic announcement of the new covenant is found in Jeremiah 31:31–34:

> "Look, the days are coming"—this is the LORD's declaration—"when I will make a new covenant with the house of Israel and with the house of Judah. This one will not be like the covenant I made with their ancestors when I took them by the hand to lead them out of the land of Egypt—my covenant that they broke even though I am their master"—the LORD's declaration. "Instead, this is the covenant I will make with the house of Israel after those days"—the LORD's declaration. "I will put my teaching within them and write it on their hearts. I will be their God, and they will be my people. No longer will one teach his neighbor or his brother, saying, 'Know the LORD,' for they will all know me, from the least to the greatest of them"—this is the LORD's declaration. "For I will forgive their iniquity and never again remember their sin."

Even though Judah and Israel are consistently described in Jeremiah as an unfaithful wife,[54] God announces a new covenant that will be fundamentally different from the one at Sinai. Primarily it is a grant treaty rather than a suzerain-vassal treaty.[55] Under this covenant, God will place knowledge of his will and his law within people ("write it on their hearts")—rather than making it an external stipulation as in the former covenant. This results in a personal relationship ("their God"/ "my people"). This new relationship is intimate ("they will all know me") based on the fact that God will forgive their sin.[56] The

---

[52] Dumbrell, *Covenant and Creation*, 240.

[53] For a longer list, see Gentry and Wellum, *Kingdom Through Covenant*, 434. It is also likely that Deut 30:11–14 is forward-looking and refers to the new covenant: see, e.g., S. R. Coxhead, "Deuteronomy 30:11–14 as a Prophecy of the New Covenant in Christ," *WTJ* (2006): 305–20; J. Sailhamer, *The Meaning of the Pentateuch: Revelation, Composition, and Interpretation* (Downers Grove, IL: InterVarsity, 2009), 290, 414, 556.

[54] See, e.g., Jer 2:20; 3:6–25; 5:7; 9:2; 13:27.

[55] Though note texts such as Jer 31:33; Ezek 36:27; Matt 28:20; John 13:34.

[56] For a formal structural outline, see S. Hafemann, "The Covenant Relationship," in *Central Themes in Biblical Theology: Mapping Unity in Diversity* (Grand Rapids, MI: Baker, 2007), 49.

older covenant was profoundly mediated through kings, priests, and prophets who spoke for God to the people. Now, however, they will all know God.[57]

This covenant is to take place at an unidentified future date. The phrase "the days are coming" is used in the immediate context to refer to a return from exile. For example, "'for look, the days are coming'—*this is* the LORD's declaration—'when I will restore the fortunes of my people Israel and Judah'—says the LORD. 'I will restore them to the land I gave to their ancestors and they will possess it'" (Jer 30:3, picked up again in 31:27). The new covenant, then, is ratified with a unified Israel and Judah only after a new exodus—something Jeremiah 32:37 makes explicit: "I will return them to this place." This second exodus is a major theme in the Prophets, especially Isaiah (Isa 11:10–16, picked up extensively in chaps. 40–66). Connected to the second exodus are references to a new creation as well (see Isa 51:3; 65:17–25; 66:22–23).[58] It is a complex sequence to come, marked by a physical return to the land, a rebuilding of the temple, and a worldwide kingdom with a new creation.

The new covenant is connected to both the Davidic King and the return from exile in Daniel's prophecy of seventy weeks. Daniel, while praying about Jeremiah's prophecy of seventy years of exile (Jer 25:11–12; 29:10), is told what is needed to complete God's purposes. "Seventy weeks are decreed about your people and your holy city—to bring the rebellion to an end, to put a stop to sin, to atone for iniquity, to bring in everlasting righteousness, to seal up vision and prophecy, and to anoint the most holy place" (Dan 9:24).

The interpretation of this passage is disputed. However, a few points will make the connection to the Davidic promise clear. First, note that the return from the exile is not exactly the same as the second exodus. The time period described is considerably longer than seventy years—at least 490 years (i.e., seventy weeks [sevens] of years—or ten jubilee cycles).[59] Most agree that it is a partial or incomplete return.

Second, the Davidic King is closely connected to the removal of sin and the establishment of righteousness. It is startling that Messiah the Prince (a reference to Jeremiah's righteous Branch of David) is vicariously cut off. Jehoiachin and the other wicked kings were cut off for their own sins of leading Israel astray; Messiah the Prince is cut off for the sins of others. It is plausible to connect this statement with "to put a stop to sin" in Daniel 9:24 in light of the Suffering Servant in Isaiah 53. As promised in the new covenant, God "will forgive their iniquity, and never again remember their sin" (Jer 31:34).

Third, the outline of history is reasonably straightforward. In the first forty-nine years, the city is rebuilt, and nothing important happens until Messiah the Prince appears 434 years later. Then, after he is cut off, the city and the sanctuary will be destroyed. This is

---

[57] Gentry and Wellum, *Kingdom Through Covenant*, 509–10.

[58] For a longer discussion, see R. Ciampa, "The History of Redemption," in *Central Themes in Biblical Theology*, 273–74.

[59] See Gentry and Wellum, *Kingdom Through Covenant*, 544. It is also notable that Jesus's Nazareth sermon interprets his appearance as the fulfillment of a significant Jubilee (Luke 4:18–19; cf. Isa 61:1–2a).

remarkably similar to the story of Jesus and the destruction of Jerusalem. In fact, most of the calculations can be interpreted as having been fulfilled in Jesus.[60]

God's purpose in creation was to subdue the whole earth under his dominion. The fall of humanity does not derail that purpose. It is pushed forward through the covenant with Abraham regarding descendants, land, and the channel through which the nations will be blessed. The Sinai covenant reveals God's will and provides a constitution for Abraham's descendants as they are formed into a holy nation. Through the covenant with David, God promises a permanent dynasty. However, it will be different from the dynasties of other kingdoms. Israel's failure to keep the Sinai covenant does not thwart God's ultimate purpose to reveal sin. Yet, because the nation breaks the covenant, Israel suffers exile to purge idolatry from her midst. In exile Israel is promised a new covenant and a new exodus, a return to the land. The OT ends with the hope of a Davidic king, a new covenant, and a return from exile. Yet it ends with much that remains unfulfilled. The second exodus has not occurred; Messiah the Prince has not come; Israel's return from exile remains incomplete. In terms of story line, the OT is a covenantal cliff-hanger.

THE COMING AND MINISTRY OF THE MESSIAH AND THE INSTITUTION OF THE NEW COVENANT

The arrival of the Son of David in the city of David is the essential first step in continuing the story line of Scripture.[61] It is important and necessary that the Messiah be manifested through human birth and life rather than merely an appearance in human form (a theophany). This is in keeping with OT expectation, once opaque but now coming into clear view, that the Messiah will be God's servant (and as such human), yet somehow be identified with Yahweh himself.[62] Yet unlike widespread expectations, the Messiah's coming would not be in victorious triumph but in vicarious suffering for God's people.[63] His completely human yet sinless life also serves as his indispensable preparation to function as our high priest. The author of Hebrews makes this clear: "After he was perfected, he became the source of eternal salvation for all who obey him, and he was declared by God a high priest to the order of Melchizedek" (Heb 5:9–10).[64] The term "perfected" seems unusual for the sinless Son of God but not in the context of high priesthood. The high priest was said to have "his hands perfected" in the LXX when he had finished his stipulations

---

[60] The text has a long history of Christian interpretations that do just this, beginning with Hippolytus of Rome. However, if we start in 457 BC with Artaxerxes's command to Ezra (Ezra 7:11–26), this timetable lands 490 years later in AD 33.

[61] For a biblical-theological treatment of Jesus's birth within the matrix of OT messianic predictions and Second Temple expectations, see A. J. Köstenberger and A. E. Stewart, *The First Days of Jesus: The Story of the Incarnation* (Wheaton, IL: Crossway, 2015).

[62] See, e.g., Psalm 110; Ezekiel 34; 36; Dan 7:13–14. See further below.

[63] See esp. Isaiah 53 in the context of the Isaianic "Servant Songs." See also the various misunderstandings regarding Jesus's identity featured in the four Gospels.

[64] The same point is made in Heb 2:10, and in Heb 7:28 the author declares Jesus to have been "perfected forever."

to be the high priest.[65] Thus, it was absolutely necessary for Jesus to be fully human and entirely sinless. This qualifies him to serve as our high priest and to sacrifice himself for God's people.

The four Gospels narrate at some length the messianic ministry of Jesus, most notably his calling, training, and commissioning of twelve apostles.[66] While each of them serves as witness to the key events in Jesus's life (the fourfold Gospel), they do so in distinctive ways, accentuating various aspects of Jesus's ministry and showcasing how messianic predictions and typology have been fulfilled in him. Matthew anchors Jesus's messianic ministry in a genealogy that prominently features Abraham and David. In the remainder of his Gospel, he shows how Jesus served as Israel's representative and fulfilled messianic prophecy.[67] He also presents Jesus as the new Moses who authoritatively teaches God's expectations for those who would enter his kingdom (Matthew 5–7). The mysteries of the kingdom are expounded in several chapters containing Jesus's parables on the kingdom (chaps. 13, 18, 25). Matthew also features Jesus as engaging in an extensive healing ministry in keeping with Isaianic prophecy. In this and other ways, Matthew weaves a fabric of messianic fulfillment of OT expectation in the person of Jesus Christ, "Immanuel," God with us (1:23), who constitutes the fulfillment of the Abrahamic promise and conveys God's presence with his followers as they set out to fulfill their risen Lord's Great Commission (28:18–20).

Mark, for his part, is primarily concerned with presenting Jesus as the authoritative, miracle-working Son of God who wields authority over nature, sickness, death, and even the supernatural.[68] He also shows Jesus engaging in a messianic ministry of healing and exorcism in keeping with Isaiah's prophecies, including those related to the Suffering Servant (cf. Isa 52:13–53:12). Jesus's teaching in (kingdom) parables is depicted as well. At the climax of Mark's Gospel, the Roman centurion testifies that Jesus is indeed the Son of God (15:39), representing the desired response to Jesus's messianic claims on part of Mark's (original Roman) readers.

Luke's Gospel, followed by the book of Acts, shows Jesus's inexorable progress from Galilee to Jerusalem, the site of his crucifixion (Luke 9:51), and subsequently the exalted Jesus's continuing ministry from Jerusalem to the ends of the earth through the Spirit-empowered new messianic community (Acts 1:1, 8). While Luke is more focused on Jesus as the Son of Adam and the church's mission to the Gentiles, he is not neglecting the fact that Jesus represents the culmination of God's promises to Israel (see esp. Luke 1–2). In fact, it is precisely through his mission to Israel that Jesus the Messiah meets rejection by the Jewish leadership and following the resurrection and ascension is proclaimed not only

---

[65] See, e.g., Exod 29:9, 29, 33, 35; Lev 4:5; 8:33; 16:32; Num 3:3 where the verb is used (exclusively) of the priesthood in the Pentateuch. Note also that twice the verb translated "perfected" is used apart from "hands" to refer to the ordained priest (Lev 8:33 and 16:32).

[66] See on this A. J. Köstenberger, *The Missions of Jesus and the Disciples According to the Fourth Gospel* (Grand Rapids, MI: Eerdmans, 1995), chap. 4.

[67] See esp. the "fulfillment" quotations in 1:23; 2:6, 15, 18; 4:15–16.

[68] See, e.g., Mark 4:35–5:43.

to Jews but also to Gentiles as full members of the NT church made up of believing Jews and Gentiles (see esp. Acts 15). In this way Israel's prophecy is fulfilled in a two-stage process in which first Jesus and then those spearheading the Gentile mission serve as "a light to the Gentiles."[69]

John, last but not least, roots Jesus's origins not merely in the virgin birth but in eternity past, presenting Jesus as the Word through whom God created the world and who now in the person of Jesus Christ had become flesh (1:1, 14). According to John, the entirety of Jesus's ministry should be viewed from the vantage point of his revelation of the Father (1:18). Like the other Gospels, John features John the Baptist's preparatory ministry, albeit under the primary category of witness to Jesus, along with other witnesses such as God the Father, the Holy Spirit, Jesus's miracles, and others. Jesus's miracles, for their part, are likewise transformed in John's Gospel to serve primarily as messianic signs pointing to Jesus's identity as Messiah and Son of God (cf. 12:37–41; 20:30–31). The universality of Jesus's mission is emphasized in the pivotal verse 3:16, which states that "whoever" believes in the Son whom God has sent will receive eternal life.[70] At the end of the Gospel, Jesus sends his followers on a mission of representing him and his message of salvation and forgiveness just as the Father had sent him (20:21; cf. 17:18).

In this way the four canonical Gospels jointly witness to the one gospel of Jesus Christ as the long-awaited Messiah and Savior, God's Son, who came, as Paul writes, in the "fullness of time . . ., born of woman, born under the law, to redeem those under the law, so that we might receive adoption as sons" (Gal 4:4–5 ESV). Yet while the Gospels spend considerable time narrating Jesus's three-year ministry, the events surrounding his death and resurrection take center stage. In particular, the Last Supper explicates the significance of Christ's death by connecting it to both the sacrifice of the Passover and the ratification of the old covenant. The original Passover constituted a consecration ritual, and the sacrifices at the ratification of the older covenant (Exodus 24) served as preparation for the establishment of the Sinai covenant. Through his transformation of one ceremonial meal into another, from Passover to the Lord's Supper, Christ connects his death to both the Passover and the old covenant.

At the institution of the Lord's Supper, Jesus declares that his body "is given for you" (Luke 22:19) and the drink is "the new covenant in [his] blood" (Luke 22:20). Although the language is slightly different in each, all three Synoptic Gospels (Matt 26:28; Mark 14:24; Luke 22:20) and Paul (1 Cor 11:25) describe the death of Jesus (represented by the bread and cup) as establishing the new covenant in the forgiveness of sins. In Exodus

---

[69] See Luke 2:32; Acts 13:47, both referencing Isa 49:6, in the first place pointing to Jesus, in the second instance extending the scope of the original prophecy to Paul and Barnabas as representatives of the mission leaders of the early church.

[70] On John 3:16, see A. J. Köstenberger, "Lifting Up the Son of Man and God's Love for the World: John 3:16 in Its Historical, Literary, and Theological Contexts," in *Understanding the Times: New Testament Studies in the 21st Century: Essays in Honor of D. A. Carson on the Occasion of His 65th Birthday*, ed. A. J. Köstenberger and R. W. Yarbrough (Wheaton, IL: Crossway, 2011), 141–59.

12:1–28, in order to avoid the death angel's work and to begin the original exodus, the Israelites must prepare for departure not merely by packing their belongings. God instituted a ceremonial meal full of meaning and purpose.

T. D. Alexander notes that the original Passover is similar to the priestly consecration rituals consisting of a sacrifice (atoning for sin), sprinkling the sacrifice's blood on their extremities (for purification), and eating the sacrificial animal and unleavened bread (for sanctification). The original Passover featured a similar process. People sacrificed a lamb, smeared its blood on the extremity of the home, and ate the roasted animal along with unleavened bread; thus, it was likely a "consecration ritual" as well.[71] As such, it allowed Holy God to dwell with the nation and consecrated them to be a priestly nation.[72] Students of the NT need not strain to see the connection to Christ's death.

The NT clearly connects the death of Christ to the Passover sacrifice.[73] Paul states at 1 Corinthians 5:7, "Clean out the old yeast so that you may be a new batch, since you are unleavened. For Christ our Passover has been sacrificed." He alludes to both the sanctification of the unleavened bread and the sacrificial foundation for it. What is more, John makes several paschal allusions at the death of Jesus in his Gospel.[74] John's image of Jesus as the Lamb of God, then, does not simply point to Jesus as a sacrifice (for many animals were used for sacrifice) but specifically to Jesus as our Passover Lamb. As such, the appropriation of his death atones, purifies, and sanctifies the believer.[75]

But there is more; at the mention of the cup, Jesus declares, "This is my blood of the covenant" (Matt 26:28). The phrase constitutes a citation of or an allusion to Exodus 24:8 where Moses declares, "This is the blood of the covenant," in explaining the sprinkling of the altar and the people. So, then, the death of Christ not merely enables consecration through sacrifice, it also inaugurates the new covenant.

The explication of the new covenant found in the book of Hebrews develops this in more detail. The author describes the logic of a covenant in relation to the cross in Hebrews 9:15–26. The death of Christ, in order to establish the new covenant, first of all atones for the sins committed under the first covenant, enabling believers to "receive the promise

---

[71] Alexander, *From Paradise to the Promised Land*, 205. See Exodus 12, 29, and Leviticus 8 for the parallels between the Passover and the consecration rituals.

[72] Ibid. The firstborn whom the death angel passed over were to be uniquely devoted to God. Later the Levites take the special place of the firstborn (see Num 3:12–13).

[73] See A. J. Köstenberger, "Was the Last Supper a Passover Meal?," in *The Lord's Supper: Remembering and Proclaiming Christ Until He Comes*, ed. T. R. Schreiner and M. R. Crawford, NAC Studies in Bible and Theology 10 (Nashville, TN: B&H, 2010), 6–30.

[74] See Alexander, *From Paradise to the Promised Land*, 207. See also A. J. Köstenberger, *John*, BECNT (Grand Rapids, MI: Baker, 2004), 552–53, who lists the lack of Jesus's bones being broken (crurifragrium), the mention of the hyssop, and the flow of blood and water as Passover allusions. C. S. Keener adds the pierced side as a possibility, calling upon rabbinic traditions (*Pesahim* 5.9; 7.1; *The Gospel of John: A Commentary* [Peabody, MA: Hendrickson, 2003], 2:1153).

[75] Some argue against attaching an atoning significance to the Passover sacrifice. However, it is likely Josephus interpreted it this way (see *Ant.* 2.312). What is more, it is clearly called the sacrifice of the Passover (Exod 12:27). Hoskins treats it as the prototypical sacrifice. P. M. Hoskins, "Deliverance from Death by the True Passover Lamb: A Significant Aspect of the Fulfillment of the Passover in the Gospel of John," *JETS* 52 (2009): 287.

of the eternal inheritance" (Heb 9:15). Under a covenant, the death of the one making the covenant must be "brought forward."[76] In other words, the one making the covenant is under obligation to keep it or suffer death (represented by dead animals in the ancient Near East). If this is not done, the covenant is invalid (Heb 9:17).[77] Therefore, the death of Christ for humanity fulfills the requirement of death because the first covenant is broken.

Second, just as the sprinkled blood purified for entrance to the first covenant (Heb 9:18–22), Christ's death purifies believers to enter the new covenant. Christ's blood purifies the heavenly sanctuary (Heb 9:23–24) and effects an eternal removal of sin (Heb 9:26; 10:10). Thus it ratifies the covenant through his representative death.[78] In chapter 10, as the author of Hebrews admonishes his readers to endurance, he alludes to the benefits of those who enter into the new covenant. They are (1) eternally forgiven and sanctified (Heb 10:1–18); (2) have boldness to enter the sanctuary before God (Heb 10:19); and (3) have eternal life through faith (Heb 10:39).

Just as the old covenant is connected to the first exodus, so is the new covenant necessary for the promised second exodus (see, e.g., Isa 11:10–16). It features the final restoration of Israel and the ingathering of the Gentiles. Two more issues that dominate the story line of the Bible are related to these twin matters: the worldwide proclamation of the gospel through the church, made up of believing Jews and Gentiles, and the consummation/final state. Much of the NT is preparing believers to participate in this worldwide proclamation and to prepare for the second coming of Christ. To conclude the description of major events, it is necessary to describe the mission and God's completion of all things.

THE TIMES OF THE GENTILES, THE MISSION TO BOTH JEWS AND GENTILES, AND THE CHURCH AS THE BODY OF CHRIST

In the Olivet discourse, Jesus outlines the contours of human history until his return.[79] Luke 21:5–28 outlines history in three overlapping stages. First will come preliminary judgments: false messiahs, war, earthquakes, famines, pestilence, and terrifying environmental sights (Luke 21:8–11).[80] These are the preliminary events surrounding the apostles

---

[76] For a defense of the translation adopted here, see S. Hahn, "A Broken Covenant and the Curse of Death: A Study of Hebrews 9:15–22," *CBQ* (2004): 416–36. See also W. Lane, *Hebrews*, WBC 47B (Nashville, TN: Thomas Nelson, 1991), 242–43. The major issue is the meaning of the word *pheresthai*, translated "established" in the CSB. However, more likely the word means "bring" or "bring forward."

[77] Hebrews 9:17 is best understood as, "For a covenant is confirmed in death (of those who break it), since it is never valid when the one making the covenant is (still) living." Thus, this represents general covenant practices. See Lane, *Hebrews*, 243.

[78] Ibid. For an accessible study of the events surrounding the cross, see A. J. Köstenberger and J. Taylor with A. Stewart, *The Final Days of Jesus: The Most Important Week of the Most Important Person Who Ever Lived* (Wheaton, IL: Crossway, 2014).

[79] Scholars generally hold to three positions regarding the Olivet Discourse (Matt 24:1–51; Mark 13:1–37; Luke 21:5–38): (1) all events refer to AD 70 (preterist position); (2) all events refer to events at the second coming of Christ; and (3) the destruction of Jerusalem refers to the events of AD 70, and the events beginning with the signs affecting the environment refer to the future. See chap. 21.

[80] These are to be distinguished from the events that end the times of the Gentiles in Luke 21:25–26.

in Luke 21:12–19. Second, this will be a time characterized by hostility, persecution, and Spirit-empowered witness. None of these is the sign that the end has come. Before these are complete, the apostles will deliver powerful witness in the midst of persecution (Luke 21:12–19).

In Luke 21:20, the discourse shifts from general occurrences to a specific event: the destruction of Jerusalem, which would happen in AD 70. Jesus tells his disciples that when armies surround Jerusalem, they must flee. The imagery in Matthew and Mark of not entering one's house to gather possessions or supplies, and the difficulty of the hurried travel of expectant mothers, serve to illustrate how quickly they must leave. There is but a small window of opportunity, and they must take it.[81] Jesus notes that the devastation is complete and enduring: "They will be killed by the sword and be led captive into all the nations, and Jerusalem will be trampled by the Gentiles until the times of the Gentiles are fulfilled" (Luke 21:24).[82] This period of time, "the times of the Gentiles," is the third and more enduring stage. It seems to be a long period of time preceding the return of Christ (Luke 21:25–31) and hints at a future restoration of Jerusalem ("until").[83]

Is there, however, more to the rather vague reference "the times of the Gentiles"? Some have suggested that it refers to the subjugation of Jerusalem and Judea by Gentiles.[84] Others have understood it to mean the worldwide proclamation of the gospel.[85] Clearly "trampled by the Gentiles" (Luke 21:24) indicates that the destruction is at the hand of the Gentiles who serve as God's instruments of judgment. Thus, it is possible that "times of the Gentiles" means little more than a lengthy occupation of Jerusalem.[86] However, more seems to be involved.

Luke's version of the Olivet Discourse does not follow Matthew or Mark verbatim, although the three versions do not materially disagree. Luke expresses certain concepts or events differently. For example, "abomination of desolation" terminology in Matthew and Mark (Matt 24:15; Mark 13:14) is expressed obliquely as "recognize that its desolation has

---

[81] Eusebius reports that this indeed happened: "Meanwhile, before the war began, members of the Jerusalem church were ordered by an oracle given by revelation to those worthy of it to leave the city and settle in a city of Perea called Pella" (*Church History*, trans. P. L. Maier [Grand Rapids, MI: Kregel, 1999], 95).

[82] Josephus notes a complete devastation: 97,000 carried off into captivity and 1.1 million people killed (Josephus, *J.W.* 6:420).

[83] The disciples' expectation in Acts 1:6 should also be noted here. See D. Bock, *Luke*, vol. 2: *9:51–24:53*, BECNT (Grand Rapids, MI: Baker, 1996), 1,681–82.

[84] See, e.g., C. S. Keener, "Luke," in *IVP Bible Background Commentary*, 2nd ed. (Downers Grove, IL: InterVarsity, 2014), 235; G. Fuller "The Olivet Discourse: An Apocalyptic Timetable," *WTJ* 28 (1966): 163; R. Stein, "Jesus, the Destruction of Jerusalem, and the Coming of the Son of Man in Luke 21:5–38," *SBJT* 16 (2012): 24; C. F. Evans, *Saint Luke*, TPINTC (Philadelphia, PA: Trinity, 1990), 752; and C. W. Stenschke, *Luke's Portrait of Gentiles Prior to Their Coming to Faith*, WUNT 2/108 (Tübingen, Germany: Mohr Siebeck, 1999), 59.

[85] See, e.g., I. H. Marshall, *The Gospel of Luke: A Commentary on the Greek Text*, NIGNTC (Grand Rapids, MI: Eerdmans, 1978), 773–75.

[86] Some have suggested that the phrase refers to Gentiles trampling Jerusalem until their kingdoms are judged as well. See, e.g., J. Nolland, *Luke*, WBC 35 (Dallas, TX: Word, 1993), 1,003–4.

come near" (Luke 21:20).[87] In the same way, Matthew and Mark report the necessity of worldwide proclamation before Christ's return (Matt 24:14; Mark 13:10). Luke, however, expresses the same reality as "until the times of the Gentiles are fulfilled" (Luke 21:24). Thus, Luke 21:24 more likely represents both judgment and proclamation.[88] While this is not a universally held interpretation, it is undisputed that a period of Gentile inclusion is the hallmark of the present time. As Paul states, "I don't want you to be ignorant of this mystery, brothers and sisters, so that you will not be conceited: A partial hardening has come upon Israel until the fullness of the Gentiles has come in" (Rom 11:25). After this Paul makes clear that "all Israel will be saved," most likely referring to the Jewish nation as a whole (though not necessarily without exception) embracing Jesus as the Messiah at his second coming prior to his millennial reign (Rom 11:26–27 citing Isa 59:20–21). This indicates that while the focus subsequent to Pentecost shifts proportionately to the Gentiles, there will be a final shift back to Israel, so that the Gentiles do not replace Israel in God's plan but Israel retains its salvation-historical distinction.

Jesus describes the events of the end in rather broad strokes. He summarizes the signs of Luke 21:25–26 simply as "the powers of the heavens will be shaken" (Luke 21:26), and he says that after this the Son of Man will come (Luke 21:27). Matthew states it in similar terms: "Immediately after the distress of those days, the sun will be darkened, and the moon will not shed its light; the stars will fall from the sky, and the powers of the heavens will be shaken" (Matt 24:29). Thus, in the Olivet Discourse the sign of the end of the times of the Gentiles consists of a series of cosmic disasters. Although the period is a time of judgment on Israel and proclamation to the Gentiles, it is a mistake to think of it as merely a time of the expansion of the church. It is an expansion bought in blood.

The book of Acts narrates the early church's mission starting in Jerusalem and moving inexorably to Judea and Samaria and to the ends of the earth as the work of the exalted Christ who sends out the Holy Spirit at Pentecost following his resurrection and ascension (Acts 1:8; chap. 2). While there are internal and external obstacles to the progression of the gospel, all these are overcome in the power of the Spirit. Foremost among these potential obstacles that are overcome by the core of the gospel message is the question: What should be the requirements for Gentiles' entrance into the church? Should Gentiles be required to adhere to Jewish identity markers such as circumcision, Sabbath, and adherence to food laws, similar to requirements for Gentile proselytes wishing to join a Jewish synagogue?[89] Or should no such requirements be placed on them in light of the fact that Jesus's death in effect fulfilled such OT stipulations, as the book of Hebrews eloquently demonstrates? In a

---

[87] In Luke the surrounding armies are the portent that Jerusalem will be left desolate. In Matthew and Mark the sign is specifically an "abomination of desolation . . . standing in the holy place" (Matt 24:15; Mark 13:14). This might refer to Titus's invasion, but the historical sequence is such that the devastation is prior to his "standing where it ought not." Instead, it is more likely that the Zealots' occupation of the temple and their atrocities match Dan 9:27.

[88] J. Green, *The Gospel of Luke*, NICNT (Grand Rapids, MI: Eerdmans, 1997), 739.

[89] See the book of Galatians, which deals with the "Judaizing controversy" and was most likely written just prior to the Jerusalem Council.

great historical and theological breakthrough, the early church at the so-called "Jerusalem Council" of Acts 15 decisively sided with the apostle Paul, who strongly advocates that no undue additional burdens be placed on Gentile converts. Even "pillars" such as James, the leader of the Jerusalem church, and the apostle Peter agree (Gal 2:9), and a decree is drafted that is subsequently circulated among the churches. With this, the path is cleared for the unhindered proclamation of the gospel all the way to Rome, the empire's capital (Acts 28).

Paul's Letters provide additional glimpses into the early church's mission, spearheaded by Paul, to Jews and Gentiles alike.[90] Paul grounds his ministry firmly in God's overarching plan, tying his mission to "all the nations" into the story line here under discussion.[91] Several of Paul's Letters are intended to follow up on Paul's successful effort of planting local churches in strategic locations such as Galatia, Thessalonica, Corinth, and Ephesus. In other cases, Paul is addressing churches originally established by others with whom he has a relationship and/or with whom he is intending to visit in his strategic church planting mission (Romans, Colossians). While in many of these correspondences Paul addresses local circumstances, Paul's Letters provide invaluable explications of the implications of Jesus's death and resurrection for believers, most comprehensively in the book of Romans. According to Paul, believers are united with Jesus in his death, burial, and resurrection, and thus enjoy the benefits of the gospel.[92] What is more, Paul unpacks the heretofore undisclosed "mystery" of the church, the "body of Christ," consisting of believing Jews and Gentiles on par with one another.[93] Importantly, Paul states that Christ is the head of the church, and she is his body, called to display spiritual unity in the midst of the diversity of its members. Paul develops this teaching on the nature of the church particularly toward the middle of his correspondence with various churches. The end of Paul's ministry finds him addressing important questions related to the continuance of his apostolic legacy, such as qualifications for church leadership and dealing with false teachers and false teachings (Letters to Timothy and Titus).[94] The body of the Pauline corpus provides an

---

[90] The formula is typically "first to the Jews, but also to the Gentiles" (see Rom 1:16; Acts 13:46; 26:23).

[91] Note the continuity of Paul's language in 2 Tim 4:17 ("But the Lord stood with me and strengthened me, so that I might fully preach the word and all the Gentiles [*panta ta ethnē*] hear it") with the language of "all the Gentiles/nations" (*panta ta ethnē*) both in the Abrahamic promises (Gen 18:18; 22:18; 26:4 LXX; Gal 3:8) and in the Great Commission (Matt 28:19) and other teachings and instructions of Jesus (Mark 13:10; Luke 24:45–47). The use of *panta ta ethnē* here and elsewhere in Paul's writings thus reflects his big-picture understanding of his mission as bringing to culmination something that was begun long ago.

[92] See the more than 200 instances where Paul refers to believers as being "in Christ." See C. R. Campbell, *Paul and Union with Christ: An Exegetical and Theological Study* (Grand Rapids, MI: Zondervan, 2012); R. Letham, *Union with Christ in Scripture, History, and Theology* (Phillipsburg, NJ: P&R, 2011).

[93] See, e.g., Gal 3:1–29, esp. v. 28; Eph 2:11–3:13; Col 1:24–29. See also Rom 12:3–8 and 1 Corinthians 12–14 where the metaphor of the church as the "body of Christ" is developed further in terms of believers possessing various God-given spiritual gifts they are to use for the edification of the entire body.

[94] For a discussion of the various heresies attested in the NT, see A. J. Köstenberger and M. J. Kruger, *The Heresy of Orthodoxy: How Contemporary Culture's Fascination with Diversity Has Reshaped Our Understanding of Early Christianity* (Wheaton, IL: Crossway, 2010), chap. 3.

indispensable deposit of theology in Scripture that ties the Gospels to the remainder of the NT, including the book of Revelation.[95]

CONSUMMATION

Scholars have long recognized that there is a notable similarity between the details of the Olivet Discourse and the seven-sealed scroll first seen in Revelation 5:1.[96] This scroll clearly recalls the scroll of judgment in Ezekiel 2:10.[97] That scroll was a book of "lamentation, mourning, and woe" (Ezek 2:10). The seven-sealed scroll is as well, but it is in the form of a first-century legal document (contract or covenant).[98] However, the opening of the seals should not be seen as the same as the content of the scroll. They are preparatory to opening the scroll.[99] The opening of the scroll can occur only after the opening of the seventh seal.[100] Instead of being the content of the book, the seven seals represent preliminary judgments leading up to the opening of the book. Interpreters should not identify the opening of the seals with the tribulation period alone.

The first four seals represent the same events that Christ describes in Matthew 24:5–9 in virtually the same order (false messiahs, war, famine, death). In fact, all three Synoptic versions of the Olivet Discourse contain the same events, although with some differences in order—and only Luke includes pestilence (these naturally follow famine, however). The fifth seal opens to reveal the martyrs under the altar (Rev 6:9). Upon their cry for justice ("How long, O Lord?"), they are told to wait until the number of martyrs is complete (Rev 6:11). This suggests persecution throughout the times of the Gentiles, not just in the apostolic age.

When the sixth seal is opened, John provides a bit more detail regarding cosmic disasters. More particularly, he describes the response of the unredeemed in light of the imminent wrath of the Lamb (Rev 6:12–17), the sealing of the 144,000 (Rev 7:1–8), and the great multitude in heaven (Rev 7:9–17). The first group is the unrepentant people of the earth, who recognize that the end is near. Notably, they still do not repent but call for the rocks of the mountains to fall on them so they can die (Rev 6:16).[101] Without entering the debate regarding the details of this passage, suffice it to say the present time is not raging

---

[95] For purposes of this survey, we mostly bypass smaller NT contributions such as James, Jude, and the Letters of Peter and John, since, while important NT voices, they contribute perhaps less centrally to the overall story line.

[96] See, e.g., C. M. Pate, "Revelation 6: An Early Interpretation of the Olivet Discourse," *CTR* 8 (2011), 44–55; G. Beale, *The Book of Revelation*, NIGTC (Grand Rapids, MI: Eerdmans, 1999), 376.

[97] S. Smalley notes that the word translated "scroll" here is the diminutive form that has fallen out of use by the first century (Gr. *biblion*; *The Revelation of John: A Commentary on the Greek Text of the Apocalypse* [Downers Grove, IL: InterVarsity, 2005], 127). The LXX of Ezek 2:9 also uses the diminutive form (Gr. *bibliou*). The usage in the Apocalypse is best seen as an intentional allusion to an OT reference.

[98] G. R. Osborne, *Revelation*, BECNT (Grand Rapids, MI: Baker, 2002), 251.

[99] G. E. Ladd, *A Commentary on the Revelation of John* (Grand Rapids, MI: Eerdmans, 1972), 80; R. Bauckham, *The Climax of Prophecy: Studies on the Book of Revelation* (Edinburgh, Scotland: T&T Clark, 1993), 247.

[100] See Beale, *Revelation*, 532.

[101] Beale notes based on parallels to Isa 2:10, 18–21 that these are idolaters (*Revelation*, 399). This may be borne out by the fact that they commit one last act of idolatry and pray to the mountains and rocks (nature) for relief from the wrath of the Lamb.

anarchy against the cosmic foundations. Instead, God is totally in charge. His coming wrath is undeniable. His angels hold back the storm clouds of wrath until his elect are sealed (Rev 7:1–3), and their spiritual security through the tribulation is firm because of their redemption in the blood of the Lamb (Rev 7:14). As the angel reports,

> For this reason they are before the throne of God, and they serve him day and night in his temple. The one seated on the throne will shelter them. They will no longer hunger; they will no longer thirst; the sun will no longer strike them, nor will any scorching heat. For the Lamb who is at the center of the throne will shepherd them; he will guide them to springs of the waters of life, and God will wipe away every tear from their eyes. (Rev 7:15–17)

When the seventh seal is opened, all of heaven is silent for about half an hour (Rev 8:1). The silence builds anticipation, but if we understand that the book of judgment is now open, it is not difficult to see that even the angels' breath is taken away at the prospect of the Lamb's wrath. The final seal releases seven angels holding trumpets. Each angel blows his trumpet, releasing ever-increasing judgments. In Revelation 8:4, it is clear that these last judgments are underway. These seem to be in response to the martyrs, "How long, O Lord?" The answer is clearly, "Not much longer."[102] The last great judgments are now progressing.[103] Justice and vengeance are coming on those who have persecuted believers.

The final trumpets (the woes) are like a firework finale of wrath including seven intense "bowl judgments." All the enemies of God and his people, those still refusing to repent (Rev 9:21; 16:9, 11, 21), are devastated, so that the angel announces, "It is done" (Rev 16:17). The harlot of Babylon who made the world drunk in her immorality (Rev 18:2) will drink the wine of God's wrath (Rev 17:19). The beast that supplanted her (Rev 17:17) arrays its armies against the Lamb and is instantaneously defeated by the Lamb and his warrior-saints (Rev 19:19–21).[104] This leads to the OT expectation of the kingdom of God on earth, commonly known as the millennium (Rev 20:1–6).[105]

The Apocalypse reveals four stages to remove the presence of sin. First, Revelation 19:19–21 notes the defeat of the Beast, the false prophet, and their forces as well as their punishment. Second, in Revelation 20:4–6, believers, dead and alive, receive resurrection bodies. At long last believers will know what it is like not to feel the presence of sin. Third,

---

[102] This is expressly stated in Rev 10:6–7: "He swore by the one who lives forever and ever, who created heaven and what is in it, the earth and what is in it, and the sea and what is in it: 'There will no longer be a delay, but in the days when the seventh angel will blow his trumpet, then the mystery of God will be completed, as he announced to his servants the prophets.'"

[103] Beale, *Revelation*, 455.

[104] For a fuller summary, see the Unit-by-Unit Discussion of the Book of Revelation in chap. 20.

[105] While the writers of this book are premillennialists, the debate is far from settled. Fortunately, the story line of the Bible is not drastically altered whether or not a millennium will literally take place. Ultimately, we agree with Osborne: "This issue will not be solved until the events take place, and then we will see who is 'right.' Until then, we should not fight over these issues but be 'iron sharpening iron' as we work together for the kingdom" (*Revelation*, 697).

Revelation 20:10 reports that after the millennium rebellion, the Devil is thrown into the lake of fire.[106] Finally, Revelation 20:11–15 presages the "great white throne judgment" where all are judged according to their works. Ultimately, "anyone not found written in the book of life was thrown into the lake of fire" (Rev 20:15). Thus, the problem that began in the garden is finally eradicated, and Daniel's promise that Messiah the Prince will "make an end of sin" (Dan 9:24) is fully realized. The serpent has been cast out of the garden. All that remains is for the garden to be reopened.

THE FINAL STATE

In the West much of our evangelism centers on the question of personal eschatology: Do you want to go to heaven when you die? This is an all-important question we should constantly ask. However, the reference is at best incomplete.[107] It might lead one to assume that what we experience is the normal human existence. As we have seen, however, our current way of life is not normal, even though it is the only one we have ever known. The Christian worldview is not that we live, die, leave this world to go to heaven, and the world continues on its course. Instead, we must understand that we live in the "times of the Gentiles" that look forward to a final permanent state in which God and humanity are reunited. Yes, the present departure of the believer is to an "intermediate state" of existence in the presence of the Lord (see 2 Corinthians 5). However, this existence is only temporary. The final hope of believers is what is known as "the final state." This final state concludes the biblical story line.

At the end of the book of Revelation, John is shown the new heavens and the new earth, but especially the new Jerusalem. Most of the symbolism regarding the city points to the security, peace, and wealth of this new plane of reality with God and redeemed humanity living in fellowship akin to that first experienced in Eden. It has massive fortified walls conveying the health and security of the city. The gates are open, signifying the lack of any threat. The city is constructed of the most precious of materials, signifying the wealth of the King.

The description of the new Jerusalem is reminiscent of the garden but not precisely equivalent. Angels are posted at the entrances (Rev 21:12), but they are not preventing entrance (as in Gen 3:24). The shape of the city is a perfect, massive cube. The shape is suggestive of the holy of holies. John notes that there is no temple in the city (Rev 21:22). This is the case because the city itself is the holy of holies.[108] Thus, like the garden, it is a sanctuary, but unlike it there is no three-fold temple hierarchy. To be in the city is to be in the presence of God.

---

[106] We are told the Devil's purpose for going out ("to deceive the nations," Rev 20:8). We are not told the reason God would allow such a thing. R. Mounce proposes that it is "to make plain that neither the designs of Satan nor the waywardness of the human heart will be altered by the mere passing of time" (*The Book of Revelation*, rev. ed., NICNT [Grand Rapids, MI: Eerdmans, 1997], 371). Clearly, no rehabilitation is possible. However, there is also a demonstration of the wickedness of the unredeemed here as well. After a thousand-year reign of Christ on earth featuring peace, abundance, and security, the unredeemed still align themselves with the serpent.

[107] See N. T. Wright, "New Heavens, New Earth," in *Called to One Hope*, ed. John Colwell (Carlisle, UK: Paternoster, 2000), 33.

[108] Osborne, *Revelation*, 760.

As John describes the inside of the city, additional Edenic similarities appear. First, a river ran out of Eden to water the garden (Gen 2:10), but here a river of life flows from the throne of God and the Lamb (Rev 21:10). Like in the garden (Gen 2:9), the tree of life is in the city. It is described as growing on both sides of the river. In English we get the picture of a tree so large that the river flows through it (like the iconic road through the California redwood). However, the Greek term (*xulon*) is neuter and is likely a collective singular.[109] In other words, instead of one tree the tree of life in the new Jerusalem is a grove of trees on both sides of the river. This picture of abundance of life is multiplied even more in that these trees produce twelve kinds of fruit per month (Rev 22:2). That its leaves produce healing for the nations suggests not only life but health as well.

The comparison with the garden does not end there. The passage invites comparison with the garden narrative. In doing so, at least four elements in the first creation are missing in the new. First, there is no tree of the knowledge of good and evil. This suggests there is no opportunity to rebel against God again.

Second, there is no curse (Rev 22:3). Adam and Eve were banished from the garden and expelled from God's presence. It has been the lot of humanity to be unable to endure the direct presence of God due to sin, but now believers can live in God's presence once again: "The throne of God and of the Lamb will be in the city, and His servants will serve Him" (Rev 22:3). Since the new creation knows no curse, humankind may enjoy the presence of God directly: "They will see his face, and his name will be on their foreheads (Rev 22:4).

Third, there is no sun or night "because the Lord God will give them light" (Rev 22:5). Earlier it was noted that God and the Lamb are the light. His glory will replace the celestial bodies as he shines on his people. This recalls the great benediction of Numbers 6:25: "May the LORD make his face shine on you."[110]

Fourth, Adam and Eve were given a grand adventure to subdue the earth and extend the rule of God throughout the earth. However, in the recreated garden, there is no such commission. It is done. The kingdom does not need to be extended. All that remains is an eternal reign (Rev 22:5).

CONCLUSION

The story line of the Bible moves the reader from paradise lost to paradise regained (and more). The story takes (and will take) longer than anyone could have possibly imagined. Progress, however, is undeniable. The narrative unity of the Scriptures is seen in the progress of the story line to ultimately fulfill God's original purposes in creation. What is more,

---

[109] See, e.g., Mounce, *Revelation*, 399; Osborne, *Revelation*, 771; I. T. Beckwith, *The Apocalypse of John* (New York, NY: Macmillan, 1919), 765.

[110] Smalley, *Revelation*, 566. In fact, the new creation covers all the blessings of the righteous: "May the LORD bless you and protect you; may the LORD make his face shine on you, and be gracious to you; may the LORD look with favor on you and give you peace" (Num 6:24–26).

the contours of biblical theology run along the arc of this story so that all the multifaceted themes of the Scriptures can be placed in this narrative sweep.[111]

The result is that recognizing this story line is important in three major areas. First, it impacts how the unity of the Scriptures is perceived.[112] The presence of this story line unites the OT with the NT. The declarations of the OT regarding Abraham, David, his coming eschatological Son, and the new covenant (to name but a few) pave the way for the NT in the fulfillment of these promises in Christ. This story line calls into question evolutionary models of Israel's religion and of Christian theology.

Second, an understanding of the story line is helpful in the defense of the inspiration of the Scriptures. The plot develops and unfolds across many thousands of years, so much so that it is difficult to maintain an evolutionary, progressive, thoroughgoing natural development. How could successive generations move the story along without writing accounts with numerous dead ends? It is unlikely that the story line only appears to exist in retrospect. Understanding the metanarrative helps one defend a transcendent intelligent divine being moving along the story.

Third, the story line should be kept in mind as the Scriptures are interpreted and applied. Not every text moves the story forward to the same extent as the promises to Abraham and David. However, every text has a purpose in the overall structure. For example, understanding the story line helps us see more depth in the inauguration of the new covenant but changes little with regard to the substitutionary nature of the death of Christ. Other texts, such as Hebrews 9:15–26, as discussed above, are brought into sharper clarity when interpreted in light of the covenant's relationship to the story line.

The NT, then, gloriously reveals the identity of the Messiah that remained hidden in OT times (1 Pet 1:10–12). It also reveals what likewise had remained a mystery up until this point: that God would establish his new messianic community consisting of believing Jews and Gentiles based on faith in the Messiah (Gal 3:28). We have seen that the promise to Abraham is fulfilled in the life and death of Christ. The promised new covenant is established by Christ. And the promise to David that his would be an eternal kingdom is fulfilled through the restoration of Eden and Christ's rule. Thus, the contents of the NT conclude the story arc begun in Genesis, but it does much more. Just as the OT contains more than narrative (e.g., Wisdom literature, Psalms, etc.), so, too, does the NT. The doctrine, reproof, correction, and instruction in righteousness contained in the NT (2 Tim 3:16) consist of much more than the mere metanarrative of Scripture. Yet understanding the "big picture" may serve as the overall framework that enables us to place our existence in this world in the context of Scripture so that we may live lives full of meaning and purpose, joining God on his mission to rescue a representative portion of humanity and to move history ever closer toward the final consummation of his purposes in the Lord Jesus Christ.

---

[111] See Klink and Lockett's description of biblical theology they call "BT2": E. Klink and D. Lockett, *Understanding Biblical Theology: A Comparison of Theory and Practice* (Grand Rapids, MI: Zondervan, 2012), chap. 3.

[112] The question of the unity and diversity of the NT is treated in the previous chapter of this volume.

Glossary

agraphon (pl. *Agrapha*): words of Jesus not recorded in the canonical NT Gospels (e.g., Acts 20:35: "It is more blessed to give than to receive")

Agrippa I: grandson of Herod the Great (s.v.) and ruler of Judea (AD 37–44); called "Herod" in the book of Acts (see Acts 12:1–4,19–23); not to be confused with his son Agrippa II before whom Paul pleaded his case (see Acts 26)

Akhmim Codex, Manuscript, or Fragment: manuscript discovered in Akhmim, Egypt in the nineteenth century allegedly containing the apocryphal Gospel of Peter

Aleppo Codex: OT manuscript (c. AD 900)

Alexandrian text type: group of manuscripts that form the basis for the modern eclectic Greek text of the NT (e.g., Codex Sinaiticus)

Alexandrinus: s.v. Codex Alexandrinus

allegory: form of extended metaphor

allepigraphy: from *allos* ("other"), *epi* ("upon"), and *graphō* ("to write"); notion that a piece of writing was authored by someone other than the person to whom authorship is explicitly ascribed in the document

alliteration: repetition of initial letters

allonymity: from *allos* ("other") and *onoma* ("name"); notion that a person other than the one explicitly named is the author of a given piece of writing

allusion: indirect identifiable intentional reference to another text or statement

***alogi*:** group of Christian heretics that flourished in Asia Minor around AD 170

amanuensis: scribe or secretary used by a biblical author to write down his message

American Standard Version (ASV): translation of the Bible first published in 1901

amillennialism: belief that the biblical references to the thousand-year reign of Christ are symbolic in nature (s.v. Millennium)

amoraim: from Aramaic *amar* ("to say, comment"); commentators of Tannaitic teachings

Amphilochius of Iconium (c. AD 340–395): bishop of Iconium, cousin of Gregory Nazianzus, and theologically close to the Cappadocian Fathers

anachronism: imposition of a later development onto an earlier period

anaphora: from *anapherō* ("I repeat"); series of sentences beginning with the same word

Ancient of Days: designation for God in Dan 7:13 in conjunction with the divine-human figure of a "One like a son of man" (s.v. "Son of man")

Annas: influential Jewish high priest (AD 6–15) and father-in-law of Caiaphas, high priest in the year of Jesus' crucifixion (see John 18:13–14)

anthropomorphism: speaking of God in human terms (e.g., that God would change his mind; see Exod 32:14; Jonah 3:10)

anti-chiliast: position rejecting the notion of a thousand-year reign of Christ at the end of human history (held by Eusebius and others)

Antichrist: end-time figure setting himself against God and the Lord Jesus Christ (e.g., 1 John 2:18; 2 John 7; s.v. man of lawlessness)

***antilegomena*:** works whose canonicity was disputed in the early church

Anti-Marcionite Prologues: despite their name, these prefaces to Mark, Luke, and John (Matthew is lost) were most likely not written against Marcion and may date to the fourth century AD; except for the prologue to Luke (which may date to around AD 160–180), they only exist in Latin

antinomianism: an "antilaw" bias, frequently resulting in licentiousness

Antiochus Epiphanes IV (reigned 175–164 BC): Seleucid (Greek) ruler who sought to impose Greek culture onto the Jews, erecting the "abomination of desolation" in the Jerusalem temple by setting up an altar to the supreme Greek god Zeus and sacrificing swine on it around 167 BC; in his opposition to God's people, he served as a precursor of the Antichrist (see Dan 9:27; 11:31; 12:11; 1 Macc 1:54; Matt 24:15; Mark 13:14)

Antipas: s.v. Herod Antipas

antiquity: criterion of canonicity pertaining to a document's writing during the apostolic period

antithesis: contrasting idea

apocalypse: a literary work containing symbolic depictions of end-time events

***Apocalypse of Peter*:** a gnostic document found in the Nag Hammadi library in Egypt

apocalyptic: a worldview that describes end-time events in symbolic terms

apocalypticism: the sociological phenomenon of a group steeped in an end-time perspective

Apocrypha: the OT Apocrypha, accepted as canonical by the Roman Catholic Church but not by those in the Protestant tradition, comprising writings such as 1 and 2 Esdras, 1, 2, 3, and 4 Maccabees, Tobit, Judith, and other writings produced subsequent to the OT prophetic period; the NT Apocrypha contains various Gospels, Acts, Epistles, and Apocalypses produced during the subapostolic period (s.v.) and are recognized by neither Roman Catholics nor Protestants as part of the NT canon

apocryphal: obscure or hidden; pertaining to the Apocrypha

***Apocryphon of John*:** a gnostic document found in the Nag Hammadi library in Egypt

aporia: apparent incongruity or literary seam indicating an author's use of written sources

apostle: in a narrow, technical sense, a member of the Twelve (see Matt 10:1–4 and parallels); slightly extended in the NT to include others also such as Paul and Barnabas; in a broader sense, also includes missionaries and other emissaries (e.g., Rom 16:7; 2 Cor 8:23; Phil 2:25)

apostolic eyewitness: the firsthand testimony of the Twelve recorded in the four canonical Gospels

Apostolic Fathers: group of writings produced during the early patristic period comprising *1 and 2 Clement*; The Letters of Ignatius; *The Letter of Polycarp to the Philippians* and *The Martyrdom of Polycarp*; *The Didache*; *The Epistle of Barnabas*; *The Shepherd of Hermas*; *The Epistle to Diognetus*; the Fragment of Quadratus; and Fragments of Papias

apostolic period: lifetime of those who were eyewitnesses of Jesus' ministry and had been specially appointed by him to serve as his messengers; normally viewed as ending with the writing of the last NT book, the book of Revelation (c. AD 95; s.v. also subapostolic period)

apostolicity: direct or indirect association of a given NT work with an apostle

Appian: second-century AD Greek historian from Alexandria, author of the *Roman History*

Aquinas: s.v. Thomas Aquinas

Aramaic: ancient near Eastern language akin to Hebrew; in the OT, featured in portions of Daniel and Esther; also found in the Targums (s.v.); Jesus spoke Aramaic, and the NT Gospels preserve several authentic sayings of Jesus in Aramaic (e.g., Matt 27:46)

***argumentatio*:** section containing the writer's main argument

Ark of the Covenant: a sacred chest made of acacia wood and covered with gold containing the tablets of stone with the Ten Commandments and other important religious objects (see, e.g., Heb 9:4)

Armageddon: from Hb. *har megido* ("Mount Megiddo"); site of battle in OT times near the city of Meggido (2 Kgs 23:28–30; 2 Chr 35:20–25) and location of the final battle between the forces of God and Satan prior to the return of Christ (Rev 16:16)

Armenian manuscripts: biblical copies written in an Indo-European language spoken in the Caucasus mountains and the Armenian diaspora

ascension (of Christ): Christian belief that the Lord Jesus Christ, subsequent to his resurrection from the dead, was taken up to heaven (see Luke 24:51; Acts 1:9)

asceticism: the suppression of bodily passions

assonance: resemblance of sound

asyndeton: deliberate omission of conjunctions

Athanasius of Alexandria (c. AD 296–373): fourth-century AD bishop of Alexandria, best known for his Festal Letter in AD 367 listing all 27 canonical books of the NT

Athenagoras of Athens (c. AD 180): Christian philosopher and apologist and author of *Supplication*

atonement: blood sacrifice rendered for sin

Attic: ancient Greek dialect

Augustine of Hippo (AD 354–430): North African church father and bishop of Hippo, son of the pious Monica and author of *Confessions* and *The City of God*

Augustinian view of the Synoptic Problem (s.v.): belief that the Gospels were written in the canonical order Matthew first, then Mark, and then Luke, with Mark using Matthew, and Luke using Matthew and Mark; some question whether Augustine actually held this view

Augustus: Roman emperor who ruled in 31/27 BC–AD 14

Authorized Version (AV): s.v. King James Version

autographs: the original OT and NT manuscripts

"Babylon": code name for the Roman Empire (e.g., 1 Pet 5:13)

Babylonian Talmud: s.v. Talmud

Bar Kokhba revolt: Jewish rebellion against the Romans (AD 132–135)

Basil of Caesarea (c. AD 330–379): fourth-century AD church father

Basilides (c. AD 117–138): second-century gnostic teacher

Book of Life: metaphorical depiction of a heavenly record of all who have received eternal life by faith in the Lord Jesus Christ (see Rev 20:12)

British Museum Codex: OT manuscript (AD 950)

Byzantine text type: also called the Majority Text, text form found in the majority of biblical manuscripts that also underlies the Textus Receptus translation (e.g., KJV)

Caesar: title of Roman emperors, harking back to Julius Caesar (born 100 BC and served as virtual dictator 46–44 BC, assassinated in 44 BC by Brutus and others in the Senate)

Caiaphas, Joseph: Jewish high priest (c. AD 18–36) in the year of Jesus' crucifixion

Cairo Geniza: repository of OT manuscripts (AD 895)

Caligula: Roman emperor (AD 37–41)

canon: from *kanōn* ("rule" or "standard"); collection of Christian Scriptures

"Canonical Edition" of the NT: theory by D. Trobisch according to which the NT was produced by the mid-second century AD as a published book by a canonical editor

canonicity: a book's status as to its inclusion in the collection of Christian Scriptures

Cassiodorus: sixth-century AD Roman statesman and writer who served in the administration of Theodoric the Great, king of the Ostrogoths

catholic: universal; later used for the Roman Catholic Church

centurion: Roman military official, from Lat. meaning "commander of 100"

Cephas: Aramaic name for the Greek name Peter (both mean "rock"; see Matt 16:18; John 1:42)

Cerinthianism: early Christian heresy attributed to Cerinthus, a gnostic teacher who held that the "Christ spirit" descended on Jesus at his baptism and left him at the cross

Cerinthus: s.v. Cerinthianism

chain quotations: s.v. pearl stringing

Chaldean: Babylonian

chiasm: from name of Greek letter c; cross-wise arrangement of phrases in such a way that the second expression is in reverse order than the first (A B B' A')

***chiliasm*:** the belief in the millennial (thousand-year) reign of Christ

Christ: from Greek *Christos* ("anointed"); equivalent to Hebrew "Messiah" (s.v.)

Christology: doctrine of (Jesus) Christ

Christophany: (preincarnate) appearance of Christ

Chrysostom: s.v. John Chrysostom

Church Fathers: church leaders, writers, and theologians of the first few centuries of the Christian era (s.v. also patristic)

Cicero, Marcus Tullius (born 65 BC): first-century BC Roman statesman and philosopher

Claudius: Roman emperor (AD 41–54); s.v. also Edict of Claudius

Clement of Alexandria (c. AD 150–215): early church father and member of the Alexandrian school; author of *Stromateis* ("Miscellanies")

Clement of Rome: bishop of Rome and author of *1 Clement* (c. AD 96)

codex: the ancient equivalent of a book, consisting of sheets bound together

Codex Alexandrinus: fifth-century AD manuscript of the Greek Bible, containing most of the Septuagint and NT

Codex Babylonicus Petropalitanus: OT manuscript (AD 1008)

Codex Bezae: fifth-/sixth-century AD biblical manuscript

Codex Montfortianus (Britanicus): late manuscript used by Erasmus in the third edition of his Greek NT published in 1522 that contains the "Johannine comma" in 1 John 5:7, almost certainly a later addition not found in the original manuscript

Codex Sinaiticus: fourth-century AD manuscript containing the Christian Bible in Greek, including the complete NT

Codex Vaticanus: fourth-century AD Greek manuscript containing most of the Septuagint and NT

Colossian heresy: unique eclectic mix of false teachings prevalent in first-century Colossae (see esp. Colossians 2)

composition criticism: method of study focusing on documents (such as the NT Gospels) as a whole and seeking to identify patterns and emphases

conflation: the merging of two or more elements into one

Coptic: last stage of written Egyptian language

corpus: body of writings (e.g., Pauline or Johannine corpus)

Corpus Hermeticum or Hermetic corpus: ancient group of writings harking back to the mythological Greek messenger of the gods, Hermes, that is gnostic (if not occult) in character

Council of Carthage: s.v. Third Council of Carthage

Council of Hippo Regius: meeting of church leaders in North Africa (AD 393)

Council of Laodicea: local meeting of bishops (AD 363–64)

Council of Nicea: first ecumenical council convened by the Roman emperor Constantine I in Nicea, Bithynia, which is modern Turkey (AD 325)

Council of Trent: Roman Catholic ecclesiastical gathering that convened between 1545 and 1563 as part of the Counter-Reformation, an effort to push back the effects of the Protestant Reformation (s.v. Reformation)

covenant: (sacred) contract

covenant community: group of people whose existence is based on an agreement with God through a covenant (s.v.)

covenantal nomism: s.v. nomism

Coverdale Bible: translation of the Bible produced by Miles Coverdale (1535)

Cynic philosophy: set of beliefs holding that a virtuous life was to be lived in accordance with nature and free from the bondage to material possessions

Cyril of Jerusalem (c. AD 315–387): fourth-century AD church father and author of *Catecheses*

Damascus: ancient and modern capital of Syria (s.v.)

Damasus: fourth-century AD bishop (considered pope by the Roman Catholic Church) who commissioned Jerome to translate the Bible into Latin, now called the Vulgate (s.v.)

Day of Atonement: *Yom Kippur*, the most sacred holiday in the Jewish calendar (see Leviticus 16; s.v. atonement)

Day of the Lord: time of final divine judgment predicted by the OT prophets

deacon: from *diakonos* ("servant"); NT nonteaching, nongoverning church office (see 1 Tim 3:8–12)

deaconess: female deacon (s.v. deacon; see 1 Tim 3:11; Rom 16:1)

Dead Sea Scrolls (DSS): a body of Jewish sectarian literature found near the Dead Sea in the years following 1947, including the *Community Rule* (1QS), the *War Scroll* (1QM), and the *Damascus Document* (CD)

Decalogue: the Ten Commandments (see Exodus 20; Deuteronomy 5)

Decapolis: from *deka* ("ten") and *polis* ("city"), a group of 10 cities in the territory of Syria, Jordan, and Palestine bound together by a common location, language, and culture (including Gerasa, Gadara, Pella, Scythopolis, and Damascus)

Deism: belief that there is a God who created the universe but does not interfere with it

deliberative rhetoric: any communication arguing for or against a contemplated future action

Delphi Inscription: inscription in the ancient Greek city of Delphi supposedly containing the maxims "know yourself" and "nothing in excess"

Deutero-Pauline: not authentically Pauline, that is, writing falsely or traditionally attributed to the apostle Paul

Diaspora: for "dispersion," the scattering of Jews beyond the region of Palestine subsequent to the Assyrian and Babylonian exiles

***Diatessaron*:** Greek "through four," name for the first-known synopsis of the Gospels compiled by the church father Tatian (c. AD 150–160)

***Didache*:** church manual from the late first or early second century AD providing information about early church practice regarding the administration of baptism, the Lord's Supper, etc.

Didymus the Blind (c. AD 313–389): ecclesiastical writer and leader of a famous catechetical school in Alexandria, Egypt

Dio Cassius: noted third-century AD Roman historian and public servant who published a multivolume history of Rome

Dio Chrysostom: first-century AD Greek orator (not to be confused with the fourth-century AD bishop John Chrysostom of Antioch)

Diocletian: Roman Emperor (AD 284–305) who launched a major persecution against Christians (AD 302–3)

Dionysius: Greek god of wine

Dionysius bar Salibi: twelfth-century Syrian bishop

Dionysius of Alexandria: mid-third-century AD bishop of Alexandria

Dionysius of Corinth: second-century AD bishop of Corinth

disciple Jesus loved, the: Johannine epithet for the disciple closest to Jesus during his earthly ministry (see John 13:23) who was also the author of John's Gospel (21:20,24); traditionally identified as John, the son of Zebedee

discourse: linguistic units composed of several sentences

discourse analysis: academic discipline devoted to the analysis of discourses (s.v. discourse)

dispensationalism: theological system dividing salvation history into distinct periods (called "dispensations"); falling into classic, revised, and progressive dispensationalism

Dispersion: s.v. Diaspora

ditheism: belief in two gods

docetism: from *dokeō* ("to seem"); the teaching that Jesus only *appeared* to be human

Domitian: Roman emperor (AD 81–96)

doxology: from *doxa* ("glory") and *logos* ("word" or "saying"); a short statement or hymn in praise of God

early Catholicism: second-century AD formation of orthodox doctrine, ecclesiastical authority, and three-tiered church leadership structure

early Christian Gentile mission: the Christian outreach to non-Jews narrated in the book of Acts

Eastern Church: part of the worldwide church that gravitated toward the Eastern Empire at Constantinople and the patriarchate there; distinct from the Western Church (s.v.)

Eastern manuscripts: copies of the Bible from the Eastern Church (s.v.) including the Peshitta (s.v.)

Eastern Orthodox Church: distinct from the Roman Catholic Church, which was centered in the West; an ecclesiastical body tracing its origin back to apostolic times and consisting of national bodies such as the Russian or the Greek Orthodox Church

***Ecclesiastical History*:** famous work by Eusebius (s.v.) in which he referred to many no longer extant works of early church fathers, such as Papias (s.v.)

ecclesiastical usage: criterion of canonicity stressing the widespread use of a given NT document in the early church

ecclesiology: doctrine of the church

echo(es): portions of text resonating with antecedent texts in forms less conspicuous than allusions; while allusions are deliberate, echoes may or may not be intended by the author

eclectic: approach to the book of Revelation that seeks to combine elements of the preterist, historicist, idealist, and futurist interpretations

Edict of Claudius: decree by the Roman Emperor Claudius in AD 49 expelling the Jews from Rome; mentioned in Acts 18:2 (s.v. Claudius)

egalitarian: pertaining to the belief in men's and women's equal right to positions of leadership, including the church offices of pastor and elder

elder: originally referring to an older man, the term also refers to the governing and teaching office of the NT church occupied by a plurality of men (e.g., 1 Tim 3:1–7; 4:14; 5:17)

election: biblical doctrine that God chose certain individuals to salvation

ellipsis: deliberate omission of one or more words of a sentence

emperor cult: worship of the Roman emperor as a god

end time: the period inaugurated by the coming of the Messiah, Jesus Christ, which will be consummated at his return or the Second Coming; also referred to as "the last days"

English Standard Version (ESV): revision of the Revised Standard Version published in 2001

Enlightenment, the: an intellectual movement in the seventeenth and eighteenth centuries advocating the primacy of reason as the basis of authority

Epicureanism: philosophy based on the teachings of Epicurus (c. 341–c. 270 BC), a form of hedonism holding pleasure to be the supreme human good and teaching the pursuit of a virtuous and temperate life so one can enjoy life's simple pleasures

epideictic rhetoric: type of speech assigning praise or blame

Epiphanius of Salamis (c. AD 315–403): fourth-century AD church father and author of *Refutation of All the Heresies* (also known as *Panarion*)

epiphany: revelation; from *epiphaneia* ("appearing"), one of the technical terms for the second coming of Christ (s.v. also *parousia*)

Epistle of Barnabas: s.v. Pseudo-Barnabas

Epistle to Diognetus: anonymous apologetic letter defending Christianity against its accusers dating to the second or third century AD

***Epistula Apostolorum*:** Latin for "Letter of the Apostles," second-century AD document that is part of the NT Apocrypha, falsely ascribed to the apostles and ultimately declared heretical

eschatology: doctrine of the end time

***eschaton*:** Gk. term meaning "last"; usually refers to end-time events related to Christ's return

ethnarch: title of ancient ruler such as Archelaus, who was ethnarch of Judea, Samaria, and Edom (4 BC–AD 6)

etymology: study of the history of the meaning of a word

Euripides: fifth-century BC Athenian dramatist

Eusebius of Caesarea (c. AD 260–c. 340): fourth-century church father and emininent historian of the early church best known for his important work *Ecclesiastical History*

***exhortatio*:** Lat. term for rhetorical section containing an exhortation

exile, the: the subjugation or deportation of the Jewish people by the Assyrians in 721 BC and the Babylonians in 605, 597, and 586 BC; also called "captivity"

***exordium*:** Lat. for "beginning"; introductory portion of an oration or argument

experts in the Law: NT designation for Jewish scribes and Scripture scholars; often referred to as "scribes"

extant reference: passage available in an existing manuscript

external evidence: attestation of a given piece of writing by a source outside of that document, such as by a patristic writer; in contrast to internal evidence (s.v.)

Felix: Roman procurator of Judea (AD 52–59; see Acts 24)

Festus, Porcius: Roman procurator of Judea (AD 60–62; see Acts 25)

Florus, Gessius: Roman procurator of Judea (AD 64–66)

forensic rhetoric: type of speech used in a courtroom setting

form criticism: method of biblical criticism that classifies units of Scripture by literary genre or pattern

formal equivalence: word-for-word approach to Bible translation (e.g., NASB)

fourfold Gospel: the notion that, properly understood, the four canonical Gospels constitute *one* gospel "according to" the four witnesses Matthew, Mark, Luke, and John

fulfillment quotations: statements by the authors of the four Gospels, especially Matthew and John, highlighting the fulfillment of various messianic passages in Jesus; introduced with a formula such as "to fulfill what was spoken by the Lord through the prophet" (e.g., Matt 1:22; 2:5,15,17,23)

functional equivalence: phrase-by-phrase approach to Bible translation (e.g., NLT)

futurist: an interpretation of the book of Revelation that sees chaps. 4–22 as referring to future events

Galba: Roman emperor (June AD 68–January AD 69)

Galilee: region in the north of Palestine surrounding the Sea of Galilee

Gallio Inscription: inscription found in Delphi, Greece, that confirms that Gallio was the governor of Achaia when Paul was in Corinth in AD 51–52 (see Acts 18:12)

Gamaliel I the Elder, Rabbi: a preeminent first-century Jewish rabbi and teacher of Paul prior to the latter's conversion to Christianity (see Acts 22:3; cf. Acts 5:34–39; Phil 3:4–6)

Gemara: part of the Talmud that contains rabbinic commentary and analysis of the Mishnah; s.v. also Jerusalem Talmud, Talmud

gematria: numerical symbolism (e.g., Jesus' genealogy in Matt 1:1–17 in three groups of 14 generations since 14 is the total of the value of the three Hebrew letters in the name "David")

General Epistles: collective expression for a body of NT writings that contains Hebrews, James, 1–2 Peter, 1–3 John, and Jude; called "general" because they are addressed to a wide, varied, and often unspecified audience

Geneva Bible: translation of the Bible into English from the original languages published in 1560

Georgian manuscripts: ancient manuscripts dating back as far as the fifth century AD written in Georgian, the language spoken in Georgia, a region between the Black and Caspian Seas on the Caucasian mountain chain

***gĕzērâ šāwâ*:** use of verbally analogous words to draw attention to the relationship between two passages

Gnostic Gospels: body of literature produced by the adherents to an early Christian heresy called "Gnosticism" (s.v.) including the Gospel of Thomas, the so-called Gospel of Truth, and others

Gnosticism: from Greek *gnōsis* ("knowledge"), a second-century religion pitting spirit against matter, considering the former good and the latter evil; precursors may be attested in the later NT (e.g., 1 Tim 6:20–21)

God-fearer: Gentile (non-Jew) attracted to Jewish worship who participates in synagogue worship while not submitting to circumcision (s.v. also proselytes)

Good News Bible (GNB): also known as Today's English Version (TEV), produced in 1978

Gospel of Mary (Magdalene): second-century AD Gnostic Gospel falsely attributed to Mary Magdalene

Gospel of Peter: apocryphal Gospel falsely attributed to the apostle Peter, most likely dated to the second half of the second century AD

Gospel of Philip: apocryphal Gospel falsely attributed to the apostle Philip, most likely dated to the second half of the second century AD

Gospel of Thomas: late second-century AD Gnostic Gospel, falsely attributed to the apostle Thomas, found in the Nag Hammadi library in Egypt

Gospel tradition: oral and/or written material underlying the written Gospels (s.v. also Synoptic tradition)

Greco-Roman: pertaining to Greek and Roman culture

Greek: *lingua franca* of the first-century world and original language of the NT

Gregory of Nazianzus (c. AD 329–390): major theologian, one of the Cappadocian Fathers, and author of *Five Theological Orations*

Gregory the Great: also known as Pope Gregory I (AD 590–604), one of the four great Latin Fathers of the church together with Ambrose, Augustine, and Jerome

Griesbach (or Two-Gospel) Hypothesis: the view, named after the German scholar J. J. Griesbach, that Matthew and Luke wrote first and Mark used both of these earlier Gospels

Hades: the abode of the dead awaiting final judgment

Halakhah (halakhic): Jewish body of law regulating all aspects of life

Hanina ben Dosa: first-century AD miracle worker and student of the Jewish rabbi Yohanan ben Zakkai

hapax legomenon **(pl.** ***hapax legomena*****):** word occurring only once in a given piece of writing

hasid **(pl.** ***hasidim*****):** Hb. "pious" or "righteous"; a Jewish religious party mentioned in 1 Maccabees that emerged during the Maccabean period (s.v. Maccabees)

Hasmoneans: Jewish ruling dynasty established during the Maccabean period

Hebrew: ancient Near Eastern language spoken by the Jewish people and original language of the OT

Hegelian: pertaining to the thought of the German philosopher G. W. F. Hegel, who posited that history progressed along the course of a dialectic from thesis to antithesis to synthesis

Hegesippus (c. AD 110–180): second-century AD chronicler of the history of the church who wrote against the Gnostics

Hellenism: Greek culture

Hellespont: the ancient term for a narrow strait now known as the Dardanelles dividing the Balkans from Asia Minor

hendiadys: two nouns linked by conjunction to express a single concept or idea

Herod: this may refer to the head of the Herodian dynasty, Herod the Great (37–4 BC) or one or his descendants, such as his sons Archelaus (s.v. Herod Archelaus), Antipas (s.v. Herod Antipas), and Philip

Herod Antipas: tetrarch of Galilee and Perea (4 BC–AD 39)

Herod Archelaus: one of the sons of Herod the Great (s.v.) who was ethnarch of Judea, Samaria, and Idumea (4 BC–AD 6)

Herod the Great: s.v. Herod

Hilary of Poitiers (c. AD 315–368): most respected Latin theologian of his day in the West; wrote major work on the Trinity

Hippolytus of Rome (c. AD 170–236): presbyter of the church at Rome and prolific author of works such as *Refutation of All Heresies* and *Antichrist*

historical Jesus: the product of scholarly research into the background of the person of Jesus Christ

historicist: approach to the interpretation of the book of Revelation according to which John's visions forecast the course of history in Western Europe with particular emphasis on popes, kings, and wars

historiography: a particular approach to writing history

history-of-religions school: approach that views history primarily in terms of the evolution of human religious consciousness and uses a comparative-religions approach seeking to understand Judaism and Christianity in relation to other ancient religions

Holman Christian Standard Bible (HCSB): English Bible translation published in 2004

Homer: ninth- or eight-century BC classic Greek epic poet; author of *The Iliad* and *The Odyssey*

homiletical midrash: interpretation of biblical text in preaching

***homolegoumena*:** NT books widely recognized as authoritative in Eusebius's day (c. AD 260–340)

hook word: word at the beginning of a paragraph repeated from the end of the preceding paragraph linking two units together

Horace: first-century BC Roman poet; author of *Odes* or *Carmina*

hyperbaton: departure from normal word order for emphasis or effect

hyperbole: exaggeration for rhetorical effect

idealist: approach to the interpretation of the book of Revelation according to which the book symbolically portrays the spiritual and timeless nature of the battle between good and evil

Ignatius of Antioch (c. AD 35–110): bishop of Antioch and early church father who wrote letters to the Ephesians, Magnesians, Philadelphians, and others

Immanuel: Hb. meaning "God with us"; identification of Jesus in Matt 1:23 alluding to Isa 7:14

imperial cult: s.v. emperor cult

***inclusio*:** an ancient literary device bracketing a section by placing one and the same word or phrase at the beginning and at the end of that section

***inclusio* of eyewitness testimony:** the literary practice of indicating the major eyewitness source of an account by featuring this person as the first and the last named character in the narrative

inerrancy: the doctrine affirming Scripture to be free from error

inspiration: the doctrine of God's determinative spiritual influence on the writers of Scripture resulting in an inerrant Bible

internal evidence: data derived from a given document itself (in contrast to external evidence, s.v.)

interpolation: insertion of text

inviolate: prohibition against altering the text of Scripture either by adding or by taking away (e.g., Rev 22:18–19)

***ipsissima verba*:** exact words

***ipsissima vox*:** exact voice, true sense

Irenaeus of Lyons (c. AD 130–200): bishop of Lyons, France, and early church father who wrote the important work *Against Heresies* refuting Gnosticism

isocolon: succession of phrases of approximately equal length and corresponding structure

Jerome (c. AD 345–420): fourth-century AD church father and translator of the Lat. Vulgate (s.v.)

Jerusalem Bible: Roman Catholic translation of the Bible published in 1966

Jerusalem Council: traditional designation for meeting of leaders in the early church in Jerusalem as narrated in Acts 15

Jerusalem Talmud: also called Palestinian Talmud; a collection of Jewish rabbinic traditions consisting of the Mishnah (c. AD 200) and the Gemara (in two versions, dated c. AD 350–400 and 500, respectively)

"Jesus of faith": Jesus as the object of the early church's faith in distinction from Jesus during his earthly ministry (a distinction upheld by the German scholars Martin Kähler, Rudolf Bultmann, and others)

"Jesus of history": s.v. historical Jesus

Jesus, Mara bar Serapion: non-Christian man in a Syrian prison who wrote a letter to his son in the first or second century AD, making mention of "the Jews . . . executing their wise King," a possible reference to Jesus outside the Bible

Jesus Seminar: group of scholars engaged in a critical "quest for the historical Jesus" (s.v.) and typically arriving at negative conclusions regarding the historicity of the information regarding Jesus in the four canonical Gospels

Jewish mysticism: s.v. merkabah mysticism

Jewish War: usually refers to the first Jewish-Roman war (AD 66–73) during which Jerusalem and the temple were destroyed

Johannine: related to (the apostle) John (s.v. also Johannine corpus)

Johannine comma: embellishment of 1 John 5:7 not found in any Greek manuscript prior to the Reformation period; s.v. also Codex Montfortianus

Johannine corpus: body of John's writings included in the Bible (i.e., Gospel of John, 1–3 John, Revelation)

John Chrysostom ("gold-mouthed"; c. AD 347–407): archbishop of Constantinople and Christian preacher and writer; best known for his *Homilies*

John Wycliffe (1330–1384): produced an English translation of the Bible from the Lat. Vulgate (s.v.)

Josephus (AD 37–100): Jewish historian; author of *Jewish Wars*, *Jewish Antiquities*, and *Against Apion*

Judaizers: first-century Jewish movement that wanted to require Gentiles to submit to circumcision as a condition for allowing them into the Christian church (see especially the book of Galatians)

Julian calendar: a reform of the Roman calendar implemented by Julius Caesar (hence the name "Julian") in 45 BC; the Julian calendar has now largely been replaced by the Gregorian calendar

Julius Africanus: early third-century AD Christian traveler and historian who wrote a history of the world

Justin Martyr (c. AD 100–165): early Christian apologist; best known for his works *Dialogue with Trypho* and *First Apology*

Juvenal: late first- and early second-century AD Roman poet; author of the *Satires*

Kabiros: ancient Greek god

***kerygma*, the:** Gk. term used in a technical sense for the core content of NT preaching

King James Version (KJV): Bible published in 1611; also known as the Authorized Version (AV)

***lacuna* (pl. *lacunae*):** gap in a manuscript, inscription, or text

Lapis Tiburtinus Inscription: a first-century tombstone found in the eighteenth century recording the career of a distinguished Roman official, possibly Quirinius

Latinism: a Latin term or phrase

Law: God-given requirements for Israel centered on the Decalogue (the Ten Commandments); the code given through Moses at Mount Sinai

legalism: a pejorative term denoting the improper fixation on laws or codes of conduct

Leningrad Codex: OT manuscript (AD 916)

***lex talionis*:** the OT principle of "eye for an eye, tooth for a tooth" (see Exod 21:22–25)

libertinism: indulgence of bodily passions, involving immoral behavior

***lingua franca*:** universal language

literary integrity: authorship of a given piece of writing by one author, denoting its authenticity, cohesion, and coherence

litotes: affirming a truth by denying its opposite (e.g., Rom 1:16: "I am not ashamed of the gospel," indicating that Paul is proud of the gospel; cf. John 6:37)

***logion* (plural *Logia*):** saying or oracle

***logos*:** Gk. *logos* ("word"), the designation for the preexistent Lord Jesus Christ in John 1:1,14 in keeping with passages such as Isa 55:11–12

Lord's Prayer, the: s.v. Model Prayer

Lost Gospels: general reference to apocryphal Gospels, that is, Gospels falsely attributed to an apostle or another figure mentioned in the NT (such as Mary Magdalene) that were written subsequent to the apostolic era; while referred to as "Lost Gospels," most of these documents are actually extant, though often in late copies and often fragmentary (s.v. also Gospel of Mary, Peter, Thomas, etc.)

Lucian of Samosata: second-century AD satirist writing in Greek; author of *The Passing of Peregrinus*

LXX: s.v. Septuagint

Maccabean martyrs: Jews who lost their lives during the Maccabean uprising against the Seleucids in the second century BC (see 2 Maccabees)

Maccabees: a Jewish family that led the second-century BC revolt against the Seleucids issuing in a period of Jewish independence

"man of lawlessness": the Antichrist (see 2 Thess 2:1–12)

manuscript (ms.; pl. mss.): anything written by hand (a text or document)

manuscript tradition: history of the transmission of (biblical) manuscripts

Marcion of Sinope (died c. AD 160): heretic best known for his truncated canon of the NT consisting of an edited version of Luke's Gospel and 10 letters of Paul (he rejected the Pastoral Epistles)

Mar Saba manuscript: a forged epistle attributed to Clement of Alexandria and "discovered" by Morton Smith in 1958, containing the only known references to the Secret Gospel of Mark

Markan priority: the view that Mark wrote first and was used by the other two Synoptic writers (Matthew and Luke)

Masoretes: Jewish scribes responsible for the preservation of the OT text

Masoretic text (MT): s.v. Masoretes

Matthean priority: the view that Matthew was the first among the Synoptic Gospel writers to write his Gospel and that Mark and Luke used Matthew

Matthew's Bible: translation of the entire Bible in the wake of John Wycliffe's translation and produced under the pseudonym "Thomas Matthew" in 1537

Melito of Sardis (died c. AD 190): bishop of Sardis near Smyrna in Asia Minor

merkabah **mysticism:** from Hb. *merkabah* ("chariot," see Ezek 1:4–26); an ancient Jewish tradition of interpretation that holds that the biblical images of God are analogies for the basic ways in which God reveals himself in the world

Messiah: from Hb. *meshshiach* ("anointed"); promised deliverer sent by God to save his people; identified in the NT as the Lord Jesus Christ (e.g., John 20:30–31)

messianic secret: term conventionally used to describe Jesus' reluctance to identify himself publicly as the Messiah, possibly due to the prevailing misunderstanding associated with the term (at least in part)

Middle Ages: period of time commonly dated from the fall of the Western Roman Empire in the fifth century AD to the rise of nation states and the Christian Reformation in the sixteenth century

Middle Platonism: a set of philosophical tenets associated with Plato that developed from c. 130 BC until the late second century AD

***midrash*:** ancient Jewish commentary, including interpretation of selected passages of Scripture, with a view toward pointing out their contemporary relevance

millennium: thousand-year reign of Christ (see Revelation 20)

minuscules: ancient manuscripts written in small cursive-like script

Mishnah: collection of Jewish rabbinic traditions compiled c. AD 200

Model Prayer: also called "The Lord's Prayer" (see Matt 6:9–11; Luke 11:2–4)

Monarchian Prologues: short introductions prefixed in many Vulgate (s.v.) mss. to the four Gospels, probably written in the fourth or fifth century AD

monism: philosophical view positing one underlying unifying principle, blurring the distinction between the Creator and the created universe

monotheism: belief in one God characteristic of Judaism, Christianity, and Islam

Montanism: mid-second century AD sect named after its founder, Montanus, who claimed to have received a series of special divine revelations and who claimed to be the *Paraclete* mentioned in John's Gospel

ms(s).: abbreviation for manuscript(s)

Muratorian Canon: an early canonical list probably dating to the later second century AD

mystery religions: Greco-Roman cults conceiving of religion primarily in terms of mystical union with the divine

mysticism: various approaches to spirituality focusing on human union with the divine, as in *merkabah* mysticism (s.v.) or mystery religions (s.v.)

myth: sacred story, particularly of human origins, that is of human fabrication rather than being rooted in actual history

Nag Hammadi Library: collection of gnostic writings found in Nag Hammadi in Upper Egypt in 1945

***narratio*:** presentation of essential facts explaining the nature of a matter

narrative criticism: study of the literary aspects of a given piece of narrative writing (e.g., the canonical Gospels)

Nazarene: an inhabitant of Nazareth, the town where Jesus was raised; hence Jesus was called a "Nazarene" in fulfillment of prophecy (Matt 2:23)

Nero: Roman emperor (AD 54–68); responsible for the fire of Rome (AD 64) and the martyrdom of many Christians, including the apostles Peter and Paul (AD 65 or 66)

"Nero *redivivus* myth": the belief that the Roman emperor Nero had not actually died but was going to return to Rome with the Parthian army (a.k.a. Nero *redux*)

New American Bible (NAB): Bible translation published in 1966

New American Standard Bible (NASB): Bible translation published in 1970

New Century Version (NCV): Bible translation published in 1987

New English Bible (NEB): Bible translation published in 1966

New International Version (NIV): Bible translation published in 1978

New King James Version (NKJV): revision of the King James Version published in 1982

New Living Translation (NLT): revision of the Living Bible (a paraphrase) published in 1996

New Perspective, the: challenge to the traditional view of Paul as opposing Jewish legalism in his day first articulated by E. P. Sanders in *Paul and Palestinian Judaism*

New Revised Standard Version (NRSV): revision of the Revised Standard Version published in 1989

New Testament Apocrypha: s.v. NT Apocrypha

***nomina sacra*:** standardized abbreviations for the names of God in early Christian manuscripts, typically consisting of the first and the last letter of a given name with a horizontal bar over the abbreviation (e.g., QS for Qeo~, "God")

nomism: term coined by E. P. Sanders referring to Jewish adherence to the Law *(nomos)* as the path of righteousness; a.k.a. covenantal nomism

NT Apocrypha: various writings produced during the subapostolic period (s.v.) that imitate the canonical Gospels, Acts, Epistles, and Revelation (e.g., the Gospel of Thomas, the Acts of Thecla, or the Apocalypse of Peter)

Old Testament Apocrypha: s.v. OT Apocrypha

Olivet Discourse: Jesus' teaching on the end time recorded in Matthew 24–25 with parallels in Mark 13 and Luke 21

oracle: vision

ordinance: church observance commanded by Christ, in particular baptism (Matt 28:18–20) and the Lord's Supper (1 Cor 11:23–26; see Matt 26:26–30 and parallels)

Origen (c. AD 185–c. 254): early church father, noted scholar, and member of the Alexandrian school of interpretation

Orosius (c. AD 385–420): disciple of Augustine best known for his *Seven Books of History against the Romans*

orthodoxy: conformity of a given document with apostolic teaching (see Acts 2:42)

orthopraxy: right practice (s.v. also orthodoxy)

Ostian Way: a famous road that connected Rome with the port city of Ostia; traditional site of Paul's tomb

ostraca: potsherds with inscriptions

OT Apocrypha: body of literature included in the canon by Roman Catholics but not Protestants; contains 1 and 2 Esdras, Tobit, Judith, Additions to Esther, Wisdom of Solomon, Sirach, Baruch, Letter of Jeremiah, Prayer of Azariah and the Song of the Three Young Men, Susanna, Bel and the Dragon, Prayer of Manasseh, 1 and 2 Maccabees

Otho: Roman emperor during part of AD 68

overseer: church office designated by the word *episkopos* (e.g., 1 Tim 3:2), a NT term used synonymously with *presbyteros* ("elder"; see Titus 1:5,7) and *poimēn* ("shepherd" or "pastor"; see Eph 4:11)

Oxyrhynchus papyri: artifacts found at an archeological site in Egypt where a large collection of ancient papyri was discovered, including fragments of several Christian texts

paganism: a variety of animistic or other non-Christian religious beliefs and practices

Pantaenus: a Christian theologian from Alexandria (died c. AD 190) mentioned by Eusebius

Papias of Hierapolis (c. AD 60–130): church father whose *Expositions of the Lord's Sayings* are cited by Eusebius (s.v.) in his *Ecclesiastical History*

papyrus: ancient writing material or scroll on which some of the earliest NT manuscripts are found (e.g., Π^{52}, a fragment of John's Gospel dating to c. AD 125)

Paraclete: from Gk. *paraklētos*; Jesus' title for the Holy Spirit ("Counselor," John 14:16,26; 15:26; 16:7); John used it for Jesus Christ ("advocate," 1 John 2:1)

paraenesis: exhortation

parallelomania: the almost compulsive tendency to find parallels even where such are not present

parataxis: the juxtaposition of two phrases

parchment: ancient scroll made from animal skins (s.v. vellum)

paronomasia: from Gk. *para* ("beside") and *onoma* ("name"); play on words exploiting confusion between similar-sounding words

***parousia*:** from Gk. *parousia* ("presence"); technical term for Jesus' second coming

***partitio*:** in Greek rhetoric, section following the *narratio* (s.v.) that outlines what will follow

passion narrative: account of events surrounding Jesus' crucifixion in the four Gospels

passion, the: the events surrounding Jesus' crucifixion

Passover: Jewish religious festival instituted on the eve of Israel's exodus from Egypt (see Exodus 12)

Pastoral Epistles: conventional designation for Paul's letters to Timothy and Titus (1–2 Timothy, Titus)

Patmos, Isle of: place of exile where the apostle John received the visions recorded in the book of Revelation (see Rev 1:9)

patristic: related to the church fathers

Pauline: related to (the apostle) Paul (s.v. also Pauline circle, Pauline corpus)

Pauline circle: group of early Christians associated with the apostle Paul in his mission; includes coworkers such as Timothy, Titus, Luke, John Mark, Silas, Barnabas, and others

Pauline corpus: body of Paul's writings included in the Bible (i.e., his 13 letters)

pearl stringing: rabbinic practice of grouping together a series of related scriptural passages; imitated by Christian writers (e.g., Rom 3:10–18; Heb 1:5–14)

Pentateuch: from Gk. *penta* ("five"); the five books of Moses—Genesis, Exodus, Leviticus, Numbers, and Deuteronomy

Pentecost: from Gk. for "fiftieth"; Jewish festival described in Lev 23:5–21 and Deut 16:8–10; term used only in Acts 2:1; 20:16; 1 Cor 16:8

pericope: self-contained unit of narrative (in the Gospels; e.g., Mark 2:1–12)

***peroratio*:** conclusion of rhetorical argument

***pesher*:** Jewish interpretive technique by which the contemporary application of a biblical reference is highlighted

Peshitta: Syriac translation of the Bible

Petronius: first-century AD Roman writer during the reign of Nero (s.v.); author of the *Satyricon*

Pharisees: influential Jewish sect known for its emphasis on the law; set itself in opposition to Jesus and, together with the Sadducees (s.v.), had him crucified

Philaster (died c. AD 397): bishop of Brescia

Philip Sidetus: early fifth-century AD Christian historian who wrote a history of the Christian church of which only fragments survive; shows at least partial dependence on Eusebius

Philo (c. 20 BC–AD 50): Jewish thinker, author, and exegete from Alexandria, Egypt, who practiced an allegorical method of interpreting Scripture

Philostratus the Athenian: Greek sophist (first half of the third century AD) of the Roman period; author of *Life of Apollonius of Tyana*

Philoxenian Version: revision of the Peshitta (s.v.) commissioned by Philoxenos of Mabbug in AD 508

Phoenician: ancient civilization centered in the north of ancient Canaan that spread between 1200 and 900 BC

Photius: ninth-century AD patriarch of Constantinople

Platonism: a philosophical system deriving its origin from the Greek philosopher Plato (c. 429–347 BC); influenced Christianity through the writings of Clement of Alexandria, Origen, and Augustine

plenary inspiration: the full or complete inspiration of every part of Scripture

pleonasm: use of more words than necessary to express an idea

Pliny the Elder: first-century AD Roman natural philosopher; author of *Natural History*

Pliny the Younger: son of Pliny the Elder and proconsul of the province of Bithynia in Asia Minor in the early second century AD

plural-to-singular device: shift from plural (group) to singular (individual) usage indicating eyewitness testimony (described by R. Bauckham in *Jesus and the Eyewitnesses*)

Plutarch: first-century AD Greek historian, biographer, and essayist; author of *Parallel Lives* and *Moralia*

pneumatic: from Greek *pneuma* ("Spirit" or "spirit"); related to spiritual matters, the human spirit, or the Holy Spirit

Polybius: second-century BC Greek historian; author of *The Histories*

Polycarp of Smyrna (c. AD 69–155): disciple of the apostle John, companion of Papias, bishop of Smyrna; author of *To the Philippians*; martyred by being burned at the stake

Polycrates: an early Christian leader who flourished in Ephesus in the second half of the second century AD

Pontius Pilate: Roman procurator of Judea (AD 26–36); together with the Jewish leaders, responsible for the crucifixion of Jesus as explained in all four Gospels

posttribulational rapture: belief that Christ will return at the end of the tribulation (s.v.)

prefect: Roman government official

premillennialism: Christian belief that the Lord Jesus Christ will return prior to ("pre") his thousand-year reign on earth; *millennium* is from Lat. *mille* ("thousand") and *annus* ("year")

presbyter: from Gk. *presbyteros* ("elder"); term sometimes used for a local church leader

preterist: approach to the interpretation of the book of Revelation according to which the events prophesied in the book were fulfilled in the first century

pretribulational rapture: belief that Christ will return prior to the tribulation (s.v.)

Prison Epistles: conventional designation for Paul's four letters written from his first Roman imprisonment—Ephesians, Philippians, Colossians, and Philemon

***probatio*:** in classic rhetoric, section denoting proofs in marshaling a given argument

proconsul: Roman office akin to governor of a province

procurator: Roman government official

proselyte: Gentile attracted to Jewish worship who submitted to circumcision and the keeping of Jewish Sabbath observances and food laws

Protestant: non-Roman Catholic evangelicals; term coined during the Christian movement called "The Protestant Reformation" sparked by protests against abuses in the Roman Catholic Church

Protestant Reformers: leaders such as Martin Luther or John Calvin who sought to return the church to its biblical foundations and who challenged unscriptural church traditions with the battle cry *sola Scriptura* ("Scripture alone")

Protevangelium of James: influential apocryphal Gospel most likely dated to the second half of the second century AD

protreptic literature: hortatory literature encouraging people to take up the philosophical life (e.g., the Epistle to Diognetus)

provenance: place of writing

Pseudepigrapha: from Gk. meaning "false title"; a collective term for Jewish Second Temple literature not included in the Apocrypha

Pseudo-Barnabas: ancient letter falsely attributed to Barnabas (dated around AD 135?)

pseudonymity: an author's attribution of a given piece of writing to someone other than the true author

"Q": a hypothetical source common to Matthew and Luke, possibly abbreviating the German word *Quelle* ("source")

***qal wāhômer*:** argument from the lesser to the greater

Quest of (or for) the historical Jesus: modern waves of historical research into the background of the person of Jesus (distinguished as "first quest," "second quest," and "third quest")

Quirinius: governor of, or holder of administrative office in, Syria mentioned in Luke's birth narrative of Jesus in Luke 2:2

Qumran: region near the Dead Sea and site where the Qumran literature was found

Qumran literature: s.v. Dead Sea Scrolls

rabbinic literature: body of literature compiling the teachings of ancient Jewish rabbis, including the Mishnah (e.g., *m. Avot*), the Babylonian and Jerusalem Talmuds (e.g., *b. Sanh.*; *y. Yeb.*), and the Tosefta (*t. Zer.*)

rapture: from Lat. *raptura*, the Vulgate (s.v) rendering of "caught up" in 1 Thess 4:17; Christians' reunion with their Lord at the time of the Second Coming in connection with the tribulation (s.v.)

realized eschatology: aspects of the end time that have already been fulfilled in Christ and in the lives of believers (e.g., eternal life in John 5:24)

redaction criticism: an approach to the study of Scripture that compares similar documents (such as one or several of the Synoptic Gospels) to detect different emphases by the respective authors in order to assess their distinctive contribution

Reformation, the: sixteenth-century movement originating as a reform within the Roman Catholic Church spearheaded by men such as Martin Luther, John Calvin, and others that gave rise to the Protestant and evangelical movement

***refutatio*:** in ancient rhetoric, refutation containing counterarguments

***regula fidei*:** Lat. "rule of faith" (s.v.)

Reuchlin Codex: OT manuscript (AD 1105)

Revised Standard Version (RSV): Bible translation published in 1952

rhetoric: study and practice of effective communication; type of discourse

rhetorical criticism: a study of the rhetorical (communicative) features in a given document (such as the book of Romans)

Rufinus (c. AD 345–411): historian and translator, contemporary of Jerome, and translator of Greek theological works into Latin

rule of faith: orthodox apostolic teaching

sacrament: a religious rite believed by Roman Catholics to mediate grace, constituting a sacred mystery

sacramentalism: the notion that a religious rite can convey divine grace

sacramentarianism: the belief that the elements of the Lord's Supper are merely symbolic of the body and blood of Jesus Christ

Sadducees: Jewish aristocratic sect generally supportive of the political status quo in Palestine; together with the Pharisees (s.v.), they were responsible for Jesus' crucifixion

salvation history: the progressive unfolding of God's provision of salvation for humanity

Samaria: region in Palestine north of Judea

Samaritan Pentateuch: the text of the five books of Moses (Genesis, Exodus, Leviticus, Numbers, Deuteronomy) used by the Samaritans

Samaritans: inhabitants of Samaria who claimed descent from the northern Israelite tribes of Ephraim and Manasseh (s.v.)

Sanhedrin: Jewish ruling council made up of Sadducees and Pharisees that delivered Jesus to Pontius Pilate to be crucified

Sarapis: Egyptian-Hellenistic god

Saul of Tarsus: alternate name of the apostle Paul (Tarsus refers to his hometown)

Savior: religious deliverer; the NT claims that Jesus is the Savior of the world (John 4:42); the term was also used for emperors in the Greco-Roman world

scholasticism: medieval method of learning that prized dialectical reasoning (the exchange of arguments and counterarguments); exhibited in Thomas Aquinas' *Summa Theologica*

scribal assimilation: copyist's alteration of a source text in order to conform a given reading to a reading elsewhere in the same text

Scripture: a written religious document that is viewed as authoritative by a given community of faith (e.g., the Hebrew Scriptures, the Christian Scriptures)

secessionists: divisive heretics who left the congregation, suggesting they were never truly saved in the first place (see esp. 1 John 2:19)

Second Temple Judaism: the religion of the Jewish people during the Second Temple period (s.v. Second Temple period below)

Second Temple period: span between the reconstruction of the temple in 516 BC and the destruction of the temple by the Romans in AD 70

Secret Mark: forged document falsely attributed to Clement of Alexandria

self-attestation of Scripture: the Bible's claims regarding its own nature

Semitic: Jewish, with reference to one of the sons of Noah, Shem (see Gen 6:10)

Semitism: also called Hebraism; a Jewish thought pattern or expression reflected in a Jewish writer's Greek document

Septuagint: Greek translation of the OT Hebrew Scriptures (abbreviated LXX)

sepulcher: type of tomb

Serapion of Antioch: patriarch of Antioch (died in AD 211) mentioned by Eusebius

Sermon on the Mount: body of Jesus' teaching presented in Matthew 5–7 (see Matt 5:1, "on the mountain")

Sermon on the Plain: Luke's equivalent to the Sermon on the Mount in Luke 6:17–49 (see Luke 6:17: "level place")

shekel: ancient Jewish coin

***shekinah*:** the glorious presence of God, especially in the temple

***Shema*:** from Hb. *shema* ("to hear" or "to listen"), the first word in Deut 6:4, "*Listen*, Israel: The Lord our God, the Lord is one"; the central Jewish affirmation of monotheism

***Shepherd of Hermas*:** early second-century AD (?) Christian document

***Sibylline Oracles*:** collection of oracles ascribed to a sibyl, a prophetess who uttered alleged divine revelation in a frenzied state

Sinaiticus: s.v. Codex Sinaiticus

Sirach: second-century BC OT apocryphal book also known as *The Wisdom of Ben Sira* or *Ecclesiasticus* (not the OT book of Ecclesiastes)

Socrates (469–399 BC): classical Greek philosopher, teacher of Plato, and one of the founders of Western philosophy

solecism: (apparent) grammatical incongruity (characteristic of the book of Revelation)

Son of God: messianic title, applied to Jesus in the NT

Son of Man: messianic title, favorite self-designation of Jesus

sons of Zebedee: the apostles John and James

source criticism: discipline devoted to discerning the underlying (literary) source(s) of a given document (s.v., e.g., Two-Source Theory)

Strabo (born c. 64 BC, died after AD 21): eminent first-century BC and AD Greek geographer and author of a *Geographia* in 17 books

stratum: Lat. for "layer," figuratively used for one of a succession of written sources incorporated into a given document

subapostolic period: era subsequent to the apostolic era

substitutionary atonement: blood sacrifice on behalf of another

Suetonius (c. AD 70–AD 130): Roman historian and author of *Lives of the Twelve Caesars*

Suffering Servant, the: figure in the second part of Isaiah (esp. 52:13–53:12) identified as Jesus the Messiah by the NT writers (e.g., 1 Pet 2:21–25)

syllogism: form of argument containing a major and a minor premise and a conclusion (e.g., Scripture is the Word of God; God does not err; Scripture is inerrant)

syncretism: eclectic mix of religious beliefs and practices

Synoptic: pertaining to Matthew, Mark, and Luke

Synoptic Gospels: from Gk. *sunopsis* (lit. "seeing together"), technical designation for Matthew, Mark, and Luke because of their common viewpoint on Jesus' life

Synoptic parallels: related passages in the Synoptic Gospels

Synoptic problem: the nature of the relationship between the Gospels of Matthew, Mark, and Luke, deemed by some a "problem" due to alleged discrepancies in chronology and wording

Synoptic tradition: oral and/or written material underlying an account in the Gospels of Matthew, Mark, and/or Luke

Syria: ancient Near Eastern region north of Israel (capital: Damascus)

Syriac language: Aramaic language that spawned its own set of literature and version of the Bible

Syriac manuscripts: copies of biblical texts written in the Syriac language (s.v.)

Tacitus (born c. AD 56; died after AD 118): Roman historian and author of *The Annals* and *The Histories*

Talmud: compilation of Jewish writings in the Babylonian and Palestinian traditions

Tannaim: from Aramaic *tanna* ("to repeat, learn"); masters of teaching transmitted by oral repetition

Tannaitic period (AD 70–200): s.v. Tannaim

Targum (pl. Targums): Aramaic paraphrase of and commentary on the Hebrew Scriptures

Tatian: early church father and compiler of the synopsis of the Four Gospels called *The Diatessaron* (c. AD 150–160)

tax collectors: local residents in NT times who collected revenues for the Roman authorities and thus were despised by their fellow citizens as traitors

temple cult: religious rites and sacrifices offered in the Jerusalem sanctuary

temple, the: usually, shorthand for the Jerusalem temple, originally built by Solomon

Tertullian (c. AD 160–225): important early Christian apologist; author of *Against Marcion*, *Apology*, and *On Baptism*

Terumah: section of the Mishnah containing tithing regulations

***testimonia*:** common OT messianic texts adduced by the early Christians to prove that Jesus was the Christ

***Testimonium Flavianum*:** disputed portion in *Jewish Antiquities* by the Jewish historian Josephus that refers to Jesus, at least part of which is believed to be a later Christian interpolation

tetragrammaton: from Gk. meaning "four letters," referring to the OT name for God, "YHWH" (likely pronounced "Yahweh" but in most translations represented as "Lord")

tetrarch: "ruler of a quarter," title of governors such as Herod Antipas (s.v.)

text types: the four major Gk. manuscript text types of the NT books are commonly classified as Alexandrian, Caesarean, Byzantine, and Western

textual criticism: the science of adjudicating between variant manuscript readings through specific criteria such as dating, text type or geographic distribution, attested readings, and possible reasons for variants

textual witnesses: readings attested in particular manuscripts

Textus Receptus: Lat. for "received text," a form of the Byzantine text type also attested in the Majority Text, which constituted the textual base for the translations by Wycliffe and Luther and for the KJV

Thallus: historian who wrote in Greek and flourished during the first and/or second century AD

theodicy: from Gk. *theos* ("God") and *dikaios* ("righteous"); an attempt at justifying God's actions (e.g., see Job, Romans, and Revelation)

Theodore of Mopsuestia (c. AD 350–428): Antiochene theologian and biblical exegete

Theodoret: fifth-century AD Syrian bishop who played pivotal role in several Byzantine church controversies

Theodotion: Hellenistic Jewish scholar (c. AD 200) who translated the Hebrew Bible into Greek, whether revising the Septuagint or directly from the Hebrew original

theophany: from Gk. *theos* ("God") and *phainō* ("appear"); an appearance of God to humans

Theophilus of Antioch: patriarch of Antioch; author of *To Autolycus* (later second century AD)

Theophrastus (c. 371–286 BC): Greek philosopher and associate and successor of Aristotle at the Lyceum, a school founded by Aristotle

Third Council of Carthage: meeting of church leaders convened in AD 397

Thomas Aquinas: thirteenth-century Dominican priest and Roman Catholic theologian; author of *Summa Theologica*

Thucydides: fifth-century BC Greek historian and author of *The History of the Peloponnesian War*

Tiberius: Roman emperor (AD 14–37)

Today's English Version (TEV): s.v. Good News Bible

tongues: the manifestation described at the occasion of the coming of the Holy Spirit at Pentecost in Acts 2 and the spiritual gift mentioned in 1 Corinthians 12–14

Torah: translation of Hebrew word for "doctrine" or "teaching"; broadly, the Jewish law encompassing both oral and written teachings; narrowly, the five books of Moses (the Pentateuch)

Tosefta: from Aram. *tosefta* ("addition, supplement"); additional teaching supplementing the Mishnah

tractate: treatise or essay, designating units in Jewish collections such as the Talmud

Trajan: Roman emperor (AD 98–117)

transfiguration: event at which Jesus' outward appearance was transformed in anticipation of his heavenly glory (see Matt 17:1–8 and parallels)

transmission: the process of copying and preserving a text (Scripture)

treatise: essay (s.v. tractate)

tribulation: a period of great suffering and affliction in relation to the return of Christ

triumphal entry: Jesus' arrival in Jerusalem and his popular acclaim as Messiah during Passion week (Palm Sunday; see Matt 21:1–11 and parallels)

Tübingen School: nineteenth-century theological movement spawned by F. C. Baur (1792–1860) at the University of Tübingen, Germany, engaging in historical-critical research and questioning many of the traditional positions in biblical scholarship

Twelfth Benediction, the: part of the liturgy of the *Shemoneh 'Esreh*, the chief prayer of Judaism consisting of 19 supplications, to which at some point a curse of heretics (Christians?) was added

Two-Document Hypothesis: s.v. Two-Source Theory

Two-Gospel Hypothesis: s.v. Griesbach Hypothesis

Two-Source Theory: hypothesis that Matthew and Luke both independently used two written sources, Mark and "Q" (s.v.)

typology: biblical pattern of correspondence along salvation-historical lines (e.g., John 3:14, where Jesus elaborated on the relationship between the serpent lifted up by

Moses in the wilderness and Jesus being lifted up at the crucifixion, in both cases giving life to the one who looks in faith)

uncial: ancient manuscript written in all capital letters without spaces or punctuation

universalism: erroneous belief that all eventually will be saved

Vaticanus: s.v. Codex Vaticanus

vaticinium ex eventu: prophecy after the fact

vellum: animal skins used for making parchment (s.v.)

verbal inspiration: the divine nature of the very words of Scripture

Vergil or Virgil: first-century BC classical Roman poet; author of *The Aeneid*

Vespasian: Roman emperor (AD 69–79)

Victorinus of Pettau (died c. AD 304): church bishop and commentator

Vitellius: Roman emperor for part of AD 68

Vulgate: Jerome's fourth-century AD Lat. translation of the Bible

"we" passages: portions of narrative in the book of Acts written in the first person plural, in all likelihood indicating that the author of Acts participated in the travels narrated in those portions of his account (Acts 16:10–17; 20:5–15; 21:1–18; 27:1–28:16)

Western Church: churches that gravitate(d) around Rome or broke away from it during the Reformation

Western manuscripts: s.v. Western Church; contrast with Eastern manuscripts

Western text type: distinctive family of manuscripts (e.g., the Codex Bezae for the Gospels and Acts) in contrast to the Alexandrian and Byzantine text types (s.v. entries there)

William Tyndale (c. 1494–1536): published the first English NT based on the Greek text in 1526

works of the law: ritual observance of OT legal requirements

Yahweh: approximate transliteration from the Hebrew consonants *yhwh* (s.v. tetragrammaton); OT name for God based on the divine self-reference in Exod 3:14 to Moses, "I AM WHO I AM"

YHWH: tetragrammaton (s.v.); Yahweh

Zion: holy mountain in Jerusalem (e.g., 2 Sam 5:7; Ps 2:6; Isa 28:16)

Name Index

Subject Index

F

G

H

I

J

R

S

T

U

V

W

Z

Scripture Index

Leviticus

Numbers

Deuteronomy

Joshua

Judges

1 Samuel

2 Samuel

1 Kings

2 Kings

Jeremiah

Ezekiel

Daniel

Hosea

Joel

Amos

Obadiah

Mark

Luke

John

Acts

Romans

1 Corinthians

2 Corinthians

Galatians

Ephesians

Philippians

Colossians

1 Thessalonians

2 Thessalonians

1 Timothy

2 Timothy

Titus

Philemon

Hebrews

James

1 Peter

2 Peter

1 John

2 John

3 John

Jude

Revelation

JEWISH EXPANSION UNDER THE HASMONEAN DYNASTY
City
City (uncertain location)
Mountain peak
Judea before the Maccabean revolt
Conquests of Jonathan
Conquests of Simon
Conquests of Hyrcanus I
Conquests of Aristobulus I
Conquests of Alexander Jannaeus
MEDITERRANEAN SEA
Aristobulus completes the conquest of Upper Galilee by defeating the Itureans (104 B.C.)
Jannaeus subdues the attack of Demetrius III and executes 800 Pharisees in reprisal (88 B.C.)
Hyrcanus I destroys Samaritan temple (128 B.C.)
Simon is murdered in a palace coup (135 B.C.)
John Hyrcanus attacks and conquers Medeba in 129 B.C.
Coele-Syria
ITUREA
PHOENICIA
GALILEE
SAMARIA
JUDEA
PEREA
Gilead
PHILISTIA
IDUMEA
NABATEA
Arabah
DEAD SEA
Sea of Galilee
Sidon
Damascus
Tyre
Panias
Mt. Hermon
Cadasa (Kedesh)
Gischala (Gush Halav)
Asor (Hazor)
Seleucia
Ptolemais (Acco)
Gennesaret
Bethsaida
Taricheae (Magdala)
Jotapata
Asochis (Hannathon)
Cana
Arbela
Dathema
Gamala
Mt. Carmel
Sepphoris
Hippos
Geba
Mt. Tabor
Philoteria (Beth-Yerah)
Abila
Gadara
Dora
Legio (Megiddo)
Strato's Tower
Scythopolis (Beth-shan)
Pella
Dion
Narbata
Samaria
Mt. Ebal
Shechem
Mt. Gerizim
Gerasa (Jerash)
Amathus
Apollonia
Pegae (Aphek)
Pharathon
Acrabeta
Coreae
Alexandrium
Joppa
Arimathea
Lebonah
Zeredah
Gedor (Gadara)
Jazer
Adida
Lydda
Modein
Ber-zetha
Gophna
Bethel
Apherema
Tyrus
Philadelphia (Amman)
Abila
Jamina
Gazara (Gezer)
Beth-horon
Mizpah
Doc
Adasa
Michmash
Jericho
Esbus (Heshbon)
Kidron
Emmaus
Beth-ramatha
Azotus (Ashdod)
Accaron (Ekron)
Mt. Nebo
Samaga
Beth-haccherem
Jerusalem
Medeba
Hyrcania
Ascalon (Ashkelon)
Adullam
Bethlehem
Beth-basi
Herodium
Marisa (Mareshah)
Keilah
Tekoa
Nezib
Beth-zur
Asphar
Lemba
Machaerus
Lachish
Hebron
Anthedon
Adora (Adoraim)
Gaza
En-gedi
Gerar
Orda
Masada
Eglaim
Raphia
Beersheba
Malatha
Kir-Moab
Rhinocorura
Oronaim (Horonaim)
Gabalis
Elusa
Zoar
Sela
Abana R.
Pharpar R.
Litani R.
Yarmuk R.
Jordan R.
Jabbok R.
Yarkon R.
Arnon R.
Zered R.
N. Besor
W. el-Arish
34 E
35 E
36 E
33 N
32 N
31 N
0 10 20 30 40 50 Miles
0 10 20 30 40 50 Kilometers

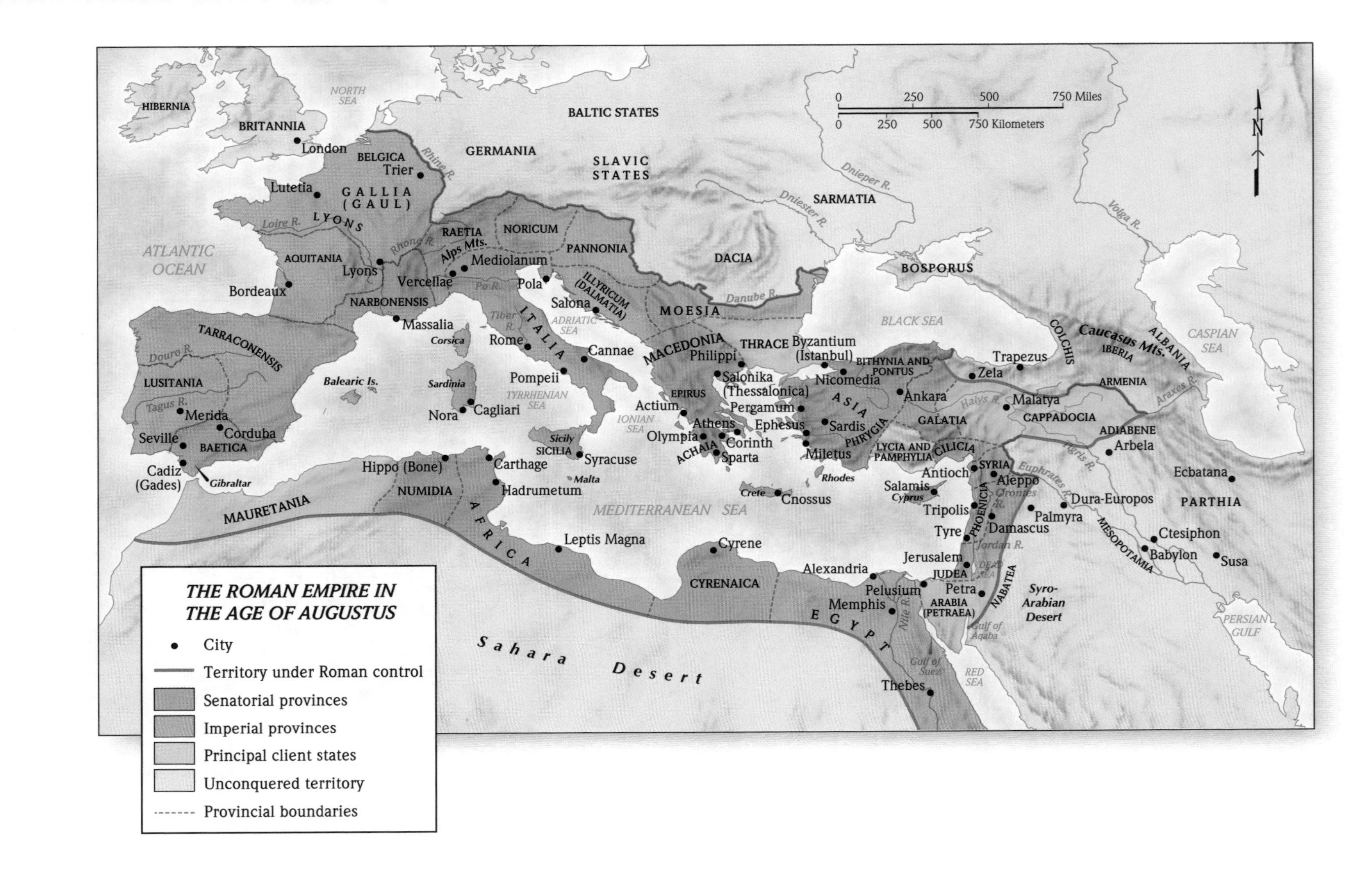
THE ROMAN EMPIRE IN THE AGE OF AUGUSTUS
City
Territory under Roman control
Senatorial provinces
Imperial provinces
Principal client states
Unconquered territory
Provincial boundaries
0 250 500 750 Miles
0 250 500 750 Kilometers
N
HIBERNIA
BRITANNIA
London
NORTH SEA
BALTIC STATES
GERMANIA
SLAVIC STATES
SARMATIA
Dnieper R.
Dniester R.
Volga R.
BELGICA
Trier
Rhine R.
Lutetia
GALLIA (GAUL)
LYONS
Loire R.
Rhone R.
ATLANTIC OCEAN
AQUITANIA
Lyons
Bordeaux
NARBONENSIS
Massalia
RAETIA
Alps Mts.
NORICUM
PANNONIA
Mediolanum
Vercellae
Po R.
Pola
ILLYRICUM (DALMATIA)
Salona
ADRIATIC SEA
MOESIA
DACIA
Danube R.
BOSPORUS
BLACK SEA
TARRACONENSIS
Douro R.
LUSITANIA
Tagus R.
Merida
Corduba
Seville
BAETICA
Cadiz (Gades)
Gibraltar
Balearic Is.
Corsica
Sardinia
Nora
Cagliari
Tiber R.
Rome
ITALIA
Pompeii
Cannae
TYRRHENIAN SEA
IONIAN SEA
Sicily
SICILIA
Syracuse
Malta
MACEDONIA
Philippi
THRACE
Byzantium (Istanbul)
Salonika (Thessalonica)
EPIRUS
Actium
Olympia
Athens
Corinth
ACHAIA
Sparta
Pergamum
Ephesus
Miletus
Sardis
ASIA
PHRYGIA
BITHYNIA AND PONTUS
Nicomedia
Ankara
GALATIA
LYCIA AND PAMPHYLIA
CILICIA
Rhodes
Crete
Cnossus
Salamis
Cyprus
COLCHIS
Caucasus Mts.
IBERIA
ALBANIA
CASPIAN SEA
Trapezus
Zela
ARMENIA
Araxes R.
Halys R.
Malatya
CAPPADOCIA
ADIABENE
Arbela
Tigris R.
Euphrates R.
SYRIA
Antioch
Aleppo
Orontes R.
PHOENICIA
Tripolis
Tyre
Damascus
Jordan R.
Palmyra
Dura-Europos
MESOPOTAMIA
Ecbatana
PARTHIA
Ctesiphon
Babylon
Susa
PERSIAN GULF
Jerusalem
JUDEA
DEAD SEA
NABATEA
Petra
ARABIA (PETRAEA)
Syro-Arabian Desert
Gulf of Aqaba
Hippo (Bone)
NUMIDIA
Carthage
Hadrumetum
MAURETANIA
AFRICA
MEDITERRANEAN SEA
Leptis Magna
Cyrene
CYRENAICA
Alexandria
Pelusium
Memphis
EGYPT
Nile R.
Gulf of Suez
RED SEA
Thebes
Sahara Desert

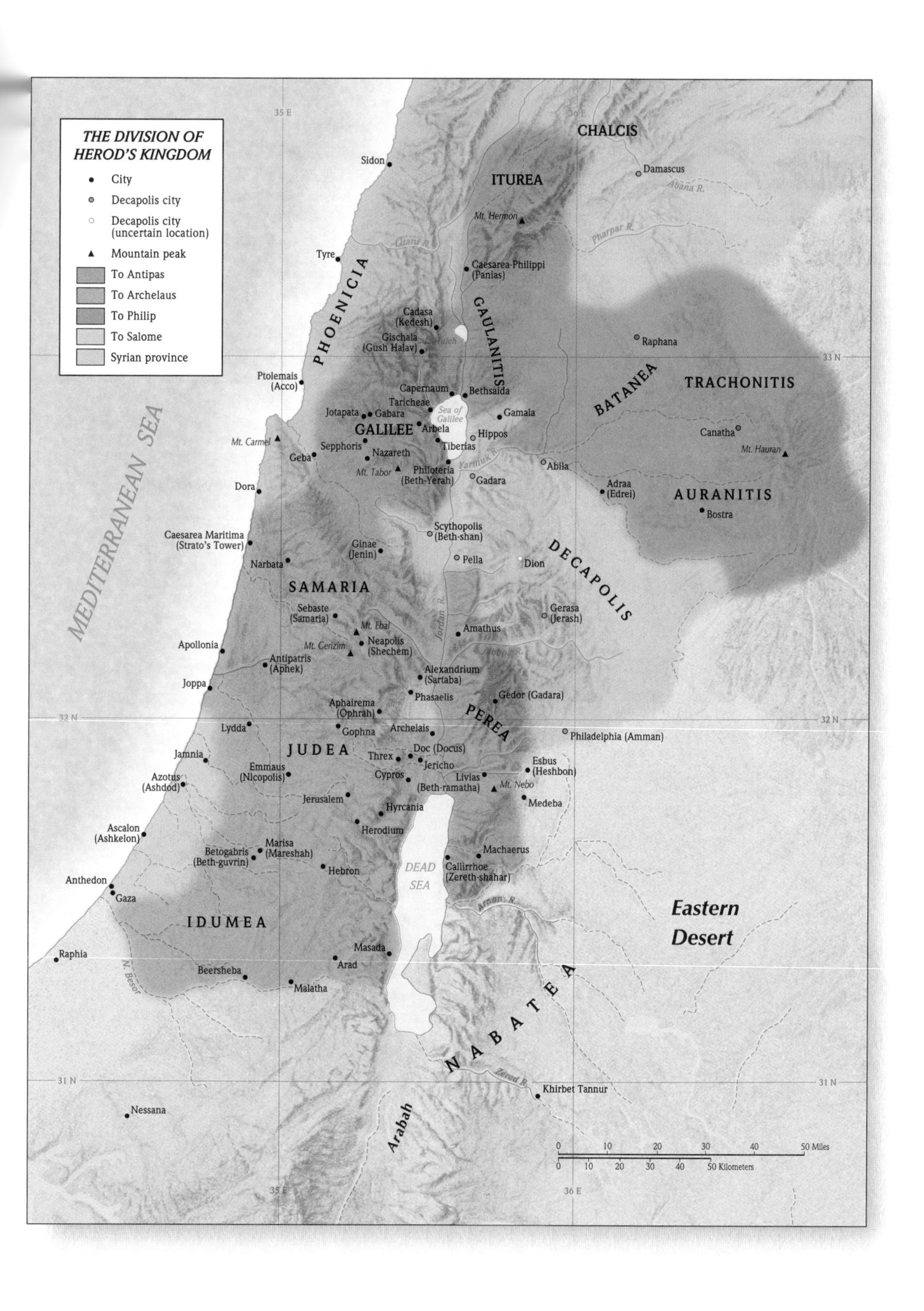

THE DIVISION OF HEROD'S KINGDOM
City
Decapolis city
Decapolis city (uncertain location)
Mountain peak
To Antipas
To Archelaus
To Philip
To Salome
Syrian province
MEDITERRANEAN SEA
CHALCIS
ITUREA
PHOENICIA
GAULANITIS
GALILEE
BATANEA
TRACHONITIS
AURANITIS
DECAPOLIS
SAMARIA
PEREA
JUDEA
IDUMEA
NABATEA
Eastern Desert
Arabah
Sidon
Damascus
Abana R.
Mt. Hermon
Pharpar R.
Litani R.
Tyre
Caesarea-Philippi (Panias)
Cadasa (Kedesh)
Gischala (Gush Halav)
Raphana
Ptolemais (Acco)
Capernaum
Bethsaida
Taricheae
Jotapata
Gabara
Sea of Galilee
Gamala
Arbela
Hippos
Canatha
Mt. Carmel
Sepphoris
Tiberias
Mt. Hauran
Geba
Nazareth
Yarmuk R.
Abila
Mt. Tabor
Philoteria (Beth-Yerah)
Gadara
Dora
Adraa (Edrei)
Bostra
Scythopolis (Beth-shan)
Caesarea Maritima (Strato's Tower)
Ginae (Jenin)
Pella
Dion
Narbata
Sebaste (Samaria)
Mt. Ebal
Gerasa (Jerash)
Jordan R.
Amathus
Apollonia
Mt. Gerizim
Neapolis (Shechem)
Jabbok R.
Antipatris (Aphek)
Alexandrium (Sartaba)
Joppa
Phasaelis
Gedor (Gadara)
Aphairema (Ophrah)
Lydda
Gophna
Archelais
Philadelphia (Amman)
Doc (Docus)
Jamnia
Threx
Jericho
Esbus (Heshbon)
Emmaus (Nicopolis)
Azotus (Ashdod)
Cypros
Livias (Beth-ramatha)
Mt. Nebo
Jerusalem
Medeba
Hyrcania
Ascalon (Ashkelon)
Herodium
Marisa (Mareshah)
Machaerus
Betogabris (Beth-guvrin)
Hebron
DEAD SEA
Callirrhoe (Zereth-shahar)
Anthedon
Gaza
Arnon R.
Masada
Raphia
Arad
N. Besor
Beersheba
Malatha
Zered R.
Khirbet Tannur
Nessana
35 E
36 E
33 N
32 N
31 N
0 10 20 30 40 50 Miles
0 10 20 30 40 50 Kilometers

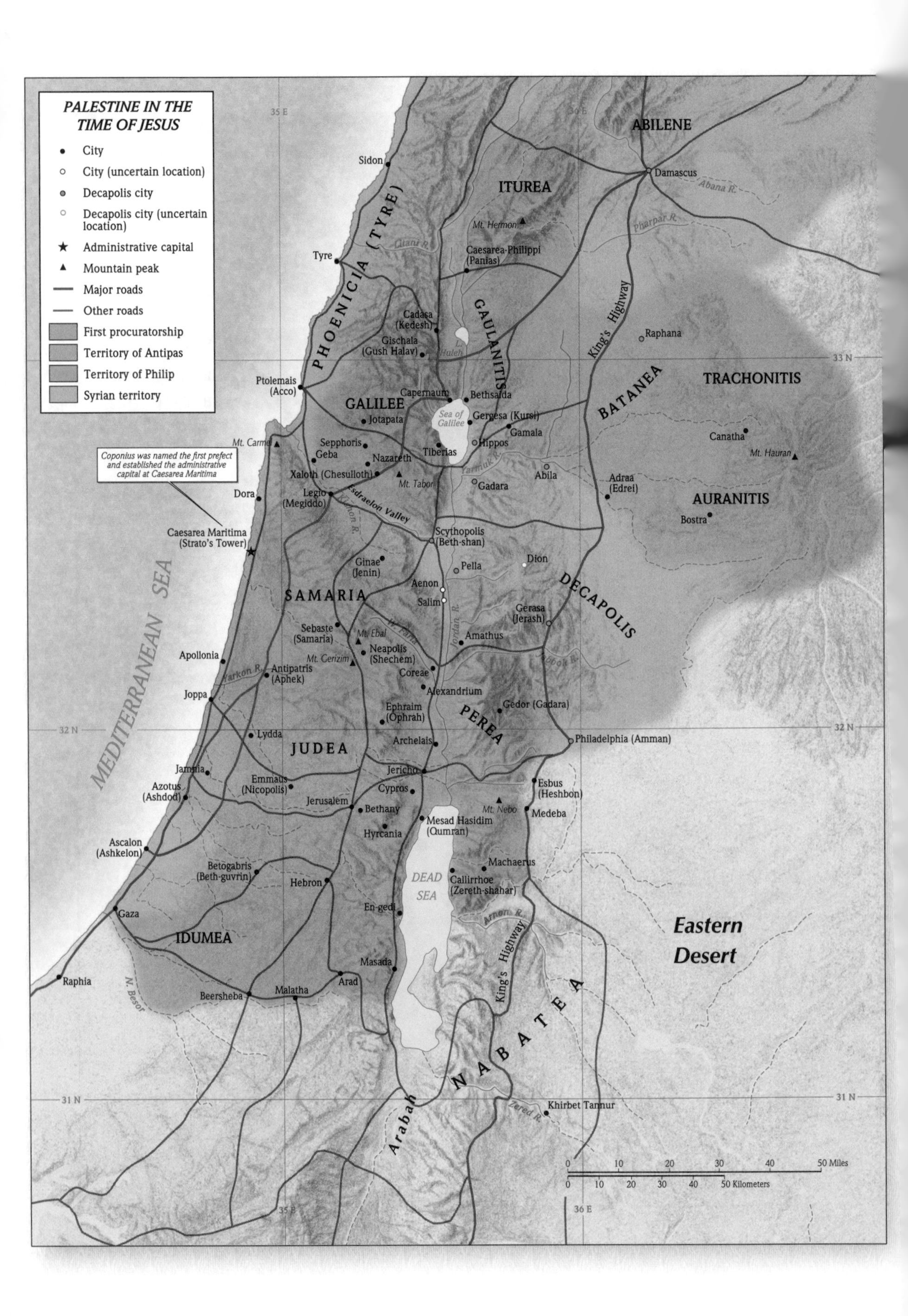

PALESTINE IN THE TIME OF JESUS
City
City (uncertain location)
Decapolis city
Decapolis city (uncertain location)
Administrative capital
Mountain peak
Major roads
Other roads
First procuratorship
Territory of Antipas
Territory of Philip
Syrian territory
Coponius was named the first prefect and established the administrative capital at Caesarea Maritima
ABILENE
ITUREA
Damascus
Sidon
Tyre
PHOENICIA (TYRE)
Mt. Hermon
Caesarea-Philippi (Panias)
GAULANITIS
Cadasa (Kedesh)
Gischala (Gush Halav)
Raphana
King's Highway
TRACHONITIS
BATANEA
Ptolemais (Acco)
GALILEE
Capernaum
Bethsaida
Sea of Galilee
Gergesa (Kursi)
Gamala
Jotapata
Sepphoris
Geba
Nazareth
Tiberias
Hippos
Xaloth (Chesulloth)
Mt. Tabor
Mt. Carmel
Canatha
Mt. Hauran
Abila
Gadara
Adraa (Edrei)
Dora
Legio (Megiddo)
Esdraelon Valley
AURANITIS
Bostra
Caesarea Maritima (Strato's Tower)
Scythopolis (Beth-shan)
Ginae (Jenin)
Pella
Dion
Aenon
Salim
SAMARIA
DECAPOLIS
MEDITERRANEAN SEA
Gerasa (Jerash)
Sebaste (Samaria)
Mt. Ebal
Amathus
Neapolis (Shechem)
Mt. Gerizim
Apollonia
Antipatris (Aphek)
Coreae
Alexandrium
Joppa
Ephraim (Ophrah)
Gedor (Gadara)
PEREA
Lydda
JUDEA
Archelais
Philadelphia (Amman)
Jamnia
Jericho
Azotus (Ashdod)
Emmaus (Nicopolis)
Esbus (Heshbon)
Cypros
Jerusalem
Bethany
Mt. Nebo
Medeba
Mesad Hasidim (Qumran)
Hyrcania
Ascalon (Ashkelon)
Machaerus
Betogabris (Beth-guvrin)
Hebron
DEAD SEA
Callirrhoe (Zereth-shahar)
Gaza
En-gedi
Arnon R.
Eastern Desert
IDUMEA
Masada
Raphia
Arad
Beersheba
Malatha
NABATEA
Arabah
Khirbet Tannur
Zered R.
33 N
32 N
31 N
35 E
36 E
0 10 20 30 40 50 Miles
0 10 20 30 40 50 Kilometers

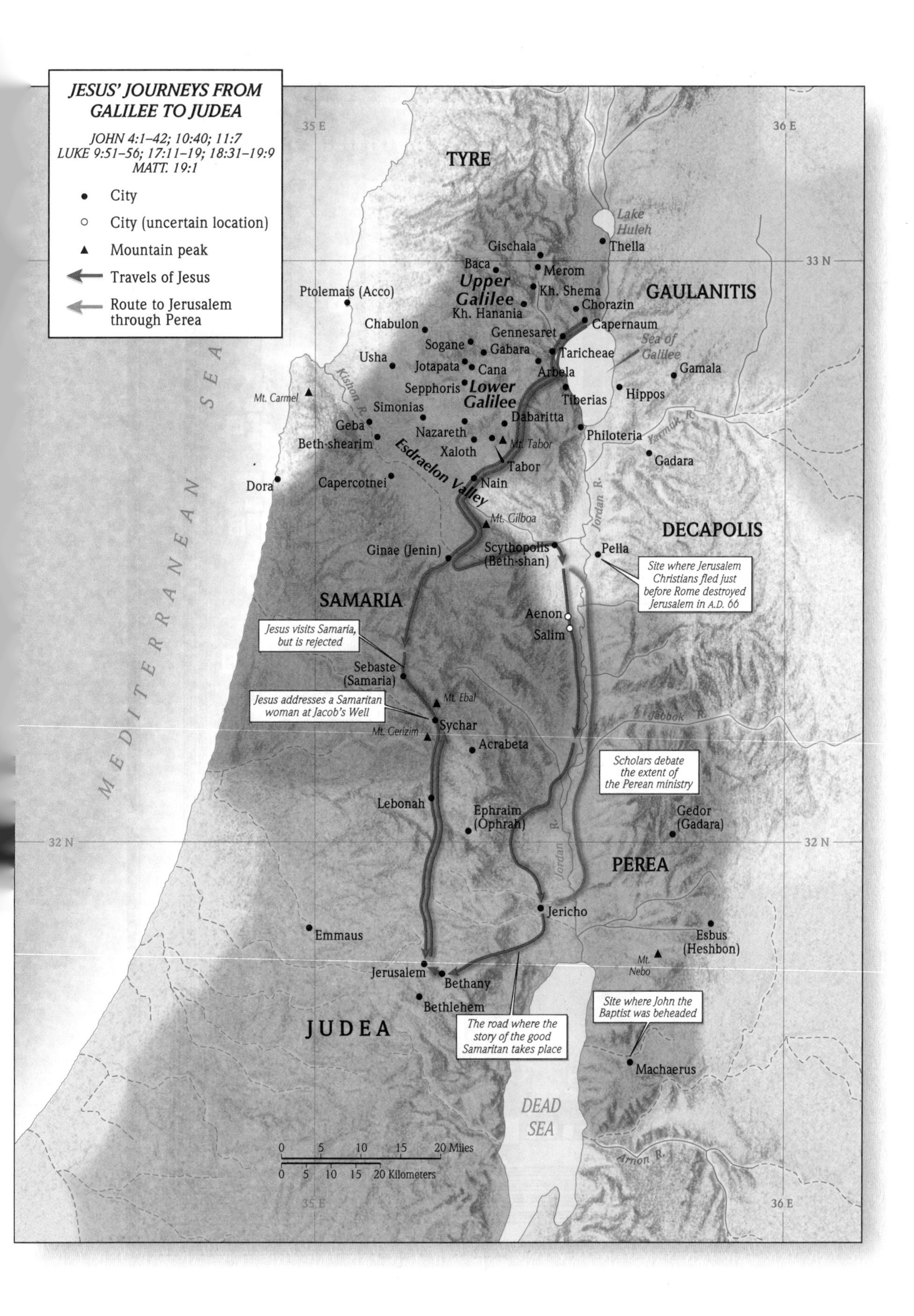

JESUS' JOURNEYS FROM GALILEE TO JUDEA
JOHN 4:1–42; 10:40; 11:7
LUKE 9:51–56; 17:11–19; 18:31–19:9
MATT. 19:1
City
City (uncertain location)
Mountain peak
Travels of Jesus
Route to Jerusalem through Perea
35 E
36 E
33 N
32 N
TYRE
Lake Huleh
Thella
Gischala
Baca
Merom
Upper Galilee
Kh. Shema
GAULANITIS
Ptolemais (Acco)
Kh. Hanania
Chorazin
Capernaum
Chabulon
Gennesaret
Sogane
Gabara
Sea of Galilee
Usha
Jotapata
Taricheae
Cana
Arbela
Gamala
Sepphoris
Lower Galilee
Tiberias
Hippos
Mt. Carmel
Kishon R.
Simonias
Geba
Dabaritta
Nazareth
Philoteria
Yarmuk R.
Beth-shearim
Mt. Tabor
Xaloth
Esdraelon Valley
Tabor
Gadara
Dora
Capercotnei
Nain
Jordan R.
Mt. Gilboa
DECAPOLIS
Ginae (Jenin)
Scythopolis (Beth-shan)
Pella
Site where Jerusalem Christians fled just before Rome destroyed Jerusalem in A.D. 66
SAMARIA
Aenon
Salim
Jesus visits Samaria, but is rejected
Sebaste (Samaria)
Mt. Ebal
Jesus addresses a Samaritan woman at Jacob's Well
Sychar
Jabbok R.
Mt. Gerizim
Acrabeta
Scholars debate the extent of the Perean ministry
Lebonah
Ephraim (Ophrah)
Gedor (Gadara)
PEREA
Jericho
Esbus (Heshbon)
Emmaus
Mt. Nebo
Jerusalem
Bethany
Bethlehem
Site where John the Baptist was beheaded
JUDEA
The road where the story of the good Samaritan takes place
Machaerus
DEAD SEA
MEDITERRANEAN SEA
0 5 10 15 20 Miles
0 5 10 15 20 Kilometers
Arnon R.

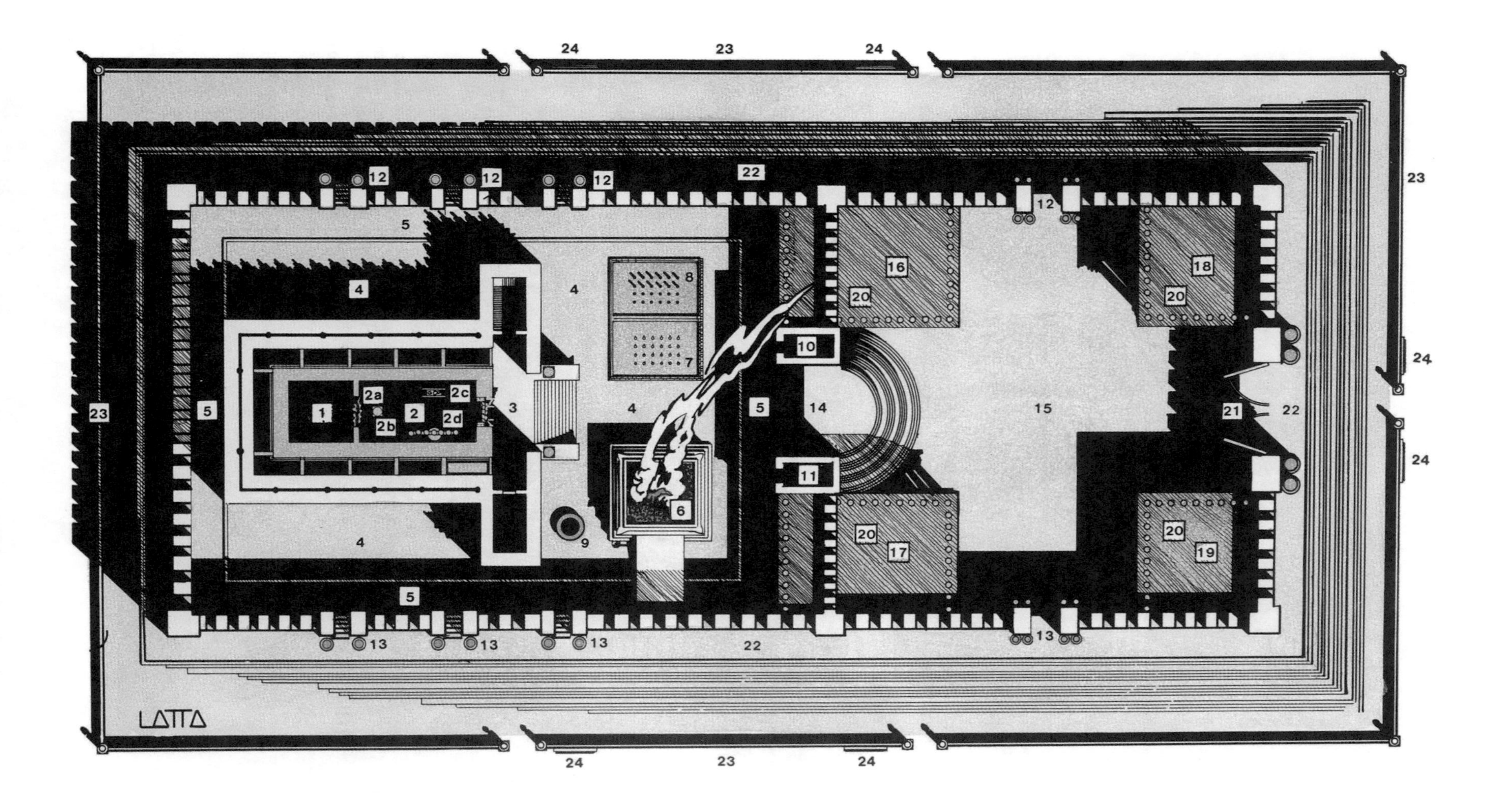

LATTA
1
2a
2b
2
2c
2d
3
4
5
6
7
8
9
10
11
12
13
14
15
16
17
18
19
20
21
22
23
24

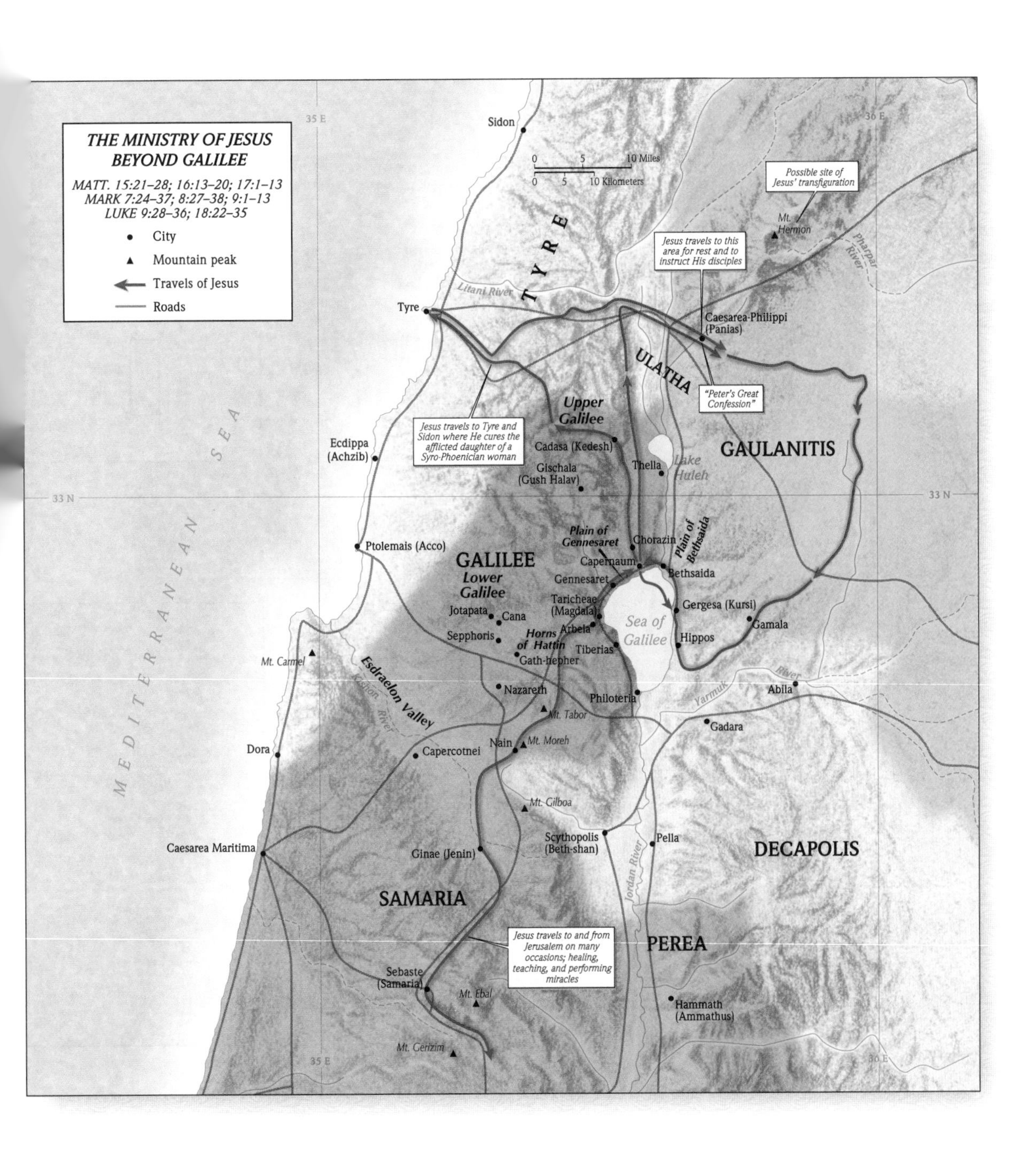
THE MINISTRY OF JESUS BEYOND GALILEE
MATT. 15:21–28; 16:13–20; 17:1–13
MARK 7:24–37; 8:27–38; 9:1–13
LUKE 9:28–36; 18:22–35
City
Mountain peak
Travels of Jesus
Roads
Sidon
Tyre
TYRE
Litani River
Possible site of Jesus' transfiguration
Mt. Hermon
Pharpar River
Jesus travels to this area for rest and to instruct His disciples
Caesarea-Philippi (Panias)
ULATHA
"Peter's Great Confession"
Jesus travels to Tyre and Sidon where He cures the afflicted daughter of a Syro-Phoenician woman
Upper Galilee
Cadasa (Kedesh)
Gischala (Gush Halav)
Thella
Lake Huleh
GAULANITIS
Ecdippa (Achzib)
MEDITERRANEAN SEA
Ptolemais (Acco)
Plain of Gennesaret
Chorazin
Plain of Bethsaida
GALILEE
Lower Galilee
Capernaum
Bethsaida
Gennesaret
Taricheae (Magdala)
Gergesa (Kursi)
Jotapata
Cana
Arbela
Sea of Galilee
Gamala
Sepphoris
Horns of Hattin
Tiberias
Hippos
Mt. Carmel
Esdraelon Valley
Kishon River
Gath-hepher
Nazareth
Philoteria
Yarmuk River
Abila
Mt. Tabor
Gadara
Dora
Capercotnei
Nain
Mt. Moreh
Mt. Gilboa
Scythopolis (Beth-shan)
Pella
Caesarea Maritima
Ginae (Jenin)
Jordan River
DECAPOLIS
SAMARIA
Jesus travels to and from Jerusalem on many occasions; healing, teaching, and performing miracles
PEREA
Sebaste (Samaria)
Mt. Ebal
Hammath (Ammathus)
Mt. Gerizim
0 5 10 Miles
0 5 10 Kilometers
35 E
36 E
33 N

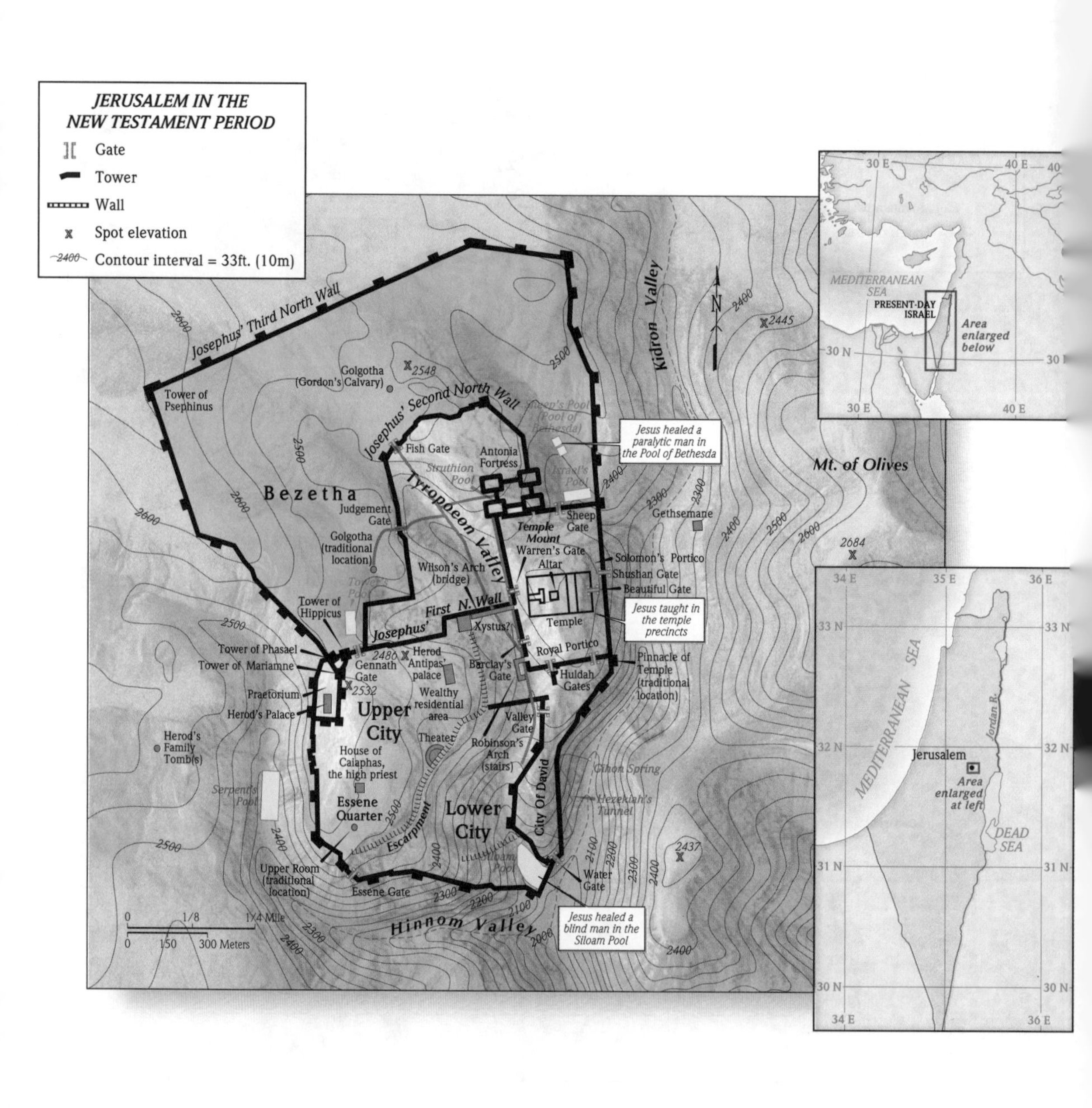
JERUSALEM IN THE NEW TESTAMENT PERIOD
Gate
Tower
Wall
Spot elevation
Contour interval = 33ft. (10m)
Josephus' Third North Wall
Tower of Psephinus
Golgotha (Gordon's Calvary)
Josephus' Second North Wall
Sheep's Pool (Pool of Bethesda)
Jesus healed a paralytic man in the Pool of Bethesda
Kidron Valley
Mt. of Olives
Bezetha
Fish Gate
Antonia Fortress
Struthion Pool
Israel's Pool
Tyropoeon Valley
Judgement Gate
Golgotha (traditional location)
Sheep Gate
Gethsemane
Temple Mount
Warren's Gate
Altar
Solomon's Portico
Shushan Gate
Beautiful Gate
Wilson's Arch (bridge)
Temple
Jesus taught in the temple precincts
Tower of Hippicus
Josephus' First N. Wall
Xystus?
Tower of Phasael
Tower of Mariamne
Gennath Gate
Herod Antipas' palace
Barclay's Gate
Royal Portico
Pinnacle of Temple (traditional location)
Huldah Gates
Praetorium
Herod's Palace
Upper City
Wealthy residential area
Valley Gate
Herod's Family Tomb(s)
Theater
Robinson's Arch (stairs)
House of Caiaphas, the high priest
Gihon Spring
Serpent's Pool
Essene Quarter
Escarpment
Lower City
City Of David
Hezekiah's Tunnel
Siloam Pool
Upper Room (traditional location)
Essene Gate
Water Gate
Jesus healed a blind man in the Siloam Pool
Hinnom Valley
0 1/8 1/4 Mile
0 150 300 Meters
2600
2548
2500
2480
2532
2445
2400
2300
2200
2100
2000
2684
2437
MEDITERRANEAN SEA
PRESENT-DAY ISRAEL
Area enlarged below
30 E
40 E
30 N
34 E
35 E
36 E
33 N
32 N
31 N
30 N
Jordan R.
Jerusalem
Area enlarged at left
DEAD SEA

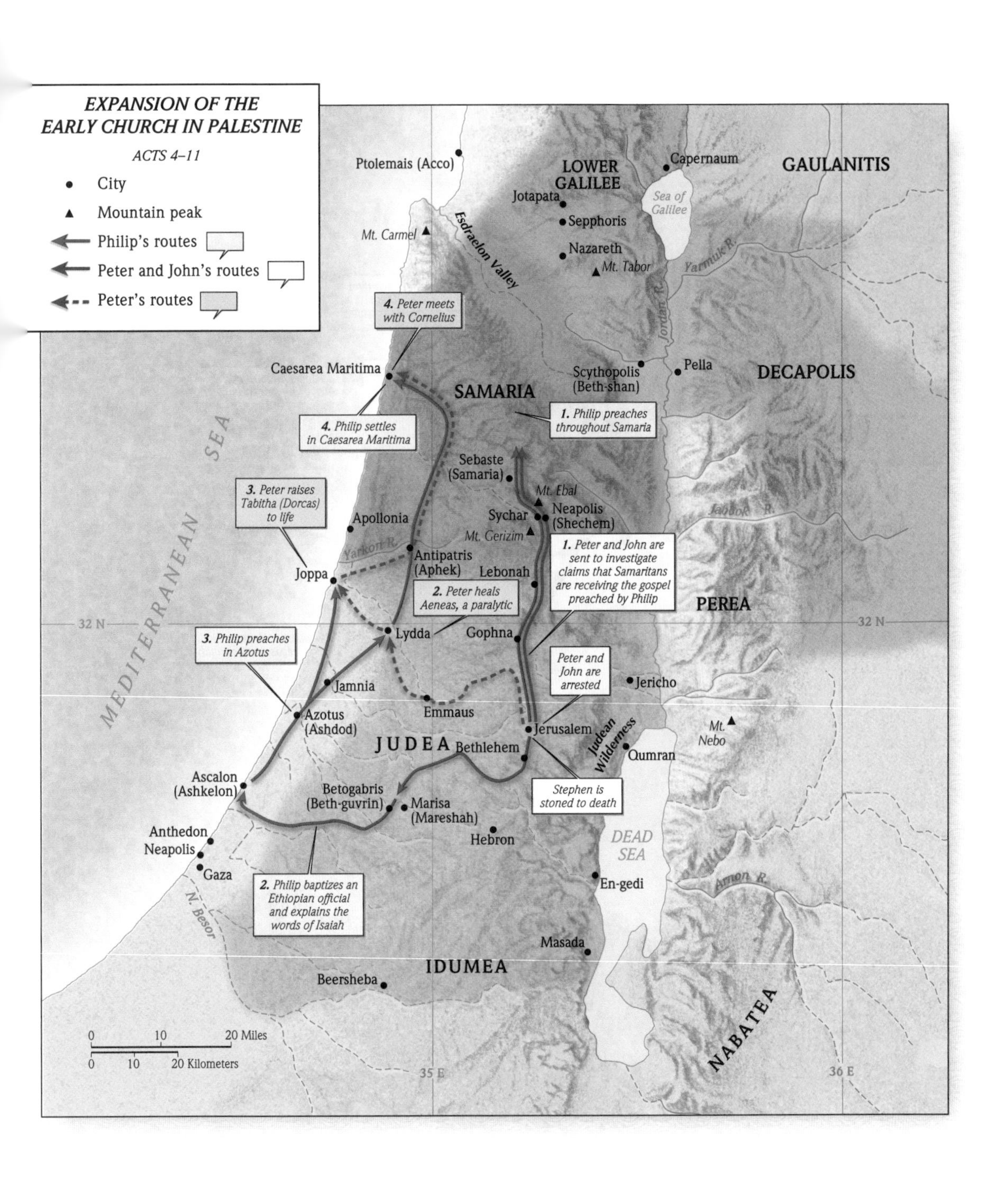
EXPANSION OF THE EARLY CHURCH IN PALESTINE
ACTS 4–11
City
Mountain peak
Philip's routes
Peter and John's routes
Peter's routes
Ptolemais (Acco)
LOWER GALILEE
Capernaum
GAULANITIS
Jotapata
Sea of Galilee
Sepphoris
Mt. Carmel
Esdraelon Valley
Nazareth
Mt. Tabor
Yarmuk R.
Jordan R.
4. Peter meets with Cornelius
Caesarea Maritima
Scythopolis (Beth-shan)
Pella
DECAPOLIS
SAMARIA
1. Philip preaches throughout Samaria
4. Philip settles in Caesarea Maritima
SEA
Sebaste (Samaria)
3. Peter raises Tabitha (Dorcas) to life
Mt. Ebal
Neapolis (Shechem)
Sychar
Jabbok R.
Apollonia
Mt. Gerizim
Yarkon R.
Antipatris (Aphek)
1. Peter and John are sent to investigate claims that Samaritans are receiving the gospel preached by Philip
Joppa
Lebonah
2. Peter heals Aeneas, a paralytic
PEREA
32 N
Lydda
Gophna
MEDITERRANEAN
3. Philip preaches in Azotus
Peter and John are arrested
Jericho
Jamnia
Azotus (Ashdod)
Emmaus
Jerusalem
Judean Wilderness
Mt. Nebo
JUDEA
Bethlehem
Qumran
Ascalon (Ashkelon)
Betogabris (Beth-guvrin)
Marisa (Mareshah)
Stephen is stoned to death
Anthedon
Neapolis
Gaza
Hebron
DEAD SEA
En-gedi
Arnon R.
N. Besor
2. Philip baptizes an Ethiopian official and explains the words of Isaiah
Masada
IDUMEA
Beersheba
NABATEA
0 10 20 Miles
0 10 20 Kilometers
35 E
36 E

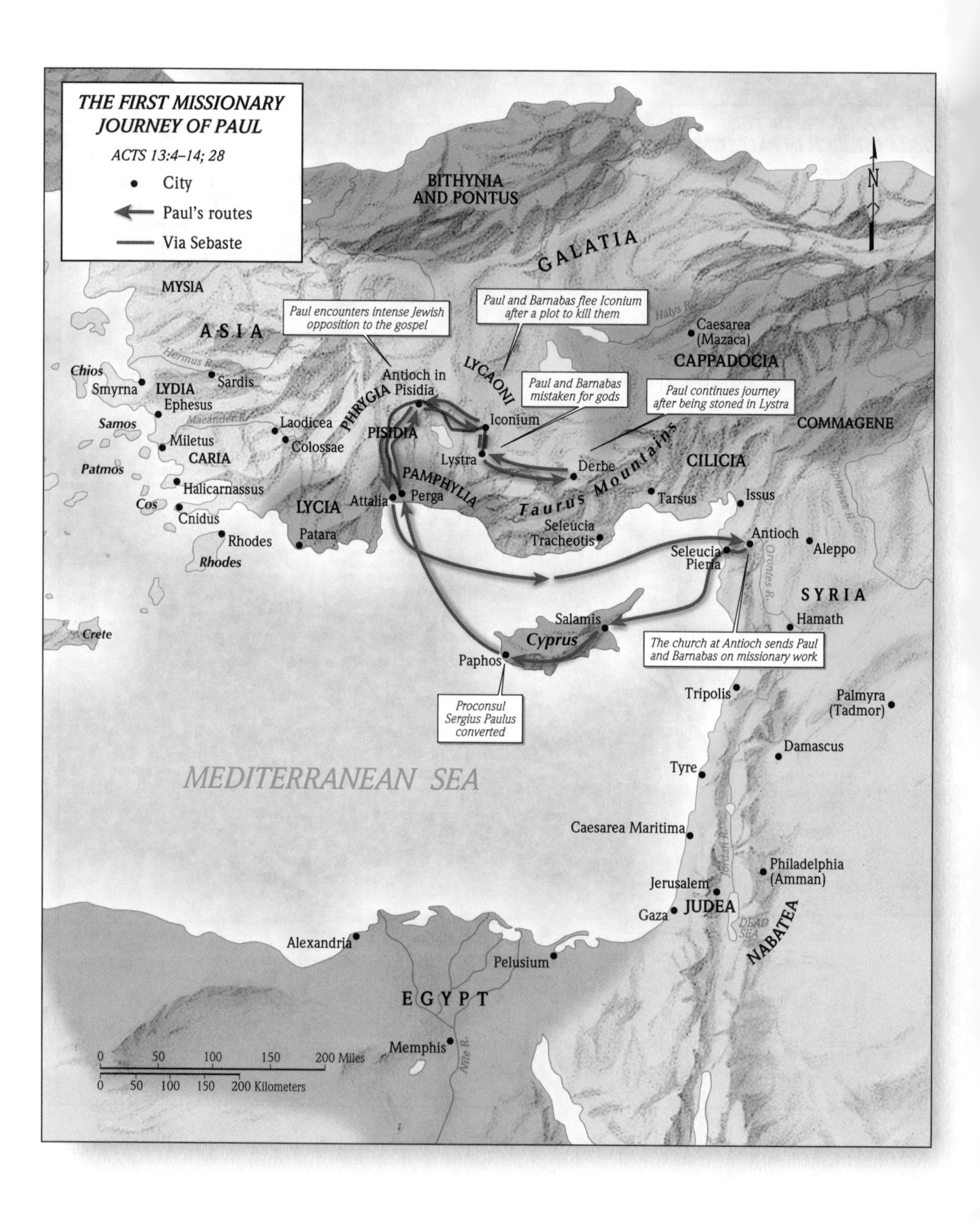

THE FIRST MISSIONARY JOURNEY OF PAUL
ACTS 13:4–14; 28
City
Paul's routes
Via Sebaste
BITHYNIA AND PONTUS
GALATIA
MYSIA
ASIA
Paul encounters intense Jewish opposition to the gospel
Paul and Barnabas flee Iconium after a plot to kill them
Paul and Barnabas mistaken for gods
Paul continues journey after being stoned in Lystra
Halys R.
Caesarea (Mazaca)
CAPPADOCIA
LYCAONIA
Chios
Smyrna
LYDIA
Sardis
Hermus R.
Ephesus
Maeander R.
Samos
Miletus
CARIA
Patmos
Halicarnassus
Cos
Cnidus
Rhodes
Rhodes
Laodicea
Colossae
PHRYGIA
Antioch in Pisidia
PISIDIA
Iconium
Lystra
Derbe
COMMAGENE
CILICIA
Taurus Mountains
Euphrates R.
PAMPHYLIA
Attalia
Perga
LYCIA
Patara
Tarsus
Issus
Seleucia Tracheotis
Antioch
Seleucia Pieria
Aleppo
Orontes R.
SYRIA
Hamath
Crete
Salamis
Cyprus
Paphos
The church at Antioch sends Paul and Barnabas on missionary work
Proconsul Sergius Paulus converted
Tripolis
Palmyra (Tadmor)
Damascus
MEDITERRANEAN SEA
Tyre
Caesarea Maritima
Jordan R.
Philadelphia (Amman)
Jerusalem
Gaza
JUDEA
DEAD SEA
NABATEA
Alexandria
Pelusium
EGYPT
Memphis
Nile R.
0 50 100 150 200 Miles
0 50 100 150 200 Kilometers
N

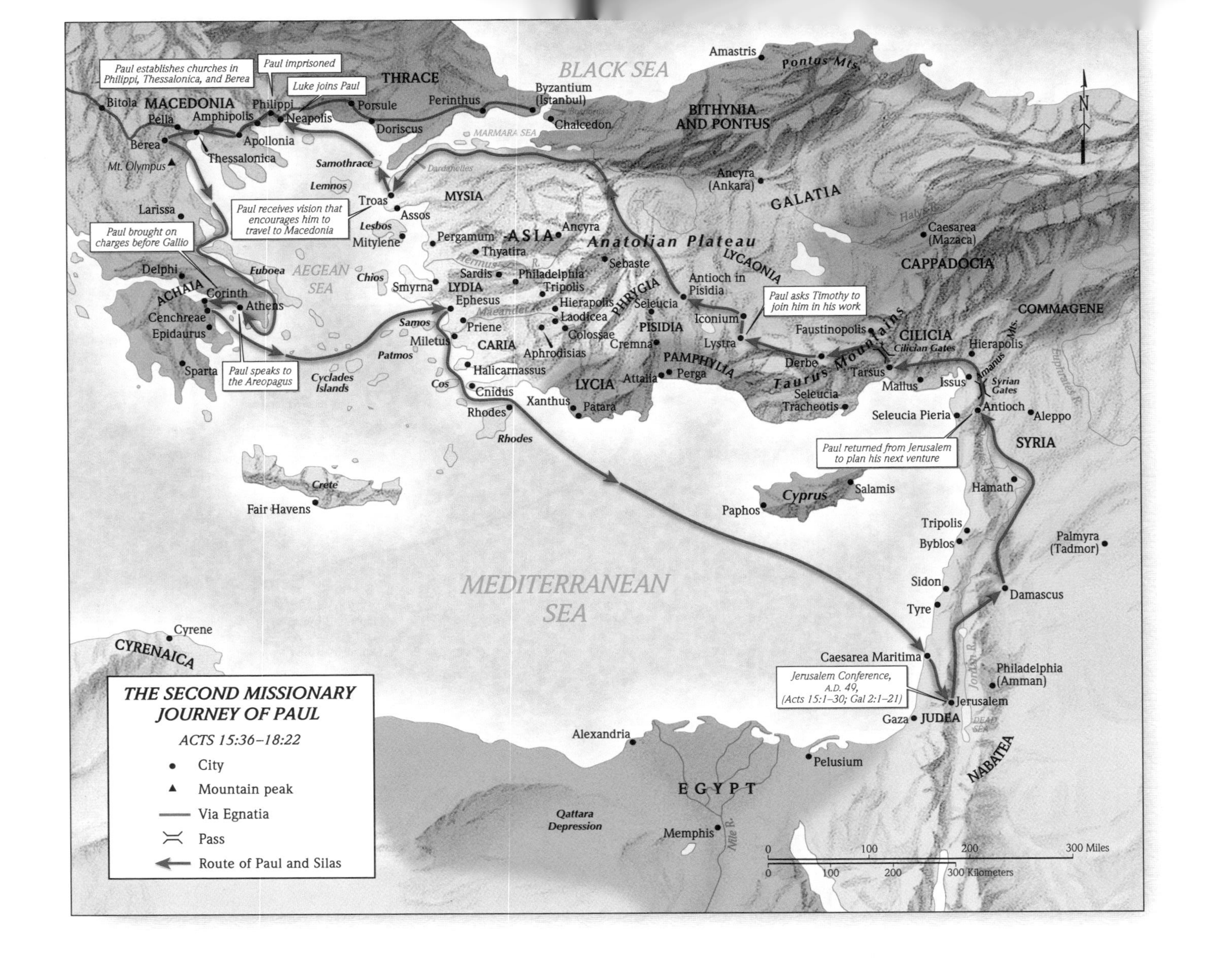

THE SECOND MISSIONARY JOURNEY OF PAUL
ACTS 15:36–18:22
City
Mountain peak
Via Egnatia
Pass
Route of Paul and Silas
Paul establishes churches in Philippi, Thessalonica, and Berea
Paul imprisoned
Luke joins Paul
Paul receives vision that encourages him to travel to Macedonia
Paul brought on charges before Gallio
Paul speaks to the Areopagus
Paul asks Timothy to join him in his work
Paul returned from Jerusalem to plan his next venture
Jerusalem Conference, A.D. 49, (Acts 15:1–30; Gal 2:1–21)
BLACK SEA
AEGEAN SEA
MEDITERRANEAN SEA
MARMARA SEA
THRACE
MACEDONIA
ACHAIA
MYSIA
ASIA
LYDIA
CARIA
LYCIA
PHRYGIA
PISIDIA
PAMPHYLIA
LYCAONIA
GALATIA
BITHYNIA AND PONTUS
CAPPADOCIA
CILICIA
COMMAGENE
SYRIA
JUDEA
NABATEA
EGYPT
CYRENAICA
Anatolian Plateau
Pontus Mts.
Taurus Mountains
Amanus Mts.
Cilician Gates
Syrian Gates
Bitola
Pella
Berea
Mt. Olympus
Amphipolis
Thessalonica
Apollonia
Philippi
Neapolis
Porsule
Doriscus
Perinthus
Byzantium (Istanbul)
Chalcedon
Amastris
Samothrace
Lemnos
Troas
Assos
Lesbos
Mitylene
Larissa
Delphi
Corinth
Athens
Cenchreae
Epidaurus
Sparta
Euboea
Chios
Samos
Patmos
Cyclades Islands
Cos
Rhodes
Crete
Fair Havens
Pergamum
Thyatira
Sardis
Philadelphia
Smyrna
Ephesus
Priene
Miletus
Halicarnassus
Cnidus
Xanthus
Patara
Ancyra
Tripolis
Hierapolis
Laodicea
Colossae
Aphrodisias
Sebaste
Seleucia
Cremna
Attalia
Perga
Antioch in Pisidia
Iconium
Lystra
Derbe
Faustinopolis
Tarsus
Mallus
Issus
Seleucia Tracheotis
Ancyra (Ankara)
Caesarea (Mazaca)
Hierapolis
Antioch
Aleppo
Seleucia Pieria
Cyprus
Salamis
Paphos
Hamath
Tripolis
Byblos
Sidon
Tyre
Damascus
Palmyra (Tadmor)
Caesarea Maritima
Jerusalem
Gaza
Philadelphia (Amman)
Jordan R.
Euphrates R.
Hermus R.
Maeander R.
Halys R.
Nile R.
Dardanelles
Bosporus
Pelusium
Alexandria
Memphis
Qattara Depression
Cyrene
0 100 200 300 Miles
0 100 200 300 Kilometers

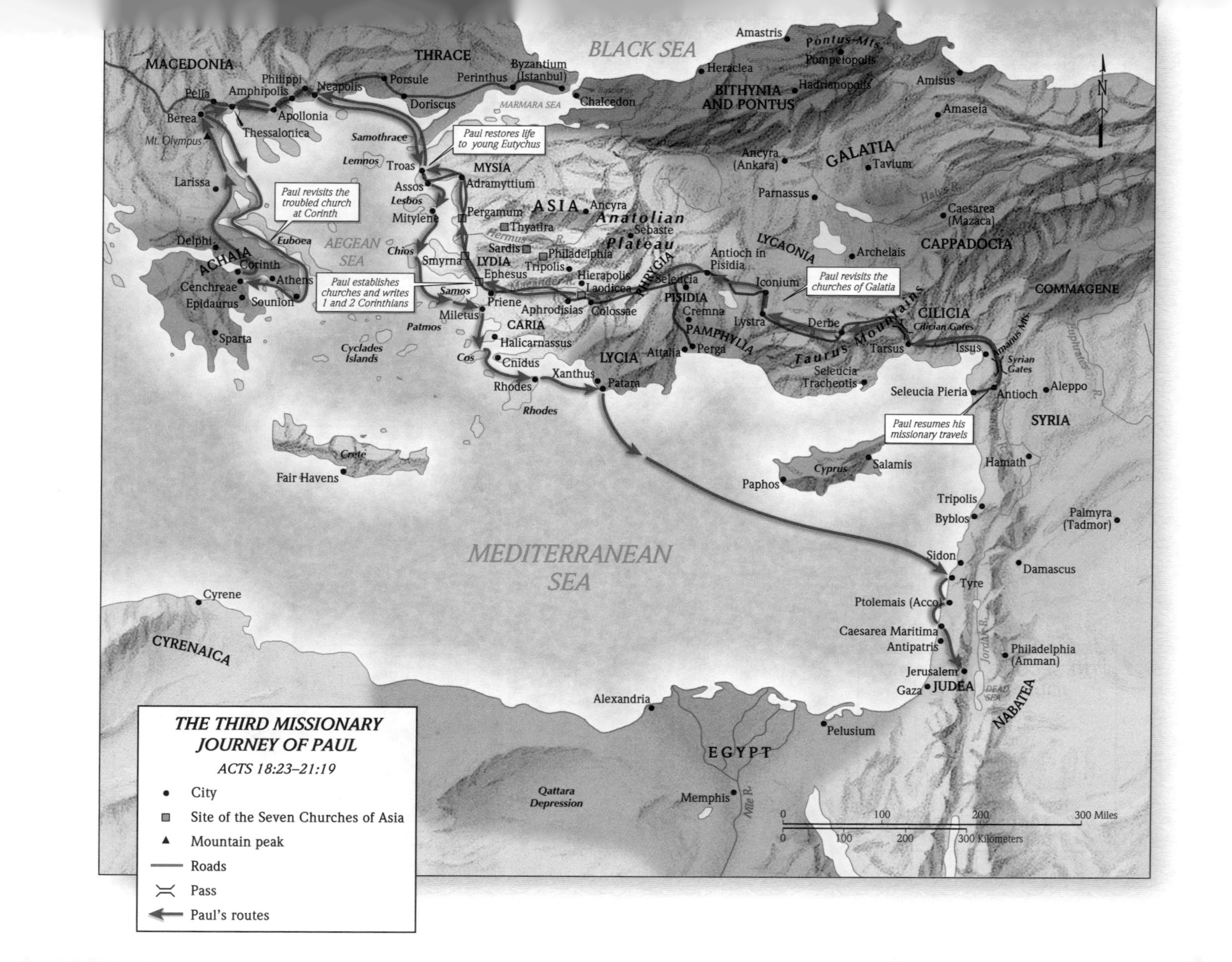

THE THIRD MISSIONARY JOURNEY OF PAUL
ACTS 18:23–21:19
City
Site of the Seven Churches of Asia
Mountain peak
Roads
Pass
Paul's routes
Paul revisits the troubled church at Corinth
Paul restores life to young Eutychus
Paul establishes churches and writes 1 and 2 Corinthians
Paul revisits the churches of Galatia
Paul resumes his missionary travels
MACEDONIA
THRACE
BLACK SEA
MARMARA SEA
AEGEAN SEA
MEDITERRANEAN SEA
ACHAIA
MYSIA
ASIA
LYDIA
CARIA
LYCIA
PHRYGIA
PISIDIA
PAMPHYLIA
LYCAONIA
GALATIA
CAPPADOCIA
CILICIA
COMMAGENE
BITHYNIA AND PONTUS
SYRIA
JUDEA
NABATEA
EGYPT
CYRENAICA
Anatolian Plateau
Taurus Mountains
Pontus Mts.
Amanus Mts.
Cilician Gates
Syrian Gates
Philippi
Amphipolis
Pella
Berea
Apollonia
Thessalonica
Neapolis
Porsule
Doriscus
Perinthus
Byzantium (Istanbul)
Chalcedon
Mt. Olympus
Larissa
Delphi
Corinth
Athens
Cenchreae
Epidaurus
Sounion
Sparta
Euboea
Samothrace
Lemnos
Troas
Assos
Lesbos
Mitylene
Chios
Samos
Patmos
Cos
Rhodes
Crete
Fair Havens
Cyclades Islands
Adramyttium
Pergamum
Thyatira
Sardis
Philadelphia
Smyrna
Ephesus
Tripolis
Hierapolis
Laodicea
Colossae
Aphrodisias
Priene
Miletus
Halicarnassus
Cnidus
Xanthus
Patara
Attalia
Perga
Cremna
Seleucia
Antioch in Pisidia
Iconium
Lystra
Derbe
Tarsus
Issus
Antioch
Seleucia Pieria
Aleppo
Seleucia Tracheotis
Ancyra
Ancyra (Ankara)
Sebaste
Parnassus
Tavium
Archelais
Caesarea (Mazaca)
Amastris
Heraclea
Pompeiopolis
Hadrianopolis
Amisus
Amaseia
Halys R.
Hermus R.
Maeander R.
Euphrates R.
Cyprus
Paphos
Salamis
Hamath
Tripolis
Byblos
Palmyra (Tadmor)
Sidon
Damascus
Tyre
Ptolemais (Acco)
Caesarea Maritima
Antipatris
Philadelphia (Amman)
Jerusalem
Gaza
Jordan R.
Dead Sea
Cyrene
Alexandria
Pelusium
Memphis
Nile R.
Qattara Depression
0 100 200 300 Miles
0 100 200 300 Kilometers
N

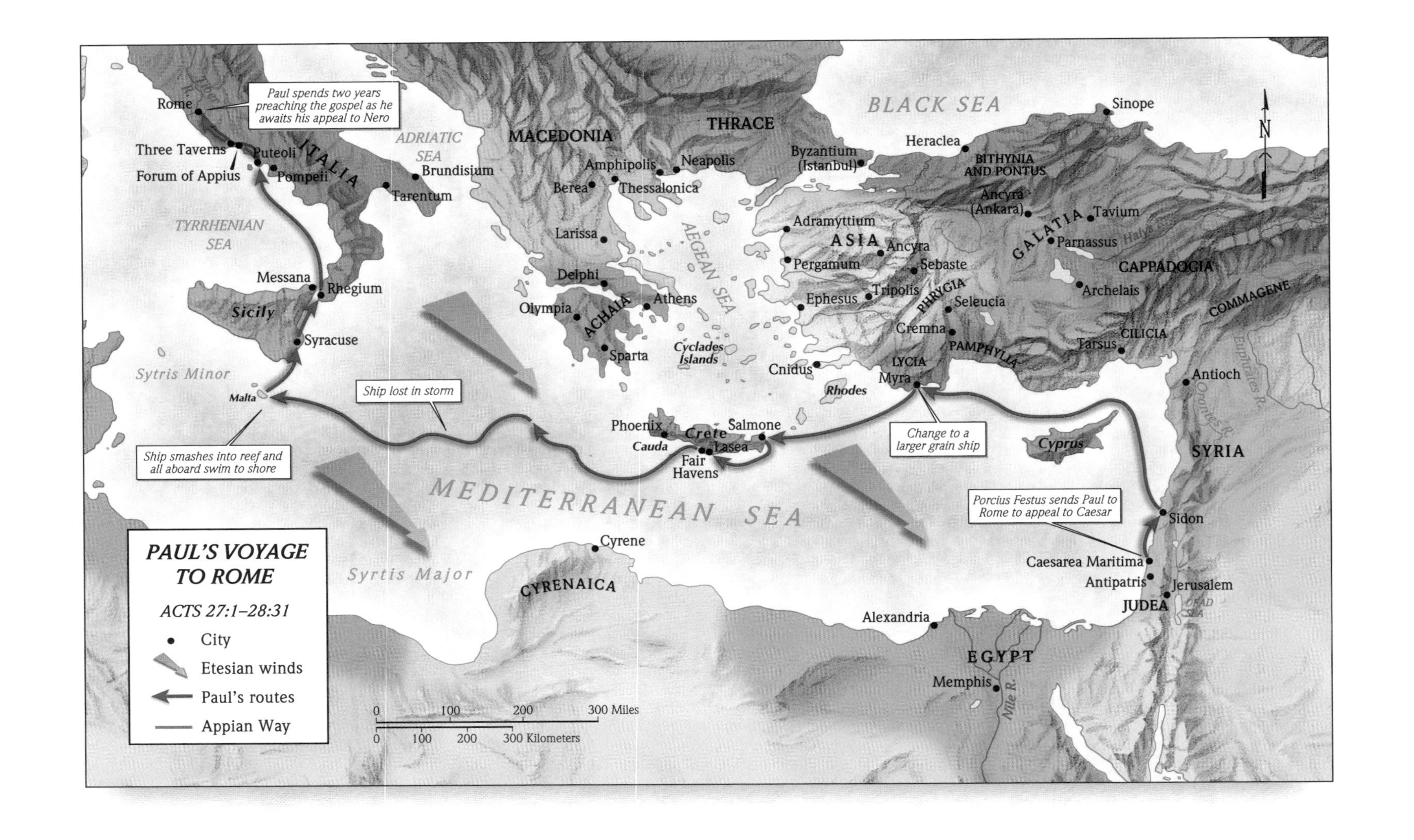
PAUL'S VOYAGE TO ROME
ACTS 27:1–28:31
City
Etesian winds
Paul's routes
Appian Way
0
100
200
300 Miles
0
100
200
300 Kilometers
N
Paul spends two years preaching the gospel as he awaits his appeal to Nero
Ship lost in storm
Ship smashes into reef and all aboard swim to shore
Change to a larger grain ship
Porcius Festus sends Paul to Rome to appeal to Caesar
Rome
Tiber R.
Three Taverns
Forum of Appius
Puteoli
Pompeii
ITALIA
ADRIATIC SEA
Brundisium
Tarentum
TYRRHENIAN SEA
Messana
Rhegium
Sicily
Syracuse
Sytris Minor
Malta
MACEDONIA
THRACE
Amphipolis
Neapolis
Berea
Thessalonica
Larissa
Delphi
Olympia
ACHAIA
Athens
Sparta
AEGEAN SEA
Cyclades Islands
BLACK SEA
Byzantium (Istanbul)
Heraclea
Sinope
BITHYNIA AND PONTUS
Ancyra (Ankara)
GALATIA
Tavium
Parnassus
Halys
Adramyttium
ASIA
Ancyra
Pergamum
Sebaste
Ephesus
Tripolis
PHRYGIA
Seleucia
Cremna
PAMPHYLIA
LYCIA
Myra
Cnidus
Rhodes
CAPPADOCIA
Archelais
COMMAGENE
CILICIA
Tarsus
Euphrates R.
Antioch
Orontes R.
SYRIA
Cyprus
Phoenix
Crete
Salmone
Cauda
Lasea
Fair Havens
MEDITERRANEAN SEA
Sidon
Caesarea Maritima
Antipatris
Jerusalem
JUDEA
DEAD SEA
Cyrene
CYRENAICA
Syrtis Major
Alexandria
EGYPT
Memphis
Nile R.

CHURCHES OF THE REVELATION
REV. 2–3
City
Cities of the Seven Churches
Major road
THRACE
Heraclea
Byzantium (Istanbul)
Bosporus
Chalcedon
MARMARA SEA
Samothrace
Nicomedia
BITHYNIA AND PONTUS
Cyzicus
Imbros
Dardanelles
Nicaea
Abydos
Lemnos
Prusa
MYSIA
Troas
Assos
Adramyttium
Dorylaeum
AEGEAN SEA
Lesbos
Mitylene
Cotiaeum
Skiros
Pergamum
ASIA
Ancyra
Nacoleia
Thyatira
Appia
Euboea
Hermus R.
Temenothyrae/ Flaviopolis
Chios
Sebaste
Smyrna
Sardis
Philadelphia
LYDIA
Tripolis
PHRYGIA
Andros
Ephesus
Hierapolis
Apamea
Laodicea
Samos
Samos
Tralles
Tinos
Magnesia
Maeander R.
Ikaria
Trogyllium
Colossae
Alabanda
Delos
Heraclea
Aphrodisias
PISIDIA
Cyclades
Miletus
Patmos
Paros
Naxos
CARIA
Islands
John writes Revelation encouraging Christians to remain faithful.
Halicarnassus
Cibyra
Idyma
PAMPHYLIA
Cos
Cos
Perga
Santorini
Cnidus
LYCIA
Rhodes
Rhodes
Xanthus
Patara
Myra
MEDITERRANEAN SEA
Crete

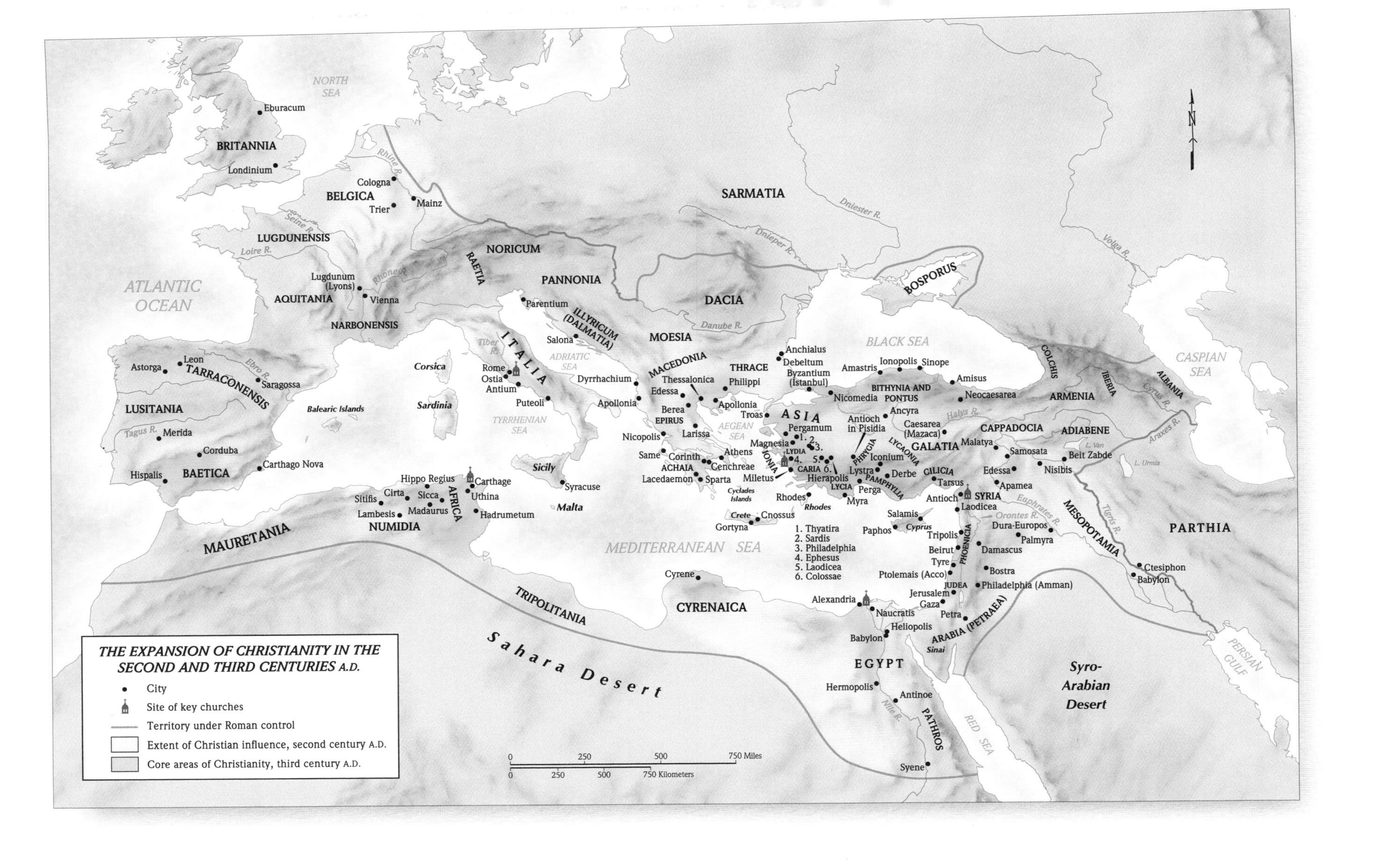
THE EXPANSION OF CHRISTIANITY IN THE SECOND AND THIRD CENTURIES A.D.
City
Site of key churches
Territory under Roman control
Extent of Christian influence, second century A.D.
Core areas of Christianity, third century A.D.
0 250 500 750 Miles
0 250 500 750 Kilometers
NORTH SEA
ATLANTIC OCEAN
Eburacum
BRITANNIA
Londinium
Cologna
BELGICA
Trier
Mainz
Rhine R.
Seine R.
LUGDUNENSIS
Loire R.
Lugdunum (Lyons)
AQUITANIA
Vienna
NARBONENSIS
Rhone R.
NORICUM
RAETIA
PANNONIA
SARMATIA
Dniester R.
Dnieper R.
Volga R.
DACIA
Danube R.
BOSPORUS
Astorga
Leon
TARRACONENSIS
Ebro R.
Saragossa
LUSITANIA
Tagus R.
Merida
Corduba
Hispalis
BAETICA
Carthago Nova
Balearic Islands
Corsica
Sardinia
Tiber R.
ITALIA
Rome
Ostia
Antium
Puteoli
Parentium
ILLYRICUM (DALMATIA)
Salona
ADRIATIC SEA
TYRRHENIAN SEA
Sicily
Syracuse
Malta
MOESIA
MACEDONIA
Thessalonica
Edessa
Berea
EPIRUS
Dyrrhachium
Apollonia
Nicopolis
Larissa
THRACE
Philippi
Apollonia
AEGEAN SEA
Same
Corinth
Athens
Cenchreae
ACHAIA
Lacedaemon
Sparta
Cyclades Islands
Crete
Cnossus
Gortyna
Anchialus
Debeltum
Byzantium (Istanbul)
BLACK SEA
Amastris
Ionopolis
Sinope
Amisus
Nicomedia
BITHYNIA AND PONTUS
Neocaesarea
Troas
ASIA
Pergamum
Magnesia
LYDIA
IONIA
CARIA
Miletus
Hierapolis
LYCIA
Rhodes
Antioch in Pisidia
PHRYGIA
Ancyra
LYCAONIA
Iconium
Lystra
Derbe
PAMPHYLIA
Perga
Myra
Caesarea (Mazaca)
GALATIA
Halys R.
CAPPADOCIA
Malatya
CILICIA
Tarsus
COLCHIS
ARMENIA
IBERIA
ALBANIA
Cyrus R.
Araxes R.
CASPIAN SEA
ADIABENE
L. Van
L. Urmia
Beit Zabde
Nisibis
Samosata
Edessa
Apamea
Antioch
SYRIA
Laodicea
Euphrates R.
Orontes R.
Tigris R.
MESOPOTAMIA
PARTHIA
Ctesiphon
Babylon
Dura-Europos
Palmyra
Damascus
Bostra
Salamis
Cyprus
Paphos
Tripolis
PHOENICIA
Beirut
Tyre
Ptolemais (Acco)
JUDEA
Jerusalem
Gaza
Philadelphia (Amman)
Petra
ARABIA (PETRAEA)
Sinai
1. Thyatira
2. Sardis
3. Philadelphia
4. Ephesus
5. Laodicea
6. Colossae
Sitifis
Cirta
Hippo Regius
Sicca
Madaurus
Lambesis
AFRICA
Carthage
Uthina
Hadrumetum
NUMIDIA
MAURETANIA
TRIPOLITANIA
MEDITERRANEAN SEA
Cyrene
CYRENAICA
Sahara Desert
Alexandria
Naucratis
Heliopolis
Babylon
EGYPT
Hermopolis
Antinoe
Nile R.
PATHROS
Syene
RED SEA
PERSIAN GULF
Syro-Arabian Desert